RadioTimes Guide to Science Fiction

Introduction by **Brian W Aldiss**

Edited by **Kilmeny Fane-Saunders**

BBC WORLDWIDE LIMITED

Published by BBC Worldwide Limited 80 Wood Lane London W12 0TT
ISBN 0 563 53460 5
First published in the United Kingdom 2001

Printed in the United Kingdom by Polestar Wheatons

Cover design by Matthew Bookman
Cover illustration by Max Ellis

Cover picture credits Star background *Images Colour Library* ● Thunderbirds *London Features International/ITC* ● Star Trek *Kobal Collection/Paramount Television* ● Flash Gordon *Kobal Collection/Universal Pictures* ● Forbidden Planet *Kobal Collection/MGM-UA* ● Star Wars *Courtesy of LucasFilm Ltd/Kobal Collection* ● Alien3 *Ronald Grant Archive/Twentieth Century Fox* ● The Matrix *Warner Bros* ● Doctor Who *BBC*

Contents

Introduction

by Brian W Aldiss

Movies are the great popular art form. The highbrow end may specialise in philosophical questions, as we see in the work of such masters as Ingmar Bergman and Andrei Tarkovsky, but for the rest of the wide spectrum, tricks, surprises and delusions are the essence of the thing. For such techniques, science fiction in its many guises is ideally suited.

At the beginning of the movie business stands the ingenious French director, Georges Méliès, whose *Le Voyage dans la Lune*, all of 21 minutes long, was first shown in 1902. Later, Méliès adapted Jules Verne's *20,000 Leagues under the Sea* (1907), the novel destined to become a Disney film in 1954, starring James Mason. In 1907 Méliès's *Le Tunnel sous la Manche* foresaw France and Britain being connected by the undersea tunnel that opened almost 90 years later.

Should we therefore credit these films with a predictive ability? They dramatise a possibility, a theory, already in the air. This is hardly the case with *The Tunnel* (or *Transatlantic Tunnel*), released in 1936; here the tunnel links Britain with the USA. The sets are striking, but such a proposition verges on engineering fantasy.

As Méliès knew, the fantastic sells tickets. The cinema's upstart sister, television, had the same idea. BBC TV, in its early black-and-white days, was strong on science fiction. *The Quatermass Experiment* in 1953 and *Nineteen Eighty-Four* a year later sold many television sets and brought thousands of new viewers to the new medium. Both stories were later turned into films.

Most science-fiction movies are escapes from reality, even if based on scientific theory. Although Kevin Costner's *Waterworld* has a basis in global warming, it serves merely as an excuse for watery adventures. The great freedom that science fiction allows is that the future is Tom Tiddler's Ground, where almost anything can happen. And, increasingly, where anything can happen which calls for special effects. In this respect, movies in general have become technology-led.

In its various guises, science fiction has always been popular, and will continue to be, as long as we continue to live in a technology-driven culture. Change and strangeness will continue to fascinate.

The science-fiction cinema was once decidedly low-budget, despite occasional exceptions such as Fritz Lang's *Metropolis* and Alexander Korda's *Things to Come*. We relied on repetitions of staples like *Frankenstein*. Such films drew on written science fiction. But minor masterpieces still appeared, such as *Dr Cyclops* and *The Incredible Shrinking Man* – of which latter film Vivian Sobchack, the authority on American film, points out, "Its entire visual movement is toward a transformation of the absolutely familiar into the absolutely alien." We thus constantly re-evaluate our responses to what we have previously regarded as normal.

Introduction

Hollywood separated science fiction from B-feature horror flicks in the fifties, with films such as *The Day the Earth Stood Still*, *When Worlds Collide*, *Them!*, *Invasion of the Body Snatchers*, *It Came from Outer Space* and *War of the Worlds*.

Slowly science-fiction movies became bigger and, frequently, better. *Planet of the Apes* in 1968 strikingly illustrates not only the re-orientation necessary for us to accept the superiority of ape civilisation over mankind's destructive culture, but a new rapport among media. *Planet* spawned sequels, working between cinema, TV and video. Now a blockbuster version is upon us. Video and DVD have widened our horizons.Such developments have enabled us to become students of film as never before. *Star Trek* also exploits these liaisons, beginning as a TV series, and now seemingly a permanent fixture on the big screen, in video and DVD, and in endless books, fiction and non-fiction.

Such fertilising liaisons will increasingly affect future productions. The day of the SF auteur is yet to dawn. With the blockbusters will go films more consciously developed as art forms, raising metaphysical questions. This became clear in director Peter Weir's 1998 *The Truman Show*. Weir has long been interested in "the mysterious fears of our nature" to quote a phrase of Mary Shelley's.

But the trailblazer here is clearly Stanley Kubrick, with his three science fiction works of startling originality: *Dr Strangelove*, *2001: a Space Odyssey*, and *A Clockwork Orange*. Kubrick's employment of music, silence and adapted speech reinforce and forge estranging images into a new unitary philosophy, which carries the perception – in direct conflict with most other future forays – that tomorrow is unknowable.

Kubrick's inheritance is carried on by another independent-minded film-maker, Steven Spielberg, whose film *AI* is the film Kubrick did not live to make.

It is this kind of creativity we hope to see flourish in the future: where the screen carries not merely special effects but a hard speculative core, reflecting the problems, fears and hopes of the present day.

How to use this guide

This guide to science fiction is the first major spin-off from the *Radio Times* film database, which is the source for the *Radio Times Guide to Films*. But this book isn't just about movies – we've also included more than 300 television series, serials and one-off dramas, plus highlights from radio science-fiction broadcasting.

The *Radio Times Guide to Science Fiction* is a book for all-round fans of the genre, covering a broad range of entries, but not attempting rival the depth of the hundreds (if not thousands) of specialist books on shows such as *Doctor Who* and *Star Trek*.

I've been a fan of science fiction since the age of ten, but in spite of all those years of reading, watching and listening to sci-fi, deciding what to include and exclude was a surprisingly difficult task. Every fan has their own definition of what is – or is not – science fiction. Space travel, aliens from Mars and time machines don't cause a problem; it's those murky grey areas that border the worlds of fantasy and horror that cause the arguments begin. I've tried to include films and programmes in which the science-fiction element – the element of speculation, of "what if", of man imposing his technical creativity on the world – is key. Mary Shelley's creation, Dr Frankenstein and his monster (a prime example of speculative fiction on the consequences of using science to transcend the "normal") is included. But Bram Stoker's Dracula, that terrifying figure of supernatural horror, is not.

Within the broad spectrum of science fiction are many sub-genres – futuristic fantasy or dystopian worlds, mad scientists on the rampage, "creature-features" when nature decides to bite back. *King Kong* is, perhaps controversially, included, as loosely part of the latter catergory; James Bond and similiar techno/gizmo fantasies are, perhaps equally controversially, excluded (except, of course, for 1979's *Moonraker*). Also not included are animated TV series, simply because the number would overwhelm the book!

While you may agree or disagree with what's been listed and what's been left out, I hope you'll enjoy browsing through the more than 1,900 entries presented here. While other specialist guides to science-fiction films, television and radio may give more detail on specific areas of interest, none – we believe – allows you to peruse all in one volume.

For the movie entries, you can access the film database (in its entirety) and current cinema information via the *Radio Times* website: **www.radiotimes.com/film.**

We'd like to hear your comments and suggestions about what you want to see on the film database and in future editions of this book and other related film books. You can write to: *Radio Times Guide to Films*, Room A1189, BBC Worldwide Ltd, 80 Wood Lane, London, W12 0TT, or e-mail us at films.radiotimes@bbc.co.uk. **KFS**

How to use this guide

The A–Z entries

FILM OR TV?

Made-for-TV movies are listed as films, except for UK one-off television dramas, which are listed as TV entries.

TITLE

Entries are listed under the titles by which we consider them to be best known in the United Kingdom and these titles are listed as they appear on screen. While many foreign-language movies are listed under their English title, others are listed under their original title, especially if they are particularly famous, or were released theatrically or on video under that title.

Alternative titles If you cannot find the entry you are looking for in the main A–Z section, refer to the appendix of alternative titles at the back of the book. You should find a cross-reference to the film you're seeking there. The alternative-title appendix is not a complete index of all the alternative titles and/or foreign-language titles by which a film or programme might be known – it is a selective appendix, designed to help you find the film you're looking for.

Alphabetisation Titles are listed alphabetically, ignoring definite and indefinite articles (a, the, an, including foreign-language articles such as les, das, il, el, place names being the exception, eg Los Angeles, El Dorado). Titles are also listed alphabetically by word, with initials counting as an individual word. For example, *ET the Extra-Terrestrial* comes before *Earth Angel*; *Earth: Final Conflict* before *Earthbound*.

STAR RATING

The star rating assigned an entry reflects the opinion of the reviewer. Many older films may be considered "difficult" or even virtually unwatchable by today's audiences but will still have a high star rating because of their importance and/or their technical excellence.

The star ratings also help rank a movie within its category. For example, a made-for-TV movie may be granted five stars in comparison to other TV movies, but you wouldn't compare it to *A Clockwork Orange*. The television sitcom *My Favorite Martian* rates four stars when compared to *Homeboys in Outer Space*, but you wouldn't compare it to the original BBC serial *The Quatermass Experiment*. And, within each star rating (since we don't give half stars) there may be a band of quality, some two-star entries being better than others.

As a guideline, the star ratings mean:

★ poor

★★ fair/average

★★★ good/better than average

★★★★ very good

★★★★★ outstanding

BRITISH BOARD OF FILM CLASSIFICATION CERTIFICATES

Where possible we give the current BBFC video certificate. For post-1982 films not on video in the UK, we list the original UK cinema certificate. Definitions of the current certificates appear at the foot of each page in the A–Z section of films. We haven't included older cinema certificates (X, AA, A), since we consider them no longer a useful guide. However, films that received a U certificate pre-1982 are listed with that certificate (once a U always a U, but the fact that *Abbott and Costello Meet Dr Jekyll and Mr Hyde* rated an X back in 1953 is amusing but not very helpful). There may be no certificate at all for foreign-language films, made-for-TV movies and films that received only a festival, rather than a theatrical, release in this country. For television series, if any, some or all of the episodes have been released on video, the certificate is given. For some series, the certification varies from episode to episode and in these cases all the certificates assigned are listed.

YEAR

Wherever possible, this is the copyright year of the film, not the year in which it was released. When we have been unable to confirm a copyright year, we have used the year of production; if that cannot be confirmed, we have used the year of first release. TV entries for series or serials are listed with the year in which the programme first began to the year in which it concluded. Open-ended years (eg *The*

X Files, 1993 –) indicate that the series was still on air at the time of going to press.

COLOUR

This refers to the original colour of the film or programme, ie the colour in which it was made: black and white, colour, tinted, sepia or a combination of these. Films that were originally made in black and white but now exist in colourised versions will still be listed as "BW", ie black and white.

RUNNINGTIME

Where there is a certificate, the running time relates to that certificate: that is, a video running time if the film is available on video in the UK, or the theatrical running time if not. Made-for-TV movies, unless they have been released on video, are not given with a running time; and for some more obscure films, it may not have been possible to ascertain the running time so none has been given. In the case of some silent films, we may only have been able to obtain information regarding the number of reels; and since the actual running length could vary dramatically depending on the speed at which the film is screened, no running time is listed. TV series are listed with the number of episodes and the running time per episode (eg 26x30mins).

REVIEWS

These have been written by our team of reviewers, and the opinions expressed in them are their own, based on their expertise and critical judgement.

LANGUAGE INFORMATION

Where applicable, language information has been added to the end of the review. If we have been able to confirm whether a film is available in subtitled or dubbed versions, we have specified. If we have been unable to confirm this information, or if different versions of a film may be available, we have given the language of the film only (ie "A German language film", versus "In French with English subtitles" and "Italian dialogue dubbed into English").

FAMILYVIEWING

Where available and appropriate, we have included a content warning at the end of the review. Where no advice as to the entry's suitability has been given, please be guided by the BBFC certificate and the content of the review itself. For those entries without a certificate, the reviewers' comments should give an indication of the content of the programme.

VIDEOAND DVDAVAILABILITY

[video symbol] = available on video
DVD = available on DVD

The information is correct at the time of going to press and is based on availability in the UK only. Video availability means that at some point the film was released on video and does not mean that it is currently on a distributor's list. More detailed information can be found via **www.radiotimes.com/film**, or in your local video store.

Encryption technology means that videos and DVDs released in other countries may not be playable on standard equipment in the United Kingdom.

CAST LIST

For each entry we have included a selected cast list of actors followed by the characters they play (where known). Famous people, when playing themselves, appear with no character name. Very rarely, and mostly in the case of less mainstream foreign films or obscure movies, we have been unable to obtain the character names.

Some actors are occasionally credited in different ways on different films or programmes. For example, early in his career, Charles Bronson used his real surname and was credited as Charles Buchinski. In these cases, we have printed the actor's name as he/she was credited on that film, followed in square brackets by the name under which that actor is listed in our index: eg Charles Buchinski [Charles Bronson].

In the case of animated films, it is assumed that the actor credited to a character is providing the voice only.

COUNTRY OF ORIGIN

The country, or countries, of origin is determined by which

How to use this guide

country/countries financed the film or show, not where it was made.

CREDITS

Each film entry includes a director credit and a writer credit. In a small number of cases, we were unable to confirm the writer credit, and so none appears. In some cases we have given additional names of those who have contributed to a screenplay, such as the person responsible for the adaptation or for additional dialogue.

There may also be additional credits for cinematography, music, costume design, art direction and others. These have been included if the reviewer has singled out this aspect of a film for special commendation, or if it received an award. Again, if a person was credited on a particular film in a variation of the name by which they are best known, then their printed credit appears first, followed in square brackets by their "real" or best-known name.

Television credits are listed as available. For long running series it has not been possible to include every director and writer, because of the sheer number of people involved. (Note: for very early television dramas and series, the producer was in fact the person we would now list as director.)

DIRECTORS', ACTORS' AND WRITERS' INDEXES

These are indexes to the films and programmes of the actors, directors and writers that appear in this book, not complete filmographies. If an actor does not appear in the cast list for an entry in the A–Z, then that show will not appear after the actor's name in the index. In the writers' index, if the person wrote the screenplay, teleplay, TV/radio programme or series, no note is included in the entry, just the title and the year. If, however, they were a source, rather than the writer, a note indicates the nature of his or her contribution (eg novel, characters, story, idea).

List of country abbreviations

US - United States
UK - United Kingdom
Alg - Algeria
Arg - Argentina
Arm - Armenia
A - Austria
Aus - Australia
Ban - Bangladesh
Bel - Belgium
Bra - Brazil
Bul - Bulgaria
Can - Canada
Chi - China
Chil - Chile
Col - Colombia
Cos R - Costa Rica
Cro - Croatia
Cub - Cuba
Cur - Curaçao
Cyp - Cyprus
Cz - Czechoslovakia (up to 1993)
Cz Rep - Czech Republic (1993 and onwards)
Den - Denmark
E Ger - East Germany (1945–90)
Egy - Egypt
Fin - Finland
Fr - France
Ger - Germany (pre-1945, post-1990)
Gr - Greece
HK - Hong Kong
Hun - Hungary
Ind - India
Ire - Republic of Ireland
Is - Israel
It - Italy
Iv C - Ivory Coast
Jam - Jamaica
Jap - Japan
Kaz - Kazakhstan
Ken - Kenya
Lux - Luxembourg
Mex - Mexico
Nep - Nepal
Neth - Netherlands
NZ - New Zealand
Nic - Nicaragua
Nor - Norway
Pak - Pakistan
Pan - Panama
Phil - Philippines
Pol - Poland
Por - Portugal
P Ric - Puerto Rico
Rus - Russia (pre-1922, post-1996)
S Afr - South Africa
S Kor - South Korea
Ser - Serbia
Slov - Slovakia (since 1993)
Sp - Spain
Swe - Sweden
Swi - Switzerland
Tai - Taiwan
Thai - Thailand
Tun - Tunisia
Tur - Turkey
Urug - Uruguay
USSR - Soviet Union (post-1922, pre-1996)
Viet - Vietnam
W Ger - West Germany (1945–90)
Yug - Yugoslavia
Zim - Zimbabwe

Reviewers

DAVE ALDRIDGE is a former crime reporter who has spent the past 25 years watching square and rectangular screens. A former editor of *Film Review* magazine, he is currently film and video reviewer for BBC Radio 5 Live and a regular contributor to *Radio Times* and other entertainment magazines.

KEITH BAILEY is the creator of The Unknown Movies (www.unknownmovies.com), a web site devoted to the cataloguing and reviewing of movies that have received little or no coverage elsewhere. Engaged in freelance writing and IT work, he resides in Victoria, Canada.

DAVID BASSOM is a freelance film and TV journalist who has written reviews, features and interviews for all of the UK's leading sci-fi publications, including *SFX*, *Dreamwatch*, *Starlog* and *Starburst*. His work has also appeared in such mainstream titles as *Cinescape*, *Film Review* and *Heat*, while his seven book credits include *Creating Babylon 5* and biographies of Ewan McGregor, George Clooney and *X Files* stars David Duchovny and Gillian Anderson.

JOANNA BERRY began her career as a film journalist at the age of 18, and was reviews editor for *Empire* magazine. Since leaving *Empire* in 1992, she has written movie features and reviews, and interviewed celebrities for a variety of magazines and newspapers. She is currently film critic for *Eve* and *Sainsbury's the Magazine*.

MAJ CANTON is the author of the definitive *Complete Reference Guide to Movies and Miniseries Made for TV and Cable 1984–1994* and a second volume covering the years 1994–99. She started her career as a TV comedy writer and is now an independent producer, having completed two TV movies for ABC. She lives in Los Angeles with her two VCRs.

JASON CARO is currently Film Editor at *What's On In London*. A devotee of sci-fi, fantasy and thrillers, he is a regular contributor to *Radio Times*, *Film Review* and *Ultimate DVD*, as well as several specialist science-fiction magazines.

ALLEN EYLES is a film historian who has written career studies of such stars as Humphrey Bogart, Rex Harrison, James Stewart and John Wayne, and is at work on a two-volume history of the Odeon cinema circuit. He founded the historical magazine *Focus on Film*, was a former editor of *Films and Filming*, and currently edits *Picture House*.

JOHN FERGUSON has worked in video publishing since 1987 and was most recently editor of *Video Home Entertainment* magazine. He also spent a year at the London office of *Billboard* and has freelanced for the both the *Daily Mail* and *Daily Express*. His association with *Radio Times* goes back to 1991.

SCOTT HAMILTON is a freelance writer and co-founder (with Chris Holland) of Stomp Tokyo (www.stomptokyo.com) and Attack of the 50 Foot DVD (www.50footdvd.com), two websites devoted to B-movies.

CHRIS HOLLAND is based in Florida and is co-founder of Stomp Tokyo and Attack of the 50 Foot DVD with Scott Hamilton (see above). When not exploring the world of video, Holland works for the US federal government.

DAVID J HOWE is a journalist and author who has written and co-written around 20 books about *Doctor Who*, as well as acting as genre reviews editor for *Starburst* magazine for 16 years. He is currently commissioning editor for Telos Publishing Ltd, working on even more *Doctor Who* projects, as well as editing dark fantasy and horror anthologies for the British Fantasy Society.

TOM HUTCHINSON has been reviewing films for newspapers and trade magazines for 30 years. He worked with director J Lee Thompson on several scripts, including *The Men in the Cage*, has presented a programme about movies for Southern Television, and was a specialist question-setter for *Mastermind* on BBC TV and BBC Radio 4. His most recent book is *Rod Steiger: Memoirs of a Friendship*.

ALAN JONES has reviewed fantasy, horror and sci-fi movies for *Radio Times* since 1995 and is also London correspondent for the American magazine *Cinefantastique*. He has researched and written numerous programmes for television, including two Film Four documentaries on the Italian horror directors Mario Bava and Dario Argento. He also reviews films regularly on TV and radio.

KIM NEWMAN is a novelist, critic and broadcaster who has worked extensively in the theatre, radio and television. His novels include *The Night Mayor*, *Anno Dracula*, *The Quorum*, *Life's Lottery* and *An English Ghost Story*. His non-fiction books include *Ghastly Beyond Belief* (with Neil Gaiman), *Nightmare Movies* and *The BFI Companion to Horror*. He is a contributing editor to *Empire* and *Sight and Sound* and has written for a wide variety of publications.

ROBERT SELLERS is a lover of the horror, science-fiction, fantasy and action movie genres. He has written biographies of Sean Connery, Tom Cruise, Sigourney Weaver and Harrison Ford and has worked as a contributor for many newspapers and magazines including *NME*, *The Guardian*, *Film Review* and *She*.

DAVID PARKINSON has been reviewing for *Radio Times* since 1995 and is currently compiling a comprehensive dictionary of world cinema. Specialising in foreign-language films, he is also a contributing editor on *Empire* and broadcasts regularly on BBC national and local radio. Among his books are *A History of Film*, *The Young Oxford Book of Cinema* and *Mornings in the Dark: the Graham Greene Film Reader*.

TONY SLOMAN works as a producer, screenwriter, editor and occasionally director. His film credits range from *Radio On*, *Cross of Iron* and *Chitty Chitty Bang Bang* to the cult TV series *The Prisoner*. Sloman is also a lecturer and broadcaster, and has recently completed a ten-year period as a governor of the British Film Institute. In addition, he holds a rare life membership of Bafta.

Contributing reviewers

Andrew Collins (*Radio Times* film editor), Brian Baxter, Ronald Bergan, Angie Errigo, Dick Fiddy, Peter Freedman, John Gammon, Lorien Haynes, Robyn Karney, John Marriott

Editorial team

Writer/researcher Matthew McGuchan
Sub-editors Samantha Dunthorne, David Oppedisano
Additional research Jeremy Aspinall, Siobhan O'Neill
Designer Ranjika DeSilva
Picture research Frances Topp
Database designed by Mark Ginns

Sources

Certain data published under licence from Baseline II Inc.
Certain data published under licence from the British Board of Film Classification. Some material is verified from the *Motion Picture Guide*, published by Cinebooks, New York, with kind permission.

A

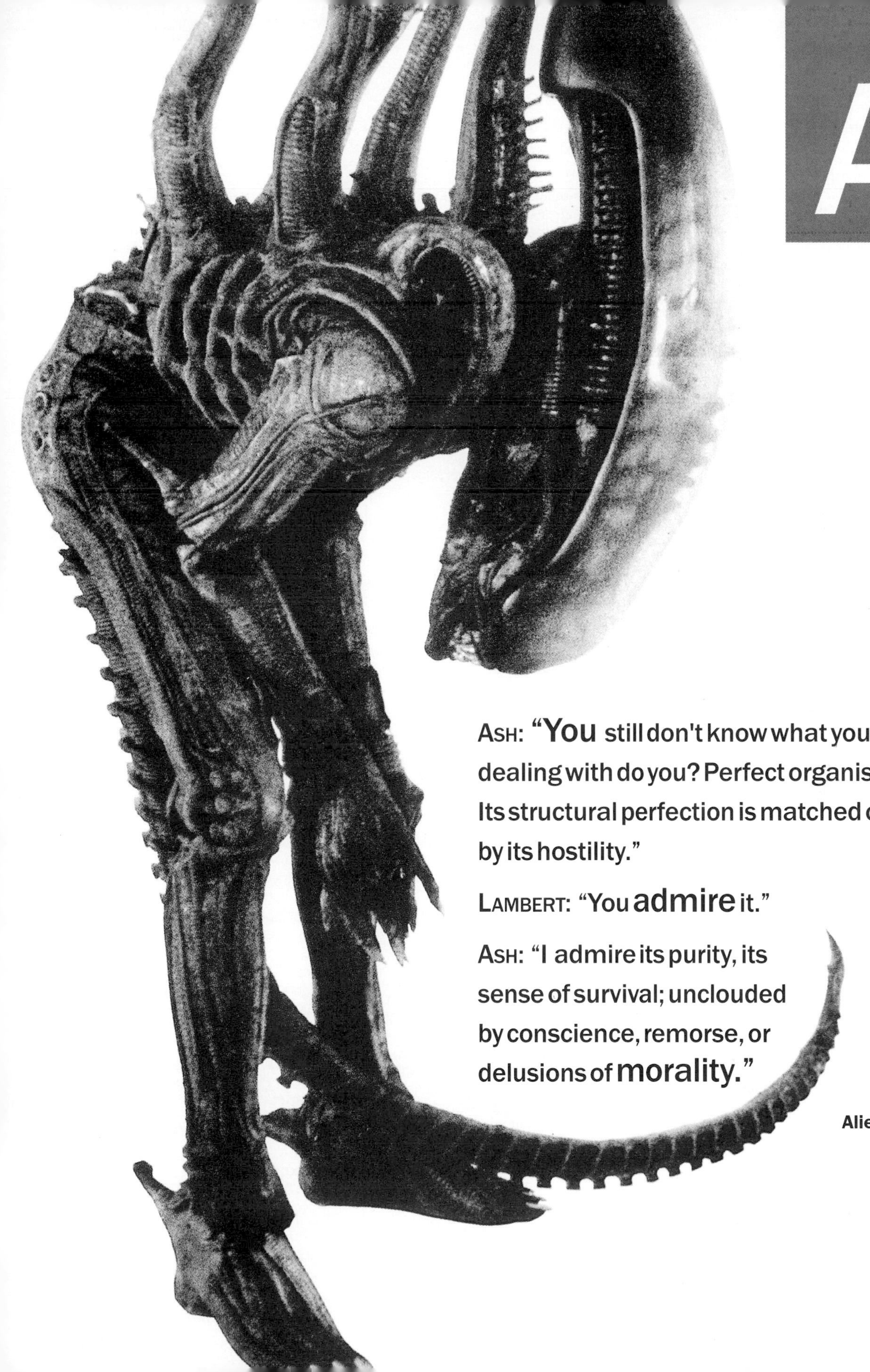

Ash: "**You** still don't know what you're dealing with do you? Perfect organism. Its structural perfection is matched only by its hostility."

Lambert: "You **admire** it."

Ash: "I admire its purity, its sense of survival; unclouded by conscience, remorse, or delusions of **morality**."

Alien 1979

A for Andromeda ★★★★

TV 1961 UK BW 7x45mins

An intelligent and thought-provoking drama from Cambridge astronomer and novelist Fred Hoyle, this is notable for being the BBC's first adult science-fiction serial since the heady days of *Quatermass* and for giving young drama school student Julie Christie her first starring role. Radio signals hailing from the constellation of Andromeda are interpreted by scientist Peter Halliday as plans for a super computer, which is duly built at a secret government research establishment. Christie is the lab assistant destined to play a pivotal role in the experiment. A less successful sequel, *The Andromeda Breakthrough*, followed a year later with Susan Hampshire in the Christie role.

Esmond Knight Professor Reinhart • **Mary Morris** Professor Dawnay • **Peter Halliday** John Fleming • **Patricia Kneale** Judy Adamson • **Noel Johnson** JM Osborne • **Julie Christie** Christine
Written by *Fred Hoyle, John Elliot*
Producer *Michael Hayes, Norman James*
Designer *Norman James*

AI: Artificial Intelligence ★★★★

2001 US Colour 140mins

Steven Spielberg's dark-toned fable for the new millenium takes the story of Pinocchio and gives it a superb twist, decked out in super special effects. Based on a story by Brian W Aldiss that caught the imagination of Stanley Kubrick more than two decades ago, *AI* (artificial intelligence) was, as Kubrick agreed, more suited to Spielberg's style than his own. As the prototype android child, programmed to love parents who then reject him, Haley Joel Osment (*The Sixth Sense*) proves once again that he is the outstanding actor of his generation, while Jude Law is charismatically good as his guide-cum-protector in the world of robot outcasts. However, it's the talking, super teddy bear who almost steals the show from the two leads. But this is no feel-good romp in the *ET* vein, and Osment's quest to become a "real" boy and win back the love of his human "mother" is a disturbing journey.

Haley Joel Osment David • **Jude Law** Gigolo Joe • **Sam Robards** Henry Swinton • **Frances O'Connor** Monica Swinton • **Jake Thomas** Martin Swinton • **Brendan Gleeson** Lord Johnson-Johnson • **William Hurt** Prof Hobby • **Ben Kingsley** Narrator
Director *Steven Spielberg*
Screenplay *Steven Spielberg, from the story by Ian Watson, from the short story "Super-Toys Last All Summer Long" by Brian W Aldiss*

Abbott and Costello Go to Mars ★ U

1953 US BW 73mins

Bud and Lou actually go to Venus – not Mars. Having run out of exotic backgrounds on Earth, the duo board a spaceship and think they've landed on Mars when they're in the middle of the New Orleans Mardi Gras. Hijacked by a couple of bank robbers, they escape to Venus, which is populated solely by former Miss Universe contestants under Mari Blanchard as Queen Allura. No matter how far they travelled, the stars' comic inventiveness was at a standstill and this film's tired and mechanical routines won't have improved with age.

Bud Abbott Lester • **Lou Costello** Orville • **Robert Paige** Dr Wilson • **Mari Blanchard** Allura • **Martha Hyer** Janie • **Anita Ekberg** Venusian woman
Director *Charles Lamont*
Screenplay *DD Beauchamp, John Grant, from a story by Howard Christie, DD Beauchamp*

Abbott and Costello Meet Dr Jekyll and Mr Hyde ★★★ PG

1953 US BW 73mins

It sounds like the double date from hell, but this is one of Bud and Lou's livelier outings. The boys play a couple of sacked cops who hope to impress Inspector Reginald Denny by capturing the monster that is terrorising London. There are even a couple of laughs in the wax museum and rooftop chase scenes, but the romance between Helen Wescott and Craig Stevens slows things down a touch. Boris Karloff hams up the role of the mad scientist.

Bud Abbott Slim • **Lou Costello** Tubby • **Boris Karloff** Dr Jekyll/Mr Hyde • **Helen Wescott** Vicky Edwards • **Craig Stevens** Bruce Adams • **Reginald Denny** Inspector
Director *Charles Lamont*
Screenplay *Lee Loeb, John Grant*

Abbott and Costello Meet Frankenstein ★★★

1948 US BW 83mins

Bud and Lou often weren't funny enough by themselves. So Universal International set up a series of confrontations from the horror films that had been such a success for the studio in the thirties. This was one of the funniest, with the boys delivering crates to a wax museum, unaware that they contain Count Dracula and Frankenstein's monster. Bela Lugosi as Dracula and Lon Chaney Jr as the Wolf Man play it straight enough to be naturally comic, so the real comedians end up as stooges. Vincent Price is the voice of the Invisible Man and Glenn Strange is the Monster.

Bud Abbott Chick • **Lou Costello** Wilbur • **Lon Chaney Jr** Lawrence Talbot/the Wolf Man • **Bela Lugosi** Dracula • **Glenn Strange** The Monster • **Lenore Aubert** Sandra Mornay • **Jane Randolph** Joan Raymond • **Frank Ferguson** Mr McDougal • **Charles Bradstreet** Dr Steven
Director *Charles T Barton [Charles Barton]*
Screenplay *Robert Lees, Frederic Rinaldo, John Grant*

Abbott and Costello Meet the Invisible Man ★★ U

1951 US BW 82mins

Bungling private eyes Bud and Lou are hired by boxer Arthur Franz to get him off a murder rap in this acceptable timepasser from the team's regular director Charles Lamont. There is a modicum of mystery beneath the thin layer of comedy, with the highlight a boxing bout in which Bud gets an invisible hand to hold off the champ.

Bud Abbott Bud Alexander • **Lou Costello** Lou Franci • **Nancy Guild** Helen Gray • **Arthur Franz** Tommy Nelson • **Adele Jergens** Boots Marsden • **Sheldon Leonard** Morgan • **William Frawley** Detective Roberts
Director *Charles Lamont*
Screenplay *Robert Lees, Frederic I Rinaldo, John Grant, from the novel "The Invisible Man" by HG Wells*

Aberration ★★ 18

1997 Aus/NZ Colour 89mins

This chiller about lethal lizards is a formulaic affair. The setting is a remote wooded area, where the local wildlife has been wiped out by a mysterious force. The guilty culprits turn out to be cunning, mutant reptiles who soon start tucking into human meat as well. Only Pamela Gidley and Simon Bossell stand in their way. Director Tim Boxell lays on lashings of gags and gore, but it is all very derivative. Contains some swearing, nudity and violence.

Pamela Gidley Amy • **Simon Bossell** Marshall • **Valery Nikolaev** Uri • **Norman Forsey** Mr Peterson • **Helen Moulder** Mrs Miller
Director *Tim Boxell*
Screenplay *Darrin Oura, Scott Lew*

Abraxas ★ 15

1991 Can Colour 86mins

Wrestler-turned-politician Jesse "the Body" Ventura is a 10,000-year-old law enforcer from the future in this cut-rate *Terminator*. His quest is to find renegade cop Sven-Ole

U = SUITABLE FOR ALL   Uc = SUITABLE FOR ALL, ESPECIALLY YOUNG CHILDREN (VIDEO ONLY)   PG = PARENTAL GUIDANCE

Thorsen (doing a terrible Arnold Schwarzenegger impersonation) before he can kill his son who holds the key to universal peace. Aside from a lot of grunting, fighting and laser-gun shoot-outs in snowy landscapes, there's little on offer to either engage or entertain in this Canadian-made time-waster.

Jesse Ventura Abraxas • **Sven-Ole Thorsen** Secundus • **Damian Lee** Dar • **Jerry Levitan** Hite • **Marjorie Bransfield** Sonia • **Ken Quinn** Carl • **Marilyn Lightstone** Abraxas's Answer Box • **Moses Znaimer** Secundus's Answer Box • **Robert Nasmith** Father • **Kris Michaels** Mother
Director *Damian Lee*
Screenplay *Damian Lee, David Mitchell*

The Absent-Minded Professor

★★★ U

1961 US BW 98mins

With its second remake, *Flubber*, recently released on video, here's a chance to see the original, a warm-hearted slice of Walt Disney-style Americana starring likeable Fred MacMurray as the inventor of flying rubber. Wicked Keenan Wynn wants to steal it and that's about the nub of the flub. As always in Disney films of this period, there's much pleasure to be had from the supporting cast, which includes veteran clown Ed Wynn (father of Keenan), *Meet Me in St Louis's* Leon Ames and Elliott Reid, the long-forgotten leading man of *Gentlemen Prefer Blondes*. It's a shame the budget didn't stretch to colour, but the marvellous black-and-white image of the flubber-driven family car crossing the moon so inspired a young Steven Spielberg that he copied it to provide the most potent shot in *ET*, and eventually used it as the logo of his company, Amblin.

Fred MacMurray Professor Ned Brainard • **Nancy Olson** Betsy Carlisle • **Keenan Wynn** Alonzo Hawk • **Tommy Kirk** Bill Hawk • **Leon Ames** Rufus Daggett • **Elliott Reid** Shelby Ashton • **Edward Andrews** Defence Secretary • **Wally Brown** Coach Elkins • **Forrest Lewis** Officer Kelly • **James Westerfield** Officer Hanson • **Ed Wynn** Fire chief • **David Lewis** Gen Singer
Director *Robert Stevenson*
Screenplay *Bill Walsh, from the short story "A Situation of Gravity" by Samuel W Taylor*

The Absent-Minded Professor ★★

TV 1988 US Colour 50mins

Sandwiched between the Fred MacMurray original and the Robin Williams remake, this TV movie began life as a two-part Disney special. Based on Samuel Taylor's short story *A Situation of Gravity*, it stars Harry Anderson as the preoccupied professor whose latest invention – flying rubber, or "flubber" – makes him a target for an unscrupulous tycoon. The effects may not be up to today's standards, but they're more sophisticated than those of the 1961 version. However, Anderson can't hold a candle to either MacMurray or Williams.

Harry Anderson Professor Henry Crawford • **Cory Danziger** Gus • **Mary Page Keller** Ellen Whitley • **Tom Callaway** Professor Donald Stillman • **Bibi Osterwald** Mrs Nakamura • **David Paymer** Mr Oliphant • **Stephen Dorff** Curtis • **Jason Zahler** Greg • **David Florek** Art
Director *Robert Scheerer*
Written by *Richard Chapman, Bill Dial, from the short story "A Situation of Gravity" by Samuel Taylor*

The Abyss ★★★ 15

1989 US Colour 163mins DVD

For some, prior to *Titanic*, this was James Cameron's *Waterworld*, a bloated, sentimental epic from the king of high-tech thrillers. Some of the criticism was deserved, but it remains a fascinating folly,

On a quest: Jude Law and Haley Joel Osment are the androids on the run in Steven Spielberg's *AI: Artificial Intelligence*

a spectacular and often thrilling voyage to the bottom of the sea. Ed Harris is the leader of an underwater team working for an oil company that is pressed into service to rescue the crew of a crippled submarine. But they soon begin to wonder if they are the only life-forms in the vicinity. Harris is great in a rare leading man role and there is first-rate support from both Mary Elizabeth Mastrantonio as his estranged partner and *The Terminator's* Michael Biehn as the unstable marine commander. Cameron excels in cranking up the tension within the cramped quarters, while at the same time the effects are awe-inspiring and deservedly won an Oscar. It's only marred by being overlong and by its sentimental attachment to aliens. Contains violence and swearing.

Ed Harris Bud Brigman • **Mary Elizabeth Mastrantonio** Lindsey Brigman • **Michael Biehn** Lieutenant Coffey • **Leo Burmester** Catfish De Vries • **Todd Graff** Alan "Hippy" Carnes • **John Bedford Lloyd** Jammer Willis • **J C Quinn** "Sonny"Dawson • **Kimberly Scott** Lisa "One Night" Standing • **Captain Kidd Brewer Jr** Lew Finler • **George Robert Klek** Wilhite • **Christopher Murphy** Schoenick • **Adam Nelson** Ensign Monk
Director/Screenplay *James Cameron*
Special effects *Joe Unsinn, Joseph Viskocil*

Acción Mutante ★★ 18

1993 Sp Colour 94mins

A terminally camp paella of *Battle Beyond the Stars* and Patty Hearst, Spanish director Alex de la Iglesia's debut feature begins in crackerjack comic book style as members of a disabled terrorist group in 2012 kidnap a debutante's daughter and hold her to ransom on a distant mining planet. But although gory, nasty and sexy in equal proportion, this Pedro Almodóvar-produced trash peters out into science-fiction on the verge of a nervous breakdown. By the time the dragged-out ending is reached, de la Iglesia has scraped the bottom of the *Spacehunter* barrel once too often in the effort to disguise his intergalactic *No Orchids for Miss Blandish*, where the hostage falls for her captor and takes charge of her fate. In Spanish with English subtitles.

Antonio Resines Ramón Yarritu • **Alex Angulo** Alex • **Frédérique Feder** Patricia Orujo • **Fernando Guillén** Orujo • **Enrique San Francisco** Novio Ultrajado • **Juan Viadas** Juanito • **Saturnino García** Quimicefa • **Karra Elejalde** Manitas
Director *Alex de la Iglesia*
Screenplay *Alex de la Iglesia, Jorge Guerricaechevarria*
Producer *Agustín Almodóvar, Pedro Almodóvar*

Ace of Wands ★★★

TV 1970-1972 UK Colour 46x30mins

A sort of children's TV stab at *The Avengers*, this copped the old Mandrake the Magician format of pitting a stage conjurer, Richard O'Sullivan-lookalike Tarot (Michael Mackenzie), against baffling and sometimes fantastical mysteries. Accompanied (like Doctor Who) by a succession of more two-fisted (Tony Selby, Roy Holder) or girly (Judy Loe, Petra Markham) assistants (and Ozymandias, a pet owl), Tarot tackled a succession of diabolical masterminds. Also like Doctor Who, Tarot's aventures were spread out through a clutch of three- or four-part serials and the show broke down fairly evenly between *Department S*-style rationalised but far-fetched solutions, science-fictional devices and the genuine supernatural. Plot gimmicks included resurgent techno-Nazis, nightmare-provoking gas, a diamond that turned people into chalk, a hospital where people were turned into dolls, several megalomaniacal computers and, in the final serial, an alien invasion. Imaginative and pulpy, with an occasional scary moment, this was filmed in colour to show off the fab seventies fashions.

Michael Mackenzie Tarot • **Donald Layne-Smith** Mr Sweet • **Judy Loe** Lulli • **Tony Selby** Sam Maxted • **Petra Markham** Mikki Diamond • **Roy Holder** Chas Diamond
Created by *Trevor Preston*
Producer *Pamela Lonsdale, John Russell*

Adam Adamant Lives! ★★★ PG

TV 1966-1967 UK BW 29x50mins

This was the BBC's answer to *The Avengers* and the creation of Canadian-born TV genius Sydney Newman, the man behind *Doctor Who*. The fantastic premise – to which Mike Myers' Austin Powers owes a huge debt – has dashing Edwardian adventurer Adam Adamant, played by Gerald Harper (who initially turned the role down) injected with an "eternal life" drug and frozen in ice by his arch foe "The Face" only to be revived in 1966, the era of mini skirts and early psychedelia. Aided by swinging London teen companion Juliet Harmer, Adamant carries on his crusading fight against crime. Much of the fun of the show was in the collision of old-fashioned morals with the permissive attitudes prevalent in the sixties. Adamant's only concession to the modern age was, amusingly, the purchase of a Mini Cooper. However, despite pulling in eight million viewers a week, Newman felt the show's disparate elements failed to gel and cancelled it after 29 episodes, some of which were directed by Ridley (*Alien, Gladiator)* Scott. (Two episodes were released on video in the early 1990s.)

Gerald Harper Adam Llewellyn de Vere Adamant • **Juliet Harmer** Georgina Jones • **Jack May** William E Simms • **Peter Ducrow** The Face
Script consultant *Tony Williamson*
Producer *Verity Lambert*

SFacts

The successful punk band from the seventies and early eighties, Adam and the Ants, took its name from the charismatic leading character of this popular series.

Addicted to Love ★★

1995 US Colour 96mins

Jeff Fahey is zapped straight back to *Lawnmower Man* territory in this intriguing, if flawed, sci-fi chiller. Depressed by the death of his girlfriend, Fahey employs a sinister new invention in an attempt to summon up a foolproof re-creation of his dead partner. However, he soon discovers that the path of computer-generated love runs far from smoothly. Sadly, despite the excellent playing of the ever-reliable Fahey, the project is let down by the formulaic direction of Paul Ziller. Also released under the title *Virtual Seduction*. Contains violence and swearing.

Jeff Fahey Liam Bass • **Ami Dolenz** Laura • **Meshach Taylor** Rich Anderson • **Carrie Genzel** Paris
Director *Paul Ziller*
Screenplay *William Widmaier, Michelle Gambel Bisley, Paul Ziller*

Adrenalin: Fear the Rush ★★ 18

1995 US Colour 93mins

Species babe Natasha Henstridge and *Highlander* star Christopher Lambert (credited here as Christophe) join forces as two cops on the trail of a plague-infected serial killer in a so-so science-fiction effort scripted and directed by direct-to-video master Albert Pyun. As viral thrillers go, it's an average action package, but the two photogenic stars add solid weight to the budget bravado. Contains swearing and violence.

Christophe Lambert [Christopher Lambert] Lemieux • **Natasha Henstridge** Delon • **Norbert Weisser** Cuzo • **Elizabeth Barondes** Wocek • **Xavier Declie** Volker • **Craig Davis** Suspect • **Nicholas Guest** Rennard • **Andrew Divoff** Sterns • **Jon Epstein** Waxman
Director/Screenplay *Albert Pyun*

The Adventures of Baron Munchausen ★★★★ PG

1988 UK/W Ger Colour 121mins DVD

John Neville plays the legendary liar to perfection in Terry Gilliam's sumptuous revision of the Rudolph Erich Raspe stories, which gives a delicious contemporary relevance to the infamous Baron's outlandish exploits as he reunites his four fantastically talented friends to fight the Turkish army. Gilliam's grandiose masterpiece visualises a warped world of chaotic Pythonesque extremes that extends from the moon (with the lunar king played by Robin Williams) to Mount Etna (where Oliver Reed gives a brilliant performance). An opulent odyssey balancing romance, comedy and thrills in one glittering, and constantly surprising, package. Contains mild swearing and brief nudity.

John Neville Baron Munchausen • **Eric Idle** Desmond/Berthold • **Sarah Polley** Sally Salt • **Oliver Reed** Vulcan • **Charles McKeown** Rupert/Adolphus • **Winston Dennis** Bill Albrecht • **Jack Purvis** Jeremy/Gustavus • **Valentina Cortese** Queen Ariadne/Violet • **Jonathan Pryce** Horatio Jackson • **Uma Thurman** Venus/Rose • **Bill Paterson** Henry Salt • **Peter Jeffrey** Sultan • **Alison Steadman** Daisy • **Sting** Heroic officer • **Robin Williams** King of the moon
Director *Terry Gilliam*
Screenplay *Charles McKeown, Terry Gilliam, from the stories by Rudolph Erich Raspe*

The Adventures of Brisco County, Jr ★★★★ PG

TV 1993-94 US Col 1x120m; 26x60m

Cult icon Bruce Campbell (of *Evil Dead* and *Hercules/Xena* fame) saddles up for this short-lived but insanely imaginative sci-fi comedy western series. Set in the 1890s, the show takes the eponymous Brisco County Jr on an anarchic ride that blends all the usual fast-shooting western scenarios with hilarious madcap comedy, *Wild Wild West*-style hi-tech technology and a time-travelling villain. Viewed in a suitably silly frame of mind, Brisco's maverick adventures are a fistful of fun. Campbell's off-the-wall charm has seldom been put to better use, and the actor is nicely partnered with a delightfully quirky supporting cast, some memorable guest stars (including Sheena Easton) and a veritable Gold Rush of smart scripting. Sadly, it only lasted one season, but well worth a shot.

Bruce Campbell Brisco County Jr • **Ashby Adams** US Attorney Ginger Breakstone • **Julius Carry** Lord Bowler • **Billy Drago** Johnny Bly • **Christian Clemenson** Socrates Poole • **John Astin** Professor Albert Wickwire • **Kelly Rutherford** Dixie Cousins
Created by *Jeffrey Boam, Carlton Cuse*
Executive producer *Carlton Cuse, Jeffrey Boam*
Producer *Tom Karnowski, Gary Schmoeller*

SFacts

How to pick a hit: "*The X Files* lead-in was *The Adventures of Brisco County Jr*, a modern-day ironic western that was a bit like *Indiana Jones*. That was the show everyone thought was going to be a hit. It was a good show, but it died very badly. A stupid science fiction show, with FBI agents investigating aliens – now that sounds bad. I wouldn't watch it."
David Duchovny, talking to *Radio Times* in 1995.

The Adventures of Buckaroo Banzai across the 8th Dimension ★★★ 15

1984 US Colour 97mins

Comic book hero and rock star Banzai (Peter Weller) crashes his Jet Car through the eighth dimension and unwittingly opens a hole in time. Unless he and his weirdo team of Hong Kong Cavaliers close it, evil aliens will overrun the Earth. Far too clever and quirky for its own good, this esoteric cult movie (the directing debut of WD Richter, writer of the 1979 *Dracula*) is a wacky spaced-out oddity. Watching it is like being on the outside of a gigantic in-joke trying desperately to understand what's so funny. An amazing cast, including Ellen Barkin, Jeff Goldblum, Christopher Lloyd and John Lithgow (as mental patient Dr Lizardo), try their best to keep it all accessible, but it wilfully degenerates into a huge impenetrable mess.

Peter Weller Buckaroo Banzai • **John Lithgow** Dr Emilio Lizardo/Lord John Whorfin • **Ellen Barkin** Penny Priddy • **Jeff Goldblum** New Jerse • **Christopher Lloyd** John Bigboote • **Lewis Smith** Perfect Tommy • **Robert Ito** Professor Hikita
Director *W D Richter*
Screenplay *Earl Mac Rauch*

The Adventures of Captain Marvel ★★★ U

1941 US BW 12x18mins

The first serial to be based on a comic book (from the *Whiz* canon, as it happens) predates *The Incredible Hulk* by having the superhero's alter egos played by different actors. Frank Coghlan Jr essays the mild-mannered scientist who only has to utter the word "Shazam" to turn into Captain Marvel (western veteran Tom Tyler), who alone can prevent the murderous Scorpion from securing the five lenses that will animate the ancient Siamese weapon that will assure him world domination. Directors William Witney and John English never pause for breath, as Tyler athletically plucks Louise Currie from endless peril during the 12 chapters. It's fast, furious and fun.

Tom Tyler Captain Marvel • **Frank Coghlan Jr** Billy Batson • **Louise Currie** Betty Wallace • **Billy Benedict** Whitey Murphy • **Robert Strange** John Malcolm • **Bryant Washburn** Henry Carlyle • **Harry Worth** Prof Bentley/The Scorpion
Director *William Witney, John English*
Screenplay *Sol Shor, Ronald Davidson, Norman S Hall, Joseph Poland, Arch B Heath*

The Adventures of Don Quick ★★

TV 1970 UK Colour 6x60mins

This space-age take on the legend of Don Quixote starred Ian Hendry as astronaut Don Quick, probably the only space hero to wear steel-rimmed glasses, who sees himself as Earth's roving ambassador, visiting planet after planet setting imaginary wrongs to right. His companion on these adventures, the Sancho Panza figure, was played by that most eccentric of British character actors Ronald Lacey, best known as the Nazi villain in *Raiders of the Lost Ark*. As a satire it had potential, but badly misfired with audiences and was taken off-air after just six episodes. A highlight of the show was Skip, an alcoholic robot with a penchant for poker. The actor in the tin box based his characterisation on north country working men's club comics. He deserved a series of his own.

Ian Hendry Captain Don Quick • **Ronald Lacey** Sergeant Sam Czopanser • **Tony Bateman** Voice of Skip
Producer *Peter Wildeblood*

The Adventures of Superman ★★★ U

TV 1952-58 US BW/Col 104x30mins

Having conquered the comics since his 1938 debut, sustained a long-running radio program and featured in two movie serials, Superman was a natural for television. In 1951, Lee Sholem directed *Superman and the Mole Men*, a brief feature film that served as a pilot for the show, introducing broad-chested, somewhat paternal George Reeves in the double role of mild-mannered reporter

Clark Kent and super-powered Kal-El, plus regulars Phyllis Coates as Lois Lane, freckle-faced Jack Larson as Jimmy Olsen and John Hamilton as editor Perry White ("Great Caesar's Ghost!"). This team stuck together for the first season, shot in black and white, but Coates was replaced by Noel Neill (who had played Lois in the serials) for the remainder of the show, which was made in colour. Conoisseurs reckon the monochrome shows – which had a *noir*-ish feel as slouch-hatted gangsters emptied tommy-guns against Superman's chest – superior to the more commonly-repeated colour episodes, which played more comedy hijinks for the kiddies and often stumbled over the milk-drinking, moralising, do-gooding that has always made Superman less interesting than his darker DC stablemate Batman. Although the first episode depicted the last days of the planet Krypton and a few subsequent cases featured science-fiction gimmickry (in *The Runaway Robot*, Superman imbied with lethal radiation after coping with an out-of-control nuclear reactor), the majority of the shows found the most powerful individual on Earth vastly overqualified as he took on the sort of crooks, counterfeiters and spies even Clark Kent could probably have handled easily if Lois wasn't nagging him all the time.

George Reeves Clark Kent/Superman • **Noel Neill** Lois Lane (1953-1957) • **Phyllis Coates** Lois Lane (1952) • **Jack Larson** Jimmy Olsen • **John Hamilton** Perry White
Source *from stories in DC Comics, from characters created by Jerry Siegel, Joe Shuster*
Producer *Whitney Ellsworth, Bernard Luber, Robert Maxwell*

The Adventures of Superman ★★★

Radio 1994 UK 150mins

Though it opens with the well-established US radio and TV narration ("Faster than a speeding bullet... It's a bird, it's a plane, it's Superman!"), writer/director Dirk Maggs's BBC Radio 1 series is based on the eighties revamp of the character artist/writer John Byrne handled in his *Man of Steel* comics mini-series, which was itself influenced by the 1979 movie. Lex Luthor (William Hootkins) is no longer a renegade mad scientist – another character, Dr Schwarz (Jon Pertwee), plays that role – but is instead an unscrupulous billionaire industrialist who takes pride in being the most powerful man in Metropolis until Superman/Clark Kent (Stuart Milligan) arrives. The show establishes the cornerstones of the franchise: Clark's Kansas background as the adopted son of Ma and Pa Kent, who at first think the crashed spaceship in their backyard is a Sputnik and that the baby inside is a Russian experimental subject; the peppery rivalry between ace reporter Lois Lane (Lorelei King) and Clark, which becomes a strange triangle as Lois is smitten with the flying, caped Superman but ignores her bespectacled workmate; and flashbacks to the last days of the planet Krypton, as Jor-El (Dick Vosburgh) sends his infant son to Earth to escape his world's destruction. Available on audio-cassette.

William Hootkins Lex Luthor • **Lorelei King** Lois Lane • **Vincent Marzello** Jimmy Olsen • **Garrick Hagon** Perry White • **Shelley Thompson** Lana Lang • **Dick Vosburgh** Jor-El • **Barbara Barnes** Lucy Lane • **Stuart Milligan** Superman • **Jon Pertwee** Schwarz • **Burt Kwouk** Doctor Teng
Director *Dirk Maggs*
Written by *Dirk Maggs, from stories in DC Comics by John Byrne, Dane Gibbons, Jerry Ordway, from characters created by Jerry Siegel, Joe Shuster*

The Adventures of Superman: Doomsday and Beyond ★★★

Radio 1995 UK 155mins

A follow-up to producer/writer Dirk Maggs's *Adventures of Superman* Radio 1 serial, this adapts a slew of DC comics that got a lot of attention because the publishers announced that their 50-year-old superhero character would die after a battle with new foe Doomsday – leading most of the non-comics-savvy press to believe that this would mean the end of the franchise, rather than an elaborate storyline designed to bring Clark Kent's alter ego back from the dead. The serial actually opens with the death of Lex Luthor (William Hootkins), of kryptonite radiation poisoning, and his reincarnation as a younger, non-bald, Australian-accented clone. Then there's a historic moment as Clark (Stuart Milligan) finally reveals his big secret to fiancée Lois Lane (Lorelei King) before dashing off to die heroically saving Metropolis from the undercharacterised alien thug Doomsday. However, four pretenders to the chest-S rise: steelworker John Henry Irons (Leon Herbert), who dons a powered armour suit like Marvel's Iron Man; the 13 per cent organic Cyborg (Kerry Shale), who claims to be what's left of Supes; bumptious teenage clone Superboy (Shale), who has the funniest moments; and the Kryptonian (Milligan), who is the real deal, albeit traumatised by his post-death experiences. It's an amazingly labyrinthine show, with more characters and plot than it can cope with, but it actually streamlines the comics and delivers some emotional patches in Superman's heroic end, his funeral and triumphant return. Available on audio-cassette.

William Hootkins Lex Luthor • **Lorelei King** Lois Lane • **Vincent Marzello** Jimmy Olsen • **Garrick Hagon** Jonathan Kent • **Kerry Shale** Superboy/The Cyborg • **Eric Meyers** Guy Gardner • **Denica Fairman** Maggie Sawyer • **Liza Ross** Supergirl • **Stuart Milligan** Superman/The Kryptonian • **Burt Kwouk** Doctor Teng • **Leon Herbert** John Henry Irons
Director *Dirk Maggs*
Written by *Dirk Maggs, from stories in DC Comics by Dan Jurgens, Karl Kesel, Jerry Ordway, Louise Simonson, Roger Stern, from characters created by Jerry Siegel, Joe Shuster*

Aelita ★★★★

1924 USSR BW 81mins

Based on the story by Alexei Tolstoy and shamelessly combining propaganda with escapism, this marks Soviet cinema's entry into the realms of science fiction. Exploiting the theatrical stylisation he had discovered during his post-1917 exile, director Jakov Protazanov leavened the polemic with much good humour, as accidental astronaut Nikolai Zeretelli leads a revolution against the tyrannical queen of Mars, Yulia Solntseva. The acting is energetic, the satire assured, and yet it was Isaak Rabinovich's expressionist sets and Aleksandra Ekster's futuristic costumes that were to have the greatest impact on the genre worldwide.

Nikolai M Zeretelli Los • **Yulia Solntseva** Queen Aelita • **Igor Illinski** Busev
Director *Jakov A Protazanov*
Screenplay *Fedor Ozep, Aleksey Fajko, from the story by Alexei Tolstoy*

Agent for H.A.R.M. ★★

1966 US Colour 85mins

This lifeless spy hokum was executed on a miniscule budget that wouldn't keep James Bond in dry martinis. Mark Richman is the agent assigned by an organisation called HARM – a sort of poor man's UNCLE – to stop the Russians from getting a deadly space spore that turns human skin into rotting fungus. Director Gerd Oswald plays it tongue-in-cheek, but it's too routine an affair to grip the imagination, despite a few diverting Bond-style gadgets. Look out for love interest Barbara Bouchet, who played

Katsuhiro Otomo
AKIRA
アキラ
Basado en el comic de KATSUHIRO OTOMO
Director Artistico TOSHIHARU MIZUTANI. Animación TAKASHI NAKAMURA.
Directores de Animación YOSHIO TAKEUCHI/HIROAKI SATO.
Escenario IZO HASHIMOTO. Director de Fotografia KATSUJI MISAWA.
Director Musical SHOJI YAMASHIRO a partir de la banda original «AKIRA».
Productor Ejecutivo SAWAKO NOMA. Productores RYOHEI SUZUKI/SHUNKO KATO.
Diseño de Carácteres/Guión/Dirección KATSUHIRO OTOMO
© AKIRA COMMITTEE
ORO FILMS

Neo-Tokyo nightmare: pacey and ultra- violent, *Akira* is one of the best known of the Japanese *manga* movies

Miss Moneypenny in the 007 spoof *Casino Royale*, and cult actor Robert "Count Yorga" Quarry. Originally produced as a television pilot, the world was luckily saved from having to endure a series.

Mark Richman [Peter Mark Richman] Adam Chance • **Wendell Corey** Jim Graff • **Carl Esmond** Professor Janos Steffanic • **Barbara Bouchet** Ava Vestok • **Martin Kosleck** Malko • **Rafael Campos** Luis • **Robert Quarry** Borg
Director *Gerd Oswald*
Screenplay *Blair Robertson*

Airplane II: the Sequel ★★ 15

1982 US Colour 80mins [video] DVD

Airplane! was always going to be a hard act to follow and this time the scattergun approach to the script carries more misfires and duds than normal. Still, the two leads from the original (Robert Hays and Julie Hagerty) are back on board again and the endless silliness of it all should win people over in the end. This time the flimsy storyline revolves around the first commercial flight to the Moon, but most of the fun to be had is in watching veteran actors taking turns in sending up their screen personae. Newcomers include William Shatner, Sonny Bono, Chuck Connors and Raymond Burr, although it is two stars from the original, Lloyd Bridges and Peter Graves, who once again shine. Contains some swearing and brief nudity.

Robert Hays Ted Striker • **Julie Hagerty** Elaine • **Lloyd Bridges** McCroskey • **Peter Graves** Captain Oveur • **William Shatner** Murdock • **Chad Everett** Simon • **Stephen Stucker** Jacobs • **Oliver Robins** Jimmie • **Sonny Bono** Bomber • **Raymond Burr** Judge • **Chuck Connors** Sarge • **John Dehner** Commissioner • **Rip Torn** Kruger • **Jack Jones** Singer
Director/Screenplay *Ken Finkleman*

The Airship Destroyer ★★★

1909 UK BW 20mins

Made hard on the heels of the publication of HG Wells's novel *The War in the Air*, this stands as Britain's first sci-fi drama, although its director, Walter R Booth, had been creating futuristic trick films for some years, most famously *The "?" Motorist*, which featured a car driving around Saturn's rings. This three-act saga opens with an inventor proposing to his sweetheart just as enemy bombers take to the skies. The depiction of the devastation wrought by aerial bombardment is surprisingly sophisticated, as is the boffin's remote-controlled retaliation. The wedding finale, however, is pure corn. The film was renamed *The Aerial Torpedo* for its 1915 reissue as a wartime morale-booster.
Director *Walter R Booth*
Screenplay *Walter R Booth, from the novel "The War in the Air" by HG Wells*

Akira ★★★★ 15

1988 Jap Colour 119mins [video]

One of the jewels of the genre, this is perhaps the best known *manga* movie in this country. Directed, co-scripted and designed by Katsuhiro Otomo from his own comic-strip, it's a pacey, unrelentingly violent post-apocalyptic adventure, in which a gang of Neo-Tokyo slum kids attempts to counter the telekinetic machinations of a rogue buddy. Yet, for all its futuristic elements, this is also a dark and disturbing portrait of contemporary urban life that seeks to expose the lack of empathy between the establishment and modern youth. The cityscapes are awesome and the camerawork is dizzying. If you're new to *manga*, prepare to be converted. In Japanese with English subtitles. Contains swearing.

Director *Katsuhiro Otomo*
Screenplay *Izo Hashimoto, Katsuhiro Otomo*

The Alchemists ★★★

TV 1999 UK Colour 2x90mins

Channel 5 successfully conjures up a heady brew of emotions with its exploration of genetic engineering. Veteran British actor Edward Hardwicke (memorably Watson to Jeremy Brett's Holmes in TV's *The Adventures of Sherlock Holmes*) trades his familiar Victorian attire for a lab coat and plays Dr Richard Bannerman, an award-winning geneticist who reluctantly accepts a job with a giant pharmaceutical firm, only to discover that it is behind a series of horrific experiments. Faced with the truth behind his employer's medical breakthroughs, Bannerman must ask if the ends can ever justify the means. After a slow start, Bannerman's modern-day alchemy becomes an engrossing and thought-provoking tale, which is dominated by a strong central performance from the ever-excellent Hardwicke.

Grant Show Connor Molloy • **Ruth Gemmell** Julia Bannerman • **Edward Hardwicke** Dr Richard Bannerman • **Aneirin Hughes** Sam Wentworth • **Ken Drury** Tony Hoggin
Director *Peter Smith*
Written by *Laura Lamson, from the novel "Alchemist" by Peter James*
Producer *Jill Green*

ALF ★★★★ U

TV 1986-1990 US Colour 102x30mins

An ordinary American family plays host to a wise-cracking Alien Life Form (nicknamed "Alf") in this delightful sci-fi sitcom. While Max Wright and Andrea Elson head the likeable cast, the undisputed star of the show is its titular character. A native of the planet Melmac, the 202-year-old aardvark-like Alf (real name: Gordon Shumway) is vividly brought to life thanks to a combination of witty dialogue, puppetry and a man in a furry suit. In-between trying to eat the family cat, Alf ensures that even the lamest scenarios raise a hearty chuckle and his good-natured exploits are a treat for kids of all ages. The show spawned an animated series and even a revival telemovie, 1996's *Project ALF*.

Max Wright Willie Tanner • **Anne Schedeen** Kate Tanner • **Andrea Elson** Lynn Tanner • **Benji Gregory** Brian Tanner • **John LaMotta** Trevor Ochmonek • **Liz Sheridan** Raquel Ochmonek
Created by *Paul Fusco, Tom Patchett*
Executive producer *Bernie Brillstein, Tom Patchett* ***Producer*** *Paul Fusco*

SFacts

Producer and series creator Paul Fusco also provided Alf's voice.

Alien ★★★★ 18

1979 US/UK Colour 116mins DVD

Top-notch acting (super-astronaut Sigourney Weaver), imaginative bio-mechanical production design (with the alien created by Swiss artist HR Giger), plus director Ridley Scott's eye for detail and brilliant way of alternating false scares with genuine jolts, all succeed in flattering a script culled from many cult sci-fi movies including *It! The Terror from beyond Space* and *Planet of the Vampires*. As a seamless blend of gothic horror and harrowing science fiction, this revolutionary "haunted house in space" thrill-ride is the classic business, stunning you with shock after shock, even when the fascinating creature is exposed in all its hideous glory. Contains violence and swearing.

Sigourney Weaver Ripley • **Tom Skerritt** Captain Dallas • **Veronica Cartwright** Lambert • **Harry Dean Stanton** Brett • **John Hurt** Kane • **Ian Holm** Ash • **Yaphet Kotto** Parker • **Helen Horton** "Mother"
Director *Ridley Scott*
Screenplay *Dan O'Bannon, from a story by Dan O'Bannon, Ronald Shusett*
Music *Jerry Goldsmith* • ***Art director*** *Roger Christian, Les Dilley [Leslie Dilley]*

Alien Cargo ★★ PG

1999 US Colour 85mins

An unremarkable variation on the *Alien* paradigm, as yet another isolated spacecraft is invaded by a sinister life-form while the best part of its crew is in hypersleep. Jason London and Missy Crider are the two crew members who awaken for a prearranged tryst only to discover that the previous shift is dead and something nasty has hitched a ride with them. The storyline is overly familiar, but director Mark Haber still manages to wring a few surprises from the material and the two leads deliver gutsy performances.

Jason London Chris • **Missy Crider** Theta
Director *Mark Haber*
Screenplay *Carla Jean Wagner*

Alien Contamination ★

1981 It Colour 90mins

Originally titled *Alien 2* in Italy, until the lawsuits flew, this atrocious shocker takes the "extra-terrestrial egg" concept a stage further. Here the eggs are being distributed across the Earth by an ex-astronaut under the control of a giant Martian cyclops, and people who get squirted with the sticky contents have a tendency to explode. Directed by Luigi Cozzi without an iota of the camp style that would have made it palatable, this badly-dubbed disaster is laughably gory, with a lame plastic-bag monster dragged out for the climax. Only the atmospheric score by composer team Goblin makes any real impression. Italian dialogue dubbed into English.

Ian McCulloch Hubert • **Louise Monroe [Louise Marleau]** Colonel Stella Holmes • **Martin Mase [Marino Mase]** Lieutenant Tony Aris • **Siegfried Rauch** Hamilton
Director/Screenplay *Lewis Coates [Luigi Cozzi]*

The Alien Dead ★

1980 US Colour 73mins

The first movie directed by hack-meister Fred Olen Ray was Buster Crabbe's last. It couldn't be a sadder epitaph for the thirties *Flash Gordon* star if it tried. Crabbe plays Sheriff Kowalski, who investigates a crash-landed meteorite in Florida, apparently responsible for turning a houseboat-full of teens into raving ghouls. A pretty awful load of old zombie nonsense, complete with cheap special effects. Look out for the numerous references to the cult movies of Roger Corman (including the character names), but even such clever touches don't make it any less static.

Buster Crabbe [Larry "Buster" Crabbe] Sheriff Kowalski • **Ray Roberts** Tom Corman • **Linda Lewis** Shawn Michaels • **George Kelsey** Emmett Michaels • **Mike Bonavia** Miller Haze
Director *Fred Olen Ray*
Screenplay *Martin Alan Nicholas, Fred Olen Ray*
Producer *Fred Olen Ray*

The Alien Factor ★

1977 US Colour 80mins

A rock-bottom alien invasion disaster made on a shoestring budget on 16mm by Baltimore film-maker Don Dohler. Three outer space monsters terrorise the Perry Hill area when they escape from their spaceship bound for an intergalactic zoo. The local authorities attempt a *Jaws*-type cover-up – difficult when locals keep turning up mutilated. Pitiful special effects, lousy acting and a droning synthesiser soundtrack make it a chore to sit through. One of the creatures, the zagatile, looks like a furry toy wearing platform boots!

Tom Griffith Ben Zachary • **Richard Dyszol** Mayor Wicker • **Tom Griffith** Sheriff • **Mary Mertens** Edie
Director/Screenplay *Don Dohler*

Alien from LA ★★ PG

1987 US Colour 83mins

More a modern retelling of *Journey to the Centre of the Earth* but, hey, anything with "alien" in the title works well in the video shop. Produced by the dreaded Golan-Globas team, this is an entertainingly naff fantasy tale with Kathy Ireland discovering all sorts of strange folk beneath the Earth's surface when she goes looking for her missing archaeologist father. Director Albert Pyun and writer Regina Davies reteamed in 1989 for a rather more family-oriented version that acknowledged the Jules Verne connectionand retained the title.

Kathy Ireland Wanda Sakneussemm • **Thom Mathews** Charmin' • **Don Michael Paul** Robbie • **Linda Kerridge** Auntie Pearl/Freki • **Richard Haddon Haines** Prof Arnold Saknussem • **William R Moses** Gus • **Janie DuPlessis** General Rykov/Shank
Director *Albert Pyun*
Screenplay *Debra Ricci, Regina Davis, Albert Pyun*
Producer *Menahem Golan, Yoram Globus*

Alien Intruder ★★ 15

1993 US Colour 90mins

A steamy play on the themes of *Westworld* with a touch of the *Dirty Dozen* thrown in for good measure. The crew losers aboard a space craft on a rescue mission find their fantasies being invaded by a mysterious being (Tracy Scoggins) when they log on to a virtual reality machine. Billy Dee Williams and Maxwell Caulfield add some credibility and director Ricardo Jacques Gale manages to spoof a few other genres in the fantasy sequences. However, it's more soft-core than sci-fi.

Billy Dee Williams Commander Skyler • **Tracy Scoggins** Ariel • **Maxwell Caulfield** Nick • **Gary Roberts** Lloyd • **Richard Cody** DJ • **Stephen Davies** Peter • **Jeff Conaway** Borman
Director *Ricardo Jacques Gale*
Screenplay *Nick Stone*

Alien Nation ★★★★ 18

1988 US Colour 86mins

This is the ultimate in buddy-buddy cop movies, but with a difference, as this time the mismatched detectives come from different planets. In the near future, an alien race has been uncomfortably integrated into American society and, against this backdrop, Earthling cop James Caan and alien cop Mandy Patinkin are reluctantly paired together to track down the killers of Caan's old partner. Director Graham Baker expertly combines the sci-fi and thriller elements and is well served by the two leads, particularly Patinkin, who manages to create a moving character while operating under a ton of latex. The movie went on to inspire a rather more humdrum but still popular TV series. Contains violence, swearing, drug abuse and sex scenes.

James Caan Matthew Sykes • **Mandy Patinkin** Sam Francisco, "George" • **Terence Stamp** William Harcourt • **Kevyn Major Howard** Rudyard Kipling • **Leslie Bevis** Cassandra • **Peter Jason** Fedorchuk • **George Jenesky** Quint • **Jeff Kober** Josh Strader • **Roger Aaron Brown** Bill Tuggle • **Tony Simotes** Wiltey • **Michael David Simms** Human dealer • **Ed Krieger** Alien dealer • **Tony Perez** Alterez • **Brian Thompson** Trent Porter • **Frank McCarthy** Captain Warner • **Keone Young** Winter • **Don Hood** Maffet • **Earl Boen** Duncan Crais
Director *Graham Baker*
Screenplay *Rockne S O'Bannon*

Alien Nation ★★★★ 12

TV 1989-90 US Col 1x120m; 21x60m

Produced by *V* creator Kenneth Johnson, this reworking of the 1988 movie follows the weekly adventures of hard-nosed LA cop Matthew Sikes and his idealistic Tenctonese partner, George Francisco. As a member of a newly-arrived alien species, Francisco struggles to overcome the prejudices of many humans around him, including Sikes. Like the original movie, the series combines thrilling high-tech cops 'n' robbers capers with a provocative commentary on racial discrimination. But where the series surpasses its predecessor is in its fascinating depiction of the complex Tenctonese culture. Gary Graham and Eric Pierpoint make the roles of Sikes and Francisco their own and the warm interplay between the show's regular cast members is a treat. Although the series was controversially cancelled after an award-winning first season, the fate of its characters was subsequently resolved by five telemovies, three of which are available on video in the UK.

Gary Graham Detective Matthew Sikes • **Eric Pierpoint** Detective George Francisco • **Michele Scarabelli** Susan Francisco • **Terri Treas** Cathy Frankel • **Sean Six** Buck Francisco • **Lauren Woodland** Emily Francisco
Created by *Rockne O'Bannon, Kenneth Johnson*

SFACTS

Loyal fans, like Pete Chambers, President of the Alien Nation Appreciation Society, hope for a return, or at least another TV movie. Chambers owns what he claims is the world's largest Alien Nation collection, which is housed in his museum (open to the public by appointment), located in the attic of his house in Coventry.

Alien Predator ★ 18

1984 Sp/US Colour 90 mins

Understandably shelved for several years, this feeble horror tale is filled with annoying characters spouting equally annoying dialogue. Former teen idols Dennis Christopher, Lynn-Holly Johnson and Martin Hewitt are touring Spain in their RV when they come upon a small town where the local inhabitants are under attack from alien microbes, brought back to Earth by the fallen Skylab space-station. Despite the promise of extra-terrestrial action in the title, audiences hoping to spot an alien or two will have to wait until the very end for a disappointing burst of latex puppet action. (Released on video in the UK as *Mutant 2*.)

Dennis Christopher Damon • **Martin Hewitt** Michael • **Lynn-Holly Johnson** Samantha • **Luis Prendes** Professor Tracer
Screenplay *Deran Sarafian, from the unproduced screenplay "Massacre at RV Park" by Noah Blogh*

Alien: Resurrection ★★★★ 18

1997 US Colour 104mins DVD

This enticing helter-skelter ride through space-opera clichés cleverly conceals the fact that there really isn't anything new of note here, just neat tangents off the basic *Alien* concept. Sigourney Weaver's Ripley is cloned 200 years after the action of *Alien 3* because she's carrying a queen fetus. French director Jean-Pierre Jeunet's thrill-ride showcases such scintillating set pieces as an underwater battle and a gallery of grotesque clones-gone-wrong. It's tense, mordantly funny, very graphic and bloody, with Weaver on great form as clone number eight who's gained some interesting alien influences on her personality. Rumours of *Alien 5* continue to circulate: will $15 million be enough to get Sigourney Weaver back as Ripley?

Sigourney Weaver Ripley • **Winona Ryder** Call • **Dominique Pinon** Vriess • **Ron Perlman** Johner • **Gary Dourdan** Christie • **Michael Wincott** Elgyn • **Kim Flowers** Hillard • **Dan Hedaya** General Perez
Director *Jean-Pierre Jeunet*
Screenplay *Joss Whedon, from characters created by Dan O'Bannon, Ronald Shusett*
Producer *Bill Badalato, Gordon Carroll, David Giler, Walter Hill*
Executive producer *Amy Jupiter*

Alien Space Avenger ★★★

1989 US Colour 80mins

This fun B-movie from director Richard W Haines melds science-fiction, soft-core porn, gangster chronicle and prison saga together for a cleverly-constructed action thriller packed with gore, laughs and quirky acting. Outlaw aliens take over a pair of flapper-era couples in the thirties, hide out in a space sphere for 50 years, then emerge in late eighties Manhattan looking for plutonium to return home. As intergalactic bounty hunters close in, a comic-book artist uses their exploits for inspiration in a "Space Avenger" series. A hugely entertaining collision of fantasy and reality, paying homage to fifties cult movies in the deftest – and daftest – fashion.

Robert Prichard • **Mike McClerie** • **Charity Staley** • **Gina Mastrogiacomo** • **Angela Nicholas**
Director *Richard W Haines*
Screenplay *Richard W Haines, Linwood Sawyer, Leslie Delano*
Producer *Robert A Harris, Richard W Haines, Ray Sundlin*

Alien Terror ★★ 18

1969 Mex/US Colour 73mins

The last movie made by veteran horror icon Boris Karloff was also the last of a shoddily assembled quartet of creature features made back-to-back in Los Angeles and Mexico. Barely directed by schlock maestro Jack Hill (the Mexico scenes were the work of Juan Ibanez) and badly edited – Karloff is clearly emoting to actors in another time and country – the film involves a molecular ray gun which freaks out observing aliens when its inventor (Karloff) accidentally blows a hole in his laboratory roof. Enter a blond ET in a silver lurex suit who inhabits the body of a psycho killer to stop humanity committing suicide. A weird and wacky mess that has to be seen to be believed.

Boris Karloff Professor John Meyer • **Enrique Guzman** Paul • **Christa Linder** Laura • **Yerye Beirute** Convict • **Maura Monti** Isabel
Director *Jack Hill, Juan Ibanez*
Screenplay *Karl Schanzer, Luis Vergara*

Alien³ ★★★ 18

1992 US Colour 109mins DVD

Given that the first two films stand up as sci-fi classics in their own right, *Seven* director David Fincher, in his feature film debut, had an impossible act to follow with this second sequel. He makes a surprisingly good job of it, developing the maternal themes of first sequel *Aliens* and providing an exhilarating final showdown. Sigourney Weaver returns as Ripley, who this time crash-lands on a prison colony where another lethal alien is let loose. A familiar cast of Brits (Charles Dance, Paul McGann, Brian Glover) provides the alien fodder and, while it isn't in the same class as the first two films, this provides a satisfactory addition to the series. Still, it would have been interesting to see what second choice director Vincent Ward (of *The Navigator: a Medieval Odyssey* fame) would have made of it – he was brought in when Renny Harlin left after script disagreements, but was himself replaced when it emerged that his version of the movie would be set in a monastery and the alien itself wouldn't be appearing. Contains violence and swearing.

Sigourney Weaver Ripley • **Charles S Dutton** Dillon • **Charles Dance** Clemens • **Paul McGann** Golic • **Brian Glover** Superintendent Andrews • **Ralph Brown** Aaron • **Danny Webb [Daniel Webb]** Morse • **Christopher John Fields** Rains • **Holt McCallany** Junior • **Lance Henriksen** Bishop II
Director *David Fincher*
Screenplay *David Giler, Walter Hill, Larry Ferguson, from a story by Vincent Ward, from characters created by Dan O'Bannon, Ronald Shusett*

The Alien Within ★★ 18

1995 US Colour 82mins

The Thing goes underwater in this fun, if hackneyed, production from veteran genre maestro Roger Corman. Roddy McDowall heads the scientific team fighting a parasitic alien during the construction of a deep sea colony. Lots of cheap thrills ensue as his crew (which includes William Shatner's daughter Melanie) tries to discover who's hiding the shape-shifter.

Roddy McDowall Dr Henry Lazarus • **Alex Hyde-White** Jedidiah Pickett • **Melanie Shatner** Catherine Harding • **Roger Halston** Wyatt • **Emile Levisetti** Brill • **Richard Biggs** Samuel Hawkes
Director *Scott P Levy [Scott Levy]*
Screenplay *Alex Simon, from a story by Rob Kerchner*
Executive producer *Roger Corman*

Alienator ★★

1989 US Colour 93mins

Fred Olen Ray, a poor man's Roger Corman for the video era, brings his usual trashy style to this cheapo futuristic thriller, which finds a busty alien hit-woman travelling to Earth to track down a convict who has escaped from a distant prison space shuttle. Caught in between are an unappealing group of teenagers. *Air Wolf*'s Jan-Michael Vincent pops up briefly and straight to video connoisseurs will recognise B-movie stalwarts such as PJ Soles, but there is little in the way of special effects or excitement.

Jan-Michael Vincent Commander • **John Phillip Law** Ward • **Ross Hagen** Kol • **Dyana Ortelli** Orrie • **Jesse Dabson** Benny • **Dawn Wildsmith** Caroline • **P J Soles** Tara
Director *Fred Olen Ray*
Screenplay *Paul Garson*

Aliens ★★★★★ 18

1986 US Colour 131mins DVD

Now that there are four *Aliens* in the franchise – from the 1979 original to 1997's *Alien: Resurrection* – debate rages about the superiority of one over the other. But there is a consensus about the second one: it's even better than the first. *Alien*, directed by *Gladiator* Oscar-winner Ridley Scott, had such an impact it quickly became hard to imagine a time when claustrophobic corridors, grimy space truckers and gooey extra-terrestrial saliva were not the sci-fi norm. When 20th Century Fox belatedly rubber-stamped a 1986 sequel, it was with an entirely different crew (under 31-year old ingénue James Cameron), yet the iconic aura of both sole human survivor Lt Ripley (Sigourney Weaver) and the lithe, skeletal monster itself was such that *Aliens* felt like a natural progression. That said, it is a very different prospect: bigger, louder, longer and more militaristic (at $20 million, it cost twice as much as its predecessor). Ripley accompanies a crack team of Marines (led by Cameron favourites Michael Biehn and Bill Paxton) to the now-colonised planet LV426 where the alien-infected ship from the first film was discovered. Surprise! The beasts have incubated using the colonists' bodies and now run rampant. Trust the man who made *Titanic* to up the alien-count from one to a couple of hundred. It's gung-ho, hardware-heavy stuff, but brilliantly stage-managed by Cameron, who treats it as a super-charged Vietnam flick. Don't forget to join in when Weaver shouts her immortal line at the mother alien: "Get away from her, you bitch!" Contains violence and swearing.

Sigourney Weaver Ripley • **Carrie Henn** Rebecca Jorden, "Newt" • **Michael Biehn** Corporal Hicks • **Paul Reiser** Carter J Burke • **Lance Henriksen** Bishop • **Bill Paxton** Private Hudson • **William Hope** Lieutenant Gorman • **Jenette Goldstein** Private Vasquez • **Al Matthews** Sergeant Apone • **Mark Rolston** Private Drake • **Ricco Ross** Private Frost • **Colette Hiller** Corporal Ferro • **Daniel Kash** Private Spunkmeyer • **Cynthia Scott** Corporal Dietrich • **Tip Tipping** Private Crowe • **Trevor Steedman** Private Wierzbowski •
***Director** James Cameron*
***Screenplay** James Cameron, from a story by James Cameron, David Giler, Walter Hill, from characters created by Dan O'Bannon, Ronald Shusett*

The Aliens Are Coming ★★ PG

1979 US Colour 97mins

Harvey Hart directed one of the early episodes of *Star Trek* ("Mudd's Women"), but it has to be said he's nothing more than a footnote to the sci-fi genre. He was gainfully employed in a whole range of genres and there's certainly little spark of imagination in this plodding alien invasion tale about the Earth being threatened by creatures from another world. *Party of Five* regular Tom Mason has a lead role and the sharp-eyed will spot Ed Harris in an early role.

Tom Mason Dr Scott Dryden • **Max Gail** Russ Garner • **Laurence Haddon** Bert Fowler • **Fawne Harriman** Joyce Cummings • **Melinda Fee** Gwen O'Brien • **Caroline McWilliams** Sue Garner • **Eric Braeden** Leonard Nero • **Matthew Laborteaux** Timmy Garner • **Ed Harris** Chuck Polchek
***Director** Harvey Hart*
***Screenplay** Robert W Lenski*

Aliens from Spaceship Earth ★

1977 US Colour 70mins

Are UFO sightings by members of the public real? Has Earth been visited by aliens from other galaxies? Does anyone want to sit through this poorly-conceived investigative report to find out? Over-used documentary fact meets Hollywood fiction in this ho-hum hokum featuring dramatic re-enactments of well-known close encounters given a speculative *Chariots of the Gods*-inspired portentousness by director Don Como. Even sixties hippie singer Donovan gets in on the alien *Sunshine Superman* act.

Donovan • **Lynda Day George** • **Leigh Taylor-Young**
***Director** Don Como*

Alligator ★★★★ 15

1980 US Colour 87mins DVD

The old urban myth about baby alligators thriving in city sewers after being discarded as pets inspires this turbo-driven eco-chiller, thanks to the genuine wit and sardonic wisdom of John Sayles's superb script. Just as he did with *Piranha* and *The Howling* (written with Terence H Winkless), Sayles crafts a monster-on-the-loose scenario that's better than the best of the fifties movies it resembles. The cast (especially tough detective Robert Forster) is highly believable and treats the in-jokes with the right amount of tongue-in-cheek deference. Director Lewis Teague (*Cujo*) brings subtle irony to the carnage and infuses the whole radical re-packaging of mutant monster clichés with an immensely likeable sense of insolent fun.

Robert Forster Detective David Madison • **Robin Riker** Marisa Kendall • **Dean Jagger** Slade • **Michael Gazzo [Michael V Gazzo]** Police Chief Clark • **Sidney Lassick [Sydney Lassick]** Lou • **Jack Carter** Mayor Ledoux • **Perry Lang** Kelly • **Henry Silva** Col Brock • **Bart Braverman** Reporter
***Director** Lewis Teague*
***Screenplay** John Sayles*

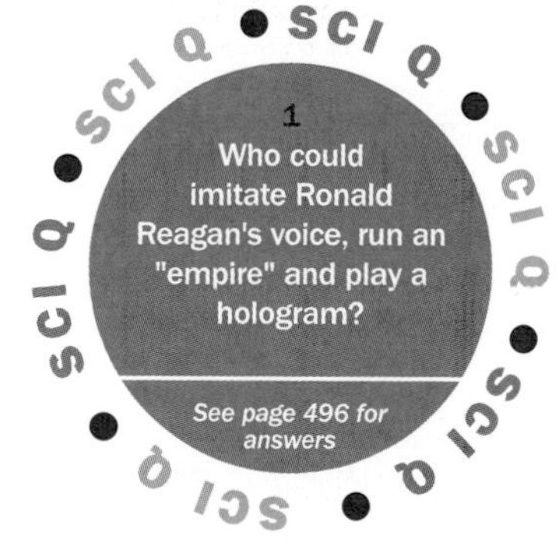
SCI Q
1
Who could imitate Ronald Reagan's voice, run an "empire" and play a hologram?
See page 496 for answers

Alligator II: the Mutation ★★ 15

1991 US Colour 90mins

The original *Alligator* was a cult delight: John Sayles had a hand in the witty dialogue, while the actors kept theirs tongues firmly in cheek. This sequel reprises the basic plot – mutant reptile wreaks havoc in suburbia (tagline: "It crashed out of the sewers... now there's hell to pay") – but it's tame stuff, despite a pretty good cast that includes Joseph Bologna, Dee Wallace Stone and Richard Lynch. And the creature isn't that scary, either.

Joseph Bologna David Hodges • **Brock Peters** Chief Speed • **Dee Wallace Stone** Christine Hodges • **Woody Brown** Rich Harmon • **Holly Gagnier** Sheri • **Richard Lynch** Hawkins • **Bill Daily** Anderson • **Steve Railsback** Vincent Brown
***Director** Jon Hess*
***Screenplay** Curt Allen*

The Alligator People ★★

1959 US BW 74mins

Fifties "creature features" don't come any sillier or more insane than this last-gasp effort from former musicals director Roy Del Ruth. Down in the Louisiana swamplands, doctor George Macready experiments with an alligator serum intended to help amputee victims grow new limbs. Bruce Bennett is a wounded man who takes the serum and turns into an upright reptile, with the help of an ill-fitting scaly rubber suit. Inept in practically every area, Del Ruth's ill-at-ease direction simply makes matters worse as the heavies slowly turn into walking handbags. That said, Beverly Garland does her usual spunky heroine routine to perfection.

Beverly Garland Jane Marvin • **Bruce Bennett** Dr Erik Lorimer • **Lon Chaney Jr** Mannon • **George Macready** Dr Mark Sinclair • **Frieda Inescort** Mrs Henry Hawthorne • **Richard Crane** Paul Webster • **Douglas Kennedy** Dr Wayne McGregor • **Vince Townsend Jr** Toby
***Director** Roy Del Ruth*
***Screenplay** Orville H Hampton, from a story by Charles O'Neal*

The Alpha Incident ★

1977 US Colour 92mins

A microbe from Mars terrorises people at a rural Wisconsin railroad depot managed by dim-witted Ralph Meeker. Only in sleep does the alien germ take control and destroy the body, so they must stay awake by playing cards and having sex. A micro-budget bore from director Bill Rebane, he of *The Giant Spider Invasion* and *Monster a-Go-Go* infamy, so you can't say you weren't warned. Apart from Meeker's messy death scene where his head turns to jelly, there's little incident worth commenting on in this over-talky feeble fable, which should never have left the drive-in.

John Alderman Dr Rogers • **John F Goff** Jack Tiller • **Ralph Meeker** Charlie • **Stafford Morgan** Ted Sorenson • **Carol Irene Newell** Jenny
***Director** Bill Rebane*
***Screenplay** Ingrid Neumayer*

Alphaville ★★★★ PG

1965 Fr BW 94mins

The winner of the prestigious Golden Bear at the Berlin Festival, this assured blend of sci-fi and *film noir* is perhaps Jean-Luc Godard's most accessible picture: a chilling peek into the future inspired as much by poetry and mythology as pulp fiction. Playing fast and loose with genre conventions, Godard explores themes more readily associated with Michelangelo Antonioni, as wonderfully world-weary private eye Eddie Constantine searches the far-off metropolis of Alphaville for missing scientist Akim Tamiroff. Anna Karina is genuinely affecting as the robot who discovers emotion, while cinematographer Raoul Coutard miraculously turns Paris into a soulless hell. A French language film

Eddie Constantine Lemmy Caution • **Anna Karina** Natacha Von Braun • **Akim Tamiroff** Henri Dickson • **Howard Vernon** Professor Leonard Nosferatu/Von Braun • **Laszlo Szabo** Chief engineer • **Michel Delahaye** Von Braun's assistant • **Jean-André Fieschi** Professor Heckel • **Jean-Louis Comolli** Professor Jeckell
Director/Screenplay *Jean-Luc Godard*
Producer *André Michelin*
Cinematographer *Raoul Coutard*

Alraune ★★★★

1927 Ger BW

Twice filmed in 1918 (by Eugen Illes and Michael Curtiz), the first adaptation of Hanns Heinz Ewers's Promethean novel to survive reunited the director and star of the 1914 German horror classic *The Golem*. Indeed, it shares many of that film's Frankensteinian features, as Paul Wegener's crazed scientist unleashes a monster of savage beauty by inseminating a prostitute with the sperm of an executed killer. Having played Maria in *Metropolis*, Brigitte Helm gives another entrancing performance, as Henrik Galeen (who had co-scripted *The Student of Prague* with Ewers in 1926) exploits the incestuous father-daughter liaison to explore the nature of evil.

Brigitte Helm Alraune • **Paul Wegener** Prof ten Brinken • **Ivan Petrovich** Frank Braun
Director *Henrik Galeen*
Screenplay *Henrik Galeen, from the novel by Hanns Heinz Ewers*

Alraune ★★

1930 Ger BW 103mins

Although Brigitte Helm reprised the title role of the murderous beauty whose crimes both fascinate and appal the scientist who fashioned her, Richard Oswald's reworking of Hanns Heinz Ewers's sensationalist novel has little else to recommend it. Made primarily to showcase the new medium of sound, the action is unfeasibly talky and woefully static in comparison to the atmospheric fluidity of Henrik Galeen's 1927 version. Helm once again entices, but Albert Basserman falls short of Paul Wegener's sens of awe and dismay at the cruelty of his creation. Moreover, Oswald's inquiry into sex, sin and social conditioning lacks intellectual rigour. A German language film

Brigitte Helm Alraune ten Brinken/Alma • **Albert Bassermann [Albert Basserman]** Geheimrat ten Brinken • **Harald Paulsen** Frank Braun • **Agnes Straub** Fürstin Wolkonski • **Liselotte Schaak** Olga Wolkonski • **Bernhard Goetzke** Dr Petersen
Director *Richard Oswald*
Screenplay *Charles Roellinghoff, Richard Weisbach, from the novel by Hanns Heinz Ewers*

Alraune ★★

1952 W Ger BW 90mins

According to legend, the mandrake root or mandragora is the humanoid shape that forms in semen beneath a hanged man. Such is the delightful premise of Hanns Heinz Ewers's controversial novel, which was remade for the fifth time by Arthur Maria Rabenalt, an Austrian hack who formerly made propaganda pictures for the Nazis. The notion of racial and genetic purity might have taken on even more sinister overtones in his hands were it not for his utter detachment from the project. Thus, Erich Von Stroheim is allowed to run riot as the scientist responsible for the husky Hildegarde Neff's psychotic existence. A German language film.

Hildegarde Neff Alraune • **Erich von Stroheim** Ten Brinken • **Karl Boehm [Karlheinz Böhm]** Frank Braun
Director *Arthur Maria Rabenalt*
Screenplay *Fritz Rotter, from the novel by Hanns Heinz Ewers*

Altered States ★★★ 18

1980 US Colour 98mins

Scientist William Hurt tinkers with tribal drug rituals and sensory deprivation tanks until they cause him to regress to a primitive killer-simian state of altered consciousness. The deer-eating Neanderthal man mid-section may seem too over-the-top considering the deliberately over-the-top whole, but, in general, director Ken Russell power-drives his mad doctor update with trademark visual excess. Even if celebrated screenwriter Paddy Chayefsky, who also wrote the novel on which this is based, removed his name from the film in disgust, Russell's razzle-dazzle hallucinogenic style certainly scores the freaked-out bullseye. Contains violence, swearing and nudity.

William Hurt Eddie Jessup • **Blair Brown** Emily Jessup • **Bob Balaban** Arthur Rosenberg • **Charles Haid** Mason Parrish • **Thaao Penghlis** Eccheverria • **Miguel Godreau** Primal man • **Dori Brenner** Sylvia Rosenberg • **Peter Brandon** Hobart • **Charles White Eagle** The Brujo • **Drew Barrymore** Margaret Jessup • **Megan Jeffers** Grace Jessup
Director *Ken Russell, Sidney Aaron [Paddy Chayefsky]*
Screenplay *Sidney Aaron [Paddy Chayefsky], from his novel*

Amanda & the Alien ★

1995 US Colour 95mins

If ever there was a movie crying out for a negative rating, it's this one. Nicole Eggert plays Amanda, who befriends an escaped human-eating alien on the run from the government. The alien keeps switching its human hosts – saving the producers money in special effects, and fitting well with the movie's other cheap aspects. All attempts at humour in this alleged comedy, when not making hah-hah references to other science fiction productions, are deplorably juvenile. Co-stars Michael Dorn and Stacey Keach try their best, but are visibly embarrassed just by being there.

Nicole Eggert Amanda • **Michael Dorn** Vint • **Stacy Keach** Emmitt Mallory • **Michael Bendetti** Charlie Nobles • **Alex Meneses** Connie Flores • **John Diehl** Colonel Rosencrans
Director *Jon Kroll*
Screenplay *Jon Kroll, from the story "Amanda & the Alien" by Robert Silverberg*

The Amazing Captain Nemo ★ U

TV 1978 US Colour 98mins

Seven writers including Robert Bloch, who penned the original *Psycho* novel, without a worthwhile idea between them, collaborated on the script for this ludicrous three-part TV series. José Ferrer brings nothing new to the part of the captain, who is awakened after a century in suspended animation and pitched into battle with a mad professor (Burgess Meredith) bent on world domination. Although Meredith had experience of playing arch villains (having excelled as the Penguin in the *Batman* TV series), even he is upstaged by his robot crew. A far cry from James Mason, let alone Jules Verne.

José Ferrer Captain Nemo • **Burgess Meredith** Professor Waldo Cunningham • **Tom Hallick** Commander Tom Franklin • **Burr DeBenning** Lieutenant Jim Porter • **Lynda Day George** Kate • **Mel Ferrer** Dr Robert Cook • **Richard Angarola** Trog • **Chip Fields** Rita Conway
Script consultant *Stan Lee*
Producer *Robert Janes, Ron Satlof*

SFacts

Sam Raimi's 21st-century take on the arachnid hero stars Tobey Maguire, Willem Dafoe and Kirsten Dunst, and is scheduled for release in spring 2002.

Director Alex March
Screenplay *Norman Katkov, Preston Wood, Robert C Dennis, William Keys, Mann Rubin, Robert Bloch, Larry Alexander*

The Amazing Colossal Man ★ PG

1957 US BW 79mins (video)

After being exposed to plutonium radiation, Lieutenant Colonel Glen Langan grows ten feet taller per day, puts on his best nappy and rampages through cardboard miniatures on the way to Las Vegas. Truly amazing, because this shoddy *Incredible Shrinking Man* in reverse is considered supremo schlock producer/director Bert I Gordon's best effort. And colossal, because that's exactly what it is – a colossal bore, although the giant syringe will raise hoots of derisive laughter. Sadly, little else will. The colonel was back a year later (played by Dean Parkin) in the even worse *War of the Colossal Beast*.

Glen Langan [Glenn Langan] Lieutenant Colonel Glenn Manning • **Cathy Downs** Carol Forrest • **William Hudson** Dr Paul Lindstrom • **James Seay** Colonel Hallock • **Larry Thor** Dr Eric Coulter
Director *Bert I Gordon*
Screenplay *Bert I Gordon, Mark Hanna*
Producer *Bert I Gordon*

The Amazing Spider-Man ★★ U

TV 1978-79 US Col 1x120m; 13x60m (video)

Marvel Comics' web-slinging, wall-climbing superhero swings on to the small screen, with modestly effective but far from amazing results. Former *Sound of Music* child star Nicholas Hammond likeably toplines as Peter Parker, a mild-mannered photojournalist who inherits super powers via a bite from a radioactive spider and battles crime in the heroic guise of Spider-Man. While the series lacks the energy and imagination of the original comic (and, indeed, its animated spin-offs), its routine and lightweight storylines always swing along reasonably well thanks to some competent aerial photography and action scenes, a groovy theme tune and the sheer novelty of the Spider-Man concept. The series' feature-length pilot was released theatrically in the UK and on video, as were various edited versions.

Nicholas Hammond Peter Parker/Spider-Man • **Irene Tedrow** Aunt May • **Robert F Simon** J Jonah Jameson • **Ellen Bry** Julie Masters • **Michael Pataki** Captain Barbera

The Amazing Spider-Man ★★★

Radio 1995 UK 150mins

The Marvel Comics renaissance of the early sixties came too late for the Golden Age of American radio, so characters like Spider-Man and the Fantastic Four went straight to TV cartoons without detouring to the wireless. However, in 1995, the BBC remedied the omission by broadcasting Dirk Maggs's adaptation of the classic Stan Lee-Steve Ditko *Spider-Man* comics as a serial within the Mark Goodier Show on Radio1. Ambitiously, writer/director Maggs not only covers the early career of Peter Parker (William Dufris), a teenager who gains super-powers after being bitten by a radioactive spider, but also of other Marvel stalwarts such as the Fantastic Four and Prince Namor, the Sub-Mariner (Garrick Hagon). The serial straddles a lot of sixties Marvel plotlines, and it's all a bit busy, with crashing music (theme by Brian May, incidental score by Mark Russell) and bravura American or cod-American performances, conveying all the excitement of the comics but missing out a little on the quirkier moments that made them distinctive. Available on audio-cassette and CD.

William Dufris Peter Parker/Spider-Man • **Lorelei King** Sue Storm/Betty Brant • **William Roberts** J Jonah Jameson/Uncle Ben • **Peter Marinker** Reed Richards • **Buffy Davis** Aunt May • **Jonathan Kydd** The Green Goblin • **Gary Martin** The Thing/Ben Grimm/The Dread Dormammu • **Garrick Hagon** Prince Namor • **Eric Meyers** Johnny Storm/The Human Torch • **David Bannerman** Flash Thompson • **Michael Roberts** Doctor Doom/Sandman • **Simon Treves** Doctor Octopus • **Anita Dobson** Liz Allan
Director *Dirk Maggs*
Written by *Dirk Maggs, from Marvel Comics characters created by Stan Lee*
Theme music *Brian May*

Amazing Stories ★★ U PG 15

TV 1985-1987 US Colour 45x30mins (video)

Cruelly nicknamed "unamazing stories" by critics, Steven Spielberg's first anthology series is certainly no match for *The Twilight Zone* or *The Outer Limits*, but it remains an agreeable slice of glossy entertainment. Although the show's selection of sci-fi, fantasy and horror stories tend to be a bit too conservative and unimaginative for their own good, each script is exceptionally well-realised, thanks to the series' no-expense-spared production values and ability to attract A-list talent. The show's big-name guest list is headed by the likes of Kevin Costner, Patrick Swayze, Carrie Fisher, Danny DeVito and Christopher Lloyd, while its directors include Martin Scorsese, Robert Zemeckis, Clint Eastwood, Tim Burton and Spielberg himself. Incidentally, one of the show's most popular episodes, *Family Dog*, spawned a spin-off animated series.

Ray Walston Fireside storyteller
Creative consultant *Richard Matheson*
Executive producer *Steven Spielberg*

The Amazing Transparent Man ★ U

1960 US BW 58mins

Bank robber Douglas Kennedy may be transparent, but B-movie maverick Edgar G Ulmer's low-grade *Invisible Man* is hardly amazing. Scientist Ivan Triesault invents a serum to create an army of invisible zombies, but when he experiments on convict Kennedy, he unleashes a one-man crime spree. Little of the style Ulmer brought to his cult classic *Detour* is in evidence in this impoverished quickie filmed back-to-back with Ulmer's *Beyond the Time Barrier*.

Marguerite Chapman Laura • **Douglas Kennedy** Joey Faust • **James Griffith** Krenner • **Ivan Triesault** Dr Ulof • **Boyd "Red" Morgan** Julian • **Carmel Daniel** Maria • **Edward Erwin** Drake
Director *Edgar G Ulmer*
Screenplay *Jack Lewis*

Amazon Women on the Moon ★★ 15

1987 US Colour 80mins (video)

This collection of comedy sketches spoofing commercials, sexual mores, tabloid television and old movies misses more targets than it hits. However, it's the fabulous cast of cult icons (director Russ Meyer), camp starlets (Sybil Danning) and Hollywood veterans (Ralph Bellamy) that makes this follow-up to *Kentucky Fried Movie* such a delight for cinema trainspotters. Ed Begley Jr plays a naked Invisible Man in the funniest segment.

Michelle Pfeiffer Brenda • **Rosanna Arquette** Karen • **Steve Guttenberg** Jerry • **Steve Forrest** Captain Nelson • **Joey Travolta** Butch • **David Alan Grier** Don Simmons •

Archie Hahn Harvey Pitnik • **Ed Begley Jr** Griffin • **Matt Adler** George • **Ralph Bellamy** Mr Gower • **Carrie Fisher** Mary Brown • **Sybil Danning** • **Russ Meyer**
Director *Joe Dante, Carl Gottlieb, Peter Horton, John Landis, Robert K Weiss*
Screenplay *Michael Barrie, Jim Mulholland*

America 3000 ★ 15

1986 US Colour 89mins

A typical example of the sub-standard exploitation product Cannon Films cranked out in the mid-eighties when the market for low-budget movies was at its highest. Essentially, this is an update of those chauvinistic all-female tribe movies of the fifties, with women in charge of the post-apocalypse society who treat men as slaves. Although billed as a comedy, most of it is taken so unenergetically and seriously that there's hardly any fun to be found. The few attempts at humour are remarkably heavy-handed, while redundant narration from a secondary character points to a last-ditch effort at saving the movie in the editing room.

Chuck Wagner Korvis • **Laurene Landon** Vena • **Camilla Sparv** Rhea • **Victoria Barrett** Lakella • **William Wallace** Gruss • **Sue Giosa** Morha • **Galyn Gorg** Lynka
Director/Screenplay *David Engelbach*

American Cyborg: Steel Warrior ★ 18

1993 US Colour 90mins

Yawn-inducing retread of *The Terminator* from prolific straight-to-video man Boaz Davidson. In this one, a ruthless killing machine (John P Ryan) cuts a swathe through a dreary post-apocalyptic world in a bid to find a woman (Nicole Hansen), who may be the only person capable of procreation. Joe Lara, as her kickfighting protector, is as uncharismatic as the rest of the cast and even the most dedicated genre fan will wince at the clichés.

Joe Lara Austin • **Nicole Hansen** Mary • **John P Ryan** Cyborg • **Yoseph Shiloa [Joseph Shiloach]** Akmir • **Uri Gavriel** Leech • **Hellen Lesnick** Carp • **Andrea Litt** Arlene • **Jack Widerker** Dr Buckley
Director *Boaz Davidson*
Screenplay *Brent V Friedman, Bill Crounse, Don Pequignot, from a story by Boaz Davidson, Christopher Pearce*

American Ninja 2: The Confrontation ★ 18

1987 US Colour 85mins

More formulaic martial arts mayhem, with army buddies Michael Dudikoff and Steve James reuniting to fight even more black-clad ninja hoods. Why more? Well, the bad guys have come up with a cloning machine to produce endless numbers of robotic martial arts experts and are kidnapping American marines for their nasty experiments. The performances are as wooden as ever, but the real disappointment is in the clumsy direction of the all-important biffing scenes.

Michael Dudikoff Joe • **Steve James** Jackson • **Larry Poindexter** Sergeant Charlie McDonald • **Gary Conway** Leo "The Lion" Burke • **Jeff Weston** Colonel "Wild Bill" Woodward • **Michelle Botes** Alicia Sanborn • **Michael Stone** Tojo Ken •
Director *Sam Firstenberg*
Screenplay *Gary Conway, James Booth, from a story by Gary Conway, from characters created by Avi Kleinberger, Gideon Amir*
Producer *Yoram Globus, Menahem Golan*

SCI Q

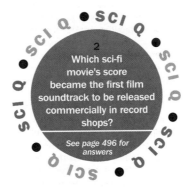

2
Which sci-fi movie's score became the first film soundtrack to be released commercially in record shops?

See page 496 for answers

Amour de Poche ★★★

1957 Fr BW 88mins

A former critic and onetime assistant to such luminaries as René Clément, Jean Renoir, Preston Sturges and Jean Grémillon, Pierre Kast made his feature debut with this adaptation of Waldemar Kaempfert's 1918 short story *The Diminishing Draft*. A variation on *The Incredible Shrinking Man* theme, it's basically a witty comedy of manners, as lab assistant Agnès Laurent is transformed into a statuette after she guzzles down Jean Marais's suspended animation formula to prevent his fiancée, Geneviève Page, from discovering their affair. The ocean-going denouement is just a tad silly, however, as the change of pace causes Kast to lose control. A French language film

Jean Marais Prof Jérôme Nordmann • **Geneviève Page** Edith Guérin • **Agnès Laurent** Simone "Monette" Landry • **France Roche** Anne-Lise Lasalle • **Régine Lovi** Brigitte, Monette's friend
Director *Pierre Kast*
Screenplay *France Roche, Pierre Kast, from the story "The Dimishing Draft" by Waldemar Kaempfert*

Amphibian Man ★★

1962 USSR Colour 77mins

One of Russia's biggest home-grown box-office hits, director Gennadi Kazansky's cross between *The Creature from the Black Lagoon* and *Romeo and Juliet* can't escape the typical Cold War atmosphere or moralising so prevalent in Soviet cinema of the day. Marine biologist Nikolai Simonov transforms his son into an amphibious creature and after "the sea devil" rescues drowning Anastasia Vertinskaya they fall in love. But she must marry a rich fisherman, so aqua boy goes into lovesick decline and finds his destiny in the oceans of the world rather than on land. A curious mixture of sternness and sentimentality. In Russian with English subtitles

Vladimir Korenev Ichthyander • **Anastasia Vertinskaya** Guttiere • **Mikhail Kozakov** Zurita • **Nikolai Simonov** Dr Salvator
Director *Gennadi Kazansky*
Screenplay *Alexei Kapler, from a novel by Alexander Belyzev*

Anchor Zone ★★

1994 Can Colour 82mins

An obscure sci-fi thriller that is reminiscent of 1997's critically acclaimed futuristic chiller *Gattaca*. Nicole Stoffman plays a member of a young elite trained into the ways of the sinister corporation that controls all aspects of life in the future. However, she begins to rebel against her regimented life, and falls in with a group of young runaways. In a largely unknown cast, Henry Czerny, of *Clear and Present Danger* fame, is suitably menacing in a smoothly villainous role.

Henry Czerny Lawson Hughes • **Nicole Stoffman** Robin • **Mark Critch** Radd • **Phelim Martin** Dogface
Director *Andrée Pelletier*
Screenplay *TH Hatte*

And Millions Will Die! ★★

1973 US Colour 93mins

An undistinguished thriller from the days when Leslie Nielsen's air of authority was still used for dramatic rather than comic purposes. He joins another TV regular, Richard Baseheart (*Voyage to the Bottom of the Sea*), in this story about an unknown force that threatens to unleash poison gas on the population of Hong Kong. It attempts to cash in on the early seventies demand for disaster movies, but there is little in the way of either star charisma or suspense. Contains violence and swearing.

Richard Basehart Dr Pruitt • **Leslie Nielsen** Gallagher • **Joseph First** Franz Kessler • **Susan Strasberg** Heather Kessler

U = SUITABLE FOR ALL Uc = SUITABLE FOR ALL, ESPECIALLY YOUNG CHILDREN (VIDEO ONLY) PG = PARENTAL GUIDANCE

Director *Leslie Martinson [Leslie H Martinson]*
Screenplay *Michael Fisher*
Producer *Mende Brown*

And You Thought Your Parents Were Weird ★★ PG

1991 US Colour 87mins

A low-budget and fairly weak family sci-fi comedy, rehashing a variety of ideas and gimmicks familiar from films including *Star Wars*, *Short Circuit* and *Forbidden Planet*. The action focuses on two boys who build a multi-talented robot from everyday household items, only to find it contains the spirit of their late father. Inoffensive, but eventually mediocre.

Marcia Strassman Sarah Carson • **Joshua Miller** Josh Carson • **Edan Gross** Max Carson • **John Quade** Irwin Kotzwinkle • **Sam Behrens** Steve Franklin • **Richard Libertini** Matthew Carson • **Alan Thicke** Newman the Robot • **Erik Walker** Dwayne Franklin • **A J Langer** Beth Allen
Director/Screenplay *Tony Cookson*

Android ★★★ 15

1982 US Colour 76mins

Three space convicts upset the plans of mad scientist Klaus Kinski to replace his companion android, Max 404, with a perfect female version in a low-key slice of cult science-fiction from the Roger Corman factory. Don Opper's portrayal of Max as a nerdy movie buff clone adds extra pop culture playfulness to the enjoyably exciting and charming proceedings, which were filmed on the same sets as *Battle beyond the Stars*. Neat suspense, a few final reel twists and another eccentric Kinski performance make this low-budget gem a high-energy winner. Contains some swearing and violence.

Klaus Kinski Dr Daniel • **Don Opper** Max 404 • **Brie Howard** Maggie • **Norbert Weisser** Keller • **Crofton Hardester** Mendes • **Kendra Kirchner** Cassandra
Director *Aaron Lipstadt*
Screenplay *Don Opper, James Reigle*

The Android Affair ★★ 12

1995 US Colour 85mins

Director Richard Kletter plumbs new depths of slow-moving mediocrity in bringing his short story *Teach 109* – co-written with sci-fi legend Isaac Asimov – to the screen. In a depressingly predictable futuristic tale, gorgeous robotics expert Harley Jane Kozak falls in love with an android called Teach 905 (played by Griffin Dunne) under the watchful eye of evil professor Ossie Davis and his assistant Saul Rubinek (wearing a ludicrous wig). Don't blame the members of the cast, though, who gamely struggle with the script, but tedium wins out in the end. Contains violence and swearing.

Harley Jane Kozak Dr Karen Garret • **Griffin Dunne** Teach 905 • **Ossie Davis** Dr Winston • **Saul Rubinek** Fiedler
Director *Richard Kletter*
Screenplay *Richard Kletter, from a short story by Isaac Asimov, Richard Kletter*

Andromeda ★★★

TV 2000 – Can/US Colour

Inspired by the work of the late Gene Roddenberry, this sci-fi action series draws from numerous Roddenberry projects, including *Planet Earth*, *Genesis II* and, of course, *Star Trek*. The show was developed as Kevin Sorbo's follow-up to *Hercules* and propels his character, noble starship captain Dylan Hunt, on a quest to rebuild the utopian galactic Commonwealth. Given the series' origins, it's hardly surprising that the second posthumous Roddenberry offering (after 1997's *Earth: Final Conflict*) feels dated, thanks to its hackneyed plotlines and unconvincing special effects. But Captain Hunt's action-packed exploits still have plenty of cheesy charm, much of which comes from Sorbo's unmistakably "Shatner-esque" central performance. The show's gorgeous female leads, Lisa Ryder and Lexa Doig, help to make the prospect of joining Hunt's quest more appealing.

Kevin Sorbo Captain Dylan Hunt • **Lisa Ryder** Beka Valentine • **Keith Hamilton Cobb** Tyr Anasazi • **Laura Bertram** Trance Gemini • **Brent Stait** Rev Bem • **Gordon Michael Woolvett** Seamus Harper • **Lexa Doig** Andromeda
Created by *Gene Roddenberry*
Executive producer *Majel Roddenberry [Majel Barrett], Allan Eastman, Adam Haight, Jay Firestone*

The Andromeda Strain ★★★★ PG

1970 US Colour 123mins

Way before the similarly themed *Outbreak* and his own blockbuster *Jurassic Park*, novelist Michael Crichton came up with a super combination of high-tech thrills and against-the-clock suspense. Robert Wise's near-documentary direction keeps tension mounting as scientists race to isolate a fatal alien virus from a fallen satellite. More science fact than fiction and still powerfully relevant, it's a faithful account of Crichton's biological invasion bestseller, layered with sophisticated special effects by Douglas Trumbull, who had helped Stanley Kubrick towards a special effects Oscar two years earlier for *2001: a Space Odyssey*.

Arthur Hill Dr Jeremy Stone • **David Wayne** Dr Charles Dutton • **James Olson** Dr Mark Hall • **Kate Reid** Dr Ruth Leavitt • **Paula Kelly** Karen Anson • **George Mitchell** Jackson • **Ramon Bieri** Major Mancheck • **Kermit Murdock** Dr Robertson • **Richard O'Brien** Grimes
Director *Robert Wise*
Screenplay *Nelson Gidding, from the novel by Michael Crichton*

The Angry Red Planet ★★ PG

1959 US Colour 79mins

A female astronaut under the influence of drugs recalls an expedition to Mars where her team are greeted by giant man-eating plants, three-eyed Martians, Cyclopean blobs, giant bat-spiders and assorted bad vibes. The cartoon-like, expressionistic special effects are red-tinted thanks to the film process "Cinemagic" to approximate the distorted, dream-like quality of Nora Hayden's drug-addled reminiscences. Renowned science-fiction director Ib Melchior gives a diverting spin to the familiar Saturday morning serial antics.

Gerald Mohr O'Banion • **Nora Hayden** Iris Ryan • **Les Tremayne** Professor Gettell • **Jack Kruschen** Sergeant Jacobs • **Paul Hahn** General Treegar • **J Edward McKinley** Professor Weiner • **Tom Daly** Dr Gordon • **Edward Innes** General Prescott
Director *Ib Melchior*
Screenplay *Ib Melchior, Sid Pink, from a story by Sid Pink*
Producer *Sid Pink*

SFacts

The "Cinemagic" process was a happy accident. Because of budget restrictions, the film was to be released in black and white and one reel came back double-exposed, with an eerie shimmer that, when tinted, made up for the minimal special effects.

Animorphs ★★★ U PG

TV 1998-2000 US/Can Col 26x30mins

KA Applegate's popular series of children's books morphs into a kiddie-pleasing live-action show. A cross between *Invasion of the Body Snatchers*, *Manimal* and *Powers Rangers*, the series follows the exploits of five ordinary youngsters who are given the ability to shape-shift into different animals and are charged with the task of saving the world from a group of parasitic aliens. The show makes the most of its capable cast and all-important animals, whose transformations are reasonably well rendered by the special effects department. And while its storylines may seem excessively well-meaning at times, the series always retains its animal attraction.

Shawn Ashmore Jake • **Brooke Nevin** Rachel • **Boris Cabrera** Marco • **Nadia-Leigh Nascimento** Cassie • **Christopher Ralph** Tobias • **Paulo Costanzo** Aximili-Esgarrouth-Isthill, "Ax" • **Richard Sali** Principal Chapman
Source *stories by KA Applegate*
Executive producer *Deborah Forte, Bill Siegler*

The Annihilator ★★★ 15

1986 US Colour 89mins

Not to be confused with *The Annihilators* (the distasteful post-Vietnam reworking of *Yojimbo* made the previous year), this is a pilot for a TV series that never saw the light of day. Directed by Michael Chapman, whose work as a cinematographer includes Martin Scorsese's *Taxi Driver* and *Raging Bull*, this suitably sinister story centres on the discovery by newspaper editor Mark Lindsay Chapman that his girlfriend has been possessed by killer humanoids during a routine flight from Hawaii. Susan Blakely and Lisa Blount lead a respectable supporting cast, which also contains the ever-dubious Brion James and Geoffrey Lewis.

Mark Lindsay Chapman Richard Armour • **Susan Blakely** Layla • **Lisa Blount** Cindy • **Brion James** Alien leader • **Earl Boen** Sid • **Geoffrey Lewis** Professor Alan Jeffries • **Catherine Mary Stewart** Angela Taylor •
Director *Michael Chapman*
Screenplay *Roderick Taylor, Bruce A Taylor*

Another Flip for Dominick ★★

TV 1982 UK Colour 85mins

A less satisfying sequel to the 1980 time-travel drama, *The Flipside of Dominick Hide*, this sends time traveller Dominick (Peter Firth) back into from the future to 1982 in search of time-lost colleague Pyrus Bonnington (Ron Berglas), whereupon he re-encounters his ancestress/lover Jane (Caroline Langrishe) and is forced to tinker with the timelines to prevent catastrophe. A refreshing aspect of the original was the oddly happy triangular relationship between Dominick and two women in different times, a precursor of *Goodnight Sweetheart*, but this follow-up gets bogged down in moralising, and both Jane and Ava (Pippa Guard) are stuck with too many nagging speeches. Among the supporting cast are Sylvia Coleridge and Michael Gough, as a professor who confuses Dominick by mistaking him for a journalist from *Time Out* magazine.

Peter Firth Dominick Hide • **Pippa Guard** Ava • **Caroline Langrishe** Jane • **Patrick Magee** Caleb Line
Director *Alan Gibson*
Written by *Jeremy Paul, Alan Gibson*
Producer *Chris Cherry*

Ape and Essence ★★★

TV 1966 UK BW 75mins

A feature-length adaptation (by John Finch) of Aldous Huxley's darkly satirical 1948 post-holocaust novel, which is written in the form of a screenplay. This stars Alec McCowen as a member of an expedition from New Zealand to a blasted Great Britain of 2048, to discover that the dominant religion is Satanism, as preached by the Arch-Vicar of Belial (Robert Eddison), and that human sacrifice is common. Women are known as "vessels" and are available for orgiastic sex, but McCowen introduces Hazel Douglas to the joys of monogamy – similar in tone to the play and film *The Bed-Sitting Room*.

Alec McCowen Alfred Poole • **Robert Eddison** Arch-Vicar • **Derek Sydney** Chief • **Petra Markham** Loola • **Hazel Douglas** Miss Hook • **Jenny Lee** Flossie
Director *David Benedictus*
Dramatisation *John Finch, from the novel by Aldous Huxley*
Producer *Peter Luke*

SCI Q

3

Who was the child star from *The Sound of Music* who went on to portray a Marvel Comics' superhero?

See page 496 for answers

A.P.E.X. ★★★ 15

1994 US Colour 98mins

Back to the Future meets *The Terminator* in another undistinguished B-movie from Phillip J Roth, the doyen of Nevada-shot sci-fi schlock (*Digital Man*). Richard Keats visits the past, gets trapped there, makes alterations and returns to 2073, with a killer cyborg in hot pursuit, to find an alternate universe thanks to a deadly virus he may have unleashed. Although efficiently directed with some notable moments (the best being the cyborg mating with a heavy metal CD), Roth doesn't have the budget, wit or imagination to pull off the ambitious concept and it quickly degenerates into a grab-bag of crude effects and amateur theatrics. Contains violence and swearing.

Richard Keats Nicholas Sinclair • **Mitchell Cox** Shepherd • **Lisa Ann Russell** Natasha Sinclair • **Marcus Aurelius** Taylor • **Adam Lawson** Rasheed • **David Jean Thomas** Dr Elgin
Director *Phillip J Roth*
Screenplay *Phillip J Roth, Ronald Schmidt, from a story by Gian Carlo Scandiuzzi, Phillip J Roth*

The Apple ★

1980 US Colour 91mins

Written and directed by Menahem Golan and co-produced with his longtime partner, Yoram Globus, this is one of the low points of Cannon's chequered history. Set in the New York of the future (well, 1994) and borrowing shamelessly from *The Rocky Horror Picture Show*, it follows the foot-tapping efforts of tunesmiths Catherine Mary Stewart and George Gilmour to deliver the world from drug-peddling villain Mr Boogalow and his demonic dance craze, The Bim. Discordant drivel best forgotten.

Catherine Mary Stewart Bibi • **George Gilmour** Alphie • **Joss Ackland** Mr Topps • **Vladek Sheybal** Mr Boogalow
Director *Menahem Golan*
Screenplay *Menahem Golan, Coby Recht, Iris Recht, from a story by Coby Recht, Iris Recht*

Arcade ★★ 15

1993 US Colour 80mins

A hot new virtual reality video game over at the Dante's Inferno arcade, run by sinister John DeLancie, feeds on teenage souls and traps them in a seven-level hell. In straight-to-video director Albert Pyun's cheap take on *Tron*, Megan Ward and Peter Billingsley must work their way to the final level of the game in order to save their friends. An assortment of digitally-enhanced landscapes and a computer brain uttering Freddy Krueger-style lines stop Pyun's cyberspace snoozer from being a complete dead loss.

Peter Billingsley Nick • **John DeLancie** Difford • **Megan Ward** Alex Manning • **Sharon Farrell** Alex's Mom • **Seth Green** Stilts • **Humberto Ortiz** Boy • **Jonathan Fuller** Arcade • **Norbert Weisser** Albert • **John DeLancie** Difford
Director *Albert Pyun*
Screenplay *David S Goyer, from an idea by Charles Band*
Executive producer *Charles Band* • ***Producer*** *Cathy Gesualdo*

Arena ★★ 15

1989 US Colour 93mins [video]

The writing and directing team behind *Eliminators* reteam for this modestly entertaining futuristic gladiator flick. Paul Satterfield plays the gentle giant whose dreams come true when he is recruited by the promoter of a no-holds-barred fight competition in space, featuring aliens from around the galaxy. Director Peter Manoogian makes the most of Danny Bilson and Paul DeMeo's knowing script and works wonders with a minimal budget. Claudia Christian in her pre-*Babylon 5* days, is the best known face in the cast.

Paul Satterfield Steve Armstrong • **Claudia Christian** Quinn • **Hamilton Camp** Shorty • **Marc Alaimo** Rogor • **Armin Shimerman** Weezil • **Shari Shattuck** Jade
Director *Peter Manoogian*
Screenplay *Danny Bilson, Paul DeMeo*

Ark II ★★

TV 1976 US Colour 15x25mins

Unimaginative and preachy Saturday morning kids show set on a 25th-century Earth devastated by war and ecological disaster. A group of squeaky-clean Americans and a talking chimp all dressed in dodgy red and silver body suits travel the land in a souped-up recreational vehicle delivering a weekly pro-eco message. Guest stars included Jonathan Harris (Dr Zachary Smith in *Lost in Space*); look out for a 13-year-old Helen Hunt in an early screen role.

Terry Lester Jonah • **Jose Flores** Samuel • **Jean Marie Hon** Ruth
Created by *Martin Roth*
Producer *Dick Bloom [Richard M Rosenbloom]*

Armageddon ★★★ 12

1998 US Colour 144mins [video] DVD

In light of 2001's *Pearl Harbor*, this megabucks popcorn-spiller from producer Jerry Bruckheimer and director Michael Bay is revealed to be a witty, post-modern exercise (by comparison anyway). There's a meteor "the size of Texas" heading for Earth – as indeed there was in *Deep Impact*, released the same year – and it's up to Bruce Willis and his motley oil-drilling gang ("the Wrong Stuff") to blast off and save us all. In hallmark Bruckheimer style, it's flashy, overwrought and excessive, but there's a knowing irony in the committee-written script and in the performances of Willis, Billy Bob Thornton and Steve Buscemi. The love subplot is a low-point, but within such an expert thrill-ride, it's not the end of the world. Contains some swearing and violence.

Bruce Willis Harry S Stamper • **Billy Bob Thornton** Dan Truman • **Ben Affleck** A J Frost • **Liv Tyler** Grace Stamper • **Keith David** General Kimsey • **Chris Ellis** Walter Clark • **Jason Isaacs** Ronald Quincy • **Will Patton** Charles "Chick" Chapple • **Steve Buscemi** Rockhound • **Ken Campbell** Max Lennert • **Charlton Heston** Narrator
Director *Michael Bay*
Screenplay *Jonathan Hensleigh, Jeffrey Abrams, from a story by Jonathan Hensleigh, Robert Roy Pool*
Producer *Jerry Bruckheimer, Gale Anne Hurd, Michael Bay*

Around the World under the Sea ★★ U

1966 US Colour 110mins

Lloyd Bridges, master scuba diver in the TV series *Sea Hunt*, spits into his mask again before investigating a series of underwater volcanic eruptions. There's some scientific chat about earthquakes and the end of the world, but mostly it's a daft yarn with a giant squid, a friendly dolphin and Shirley Eaton as the only woman in sight. It was filmed on the Great Barrier Reef and in the Bahamas by veteran director Andrew Marton, the man responsible for the chariot race sequence in *Ben-Hur*.

Lloyd Bridges Dr Doug Standish • **Shirley Eaton** Dr Maggie Hanford • **Brian Kelly** Dr Craig Mosby • **David McCallum** Dr Phil Volker • **Keenan Wynn** Hank Stahl • **Marshall Thompson** Dr Orin Hillyard • **Gary Merrill** Dr August Boren
Director *Andrew Marton*
Screenplay *Arthur Weiss, Art Arthur*

The Arrival ★★★ 18

1996 US Colour 103mins [video]

Although not in the same league as *Independence Day* or *The X Files*, director David Twohy skilfully reworks a number of science fiction clichés (as well as ideas from his *Waterworld* and *The Fugitive* scripts) to deliver a polished entry in the alien invasion sweepstakes. Charlie Sheen plays an astronomer who goes on the run after he discovers an extraterrestrial conspiracy to change the Earth's climate and prepare it for colonisation. He faces some stylish computer-generated effects at every turn, but still emerges as the winner in this pleasing, if low-key, B-movie. Contains swearing and brief nudity.

Charlie Sheen Zane Ziminski • **Ron Silver** Gordian • **Lindsay Crouse** Ilana Green • **Teri Polo** Char • **Richard Schiff** Calvin • **Tony T Johnson** Kiki
Director/Screenplay *David Twohy [David N Twohy]*

Artemis 81 ★★

TV 1981 UK Colour 185mins

David Rudkin's three-hour-long Armageddon epic is arguably one of the most arcane and baffling, some would say pretentious, productions the BBC ever committed to celluloid. Hywel Bennett plays Gideon, a student of the paranormal who discovers that an ancient pagan relic stolen from a museum contains the power to destroy the world. A convoluted narrative that worked on several levels, most of which were lost on critics and viewers, the film is notable today for its eclectic cast featuring fifties matinée idol Anthony Steel, fledgling pop star Sting, who plays Helith, the angel of love, Hammer horror siren Ingrid Pitt and the first credited screen appearance of Daniel Day-Lewis. Directed on visual overload by Alastair Reid, who found better fortune with Channel 4's controversial 1989 drug drama *Traffik*.

Hywel Bennett Gideon Harlax • **Dinah Stabb** Gwen Meredith • **Dan O'Herlighy** Von Drachenfels • **Sting** Helith • **Anthony Steel** Tristram Guise • **Margaret Whiting** Laura Guise • **Roland Curram** Asrael • **Ingrid Pitt** Hitchcock blonde
Director *Alastair Reid*
Written by *David Rudkin*
Producer *David Rose*

As Time Goes By ★

1987 Aus Colour 96mins

When the Australian film industry does science fiction well, it comes up with classics such as the *Mad Max* series. But when it misses by miles, the result is something akin to this unearthly, "adult" sci-fi spoof depicting a surfer's close encounter with an alien travelling in a UFO disguised as a forties diner (honestly!). Max Gillies plays extra-terrestrial Joe Bogart, spouting lines from old fifties space movies and also doing impressions of famous Hollywood actors. As a one-joke premise stretched extremely thinly, this quickly outstays its welcome. Contains mild swearing.

Bruno Lawrence Ryder • **Max Gillies** Joe Bogart • **Nique Needles** Mike • **Ray Barrett** J L Weston • **Marcelle Schmitz** Connie Stanton • **Deborah Force** Cheryl • **Christine Keogh** Margie • **Mitchell Faircloth** James McCauley
Director/Screenplay *Barry Peak*

The Asphyx ★★★★ 15

1972 UK Colour 82mins [video]

A thoughtful and convincing British horror oddity exploring aspects of immortality with a unique sci-fi spin. The title refers to a soul-snatching being from another dimension that approaches the body at the moment of death. Photographer Robert Stephens captures one such life form in the hope he can claim eternal life. Morbid, intriguing and acted with sensitive conviction (by Stephens, Robert Powell and Jane Lapotaire), director Peter Newbrook's cerebral chiller is a wordy Gothic drama masquerading as a supernatural terroriser. Contains violence.

Robert Stephens Hugo Cunningham • **Robert Powell** Giles Cunningham • **Jane Lapotaire** Christina Cunningham • **Alex Scott** President • **Ralph Arliss** Clive Cunningham • **Fiona Walker** Anna Cunningham • **Terry Scully** Pauper • **John Lawrence** Mason • **David Grey** Vicar • **Tony Caunter** Warden
Director *Peter Newbrook*
Screenplay *Brian Comfort*

Assassin ★★ PG

1986 US Colour 90mins

A rather dated mix of sci-fi and thrills, with Robert Conrad as the ageing agent on the trail of a robotic killer who has been reprogrammed to eliminate lots of important people. Karen Austin is the scientist whose creature has been put to misuse. Conrad does his best, but he is hardly helped by an uncharismatic supporting cast and insipid direction from TV-movie specialist Sandor Stern. Contains some violence

Robert Conrad Henry Stanton • **Karen Austin** Mary Casallas • **Richard Young** Robert Golem • **Jonathan Banks** Earl Dickman • **Robert Webber** Calvin Lantz • **Ben Frank** Franklin • **Jessica Nelson** Ann Walsh • **Nancy Lenehan** Grace Decker
Director/Screenplay *Sandor Stern*

Assignment Terror ★★

1970 Sp/It/W Ger Colour 86mins

The fourth (of nine films to date) to feature werewolf Waldemar Daninsky (portrayed by Hispanic horror star Paul Naschy) has a great central conceit, but it's ruined by Tulio Demicelli's leaden direction and Jacinto Molina's (Naschy's real name) banal script. Aliens, led by Michael Rennie, decide to conquer Earth by reviving the famous monsters of mankind's fears so they'll be too scared to fight back. Along with Daninsky, the Frankenstein Monster, Dracula and the Mummy spearhead the plan. Rennie's assistant Karin Dor (star of Hitchcock's *Topaz*) and change-of-heart Daninsky eventually scupper the eccentric invasion. Charming for five minutes, terminally boring for the remaining 80. Spanish dialogue dubbed into English.

Michael Rennie Dr Odo Warnoff • **Karin Dor** Maleva Kerstein • **Craig Hill** Kirian • **Paul Naschy** Waldemar Daninsky
Director *Tulio Demichelli, Hugo Fregonese*
Screenplay *Jacinto Molina [Paul Naschy] from his story*

Asteroid ★★

TV 1997 US Colour 2x105mins

The discovery of an asteroid on a collision course with Earth cues a four-hour scramble for survival in Bradford May's small screen rocky horror show. Genre favourite Michael Biehn and Annabella Sciorra lead a reasonable cast through all the usual tried-and-tested disaster movie conventions and some spectacular *Independence Day*-inspired special effect set pieces. Although it's poorly paced and lacks both the emotional resonance of *Deep Impact* and the sheer adrenaline rush of *Armageddon*, the mini-series generally makes for rock-solid and believable sci-fi drama. Tellingly, however, the production's running time was cut by about an hour for its US DVD release.

Michael Biehn Director Jack Wallach • **Annabella Sciorra** Dr Lily McKee • **Jensen Daggett** Dr Valerie Brennan • **Don Franklin** Ben Dodd • **Zachary B Charles** Elliot McKee • **Carlos Gomez** Adam Marquez • **Anne-Marie Johnson** Karen Dodd
Director *Bradford May*
Written by *Robbyn Burger, Scott Sturgeon*

The Astounding She-Monster ★★

1958 US BW 59mins

A super-tall female alien in a skin-tight metallic spacesuit, spangled tights and high heels lands on Earth and uses her glow-in-the-dark touch to kill. A group of loyal citizens band together to fight the intergalactic menace in a prime example of ultra-cheap fifties trash, which is so bad it's actually quite good fun. Pitiful special effects and deadly dull nocturnal strolls through the forest by the extraordinary-looking She-Monster (Shirley Kilpatrick) only add to its camp charm. Astounding it certainly is!

Robert Clarke Dick Cutler • **Kenne Duncan** Nat Burdell • **Marilyn Harvey** Margaret Chaffee • **Jeanne Tatum** Esther Malone • **Shirley Kilpatrick** Monster
Director *Ronnie Ashcroft*
Screenplay *Frank Hall*

The Astro-Zombies ★

1968 US Colour 90mins

One of the all-time worst science-fiction camp classics directed by Ted V Mikels, purveyor of the execrable exploitation films *The Corpse Grinders* and *Blood Orgy of the She-Devils*. Produced and co-scripted by Wayne Rogers (of television *MASH* fame), veteran horror actor John Carradine phones in his performances as the demented Dr DeMarco murdering for body parts in order to create skeletal zombies. Tura Satana is an agent trying to steal DeMarco's scientific secrets for a foreign power. They're welcome to them – and the one claustrophobic set the micro-budget could afford – in this truly terrible turkey.

Wendell Corey Holman • **John Carradine** Dr DeMarco • **Tom Pace** Eric Porter • **Joan Patrick** Janine Norwalk • **Rafael Campos** Juan • **Tura Satana** Satanna • **William Bagdad** Franchot • **Vincent Barbi** Tiros • **Joseph Hoover** Chuck Edwards
Director *Ted V Mikels*
Screenplay *Ted V Mikels, Wayne Rogers*

Astronauts ★★

TV 1981/1983 UK Colour 7x30mins

This seven-episode sit-com, written by ex-Goodies Graeme Garden and Bill Oddie, prefigured the theme of *Red Dwarf* with three contrasting characters – pukka RAF officer Malcolm Mattocks (Christopher Godwin), slobbish techie David Ackroyd (Barrie Rutter) and semi-vamp doctor Gentian Foster (Carmen Du Sautoy), plus dog (Bimbo) – spending a long time in close confinement in what was described as "a tin bed-sit", the orbiting Sky Lab. Their mission commander, blimpish Yank Colonel Beadle (Bruce Boa), keeps constant surveillance on the crew as they get on each others' nerves, come close to cracking up and more or less cope with routine crises. It could have been funnier.

Christopher Godwin Cmdr Malcolm Mattocks • **Carmen Du Sautoy** Dr Gentian Foster • **Barrie Rutter** Technical Officer David Ackroyd • **Bruce Boa** Beadle
Director *Douglas Argent*
Written by *Graeme Garden, Bill Oddie*
Executive producer *Alan McKeown*

The Astronaut's Wife ★★★★ 18

1999 US Colour 109mins DVD

Rand Ravich's directorial debut is a psychological thriller that's refreshingly free of shock clichés and the usual baggage associated with *Quatermass*-inspired science fiction. Charlize Theron is wonderful as Johnny Depp's distressed and puzzled spouse, who notices alarming differences in her husband's behaviour after he survives a space mission accident. Enhanced by inventive camera angles and stunning production design (by *Gattaca*'s Jan Roelfs), this stylish entry into insidious invasion territory is an engrossing nightmare that is alarmingly believable. Contains sex scenes and swearing.

Johnny Depp Spencer Armacost • **Charlize Theron** Jillian Armacost • **Joe Morton** Sherman Reese • **Clea DuVall** Nan • **Samantha Eggar** Doctor • **Donna Murphy** Natalie Streck • **Nick Cassavetes** Alex Streck • **Gary Grubbs** NASA director
Director/Screenplay *Rand Ravich*
Cinematographer *Allen Daviau*
Production designer *Jan Roelfs*

At the Earth's Core ★★ PG

1976 UK Colour 86mins

Victorian explorer Doug McClure and fidgety scientist Peter Cushing encounter all manner of rubber monsters as they burrow through the earth with a giant boring device – yes, there is another apart from the film itself – to the subterranean kingdom of Pellucidar. This childish and chintzy Edgar Rice Burroughs adaptation would be an even bigger patience-tester if not for sultry heroine Caroline Munro and the truly awful man-in-suit special effects, which will inspire hoots of laughter rather than the intended sense of wonder.

Doug McClure David Innes • **Peter Cushing** Dr Abner Perry • **Caroline Munro** Dia • **Cy Grant** Ra • **Godfrey James** Ghak • **Sean Lynch** Hooja • **Michael Crane** Jubal
Director *Kevin Connor*
Screenplay *Milton Subotsky, from the novel by Edgar Rice Burroughs*

Atlantis, the Lost Continent ★★

1961 US Colour 90mins

Famed producer/director George Pal came unstuck with this silly fantasy adventure after winning praise for his *The War of the Worlds* and *The Time Machine*. Anthony Hall is the young Greek sailor facing danger, intriguing animal men and atomic death rays in the final days of the fabled city before it slips into the deep thanks to a volcanic eruption. Even the special effects are below sea level in this uneasy mix of comic-book science fiction and tacky sand-and-sandal epic that Pal set at the time of the Roman Empire so he could borrow footage from *Quo Vadis* to pep it up.

Anthony Hall [Sal Ponti] Demetrios • **Joyce Taylor** Antillia • **John Dall** Zaren • **Bill Smith [William Smith]** Captain of the guard • **Edward Platt** Azor • **Frank DeKova** Sonoy • **Berry Kroeger** Surgeon • **Edgar Stehli** King Kronas • **Wolfe Barzell** Petros
Director *George Pal*
Screenplay *Daniel Mainwaring, from a play by Gerald Hargreaves*

Atom Age Vampire ★★

1960 It/Fr BW 87mins

Although shoddily staged and directed by Anton Giulio Majano, this routine guilty pleasure reaches heights of sleazy delirium because of its disfigurement plot. Mad doctor Alberto Lupo (specialising in Hiroshima bomb victims) falls in love with scarred stripper Susanne Loret and restores her beauty via a serum formulated from the glands of women he murders when transformed into a rampaging hideous monster. Spuriously linked to the late fifties trendy "atomic horror" angle by pre-credits nuclear blast documentary footage, Majano's badly-dubbed Sadean shocker boasts impressive black-and-white atmospherics making it a worthwhile time-waster for Italian genre addicts. An Italian language film

Alberto Lupo Prof Alberto Levin • **Susanne Loret** Jeannette • **Sergio Fantoni** Pierre
Director *Anton Guilio Majano*
Screenplay *Anton Guilio Majano, Piero Monviso, Gino De Santis, Alberto Bevilacqua*

Atom Man vs Superman ★★★ U

1950 US BW 15x16mins

This proficient chapter-play from veteran B-hiver Spencer Gordon Bennet is notable for the introduction of the Man of Steel's arch-nemesis, Lex Luthor. Bestriding the screen, Lyle Talbot is magnificent as the Atom Man, who uses a hunk of synthetic kryptonite to diminish Superman's powers, while he runs riot around Metropolis with a disintegrator that can reduce people to their basic atoms to be reassembled at his whim. Moreover, he also plans to kidnap Lois Lane and sweep her off into outer space. Naturally, Kirk Alyn triumphs in the end. But there's no doubting who wins in the acting stakes.

Kirk Alyn Clark Kent/Superman • **Noel Neill** Lois Lane • **Lyle Talbot** Luthor/Atom Man • **Pierre Watkin** Perry White • **Tommy Bond** Jimmy Olsen
Director *Spencer Gordon Bennet*
Screenplay *George H Plympton, Joseph Poland, David Mathews*

Atom Squad ★★

TV 1953-1954 US BW 125x15mins

Broadcast live from Philadelphia in 15-minute episodes every weekday for six months, this series followed the efforts of a counter-intelligence agency charged with protecting America's super-scientific secrets from evil foreigners – mostly sneaky Soviets, with a few leftover Nazis in the mix. Our square-jawed, hat-wearing heroes were Robert Courtleigh and Bob Hastings, while their laconically-named chief was Bram Nossen. Although their usual quarry was spies and mad scientists, a few flying saucers and aliens popped up (*Stranger from Outer Space*, *The Fugitives from Galaxy 29*). The duo were always after villains who sought to use devices that could stop the moon in its orbit or melt the polar ice caps, and they would always catch them well before there was any risk of such gadgets being turned on and expensive special effects being required. One episode, *The Trouble at Fort Knox*, prefigured the plot of *Goldfinger* as villains irradiate rather than steal the nation's gold reserve.

Robert Courtleigh Steve Elliott • **Bob Hastings** Dave Fielding • **Bram Nossem** Chief
Producer *Adrian Samish*

SCI Q

4
What was the first sci-fi TV series to spawn a movie?

See page 496 for answers

The Atomic Kid ★★ U

1954 US BW 85mins

Made at a time when nuclear power could be treated as a joke, this happy-go-lucky tosh has Mickey Rooney as a prospector who survives an atomic test in the desert and finds he's immune to radiation. His special powers come in handy when he helps the FBI catch a ring of communist spies. The story is by Blake Edwards, who went on to make such comic gems as *10*. This film, however, is more of a four.

Mickey Rooney Blix Waterberry • **Robert Strauss** Stan Cooper • **Elaine Davis** Audrey Nelson • **Bill Goodwin** Dr Rodell • **Whit Bissell** Dr Edgar Pangborn • **Joey Forman** MP in Hospital • **Hal March** Ray
Director *Leslie H Martinson*
Screenplay *Benedict Freedman, John Fenton Murray, from a story by Blake Edwards*

The Atomic Submarine ★★ PG

1960 US BW 67mins

Endearing hokum about an underwater alien, with a nicely-sustained tense atmosphere from director Spencer Gordon Bennet. But the real star of this B-movie is producer Alex Gordon, who assembled a memorable cast for movie buffs. The nominal star is Arthur Franz (*The Sniper*, *Invaders from Mars*) and in support are a veritable clutch of familiar faces, all past their sell-by date, including amiable veteran Dick Foran from *The Petrified Forest*, George Sanders's older brother Tom Conway and former cowboy star Bob Steele. The obligatory blonde is Frank Sinatra's one-time girlfriend Joi Lansing.

Arthur Franz Reef • **Dick Foran** Wendover • **Brett Halsey** Carl • **Tom Conway** Sir Ian Hunt • **Paul Dubov** Dave • **Bob Steele** Griff • **Victor Varconi** Kent • **Joi Lansing** Julie • **Selmer Jackson** Admiral • **Jack Mulhall** Murdock • **Jean Moorhead** Helen

Director *Spencer G Bennet [Spencer Gordon Bennet]*

Screenplay *Orville H Hampton*

Atragon ★★ U

1963 Jap Colour 89mins

The Atlantis myth goes Oriental in this reasonable slice of Jules Verne-slanted sci-fi action from director Inoshiro (*Godzilla*) Honda. The ancient undersea kingdom of Mu has harnessed energy from the centre of the Earth and intends to conquer the surface world by causing devastating earthquakes and tidal waves. The world's only hope is Captain Shinguji's atomic powered super-submarine *Atragon*, built during the Second World War but never used during that conflict, which also has the ability to fly and traverse land. Special effects maestro Eiji Tsuburaya provides the *Nautilus*-inspired sub, sea serpent and final orgy of epic noisy destruction. Japanese dialogue dubbed into English.

Tadao Takashima Commercial photographer Susumu Hatanaka • **Yoko Fujiyama** Makoto Shinguji, the captain's daughter • **Yu Fujiki** Captain Shinguji • **Kenji Sahara** Mu agent Uchino • **Akemi Kita** • **Tetsuko Kobayashi** Empress of Mu • **Jun Tazaki**

Director *Inoshiro Honda*

Screenplay *Shinichi Sekizawa*

Attack of the Crab Monsters ★★★

1957 US BW 62mins

Atomic testing on a remote Pacific island causes the crab population to mutate into giant monsters in one of cult director Roger Corman's earliest successes. The *King Kong* crustaceans look shoddy and laughable (you can often glimpse the stuntmen's feet under the costumes), but Charles Griffith's script successfully mines the concept for keen menace and gruesome shock. (The crabs decapitate victims and eat the heads in order to assimilate their brain power.) Lunatic but fast-moving fun.

Richard Garland Dale Drewer • **Pamela Duncan** Martha Hunter • **Russell Johnson** Hank Chapman • **Leslie Bradley** Dr Karl Weigand • **Mel Welles** Jules Deveroux • **Richard Cutting** Dr James Carson • **Beach Dickerson** Ron Fellows

Director *Roger Corman*

Screenplay *Charles Griffith*

Producer *Roger Corman*

Attack of the 50 Ft Woman ★★

1958 US BW 65mins

Although it's no more than a barely competent example of low-budget fifties sci-fi, this poverty-row cheapie directed by Nathan Hertz (more usually known as Nathan Juran) has come to be regarded as a legendary absurd classic. There's a strangely contemporary feminist slant to the tale, with Allison Hayes teaching her cheating husband a major lesson after a bald alien turns her into a giantess, clothed in a bedsheet bikini. However, with the effects at their least special, Hayes's accelerating voluptuousness also exerts a curious fascination, proving once and for all that size isn't everything.

Allison Hayes Nancy Archer • **William Hudson** Harry Archer • **Roy Gordon** Dr Cushing • **Yvette Vickers** Honey Parker • **Ken Terrell** Jessup Stout • **George Douglas** Sheriff Dubbitt • **Otto Waldis** Dr von Loeb • **Frank Chase** Charlie • **Eileene Stevens** Nurse

Director *Nathan Hertz [Nathan Juran]*

Screenplay *Mark Hanna*

Attack of the 50 Ft Woman ★★ 12

1993 US Colour 89mins

A pointless revamp of the beloved 1958 cult classic that often looks cheesier than its inspiration. Daryl Hannah narrates and stars as the rich, unhappy wife, abused by both her unfaithful husband and her uncaring father, who takes revenge when she grows to monstrous proportions after being zapped by an alien ray. Christopher Guest (best known for *This Is Spinal Tap* and for being Jamie Lee Curtis's husband) directs half-heartedly, missing more satirical targets than he hits in an attempt to match the fun incompetence of the original – only in the special effects area does he manage that! Contains mild swearing and brief nudity.

Daryl Hannah Nancy Archer • **Daniel Baldwin** Harry Archer • **William Windom** Hamilton Cobb • **Frances Fisher** Dr Cushing • **Christi Conaway** Honey • **Paul Benedict** Dr Loeb • **O'Neal Compton** Sheriff Denby • **Victoria Haas** Deputy Charlie Spooner

Director *Christopher Guest*

Screenplay *Joseph Dougherty, from the 1958 film*

Attack of the Killer Tomatoes ★ PG

1978 US Colour 86mins

Behind an irresistible title lurks one of the worst movies ever made. Deliberately planned as a bad movie from the start, the fact that director John DeBello totally achieves his aim is the only good thing to say about this dire spoof, in which giant tomatoes rampage through San Diego to avenge fruit mistreatment. It's all downhill after the fun title song, as intentionally awful special effects (the tomatoes are beach balls), ludicrous dialogue and low camp turns this parody of monster movies into a mind-numbing splatter bore. Still, it did spawn three sequels (one of which starred George Clooney) and a television cartoon show.

David Miller Mason Dixon • **George Wilson** Jim Richardson • **Sharon Taylor** Lois Fairchild • **Jack Riley** Agricultural official • **Rock Peace** Wilbur Finletter • **Eric Christmas** Senator Polk • **Al Sklar** Ted Swan • **Ernie Meyers** President

Director *John DeBello*

Screenplay *Costa Dillon, John DeBello, Steve Peace*

Producer *Steve Peace, John DeBello*

Attack of the Puppet People ★★

1958 US BW 78mins

Doll manufacturer John Hoyt gets lonely and starts reducing people to marionette size so they'll be his obedient "friends" in this routine riff on *The Incredible Shrinking Man* from veteran copycat exploitation director Bert I Gordon. John Agar is the rebel rocker who leads five other miniature companions on a mission to return to normal dimensions. Featuring better special effects than usual for a Gordon groaner (for example *Earth vs the Spider*) and a nice tongue-in-cheek flavour, Agar and June Kenney border on the annoying as plucky puppet folk, while Hoyt does a side-splitting turn as the kindly maniac.

John Agar Bob Westley • **John Hoyt** Mr Franz • **June Kenney** Sally Reynolds • **Michael Mark** Emil • **Kenny Miller** Stan

Director *Bert I Gordon*

Screenplay *George Worthing Yates, from a story by Bert I Gordon*

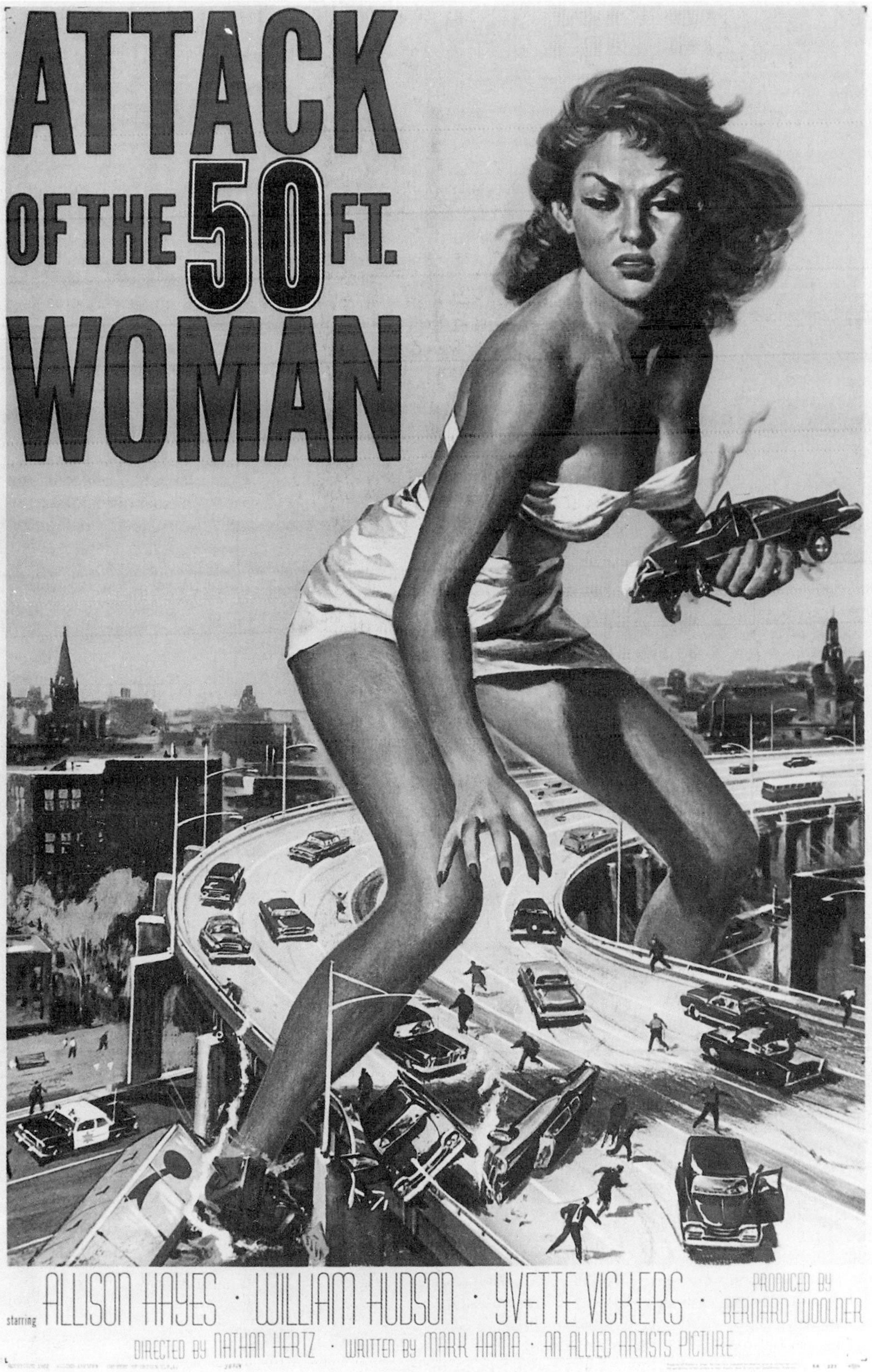

Tall story: despite a small budget and absurd storyline, *Attack of the 50 Ft Woman* has become a cult classic

August in the Water ★★★

1995 Jap Colour 117mins

As Fukuoka City swelters in drought-inducing heat and its citizens fall prey to a mysterious epidemic, champion diver Rena Komine emerges from a coma and begins to experience visions of a rock face which resembles the meteorites that have recently been falling to earth. A hybrid of Leni Riefenstahl's *Olympia* and Andrei Tarkovsky's *Solaris*, Sogo Ishii's visually sumptuous sci-fi puzzle could all too easily be dismissed as mystical tosh. It's certainly self-consciously obscure. While so many films hammer home their messages, however, it's rather refreshing to watch something that makes you search for enlightenment. A Japanese language film.

Shinsuke Aoki Mao • **Rena Komine** Izumi • **Reiko Matsuo** Miki • **Masaaki Takarai** Ukiya • **Naho Toda** Yo

Director/Screenplay *Sogo Ishii*

The Aurora Encounter ★★★ U

1985 US Colour 86mins

Good performances and some neat special effects lift this drama from being yet another run-of-the-mill alien-on-Earth fantasy. It's the Old West at the end of the last century when a powerful but cute little alien turns up to give the locals a scare. Not exactly brain-straining stuff, but an entertaining watch for fantasy fans just the same. Contains mild swearing.

Jack Elam Charlie • **Peter Brown** Sheriff • **Carol Bagdasarian** Alain • **Dottie West** Irene • **Will Mitchell** Ranger • **Charles B Pierce** Preacher • **Mickey Hays** Aurora spaceman • **Spanky McFarland** Governor

Director *Jim McCullough Sr*

Screenplay *Jim McCullough Jr*

Automan ★★

TV 1983-1984 US Colour 1x90m; 12x60m

Although its science-fiction premise was ahead of the wave, this was still a vacuous one-season Glen A Larson superhero series of no particular distinction. Police computer expert Walter Nebicher (Desi Arnaz Jr) creates a crime-fighting hologram called Automan (Chuck Wagner), which partners him in the pursuit of the usual round of crooked politicians, big-time gangsters, mad geniuses and petty hoods. Wagner's character seems visually patterned after the creations of the film *Tron*, but the world he inhabits is mundane, miring the show in the tradition established by the fifities *Superman* TV show: that the hero could be a fantastical, super-powered creation, but the villains were just ordinary criminals.

Desi Arnaz Jr Walter Nebicher • **Chuck Wagner** Automan • **Robert Lansing** Lt Jack Curtis • **Gerald S O'Loughlin** Capt EG Boyd • **Heather McNair** Roxanne Caldwell

Producer/Created by *Glen A Larson*

Automatic ★★★ 15

1994 US Colour 86mins

A cutting-edge electronics corporation tries to hush up a homicidal fault that develops within its top secret prototype, a cyborg bodyguard/servant called J269 (Oliver Gruner), by sending in a SWAT team to eliminate it. Unfortunately lowly secretary (Daphne Ashbrook) has witnessed the murderous glitch and will have to be erased, too. An effective, well-mounted action thriller in the *Die Hard* mould that treads old ground with fresh verve. Contains swearing and violence.

Olivier Gruner J269 • **Daphne Ashbrook** Nora Rochester • **John Glover** Goddard Marx • **Jeff Kober** Major West • **Penny Johnson** Julia Rodriguez • **Marjean Holden** Epsilon leader • **Dennis Lipscomb** Raymond Hammer

Director *John Murlowski*

Screenplay *Susan Lambert, Patrick Highsmith*

The Avengers ★★★★★ U PG

TV 1960-1968 UK BW and Colour

One of the all-time cult shows and one of the few British TV exports to hit it big in America, this pre-Bond slice of spy hokum started life with Ian Hendry in the lead role of a crusading doctor out to "avenge", hence the show's title, the death of his fiancée, ably assisted by mysterious agent John Steed. When Hendry left to pursue a cinema career Patrick Macnee's Steed character took centre stage and then the series really hit its stride with the introduction of leather-clad, judo expert Cathy Gale (Honor Blackman), while Blackman's replacement, the unknown Diana Rigg, made an instant impact as Emma Peel. The show's emphasis changed, too, from standard thriller plotlines to a more sci-fi orientated approach with mad scientists, man-eating plants and killer robots, a formula that reached even giddier heights of psychedelic excess in the Linda Thorson post-Rigg era. Combining surreal humour, quintessential English charm and a plethora of guest stars, *The Avengers* was sold to over 70 countries and remains just about unsurpassed in British fantasy drama.

Patrick Macnee Steed • **Honor Blackman** Cathy Gale • **Diana Rigg** Emma Peel • **Linda Thorson** Tara King • **Ian Hendry** Dr David Keel

Devised by *Leonard White*

The Avengers ★ 12

1998 US Colour 85mins DVD

The cult sixties TV series gets royally shafted by Hollywood in a stunningly designed blockbuster that's stunningly awful in every other department. Ralph Fiennes and Uma Thurman couldn't be more miscast as John Steed and Emma Peel, here trying to stop Sean Connery holding the world's weather to ransom and freezing London to an arctic standstill. Ruthlessly edited before release and packed with arch one-liners, bad puns and vulgar double entendres, this is misguided and misbegotten to a simply staggering degree, while Jeremiah Chechik's mannered direction screeches the action to an unexciting halt at every flat turn. Contains some violence and swearing.

Ralph Fiennes John Steed • **Uma Thurman** Doctor Emma Peel • **Sean Connery** Sir August De Wynter • **Jim Broadbent** Mother • **Fiona Shaw** Father • **Eddie Izzard** Bailey • **Eileen Atkins** Alice • **John Wood** Tribshaw • **Carmen Ejogo** Brenda • **Keeley Hawes** Tamara • **Shaun Ryder** Donavan • **Patrick Macnee** Invisible Jones

Director *Jeremiah Chechik*

Screenplay *Don MacPherson*

Producer *Jerry Weintraub*

Production designer *Stuart Craig*

The Awful Dr Orloff ★★ 15

1962 Sp/Fr BW 90mins

Trash-meister Jess Franco's incredible directing career took off with this graphic Spanish shocker (which credits the director as Norbert Moutier, one of many pseudonyms he has taken to avoid France's strict quota laws), in which demented Howard Vernon kidnaps starlets to perform skin-graft operations on his disfigured daughter. Franco's early gore landmark is rather talky by today's standards, but the expressionistic black-and-white photography still impresses even if the tacky tinsel terror charts familiar sixties territory. It spawned four sequels. Contains violence and nudity.

Howard Vernon Dr Orloff • **Conrado San Martin** Inspector Tanner • **Diana Lorys** Wanda Bronsky • **Perla Cristal** Arne

Director *Norbert Moutier [Jesus Franco]*

Screenplay *Jesus Franco, from the novel "Gritos en la Noche " by David Khune [Jesus Franco]*

B

"If only you could see what I've seen with your eyes..."

"I've seen things you people wouldn't believe. Attack ships on fire off the shoulder of Orion. I watched C-beams glitter in the dark near the Tannhauser gate. All those moments will be lost in time, like tears in rain."

Blade Runner 1982

Babylon 5 ★★★★★ PG 12

TV 1993-1999 US 110x60mins

Imaginatively conceived as a "five-year novel for television", J Michael Straczynski's 23rd-century space station saga charts Babylon 5's mission to keep the peace in a galaxy on the verge of war. A sumptuous feast of clever plot development, compelling characterisation and strong special effects, the series successfully forms one of TV's most sweeping and exhilarating sci-fi adventures to date. The extremely likeable Bruce Boxleitner assumes command in season two and comfortably leads an intriguing ensemble of diverse performers through a sequence of cataclysmic cosmic changes. Not even the comic-book dialogue, clumsy humour or extremely lacklustre fifth season can undermine the sheer brilliance of Straczynski's vision, or the enormous impact of watching the consistently surprising and rewarding saga unfold. Followed by four lacklustre telemovies and the equally disappointing *Crusade*.

Bruce Boxleitner John Sheridan • **Claudia Christian** Susan Ivanova • **Jerry Doyle** Michael Garibaldi • **Mira Furlan** Delenn • **Richard Biggs** Dr Stephen Franklin • **Bill Mumy** Lennier • **Stephen Furst** Vir Cotto • **Andreas Katsulas** G'Kar • **Peter Jurasik** Mollari • **Walter Keonig** Alfred Bester • **Pat Tallman** Lyta Alexander • **Michael O'Hare** Jeffrey Sinclair/Valen
Created by *J Michael Straczynski*
Executive producer *J Michael Straczynski, Douglas Netter* • ***Producer*** *John Copeland*

Back to the Future ★★★★★ PG

1985 US Colour 111mins

This irresistible combination of dazzling effects and sly comedy propelled Michael J Fox to stardom and Robert Zemeckis to the front rank of Hollywood directors. And time has not robbed it of any of its vitality. Fox plays the young student who travels back in time to the fifties and acts as matchmaker for his future parents, who are showing no signs of falling in love. It's beautifully played by the cast (honourable mentions to Christopher Lloyd, Lea Thompson and Crispin Glover), making the most of an ingenious script from Bob Gale and Zemeckis, which finds time to poke fun at fifties icons and lifestyles between time travelling. Zemeckis's direction is equally adroit and he never lets the effects swamp the film. Contains some swearing.

Michael J Fox Marty McFly • **Christopher Lloyd** Dr Emmett Brown • **Lea Thompson** Lorraine Baines • **Crispin Glover** George McFly • **Thomas F Wilson** Biff Tannen • **Claudia Wells** Jennifer Parker • **Marc McClure** Dave McFly • **Wendie Jo Sperber** Linda McFly • **George DiCenzo** Sam Baines • **James Tolkan** Mr Strickland
Director *Robert Zemeckis*
Screenplay *Robert Zemeckis, Bob Gale*

Back to the Future Part II

★★★ PG

1989 US Colour 103mins

After the success of the first time-travelling caper a sequel was inevitable, although this time around director Robert Zemeckis is guilty of over-gilding the lily. Stars Michael J Fox and Christopher Lloyd are back, along with Lea Thompson and Thomas F Wilson, but the film gets bogged down by trying to cram in too many ideas and settings. The effects, however, are even better than in the first film, and the cast certainly enjoys itself in a baffling array of roles. Contains some swearing and violence.

Michael J Fox Marty McFly/Marty McFly Jr /Marlene McFly • **Christopher Lloyd** Dr Emmett Brown • **Lea Thompson** Lorraine • **Thomas F Wilson** Biff Tannen/Griff Tannen • **Harry Waters Jr** Marvin Berry • **Charles Fleischer** Terry • **Joe Flaherty** Western Union Man • **Elisabeth Shue** Jennifer • **James Tolkan** Strickland • **Jeffrey Weissman** George McFly
Director *Robert Zemeckis*
Screenplay *Bob Gale, from a story by Bob Gale, Robert Zemeckis*

Back to the Future Part III

★★★★ PG

1990 US Colour 113mins

Director Robert Zemeckis's blockbusting trilogy went slightly off the rails with the second segment, but it got right back on

Last great hope: compelling characters made the gripping saga of *Babylon 5* an enduring success

track (literally) with the concluding instalment. Shot back-to-back with *Part II*, the film is set predominantly in the old West and offers Michael J Fox the chance to indulge in all the sharpshooting situations that made Saturday matinée western serials such a treat for millions of children (including, one suspects, Zemeckis and screenwriter Bob Gale). As before, the plot revolves around the need to tinker with time and the problem of how to power the trusty DeLorean car so that Fox can get back to the present. And once more Gale and Zemeckis have come up with an ingenious plot and a clutch of in-jokes, including the casting of western favourites Dub Taylor, Harry Carey Jr and Pat Buttram as a trio of old timers in the saloon. The inimitable Fox is again on cracking form as Marty McFly and Christopher Lloyd's romance with Mary Steenburgen is surprisingly touching. Using the special effects intelligently, Zemeckis stages a spectacular steam-train finale and neatly ties up the trilogy's loose ends. Look out for a cameo appearance from ZZ Top. Contains some swearing.

Michael J Fox Marty McFly/Seamus McFly • **Christopher Lloyd** "Doc" Emmett Brown • **Mary Steenburgen** Clara Clayton • **Thomas F Wilson** Buford "Mad Dog" Tannen/Biff Tannen • **Lea Thompson** Maggie McFly/Lorraine McFly • **Elisabeth Shue** Jennifer • **Matt Clark** Bartender • **Richard Dysart** Barbed wire salesman • **James Tolkan** Marshal Strickland • **Pat Buttram** Saloon old timer • **Harry Carey Jr** Saloon old timer • **Dub Taylor** Saloon old timer

Director *Robert Zemeckis*

Screenplay *Bob Gale, from a story by Bob Gale, Robert Zemeckis*

Bad Channels ★ 15

1992 US Colour 78mins [video]

Disc jockey "Dangerous" Dan O'Dare (Paul Hipp) is held hostage by a bug-like alien and its cute robot sidekick, during a record marathon at Radio 666 in this straight-to-video rock satire from director Ted Nicolaou, an in-house director of producer Charles Band's Full Moon video company. Lame spoofs of pop promos – two featuring forgettable songs by Blue Oyster Cult – battle with the terrible special effects and the dumb comedy for what really lies at the bottom of this boring barrel.

Paul Hipp Dan O'Dare • **Martha Quinn** Lisa • **Michael Huddleston** Corky • **Charlie Spradling** Cookie • **Daryl Strauss** Bunny • **Melissa Behr** Ginger • **Victor Rogers** Sheriff Hickman

Director *Ted Nicolaou*

Screenplay *Jackson Barr, from an idea by Charles Band*

Bad Taste ★★★★ 18

1987 NZ Colour 87mins [video]

Director Peter Jackson is making an epic live-action version of *The Lord of the Rings* in his native New Zealand, but this cheerfully disgusting horror comedy was his first full-length feature. Jackson, who received an Oscar nomination for 1994's psychological drama *Heavenly Creatures* (the film that launched the screen career of Kate Winslet), here directs in chaotic fashion, with large quantities of gore, flying viscera, macabre humour and wild special effects. Indeed, this man-eating alien invasion, made over a five-year period, remained the bloody benchmark of sci-fi horror until Jackson topped it himself five years later with *Braindead*. The title says it all, so those of a sensitive nature be warned.

Peter Jackson Derek/Robert • **Mike Minett** Frank • **Peter O'Herne** Barry • **Terry Potter** Ozzy • **Craig Smith** Giles • **Doug Wren** Lord Crumb

Director/Screenplay *Peter Jackson*

The Bamboo Saucer ★★★

1968 US Colour 100mins

The great Dan Duryea swansonged with this cut-price thriller, which was re-released a year later as *Collision Course*. With Vietnam rather than the usual Cold War providing the political impetus, US Secret Service official Duryea is prepared to collaborate with Lois Nettleton's Soviet mission in order to locate an alien spaceship that appears to have crash-landed in the mountains of Maoist China. The decision to take the craft for a spin seems far-fetched, but it furnishes Frank Telford (who has built the suspense steadily) with the opportunity for a grandstand finish.

Dan Duryea Hank Peters • **John Ericson** Fred Norwood • **Lois Nettleton** Anna Karachev • **Bob Hastings** Garson • **Vincent Beck** Zagorsky • **Bernard Fox** Ephram • **Robert Dane** Miller • **Rico Cattani** Dubovsky • **James Hong** Sam Archibald

Director *Frank Telford*

Screenplay *Frank Telford, from a story by Rip Von Ronkel, John P Fulton*

Barb Wire ★ 18

1995 US Colour 100mins [video]

"Don't call me babe!" scowls Pamela Anderson Lee, as she roves around Steel Harbor zapping agents of the Congressional Directorate. OK, providing you don't ask us to call this insulting reworking of *Casablanca* a film. Betraying his pop-video background with just about every shot, director David Hogan clearly isn't interested in storytelling, which is just as well as he doesn't have much of a tale to tell. Even amid the devastation of a second American civil war, surely more will stand between the people and tyranny than magical contact lenses? Despite being treated like a computer generated cartoon, Pam takes it all in surprisingly good part. Contains violence, swearing and nudity.

Pamela Anderson Lee [Pamela Anderson] Barb Wire • **Temuera Morrison** Axel Rood • **Victoria Rowell** Cora D • **Jack Noseworthy** Charlie • **Xander Berkeley** Alexander Willis

Director *David Hogan*

Screenplay *Chuck Pfarrer, Ilene Chaiken, from a story by Ilene Chaiken*

Barbarella ★★★ 15

1967 Fr/It Colour 93mins [video]

The famed French comic strip comes to glorious psychedelic life in director Roger Vadim's 40th-century space opera. Once you get past Jane Fonda's infamous anti-gravity striptease however, the script turns rather dull and the imaginative sets steal the whole show as Fonda's nubile intergalactic bimbo experiences close encounters of the sexually bizarre kind. A pleasure machine, cannibalistic dolls and Anita Pallenberg's Black Queen help ease the verbal vacuum in Vadim's relentless visual assault, which is sure to delight some and prove tiresome to others. Contains violence and sex scenes.

Jane Fonda Barbarella • **John Phillip Law** Pygar • **Anita Pallenberg** Black Queen • **Milo O'Shea** Concierge/Durand-Durand • **David Hemmings** Dildano • **Marcel Marceau** Professor Ping • **Ugo Tognazzi** Mark Hand • **Claude Dauphin** President of Earth • **Catherine Chevalier** Stomoxys • **Marie Therese Chevalier** Glossina • **Serge Marquand** Captain Sun • **Veronique Vendell** Captain Moon • **Sergio Ferrero** Black Queen's messenger

Director *Roger Vadim*

Screenplay *Terry Southern, Brian Degas, Claude Brulé, Jean-Claude Forest, Clement Biddle Wood, Tudor Gates, Vittorio Bonicelli, Roger Vadim, from the comic by Jean-Claude Forest*

Producer *Dino De Laurentiis*

Barney's Great Adventure ★★★ U

1998 US Colour 73mins [video]

Television's popular purple dinosaur magically appears to teach three vacationing youngsters all about the worlds of the farmyard and the circus as they undertake a quest to find a nearly-hatched alien egg. Devoid of the usual Hollywood special effects razzmatazz, but not so sugary that it will cause tooth decay, this nursery rhyme-style fantasy will have children hitting the rewind button for ever.

George Hearn Grandpa Greenfield • **Shirley Douglas** Grandma Greenfield • **Trevor Morgan** Cody Newton • **Kyla Pratt** Marcella • **Diana Rice** Abby Newton • **Jeff Ayers** Baby Bop • **Jeff Brooks** BJ • **Julie Johnson** Baby Bop • **David Joyner** Barney • **Bob West** Barney • **Patty Wirtz** BJ

Director *Steve Gomer*

Screenplay *Stephen White, from a story by Sheryl Leach, Dennis DeShazer, Stephen White, from characters created by Kathy Parker, Sheryl Leach, Dennis DeShazer*

Baron Munchhausen ★★★

1961 Cz Colour 81mins

Czech animator Karel Zeman tackled the fantastic adventures of the notorious mythomaniac by using puppets, cartoons, special effects and live action against painted backdrops. Zeman's inspiration sprang from the 1862 edition of Gottfried Burger's novel, with its drawings by Gustave Doré, and the turn-of-the-century films of conjurer and cinema pioneer Georges Méliès. Yet, fascinating as it is visually, it is stilted and uninvolving. Both the sumptuous 1943 German epic and Terry Gilliam's overblown but under-rated 1988 version are more enjoyable. A Czech language film.

Milos Kopecky Baron Munchhausen • **Jana Brejchova** Bianca • **Rudolf Jelinek** Tonik • **Jan Werich** Captain of Dutch ship • **Rudolf Hrusinsky** Sultan • **Eduard Kohout** Commander of the fortress • **Karel Hoger** Cyrano de Bergerac

Director *Karel Zeman*

Screenplay *Karel Zeman, Jiri Brdecka, Josef Kainar, from the novel "Baron Prásil" by Gottfried Burger and the illustrations by Gustave Doré*

Batman ★★★ U

1943 US BW 15x16mins

Created by Bob Kane in 1939, the Caped Crusader made his movie debut in this high-camp serial. A 26-year western veteran, director Lambert Hillyer never gets to grips with the gleefully implausible story of Dr Daka, an undercover agent who plans to use his zombie army to deliver Gotham's radium supply to the Axis. He's not helped by the unheroic antics of Lewis Wilson and Douglas Croft as the eponymous duo. But J Carrol Naish makes a splendid villain and so, at the height of the sixties TV show's popularity, this was reissued as *An Evening with Batman and Robin*.

Lewis Wilson Bruce Wayne/Batman • **Douglas Croft** Dick Grayson/Robin • **J Carrol Naish** Dr Tito Daka • **Shirley Patterson** Linda • **William Austin** Alfred • **Charles C Wilson** Captain Arnold • **Charles Middleton** Ken Colton

Director *Lambert Hillyer*

Screenplay *Victor McLeod, Leslie Swabacker, Harry Fraser [Harry L Fraser], from characters created by Bob Kane*

Batman ★★★★ U

1966 US Colour 104mins

Forget Michael Keaton, Val Kilmer and George Clooney; this is the movie spin-off from the hit TV series of the sixties, with

Holy superheroes! Adam West and Burt Ward scaled new heights of flamboyant fun in TV's *Batman*, appealing to adults and children alike

Adam West as the Caped Crusader and Burt Ward as the Boy Wonder. Lee Meriwether, the least well known of the three actresses who played Catwoman in the sixties (the others were Julie Newmar and Eartha Kitt), takes on the role here, while Cesar Romero, Burgess Meredith and Frank Gorshin show Jack Nicholson, Danny DeVito and Jim Carrey just how to play the Joker, the Penguin and the Riddler. Director Leslie H Martinson allows the pace to slacken occasionally, but Lorenzo Semple Jr's script overflows with the kind of throwaway gags that Joel Schumacher's *Batman and Robin* cried out for.

Adam West Batman/Bruce Wayne • **Burt Ward** Robin/Dick Grayson • **Lee Meriwether** Catwoman/Kitka • **Cesar Romero** Joker • **Burgess Meredith** Penguin • **Frank Gorshin** Riddler • **Alan Napier** Alfred • **Neil Hamilton** Commissioner Gordon • **Stafford Repp** Chief O'Hara • **Madge Blake** Aunt Harriet Cooper • **Reginald Denny** Commodore Schmidlapp
Director *Leslie H Martinson*
Screenplay *Lorenzo Semple Jr, from characters created by Bob Kane*

Batman ★★★★ U

TV 1966-1968 US Colour 120x30mins

An extraordinarily successful but short-lived cult phenomenon, this played on two levels – delivering old-fashioned, comic-book-style thrills for children (who would eagerly tune in "same Bat-time, same Bat-channel" to see how the Caped Crusader escaped this week's absurd death trap) while pitching slyly camp, archly comic spoof to older teens and adults. Adam West and Burt Ward played Batman and Robin with an overly earnest refusal to admit the characters' absurdity, while regulars Alan Napier (butler Alfred), Neil Hamilton (Commissioner Gordon), Stafford Repp (Chief O'Hara) and Madge Blake (Aunt Harriet) fussed around. The source of most fun, however, was a succession of flamboyant, cackling "special guest villains" – the core baddies were Frank Gorshin (the Riddler), Burgess Meredith (the Penguin), Cesar Romero (the Joker), Julie Newmar (Catwoman), Victor Buono (King Tut) and Vincent Price (Egghead), but there were equally committed and eccentric turns from George Sanders, Eli Wallach and Otto Preminger (all as Mr Freeze), Roddy McDowall (the Bookworm), Shelley Winters (Ma Parker) and Cliff Robertson (Shame), not to mention goodness-knows-what-they-were-thinking-of fiendishness from Liberace, Eartha Kitt (a replacement Catwoman), Tallulah Bankhead, Joan Collins and Zsa Zsa Gabor. The sound effects captions laid over frenetic fights, tilted camera angles of pop art sets, super-cool design of the Batmobile and other accessories, jazzy Neal Hefti score and occasionally witty scripts made this a truly happening show in its first season, but the joke wore thin swiftly. In its third year, Yvonne Craig joined the regulars as a mod Batgirl, but didn't lift the ratings to the point of saving the show. A second-season two-parter crossed over with producer William Dozier's other, less successful superhero camp exercise, partnering Gotham City's dynamic duo with fellow crimefighters the Green Hornet

Hero with a dark side: Michael Keaton is the brooding caped crusader in Tim Burton's stunning version of the Bob Kane creation, *Batman*

(Van Williams) and Kato (Bruce Lee). Later, a darker knight appeared in Tim Burton's *Batman* films – and a run of terrific animated shows from *Batman: The Animated Series* to *Batman Beyond* (also known as *Batman of the Future*) – but the Joel Schumacher *Batman* films resurrected some of the worst of this incarnation of the character.

Adam West Bruce Wayne/Batman • **Burt Ward** Dick Grayson/Robin • **Alan Napier** Alfred • **Neil Hamilton** Commissioner Gordon • **Stafford Repp** Chief O'Hara • **Yvonne Craig** Barbara Gordon/Batgirl • **Madge Blake** Aunt Harriet
Executive producer *William Dozier* •
Producer *Howie Horwitz*

Batman ★★★★★ 15

1989 US Colour 121mins DVD

Holy tour de force! Only director Tim Burton could take the caped crusader into the darkest realms of comic-strip nightmare yet still manage to weave an arresting tale full of doomy Shakespearean irony. From the camera crawling around the Bat symbol under the opening credits to the *Hunchback of Notre Dame*-inspired finale, Burton captures the spirit of artist Bob Kane's creation to produce a sophisticated *film noir* full of black humour and creepy images. With Michael Keaton's brooding Batman/Bruce Wayne and Jack Nicholson's superlative Joker/Jack Napier on the knife-edge of good and evil, Burton cleverly places both tragic characters within the same psychotic bracket, making the film the *Blue Velvet* of superhero movies. Shot on 18 sound stages at Britain's Pinewood Studios, the Gotham City set was the largest construction since 1963's *Cleopatra*, costing $5.5 million and using 60 miles of scaffolding; its designer said he wanted Gotham City to look like a New York that had gone without planning permission for 300 years. This marvellous original is still the best of the entire series, knocking its dismal sequels into a cocked cape. Contains some swearing.

Michael Keaton Batman/Bruce Wayne • **Jack Nicholson** Joker/Jack Napier • **Kim Basinger** Vicki Vale • **Robert Wuhl** Alexander Knox • **Pat Hingle** Commissioner Gordon • **Billy Dee Williams** Harvey Dent • **Michael Gough** Alfred • **Jack Palance** Carl Grissom • **Jerry Hall** Alicia • **Tracey Walter** Bob the Goon • **Lee Wallace** Mayor • **William Hootkins** Eckhardt • **Richard Strange** Goon • **John Sterland** Accountant • **Edwin Craig** Rotelli • **Vincent Wong** First crimelord • **Joel Cutrara** Second crimelord • **John Dair** Ricorso • **Christopher Fairbank** Nic • **George Roth** Eddie • **Kate Harper** Anchorwoman • **Bruce McGuire** Anchorman • **Richard Durden** TV director • **Kit Hollerbach** Becky
Director *Tim Burton*
Screenplay *Sam Hamm, Warren Skaaren, from a story by Sam Hamm, from characters created by Bob Kane*
Production designer *Anton Furst*

Batman and Robin ★ U

1949 US BW 15x16mins

If the original Lambert Hillyer serial was a disappointment, its sequel was nigh on a disaster. With Lewis Wilson and Douglas Croft consigned to well-merited obscurity, Robert Lowery and John Duncan assumed the mantles of Bruce Wayne and Dick Grayson, while Lyle Talbot stepped in as Commissioner Gordon. However, there's little suspense in their pursuit of the Wizard, a master criminal out to secure the diamonds needed to operate the ray gun he's stolen from eccentric professor, William Fawcett. Made in a hurry and on the cheap, this is the undoubtedly the nadir of the Caped Crusader's screen career.

Robert Lowery Bruce Wayne/Batman • **John Duncan** Dick Grayson/Robin • **Jane Adams** Vicki Vale • **Lyle Talbot** Commissioner Gordon • **Ralph Graves** Harrison • **Don Harvey** Nolan • **Leonard Penn** Carter • **William Fawcett** Professor Hammil
Director *Spencer Gordon Bennet*
Screenplay *George H Plympton, Joseph F Poland, Royal K Cole, from characters created by Bob Kane*

Batman and Robin ★★ U

1997 US Colour 245mins DVD

With the Batman franchise looking decidedly tired, Caped Crusader Mark 3 was introduced in the shape of *ER's* George Clooney in an attempt to pep up the flagging formula. The rugged former medic doesn't disgrace himself in this wild special effects extravaganza that is as close to a cartoon adventure as director Joel Schumacher could get. There's a decidedly two-dimensional Arnold Schwarzenegger as a heavily accented Mr Freeze, while Uma Thurman gave birth to a million copycat hairstyles as villainess Poison Ivy. Compared to the first two films, however, this is a major disappointment. Contains violence and swearing.

Arnold Schwarzenegger Mr Freeze/Dr Victor Fries • **George Clooney** Batman/Bruce Wayne • **Chris O'Donnell** Robin/Dick Grayson • **Uma Thurman** Poison Ivy/Pamela Isley • **Alicia Silverstone** Batgirl/Barbara Wilson • **Michael Gough** Alfred Pennyworth • **Pat Hingle** Commissioner Gordon • **John Glover** Dr Jason Woodrue • **Elle Macpherson** Julie Madison • **Vendela K Thommessen** Nora Fries • **Coolio** Banker
Director *Joel Schumacher*
Screenplay *Akiva Goldsman, from characters created by Bob Kane*
Project consultant *Bob Kane*

Batman Forever ★★★★ PG

1995 US Colour 114mins DVD

Although it performed well at the box office, the critics were less than convinced by the gloomy turn taken by *Batman Returns*. So, when Tim Burton said no to a third outing at the helm of this lucrative franchise, Warners brought in the flamboyant Joel Schumacher to return the series to its comic-book roots. Even though the director boasted several hours spent researching old DC comics, there were those who felt he had been more influenced by the camp quirkiness of the sixties' TV series than the original Bob Kane artwork. There's no doubting that this entry is nowhere near as dark as its predecessors, even though the famously brooding Val Kilmer took over the Dark Knight's mantle from Michael Keaton. But it's easily the funniest of the quartet to date, with Chris O'Donnell's Robin and Michael Gough's Alfred having as many quotable quips as Jim Carrey's Riddler. It's also the fastest, with the action hurtling along at a breakneck pace as Batman tries to prevent the Riddler from stealing the collective IQs of Gotham City, while Robin seeks to settle his own private score with crooked lawyer Two-Face (an underused Tommy Lee Jones). Finally, it's unquestionably the sexiest, with Drew Barrymore and Debi Mazar teasingly wicked as Sugar and Spice, and Nicole Kidman oozing class as psychologist Chase Meridian. With the special effects team including John Dykstra and Oscar-nominated photography from Stephen Goldblatt, it's an undemanding piece of popcorn fodder. Contains some swearing.

Val Kilmer Batman/Bruce Wayne • **Tommy Lee Jones** Harvey Two-Face/Harvey Dent • **Jim Carrey** The Riddler/Edward Nygma • **Nicole Kidman** Dr Chase Meridian • **Christopher O'Donnell [Chris O'Donnell]** Robin/Dick Grayson • **Michael Gough** Alfred Pennyworth • **Pat Hingle** Commissioner James Gordon • **Debi Mazar** Spice • **Drew Barrymore** Sugar • **Ed Begley Jr** Fred Stickley
Director *Joel Schumacher*
Screenplay *Lee Batchler, Janet Scott Batchler, Akiva Goldsman, from a story by Lee Batchler, Janet Scott Batchler, from characters created by Bob Kane*

Batman: Knightfall ★★★

Radio 1995 UK 180mins

Broadcast first as three serials (*A Knight's Fall, A Hero's Quest, A Batman Reborn*), this was adapted from a year's run of DC's *Batman* titles by producer Dirk Maggs, chronicling a difficult patch of Batman's career. Having encountered Jean-Paul Valley (Kerry Shale), a young man raised from birth to be a fanatical assassin, Bruce Wayne (Bob Sessions) is forced to ask the junior hero to assume the identity of the Batman when he is put in a wheelchair after his back is broken by Bane (Peter Marinker), a new villain who has also staged a rocket attack on Arkham Asylum and released all of Batman's traditional enemies. It may well be a little too epic even for its length, with more plots and characters than it can quite cope with, including a trans-Atlantic distraction.
Released on audio-cassette.

Bob Sessions Batman/Bruce Wayne • **Michael Gough** Alfred • **Peter Marinker** Bane • **Kerry Shale** Jean Paul Valley/The Joker • **William Roberts** Commissioner Gordon • **Lorelei King** Officer Montoya • **Eric Meyers** Sergeant Harvey Bullock • **Michael Roberts** The Ventriloquist/ Scarface • **Alibe Parsons** Dr Shondra Kinsolving • **James Goode** Scarecrow/ Nightwing • **Daniel Marinker** Tim Drake/Robin • **Chris Emmett** The Mad Hatter • **Vincent Marzello** Mayor Krol • **Stuart Milligan** The Riddler

Director *Dirk Maggs*

Written by *Dirk Maggs, from the "DC Comics" stories by Chuck Dixon, Alan Grant, Doug Moench, Dennis O'Neil, from characters chreated by Bob Kane*

Batman: Mask of the Phantasm ★★★★ PG

1993 US Colour 73mins [video]

Released in cinemas after the TV animated series took off, this cartoon feature expertly captures the feel of the Batman comics. The Phantasm is a formidable vigilante, who painstakingly executes Gotham's most powerful criminals. After both the police and the underworld mistakenly hold the Dark Knight responsible, Batman must unmask the real culprit and at the same time Bruce Wayne has to deal with a woman from his shadowy past. Stylishly drawn, and powerfully driven, with a strong cast of voices – including Stacy Keach and *Star Wars*'s Mark Hamill – this is a spirited riposte to the live-action film series.

Kevin Conroy Batman/Bruce Wayne • **Dana Delany** Andrea Beaumont • **Hart Bochner** Councilman Arthur Reeves • **Stacy Keach** Phantasm/Carl Beaumont • **Abe Vigoda** Salvatore Valestra • **Dick Miller** Chuckie Sol • **John P Ryan** Buzz Bronski • **Efrem Zimbalist Jr** Alfred the butler • **Bob Hastings** Commissioner Gordon • **Mark Hamill** The Joker

Director *Eric Radomski, Bruce W Timm*

Screenplay *Alan Burnett, Paul Dini, Martin Pasko, Michael Reaves, from a story by Alan Burnett, from characters created by Bob Kane*

Batman Returns ★★★★ 15

1992 US Colour 121mins [video] DVD

Director Tim Burton refused to lighten up for the second of the Batman movies (we would have to wait for the Joel Schumacher-directed *Batman Forever* for that) and the result is another moody, gloomy and occasionally perverse portrait of the dark knight. As with the first of the series, the sets are suitably stunning, and, while action may not be Burton's strongest suit, there are still some dazzling set pieces and a whole range of new gadgets. The only real problem is that, as in *Batman*, the villains bag all the best lines – Danny DeVito's tragic Penguin, Michelle Pfeiffer in that suit as Catwoman – with poor old Michael Keaton's Bruce Wayne left to look vaguely troubled while his alter ego Batman bashes up the baddies. Even though some fans of the well-loved sixties TV show may reject its brooding atmosphere, this is still impressive stuff. Contains some violence.

Michael Keaton Batman/Bruce Wayne • **Danny DeVito** Oswald Cobblepot/The Penguin • **Michelle Pfeiffer** Catwoman/Selina Kyle • **Christopher Walken** Max Shreck • **Michael Gough** Alfred • **Michael Murphy** Mayor • **Cristi Conaway** Ice princess • **Andrew Bryniarski** Chip • **Pat Hingle** Commissioner Gordon • **Vincent Schiavelli** Organ grinder • **Steve Witting** Josh • **Jan Hooks** Jen

Director *Tim Burton*

Screenplay *Daniel Waters, from a story by Daniel Waters, Sam Hahm, from characters created by Bob Kane*

Bats ★ 15

1999 US Colour mins

Genetically enhanced killer bats are released upon an unsuspecting Texas town by a mad genius, whose only defence is: "I'm a scientist! That's what we do!" A perky zoologist, her cowardly sidekick and the town's sheriff fight to fend off the flying monsters in this by-the-numbers monster movie. The bats could make effective villains in a better picture, but the lead characters never say or do anything remotely interesting. One might complain that the mad genius disappears too quickly, but he's pretty boring, too. When will they ever learn to genetically enhance formula film-making?

Lou Diamond Phillips Emmett Kimsey • **Dina Meyer** Dr Sheila Casper • **Bob Gunton** Dr Alexander McCabe • **Leon** Jimmy Sands • **Carlos Jacott** Dr Tobe Hodge • **David Shawn McConnell** Deputy Munn • **Marcia Dangerfield** Mayor Branson • **Oscar Rowland** Dr Swanbeck

Director *Louis Morneau*

Screenplay *John Logan*

*batteries not included ★★★ PG

1987 US Colour 102mins [video]

The presence of the distinguished Hume Cronyn and Jessica Tandy makes this saccharine-sodden retread of *Cocoon* worth watching. They play residents of a doomed New York block of flats who find unlikely allies in a friendly group of alien space creatures. It's made by Steven Spielberg's production company Amblin, but there is little of his magic touch here (even though it's based on one of his scripts for his *Amazing Stories* TV series), and director Matthew Robbins lets sentimentality run supreme. Nevertheless, children and soft-hearted adults will be enchanted.

Hume Cronyn Frank Riley • **Jessica Tandy** Faye Riley • **Frank McRae** Harry Noble • **Elizabeth Pena** Marisa • **Michael Carmine** Carlos • **Dennis Boutsikaris** Mason • **Tom Aldredge** Sid • **Jane Hoffman** Muriel • **John DiSanti** Gus • **John Pankow** Kovacs • **MacIntyre Dixon** DeWitt

Director *Matthew Robbins*

Screenplay *Brad Bird, Matthew Robbins, Brent Maddock, SS Wilson, from a story by Mick Garris, Steven Spielberg*

Battle beneath the Earth ★★ U

1968 UK Colour 91mins

Now *here's* an idea. The Red Chinese have dug a series of tunnels beneath the United States. In go Chinese H-bombs and lasers, and in after them goes Kerwin Matthews, the Harrison Ford of British cinema back in the sixties, to do a job even 007 might have found taxing. Everyone takes it very seriously and, as a result, it's hugely enjoyable rubbish.

Kerwin Mathews Commander Jonathan Shaw • **Viviane Ventura** Tila Yung • **Robert Ayres** Admiral Felix Hillebrand • **Peter Arne** Arnold Kramer • **Al Mulock** Sergeant Marvin Mulberry • **Martin Benson** General Chan Lu • **Peter Elliott** Kengh Lee • **Earl Cameron** Sergeant Seth Hawkins

Director *Montgomery Tully*

Screenplay *Lance Z Hargreaves*

Executive producer *Charles Vetter*

Battle beyond the Stars ★★★ PG

1980 US Colour 98mins

Roger Corman always had a great eye for angles, and this entertaining slice of hokum from his production company is great B-movie fodder. Essentially, it's *The Magnificent Seven* in space – Corman even manages to rope in one of the original cast, Robert Vaughn, to take his place alongside the likes of John Saxon (as the baddie), George Peppard and Richard Thomas from *The Waltons*. The special effects aren't bad, given the constraints of the budget, and Jimmy T Murakami directs the proceedings efficiently enough. The knowing script is by John Sayles, now better known as the writer/director of such critically acclaimed films as *Passion Fish* and *Lone Star*.

Richard Thomas Shad • **Robert Vaughn** Gelt • **John Saxon** Sador • **George Peppard** Cowboy • **Darlanne Fluegel** Nanelia • **Sybil Danning** St Exmin • **Sam Jaffe** Dr Hephaestus • **Morgan Woodward** Cayman • **Steve Davis** Quopeg

Director *Jimmy T Murakami*

Screenplay *John Sayles, from a story by John Sayles, Ann Dyer*

Battle beyond the Sun ★

1959 USSR/US Colour 67mins

This version of the space race to Mars between the Russians and the Americans is constructed by cult director Roger Corman out of special effects and footage from an existing Russian sci-fi movie, *Nebo Sovyot*, combined with new footage. This includes the major highlight – a notoriously kitsch battle between a penis-shaped monster and a vagina-shaped alien. Otherwise it's a deadly dull combination of conflicting styles and hasty edits.

Edd Perry [Ivan Pereverzev] Kornev • **Andy Stewart [A Shvorin]** Gordiyenko • **Kirk Barton [K Bartashevich]** Klark • **Gene Tonner [G Tonunts]** Verst • **Barry Chertok [V Chernyak]** Somov • **V Dobrovolskiy** Demchenko • **Arla Powell [A Popova]** Korneva • **T Litvinenko** Lena

Director *Thomas Colchart [A Kozyr], M Karyukov*

Screenplay *M Karyukov, Nicholas Colbert [A Sazonov], Edwin Palmer [Yevgeny Pomeshchikov], Francis Ford Coppola (English version adaptation)*

Executive producer *Roger Corman*

Battle for the Planet of the Apes ★ PG

1973 US Colour 86mins

The fifth, final and least effective entry in the series. It's good apes versus guerrilla gorillas as our heroes attempt to restore racial harmony to Earth and make humans social equals. Spotting who's who under the hairy masks will while away the time as this threadbare monkey business wends its time-warp way back to the beginning of the original *Planet of the Apes*. Endless action can't disguise the cheapness of the production or the lack of novelty and story values in a rather desperate effort to milk the idea one time too many.

Roddy McDowall Caesar • **Claude Akins** Aldo • **John Huston** Lawgiver • **Natalie Trundy** Lisa • **Severn Darden** Kolp • **Lew Ayres** Mandemus • **Paul Williams** Virgil • **Austin Stoker** MacDonald

Director *J Lee Thompson*

Screenplay *John William Corrington, Joyce Hooper Corrington, from a story by Paul Dehn, from characters created by Pierre Boulle*

Battle in Outer Space ★ U

1959 Jap Colour 90mins

Nowhere near as good as director Inoshiro Honda's first space adventure *The Mysterians*, this aimless spectacle resembles an episodic *Flash Gordon* serial more than a fully-fledged fantasy. The mediocre, cardboard-looking special effects by *Godzilla* grand master Eiji Tsuburaya don't help much either in the all-out space battle between earth and pint-sized Natalian aliens. It's 1965 and after flooding Venice, burning New York and destroying the Golden Gate Bridge, earth sends two spaceships to fight the enemy on their own moon turf. More wholesale destruction against futuristic landscapes later and the aliens are vanquished by the usual trusty ray gun. Frenetic and over-acted, Honda's wandering grip on the scattershot narrative will echo most viewers' attention spans. Japanese dialogue dubbed into English.

Ryo Ikebe Major Ichiro Katsumiya • **Kyoko Anzai** Etsuko Shiraishi • **Koreya Senda** Professor Adachi • **Harold Conway** Dr Immerman

Director *Inoshiro Honda*

Screenplay *Shinichi Sekizawa, from a story by Jojiro Okami*

Special effects *Eiji Tsuburaya*

Battle of the Worlds ★★★

1961 It Colour 84mins

A dead planet still run by computers is trying to annihilate mankind. When a pre-programmed meteor looks set to collide with Earth, but stops in space and launches attacking flying saucers instead, fascinated Professor Benson (Claude Rains) gains access to it in order learn as much about the extinct alien race as possible. But the military want the alien-made meteor destroyed even if it means blowing up Benson as well. Inventively visual direction, an ironic script with an adept philosophical core, great set design and 72-year-old Rains turning in an effective performance make this one of the best sci-fi efforts from journeyman stylist Antonio Margheriti.

Claude Rains Prof Benjamin Benson • **Bill Carter** Fred Steel • **Maya Brent** Eva • **Umberto Orsini** Bob Cole • **Jacqueline Derval** Cathy • **Renzo Palmer** General Verrick • **Carol Danell** Mrs Collins

Director *Anthony Dawson [Antonio Margheriti]*

Screenplay *Vassily Petrov*

Battlefield Earth ★ 12

2000 US Colour 117mins

Based on the novel by L Ron Hubbard, founder of Scientology, this expensive stinker is very much a labour of love for its producer and star, John Travolta. In the year 3000, Earth is controlled by ten-foot-tall aliens from the planet Psychlo; the few remaining humans either hide out in the mountains or live and die as slaves. One man, Jonnie Goodboy Tyler (Barry Pepper), dares to rebel against the invaders, a course of action that brings him into conflict with fearsome chief of security Terl (a dreadlocked Travolta). With futuristic designs redolent of *Blade Runner* and *Independence Day*-style space battles, Roger Christian's epic looks and sounds like your average sci-fi blockbuster. Yet the emphasis placed on indoctrination, enslavement and superior alien intelligence brings the film troublingly close to subliminal propaganda, while the script is so unfeasibly banal you'd have to be brainwashed to enjoy it.

John Travolta Terl • **Barry Pepper** Jonnie Goodboy Tyler • **Forest Whitaker** Ker • **Kim Coates** Carlo • **Richard Tyson** Robert the Fox • **Sabine Karsenti** Chrissie • **Michael Byrne** Parson Staffer • **Sean Hewitt** Heywood

Director *Roger Christian*

Screenplay *Corey Mandell, JD Shapiro, from the novel by L Ron Hubbard*

Battlestar Galactica ★★★ U PG

TV 1978-1979 US Colour 24x60mins

Launched in the wake of *Star Wars* mania (much to the suspicion of George Lucas, who unsuccessfully sued the series' makers for plagiarism), Glen A Larson's lavish sci-fi saga is pure "Cowboys and Indians" in space. *Bonanza*'s Lorne

Greene, sombre Richard Hatch and show-stealing Dirk Benedict lead the remnants of humanity on an epic quest for a mythical planet known as Earth, where they hope to find deliverance from the evil Cylons. It may be derivative, repetitive and over-earnest a lot of the time, but small-screen sci-fi shoot-'em-ups are seldom more enjoyable, star-studded or visually stunning than this. In fact, the production values were so strong that they enabled the series to spawn two "movies" in Europe, *Battlestar Galactica* (based on the series' three-hour pilot, *Saga of a Star World*) and *Mission Galactica: The Cylon Attack* (based on the two-part tale, *The Living Legend*).

Lorne Greene Cmdr Adama • **Richard Hatch** Capt Apollo • **Dirk Benedict** Lt Starbuck • **Herbert Jeffferson Jr** Lt Boomer • **Terry Carter** Col Tigh • **Maren Jensen** Athena • **Noah Hathaway** Boxey • **John Colicos** Balthar • **Laurette Spang** Cassiopeia • **Anne Lockhart** Sheba
Created by *Glen A Larson*
Executive producer *Glen A Larson* •
Producer *Donald P Bellisaro*
Visual effects supervisor *John Dykstra*

SFacts

The series managed to attract some interesting guest stars, including Jane Seymour, who featured in the pilot and first episode as Serena, love interest of Apollo and mother of Boxey. She conveniently died, leaving her offspring to fulfil the "cute kid" niche in the series. Other notable guest stars were Fred Astaire, Ray Milland, Lloyd Bridges, Roy Thinnes, Britt Ekland and Patrick Macnee.

Richard "Apollo" Hatch has been keeping the *Galactica* fires burning: in 1999 he produced a trailer, *Battlestar Galactic: the Second Coming*, set 20 years after the close of the original series. And Tom DeSanto and Bryan Singer (*X-Men*) announced in February 2001 that they are planning a new *Battlestar Galactica* series, to air possibly in 2002.

Battletruck ★★★ 15

1982 US Colour 88mins [video]

Lone warrior hero Michael Beck takes on bloodthirsty pirates and their super truck after 21st-century oil wars cause a fuel shortage. Further friction occurs when Annie McEnroe, the villain's daughter, is caught between the opposing camps. This may seem to be a rather juvenile *Mad Max* clone, but director Harley Cokliss ensures that the subtle ecological messages don't get in the way of the fast-paced mayhem. The New Zealand locations provide an intriguingly atmospheric background to the irony and sharp wit of the screenplay.

Michael Beck Hunter • **Annie McEnroe** Corlie • **James Wainwright** Straker • **John Ratzenberger** Rusty • **Randolph Powell** Judd • **Bruno Lawrence** Willie • **Diana Rowan** Charlene • **John Bach** Bone
Director *Harley Cokliss*
Screenplay *Irving Austin, Harley Cokliss, John Beech*

Beach Babes from Beyond ★ 18

1993 US Colour 76mins [video]

Kitsch fans will be in seventh heaven over this. Not only does it boast a trio of non-famous siblings (Joe Estevez, brother of Martin; Don Swayze, brother of Patrick and Joey Travolta, brother of John) but you also get Sly's mum Jacqueline Stallone and Burt Ward, better known as Robin from the *Batman* TV series. Of course, it's rubbish – it's basically a softcore teen comedy, with a bunch of alien bimbos in bikinis coming to the aid of a beach bum, while taking on a nasty swimwear manufacturer (Ward). But the awfulness of the playing will keep you transfixed.

Joe Estevez Uncle Bud • **Don Swayze** Gork • **Joey Travolta** Dr Veg • **Burt Ward** Mr Bun • **Jacqueline Stallone** Yanna • **Linnea Quigley** Sally • **Sara Bellomo** Xena • **Tamara Landry** Luna • **Nicole Posey** Sola
Director *Ellen Cabot [David DeCoteau]*
Screenplay *Alexander Sachs*

The Beast from 20,000 Fathoms ★★★★

1953 US BW 79mins

The first prehistoric-monster-on-the-rampage feature and arguably the best. Based on the Ray Bradbury story *The Fog Horn*, it also marked the solo debut of special effects genius Ray Harryhausen, who would refine his stop-motion puppetry in the Sinbad fantasies and *Jason and the Argonauts*. Freed from a prehistoric hibernation by an atomic blast at the North Pole, the peeved monster effectively tramples through New York and ends up taking a bite out of the Coney Island roller coaster. Tense and ferocious, this was the *Jurassic Park* of its day and spawned countless imitations.

Paul Christian Tom Nesbitt • **Paula Raymond** Lee Hunter • **Cecil Kellaway** Professor Elson • **Kenneth Tobey** Colonel Evans • **Jack Pennick** Jacob • **Donald Woods** Captain Jackson • **Lee Van Cleef** Corporal Stone
Director *Eugène Lourié*
Screenplay *Lou Morheim, Fred Freiberger, from the story "The Fog Horn" by Ray Bradbury*

The Beast of Hollow Mountain ★★

1956 US/Mex Colour 46mins

A full 13 years before his story *Valley of the Mist*, on which this film was based, turned up posthumously in *The Valley of the Gwangi* (executed by his disciple Ray Harryhausen) Willis O'Brien tried out his cowboys versus prehistoric monster idea in this hokey dud shot in Mexico. Sadly, the low budget producers couldn't afford to hire O'Brien, the animator on the original *King Kong*, to animate the combat scenes between Guy Madison and the tyrannosaurus once they'd bought the story. When it finally makes its long-awaited appearance, within a typically fifties western scenario about greedy land barons, the dinosaur is sub-standard and a crashing disappointment.

Guy Madison Jimmy Ryan • **Patricia Medina** Sarita • **Eduardo Noriega** Enrique Rios • **Carlos Rivas** Felipe Sanchez • **Mario Navarro** Panchito
Director *Edward Nassour, Ismael Rodriguez*
Screenplay *Robert Hill, Jack DeWitt, from the story "Valley of the Mist" by Willis H O'Brien*

The Beast with a Million Eyes ★★

1955 US BW 79mins

Made for a paltry $23,000, this Roger Corman executive-produced allegory has been written off because of its peculiar premise and its bargain-basement effects. The prospect of watching birds and barnyard animals turning on humans at the behest of a malevolent alien force may, indeed, seem preposterous. As does the rationale that this evil entity can be tamed by folksy, white middle-American love. But the notion that we are being watched over by a potentially malicious presence (whether it be deity or authority) is actually rather provocative. Flawed, but laudably unconventional, this proved to be director David Karmansky's only film.

Paul Birch Allan Kelley • **Lorna Thayer** Carol Kelley • **Dona Cole** Sandy Kelley • **Dick Sargent** Deputy Larry Brewster
Director *David Kramarsky*
Screenplay *Tom Filer*

The Bed Sitting Room ★★★

1969 UK Colour 91mins

One of comic genius Spike Milligan's two great West End hits, the other being *Son of Oblomov*, this anti-war play by Milligan and John Antrobus seemed ideal screen material. Set three years after the great nuclear holocaust, its cast gradually transmutes into various altered physical states: Ralph Richardson plays the title role, while Arthur Lowe becomes a parrot. The rest of the cast is peopled by priceless British eccentrics, including Milligan's *Goon Show* pal Harry Secombe and Peter Cook and Dudley Moore. Top-billed is the 17-month pregnant Rita Tushingham, who also starred in director Richard Lester's *The Knack... and How to Get It*. Lester is quite at home in this surreal world, having pressed the anti-war button earlier with *How I Won the War* and having made his big screen bow with the silent two-reeler *The Running, Jumping and Standing Still Film*. Yet this type of farrago sorely tried the patience of paying punters and, despite its undoubted originality, *The Bed Sitting Room* failed to transfer successfully from stage to screen. Watch carefully for Marty Feldman in his movie debut.

Ralph Richardson Lord Fortnum • **Rita Tushingham** Penelope • **Peter Cook** Inspector • **Dudley Moore** Sergeant • **Arthur Lowe** Father • **Roy Kinnear** Plastic Mac Man • **Mona Washbourne** Mother • **Michael Hordern** Captain Bules Martin • **Spike Milligan** Mate • **Harry Secombe** The Shelter Man • **Ronald Fraser** Field Marshal Sergeant • **Jimmy Edwards** Nigel • **Richard Warwick** Allan • **Frank Thornton** Newscaster • **Dandy Nichols** Ethyl Shroake • **Henry Woolf** Electricity man • **Ron Brody** Dwarf • **Gordon Rollings** Patient • **Marty Feldman** Nurse Arthur

Director *Richard Lester*

Screenplay *John Antrobus, from the play by Spike Milligan, John Antrobus*

The Bees ★

1978 US Colour 85mins

This feeble "killer bee" movie is an equal disaster in terms of its stupid wandering plot and lame dialogue. A cash-hungry corporation invests in a mutant strain of Amazon bees, only for the insects escape and set about devastating America as a plea to the world to be more environmentally friendly. Horror veteran John Carradine, sporting a terrible German accent, is stung to death at the hilarious high point, while hero John Saxon tries to eliminate the threat by making all the male insects homosexual. Seeing is bee-lieving! Even President Gerald Ford gets in on the act as documentary footage is spliced into this desperately tacky misfire.

John Saxon John Norman • **Angel Tompkins** Sandra Miller • **John Carradine** Dr Sigmund Humel • **Claudio Brook** Dr Miller • **Alicia Encinias** Alicia

Director/Screenplay *Alfredo Zacharias*

Before I Hang ★★★

1940 US BW 62mins

A short and sweet programme filler allowing Boris Karloff to veer superbly between brilliant scientist and rabid madman. This time he's dabbling in serums to combat old age and uses a criminal's blood for some behind bars experimentation after he's imprisoned for a "mercy killing". There's loads of fun psychobabble about medicine being for the good of mankind, but what it and many of the King of Horror's potboilers from the period eventually turns into is another twist on the *Frankenstein* theme. Yet Karloff glues it all together as ever.

Boris Karloff Dr John Garth • **Evelyn Keyes** Martha Garth • **Bruce Bennett** Dr Paul Ames • **Edward Van Sloan** Dr Ralph Howard • **Ben Taggart** Warden Thompson • **Pedro De Cordoba** Victor Sondini • **Wright Kramer** George Wharton • **Barton Yarborough** Stephen Barclay • **Don Beddoe** Captain McGraw • **Robert Fiske** District Attorney • **Kenneth MacDonald** Anson

Director *Nick Grinde*

Screenplay *Robert D Andrews*

Beginning of the End ★

1957 US BW 72mins

Rubbishy schlock horror about an atomic radiation leak that kills off scores of farmers in the Midwest and produces giant grasshoppers that march in formation on Chicago, slaughtering everyone who stands in their way. Peter Graves is the baffled boffin, while Peggy Castle plays a boggled journalist. Cheesy effects and hammy performances may delight fans of the genre, but 15 minutes is as much as most people can take before boredom sets in. Director Bert I Gordon specialised in this sort of thing, and was still churning out dross like *Empire of the Ants* in the seventies.

Peggie Castle Audrey • **Peter Graves (1)** Ed Wainwright • **Morris Ankrum** General Hanson • **Richard Benedict** Corporal Mathias • **James Seay** Captain Barton • **Thomas B Henry [Thomas Browne Henry]** Colonel Sturgeon • **John Close** Major Everett

Director *Bert I Gordon*

Screenplay *Fred Freiberger, Lester Gorn*

Producer *Bert I Gordon*

Bela Lugosi Meets a Brooklyn Gorilla ★

1952 US BW 74mins

The last film Bela Lugosi made before he fell into the clutches of Ed Wood, this cheapie was produced (and in just two weeks) to cash in the "success" of the Lon Chaney Jr vehicle, *Bride of the Gorilla*. Although Lugosi was the nominal star (and his mad scientist's simmering menace turns out to be the film's sole virtue), producer Jack Broder was much more interested in showcasing the negligible talents of his Martin and Lewis lookalikes, Duke Mitchell and Sammy Petrillo. The latter's convulsed mugging is often embarrassing to watch, none more so than in a scene that is designed to lampoon Lugosi's vampiric past.

Bela Lugosi Dr Zabor • **Duke Mitchell** • **Sammy Petrillo** • **Charlita** Nona • **Muriel Landers** Salome • **Al Kikume** Chief Rakos • **Mickey Simpson** Chula • **Milton Newberger** Bongo

Director *William Beaudine*

Screenplay *Tim Ryan, "Ukie" Sherin, Edmond Seward*

Beneath the Planet of the Apes ★★★ 15

1969 US Colour 0mins

The first sequel to the enormously successful and popular *Planet of the Apes* is also the best. Although less subtle and profound than its predecessor, it's still an exciting and colourful action adventure. This time around, astronaut James Franciscus and chimpanzee scientist Kim Hunter search for Charlton Heston (star of the first film) in the nuclear-devastated future, evading militaristic apes only to stumble upon an underground community of mutant, telepathic humans. It ends somewhat hammily in the buried ruins of Grand Central Station, but the ensuing total destruction of the world didn't stop three more progressively silly sequels from appearing. In fact, the finale here still manages a quite startling impact considering the film's tendency to wallow in the camper aspects of its taut material. Contains violence.

Charlton Heston George Taylor • **James Franciscus** Brent • **Kim Hunter** Dr Zira • **Maurice Evans** Dr Zaius • **Linda Harrison** Nova • **Paul Richards** Mendez • **Victor Buono** Fat man • **James Gregory** Ursus • **Jeff Corey** Caspay • **Natalie Trundy** Albina • **Thomas Gomez** Minister • **David Watson** Cornelius • **Don Pedro Colley** Negro • **Tod Andrews** Skipper • **Lou Wagner** Lucius

Director *Ted Post*

Screenplay *Paul Dehn, Mort Abrahams, from characters created by Pierre Boulle*

Beware! The Blob ★ 15

1971 US Colour 86mins [video]

Noteworthy only for being directed by Larry (*Dallas*) Hagman – it was actually re-released in the eighties with the tag line "The film that JR shot!" – this pointless sequel to the 1958 classic rehashes virtually the same plot, but dumbs it down with amateurish special effects and strained acting. Godfrey Cambridge brings a globule of alien jelly back from the Arctic, which thaws out to become a homicidal protoplasm that increases its size by attacking partygoers and bowling alleys. The interesting cameo cast exists solely to get eaten by the red mass. Not scary or campy, just boring.

Robert Walker Jr Bobby Hartford • **Gwynne Gilford** Lisa Clark • **Godfrey Cambridge** Chester • **Richard Stahl** Edward Fazio • **Richard Webb** Sheriff Jones • **Carol Lynley** Leslie • **Shelley Berman** Hairdresser • **Burgess Meredith** Hobo • **Graham Gerrit** Joe • **Marlene Clark** Marian • **JJ Johnson** Deputy • **Larry Hagman** Cop
Director *Larry Hagman*
Screenplay *Anthony Harris, Jack Woods, from a story by Richard Clair, Anthony Harris*

Beyond the Stars ★★★ PG

1988 Can/US Colour 87mins [video]

A charming drama in which a very young-looking Christian Slater stars as a teenager who dreams of becoming an astronaut. His life changes for ever when he discovers that a reclusive neighbour (Martin Sheen) actually took part in a Moon landing and the two form an uneasy friendship. Both Slater and Sheen are delightful in this enjoyable tale, and they are joined by an impressive cast, which includes F Murray Abraham, *Falcon Crest*'s Robert Foxworth and a pre-*Basic Instinct* Sharon Stone. Contains some mild swearing.

Martin Sheen Paul Andrews • **Christian Slater** Eric Mason • **Robert Foxworth** Richard Michaels • **Sharon Stone** Laurie McCall • **Olivia D'Abo** Mara Simons • **F Murray Abraham** Harry • **Don Davis [Don S Davis]** Phil
Director/Screenplay *David Saperstein*

Beyond the Time Barrier ★★ U

1960 US BW 75mins

Pilot Robert Clarke breaks the time barrier in an experimental hypersonic aircraft, crosses the fifth dimension and finds himself on post-World War III Earth where the underground civilisation is menaced by mutants caused by "the cosmic nuclear plague of 1971". A flimsy fantasy from cult director Edgar G Ulmer (shot back to back with *The Amazing Transparent Man*), saddled with a dreadful script, amateur acting and a crudely expressed "ban the bomb" political message. What little minimalist atmosphere Ulmer does manage to achieve comes courtesy of the 1959 Texas State Fair in Dallas as the futuristic exhibits were used as cheap and cheerfully weird backdrops.

Robert Clarke Maj William Allison • **Darlene Tompkins** Trirene • **Arianne Arden** Markova • **Vladimir Sokoloff** The Supreme • **Stephen Bekassy** Karl Kruse • **John Van Dreelen** Dr Bourmane • **Boyd "Red" Morgan** Captain
Director *Edgar G Ulmer*
Screenplay *Arthur C Pierce*

Bicentennial Man ★★ 12

1999 US Colour 125mins [video] DVD

Based on the work of two of science fiction's literary giants, Isaac Asimov and Robert Silverberg, this admirably treats its robot hero as a suitable case for dramatic treatment. Unfortunately, Robin Williams plays it for tears as Andrew, the android butler who has been assembled to serve one family over four generations. Programmed to follow Asimov's three laws of robotics (a robot may not harm a human being and must obey his or her orders while protecting its own existence), Andrew is treated well by his owner (Sam Neill), but later has himself reconstructed as a human being for the sake of his true love (Embeth Davidtz). Directed by Chris Columbus from a Nicholas Kazan script, the film makes Andrew irritatingly cute (as does the star), undermining Asimov's original analogy with black outsiders. With marvellous effects and ideas scuppered by sentimentality, it's really enough to make a mechanical man weep.

Robin Williams Andrew • **Embeth Davidtz** Little Miss/Portia • **Sam Neill** Sir • **Oliver Platt** Rupert Burns • **Wendy Crewson** Ma'am • **Hallie Kate Eisenberg** Little Miss, 7 years old • **Stephen Root** Dennis Mansky • **Lynne Thigpen** Female president • **Kiersten Warren** Galatea robotic/Human
Director *Chris Columbus*
Screenplay *Nicholas Kazan, from a short story by Isaac Asimov and from the novel "The Positronic Man" by Isaac Asimov, Robert Silverberg*

Big Meat Eater ★★★ 18

1982 Can Colour 78mins [video]

A maniac has killed the mayor of a Canadian small town, only for aliens to arrive and reanimate the corpse as their slave. Meanwhile, a genius transvestite uses the "Baloney-um" fluid fermenting under the local butcher's shop to propel his car-turned-spaceship into orbit. Confused? You still will be after watching this bizarre cult oddity, which combines cheap-and-cheerful special effects (the aliens are toy robots shot in extreme close-up) with songs like *Baghdad Boogie* and *Chemical World*. Director Chris Windsor's quirky genre references and canny awareness of all things Rocky Horror make this a warped one-off that's worth catching.

George Dawson Bob Sanderson • **Andrew Gillies** Jan Wczinski • **Big Miller [Clarence "Big" Miller]** Abdulla • **Stephen Dimopoulos** Joseph Wczinski • **Georgina Hegedos** Rosa Wczinski • **Ida Carnevali** Babushka • **Howard Taylor** Mayor Carmine Rigatoni • **Heather Smith-Harper** Secretary
Director *Chris Windsor*
Screenplay *Phil Savath, Laurence Keane, Chris Windsor*

The Big Mess ★★★★

1970 W Ger BW and Colour 86mins

Set in 2034 and inspired by Baran and Sweezy's book, *The Monopole Capitalism*, this is the antidote to all tales of heroic space adventure. Widely seen as a riposte to the optimistic, yet antiseptic futurism of *2001: a Space Odyssey*, Alexander Kluge's cosmos is littered with rust-bucket spaceships and unscrupulous astronauts ruled totally by profit. His Earth is no better, with multinational conglomerates controlling every aspect of life and keeping nations in a permanent state of war. Yet while this assault on the consumer society is bitingly sharp, it takes pity on the hapless humans whose indifference allowed it to develop. A German language film.

Siegfried Graue • **Hark Bohm** • **Maria Sterr** • **Vincent Sterr**
Director/Screenplay *Alexander Kluge*

The Big Pull ★★

TV 1962 UK BW 6x30mins

A six-part BBC television serial scripted by Robert Gould, produced (that is, directed) by Terence Dudley, this is heavily derivative of the first and second *Quatermass* serials. Sklorski (Frank Fenter), an American astronaut, orbits the Earth in parallel with the real-life Mercury program, but his capsule – like that of Victor Caroon in *The*

Quatermass Experiment, and Marvel Comics's then-new Fantastic Four – picks up strange radiation in the Van Allen belt and he returns to Earth changed, combining his body with that of scientist Weatherfield (Felix Deebark). The effect spreads in a series of "fusions", in which two men become one alien entity, and *Quatermass*-style rocket boffin Sir Robert Nailer (William Dexter) gets on the case to thwart the invasion. In a large cast, Frederick Treves is the most familiar player, popping up towards the end as one of the "fusions". Music and sound effects were by the BBC Radiophonic Workshop, a year away from its association with a show that would also fill a slot early on Saturday evening, *Doctor Who*.

William Dexter Sir Robert Nailer • **June Tobin** Lady Nailer • **Ray Roberts** Dr Alan Tullis • **George Street** Chief Supt Stroud • **Fred Ferris** Det Supt Allison • **Frederick Treves** Bruton-Anderson • **Felix Deebark** Dr Weatherfield • **Frank Fenter** Sklorski • **Helen Horton** Mrs Weatherfield
Written by *Robert Gould*
Producer *Terence Dudley*
Designer *Lionel Radford*

Biggles ★ PG

1986 UK Colour 88mins

A hero to a generation of young readers, Captain WE Johns's immortal flying ace is made to look very foolish in this ghastly spoof, directed with a leaden touch by John Hough. Neil Dickson does his best to give Biggles his customary gung-ho cheeriness, but his efforts are shot to pieces by a shambles of a story in which burger-bar boss Alex Hyde-White is whisked from modern America back to the First World War to join his time-twin the flying ace on a secret mission. However, the saddest aspect of this sorry episode is that it was Peter Cushing's final film. Not even one for entertaining the children.

Neil Dickson James "Biggles" Bigglesworth • **Alex Hyde-White** Jim Ferguson • **Fiona Hutchison** Debbie Stevens • **Peter Cushing** Colonel Raymond • **Marcus Gilbert** Eric von Stalhein • **William Hootkins** Chuck • **Michael Siberry** Algy • **Daniel Flynn** Ginger
Director *John Hough*
Screenplay *John Groves, Ken Walwin, from characters created by Captain WE Johns*

Bill & Ted's Bogus Journey

★★★★ PG

1991 US Colour 89mins

Wayne's World heroes Wayne and Garth may have won out at the box office, but Bill and Ted remain the original and best dudes. This time around the two airheads (played with enormous energy by Alex Winter and Keanu Reeves) are still trying to get their band together when they are murdered by their robotic doppelgängers sent from the future by the evil Joss Ackland. They must then face the Grim Reaper if they are to become the saviours of mankind. This sequel lacks the inspired stupidity of the first, but it is still a hoot, especially the knowing nods to Ingmar Bergman's classic *The Seventh Seal* as the gormless duo play battleships with the Grim Reaper. Reeves and Winter are once again cheerfully inept and British director Peter Hewitt manages to stage the spectacular set pieces with some panache. Mostly excellent. Contains swearing.

Keanu Reeves Ted/Evil Ted • **Alex Winter** Bill/Evil Bill • **George Carlin** Rufus • **Joss Ackland** De Nomolos • **Sarah Trigger** Joanna • **Annette Azcuy** Elizabeth • **Hal Landon Jr** Captain Logan • **Amy Stock-Poynton** Missy • **Chelcie Ross** Colonel Oats • **William Sadler** Grim Reaper • **Jeff Miller** Bill Double • **David Carrera** Ted Double
Director *Peter Hewitt*
Screenplay *Ed Solomon, Chris Matheson*

Bill & Ted's Excellent Adventure

★★★★ PG

1988 US Colour 85mins

A nonstop giggle from start to finish, this beguiling grab-bag of time-travel clichés, hard-rock music and Valley-speaking cool dudes is a flawless, purpose-built junk movie. Director Stephen Herek's scattershot style perfectly complements the wayward cosmic capers, while Keanu Reeves (in his pre-sex symbol days) bravely takes on comedian Alex Winter for the "Most Witlessly Appealing Airhead" crown. Reeves resembles a moronic puppet with loose strings ambling amiably through this happy-go-lucky voyage into the short circuits of history. Engaging to the max. Contains some swearing.

Keanu Reeves Ted "Theodore" Logan • **Alex Winter** Bill S Preston • **George Carlin** Rufus • **Terry Camilleri** Napoleon • **Dan Shor** Billy the Kid • **Tony Steedman** Socrates • **Rod Loomis** Sigmund Freud • **Al Leong** Genghis Khan • **Jane Wiedlin** Joan of Arc • **Robert V Barron** Abraham Lincoln • **Clifford David** Ludwig van Beethoven • **Hal Langdon Jr** Captain Logan • **Bernie Casey** Mr Ryan • **Amy Stock-Poynton** Missy/Mom
Director *Stephen Herek*
Screenplay *Chris Matheson, Ed Solomon*

Biohazard ★ 18

1984 US Colour 75mins

This film gives new meaning to the words "low budget". Shot for just $250,000, Fred Olen Ray's film slavishly imitates *Alien*, like so many video fodder monster movies of the early eighties and, while welcomingly short, still succeeds in dulling the viewer's senses. It concerns top secret experiments in matter transference that opens a doorway to another dimension, letting in a face-ripping lizard-like creature which proceeds to chew on the amateurish cast. And not a moment too soon, either. There's gore galore and a few in-jokes, like the alien tearing up a poster of ET, but the real highlight comes at the end with a series of out-takes, including an actress's blonde wig slipping off during a love scene. Followed by a sequel, ye gods (1995's *Biohazard: the Alien Force*).

Aldo Ray General Randolph • **Angelique Pettyjohn** Lisa Martyn • **William Fair** Mitchell Carter • **Frank McDonald** Mike • **Christopher Ray** Bio-monster • **Carroll Borland** Rula Murphy • **Richard Hench** Roger
Director/Screenplay *Fred Olen Ray*

SFacts

Typecasting: the director's five-year-old son plays the monster; young Ray appeared as the "special guest bio-monster" in the 1995 sequel, and went on two years later to play the monster in 1997's *Hybrid*.

The Bionic Boy ★

1977 HK/Phil Colour 95mins

The exploitation industry's riposte to American television's *The Six Million Dollar Man* and *The Bionic Woman* was this appalling mix of adolescent sci-fi and martial arts. Johnson Yap, a Singapore karate prodigy, stars as the 11-year-old kid who dies in a car crash only to be revived and kitted out with electronic artificial limbs. He then goes on a revenge spree to nail the gangsters who murdered his Interpol agent father for saving a wealthy industrialist's life. A complete wash out in every artistic area, even the fight sequences are unimaginative and lethargically staged considering Yap's supposed prowess. Incredibly, *Dynamite Johnson*, an equally terrible sequel, followed in 1978.

Johnson Yap • **Ron Rogers** • **Susan Beacher** • **Clem Parsons** • **David McCoy** • **Steve Nicholson**
Director *Leody M Diaz*
Screenplay *Romeo N Galang*

Bionic Ever After? ★★ PG

1994 US Colour 86mins

If you're looking for undemanding viewing, this frivolous TV movie reuniting Six Million Dollar Man (Lee Majors) with the Bionic Woman (Lindsay Wagner) is just the ticket. The story has the bionic duo coming out of retirement to foil a terrorist who is about to launch a nuclear-tipped missile; they also must free the ambassador to the Bahamas, whose embassy has been hijacked. After the daring heroics, the couple finally get hitched. Fans of the TV shows will like seeing how their heroes have aged, but this sombre version is sorely lacking in the originals' comic-book elements.

Lee Majors Steve Austin • **Lindsay Wagner** Jaime Sommers • **Richard Anderson** Oscar Goldman • **Farrah Forke** Kimberly • **Martin E Brooks** Dr Rudy Wells • **Alan Sader** John McNamara • **Geordie Johnson** Miles Kendrick
Director *Stephen Stafford*
Screenplay *Michael Sloan, Norman Morill, from a story by Michael Sloan*

Bionic Showdown: the Six Million Dollar Man and the Bionic Woman ★★★ PG

1989 US Colour 92mins

Before you start worrying, Lee Majors and Lindsay Wagner are not about to beat the bionic daylights out of each other. After all, if you remember, they were once lovers before his disastrous test flight and her sky-diving mishap. No, the bionic baddie belongs to a secret government organisation intent on disrupting the Russian/American unity games. What with Steve Austin's eyes, Jaime Sommers's ears, a couple of phenomenal right arms and four of the fastest legs on the planet, who's going to bet against them? Look out for a young hopeful by the name of Sandra Bullock.

Lee Majors Steve Austin • **Lindsay Wagner** Jaime Sommers • **Richard Anderson** Oscar Goldman • **Martin E Brooks** Dr Rudy Wells • **Sandra Bullock** Kate Mason • **Jeff Yagher** Jim Goldman • **Geraint Wyn Davies** Devlin • **Robert Lansing** General McAllister • **Josef Sommer** Esterman
Director *Alan J Levi*
Screenplay *Michael Sloan, Ted Mann, from a story by Michael Sloan, Robert DeLaurentiis*

The Bionic Woman ★★★ U

TV 1976-1978 US Colour 58x60mins

This spin-off from *The Six Million Dollar Man* pulled off the trick not managed a decade earlier by *The Girl from U.N.C.L.E.*, introducing a series stablemate and extending the franchise beyond the cancellation of both shows. Introduced in a two-part *Six Million Dollar Man* story in 1975, Jamie Sommers (Lindsay Wagner) was the athletic girlfriend of bionic Steve Austin (Lee Majors), cyborged up after a parachuting accident. She died in that show, but was popular enough to rate a season-opening *Return of the Bionic Woman* and a few more featured spots in the 1975-76 season before debuting on her own show in 1976, which ran for three seasons – then popped up again the reunion shows *The Return of the Six Million Dollar Man and the Bionic Woman* (1987), *Bionic Showdown* (1989 – with Sandra Bullock as the new Bionic Woman!) and *Bionic Ever After?* (1994). Recurring villains were the Fembots (later name-checked in the *Austin Powers* films), created by John Houseman in *Kill Oscar, Part 1*, and ideas ran so thin that there were several episodes featuring Max, "the bionic dog". Like Leo G. Carroll before him, Richard Anderson hopped between both shows as the bionic agents' boss Oscar Goldman, while Lee Majors made frequent guest appearances in return for Wagner crossing over to the parent programme once in a while.

Lindsay Wagner Jaime Sommers • **Richard Anderson** Oscar Goldman • **Martin E Brooks** Dr Rudy Wells
Source *Inspired by characters from the novel "Cyborg" by Martin Caidin*
Executive producer *Lionel E Siegel*

SFacts

Notable guests include Andy Griffith, Tippi Hedren, Donald O'Connor, Kristy McNichol, Hoyt Axton, Julie Newmar, Robert Loggia, Evel Knievel, Keenan Wynn and Helen Hunt (who has claimed she would like to burn *Sanctuary: Earth*, in which she plays an alien princess).

The Birds ★★★★★ 15

1963 US Colour 113mins

Alfred Hitchcock followed-up *Psycho* with this shock classic, based on Daphne du Maurier's ambiguous "nature turns on mankind" story, in which our feathered friends turn into formidable foes and launch an attack an isolated Californian community. The Master of Suspense purposely begins at a somewhat leisurely pace, focusing on Tippi Hedren's romantic game of one-upmanship with lawyer Rod Taylor, but soon builds towards some of his most terrifying sequences. Using electronically treated recordings of bird squawks instead of music, Hitch unleashes menace and mayhem to often spine-tingling effect.

Tippi Hedren Melanie Daniels • **Rod Taylor** Mitch Brenner • **Suzanne Pleshette** Annie Hayworth • **Jessica Tandy** Lydia Brenner • **Veronica Cartwright** Cathy Brenner • **Ruth McDevitt** Mrs MacGruder
Director *Alfred Hitchcock*
Screenplay *Evan Hunter, from the short story by Daphne du Maurier*
Producer *Alfred Hitchcock*

The Birds II: Land's End ★ 15

1994 US Colour 82mins

Unhappily married Brad Johnson and Chelsea Field take their two kids on vacation to Gull Island, only to become pecking targets in this vapid TV movie sequel to Alfred Hitchcock's classic 1963 shocker. More concerned with soap-opera squabbles than any avian horror, this slice of schlock offers an ecological explanation of the bird attacks that simply doesn't ring true. Tippi Hedren supplies a cameo, to little effect, while director Rick Rosenthal was so distressed by the whole farrago that he used the significant "bad movie" pseudonym, Alan Smithee, on the credits.

Brad Johnson Ted Hocken • **Chelsea Field** May Hocken • **James Naughton** Frank Irving • **Tippi Hedren** Helen Matthews • **Jan Rubes** Karl
Director *Alan Smithee [Rick Rosenthal]*
Screenplay *Ken Wheat, Jim Wheat, Robert Eisele, from the short story by Daphne du Maurier*

The Black Hole ★★★ PG

1979 US Colour 97mins

There was a time in the seventies when Disney seemed to have lost its magic touch and this unwieldy sci-fi epic didn't really succeed in halting the decline of the period. It's actually not too bad, boasting some stunning special effects and an intriguing story about a disturbed scientist (Maximilian Schell) who is about to go boldly where no man has been before into a black hole in space. The cast is dependable but it's all a bit staid.

Maximilian Schell Dr Hans Reinhardt • **Anthony Perkins** Dr Alex Durant • **Robert Forster** Capt Dan Holland • **Joseph Bottoms** Lt Charles Pizer • **Yvette Mimieux** Dr Kate McCrae • **Ernest Borgnine** Harry Booth
Director *Gary Nelson*
Screenplay *Jeb Rosebrook, Gerry Day, from a story by Bob Barbash, Richard Landau, Jeb Rosebrook*
Special effects *Peter Ellenshaw, Art Cruickshank, Eustace Lycett, Danny Lee, Harrison Ellenshaw, Joe Hale*

Black Moon ★★★

1974 Fr Colour 100mins

Beautifully photographed by Sven Nykvist, Louis Malle's first film in English is a weird, futuristic fantasy set in a countryside where symbols abound. Not all of this enigmatic movie comes off, but Malle's Wonderland is full of surprising things, including talking rats, unicorns and ex-Andy Warhol hunk Joe Dalessandro. Cathryn Harrison, Rex's granddaughter, is adequate as the Alice figure; the title refers to the time of chaos that preludes some cataclysmic change.

Cathryn Harrison Lily • **Thérèse Giehse** The old lady • **Alexandra Stewart** Sister • **Joe Dallesandro** Brother
Director *Louis Malle*
Screenplay *Louis Malle, Ghislain Uhry, Joyce Buñuel*
Producer *Louis Malle*
Cinematographer *Sven Nykvist*

The Black Scorpion ★★★

1957 US BW 87mins

The slumber of giant scorpions is disturbed due to volcanic activity, in director Edward Ludwig's low-budget sci-fi drama. The leader of the angry arachnids takes one look at the desert and heads straight for Mexico City and a showdown with a cast headed by B-movie regulars Richard Denning and Mara Corday. Special effects come courtesy of Willis O'Brien, who helped give life to King Kong, and there's a scene in the insects' lair that might have provided some inspiration for *Starship Troopers*. The climax,taking place in the Mexico City stadium, is wonderfully schlocky.

Richard Denning Henry Scott • **Mara Corday** Teresa • **Carlos Rivas** Arturo Ramos • **Mario Navarro** Juanito • **Carlos Muzquiz** Doctor Velasco • **Pascual Garcia Pena** Jose de la Cruz
Director *Edward Ludwig*
Screenplay *David Duncan, Robert Blees, from a story by Paul Yawitz*

The Black Sleep ★

1956 US BW 82mins

In order to cure his wife's catalepsy, mad doctor Basil Rathbone performs surgery on innocent victims to unlock the secrets of the brain. His failed lobotomy experiments eventually escape their cellar prison and rebel against him. Aside from the unique spectacle of seeing such horror heavies as Rathbone, Bela Lugosi (a mute butler), Lon Chaney Jr (Mungo the idiot), John Carradine (a poetry-spouting nutcase), Tor Johnson (a blind retard) and Akim Tamiroff (Odo the gypsy), this wasted opportunity is barely watchable.

Basil Rathbone Sir Joel Cadman • **Akim Tamiroff** Odo • **Lon Chaney Jr** Mungo • **John Carradine** Borg • **Bela Lugosi** Casimir • **Herbert Rudley** Dr Gordon Ramsay • **Patricia Blake** Laurie • **Phyllis Stanley** Daphne • **Tor Johnson** Curry
Director *Reginald Le Borg*
Screenplay *John C Higgins*

Blade ★★★ 18

1998 US Colour 115mins [video] DVD

Wesley Snipes is the half-mortal, half-vampire who hunts down creatures of the night in this flashy action adventure based on the popular comic. Aided by gruff-and-tough Kris Kristofferson, he finally meets his match when he flashes fangs at vampire Stephen Dorff, whose evil plans include running a nightclub that will supply humans for his fiendish pals to feed on. Daft stuff indeed, but snappily paced and performed with tongue firmly in cheek. Plus Snipes looks great in leather strides and coat. Contains swearing and violence.

Wesley Snipes Blade • **Stephen Dorff** Frost • **Kris Kristofferson** Whistler • **Kevin Patrick Walls** Krieger • **N'Bushe Wright** Karen • **Donal Logue** Quinn • **Arly Jover** Mercury • **Udo Kier** Dragonetti • **Traci Lords** Raquel • **Eric Edwards** Pearl • **Tim Guinee** Curtis Webb • **Sanaa Lathan** Vanessa
Director *Stephen Norrington*
Screenplay *David S Goyer, from characters created for Marvel Comics by Marv Wolfman, Gene Colan*
Producer *Peter Frankfurt, Wesley Snipes, Robert Engelman* • ***Co-producer*** *Andrew J Horne, Jon Divens* • ***Executive producer*** *Stan Lee, Avi Arad*

Blade Runner ★★★★★ 15

1982 US Colour 112mins [video] DVD

A super Philip K Dick story about a superdick searching for rebellious replicants translates here into a violent visual eye-popper, based in a futuristic Los Angeles, which set the acid rain/neon-drenched metropolis design standard for eighties sci-fi. As influential as *2001: a Space Odyssey* and *Star Wars*, and as thought-provoking as the former Kubrick classic, Ridley Scott's atmospheric downer is a compelling *noir* thriller that pleads for harmony between man and machine. Harrison Ford stars as the former cop assigned to track down android Rutger Hauer and his three associates. Hauer gives an exceptional performance as the blond humanoid who, like the others, has been implanted with memories of a nonexistent youth. *The Director's Cut*, which drops Ford's voice-over, actually adds more depth to the 1982 original, so the full masterpiece can shine through. Contains violence, swearing and brief nudity.

Harrison Ford Rick Deckard • **Rutger Hauer** Roy Batty • **Sean Young** Rachael • **Edward James Olmos** Gaff • **M Emmet Walsh** Bryant • **Daryl Hannah** Pris • **William Sanderson** Sebastian • **Brion James** Leon • **Joe Turkel [Joseph Turkel]** Tyrell • **Joanna Cassidy** Zhora
Director *Ridley Scott*
Screenplay *Hampton Fancher, David Peoples, from the story "Do Androids Dream of Electric Sheep?" by Philip K Dick*
Cinematographer *Jordan Cronenweth* • ***Music*** *Vangelis* • ***Production design*** *Lawrence G Paull* • ***Special effects*** *Douglas Trumbull*

Blake of Scotland Yard ★★★

1927 US BW

Alchemy had been only an occasional theme in cinema since George Méliès's *The Philosopher's Stone* (1900). But this serial sure turned base material into gold for Universal, as producer Carl Laemmle bought all 12 episodes for just US$97,000 and it went on to gross over US$3.5 million worldwide. Hayden Stevenson's dogged pursuit of the avaricious Monty Montague proved compelling. But the main reason lies in the imaginative direction of Robert F Hill, whose atmospheric gothic manor sets harked back to Feuillade's heyday, while his emphasis on drama rather than breakneck action gave the audience more than a mere visceral thrill. Hill remade this serial in 1937, expanding it to 15 chapters, with Ralph Byrd (*Dick Tracy*) taking over the role of Blake.

Hayden Stevenson Angus Blake • **Gloria Grey** Lady Diane Blanton • **Herbert Prior** Lord Blanton • **Monty Montague** Jarvis • **Wilbur Mack** Albert Drexel • **Albert Hart** The Spider • **Grace Cunard** Queen of Diamonds
Director *Robert F Hill*
Screenplay *William Lord Wright*

Blake's 7 ★★★★

TV 1978-1981 UK Colour 39x50mins

After *Doctor Who*, this has to be the biggest cult sci-fi show the BBC ever made. Created by Terry Nation, the man who gave us the Daleks, it featured gritty plotlines, where regular characters were courageously killed off and the good guys didn't always win. *Blake's 7* endeared itself to both serious genre fans and also to those who

Magnificent seven: with its combination of gritty plotlines, compelling characters and high camp appeal, *Blake's 7* became one of the BBC's biggest sci-fi successes

watched for its high camp appeal or simply to have a good laugh at the sloppy effects and fashion disasters that were constantly on display. Set in the far future, a small group of outlaws led by Blake (Gareth Thomas) and later the hysterically smug Avon (Paul Darrow) battle with a corrupt and totalitarian galactic federation. Over ten million viewers tuned in for the final episode that proved as dramatic and shocking as anything a modern-day soap opera story editor could ever dream of devising. Thirteen 55-minute episodes were also made, giving viewers five minutes more to marvel at the space sets.

Gareth Thomas Blake • **Sally Knyvette** Jenna • **Paul Darrow** Avon • **David Jackson** Gan • **Jan Chappell** Cally • **Michael Keating** Vila • **Glyn Owen** Leylan • **Peter Tuddenham** Zen/Orac • **Stephen Greif** Travis • **Brian Croucher** Travis • **Jacqueline Pearce** Servalan • **Josette Simon** Dayna • **Steven Pacey** Tarrant • **Glynis Barber** Soolin

Created by *Terry Nation*
Script editor *Chris Boucher*
Producer *David Maloney*

SFacts

Creator Terry Nation was a gag writer for Tony Hancock, but it wasn't until he fell out with the ill-starred comedian that the opportunity arose to work on the first series of *Doctor Who*.

Blake's 7: The Sevenfold Crown ★★

Radio 1998 UK 110mins

Broadcast on Radio 4, this original story – written by Barry Letts – is an example of why cross-media transfers can often be a mistake. Many of the original cast of the popular TV series reprise their roles (Paul Darrow, Jacqueline Pearce, Michael Keating and Peter Tuddenham) but they fail to rekindle the sparky interaction that made the original such a success. The rather clichéd plot has the band of renegades on the trail of a diadem of power, which the over-the-top villainess Servalan (Pearce) also covets. Paul Darrow is as arrogant as ever, and also display more than a touch of meglomania, while the female leads are very much background characters here. However, there's enough action to keep diehard fans of the series happy. Available on audio-cassette.

Paul Darrow Avon • **Jacqueline Pearce** Servalan • **Michael Keating** Vila • **Steven Pacey** Tarrant • **Paula Wilcox** Soolin • **Angela Bruce** Dayna • **Peter Tuddenham** Orac/Slave • **Pip Donaghy** King Gheblakon • **Janet Dale** Jelka • **Christian Rodska** Dr Kapple

Director *Barry Lighthill*
Written by *Barry Letts*

Blake's 7: The Syndeton Experiment ★★★

Radio 1998 UK 60mins

Set shortly after the events of *The Sevenfold Crown*, this follow-up Radio 4 *Blake's 7* drama is more successful than the first effort. This time the evil Servalan (Jacqueline Pearce) and the renegades led by Paul Darrow are in hot pursuit of nanochip that, when implanted in the brain, gives the controller total power over the unfortunate person in whom it is embedded. Once again the action is fast-paced, if a tad confusing, while the sound effects often irritate. Available on CD.

Paul Darrow Avon • **Michael Keating** Vila • **Steven Pacey** Tarrant • **Jacqueline Pearce** Servalan • **Angela Bruce** Dayna • **Paula Wilcox** Soolin • **Peter Tuddenham** Orac • **Judy Cornwell** Gaskia • **Peter Jeffrey** Doctor Rossum • **Graham Padden** Vledka

Written by *Barry Letts*
Producer *Brian Lighthill*

Blast from the Past ★★★ 12

1998 US Colour 108mins [video] DVD

Convinced that an atomic bomb is about to drop on sixties America, married couple Sissy Spacek and Christopher Walken seal themselves in an elaborate fallout shelter for 35 years. What will their naive son (Brendan Fraser) make of the cynical nineties when he's sent out into the world for the first time? Not quite enough, unfortunately, in Hugh Wilson's somewhat laboured "culture clash" romantic comedy, as Fraser enlists the aid of streetwise Alicia Silverstone in his quest for supplies. Though the tone is sweet, the gags fail to bite and there's little innovation on offer beyond the initial premise. But it's pleasant enough, with Fraser's goofy charm particularly winning. Contains swearing and some sexual references.

Brendan Fraser Adam • **Christopher Walken** Calvin • **Sissy Spacek** Helen • **Alicia Silverstone** Eve • **Dave Foley** Troy • **Joey Slotnick Soda jerk** • **Rex Linn** Dave
Director *Hugh Wilson*
Screenplay *Bill Kelly, Hugh Wilson, from a story by Bill Kelly*

A Blind Bargain ★★★

1922 US BW 5 reels

The fourth of the five films Lon Chaney made for Wallace Worsley is a Dr Moreau-style melodrama in which Chaney's misguided surgeon plans to perform a glandular operation on penniless soldier Raymond McKee, only to be confounded by one of his hideously deformed cast-offs, a piteous simian hunchback. Typically, the Man of a Thousand Faces plays both creator and creation and it's worth noting the similarity between his apeman make-up and that of Fredric March's alter ego in the 1931 version of *Dr Jekyll and Mr Hyde*.

Lon Chaney Dr Arthur Lamb/Hunchback • **Raymond McKee** Robert Sandell • **Virginia True Boardman** Mrs Sandell
Director *Wallace Worsley*
Screenplay *J G Hawks, from the novel "The Octave of Claudius" by Barry Pain*

Bliss ★★★ 12 15

TV 1995-1997 UK Colour 5x90mins

Simon Shepherd plays Dr Sam Bliss, a brilliant Cambridge scientist who lives life to the full and investigates phenomena that defy traditional scientific boundaries in between pursuing his love for fine wine, elegant women and classical song. While Bliss's exploits aren't quite the divine blend of *The X Files* and *Inspector Morse* that it makers seem to be aiming for, they still provide the basis of a skilfully acted and respectable sci-fi drama occasional series.

Simon Shepherd Dr Sam Bliss • **Sian Webber** Dr Melanie Kilpatrick • **Zoe Hart** Louise Bliss • **Sarah Smart** Zoe Bliss • **Anthony Smee** Graham Fairfax
Director *Marc Evans, Richard Standeven, Simon Shore, Crispin Reece*
Written by *Michael Stewart, Richard McBrien, Charles Brent, Simon Eden, from an idea by Michael Stewart*
Producer *Jacky Stoller*

The Blob ★★★★★ 15

1958 US Colour 82mins

Steve McQueen got his first starring role in this musty delight about a giant red alien jelly terrorising small-town America and absorbing the population. A quintessential fifties classic (which spawned an equally successful 1988 remake), its gaudy colours, self-mocking tone and neat title creature add up to loads of unsettling fun. The scene where the outer-space ooze invades a local cinema has become one of science fiction's key images. The title song, was written by Burt Bacharach and Mack David, brother of Hal, Bacharach's longtime collaborator. Contains some violence.

Steven McQueen [Steve McQueen] Steve • **Aneta Corseaut** Judy • **Earl Rowe** Police lieutenant • **Olin Howlin** Old man • **Steven Chase [Stephen Chase]** Doctor • **John Benson** Sergeant Jim Bert ***Director*** *Irvin S Yeaworth Jr*
Screenplay *Irvin S Yeaworth Jr, Theodore Simonson, Ruth Phillips, from an idea by Irvine H Millgate*

The Blob ★★★★ 18

1988 US Colour 90mins

The Space Sponge returns in a super remake of the cult monster movie from sci-fi's golden era. As with John Carpenter and his remake of *The Thing*, director Chuck Russell (*The Mask*) gets his revamp exactly right. By re-interpreting all the potent moments from the Steve McQueen original in today's sophisticated special-effects terms, and updating the plot to include contemporary mores and political issues, Russell creates a breakneck monster-on-the-loose crowd-pleaser with a fun nostalgic pulse. Co-writer Darabont would achieve greater fame with *The Shawshank Redemption* six years later.

Shawnee Smith Meg Penny • **Donovan Leitch** Paul Taylor • **Kevin Dillon** Brian Flagg • **Ricky Paull Goldin** Scott Jeskey • **Billy Beck** Can man • **Jeffrey DeMunn** Sheriff Herb Geller • **Candy Clark** Fran Hewitt • **Beau Billingslea** Moss Woolsey • **Art La Fleur [Art LaFleur]** Mr Penny • **Del Close** Reverend Meeker • **Douglas Emerson** Eddie Beckner • **Michael Kenworthy** Kevin Penny • **Sharon Spelman** Mrs Penny
Director *Chuck Russell*
Screenplay *Chuck Russell, Frank Darabont*

The Blood Beast Terror ★

1967 UK Colour 87mins

Peter Cushing considered this clumsy chiller the worst picture he ever made. In many respects he was right. He's the policeman investigating vampiristic murders carried out by a giant death's-head moth masquerading as the "daughter" of a renowned Victorian entomologist. Vernon Sewell's direction barely papers over the pedestrian cracks in an equally moth-eaten screenplay decked out with dodgy horror clichés.

Peter Cushing Inspector Quennell • **Robert Flemyng** Professor Mallinger • **Wanda Ventham** Clare Mallinger • **Vanessa Howard** Meg Quennell • **Roy Hudd** Morgue attendant • **David Griffin** William • **Kevin Stoney** Grainger • **Glynn Edwards** Sergeant Allan • **John Paul** Warrander • **Russell Napier** Landlord
Director *Vernon Sewell*
Screenplay *Peter Bryan*

Blue Flame ★ 15

1995 US Colour 87mins

A hard-boiled detective goes on a search-and-destroy mission when two aliens kidnap his daughter, in the writing/directing debut of former William Morris agent Cassian Elwes. With its threadbare plot and terrible dialogue, this excruciating low-budget disaster is bearable only thanks to cinematographer Daniele Massaccesi's keen eye, which does at least make it visually interesting. The story apparently came to Elwes while he was high on medicinal drugs during an operation – worth bearing in mind if you're considering whether to watch this psychedelic-tinged fiasco.

Brian Wimmer Flemming • **Kerri Green** Rain • **Jad Mager** Fire • **Cecilia Peck** Jessie
Director/Screenplay *Cassian Elwes*
Cinematographer *Daniele Massaccesi*

Blue Monkey ★★★

1987 US Colour 98mins

Silly, scary and lots of fun, director William (*Death Weekend*) Fruet's throwback to fifties monster movies creates a constant stream of knowing chuckles and disturbing horror in roughly equal proportion. A gardener cuts himself on an exotic plant and promptly vomits up a larva and steroids turn the insect into a giant mutant bug in this nostalgia-tinged hokum unashamedly stealing ideas from *Aliens*, *Jaws* and *The Fly*. Hard-boiled detective Steve Railsback creeps through dark

Sticky situation: with its sophisticated special effects, Chuck Russell's 1988 remake of alien jelly cult hit *The Blob* successfully updated the fifties original

tunnels to eradicate the latest threat to mankind. Camp dialogue ("We still have a few bugs to iron out"), cardboard creatures and gleeful schlock all combine to make this an enjoyably slime-encrusted B movie.

Steve Railsback Detective Jim Bishop • **Gwynyth Walsh** Dr Rachel Carson • **Susan Anspach** Dr Judith Glass • **John Vernon** Roger Levering • **Joe Flaherty** George Baker • **Robin Duke** Sandra Baker • **Don Lake** Elliot Jacobs • **Sandy Webster** Fred Adams • **Joy Coghill** Dede Wilkens • **Bill Lake** Paramedic • **Stuart Stone** Joey • **Sarah Polley** Ellen

Director *William Fruet*

Screenplay *George Goldsmith*

Blue Sunshine ★★★★ 18

1976 US Colour 94mins [video]

One of the best shockers produced in the seventies, director Jeff Leiberman's cult classic is a psychedelic chiller of the highest order. Intriguing pulp fiction invades subversive David Cronenberg territory as the ten-year-delayed after-effects of an LSD derivative result in a group of former Stanford University students to losing their hair, then their cool, before turning into crazed, vicious killers. Directed with economic flair and sly black humour by Leiberman, this drug-culture allegory sizzles with invention and frenetically potent horror.

Zalman King Jerry Zipkin • **Deborah Winters** Alicia Sweeney • **Mark Goddard** Edward Flemming • **Robert Walden** David Blume • **Charles Siebert** Detective Clay • **Ann Cooper** Wendy Flemming • **Ray Young** Wayne Mulligan • **Brion James** Tony

Director/Screenplay *Jeff Lieberman*

The Body Disappears ★★ U

1941 US BW 72mins

Warner Bros sought to cash in on Universal's continuing *Invisible Man* series with this rough 'n' ready comedy. One of the studio era's more memorable character actors, Edward Everett Horton proves what a practised farceur he was as the dotty scientist who views comatose playboy Jeffrey Lynn as the ideal cadaver for his resurrection serum. However, the concoction succeeds only in rendering Lynn invisible. There's some suggestively imperceptible nudity from Jane Wyman and much regrettably racist grimacing from Willie Best.

Jeffrey Lynn Peter DeHaven III • **Jane Wyman** Joan Shotesbury • **Edward Everett Horton** Prof Shotesbury • **Herbert Anderson** George "Doc" Appleby • **Marguerite Chapman** Christine

Lunceford • **David Bruce** Jimmy Barbour • **Willie Best** Willie • **Natalie Schafer** Mrs Lunceford • **Sidney Bracey** Barrett • **Craig Stevens** Robert Struck
Director *D Ross Lederman*
Screenplay *Scott Darling, Erna Lazarus*

Body Parts ★★★ 18

1991 US Colour 84mins

From the writers of novels that inspired the film classics *Diabolique* and *Vertigo* comes this not-so-classic sci-fi horror, blending high-tech surgery with low-grade shocks. After a car accident, prison psychiatrist Jeff Fahey has the arm of an executed killer grafted on to his shoulder, which develops a murderous life of its own. Then he meets other recipients of the psycho's body parts suffering similar symptoms. *Near Dark* screenplay writer Eric Red directs all this sinister lunacy with a sure hand . Contains swearing and violence.

Jeff Fahey Bill Chrushank • **Lindsay Duncan** Dr Webb • **Kim Delaney** Karen Chrushank • **Brad Dourif** Remo Lacey • **Zakes Mokae** Detective Sawchuk • **Peter Murnik** Mark Draper • **Paul Ben-Victor** Ray Kolberg • **John Walsh** Charlie Fletcher • **Nathaniel Moreau** Bill Jr • **Sarah Campbell** Samantha
Director *Eric Red*
Screenplay *Eric Red, Norman Snider, from a story by Patrica Herskovic, Joyce Taylor, from the novel "Choice Cuts" by Thomas Narcejac, Pierre Boileau*

Body Snatchers ★★★★ 15

1993 US Colour 83mins

Those interstellar pods capable of duplicating humans return for a third sinister attempt on mankind's individual identities in director Abel Ferrara's masterly reinterpretation of the classic Jack Finney terror tale. Easily on an empathic par with the 1956 original chiller *Invasion of the Body Snatchers*, Ferrara's keen contemporary eye, controlled vision and heartless shock tactics make the underlying message seem more pertinent and vital than ever. Meg Tilly and Gabrielle Anwar make indelible impressions as they take on the horrifying enemy infiltrating their military home base. Contains violence, swearing and nudity.

Terry Kinney Steve Malone • **Meg Tilly** Carole Malone • **Gabrielle Anwar** Marty Malone • **Forest Whitaker** Doctor Collins • **Reilly Murphy** Andy Malone • **Billy Wirth** Tim Young • **Christine Elise** Jenn Platt • **R Lee Ermey** General Platt • **Kathleen Doyle** Mrs Platt • **G Elvis Phillips** Pete • **Stanley Small** Platt's aide • **Tonea Stewart** Teacher
Director *Abel Ferrara*
Screenplay *Stuart Gordon, Dennis Paoli, Nicholas St John, from a story by Larry Cohen, Raymond Cistheri, from the novel "Invasion of the Body Snatchers" by Jack Finney*

The Body Stealers ★

1969 US/UK Colour 91mins

Parachutists pass through a red mist and disappear into thin air. And before long you will, too! Is there any point in sticking around to find out it's alien Maurice Evans putting sky divers in suspended animation and substituting duplicates? Not really. A shame top agents Patrick Allen and Neil Connery (Sean's kid brother) don't reach the same conclusion after investigating a top secret space research lab, in this talky, low budget and hopelessly inept clone of *Invasion of the Body Snatchers*.

George Sanders General Armstrong • **Maurice Evans** Dr Matthews • **Patrick Allen** Bob Megan • **Neil Connery** Jim Radford • **Hilary Dwyer** Julie Slade • **Robert Flemyng** WC Baldwin • **Lorna Wilde** Lorna • **Allan Cuthbertson** Hindesmith • **Michael Culver** Lieutenant Bailes • **Sally Faulkner** Joanna
Director *Gerry Levy*
Screenplay *Mike St Clair, Peter Marcus*
Producer *Tony Tenser*

Bog ★

1978 US Colour 85mins

Veteran musical comedy actress Gloria DeHaven plays two terribly written roles in director Don Keeslar's hopeless monster farrago filmed in Wisconsin. She's a pathologist investigating a blood-draining creature sighted at Bog Lake and also an old witch with a psychic link to the fabled bayou Big Foot with a predilection for female victims. Doctor Marshall (*Fiend without a Face*) Thompson and sheriff Aldo Ray are also baffled by the slime creature's habits in this lacklustre micro-budget Z-movie bogged down by freeze frames and amateur production values.

Gloria DeHaven Ginny Glen/Adrianna • **Aldo Ray** Sheriff Neal Rydholm • **Marshall Thompson** Doctor Brad Wednesday
Director *Don Keeslar*
Screenplay *Carl N Kitt*

Bombshell ★

1997 US Colour 95mins

Beware any film that has "bomb" in the title, as it may live up to its unfortunate moniker. That's the case with this lame sci-fi thriller. Henry Thomas (still best known, over a decade later, as Elliott in *ET*) is one of two scientists in the near future (the other being Frank Whaley). They are using nanotechnology to fight cancer, but discover that their miracle cure could actually cause the disease. Of course, big business is involved so it's not long before poor old Henry finds himself at the mercy of mysterious people, and missing a kidney to boot. Daft fare that was originally made for the Sci-Fi Channel in the US, this is insulting for sci-fi fans and boring twaddle for everyone else. Matters are further hindered by such a wooden performance from Mädchen Amick (*Twin Peaks*) that you start to wonder whether the bad guys removed her acting ability at the same time as they whipped out Thomas's kidney.

Henry Thomas Buck Hogan • **Mädchen Amick** Angeline • **Frank Whaley** Malcolm • **Brion James** Donald • **Pamela Gidley** Melinda • **Michael Jace** Detective Jefferson • **Martin Hewitt** Adam • **David Packer** Brad • **Victoria Jackson** Waitress
Director *Paul Wynne*
Screenplay *Paul Wynne, from a story by Vicky Pike, Paul Wynne*

The Boogie Man Will Get You ★★★

1942 US BW 66mins

Here's a fun cast in a lively programme filler that cheered up many a wartime audience. Boris Karloff plays a demented (what else?) scientist who attempts to turn salesmen into supermen in a crazy plot, which also involves the wonderful Peter Lorre. Larry Parks is the juvenile lead – a long way from his performance in *The Jolson Story* – with Jeff Donnell aboard to add romantic interest. Lew Landers, who, as Louis Friedlander, made his directorial feature debut with the 1935 Karloff classic *The Raven*, successfully juggles the lunatic elements of plot and action.

Boris Karloff Professor Nathaniel Billings • **Peter Lorre** Dr Lorentz • **Maxie Rosenbloom** Maxie • **Larry Parks** Bill Leyden • **Jeff Donnell** Winnie Leyden • **Maude Eburne** Amelia Jones • **Don Beddoe** J Gilbert Brampton • **George McKay** Ebenezer • **Frank Puglia** Silvio Baciagalupi • **Eddie Laughton** Johnson
Director *Lew Landers*
Screenplay *Edwin Blum, Paul Gangelin (adaptation), from a story by Hal Fimberg, Robert E Hunt*

Born in Flames ★★★ 15

1983 US Colour 79mins

In a futuristic New York, ten years after a peaceful revolution has made all men

U = SUITABLE FOR ALL Uc = SUITABLE FOR ALL, ESPECIALLY YOUNG CHILDREN (VIDEO ONLY) PG = PARENTAL GUIDANCE

equal, three feminists from different backgrounds (the army, radio and performance arts) join together to fight for the rights of women irrespective of their race or sexual preference. A classic women's rights movie that utilises an in-your-face, cinéma vérité style, poignant arguments and razor-sharp humour to put across the hopeful fantasy of liberation against oppression. Among the cast is future director Kathryn (*Strange Days*) Bigelow.

Honey • **Adele Bertei** Isabel • **Jeanne Satterfield** Adelaide • **Flo Kennedy** Zella • **Pat Murphy** Newspaper editor • **Kathryn Bigelow** Newspaper editor • **Becky Johnston** Newspaper editor • **Hillary Hurst** Leader of women's army • **Sheila McLaughlin** Other leader • **Marty Pottenger** Other leader/Woman at site
Director *Lizzie Borden*
Screenplay *Hisa Tayo, from a story by Lizzie Borden*

The Borrower ★★★ 18

1989 US Colour 87mins

John McNaughton's follow-up to the hugely controversial *Henry: Portrait of a Serial Killer* finds him in more straightforward sci-fi horror territory. The story tracks an alien creature with a penchant for ripping the heads off unsuspecting humans and plonking them on his own neck. Rae Dawn Chong and Don Gordon are the puzzled detectives on its trail. McNaughton has some fun playing around with genre conventions and, while it's a long way from the bleak dread of *Henry*, it offers enough scares to keep horror fans happy. Contains swearing and sexual situations.

Rae Dawn Chong Diana Pierce • **Don Gordon** Charles Krieger • **Antonio Fargas** Julius Caesar Roosevelt • **Tom Towles** Bob Laney • **Neil Giuntoli** Scully • **Pam Gordon** Connie • **Mädchen Amick** Megan • **Larry Pennell** Captain Scarcelli
Director *John McNaughton*
Screenplay *Sam Egan [Mason Nage], Richard Fire, from a story by Sam Egan [Mason Nage]*

The Bowery Boys Meet the Monsters ★★★

1954 US BW 65mins

In 1946 surviving members of the Dead End Kids, who'd come to prominence in films such as in *Angels with Dirty Faces*, became the Bowery Boys to conveyor-belt feed the nation's adolescents with juvenile slapstick comedies of which this was the most commercially successful. A monster spoof, in the vein of those perpetrated by Abbott and Costello, this has the Boys running foul of a family that makes the Addams clan look like something out of Enid Blyton and, in the process getting tangled up with man-eating trees, gorilla transplants, robots and vampires. Although not particularly funny, it's directed by Edward Bernds, who'd previously worked with the Three Stooges.

Leo Gorcey Slip • **Huntz Hall** Sach • **Bernard Gorcey** Louie • **Lloyd Corrigan** Anton • **Ellen Corby** Amelia • **John Dehner** Derek • **Laura Mason** Francine • **Paul Wexler** Grissom
Director *Edward Bernds*
Screenplay *Elwood Ullman, Edward Bernds*

SCI Q

5

In which TV sci-fi thriller did *Darling* Julie Christie make her professional debut?

See page 496 for answers

A Boy and His Dog ★★★★ U

1975 US Colour 87mins

Featuring a very early screen appearance by Don Johnson, this film remains one of his best. He's actually not particularly brilliant in it as he is upstaged by his canine co-star, but this offbeat sci-fi comedy has deservedly become a cult favourite. Set in a post-apocalyptic world, the story follows the adventures of Johnson and his super intelligent dog when they get mixed up with a strange subterranean community, unable to reproduce sexually. Director LQ Jones (best known as a western character actor) works wonders with a tiny budget and maintains a pleasingly black tone throughout.

Don Johnson Vic • **Susanne Benton** Quilla June • **Jason Robards [Jason Robards Jr]** Mr Craddock • **Alvy Moore** Dr Moore • **Helene Winston** Mez • **Charles McGraw** Preacher • **Hal Baylor** Michael
Director *LQ Jones*
Screenplay *LQ Jones, from the novella by Harlan Ellison*

The Boy from Andromeda ★★★

TV 1991 NZ/Can Colour 6x30mins

A six-part serial for children, filmed in New Zealand before it became a fashionable locale for international co-productions. Teenage heroes Katrina Hobbs, Fiona Kay and Anthony Samuels discover fragments of a 100-year-old crashed spaceship near a volcano that turns out to be an alien device that could destroy the planet. The space debris prompts flashback-like visions which reveal that the volcano is protected by an invisible Guardian, but the children join up with Drom (played by a female, Jane Cresswell, but with a male voice, John Watson), survivor of the crashed ship, to thwart the creature. Nice scenery and above-average effects.

Katrina Hobbs Jenny • **Jane Creswell** Drom • **Fiona Kay** Tessa • **Anthony Samuels** Lloyd • **Heather Bolton** Shirley • **Paul Gittins** Ralph • **John Watson** Voice of Drom
Director *Wayne Tourell*
Written by *Ken Catran*

The Boy Who Turned Yellow ★★

1972 UK Colour 55mins

It is a film-making tragedy that after 1960's *Peeping Tom*, director Michael Powell's reputation took a serious nose dive. This peculiar little film for children, which was the final teaming of Powell with longtime collaborator Emeric Pressburger, sadly did nothing to resurrect the great man's career. Here, schoolboy John (Mark Dightman) takes a trip to the Tower of London and loses his pet mouse. Sent home from school later for falling asleep in a class on electricity, he dreams (or does he?) that the people on the tube and in the street have turned yellow.

Mark Dightman John • **Robert Eddison** Nick • **Helen Weir** Mrs Saunders • **Brian Worth** Mr Saunders • **Esmond Knight** Doctor • **Laurence Carter** Schoolteacher • **Patrick McAlinney** Supreme Beefeater
Director *Michael Powell*
Screenplay *Emeric Pressburger*
Producer *Roger Cherrill*

The Boys from Brazil ★★★ 18

1978 US Colour 118mins

Ira Levin's ingenious novel about the cloning of Hitler's body tissue, producing identical little boys who might revive the Third Reich, is given the epic treatment by director Franklin J Schaffner. Masterminding the genetic engineering is the infamous Dr Mengele, played by Gregory Peck in a convincing departure from his usual good-guy roles. James Mason is his accomplice and Laurence Olivier is the Nazi hunter modelled on Simon Wiesenthal who tracks them down. More plausible now than it was in the late seventies and still an accomplished, globe-trotting thriller, with the added appeal of Peck, Mason and Olivier all scoring points off each other. Contains violence.

Gregory Peck Dr Josef Mengele • **Laurence Olivier** Ezra Lieberman • **James Mason** Eduard Seibert • **Lilli Palmer** Esther Lieberman • **Uta Hagen** Frieda Maloney • **Rosemary Harris** Herta Doring • **Jeremy Black** Bobby/Jack/Erich/Simon • **Steve Guttenberg** Barry Kohler • **John Rubinstein** David Bennett • **Michael Gough** Mr Harrington • **Linda Hayden** Nancy • **Bruno Ganz** Professor Bruckner • **John Dehner** Henry Wheelock • **Denholm Elliott** Sidney Beynon • **Prunella Scales** Mrs Harrington • **Gunter Meisner** Farnbach • **Wolf Kahler** Schwimmer
Director *Franklin J Schaffner*
Screenplay *Heywood Gould, from the novel by Ira Levin*

The Brain ★★ 12

1962 W Ger/UK BW 83mins

Hammer Horror veteran Freddie Francis does a decent job directing the third version of Curt Siodmak's *Donovan's Brain*. Peter Van Eyck is the scientist controlled by the power-crazed organ of a sadistic tycoon kept alive after a plane crash. More of a mystery than an all-stops-out horror, the moody tale has some eerie moments and is efficiently involving. A competent cast, including producer Raymond Stross's wife Anne Heywood, injects new life into a familiar story.

Anne Heywood Anna • **Peter Van Eyck** Doctor Peter Corrie • **Cecil Parker** Stevenson • **Bernard Lee** Frank Shears • **Ellen Schwiers** Ella • **Maxine Audley** Marion • **Jeremy Spenser** Martin • **Ann Sears** Secretary • **Victor Brooks** Farmer • **Alistair Williams** Inspector Pike • **Kenneth Kendall** Newscaster • **John Junkin** Frederick • **Frank Forsyth** Francis • **Bandana Das Gupta** Miss Soong • **Allan Cuthbertson** Doctor Silva
Director *Freddie Francis*
Screenplay *Robert Stewart, Phil Macki, from the novel "Donovan's Brain" by Curt Siodmak*
Producer *Raymond Stross*

Brain Damage ★★★★ 18

1988 US Colour 85mins

An outrageously gory and excessively violent fable infused with the junk culture and trash aesthetic of cult director Frank Henenlotter's demented imagination. *The Muppet Show* meets *The Tingler* in this spaced-out gore joke about Elmer, the all-singing, all-dancing alien parasite, who injects a euphoric hallucinogenic fluid into his host, Rick Herbst, in return for donors it can suck brains from. The more Herbst gets addicted to Elmer's secretion, the more dangerous the risks he's prepared to take to satisfy his vicious pet's bloodlust. Quirky, inventive and completely offensive – some death scenes deliberately use pornographic imagery – this wickedly humorous slice of warped genius couldn't have come from anyone other than the perpetrator of *Basket Case*.

Rick Herbst Brian • **Gordon MacDonald** Mike • **Jennifer Lowry** Barbara • **Theo Barnes** Morris Ackerman • **Lucille Saint-Peter** Martha Ackerman • **Vicki Darnell** Blonde in Hell Club • **Joe Gonzales** Guy in shower • **Bradlee Rhodes** Night watchman • **Don Henenlotter** Policeman
Director/Screenplay *Frank Henenlotter*

Brain Dead ★★★ 15

1990 US Colour 80mins

Neurologist Bill Pullman is blackmailed by business friend Bill Paxton into studying the case history of paranoid accountant-turned-serial-killer Bud Cort in order to unlock the secrets in his mind. After brain surgery and shock therapy, however, Cort switches personalities with Pullman, turning director Adam Simon's enjoyably quirky *Twilight Zone* update into a crazed splatter romp. Dreams within dreams, nightmare flashbacks, terrifying visions and people running around with brains in jars keep the pace lively and interesting, even if it is hard to follow exactly what's going on.

Bill Pullman Rex Martin • **Bill Paxton** Jim Reston • **Bud Cort** Jack Halsey • **Patricia Charboneau** Dana Martin • **Nicholas Pryor** Conklin/Ramsen • **George Kennedy** Vance • **Brian Brophy** Ellis
Director *Adam Simon*
Screenplay *Charles Beaumont, Adam Simon, from a story by Charles Beaumont*

The Brain Eaters ★★ PG

1958 US BW 60mins

Based on Robert Heinlein's landmark alien invasion novel *The Puppet Masters* (which Disney remade in 1999), this routine B-movie exemplifies the atomic-era paranoia genre. Yet, despite the laughable, hairy, neck-burrowing parasites and the stock scientist-versus-the-military scenario, director Bruno VeSota creates an imaginatively bleak atmosphere through tilted camera angles and crisp black-and-white photography. No great shakes, but it is only an hour long and *Star Trek* fanatics can see their beloved Spock (Leonard Nimoy) in an early intergalactic role.

Edwin Nelson Dr Kettering • **Joanna Lee** Alice • **Jody Fair** Elaine • **Alan Frost** Glenn • **Jack Hill** Senator Powers • **David Hughes** Dr Wyler • **Robert Ball** Dan Walker • **Greigh Phillips** Sheriff • **Orville Sherman** Cameron • **Leonard Nimoy** Protector • **Doug Banks** Doctor • **Henry Randolph** Telegrapher
Director *Bruno VeSota*
Screenplay *Gordon Urquhart*

The Brain from Planet Arous ★★ PG

1958 US BW 70mins

An all-time camp schlock classic, with bad-movie icon John Agar an absolute hoot as the nuclear physicist possessed by a floating alien brain called Gor, in its first step towards Earth domination. Soon Agar is sporting silver contact lenses and setting model planes on fire with a glance, while his pet dog is taken over by Gor's rival for the final axe battle. What were they thinking? Unsurprisingly, director Nathan Hertz changed his name to Nathan Juran for *The 7th Voyage of Sinbad* later the same year.

John Agar Steve • **Joyce Meadows** Sally Fallon • **Robert Fuller** Dan • **Thomas Browne Henry** John Fallon • **Henry Travis** Colonel Grogley • **Ken Terrell** Colonel • **Tim Graham** Sheriff Paine • **E Leslie Thomas** General Brown • **Bill Giorgio** Russian
Director *Nathan Hertz [Nathan Juran]*
Screenplay *Ray Buffum*

The Brain Machine ★★ U

1954 UK BW 79mins

A British B-movie which begins promisingly in sci-fi mode, but soon lapses into routine thrillerdom, a typical product of the old Merton Park studios. The machine of the title, known as an "electroencephalograph", is attached to an accident victim who may also be a psychopath. Despite its cheap production values and leaden acting from Patrick Barr, Elizabeth Allan and Maxwell Reed, the picture has a trashy energy that can be enjoyed if you disengage your own brain. Writer/director Ken Hughes went on to bigger things such as *The Trials of Oscar Wilde* and *Cromwell*.

Patrick Barr Dr Geoffrey Allen • **Elizabeth Allan** Dr Philippa Roberts • **Maxwell Reed** Frank Smith • **Russell Napier** Inspector Durham • **Gibb McLaughlin** Spencer Simon • **Edwin Richfield** Ryan • **Neil Hallett** Sergeant John Harris • **Vanda Godsell** Mae • **Bill Nagy** Charlie
Director/Screenplay *Ken Hughes*

The Brain Machine ★

1972 US Colour 92mins

Reverend James Best (Sheriff Rosco from *The Dukes of Hazzard*) is one of four people who volunteer for a secret government experiment in this sloppy metaphysical thriller. The human guinea pigs are incarcerated in the "E-Box" and bombarded with questions concerning immortality, truth and desire. But dredging up their terrifying memories causes madness and homicide. The point of the apparently illegal research is never explained in director/co-writer Joy N Houck Jr's confused scenario and, coupled with the mediocre acting, cheap production values and poor special effects, it is hardly worth anyone's time or effort trying to figure it all out.

James Best • **Barbara Burgess** • **Gil Peterson** • **Gerald McRaney**
Director/Screenplay *Joy N Houck Jr*

Brain Smasher . . . a Love Story ★★ PG

1993 US Colour 81mins (video)

In straight-to-video director Albert Pyun's mildly amusing action comedy, bouncer Ed Malloy (Andrew Dice Clay) joins supermodel Teri Hatcher and her botanist sister to stop a sacred mystical lotus flower, which holds the key to unlimited power over matter, from falling into the hands of a suave band of Chinese ninja monks. Although described as Rambo, Superman and the Terminator all rolled into one, Malloy (as played by wild comedian Clay) prefers dropping one-liners to participating in any kick-boxing fight. The romance between Clay and Hatcher looms larger than any of the anticipated "brain smashing" mayhem.

Andrew Dice Clay Ed Malloy • **Teri Hatcher** Samantha Crain
Director/Screenplay *Albert Pyun*
Producer *Tom Karnowski*

The Brain That Wouldn't Die ★★

1959 US BW 0mins

After decapitating his fiancée Virginia Leith in a car crash, demented surgeon Jason Evers decides to transplant her still living head onto the body of a facially scarred stripper. But Leith wants to die and telepathically manipulates the giant pinhead mutant locked up in Evers' cupboard to go on the rampage. This rock bottom fantasy exploitation pic reaches high levels of engaging absurdity through poverty-row production values and ludicrous, blood-soaked action. Left on the shelf for three years (Evers had changed his name from Herb to Jason by then), this appalling cheapie has nonetheless become a brainless cult classic.

Jason Evers Dr Bill Cortner • **Leslie Daniel** Kurt • **Paula Maurice** B-Girl • **Virginia Leith** Jan Compton • **Adele Lamont** Doris • **Bruce Brighton** Doctor • **Lola Mason** Donna Williams • **Audrey Devereau** Jeannie • **Eddie Carmel** Monster • **Bruce Kerr** Announcer
Director *Joseph Green*
Screenplay *Joseph Green, from a story by Rex Carlton, Joseph Green*
Producer *Rex Carlton*

SCI Q • SCI Q • SCI Q • SCI Q •

6

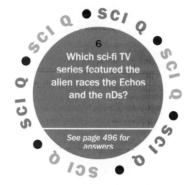

Which sci-fi TV series featured the alien races the Echos and the nDs?

See page 496 for answers

Braindead ★★★★★ 18

1992 NZ Colour 99mins (video)

Kiwi director Peter Jackson's horrendously funny gross-out shocker is a brilliant black comedy, and the ultimate gore movie. Timothy Balme's mother gets bitten by a Sumatran "rat monkey" carrying a living-dead virus and turns into a rabid zombie with terrible table manners. Cue zombie sex, kung fu priests, reanimated spinal columns and half-eaten craniums, all building towards a final, gore-drenched massacre. Jackson's outrageously sick groundbreaker is a virtuoso *Grand Guignol* masterpiece. You really won't believe your eyes! Contains graphic violence, swearing and sex scenes.

Timothy Balme Lionel • **Diana Penalver** Paquita • **Liz Moody** Mum • **Ian Watkin** Uncle Les • **Brenda Kendall** Nurse McTavish • **Stuart Devenie** Father McGruder • **Jed Brophy** Void • **Elizabeth Brimilcombe** Zombie mum • **Peter Jackson** Undertaker's assistant
Director *Peter Jackson*
Screenplay *Peter Jackson, Stephen Sinclair, Francis Walsh*

Brainscan ★★★ 15

1994 Can/US/UK Colour 90mins (video)

Misfit loner Edward Furlong sends off for the virtual reality game *Brainscan*, advertised as the ultimate in terror, only to wake up with memory loss and a severed foot in the refrigerator. Frank Langella is the cop on his trail. But will he believe the murder is really the work of the Trickster, a vile demon who represents the dark side of anybody playing the game? Despite some inferior special effects, this unusually bleak and intense chiller is one of the best horror films to use the virtual reality hook.

Edward Furlong Michael Brower • **Frank Langella** Detective Hayden • **T Rider-Smith** Trickster • **Amy Hargreaves** Kimberly • **Jamie Marsh** Kyle • **Victor Ertmanis** Martin • **David Hemblen** Dr Fromberg • **Vlasta Vrana** Frank
Director *John Flynn*
Screenplay *Andrew Kevin Walker, from a story by Brian Owens*

Brainstorm ★★★★ 15

1983 US Colour 101mins (video)

Today, in films like *The Lawnmower Man* and *Strange Days*, it's called "virtual reality". But when *2001* special effects genius Douglas Trumbull directed this film (which turned out to be Natalie Wood's last), he termed it "telepathic engineering". Louise Fletcher (giving an outstanding performance) and Christopher Walken invent a headset enabling the wearer to experience the sensory recordings of others. Then Fletcher has a coronary and leaves behind a recording of her death experience which the military seizes for its own misuse. Although flawed and naive, Trumbull's metaphysical odyssey is a technically dazzling triumph packing the same pseudo-religious punch as *Close Encounters*.

Christopher Walken Michael Brace • **Natalie Wood** Karen Brace • **Cliff Robertson** Alex Terson • **Louise Fletcher** Lillian Reynolds • **Donald Hotton** Landon Marks • **Joe Dorsey** Hal Abramson • **Darrell Larson** Security technician
Director *Douglas Trumbull*
Screenplay *Robert Statzel, Phillip Frank Messina, from a story by Bruce Joel Rubin*

Brainwaves ★★ 18

1982 US Colour 76mins (video)

This suffers from a combination of a low budget and some clumsy writing and direction. Suzanna Love plays a woman who regains consciousness after a coma only to discover that, thanks to some ground-breaking surgery, she has inherited the brainwaves of a murdered woman. There are some nifty moments but the main point of interest is the eclectic casting – as well as Vera Miles and Keir Dullea (*2001: a Space Odyssey*), there is Tony Curtis in a ripe cameo as an improbable brain surgeon.

Keir Dullea Julian Bedford • **Suzanna Love** Kaylie Bedford • **Vera Miles** Marian • **Percy Rodrigues** Dr Robinson • **Tony Curtis** Dr Clavius • **Paul Wilson [Paul Willson]** Dr Schroder • **Ryan Seitz** Danny Bedford • **Nicholas Love** Willy Meiser
Director *Ulli Lommel*
Screenplay *Ulli Lommel, Suzanna Love*
Producer *Ulli Lommel*

Brasil Ano 2000 ★★★

1969 Bra Colour 95mins

A realistic approach to poverty and an emphasis on indigenous folklore had been key elements of the *cinemo novo* movement in the early sixties. But, as the precariousness of civilian democracy became readily apparent, the Brazilian new wave was forced to enter into its more allegorical, "cannibalist-tropicalist" phase. This post-apocalyptic fantasy dates from the end of that period and shows a society so literally turned upside down that the despised natives are now atop the pecking order. But life in this desolate utopia is far from easy, as Annecy Rocha and her mother Iracema de Alencar discover on their desperate journey. A Portuguese language film.

Annecy Rocha • **Enio Goncalves** • **Iracema de Alencar** • **Ziembinsky**
Director/Screenplay *Walter Lima Jr*

Brave New World ★★★

TV 1980 US Colour 2x95mins

Surprisingly, Aldous Huxley's 1932 novel didn't make it to the big or the small screen until 1980, by which time its rickety science had been invalidated by real-life genetics, its rebel-against-the-awful-world-of-the-future plot had been used too many times and the targets of its satirical barbs (like Henry Ford) had become passé. This two-part miniseries retains much of the memorable language of the book, but stirs in a few late-seventies elements that have themselves now become quaint – disco-style costumes, character names like "Lenina Disney", references to cloning, fast foods and musak – but Robert E Thompson's script mostly sticks faithfully to the novel's texts. In a bland, sleek future that seems too close to the worlds of second-rate TV sci-fi like *Logan's Run*, a mishap at the eugenics factory produces a Shakespeare-spouting throwback (Kristoffer Tabori,) who is briefly a craze and then an embarrassment to the privileged but empty society. The casting is pretty good, with everyone except Tabori managing a creepily happy TV commercial tone that conveys the doped, distracted zombie haze of these futuristic lotus-eaters – Bud Cort is the slight misfit, Kier Dullea the perfect citizen who commands the Hatcheries, Julie Cobb the "pneumatic" girl who discovers the horrors of the wild life and Ron O'Neal the smoothly manipulative Big Brother-type leader Mustapha Mond. A 1998 TV remake with Leonard Nimoy as Mond and Peter Gallagher as the rebel Bernard Marx, hammered the story into a conventional against-the-system diatribe with a ridiculous happy ending.

Julie Cobb Linda Lysenko • **Bud Cort** Bernard Marx • **Keir Dullea** Thomas Grahmbell • **Ron O'Neal** Mustapha Mond • **Marcia Strassman** Lenina Disney • **Kristoffer Tabori** John Savage • **Dick Anthony Williams** Helmholtz Watson
Director *Burt Brinckerhoff*
Written by *Robert E Thompson, from the novel by Aldous Huxley*

SFacts

There once was a plan to turn this into a Broadway musical, with either Leonard Bernstein or Rodgers and Hammerstein providing the score. Huxley wrote the story intending, he is reported to have said, "to have a little fun pulling the leg of HG Wells".

Brazil ★★★★★ 15

1985 US/UK Colour 137mins

In Terry Gilliam's extraordinary vision of a futuristic bureaucratic hell, Jonathan Pryce stars as the Orwellian hero, a permanently harrassed clerk at the all-seeing Department of Information Retrieval, who is only kept sane by his vivid daydreams, which see him as a heroic flying warrior coming to the aid of a beautiful woman (Kim Griest). As unpredictable as Gilliam's Monty Python animations, this daring and dazzling take on *1984* creates a weird world inhabited by crazy characters, including Robert De Niro, in an inspired but brief cameo as an SAS-style repairman. The movie's sledgehammer conclusion gave studio executives sleepless nights. Expect the same.

Jonathan Pryce Sam Lowry • **Robert De Niro** Archibald "Harry" Tuttle • **Katherine Helmond** Mrs Ida Lowry • **Ian Holm** Mr Kurtzmann • **Bob Hoskins** Spoor • **Michael Palin** Jack Lint • **Ian Richardson** Mr Warrenn • **Peter Vaughan** Mr Eugene Helpmann • **Kim Greist** Jill Layton • **Jim Broadbent** Dr Jaffe • **Barbara Hicks** Mrs Terrain • **Charles McKeown** Lime
Director *Terry Gilliam*
Screenplay *Terry Gilliam, Tom Stoppard*

Brick Bradford ★★★★ U

1947 US BW 15x18mins

Cracking fun from start to finish, this rollicking serial opens with Kane Richmond striving to prevent a UN interceptor ray falling into the hands of evil Charles Quigley. But then the anti-guided missile device runs short of Lunarium. So Brick has to travel to the Moon (via the Crystal Door – cheaper special effects than a rocket) and help a band of rebels overthrow the tyrannical Lunarians before he can board the Time Top to find an 18th-century Englishman in the depths of Central America to secure another missing formula element. And only then (!) can he rescue Linda Johnson from Quigley. Marvellous.

Kane Richmond Brick Bradford • **Linda Johnson** June • **Rick Vallin** Sandy Sanderson • **Pierre Watkin** Prof Salisbury • **Charles Quigley** Laydron • **Jack Ingram** Albers • **Carol Forman** Queen Khana
Director *Spencer Gordon Bennet*
Screenplay *Lewis Clay, Arthur Hoerl, George H Plympton, from the comic strip by Clarence Gray, William Ritt*

Bride of Frankenstein ★★★★★ PG

1935 US BW 74mins

James Whale's extravagantly produced sequel to his own *Frankenstein* still ranks as one of horrordom's greatest achievements. From his wittily eccentric direction and Elsa Lanchester's electric hairdo, to Ernest Thesiger's ingenious portrayal of the perverse Dr Pretorius and Boris Karloff's alternately poignant and pushy monster, it's a class act from amazing start to religious-slanted finish. They don't get any better than this one and some scenes – the unveiling of the bride to the sound of wedding bells, the miniature people in bell jars – are of emphatic classic status.

Boris Karloff The monster • **Colin Clive** Henry Frankenstein • **Valerie Hobson** Elizabeth • **Ernest Thesiger** Doctor Pretorius • **Elsa Lanchester** Mary Shelley/The Bride • **Gavin Gordon** Lord Byron • **Douglas Walton** Percy Bysshe Shelley • **Una O'Connor** Minnie • **EE Clive** Burgomaster • **Lucien Prival** Butler • **OP Heggie** Hermit • **Dwight Frye** Karl • **Reginald Barlow** Hans
Director *James Whale*
Screenplay *William Hurlbut, John L Balderston, from the novel "Frankenstein" by Mary Shelley*
Cinematographer *John Mescall* • ***Art director*** *Charles D Hall* • ***Special effects*** *John P Fulton* • ***Make-up*** *Jack Pierce* • ***Music*** *Franz Waxman*

Bride of Re-Animator ★★ 18

1991 US Colour 92mins [video]

Nowhere near as impactful, witty or fresh as the original HP Lovecraft-based cult movie *Re-Animator*, director Brian Yuzna's gloriously gory sequel (he produced the first outing) sadly ventures more into standard Frankenstein territory. Jeffrey Combs is good value as Herbert West, the mad doctor with the luminous green serum that revives dead tissue to create a living woman out of assorted body parts (the feet of a ballet dancer, the womb of virgin and so on). This has the usual dire consequences and it's all gruesomely over-the-top, with a nightmarishly surreal climax. Contains violence, and some swearing.

Jeffrey Combs Herbert West • **Bruce Abbott** Dan Cain • **Claude Earl Jones** Lieutenant Leslie Chapham • **Fabiana Udenio** Francesca Danelli • **David Gale** Doctor Carl Hill • **Kathleen Kinmont** Gloria/The Bride
Director *Brian Yuzna*
Screenplay *Woody Keith, Rick Fry, from a story by Brian Yuzna, Woody Keith, Rick Fry, from the story "Herbert West – the Re-Animator" by HP Lovecraft*
Producer *Brian Yuzna*

Bride of the Monster ★ PG

1955 US BW 68mins [video]

Many will know about this movie purely because Tim Burton expertly re-created key scenes in his superb *Ed Wood* biopic. The movie itself is pure torture to watch, but has to be seen to be believed. Bela Lugosi, in his only true starring role in an Ed Wood exploiter, is a fugitive Russian scientist trying to create a race of super-beings in his swamp-based hideout. *Plan 9 from Outer Space* star Tor Johnson is his moronic, mute assistant, while bland hero Tony McCoy only got the role because his Arizona rancher father financed the film. The whole sorry affair comes complete with light-bulb special effects and the infamous pit fight between Lugosi and a lifeless rubber octopus stolen from a John Wayne movie.

Bela Lugosi Dr Eric Vornoff • **Tor Johnson** Lobo • **Tony McCoy** Lieutenant Dick Craig • **Loretta King** Janet Lawton • **Harvey Dunn** Captain Robbins • **George Becwar** Professor Strowski • **Paul Marco** Kelton • **Don Nagel** Martin • **Bud Osborne** Mac
Director *Edward D Wood Jr*
Screenplay *Edward D Wood Jr, Alex Gordon*
Producer *Edward D Wood Jr*

Bridge of Dragons ★★ 18

1999 US Colour 87mins [video]

Dolph Lundgren's star may have faded a little since the heady days of *Rocky IV* and *Universal Soldier*, but he remains a popular draw in video-land and this won't disappoint his fans. Set in a post-apocalyptic future, it stars Lundgren as a programmed killing machine – an always helpful plot device since it explains the wooden acting. When he comes to the rescue of a princess, he incurs the wrath of evil warlord Cary-Hiroyuki Tagawa. While this offers plenty of high-quality biffing and loud explosions, it's the charismatic Tagawa who steals the show.

Dolph Lundgren Warchyld • **Cary-Hiroyuki Tagawa** Ruecheng • **Rachel Shane[Valerie Chow]** Halo
Director *Isaac Florentine*
Screenplay *Carlton Holder*

Bridge of Time ★ U

1997 US Colour 102mins

This asinine science-fiction adventure was filmed entirely in South Africa. Forced to crash-land their plane, a UN relief worker (*LA Law*'s Susan Dey), her photojournalist ex-husband and an opportunistic fortune hunter are rescued and brought to a mystical city where the people live in harmony and youth springs eternal. Although the visitors are not held captive, their departure becomes increasingly complicated when the city's spiritual leader (Cicely Tyson) convinces them it is their destiny to be the custodians of the human race. If you enjoy terrible acting and really bad dialogue, this brainless TV movie is not to be missed.

Susan Dey Madeline Armstrong • **Cotter Smith** Robert Creighton • **Nigel Havers** Halek • **Cicely Tyson** Guardian • **Robert Whitehead** Maxwell Spring • **Kimberleigh Stark** Keza • **Todd Jensen** William
Director *Jorge Montesi*
Screenplay *Drew Hunter, Christopher Canaan*

Britannia Hospital ★★★ 15

1982 UK Colour 111mins [video]

Director Lindsay Anderson's top-heavy symbolism all but crushes the satirical life out of this attempt to lampoon the state of the nation, with a run-down hospital expecting a royal visit to celebrate its 500th anniversary used as a metaphor for Britain's moral decay. Media hacks, strike-bent workers, bureaucratic chaos and sinister laboratory experiments are Anderson's targets, although the burlesque humour makes it seem closer to "Carry On Casualty". Malcolm McDowell, Anderson's favourite hero in such films as *If...* and *O Lucky Man!*, is the journalist who wanders through NHS chaos in a film saved by some of Britain's finest character actors, including Leonard Rossiter, Graham Crowden, Jill Bennett and cherubic Joan Plowright. Don't expect to find wit as sharp as a hospital scalpel; this seems much happier using a meat cleaver. Contains violence, swearing and nudity.

Leonard Rossiter Potter • **Graham Crowden** Millar • **Malcolm McDowell** Mike • **Joan Plowright** Phyllis • **Marsha A Hunt** Amanda • **Frank Grimes** Fred • **Jill Bennett** MacMillan • **Robin Askwith** • **John Bett** • **Peter Jeffrey** • **Fulton Mackay** • **John Moffatt** • **Dandy Nichols** • **Alan Bates**
Director *Lindsay Anderson*
Screenplay *David Sherwin*

The Bronx Executioner ★

1989 It Colour 92mins

Director "Bob Collins" (Vanio Amici) took a lot of footage from Romolo Guerrieri's *The Final Executioner*, redubbed it, and inserted some newly-shot footage starring Gabriele Gori, resulting in this movie. Needless to say, the end result is an utter mess. Formerly a post-holocaust movie, the futuristic story now concerns sheriff Woody Strode training Gori to keep the peace between leather-clad androids and humanoids fighting among the green fields and gravel pits the Bronx is well known for. Though Italians never were very good at ripping off *Mad Max* and *Escape from New York*, this reaches new levels of ineptness, being not only incredibly cheap and dumb, but having some of the worst and passionless action scenes anywhere. Italian dialogue dubbed into English.

Gabriele Gori • **Margit Evelyn Newton** • **Chuck Valenti** • **Rod Robinson** • **Alex Vitale** Dakar • **Woody Strode** Sheriff
Director *Bob Collins [Vanio Amici]*
Screenplay *Piero Regnoli, from a story by Vanio Amici*

The Brood ★★★★ 18

1979 Can Colour 88mins [video] DVD

Oliver Reed, a doctor experimenting with the new science of psychoplasmics, persuades Samantha Eggar to "shape her rage" and give birth to deformed children with killer instincts in another of director David Cronenberg's disturbing shockers. An intriguing metaphor for both unexplained bodily changes and the

Hero worship: Buck Rogers (Buster Crabbe) and sidekick Wilma Deering (Constance Moore) begin a battle against interplanetary baddies that captured the public's imagination for decades

U = SUITABLE FOR ALL Uc = SUITABLE FOR ALL, ESPECIALLY YOUNG CHILDREN (VIDEO ONLY) PG = PARENTAL GUIDANCE

mental abuse some parents heap on their offspring, this genuinely creepy and upsetting stomach churner is a modern horror classic. In one of her best performances, Eggar gives a poignant emotional depth to Cronenberg's complex chiller.

Oliver Reed Dr Hal Raglan • **Samantha Eggar** Nola Carveth • **Art Hindle** Frank Carveth • **Cindy Hinds** Candice Carveth • **Nuala Fitzgerald** Julianna Kelly • **Henry Beckman** Barton Kelly • **Susan Hogan** Ruth Mayer • **Michael McGhee** Inspector Mrazek
Director/Screenplay *David Cronenberg*

The Brother from Another Planet

★★★ 15

1984 US Colour 108mins [video]

A beguiling and thoughtful example of science fiction as social satire from independent writer/director John Sayles, the best purveyor of refreshingly new gritty comedies in the business. As the mute ET wandering Harlem streets in a daze, Joe Morton gives a *tour de force* performance. Despite a "magical touch" enabling him to mend any household object, Sayles mainly uses his alien hero's inability to speak as an object lesson in human behaviour. The provocative device provides opportunities for a fine roster of supporting characters to pour out their hearts and be spiritually "fixed". Contains violence, swearing and drug abuse.

Joe Morton The Brother • **Daryl Edwards** Fly • **Steve James** Odell • **Leonard Jackson** Smokey • **Bill Cobbs** Walter • **Maggie Renzi** Noreen • **Tom Wright** Sam • **Ren Woods** Bernice • **Reggie Rock Bythewood** Rickey
Director/Screenplay *John Sayles*

Bruce Gentry – Daredevil of the Skies ★★★ U

1948 US BW 15x16mins

Tom Neal spent much of his career playing humourless baddies (a fact that off-screen acquaintances considered typecasting – Neal was later jailed for the manslaughter of his wife). However, he's very much the hero of this lively chapter-play, in which he teams with rancher Ralph Hodges and his sister Judy Clark to confound a master criminal known as the Recorder because (yes, you guessed it), he communicates only via recorded messages. The effects for the flying disc that can pinpoint targets with unerring accuracy are pinched to the last penny. But Neal's flight to save the Panama Canal is white-knuckle stuff.

Tom Neal Bruce Gentry • **Judy Clark** Juanita Farrell • **Ralph Hodges** Frank Farrell • **Tristram Coffin** Krendon • **Terry Frost** Chandler • **Jack Ingram** Allen
Director *Spencer Gordon Bennet, Thomas Carr*
Screenplay *George H Plympton, Joseph F Poland, Lewis Clay*

The Bubble ★★

1966 US Colour 93mins

Arch Oboler is not a name instantly identifiable among cinemagoers, yet it was he who brought us the first ever 3-D movie, *Bwana Devil* in 1952. While Hollywood lost interest in the costly process, Oboler persisted and finally perfected Space-Vision (his own 3-D system) and released *The Bubble*. Ironically, this overly talky movie about three people trapped in a town populated by zombies and surrounded by an energy shield – a strained indictment of small-town mentality that demands conformity – hardly merited or benefitted from 3-D exposure. Perhaps more imagination should have been invested in the plot and characterisations rather than in the technical angle.

Michael Cole Mark • **Deborah Walley** Catherine • **Johnny Desmond** Tony • **Kassid McMahon** • **Barbara Eiler**
Director/Screenplay *Arch Oboler*
Cinematographer *Charles Wheeler*

Buck Rogers ★★ U

1939 US BW 12x20mins

Created by Philip F Nowlan in 1929, Buck Rogers was America's first sci-fi comic-strip hero. However, it took the success of *Flash Gordon* to lure him on to the screen and, ironically, in the form of Buster Crabbe himself. Awakening from a five-century Nirvano gas-induced slumber, Crabbe is detailed by the citizens of Hidden City to accompany Constance Moore on a mission to Saturn to enlist its inhabitants in a war against the despicable Killer Kane (Anthony Warde). Overdependent on interplanetary shuttling and low-impact battle sequences, the serial was later re-edited into the features *Planet Outlaws* (1953) and Destination Saturn (1965).

Buster Crabbe [Larry "Buster" Crabbe] Buck Rogers • **Constance Moore** Wilma Deering • **C Montague Shaw** Dr Huer • **Jackie Moran** Buddy Wade • **Anthony Warde** Killer Kane
Director *Ford Beebe, Saul A Goodkind*
Screenplay *Norman S Hall, Ray Trampe, from the character created by Philip F Nowlan*

Buck Rogers in the 25th Century

★★★ U PG 15

TV 1979-81 US Col 4x120m; 33x60m [video]

For his follow-up to *Battlestar Galactica*, writer/producer Glen A Larson revived one of the sci-fi genre's most enduring heroes and made him the star of this lightweight but surprisingly enjoyable series. Gil Gerard heads the cast as the titular Captain William "Buck" Rogers, a contemporary Nasa astronaut who is thrown 500 years into the future, where he becomes the galaxy's greatest hero. Buck is at his best during the show's Earth-based first season, which is far more fun than its *Star Trek*-style second year of deep space exploration. Yet even when its plotlines are at their most frivolous or tedious, the series doesn't stint on exciting action sequences, impressive special effects or famous guest stars, and it is always well served by the agreeably macho Gerard and the sensationally slinky Erin Gray, who plays sidekick Colonel Deering. The series' pilot episode, *Awakening*, received a theatrical release in Europe.

Gil Gerard Buck Rogers • **Erin Gray** Colonel Wilma Deering • **Tim O'Connor** Dr Elias Huer • **Wilfrid Hyde White** Dr Goodfellow • **Jay Garner** Admiral Asimov • **Thom Christopher** Hawk • **Mel Blanc** Voice of Twiki • **Felix Silla** Twiki • **Pamela Hensley** Princess Ardala
Executive story consultant *Stephen McPherson*
Executive producer *Glen A Larson* • ***Supervising producer*** *Leslie Stevens*

Buffy the Vampire Slayer

★★★★★ PG 12 15

TV 1997– US Colour [video]

Dissatisfied with the way Buffy Summers's 1992 big screen debut was primarily played for laughs, executive producer Joss Whedon took a second stab at the Slayer's adventures and produced a mesmerising blend of drama, comedy, horror, action and sci-fi. Picking up from events in the movie, the series pits Sarah Michelle Gellar's Buffy against both an array of monsters and an assortment of personal demons. Infinitely better than it sounds, this cross between *The X Files* and *Clueless* excels thanks to its smart and inventive plotting and unbeatable characterisation. The beguiling Gellar is simultaneously strong and vulnerable as the Slayer, and heads an outstanding cast of eclectic performers. Although the show loses some of its focus during its sci-fi-orientated fourth season, it remains a unique and thoroughly marvellous piece of television. The series has also spawned a successful spin-off show, *Angel*, and an animated *Buffy* series is currently in the works.

Sarah Michelle Gellar Buffy Summers • **Nicholas Brendon** Alexander "Xander" Harris • **Alyson Hannigan** Willow Rosenberg • **Anthony Stewart Head [Anthony Head]** Rupert Giles • **Charisma Carpenter** Cordelia Chase • **David Boreanaz** Angel • **Kristine Sutherland** Joyce Summers • **Emma Caulfield** Anya Emerson/Anyanka
Created by *Joss Whedon*
Executive producer *Joss Whedon*

Bug ★★ 15

1975 US Colour 95mins

The last film produced by William Castle, the king of gimmick cinema (*The Tingler*, *Macabre*), is one of his better efforts. An earthquake unleashes a swarm of fire-making insects, which scientist Bradford Dillman mates with the common cockroach in order to communicate with them. The initial nature-revenge plot tends to get lost once the routine mad doctor thread takes over, but zestful direction and tongue-in-cheek acting eke out some decent thrills and chills from the implausible tale. Castle originally wanted to present this in "Feel-O-Vision", with windscreen wiper-style brushes attached to every cinema seat, but was prevented by the huge costs involved.

Bradford Dillman James Parmiter • **Joanna Miles** Carrie Parmiter • **Richard Gilliland** Metbaum • **Jamie Smith Jackson** Norma Tacker • **Alan Fudge** Mark Ross • **Jesse Vint** Tom Tacker • **Patty McCormack** Sylvia Ross • **Fred Downs** Henry Tacker • **James Greene** Reverend Kern • **Jim Poyner** Kenny Tacker • **Sam Jarvis** Taxi Driver • **Brenden Dillon** Charlie
Director *Jeannot Szwarc*
Screenplay *Thomas Page, William Castle, from the novel "The Hephaestus Plague" by Thomas Page*
Producer *William Castle*

The Bulldog Breed ★★ PG

1960 UK BW 93mins

There is no doubt where the fun lies in this merely adequate comedy, and that is in the brief sight of hopefuls Michael Caine and Oliver Reed playing second fiddle to Norman Wisdom. Coming towards the end of his purple patch, Wisdom is not at his best as the fumbling shop assistant whose career in the navy culminates in an ill-fated moonshot. The script does him few favours, however, restricting the opportunities for sentimental slapstick in order to accommodate the surplus plot.

Norman Wisdom Norman Puckle • **Ian Hunter** Admiral Sir Bryanston Blyth • **David Lodge** CPO Knowles • **Robert Urquhart** Commander Clayton • **Edward Chapman** Mr Philpots • **Eddie Byrne** PO Filkins • **Peter Jones** Diving instructor • **John Le Mesurier** Prosecuting counsel • **Terence Alexander** Defending counsel • **Sydney Tafler** Speedboat owner • **Liz Fraser** Naafi Girl • **Penny Morrell** Marlene • **Michael Caine** Sailor • **Oliver Reed**
Director *Robert Asher*
Screenplay *Jack Davies, Henry Blyth, Norman Wisdom*

The Burning Glass ★★

TV 1960 UK BW 90mins

Charles Morgan's 1953 stage play deals with an innocent scientist who discovers a super-weapon and is unsure whether to turn it over to the British government. The McGuffin is a machine that can harness the powers of the sun and focus light like a magnifying glass, burning any city it happens to be pointed at. The property was adapted twice for British television, as an hour-long *Television Playhouse* special in 1956, with John Robinson (the second TV *Quatermass*) as the conscience-stricken scientist and Robert Rietty as the agent of a foreign power (which, unusually, seems to be America rather than Russia) out to get hold of the device. This 1960 90-minute *Play of the Week* version cast Michael Atkinson and a more eastern Peter Reynolds in the leads. An attempt to debate the issues surrounding the atom bomb, the play sticks mostly to the drawing room for its conscience-wrangling and spy plotting. The actual sci-fi elements are slight, and improbable.

Michael Atkinson Christopher Terriford • **Daphne Slater** Mary Terriford • **Anthony Newlands** Tony Locke • **Roger Livesey** Montague Winthropp • **Peter Reynolds** Tamas Domokos Hardlip
Director *David Boisseau*
Adapted by *Elizabeth Lincoln, from the play by Charles Morgan*

The Burning Zone ★

TV 1996-1997 US Colour 19x60mins

Outbreak is infected with a touch of *The X Files* here and breeds a less than catchy viral thriller series. The show revolves around a specialised task force that investigate biological disasters, and secretly attempt to expose a mysterious global conspiracy known as "The Dawn". In a further *X Files* parallel, their missions are initially led by unorthodox scientist Jeffrey Dean Morgan and his sceptical sidekick, Tamlyn Tomita. Thanks to its "virus-of-the-week" format and hackneyed characters, the series proves to be a formulaic and repetitive affair and it struggles to sustain viewer interest beyond its first episode. Not even Morgan and Tomita's mid-season disappearance could save this small screen scourge from a justly early demise.

Jeffrey Dean Morgan Dr Edward Marcase • **Tamlyn Tomita** Dr Kimberly Shiroma • **James Black** Agent Michael Hailey • **Michael Harris** Dr Daniel Cassian • **Bradford Tatum** Dr Brian Taft
Created by *Coleman Luck*
Executive producer *Coleman Luck, James D McAdams*

Buttoners ★★★★

1997 Cz Rep Colour 108mins

Although this ingeniously structured portmanteau picture often recalls the surrealist antics of Luis Buñuel, Petr Zelenka's astute mix of satire, sci-fi and historical supposition owes more to the eccentric strain of Czech comedy that also inspires the likes of Jan Svankmajer. Starting with the atomic assault on Hiroshima, Zelenka relates six stories that gradually link together to form a mischievous thesis on the role of chance, coincidence, fate and forgiveness in everyday life. Featuring a gallery of offbeat characters, including a man who spits at trains and another who snips buttons off furniture, this is a gleefully quirky and superbly controlled film. In Czech with English subtitles.

Pavel Zajicek Radio 1 moderator • **Jan Haubert** Guest • **Seisuke Tsukahara** Japanese man with spectacles • **Motohiro Hosoya** Japanese man with beard • **Junzo Inokuchi** Young Japanese man • **Svetlana Svobodova** Japanese woman • **Frantisek Cerny** Franta, taxi driver • **Michaela Pavlatova** Woman in taxi • **Jan Cechticky** Man in taxi • **Vladimir Dlouhy** Psychiatrist • **Marek Najbrt** Patient • **Jiri Kodet** Honza, host • **Inka Brendlova** Sylvia, hostess • **Rudolf Hrusinsky Jr** Unsuccessful man • **Eva Holubova** His wife • **Mariana Stojlovova** Girl at seance • **Bára Brodska** Girl at seance • **Julie Stalpovskich** Girl at seance • **Barbora Johnova** Girl at seance
Director/Screenplay *Petr Zelenka*

C

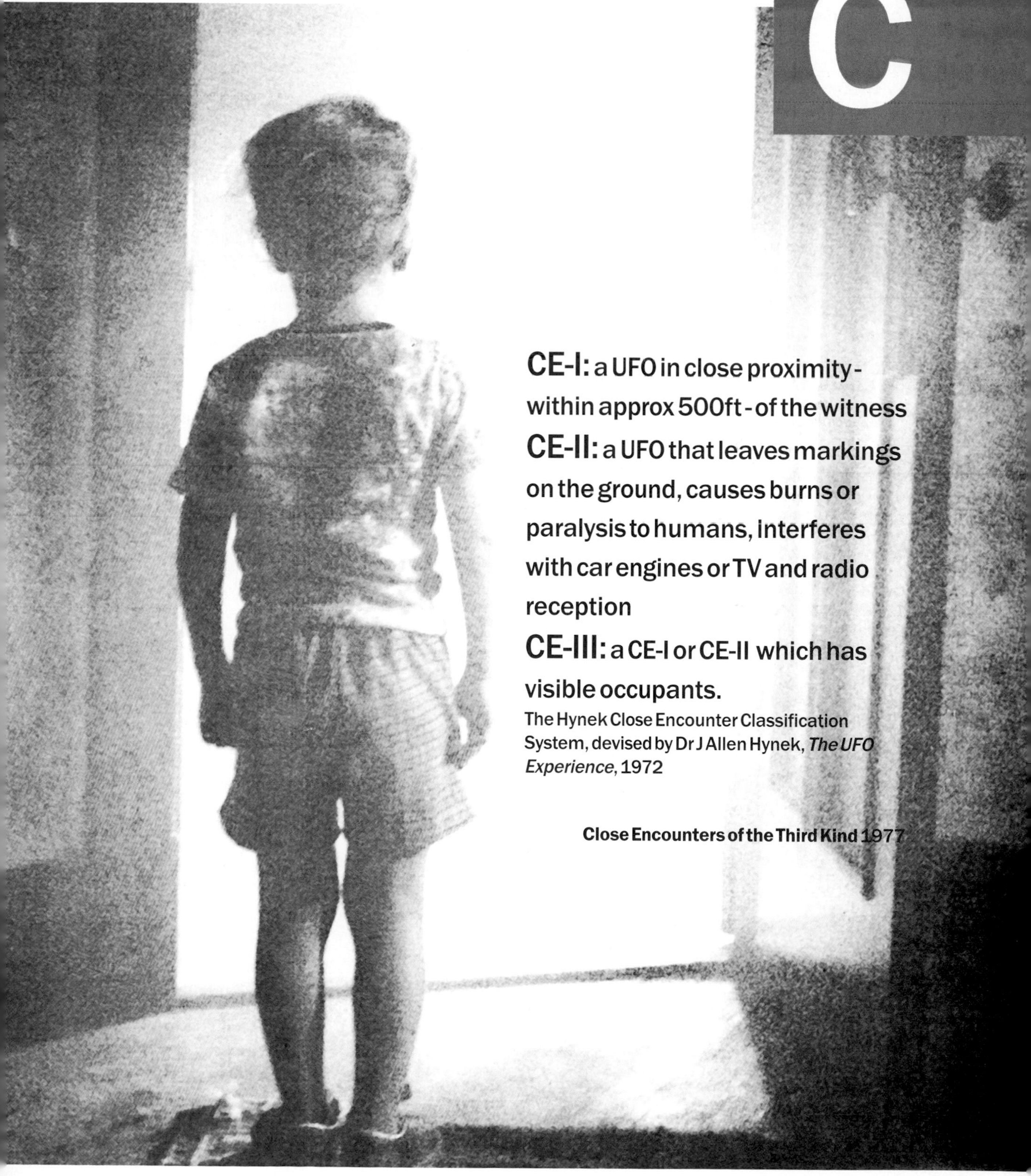

CE-I: a UFO in close proximity - within approx 500ft - of the witness
CE-II: a UFO that leaves markings on the ground, causes burns or paralysis to humans, interferes with car engines or TV and radio reception
CE-III: a CE-I or CE-II which has visible occupants.

The Hynek Close Encounter Classification System, devised by Dr J Allen Hynek, *The UFO Experience*, 1972

Close Encounters of the Third Kind 1977

The CBS Radio Mystery Theater ★★★

Radio 1974-1982 US 1500x45-60mins

The sound of a creaking door opened each episode of this long-running anthology series. The stories were a mix of mystery, horror, suspense, the supernatural and science-fiction, and were frequently introduced by the actor EG Marshall. Created by Hiram Brown, the legendary radio drama producer responsible for *Inner Sanctum*, at its peak it was heard on 350 stations in the United States. The series lives on via the legion of fans who swap favourite episodes via the Internet and conventions. They do so illegally, however, as the rights to all episodes are still owned by Brown, who has never agreed to publish them on tape.

Created by *Himan Brown*
Producer *Himan Brown*

CIA – Codename Alexa ★★ 18

1992 US Colour 94mins

From the days when OJ Simpson was better known as the sportsman-turned-aspiring-actor rather than the infamous murder suspect, this is a strictly by-the-numbers affair that grafts some sci-fi elements on to a fairly standard action plot. Kathleen Kinmont is the top-notch terrorist courted by moody CIA agent Lorenzo Lamas, who wants her to betray crime boss Alex Cord. Director Joseph Merhi makes sure all the ingredients for a straight-to-video success are present and correct, although mainstream film fans are unlikely to be impressed.

Lorenzo Lamas Mark Graver • **Kathleen Kinmont** Alexa • **Alex Cord** Victor Mahler • **O J Simpson** Nick Murphy • **Stephen Quadros** Max • **Pamela Dixon** Chief • **Michael Bailey Smith** Benedetti
Director *Joseph Merhi*
Screenplay *John Weidner, Ken Lamplugh*
Producer *Joseph Merhi, Richard Pepin*

California Man ★★ PG

1992 US Colour 88mins

A belated attempt to cash in on *Bill and Ted*-style comic capers, although by this stage the Californian teen speak was becoming more irritating than funny. Sean Astin and Pauly Shore are the two nerdish teenagers who gain a ticket to "cooldom" when they dig up a deep-frozen caveman (*George of the Jungle's* Brendan Fraser) and educate him in the ways of adolescent etiquette. There are some amusing moments, Fraser makes for a pleasingly gormless hunk and the reliable Richard Masur is among the supporting players. However, the comic posturing of Shore, who rose to fame on MTV, quickly grates and ultimately it lacks the winning stupidity of Bill and Ted's two adventures. Released in the USA as *Encino Man*. Contains drug use.

Sean Astin Dave Morgan • **Brendan Fraser** Link • **Pauly Shore** Stoney Brown • **Megan Ward** Robyn Sweeney • **Robin Tunney** Ella • **Michael DeLuise** Matt • **Patrick Van Horn** Phil • **Dalton James** Will • **Rick Ducommun** Mr Brush • **Jonathan Quan [Ke Huy Quan]** Kim • **Mariette Hartley** Mrs Morgan • **Richard Masur** Mr Morgan • **Ellen Blain** Teena Morgan •
Director *Les Mayfield*
Screenplay *Shawn Schepps, from a story by Shawn Schepps, George Zaloom*

Caltiki, the Immortal Monster ★★

1959 It BW 76mins

Future horror maestro Mario Bava directed 70 per cent of this endearing Italian-style mixture of *The Quatermass Experiment* and *The Blob* when credited director Riccardo Freda walked off the film and left his cinematographer in confused charge. Freda was probably exaggerating when he stated he took such action to make the indecisive Bava take the plunge into directing. Yet this purported Mayan legend, about a radioactive monster unleashed when explorers defile its holy lair, nevertheless demonstrates how Bava's technica genius overcame the micro-budgets he was to suffer throughout his long and illustrious career.

John Merivale Dr John Fielding • **Didi Sullivan [Didi Perego]** Ellen Fielding • **Gerard Herter** Max Gunther • **Daniela Rocca** Linda • **Giacomo Rossi-Stuart** Professor Rodriguez
Director *Robert Hampton [Riccardo Freda], Mario Bava*
Screenplay *Filippo Sanjust*

Cape Canaveral Monsters ★

1960 US BW 69mins

As one would expect from the legend that is Phil Tucker, the man responsible for *Robot Monster* (1953), one of the all-time great sci-fi clangers, large doses of unintentional humour are on the cards, but that's about all you get from this lame reds-under-the-beds Z-feature. For Communist agitators read instead invading aliens who inhabit the bodies of a pair of car crash victims and set about sabotaging America's space missile programme with the aid of a cheapo secret lab and a bazooka-type gun. Having had the nerve to blame the failure of *Robot Monster* on the script, this time Tucker personally undertook the writing chores himself on what turned out to be his directorial swan song, although he still plagued the industry briefly as a producer.

Scott Peters Tom Wright • **Linda Connell** Sally Markham • **Jason Johnson** Haroun • **Katherine Victor** Nadja
Director/Screenplay *Phil Tucker*

Capricorn One ★★★★ PG

1978 US Colour 118mins DVD

Did the Americans really land on the Moon, or did they fake it in a TV studio? That's the premise of this ingenious thriller, in which three men are bound for Mars until there's a technical slip-up on the launch pad. The astronauts end up faking the mission to save face, but their space capsule (which went without them) burns up on re-entry. Problem one: three embarrassingly alive astronauts. Problem two: their distraught families. Problem three: Elliott Gould as a nosey reporter. Directed by Peter Hyams with real flair, this is hugely enjoyable, all the way to the gripping finale with Telly Savalas relishing his fun role as an old-time crop-dusting pilot who's got the right stuff.

Elliott Gould Robert Caulfield • **James Brolin** Charles Brubaker • **Sam Waterston** Peter Willis • **Brenda Vaccaro** Kay Brubaker • **O J Simpson** John Walker • **Hal Holbrook** Dr James Kelloway • **Karen Black** Judy Drinkwater • **Telly Savalas** Albain • **David Huddleston** Hollis Peaker • **David Doyle** Walter Loughlin
Director/Screenplay *Peter Hyams*

Captain America ★★★

1944 US BW

A weapon powered by dynamic vibrations, a deadly purple poison, a resurrection machine, a Mayan treasure map and a villain called the Scarab, who plans to murder the heroine by mummification – and all this in just 15 chapters. It was clearly all too much for Dick Purcell, who died shortly after playing the titular hero (who was changed from the comic-book's battling GI to a crusading DA). But then the misdemeanours of Lionel Atwill would have taxed even the heartiest of souls. Directing his last serial for Republic, John English brings his customary brio to the predictable, but nevertheless highly enjoyable proceedings.

Dick Purcell Grant Gardner/Captain America • **Lorna Gray** Gail Richards • **Lionel Atwill** Dr Maldor/Scarab • **Charles**

Trowbridge Commissioner Dryden • **George J Lewis** Matson • **John Davidson** Gruber • **Russell Hicks** Mayor Randolph
Director *John English, Elmer Clifton*
Screenplay *Royal Cole, Ronald Davidson, Basil Dickey, Jesse Duffy, Harry Fraser, Joseph F Poland*

Captain America ★★ U

1979 US Colour 93mins

It's odd that the most patriotic superhero of all, in the United States at least, is the one who has failed to take off. In this TV movie, Reb Brown has the necessary physique but little else as he dons the stars-and-stripes costume to save Phoenix from being blown up by a neutron bomb. An even sillier sequel followed, and there was a movie version in 1990, but in both cases the concept failed to grab the public's imagination.

Reb Brown Steve Rogers/Captain America • **Len Birman** Dr Simon Mills • **Heather Menzies** Dr Wendy Day • **Steve Forrest** Lou Brackett • **Robin Mattson** Tina Hayden • **Joseph Ruskin** Rudy Sandrini
Director *Rod Holcomb*
Screenplay *Don Ingalls, from a story by Chester Krumholz, Don Ingalls*

Captain America ★★ PG

1990 US Colour 93mins

This is another botched attempt to revive the popular American cartoon character, with Matt Salinger taking the title role, battling the evil Red Skull. Albert Pyun is a competent director of sci-fi and martial arts action movies, but this tough, brooding comic-book fantasy suffers in comparison to other big-budget superhero adventures, and Salinger lacks charisma as the hero. There is, however, solid support from old hands such as Ned Beatty, Ronny Cox and Darren McGavin. Contains comic-book violence and mild swearing.

Matt Salinger Steve Rogers/Captain America • **Ned Beatty** Sam Kolawetz • **Scott Paulin** Red Skull • **Ronny Cox** President Tom Kimball • **Darren McGavin** General Fleming • **Kim Gillingham** Bernice/Sharon • **Michael Nouri** Lieutenant Colonel Louis • **Melinda Dillon** Mrs Rogers • **Francesca Neri** Valentina De Santis • **Bill Mumy** Young Fleming • **Carla Cassola** Dr Maria Vaselli
Director *Albert Pyun*
Screenplay *Stephen Tolkin*

Captain Midnight ★★

1942 US BW

Directed by one of Laurel and Hardy's favourite collaborators (James W Horne) and fronted by the face of MGM's hilarious Pete Smith Specialities (Dave O'Brien), this 15-part chapterplay was based on a popular radio show. However, it's so loaded down with wartime propaganda (to alert Americans to the dangers of fifth columnists like James Craven and his evil daughter, Luana Walters), that its entertainment value is now strictly limited. As you'd expect of a veteran of Tex Ritter's Texas Rangers horse operas, O'Brien is more at home in the action sequences, although many of these rely on bargain-basement aerial effects.

Dave O'Brien Captain Midnight • **Dorothy Short** Joyce • **James Craven** Ivan Shark • **Bryant Washburn** Edwards • **Luana Walters** Fury • **Sam Edwards** Chuck
Director *James W Horne*
Screenplay *Basil Dickey, George H Plympton, Jack Stanley, Wyndham Gitten*

Captain Midnight ★★

TV 1954-1956 US BW 39x30mins

Captain Midnight, a masked aviator who had earned his nickname in the First World War, made his US radio debut in 1938 and flew dangerous, sometimes fantastical missions until 1949, popping up in a film serial in 1942. His TV debut came in 1951 in *Captain Midnight's Adventure Theatre*, in which he merely introduced episodes of old serials, but in 1954, Richard Webb was cast as the Ovaltine-drinking (and promoting) commander of the Secret Squadron, taking to the skies to combat spies and subversives, and keep powerful new weapons out of evil hands, although the more fantastical episodes did yank in some sci-fi stuff. Because Screen Gems, Inc, the production company, foresaw that Ovaltine, owner of the franchise from the radio days, might withdraw sponsorship, they prepared alternate soundtracks in which Captain Midnight was overdubbed as Jet Jackson and the show entered syndication under the title *Jet Jackson, the Flying Commando*.

Richard Webb Captain Midnight • **Sid Melton** Ichabod "Ikky" Mudd • **Olan Soule** Aristotle "Tut" Jones
Director *D Ross Lederman*

Captain Nemo and the Underwater City ★ U

1969 UK Colour 105mins

MGM steered well clear of Jules Verne novels after its disastrous early talkie adaptation of *Mysterious Island* in 1929. Undoubtedly, the success of Disney's *20,000 Leagues under the Sea* influenced this change of heart, but the 15-year gap between the films and the fact that this was made by MGM's British operation suggest that no one had any real faith in the project. Robert Ryan as Nemo looks as if experiencing the "bends" would be preferable to participating in the picture, which has barely adequate effects and a shoddy script made up of borrowed ideas.

Robert Ryan Captain Nemo • **Chuck Connors** Senator Robert Fraser • **Nanette Newman** Helena • **John Turner** Joab • **Luciana Paluzzi** Mala • **Bill Fraser** Barnaby • **Kenneth Connor** Swallow • **Allan Cuthbertson** Lomax • **Christopher Hartstone** Philip
Director *James Hill*
Screenplay *Jane Baker, R Wright Campbell, from characters created by Jules Verne*

Captain Nice ★★

TV 1967 US Colour 15x30mins

Despite the proven wit of creator Buck Henry, fresh from *Get Smart*, this sit-com superhero parody lasted only half a season, perhaps because *Batman* was already quite parodic enough. Mild-mannered police scientist Carter Nash (William Daniels), a character loosely based on the Silver Age Flash's civilian identity, hits on a formula that transforms him into the super-powered but still mild-mannered Captain Nice. The Captain only fought crime because his overbearing sit-com mother (Alice Ghostley) nagged him and she also sewed his ill-fitting costume. Ann Prentiss was the cop love interest, more stereotypically aggressive than the hero. The very similar *Mr Terrific* was first telecast on the same day that *Captain Nice* appeared; Canadian and British variants, *My Secret Identity* and *My Hero*, came along decades later.

William Daniels Carter Nash/Captain Nice • **Ann Prentiss** Sgt Candy Kane • **Alice Ghostley** Mrs Nash • **Liam Dunn** Mayor Finney • **Bill Zuckert** Chief Segal • **Byron Foulger** Mr Nash
Created by *Buck Henry*

Captain Power and the Soldiers of the Future ★★ PG

TV 1987-1988 US 22x30mins

The twist of this regulation future war series was that it was backed by the toy company Mattel and featured bogus interaction between the on-screen action and kids watching at home, who could zap evil robots if they purchased and used the tie-in toys, which were sometimes activated by signals within the programme. The device proved unwieldy and the toys didn't shift enough units, so the show was cancelled after a season, to the delight of parents who resented relentless product-plugging and fortunes spent on batteries. Set in the year 2147, after humankind has almost lost the Metal Wars, the show followed the adventures of a team of super-soldiers led by Tim Dunigan as they fought off the Bio-Dreads, mechanical servants of the Volcanian Empire of David Hemblen. Created by Gary Goddard, who had made the *Masters of the Universe* feature, the show was script-edited by J Michael Straczynski (who carried over some of the ideas into his own *Babylon 5*) and Larry DiTillio. Shot in Canada, it was a busy, noisy effort, torn between the kiddie-level shoot 'em ups demanded by the toy tie-in and more standard sci-fi militarism.

Tim Dunigan Capt Jonathan Power • **Peter MacNeill** Maj Matthew "Hawk" Masterson • **Sven-Ole Thorsen** Lt Michael "Tank" Ellis
Director *Ken Girotti*
Created by *Garry Goddard*

Captain Scarlet and the Mysterons ★★★★★ U

TV 1967-1968 UK Colour 32x30mins

Thunderbirds may be Gerry Anderson's most popular and successful show but *Captain Scarlet* remains his supermarionation masterpiece. The indestructible Captain Scarlet, voiced by actor Francis Matthews, who got the job after Anderson heard him impersonating Cary Grant, is the top agent of Spectrum, Earth's first line of defence in their 21st-century war against the Mysterons, aliens from the planet Mars who have the power to create duplicate human beings. Full of memorable characters including Captain Black and the Angels, a team of female pilots who protect Cloudbase, Spectrum's orbiting HQ. An intriguing idea to have guest star puppets every week, voiced by a celebrity, starting with *The Prisoner*'s Patrick McGoohan, was sadly ruled out for being too costly. Watching the show today it's startling how dark and violent the subject matter is, considering this was a puppet show meant for kids.

Francis Matthews Captain Scarlet • **Ed Bishop** Captain Blue • **Donald Gray** Colonel White/Captain Black • **Janna Hill** Symphony Angel • **Cy Grant** Lt Green • **Jeremy Wilkin** Captain Ochre • **Liz Moran** Rhapsody Angel/Destiny Angel • **Paul Maxwell** Captain Grey • **Sylvia Anderson** Melody Angel
Created by *Gerry Anderson*
Music *Barry Gray* • ***Special effects supervisor*** *Derek Meddings*

Captain Video and His Video Rangers ★★★★

TV 1949-1955 US BW 1537x15/30mins

The first major success of television science fiction, *Captain Video* inspired numerous imitations in the 1950s. Initially created as the host of a series which would repackage old western B-movies for a kid audience, Captain Video became an action star in his own right, working out of his super-scientific secret base to thwart the evil plans of Dr Pauli, assisted by the loyal teenage Video Ranger, an audience stand-in who was supposed to be just one of a vast but rarely-seen army of Rangers. At first, Captain Video stayed in his cardboard lab and tinkered with gadgets, but when word reached the producers that a rival network was reviving Buck Rogers, Video had to take to space in his ships, the *X-9* and the *Galaxy II*. The first Video was Richard Coogan, who was replaced by Al Hodge after a year, while Don Hastings was the Video Ranger throughout the run, with Bram Nossem and Hal Conklin playing Dr Pauli. As a cost-saving measure, chunks of westerns were inserted into the program, purportedly so that the Captain could check up on the heroic activities of his Video Rangers Out West while he was taking care of the rest of the universe of the 22nd century. Surprisingly distinguished guest writers included Jack Vance, Damon Knight, Cyril Kornbluth, James Blish and Robert Sheckley, while among the many villains was Ernest Borgnine as the thuggish Nargola. The Lone Ranger used Rossini, but the Video Rangers had a Wagner theme (the *Flying Dutchman* overture). The show, which ran serial stories on weekdays, spun off a film serial, *Captain Video Master of the Stratosphere* (1951, with Judd Holdren), and a half-hour non-serial show, *The Secret Files of Captain Video*. The Captain went down with the ship, the show being cancelled when the struggling DuMont network disappeared.

Al Hodge Captain Video • **Richard Coogan** Captain Video • **Don Hastings** Ranger • **Hal Conklin** Dr Pauli • **Bram Nossem** Dr Pauli • **Fred Scott** Ranger Rogers/Announcer
Concept creator *James L Caddigan*

Captain Z-Ro ★★

TV 1951-1956 US BW 77x30mins

A kids' adventure series on the model of the amazingly successful *Captain Video*, this had three incarnations, on local stations in San Francisco (1951) and Los Angeles (1953) as a five-days-a-week, 15-minute live program and then in syndication (1955-56) as a filmed half-hour show. Creator/writer Roy Steffens played Captain Z-Ro, a villainous-looking (goatee and black moustache) hero who was the proprietor of a secret laboratory equipped with a remote viewer for observing historical events and a time machine for popping back and straightening things out whenever it looked like history was about to run off course – rescuing Robin Hood, George Washington, William Tell, Genghis Khan(!) or King Alfred when it seemed as if their victories were about to be rewritten as defeats. It never occurred to the Captain that it might have been more fun to tinker with history to the advantage of the present, but the show was stuck with a notional educational content as Z-Ro's young pal Jet (Bobby Trumbull, Jeff Silvers, Bruce Haynes) learned history lessons. Like the later TV time traveller Doctor Who, Captain Z-Ro sometimes got away from the schoolbook stuff to deal with more sci-fi material, such as battling a renegade android or taking to space.

Roy Steffins Captain Z-Ro • **Bob Turnbull** Jet • **Jeff Silvers** Jet • **Bruce Haynes** Jet
Created by *Roy Steffins*

Captain Zep – Space Detective ★★

TV 1983-1984 UK Colour 12x30mins

This interactive science-fiction series for children followed the adventures of the eponymous hero, a sort of galactic Sherlock Holmes, as he tackled weird mysteries. A teacher at the Solve Academy for would-be space detectives, he would set a mystery a week, which the students would try to solve. Young viewers were encouraged to write in with answers to questions set, and those lucky ones with the correct answer received a badge. The show ran for two series, with Paul Greenwood, followed by Richard Morant, as the cleverest detective in the galaxy.

Paul Greenwood Captain Zep (series 1) • **Richard Morant** Captain Zep (series 2) • **Ben Ellison** Jason Brown • **Harriet Keevil** Professor Spiro • **Tracey Childs** Professor Vana
Written by *Dick Hills, Colin Bennett*
Producer *Christopher Pilkington*

Captive Women ★

1952 US BW 67mins

A laughably bad Armageddon fiasco from Grade Z producer Albert Zugsmith showing

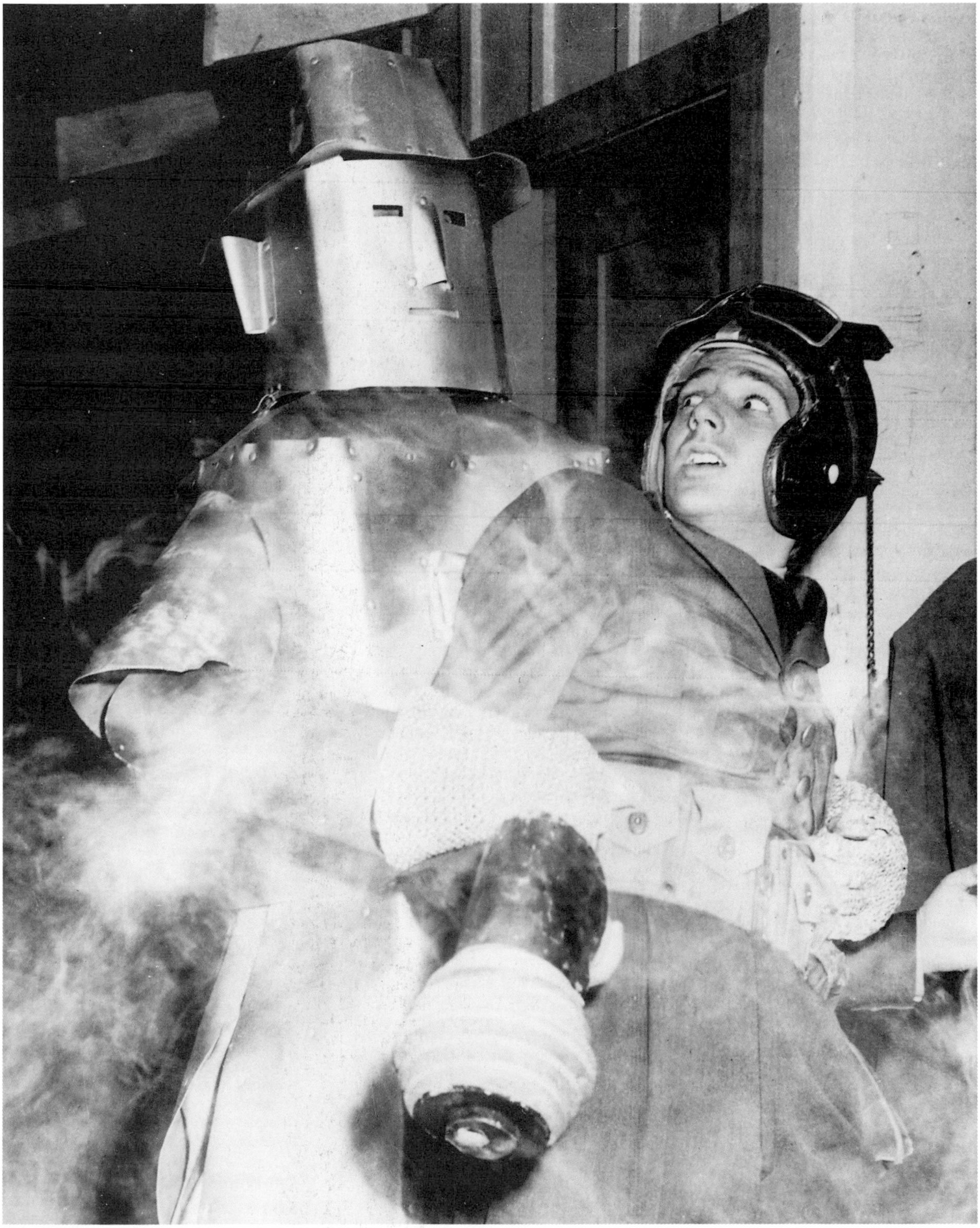

Video nasty: tin terrors lurked on every corner as villains lined up to do battle with *Captain Video and His Video Rangers* as they sought to save the world throughout the early fifties

29th-century New York as an over-grown jungle in the wake of atomic war. Three warring factions populate the Manhattan rubble – the handsome Norms, the disfigured Mutates and the devil-worshipping Upriver people – and the story, such as it is, kicks in when the Mutates start kidnapping the Norms' women for breeding purposes. Inept special effects scupper director Stuart Gilmore's few imaginative touches in the plodding plot, and bland acting renders the serial-like suspense virtually ineffectual. Most of the cast appeared in Zugsmiths's far superior *The Man from Planet X.*

Robert Clarke Rob • **Margaret Field** Ruth • **Gloria Saunders** Catherine • **Ron Randell** Riddon • **Stuart Randall** Gordon • **Paula Dorety** Captive • **Robert Bice** Bram • **Chili Williams** Captive

Director *Stuart Gilmore*

Screenplay *Aubrey Wisberg, Jack Pollexfen*

Carnosaur ★★

1993 US Colour 82mins

Executive producer Roger Corman's cheap answer to *Jurassic Park* finds evil scientist Diane Ladd developing a virus in chicken eggs that makes women give birth to savage dinosaurs. It's ably directed by Adam Simon, whose *Brain Dead* was better, and delivers the copious blood and gore the child-friendly Steven Spielberg blockbuster couldn't, via stomach-bursting birth scenes and prehistoric carnage. However, the dreadful model monsters, dodgy animatronics and overly talky script quickly, and rightly, made this extinct in movie houses. *Carnosaur 2* (1995) used the same tacky models in a script inspired more by *Aliens* than *The Lost World.*

Diane Ladd Dr Jane Tiptree • **Raphael Sbarge** "Doc" Smith • **Jennifer Runyon** Thrush • **Harrison Page** Sheriff • **Clint Howard** Trucker • **Ned Bellamy** Fallon • **Scott Levy** Soldier

Director *Adam Simon*

Screenplay *Adam Simon, from a novel by Harry Adam Knight*

Carry On Screaming ★★★★ PG

1966 UK Colour 92mins

This is one of the finest entries in Britain's most popular comedy series. Mocking that other bastion of British cinema in the sixties, the Hammer horror film, Talbot Rothwell's script positively bristles with classic one-liners, the most memorable being Kenneth Williams's gleeful "Frying tonight!" as he sinks into a bubbling cauldron. In his only *Carry On*, Harry H Corbett is superb as the Holmesian detective and Fenella Fielding revels in her role as a vampish vampire, but the picture belongs to Williams as the undead Dr Watt, an amalgam of every mad scientist who ever set foot in a lab.

Kenneth Williams Dr Watt • **Harry H Corbett** Detective Sergeant Bung • **Fenella Fielding** Valeria • **Jim Dale** Albert Potter • **Charles Hawtrey** Dan Dann • **Joan Sims** Emily Bung • **Angela Douglas** Doris Mann • **Bernard Bresslaw** Sockett • **Peter Butterworth** Detective Constable Slobotham • **Jon Pertwee** Dr Fettle • **Tom Clegg** Oddbodd • **Billy Cornelius** Oddbodd Jr

Director *Gerald Thomas*

Screenplay *Talbot Rothwell*

The Cars That Ate Paris ★★★★ 15

1974 Aus Colour 84mins

Peter Weir achieved a career high as the Oscar-nominated director of *The Truman Show.* His directorial debut, however, could not be more different from films such as *Picnic at Hanging Rock* and *Witness*, with which he made his reputation. It's a darkly comic tale of a small Australian town that feeds on passing travellers for their car parts; Terry Camilleri is the newcomer who decides to fight back. Rough edges notwithstanding, it's a sharp, vaguely unsettling affair and fortunately free of some of the portentous imagery that occasionally mars Weir's later works. Among the well known faces in the cast is John Meillon, familiar as Walter Reilly in the *Crocodile Dundee* films. Contains swearing.

Terry Camilleri Arthur • **John Meillon** Mayor • **Melissa Jaffa** Beth • **Kevin Miles** Dr Midland • **Max Gillies** Metcalfe • **Peter Armstrong** Gorman

Director *Peter Weir*

Screenplay *Peter Weir, Keith Gow, Piers Davies*

Carver's Gate ★★ 15

1995 US Colour 93mins

Fans of *The Matrix* should keep an eye out for this ambitious, if not wholly convincing, sci-fi thriller, which explores the blurring lines between real life and virtual reality. In the near future, the population is kept sedated by realistic and sophisticated computer games – until characters in the games start invading the real world. Director Sheldon Inkol displays some nice touches, although a bigger budget and a more charismatic lead would have helped.

Michael Paré Carver • **Tara Maria Manuel** Dinah

Director *Sheldon Inkol*

Screenplay *Doug Bagot, Timothy Lee, Sheldon Inkol*

Castle of Evil ★

1966 US Colour 80mins

Relatives of a dead, mad scientist gather in his creepy castle for the reading of the will, only to be systematically murdered by a robot fashioned in the image of the deceased. The result is a ridiculously bad mixture of Agatha Christie and schlock horror, featuring forties sex goddess Virginia Mayo as the madman's ex-mistress. A free funeral was promised if you died of fright while watching this amateur exploiter, though one is more likely to die laughing.

Scott Brady Matt Granger • **Virginia Mayo** Sable • **Lisa Gaye** Carol Harris • **David Brian** Robert Hawley • **Hugh Marlowe** Dr Corozal • **William Thourlby** The robot • **Shelley Morrison** Lupe Tekal d'Esperanza • **Natividad Vacio** Machado • **Ernest Sarracino** Tunki

Director *Francis D Lyon*

Screenplay *Charles A Wallace*

Producer *Earle Lyon*

The Cat from Outer Space ★★ U

1978 US Colour 94mins

Harmless Disney matinée fodder, with alien feline "Jake" grounded on Earth and in need of human dexterity to repair its disabled spacecraft in order to rejoin the mothership. Startling similarities to *ET* (still four years in the future) add an unforeseen layer of entertainment value to a bland package that could have done with a bit of Spielberg magic. Other than Jake's "wonder collar" that levitates people and places them in suspended animation, plus some climactic daredevil stuntwork, it's a pretty uninspired juvenile romp.

Ken Berry Dr Frank Wilson • **Sandy Duncan** Dr Liz Bartlett • **Harry Morgan** General Stilton • **Roddy McDowall** Stallwood • **McLean Stevenson** Dr Carl Link • **Jesse White** Earnest Ernie • **Alan Young** Dr Wenger • **Hans Conried** Dr Heffel • **Ronnie Schell** Sergeant Duffy • **James Hampton** Captain Anderson • **Howard T Platt** Colonel Woodruff • **William Prince** Mr Olympus

Director *Norman Tokar*

Screenplay *Ted Key*

Cat-Women of the Moon ★ U

1953 US BW 63mins

"You've Never Seen Anything Like It," screamed the posters for this delightfully abysmal camp classic. Astronaut Sonny

Tufts leads a dim-witted expedition to the dark side of the moon and discovers a bevy of telepathic feline beauties out to steal his spaceship and invade Earth. With a set left over from a submarine movie, cat-women dancers in black wigs and leotards, toy zap guns, a tacky giant spider and the wooden Tufts making the absolute least of his screen time, this is lunar lunacy of the worst kind. Originally shown in 3-D, a process that only magnified the threadbare production values, it was remade as *Missile to the Moon* in 1958.

Sonny Tufts Grainger • **Victor Jory** Kip • **Marie Windsor** Helen • **William Phipps** Doug • **Douglas Fowley** Walter • **Carol Brewster** Alpha • **Suzanne Alexander** Zeta • **Susan Morrow** Lambda
Director *Arthur Hilton*
Screenplay *Roy Hamilton, from a story by Al Zimbalist, Jack Rabin*

The Caves of Steel ★★★

TV 1964 UK BW 75mins

Writer Terry Nation takes a more benevolent look at robotics here than in his Dalek serials for *Doctor Who*, adapting Isaac Asimov's 1954 science-fiction mystery novel. Human detective Elijah Bailey (Peter Cushing) is partnered by robot policeman R Daneel Olivaw (John Carson) to investigate the murder of an arrogant offworld scientist in a New York that has become a vast, overpopulated hive-like dome. Directed by Peter Sasdy (*The Stone Tape*), this was first broadcast on BBC2 in a series called *Story Parade*, which presented adaptations of modern novels.

Peter Cushing Elijah Baley • **John Carson** R Daneel Olivaw • **Kenneth J Warren** Commissioner Enderby • **Ellen McIntosh** Jessie Baley • **Richard Beale** Controller • **John Boyd-Brent** Clousar • **John Wentworth** Dr Fastolfe • **Naomi Chance** Dr Gerrigel
Director *Peter Sasdy*
Dramatised by *Terry Nation, from the novel by Isaac Asimov*
Producer *Eric Tayler*
Special Effects *Jack Kine, Bernard Wilkie* • ***Design*** *Richard Henry, Peter Seddon*

The Cell ★★★ 18

2000 US/Ger Colour 109mins [video]

Music-video maestro Tarsem Singh makes a visually audacious debut with this hybrid of *The Silence of the Lambs* and *What Dreams May Come*. The sci-fi chestnut of a plot has psychotherapist Jennifer Lopez employing cutting-edge brain-jaunting paraphernalia to enter the subconscious of comatose serial killer Vincent D'Onofrio and help rescue his latest victim. Tarsem reinforces his credentials as a magpie imagist, employing a veritable barrage of digital trickery to conjure up the nightmarish mindscape of a psychopath. But his grasp of plotting and pacing is less assured, while the stylised sections occasionally sit uncomfortably within the generic thriller framework. That said, this remains an often dazzling showcase for his imagination.

Jennifer Lopez Catherine Deane • **Vince Vaughn** Agent Peter Novak • **Vincent D'Onofrio** Carl Stargher • **Marianne Jean-Baptiste** Dr Miriam Kent
Director *Tarsem Singh*
Screenplay *Mark Protosevich*

The Chain Reaction ★★★ 15

1980 Aus Colour 88mins [video]

Boasting chase sequences by *Mad Max*'s George Miller, this hefty chunk of Australian exploitation knocks spots off similar big-budget Hollywood offerings. Director Ian Barry's smart use of both camera and sound effects transforms many of the action set pieces. But, unfortunately, his delineation of character never rises above the comic-book level and there's a wasteful predictability about Steve Bisley and Arna Maria Winchester's bid to expose a leak at a nuclear plant. Great things were forecasted for Barry after this, but nine years were to pass before he directed the little-seen *Minnamurra*.

Steve Bisley Larry • **Arna Maria Winchester** Carmel • **Ross Thompson** Heinrich • **Ralph Cotterill** Grey • **Hugh Keays-Byrne** Eagle • **Lorna Lesley Constable** Gloria • **Richard Moir** Piggott • **Patrick Ward** Oates • **Laurie Moran** Sergeant McSweeney • **Michael Long** Doctor
Director/Screenplay *Ian Barry*

Chain Reaction ★★★ 12

1996 US Colour 102mins [video] DVD

Watching Keanu Reeves play a scientist seeking to make cheap power out of water is a little hard to take. But after he and fellow researcher Rachel Weisz go on the run from mysterious saboteurs after cracking the formula, *The Fugitive* director Andrew Davis's muddled suspense tale finally takes flight. With an unfocused script that's hazy on explanations, the film survives thanks to the pell-mell action that papers over the weak links in the convoluted plot. Don't think, just panic, as Reeves tries to cash in on his *Speed* hero persona in a running, jumping slice of escapism. Contains some violence and swearing.

Keanu Reeves Eddie Kasalivich • **Morgan Freeman** Paul Shannon • **Rachel Weisz** Lily Sinclair • **Fred Ward** FBI Agent Ford • **Kevin Dunn** FBI Agent Doyle • **Brian Cox** Lyman Earl Collier • **Joanna Cassidy** Maggie McDermott • **Chelcie Ross** Ed Rafferty
Director *Andrew Davis*
Screenplay *Josh Friedman, JF Lawton, Michael Bortman, Arne L Schmidt, Rick Seaman*
Producer *Arne L Schmidt, Andrew Davis*

The Champions ★★ U PG

TV 1968-1969 UK Colour 30x60mins [video]

Returning from a secret mission, three agents of Nemesis, an international crime fighting organisation, crash-land in Tibet and are rescued by a lost race of people that look like rejects from *Lost Horizon* who endow them with super-human attributes including increased strength and the ability to communicate telepathically with each other. Sounds great – alas, this awkward clash between the worlds of science fiction and espionage lacks the quality of similarly themed shows of the time like *The Avengers* and *Randall and Hopkirk (Deceased)*, while the three leads, American Stuart Damon, Britisher William Gaunt and exotic Alexandra Bastedo lack spark. The comic strip plots revolving around madmen out to take over the world plus budget restrictions make the show look dated before its time. After a poor run on American television it was cancelled after 30 episodes.

Stuart Damon Craig Stirling • **William Gaunt** Richard Barrett • **Alexandra Bastedo** Sharron Macready • **Anthony Nicholls** Cmdr Tremayne
Screenplay *Monty Berman, Dennis Spooner*
Producer *Monty Berman*

Charleston ★★★

1927 Fr BW 17mins

Still reeling from the commercial calamity of *Nana* (1926), Jean Renoir decided to use up the celluloid left over from his lambasted Zola adaptation to shoot this silent sci-fi curio. Having recently become a passionate jazz fan, he hired touring African-American dancer Johnny Huggins to play an alien who lands in a post-apocalyptic Paris of 2028 to encounter Europe's sole surviving human, Catherine Hessling, with whom he can only comunicate through dance. Renoir (who appears in cameo as an angel) always claimed this was an unfinished project – it was shot in three days on a single set – that was never intended for release.

Catherine Hessling Dancer • **Johnny Huggins** Explorer • **Pierre Braunberger** Angel • **Pierre Lestringuez** Angel • **Jean Renoir** Angel

Director *Jean Renoir*

Screenplay *Pierre Lestringuez, from an idea by André Cerf*

Producer *Jean Renoir*

Cinematographer *Jean Bachelet*

Editor *Jean Renoir*

Charly ★★★★ PG

1968 US Colour 99mins

Cliff Robertson found himself cast as heroic types after he played the young John F Kennedy in *PT 109*, but the most rewarding role of his career came with this Oscar-winning portrayal of a mentally disabled man whose life is transformed by a brain operation. The scenes between Robertson and Claire Bloom are touching, and Algernon the mouse is unforgettable, so director Ralph Nelson can be forgiven for playing down some of the fascinating possibilities raised by Stirling Silliphant's shrewd script. The film may feel a little twee in this more cynical age, but it remains an unassuming charmer.

Cliff Robertson Charly Gordon • **Claire Bloom** Alice Kinian • **Leon Janney** Dr Richard Nemur • **Lilia Skala** Dr Anna Straus • **Dick Van Patten** Bert • **William Dwyer** Joey • **Ed McNally** Gimpy • **Dan Morgan** Paddy

Director *Ralph Nelson*

Screenplay *Stirling Silliphant, from the short story and novel "Flowers for Algernon" by Daniel Keyes*

Producer *Ralph Nelson*

Chase Morran ★ 18

1996 US Colour 89mins

A cult cast – *The Evil Dead*'s Bruce Campbell, *Eraserhead*'s Jack Nance, *Blade Runner*'s Brion James – supply the sole points of interest in this by-the-numbers exploiter. Campbell plays a terrorist who takes over the small intergalactic settlement of Dome 4 and forces its residents to make bombs. Luckily, Chase Morran (Joseph Culp, son of Robert) is on hand to save the day. Cheap nonsense with little imagination or credibility in its corner. Contains violence, sexual references and swearing.

Bruce Campbell Alex Windham • **Joseph Culp** Chase Morran • **Jocelyn Seagrave** Lily Moran • **Brion James** Chairman • **Jack Nance** Mellow

Director *Gilbert Po*

Screenplay *Hesh Rephun*

Cherry 2000 ★★ 15

1988 US Colour 94mins

Melanie Griffith's career has certainly had its ups (*Working Girl*) and its downs (*The Bonfire of the Vanities*), and *Cherry 2000* falls firmly into the latter category. In this futuristic tale, set in the year 2017, sexual partners have been replaced by robot playmates. When his mechanical dream girl breaks down, Sam Treadwell (David Andrews) heads off into the desert for spare parts with expert scavenger E Johnson (Griffith). Although there are some nice effects, they can't hide the B-movie performances or the utterly ludicrous plot.

Melanie Griffith E Johnson • **David Andrews** Sam Treadwell • **Ben Johnson** Six Finger Jake • **Tim Thomerson** Lester • **Brion James** Stacy • **Pamela Gidley** Cherry 2000 • **Harry Carey Jr** Snappy Tom •

Author, author

10 top science-fiction writers who have been a hit with film-makers and audiences alike.

ISAAC ASIMOV This Russian-born professor of biochemistry is widely regarded as the most scientific of all sci-fi writers. Indeed, he wrote over 30 non-fiction books in his bid to popularise science. Convinced of technology's potential to improve life, he made his reputation with the short story collection *I, Robot* (1950), for which he conceived the famous Three Laws of Robotics. His novel (with Robert Silverberg) *The Positronic Man* became the Robin William's vehicle *Bicentennial Man*, while his short stories have been adapted frequently in TV anthology series and also as the film *The Android Affair* (1995). Asimov pioneered the sci-fi detective story with *The Caves of Steel* (filmed for television), and also created the innovative but short-lived TV series *Probe*. His most enduring achievement, complete with its theory of "psycho-history", is the *Foundation* trilogy which has been adapted for BBC Radio 4.

RAY BRADBURY Ray Bradbury was working as a newspaper vendor when he published his first story in 1938. Often considered the poet of science fiction, his filmed works include *The Martian Chronicles*, *The Illustrated Man* (1951), and *Fahrenheit 451*. The story *The Meteor* was the source for two versions of *It Came from Outer Space*, while *The Fog Horn* was filmed as *The Beast from 20,000 Fathoms*. His TV anthology series, featuring his stories exclusively, ran from 1985 to 1992.

ARTHUR C CLARKE Arthur Charles Clarke published his first short story, *Travel By Wire!*, in 1937. His short story *Breaking Strain* was filmed as *Trapped in Space*, and his work appeared frequently in TV anthology series. He remains best known, however, for *The Sentinel*, which inspired Stanley Kubrick's film, *2001: a Space Odyssey*.

MICHAEL CRICHTON Having started writing during his medical studies (occasionally resorting to suchpseudonyms as John Lange and Jeffrey Hudson), Crichton debuted on the bestseller lists with *The Andromeda Strain* (1969), which was filmed, the following year, by Robert Wise. The little-seen *The Terminal Man*, *Looker* and the unsuccessful *Sphere* were also adapted from his books. He scripted *Westworld* (which he also directed), *Looker*, *Coma* and *Runaway*, but it's the adaptations of his hit novel *Jurassic Park* and its sequel *The Lost World* that have been most successful.

PHILIP K DICK Early in his career, unable to place his "serious" novels, Dick began churning out sci-fi for Ace Books. His quirky, paranoid fictions are at the root of modern sci-fi masterpieces *Blade Runner* (*Do Androids Dream of Electric Sheep?*) and *Total Recall* (*We Can Remember It for You Wholesale*). Touted as the inspiration behind *The Terminator*, his short story *Second Variety* formed the basis of 1995's

Cameron Milzer Ginger • **Michael C Gwynne** Slim • **Jennifer Mayo** Randa • **Marshall Bell** Bill • **Jeff Levine** Marty • **Howard Swaim** Skeet
Director *Steve De Jarnatt*
Screenplay *Michael Almereyda, from a story by Lloyd Fonvielle*

Childhood's End ★★★

Radio 1997 UK 115mins

A Radio 4 *Classic Serial* dramatisation (scripted by Tony Mulholland) of Arthur C Clarke's 1954 novel, which does its best to cope with the clod-hopping structure of the influential but over-rated original book, which delivers some moments of un-Clarkeian character and emotion amid his tangled but unquestionably mind-stretching Big Ideas. The whole story is filtered through Jan Rodricks (Steven Pacey), the last real human being, with the destruction of the Earth as an impressive aural backdrop and a plot that lurches over several centuries with new characters and entire social movements hauled onstage and tossed away within minutes of airtime. The premise is that humanity is finally contacted by an alien species, the Overlords, who organise a New World Order with the help of sympathetic United Nations General Secretary Stormgren (Philip Voss), some incipient telepaths (notably Russian Alison Pettitt), vanquishing a resistance movement led by an irrational Welshman (Bernard Lloyd). The sound effects (especially the augmented, squelchy alien demon voices) convey an interstellar epic feel and good, intense performances (including Peter Jeffrey as the lead Overlord) deliver much of Clarke's gosh-wow consciousness-expanding cosmology. Available on audio-cassette.
Steven Pacey Jan Rodricks • **Peter Jeffrey** Karellen • **Philip Voss** Stormgren • **Alison Pettitt** Katerina • **Yana Weinstein** Young Katerina • **Patricia Perry** Dr Ivanovna • **Bernard Lloyd** Wainwright • **Lynne Farleigh** Katya • **Paul Webster** Sir Kenneth
Director *Brian Lighthill*
Dramatised by *Tony Mulholland, from the novel by Arthur C Clarke*
Music *Jeff Mearns*

Children of the Damned ★★

1964 UK BW 80mins

In this less-than-thrilling sequel to *Village of the Damned*, six children of assorted nationalities with deadly extra-sensory powers, escape from their respective London embassies. The alien kids demonstrate their lethal gifts against the armed forces who are trying to destroy them, in the name of world security. However, despite a literate script (based on John Wyndham's novel *The Midwich Cuckoos*) and thoughtful direction by Anton M Leader, the film has nowhere to go and quickly runs out of steam.
Ian Hendry Colonel Tom Lewellin • **Alan Badel** Dr David Neville • **Barbara Ferris** Susan Eliot • **Alfred Burke** Colin Webster • **Sheila Allen** Diana Looran • **Clive Powell** Paul • **Frank Summerscales** Mark • **Mahdu Mathen** Rashid • **Gerald Delsol** Aga Nagalo • **Roberta Rex** Nina • **Franchesca Lee** Mi-Ling • **Harold Goldblatt** Harib
Director *Anton M Leader*
Screenplay *John Briley, from the novel "The Midwich Cuckoos" by John Wyndham*

Chimera ★★★ 15

TV 1991 UK Colour 4x60mins 📼

Adapted by Stephen Gallagher from his own *mess-with-nature-and-it'll-bite-you-in-the-arse* novel, this four-part ITV mini-series

Screamers. The upcoming Tom Cruise/Steven Spielberg collaboration *Minority Report* (based on his story first published in 1956) will only consolidate his reputation.

ROBERT A HEINLEIN Having launched his short story career with *Lifeline* (1939), he adopted the pen name Anson MacDonald for his debut novel, *Beyond This Horizon* (1948). Always a proponent of right-of-centre attitudes, Heinlein tended to focus on self-confident individuals with a burning need to belong to a unit with a mission – such as the young cadet in *Starship Troopers*, which was so audaciously filmed by Paul Verhoeven in 1997. Other of his filmed works include *The Puppet Masters* (filmed under that title and also as *The Brain Eaters*), while his *Space Cadet* was the basis for the fifties TV series *Tom Corbett, Space Cadet*. In addition, Heinlein scripted the landmark *Destination Moon* and *Project Moonbase*.

RICHARD MATHESON Stephen King's hero published his first story, *Born of Man and Woman* in 1950. Several early novels were adapted for the screen, notably *The Shrinking Man* (as *The Incredible Shrinking Man*) and *I Am Legend* (as *The Last Man on Earth* and *The Omega Man*). He quickly adapted to screenwriting himself, becoming a regular contributor to *The Twilight Zone*, as well as *The Invaders* and *Star Trek*. He also produced some striking teleplays, including Steven Spielberg's debut, *Duel* (1971).

JULES VERNE From the publication of *Five Weeks in a Balloon* (1863), Verne's work combined a fascination for technology with an explorer's curiosity and a prophet's intuition. Frequently adapted for the screen, his stories ranged from such subterranean adventures as *Journey to the Centre of the Earth* to globe-trotting travelogues like *Around the World in 80 Days* (1873). His grasp of science may have been shaky, but he certainly had the knack of creating compelling anti-heroes, including, most famously, Captain Nemo in *20,000 Leagues Under the Sea*.

HG WELLS Although this ex-draper's assistant published literary novels, it's his science-fiction that's had the greatest impact. Among his works filmed are *The Invisible Man*, *Things to Come*, *Food of the Gods*, *The War of the Worlds* and *The Island of Dr Moreau*. But more intriguing were his sinister visions of future societies, like those populated by the Eloi and Morlocks in *The Time Machine* (filmed in 1960) and the Selenites in *The First Men in the Moon* (1964).

JOHN WYNDHAM Often using the pseudonymous surnames Benyon and Harris, Wyndham began writing in 1931. But it was only after war service that he started to make an impact. He tapped into Cold War unease for his best-known novel, *The Day of the Triffids*, which was brought to the screen in 1963 and later adapted for television. He caught the mood of the times once more with *The Midwich Cuckoos*, which was twice filmed as *Village of the Damned* in 1960 and 1995. His short story *Random Quest* was the basis for 1971's *Quest for Love*. Many novels, including *The Kraken Wakes*, have also been adapted for radio. Tending to pessimism and inconsistency, later works like *Chocky* (filmed for television) were not as successful.

follows the well-worn path of more traditional monster fare: teasing the viewer with haphazard glimpses of the titular creature until the final reel, a neat job of anamatronics when it arrives, and casting the scientific fraternity as the villains, the real monsters. John Lynch is the journalist investigating the death of his girlfriend at an isolated fertility clinic, who discovers that obscene genetic experiments have spawned a hybrid monster that is on the rampage. A classy production, cleverly intermingling genres from whodunit to dark horror with sci-fi trimmings, but in the end a rather ponderous one that takes far too long to reach its inevitable conclusion. Later released on video in an edited, 104-minute version.

John Lynch Peter Carson • **Christine Kavanagh** Alison Wells • **Kenneth Cranham** Hennessey • **David Calder** Dr Jenner
Director *Lawrence Gordon Clark*
Written by *Stephen Gallagher, from his novel*
Producer *Nick Gillott*

Chocky ★★★ U

TV 1984-1986 UK Colour 18x30mins

John Wyndham's 1963 novella (published as a book in 1969) had been done several times on the radio – a suitable medium for a story in which the alien is a disembodied voice whispering inside the mind of young Matthew Gore – before ITV had Anthony Read adapt it as a six-part serial in 1984. For television, Chocky, who is mistaken by Matthew's family for an "imaginary friend" is reimagined as a blob of green light. The serial was so popular that Read scripted two sequels, *Chocky's Children* (1985) and *Chocky's Challenge* (1986), in which Matthew discovers other "befriended" children who – like benevolent versions of the alien kids from Wyndham's *The Midwich Cuckoos* – set about reforming the adult world with science. Guest stars, mostly as unsympathetic adults, include Jeremy Bulloch, John Grillo, Ed Bishop, Richard Wordsworth and Joan Blackham.

Andrew Ellams Matthew Gore • **James Hazeldine** David Gore • **Carol Drinkwater** Mary Gore • **Glynis Brooks** Voice of Chocky • **Zoe Hart** Polly Gore
Adapted by *Anthony Read, from the novels by John Wyndham*

Chocky ★★★

Radio 1998 UK

A feature-length BBC Radio 4 production of the often-adapted John Wyndham story, neatly updated to make the "average" family less fifties upper middle-class (Mum is no longer a housewife, but a website designer; they all have regional accents) and incorporating subtle uses of new technology (the young hero wins a prize for a sampled music piece co-composed with his alien visitor). Accountant Owen Teale and his wife Kathy Tyson are disturbed when their adopted 12-year-old son (Sasha Dhawan) enters into communication with Chocky (Kathryn Hunt), an entity variously interpreted as an imaginary friend, a possessing demon, a guardian angel and (correctly) an alien explorer. Worries about child abuse, with the possibility that Dhawan is projecting to cover some horrible pre-adoption experience, and the tabloid media frenzy, add a modern sheen to Wyndham's striking plot nugget, rescuing him from seeming old-fashioned without fully embracing the trendy eco-speak that dominated the ITV *Chocky* serials. Available on audio-cassette.

Owen Teale David Gore • **Kathy Tyson** Mary Gore • **Sacha Dhawan** Matthew Gore • **Kathryn Hunt** Chocky • **Holly Grainger** Polly Gore • **John Lloyd Fillingham** Alan • **John Branwell** Sir William Thorbe • **William Oxborrow** Roy Landis • **Melissa Sinden** Denise Clutterbuck
Director *Melanie Harris*
Dramatised by *John Constable, from the novel "Chocky" by John Wyndham*
Music *Paul Cargill*

C.H.O.M.P.S. ★★ PG

1979 US Colour 86mins

Based on a story by Joseph Barbera (of Hanna-Barbera cartoon fame), this film falls between two stools – it's a bit gritty for younger children and too simplistic for the pre-teens, so its mix of crime and comedy won't find many takers. The title refers to the Canine Home Protection System designed in the shape of a robotic dog by inventor Wesley Eure in a bid to save Conrad Bain's struggling security company. The slapstick has the feel you'd expect of the man who helped create Tom and Jerry, but it's nothing for the cartoon's guard dog, Spike, to worry about. Contains some swearing.

Wesley Eure Brian Foster • **Valerie Bertinelli** Casey Norton • **Conrad Bain** Ralph Norton • **Chuck McCann** Brooks • **Red Buttons** Bracken • **Larry Bishop** Ken Sharp • **Hermione Baddeley** Mrs Flower • **Jim Backus** Mr Gibbs • **Robert Q Lewis** Merkle • **Regis Toomey** Chief Patterson
Director *Don Chaffey*
Screenplay *Dick Robbins, Duane Poole, Joseph Barbera, from a story by Joseph Barbera*

Chosen Survivors ★★

1974 US/Mex Colour 98mins

Jackie Cooper and Bradford Dillman are among a group of specially selected citizens who are carted off to a deep underground bunker to test individual reactions to probable nuclear war. Unfortunately a horde of killer vampire bats are locked in with them, and it's supper time. Sutton Roley's ecological revenge thriller is clearly inspired by Hitchcock's *The Birds* and the bat effects are wholly convincing, but his protagonists are obvious clichés and the direction has a TV-movie feel and ambition about it. Best thing here is waiting to see which member of the cast, who all had to be inoculated against rabies, is going to get bat-erred to death next.

Jackie Cooper Raymond Couzins • **Alex Cord** Steven Mayes • **Richard Jaeckel** Gordon Ellis • **Bradford Dillman** Peter Macomber • **Pedro Armendariz Jr** Luis Cabral • **Diana Muldaur** Alana Fitzgerald • **Lincoln Kilpatrick** Woody Russo • **Gwen Mitchell** Carrie Draper • **Barbara Babcock** Lenore Chrisman • **Christina Moreno** Kristin Lerner • **Nancy Rodman** Claire Farraday • **Kelly Lange** Mary Louise Borden
Director *Sutton Roley*
Screenplay *HB Cross, Joe Reb Moffley, from a story by HB Cross*

The Christmas Martian ★★

1971 Can Colour 86mins

Made a decade before *ET*, this French-Canadian children's film centres on a couple of youngsters who befriend an amiable alien after he gets lost in the wintry woods. The fact that it's set during the festive season provides director Bernard Gosselin with the opportunity to pile on not only the sentiment, but also the spurious allusions to both the Nativity and Santa. The pace picks up slightly once the grown-ups decide that their kids' new intergalactic chum has outstayed his welcome, but it's still unlikely that today's children will stay the course. A French language film.

Marcel Sabourin Martian • **Catherine Leduc** Katou • **Francois Gosselin** Francois • **Roland Chenail** Chief of police
Director *Bernard Gosselin*
Screenplay *Roch Carrier*

Chronopolis ★★★★

1982 Fr Colour 70mins

Associated with sci-fi since *The Green Planet* in 1968, the Polish-born animator Piotr Kamler created his masterpiece with this surreal, rhythmic stop-motion fantasy.

The result of five years' painstaking labour and shot wholly with a 1920 Debrie camera, its refusal to indulge in cutting-edge visual trickery not only enhances its charm, but also demands that it's viewed as a work of art and not a mere exercise in futurism. Once Michel Lonsdale's introduction has guided you around this city lost in space, you are left to watch and wonder at its inhabitants gleeful games with time. They are unique and utterly beguiling. A French language film.

Michel Lonsdale Commentator
Director/Screenplay *Piotr Kamler*
Animator *Piotr Kamler*

CHUD ★ 18

1984 US Colour 83mins [video]

Thanks to toxic waste dumped in the Manhattan sewage system, tramps and derelicts have mutated into "Cannibalistic Humanoid Underground Dwellers". That's according to this lamentable urban horror movie, which is neither gory nor exciting enough to warrant much attention. A photographer, the head of a soup kitchen and a police captain whose wife has fallen prey to the zombies join forces to get to the bottom of the cover-up. Ridiculous monsters, unappealing main characters and an inevitable twist ending only add insult to injury in this crass exploiter.

John Heard George Cooper • **Kim Greist** Lauren Daniels • **Daniel Stern** The Reverend • **Christopher Curry** Captain Bosch • **George Martin** Wilson • **John Ramsey** Commissioner • **Eddie Jones** Chief O'Brien • **Laure Mattos** Flora Bosch • **JC Quinn** Murphy • **John Goodman** Cop in diner
Director *Douglas Cheek*
Screenplay *Parnell Hall*

Circuit Breaker ★

1996 US Colour 90 mins

Intergalactic repairman Corbin Bernsen and wife Lara Harris come across a broken-down spaceship in this cable TV movie, which is essentially *Dead Calm* in space. On board the craft is android Richard Grieco who, in time honoured genre tradition, is planning to create a new breed of human. Slow-moving and predictable, this tepid thriller relies more on gratuitous sex and violence than anything of a science-fiction nature.

Lara Harris Katrina Carver • **Richard Grieco** Adam • **Corbin Bernsen** Foster Carver • **Edie McClurg**
Director/Screenplay *Victoria Muspratt*
Executive producer *Roger Corman*

Circuitry Man ★★ 15

1990 US Colour 88mins [video]

Co-scripted by director Steven Lovy and his brother Robert, this is a futuristic patchwork made up of snippets from a range of sci-fi films, most notably *Blade Runner*, *Logan's Run* and *Mad Max*. More time spent at the typewriter and a little less playing with special effects might have resulted in a better (and certainly more coherent) picture. As it is, Dana Wheeler-Nicholson's flight from the villainous Lu Leonard, carrying a case full of pleasure-inducing computer chips, is little more than a string of clichés and pompous pronouncements. A scenery-chewing cameo from Dennis Christopher is a rare highlight. Contains swearing and violence.

Jim Metzler Danner • **Dana Wheeler-Nicholson** Lori • **Lu Leonard** Juice • **Vernon Wells** Plughead • **Barbara Alyn Woods** Yoyo • **Dennis Christopher** Leech
Director *Steven Lovy*
Screenplay *Steven Lovy, Robert Lovy*

City beneath the Sea ★★★

TV 1962 UK BW 7x30mins

A sequel to the nuclear-themed *Plateau of Fear*, this serial has reporter Gerald Flood and boy sidekick Stewart Guidotti involved in a *20,000 Leagues under the Sea*-style plot. Underwater megalomaniac Aubrey Morris, who doesn't know the meaning of the expression "underplaying", wants to conquer the world, operating out of the underwater city of Aegira, with the usual clutch of kidnapped geniuses on his team, plus a Nazi U-boat captain-turned-pirate (Dennis Goacher). More trouble at Aegira featured in a 1963 follow-up, *Secret Beneath the Sea*.

Gerald Flood Mark Bannerman • **Stewart Guidotti** Peter Blake • **Caroline Blakiston** Dr Ann Boyd • **Aubrey Morris** Prof Ludwig Ziebrecken • **Dennis Goacher** Kurt Swendler
Director *Kim Mills*
Written by *John Lucarotti*
Producer *Guy Verney*

City beneath the Sea ★★ U

1971 US Colour 89mins [video]

Irwin Allen, Mr Disaster Movie himself, took a dive in this pilot for a TV series that was never made, and it's easy to see why, as each crisis facing the vast submerged 21st-century metropolis of Pacifica had been done better in previous Allen sci-fi shows. Even the cast was familiar: Richard Basehart from *Voyage to the Bottom of the Sea* and *The Time Tunnel*'s James Darren. Asteroids on a collision course, sea monsters, internal dissension and bullion robberies are piled on in the desperate effort to build excitement. But it's all too much, the performances too wooden and the waterlogged effects absurd.

Stuart Whitman Admiral Michael Matthews • **Robert Wagner** Brett Matthews • **Rosemary Forsyth** Lia Holmes • **Robert Colbert** Commander Woody Patterson • **Susana Miranda** Elena • **Burr DeBenning** Dr Aguila • **Richard Basehart** President • **Joseph Cotten** Dr Ziegler • **James Darren** Dr Talty • **Sugar Ray Robinson** Captain Hunter • **Edward G Robinson Jr** Dr Burkson
Director *Irwin Allen*
Screenplay *John Meredyth Lucas, from a story by Irwin Allen*
Producer *Irwin Allen*

SFacts

Budget-conscious producer Irwin Allen recycled his props: one of the underwater crafts seen in this TV movie also appeared in episodes of *Voyage to the Bottom of the Sea*.

City Limits ★★ 15

1985 US Colour 81mins [video]

Set in a futuristic world where most adults have been eradicated by plague, this post-apocalyptic action adventure depicts a Los Angeles divided between two motorbike gangs – the DAs and the Clippers. Orphaned Lee (John Stockwell) comes to town to join the latter, only to uncover a plot to take control of the city by the sinister Sunya Corporation, whose head honcho is none other than Robby Benson! Rae Dawn Chong and Kim Cattrall co-star in this low-budget film that has some entertaining moments.

Darrell Larson Mick • **John Stockwell** Lee • **Kim Cattrall** Wickings • **Rae Dawn Chong** Yogi • **John Diehl** Whitey • **Danny De La Paz** Ray • **Don Opper** Sammy • **Norbert Weisser** Bolo • **Dean Devlin** Ernie • **Robby Benson** Carver • **James Earl Jones** Albert
Director *Aaron Lipstadt*
Screenplay *Don Opper, from a story by James Reigle, Aaron Lipstadt*
Producer *Rupert Harvey, Barry Opper*

The City of Lost Children ★★★★ 15

1995 Fr/Sp/Ger Colour 107mins [video]

Ron Perlman, still best known as Vincent in the TV series *Beauty and the Beast*, stars in this sinister fantasy adventure from French directors Jean-Pierre Jeunet and Marc Caro, who, with their extraordinary *Delicatessen*, set new standards for dark

The future's orange: Stanley Kubrick's highly controversial dystopian fantasy *A Clockwork Orange* follows the sadistic adventures of Alex, played with disturbing intensity by Malcolm McDowell

fables. This surreal tale is an astonishing eye-opener from its nightmare opening to the climactic battle, as carnival strongman One (Perlman) leads the fight against the evil Krank (Daniel Emilfork), who steals children's dreams. For those who thought films could do nothing new, prepare to be surprised. In French with English subtitles.

Ron Perlman One • **Daniel Emilfork** Krank • **Judith Vittet** Miette • **Dominique Pinon** Clones/Diver/Stocle • **Jean-Claude Dreyfus** Marcello, the flea tamer • **Mireille Mossé** Mademoiselle Bismuth
Director *Marc Caro, Jean-Pierre Jeunet*
Screenplay *Gilles Adrien, Jean-Pierre Jeunet, Marc Caro, Guillaume Laurant*

City under the Sea ★★★ U

1965 UK Colour 83mins

Tenuously based on Edgar Allan Poe, with Jules Verne being the main uncredited inspiration, director Jacques Tourneur's final feature (Poe regular Roger Corman turned it down) is a fanciful mix of comedy adventure and submarine suspense. Vincent Price enjoyably camps it up as the immortal underwater leader of a Cornish contingent of smugglers-turned-gillmen, and the whole subterranean soufflé is highly watchable even if it does slide from the poetic to the pathetic in the second half.

Vincent Price Captain • **David Tomlinson** Harold • **Tab Hunter** Ben • **Susan Hart** Jill • **John Le Mesurier** Ives • **Henry Oscar** Mumford • **Derek Newark** Dan
Director *Jacques Tourneur*
Screenplay *Charles Bennett, Louis M Heyward*

Class of 1999 ★★ 18

1990 US Colour 91mins

This sequel to *Class of 1984* – directed, like the original, by Mark L Lester – presents the high school of the future as a violent battleground where teachers have been replaced by robots who can supposedly handle the psychopathic kids. Obviously the robots' programmers had never seen *Westworld* and it's not long before the machines malfunction and things get ugly. Brutal and camp at the same time, it falls down because Lester actually thinks he can insert some sort of message into the mayhem.

Malcolm McDowell Dr Miles Langford • **Bradley Gregg** Cody Culp • **John P Ryan** Mr Hardin • **Pam Grier** Ms Connors • **Stacy Keach** Dr Bob Forrest • **Traci Lin** Christine Langford • **Patrick Kilpatrick** Mr Bryles • **Darren E Burrows [Darren Burrows]** Sonny
Director *Mark L Lester*
Screenplay *C Courtney Joyner, from a story by Mark L Lester*
Producer *Mark L Lester*

Class of 1999 II: The Substitute

★ 18

1993 US Colour 86mins (video)

Cyborg substitute teacher Sasha Mitchell starts killing his high school students when they turn delinquent in a boring follow-up to the original video hit. Part *Blackboard Jungle*, part bloodthirsty war movie, this cynical sequel is a badly-structured, sleazy shambles, which incorporates footage from *Class of 1999* to beef up its running time. A film that relentlessly plumbs the depths of unpleasantness.

Sasha Mitchell John Bolen • **Nick Cassavetes** Emmett Grazer • **Caitlin Dulany** Jenna McKensie
Director *Spiro Razatos*
Screenplay *Mark Sevi*

Class of Nuke 'Em High ★ 18

1986 US Colour 81mins (video)

This typically bargain-basement production from Troma, the no-frills company who brought us the cult-ish *Toxic Avenger* movies, follows a bunch of high school kids who suffer radiation mutation from a local nuclear plant that makes the one in *The Simpsons* look like a model of health and safety. Yes, it's awfully acted, insanely scripted and cluelessly directed, but criticising a Troma movie is somewhat pointless, since they don't pretend to produce anything other than sick, silly, slimy entertainment for beered-up horror fans. Anybody else should steer clear.

Janelle Brady Chrissy • **Gilbert Brenton** Warren • **Robert Prichard** Spike • **R L Ryan** Mr Paley • **James Nugent Vernon** Eddie • **Brad Dunker** Gonzo • **Gary Schneider** Pete • **Theo Cohan** Muffey
Director *Richard W Haines, Samuel Weil [Lloyd Kaufman]*
Screenplay *Richard W Haines, Mark Rudnitsky, Samuel Weil [Lloyd Kaufman], Stuart Strutin, from a story by Richard W Haines*

Cleopatra 2525 ★★

TV 2000-2001 US Colour 22x30mins

The makers of *Xena: Warrior Princess* give the Buck Rogers story an oestrogen-charged spin, with predictably flashy, trashy results. Former soap star Jennifer Sky plays the titular Cleopatra, an "exotic dancer" who is cryogenically frozen in 2001 and reawakens five centuries later. On learning that the Earth has been enslaved by robots, Cleo reluctantly joins forces with two female freedom fighters to save the world. With plotlines as flimsy as its outfits and little in the way of surprises or character development, this tongue-in-cheek sci-fi action romp is at best a guilty pleasure for admirers of its three enchanting leads. After an opening season of half-hour episodes, the show was extended to six hour-long instalments, but that wasn't enough to give the series any real substance or to prevent its demise.

Gina Torres Hel • **Jennifer Sky** Cleopatra • **Victoria Pratt** Sarge • **Patrick Kake** Mauser • **Danielle Cormack** Raina • **Joel Tobeck** Creegan
Executive producer *Sam Raimi*

A Clockwork Orange ★★★ 18

1971 UK Colour 136mins

Unseen between 1974 (when Stanley Kubrick himself quietly withdrew it) and 2000 (after his death), it is little wonder that an inflated degree of mythology surrounds *A Clockwork Orange*. Adapted from the 1962 Anthony Burgess novella about anarchic yobs ("droogs") in a dystopian future, it was shocking then and it's shocking today, particularly the scenes of rape and sadistic "ultaviolence" in the first half. Burgess and Kubrick may have been making intellectual points about the state and free will – Alex (Malcolm McDowell) is brainwashed into submission in the film's slower second half – but the film is not quite the masterpiece unattainability has bestowed on it. Fascinating and prescient, yes, and its moral ambiguity is brave, but essential viewing only really for film students and voyeurs.

Malcolm McDowell Alex • **Patrick Magee** Mr Alexander • **Michael Bates** Chief Guard • **Warren Clarke** Dim • **John Clive** Stage Actor • **Adrienne Corri** Mrs Alexander • **Carl Duering** Dr Brodsky • **Paul Farrell** Tramp • **Miriam Karlin** Cat Lady • **Aubrey Morris** Deltoid • **Steven Berkoff** Constable • **David Prowse [Dave Prowse]** Julian
Director *Stanley Kubrick*
Screenplay *Stanley Kubrick, from the novel by Anthony Burgess*
Cinematographer *John Alcott* • ***Editor*** *Bill Butler* • ***Production designer*** *John Barry* • ***Music*** *Walter Carlos*

A Clockwork Orange ★★★

Radio 1998 UK 90mins

This Radio 4 dramatisation of Anthony Burgess's 1962 novel isn't quite able to crawl out from under the footprint of Stanley Kubrick's 1971 film version – though it does include the surprisingly upbeat ending (in which Alex grows out of juvenile delinquency) omitted by mistake from the film. Jason Hughes plays a Welsh-accented Alex, spieling nadstat fluently, with Struan Rodger, Jack Davenport, John McArdle and Dorien Thomas as the minions of the state and Bill Stewart as the dissident writer. The production uses a lot of chanting and music, with lyrics written for Beethoven's *Ode to Joy*, to give an impression of the brutal world of the novel, but the mix of satire and horror doesn't quite gel. Available on audio-cassette and CD.

Jason Hughes Alex • **Struan Rodger** Dr Brodsky • **John McArdle** Chaplain • **Jack Davenport** Minister • **Bill Stewart** Alexander • **Clare Isaac** Dr Branom • **Dorien Thomas** Mr Deltoid • **Rhodri Hugh** Dim • **Robert Harper** Pete • **Wayne Forester** Georgie
Director *Alison Hindell*
Adapted by *Alison Hindell, from Anthony Burgess's own stage version of his novella*
Music *John Hardy*

Cloned ★★

1997 US Colour

An intriguing made-for-TV sci-fi thriller, which unfortunately lacks killer punch. Set in the near future, the under-rated Elizabeth Perkins plays a grieving mother still trying to come to terms with the death of her young boy. When she spots another youngster who is the spitting image of her dead child, she learns that her baby was cloned, opening up all sorts of moral dilemmas. Perkins is as good as ever in a largely unknown cast, but this can't seem to make up its mind whether it's a chiller or a weepie. Contains some strong language and violence.

Elizabeth Perkins Skye Weston • **Alan Rosenberg** Dr Wesley Kozak • **Bradley Whitford** Rick Weston • **Enrico Colantoni** Steve Rinker • **Scott Paulin** John Gryce • **Tina Lifford** Claire Barnes • **Hrothgar Mathews** Dr Richard Mason
Director *Douglas Barr*
Screenplay *Carmen Culver, David Taylor, from a story by Perri Klass, Carmen Culver*

The Cloning of Joanna May

★★★ 15

TV 1992 UK Colour 151mins (video)

This two-part dramatisation of Fay Weldon's 1989 novel, reuniting writer Ted Whitehead and director Philip Saville – who had done the more successful TV version of Weldon's *The Life and Loves of a She-Devil*. Although it drops a lot of genetics-speak, it's actually a twisted study of a seriously skewed relationship as ice maiden Patricia Hodge discovers that her obsessive ex-husband Brian Cox – "You may be a brilliant businessman, but you're a sentimental psychopath – "took precautions against their inevitable break-up by surreptitiously having her cloned, which means that there are a pack of 22-year-old knock-offs around for Cox to choose from, though they turn out to have unexpected psychic powers and are able to give him a fatal heart attack. The finale finds Hodge cloning Cox, and vowing to give him a healthy upbringing rather than the hideous childhood (he was kept in a dog kennel) that made him a madman in the first place. The plot makes little sense, but the lead performances and characters are fascinating.

Patricia Hodge Joanna May • **Brian Cox** Carl May • **Billie Whitelaw** Mavis • **James Purefoy** Oliver • **Jean Boht** Mrs Love • **Peter Capaldi** Isaac • **Sarah Badel** Angela • **Oliver Ford Davies** Gerald • **Siri Neal** Bethany • **Peter Guinness** Phillip
Director *Phillip Saville*
Written by *Ted Whitehead, from the novel by Fay Weldon*
Producer *Gub Neal*

The Clonus Horror ★★

1978 US Colour 90mins

Robert S Fiveson's would-be future shocker is a prime example of an intelligent premise, poorly realised. Borrowing its atmosphere from Georges Orwell and Lucas (in the shape of *THX 1138*), the story focuses on a top-secret government cloning operation, the novel twist being that the film's hero (a moderately convincing Tim Donnelly) is actually one of the clones, who escapes his laboratory prison in an attempt to warn the outside world. Although the film is dull, there's curiosity value in its handling of a story that was pure sci-fi back in the seventies, yet today is depressingly closer to fact.

Tim Donnelly Richard Knight Jr • **Dick Sargent** Dr Jameson • **Peter Graves** Jeff Knight • **Paulette Breen** Lena • **David Hooks** Prof Richard P Knight • **Keenan Wynn** Jake Noble
Director *Robert S Fiveson*
Screenplay *Myrl A Schreibman, Robert S Fiveson, from a story by Bob Sullivan*

Close Encounters of the Third Kind ★★★★★ PG

1977 US Colour 126mins DVD

Remember the time when aliens were friendly? Here's the reverse of sci-fi smash hits *Independence Day* and *Men in Black* – a delightfully optimistic parable about secret government communications with a visiting spacecraft. Richard Dreyfuss plays the power worker who gets caught up in all the UFO phenomena in a Steven Spielberg fantasy that's truly suspenseful and genuinely felt, rather than just sweet and sentimental. Yet it's the awesome special effects (such as the glittering mother ship) that really fuel this uplifting tale. Contains some swearing.

Richard Dreyfuss Roy Neary • **Francois Truffaut** Claude Lacombe • **Teri Garr** Ronnie Neary • **Melinda Dillon** Jillian Guiler • **Bob Balaban** David Laughlin • **J Patrick McNamara** Project leader • **Warren Kemmerling** Wild Bill • **Roberts Blossom** Farmer • **Philip Dodds** Jean Claude • **Cary Guffey** Barry Guiler
Director/Screenplay *Steven Spielberg*
Cinematographer *Vilmos Zsigmond* • ***Editor*** *Michael Kahn* • ***Music*** *John Williams* • ***Production designer*** *Joe Alves* • ***Art director*** *Dan Lomino* • ***Set designer*** *Phil Abramson* • ***Special effects*** *Douglas Trumbull, Roy Arbogast, Gregory Jein, Matthew Yuricich, Richard Yuricich*

SFacts

The original version of this film won an Oscar for cinematography and a Special Achievement Award for sound effects editing, and received seven other nominations. The film was re-released as a Special Edition in 1980. This has a new ending in which we see inside the spaceship, and there are extra special effects, such as the UFO depositing an ocean freighter in the Gobi desert. Director Steven Spielberg is said to prefer the Special Edition to the original.

Cocoon ★★★★ PG

1985 US Colour 111mins

Director Ron Howard hit the big time with this blockbuster about pensioners finding a new lease of life after stumbling across aliens on a rescue mission from another planet. What saves it from a complete wallow in sentimentality is the sharp and sassy playing of a distinguished cast of Hollywood legends – Oscar-winning Don Ameche, Wilford Brimley, real-life husband and wife Jessica Tandy and Hume Cronyn – all of whom easily steal the show from the bland but youthful Steve Guttenberg and Tahnee Welch. Howard handles the human drama and sci-fi with equal aplomb and the feel-good sentiments certainly struck a chord – a sequel followed three years later. However, a dash of Victor Meldrew's *One Foot in the Grave*-style cynicism would not have gone amiss. Contains swearing and brief nudity.

Steve Guttenberg Jack Bonner • **Brian Dennehy** Walter • **Don Ameche** Art Selwyn • **Wilford Brimley** Ben Luckett • **Hume Cronyn** Joe Finley • **Jack Gilford** Bernie Lefkowitz • **Maureen Stapleton** Mary Luckett • **Jessica Tandy** Alma Finley • **Gwen Verdon** Bess McCarthy • **Herta Ware** Rose Lefkowitz • **Tahnee Welch** Kitty • **Barret Oliver** David • **Linda Harrison** Susan • **Tyrone Power Jr** Pillsbury • **Clint Howard** John Dexter • **Charles Lampkin** Pops • **Mike Nomad** Doc • **Jorge Gil** Lou Pine
Director *Ron Howard*
Screenplay *Tom Benedek, from a story by David Saperstein*

Cocoon: the Return ★★ PG

1988 US Colour 114mins

Straining far too hard to recapture the touching whimsy of Ron Howard's original film, director Daniel Petrie has succeeded only in producing a mawkish melodrama. Although the ever-dapper Don Ameche reprises his Oscar-winning role of Art Selwyn, there is much less of a spring in his step, and fellow old folks Wilford Brimley and Hume Cronyn are clearly equally uncomfortable with a script in which an emphasis on the joy of living has been overlaid with a glum resignation to the consolation prizes of old age. The performances remain endearing, however, and it can still raise a tear if you're in the mood. Contains swearing.

Don Ameche Art Selwyn • **Hume Cronyn** Joe Finley • **Wilford Brimley** Ben Luckett • **Courteney Cox** Sara • **Jack Gilford** Bernie Lefkowitz • **Steve Guttenberg** Jack Bonner • **Barret Oliver** David • **Maureen Stapleton** Mary Luckett • **Elaine Stritch** Ruby • **Jessica Tandy** Alma Finley • **Gwen Verdon** Bess McCarthy
Director *Daniel Petrie*
Screenplay *Stephen McPherson, from a story by Stephen McPherson, Elizabeth Bradley, from characters created by David Saperstein*

Cold Lazarus ★★★★

TV 1996 UK Colour 275mins

Having worked on the edges of fantasy and horror for most of his career, Dennis Potter finally took the plunge into science fiction with his last produced work. The writer's dying wish was that two linked serials, *Karaoke* and *Cold Lazarus*, be co-produced by the BBC and the independent Channel 4; *Karaoke* played first on BBC1 and was repeated on Channel 4, but *Cold Lazarus* debuted on Channel 4 with repeats on BBC1. Daniel Feeld (Albert Finney), the contemporary author's stand-in who was the protagonist of *Karaoke*, survives into 2368 in this sequel, as a frozen severed head whose memories are probed by a team of scientists who find the rights to the project absorbed by sinister media interests. An example of science fiction as satire, a surprisingly rare television genre, *Cold Lazarus* doesn't try to hang together as a sensible extrapolation of a future the terminally-ill Potter didn't believe in, but is instead a despairing cartoon of the late nineties, with issues of political control of scientific advance, media irresponsibility and the fragmentation of society put forward in a highly-coloured, extremely bitter vision that owes a little to Terry Gilliam's *Brazil*. Unusual actresses Frances de la Tour and Diane Ladd tear into the roles of dedicated scentist and crass tycoon with spirit, while director Renny Rye seems equally influenced by cyberpunk misery and the cheery tat of vintage *Doctor Who*. Shown in four parts.

Albert Finney Daniel Feeld • **Frances de la Tour** Emma Porlock • **Diane Ladd** Martina Masdon • **Ciaran Hinds** Fyodor • **Henry Goodman** David Siltz • **Ganiat Kasumu** Luanda • **Grant Masters** Tony Watson • **Saffron Burrows** Sandra Sollars • **Claudia Malkovich** Kaya
Director *Renny Rye*
Written by *Dennis Potter*
Producer *Kenith Trodd, Rosemarie Whitman*

The Colossus of New York ★

1958 US BW 71mins

When Otto Kruger stays late at the lab to transplant his brother's brain into a robot, he ends up with a combination of Frankenstein's monster and *The Wrong Trousers*. Man-made monsters are not noted for their gratitude, however, and the big lad is soon biting chunks out of the Big Apple. The dialogue and effects are wretched, Kruger and Ross Martin are lifeless, while Eugène Lourié's direction is more leaden than the creature's footwear. That said, there is a nice turn from B-movie queen Mala Powers.

Ross Martin Dr Jeremy Spensser • **Mala Powers** Anne Spensser • **Charles Herbert** Billy Spensser • **John Baragrey** Dr Henry Spensser • **Otto Kruger** Dr William Spensser • **Robert Hutton** Professor John Carrington • **Ed Wolff** Colossus
Director *Eugène Lourié*
Screenplay *Thelma Schnee, from a story by Willis Goldbeck*

Colossus: the Forbin Project ★★★

1969 US Colour 99mins

This chilling suspense film had the misfortune to be made around the same time as *2001: a Space Odyssey*, diluting its depiction of machines turning against humankind. Fortunately, the intervening years have been kind to Joseph Sargent's thinking man's sci-fi entry, which imagines a time when one super computer has total control over all western defence systems. When it decides to link terminals with its Soviet counterpart in a bid for world domination, its human masters discover they can't switch the damn thing off. Cleverly playing up the thriller aspects of the story and cannily making the computer the film's central character, this well-acted and utterly persuasive shocker provides a cautionary warning regarding man's dependency on technology.

Eric Braeden Dr Charles Forbin • **Susan Clark** Dr Cleo Markham • **Gordon Pinsent** The President • **William Schallert** Grauber • **Leonid Rostoff** 1st Chairman • **Georg Stanford Brown** Fisher • **Tom Basham** Harrison
Director *Joseph Sargent*
Screenplay *James Bridges, from the novel "Colossus" by D F Jones*
Producer *Stanley Chase*

Coma ★★★★ 15

1977 US Colour 108mins [video]

Doctor Geneviève Bujold and sinister surgeon Richard Widmark clash memorably in this taut medical thriller, faithfully adapted from Robin Cook's bestseller by doctor-turned-novelist Michael Crichton. The *ER*/ *Jurassic Park* creator also directs and expertly turns the ample suspense screws in the gripping way that has become his trademark. It's Crichton's assured sense of creepy paranoia within the absorbing central mystery that gives an extra disturbing edge to the hospital horrors.

Geneviève Bujold Dr Susan Wheeler • **Michael Douglas** Dr Mark Bellows • **Elizabeth Ashley** Mrs Emerson • **Rip Torn** Dr George • **Richard Widmark** Dr George A Harris • **Lois Chiles** Nancy Greenly • **Harry Rhodes** Dr Morelind • **Gary Barton** Computer technician • **Frank Downing** Kelly • **Richard Doyle** Jim • **Alan Haufrect** Dr Marcus • **Lance Le Gault** Vince • **Michael MacRae** Chief resident • **Tom Selleck** Sean Murphy
Director *Michael Crichton*
Screenplay *Michael Crichton, from the novel by Robin Cook*

Come Back Mrs Noah ★★

TV 1977-1978 UK Colour 6x30mins

Jeremy Lloyd and David Croft, creators of *Are You Being Served?* and *'Allo 'Allo*, threw together this less successful sit-com, cast with survivors of earlier comedy hits, but failed to make the comedy-in-space hit that *Red Dwarf* would eventually become. In the 21st century, housewife Mrs Gertrude Noah (Molly Sugden) wins a trip to the *Britannia Seven* space station, but is blasted into an erratic orbit and finds herself stuck in a ship with journalist Clive Cunliffe (Ian Lavender), as the ground control spend six episodes trying to rescue her from a peril she barely recognises. It wasn't very funny.

Mollie Sugden Mrs Noah • **Ian Lavender** Clive Cunliffe • **Donald Hewlett** Carstairs • **Michael Knowles** Fanshaw
Written by *Jeremy Lloyd, David Croft*
Producer *David Croft*

Commando Cody: Sky Marshal of the Universe ★★

1953 US Colour 12x30mins

As much an exercise in conservation as anything else, this show about a superhero who flies with a jetpack and wears a distinctive helmet was constructed around extensive use of exciting footage from the Republic film serial archive. The character Commando Cody (played by George Wallace) first appeared in a serial, *Radar Men from the Moon* (1952), which was itself the third usage of the hero costume (and flight sequences) that had appeared in *King of the Rocket Men* (1949) and *Zombies of the Stratosphere* (1952). *Commando Cody, Sky Marshal of the Universe*, with Judd Holdren – who had played a different character with the same costume in *Zombies of the Stratosphere* – in the lead, was shot as a TV series in 1953, but first released as a movie serial before making its actual television bow in 1955. Cody works for the Interplanetary Commission to defeat the alien ruler of Planet M-27 (Gregory Gay), who is intent on taking over the Earth, His sober sidekick William Schallert is swiftly ditched in favour of the more comical Richard Crane, while his no-kissy-stuff spunky girl assistant is Aline Towne.

Judd Holdren Commando Cody • **Aline Towne** Joan Gilbert • **Gregory Gaye** The Ruler • **Richard Crane** Dick Preston • **William Schallert** Ted Richards • **Craig Kelly** Commissioner Henderson
Director *Franklin Adreon, Fred C Brannon, Harry Keller*

Communion ★★ 15

1989 US Colour 104mins [video]

Was author Whitley Strieber abducted by aliens as outlined in his bestselling book *Communion*? Or was his close encounter and subsequent medical probing just a bizarre hallucination, or even a cynical marketing ploy as his detractors have claimed? You really won't be any the wiser after watching this ponderous, pompous and cost-cutting quasi-documentary, despite an enormous amount of conviction from Christopher Walken as the traumatised novelist. When it plays the game and goes for cheap sci-fi scares, this earnest treatise is reasonable fun. But, compared to *The X Files*, it's old UFO news indeed. Contains violence and swearing.

Christopher Walken Whitley Strieber • **Lindsay Crouse** Anne Strieber • **Joel Carlson** Andrew Strieber • **Frances Sternhagen** Dr Janet Duffy • **Andreas Katsulas** Alex • **Terri Hanauer** Sara • **Basil Hoffman** Dr Friedman • **John Dennis Johnston** Fireman • **Dee Dee Rescher** Mrs Greenberg • **Aileen Fitzpatrick** Mother
Director *Philippe Mora*
Screenplay *Whitley Strieber, from his book*

The Computer Wore Tennis Shoes ★★ U

1970 US Colour 90mins

What might have been a nifty idea for a half-hour TV show is stretched to breaking point in this Disney comedy. The ever-willing Kurt Russell stars as the teenager who becomes a genius after a computer downloads its memory system into his brain. Suddenly, our hero is winning game shows and taking on Cesar Romero's inept crime ring. It's as engaging as it is predictable, although we could have done without the inevitable comic car chase. The majority of the cast reassembled a couple of years later for the lacklustre sequel, *Now You See Him, Now You Don't*.

Cesar Romero A J Arno • **Kurt Russell** Dexter • **Joe Flynn** Dean Higgins • **William Schallert** Professor Quigley • **Alan Hewitt** Dean Collingsgood • **Richard Bakalyan** Chillie Walsh • **Debbie Paine** Annie • **Frank Webb** Pete • **Michael McGreevey** Schuyler • **Jon Provost** Bradley
Director *Robert Butler*
Screenplay *Joseph L McEveety*

The Computer Wore Tennis Shoes ★★ U

1995 US Colour 86mins

Made 25 years after Kurt Russell starred in the original, this TV movie continues Disney's trend of updating its old hits for a new generation. Indeed, one of the executive producers is Les Mayfield, director of another recent retread, *Flubber*. Sure, the computer is a lot snazzier than the one Russell interfaced with, but Kirk Cameron has none of Russell's boyish charm. Once again, our hero makes a name for himself on the college quiz show circuit, but this time the focus falls on a jealous rival setting out to discredit the mega-byte brainbox.

Kirk Cameron Dexter Riley • **Larry Miller** Dean Valentine • **Jason Bernard** Professor Miles Quigley • **Jeff Maynard** Gozin • **Anne Marie Tremko** Sarah Matthews • **Andrew Woodworth** Will • **Mathew McCurley** Norwood • **Dean Jones** Dean Carlson • **Charles Lane** Regent Yarborough • **Paul Dooley** Senator Thatch
Director *Peyton Reed*
Screenplay *Joseph L McEveety, Ryan Rowe*

Coneheads ★★ PG

1993 US Colour 86mins

The American satirical series *Saturday Night Live* has spawned some blockbuster movies – *The Blues Brothers* and *Wayne's World*, for instance – but this Dan Aykroyd creation sank without trace. Aykroyd is reunited with old TV colleagues Jane Curtin, best known over here for the sitcom *3rd Rock from the Sun*, and Laraine Newman for this dismal comedy about a family of aliens (Aykroyd, Curtin and Michelle Burke) trying to get to grips with life on earth. Despite cameos from younger generation *Saturday Night Live* comics, such as *The Wedding Singer*'s Adam Sandler and Chris Farley, plus an appearance from *Spinal Tap*'s Michael McKean, the characters are long past their sell-by date, and Aykroyd and co sadly fail to recapture past glories. Contains some swearing and sex scenes.

Dan Aykroyd Beldar • **Jane Curtin** Prymaat • **Michael McKean** Seedling • **Michelle Burke** Connie • **David Spade** Turnbull •

The proof is out there: astronomer Jodie Foster prepares to meet the neighbours in *Contact*

Chris Farley Ronnie • **Jason Alexander** Larry Farber • **Lisa Jane Persky** Lisa Farber • **Sinbad** Otto • **Shishir Kurup** Khoudri • **Jon Lovitz** Dr Rudolf • **Phil Hartman** Marlax • **Laraine Newman** Laarta • **Ellen DeGeneres** Coach • **Michael Richards** Motel clerk • **Dave Thomas** Highmaster
Director *Steve Barron*
Screenplay *Tom Davis, Dan Aykroyd, Bonnie Turner, Terry Turner*

Conquest of Space ★★★ U

1955 US Colour 77mins [video]

Paramount slashed the budget and added soap-opera bubbles to George Pal's sequel to *Destination Moon*, hastening the end of the producer's relationship with the studio. With the accent more on science than on fiction, *Conquest of Space* aims to offer an accurate reflection of what a trip to Mars would be like technically and how it would affect the crew psychologically. Despite an out-of-sync religious tone and the sight of snow falling on the red planet when the astronauts land on Christmas Day, Pal's reverential approach still manages to evoke a sense of wonder. Look out for the orbiting space station wheel and the Martian landscapes.

Walter Brooke Samuel Merritt • **Eric Fleming** Barney Merritt • **Mickey Shaughnessy** Mahoney • **Phil Foster** Siegle • **William Redfield** Cooper • **William Hopper** Fenton • **Benson Fong** Imoto • **Ross Martin** Fodor • **Vito Scotti** Sanella • **John Dennis** Donkersgoed
Director *Byron Haskin*
Screenplay *Philip Yordan, Barre Lyndon, George WorthingtonYates, from the book "The Mars Project" by Chesley Bonestell, Willy Ley*

Conquest of the Planet of the Apes ★★★ 15

1972 US Colour 86mins [video]

The fourth film in the sci-fi saga illustrates how the ape revolt happened in the first place. Caesar, played by series regular Roddy McDowall, gains the power of speech, forms enslaved fellow simians into guerrilla groups and leads them against the evil human race who have adopted them as household pets. Gritty direction from J Lee Thompson and plenty of fun philosophising, complete with intriguing moral lessons and neat ape/man role reversals (take a bow, Paul Dehn, for an uncommonly fine script), make this episode a compelling outing into futuristic monkey business. Contains violence.

Roddy McDowall Caesar • **Don Murray** Breck • **Ricardo Montalban** Armando • **Natalie Trundy** Lisa • **Hari Rhodes** MacDonald • **Severn Darden** Kolp • **Lou Wagner** Busboy • **John Randolph** Commission chairman • **Asa Maynor** Mrs Riley • **HM Wynant** Hoskyns
Director *J Lee Thompson*
Screenplay *Paul Dehn, from characters created by Pierre Boulle*

Contact ★★★ PG

1997 US Colour 143mins [video] DVD

A rather over-zealous take on New Age spirituality mars this otherwise impressive adaptation of Carl Sagan's bestselling novel. Jodie Foster stars as the dedicated astronomer who receives a message from extraterrestrials explaining how humble humans can build a spacecraft and go to meet them. Matthew McConaughey plays the religious adviser who is battling for her soul, while Tom Skerritt and James Woods portray sceptical presidential aides. Along with the always reliable Foster, they all deliver excellent performances. The digital effects, meanwhile, are stunning and director Robert Zemeckis is at home with the action sequences. If only he'd stuck to the sci-fi.

Jodie Foster Dr Eleanor "Ellie" Arroway • **Matthew McConaughey** Palmer Joss • **Tom Skerritt** Dr David Drumlin • **Angela Bassett** Rachel Constantine • **John Hurt** SR Hadden • **David Morse** Theodore "Ted" Arroway • **Rob Lowe** Richard Rank • **William Fichtner** Kent • **James Woods** Michael Kitz • **Larry King** • **Jay Leno** • **Jake Busey** Joseph
Director *Robert Zemeckis*
Screenplay *James V Hart, Michael Goldenberg, from a story by Ann Druyan, Carl Sagan, from the novel by Carl Sagan*
Producer *Robert Zemeckis, Steve Starkey*

Convict 762 ★ 18

1997 US Colour 91mins [video]

"The more he kills, the stronger he gets!" runs the tagline. And the longer you watch this utter claptrap, the weaker your will to live will become. When a spaceship full of women conveniently crash-lands on a prison planet, they discover just two inhabitants left alive: a guard and Convict 762, the man responsible for massacring the entire prison population. The only problem is that *both* claim to be the warden. Directed by Luca Bercovici, this inexplicably bad sci-fi movie would have been a waste of talent, if only there had been some talent involved in the first place. Contains violence, nudity and some swearing.

Frank Zagarino Vigo • **Billy Drago** Mannix • **Shannon Sturges** Nile • **Michole White** Austin • **Tawny Ellis** Reno • **Shae D'Lyn** Sheridan • **Charlie Spradling** Helena • **Merle Kennedy** Lincoln
Director *Luca Bercovici*
Screenplay *J Reifel*

The Cosmic Man ★ U

1959 US BW 69mins [video]

John Carradine is the mysterious creature from another planet who arrives on Earth in a huge weightless globe. His presence unleashes a debate between the military authorities who want to blow him up, and the scientific establishment who want to keep him alive. This dismal science-fiction programme-filler is mercifully short in length and equally short of action and ideas. In these days of special effects blockbusters and advanced scientific knowledge, it's deader than a Dodo.

Bruce Bennett Dr Karl Sorenson • **John Carradine** Cosmic man • **Angela Greene** Kathy Grant • **Paul Langton** Colonel Mathews • **Scotty Morrow** Ken Grant • **Lyn Osborn** Sergeant Gray • **Walter Maslow** Dr Richie • **Robert Lytton** General Knowland
Director *Herbert Greene*
Screenplay *Arthur C Pierce*

Cosmic Slop ★★

1994 US Colour 84mins

A marked change of pace for the Hudlin brothers, Reginald and Warrington, who are best known for the hip-hop humour of *House Party* and the Eddie Murphy vehicle *Boomerang*. Here, three heavily ironic tales tackle the thorny issues of race and religion. The first poses a moral dilemma for a black politician facing an alien invasion, the second finds a priest facing up to a miracle vision, while the final segment is a cautionary tale of revolution. It doesn't quite hang together, but the Hudlins deserve credit for their refreshingly imaginative approach, although the movie was dropped by HBO in America after one screening due to bomb threats. Contains violence, swearing and drug abuse.

George Clinton Host • **Robert Guillaume** Gleason Golightly • **Michele Lamar Richards** Gail Golightly • **Jason Bernard** Bernard Shields • **Edward Edwards** Chief of staff • **Chi McBride** T-Bone • **Paula Jai Parker** Tang • **Efrain Figueroa** Padrino • **Nicholas Turturro** Father Carlos • **Richard Herd** Cardinal
Director *Reginald Hudlin, Warrington Hudlin, Kevin Rodney Sullivan*
Screenplay *Kyle Baker, Warrington Hudlin, Trey Ellis, from the short stories "Faces at the Bottom of the Well" by Derrick Bell and "Tang" by Chester Himes*

SFacts

Cosmic Slop **was the name of a ground-breaking album from seventies band Funkadelic – founder and funk icon George Clinton hosts the film, and Clinton and fellow band member Bernard Worrell had a hand in the soundtrack.**

Countdown ★★★★ U

1968 US Colour 97mins

A fascinating early work from Robert Altman about the planning of a mission to the Moon and its effect on the lives of those involved. There are early signs of what would become Altman trademarks (the large cast; the cool, documentary air) and he coaxes fine, naturalistic performances from a pre-stardom James Caan and Robert Duvall – later to be reunited in *The Godfather* – as the two astronauts, only one of whom will go on the mission.

James Caan Lee Stegler • **Joanna Moore** Mickey Stegler • **Robert Duvall** Chiz • **Barbara Baxley** Jean • **Charles Aidman** Gus • **Steve Ihnat** Ross Lewellyn • **Michael Murphy** Rick • **Ted Knight** Walter Larson • **Stephen Coit** Dr Ehrman • **John Rayner** Dunc • **Charles Irving** Seidel • **Bobby Riha Jr** Stevie
Director *Robert Altman*
Screenplay *Loring Mandel, from the novel "The Pilgram Project" by Hank Searls*

Countdown at Woomera ★★

TV 1961 UK BW 90mins

This ambitious feature-length one-off (scripted by Henry Bentinck) was broadcast live from Associated-Rediffusion's Wembley Studios in 1961, trying for a more serious monster-free approach to outer space than the *Quatermass* serials, but coming across as mostly undigested textbook speeches and bland political intrigue. It has the first man (Neil McCallum) landing on the moon in 1968 (close call), but is mostly about the boys at Mission Control in the Australian outback, where Patrick Barr is the gruff commanding officer, Sylvia Kay the fiancée in telepathic contact with her man in space, and Allan Cuthbertson (possessor of the finest toothbrush moustache in *Spotlight*) as the officious security chief. The menace was added by a bioweapon that could wipe out all life on earth.

Neil McCallum Robert McKerrell • **Sylvia Kay** Margaret Paisley • **John Welsh** Sir Robert Trevelyan • **Patrick Barr** General O'Connor • **John Glyn-Jones** Dr Newton • **John Tate** Professor Leighton • **Allan Cuthbertson** Superintendent Steel
Director *Cyril Coke*
Written by *Harry Bentinck*

Counterblast ★★

1948 UK BW 99mins

Among the first films to consider Nazi experiments into germ warfare, this brisk British thriller boasts the interesting premise of turning a wanted war criminal into an accidental hero. Having killed an Australian doctor to escape a death camp, Mervyn Johns arrives in England to develop a lethal serum for his indefatigable controller, Sybilla Binder. However, a secret fondness for lab assistant Nova Pilbeam and the growing suspicions of scientist Robert Beatty cause him to rethink his tactics. Considered overly violent on its 1953 US release, this was an ambitious picture for its time and still entertains, despite its flaws.

Robert Beatty Dr Rankin • **Mervyn Johns** Dr Bruckner • **Nova Pilbeam** Tracy Shaw • **Margaretta Scott** Sister Johnson • **Sybilla Binder** Martha • **Marie Lohr** Mrs Coles • **Karel Stepanek** Prof Inman • **Alan Wheatley** Kennedy
Director *Paul L Stein*
Screenplay *Jack Whittingham, from a story by Guy Morgan*

Counterstrike ★★★

TV 1969 UK BW 10x50mins

This *Avengers*-type thriller was typical of the kind of science fantasy the BBC excelled at in the sixties and seventies. Brooding Jon Finch, just two years away from a modest shot at stardom with lead roles in Roman Polanski's *Macbeth* and Alfred Hitchcock's *Frenzy*, plays Simon King, an intergalactic secret agent sent to Earth by a sort of cosmic United Nations to prevent an alien invasion. Referred to as Centaurans, they hail from a dying planet and hope to make the Earth their own by infiltrating and wrecking society from within. A clever premise that avoided the need for the costly effects that the standard BBC budget couldn't have matched – *Independence Day*, it is not.

Jon Finch Simon • **Sarah Bracket** Mary • **Kate Fitzroy** Control
Created by *Tony Williamson*
Script editor *David Rolfe*
Producer *Patrick Alexander*

Crack in the World ★★★ U

1965 US Colour 95mins

Scientists attempt to harness the inner energy of the earth and get it all wrong in this moderate sci-fi thriller. Director Andrew Marton – who was responsible for the chariot race in *Ben-Hur* – knows how to milk this kind of thing, and no one looks more worried about the end of the world than tight-lipped Dana Andrews, who had to deal with a similar scale of problem in *The Satan Bug* the same year. Among the cast, Alexander Knox brings a touch of class to the proceedings, while Janette Scott and Kieron Moore reprise their double act from *The Day of the Triffids*. The effects just about pass muster, although they may look familiar to fans of other movies in the genre, notably

Master of the World.

Dana Andrews Dr Stephen Sorensen • **Janette Scott** Maggie Sorensen • **Kieron Moore** Ted Rampion • **Alexander Knox** Sir Charles Eggerston • **Peter Damon** Masefield • **Gary Lasdun** Markov • **Mike Steen** Steele • **Todd Martin** Simpson • **Jim Gillen** Rand
Director *Andrew Marton*
Screenplay *Jon Manchip White, Julian Halevy [Julian Zimet], from a story by Jon Manchip White*

Crash and Burn ★★ 15

1990 US Colour 81mins

With his Empire Pictures company, Charles Band was behind some of the sharpest, smartest slices of low budget sci-fi (*Trancers, Zone Troopers*). However, stepping behind the lens himself didn't prove to be one of his brightest moves with this derivative post apocalypse thriller. In a new low-tech world ruled over by a sinister corporation, a disparate group of people at a community TV station find themselves up against a lethal android. The climactic battle has its moments but the derivative script is riddled with clichés and budget constraints (usually not a problem for Band) this time count against him. Notable mainly for a then rare appearance by *The Waltons* star Ralph Waite.

Paul Ganus Tyson Keen • **Megan Ward** Arrin Hooks • **Ralph Waite** Lathan Hooks • **Bill Moseley** Quinn
Director *Charles Band*
Screenplay *JS Cardone*

The Crater Lake Monster ★

1977 US Colour 85mins

Though the title suggests a story about a rampaging beast, the movie is actually more concerned with two idiots who live around the lake, getting into endless inane bouts of comic chatter and slapstick situations. Occasionally we get a few seconds of stop-motion dinosaur mayhem (by David Allen), but it's not up to Ray Harryhausen standard – shots of the monster are often a phoney-looking close-up of a rubber head. This account of a meteorite thawing a frozen dinosaur egg at the bottom of a lake is so slow and shoddy, it makes some of the worst fifties monster movies look like masterpieces.

Richard Cardella Sherriff Steve Hanson • **Glen Roberts** Arnie Chabot • **Mark Siegel** Mitch Kowalski • **Kacey Cobb** Susan Patterson • **Richard Garrison** Dan Turner • **Michael Hoover** Ross Conway • **Bob Hyman** Richard Calkins • **Suzanne Lewis** Paula Conway
Director *William R Stromberg*
Screenplay *William R Stromberg, Richard Cardella*

The Crawling Hand ★★★

1963 US BW 88mins

The dismembered hand of an alien-possessed astronaut lands on a beach in California, where a student finds it and discovers its evil, strangulating powers. A canny science-fiction reworking of *The Beast with Five Fingers*, Herbert (*I Was a Teenage Frankenstein*) Strock's skilful direction, and a game cast rising to the illogical occasion, make this a delightfully schlocky exploitation film that successfully goes for the jugular with effective shock cuts and a demented drive verging on the delirious.

Peter Breck Steve Curan • **Kent Taylor** Doc Weitzberg • **Rod Lauren** Paul Lawrence • **Sirry Steffen** Marta Farnstrom • **Alan Hale [Alan Hale Jr]** Sheriff • **Arline Judge** Mrs Hotchkiss • **Richard Arlen** Lee Berrenger
Director *Herbert L Strock*
Screenplay *Herbert L Strock, William Idelson, from a story by Robert Young*

The Crazies ★★★ 18

1973 US Colour 102mins

A commendable, if unsuccessful attempt by director George A Romero to repeat the success of his revolutionary horror classic *Night of the Living Dead*. This time around, panic and paranoia prevail when an army plane carrying a bio-chemical virus crashes in Pennsylvania and turns the locals into killers. Consistently shifting points-of-view keep involvement to a minimum and greatly undercut the suspense, despite the sudden acts of shocking violence and some effective gore moments.

Lane Carroll Judy • **WG McMillan [Will MacMillan]** David • **Harold Wayne Jones** Clank • **Lloyd Hollar** Col Pockem • **Richard Liberty** Artie • **Lynn Lowry** Kathie • **Richard France** Dr Watts • **Harry Spillman** Maj Ryder
Director *George A Romero*
Screenplay *George A Romero, from a story by Paul McCollough*
Editor *George A Romero*

The Creation of the Humanoids ★★

1962 US Colour 75mins

This was, reputedly, pop icon Andy Warhol's favourite movie. His opinion aside, this is a rather run-of-the-mill tale of a post-Holocaust world in which the androids built to help mankind soon outnumber the humans. Don Megowan is the hero who tries to remedy the situation. Certainly not in *The Terminator* league, but a curio, if only for its cult associations.

Don Megowan Capt Kenneth Craigus • **Erica Elliott** Maxine Megan • **George Milan** Acto • **Dudley Manlove** Lagan • **Frances McCann** Esme Craigus Milos
Director *Barry E Wesley*
Screenplay *Jay Simms*

Creator ★★ 15

1985 US Colour 103mins

Based on Jeremy Leven's novel, this jumbled comedy drama involves a Nobel Prize-winning-scientist-turned-college-professor who tries to resurrect his long-dead wife via cloning. Peter O'Toole brings his customary God-like grandeur to the lead role, complemented by the young, amiable supporting cast that includes Mariel Hemingway, Virginia Madsen and Vincent Spano. The film's chief handicap is an excess of soap opera-style plot strands: the intervention of O'Toole's scientist rival (David Ogden Stiers), a pair of budding romances and an incurable illness. Naturally, they all intertwine in the implausible finale.

Peter O'Toole Dr Harry Wolper • **Mariel Hemingway** Meli • **Vincent Spano** Boris • **Virginia Madsen** Barbara Spencer • **David Ogden Stiers** Sid Kuhlenbeck • **John Dehner** Paul • **Karen Kopins** Lucy Wolper • **Kenneth Tigar** Pavlo
Director *Ivan Passer*
Screenplay *Jeremy Leven, from his novel*

Creature from the Black Lagoon ★★★★ PG

1954 US BW 75mins

It's horribly dated, the acting's lousy, the 3-D effects are worthless and the monster is a man in a rubber suit. Yet *Creature from the Black Lagoon* remains one of the all-time classic monster movies. The by-the-numbers plot – explorers encounter a half-man, half-fish that has the hots for Julia Adams – is enlivened by director Jack Arnold's atmospheric use of the Florida Everglades locations and a sympathetic portrait of the "Gill-Man". (Champion swimmer Ricou Browning was picked for the role because he could hold his breath for four minutes at a time.) The underwater sequences are particularly memorable, while the scene where Adams swims alone with the creature watching from below plays upon all our fears of what may lurk beneath the sea. (That same fear was brilliantly exploited decades later in *Jaws*.) A massive hit in its day, the Gill-Man justly entered the horror hall of fame alongside

Universal's other great monsters, Dracula and Frankenstein. Avoid the two turgid sequels that followed.

Richard Carlson David Reed • **Julia Adams [Julie Adams]** Kay Lawrence • **Richard Denning** Mark Williams • **Antonio Moreno** Carl Maia • **Nestor Paiva** Lucas • **Whit Bissell** Edwin Thompson • **Ben Chapman** Gill-Man • **Harry Escalante** Chico • **Ricou Browning** Gill-Man (underwater sequences only)
Director *Jack Arnold*
Screenplay *Harry Essex, Arthur Ross, from a story by Maurice Zimm*

The Creature Walks among Us ★★

1956 US BW 78mins

The third and final outing for *The Creature from the Black Lagoon*. Captured in the Everglades by scientists Jeff Morrow and Rex Reason, the famous Gill-Man is mutated so he can live on land. Blamed for a crime he didn't commit, the transformed semi-human (Don Megowan) breaks out of his cage to bring his tormentors to justice while falling under the spell of Leigh Snowden's sexy charms. Directed by John Sherwood as just another conventional monster movie, in complete contrast to director Jack Arnold's subtle "Beauty and the Beast" shadings prevalent in the first two episodes, this disappointment only achieves a modicum of Arnold's resonance in the climax when the altered fish-out-of-water lumbers back to the sea doomed to drown.

Jeff Morrow Dr William Barton • **Rex Reason** Dr Thomas Morgan • **Leigh Snowden** Marcia Barton • **Gregg Palmer** Jed Grant • **Maurice Manson** Dr Borg • **James Rawley** Dr Johnson • **David McMahon** Capt Stanley • **Paul Fierro** Morteno • **Don Megowan** Creature (on land)
Director *John Sherwood*
Screenplay *Arthur Ross*

The Creature Wasn't Nice ★ PG

1981 US Colour 77mins

This is a painfully lame spoof of *Alien* from writer/director Bruce Kimmel. *Laverne and Shirley* star Cindy Williams, Leslie Nielsen and Steed himself, Patrick Macnee, are among the mismatched crew who must deal with a stowaway monster on board their spaceship. The "highlight" is the alien monster's musical number, *I Want to Eat Your Face*, but in the main this is a misbegotten enterprise that smothers its decent cast with camp gags and idiotic dialogue. Kimmel and Williams also worked together on the far superior *First Nudie Musical*.

Cindy Williams McHugh • **Bruce Kimmel** John • **Leslie Nielsen** Jameson • **Gerrit Graham** Rodzinski • **Patrick Macnee** Stark • **Ron Kurowski** Creature
Director/Screenplay *Bruce Kimmel*

Creature with the Atom Brain ★

1955 US BW 69mins

"He comes from beyond the grave!" hailed the poster, and you'll feel like crawling into one after watching this laboured comic strip-style hokum. Back in the fifties, mad nuclear scientists were as American as Coca-Cola and Mom's apple pie. Here a suitably bonkers Richard Denning uses atomic energy to create zombie-like robots as instruments of his tortured revenge. Curt Siodmak, who wrote the classic *I Walked with a Zombie* in 1943, really seems to be slumming it here. However, the real surprise is how a film combining gangsters, zombies and Nazis could turn out to be such a monotonous watch.

Richard Denning Dr Chet Walker • **Angela Stevens** Joyce Walker • **S John Launer** Captain Dave Harris • **Michael Granger** Frank Buchanan • **Gregory Gaye** Professor Steigg • **Linda Bennett** Penny Walker • **Tristram Coffin** District Attorney MacGraw • **Harry Lauter** Reporter • **Larry Blake** Reporter
Director *Edward L Cahn*
Screenplay *Curt Siodmak*

SCI Q • SCI Q • SCI Q • SCI Q •

7

Which movie spacecraft's design was inspired by a hamburger with an olive next to it?

See page 496 for answers

The Creeping Terror ★

1964 US Colour 75mins

In one of the cheapest films you'll ever see: a spaceship crashes in a western US desert and produces a monstrous alien with an appetite for teenagers of the American and screaming variety. You don't have to be Einstein to deduce that the producer's cash wasn't spent on the title creature, which resembles a disgruntled shaggy quilt with five men propped inside to make it crawl. One hilarious blooper features a pair of tennis shoes poking out from underneath. This must rank as one of the all-time dumb monster flicks. Add to that diabolical acting, abysmal dialogue and laughable sets, and you have a Grade-Z experience. Film-maker Art J Nelson, who also plays the lead, never directed another film.

Vic Savage [Art J Nelson] Martin Gordon • **Shannon O'Neill** Brett Gordon • **William Thourlby** Dr Bradford
Director *Art J Nelson*
Screenplay *Robert Silliphant, Alan Silliphant*

Creepozoids ★ 18

1987 US Colour 68mins

Prolific hack director David DeCouteau strikes again with this substandard *Alien* copy set in post-nuclear 1998. Five army deserters shelter from acid rain in an abandoned laboratory where they are terrorised by bad muppet mutants including a shockingly awful giant rat and a baby monster. Trash scream queen Linnea Quigley takes a nude shower while the rest of the cast, including porno star Ashlyn Gere (Kim McKamy), run around dark endless tunnels. Although originally only 71 minutes long, this vapid groan-inducer feels twice its length.

Linnea Quigley Bianca • **Ken Abraham** Butch • **Michael Aranda** Jesse • **Richard Hawkins** Jake • **Kim McKamy** Kate • **Joi Wilson** Scientist • **Kim McKamy** Kate
Director *David DeCoteau*
Screenplay *David DeCoteau, Burford Hauser*

Crime Traveller ★★★

TV 1997 UK Colour 8x50mins

This lightweight BBC action fantasy drama was semi-nostalgic in its style and reminiscent of sixties classics such as *The Champions* and *The Saint*. Unfortunately, the reality-based TV agenda of the nineties and beyond consigned it to an early grave after just one series. It was the creation of Anthony Horowitz, who got the idea while writing an episode of *Poirot*. The challenge was to bring a completely new dimension to the detective drama, and what better than a cop who can go back in time and solve crimes before they've even happened. *EastEnder*'s star Michael French was the time-travelling sleuth, ably partnered by police scientist Chloë Annett, best known as Kochanski in *Red Dwarf*. The duo's boss, increasingly baffled by the miraculous way they solve crimes, was originally written for a man but instead given a hard-edged sheen by *The Royle Family*'s Sue Johnston.

Michael French Jeff Slade • **Chloë Annett** Holly Turner • **Sue Johnston** Grisham •

Paul Trussell Morris • **Richard Dempsey** Nicky • **Bob Goody** Danny
Written by *Anthony Horowitz*
Producer *Brian Eastman*

Crime Zone ★★ 15

1989 US Colour 92mins [video]

If Roger Corman is remembered for anything, it will be his ability to spot talent in the unlikeliest of places. This was an early directorial assignment for Luis Llosa, who later would go on to direct big bucks blockbusters such as *The Specialist* and *Anaconda*, and there are flashes of style among the usual B-movie clichés in this rollicking tale about two youngster who rebel against the autocratic rules of their futuristic society. David Carradine lends his experience and there is also an early role for future *Twin Peaks* star Sherilyn Fenn.

David Carradine Jason • **Peter Nelson** Bone • **Sherilyn Fenn** Helen • **Michael Shaner** Creon • **Orlando Sacha** Alexi
Director *Luis Llosa*
Screenplay *Daryl Haney*
Executive producer *Roger Corman*

Crimes of the Future ★★

1970 Can BW 63mins

Canadian cult director David Cronenberg's second underground feature – a companion piece to his debut *Stereo* (1969) – deals with deadly cosmetics wiping out the female race and how the male population sublimate their sexual desires by becoming paedophiles because the adult women are all dying. All the diverse themes Cronenberg expands on in his later works are here in seminal form, but the film is rather a pretentious, eccentric and over-stylised black satire. The soundtrack, a mix of disembodied marine-life sounds and techno-babble, doesn't help matters. For die-hard completists only.

Ronald Mlodzik Adrian Trilpod • **Jon Lidolt** • **Tania Zolty** • **Paul Mulholland**
Director/Screenplay *David Cronenberg*
Producer *David Cronenberg*

The Crimson Ghost ★★

1946 US BW

Where would serials have been without fantastical villains and top secret weapons? The gadget here is the Cyclotrode (a counteratomic device capable of shorting any electrical circuit), while the criminal mastermind is a skeletal figure shrouded in monastic garb. The Ghost was played by Bud Geary to prevent viewers spotting which one of inventor Keene Duncan's associates was a traitor, while his chief sidekick, Ashe, was played by TV's Lone Ranger, Clayton Moore. Charles Quigley's criminologist is a somewhat doltish hero, but Linda Stirling makes her increasingly preposterous perils seem suitably scary. A highlights feature, *Cyclotrode X*, was released in 1966.

Charles Quigley Duncan Richards • **Linda Stirling** Diana Farnsworth • **Joe Forte** Prof Parker / Crimson Ghost • **Clayton Moore** Ashe • **Keene Duncan** Prof Chambers
Director *William Witney, Fred Brannon [Fred C Brannon]*
Screenplay *Albert DeMond, Basil Dickey, Jesse Duffy, Sol Shor*

Critters ★★★ 15

1986 US Colour 82mins [video]

Stephen Herek, later to hit the jackpot with *Bill and Ted's Excellent Adventure*, directs a cheeky smash-and-grab raid on *Gremlins* and comes up with a crude but entertaining horror comedy. The "critters" of the title are a race of nasty hedgehog-like alien creatures who invade a small American town and proceed to wreak havoc until two intergalactic bounty hunters arrive to save the day. The cast, which includes Dee Wallace Stone, M Emmet Walsh and a young Billy Zane, remains stoically straight-faced throughout, the creatures nab the best lines (in subtitles), and Herek keeps his tongue stuck firmly in his cheek. It went on to spawn three sequels. Contains violence and swearing.

Dee Wallace Stone Helen Brown • **M Emmet Walsh** Harv • **Billy Green Bush** Jay Brown • **Scott Grimes** Brad Brown • **Nadine Van Der Velde** April Brown • **Don Opper** Charlie McFadden • **Terrence Mann** Johnny Steele • **Billy Zane** Steve Elliot • **Ethan Phillips** Jeff Barnes
Director *Stephen Herek*
Screenplay *Stephen Herek, Dominic Muir*

Critters 2: the Main Course ★★ 15

1988 US Colour 82mins [video]

Critters was cheap but hugely entertaining junk food, a cash-in on *Gremlins*. Quite how it manage to spawn so many sequels beggars belief, but this at least sticks pretty close to the original and manages to hold on to much of the cast. Scott Grimes is once again pressed back into action when he discovers that two of the evil, spiny space scum have survived and are now a family, while Don Opper and Terrence Mann beam in from outer space to help the townfolk. Director Mick Garris adeptly mixes the gags with the gore, but it doesn't quite satisfy the appetite as much as the first course.

Scott Grimes Brad Brown • **Liane Curtis** Megan Morgan • **Don Opper** Charlie McFadden • **Terrence Mann** Ug
Director *Mick Garris*
Screenplay *DT Twohy, Mick Garris*

Critters 3 ★★ 15

1991 US Colour 81mins [video]

This largely forgotten entry in a largely forgettable B-movie franchise has received a new lease of life thanks to the presence of Leonardo DiCaprio in the cast. The *Titanic* hero reveals little star potential in this cheap and cheerful caper, which finds the man-eating space critters hitting the city for the first time and laying siege to a tenement building. Contains violence and swearing.

Aimee Brooks Annie • **John Calvin** Clifford • **Katherine Cortez** Marcia • **Leonardo DiCaprio** Josh • **Geoffrey Blake** Frank • **Don Opper** Charlie McFadden
Director *Kristine Peterson*
Screenplay *David J Schow*

Critters 4 ★★★ 15

1992 US Colour 90mins [video]

The *Critters* series has provided a few skeletons in the closet for now famous stars. Part three offered an early role for Leonardo DiCaprio, and part four – actually shot back to back with number three – features Angela Bassett, later to find fame and acclaim in the Tina Turner biopic *What's Love Got to Do with It*. This one's set in outer space, allowing for some gags at the expense of slightly bigger budget sci-fi fare. Otherwise, it's as cheap and cheerful as ever. Contains swearing and violence.

Don Keith Opper [Don Opper] Charlie McFadden • **Angela Bassett** Fran • **Brad Dourif** Al Bert • **Paul Whitthorne** Ethan • **Terrence Mann** Ug/Counselor Tetra • **Anders Hove** Rick • **Eric DaRe** Bernie • **Martine Beswick** Angela • **Anne Elizabeth Ramsay** Dr McCormick
Director *Rupert Harvey*
Screenplay *Joseph Lyle, David J Schow*

Croisières Sidérales ★★

1941 Fr BW and Colour 95mins

It's Sleeping Beauty in space in this curio from the debuting André Zwoboda, which has the distinction of being the only sci-fi movie made during the Nazi Occupation. On the surface, the story of an inventor (Jean Marchat) who sees his wife (Madeleine Sologne) age 25 years during a 14-day stratospheric mission and then blasts off to undergo the same process, seems trite and sentimental. But Zwoboda's study in relativity got him into all sorts of trouble with the Vichy authorities, who were

Square roots: six strangers awaken to find themselves in a nightmare world in Vincenzo Natali's chilling debut feature *Cube*

convinced that his allusion to the work of the Jewish Einstein was a deliberate act of subversion. A French language film.

Madeleine Sologne Francoise Monier • **Julien Carette** Lucien Marchand • **Suzanne Dehelly** Georgette Marchand • **Robert Arnoux** Antoine • **Jean Marchat** Robert Monier • **Suzanne Dantès** Camille
Director *André Zwobada*
Screenplay *Pierre Guerlais, Pierre Bost*
Cinematographer *Jean Isnard*

Crosstalk ★★

1982 Aus Colour 83mins

A dated but still interesting techno-chiller from Down Under that owes a huge debt to the Hitchcock classic *Rear Window*. Gary Day is the house-bound boffin who begins to wonder why his artificially intelligent computer has become obsessed with the goings-on of his neighbour (John Ewart). The film's vision of the future is quaintly anachronistic and the clumsy acting doesn't help, but director Mark Egerton still manages the odd chilling moment.

Gary Day Ed Ballinger • **Penny Downie** Cindy • **Brian McDermott** Whitehead • **Peter Collingwood** Hollister • **Kim Deacon** Jane • **Jill Forster** Mrs Stollier
Director *Mark Egerton*
Screenplay *Mark Egerton, Linda Lane*

Crossworlds ★★★ 15

1996 US Colour 87mins

Cheap and cliché-ridden it may be, but this *Stargate* meets *Star Wars* hybrid is an enjoyably unpretentious fantasy romp. All-American Josh Charles learns from a mysterious stranger that the crystal around his neck is the key to a trans-dimensional portal where time and space have no meaning. In this crossworld, where everyone is red-hued and moves in slow motion, he teams up with Ben Kenobi clone Rutger Hauer in a battle for survival against megalomaniac Stuart Wilson, who not only has designs on the universe but also killed Charles's father years earlier. If you can get over the slow start and revel in the low-rent George Lucas homages, this will be an entertaining experience. Contains violence and some swearing.

Rutger Hauer AT • **Josh Charles** Joe Talbot • **Stuart Wilson** Ferris • **Andrea Roth**

Laura • **Perry Anzilotti** Rebo
Director *Krishna Rao*
Screenplay *Krishna Rao, Raman Rao*

Crusade ★★ U PG 12

TV 1999 US Colour 13x60mins

A short-lived spin-off from *Babylon 5*, *Crusade* seemingly aimed to beat *Star Trek* at its own game, but instead was cancelled midway through the production of its opening season. Set in 2267, the starship-based series sees Captain Matthew Gideon (Gary Cole) and the crew of the *Excalibur* attempting to find a cure for an alien plague that is about to destroy all life on Earth. Series creator J Michael Straczynski doubtless had some clever twists planned for the show's long-term "story arc", but without those surprises, *Crusade*'s 13-episode run produces little more than a routine *Trek* wannabe. Cole's compulsive central performance and the superb visuals are the only antidotes to an otherwise bland concoction.

Gary Cole Captain Matthew Gideon • **Carrie Dobro** Dureena Nafeel • **Daniel Dae Kim** Lt John Matheson • **Marjean Holden** Dr Sarah Chambers • **David A Brooks** Max Eilerson • **Tracy Scoggins** Captain Elizabeth Lochley
Created by *J Michael Straczynski*
Executive producer *J Michael Straczynski, Douglas Netter*

Cube ★★★★ 15

1997 Can Colour 86mins DVD

Six strangers wake up to find themselves in a 14ft by 14ft cube. When they try to get out of their prison, they find they are snared in a seemingly endless maze of interlocking cubicles armed with lethal booby traps. How did they get there? Why have they been incarcerated? Director Vincenzo Natali's extraordinary debut feature takes a unique idea and milks its potential to the maximum with dark panache. Genuinely creepy and gory, with the discernible influence of David Cronenberg, this science-fiction horror puzzler is awash with bold ideas and unsettling tension. Natali keeps the enigma puzzling anew at every sharp twist and turn. Contains swearing and violence.

Nicole deBoer Leaven • **Nicky Guadagni** Holloway • **David Hewlett** Worth • **Andrew Miller** Kazan • **Julian Richings** Alderson • **Wayne Robson** Rennes • **Maurice Dean Wint** Quentin
Director *Vincenzo Natali*
Screenplay *Vincenzo Natali, André Bijelic, Graeme Manson*

SFacts

All the characters are named after prisons in the United States (Leavenworth, Alderson, San Quentin), England (Holloway), France (Rennes) and Russia (Kazan).

Curious Dr Humpp ★★★

1967 Arg BW 85mins

This oddity is one of the most bizarre mixes of sex, horror and sci-fi ever made. Forget the story – something about a voyeuristic mad scientist giving kidnapped girls aphrodisiacs – it's the fusion of paranoid fantasy, horrific morality and softcore banality that makes this exploitation movie by director Emilio Vieyra such a gob-smacker. The film is packed with striking black-and-white imagery– misshapen monsters in metal boots going to strip clubs, black-faced mutants with lights in their heads. Curiously unforgettable. Spanish dialogue dubbed into English.

Ricardo Bauleo • **Gloria Prat** • **Aldo Barbero** • **Susan Beltran** • **Justin Martin**
Director *Emilio Vieyra*
Screenplay *Emilio Vieyra, Raul Zorrilla*

The Curse of Frankenstein ★★★★ 15

1957 UK Colour 79mins

This was the classic that single-handedly revived traditional British Gothic and firmly placed the "Hammer House of Horror" on the global gore map. Peter Cushing is the demented Baron who yearns to resurrect the dead, while Christopher Lee plays the hideous creature who proves his mad theories correct. With its gruesome atmosphere, unflinching direction and outstanding design, this phenomenally successful film was the first colour version of Mary Shelley's tale, setting a standard Hammer found it hard to live up to.

Peter Cushing Baron Victor Frankenstein • **Christopher Lee** The Creature • **Hazel Court** Elizabeth • **Robert Urquhart** Paul Krempe
Director *Terence Fisher*
Screenplay *Jimmy Sangster, from the novel "Frankenstein" by Mary Shelley*

Curse of the Fly ★★

1965 UK BW 86mins

Brian Donlevy takes over from Vincent Price as the mad doctor experimenting with teleportation through the fourth dimension in this average second sequel to monster hit *The Fly*. Unfortunately, he still can't get the matter transmissions right, and the mutant results of his labours are locked in a closet, ready to scare his son's unbalanced wife (Carole Gray). Journeyman director Don Sharp's talent for shock effects gets lost amid the stiff acting and slow pacing.

Brian Donlevy Henri Delambre • **George Baker** Martin Delambre • **Carole Gray** Patricia Stanley • **Yvette Rees** Wan • **Bert Kwouk** Tai • **Michael Graham** Albert Delambre • **Jeremy Wilkin** Inspector Ronet
Director *Don Sharp*
Screenplay *Harry Spalding, from characters created by George Langelaan*

Cyber Bandits ★★

1995 US Colour 86mins

Full marks for brazen originality goes to director Erik Fleming's virtual reality thriller even if it scores low points for not making much sense. Pop stars Adam Ant, Grace Jones and Martin Kemp are featured in this weirdly off-putting action adventure revolving around the search for a super-weapon invented by German scientist Henry (*Rowan and Martin's Laugh-In*) Gibson. The tubular device has the ability to send victims into a permanent state of virtuality where they must spend the rest of their lives jumping through suggested fantasy hoops by the person who fired it. The overly bizarre plot, and the unique atmosphere Fleming brings to it, is all there is to this real curiosity.

Martin Kemp Jack Morris • **Alexandra Paul** Rebecca Snow • **Adam Ant** Manny • **James Wong** Tojo • **Robert Hays** Morgan • **Henry Gibson** Dr Knutsen • **Grace Jones** Masako Yokohama
Director *Erik Fleming*
Screenplay *James Robinson, Winston Beard, from a story by James Robinson*

Cyber-Tracker ★★ 18

1994 US Colour 90mins

Don "The Dragon" Wilson looks uncomfortable in the suit and tie he's forced to wear while playing a Secret Service agent and loyal servant of a future American government. But it looks like he's about to be made obsolete by the new "robotic justice" programme, which hunts down escaped criminals and carries out their executions in public. Of course, there's an evil conspiracy behind it all. Die-hard sci-fi fans might enjoy this generic action thriller.

Don "The Dragon" Wilson Eric Phillips • **Joseph Ruskin** J Craig Round • **Richard Norton** Mike Ross • **Stacie Foster** Griff
Director *Richard Pepin*
Screenplay *Jacobsen Hart*

Cyberzone ★

1995 US Colour 95mins

B-movie auteur Fred Olen Ray does *Blade Runner* with his typically dismal low budget technique, with bounty hunter Marc Singer hired to track down four female androids that have been smuggled to Earth. There is some occasional distraction with some nudity and humor, thanks to the fact the androids were programmed in the art of prostitution, but it's still pretty rough going.

Marc Singer Jack Ford • **Matthias Hues** Hawkes • **Rochelle Swanson** Beth Enright
Director *Fred Olen Ray*
Screenplay *William C Martell*

Cyborg ★★★ 18

1989 US Colour 79mins DVD

Mad Max meets *Escape from New York* in director Albert Pyun's cheap and cheerful science-fiction adventure where all the characters are named after electric guitars (Fender, Rickenbacker). Jean-Claude Van Damme is a futuristic mercenary hired to escort a cyborg carrying the antidote to a deadly plague that has almost wiped out mankind in the 21st century. On the journey they fall foul of the Flesh Pirates, torturers and crucifixion as genre master Pyun piles on the trash, panache and gratuitous violence with cut-price style.

Jean-Claude Van Damme Gibson Rickenbacker • **Deborah Richter** Nady Simmons • **Vincent Klyn** Fender Tremolo • **Alex Daniels** Marshall Strat • **Dayle Haddon** Pearl Prophet • **Blaise Loong** Furman Vox • **Rolf Muller** Brick Bardo • **Haley Peterson** Haley
Director *Albert Pyun*
Screenplay *Kitty Chalmers*

Cyborg 2: Glass Shadow ★★★ 18

1993 US Colour 95mins

A martial-arts-fighting cyborg (Angelina Jolie) is created by a sinister US corporation to destroy a Japanese rival in an action-packed futuristic adventure with a fun cast. Hero Elias Koteas falls for the sexy humanoid, and together they fight bounty hunter Billy Drago and mercenary storm troopers sent out by evil president Allen Garfield to foil their plan. Writer/ director Michael Schroeder keeps it all bubbling along neatly in this violent fantasy, which has flashbacks to the Van Damme original. Jack Palance provides some surreal philosophical subtext as a techno-God.

Elias Koteas Colson "Colt" Ricks • **Angelina Jolie** Casella "Cash" Reese • **Billy Drago** Danny Bench • **Jack Palance** Mercy • **Allen Garfield** Martin Dunn
Director *Michael Schroeder*
Screenplay *Ron Yanover, Mark Gelman, Michael Schroeder, from a story by Ron Yanover, Mark Gelman*

Cyborg 3: The Recycler ★★★ 18

1994 US Colour 87mins

Director Michael Schroeder climbs aboard the *Cyborg* franchise once more to even greater effect. Here, a *Mad Max*-inspired apocalyptic landscape becomes the stomping ground for despicable "recycler" (bounty hunter) Richard Lynch who preys on the comfort of benevolent humanoids. Scientist Zach Galligan and reproductive replicant Khrystyne Haje are caught up in the battle between bloodthirsty mankind and innocent robots for the right to procreate. It's veteran bad guy Lynch you'll remember as he takes magnetic evil to a superb new level of villainy.

Zach Galligan Evans • **Malcolm McDowell** Lord Talon • **Michael Bailey Smith** Donovan • **Rebecca Ferratti** Elexia • **Khrystyne Haje** Cash • **Andrew Bryniarski** Jocko • **Richard Lynch** Lewellyn
Director *Michael Schroeder*
Screenplay *Barry Victor, Troy Bolotnick*
Producer *Alan Mehrez*

Cyborg Cop ★ 18

1993 US Colour 92mins

David Bradley heads off to a Caribbean island in search of his missing brother. There he uncovers a secret organisation run by John Rhys-Davies (*Raiders of the Lost Ark*) that kidnaps innocent people and converts them into killer cyborgs. Seemingly filmed in abandoned buildings, this is a cheesy *Terminator* rip-off with unexceptional action scenes.

David Bradley Jack Ryan • **John Rhys-Davies** Kessel • **Alonna Shaw** Cathy • **Todd Jensen** Phillip • **Rufus Swart** Cyborg • **Ron Smerczak** Callan • **Anthony Fridjohn** Hogan • **Shalom Kenan** Steve
Director *Sam Firstenberg*
Screenplay *Greg Latter*
Producer *Danny Lerner*

Cyborg Cop II ★ 18

1994 US Colour 93mins

David Bradley returns to track down psycho serial killer Morgan Hunter, who tricks prison authorities into making him a cyborg in a lazy rip-off of all the far better half-man/half-machine fantasy adventures around. Because Bradley is etched as chauvinistically arrogant and no less sadistic than his criminal prey, there's no tension generated or character empathy.

David Bradley Jack Ryan • **Morgan Hunter** Starkraven • **Jill Pierce** Liz McDowell
Director *Sam Firstenberg*
Screenplay *Jon Stevens, from a story by Sam Firstenberg*

The Cyclops ★

1957 US BW 75mins

Gloria Talbott plays a woman searching for her fiancé, who goes missing after his plane crashes in a radiation-polluted area. He subsequently turns up as a 50ft tall, one-eyed mutant. Guess the wedding's off, then. Bargain basement tosh that relies on a risible array of special effects, including giant spiders, lizards and rodents.

James Craig Russ Bradford • **Gloria Talbott** Susan Winter • **Lon Chaney Jr** Martin Melville • **Tom Drake** Lee Brand • **Duncan "Dean" Parkin** Bruce Barton/The Cyclops • **Vincente Padula [Vincent Padula]** The Governor
Director/Screenplay *Bert I Gordon*

"It can do many things, Lesterson. But the thing it does most efficiently is exterminate human beings."

Patrick Troughton, the Second Doctor

Doctor Who, 1966-1969

D

DNA ★★★ 15

1996 US Colour 93mins

Mark Dacascos is one of the more interesting and charismatic action heroes to have emerged in recent years. He remains best known for the flawed live-action *manga* feature *Crying Freeman*, but his talent is also well deployed in this otherwise formulaic thriller. He plays a doctor who is reluctantly coerced into tracking down mad scientist Jürgen Prochnow, who left him for dead years ago and has now regenerated an ancient, possibly alien, killing machine. Director William Mesa, who designed the stunning visual effects for *The Fugitive*, splices together elements of *Jurassic Park* and *Predator* into an entertaining low-budget thriller. Contains violence and swearing.

Mark Dacascos Ash Mattley • **Jürgen Prochnow** Dr Carl Wessinger • **Robin McKee** Claire Sommers • **Roger Aaron Brown** Loren Azenfeld • **John H Brennan** Halton • **Thomas Taus Jr** Matzu • **Joel Torre** Taka • **Susan Africa** Nurse • **Mark McCracken** Balacau • **Kris Aguilar** Kasala
Director *William Mesa*
Screenplay *Nick Davis*

Daleks – Invasion Earth 2150 AD ★★★ U

1966 UK Colour 83mins

The second feature starring Peter Cushing as Doctor Who has the BBC's Time Lord aiding human survivors in their future war against the diabolical Daleks. *Independence Day* it's not, but director Gordon Flemyng keeps the colourful action moving swiftly along to cheap and cheerful effect. Youngsters will love it, while adults will want to E-X-T-E-R-M-I-N-A-T-E Bernard Cribbins, who provides comic relief as the bumbling bobby. Yet, through all the mayhem roll the ever-impressive Daleks, truly one of science fiction's greatest alien creations.

Peter Cushing Doctor Who • **Bernard Cribbins** Tom Campbell • **Ray Brooks** David • **Jill Curzon** Louise • **Roberta Tovey** Susan • **Andrew Keir** Wyler • **Godfrey Quigley** Dortmun • **Roger Avon** Wells • **Keith Marsh** Conway • **Geoffrey Cheshire** Roboman • **Steve Peters** Roboman leader
Director *Gordon Flemyng*
Screenplay *Milton Subotsky*

Damnation Alley ★ PG

1977 US Colour 87mins

An utterly pedestrian adaptation of Roger Zelazny's much-admired novel, a science-fiction tale that takes place after a nuclear holocaust. This film version features psychedelic visual effects that are really quite awful as five survivors of the Third World War cross America in a futuristic tank driven by George Peppard, looking for others after receiving mystery radio signals. Lacklustre acting, tedious exposition and laughable rubber monsters – giant cockroaches and scorpions, if you please – damn this forgettable, regrettable misfire. Contains swearing.

Jan-Michael Vincent Tanner • **George Peppard** Denton • **Dominique Sanda** Janice • **Paul Winfield** Keegan • **Jackie Earle Haley** Billy • **Kip Niven** Perry
Director *Jack Smight*
Screenplay *Alan Sharp, Lukas Heller, from the novel by Roger Zelazny*

The Damned ★★

1961 UK BW 94mins

A downbeat financial disaster from Hammer, this clearly reflects the troubled shoot, the creative differences between director Joseph Losey and the cost-conscious House of Horror, and the delayed release in butchered form. While on holiday in Weymouth, and after being mugged by biker gang leader Oliver Reed, American boat owner Macdonald Carey stumbles on a secret government programme in which radioactive children are being schooled to repopulate the planet after a nuclear war. The plot – which mixes romance, doom-laden science-fiction, elements of a British Hells Angels exploitation movie and a state conspiracy potboiler – never really fuses to create the powerful Orwellian fable the film was once acclaimed as.

Macdonald Carey Simon Wells • **Shirley Anne Field** Joan • **Viveca Lindfors** Freya Nelson, sculptress • **Alexander Knox** Bernard, scientist • **Oliver Reed** King • **Walter Gotell** Maj Holland • **Brian Oulton** Mr Dingle • **Kenneth Cope** Sid
Director *Joseph Losey*
Screenplay *Evan Jones, from the novel "The Children of Light" by HL Lawrence*

Danger: Diabolik ★★★

1967 It/Fr Colour 98mins

Based on a cult comic strip, this mix of fantasy and madcap criminality is directed with michievous glee by horror specialist Mario Bava. utilising stylised sets and encouraging his multi-national cast to camp it up something rotton, Bava arrives at a *Barbarella*-style romp, a comparison that is reinforced by the presence of John Phillip Law as the master criminal who curries favour with the populace by destroying Italy's tax records. The finale, with its radioactive gold shower, is justifiably famous, and the press conference given by pompous minister Terry-Thomas, under the influence of laughing gas, is riotously funny.

John Phillip Law Diabolik • **Marisa Mell** Eva Kant • **Michel Piccoli** Insp Ginko • **Adolfo Celi** Ralph Valmont • **Terry-Thomas** Minister of Finance
Director *Mario Bava*
Screenplay *Mario Bava, Dino Maiuri, Brian Degas, Tudor Gates, from a story by Angela Giussani, Luciana Giussani, Dino Maiuri, Adriano Baracco*

The Dark ★★ 15

1979 US Colour 86mins

This disjointed sci-fi horror movie was started by director Tobe Hooper as a fully fledged horror, then completed by John "Bud" Cardos when something more *Alien*-inspired was required. No wonder the end result is a confusing mix of supernatural slasher and intergalactic monster movie. A seven-foot alien in blue jeans stalks Los Angeles, ripping the heads off its victims and mutilating them with laser vision. Author William Devane, TV reporter Cathy Lee Crosby and cop Richard Jaeckel set out to track it down. Little happens between the murderous attacks, all predicted by a mystic, and the murders themselves have minimal impact thanks to Cardos's unimaginative restraint. Contains violence, swearing and a sex scene.

William Devane Ray Warner • **Cathy Lee Crosby** Zoe Owens • **Richard Jaeckel** Detective Mooney • **Warren Kemmerling** Captain Speer • **Biff Elliot** Bresler • **Jacquelyn Hyde** DeRenzey • **Casey Kasem** Pathologist • **Vivian Blaine** Courney Floyd
Director *John "Bud" Cardos*
Screenplay *Stanford Whitmore*

Dark Angel ★★★ 18

1989 US Colour 87mins

Dolph Lundgren gives his best performance to date as a Houston detective on the trail of an intergalactic drug dealer in this smartly scripted and crisply directed (by Craig R Baxley of *Action Jackson* fame) science-fiction spin on the buddy cop movie. The alien pusher has come to Earth to obtain a substance produced within the human body that is much sought after as a narcotic on his planet. Owing debts to *Predator*, *Alien Nation* and *Miami Vice*, the stock ingredients are all well proportioned in a cracking yarn that's exciting to watch thanks to the extra twists added by Baxley. Brian Benben scores as Lundgren's by-the-book FBI sidekick, while the inventive alien weaponry provides graphic thrills.

Dolph Lundgren Jack Caine • **Brian Benben** Laurence Smith • **Betsy Brantley** Diane Pollon • **Matthias Hues** Talec • **David Ackroyd** Switzer • **Jim Haynie** Captain Malone
Director *Craig R Baxley*
Screenplay *Jonathan Tydor, Leonard Maas Jr*

Dark Angel ★★★

TV 2000 – US Colour

Co-created by *Titanic* and *Terminator* über-director James Cameron, this post-apocalyptic sci-fi action series centres around the weekly heroics of a genetically-engineered young woman. While fleeing from her "creators", Max (Jessica Alba) teams up with a wheelchair-bound cyberjournalist to help the helpless and fight corruption. The scenario might be extremely familiar, but it is vibrantly realised thanks to some bright scripting, divine visuals and high impact *Matrix*-inspired action sequences. Although the dazzlingly beautiful Jessica Alba can't always disguise her limited acting range, she remains an attractive lead and generally interacts well with her co-stars, especially the engaging Michael Weatherly.

Jessica Alba Max Guevara • **Michael Weatherly** Logan Cale • **Alimi Ballard** Herbal Thought • **Jennifer Blanc** Kendra Maibaum • **Richard Gunn** Sketchy • **J C MacKenzie** Ray Reagan, Normal • **John Savage** Colonel Donald Lydecker • **Valerie Rae Miller** Original Cindy
Created by *James Cameron*
Executive producer *James Cameron, Charles H Eglee*

SFacts

The series has swept recent awards, including the People's Choice award in 2001 for Favorite TV New Dramatic Series, while star Jessica Alba (despite our reviewer's reservations) won Breakout Star of the Year from the TV Guide Awards, as well as being nominated for best actress by Young Artist Awards, TV Guide Awards and the Golden Globe Awards.

Dark City ★★★★ 15

1998 US Colour 96mins [video] DVD

Director Alex Proyas lends a potent gothic atmosphere to this dreamlike *film noir* fantasy about a race of mysterious bald figures who continually reconfigure a surreal, gloomy city and its inhabitants as some sort of weird experiment. As with *The Crow*, Proyas employs every striking camera angle in his visual vocabulary, breathing dread into the overhanging *Batman*-style architecture. The effects are impressively realised, too, as buildings stretch and widen before our eyes. Although overshadowed by the film's visual flair, the eclectic cast – including Rufus Sewell, Kiefer Sutherland, William Hurt and Ian Richardson – adds a splash of colour to the shadowy surroundings.

Rufus Sewell John Murdoch • **Kiefer Sutherland** Dr Daniel Schreber • **Jennifer Connelly** Emma Murdoch • **Richard O'Brien** Mr Hand • **Ian Richardson** Mr Book • **Colin Friels** Walenski • **Mitchell Butel** Husselbeck • **Frank Gallacher** Stromboli • **Melissa George** May • **William Hurt** Inspector Frank Bumstead
Director *Alex Proyas*
Screenplay *Alex Proyas, Lem Dobbs, David S Goyer, from a story by Alex Proyas*
Producer *Alex Proyas*
Cinematographer *Dariusz Wolski*

Dark Planet ★★ 15

1997 US Colour 92mins [video]

"Dark" is an appropriate word for this cheap science-fiction effort, in which the lighting is so bad it's hard to determine what's happening. On a deep space mission, Michael York and Harley Jane Kozak represent two sides at war on earth who have called a truce in order to find the eponymous planet, which may provide sanctuary for the survivors of their dying world. Slow and shabby, the film still generates interest thanks to decent performances from most of the cast. Contains some swearing, violence and sexual references.

Paul Mercurio Anson Hawke • **Harley Jane Kozak** Commander Brendan • **Michael York** Commander Winter • **Maria Ford** Salera • **Ed O'Ross** Byron • **Phil Morris** Fletcher
Director *Albert Magnoli*
Screenplay *SO Lee, J Reifel*

Dark Season ★★

TV 1991 UK Colour 6x25mins

This adventure series set in a school is most notable for an early appearance of the future *Titanic* superstar Kate Winslet, who plays one of the teenagers battling against mind-controlling computers that have been installed in classrooms. "Fantasy is back in vogue," said director Colin Cant. "I think it's a rebellion against all the realism that we have on TV at the moment... Young people want a bit more excitment and heroism in their lives, the chance to imagine what it would be like to be face to face with danger, to be in a situation where they're fighting for their lives."

Tim Barker Dr Osley • **Samantha Cahill** Olivia • **Ben Chandler** Thomas • **Rosalie Crutchley** Mrs Polzinski • **Brigit Forsyth** Miss Maitland • **Victoria Lambert** Marcle • **Grant Parsons** Mr Eldritch • **Cyril Shaps** Mr Polzinski • **Kate Winslet** Reet
Director *Colin Cant*
Written by *Russell T Davies*

Dark Side of the Moon ★★ 18

1990 US Colour 87mins [video]

Intriguing, if far fetched, variation on the *Alien* theme, in which a spaceship comes across an old shuttle, which went missing in the previous century. It soon become apparent that the old craft wasn't uninhabited and that the mystery somehow involves the Bermuda Triangle. Will Bledsoe is uninspiring as the heroic crew member, but there is solid support from Joe Turkel (*Blade Runner*) and DJ Webster's direction is moderately atmospheric. Contains violence, swearing and sex scenes.

Robert Sampson Capt Flynn • **Will Bledsoe** Giles • **Joe Turkel** Paxton • **Camilla More** Lesli • **John Diehl** Jennings • **Wendy MacDonald** Alex • **Alan Blumenfeld** Dreyfuss
Director *DJ Webster*
Screenplay *Chad Hayes, Carey W Hayes*

Dark Skies ★★★ 12

TV 1996-97 US Col 1x120m; 18x60m [video]

Best described as *The Invaders* meets *JFK*, Bryce Zabel's novel blend of sci-fi adventure and pseudo-historical drama aimed to chart a covert alien invasion of America from the sixties to the present day. Unfortunately, however, the series was shot down during the opening season of its anticipated multi-year run, leaving Zabel's long-term plans and lofty ambitions for the saga up in the smoke. Even as an unfinished tale, though, the series remains an intriguing and nicely mounted – if frequently ridiculous – offering. Much like *Babylon 5*, the show's story arc delivers some clever surprises and radical format changes, including a major character's mid-season transformation from hero to villain. The performances are equally strong, with Eric Close and JT Walsh ably leading a talented cast. Clearly, it's an enormous pity that the curtain fell on

Dark Skies long before its story had been completed.

Eric Close John Loengard • **Megan Ward** Kimberly Sayers • **J T Walsh** Frank Bach • **Conor O'Farrell** Phil Albano • **Tim Kelleher** Jim Steele • **Charley Lang** Dr Charlie Halligan
Created by *Bryce Zabel*
Executive producer *James D Parriott, Joseph Stern, Bryce Zabel* • ***Producer*** *Brad Markowitz*

Dark Star ★★★★ PG

1973 US Colour 79mins

Produced as a film project at the University of Southern California for just $60,000, this sly space parody begins as a satire on *2001: a Space Odyssey*. However, it quickly moves into original territory as the cabin-fevered crew copes with an alien stowaway, a nagging computer, its late commander's cryogenically-preserved brain and a thermo-nuclear device that's all set to explode. Witty, profound and cleverly scored by its producer/director John Carpenter, this cult favourite was co-written (with Carpenter) by cast member Dan O'Bannon, who later worked on *Alien*. Contains some swearing.

Brian Narelle Doolittle • **Andreijah Pahich** Talby • **Carl Kuniholm** Boiler • **Dan O'Bannon** Pinback • **Joe Sanders** Powell • **Miles Watkins** Mission Control • **Cookie Knapp** Computer
Director *John Carpenter*
Screenplay *John Carpenter, Dan O'Bannon*

Dark Universe ★★ 15

1993 US Colour 82mins

Another shlocker from Fred Olen Ray, although this time he is content to sit on the sidelines as co-producer. Steve Latshaw instead is given the thankless task of marshalling this tired tale of an astronaut who is taken over by an alien lifeform and proceeds to wreak havoc on earth. The zero-budget effects will raise an unintentional giggle, but the amateur writing and playing really try the patience. Martin Sheen's brother Joe Estevez is the closest thing to a familiar face.

Blake Pickett Kim Masters • **Cherie Scott** Judy Lawson • **Bently Tittle** Tom Hanning • **John Maynard** Frank Norris • **Patrick Moran** Carlson • **Joe Estevez** Rod Kendrick
Director *Steve Latshaw*
Screenplay *Patrick Moran*

Darkbreed ★★★ 18

1996 US Colour 91mins

Jack Scalia wages a one-man war against an alien invasion force in a mindlessly enjoyable blend of *The X-Files*, *The Invaders* and *The A-Team*. The former astronaut learns Earth is about to be taken over by the dark breed, a deadly race of parasites, so he embarks on a mission to destroy a canister containing their eggs. Wall-to-wall violence, action and mayhem ensue in a cliché-ridden plot that contains the odd flash of impressive special effects. Reliable B-movie action man Scalia gives this okay thriller a touch of extraclass. Contains violence and some swearing.

Jack Scalia Nicholas Saxon • **Donna W Scott** Deborah • **Jonathan Banks** Joseph Shay • **Robin Curtis** Marian
Director *Richard Pepin*
Screenplay *Richard Preston Jr*
Producer *Richard Pepin, Joseph Merhi*

The Darker Side of Terror ★ 15

1979 US Colour 91mins

Research scientist Robert Forster doesn't get the important job he was angling for, so he clones himself to prove he was right for the appointment. Unfortunately, his trouble-making duplicate sets his sights on seducing his creator's wife (Adrienne Barbeau). A deranged TV movie with little to offer in the thrill or surprise departments, though there is plenty to scoff at in disbelief.

Robert Forster Prof Paul Corwin/Clone • **Adrienne Barbeau** Margaret • **Ray Milland** Prof Meredith • **John Lehne** Lt Merholz • **David Sheiner** Prof Hillstrom • **Denise DuBarry** Ann Sweeney
Director *Gus Trikonis*
Screenplay *John Herman Shaner, Al Ramrus*

Darkman ★★★★ 18

1990 US Colour 91mins DVD

Independent director Sam Raimi's first studio movie is a splashy amalgam of *The Phantom of the Opera* and *Doctor X*, with a perfectly cast Liam Neeson donning synthetic flesh masks to take revenge on the mob who disfigured him. Pathos and tragedy are always lurking beneath the horrific surface of *The Evil Dead* creator's kaleidoscopic take on classic thirties *Grand Guignol*, given a nifty nineties spin by exaggerated camera moves and psychedelic visuals. This tasty buffet of gothic moodiness, startling make-up effects and expressionistic artifice sees the frenetic Raimi on vibrant virtuoso form. Contains swearing and violence.

Liam Neeson Peyton Westlake/Darkman • **Frances McDormand** Julie Hastings • **Colin Friels** Louis Strack Jr • **Larry Drake** Robert G Durant • **Nelson Mashita** Yakitito • **Jessie Lawrence Ferguson** Eddie Black • **Rafael H Robledo** Rudy Guzman • **Danny Hicks** Skip • **Theodore Raimi** Rick • **Dan Bell** Smiley • **Nicholas Worth** Pauly • **Aaron Lustig** Martin Katz • **Arsenio "Sonny" Trinidad** Hung Fat • **Bruce Campbell** Final Shemp • **Jenny Agutter** Doctor
Director *Sam Raimi*
Screenplay *Chuck Pfarrer, Sam Raimi, Ivan Raimi, Daniel Goldin, Joshua Goldin, from a story by Sam Raimi*

Darkman II: the Return of Durant ★★★ 18

1995 US/Can Colour 88mins

It more or less covers the same ground as the original, but this direct-to-video sequel is just as dynamic and fast-paced as its predecessor, with director Bradford May taking more than a few leaves out of the Sam Raimi style book. Arnold Vosloo – wrapped in bandages in 1999's *The Mummy* – takes over from Liam Neeson as the synthetic mask-wearing Dr Peyton Westlake, battling his resurrected nemesis Durant (Larry Drake) who has taken over the city's rackets with the help of a high-tech ray gun. The formula is forties pulp fiction with a twist of black comedy and some superior special effects, but it all works like a charm in this effective reprise. Contains violence and swearing.

Arnold Vosloo Dr Peyton Westlake/Darkman • **Larry Drake** Robert G Durant • **Renee O'Connor** Laurie Brinkman • **Kim Delaney** Jill Randall • **Lawrence Dane** Dr Alfred Hathaway • **Jesse Collins** Dr David Brinkman • **David Ferry** Eddie • **Rod Wilson** Ivan Druganov • **Jack Langedijk** Rollo Latham • **Sten Eirik** Whitey • **Steve Mousseau** Roy • **James Millington** Mr Perkins
Director *Bradford May*
Screenplay *Steve McKay, from a story by Robert Eisele, from characters created by Sam Raimi,*

Darkman III: Die Darkman Die ★★★ 15

1996 US Colour 83mins

Arnold Vosloo dons synthetic flesh once more as deformed superhero Peyton Westlake in the second sequel to the 1990 fantasy horror. This time he is pitted against evil drug baron Jeff Fahey, who is determined to learn the secret of Westlake's strength. With executive producer Sam Raimi (who directed the original *Darkman*) and returning director/cameraman Bradford May maintaining the quality and integrity of both previous adventures, and a well-realised script accenting character as much as explosive gimmicks, this comic-strip horror escapade is a worthwhile addition to the series. Contains violence and swearing.

Jeff Fahey Peter Rooker • **Arnold Vosloo** Dr Peyton Westlake/Darkman • **Roxann Biggs-Dawson** Angela Rooker • **Darlanne Fluegel** Dr Bridget Thorne • **Alicia Panetta** Jenny Rooker • **Nigel Bennett** Nico • **Von Flores** Johnny Lee • **Ronn Sarosiak** Mack
Director *Bradford May*
Screenplay *Mike Werb, Michael Colleary, from characters created by Sam Raimi*

DARYL ★★★ PG

1985 US Colour 95mins [video]

This new-age fairy tale is a charming, lightweight diversion about a Florida couple whose lives are transformed after fostering a young boy suffering from what they believe to be amnesia. When they learn Daryl actually stands for Data Analysing Robot Youth Lifeform, the real drama unfolds as they fight to stop his termination by Pentagon intelligence agents because his computer brain has become clouded by human emotions. Well acted and well written considering it has such a formula sci-fi plot, director Simon Wincer's popcorn picture with heart echoes his later success with *Free Willy*. Perfect family viewing.

Mary Beth Hurt Joyce Richardson • **Michael McKean** Andy Richardson • **Barret Oliver** Daryl • **Colleen Camp** Elaine Fox • **Kathryn Walker** Ellen Lamb • **Josef Sommer** Dr Jeffrey Stewart • **Ron Frazier** General Graycliffe • **Steve Ryan** Howie Fox • **Danny Corkill** Turtle Fox • **David Wohl** Mr Nesbitt
Director *Simon Wincer*
Screenplay *David Ambrose, Allan Scott, Jeffrey Ellis*

Daughter of Dr Jekyll ★

1957 US BW 69mins

One of the more unusual takes on Robert Louis Stevenson's seminal gothic classic, in that Dr Jekyll doesn't actually appear. Instead, the film tells of his less well-known daughter, who, upon landing in England to claim her father's inheritance, is blamed for a series of grisly murders. The result is a hotchpotch of vampire, werewolf and Jekyll-and-Hyde elements, all searching in vain for a coherent storyline. Shot not at a studio but in an authentic crumbling mansion in the suburbs of Hollywood, this is a masterclass of abysmal acting.

John Agar George Hastings • **Gloria Talbott** Janet Smith • **Arthur Shields** Dr Lomas • **John Dierkes** Jacob • **Martha Wentworth** Mrs Merchant
Director *Edgar G Ulmer*
Screenplay *Jack Pollexfen*

Dawn of the Dead ★★★★ 18

1979 US Colour 139mins [video] DVD

The *Citizen Kane* of gore. Some see George A Romero's astoundingly violent sequel to his classic *Night of the Living Dead* as a satirical attack on American consumerism and shallow materialistic values, as it continues the premise of the reawakened dead stalking the living with cannibal intent through a shopping mall. Others merely see it as the greatest zombie fantasy of all time. Cynical, devastating and relentless, Romero's gruelling masterpiece about the American Dream turning into a terrifying nightmare is an ideal blend of black comedy and hip, if harrowing, carnage. Contains swearing and violence.

David Emge Stephen • **Ken Foree** Peter • **Scott Reiniger** Roger • **Gaylen Ross** Francine • **David Crawford** Dr Foster • **David Early** Mr Berman • **George A Romero** TV director
Director/Screenplay *George A Romero*
Music *Dario Argento and the Goblins*

The Day After ★★★ 12

1983 US Colour 115mins [video]

The effect of nuclear war and its aftermath on several Kansas families makes for a mild diversion in this lavish television movie directed by Nicholas Meyer. The impact of the twin explosions, subsequent radiation poisoning, looting and firing squads moving in to assess the damage, is lessened due to network-imposed soft-pedalling of the true horrors. But the keen eye kept on the more personally-felt traumas of the grim situation gives a better than average focus as the apocalypse victims try to rebuild society. The A-list cast, including Steve Guttenberg, John Lithgow and Jason Robards, rise to the often heavy-handed occasion.

Jason Robards [Jason Robards Jr] Dr Russell Oakes • **JoBeth Williams** Nancy Bauer • **Steve Guttenberg** Stephen Klein • **John Cullum** Jim Dahlberg • **John Lithgow** Joe Huxley • **Bibi Besch** Eve Dahlberg • **Lori Lethin** Denise Dahlberg • **Amy Madigan** Alison Ransom
Director *Nicholas Meyer*
Screenplay *Edward Hume*

Day of the Animals ★★★ 15

1977 US Colour 92mins [video]

One of the best movies made by horror hack William Girdler, who died in a tragic helicopter accident just as he was about to hit the big time with *The Manitou*. Ecological erosion of the ozone layer causes wild creatures to attack a group of Californian mountain hikers in this creditable effort tautly streamlined by a top-flight B-movie cast including Leslie Nielsen before he turned *Airplane!* comedian. Bears, wolves, vultures, snakes, dogs and rats (in a truly amazing forest ranger attack) all get in on the menacing act that's beautifully photographed and directed for lively shock value and welcome chuckles between the carnage.

Christopher George Steve Buckner • **Leslie Nielsen** Paul Jensen • **Lynda Day George** Terry Marsh • **Richard Jaeckel** Taylor MacGregor • **Michael Ansara** Daniel Santee • **Paul Mantee** Roy Moore • **Jon Cedar** Frank Young • **Paul Barnes** Forest ranger • **Andrew Stevens** Bob Denning • **Kathleen Bracken** Beth Hughes • **Bobby Porter** Jon Goodwyn • **Susan Blacklinie** Mandy Young • **Michelle Stacy** Little girl • **Garrison True** Newscaster • **Michael Clifford** Sheriff • **Michael Rougas** Military officer
Director *William Girdler*
Screenplay *William Norton, Eleanor Norton, from a story by Edward E Montoro*
Producer *Edward E Montoro*

The Day of the Dolphin ★★ PG

1973 US Colour 100mins [video]

George C Scott takes on one of the biggest challenges of his career by conducting meaningful conversations with dolphins. He even teaches his pet dolphin endearments like "Fa" and "Pa". Aaah, isn't that cute? But this isn't a Flipperish, Disney-pic. Indeed, things get decidedly bleak when it's revealed that Scott's dolphins are destined to be used as sentient torpedoes in a plot to assassinate the President aboard his yacht. Georges Delerue's score is a high point.

George C Scott Dr Jake Terrell • **Trish Van Devere** Maggie Terrell • **Paul Sorvino** Mahoney • **Fritz Weaver** Harold DeMilo • **Jon Korkes** David • **Edward Herrmann** Mike • **Leslie Charleson** Maryanne • **John David Carson** Larry • **Victoria Racimo** Lana • **John Dehner** Wallingford • **Severn Darden** Schwinn • **William Roerick** Dunhill • **Elizabeth Wilson** Mrs Rome
Director *Mike Nichols*
Screenplay *Buck Henry, from a novel by Robert Merle*
Music *Georges Delerue*

The Day of the Triffids ★★★ 15

1962 UK Colour 94mins [video]

A meteor shower blinds all but a few Earthlings, leaving society in a state of hysteria and at the mercy of carnivorous plants from outer space in this rather disappointing version of John Wyndham's classic sci-fi novel. While the Triffids themselves are efficiently bizarre and menacing, Steve Sekely's barely competent direction hardly provides the sinister spores with a shining showcase. That was left to Freddie Francis, director of the lighthouse scenes added later in a bravura effort to beef up the chills and thrills.

Howard Keel Bill Masen • **Janette Scott** Karen Goodwin • **Nicole Maurey** Christine Durrant • **Kieron Moore** Tom Goodwin • **Mervyn Johns** Mr Coker • **Alison Leggatt** Miss Coker • **Janina Faye** Susan • **Geoffrey Matthews** Luis de la Vega • **Gilgi Hauser** Teresa de la Vega

Director *Steve Sekely, Freddie Francis*
Screenplay *Philip Yordan, from the novel by John Wyndham*

The Day of the Triffids ★★★

TV 1981 UK/Aus/US Colour 6x30mins

A polished and faithful adaptation of John Wyndham's classic novel that thankfully puts to rest the memories of the 1962 Howard Keel film version. Not a period piece, the makers ditched the book's original setting of the early fifties for a more topical approach, in the hope of lending the production a frightening immediacy, as if it could all really happen tomorrow. Ironically, looking at the serial today, it is itself now horribly dated. Ken Hannam's direction consciously aims more for dramatic realism than outright fantasy. John Duttine is Wyndham's Everyman hero temporarily blinded and hospitalisedwhen the rest of the world is watching a strange light show in the sky which renders them blind and easy prey for Triffids, hulking man-eating plants.

John Duttine Bill Mason • **Emma Relph** Jo • **Maurice Colbourne** Jack Coker • **Jonathan Newth** Dr Soames • **Stephen Yardley** John • **David Swift** Beadley • **Perlita Neilson** Miss Durrant

Director *Ken Hannam*
Adapted by *Douglas Livingstone, from the novel by John Wyndham*
Producer *David Maloney*
Visual effects *Steve Drewett*

The Day the Earth Caught Fire ★★★

1961 UK BW 98mins

Atomic explosions at the two poles put the Earth on a collision course with the Sun in this bleak British doomsday vision. With the emphasis on the reactions of some London journalists to the impending catastrophe rather than elaborate special effects, this tautly intelligent sci-fi thriller hits all the right buttons, helped by a script full of fatalistic quips and apocalyptic cynicism. Engrossing, with a memorable fade-out on two possible newspaper headlines.

Leo McKern Bill Maguire • **Janet Munro** Jeannie • **Edward Judd** Peter Stenning • **Michael Goodliffe** Night editor • **Bernard Braden** News editor • **Reginald Beckwith** Harry • **Gene Anderson** May • **Arthur Christiansen** Editor • **Austin Trevor** Sir John Kelly • **Renée Asherson** Angela • **Michael Caine** Policeman

Director *Val Guest*
Screenplay *Val Guest, Wolf Mankowitz*

The Day the Earth Stood Still ★★★★★ U

1951 US BW 88mins

The sight of a flying saucer hovering over Washington in 1951 would have confirmed the fears of many Americans that the end was nigh. But, coming just four months after Christian Nyby and Howard Hawks had unleashed *The Thing from Another World* upon a petrified Cold War public, director Robert Wise's sci-fi classic was actually a welcome sign of hope. This was also a bold attempt to increase the genre's credibility. From Bernard Herrmann's otherworldly score to Lyle Wheeler and Addison Hehr's deceptively simple designs, *The Day the Earth Stood Still* has had an incalculable influence on big screen science-fiction. Edmund H North's script deftly pokes fun at the Red-baiters and Robert Wise slickly blends the docudramatic and the melodramatic without ever lapsing into pomposity or hysteria. Michael Rennie is a revelation as Klaatu, exuding dignity, sympathy and authority in a role that was originally intended for Spencer Tracy.

Michael Rennie Klaatu • **Patricia Neal** Helen Benson • **Hugh Marlowe** Tom Stevens • **Sam Jaffe** Dr Barnhardt • **Billy Gray** Bobby Benson • **Frances Bavier** Mrs Barley • **Lock Martin** Gort • **Drew Pearson** Drew Pearson • **Frank Conroy** Harley • **Carleton Young** Colonel

Director *Robert Wise*
Screenplay *Edmund H North, from the short story "Farewell to the Master" by Harry Bates*
Music *Bernard Herrmann*
Costume Designer *Travilla*

The Day the Fish Came Out ★★

1967 UK/Gr Colour 109mins

Michael Cacoyannis's follow-up to his highly acclaimed *Zorba the Greek* couldn't have been more different, or more of a disappointment: a ham-fisted satire that falls prisoner to the modish mood of its time. Tom Courtenay and Colin Blakely play NATO airmen whose plane, carrying a pair of H-bombs and a doomsday weapon, ditches in the sea near a Greek island. As you can imagine, the laugh quota substantially drops when locals start getting contaminated. Cacoyannis, who not only directs but also wrote the screenplay, struggles to integrate the clashing styles of farce and realism into any coherent whole. Amid all the fake psychedelia, you can spot a fresh-faced Candice Bergen and a pre-*Saint* Ian Ogilvy.

Tom Courtenay Navigator • **Sam Wanamaker** Elias • **Colin Blakely** Pilot • **Candice Bergen** Electra • **Ian Ogilvy** Peter • **Dimitris Nicolaides** Dentist • **Nikos Alexiou** Goatherd • **Patrick Burke** Mrs Mavroyannis

Director/Screenplay *Michael Cacoyannis*
Producer *Michael Cacoyannis*
Cinematographer *Walter Lassally*

The Day the Sky Exploded ★★

1958 It/Fr BW 85mins

A ragbag assortment of Space Age clichés are marshalled with little care or attention by director Paolo Heusch in this routine disaster picture made bearable by the genius cinematography of future genre maestro Mario Bava. Astronaut Paul Hubschmid is forced to abort the first US/USSR/UK space mission, but the rocket debris crashes into the sun, sending a meteor shower hurtling towards earth causing massive tidal waves, typhoons and earthquakes. Hubschmid then organises world powers to fire all their atomic weapons into space and destroy the threat to mankind. Fluffed suspense, poor scripting and robotic acting doom this *When Worlds Collide*-Italian style. Dubbed into English.

Paul Hubschmid John MacLaren • **Madeleine Fischer** Katy Dandridge • **Fiorella Mari** Mary MacLaren • **Ivo Garrani** Herbert Weisser • **Dario Michaelis** Pierre Leducq • **Sam Galter** Randowsky • **Jean-Jacques Delbo** Sergei Boetnikov

Director *Paolo Heusch*
Screenplay *Alessandro Continenza, Marcello Coscia, from a story by Virgilio Sabel*
Cinematographer *Mario Bava*

The Day the World Ended ★★

1956 US BW 81mins

The first science-fiction film from cult director Roger Corman has seven survivors of a nuclear war fighting off atomic radiation mutants from their mountain retreat. Not much else happens in this cheesy yet ludicrously entertaining fright flick, which transposes the Garden of Eden

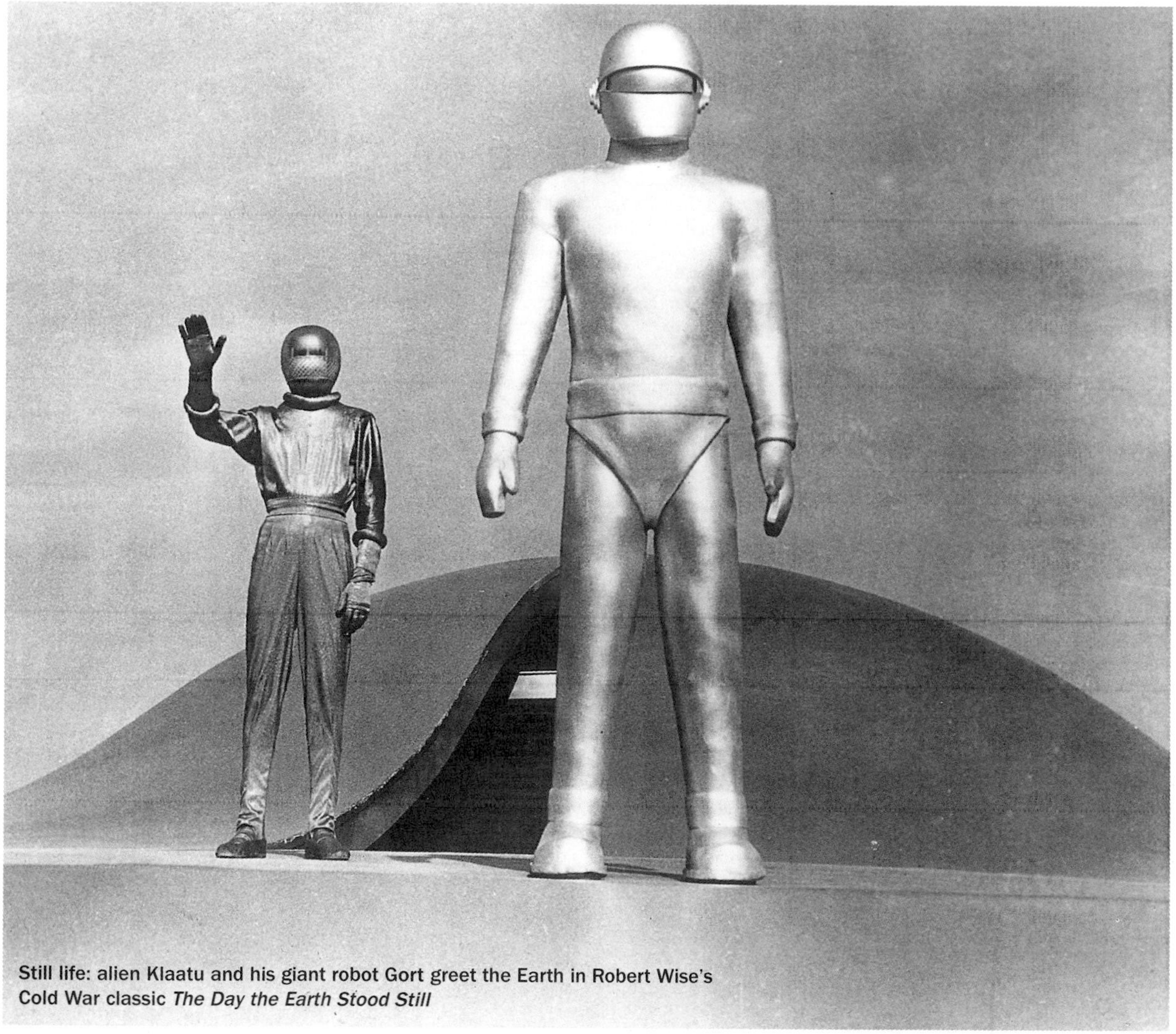

Still life: alien Klaatu and his giant robot Gort greet the Earth in Robert Wise's Cold War classic *The Day the Earth Stood Still*

myth into an uncertain future. The ads at the time promised "a new high in naked shrieking terror", but the only shrieks to be heard now will be ones of laughter at the three-eyed, four-armed monster suits.

Richard Denning Rick • **Lori Nelson** Louise • **Adele Jergens** Ruby • **Touch Connors [Mike Connors]** Tony • **Paul Birch** Maddison • **Raymond Hatton** Pete • **Paul Dubov** Radek • **Jonathan Haze** Contaminated man • **Paul Blaisdell** Mutant
Director *Roger Corman*
Screenplay *Lou Rusoff, from his story*
Producer *Roger Corman*

The Day Time Ended ★

1980 US/Sp Colour 80mins

The Day Time Ended can't end soon enough! Jim Davis's family moves into a solar-powered desert home, only to find they're slap-bang in the middle of a time vortex that lures visiting aliens to warn them about earth's imminent destruction. A nonsensical blend of cardboard special effects, *Close Encounters* aliens and weird prehistoric monsters, this crudely-assembled affair is directed by low-budget genius John "Bud" Cardos with little of the knowing jauntiness or exploitation smarts that exemplifies his best work (*Kingdom of the Spiders*, *The Dark*).

Jim Davis Grant • **Christopher Mitchum** Richard • **Dorothy Malone** Ana • **Marcy Lafferty** Beth • **Scott Kolden** Steve • **Natasha Ryan** Jenny
Director *John "Bud" Cardos*
Screenplay *Wayne Schmidt, J Larry Carroll, David Schmoeller, from a story by Steve Neill*

Daybreak ★★ 18

1993 US Colour 87mins

Based on Alan Browne's off-Broadway success, *Beirut*, this provocative parable is set in a crumbling New York of the future, where an Aids-like epidemic has persuaded the government to keep the afflicted in quarantine centres that are tantamount to concentration camps. Opposing the green shirts who mercilessly round up suspects are rebels Cuba Gooding Jr and Moira Kelly, whose brother is the most fanatical of the fascists. The commitment of the cast can't be faulted and writer/director Stephen Tolkin ensures the action never lets up. But both his symbolism and his plea for increased tolerance are regrettably heavy-handed.

Cuba Gooding Jr Torch • **Martha Plimpton**

Lauri • **Moira Kelly** Blue • **Omar Epps** Hunter • **David Eigenberg** Bucky
Director *Stephen Tolkin*
Screenplay *Stephen Tolkin, from the play "Beirut" by Alan Browne*

Dead & Buried ★★ 18

1981 US Colour 93mins

Disappointing collaboration between the director of British cult horror movie *Death Line* Gary Sherman and *Alien* writers Dan O'Bannon and Ronald Shusett. In his final film role, Jack Albertson plays a mad mortician who revives the dead in a sleepy New England town, who then murder people to supply him with fresh corpses. James Farentino is the perplexed local sheriff. Uneven but pleasingly gory with standout make-up effects from Stan Winston – the zombies have to return to Albertson for weekly touch-ups. Winston later did pioneering work on *Terminator 2* and *Jurassic Park*.

James Farentino Sheriff Dan Gillis • **Melody Anderson** Janet Gillis • **Jack Albertson** G William Dobbs • **Dennis Redfield** Ron • **Nancy Locke** Linda • **Lisa Blount** Girl on the beach • **Robert Englund** Harry
Director *Gary A Sherman [Gary Sherman]*
Screenplay *Ronald Shusett, Dan O'Bannon, from a story by Jeff Miller*

SFacts

This film became one of many caught up in the UK's video nasties controversy and was denied a certificate for almost ten years.

The Dead Don't Die ★★

1975 US Colour 90mins

Robert Bloch (*Psycho*) wrote this peculiar TV movie as an homage to the pulp thrillers of the thirties and B-horror veteran Curtis Harrington roped in an all-star cast to play up its knowingly camp nostalgia. In Depression-hit Chicago, George Hamilton uncovers a plot by mad scientist Ray Milland to create an army of zombies and take over the world. Shot entirely at night, and using the surreal "anything goes" atmosphere inherent in the Republic serial format, Harrington's reliance on overstated acting and overheated melodrama turns all the disparate elements into a sinister, heady cocktail, almost by default.

George Hamilton Don Drake • **Ray Milland** Jim Moss • **Linda Cristal** Vera Lavalle • **Joan Blondell** Levenia Hatcher • **Ralph Meeker** Lieutenant Reardon • **James McEachin** Frankie Specht
Director *Curtis Harrington*
Screenplay *Robert Bloch*

Dead Man Walking ★★ 18

1988 US Colour 86mins

A rare foray into a more mainstream genre for Gregory Hippolyte, best known for his erotic thriller franchises such as *Animal Instincts*. It's a pretty unremarkable post-apocalypse tale, in which a disparate duo team up to rescue a woman who has been kidnapped by a gang of disease-infected crazies. Connoisseurs of B-grade hokum will enjoy the over-the-top performances of hardworking genre experts such as Brion James, Wings Hauser and Jeffrey Combs.

Wings Hauser John Luger • **Brion James** Dekker • **Jeffrey Combs** Chaz • **Pamela Ludwig** Lelia • **Sy Richardson** Snake •
Director *Gregory Brown [Gregory Hippolyte]*
Screenplay *John Weidner, Rick Marx*

The Dead Mountaineer Hotel ★★★

1979 USSR Colour 90mins

Having already penned Andrei Tarkovsky's 1979 sci-fi masterpiece, *Stalker*, Arkady and Boris Strugatsky produced this genre-bending mystery, which intrigues both in terms of plot and concept. Refuting the accepted wisdom that visiting aliens instantly adopt an earthly mindset, the action chronicles the attempts of a police inspector to fathom the psychology and aspirations of the group of eccentric "visitors" he finds taking refuge in an isolated hotel in the Ala-Tau mountains of Kazakhstan. Although director Grigory Kromarov doesn't wholly succeed in his bid to put traditional narrative structure through the interstellar wringer, it's a fiercely intelligent picture all the same. A Russian language film.

Juri Jarvet • **Uldis Pucitis** • **Lembit Peterson** • **Mikk Mikiver**
Director *Grigory Kromanov*
Screenplay *Arkady Strugatsky, Boris Strugatsky*

Dead-End Drive-In ★★★ 18

1986 Aus Colour 86mins

In the retro-fitted Republic of Australia, authorities designate drive-in movie houses as makeshift prison camps to control rebellious youth. Once inside, the trapped teens find life too easy (junk food rations and endless junk movies) so they don't want to break out. Everyone, that is, except born outsider Ned Manning and his girlfriend Natalie McCurry who refuse to conform and set in motion explosive events. *A Clockwork Orange* meets *Mad Max* in director Brian (*Turkey Shoot*) Trenchard-Smith's under-rated futuristic fantasy, mixing cerebral political allegory with highly commercial action adventure trappings.

Ned Manning Crabs • **Natalie McCurry** Carmen • **Peter Whitford** Thompson • **Wilbur Wilde** Hazza • **Dave Gibson** Dave
Director *Brian Trenchard-Smith*
Screenplay *Peter Smalley, from the short story "Crabs" by Peter Carey*

The Deadly Bees ★

1967 UK Colour 83mins

Suzanna Leigh is the pop singer who visits a remote island to recover from exhaustion. There she meets an insane beekeeper who breeds a strain of mutant bee that attacks a certain scent. This is one of the worst films Oscar-winning cinematographer-turned-director Freddie Francis ever made for Hammer rivals Amicus. More a routine whodunnit than a horror film – despite a couple of gruesome sting deaths – this heavy-handed adaptation of HF Heard's novel *A Taste for Honey*, heavily influenced by Alfred Hitchcock's *The Birds*, is a lacklustre plod through obvious red herrings and banal dialogue complete with laughable stiff-upper-lip cast.

Suzanna Leigh Vicki Robbins • **Frank Finlay** Manfred • **Guy Doleman** Hargrove • **Catherine Finn** Mrs Hargrove • **John Harvey** Thompson • **Michael Ripper** Hawkins • **Anthony Bailey** Compere • **Tim Barrett** Harcourt
Director *Freddie Francis*
Screenplay *Robert Bloch, Anthony Marriott, from the novel "A Taste of Honey" by HF Heard*

Deadly Friend ★★ 18

1986 US Colour 86mins

In this daft horror yarn from *Nightmare on Elm Street* director Wes Craven, Matthew Laborteaux is the teen genius whose robot is destroyed shortly before his girlfriend is killed. Naturally, he decides to plant the robot's brain into his girl's head – but things don't go as planned. The plot bears a remarkable resemblance to cult shocker *Re-Animator*, made the year before. Despite this, *Deadly Friend* is still an enjoyable, if unscary piece of entertainment.

Matthew Laborteaux Paul • **Kristy Swanson** Samantha • **Anne Twomey** Jeannie Conway • **Michael Sharrett** Tom • **Richard Marcus** Harry • **Anne Ramsey** Elvira Williams • **Russ Marin** Dr Johanson • **Andrew Roperto** Carl Denton
Director *Wes Craven*
Screenplay *Bruce Joel Rubin, from the novel "Friend" by Diana Henstell*

The Deadly Mantis ★★

1957 US BW 78mins

The dawning of the atomic age gave rise to an invasion of big bug movies, but this perfunctorily-directed, would-be sci-fi epic from Nathan Juran isn't in the same league as *Them!* or *Tarantula*. Still, there's something cathartic about watching a giant praying mantis, awoken from its arctic slumber by nuclear testing, laying waste to tourist attractions in New York and Washington DC. The love story featuring Craig Stevens (TV's Peter Gunn), critically shifts focus from some good effects sequences. **Craig Stevens** Colonel Joe Parkman • **William Hopper** Dr Ned Jackson • **Alix Talton** Marge Blaine • **Donald Randolph** General Mark Ford • **Pat Conway** Sergeant Pete Allen • **Florenz Ames** Professor Anton Gunther • **Paul Smith** Corporal

Director *Nathan Juran*
Screenplay *Martin Berkeley, from a story by William Alland*

Deadly Reactor ★★ 18

1989 US Colour 84mins

Another lame attempt to splice the western with sci-fi – and you donfit have to look far to find out whofis at fault. Step forward, David Heavener, who not only stars, but takes a writing and directing credit. He plays a mysterious quiet man who comes to the aid of a peace-loving people who are threatened by post-apocalyptic outlaws led by Darwyn Swalve. Veteran Stuart Whitman is the best known face in the cast.

Stuart Whitman Duke • **David Heavener** Cody • **Darwyn Swalve** Hog
Director/Screenplay *David Heavener*

Deadly Weapon ★★ 15

1989 US Colour 86mins

Michael Miner had a hand in the script for the splendid *RoboCop*, although unsurprisingly this genre tale isn't really in the same league. However, put-upon teens will probably be cheering on Rodney Eastman, who stumbles upon a lethal new weapon and starts putting it to distinctly un-military uses against his tormentors. Sci-fi fans will take delight in spotting stars of the small screen old and new, including Gary Frank (*Deep Space 9*) and *Star Trek* veteran Walter Koenig.

Rodney Eastman Zeke • **Kim Walker** Tracey • **Gary Frank** Lt Dalton • **Michael Horse** Indian Joe • **William Sanderson** Reverend Smith • **Walter Koenig**
Director *Michael Miner*
Screenplay *Michael Miner, from a story by George Lafia, Michael Miner*

Death Line ★★★★ 18

1972 UK Colour 83mins

Reactionary cop Donald Pleasence investigates mysterious disappearances in the London Underground and makes the startling discovery that a colony of cannibals has existed in the creepy tunnels since a Victorian cave-in disaster. Strong stuff in its day, Gary Sherman never directed a better movie than this grisly frightener, which provides dark scares while presenting an effective commentary on violence. A criminally under-rated slice of British horror, this manages to be eerie, touching, melancholic and imaginative to a degree rarely seen in the genre. Highly recommended, and remember, "Mind the gap"!

Donald Pleasence Inspector Colquhoun • **Christopher Lee** Stratton-Villiers • **Norman Rossington** Detective Rogers • **David Ladd** Alex Campbell • **Sharon Gurney** Patricia Wilson • **Hugh Armstrong** The man • **James Cossins** Manfred • **Clive Swift** Inspector Richardson
Director *Gary Sherman*
Screenplay *Ceri Jones, from the story "Death Line" by Gary Sherman*

Death Machine ★★★ 18

1994 UK Colour 111mins

Cheerfully lifting from the likes of *The Terminator*, *Alien* and *Die Hard*, homegrown director Stephen Norrington fashions a distinctly un-British but hugely entertaining techno thriller. Set in the near future, the story pits hi-tech weapons firm executive Ely Pouget and a gang of terrorists against barmy scientist Brad Dourif and his bone-crunching killing machine in a deserted office building. There's little in the way of character development, but former effects man Norrington never lets the pace slacken for a minute and designs some ingenious action sequences.

Brad Dourif Jack Dante • **Ely Pouget** Hayden Cale • **William Hootkins** John Carpenter • **John Sharian** Sam Raimi • **Martin McDougall** Yutani • **Richard Brake** Scott Ridley • **Andreas Wisniewski** Weyland • **Rachel Weisz** A N Other personnel manager
Director/Screenplay *Stephen Norrington*

The Death of the Incredible Hulk ★★ PG

1990 US Colour 94mins

One of a number of TV movie spin-offs from the wearisome series, this has Bill Bixby still searching for a way of ridding himself of the alter ego who ruins all his clothes. Here, he finds a sympathetic scientist (Philip Sterling) to help reverse the genetic process only to find himself the target of evil terrorists out to build the perfect soldier. Green-dyed Lou Ferrigno once again gets a chance to ripple his muscles, but the playing and the direction are as bland as usual. This is for people who like reading the final chapter of a book first.

Bill Bixby Dr David Banner • **Lou Ferrigno** The Hulk • **Elizabeth Gracen** Jasmin • **Philip Sterling** Dr Ronald Pratt • **Andreas Katsulas** Kasha • **Barbara Tarbuck** Amy Pratt • **Carla Ferrigno** Bank clerk • **John Novak** Zed • **Anna Katarina** Bella • **Chilton Crane** Betty • **Duncan Fraser** Tom • **Dwight McFee** Brenn
Director *Bill Bixby*
Screenplay *Gerald DiPego, from the comic strip "The Incredible Hulk" by Stan Lee*

Death Race 2000 ★★★★ 18

1975 US Colour 76mins

An action-packed satire set in the future when a fascist American government sponsors a nationally-televised road race in which drivers score points for ramming pedestrians. The event is staged to pacify the ravenous public's lust for blood and prevent the overthrow of the President. The light-hearted direction by Paul Bartel keeps this demolition derby on an amusing track, despite the graphic violence, and there are digs at US political apathy and the nation's obsession with sports. With its cast of cartoon caricatures – David Carradine is a bionic Frankenstein, Sylvester Stallone is Machine Gun Joe Viterbo – this Roger Corman production is a lot more entertaining than its more serious and expensive contemporary, *Rollerball*. Contains violence, swearing and brief nudity.

David Carradine Frankenstein • **Simone Griffeth** Annie • **Sylvester Stallone** Machine Gun Joe Viterbo • **Mary Woronov** Calamity Jane • **Roberta Collins** Mathilda the Hun • **Martin Kove** Nero the Hero • **Louisa Moritz** Myra • **Don Steele** Junior Bruce
Director *Paul Bartel*
Screenplay *Robert Thom, Charles B Griffith, from a story by Ib Melchior*
Producer *Roger Corman*

Deathsport ★★

1978 US Colour 82mins

Ranger guides David Carradine and Claudia Jennings battle the evil Statesmen, futuristic Hell's Angels who ride cycles called Death Machines, in a banal reworking of *Death Race 2000*. It's set in the post-apocalyptic year 3000, and mixes cheap *Star Wars* tricks and cannibal mutants into the vehicular violence. There's lots of fiery crashes and gory comedy, but little sense in a movie shot separately by directors Henry Suso and Allan Arkush and then literally stuck together. It shows! Jennings was *Playboy* playmate of the year in 1970, and died in a car accident less than a year after this film was completed.

David Carradine Kaz Oshay • **Claudia Jennings** Deneer • **Richard Lynch** Ankar Moor
Director *Roger Corman, Henry Suso, Allan Arkush*
Screenplay *Henry Suso, Donald Steward, from a story by Frances Doel*

Deathwatch ★★★ 15

1980 Fr/W Ger Colour 124mins

Inspired by a novel by David Compton, this futuristic discourse on the intrusiveness of television is much bleaker and censorious than either Didier Grousset's *Kamikaze* or *The Truman Show*. With Glasgow providing the desolate backdrop, this shows how easy it is to commit acts of psychological trespass, as Harvey Keitel uses a miniature camera implanted in his skull to record the final days of the terminally ill Romy Schneider for unscrupulous Harry Dean Stanton's TV show. Had the focus remained on the docu-soap mentality, this might have packed more of a punch, but Bertrand Tavernier's instinctive humanism deflects his purpose.

Romy Schneider Katherine Mortenhoe • **Harvey Keitel** Roddy • **Harry Dean Stanton** Vincent Ferriman • **Thérèse Liotard** Tracey • **Max von Sydow** Gerald Mortenhoe
Director *Bertrand Tavernier*
Screenplay *Bertrand Tavernier, David Rayfiel, from the novel "The Continuous Katherine Mortenhoe (The Unsleeping Eye)" by David Compton*

Deceit ★★ 18

1989 US Colour 88mins

Not one of the better efforts from prolific director-producer Albert Pyun, best known for helping Jean-Claude Van Damme to break out of straight-to-video land with *Cyborg*. This lurid slice of exploitation was made in the same year and finds a plucky prostitute fighting back against two alien invaders out on the town before destroying the world. The plotting raises some chuckles, but it's forgettable stuff.

Samantha Phillips Eve Bendibuckle • **Diane Defoe** Wilma Fernbacker
Director *Albert Pyun*
Screenplay *Kitty Chalmers*

Deep Blue Sea ★★★ 15

1999 US Colour 100mins DVD

The disaster movie genre meets *Jaws* in director Renny Harlin's popcorn screamer about three genetically mutated, brainy sharks stalking the marooned members of an underwater research facility. Despite a waterlogged script, and the failure of the B-movie cast to rise above it, Harlin's submerged *Cliffhanger* remains afloat through sheer nerve, technical prowess and some truly spectacular shock moments involving computer special effects. The tricks-of-the-trade invented by Steven Spielberg for *Jaws* are all present and correct, but merely placed on a far bigger hi-tech canvas in an effectively trashy blockbuster with a high quota of grisly gore and hopelessly mundane dialogue. Saffron Burrows's wet-suit strip is the hilarious high point in this dumbed-down shark lark. Contains horror and swearing.

Saffron Burrows Dr Susan McAlester • **Thomas Jane** Carter Blake • **LL Cool J** Sherman "Preacher" Dudley • **Jacqueline McKenzie** Janice Higgins • **Michael Rapaport** Tom "Scog" Scoggins • **Stellan Skarsgård** Jim Whitlock • **Aida Turturro** Brenda Kerns • **Samuel L Jackson** Russell Franklin
Director *Renny Harlin*
Screenplay *Duncan Kennedy, Donna Powers, Wayne Powers*

Deep Impact ★★★★ 12

1998 US Colour 116mins

A huge comet is on a collision course with Earth in director Mimi Leder's science-fiction disaster movie, which gains a certain amount of credibility by highlighting the human side of the impending catastrophe. The frightening scenario focuses on TV reporter Téa Leoni – who stumbles upon the story while tracking down what she thinks is a Presidential indiscretion – and astronaut Robert Duvall, who leads a mission to intercept the threat in space. The chilling gravity of the situation is hauntingly evoked by the national lottery instigated to choose who will "survive" in an underground retreat. Leder adds gripping immediacy to executive producer Steven Spielberg's loose remake of Rudolph Maté's 1951 movie *When Worlds Collide* and caps it all with a spectacular display of epic destruction. Contains swearing.

Robert Duvall Spurgeon Tanner • **Téa Leoni** Jenny Lerner • **Elijah Wood** Leo Biederman • **Vanessa Redgrave** Robin Lerner • **Maximilian Schell** Jason Lerner • **Morgan Freeman** President Tom Beck • **James Cromwell** Alan Rittenhouse • **Ron Eldard** Oren Monash • **Jon Favreau** Gus Partenza • **Mary McCormack** Andrea Baker
Director *Mimi Leder*
Screenplay *Michael Tolkin, Bruce Joel Rubin*
Producer *Richard D Zanuck, David Brown*

Deep Red ★ 18

1994 US Colour 121mins

Not the Dario Argento masterpiece, but a weak science-fiction thriller about a young girl whose blood is contaminated and her ageing process halted thanks to an alien close encounter. It's up to bland private eye Michael Biehn and his estranged wife Joanna Pacula to protect the girl from being kidnapped and used in weird experiments by evil shape-shifting doctor John de Lancie, who sends killer milkmen to trace her. As daft as it sounds, and cliché-ridden to the humdrum hilt, this crude chiller marks a low point in the career of director Craig R Baxley, who originally showed showed such promise with the 1990 Dolph Lungren vehicle *Dark Angel*. Contains violence.

Michael Biehn Joe Keyes • **Joanna Pacula** Monica Quik • **Steven Williams** Eldon James • **Lisa Collins** Mrs Helen Rickman • **Tobin Bell** Warren Rickman • **Lindsey Haun** Gracie Rickman • **John de Lancie** Thomas Newmeyer • **John Kapelos** Mack Waters
Director *Craig R Baxley*
Screenplay *D Brent Mote*

Deep Rising ★★ 15

1998 US Colour 101mins DVD

Tremors meets *Titanic* in a dopey sea-monster movie from director Stephen Sommers, who went on to direct *The Mummy*. In this tepid horror tale, a high-tech pleasure cruiser on its maiden voyage is overrun by modern-day pirates, then attacked by a multi-tentacled, Hydra-like creature. The film navigates an ocean of hilarious monster-movie clichés and derivative special-effects sequences, while Treat Williams does a poor Kurt Russell impression and Famke Janssen (of *Goldeneye* fame) lets her wet T-shirt do the acting. A gruesome fantasy that doesn't skimp on memorably tacky death scenes (a victim sucked through a toilet!), *Deep Rising* is sadly all at sea in terms of coherence and any vestige of credibility. Contains violence and swearing.

Treat Williams John Finnegan • **Famke Janssen** Trillian • **Anthony Heald** Simon

Canton • **Kevin J O'Connor** Joey Pantucci • **Wes Studi** Hanover • **Derrick O'Connor** Captain • **Jason Flemyng** Mulligan • **Cliff Curtis** Mamooli
Director/Screenplay *Stephen Sommers*
Producer *Laurence Mark, John Baldecchi*

Deep Space ★★★ 18

1987 US Colour 86mins (video)

Prolific hack director Fred Olen Ray assembles another cast of trash icons for his most expensive offering to date ($1.5 million) and, for once, manages to craft a halfway decent *Alien* rip-off. The American armed forces have created a monster for future warfare use, but the space lab housing it has crashed in a California junkyard. Cops Charles (*Beyond the Valley of the Dolls*) Napier and Ron (*Barney Miller*) Glass go after the man-eater. Anthony (*Dracula vs Frankenstein*) Eisley and Julie (Catwoman) Newmar are also in the line-up.

Charles Napier Det Ian McLemore • **Ann Turkel** Carla Sanbourn • **Bo Svenson** Captain Robertson • **Ron Glass** Jerry • **Julie Newmar** Elaine Wentworth •
Director *Fred Olen Ray*
Screenplay *Fred Olen Ray, TL Lankford*

Deep Station Emerald ★★★

Radio 1996 UK 4x30mins

Joe Turner's four-part science-fiction drama for Radio 4 is an effective thriller, featuring gravel-voiced Tom Georgeson and *Royle Family* star Ricky Tomlinson. The Deep Station *Emerald* of the title is a futuristic (2012) underwater petrochemical research facility, whose crew members are elated when they discover a source of cold fusion. But before they can bring this astounding discovery to the wider world, an unknown killer begins to murder his (or her) colleagues one by one. Then, to complicate matters, a deadly man-made virus begins to infect those on board. For once, the sound effects are effective, not intrusive, and the paranoia and atmospheric tension mount to a satisfying conclusion.

Maureen Beattie Rossi • **Tom Georgeson** Kettle • **Danny Webb** Capt Harris • **Ricky Tomlinson** O'Connor • **Lorelei King** Dr Beverly Crenshaw
Director *Martin Jameson*
Written by *Joe Turner*
Music *Paul Cargill*

DeepStar Six ★ 15

1989 US Colour 94mins (video)

An experimental underwater colony disturbs a prehistoric sea creature in this shallow combination of *Alien* and *Jaws*. Directed by Sean S Cunningham, the originator of the *Friday the 13th* series, this soggy farrago sinks fast in an ocean of technical mumbo jumbo, murky model work and outrageously bad acting. Cunningham is completely out of his depth in his attempts to scare up tides of terror from a laughable script.

Taurean Blacque Laidlaw • **Nancy Everhard** Joyce Collins • **Greg Evigan** McBride • **Miguel Ferrer** Snyder • **Nia Peeples** Scarpelli • **Matt McCoy** Richardson • **Cindy Pickett** Diane Norris • **Marius Weyers** Van Gelder
Director *Sean S Cunningham*
Screenplay *Lewis Abernathy, Geof Miller, from a story by Lewis Abernathy*

SCI Q • SCI Q • SCI Q • SCI Q •

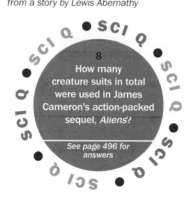

8
How many creature suits in total were used in James Cameron's action-packed sequel, *Aliens*?

See page 496 for answers

Deepwater Black ★★

TV 1997 Can/US Colour 13x30mins

The Earth's population is being wiped out by a deadly virus and the future of humanity lies in the hands of six teenage clones in the US Sci-Fi Channel's first-ever original series. Based on Ken Catran's *Deepwater Black* novels, the show follows the exploits of the Deepwater's crew as they attempt to transport the gene banks of the human race to a possible new home. A pre-*Star Trek: Deep Space Nine* Nicole de Boer and a pre-*Andromeda* Gordon Michael Woolvett are among the cast of this lean but reasonably rewarding teen-orientated sci-fi show, which gives some typical plotlines a wholesome reworking.

Gordon Woolvett Reb • **Nicole de Boer** Yuna • **Jason Cadieux** Bren • **Kelli Taylor** Gret • **Craig Kirkwood** Zak • **Sara Sahr** Lise • **Julie Khaner** Gen
Source *from the novels by Ken Catran*
Executive producer *Wilf Copeland, Alex Nassar*

Def-Con 4 ★★★ 15

1984 US Colour 83mins (video)

This post-apocalyptic action film doesn't have the budget to provide too many futuristic thrills, yet what it lacks in hardware trappings it more than makes up for in imaginative staging (especially the outer space opening). While radiation-ravaged America is overrun by as many ideas lifted from better science-fiction entries (*WarGames, The Terminator*) as it is with sadistic punks and militant cannibals, this low-rent *Mad Max* remains a watchable enough potboiler before it degenerates into a routine cat-and-mouse chase. Contains violence.

Lenore Zann JJ • **Maury Chaykin** Vinny • **Kate Lynch** Jordan • **Kevin King** Gideon Hayes • **John Walsch** Walker • **Tim Choate** Howe • **Jeff Pustil** Lacey • **Donna King** Alice • **Allan MacBillivray** Boomer • **Florence Paterson** Mrs Boyd
Director/Screenplay *Paul Donovan*

Deluge ★★★

1933 US BW 68mins

Long believed lost, director Felix E Feist's feature debut was rediscoverd in 1987 and immediately hailed as one of Hollywood's earliest "disaster" movies. Based on the book by S Fowler Wright, it combined special effects work with footage of an actual Californian earthquake to depict the tidal wave that engulfs the Eastern seaboard and leaves Sidney Blackmer to romance Peggy Shannon in the belief that his wife and family have perished. Elements of *Waterworld* can be detected in their battle against evil Fred Kohler and his band of outlaws, although the sentimental resolution to Lois Wilson's unexpected reappearance was just pure melodrama.

Peggy Shannon Claire Arlington • **Lois Wilson** Helen Webster • **Sidney Blackmer** Martin Webster • **Matt Moore** Tom • **Fred Kohler** Jephson • **Ralf Harolde** Norwood • **Edward Van Sloan** Prof Carlyle • **Samuel Hinds [Samuel S Hinds]** Chief prosecutor
Director *Felix E Feist [Felix Feist]*
Screenplay *John Goodrich, Warren B Duff [Warren Duff], from the novel "Deluge: a Romance" by S Fowler Wright*
Special effects *Ned Mann*
Cinematographer *Norbert Brodine*

Demolition Man ★★★★ 15

1993 US Colour 110mins (video) DVD

This comes pretty close to being Sylvester Stallone's best ever picture: a pretension-free, futuristic thriller in which he wisely keeps his tongue stuck firmly in his cheek. Stallone is a tough cop whose unconventional methods land him in a cryogenic prison. Decades later, he is defrosted to hunt down an old sparring partner, the spectacularly psychopathic

Wesley Snipes (complete with blond thatch), who has escaped from his deep frozen state and is creating havoc in the now crime-free Los Angeles (renamed San Angeles). The writers have a lot of fun sending up modern-day political correctness in this caring vision of the future – violence, red meat and sex are among the items on the banned list – and director Marco Brambilla delivers the goods when it comes to the action set pieces. Of the supporting cast, Sandra Bullock has an early run at a role she would later perfect in *Speed*, while Nigel Hawthorne is the doctor overseeing this 21st-century Utopia. Contains swearing and violence.

Sylvester Stallone John Spartan • **Wesley Snipes** Simon Phoenix • **Sandra Bullock** Lenina Huxley • **Nigel Hawthorne** Dr Raymond Cocteau • **Benjamin Bratt** Alfredo Garcia • **Bob Gunton** Chief George Earle • **Glenn Shadix** Associate Bob • **Denis Leary** Edgar Friendly • **Grand L Bush** Young Zachary Lamb • **Steve Kahan** Captain Healy

Director *Marco Brambilla*

Screenplay *Daniel Waters, Robert Reneau, Peter M Lenkov, from a story by Peter M Lenkov, Robert Reneau*

The Demolitionist ★★ 18

1995 US Colour 85mins

Nicole Eggert acquits herself well as the star of this *RoboCop* clone, but it's an otherwise remarkably routine effort from make-up effects man-turned-director Robert Kurtzman. Former *Baywatch* babe Eggert plays an undercover police officer who undergoes a futuristic blood transplant after she's slain by villain Richard Grieco and is transformed into an enhanced human fighting machine. Kurtzman laboriously piles on the intermittently funny in-jokes, and genre enthusiasts will enjoy the cameos by such horror luminaries as *Dawn of the Dead* make-up man Tom Savini and *Evil Dead* star Bruce Campbell. Contains swearing, violence and nudity.

Nicole Eggert Alyssa Lloyd • **Richard Grieco** Mad Dog • **Bruce Abbott** Prof Jack Crowley • **Susan Tyrrell** Mayor Grimbaum • **Peter Jason** Police Chief Higgins

Director *Robert Kurtzman*

Screenplay *Brian DiMuccio, Dino Vindeni*

Demon Seed ★★★★ 15

1977 US Colour 90mins

This literate sci-fi take on *Rosemary's Baby*, based on a Dean R Koontz novel, is as weird, provocative and compelling as you would expect from Donald Cammell, the co-director of *Performance*. Julie Christie is dazzling as the victim of a power-crazed computer that decides it's greater than its genius creator and malfunctions to conceive a child, by terrifying means. A claustrophobic cautionary tale that shrouds its incredible special effects in a powerful hallucinatory atmosphere, with Robert Vaughn providing the creepily compelling voice of the machine. Contains violence and nudity.

Julie Christie Dr Susan Harris • **Fritz Weaver** Dr Alex Harris • **Gerrit Graham** Walter Gabler • **Berry Kroeger** Petrosian • **Lisa Lu** Dr Soon Yen • **Larry J Blake [Larry Blake]** Cameron • **John O'Leary** Royce • **Alfred Dennis** Mokri • **David Roberts** Warner • **Patricia Wilson** Mrs Talbert • **E Hampton Beagle** Night operator • **Dana Laurita** Amy • **Robert Vaughn** Proteus

Director *Donald Cammell*

Screenplay *Robert Jaffe, Roger O Hirson, from the novel by Dean R Koontz*

Destination Inner Space ★★★

1966 US Colour 81mins

Enjoyable low-budget monster movie from the deep hokum, despite obvious parallels to *The Thing from Another World*. When a UFO is discovered at the bottom of the sea near a marine research facility divers are sent to investigate, only to find a giant amphibian creature with a destructive agenda. Director Francis D Lyon keeps the pace lively, while the underwater scenes are especially well handled. There's also a nicely observed battle of wits between the scientists – keen to study the new species of alien – and the military, who are ever eager to drop a bomb on whatever they don't understand. Although clearly modelled on that nasty resident of the black lagoon, the monster is the film's definite highlight, even if you can spot the actor's scuba tank through the costume.

Scott Brady Cmdr Wayne • **Sheree North** Sandra • **Gary Merrill** Dr Le Satier • **Mike Road** Hugh Maddox • **Wende Wagner** Rene • **John Howard** Dr James • **William Thourlby** Tex • **Biff Elliott** Dr Wilson • **[Ron Burke]** The Thing • **James Hong** Ho Lee

Director *Francis D Lyon*

Screenplay *Arthur C Pierce*

Destination Moon ★★★ U

1950 US Colour 91mins

Intended to be the first realistic film about space exploration, producer George Pal's fun effort was beaten into cinemas by the exploitation quickie *Rocketship X-M*. But that didn't have an animated lecture on the principles of space travel hosted by Woody Woodpecker! Co-scripted by science fiction great Robert A Heinlein, the pedestrian tale of man's first lunar landing has dated badly and the corny dialogue uttered by the barely adequate cast doesn't help. Yet the enthralling look, taken straight from the pulp fiction illustrations of the day, is enchanting and colourful and the special effects (which won an Oscar) are impressive for the era.

Warner Anderson Dr Charles Cargraves • **John Archer** Jim Barnes • **Tom Powers** Gen Thayer • **Dick Wesson** Joe Sweeney • **Erin O'Brien-Moore** Emily Cargraves • **Ted Warde** Brown

Director *Irving Pichel*

Screenplay *Rip van Ronkel, Robert A Heinlein, James O'Hanlon*

Producer *George Pal*

Special effects *Lee Zavitz*

Destroy All Monsters ★★★ PG

1968 Jap Colour 85mins

Alien Kilaaks unleash Toho Studios' entire repertory company of rubber-suited, scaly behemoths to raze a selection of capital cities in this, the ultimate Japanese monster movie. Godzilla attacks New York, Mothra invades Peking and Rodan obliterates Moscow, while Wenda, Baragon and Spigas, the mega-spider from *Son of Godzilla*, all make appearances. Even three-headed Ghidrah shows up for this mighty marathon, which features a zany comic-strip plot, hilariously wooden acting, atrocious dubbing and special effects miniatures that make *Thunderbirds* look like *Terminator 2*. What are you waiting for? Japanese dialogue dubbed into English

Akira Kubo Flight Captain • **Jun Tazaki** Dr Yoshido • **Yoshio Tsuchiya** Dr Otani • **Kyoko Ai** Queen of the Kilaaks • **Yukiko Kobayashi** Kyoko • **Andrew Hughes** Dr Stevenson

Director *Ishiro Honda [Inoshiro Honda]*

Screenplay *Kaoru Mabuchi, Ishiro Honda*

Devil Bat ★★

1940 US BW 68mins

One of the better-known films from Bela Lugosi's sad years on Poverty Row. In this tedious and predictable shocker, the *Dracula* star is in his other customary role, playing a mad scientist who takes revenge on his enemies by setting his giant killer bats on them. Although hammy, fans rate his performance better than those he later gave for Monogram. The rest of the cast, is adequate, although the bat effects are amateurish in the extreme.

Bela Lugosi Dr Paul Carruthers • **Suzanne**

Kaaren Mary Heath • **Dave O'Brien** Johnny Layton • **Guy Usher** Henry Morton • **Yolande Mallott** Maxine • **Donald Kerr** One Shot Maguire • **Edward Mortimer** Martin Heath • **Gene O'Donnell** Don Morton
Director *Jean Yarbrough*
Screenplay *John Thomas Neville, from a story by George Bricker*

The Devil Commands ★★★

1941 US BW 61mins

Boris Karloff grabs the attention in one of the weirdest movies he made, playing an unhinged scientist trying to communicate with the dead (specifically, his late wife) via a brain-wave recording contraption and stolen corpses. Vastly underrated, time has been kind to director Edward Dmytryk's macabre miniature. Today, the quaint surrealist touches of wired-up bodies in robot-like diving suits give it a strangely quirky atmosphere. Anne Revere's evil spiritualist adds further chills in a must-see rarity for Karloff collectors.

Boris Karloff Dr Julian Blair • **Richard Fiske** Dr Richard Sayles • **Amanda Duff** Anne Blair • **Anne Revere** Mrs Walters • **Ralph Penney** Karl • **Dorothy Adams** Mrs Marcy • **Walter Baldwin** Seth Marcy
Director *Edward Dmytryk*
Screenplay *Robert D Andrews, Milton Gunzberg, from the novel "The Edge of Running Water " by William Sloane*

Devil Girl from Mars ★★ U

1954 UK BW 73mins [video]

If proof were needed about the gulf between British and American B-movies, it's contained in this rare UK contribution to the fifties sci-fi boom. Yet, curiously, David MacDonald's scoffably stiff drama enjoys cult status in the States. Presumably this owes much to the sight of leather-clad Martian Patricia Laffan, as she patrols the Scottish Highlands (with her robot, Chani) in search of men to repopulate her ailing planet. It certainly can't be down to the dialogue or the hammed-up performances of journalist Hugh McDermott, model Hazel Court or escaped criminal Peter Reynolds.

Hugh McDermott Michael Carter • **Hazel Court** Ellen Prestwick • **Patricia Laffan** Nyah • **Peter Reynolds** Albert Simpson
Director *David MacDonald*
Screenplay *John C Maher, James Eastwood, from their play*

Devilman Story ★★

1967 It BW 80mins

A high-ranking criminal (Italian sleaze icon Aldo Sambrell) carries out cranium transplant experiments on human guinea pigs in a secret North African laboratory in order to increase his own fiendish brainpower. Guy Madison is the scientist coerced into helping the maniac mastermind. Made solely to steal the box-office thunder from Mario Bava's exquisite *Danger: Diabolik* (it didn't!) and using a similar line in futuristic set designs and silver-helmeted Devilman costumes, this routine *Superago*-style comic strip affair has enough engaging twists – for example, Moors riding to the desert rescue – to make it an appealing time waster. Producer Gabriele Crisanti would find future notoriety with the gore classics *Giallo A Venezia*, *Patrick Lives Again*, *Malabimba*, *Satan's Baby Doll* and *Zombie 3*. Italian dialogue dubbed into English

Guy Madison Mike • **Luisa Baratto** Christine Becker • **Diana Lorys** Yasmin
Director *Paul Maxwell [Paolo Bianchini]*
Screenplay *Paul Maxwell [Paolo Bianchini], Max Caret*

The Devil's Kiss ★

1971 Sp Colour

While never on a par with his compatriots Jesus Franco and Jacinto Molina, Jorge (credited as Georges) Gigo managed to keep busy during the seventies as a director of erotic horror flicks (although, ironically, he made his two best known films, *Porno Girls* and *Trap for a Call Girl*, under the pseudonym George Lewis). However, those salubrious offerings can't hold a candle to this abysmal reworking of the Frankenstein story. The voluptuous Silvia Solar stars as a demented scientist who, with the aid of a diminutive sidekick, creates a slave male who has a problem with subservience. You've been warned. Spanish dialogue dubbed into English. Contains violence, sex scenes and nudity.

Silvia Solar Clair Grandier • **Olivier Mathot** Prof Gambler • **Jose Nieto** Duc de Haussemont • **Evelyne Scott** Loretta • **Daniel Martin** Richard • **Maria Silva** Susan
Director *Georges Gigo [Jorge Gigo]*
Screenplay *Georges Gigo [Jorge Gigo]*

Die, Monster, Die! ★★ 15

1965 US/UK Colour 74mins [video]

Supposedly, but barely, based on the HP Lovecraft story *The Colour out of Space*, former Roger Corman art director Daniel Haller's feature debut is a creditable genre effort in spite of itself. An American scientist (Nick Adams) turns up at the remote village of Arkham to visit his fiancée (Suzan Farmer) and her crippled father (Boris Karloff) only to find that a recently crash-landed meteorite is causing strange mutations. Naturally, Haller is instinctively adept at getting the most atmospheric chills from the visual components of his terror tale, rather than from the muddled script and weak acting.

Boris Karloff Nahum Witley • **Nick Adams** Stephen Reinhart • **Freda Jackson** Letitia Witley • **Suzan Farmer** Susan Witley • **Terence DeMarney** Merwyn • **Patrick Magee** Dr Henderson • **Paul Farrell** Jason
Director *Daniel Haller*
Screenplay *Jerry Sohl, from the novel "The Colour out of Space" by HP Lovecraft*

10 WAYS TO STOP AN ALIEN MONSTER

- **Freeze it** *The Blob*
- **Blast it with a fire extinguisher** *The Monster That Challenged the World*
- **Sneeze in its face – they can't stand germs** *War of the Worlds*
- **Traumatise it with a high-pitched noise** *Not of This Earth*
- **Spray it with sea-water** *The Day of the Triffids*
- **Shine your car headlights on it** *Invasion of the Saucer Men*
- **Tempt it with a poisoned cow** *Island of Terror*
- **Or offer it a poisoned Italian** *Eat and Run*
- **Play it the sound of Slim Whitman yodelling** *Mars Attacks!*
- **Or, if you're really desperate . . . feed it the cancerous liver you have just surgically removed from a terminally ill scientist** *Forbidden World*

Digby, the Biggest Dog in the World ★★ U

1973 UK Colour 88mins

While Peter Sellers was a natural before a movie camera, his fellow Goons never really found a screen niche. Spike Milligan, for example, looks singularly lost in this kiddie comedy about a nosey pooch who guzzles down a sample of miracle plant food, Project X, and just keeps growing. Even the versatile Jim Dale struggles to make a go of Michael Pertwee's script, which is essentially a one-gag shaggy dog story. Younger viewers will doubtless enjoy the sight of a king-size sheepdog, but older children and grown-ups will probably be put off by the ropey special effects.

Jim Dale Jeff Eldon • **Spike Milligan** Dr Harz • **Angela Douglas** Janine • **John Bluthal** Jerry • **Norman Rossington** Tom • **Milo O'Shea** Dr Jameson • **Richard Beaumont** Billy White • **Dinsdale Landen** Col Masters • **Garfield Morgan** Rogerson • **Victor Spinetti** Professor Ribart
Director *Joseph McGrath*
Screenplay *Michael Pertwee, from a story by Charles Isaacs, from the book "Hazel" by Ted Key*

Digital Man ★★ 15

1994 US Colour 91mins

A cyborg soldier is assigned to take out a band of high-tech terrorists and ends up with the launch codes to 250 missile silos. As his megalomania increases, he holds the world to ransom in director Phillip J Roth's scattershot sci-fi opus, which boasts good special effects and super weaponry, but little sense of structure. When things explode and spacecraft fly, Roth's futuristic one-man-army tale passes muster. But when the action grinds to a halt, so does the dumb story.

Ed Lauter General Roberts • **Ken Olandt** Sergeant Anders • **Matthias Hues** Digital Man • **Paul Gleason** Dr Parker • **Adam Baldwin** Captain West • **Sherman Augustus** Jackson • **Don Swayze** Billy • **Kristen Dalton** Gena
Director *Phillip J Roth*
Screenplay *Ken Melamed, Paul J Robbins*

Dimension of Fear ★★

TV 1963 UK BW 4x45mins

A four-part serial, scripted by John Lucarotti, this 1963 effort was another ATV stab at grabbing the *Quatermass* audience. Set in a government space research centre and a stereotypical sleepy English village, the story (conceived by Berkley Mather) deals with invaders from a fourth dimension.

Katharine Blake Dr Barbara Finch • **Peter Copley** Professor Meredith • **Robin Bailey** Colonel Alan Renton • **Richard Coleman** Inspector Truick • **Margaret Ashcroft** Miss Reynolds • **Mark Eden** Dr Leosser
Director *Don Leaver*
Written by *John Lucarotti, from a story by Berkely Mather*
Producer *Guy Verney*

Dimension X ★★★

Radio 1950-1951 US 50x30mins

This NBC series, along with its successor *X Minus One* (which recycled many of its scripts), marked the advent of "grown-up" science-fiction listening. It was one of the first to use stories from established top writers of the genre – including Kurt Vonnegut, Isaac Asimov, Ray Bradbury, Robert Heinlein and Theodore Sturgeon – and is one of the first to be recorded on tape. Despite the impact of the series, it only lasted for 50 episodes; an improvement, however, on CBS's rival attempt at an adult science-fiction series, *Beyond Tomorrow*, which only lasted for three episodes in 1950. A more obscure and less successful rival series, *2000 Plus* (1950-1952), featured stories scripted by staff writers, all set beyond the turn of the millenium.

Norman Rose Narrator
Director *Fred Wiehe, Edward King*
Adapter/Writer *Ernest Kinoy, George Lefferts*

Dinosaur Valley Girls ★

1996 US Colour 94mins

One Million Years BC meets *Playboy* magazine in director Donald F Glut's dumb caveman comedy. In post-nuclear LA, lots of hot babes in animal skin bikinis fend off Neanderthal advances, tacky stop-motion dinosaurs and blown-up lizard footage in this super-cheap exploitation item continuing the slide of one-time Oscar hopeful Karen Black's career into ever more shoddy material. Those expecting mild sexual titillation will have to make do with radiant smiles, endless sunbathing shots and the odd breast exposure.

William Marshall Tony/To-nee • **Ed Furey** Ur-so • **Jeff Rector** Tony Markham • **Denise Ames** Hea-Thor • **Karen Black** Ro-Kell • **Carrie Vanston** Karen Forster
Director/Screenplay *Donald F Glut*

Dinosaurus! ★★

1960 US Colour 82mins

Jurassic Park this ain't! A caveman, a friendly brontosaurus and a nasty T-Rex are disturbed from their slumber on a tropical island by construction workers in one of the funniest – unintentionally – monster movies ever made. Best described as a prehistoric take on the Three Stooges' brand of comedy (see the Neanderthal man have "comical" problems with modern appliances; see the T-Rex fight a steam shovel), this will be loved by youngsters, while adults will shake their heads in dismay at the cheap mindlessness. Still, lousy special effects and even worse acting do make it hilariously compulsive viewing.

Ward Ramsey Bart Thompson • **Paul Lukather** Chuck • **Kristina Hanson** Betty Piper • **Alan Roberts** Julio • **Gregg Martell** Prehistoric man • **Fred Engelberg** Mike Hacker • **Luci Blain** Chica • **Jack Younger** Jasper • **Wayne Tredway** Dumpy • **Howard Dayton** Mousey • **James Logan** O'Leary
Director *Irvin S Yeaworth Jr*
Screenplay *Jean Yeaworth, Dan E Weisburd, from an idea by Jack H Harris*

Disturbing Behaviour ★★ 15

1998 US Colour 83mins DVD

Bad kids in a small town are turning good after undergoing experimental psychological treatment in this tepid teen variation on *The Stepford Wives*. Trouble is, they turn homicidal when sexually aroused, and it seems high school student James Marsden is the only one to notice. Director David Nutter brings some of his trademark *X Files* moodiness to the material, but he can't seem to decide what sort of film he's making. A statement about individuality versus conformity? Or just another run-of-the-mill slash-fest? Sadly, the latter concept takes hold as the plot-holes become ever more glaring, and any hopes that this might turn out to be a smart, paranoid conspiracy thriller are slowly dashed. Contains swearing.

Bruce Greenwood Dr Caldicott • **Katie Holmes** Rachel Wagner • **William Sadler** Dorian Newberry • **Nick Stahl** Gavin Strick • **Steve Railsback** Officer Cox • **James Marsden** Steve Clark • **Tobias Mehler** Andy Effkin • **Katharine Isabelle** Lindsay Clark • **Bruce Greenwood** Dr Caldicott • **Katie Holmes** Rachel Wagner • **William Sadler** Dorian Newberry • **Nick Stahl** Gavin Strick • **Steve Railsback** Officer Cox • **James Marsden** Steve Clark • **Tobias Mehler** Andy Effkin
Director *David Nutter, David Nutter*
Screenplay *Scott Rosenberg*

Doc Savage: the Man of Bronze ★★ PG

1975 US Colour 96mins

George Pal was a legendary figure in the worlds of sci-fi and fantasy, but this, his swan-song film as a producer, is not the best way to remember him. The story is taken from the ever-popular Doc Savage books of the thirties, with television's Tarzan, Ron Ely, in the title role. Despite director Michael Anderson's admirable attempts to insert some knowing humour, however, it remains a rather tame and routine adventure. Contains some violence and swearing.

Ron Ely Doc Savage • **Paul Gleason** Long Tom • **Bill Lucking [William Lucking]** Renny • **Michael Miller** Monk • **Eldon Quick** Johnny • **Darrell Zwerling** Ham • **Paul Wexler** Captain Seas • **Janice Heiden** Andriana
Director *Michael Anderson*
Screenplay *George Pal, Joe Morhaim, from the novel by Kenneth Robeson*

Dr Black and Mr Hyde ★

1975 US Colour 87mins

Arguably the worst blaxploitation horror movie ever made, and with at least something to offend every race. Wealthy Afro-American Dr Henry Pride (football star Bernie Casey) is working on a cure for cirrhosis of the liver and, after using patients as research at the Watts free clinic where he volunteers his medical services, he experiments on himself and turns into a murderous white man with a phobia regarding prostitutes. Cheaply made – Casey's make-up job looks like a dusting of flour – and depressingly sleazy, director William Crain's stinker fails to offer the same hip changes to its classic source material as did his *Blacula*.

Bernie Casey Dr Henry Pride/Mr Hyde • **Rosalind Cash** Dr Billie Worth • **Marie O'Henry** Linda • **Ji-Tu Cumbuka** Lt Jackson • **Milt Kogan** Lt O'Connor • **Stu Gilliam** Silky
Director *William Crain*
Screenplay *Larry LeBron, from a story by Lawrence Woolner*

Doctor Blood's Coffin ★★

1960 UK Colour 92mins

Before he launched his mainstream career with *The Ipcress File* and *Lady Sings the Blues*, director Sidney J Furie cut his teeth on such British programme fillers as this cheap and cheerful *Frankenstein*-flavoured tale. Doctor Kieron Moore experiments in bringing the dead back to life while his fetching nurse (Hazel Court) screams a lot amid the lurid, Hammer Horror-style glossiness. Enhanced by its Cornish tin-mine setting, Furie's cardboard suspense shocker is hardly a classic, but it is great fun, and Moore is impressive as the madman torn between science and evil.

Kieron Moore Doctor Peter Blood • **Hazel Court** Linda Parker • **Ian Hunter** Doctor Robert Blood • **Fred Johnson** Mr Morton • **Kenneth J Warren** Sergeant Cook • **Andy Alston** Beale • **Paul Stockman** Steve Parker • **John Ronane** Hanson • **Gerald C Lawson** Sweeting
Director *Sidney J Furie*
Screenplay *Jerry Juran, James Kelly, Peter Miller, from a story by Jerry Juran*

Dr Coppelius ★★★ U

1966 US/Sp Colour 86mins

Itself inspired by a tale by Hoffman, Délibes's ballet *Coppelia* is the bedrock of this delightful children's fantasy. Claudia Corday of the Harkness Ballet takes the dual role of the robotic doll (created by Walter Slezak's eccentric inventor) and the simple village girl who has to rescue her beloved before he loses his heart to her mechanical lookalike. With Caj Selling of the Royal Swedish Ballet playing the bewitched swain, the extensive dance sequences are majestically realised. But sci-fi fans will enjoy Slezak's pantomimic approach to the role, whichhe reprised in the sequel, *The Mysterious House of Dr C*.

Walter Slezak Dr Coppelius • **Claudia Corday** Swanhilda/Coppelia • **Caj Selling** Franz • **Eileen Elliott** Brigitta • **Carmen Rojas** Spanish doll • **Veronica Kusmin** Roman doll • **Milorad Miskovitch** Hungarian dance champion • **Luis Prendes** Mayor
Director *Ted Kneeland*
Screenplay *Ted Kneeland, from a story by Victor Torruella, from the ballet "Coppelia" by Clément Philibert, Léo Delibes, Charles Louis Etienne Nuitter*

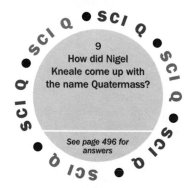

SCI Q • SCI Q • SCI Q • SCI Q • SCI Q •

9
How did Nigel Kneale come up with the name Quatermass?

See page 496 for answers

Doctor Crimen ★★★

1953 Mex BW 85mins

Chano Urueta emerged as the godfather of Mexican exploitation with this Balkan-based Beauty and the Beast fable. Jose Maria Linares Rivas stars as a disfigured plastic surgeon who creates a handsome "monster" to help him silence a snooping journalist. However, Carlos Navarro's braindead youth falls in love with Miroslava and only her editor, Fernando Wagner, can save her. A Spanish language film.

Miroslava Nora • **Carlos Navarro** Ariel/Sergei Rostov • **Jose Maria Linares Rivas** Hermann Ling • **Fernando Wagner** Gherasimos • **Alberto Mariscal** Mischa • **Stefan Berne** Crommer
Screenplay *Dino Maiuri, Chano Urueta*

Dr Cyclops ★★★

1940 US Colour 78mins

Ernest B Schoedsack, co-director of the original *King Kong*, returns to the fantasy genre with this wonderfully weird tale of a mad scientist (Albert Dekker) who miniaturises explorers in his Amazon jungle laboratory. Borrowing ideas from *Kong* special effects man Willis O'Brien, Schoedsack crafts a well-mounted science-fiction thriller, the first of its kind in vivid Technicolor. The standard plot now looks hackneyed, and the cueball-headed Dekker is stereotypically crazy. However, the impressive array of oversize props make this a lot of fun to watch.

Albert Dekker Dr Thorkel • **Janice Logan** Dr Mary Mitchell • **Thomas Coley** Bill Stockton • **Charles Halton** Dr Bulfinch • **Victor Kilian** Steve Baker • **Frank Yaconelli** Pedro • **Bill Wilkerson** Silent Indian • **AllenFox** Cab driver • **Paul Fix** Dr Mendoza • **Frank Reicher** Prof Kendall
Director *Ernest B Schoedsack*
Screenplay *Tom Kilpatrick*

Dr Frankenstein on Campus ★★★

1967 Can Colour 83mins

When Viktor Frankenstein IV (Robin Ward) arrives at a Canadian college, the other students make fun of his name. But his classmates stop laughing when he joins forces with mysterious Professor Sean Sullivan to create lethal brainwashing pills that turns them into murderous remote-controlled zombies. A stellar performance by Ward, good special effects and brisk direction by Gilbert W Taylor make this an interesting twist on the Frankenstein theme, especially when Viktor is revealed to be an android. Sub-plots involving student protest rallies and hippie drug-taking make this terror time capsule more enjoyable than ever.

Robin Ward Viktor Frankenstein • **Kathleen Sawyer** Susan Harris • **Austin Willis** Cantwell • **Sean Sullivan** Professor Preston • **Ty Haller** Tony • **Tony Moffat-Lynch** David • **Stephanie Laird** Debbie • **Ken Hagan** Reporter
Director *Gilbert W Taylor*
Screenplay *David Cobb, Bill Marshall, Gilbert W Taylor*

Dr Goldfoot and the Bikini Machine ★★ PG

1965 US Colour 84mins

Very much a product of the Swinging Sixties, this slice of tosh combines several of the elements that made AIP films so popular at the drive-ins. Vincent Price plays

Off the wall: Fredric March won the best actor Oscar for his portrayal of the tormented doctor in this classic 1931 version of Robert Louis Stevenson's oft-told tale, *Dr Jekyll and Mr Hyde*

the eponymous doctor, who creates female robots so they can marry rich men and line his coffers. Susan Hart plays the female lead and Frankie Avalon and Dwayne Hickman are also along for the ride. Even Annette Funicello drops in! It's all a little too daft, though, while the humour is positively leaden. A sequel followed in 1966.

Vincent Price Dr Goldfoot • **Frankie Avalon** Craig Gamble • **Dwayne Hickman** Todd Armstrong • **Susan Hart** Diane • **Jack Mullaney** Igor • **Fred Clark** D J Pevney • **Alberta Nelson** Reject No 12 • **Milton Frome** Motorcycle Cop
Director *Norman Taurog*
Screenplay *Elwood Ullman, Robert Kaufman, from a story by James Hartford*
Producer *James H Nicholson, Samuel Z Arkoff*

Dr Goldfoot and the Girl Bombs ★★

1966 US/It Colour 85mins

Only in the mid-sixties could you have got away with a film like this! Thanks to cult Italian horror director Mario Bava, this sequel to *Dr Goldfoot and the Bikini Machine* piles on the style, but rather loses out in the fun stakes. Still, Vincent Price is his usual hammy self as Dr Goldfoot, who gets backing from China to start a war between the Americans and the Soviets using sexy robot girls with bombs implanted in their navels. (As the advertising went: "Don't touch – she's a booby bomb!") Teen idol Fabian plays the spy out to foil the dastardly plan, while Italian comics Franco and Ciccio – arguably cinema's worst-ever comedy double act – have supporting roles. Amiable rubbish that manages to make *Austin Powers* look like *The Third Man*.

Vincent Price Dr Goldfoot • **Fabian** Bill Dexter • **Franco Franchi** Franco • **Ciccio Ingrassia** Ciccio • **Laura Antonelli** Rosanna • **Moana Tahi** Goldfoot's assistant
Director *Mario Bava*
Screenplay *Louis M Heyward, Castellano Pipolo, Robert Kaufman, from a story by James Hartford*

Dr Heckyl & Mr Hype ★★

1980 US Colour 97mins

Twenty years after his fleeting appearance in *The Two Faces of Dr Jekyll*, Hammer's version of Robert Louis Stevenson's horror classic, Oliver Reed finally gets to tackle the title role himself in a clumsy comedy that mixes the Jekyll and Hyde idea with elements of *The Nutty Professor*. Reed is engagingly grotesque – bulbous nose, mangy skin, the works – as a scientist who overdoses on an experimental diet formula and transforms into a dashing playboy with a predilection for killing. Reed enters into the rollicking spirit of the piece, but director Charles B Griffith, whose career began on such Roger Corman movies as *Little Shop of Horrors*, ruins the amusing idea with laboured dialogue and stilted slapstick.

Oliver Reed Dr Heckyl/Mr Hype • **Sunny Johnson** Coral Careen • **Maia Danziger** Miss Finebum • **Virgil Frye** Lieutenant Mack Druck "Il Topo" • **Mel Welles** Dr Hinkle • **Kedrick Wolfe** Dr Lew Hoo • **Jackie Coogan** Sergeant Fleacollar • **Corinne Calvet** Pizelle Puree
Director/Screenplay *Charles B Griffith*

Dr Jekyll and Mr Hyde ★★

1920 US Tinted 63mins

Based on Thomas Russell Sullivan's Victorian stage adaptation and steeped in the attitudes of that era, this is generally considered to be the best silent version of Robert Louis Stevenson's classic story. It's hopelessly dated by modern standards, though, while John Barrymore slices the ham far too thickly. His Jekyll isn't the villain of the piece so much as his girlfriend's father, played by Brandon Hurst. It's Hurst who suggests idealist Jekyll experiments with the good and evil sides of human nature, and he's also the one who deliberately leads him into temptation with silent goddess Nita Naldi. The initial transformation is nothing more than Barrymore twisting his face into an evil grimace, but a nightmare vision of a monstrous spider with Hyde's face is extremely well-done and still carries a potent charge.

John Barrymore Dr Henry Jekyll/Mr Edward Hyde • **Martha Mansfield** Millicent Carew • **Nita Naldi** Gina • **Brandon Hurst** Sir George Carew • **Charles Lane** Dr Richard Lanyon
Director *John S Robertson*
Screenplay *Clara S Beranger, from the novel "The Strange Case of Dr Jekyll and Mr Hyde" by Robert Louis Stevenson*

Dr Jekyll and Mr Hyde ★★★★ 12

1931 US BW 91mins [video]

Robert Louis Stevenson's oft-told split personality tale receives its most stylish, erotic and exciting treatment under Rouben Mamoulian's sure direction. Fredric March deservedly won the best actor Oscar – shared with Wallace Beery in *The Champ* – for his tormented performance; the single-take transformation scenes are particularly impressive. Also memorable is the smouldering sensuality of Miriam Hopkins as the prostitute who's the object of his evil attentions. This most enduring adaptation of the Faustian moral fable is totally satisfying.

Fredric March Dr Henry Jekyll/Mr Hyde • **Miriam Hopkins** Ivy Pearson • **Rose Hobart** Muriel Carew • **Holmes Herbert** Dr Lanyon • **Halliwell Hobbes** Brigadier General Carew • **Edgar Norton** Poole • **Arnold Lucy** Utterson • **Colonel McDonnell** Hobson • **Tempe Pigott** Mrs Hawkins
Director *Rouben Mamoulian*
Screenplay *Samuel Hoffenstein, Percy Heath, from the novel "The Strange Case of Dr Jekyll and Mr Hyde" by Robert Louis Stevenson*
Producer *Rouben Mamoulian*

Dr Jekyll and Mr Hyde ★★★

1941 US BW 126mins

Director Victor Fleming's first film after *Gone with the Wind* was this lavish MGM treatment of Robert Louis Stevenson's classic good-versus-evil cautionary tale. With the accent on the bad doctor's emotional turmoil rendered in complex Freudian terms to little dramatic effect rather than the horror of the situation, it's a poor, if at times scary, relation to the superior 1931 version, which starred Fredric March. Spencer Tracy adds scant shading to either side of his split personality, despite an impressive and sinister transformation montage. This is, however, worth seeing for the production standards and the luminescent Ingrid Bergman.

Spencer Tracy Dr Harry Jekyll/Mr Hyde • **Ingrid Bergman** Ivy Peterson • **Lana Turner** Beatrix Emery • **Donald Crisp** Sir Charles Emery • **Ian Hunter** Dr John Lanyon • **Barton MacLane** Sam Higgins • **C Aubrey Smith** The bishop • **Peter Godfrey** Poole
Director *Victor Fleming*
Screenplay *John Lee Mahin, from the novel "The Strange Case Of Dr Jekyll and Mr Hyde" by Robert Louis Stevenson*
Producer *Victor Saville*

Dr Jekyll and Ms Hyde ★ 12

1995 US Colour 86mins [video]

This dire, unfunny and completely unnecessary comic twist on Robert Louis Stevenson's classic tale stars Tim Daly as Jekyll's descendant, a gormless fellow who has the unhappy knack of turning into trampy vamp Helen Hyde (Sean Young). Neither funny nor frightening, the only really scary thing in the movie is Young's bad acting. As you would expect, this ended up in bargain video bins everywhere. Contains swearing and nudity.

Sean Young Helen Hyde • **Tim Daly [Timothy Daly]** Dr Richard Jacks • **Lysette Anthony** Sarah Carver • **Stephen Tobolowsky** Oliver Mintz • **Harvey Fierstein** Yves DuBois • **Thea Vidale** Valerie • **Jeremy Piven** Pete Walston • **Polly Bergen** Mrs Unterveldt • **Stephen Shellen** Larry • **Sheena Larkin** Mrs Mintz
Director *David F Price*
Screenplay *Tim John, Oliver Butcher, William Davies, William Osborne, from a story by David Price, from the novel "The Strange Case of Dr Jekyll and Mr Hyde" by Robert Louis Stevenson*

Dr Jekyll and Sister Hyde
★★★ 18

1971 UK Colour 93mins

Written by Brian Clemens (longtime writer and producer of *The Avengers* TV series), this bizarre bisexual take on the split personality classic even includes the grave robbers Burke and Hare and a Jack the Ripper subplot. While not quite living up to its initial sensationalist hype – "the transformation of a man into a woman will take place before your very eyes", warned the ads – it's still mid-range Hammer horror with extra heat supplied by solid Ralph Bates and Martine Beswicke as the good and evil flip sides. Contains some violence.

Ralph Bates Dr Jekyll • **Martine Beswick** Sister Hyde • **Gerald Sim** Professor Robertson • **Lewis Fiander** Howard • **Dorothy Alison** Mrs Spencer • **Neil Wilson** Older policeman • **Ivor Dean** Burke • **Paul Whitsun-Jones** Sergeant Danvers • **Philip Madoc** Byker • **Tony Calvin** Hare • **Susan Brodrick** Susan
Director *Roy Ward Baker*
Screenplay *Brian Clemens, from the novel "The Strange Case of Dr Jekyll and Mr Hyde" by Robert Louis Stevenson*

Dr M ★★ 18

1989 W Ger/It/Fr Colour 111mins

Claude Chabrol is one of the most unpredictable directors in world cinema, and even his failures make for more interesting and compelling viewing than the latest bland Hollywood sequel. *Dr M* is a case in point. Set in a futuristic Berlin, the action centres on the evil schemes of Dr Marsfeldt (Alan Bates), a media mogul who has obviously been modelled on Fritz Lang's hypnotising hoodlum Dr Mabuse. Chabrol also seems to be heading towards Lang's *Metropolis* territory, but he takes a wrong turning en route and ends up in a low budget version of Gotham City. The story is jumbled and the acting unrestrained, but it's worth a look. Contains violence and swearing.

Alan Bates Dr Marsfeldt • **Jennifer Beals** Sonja Vogler • **Jan Niklas** Klaus Hartmann • **Hanns Zischler** Moser • **Benoît Régent** Stieglitz • **William Berger** Penck • **Alexander Radszun** Engler • **Peter Fitz** Veidt • **Daniela Poggi** Kathi • **Beatrice Macola** Anna • **Jean Benguigui** Rolf • **Michael Degen** Reimar von Geldern • **Wolfgang Preiss** Kessler • **Andrew McCarthy** Assassin
Director *Claude Chabrol*
Screenplay *Sollace Mitchell, from a story by Thomas Bauermeister, from the novel "Dr Mabuse, der Spieler " by Norbert Jacques*

Doctor Renault's Secret ★★★

1942 US BW 58mins

Considering the Nazis' contemporary obsession with genetics, this remake of Richard Rosson's lost 1927 silent *The Wizard* may seem in bad taste. But George Zucco's misuse of servant J Carroll Naish to unlock the secret of evolution is played with such pantomimic glee that it's impossible to take offence. Directing his last feature before resuming his career as a painter, Harry Lachman takes the action at a regulation B-clip. But thanks to Nathan Juran's quaintly disquieting sets, there's a palpable sense of menace, while Sheppard Strudwick seeks to save Lynne Roberts from both her brain specialist uncle Zucco and his ex-convict gardener Mike Mazurki.

J Carrol Naish Mr Noel • **John Sheppered [Shepperd Strudwick]** Dr Larry Forbes • **Lynne Roberts** Madeline Renault • **George Zucco** Dr Renault • **Bert Roach** Proprietor • **Eugene Borden** Coroner • **Jack Norton** Austin • **Arthur Shields** Inspector Duval • **Ray Corrigan** Gorilla
Director *Harry Lachman*
Screenplay *William Bruckner, Robert F Metzler [Robert Metzler], Frances Hyland, from the novel "Balaoo" by Gaston Leroux*

Dr Strangelove, or How I Learned to Stop Worrying and Love the Bomb ★★★★★ PG

1963 UK BW 90mins DVD

Is this the way the world ends, not with a bang but a simper? The late Stanley Kubrick's ferocious Cold War satire makes us smile through gritted teeth as unhinged general Sterling Hayden sends a squadron of nuclear bombers to attack Russia and trigger an apocalypse-laden doomsday machine. Peter Sellers's trio of performances (bemused airman, confused president and defused US Nazi advisor, re-armed by the prospect of world annihilation) spirals from gentle humour to surreal horror. The scenes in which Hayden raves about "body fluids" and Pentagon general George C Scott rants about statistical deaths were obviously inspired by Sellers's genius. Kubrick's unsparing disgust with our warlike instincts has never been so obvious nor so grimly comic. Contains swearing.

Peter Sellers Group Captain Lionel Mandrake/President Merkin Muffley/Dr Strangelove • **George C Scott** General "Buck" Turgidson • **Sterling Hayden** General Jack D Ripper • **Keenan Wynn** Colonel "Bat" Guano • **Slim Pickens** Major TJ "King Kong • **Peter Bull** Ambassador de Sadesky • **Tracy Reed** Miss Scott • **James Earl Jones** Lieutenant Lothar Zogg • **Ray Corrigan** Gorilla
Director *Stanley Kubrick*
Screenplay *Stanley Kubrick, Terry Southern, Peter George, from the novel "Red Alert" by Peter George*
Cinematographer *Gilbert Taylor* • ***Art director*** *Ken Adam* • ***Editor*** *Anthony Harvey*

Doctor Who: the First Doctor
★★★★ U

TV 1963-1966 UK BW 134x25mins

The world's longest running TV science fiction series, featuring Doctor Who, a mysterious traveller through space and time, was originally devised largely as an educational tool for children with its mix of science, drama and history. The Daleks changed all that, broadening the show's appeal to adults as well as kids and the stories gradually shifted their emphasis from part education to all-out fantasy. Best known for TV's *The Army Game* and a stalwart of British fifties cinema, notably in the first *Carry On* movie, William Hartnell created the role of the Doctor, given near carte blanche by producers to interpret the part as he wished, playing him as a grandfatherly figure, tetchy and irritable, but soft-hearted with a quicksilver mind. "A cross between the wizard of Oz and Father Christmas" in Hartnell's own words. In 1966 ill health sadly forced Hartnell to leave the role he had loved playing so dearly.

William Hartnell Doctor Who • **William Russell** Ian Chesterton • **Jacqueline Hill** Barbara Wright • **Carole Ann Ford** Susan Foreman • **Maureen O'Brien** Vicki • **Peter Purves** Steven Taylor • **Jackie Lane**

Dorothea "Dodo" Chaplet • **Michael Craze** Able Seaman Ben Jackson • **Adrienne Hill** Katarina • **Anneke Wills** Polly Wright
Story editor *David Whitaker*
Producer *Verity Lambert*

Doctor Who: the Second Doctor

★★★★ U

TV 1966-1969 UK BW 119x30mins

With the departure of William Hartnell, the BBC were left in a quandary as to how to replace him. In the end they didn't, hitting on the brilliant idea that the Doctor was capable of changing his physical appearance and personality when close to death. This regeneration gimmick would allow for smooth transition between future actors playing the role. Former Shakespearean actor Patrick Troughton brought a more off-beat and comedic quality to the part, playing the Doctor as a cosmic hobo, scruffily dressed in an old frock coat and baggy checked trousers, with a penchant for playing the recorder. Troughton's era is synonymous with monsters – Daleks, the Yeti, Ice Warriors and the Cybermen – and for the first time we learned something of the Doctor's origins, that he was a renegade Time Lord from the planet Gallifrey who stole his time machine, the Tardis, to gallivant around the universe. Captured and put on trial by the Time Lords, he is exiled to Earth and undergoes regeneration once more. With tragic irony Troughton was to collapse and die while attending an American *Doctor Who* fans' convention in 1987.

Patrick Troughton Doctor Who • **Anneke Wills** Polly • **Michael Craze** Ben • **Frazer Hines** Jamie McCrimmon • **Deborah Watling** Victoria Waterfield • **Wendy Padbury** Zoe Heriot • **Nicholas Courtney** Brigadier Lethbridge Stewart • **John Levene** Sereant Benton
Script editors *Davis Gerry, Peter Byant, Derrick Sherwin, Terrance Dicks*
Producer *Innes Lloyd, Peter Bryant*

Doctor Who: the Third Doctor

★★★★★ U PG

TV 1970-1974 UK Colour 128x30mins

As *Doctor Who* moved into the seventies it did so for the first time in colour and with a new actor at the helm. Best known for radio's comedy hit *The Navy Lark*, Jon Pertwee was the most flamboyant and dandified Doctor, with a droll sense of humour and faultless manners. Pertwee's Doctor was truly an extension of the actor, a lover of adventure and gadgetry. This was incorporated into the show turning the character into a real man of action, a sort of interplanetary James Bond, an exponent of martial arts and fencing who also boasted his own version of 007's famous trick Aston Martin in the shape of the "Whomobile", a flying saucer-like car that actually flew. An exile on Earth, Pertwee's Doctor spent the majority of his time seconded to Unit (United Nations Intelligence Taskforce), a top secret army under the command of Brigadier Lethbridge Stewart (memorably played by Nicholas Courtney) who defended the earth against invasion from Sea Devils, the Autons and the Master. After saving the earth from destruction a few times, the Doctor did win his freedom back from the grateful Time Lords.

Jon Pertwee Doctor Who • **Caroline John** Elizabeth "Liz" Shaw • **Nicholas Courtney** Brigadier Lethbridge Stewart • **Katy Manning** Jo Grant • **Elisabeth Sladen** Sarah Jane Smith • **Richard Franklin** Captain Mike Yates • **John Levene** Sereant Benton • **Roger Delgado** The Master
Script editor *Terrance Dicks*
Producer *Derrick Sherwin, Barry Letts*

SCI Q • SCI Q • SCI Q • SCI Q • SCI Q •

10
Which 1929 film did Hitler ban because he feared the rocket sequences might harm war preparations?

See page 496 for answers

Doctor Who: the Fourth Doctor

★★★★★ U PG

TV 1974-1981 UK Colour 178x25mins

The longest-running Doctor, Tom Baker is also the fan's favourite. Along with Jon Pertwee his era probably contains the biggest bulk of best stories, and he was also largely responsible for securing the show's success overseas, particularly in America. But the beginning of his career was inauspicious. A former monk, Baker was between acting jobs and working on a building site when he was asked to play the Doctor. With his floppy hat, endless scarf, his shock of curly hair and Harpo Marx-like bulging eyes, Baker was an instant hit, particularly with children who enjoyed his off the wall humour, eccentric manners and obsession with jelly babies. Baker also collected some of the series' more memorable companions: roving journalist Sarah Jane Smith, the scantily-clad warrior Leela, the robot dog K9 and Romana, played by Lalla Ward, whom Baker later married in a blaze of publicity. Sadly the marriage didn't last, and neither did Baker, finally quitting the role. But for many, his remains the face of Doctor Who.

Tom Baker Doctor Who • **Elisabeth Sladen** Sarah Jane Smith • **Ian Marter** Harry Sullivan • **Nicholas Courtney** Brigadier Lethbridge Stewart • **John Levene** Sergeant (RSM) Benton • **Matthew Waterhouse** Adric • **Louise Jameson** Leela • **Janet Fielding** Tegan Jovanka • **Mary Tamm** Romanadvoratrelundar Mk I, "Romana" • **Lalla Ward** Romanadvoratrelundar Mk II, "Romana" • **Sarah Sutton** Nyssa
Script editors *Robert Holmes, Anthony Read, Douglas Adams, Christopher H Bidmead*
Producer *Philip Hinchcliffe, Graham Williams, John Nathan-Turner*

Doctor Who: the Fifth Doctor

★★★ U PG

TV 1982-1984 UK Colour 66x25m

Already popular with TV audiences as Tristan in the BBC family drama *All Creatures Great and Small*, Peter Davison brought a youthful exuberance and innocence to the role. A fan of the show when he was growing up, Davison drew inspiration principally from the first two Doctors, his own characterisation being a mixture of William Hartnell's brusqueness and Patrick Troughton's vulnerability – with a soupçon of English gent thrown in – reflected in the Doctor's typically dotty dress sense, cricket sweater, striped trousers and regency-style coat. Davison's era is notable for the return of some classic old monsters like the Daleks, Cybermen and the Sea Devils, and for the show losing its traditional Saturday teatime slot, going out instead twice on weekdays. Fans were kept happy with a feature length and two 45-minute specials..

Peter Davison Doctor Who • **Janet Fielding** Tegan Jovanka • **Sarah Sutton** Nyssa • **Matthew Waterhouse** Adric • **Mark Strickson** Vislor Turlough • **Nicholas Courtney** Brigadier Lethbridge Stewart • **Nicola Bryant** Perpugilliam "Peri" Brown • **Gerald Flood** Voice of Kamelion
Script editors *Eric Saward, Anthony Root*
Producer *Nathan-Turner*

Doctor Who: the Sixth Doctor

★★ 12

TV 1984-86 UK Colour 18x25m; 13x45m

Prior to playing Doctor Who, Colin Baker had already appeared in a 1983 episode

DOCTOR WHO

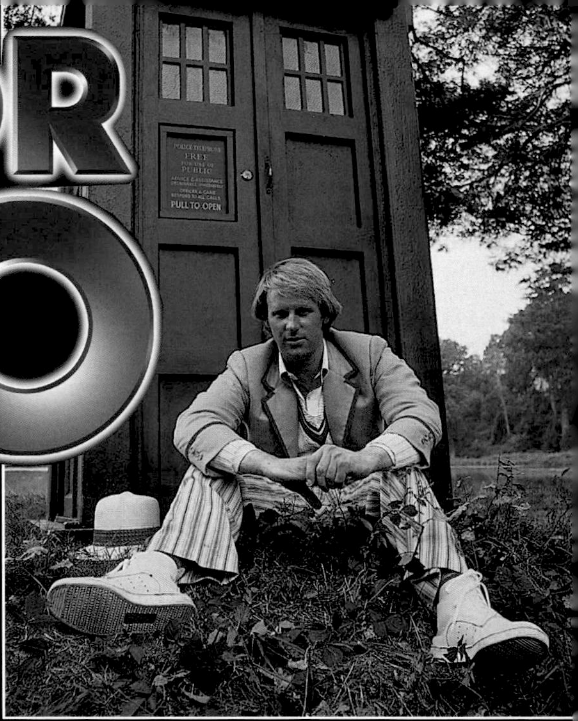

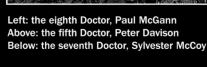

Left: the eighth Doctor, Paul McGann
Above: the fifth Doctor, Peter Davison
Below: the seventh Doctor, Sylvester McCoy

Above: the third Doctor, Jon Pertwee. Above right: the fourth Doctor, Tom Baker. Right: the first Doctor, William Hartnell
Below right: the second Doctor, Patrick Troughton
Below: the sixth Doctor, Colin Baker

where he shot the then incumbent actor in the role, Peter Davison. A year later he was offered the chance of taking over. It was a dream come true for the former solicitor who had already found TV fame as villain Paul Merroney in BBC's hit drama *The Brothers*, but Baker's reign as the Doctor turned out to be the most controversial period in the show's history. Baker's interpretation of the role – alien-like, with mood swings, traces of paranoia and an unpredictable, sarcastic nature – heavily divided fans. The fact that he was saddled with some of the worst stories ever didn't help. Finally, the show was postponed for 18 months and fans feared this was the end of their hero. But the series returned with an ambitious 14-part story that saw the Doctor standing trial for his life. It proved Baker's last gasp, and the actor was unceremoniously sacked.

Colin Baker Doctor Who • **Nicola Bryant** Perpugilliam "Peri" Brown • **Nicholas Courtney** Brigadier Lethbridge Stewart • **Bonnie Langford** Melanie
Script editor *Eric Saward*
Producer *John Nathan-Turner*

Doctor Who: the Seventh Doctor ★★★ PG

TV 1987-1989 UK Colour 42x25mins

When news broke that Sylvester McCoy would be the next Doctor Who the reaction of most fans was, Sylvester Who? Chosen out of a reported 5,000 applicants, McCoy had first applied for the role back when Peter Davison left. A highly versatile actor, with experience at the National Theatre and in comedy variety shows, McCoy's Doctor was a welcome throwback to Patrick Troughton's cosmic clown persona. But as the series progressed his portrayal grew darker and more mysterious, while the scripts began hinting that the Doctor might have an altogether different origin and purpose than previously believed. McCoy's reign must be regarded as perhaps the most uneven, encompassing some all-time great stories (*Remembrance of the Daleks*) along with some prize turkeys (*Paradise Towers*). And who can ever forget (or forgive) Bonnie Langford as companion Mel. Much better was Sophie Aldred's tough, street-wise Ace. Then in 1989 came the news that every fan had been dreading: the show's cancellation.

Sylvester McCoy Doctor Who • **Bonnie Langford** Melanie • **Sophie Aldred** Ace • **Nicholas Courtney** Brigadier Lethbridge Stewart
Script editor *Andrew Cartmel*
Producer *John Nathan-Turner*

Doctor Who ★★ 12

TV 1996 UK/US Colour 84mins

After a seven-year hiatus, the man in the Tardis was back in the shape of *Withnail & I* star Paul McGann, in what was hoped would be the first in a possible series of TV movies. The man responsible for the Time Lord's Lazarus-like return was producer Philip Segal, who got the go ahead from the BBC with backing from Steven Spielberg's Amblin company, who later backed out of the project, to be replaced by 20th Century Fox TV. Set in San Francisco, although shot in Vancouver, the Doctor, aided by a beautiful (of course) heart surgeon, is once again pitted against the Master, a miscast Eric Roberts. Although the production values are impressive, this hugely disappointing revival just wasn't worth the wait. It's not McGann's fault – given time, he might well have proved himself the best Doctor since Tom Baker. The real fault lies in the bland Americanisation of a much-loved British institution.

Paul McGann The Doctor • **Sylvester McCoy** The Old Doctor • **Eric Roberts** The Master • **Daphne Ashbrook** Dr Grace Holloway • **Yee Jee Tso** Chang Lee • **John Novak** Salinger • **Michael David Simms** Dr Swift • **Gordon Tipple** The Old Master • **Catherine Lough** Wheeler
Director *Geoffrey Sax*
Written by *Matthew Jacobs*
Executive producer *Philip David Segal Alex Beaton, Jo Wright*

Dr Who and the Daleks ★★★ U

1965 UK Colour 82mins

The first big-screen outing for the BBC's ever-popular sci-fi TV series has Peter Cushing playing the time-travelling Doctor with amiable seriousness as he pits his wits against those mobile knobbly tin cans forever shrieking "Exterminate". Set on the planet Skaro where the good Thals are trying to stop the evil Daleks detonating another neutron bomb, the cheap art direction is strictly "101 Uses for Pink Plastic Sheeting". Lacking the bite and inventiveness that set the landmark series apart, this spin-off unwisely injects humour into its sparse scenario. However, despite the many faults, it's still a slick slice of enjoyable mayhem generating loads of fun for both the uninitiated and die-hard fans alike.

Peter Cushing Dr Who • **Roy Castle** Ian • **Jennie Linden** Barbara • **Roberta Tovey** Susan • **Barrie Ingham** Alydon • **Michael Coles** Ganatus • **Geoffrey Toone** Temmosus • **Mark Peterson** Elydon • **John Brown** Antodus • **Yvonne Antrobus** Dyoni
Director *Gordon Flemyng*
Screenplay *Milton Subotsky, from the BBC TV series by Sydney Newman, from the characters created by Terry Nation*
Producer *Milton Subotsky*

Doctor Who: the Ghosts of N-Space ★★★

Radio 1996 UK 6x10mins

A follow-up to the radio serial *The Paradise of Death*, reuniting writer Barry Letts, director Phil Clarke and regular cast-members Jon Pertwee, Nicholas Courtney, Elisabeth Sladen and Richard Pearce in a very complex six-parter set in and around a Sicilian castle owned by the Brigadier's uncle, which is haunted by demonic creatures and ghosts who turn out to be bleeding through from "N-space", the parallel universe where dead souls go. A mafia don (Stephen Thorne) is trying to buy up the castle, but he turns out to be a near-immortal alchemist, the Doctor has a jaunt into the afterlife to see what the trouble is there and the Tardis takes a time trip back to the 18th century, where Sarah Jane (Sladen) finds herself involved with intrigues literally out of an Anne Radcliffe novel. The script indulges in colloquialisms ("naff", "wimp", "wally") that sit ill with the supposed seventies setting, and there is even some mild swearing. Like a lot of TV six-parters, it is stuffed with a bit too much padding – here, running jokes and funny voices – but starts and ends well. Available on audio-cassette and CD.

Jon Pertwee The Doctor • **Nicholas Courtney** Brigadier Lethbridge Stewart • **Elisabeth Sladen** Sarah Jane Smith • **Richard Pearce** Jeremy Fitzoliver • **Jonathan Tafler** Clemenza • **Don McCorkindale** Don Fabrizzio • **Stephen Thorne** Max • **David Holt** Nico • **Sandra Dickinson** Maggie
Written by *Barry Letts*
Producer *Phil Clarke*

SFacts

The Ghosts of N-Space **was Jon Pertwee's last performance as the Doctor. He died in May 1996, four months after it was broadcast.**

Doctor Who: The Paradise of Death ★★★

Radio 1993 UK 145mins

A five-part radio serial by Barry Letts, broadcast on BBC Radio 2 in 1993 and available commercially in an extended version, this brings back Jon Pertwee (the Doctor), Elisabeth Sladen (Sarah Jane Smith) and Nicholas Courtney (Brigadier Lethbridge-Stewart) from the early seventies TV incarnation of *Doctor Who* and sets them loose in an adventure that begins with the investigation of Spaceworld, a theme park on Hampstead Heath run by genuine alien businessmen, and then hops across the universe by spaceship and Tardis to an Edgar Rice Burroughs-style world of gladiatorial combat, bat-riding warriors and a voracious but insidiously attractive plant lifeform. It has the usual doses of satire, aimed at rapacious capitalism and the mind-numbing media, with a lot of comedy, courtesy of Jeremy Fitzoliver (Richard Pearce) – a new character, a posh tagalong from reporter Sarah Jane's magazine – and some dim-witted alien henchmen. It misses only the scarier aspects of the show, although there is a creepy alien sadist who enjoys the prospect of torturing Sarah Jane but never gets round it it. Available on audio-cassette and CD.

Jon Pertwee The Doctor • **Nicholas Courtney** Brigadier Lethbridge Stewart • **Elisabeth Sladen** Sarah Jane Smith • **Harold Innocent** Freeth • **Peter Miles** Tragan • **Maurice Denham** President • **Richard Pearce** Jeremy Fitzoliver
Director *Phil Clarke*
Written by *Barry Letts*

Doctor Who: Slipback ★★★

Radio 1985 UK 6x10mins

During the 18-month gap between the two troubled Colin Baker series of *Doctor Who*, this serial went some way towards slaking fans' thirst for more of the Time Lord. Scripted by *Who* script editor Eric Saward, one-upping his *Earthshock* dinosaur-exterminating-collision with a script revolving around a mad computer meddling with the Big Bang that created the universe, *Slipback* was broadcast in six ten-minute episodes, complete with cliffhangers, in the children's magazine show *Pirate Radio 4*. The story has the Tardis materialise in a spaceship where someone is tinkering with time itself, a monster is running around slaughtering the crew, and alien Captain Slarn (hollow-voiced Valentine Dyall) has either a lecherous or a culinary interest in Earth women (his sliminess is conveyed through repulsive massage sound effects). Colin Baker's Doctor and then-companion Peri (Nicola Bryant) play broadly (especially when in dire peril), with some Douglas Adams-y bits of humour, but Jane Carr as two different computer personalities carries most of the weight of the drama. Not without the camp clod-hopping that was afflicting the TV version at the time, but arguably as good as if not better than any other Colin Baker *Doctor Who* serial. Available on audio-cassette and CD.

Colin Baker The Doctor • **Nicola Bryant** Peri • **Jane Carr** Computer • **John Glover** Grant • **Nick Revell** Bates/Snatch • **Alan Thompson** Mutant/Steward • **Valentine Dyall** Slarn • **Ron Pember** Seedle
Written by *Eric Saward*
Producer *Paul Spencer*

A Dog, a Mouse and a Sputnik ★★

1958 Fr BW 94mins

This resembles the situation Norman Wisdom got himself into in *The Bulldog Breed*, as well-meaning incompetent Noël-Noël has to assume control of a rocket after his fellow astronaut becomes incapacitated. Not that the veteran funnyman was supposed to be there – he was simply trying to protect the sacrificial critters of the title from blasting off on a Franco-Russian space probe. Rushed out following the success of *A Pied, à Cheval et en Voiture* (1957), this amiable family comedy reunites Noël-Noël with the long-suffering Denise Grey, while there are welcome supporting turns from practised farceurs Mischa Auer and Darry Cowl. A French language film.

Noël-Noël Léon Martin • **Denise Grey** Marguerite Martin • **Mischa Auer** Professor • **Noël Roquevert** Mayor • **Darry Cowl** Sub-attaché • **Robert Lombard** Chief of police
Director *Jean Dréville*
Screenplay *Jean-Jacques Vital*

Dogora the Space Monster ★★★

1964 Jap Colour 83mins

Gangsters find themselves up against giant octopus-like creatures during diamond robberies in this luminous sci-fi fantasy by veteran Japanese *Kaiju Eiga* director Inoshiro Honda. The cells mutated by radiation into Dogora then use their viscous tentacles to devour the carbon from bigger objects such as trains, boats and bridges before being eliminated by wasp venom. Often cited as an allegory of Oriental exploitation by the western world, Honda's ambitious and dream-like creature feature works mainly as solid escapist fare. The only film to feature the surreal Dogora, this is an imaginative one-off. A Japanese language film

Yosuke Natsuki Inspector Kommei • **Yoko Fujiyama** Musiyo • **Akiko Wakabayashi** Nago • **Hiroshi Koizumi** Korino • **Nobuo Nakamura** Dr Munakata
Director *Inoshiro Honda*
Screenplay *Shinichi Sekizawa, from a story by Jojiro Okami*
Special effects *Eiji Tsuburaya*

Dogs ★

1976 US Colour 89mins

Where Alfred Hitchcock managed to sustain audience belief that our feathered friends had begun attacking humans in *The Birds*, this low-budget howler fails to convince with its tale of a pack of killer hounds on the loose in an isolated college campus. Ex-Man from UNCLE David McCallum struggles gamely as a biology professor whose students end up as Winalot chunks. The Hitchcock connection resurfaces in a pastiche of the *Psycho* shower scene, with one of the canine stars in the Anthony Perkins role. If movies were dogs, this one would be a shih-tzu.

David McCallum Harlan Thompson • **George Wyner** Michael Fitzgerald • **Eric Server** Jimmy Goodmann • **Sandra McCabe** Caroline Donoghue • **Sterling Swanson** Dr Martin Koppelman • **Holly Harris** Mrs Koppelman
Director *Burt Brinckerhoff*
Screenplay *O'Brian Tomalin*

Doin' Time on Planet Earth ★★ 15

1988 US Colour 79mins [video]

Nicholas Strouse is a teenager who, in the course of his search for a date for his brother's wedding, comes to believe he is an alien from outer space. Candice Azzara and Adam West are two other potential aliens who believe that Strouse holds the information that will lead them all home. And it all has something to do with the wedding being on a blue moon and in Ryan's father's revolving restaurant. Too complicated to be truly funny.

Nicholas Strouse Ryan Richmond • **Matt Adler** Dan Forrester • **Andrea Thompson** Lisa Winston • **Martha Scott** Virginia Camalier • **Adam West** Charles Pinsky • **Hugh Gillin** Fred Richmond • **Timothy Patrick Murphy** Jeff Richmond
Director *Charles Matthau*
Screenplay *Darren Star, from a story by Andrew Licht, Jeffrey A Mueller, Darren Star*

The Doll ★★★

1962 Fr Colour 95mins

Aiming a dig squarely at Peronist Argentina, this political fantasy draws on the robotic deceptions of Metropolis for its satirical inspiration. Zbigniew Cybulski and Sonne Teal take dual roles: he as the dictator of a "fictional" Latin American state and the revolutionary leader seeking to topple him; she as the dictator's wife and the mechanised doppleganger who is slyly substituted by Machiavellian banker, Claudio Gora. Jacques Baratier's direction is steady, but occasionally obfuscatory. A French language film.

Zbigniew Cybulski Col Prado Roth/The Rebel • **Sonne Teal** Marion/The Doll • **Claudio Gora** Moren, the banker
Director *Jacques Baratier*
Screenplay *Jacques Audiberti*

Donovan's Brain ★★★

1953 US BW 83mins

Directed with unnerving seriousness by MGM journeyman Felix Feist, this is the most faithful and easily the best adaptation of Curt Siodmak's fiendish novel. The tale of doctor Lew Ayres's struggle with the maniacal powers of a dead industrialist's transplanted brain is given chilling credibility by the extraordinary range of expressions Ayres assumes whenever he's gripped by the millionaire's insane desire to destroy his family and former associates. Lab assistant Gene Evans and wife Nancy Davis (Ronald Reagan's future first lady) are on hand to provide effectively uncomprehending support.

Lew Ayres Dr Patrick J Corey • **Gene Evans** Dr Frank Schratt • **Nancy Davis** Janice Cory • **Steve Brodie** Herbie Yocum • **Lisa K Howard** Chloe Donovan
Director *Felix Feist*
Screenplay *Felix Feist, from the novel by Curt Siodmak*

Don't Play with Martians ★★

1967 Fr Colour 100mins

One of France's most bankable directors, Philippe de Broca, took the time out to co-script this knockabout adaptation of Michel Labry's novel. Jean Rochefort gives of his best as the incompetent journalist, who is dispatched to an island off Brittany to cover the birth of some sextuplets, only to miss the delivery, an alien visitation and the emergence of a prehistoric creature from the depths of the Atlantic. But Henri Lanoë's direction, like the humour, is much too broad. A French language film.

Jean Rochefort René • **Macha Méril** Marie • **André Vallardy** Job
Director *Henri Lanoë*
Screenplay *Philippe de Broca, Johanna Harwood, Henri Lanoë, from the novel by Michel Labry*

Doom Runners ★★

1997 US Colour 95mins

This sci-fi adventure with an environmental message follows a group of children who undertake a perilous journey in post-apocalyptic Australia. The youngsters are looking for the unpolluted paradise known as New Eden, but the evil Dr Kao (Tim Curry) and his Doom Troopers are determined to stop them and wipe their memories. Curry makes a suitably over-the-top villain and there's enough action here to satisfy younger viewers.

Lea Moreno Jada • **Tim Curry** Dr Kao • **Dean O'Gorman** Deek • **Bradley Pierce** Adam • **Nathan Jones** Vike • **Rebecca Smart** Lizzie • **Peter Carroll** William • **David Whitney** Thorne • **Putu Winchester** Danny
Director *Brendan Maher*
Screenplay *Barney Cohen, Ken Lipman*

Doomsday Man ★★

1998 US Colour 89mins

This futuristic thriller hits all the right buttons, but still fails to excite. Yancy Butler is the feisty soldier assigned to track down mad researcher James Marshall, who has made off with a lethal biological weapon from a top-secret base. The cast is better than average, with the actors enthusiastically giving it their best shot. Director William Greenblatt may be better known as a producer, but he scores in the action sequences. Sadly, however, this is predictable fare.

Yancy Butler Kate • **Esai Morales** Mike Banks • **James Marshall** Tom Banks • **Renee Griffin** Jill • **Randell Haynes** Lyons • **Jill Galloway** Melissa • **Barry Bell** Prentiss
Director *William R Greenblatt*
Screenplay *Andrew Stein*

Doomsday Rock ★★

1997 US Colour

Although it's not exactly *Deep Impact* on a shoestring, this TV movie shows all too clearly just what a difference a budget makes. Australian Brian Trenchard-Smith has always had a sure touch with action subjects and builds up a fair head of steam here, as astronomer William Devane and his daughter Connie Sellecca occupy a nuclear silo in a bid to alert the world to the danger from an approaching giant comet. However, whereas *Deep Impact* director Mimi Leder could throw in a few computer-generated set pieces to sustain the tension, Trenchard-Smith has to rely on ominous sounding jargon and heated confrontations. Contains violence.

Connie Sellecca Katherine Sorenson • **Ed Marinaro** Richard Chase • **William Devane** Dr Carl Sorenson • **Marsha Warfield** Lisa Dillon • **Jessica Walter** Secretary of Defense McGregor
Director *Brian Trenchard-Smith*
Screenplay *David Bourla, Michael Norell*

Doomwatch ★★★★ PG

TV 1970-1972 UK Colour 37x50mins

Widely described as the first "green" drama series, this mix of sci-fi, horror and eco-drama was highly innovative. Tackling such issues as embryo research, toxic waste pollution and genetic manipulation, it was the brainchild of *Doctor Who* script editor Gerry Davis and Dr Kit Pedler, a scientist at the University of London. It told of a fictitious government agency whose job was to protect mankind and the environment from dangerous or unprincipled advances in science. The early episodes, notably one featuring intelligent man-eating rats, are the most celebrated. As the stories became more mundane and less fantastical in ambition, Pedler and Davis left the show in protest.

John Paul Dr Spencer Quist • **Simon Oates** Dr John Ridge • **Robert Powell** Tobias Wren • **Joby Blanshard** Colin Bradley • **John Nolan** Geoff Hardcastle • **Jean Trend** Dr Fay Chantry • **John Barron** Minister • **John Bown** Cmdr Neil Stafford • **Elizabeth Weaver** Dr Anne Tarrant
Devised by *Kit Pedler, Gerry Davis*
Producer *Terence Dudley*

SFacts

The *Doomwatch* series eerily predicted many newspaper headlines:

***The Plastic Eaters* (9 February 1970) featured an airplane dissolving in mid-air when its plastic components are eaten by a mystery virus. Five months later *News of the World* (5 July 1970) reports on scientists launching a research programme looking at self-destructive plastics that crumble into powder which would then be eaten by bacteria.**

***Tomorrow the Rat* (2 March 1970) looked at an experiment in rat breeding gone wrong, resulting in London being plagued with a new breed of intelligent killer rats. On 16 September 1970 the *Daily Mail* reports on a new strain of "super rat" in Shropshire, immune to Warfarin and all permitted rat poisons.**

***The Red Sky* (6 April 1970) showed the damage caused by a high-flying rocket plane. Five months later, on 3 September 1970, the *Daily Express* reports "Concorde shock waves a danger to health", as the supersonic plane's test flights split roof tiles, crack windows and disturb animals.**

Doomwatch ★★

1972 UK Colour 91mins

As a spin-off from a modish ecological BBC TV series – a more fact-based version of *The X Files* – this crash-landed unhappily in the swamp of horror instead of on the firmer ground of science fact or fiction. John Paul, Ian Bannen and Judy Geeson look suitably intense as an investigation is mounted into the effects of a sunken oil tanker on the inhabitants of an island off the Cornish coast only to discover something nastily mutated in the biological woodshed. Risibly alarmist, certainly, but the environmental dangers it pinpoints are still only too topical.

Ian Bannen Dr Del Shaw • **Judy Geeson** Victoria Brown • **John Paul** Dr Quist • **Simon Oates** Dr Ridge • **George Sanders** Admiral • **Percy Herbert** Hartwell • **Geoffrey Keen** Sir Henry Layton • **Joseph O'Conor** Vicar • **Shelagh Fraser** Mrs Straker
Director *Peter Sasdy*
Screenplay *Clive Exton, from the TV series by Kit Pedler, Gerry Davis*

Doomwatch: Winter Angel ★★★★

TV 1999 UK Colour 120mins

The fight against eco-disaster continues in Channel 5's telemovie spin-off from the ahead-of-its-time seventies sci-fi drama series. Philip Stone replaces John Paul as an aging Spencer Quist, and recruits Trevor Eve's Professor Neil Tannahill to lead an investigation into an international conspiracy involving secretly-stored toxic waste. Although the exploits of Tannahill and his new "Doomwatch" team become increasingly absurd and confusing as the story develops, they are stylishly shot and well-acted, especially by Eve. Perhaps even more impressively, the production also recaptures the spirit of the original series, and its all-important thought-provoking relevance. Despite its obvious strengths, however, the telemovie failed to spawn a proposed revival series of *Doomwatch*.

Trevor Eve Neil Tannahil • **Amanda Ooms** Meg Tannahil • **Philip Stone** Spencer Quist • **Miles Anderson** Toby Ross • **Dallas Campbell** Hugo Cox • **Allie Byrne** Teri Riley
Director *Roy Battersby*
Written by *Ian MacDonald, John Howett*
Producer *Peter Lee-Wright*

Doorways ★★★ 15

1993 US Colour 83mins

We already know from the *Mad Max* movies that oil will become a precious commodity sometime in the future. But the alien villains in this TV movie aren't just prepared to engage in a little highway robbery, they're willing to cross into a parallel Earth in order to meet their fuel needs. The premise is intriguing enough, but the film soon descends into a standard race against time as a doctor tries to help a fugitive stay out of the clutches of both the FBI and the agent of the evil Dark Lord. Derivative, but above average.

George Newbern Dr Tom Mason • **Anne Le Guernec** Cat • **Kurtwood Smith** Trager • **Robert Knepper** Thane • **Hoyt Axton** Jake • **Tisha Putman** Cissy
Director *Peter Werner*

Double Dragon ★★ 12

1994 US Colour 91mins

In the ravaged, flooded Los Angeles of 2007, Jimmy and Billy (Mark Dacascos and Scott Wolf) are streetwise youths who come upon one half of an ancient Chinese talisman, which gives awesome power to whoever possesses both halves. Unfortunately, the other portion is owned by unscrupulous gang boss Koga Shuko (Robert Patrick) and his phalanx of gigantic henchmen. Naturally, he's out to reunite the "Double Dragon" and take over the world. Nifty ideas include cars that run on any old garbage lying around, although it appears kickboxing will still be the preferred method of self-defence in 2007. Decent effects and a wisecracking screenplay lift James Yukich's movie above the usual futuristic fare.

Robert Patrick Koga Shuko • **Mark Dacascos** Jimmy Lee • **Scott Wolf** Billy Lee • **Kristina Malandro Wagner** Linda Lash • **Julia Nickson [Julia Nickson-Soul]** Sartori Imada • **Alyssa Milano** Marian Delario
Director *James Yukich*
Screenplay *Michael Davis, Peter Gould, from a story by Neal Shusterman, Paul Dini*
Producer *Ash R Shah, Sunil R Shah, Alan Schechter, Jane Hamsher, Don Murphy*

Dracula, Prisoner of Frankenstein ★

1972 Sp Colour 86mins

Spanish hack director Jesus Franco intended to make a parody of horror myths, but clearly doesn't have the talent or the budget to pull off such a cartoonish conceit. This sorry spectacle has Dr Frankenstein (a slumming Dennis Price) reviving Dracula (Franco regular Howard Vernon) with a nightclub singer's blood, so that he can use his vampire acolytes to conquer the world. Lousy make-up, shoddy special effects and practically no dialogue degrade the Transylvanian count and good doctor's names. Shot on location in Spain and Portugal, the film should really have been shot at dawn. Spanish dialogue dubbed into English

Dennis Price Dr Frankenstein • **Howard Vernon** Dracula
Director/Screenplay *Jesus Franco*

Dracula vs Frankenstein ★

1970 US Colour 90mins

Director Al Adamson surely ranks alongside Ed Wood as one of the genre's true incompetents. This is arguably his crowning glory – a hilarious mix of bad music, teenage dopeheads, beach parties and unconvincing monsters. Horror veterans J Carrol Naish and Lon Chaney Jr (who both never made another film) look thoroughly embarrassed, while the plot is a complete shambles. Hardly surprising, since the movie started life as a biker film before being turned into a monster free-for-all. A must for all bad movie lovers.

J Carrol Naish Dr Frankenstein • **Lon Chaney Jr** Groton, the Mad Zombie • **Regina Carrol** Judith • **John Bloom** The Monster • **Anthony Eisley** Mike Howard • **Zandor Vorkov** Count Dracula
Director *Al Adamson*
Screenplay *William Pugsley, Samuel M Sherman*

Dragon Fury ★★

1995 US Colour 80mins

Futuristic nonsense in which warrior Robert Chapin must travel back in time to 1999 in order bid to find a cure for an epidemic that is wiping out the human race in the present day. He is pursued by other sword-wieldiers who are happy enough with the way the future has turned out. The modern-day settings can't disguise the budget constraints, although that scarcely justifies the uninspiring action sequences and dull performances. Contains violence, nudity and swearing.

Richard Lynch Vestor • **Robert Chapin** Mason • **Chona Jason** Regina • **Deborah Stambler** Dr Ruth • **TJ Storm** Fullock
Director/Screenplay *David Heavener*

Dreamscape ★★ 15

1984 US Colour 94mins

Psychic Dennis Quaid enters the American president's guilt-plagued nuclear nightmares to save him from a paranormal assassin in a workmanlike fantasy thriller directed (and co-written) by Joseph Ruben (director of *Sleeping with the Enemy*). The perfectly-cast actors fly as high as they can with the intriguing concept, but the script is mediocre and lacks any real excitement. The real pleasure of this efficient piece of film-making comes from the dream sequences that punctuate the political thriller framework. These include a dose of sex comedy, a post-holocaust vision, an erotic interlude and, best of all, a no-holds-barred "Snake Man" nightmare.

Dennis Quaid Alex Gardner • **Max von Sydow** Dr Paul Novotny • **Christopher Plummer** Bob Blair • **Eddie Albert** President • **Kate Capshaw** Dr Jane Devries
Director *Joseph Ruben*
Screenplay *Joseph Ruben, David Loughery, Chuck Russell, from a story by David Loughery*

Drive ★★★ 18

1996 US Colour 99mins

Mark Dacascos stars in this outrageously violent martial-arts adventure with vaguely science-fiction overtones. Taking unemployed songwriter Kadeem Hardison hostage, superhuman fighter Dacascos goes on the run and battles endless acrobatic villains for no reason whatsoever. Forget the story – it's the endless parade of Jackie Chan-style stunts, hard-core gore and bizarre humour, superbly woven together by director Steve Wang – that matter in this turbo-charged *Lethal Weapon* clone. Contains swearing and violence.

Mark Dacascos Toby Wong • **Kadeem Hardison** Malik Brody • **John Pyper-Ferguson** Vic Madison • **Brittany Murphy** Deliverance Bodine • **Tracey Walter** Hedgehog • **James Shigeta** Mr Lau • **Masaya Kato** Advanced model • **Dom Magwili** Mr Chow • **Mark Dacascos** Toby Wong • **Kadeem Hardison** Malik Brody • **John Pyper-Ferguson** Vic Madison • **Brittany Murphy** Deliverance Bodine • **Tracey Walter** Hedgehog • **James Shigeta** Mr Lau • **Masaya Kato** Advanced model • **Dom Magwili** Mr Chow
Director *Steve Wang, Steve Wang*
Screenplay *Scott Phillips*

Driving Force ★★ 15

1988 Aus Colour 90mins

Wouldn't it be nice, just once, if, after an apocalyptic nuclear disaster, the Earth was ruled by ruthless, neatly dressed accountants and clerks rather than the leather-clad bikers who inevitably run riot? Sadly, it's not to be and this is another substandard excursion into *Mad Max* territory, with Sam Jones as the moody hero fighting off the bad guys led by fellow straight-to-video star Don Swayze (who is the not-nearly-so-famous younger brother of Patrick). The performances are nondescript and the requisite explosions are loud, but staged with little originality or flair. Contains violence, swearing and nudity.

Sam Jones • **Catherine Bach** • **Angel Cook** • **Don Swayze**
Director *Andrew Prowse*
Screenplay *Patrick Edgeworth*

Dune ★★★ 15

1984 US Colour 130mins DVD

Frank Herbert's mammoth cult novel, about the competition between two warring families for control of a barren planet renowned for its mind-expanding spice, is converted by director David Lynch into a dense, swirling mass of religious symbolism and mysticism. Under-rated on its release, this is a film that deserves revisiting. Lynch was, reportedly, unhappy with the final cut, but his film is visually stunning – the industrial design is truly unique – and many of the scenes are among the most memorable, and original, of the genre. Kyle MacLachlan (in his film debut) stars as the "messiah" alongside an amazing cast that includes Sean Young, Francesca Annis, Sting, Patrick Stewart and Kenneth McMillan (as the decaying, bloated Baron Harkonnen, perhaps the most repellent villian ever created). Contains violence and swearing.

Kyle MacLachlan Paul Atreides • **Francesca Annis** Lady Jessica • **Leonardo Cimino** Baron's doctor • **Brad Dourif** Piter De Vries • **José Ferrer** Padishah Emperor Shaddam IV • **Linda Hunt** Shadout Mapes • **Freddie Jones** Thufir Hawat • **Richard Jordan** Duncan Idaho • **Virginia Madsen** Princess Irulan • **Silvana Mangano** Reverend Mother Ramallo • **Everett McGill** Stilgar • **Kenneth McMillan** Baron Vladimir Harkonnen • **Jack Nance** Nefud • **Sian Phillips** Reverend Mother Gaius Helen Mohiam • **Jürgen Prochnow** Duke Leto Atreides • **Paul Smith** Beast Rabban • **Patrick Stewart** Gurney Halleck • **Sting** Feyd Rautha • **Dean Stockwell** Dr Wellington Yueh • **Max von Sydow** Dr Kynes • **Alicia Roanne Witt** Alia • **Sean Young** Chani
Director *David Lynch*
Screenplay *David Lynch, from the novel by Frank Herbert*

Dune Warriors ★★ 18

1991 US/Phil Colour 74mins

Co-produced by Roger Corman, this is typically derivative fare, mixing *The Magnificent Seven* with the third *Mad Max*. David Carradine, who first worked with Corman on Martin Scorsese's *Boxcar Bertha*, heads a gang of futuristic mercenaries who are hired to protect a village which has a valuable source of water, a much sought-after commodity in this post-nuclear world. Cirio H Santiago piles up plenty of bloody action sequences, but doesn't stint on the clichés, either. He isn' helped by the fact that Carradine sleepwalks through his role and that the only other familiar face is that of Rick *Deathstalker*) Hill.

David Carradine Michael • **Rick Hill** John • **Luke Askew** William • **Jillian McWhirter** Val • **Blake Boyd** Dorian • **Val Gary** Jason • **Joe Zucchero** Reynaldo • **Bon Vibar** Emilio
Director *Cirio H Santiago*
Screenplay *TC McKelvey*
Producer *Cirio H Santiago, Roger Corman*

Duplicates ★★ 15

1992 US Colour 87mins

Although it suffers from the constrictions of its TV-movie format, this is still a moderately chilling affair. Gregory Harrison and Kim Griest – the memorable love interest in *Brazil* – play a married couple who discover that the disappearance of their son may be connected to a sinister scientific conspiracy. Sadly, the movie's choice of title means that the "shocking" truth is hardly a surprise. The two leads are ably supported by the likes of Kevin McCarthy, Lane Smith and Cicely Tyson, while small-screen veteran Sandor Stern keeps the action moving along competently enough.

Gregory Harrison Bob Boxletter • **Kim Greist** Marion Boxletter • **Cicely Tyson** Dr Lila Randolph • **Kevin McCarthy** Dr Nelson Congemi • **Lane Smith** Fryman • **William Lucking** Chief Robinson
Director *Sandor Stern*
Screenplay *Sandor Stern, Andrew Neiderman*

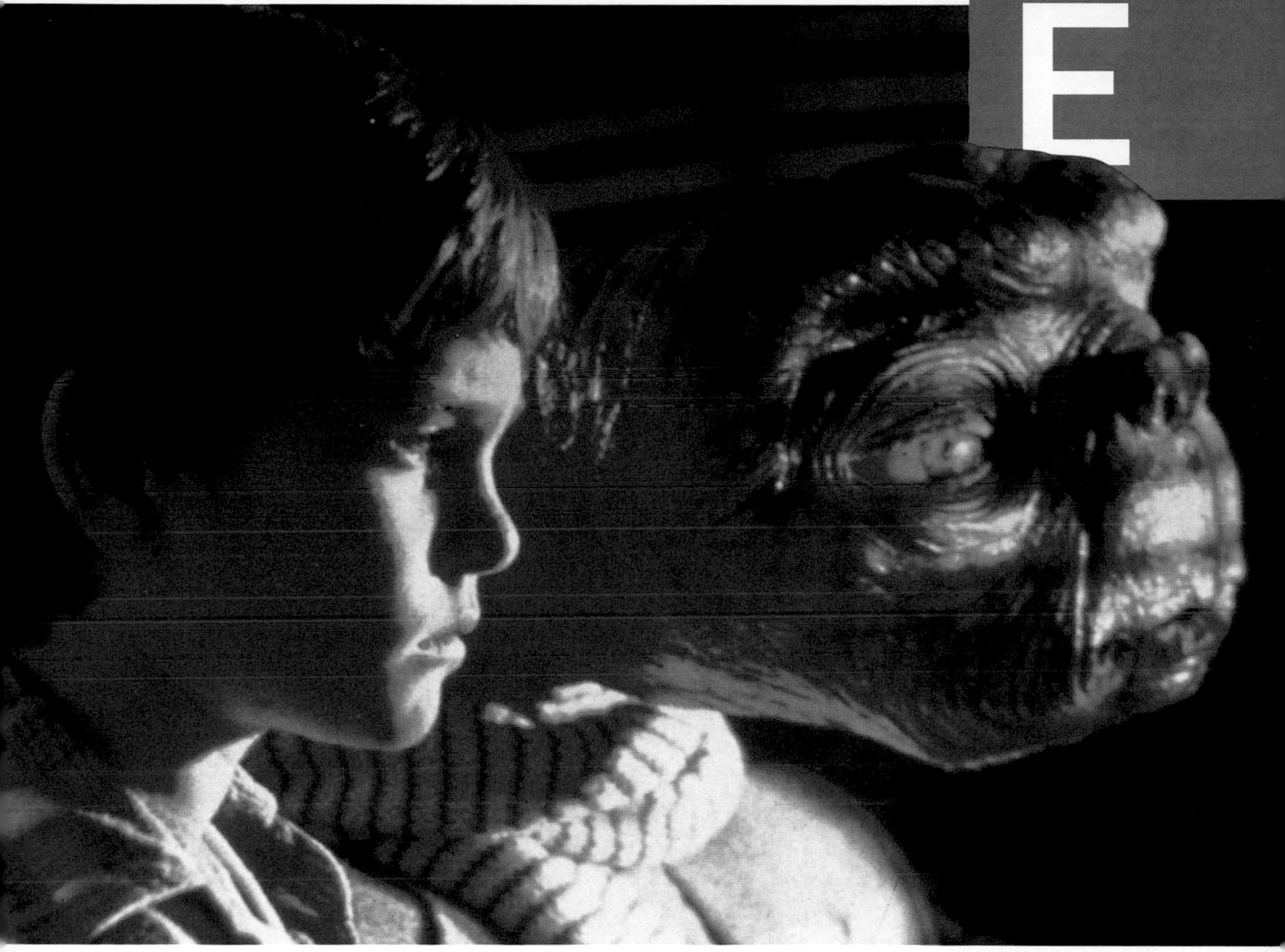

E

"**From** the very beginning, ET was a movie about my childhood – about my parents' divorce, although people haven't often seen that it's about divorce. My parents split up when I was 15 or 16 years old, and I needed a **special friend**, and had to use my **imagination** to take me to places that felt good – that helped me move beyond the problems my parents were having, and that ended our family as a whole. And thinking about that time, I thought, an extraterrestrial character would be the perfect springboard to purge the **pain** of your parents' **splitting up.**"

Steven Spielberg talking to Roger Ebert, Chicago Sun-Times, 18 December 1997

ET the Extra-Terrestrial 1982

ET the Extra-Terrestrial
★★★★★ U

1982 US Colour 109mins

Steven Spielberg's ode to aliens could also be seen as a tribute to all the loners of the world, as little ET, abandoned by his pot-bellied extra-terrestrial pals, has to cope on Earth until they can come back and rescue him. Luckily, he's befriended by an equally lonely little boy named Elliott, played by Henry Thomas, who proceeds to teach his alien chum how to talk, dress up in women's clothes and guzzle beer. Nineteen years since it was released, this is still a special, delightful adventure in which Spielberg manages to not only entertain young children, but also reach out to the child in all of us. Contains some mild swearing.

Henry Thomas Elliott • **Dee Wallace [Dee Wallace Stone]** Mary • **Peter Coyote** Keys • **Robert MacNaughton** Michael • **Drew Barrymore** Gertie • **K C Martel** Greg • **Sean Frye** Steve • **Tom Howell** Tyler • **Erika Eleniak** Pretty girl • **David O'Dell** Schoolboy • **Richard Swingler** Science teacher • **Frank Toth** Policeman • **Robert Barton** Ultrasound man • **Michael Darrell** Van driver • **Milt Kogan** Doctor
Director *Steven Spielberg*
Screenplay *Melissa Mathison*
Producer *Steven Spielberg, Kathleen Kennedy*
Cinematographer *Allen Daviau* • ***Music*** *John Williams* • ***Special effects*** *Carlo Rambaldi*

SFacts

Steven Spielberg designed ET's face by taking a photograph of a baby and superimposing scientist Albert Einstein's eyes and forehead on top. ET's voice was a combination of a heavy-smoking ex-schoolteacher and *Terms of Endearment* actress Debra Winger. The Walt Disney Studio passed on making the film because their research showed audiences wouldn't be interested in the subject matter.

Earth Angel ★★★ PG

1991 US Colour 90mins

The most fun you can have with this TV movie is to make a list of the films it has pillaged for its plot. Just to get you started, we'll give you *Back to the Future* and *The Curse of the Cat People*, but there are many more. Cathy Podewell is pleasing enough as the student who is sent back to Earth to sort out the complications that have arisen in the 30 years since she cheated on her boyfriend with the class swot. *Star Wars*'s Mark Hamill, and Roddy McDowall are among the guest stars keeping this undemanding piece of fluff in the air.

Cathy Podewell Angela • **Erik Estrada** Duke • **Cindy Williams** Judith • **Mark Hamill** Wayne Stein • **Roddy McDowall** Mr Tatum • **Rainbow Harvest** Cindy
Director *Joe Napolitano*
Screenplay *Nina Shengold*

The Earth Dies Screaming ★

1964 UK BW 66mins

Great title, boring movie. Veteran horror director Terence Fisher hit the bottom of the alien-invasion barrel with the first in his off-Hammer sci-fi trilogy that continued with the better *Island of Terror* and *Night of the Big Heat*. Test pilot Willard Parker returns to England and finds the entire population wiped out by robots that kill by touch and then re-animate their victims as zombies. Parker must find their power source that's controlled by beings from a distant planet. Hampered by a muddled script and poor characterisations, Fisher does manage to inject atmospheric menace into the village-under-siege sequence, but the rest of this workmanlike dud is a real waste of his worthy talents.

Willard Parker Jeff Nolan • **Virginia Field** Peggy Taggett • **Dennis Price** Quinn Taggett • **Vanda Godsell** Violet Courtland
Director *Terence Fisher*
Screenplay *Henry Cross [Harry Spalding]*

Earth: Final Conflict ★★ U PG 12

TV 1997- US/Can Colour

Based on an unfilmed pilot script penned by *Star Trek* creator Gene Roddenberry in the mid-seventies, this alien invasion saga sees early 21st-century Earth playing host to the mysterious and duplicitous Taelons. In its opening year, the show offers an intriguing and well-acted look at how the arrival of aliens might affect life on earth. But subsequent seasons' emphasis on action-adventure, coupled with a steady stream of inconsistent plot developments and abrupt cast changes, largely transform the series into a routine comic-book yarn. Throughout everything, though, the show's earth-shattering alien designs and ethereal music never fail to impress.

Kevin Kilner William Booone • **Robert Leeshock** Liam Kincaid • **Lisa Howard** Lili Marquette • **Jayne Heitmeyer** Renee Palmer • **Von Flores** Ronald Sandoval • **Richard Chevolleau** Augur • **David Hemblen** Jonathan Doorsl • **Leni Parker** Da'an • **Majel Barrett** Dr Belman
Created by *Gene Roddenberry*
Executive producer *Majel Roddenberry [Majel Barrett], David Kirschner*

Earth Girls Are Easy ★★★★ PG

1988 US Colour 100mins

In this enormously entertaining musical comedy, three randy aliens crash-land in LA and are given a guided tour through Planet Hollywood's craziness by two beautician Valley Girls. Geena Davis and Julie Brown, an American cult singer/comedian whose songs inspired this "Martian Beach Party", are terrific in a poppet of a popcorn movie full of bitchy one-liners and frothy fantasy. There's no attempt at a reality check in this hairsprayed *Lost in Space*, just breezy glitz, garish glamour and *Grease*-type songs in a contemporary trash setting. Fab.

Geena Davis Valerie Dale • **Jeff Goldblum** Mac • **Jim Carrey** Wiploc • **Damon Wayans** Zebo • **Julie Brown** Candy Pink • **Charles Rocket** Ted • **Michael McKean** Woody • **Larry Linville** Dr Bob
Director *Julien Temple*
Screenplay *Julie Brown, Charlie Coffey, Terrence E McNally*

Earth II ★★ U

1971 US Colour 93mins

This TV pilot was another attempt by American networks to cash in on the success of *Star Trek* – with mixed results. Gary Lockwood (*2001*) and Anthony Franciosa lead the 2,000 inhabitants of the *Earth II* space station, situated between the Earth and the Moon and declared an independent country. Peace is threatened when an atomic bomb is activated against the station. Predictable space opera with superior special effects, but little else to engage the mind – and there's no Mr Spock.

Gary Lockwood David Seville • **Scott Hylands** Jim Capa • **Hari Rhodes** Loren Huxley • **Tony Franciosa [Anthony Franciosa]** Frank Karger • **Mariette Hartley** Lisa Karger • **Gary Merrill** Walter Dietrich
Director *Tom Gries*
Screenplay *William Read Woodfield, Allan Balter*

Earth 2 ★★★ PG

TV 1994-95 US Col 1x120m; 20x60mins

A small group of late-22nd century colonists attempt to find a new home on an alien world in this acclaimed "planet trek". Produced by Steven Spielberg's Amblin Entertainment, the series successfully eschews high-concept science fantasy and mindless action in favour of believable science fiction and powerful human drama. Debrah Farentino admirably leads a strong line-up of engaging performers, which includes the likes of Clancy Brown, Sullivan Walker and Antonio Sabato Jr. The show's exceptional characterisation is matched by its superior production values and extremely effective use of New Mexico to depict the colonists' new world. Sadly, however, the series' slow-moving but rewarding storylines came to a cliffhanging end after just a season. The show inluded a two-part, feature-length pilot, *First Contact*, which made its UK debut on video.

Debrah Farentino Devon Adair • **Clancy Brown** John Danziger • **Antonio Sabato Jr** Alonzo Solace • **Jessica Steen** Dr Julia Heller • **John Gegenhuber** Morgan Martin • **Rebecca Gayheart** Bess Martin • **J Madison Wright** True Danziger • **Sullivan Walker** Yale • **Joey Zimmerman** Ulysses Adair

***Created by** Michael Duggan*

***Executive producer** Michael Duggan, Carol Flint, Mark Levin*

Earth vs the Flying Saucers ★★ U

1956 US BW 79mins

Commendable only for special-effects genius Ray Harryhausen's flying saucers trashing Washington DC's landmarks, this routine potboiler lifts most of its plot from HG Wells's *The War of the Worlds*, but does little else with its *Mars Attacks!* scenario. Hero scientist Hugh Marlowe, back in the nation's capital after surviving *The Day the Earth Stood Still*, slows down the plodding story even further by embarking on a sluggish romantic interlude with Joan Taylor. It just goes to show how little has changed in 30 years: modern blockbusters are all special effects and little story, too. For serial Harryhausen freaks only.

Hugh Marlowe Dr Russell A Marvin • **Joan Taylor** Carol Marvin • **Donald Curtis** Major Huglin • **Morris Ankrum** General Hanley • **John Zaremba** Professor Kanter • **Tom Browne Henry [Thomas Browne Henry]** Admiral Enright • **Grandon Rhodes** General Edmunds • **Larry Blake** Motorcycle officer • **Harry Lauter** Cutting • **Charles Evans** Dr Alberts • **Clark Howat** Sergeant Nash • **Frank Wilcox** Alfred Cassidy

***Director** Fred F Sears*

***Screenplay** George Worthing Yates, Raymond T Marcus [Bernard Gordon], from a story by Curt Siodmak, from the article "Flying Saucers from Outer Space" by Major Donald E Keyhoe*

Earth vs the Spider ★

1958 US BW 72mins

A high-school biology teacher finds a "dead" giant spider and puts it in the gym. But when the local rock 'n' roll band starts practising for the prom, the mutation wakes up and rampages around town sucking the vital fluids from terrified teenagers – rather like what cult schlock director Bert I Gordon has done to his favourite "oversized thing" theme! Sounds trashy fun – and it is for about five minutes – but inept Gordon soon gets wound up in a tangled web of his own when the dreadful special effects (even by rock-bottom fifties standards) and awful performances lose their camp lustre.

Edward Kemmer Mr Kingman • **June Kenny** Carol Flynn • **Gene Persson** Mike Simpson • **Gene Roth** Sheriff Cagle • **Hal Torey** Mr Simpson • **June Jocelyn** Mrs Flynn

***Director** Bert I Gordon*

***Screenplay** Laszlo Gorog*

Earthbound ★

1981 US Colour 94mins

Pandemonium breaks out in the town of Gold Rush when a disabled spaceship lands in its midst and the humanoid cargo seeks out grandfather Burl Ives for help. Evil government agent Joseph Campanella is convinced the aliens are anything but benevolent in this tiresome retread of science-fiction clichés without an iota of style to differentiate it from the rest of its Z-movie pack.

Burl Ives Ned Anderson • **Christopher Connelly** Zef • **Meredith MacRae** Lara • **Joseph Campanella** Conrad • **Todd Porter** Tommy • **Marc Gilpin** Dalem

***Director** James L Conway*

***Screenplay** Michael Fisher*

***Producer** James L Conway*

Earthsearch ★★★

Radio 1981 UK 10x30mins

In James Follet's *Star Trek* meets *2001: a Space Odyssey*, four orphaned children, born in space and cared for by androids and sinister sentient "guardian angel" computers, go on a quest to rediscover the Earth their grandparents left more than 100 years earlier. But when Sean Arnold (pompous, by-the-book commander), Amanda Murrey (sensible science officer), Haydn Wood (impetuous creative engineer) and Kathryn Hurlbutt (flightly astronomer) reach the solar system, they discover that the entire planet has disappeared – removed to an undisclosed location more than 500,000 years earlier. Turns out that really one million years have passed (near speed-of-light travel has that effect). So they begin on a quest to find their spiritual home, encountering pockets of surviving humanity with odd, and occasionally deadly, cultures along the way. The adventure in space rattles along well enough, with the appeal of the well-drawn main characters overcoming the occasional lack of originality and awkward dialogue. Available on audio-cassette.

Sean Arnold Commander Telson • **Amanda Murray** Sharna • **Kathryn Hurlbutt** Astra • **Haydn Wood** Darv • **Sonia Fraser** Angel One • **Gordon Reid** Angel Two

***Director** Glyn Dearman*

***Written by** James Follett*

Earthsearch II ★★★

Radio 1982 UK 10x30mins

Set four years after the events in *Earthsearch*, this sequel finds the foursome of Telson, Sharna, Darv and Astra (Sean Arnold, Amanda Murray, Haydn Wood and Kathryn Hurlbutt) forced to return to the spaceship *Challenger* to resume their search for the missing planet Earth. The evil organic free-willed computer "angels" (Sonia Fraser and Gordon Reid) are as manipulative as ever, but the intended comic-relief android Tidy (voiced by David Gooderson) irritates, rather than amuses. Still, those who enjoyed the dynamics of the first half will enjoy the resolution of the second. Available on audio-cassette.

Sean Arnold Commander Telson • **Amanda Murray** Sharna • **Haydn Wood** Darv • **Kathryn Hurlbutt** Astra • **Sonia Fraser** Angel One • **Gordon Reid** Angel Two • **David Gooderson** Tidy • **Stephen Garlick** George • **Michael Maloney** Bran

***Director** Glyn Dearman*

***Written by** James Follett*

Eat and Run ★★★ 15

1986 US Colour 80mins

This spoof on the "creature features" of the fifties, those sci-fi cheapies which went for the bizarre with an earnestness that now seems camp, revolves around a king-sized alien whose favourite food on Earth turns out to be Italian – or rather, Italians. This unpleasant eating habit is discovered by Irish cop Mickey McSorely (Ron Silver), but not surprisingly nobody believes him. Certain humorous interludes are just too slack to hit home, but Silver, a much underused actor, acquits himself well at the centre of this amiable nonsense.

Ron Silver Mickey McSorely • **Sharon Schlarth** Judge Cheryl Cohen • **R L Ryan** Murray Creature • **John F Fleming** Police captain • **Derek Murcott** Sorely McSorely • **Robert Silver** Pusher • **Mimi Cecchini** Grandmother • **Tony Moundroukas** Zepoli kid • **Frank Nastasi** Pick-up driver

***Director** Christopher Hart*

***Screenplay** Stan Hart, Christopher Hart*

Ebirah, Horror of the Deep

★★ U

1966 Jap Colour 83mins

Or *Godzilla versus the Sea Monster*, as it was known everywhere else. In his sixth screen outing, the king of the monsters and his one-time arch enemy, Mothra, hiss and make up to battle the evil giant lobster Ebirah, being used as a p(r)awn by the nasty Red Bamboo gang seeking world domination. Typical Japanese monster fare featuring cardboard mayhem, laughable special effects and failed comedy sees Godzilla play football. Total trash, naturally. Absolutely unmissable, of course. Japanese dialogue dubbed into English.

Akira Takarada • **Toru Watanabe** • **Hideo Sunazuka** • **Kumi Mizuno**
Director *Jun Fukuda*
Screenplay *Shinichi Sekizawa*

Eerie, Indiana ★★★★ U PG

TV 1991-1992 US Colour 19x30mins

When his family moves to Eerie, Indiana, young Marshall Teller finds himself living in the weirdest and wackiest town in the world. With the help of his friend Simon, Marshall starts to collect evidence of Eerie's crazy goings-on, and encounters everything from ghosts and aliens to time warps and alternate realities. An incredibly inventive and wonderfully whimsical blend of *Twin Peaks* and *The Twilight Zone*, this half-hour sci-fi comedy-drama is the home of magical entertainment. The show's concept is cleverly realised, while Omri Katz and Justin Shenkarow are delightfully wide-eyed as the show's central characters. Disappointingly, the serieswas cancelled after a brief but brilliant one-season run, and later spawned an inferior spin-off, 1998's *Eerie, Indiana: The Other Dimension*. Set in an alternate universe and featuring a new cast, the show followed the unmemorable adventures of Marshall and Simon's doppelgangers.

Omri Katz Marshall Teller • **Justin Shenkarow** Simon Holmes • **Mary-Margaret Humes** Marilyn Teller • **Francis Guinan** Edgar Teller • **Juli Condra** Syndi Teller
Created by *Karl Schaefer, José Rivera*
Executive producer *Karl Schaefer*

SFacts

The population of Eerie, Indiana was 16,661.

Egghead's Robot ★★ U

1970 UK Colour 56mins

Once upon a time, bodies like the Children's Film Foundation guaranteed a steady flow of entertainment for younger viewers. These days, Hollywood seems to have cornered the market in children's movies and British film-makers have given up the ghost. So, gone are amiable romps like this one, which feels like a *Beano* strip come to life. A young Keith Chegwin stars as the son of inventor Richard Wattis, who borrows a lookalike robot to do his chores and get him out of all manner of scrapes. However, despite Roy Kinnear pantomiming as a park keeper, this will seem painfully twee to today's pre-teen sophisticates.

Keith Chegwin Egghead Wentworth • **Jeffrey Chegwin** Eric • **Kathryn Dawe** Elspeth • **Roy Kinnear** Park keeper • **Richard Wattis** Paul Wentworth • **Patricia Routledge** Mrs Wentworth
Director *Milo Lewis*
Screenplay *Leif Saxon*

Electra ★★ 18

1995 US Colour 86mins

Possibly the wackiest of Shannon Tweed's many erotic thrillers, this is an absolutely barmy mix of soft-core porn and sci-fi silliness. Tweed plays a frustrated widow whose stepson holds the key to a sexually transmittable formula for creating the master race. It's all utter tosh, of course, although in the company of charisma-free unknowns such as Joe Tab and Sten Eirik, Tweed positively shines, even when she's got her clothes on.

Shannon Tweed Lorna Duncan/Electra • **Joe Tab** Billy Duncan • **Sten Eirik** Marcus Roach • **Katie Griffin** Mary Anne Parker
Director *Julian Grant*
Screenplay *Lou Aguilar, Damian Lee*

The Element of Crime ★★★★ 15

1984 Den Colour 103mins

Shouded in post-apocalyptic sepia, Lars von Trier's debut feature is a ragbag of visual allusions to everything from German Expressionism and Hollywood *noir* to the self-reflexivity of the *Nouvelle Vague* and the grim poetry of Andrei Tarkovsky. It's possible to play detective while watching this thriller, looking for the postmodernist references. But shamus Michael Elphick's quest to unmask the mathematically-minded serial perpetrator of the "Lotto murders" makes for compelling viewing. With Esmond Knight leading a first-rate multinational ensemble, this was rightly hailed as the work of a master-in-waiting.

Michael Elphick Fisher • **Esmond Knight** Osborne • **Me Me Lai** Kim • **Jerold Wells** Police Chief Kramer • **Ahmed El Shenawi** Therapist • **Astrid Henning-Jensen** Osborne's housekeeper • **Janos Hersko** Coroner • **Stig Larsson** Coroner's assistant • **Lars von Trier** Schmuck of Ages
Director *Lars von Trier*
Screenplay *Lars von Trier, Niels Vorsel*

Eliminators ★★ 15

1986 Colour 95mins

A minor entry in Charles Band Empire Pictures canon, but still sharper than most other straight-to-video fodder. Writers Danny Bilson and Paul DeMeo, who scripted *Trancers* and *Zone Troopers*, once again play fast and loose with genres, in which a crippled android collects an eclectic band (including a pet robot and a martial arts expert) to stop an evil genius who wants to start messing around with time. Not quite as funny as Bilson and DeMeo's other two flicks for Empire, but it bustles along amusingly enough. Denise Crosby, who provides the glamour, will be familiar to Trekkie fans – as well as appearing in *Next Generation*, she was also the star of the recent computer game *Star Trek Armada*.

Andrew Prine Harry Fontana • **Denise Crosby** Nora Hunter • **Patrick Reynolds** Mandroid • **Conan Lee** Kuji • **Roy Dotrice** Abbott Reeves • **Peggy Mannix** Bayou Betty
Director *Peter Manoogian*
Screenplay *Paul DeMeo, Danny Bilson*

Elves ★ 18

1989 US Colour 89mins

The credits indicate the town of Colorado Springs lent a generous hand to this videotaped backyard production, although its perverse nature makes one ask why. What there was for the budget seems to have been almost entirely spent on star Dan Haggerty, possibly explaining why there is only one stiff animatronic elf, despite the plural title. Haggerty plays a small-town department store Santa investigating his predecessor's castration, with plenty of Nazis, incest, rape, drugs, and other questionable elements popping up along the way, although played out in an almost cheerful manner.

Dan Haggerty • **Deanna Lund** • **Julie Austin** • **Borah Silver**
Director *Jeffrey Mandel*
Screenplay *Mike Griffin, Bruce Taylor, Jeff Mandel*

Embryo ★★ 15

1976 US Colour 103mins

Frankenstein rides again in director Ralph Nelson's stylish but pointless seventies update. Rock Hudson gives one of his worst performances as the scientist who invents a hormone enabling fetuses to grow rapidly to maturity outside the womb. When he develops gorgeous Barbara Carrera, she turns into a homicidal maniac looking for the formula to stop her accelerated ageing. Embarrassing dialogue – Rock teaching his artificial creation about sex and mathematics – and nauseating special effects will further test the patience of the initially interested.

Rock Hudson Dr Paul Holliston • **Diane Ladd** Martha • **Barbara Carrera** Victoria • **Roddy McDowall** Riley • **Ann Schedeen** Helen • **John Elerick** Gordon
Director *Ralph Nelson*
Screenplay *Anita Doohan, Jack W Thomas*

Empire of the Ants ★★

1977 US Colour 84mins

How the Pest was Won! Supposedly based on a story by HG Wells, this tacky tale of tepid terror is just another poverty-row, giant-insect tale from schlock director Bert I Gordon, more famous now for featuring a pre-*Dynasty* Joan Collins up to her designer khakis in mud fighting off laughably phoney mutant ants. She's the head swindler of a housing development consortium on a resort island where radiation waste has been dumped. In between the slipshod special effects, the actors bicker a lot while trying to escape the boring menace. Camp, if nothing else.

Joan Collins Marilyn Fryser • **Robert Lansing** Dan Stokely • **John David Carson** Joe Morrison • **Albert Salmi** Sheriff Art Kincade • **Jacqueline Scott** Margaret Ellis
Director *Bert I Gordon*
Screenplay *Jack Turley, from a story by Bert I Gordon, from a story by HG Wells*

Encounter at Raven's Gate ★★★★ 15

1988 Aus Colour 85mins [video]

This stand-out thriller involves a paroled ex-convict, his brother, the brother's bored wife and the strange phenomena that occur at Raven's Gate farm – perhaps the work of visiting evil aliens. Director Rolf De Heer allows the viewer's imagination to go into overdrive thanks to creepy photography and evocative use of sound – both of which create more edge-of-seat menace than using cheap UFO effects or rubber monsters. Tense, engrossing and packed with unusual incident (the sky raining dead birds), this atmospheric gem is a fine example of low-budget success.

Steven Vidler Eddie Cleary • **Celine Griffin** Rachel Cleary • **Ritchie Singer** Richard • **Vincent Gil** Felix Skinner • **Saturday Rosenberg** Annie • **Terry Camilleri** Dr Hemmings • **Max Cullen** Sergeant Taylor
Director *Rolf De Heer*
Screenplay *Marc Rosenberg, Rolf De Heer, James Michael Vernon*

The End of the World ★★

1930 Fr BW 91mins

Abel Gance's politically dubious conflagration movie was an ambitious project which clearly failed, and not just because the producers re-edited the footage without Gance's consent. It's DeMille meets the Comet, with civilisation descending into sordid debauchery as the natural order is shattered by a series of spectacular disasters. Away from the chaos, scientist Victor Francen strives to find a way to deflect the approaching projectile, while his eccentric brother (Gance) spreads a penitential message that's both messianic and fascistic. It's attention-grabbing fare, but deeply imperfect. In French with English subtitles.

Abel Gance Jean Novalic • **Victor Francen** Martial Novalic • **Georges Colin** Werster • **Colette Darfeuil** Geneviève de Murcie • **Sylvie Grenade [Sylvie Gance]** Isabelle Boilin
Director *Abel Gance*
Screenplay *Abel Gance, André Lang, from a story by Camille Flammarion*

End of the World ★

1977 US Colour 86mins

Space invaders use a Californian convent as a base of operations in their plot to blow up the Earth because mankind is polluting the universe. Christopher Lee lends a modicum of dignity to the incredibly tacky proceedings as a Catholic priest and his extra-terrestrial double who is controlling the murderous alien nuns. Tedious junk with a has-been cast, including Sue Lyon (*Lolita*).

Christopher Lee Father Pergado/Zindar • **Sue Lyon** Sylvia Boran • **Kirk Scott** Professor Andrew Boran • **Dean Jagger** Ray Collins • **Lew Ayres** Beckerman • **Macdonald Carey** John Davis • **Liz Ross** Sister Patrizia
Director *John Hayes*
Screenplay *Frank Ray Perilli*

Endless Descent ★

1990 Sp Colour 86mins

The title says it all. An attempt by Spanish hack director Juan Piquer Simon to match the thrilling sense of wonder contained in *The Abyss* doesn't have the budget, special effects know-how or acting smarts to carry it off. Nuclear submarine inventor Jack Scalia and Captain R Lee Ermey dive into uncharted seas to find out why prototype sub Siren 1 vanished in the deep. It turns out there's a giant underwater air pocket in a rift populated by multi-tentacled sea creatures and humanoid fish which are the result of a genetic engineering experiment. Unfathomable junk with soggy suspense and damp drama.

Jack Scalia Wick Hayes • **R Lee Ermey** Capt Randall Phillips • **Ray Wise** Robbins • **Deborah Adair** Nina Crowley • **Emilio Linder** Philippe • **John Toles Bey** Skeets
Director *Juan Piquer Simon*
Screenplay *David Coleman, from a story by Juan Piquer Simon, Mark Klein*
Special effects *Colin Arthur, Basilio Cortijo*

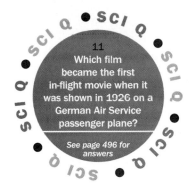

SCI Q

11
Which film became the first in-flight movie when it was shown in 1926 on a German Air Service passenger plane?

See page 496 for answers

Enemy Mine ★★★★ 15

1985 US Colour 89mins [video]

Star Wars meets *Love Thy Neighbour* as Earthman Dennis Quaid and lizard-like alien Louis Gossett Jr (virtually unrecognisable under very impressive scaly make-up) crash-land on an unknown planet and learn that co-operation equals survival. Wolfgang Petersen – director of *Outbreak* and *In the Line of Fire*, among others – makes this racial tolerance plea in outer space disguise a satisfying blend of action spills and emotional thrills. It touches both the brain and heart, remaining true to its pulp science-fiction roots while never being anything less than engrossing entertainment. Contains some violence and swearing.

Dennis Quaid Willis Davidge • **Louis Gossett Jr** Jeriba Shigan • **Brion James** Stubbs • **Richard Marcus** Arnold • **Carolyn McCormick** Morse • **Bumper Robinson** Zammis • **Jim Mapp** Old Drac • **Lance Kerwin** Wooster • **Scott Kraft** Jonathan • **Andy Geer** Bates • **Lou Michaels** Wilson • **Henry Stolow** Cates • **Herb Andress** Hoffer
Director *Wolfgang Petersen*
Screenplay *Edward Khmara, from a story by Barry Longyear*

Ernest Goes to School ★ PG

1994 US Colour 85mins

Jim Varney's unloveable creation Ernest P Worrell gets a dose of learning in yet another instalment in the dim series. Forced to return to the classroom to finish his high school diploma, the lowly janitor is transformed into an intellectual with the help of two mad scientists. However, it's not long before the whole school is plunged into chaos. Even by the low standards of the franchise, this is really feeble stuff.

Jim Varney Ernest P Worrell • **Linda Kash** Gerta • **Bill Byrge** Bobby • **Kevin McNulty** Axwell • **Corrine Koslo** Miss Flugal • **Duncan Fraser** Coach Decker • **Jason Michas** Donald • **Sarah Chalk [Sarah Chalke]** Maisy

Director/Screenplay *Coke Sams*

Escape from LA ★★ 15

1996 US Colour 96mins DVD

In John Carpenter's shambolic, big-budget sequel to his far superior *Escape from New York*, Kurt Russell returns as macho hero Snake Plissken, who this time around is blackmailed into scouring the City of Angels for a doomsday device stolen by the president's daughter. Apart from the witty, face-lifted zombie section, this inept and unexciting rehash lacks the sharp black comedy of the original. Lacklustre special effects don't help either, and this empty vessel of worn-out science-fiction ideas must go down as a major disappointment from the usually reliable genre maestro.

Kurt Russell Snake Plissken • **A J Langer** Utopia • **Steve Buscemi** "Map to the Stars" Eddie • **George Corraface [Georges Corraface]** Cuervo Jones • **Stacy Keach** Malloy • **Michelle Forbes** Brazen • **Pam Grier** Hershe • **Jeff Imada** Saigon Shadow • **Cliff Robertson** President • **Peter Fonda** Pipeline

Director *John Carpenter*

Screenplay *John Carpenter, Debra Hill, Kurt Russell, from characters created by John Carpenter, Nick Castle*

Escape from New York ★★★ 15

1981 US Colour 94mins DVD

Sullen Kurt Russell impersonates Clint Eastwood in director John Carpenter's tough futuristic western that never surpasses or fulfils the ingenuity of its premise – Manhattan Island as a maximum security prison where the president's plane has crashed. Closely resembling *Assault on Precinct 13* in tone and plot dynamics, it's certainly Carpenter's slickest looking film, with the presence of Lee Van Cleef reinforcing its Sergio Leone associations. But, despite a marvellous opening sequence, this slice of escapism often disappoints, although it still rates higher than the poor 1996 sequel *Escape from LA*.

Kurt Russell Snake Plissken • **Lee Van Cleef** Bob Hauk • **Donald Pleasence** President • **Isaac Hayes** Duke of New York • **Adrienne Barbeau** Maggie • **Harry Dean Stanton** "Brain" • **Ernest Borgnine** Cabby

Director *John Carpenter*

Screenplay *John Carpenter, Nick Castle*

Escape from Planet Earth ★

1967 US Colour 83mins

A rocket crew, led by *Incredible Shrinking Man* star Grant Williams, are on their way to Venus when earth is destroyed in an atomic war started by Red China. After much hot-tempered arguing, macho flirting and stalking through corridors, they decide to restart the human race somewhere else in space. A comatose cosmic caper fleshed out with stock footage from disaster documentaries and the Japanese *Warning from Space* (1956) and directed by schlock maestro Lee (*Superman and the Mole People*) Sholem. Completely devoid of style or sense, this was made in 1967 but not released until 1972, three years before the supposed 1975 nuclear holocaust depicted here on a papier mâché globe on a string.

Grant Williams Major Kurt Mason • **Henry Wilcoxon** Dr Christopher Perry • **Mala Powers** Major Georgianna Bronski

Director *Lee Sholem*

Escape from the Planet of the Apes ★★★★ PG

1971 US Colour 93mins

The third of the popular movie series sees Roddy McDowall and Kim Hunter land in present-day California after surviving the catastrophe that ended *Beneath the Planet of the Apes*. This is very much a film of two halves, the first being an amusing collection of observations on modern life, as seen through the eyes of the more advanced apes. The second half, however, is much darker, with the arrogant and fearful humans being driven to unspeakable cruelty to protect their future. An intelligent script, unassuming direction and solid performances add up to a fine film.

Roddy McDowall Cornelius • **Kim Hunter** Zira • **Bradford Dillman** Dr Lewis Dixon • **Natalie Trundy** Dr Stephanie Branton • **Eric Braeden** Dr Otto Hasslein • **William Windom** The President • **Sal Mineo** Milo

Director *Don Taylor*

Screenplay *Paul Dehn, from characters created by Pierre Boulle*

The Escape of RD 7 ★★★

TV 1961 UK BW 5x45mins

This BBC TV thriller from 1961 deals with genetically-engineered plagues and concerns the conflict between conscientious but cracked scientist Dr Anna Hastings (Barbara Murray) and Machiavellian but smooth financier Patrice Constantine (Patrick Cargill) over control of a disease designed to wipe out plague rats, but which might well pose a threat to humanity.

Barbara Murray Dr Anna Hastings • **Jennifer Wright** Peggy Butler • **Ellen Pollock** Dr Mary Carter • **Derek Waring** David Cardosa • **Roger Croucher** Peter Warner • **Patrick Cargill** Patrice Constantine

Written by *Thomas Clarke, from an idea by James Parish*

Producer *James Ormerod*

Escape to Witch Mountain ★★★★ U

1975 US Colour 90mins

With actors such as Ray Milland, Eddie Albert and Donald Pleasence treating this Disney children's movie as seriously as any other adult-themed movie they might tackle, the result, with a well-written narrative by Robert Malcolm Young, succeeds in being at the same time speedy, scary and sentimental. The two clairvoyant youngsters soon seem to get accustomed to being pursued, and Milland is oozingly malevolent as the villain who wants to use their powers for his own nefarious ends. Bette Davis was to loom alarmingly in the follow-up movie *Return from Witch Mountain*, but this has plenty of thrills to be going on with for grown-ups as well as children.

Kim Richards Tia Malone • **Ike Eisenmann** Tony Malone • **Ray Milland** Aristotle Bolt • **Eddie Albert** Jason O'Day • **Donald Pleasence** Lucas Deranian • **Walter Barnes** Sheriff Purdy • **Reta Shaw** Mrs Grindley • **Denver Pyle** Uncle Bene • **Alfred Ryder** Astrologer • **Lawrence Montaigne** Ubermann • **Terry Wilson** Biff Jenkins

Director *John Hough*

Screenplay *Robert Malcolm Young, from the novel by Alexander Key*

Escape to Witch Mountain ★★

1995 US Colour 87mins

John Hough's 1975 adaptation of Alexander Key's exciting children's novel was a hard act to follow, but Disney has made a fair fist of this TV-movie remake. Writer/director Peter Rader has kept the best of Robert Malcolm Young's original screenplay; Robert Vaughn replaces Ray Milland as the evil millionaire seeking to exploit the mystical powers of a pair of orphaned twins. The youngsters are played by Elisabeth Moss and Erik Von Detten – interestingly, the latter provides the voice of vicious neighbour Sid in *Toy Story*. Brad Dourif, Henry Gibson and Vincent Shiavelli are among the solid supporting cast.

Robert Vaughn Edward Bolt • **Elisabeth Moss** Anna • **Erik Von Detten** Danny • **Lynne Moody** Lindsay Brown • **Perrey Reeves** Zoe Moon • **Lauren Tom** Claudia Ford • **Vincent Schiavelli** Waldo Fudd • **Henry Gibson** Professor Ravetch • **Sam Corrigan** Xander • **Bobby Motown** Skeeto • **Brad Dourif** Luther
Director *Peter Rader*
Screenplay *Peter Rader, from the film by Robert Malcolm Young, from the novel by Alexander Key*

Escapement ★★

1958 UK BW 77mins

Also known under the more lurid title of *The Electronic Monster*, this underwhelming British thriller has Rod Cameron investigating an actor's death at a clinic specialising in electronic hypnosis. Barely mesmerising, it was one of those zero-budget British movies that gave refuge to B-picture stars from Hollywood, in this case Mary Murphy and former Fred MacMurray stand-in, Cameron.

Rod Cameron Keenan • **Mary Murphy** Ruth • **Meredith Edwards** Dr Maxwell • **Peter Illing** Zekon • **Kay Callard** Laura Maxwell • **Carl Jaffe** Dr Erich Hoff
Director *Montgomery Tully*
Screenplay *Charles Eric Maine, J MacLaren-Ross, from the novel by Charles Eric Maine*

Eve of Destruction ★ 18

1991 US Colour 95mins [video]

This female version of *The Terminator* features an eye-catching performance from Dutch star Renée Soutendijk as a scientist who creates a cyborg in her own image, which then runs amok with a thermonuclear bomb in its womb. Gregory Hines plays the cop tracking her down, while Duncan Gibbins directs with some verve. However, the interesting premise of a robotic doppelganger acting out its maker's sexual fantasies and fears isn't sufficiently explored amid the obligatory explosions and fifth-rate effects. The makers thoughtfully fill the final 15 minutes with scenes of ticking clocks, so at least you know how much longer you have to suffer.

Gregory Hines Jim McQuade • **Renée Soutendijk** Dr Eve Simmons/Eve VIII • **Michael Greene** General Curtis • **Kurt Fuller** Schneider • **John M Jackson** Peter Arnold • **Loren Haynes** Steve the robot
Director *Duncan Gibbins*
Screenplay *Duncan Gibbins, Yale Udoff*

Event Horizon ★★★ 18

1997 US/UK Colour 91mins [video] DVD

A messy (in more ways than one) but enjoyable slice of space splatter from British director Paul Anderson. Named after the area of space around a black hole beyond which matter seemingly disappears, the *Event Horizon* here is an experimental spacecraft that has been missing for years but has just reappeared off Neptune. A rescue team, led by Laurence Fishburne, is sent to retrieve it, but it soon becomes apparent that it's in the grip of a malevolent force. Fishburne, Sam Neill, Joely Richardson and Sean Pertwee bring some class to the B-movie dialogue, and Anderson delivers some eye-poppingly nasty sequences that will please horror fans. Contains swearing and disturbing scenes.

Laurence Fishburne Miller • **Sam Neill** Weir • **Kathleen Quinlan** Peters • **Joely Richardson** Starck • **Richard T Jones** Cooper • **Jack Noseworthy** Justin • **Jason Isaacs** DJ • **Sean Pertwee** Smith
Director *Paul Anderson*
Screenplay *Philip Eisner*
Producer *Lawrence Gordon, Lloyd Levin, Jeremy Bolt* • ***Executive producer*** *Nick Gillott*

SFacts

The striking interiors of the *Event Horizon* vessel were modelled on Notre Dame cathedral, complete with cruciform motif.

Evil of Frankenstein ★★

1964 UK Colour 86mins

The third of Hammer's *Frankenstein* sequels and the least interesting of all – although, because it was made for Universal, it's the only one that could use their copyrighted Boris Karloff monster look. Peter Cushing lends his usual conviction to the mad doctor part, this time bringing his brain-damaged creation back to life with the help of a mesmerist. But the crooked Zoltan (Peter Woodthorpe) hypnotises the monster into carrying out his vengeful crimes. Lumbering direction by Freddie Francis matches the gait of New Zealand wrestler Kiwi Kingston as the infamous bolted one in this stagy outing.

Peter Cushing Baron Frankenstein • **Peter Woodthorpe** Zoltan • **Sandor Eles** Hans • **Kiwi Kingston** Creature • **Duncan Lamont** Chief of Police • **Katy Wild** Beggar girl • **David Hutcheson** Burgomaster • **Caron Gardner** Burgomaster's wife
Director *Freddie Francis*
Screenplay *John Elder*

Evolution ★★★ PG

2001 US Colour 101mins

Ivan Reitman's lightweight but amiably daft science-fiction comedy is pitched as *Ghostbusters* (an earlier Reitman smash) meets *Men in Black*. Though it shares those films' laid-back performances, tongue-in-cheek approach and cute special-effects creations, it lacks some of their wit and sparkle. Fortunately, it does boast the considerable comic charm of David Duchovny and Orlando Jones (as college professors), Seann William Scott (as an aspiring fireman) and Julianne Moore (as a government scientist), while the loose Darwinian concept allows for an entertainingly mad menagerie of regenerated digital creatures. However, it says a lot about the evolution of sci-fi cinema since the fifties that Reitman's return to the genre is so reliant on computer-generated.

David Duchovny Dr Ira Kran • **Orlando Jones** Harry Block • **Seann William Scott** Wayne • **Julianne Moore** Allison • **Ted Levine** General Woodman • **Ethan Suplee** Deke • **Katharine Towne** Nadine • **Dan Aykroyd** General Lewis
Director *Ivan Reitman*
Screenplay *David Diamond, David Weissman, Don Jakoby, from a story by Don Jakoby*

Evolver ★★ 15

1994 US Colour 87mins [video]

A scrapped military project is turned into a virtual reality game named "Evolver" in director Mark Rosman's cheap TV movie. Ethan Randall plays the top laser tag champion in America who gets the chance to play it internationally, only to end up fighting for survival. A predictable science-fiction potboiler from one-time genre hopeful Rosman, director of *The House on Sorority Row*.

Ethan Randall [Ethan Embry] Kyle Baxter • **John DeLancie** Russell Bennett • **Cindy Pickett** Melanie Baxter • **Paul Dooley** Jerry Briggs • **Cassidy Rae** Jamie Saunders • **Nassira Nicola** Ali Baxter • **Chance Quinn** Zach Renzetti • **Tim Griffin** Dwight • **Michael Champion** Squad leader • **Eugene Williams** Tiny • **Jamie Marsh** Ace
Director *Mark Rosman*
Screenplay *Mark Rosman, Manny Coto*

eXistenZ ★★★★★ 15

1999 Can/UK Colour 96mins

This "body horror" shocker from cult director David Cronenberg confidently expands on the themes of his disturbing 1982 feature *Videodrome*. Jennifer Jason Leigh invents a game system – "eXistenZ" – that taps so deeply into users' fears and desires that it blurs the boundaries between escapism and reality. Security guard Jude Law is drawn into playing the game with its creator as he attempts to find out who is behind an assassination attempt on her life. Nothing is what it seems in this futuristic thriller in which games consoles are inserted directly into the spinal column, gristle guns fire human teeth instead of bullets and two-headed reptiles roam the wilds. Fiendishly clever and brilliantly audacious, this flight of surreal fantasy uses Cronenberg's patented images to disturbing effect – the virtual reality games industry made flesh. Contains violence and swearing.

Jennifer Jason Leigh Allegra Geller • **Jude Law** Ted Pikul • **Ian Holm** Kiri Vinokur • **Don McKellar** Yevgeny Nourish • **Callum Keith Rennie** Hugo Carlaw • **Sarah Polley** Merle • **Robert A Silverman** D'Arcy Nadler • **Christopher Eccleston** Levi • **Willem Dafoe** Gas
Director/Screenplay *David Cronenberg*
Producer *Robert Lantos, Andra Hamori, David Cronenberg*

Expect No Mercy ★ 18

1995 Can Colour 90mins

Wolf Larson plays Warbeck, the kind of megalomaniac who runs one of those high-tech labs/fight schools. Of course, no one running such places is ever up to any good, so it falls to Federal agents Billy Blanks and Jalal Merhi to go undercover and save the day. When not involved in countless fight sequences, Blanks depends on his undeniable screen presence, while Merhi's strong accent makes him sound goofy. The attempt to portray virtual reality and high-tech on a small budget make the movie come across as one big eyesore.

Billy Blanks Justin Vanier • **Wolf Larson** Warbeck • **Laurie Holden** Vicki • **Jalal Merhi** Eric • **Brett Halsey** Bromfield
Director *Zale Dalen*
Screenplay *J Stephen Maunder*

Explorers ★★★ U

1985 US Colour 104mins

This is a minor entry in the Joe Dante canon, but an amusing family yarn all the same. A pre-fame Ethan Hawke and River Phoenix team up with Jason Presson as a trio of kids who build their own spacecraft and set off on the adventure of a lifetime. The youngsters are uniformly excellent and the tone is refreshingly unpatronising and unsentimental. Kids will love it, while adults will enjoy spotting the in-jokes Dante could not resist including.

Ethan Hawke Ben Crandall • **River Phoenix** Wolfgang Müller • **Jason Presson** Darren Woods • **Amanda Peterson** Lori Swenson • **Dick Miller** Charlie Drake
Director *Joe Dante*
Screenplay *Eric Luke*

The Eye Creatures ★

1965 US Colour 80mins

Invasion of the Saucer Men (1957) was pretty bad in the terrorised teens department, but skid row director Larry Buchanan's uncredited remake (commissioned by AIP to complete a TV package) manages to hit absolute rock bottom. John Ashley is the heroic rebel who saves America from invasion by aliens merely by turning on his car headlights. *Invasion* at least had fun monsters, whereas this shoddy, snail-paced shocker uses extras in ill-fitting suits sporting lots of eyeball sockets. Hopeless and worthless.

John Ashley Stan Kenyon • **Cynthia Hull** Susan Rogers • **Warren Hammack** Lt Robertson • **Chet David** Mike Lawrence
Director *Larry Buchanan*
Screenplay *Robert J Burney, Al Martin*

Eyes without a Face ★★★★★ 18

1959 Fr/It BW 86mins

This is one of the most haunting horror films ever made. Director Georges Franju made his name with a series of inspired documentary shorts, and it's the realism of his approach that makes this "poetic fantasy" so unnerving. There's nothing of the hammy Hollywood mad scientist in Pierre Brasseur, as he and assistant Alida Valli resort to murder in order to rebuild the face of his daughter, Edith Scob. This is cold and calculating science, simultaneously on the verge of breakthrough and the breakdown of morality. Franju's control of atmosphere is masterly, Eugen Schüfftan's photography is outstanding, and Auguste Capelier deserves a mention for designing Scob's unforgettable mask. In French with English subtitles. Contains violence.

Pierre Brasseur Professor Génessier • **Alida Valli** Louise • **Edith Scob** Christiane • **Francois Guérin** Jacques • **Juliette Mayniel** Edna Gruber • **Béatrice Altariba** Paulette • **Alexandre Rignault** Inspector Parot • **René Genin** Bereaved father
Director *Georges Franju*
Screenplay *Jean Redon, Georges Franju, Jean Redon, Claude Sautet, Pierre Boileau, Thomas Narcejac, from the novel "Les Yeux sans Visage" by Jean Redon*
Music *Maurice Jarre* • ***Cinematographer*** *Eugen Schüfftan*

F

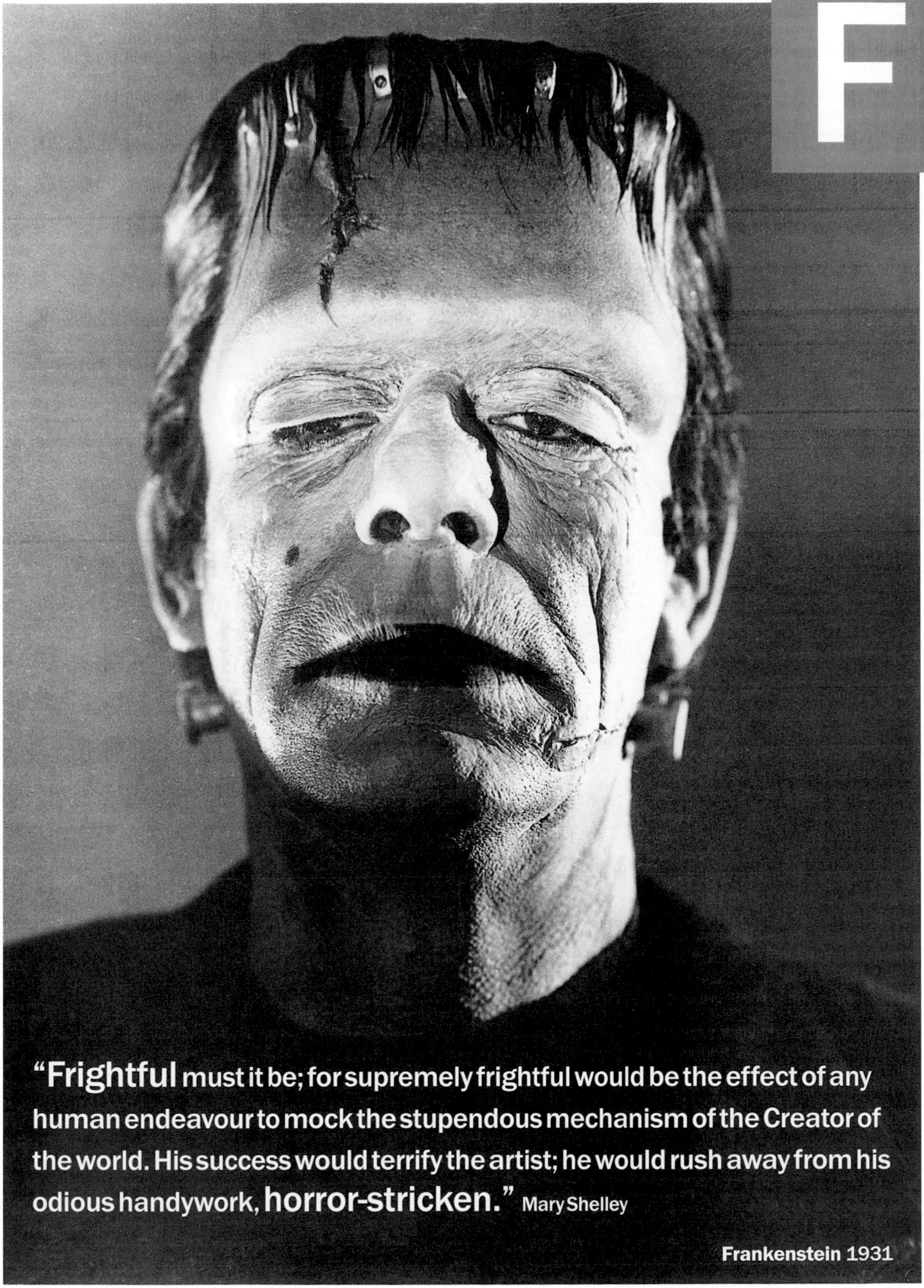

"**Frightful** must it be; for supremely frightful would be the effect of any human endeavour to mock the stupendous mechanism of the Creator of the world. His success would terrify the artist; he would rush away from his odious handywork, **horror-stricken.**" Mary Shelley

Frankenstein 1931

FP1 ★★

1932 UK/Ger BW 74mins

An early instance of tri-lingual film-making, this sci-fi melodrama was a German venture, with different casts for the German, French and English versions all under one director, Karl Hartl. The best scenes show planes using a huge floating aerodrome in the middle of the Atlantic Ocean that serves as a stopping point for flights between Europe and America. The shorter British version stars Conrad Veidt as the aviator and inventor who saves the base from a sabotage attempt. Like modern "Europuddings", it met with mixed success.

Conrad Veidt Maj Ellisen • **Leslie Fenton** Capt Droste • **Jill Esmond** Claire • **George Merritt** Lubin • **Donald Calthrop** Photographer • **Warwick Ward** 1st Officer • **Philip Manning** Doctor • **Nicholas Hannen** Matthias • **William Freshman** Konrad • **Alexander Field** Sailor • **Francis L Sullivan** Sailor
Director *Karl Hartl*
Screenplay *Walter Reisch, Kurt Siodmak, Robert Stevenson, Peter Macfarlane, from a story by Walter Reisch, Kurt Siodmak*

Face of Terror ★★

1962 Sp BW 81mins

More pharmaceutical fear and surgical shock from Spain where *Eyes without a Face*-style sensational disfigurement parables proved popular in the early sixties. Unbalanced Lisa Gaye's scarred face is repaired with a special lotion invented by plastic surgeon Fernando Rey. During an affair with a playboy, the now beautiful patient finds her visage falling apart at inopportune moments and her frenzied need for more of the restorative fluid sends her back to Rey's laboratory where mortal fate intervenes. Sleazy horror melodrama that was extensively re-cut for the American market with added footage directed by William Hole Jr.

Lisa Gaye Norma • **Fernando Rey** Dr Charles Taylor • **Virgilio Teixeira** Playboy • **Conchita Cuetos** Alma • **Gerard Tichy** Sanatorium head
Director *Isidoro Martinez Ferry, William J Hole Jr*
Screenplay *Monroe Manning*

The Faculty ★★★ 15

1998 US Colour 99mins DVD

Scream writer Kevin Williamson teams up with *From Dusk till Dawn* director Robert Rodriguez for an enjoyable reworking of alien invasion movies, bolstered by Williamson's patented in-jokes and genre subversions. Considerably less subtle than the fifties films that inspired it, *The Faculty* succeeds through assured performances from the teenage cast, zippy direction and the writer's refusal to take even the most tense moments seriously. Along the way, there's humorous homage paid to sci-fi related novels, TV and films. Despite a reliance on digital effects, this is classy, extra-terrestrial entertainment. Contains swearing and violence.

Jordana Brewster Delilah • **Clea DuVall** Stokely • **Laura Harris** Marybeth • **Josh Hartnett** Zeke • **Shawn Hatosy** Stan • **Salma Hayek** Nurse Harper • **Famke Janssen** Miss Burke • **Piper Laurie** Mrs Olson • **Robert Patrick** Coach Willis • **Elijah Wood** Casey
Director *Robert Rodriguez*
Screenplay *Kevin Williamson, from a story by David Wechter, Bruce Kimmel*

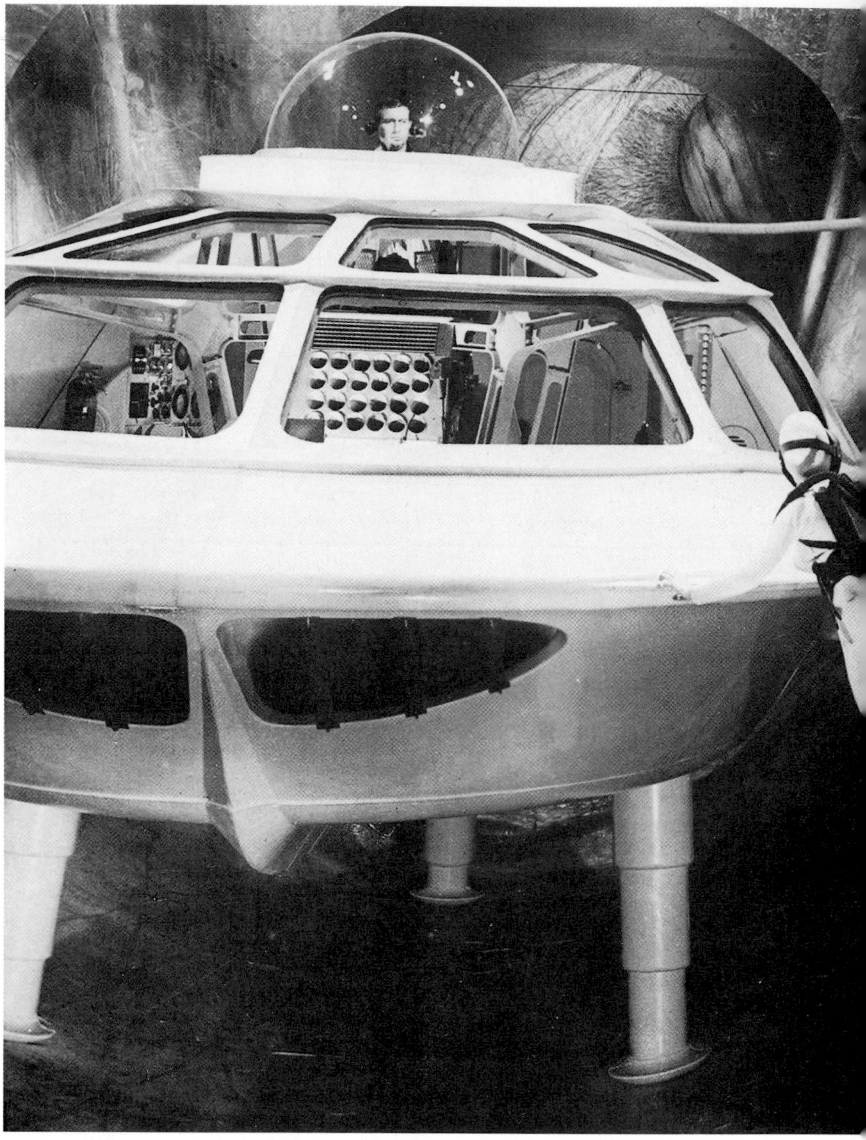

Micro-surgery: superb special effects created a *Fantastic Voyage* in the human body

Fahrenheit 451 ★★★

1966 UK Colour 107mins

This adaptation of Ray Bradbury's deeply troubling novel has to go down as one of François Truffaut's lesser efforts. The only film Truffaut directed in English, it promises much but is sadly flawed. Syd Cain's futuristic sets cleverly convey the menace and desperation of a society in which books

are banned and burned, Cyril Cusack's fire chief is hugely resistible as he unquestioningly performs his duty and Julie Christie superbly judges the contrasts in her dual role. But Oskar Werner – who starred in Truffaut's *Jules et Jim* – seems to have lost the plot, and, as he's its driving force, this is a major stumbling block. Worth watching, but not the masterpiece it should have been

Oskar Werner Montag • **Julie Christie** Linda/Clarisse • **Cyril Cusack** Captain • **Anton Diffring** Fabian
Director *Francois Truffaut*
Screenplay *Francois Truffaut, Jean-Louis Richard, David Rudkin, Helen Scott, from the novel by Ray Bradbury*

Fail-Safe ★★★★ PG

1964 US BW 107mins

Dr Strangelove by any other name! This sweaty-palmed suspense movie follows the same flight path as *Strangelove* – in fact, there was an aborted charge of literary plagiarism – as a squadron of US planes, loaded with nuclear bombs, accidentally sets off to devastate Moscow and cannot be halted from its doomsday mission. Director Sidney Lumet builds the tension from neurotic jitters (Larry Hagman as presidential interpreter) through to psychotic jeopardy (Walter Matthau's anti-Soviet professor urging the Armageddon sanction) when fail-safe devices fail and American president Henry Fonda has to warn his Soviet counterpart that the world is heading into nightmare. By telling it straight, the idea loses a certain satirical edge, but gains a hint of reality. Anyway, it's a warning we can't hear too often – that machines should never be the masters of men.

Henry Fonda The President • **Walter Matthau** Groeteschele • **Frank Overton** General Bogan • **Dan O'Herlihy** General Black • **Fritz Weaver** Colonel Cascio • **Larry Hagman** Buck • **Edward Binns** Colonel Grady • **William Hansen** Secretary Swenson • **Russell Hardie** General Stark • **Russell Collins** Knapp
Director *Sidney Lumet*
Screenplay *Walter Bernstein, from the novel by Eugene Burdick, Harvey Wheeler*

Falling Fire ★★

1998 US/Can Colour 90mins

An uninspired and astoundingly dull science-fiction thriller in which a team of specialists sent on a space mission to replenish the earth's depleted resources, discover a meglomaniac killer in among them. Scripted with a complete lack of invention by Peter *thirtysomething* Horton.

Michael Paré First Officer Daryl Boden • **Heidi Von Palleske** Marilyn Boden • **Mackenzie Gray** Flight Specialist Joe Schneider • **Zerha Leverman** Rene Lessard
Director *Daniel D'Or*
Screenplay *Daniel D'Or, Peter I Horton [Peter Horton], G Philip Jackson, from a story by Peter I Horton [Peter Horton]*

The Fantastic Journey ★★

TV 1977 US Colour 1x90mins; 9x60mins

A disparate group of travellers, lost in the Bermuda Triangle, find themselves on a mysterious island subdivided into different time zones, past, future and present all co-existing together, a clever format that allowed writers free rein to devise exciting new scenarios each week as the characters strive to reach a part of the island called Evoland (drop the "and" and it's love spelt backwards) where they can all be safely returned to their rightful time. Rushed into production to cash in on the flowering sci-fi boom of the late seventies, the show was denied time to build up an audience, despite the best efforts of an interesting cast that included the ever reliable Roddy McDowall and Jared Martin, who later starred in the TV series *War of the Worlds*.

Jared Martin Varian • **Carl Franklin** Dr Fred Walters • **Ike Eisenmann** Scott Jordan • **Katie Saylor** Liana • **Roddy McDowall** Willoway
Story consultants *Calvin Clements Jr, DC Fontana*
Producer *Leonard Katzman* • ***Executive producer*** *Bruce Lansbury*

Fantastic Planet ★★★★ PG

1973 Fr/Cz Colour 69mins

A remarkable animated French/Czech science-fiction fantasy conceived by Roland Topor and René Laloux, depicting the odd happenings on planet Yagam. There, humans, called Oms, are pets of the giant Draags, and numerous allegorical references are imaginatively drawn as a war breaks out between the two factions. A fascinating fable utilising impressive organic design, surreal composition and stunning visuals, this Cannes award-winner is highly intriguing and compulsive viewing. French dialogue dubbed into English.

Barry Bostwick • **Marvin Miller** • **Olan Soule** • **Cynthia Alder** • **Nora Heflin** • **Hal Smith** • **Mark Gruner** • **Monika Ramirez** • **Janet Waldo**
Director *René Laloux*
Screenplay *René Laloux, from the book "Oms en Serie" by Stefan Wul*

Fantastic Voyage ★★★★ U

1966 US Colour 96mins

Shrunken doctors in a mini-sub journeying through the body of a dying Czech scientist to perform interior brain surgery provide the plot for this wonderfully ludicrous sixties classic. An interesting cast (secret agent Stephen Boyd, Raquel Welch in a tight diving suit, Donald Pleasence in danger from rampaging white corpuscles), deft execution by director Richard Fleischer and tremendous special effects for the time ensure an imaginative guided tour through the bloodstream to witness the wonders of the heart, lungs and other

Space opera: lost in a galaxy far, far away... the cast of runaway hit *Farscape*

assorted organs along with the requisite doses of sex, suspense and sabotage, of course.

Stephen Boyd Grant • **Raquel Welch** Cora Peterson • **Donald Pleasence** Dr Michaels • **Edmond O'Brien** General Carter • **Arthur O'Connell** Colonel Donald Reid • **William Redfield** Captain Bill Owens • **Arthur Kennedy** Dr Duval • **Jean Del Val** Jan Benes • **Barry Coe** Communications aide • **Ken Scott** Secret serviceman • **Shelby Grant** Nurse • **James Brolin** Technician • **Brendan Fitzgerald** Wireless operator
Director *Richard Fleischer*
Screenplay *Harry Kleiner, David Duncan, from the novel by Otto Klement, Jay Lewis Bixby*
Art Director *Jack Martin Smith, Dale Hennesy* • ***Cinematographer*** *Ernest Laszlo*

Far Out Space Nuts ★★

TV 1975-1976 US Colour 16x30mins

Bob "Gilligan" Denver and Chuck McCann (who also co-wrote most of the episodes) starred in this short-lived Saturday morning kiddie effort from the Sid and Marty Krofft stable, playing Junior and Barney, a pair of goofy technicians accidentally blasted into outer space ("I said lunch, not launch!") and stuck on an uncharted planet inhabited by Honk (Patty Maloney), a horned alien. The guest villains included Robert (*Count Yorga, Vampire*) Quarry, Leo V Gordon and John Carradine. Humour consisted mostly of the pie-in-the-face variety.

Bob Denver Junior • **Chuck McCann** Barney • **Patty Maloney** Honk
Producer *Marty Krofft, Sid Krofft, Al Schwartz*

Farscape ★★★★ PG 12 15 18

TV 1999 – Aus/US Colour DVD

Far and away the most exciting, daring and visually striking sci-fi show to hit the screen in recent years, *Farscape* propels contemporary human astronaut John Crichton into a distant galaxy of dazzling Jim Henson Company-designed aliens. Its premise might sound like Buck Rogers meets the Muppets, but the show swiftly establishes itself as a distinctively imaginative, unpredictable and intelligent space opera. Ben Browder's engaging everyman hero heads a strong character line-up, and gives the series a knowing, *Scream*-style sense of fun that most genre offerings can only dream of. Although its ongoing story arcs make casual viewing rather difficult and its eclectic plotlines don't always manage to hit the target, *Farscape* remains far more hit than miss, and almost always manages to entertain and surprise.

Ben Browder Cmdr John Crichton • **Claudia Black** Officer Aeryn Sun • **Virginia Hey** Pa'u Zotoh Zhaan • **Anthony Simcoe** General Ka D'Argo • **Sean Masterson** Pilot • **Lani John Tupu** Voice of Pilot/Captain Crais • **Gigi Edgley** Chiana • **Paul Goddard** Stark • **Jonathan Hardy** Voice of Dominar Rygel XVI • **Wayne Pygram** Scorpius
Created by *Rockne S O'Bannon*
Executive Producer *Robert Halmi Jr, Brian Henson, David Kemper, Rockne S O'Bannon, Kris Noble*

Fiend without a Face ★★★

1957 UK BW 73mins

Canadian atomic experiments cause human thoughts to transform into brain-sucking creatures in a grisly little fifties number featuring unusually graphic special effects for the period. Arthur Crabtree's *Quatermass*-style shocker starts off pretty ordinarily but, once the flying spinal cords whip into throat-choking action, the screams you hear may well be your own! British to the core, despite the pseudo-American trappings and fading Hollywood actor Marshall Thompson taking centre stage.

Marshall Thompson Major Jeff Cummings • **Terence Kilburn [Terry Kilburn]** Captain Chester • **Kynaston Reeves** Professor Walgate • **Stanley Maxted** Colonel Butler • **Michael Balfour** Sergeant Kasper • **Kim Parker** Barbara • **Gil Winfield** Dr Warren • **Shane Cordell** Nurse • **James Dyrenforth** Mayor Hawkins • **Kerrigan Prescott** Atomic engineer
Director *Arthur Crabtree*
Screenplay *Herbert J Leder, from a story by Amelia Reynolds Long*

The Fifth Element ★★★★ PG

1997 Fr Colour 121mins [video] DVD

Ancient evil returns to destroy the galaxy in director Luc Besson's ultra-hip, socially conscious and clever science-fiction action comedy. Laconic former government agent Bruce Willis is forced to save the universe when the secret key to stopping this happening literally falls into his cab in 23rd-century New York. A superb flight of imagination that soars into original terrain for an inventive roller-coaster ride, Besson's instant classic in the *Blade Runner* tradition is a stunning achievement that delivers on all levels. The satire is slick, the visuals unusual and the thrills futuristic, and if the Big Apple special effects don't amaze, the camp trip to the resort planet of Fhloston Paradise certainly will. Gary Oldman is great as *haute-couture* corruption personified.

Bruce Willis Korben Dallas • **Gary Oldman** Zorg • **Ian Holm** Cornelius • **Milla Jovovich** Leeloo • **Chris Tucker** Ruby Rhod • **Luke Perry** Billy • **Brion James** General Munro • **Tommy "Tiny" Lister Jr [Tom "Tiny" Lister Jr]** President Lindberg • **Lee Evans** Fog • **Charlie Creed-Miles** David • **Tricky** Right Arm • **John Neville** General Staedert
Director *Luc Besson*
Screenplay *Luc Besson, Robert Mark Kamen*
Producer *Patrice Ledoux* • ***Co-producer*** *Iain Smith* • ***Associate producer*** *John A Amicarella*

Final Approach ★ 15

1991 US Colour 96mins [video]

This *Twilight Zone*-style science-fiction thriller tries for zest, but lacks any originality. Debut director Eric Steven Stahl emphasises technology over content in this tale, jarringly told (often in flashback) of a test pilot, played by the traditionally dour James B Sikking, who is interrogated after an accident involving a top secret plane. The always reliable Hector Elizondo plays the psychiatrist probing his past and provides some comic relief to counterbalance the dull Sikking. Gimmicky and uninvolving, this is notable only for its pioneering use of digital sound.

James B Sikking Colonel Jason J Halsey • **Hector Elizondo** Dr Dio Gottlieb • **Madolyn Smith Osborne [Madolyn Smith]** Casey Halsey • **Kevin McCarthy** General Geller • **Cameo Kneuer** Brooke Halsey
Director *Eric Steven Stahl*
Screenplay *Eric Steven Stahl, Gerald Laurence*

The Final Countdown ★★★ PG

1980 US Colour 98mins [video]

What would have happened if the Americans possessed modern aircraft carriers and nuclear weapons during the time of the attack on Pearl Harbor? That's the ingenious premise of this absorbing and never silly sci-fi thriller as Captain Kirk Douglas and Martin Sheen sail into a time-warp, and have the power to alter history at the touch of a button. Somewhat reminiscent of a *Twilight Zone* but on a big budget: the film was given unprecedented and complete access to film aboard the USS *Nimitz*.

Kirk Douglas Captain Matthew Yelland • **Martin Sheen** Warren Lasky • **Katharine Ross** Laurel Scott • **James Farentino** Commander Richard Owens • **Ron O'Neal** Commander Dan Thurman • **Charles Durning** Senator Samuel Chapman • **Victor Mohica** Black Cloud • **James C Lawrence** Lieutenant Perry
Director *Don Taylor*
Screenplay *David Ambrose, Gerry Davis, Thomas Hunter, Peter Powell*
Executive producer *Richard R St Johns* • ***Producer*** *Peter Vincent Douglas* • ***Associate producer*** *Lloyd Kaufman*

The Final Programme ★★

1973 UK Colour 83mins

The sight of the misshapen messiah will certainly send shudders down the spine of those who have stuck with the stylised imagery and apocalyptic incidents that comprise this baffling adaptation of one of Michael Moorcock's "Jerry Cornelius" stories. But many more will have long since despaired of finding any tangible meaning in this fatally flawed fantasy that ends with a cruel joke at the expense of *2001: a Space Odyssey*. Patrick Magee, Graham Crowden and George Coulouris make fearsome adversaries, but Jon Finch's bid to save both his sister and the planet are confounded by director Robert Fuest's preoccupation with look over logic.

Jon Finch Jerry Cornelius • **Jenny Runacre** Miss Brunner • **Hugh Griffith** Professor Hira • **Patrick Magee** Dr Baxter • **Sterling Hayden** Major Wrongway Lindbergh • **Harry Andrews** John • **Graham Crowden** Dr Smiles • **George Coulouris** Dr Powys
Director *Robert Fuest*
Screenplay *Robert Fuest, from the novel by Michael Moorcock*
Producer *John Goldstone, Sandy Lieberson*

The Final War ★★★

1960 Jap BW 77mins

Made just 15 years after the decimation of Hiroshima and Nagasaki and with the Cold War about to enter its frostiest phase, this terrifyingly plausible feature explores just how quickly events could spiral out of control in the wake of a nuclear accident. America may not have intended a bomb to explode over South Korea, but it's only a matter of hours before the entire planet (with the puzzling exception of Argentina) will have been reduced to radioctive rubble. Amid the mayhem, director Shigeaki Hidaka wisely inserted a human interest angle, as irradiated journalist Tatsuo Umemiya roams Tokyo looking for his beloved. A Japanese language film.

Tatsuo Umemiya Shigeo • **Yoshiko Mita** • **Yayoi Furusato** • **Noribumi Fujishima** • **Yukiko Nikaido** • **Michiko Hoshi**
Director *Shigeaki Hidaka*
Screenplay *Hisataka Kai*

The Final War ★★★

1962 Jap BW 110mins

Although director Shue Matsubayashi's apocalyptic disaster movie sometimes plays like a Japanese monster movie without any central monster, it ultimately emerges as a sobering anti-war tract clearly inspired by *On the Beach*. After a few nuclear alarms in missile bases and an increase in global tension as a result, World War III is finally caused by a misunderstanding when two Cold War superpowers' aircraft collide in mid-air. Cue Eijii (*Godzilla*) Tsuburaya's ace special effects depicting London Bridge falling down, the Arc de Triomphe collapsing and the Statue of Liberty disintegrating as earthquakes and tidal waves engulf the world, leaving the population dying of radiation sickness. Scarily believable, still relevant and efficiently directed by comedy movie master Matsubayashi. A Japanese language film.

Frankie Sakai • **Nobuko Otowa** • **Akira Takarada** • **Yumi Shirakawa**
Director *Shue Matsubayashi*
Screenplay *Takeshi Kimura, Toshio Yasumi*
Special Effects *Eiji Tsuburaya*

Fire in the Sky ★★★ 15

1993 US Colour 104mins

It's a case from *The X Files* that Scully and Mulder missed: a small-town lumberjack vanishes in the woods and his colleagues claim he was kidnapped by aliens. Problem is, the investigating officer here is sceptical James Garner and he suspects foul play. Director Robert Lieberman wisely concentrates on the emotional impact of the event on a close-knit circle of friends and family, although the eventual revelation of the abduction is genuinely scary. DB Sweeney shines in the lead role and there's good support from *Terminator 2's* Robert Patrick, *The Last Seduction's* Peter Berg and Henry Thomas of *ET* and *Legends of the Fall* fame, although old pro Garner effortlessly steals every scene in which he appears. Contains some swearing.

D B Sweeney Travis Walton • **Robert Patrick** Mike Rogers • **Craig Sheffer** Allan Dallis • **Peter Berg** David Whitlock • **Henry Thomas** Greg Hayes • **Bradley Gregg** Bobby Cogdill • **James Garner** Lieutenant Frank Watters • **Noble Willingham** Sheriff Blake Davis • **Kathleen Wilhoite** Katie Rogers • **Georgia Emelin** Dana Rogers • **Scott Macdonald** Dan Walton • **Wayne Grace** Cyrus Gilson • **Kenneth White** Buck • **Robert Covarrubias** Ray Melendez • **Bruce Wright** Dennis Clay • **Robert Biheller** Ellis • **Tom McGranahan** Dr Wilson • **Julie Ariola** Dr Cayle • **Peter Mark Vasquez** Ramon • **Gordon Scott** George
Director *Robert Lieberman*
Screenplay *Tracy Tormé, from the book "The Walton Experience" by Travis Walton*

Fire Maidens from Outer Space ★ U

1956 UK BW 79mins

Just what the world needed – an even dafter British version of the infamous space exotica romp *Cat-Women of the Moon*. Life is such a trial for the female lost civilization of Atlantis, stranded on the 13th moon of Jupiter. They wear bathing suits with little skirts, lie around in flames all day to gain some extra energy, perform dances to Borodin's music and fight a lumpy-faced creature wearing ill-fitting tights. Instant has-been Anthony Dexter is the astronaut determined to rescue the alien damsels from this terrible existence. Despite the extensive use of classical music, beating Stanley Kubrick's similar *2001* ploy by more than a decade, this is bottom-of-the-barrel lunatic nonsense that has to be seen to be believed.

Anthony Dexter Luther Blair • **Susan Shaw** Hestia • **Paul Carpenter** Larson • **Harry Fowler** Sydney Stanhope • **Jacqueline Curtiss** Duessa • **Sidney Tafler [Sydney Tafler]** Dr Higgins • **Owen Berry** Prasus • **Rodney Diak** Anderson • **Maya Koumani** Fire Maiden • **Jan Holden** Fire Maiden • **Kim Parker** Fire Maiden
Director/Screenplay *Cy Roth*

The Fire Next Time ★★

TV 1992 US Colour 2x120mins

An unremarkable but nicely played apocalyptic tale with an understated green message. The setting is the near future, where the inhabitants are paying the price for the previous generation's ecological mistakes. Struggling to survive against the forces of nature – plus the regulation post-apocalypse psychos – are an ordinary American family, headed by Craig T Nelson and Bonnie Bedelia. There are plenty of canny actors in supporting roles (Richard Farnsworth, Jürgen Prochnow, Charles Haid, John Vernon), so it's a shame that the direction from Tom McLoughlin is so formulaic. Originally screened as a two-part mini-series,

Craig T Nelson Drew Morgan • **Bonnie Bedelia** Suzanne Morgan • **Richard Farnsworth** Frank Morgan • **Jürgen Prochnow** Larry Richter • **Justin Whalin** Paul Morgan • **Ashley Jones** Linnie Morgan • **Charles Haid** Buddy Eckhard • **John Vernon** Boudreaux
Director *Tom McLoughlin*
Written by *James S Henerson*

Fireball XL5 ★★★ U

TV 1962-1963 UK BW 39x25mins

In many respects this was the puppet show that paved the way for *Thunderbirds*, *Captain Scarlet* and the rest. Following directly after *Supercar*, this was Gerry Anderson's second major supermarionation series and a major step up in technical terms, although caveman stuff by today's standards. The *Fireball XL5* of the title (named after a popular advertisement at the time for a motor oil called Castrol XL, Anderson merely added the 5) is an interplanetary rocket ship patrolling the galaxy in the 21st century, saving it from alien invaders. Commanded by Steve Zodiac, other crew members included Venus, a doctor of space medicine, voiced by Sylvia Anderson, the future voice of Lady Penelope, and Robert the Robot, which Anderson himself performed, the only time in his lengthy career that he ever lent his own voice to one of his famous characters.

Paul Maxwell Colonel Steve Zodiac • **Sylvia Anderson** Venus • **David Graham** Prof Matt Matic/Zoonie • **John Bluthal** Commander Zero • **David Graham** Lt Ninety • **Gerry Anderson** Robert the robot
Created by *Gerry Anderson*
Producer *Gerry Anderson*

Firebird 2015 AD ★

1980 US Colour 97mins

Petrol is in such short supply in the 21st century that the government orders all cars to be destroyed. However, when their owners start getting wiped out, too, it's up to illegal bands of motorcyclists to take the law into their own hands. Poorly written and directed, this *Mad Max* rip-off has minor futuristic fantasy touches, but it includes plenty of stunt action for those who like that sort of thing. Doug McClure probably wished he had stayed in *The Land That TIme Forgot*.

Darren McGavin Red • **Doug McClure** McVain • **George Touliatos** Indy • **Mary Beth Rubens** Jill
Director *David M Robertson*
Screenplay *Barry Pearson, Biff McGuire, Maurice Hurley*

Firehead ★★ 15

1991 US Colour 83mins

This dull espionage thriller with mild fantasy overtones is notable for wasting a fine cast. Scientist Chris Lemmon (sounding and acting like his father Jack) and CIA agent Gretchen Becker team up to track down Soviet defector Brett Porter, who has the ability to shoot laser beams from his eyes, move molecules and start fires. Christopher Plummer is the government bureaucrat-by-day/secret-society-leader-by-night who needs Porter to kill the president and start World War III. Martin Landau is a retired admiral and Lemmon's mentor. Peter Yuval's suspense adventure never knows quite what direction to move in and the result is a fuzzy action-powered muddle. Contains violence and swearing

Christopher Plummer Colonel Garland Vaughn • **Chris Lemmon** Warren Hart • **Martin Landau** Admiral Pendleton • **Gretchen Becker** Melia Buchanan • **Brett Porter** Ivan Tibor
Director *Peter Yuval*
Screenplay *Peter Yuval, Jeff Mandel*

Firepower ★★ 18

1993 US Colour 90mins [video]

Prolific straight-to-video director Richard Pepin (*T-Force, The Silencers*) splices together the science fiction and fight contest genres for this predictably efficient thriller. Gary Daniels and Chad McQueen play a pair of futuristic cops who are forced into the fight ring when they go undercover in a no-go crime zone in 21st-century Los Angeles. Every post-apocalypse cliché is present and correct, but the fight sequences will satisfy the more undemanding fans of the genre.

Chad McQueen • **Gary Daniels** • **George Murdock** • **Joseph Ruskin**
Director *Richard Pepin*
Screenplay *Michael January*

Firestarter ★★★ 15

1984 US Colour 109mins [video]

Stephen King's work has suffered mixed fortunes at the hands of film-makers and this early folly, it has to be said, is not one of the better adaptations. A very young Drew Barrymore is the girl with very fiery thoughts which are seemingly connected to the sinister experiments her father and mother (David Keith and Heather Locklear) underwent as students. Despite a starry cast (Martin Sheen, George C Scott, Louise Fletcher), there's little here in the way of frights or suspense.

David Keith Andrew McGee • **Drew Barrymore** Charlie McGee • **Freddie Jones** Dr Joseph Wanless • **Heather Locklear** Vicky McGee • **Martin Sheen** Captain Hollister • **George C Scott** John Rainbird • **Art Carney** Irv Manders • **Louise Fletcher** Norma Manders • **Moses Gunn** Dr Pynchot • **Antonio Fargas** Taxi Driver
Director *Mark L Lester*
Screenplay *Stanley Mann, from the novel by Stephen King*
Music *Tangerine Dream*

First Born ★★★

TV 1988 UK Colour 3x50mins

This accomplished adult fantasy drama, adapted from the novel by Maureen Duffy, stars Charles Dance as a scientist playing God with genetics. In the hope of creating a new breed of creature, Dance impregnates a female gorilla with human sperm, resulting in the birth of a hybrid child he christens Gordon, or "Gor" for short. Keeping his experiments secret Dance watches Gor grow up to be a model son, but when he reaches early manhood and discovers his true origin the consequences are devastating. Sympathetically acted and at the time scientifically too far-fetched to take seriously, the premise now looks all too horribly relevant and possible. Look out for a young Gabrielle Anwar who later hit the Hollywood big time in *Scent of a Woman* opposite Al Pacino.

Charles Dance Dr Edward Forester • **Julie Peasgood** Ann Forester • **Philip Madoc** Colonel Lancing • **Jamie Foster** Gordon "Gor" as an adult • **Peter Wiggins** Gordon "Gor" as a child • **Peter Tilbury** Chris Knott • **Rosemary McHale** Nancy Knott • **Gabrielle Anwar** Nell Forester
Director *Philip Saville*
Written by *Ted Whitehead, from the novel "The Gor Saga" by Maureen Duffy*
Producer *Sally Head* • ***Associate producer*** *Rosalind Wolfes*

First Man into Space ★★ PG

1958 UK BW 73mins [video]

Cosmic rays mutate Earth's first astronaut into a marauding monster with a taste for blood in this briskly efficient B movie from the golden era of British science fiction. In a film bearing more than a passing resemblance to Hammer's *The Quatermass Experiment* with a dash of *Dracula* thrown in for good exploitative measure, director Robert Day goes for both pity and scares by engendering sympathy for the one-eyed malformation while delivering uneasy shocks. Lacklustre acting from Marshall Thompson doesn't help his cause, but Marla Landi screaming every time the slime-encrusted alien appears does add an unintentional streak of light entertainment.

Marshall Thompson Commander CE Prescott • **Marla Landi** Tia Francesca • **Bill Edwards** Lt Dan Prescott • **Robert Ayres** Captain Ben Richards • **Bill Nagy** Wilson • **Carl Jaffe** Dr Paul von Essen • **Roger Delgado** Mexican consul • **John McLaren** State Department offical • **Richard Shaw** Witney • **Bill Nick** Clancy
Director *Robert Day*
Screenplay *John C Cooper, Lance Z Hargreaves, from a story by Wyott Ordung*

First Men in the Moon ★★★ U

1964 UK Colour 98mins [video]

Outstanding special effects from stop-motion magician Ray Harryhausen add further lustre to director Nathan Juran's colourfully engaging tale about a Victorian lunar expedition. Based on the HG Wells novel, Lionel Jeffries is splendid as the eccentric Professor Cavor using his anti-gravity paint invention to achieve lift-off into light-hearted adventure. Cavor, Edward Judd and Martha Hyer are then captured by insectoid creatures and menaced by a Moon caterpillar in this highly enjoyable flight of sheer fantasy.

Edward Judd Arnold Bedford • **Lionel Jeffries** Cavor • **Martha Hyer** Kate Callender • **Erik Chitty** Gibbs • **Betty McDowall** Maggie • **Miles Malleson** Registrar • **Laurence Herder** Glushkov • **Gladys Henson** Matron
Director *Nathan Juran*
Screenplay *Nigel Kneale, Jan Read, from the novel by H G Wells*
Special effects *Ray Harryhausen*

First Men in the Moon ★★★

Radio 1996 UK 4x30mins

This solid rendering of the HG Wells classic was an independent production for Radio 4. The rotund vowels of Donald Sinden are ideal for the eccentric Professor Cavor, and Sinden is ably supported by James Bolem, Tom Georgeson and Gary Olsen. Joe Dunlop's adaptation works well, thanks in part to the original's suitability for radio: what the listeners conjure up in their own imagination is far superior to mediocre TV special effects. Their journey to the moon is a cracking adventure and a treat for listeners. Available on audio-cassette.

Donald Sinden Professor Cavor • **James Bolam** Bedford • **Tom Georgeson** Spike • **Gary Olsen** Manson • **Jilly Bond** Elise
Director *Martin Jameson*
Adapted by *Joe Dunlop, from the novel by HG Wells*
Music *Robert Rigby*

First Spaceship on Venus ★★ U

1960 W Ger/Pol Colour 80mins

Adapted from the novel *Planet of Death* by Stanislaw Lem (who also wrote *Solaris*), this is something of a throwback to the pacifist parables churned out by Hollywood's B-wing in the mid-fifties.

However, instead of a single admonitory messenger arriving on earth, a multi-national mission heads to Venus to discover that the planet'spopulation has been wiped out during an accidental conflagration. This was clearly a prestigious project, as director Kurt Maetzig was one of the co-founders of the famous DEFA studio. But while the sets are impressive, the dialogue strains for significance and the storyline is all too predictable. A German language film.

Yoko Tani Sumiko Ogimura • **Oldrich Lukes** Harringway • **Ignacy Machowski** Orloff • **Julius Ongewe** Talua • **Michal Postnikow** Durand • **Kurt Rackelmann** Sikarna
Director *Kurt Maetzig*
Screenplay *J Barckhauer, J Fathke, W Kohlhaase, Kurt Maetzig, Guenther Reisch, Guenther Ruecker, Alexander Stenbock-Fermor, from the novel "Planet of Death" by Stanislaw Lem*

First Wave ★★★

TV 1998 – Can

Shape-shifting aliens are among us, and humanity's only hope of survival lies with the heroic Cade Foster and the prophecies of Nostradamus. Dubbed by its makers as "the world's sexiest sci-fi series" due to its gratuitous sex scenes and *Baywatch*-style hot-bods, *First Wave* gradually toned down the tackiness and established itself as a modestly engaging alien invasion saga. Even when the show is at its most slow-moving and repetitive, Sebastian Spence makes a sympathetic and agreeable hero, while co-star Rob LaBelle brings some much-needed manic charm to proceedings. The arrival of former porn star Traci Lords in season three adds further spice to the series, and heralds a slight increase in the action quotient. Incidentally, the show boasts movie legend Francis Ford Coppola as an executive producer, although signs of his input are harder to find than evidence of the Gua invasion.

Sebastian Spence Cade Foster • **Rob LaBelle** Eddie Nambulour • **Roger R Cross** Joshua/Cain • **Traci Lords** Jordan Radcliffe • **Robert Duncan** Mabus
Created by *Chris Brancato*
Executive producer *Francis Ford Coppola, Larry Sugar*

Fist of the North Star ★★ 18

1986 Jap Colour 111mins

Based on a Japanese *manga* (comic book) of the same name, it was inevitable that this animated movie would gain instant cult status because of the extremely violent and gory deaths many of the grotesque characters suffer. One "hero" aims get his girlfriend back from the brute who beat him up and left him for dead, but there is not much else going on in this story about various martial arts factions and *Mad Max*-like gangs constantly at each other's throats in a post-apocalypse world. Still, it's better and more faithful to the original comic book than the live-action version made several years later (starring Gary Daniels).

John Vickery Ken • **Melodee Spivack** Julia • **Wally Burr** Raoh • **Michael McConnohie** Shin • **Gregory Snegoff** Rei • **Tony Oliver** Bat • **Holly Sidell** Lynn
Director *Toyoo Ashida*
Screenplay *Susumu Takahisa, from the graphic novels by Buronson Hara, Tetsuo Hara*

Fist of the North Star ★★ 18

1995 US Colour 88mins

A very standard live-action version of the popular Japanese animated *manga* series written and directed by the team behind *Hellbound: Hellraiser II*. Martial arts star Gary Daniels is Kenshiro, the warrior on a mission to restore peace between the warring faction of the Northern and Southern Star, in his post-apocalyptic kingdom. Evil Southern Star chief Lord Shin (Costas Mandylor) has other ideas. Resembling a bad spaghetti western unceremoniously placed in a science-fiction setting, Tony Randel's direction fails to match the hyper-kinetic quality of the original cartoon despite plenty of goofy action spiced up with additional gore.

Gary Daniels Kenshiro • **Malcolm McDowell** Ryuken • **Costas Mandylor** Lord Shin • **Dante Basco** Bat • **Nalona Herron** Lynn • **Melvin Van Peebles** Asher • **Bill Nagel** Miner • **Clint Howard** Stalin • **Chris Penn [Christopher Penn]** Jackal
Director *Tony Randel*
Screenplay *Peter Atkins, Tony Randel, from the graphic novels by Buronson Hara, Tetsuo Hara*

Five ★★★

1951 US BW 90mins

Former radio producer turned exploitation merchant Arch Oboler has some interesting gimmick-laden films to his credit, most notably the first movie in 3-D, the notorious *Bwana Devil*. The gimmick here is both the title and the plot, which deals with the last five survivors after the Earth has been devastated by a (then topical) A-bomb blast. The trouble is, it's all rather static and cheap-looking, and it's awfully hard to care about these particular survivors, a group of unknowns who have remained as such. A story like this really needs star-power, as was the case in such post-apocalypse movies as *On the Beach* and *The World, the Flesh and the Devil*. However, the dialogue is clever and the situations, though contrived, are nonetheless intriguing. The bizarre whole is certainly a rare collector's item, although perhaps better suited to the radio.

William Phipps Michael • **Susan Douglas** Roseanne • **James Anderson** Eric • **Charles Lampkin** Charles • **Earl Lee** Barnstable
Director/Screenplay *Arch Oboler*
Producer *Arch Oboler*

The Flame Barrier ★★ U

1958 US BW 71mins

This post-Sputnik scare story was designed to cash in on public disquiet at venturing beyond the final frontier. The star of the show (or villain of the piece depending on your viewpoint) is art director James D Vance, who designed the heat-emitting cannibal protoplasm attached to the satellite that has crash-landed in the Yucatan jungle. There's a Val Lewton feel to the sequences in which explorer Arthur Franz locates the craft. But thenceforth, Paul Landres is at the mercy of his cut-price special effects and the limited talents of Robert Brown and Vincent Padula, who form a singularly incompetent search party.

Arthur Franz Dave Hollister • **Kathleen Crowley** Carol Dahlmann • **Robert Brown** Matt Hollister • **Vincent Padula** Julio • **Rodd Redwing** Waumi • **Kaz Oran** Tispe
Director *Paul Landres*
Screenplay *Pat Fielder, George Worthing Yates, from a story by George Worthing Yates*

The Flaming Disk ★★

1920 US BW 12x18mins

Elmo Lincoln, the first screen Tarzan in *Tarzan of the Apes* (1918), stars as a secret agent in this 18-chapter silent serial, with Lee Kohlmar as a professor who invents an optical lens that concentrates the sun's rays into a metal vaporiser. Villain Roy Watson steals the device before it can be handed over to the government, and starts using it to crack open safes in banks. Lincoln also plays the part of his brother – until Chapter 17 – held under hypnotic trance by Watson and forced into being his accomplice. By all contemporary accounts, this is a serviceable programme filler packed with the clichés of the format – ludicrous last-minute rescues, thrilling derring-do and damsels in distress.

Elmo Lincoln Elmo Gray/Jim Gray • **Louise Lorraine** Helen • **Monty Montague** Bat • **Lee Kohlmar** Prof Wade • **George Williams** Stanley W Barrows
Director *Robert F Hill*
Screenplay *Arthur Henry Gooden, Jerry Ash*

The Flash ★★★★ PG

TV 1990-91 US Col 1x120m; 21x60m [video]

One of the finest superhero adventure series ever made, this delightful adaptation of the DC comic toplines a pre-*Dawson's Creek* John Wesley Shipp as the titular cop-turned-fast-travelling do-gooder. Although cruelly cancelled at the end of its first season, the Flash's small-screen capers seldom put a foot wrong. The series captures a winning balance between believable superheroics, fast-moving drama and upbeat comedy, and also boasts some first-rate visuals and a fitting theme tune from Danny Elfman. Shipp is a strong and appropriately wholesome lead, while Amanda Pays provides a glamorous sidekick. The series include one feature-length episode.

John Wesley Shipp Barry Allen/The Flash • **Amanda Pays** Christina McGee • **Alex Desert** Julio Mendez • **Biff Manard** Officer Michael Frances Murphy • **Vito D'Ambrosio** Officer Bellows • **Mike Genovese** Lt Warren Garfield
Source *based on the character created by Gardner Fox, Harry Lampert*
Executive producer *Danny Bilson, Paul LeMeo*

SFacts

One of the recurring villains in *The Flash* was none other than Luke Skywalker himself, alias Mark Hamill who, as the Trickster, makes a gallant effort at slowing down the Flash.

Flash Gordon ★★★ U

1936 US BW 205mins

This is the feature-length condensation of the original 13-part *Flash Gordon* serial, which inspired director George Lucas to create *Star Wars*. Breathless cliffhangers and vintage action meets cheesy special effects and hilarious overacting as charismatic hero Flash (former Olympic athlete Larry "Buster" Crabbe), along with Dale Arden (Jean Rogers) and Dr Zarkov (Frank Shannon), prevent Ming the Merciless (Charles Middleton) of the Planet Mongo conquering Earth. It's non-stop thrill-a-minute stuff (thanks to the ruthless editing) as Flash battles one adversary after another including Lion Men, Gocko the dragon-lizard monster and King Kala's underwater aliens. The best of the Crabbe trilogy of *Flash Gordon* films.

Larry "Buster" Crabbe Flash Gordon • **Jean Rogers** Dale Arden • **Charles Middleton** Ming the Merciless • **Priscilla Lawson** Princess Aura • **John Lipson** King Vultan • **Richard Alexander** Prince Barin • **Frank Shannon** Dr Zarkov • **Duke York Jr** King Kala • **Henry MacRae** Producer
Director *Frederick Stephani*
Screenplay *Frederick Stephani, George Plympton, Basil Dickey, Ella O'Neill, from the comic strip by Alex Raymond*

Flash Gordon ★★★

TV 1954-1955 US BW 39x30mins

Already famous thanks to the long-running newspaper comic strip and three action-packed Universal film serials, Flash Gordon made his television debut in this odd series, shot in Europe (in Berlin and Marseilles) to keep the costs down, with a lot of accented guest villains bested by the Yankee heroes. The leads were male model Steve Holland as Flash, Irene Champlin as girlfriend Dale Arden and Joseph Nash as bearded scientist Dr Zarkov, and the original's contemporary setting was shifted to 3063, where Flash is an agent of the Galaxy Bureau of Investigation and tangles with menaces like Zydereen (Marie Powers), the Mad Witch of Neptune, who appeared in three episodes, and a villain simply named "Evil". Among the directors was Gunther von Fritsch, who had been replaced by Robert Wise on *The Curse of the Cat People* (1944) and found work hard to come by.

Steve Holland Flash Gordon • **Irene Champlin** Dale Arden • **Joe Nash [Joseph Nash]** Dr Zarkov • **Henry Beckman** Commander Richards
Director *Wallace Worsley Jr, Gunther von Fritsch*
Source *from the comic strip created by Alex Raymond*

Flash Gordon ★★★ PG

1980 US Colour 106mins [video] DVD

Aiming for the tongue-in-cheek frivolity of the fabulous Buster Crabbe adventures of the thirties, Mike Hodges's big-budget fantasy is great fun, providing you ignore the plot altogether and concentrate on the corny performances and cheesy special effects. Although Ornella Muti makes a wonderfully witty Princess Aura, it's Max von Sydow who runs away with the picture as the dastardly Emperor Ming. However, the sheer badness of Sam J Jones as Flash (whose dialogue had to be dubbed by another actor) and Melody Anderson as Dale Arden also adds to the charm of this expensive sci-fi pantomine.

Sam J Jones [Sam Jones] Flash Gordon • **Melody Anderson** Dale Arden • **Topol** Dr Hans Zarkov • **Max von Sydow** Emperor Ming • **Ornella Muti** Princess Aura • **Timothy Dalton** Prince Barin • **Brian Blessed** Prince Vultan • **Peter Wyngarde** Klytus • **Mariangela Melato** Kala • **John Osborne** Arborian priest • **Richard O'Brien** Fico • **John Hallam** Luro • **Suzanne Danielle** Serving girl
Director *Mike Hodges*
Screenplay *Lorenzo Semple Jr, Michael Allin, from the characters created by Alex Raymond*
Cinematographer *Gilbert Taylor* • ***Production designer*** *Danilo Donati* • ***Costume designer*** *Danilo Donati* • ***Music*** *Queen, Howard Blake*

Flash Gordon Conquers the Universe ★★ U

1940 US BW 12x20mins [video]

It's unlikely that the great GW Pabst would have been overjoyed to discover that footage from his classic mountain film *The White Hell of Piz Palu* had found its way into the third and final serial featuring Alex Raymond's interstellar hero. However, the Frigia sequences considerably enhance an otherwise lacklustre adventure in which "Buster" Crabbe heads for the Planet Mongo to prevent Charles Middleton's merciless Ming from plaguing earth with the Purple Death. Ford Beebe and Ray Taylor direct with brio, but there's an end-of-era feel about the proceedings, confirmed by Ming's obliteration in the final reel.

Buster Crabbe [Larry "Buster" Crabbe] Flash Gordon • **Carol Hughes** Dale Arden • **Charles Middleton** Emperor Ming • **Frank Shannon** Dr Zarkof • **Shirley Deane** Princess Aura • **Anne Gwynne** Sonja • **Roland Drew** Prince Barin • **Michael Mark** Karm
Director *Ford Beebe, Ray Taylor*
Screenplay *George H Plympton, Basil Dickey, Barry Shipman, from the comic strip "Flash Gordon" by Alex Raymond*

Flash Gordon's Trip to Mars ★★★

1938 US BW 15x20mins

Orson Welles was responsible for the relocation of this serial from Mongo to Mars, as Universal sought to exploit the

Master of the universe: Buster Crabbe as Flash Gordon and Carol Hughes as Dale Arden make light work of saving the earth

furore caused by his *War of the Worlds* broadcast. However, the studio only had itself to blame for the cheapness of the sets (a curious factor considering the success of the 1936 original), which undermine an otherwise lively adventure in which Charles Middleton's scheme to deprive earth of nitrogen is foiled by "Buster" Crabbe and his unlikely allies the Clay People (who've been rendered thus by the evil Queen of Magic, Beatrice Roberts). A tad self-conscious, but irresisible all the same.

Buster Crabbe [Larry "Buster" Crabbe] Flash Gordon • **Jean Rogers** Dale Arden • **Charles Middleton** Emperor Ming • **Frank Shannon** Dr Zarkov • **Richard Alexander** Prince Barin • **Beatrice Roberts** Azura, Queen of Magic • **Donald Kerr** Happy • **Montague Shaw [C Montague Shaw]** King of the Clay People
Director *Ford Beebe, Robert F Hill*
Screenplay *Ray Trampe, Norman S Hall, Wyndham Gittens, Herbert Dalmas, from the comic strip "Flash Gordon" by Alex Raymond*

Flatliners ★★★ 15

1990 US Colour 109mins [video] DVD

Is there life after death? Not with some of the acting on display here. Julia Roberts purses her bicycle-pedal lips and looks bemused in this gothic mix of old dark house and high-tech laboratory, as one of a group of medical students whose extracurricular experiments involve temporarily inducing their own deaths. Director Joel Schumacher puts more flash than flesh on the story, but still manages to deliver the expected chills with cool efficiency. But the trouble is, the after-life stuff is really rather too crudely clichéd. Contains swearing and sex scenes.

Kiefer Sutherland Nelson Wright • **Julia Roberts** Rachel Mannus • **Kevin Bacon** David Labraccio • **William Baldwin** Joe Hurley • **Oliver Platt** Randy Steckle • **Kimberly Scott** Winnie Hicks • **Joshua Rudoy** Billy Mahoney • **Benjamin Mouton** Rachel's father • **Aeryk Egan** Young Nelson • **Kesha Reed** Young Winnie •
Director *Joel Schumacher*
Screenplay *Peter Filardi*
Cinematographer *Jan De Bont*

The Flesh Eaters ★★★★

1964 US BW 89mins

Stylishly directed, well acted and featuring some spectacular gore effects for the period, director Jack Curtis's splendidly convincing comic fantasy is long overdue for discovery as one of the most accomplished and influential shockers spearheading the nasty strain of American gothic that would sublimate itself in the better known *Blood Feast.* Filmed in 1960–61 in suburban New York but not released until 1964, it features pilot Byron Sanders and two passengers, alcoholic movie star Rita Morley and her secretary Barbara Wilkin, who crash on a small island where mad Nazi scientist Martin Kosleck is creating tiny carnivorous sea creatures. After stripping the flesh off the cast (an effect realised by scratching the emulsion on the celluloid), Kosleck electrifies his deadly spawn and turns them into one giant monster in what is a very creepy climax. A must for connoisseurs of the curious and bizarre, this ambitious spine chiller is a seminal sci-fi horror spectacular.

Martin Kosleck Peter Bartell • **Rita Morley** Laura Winters • **Byron Sanders** Grant Murdock • **Ray Tudor** Omar • **Barbara Wilkin** Jan Letterman
Director *Jack Curtis*
Screenplay *Arnold Drake*
Special effects *Ray Benson* •
Cinematographer *Carson Davidson*

Flesh Feast ★

1970 US Colour 72mins

What do Hollywood glamour queens do when they retire? Play homicidal maniacs, of course. The trend started memorably with *What Ever Happened to Baby Jane?* but hit rock bottom with this tasteless and cheap mess of a movie. Lured back to the screen long after her glory days of the forties, Veronica Lake plays a scientist conducting anti-ageing experiments using live maggots that devour old skin tissue. It's an interesting approach to cosmetic surgery! This was Lake's last film and was filmed in Florida in what looks rather like director Brad F Grinter's sitting room.

Veronica Lake Dr Elaine Frederick • **Phil Philbin** Ed Casey • **Heather Hughes** Kristine • **Martha Mischon** • **Yanka Mann** • **Dian Wilhite** • **Chris Martell**
Director *Brad F Grinter*
Screenplay *Brad F Grinter, Thomas Casey*
Cinematographer *Thomas Casey*
Special effects *Doug Hobart*

Flesh for Frankenstein ★★★ 18

1974 US Colour 90mins [video]

Explicit blood-letting and violence overwhelms director Paul Morrisey's shockingly funny exposé of the venal grime behind Victorian aristocracy. Udo Kier is wonderfully arrogant and bad-tempered as the Nietzschean Baron dismembering the local townspeople to build the perfect Aryan male and his female mate. Originally shown in excellent 3-D (the reason why sharp instruments are constantly being thrust into the camera) a strong stomach is still needed to witness the flattened down lurid gore and sickening splatter. Full of camp quotable dialogue and a particularly hilarious sex scene between Joe Dallesandro and Monique van Vooren.

Joe Dallesandro Nicholas • **Udo Kier** Frankenstein • **Monique Van Vooren** Katrin • **Arno Juerging** Otto • **Srdjan Zelenovic** Man Monster
Director *Paul Morrissey*
Screenplay *Paul Morrissey, Tonino Guerra*
Producer *Andy Warhol*

Flesh Gordon ★★ 18

1974 US Colour 84mins [video]

Only in Britain would this limp sex spoof of the Flash Gordon Saturday morning pictures adventure series have become a theatrical, and then later, video hit. Jason Williams in the title role, Suzanne Fields, John Hoyt and a cameo from real-life porn star Candy Samples supply the talent. The Earth is being bombarded with a sex ray from the Planet Porno, and Flesh Gordon is the man to save us from our naughty selves. Not hilarious, but harmless all the same.

Jason Williams Flesh Gordon • **Suzanne Fields** Dale Ardor • **Joseph Hudgins** Dr Flexi Jerkoff • **John Hoyt** Professor Gordon • **William Hunt [William Dennis Hunt]** Emperor Wang • **Craig T Brandy** (uncredited) Voice of the monster • **Candy Samples**
Director *Howard Ziehm, Michael Benveniste*
Screenplay *Michael Benveniste*

Flight of the Navigator ★★★ U

1986 US Colour 85mins [video]

An appealing children's adventure that has just enough quirky touches to keep adults involved as well. Joey Cramer is the youngster who goes missing at the age of 12, only to turn up eight years later completely unchanged. It soon becomes apparent that his disappearance is linked to alien space travel. The scenes where Cramer attempts to get to grips with the fact that he has missed out on eight years of his life (his younger brother is now his elder) are neatly handled by director Randal Kleiser, who proves equally adept at the action sequences. Of the adults, Veronica Cartwright and Howard Hesseman come off best, while a pre-stardom Pee-Wee

Herman (aka Paul Reubens) provides the voice of Cramer's friendly robot.

Joey Cramer David Freeman • **Veronica Cartwright** Helen Freeman • **Cliff De Young** Bill Freeman • **Sarah Jessica Parker** Carolyn McAdams • **Howard Hesseman** Dr Faraday • **Paul Mall** Max • **Robert Small** Troy • **Matt Adler** Jeff aged 16 • **Albie Whitaker** Jeff aged eight
Director *Randal Kleiser*
Screenplay *Michael Burton, Matt MacManus, from a story by Mark H Baker*

The Flight That Disappeared
★ U

1961 US BW 72mins

A weak effort from Reginald Le Borg, the Poverty Row director responsible for such fifties trash classics as *The Black Sleep*. Three nuclear scientists are on board a plane headed for Washington, armed with plans for a powerful super-bomb. Their flight reaches an altitude that suddenly shifts them into another dimension, where a jury representing future generations subjects them to a trial for their warrior invention. A slight plea-for-pacifism ethical drama further let down by a confusing script and shoddy production values.

Craig Hill Tom Endicott • **Paula Raymond** Marcia Paxton • **Dayton Lummis** Dr Morris • **Gregory Morton** Examiner • **John Bryant** Hank Norton • **Addison Richards** Sage • **Nancy Hale** Barbara Nielsen • **Bernadette Hale** Joan Agnew
Director *Reginald Le Borg*
Screenplay *Ralph Hart, Judith Hart, Owen Harris*

Flight to Mars ★ U

1951 US Colour 71mins

A ramshackle space opera in comic-strip style about mankind's first landing on Mars and the discovery of an advanced, dying underground civilisation plotting an Earth invasion because they are running low on natural resources. Shot in 11 days by infamous quickie merchants Monogram Studios, this uninspired pulp nonsense launched star Cameron Mitchell's low budget B-movie career. Some chuckles are to be had from the Martian girls wearing silver miniskirts, but there's not much else. Mitchell's astronaut costume was a leftover from *Destination Moon*, a hit movie that this film tried to cash in on.

Marguerite Chapman Alita • **Cameron Mitchell** Steve • **Arthur Franz** Jim • **Virginia Huston** Carol • **John Litel** Dr Lane • **Richard Gaines** Prof Jackson • **Morris Ankrum** Ikron • **Lucille Barkley** Terris
Director *Lesley Selander*
Screenplay *Arthur Strawn*

The Flipside of Dominick Hide
★★★★

TV 1980 UK Colour 95mins

A 1982 *Play for Today* written by Jeremy Paul and director Alan Gibson (*Dracula AD 1972*), this rather sweet time travel story follows Dominick Hide (Peter Firth), naive inhabitant of a rare upbeat British TV future, as he journeys in a flying saucer from 2130 to the eighties in order to study London's historical transport system. While searching for an ancestor, Dominick has an affair with modern girl Jane (Caroline Langrishe) and becomes his own great-great-great grandfather – a not-unpredictable twist carried off by the charm of the playing. Firth's future man, mistaken for a priest because of his odd hat, assumes himself to be smarter than the primitives of the past, but keeps literally tripping over historical customs – used to holographic entertainers plucking Lennon and McCartney on a mandolin, he tries to walk through a guitarist in a restaurant. Dominick's future wife Ava is played by Pippa Guard, in an interesting contrast with Langrishe, while his boss Caleb Line affords Patrick Magee an opportunity to glower. Paul and Gibson delivered a 1982 sequel, *Another Flip for Dominick*.

Peter Firth Dominick Hide • **Pippa Guard** Ava • **Caroline Langrishe** Jane • **Patrick Magee** Caleb Line
Director *Alan Gibson*
Written by *Jeremy Paul, Alan Gibson*
Producer *Chris Cherry*

SFacts

Critics raved about *The Flipside of Dominick Hide*: "Funny, romantic and ingenious", said *The Observer*, while *The Times* called it "a delicious romp". It went on the win the award for Best Dramatic Script and the Special Jury Prize at the Banff Television Festival.

Flubber ★★★ U

1997 US Colour 90mins DVD

Flubber carries on Hollywood's recent obsession with souping-up the hit comedies of the sixties – in this case *The Absent Minded Professor* (1961) – with today's sophisticated special effects. Robin Williams is Philip Brainard, a scientist who becomes so immersed in creating a new energy source that he once again misses his own wedding. But this time he has an excuse, if only his long-suffering fiancée will listen, because he has invented Flubber – a substance like rubber which generates its own energy, wreaking havoc everywhere it goes. In fact it gives inanimate objects a life of their own, resulting in *Home Alone*-style attacks on baddies by everything from toy robots to bowling balls. Kids will lap it up.

Robin Williams Professor Philip Brainard • **Marcia Gay Harden** Sara Jean Reynolds • **Christopher McDonald** Wilson Croft • **Raymond J Barry** Chester Hoenicker • **Clancy Brown** Smith • **Ted Levine** Wesson • **Wil Wheaton** Bennett Hoenicker • **Edie McClurg** Martha George
Director *Les Mayfield*
Screenplay *John Hughes, Bill Walsh, from the story "A Situation of Gravity" by Samuel W Taylor*
Producer *John Hughes, Ricardo Mestres* • ***Executive Producer*** *David Nicksay* • ***Co-producer*** *Michael Polaire* • ***Associate producer*** *Nilo Rodis*

The Fly ★★★ 15

1958 US Colour 89mins

No match for the superior David Cronenberg remake, but still a slick slice of absurdist fifties' sci-fi in its own right. Based on a *Playboy* short story, with a script by *Shogun* writer James Clavell, the plot has matter-transmitter experiments giving Al Hedison (later David Hedison) the head and arm of a common house fly, while Vincent Price, as Hedison's brother, has histrionics about family curses. Enjoyably unsettling once past the inconsistencies of the premise, this plush flesh-crawler includes many marvellous moments to savour, not least of which are the fly's-eye prism view and the tiny half human/half fly trapped in a cobweb shrieking "Help me!".

Al Hedison [David Hedison] Andre • **Patricia Owens** Helene • **Vincent Price** Francois • **Herbert Marshall** Inspector Charas • **Kathleen Freeman** Emma • **Betty Lou Gerson** Nurse Andersone • **Charles Herbert** Philippe • **Eugene Borden** Dr Ejoute • **Torben Meyer** Gaston
Director *Kurt Neumann*
Screenplay *James Clavell, from a story by George Langelaan*

The Fly ★★★★ 18

1986 US Colour 91mins

It's easy to see why visceral visionary David Cronenberg wanted to remake the landmark 1958 chiller about scientific experiments in molecular teleportation. It plunges into the same primal territory he explored in *Shivers*, *Rabid* and *Videodrome* by regurgitating his deep-seated fears of ageing, disease, deformity and the beast within. Only Cronenberg can get away with working out his raw phobias on screen while being poignantly witty and repulsively entertaining at the same time. Jeff Goldblum's sensitive performance takes the edge off the grisly special effects, but many will find it hard to get past the gooey gore to the message. Contains some swearing.

Jeff Goldblum Seth Brundle • **Geena Davis** Veronica Quaife • **John Getz** Stathis Borans • **Joy Boushel** Tawny • **Les Carlson** Dr Cheevers • **George Chuvalo** Marky • **David Cronenberg** Gynaecologist • **Carol Lazare** Nurse • **Shawn Hewitt** Clerk
Director *David Cronenberg*
Screenplay *Charles Edward Pogue, David Cronenberg, from a story by George Langelaan*

The Fly II ★★ 18

1989 US Colour 100mins

Exactly what you'd expect from special effects and make-up artist-turned-director Chris Walas: too much emphasis on gore galore and scant attention paid to plot. Not that there is one, really merely sketchy broad strokes showing Son of the Fly going berserk in a labyrinthine biochemical laboratory. Eric Stoltz does what he can encased in rubber as the misunderstood larva, but it goes without saying that this obvious sequel, inspired more by *Alien*, has none of the sly subtlety, horrific elegance or poignant humour David Cronenberg brought to his superior 1986 film. Still, the Muppet-style deformed dog is a laugh. Contains swearing and violence.

Eric Stoltz Martin Brundle • **Daphne Zuniga** Beth Logan • **Lee Richardson** Anton Bartok • **John Getz** Stathis Borans • **Frank Turner** Dr Shepard • **Ann Marie Lee** Dr Jainway • **Gary Chalk** Scorby • **Saffron Henderson** Ronnie • **Harley Cross** Martin aged 10 • **Matthew Moore** Martin aged 4 • **Rob Roy** Wiley • **Andrew Rhodes** Hargis • **Pat Bermel** Mackenzie • **William Taylor** Dr Trimble • **Jerry Wasserman** Simms • **Duncan Fraser** Obstetrician • **Janet Hodgkinson** Nurse • **Sean O'byrne** Perinatologist • **Mike Winlaw** Neonatologist • **Kimelly Anne Warren** Marla • **Ken Camroux** Linder
Director *Chris Walas*
Screenplay *Mick Garris, Jim Wheat, Frank Darabont, Ken Wheat, from a story by Mick Garris*

Flying Disc Man from Mars ★★★ U

1950 US BW 12x16mins

Containing footage recycled from at least half-a-dozen episodic predecessors, Fred C Bannon's remake of *The Purple Monster Strikes* must be the most derivative serial of all time. Not only does James Craven reprise his role as the scientist who misguidedly assists a mooted Martian invasion, but Gregory Gaye was made to wear the same Mota (yes, "atom" spelt backwards) costume Roy Barcroft used in the original to preclude the need for filming new long shots! However, Mota's gravity-defying spaceship is an inspired touch and the final showdown in the lava trail of an A-bombed volcano is as rousing as it's ridiculous.

Walter Reed Kent Fowler • **Lois Collier** Helen • **Gregory Gaye** Mota • **James Craven** Dr Bryant • **Harry Lauter** Drake • **Tom Steele** Taylor
Director *Fred C Brannon*
Screenplay *Ronald Davidson*

The Flying Saucer ★★ PG

1949 US BW 75mins

Although many fifties sci-fi movies were allegories for the Red Threat, Mikel Conrad's UFO drama comes right out and accuses the Soviets of using space to compromise American security. However, he takes his time getting there both as writer-director and as the government agent who wanders round Alaska seeking witnesses to the mysterious phenomenon that has been illuminating the night sky. It's xenophobic propaganda from start to finish. But, if nothing else, the film led to the word "disc" being dropped in favour of "saucer" to describe extraterrestrial craft.

Mikel Conrad Mike Trent • **Pat Garrison** Vee Langley • **Hantz Von Teuffen** Hans • **Lester Sharpe** Col Marikoff • **Russell Hicks** Hank Thorn • **Frank Darien** Matt Mitchell • **Denver Pyle** Turner • **Roy Engel** Dr Carl Lawton • **Erl Lyon [Earle Lyon]** Alex Muller
Director *Mikel Conrad*
Screenplay *Howard Irving Young, Mikel Conrad, from a story by Mikel Conrad*
Cinematographer *Phillip Tannura*

SFacts

The term "flying saucer" was coined in June 1947 when a businessman named Kenneth Arnold, who was piloting a small plane over the Cascade Mountains in Washington State, claimed to see a group of shiny disks flying through the air at more than 1200 mph. A wave of similar sightings followed. This film was the first to deal with this phenomenon.

The Flying Saucer ★

1964 It Colour 93mins

Hardly ever shown outside its native Italy, this sci-fi tinged farce was produced as a starring vehicle for top comedian Alberto Sordi, known internationally for his minor role in *Those Magnificent Men in Their Flying Machines*. Sordi plays four different characters claiming to have seen a UFO who are each locked up in a lunatic asylum for their persistent ramblings. Very broad, very Italian and with little interest to anyone outside those shores apart from the inclusion of gorgeous Monica (*Modesty Blaise*) Vitti and the fact it was directed by future soft-porn peddler Tinto Brass (*Caligula, Salon Kitty, The Key* and *PO Box: Tinto Brass*). An Italian language film.

Alberto Sordi Vincenzo Berruti • **Monica Vitti** Dolores • **Silvana Mangano** Vittoria • **Eleonora Rossi Drago** Clelia
Director *Tinto Brass*
Screenplay *Rodolfo Sonego*

The Food of the Gods ★★ 18

1975 US Colour 84mins

This "revenge of nature" thriller owes much to big bug movies of the fifties like *Them!* but lacks the charm that made those schlock classics so memorable. Still, it's tough to dislike a movie that incorporates giant chickens and rats in its tale of a remote island where a mystery substance has caused the creatures to grow to an abnormal size. Based loosely on the HG Wells novel, the special effects that are so crucial in making a picture like this work are variable at best, but director Bert I Gordon conjures up some gruesome set-piece deaths such as a man stung to death by a giant wasp. Ultimately this wears out its welcome – once you've seen one giant chicken, you've seen them all.

Marjoe Gortner Morgan • **Pamela Franklin** Lorna Scott • **Ralph Meeker** Jack Bensington • **Ida Lupino** Mrs Skinner • **Jon Cypher** Brian • **Belinda Balaski** Rita • **Tom Stovall** Tom • **John McLiam** Mr Skinner
Director *Bert I Gordon*
Screenplay *Bert I Gordon, from the novel by HG Wells*
Producer *Bert I Gordon*

Forbidden Planet ★★★★★ U

1956 US Colour 94mins

What unknown terror roams the planet Altair-4 killing everyone apart from tormented scientist Morbius (Walter Pidgeon) and his daughter Altaira (Anne Francis)? Starship commander Leslie Nielsen (long before he turned *Airplane!* comedian) finds out in one of the finest science-fiction films ever made. Loosely based on Shakespeare's *The Tempest*, which explains its overall intelligence, this is an enthralling eye-popper. The super monster effects (created by Disney animators) and outstanding technology include the unforgettable Robby the Robot, the subterranean Krell city, Morbius's futuristic home and an impressive array of space vehicles. The *2001* of the fifties.

Walter Pidgeon Dr Morbius • **Anne Francis** Altaira • **Leslie Nielsen** Commander Adams • **Warren Stevens** Lieutenant "Doc" Ostrow • **Jack Kelly** Lieutenant Farman • **Richard Anderson** Chief Quinn • **Earl Holliman** Cook • **George Wallace [George D Wallace]** Bosun • **Bob Dix [Robert Dix]** Grey • **Jimmy Thompson** Youngerford • **Marvin Miller** Robby the Robot
Director *Fred McLeod Wilcox [Fred M Wilcox]*
Screenplay *Cyril Hume, from a story by Irving Block, Allen Adler*

SFacts

Forbidden Planet **was the first film to have a score entirely performed by electronic instruments – the soundtrack took a year to complete. *Forbidden Planet* was also the first science-fiction film to cost $1 million.**

Forbidden World ★★ 18

1982 US Colour 76mins

This Roger Corman-produced follow-up to the similarly themed *Galaxy of Terror* is typical exploitation fare and yet another in the endless line of *Alien* rip-offs. Jesse Vint plays the intergalactic troubleshooter sent to investigate when food researchers start being devoured by the fast-growing organism they have created. Thoroughly predictable from start to finish, this does at least boast decent (and plentiful!) gore effects and suitably claustrophobic set design. The Giger-esque monster is amusingly slain by feeding it the cancerous liver of a dying scientist – a cinematic first?

Jesse Vint Mike Colby • **Dawn Dunlap** Tracy Baxter • **June Chadwick** Dr Barbara Glaser • **Linden Chiles** Dr Gordon Hauser • **Fox Harris** Dr Cal Tinbergen • **Raymond Oliver** Brian Beale • **Scott Paulin** Earl Richards
Director *Allan Holzman*
Screenplay *Tim Curnen, from a story by Jim Wynorski, RJ Robertson*

Forever Young ★★ PG

1992 US Colour 97mins DVD

This humdrum romantic fantasy is no more than a minor entry in the Mel Gibson canon. The star obviously had to dig deep to find the enthusiasm to carry off his tired role, playing a cryogenic Rip Van Winkle who wakes 53 years after he has been frozen and forgotten. Hollywood used to churn out this kind of fluff with practised ease and it's a pity director Steve Miner couldn't have found the same winning formula here. That said, the reunions are touching, Jamie Lee Curtis provides charming support, and at least we're spared the usual smug time-lapse jokes.

Mel Gibson Daniel McCormick • **Jamie Lee Curtis** Claire • **Elijah Wood** Nat • **Isabel Glasser** Helen • **George Wendt** Harry • **Joe Morton** Cameron • **Nicholas Surovy [Nicolas Surovy]** John • **David Marshall Grant** Wilcox • **Robert Hy Gorman** Felix • **Millie Slavin** Susan Finley • **Michael Goorjian** Steven • **Veronica Lauren** Alice
Director *Steve Miner*
Screenplay *Jeffrey Abrams*

Fortress ★★★ 18

1992 Aus /US Colour 91mins DVD

An entertaining science-fiction thriller, with Christopher Lambert sent to a maximum security prison for conceiving a second child – a crime in director Stuart Gordon's imaginatively-rendered totalitarian future. There he suffers high-tech torture and intense corruption while planning a daring break out. Violent, inventive (watch out for the Intestinator and the Mind Wipe Chamber!) and lots of intriguing fun, *Re-Animator* man Gordon makes this fantasy *Great Escape* meets *Prisoner Cell Block H* a suspenseful roller-coaster ride, despite its pulp limitations. You can't fail to be swept away by its excess verve as the action gets continuously cranked up to ever more fast and furious levels. Contains violence, sweaing, and some nudity.

Christopher Lambert John Brennick • **Kurtwood Smith** Prison Director Poe • **Loryn Locklin** Karen Brennick • **Lincoln Kilpatrick** Abraham • **Clifton Gonzalez** Nino • **Jeffrey Combs** D-Day • **Tom Towles** Stiggs • **Vernon Wells** Maddox • **E Briant Wells** Friendly border guard • **Denni Gordon** Lydia
Director *Stuart Gordon*
Screenplay *Steve Feinberg, Troy Neighbors*

Fortress 2: Re-entry ★★ 15

1999 US/Lux Colour 92mins DVD

Eight years after the moderately successful *Fortress*, Christopher Lambert is inexplicably called back to reprise his role as a rebel imprisoned by an evil global corporation. In the first film, Lambert was banged up in a high-tech underground prison. Here, he's incarcerated aboard an orbiting space slammer. Escaping involves lots of running down corridors and much noisy mayhem, which makes it hard to work out who's doing what to whom, and why. Less glossy and violent than the original, there's nothing especially wrong with *Fortress 2*. There's just nothing here that would make it worth the trip to your local cinema.

Christopher Lambert John Brennick
Director *Geoff Murphy*
Screenplay *John Flock, Peter Doyle, from a story and characters created by Steven Feinberg, Troy Neighbors*

The Foundation Trilogy ★★★★

Radio 1973 UK 8x60mins

Adapted from Isaac Asimov's original *Foundation* trilogy – which he worked on from 1941 to 1958. Even over eight episodes, the series has trouble getting in all the galaxy-spanning action of the novels, and Asimov's preference for the broad sweep of history over individuals makes it hard to get much emotional affect from the rise and fall of whole societies. The story concerns the decay of a Galactic Empire to be replaced by the Foundation, a trans-planetary government inspired by the psycho-historical visions of maths genius Hari Seldon (William Eedle), which is itself opposed by sundry self-interested would-be rulers – notably the Mole (Wolfe Morris), a megalomaniacal telepathic mutant. With footnotes from a robotic encyclopedia (David Valla) who clearly inspired Douglas Adams' *Hitch-Hiker's Guide to the Galaxy* and a lot of radiophonic effects, this is an epic on a scale that no other medium could mount and a terrific cast of British radio voices succeed in imbuing some of Asimov's stick figures with genuine character. Available on audio-cassette.

William Eedle Harry Seldon • **Lee Montague** Salvor Hardin • **Geoffrey Beevers** Gaal Dornick • **John Hollis** Yohan Lee • **Angela Pleasence** Bayta Darell • **Maurice Denham** Ebling Mis • **Gary Watson** Toran Darell • **Nigel Anthony** Prince Dagobert • **Wolfe Morris** Magnifico the Mule • **Sarah Frampton** Arkady Darell • **Cyril Shaps** First Guardian/Preem Palver • **Peter Pratt** Lord Stettin • **Prunella Scales** Lady Callia
Dramatised by *Patrick Tull, Mike Stott, from the novels "Foundation", "Foundation and Empire" and "Second Foundation" by Isaac Asimov*
Director *David Cain*
Producer *David Cain, David H Godfrey*

4D Man ★★

1959 US Colour 85mins

Research scientist Robert Lansing discovers the secret of penetrating solid matter when he accidentally opens a fourth dimension thanks to an electric motor stirring up his brainwaves. Entering a sordid life of crime due to his power, he must keep replenishing his life force by passing through the bodies of others or else suffer from premature aging. Passable special effects make this novel effort from *The Blob* team reasonably engaging, despite some overwrought acting and plot inconsistencies.

Robert Lansing Scott Nelson • **Lee Meriwether** Linda Davis • **James Congdon** Tony Nelson • **Guy Raymond** Fred • **Edgar Stehli** Dr Carson • **Robert Strauss** Roy Parker • **Patty Duke** Marjorie Sullivan
Director *Irvin S Yeaworth Jr*
Screenplay *Theodore Simonson, Cy Chermak*

Four-Sided Triangle ★★

1953 UK BW 84mins

When scientists Stephen Murray and John Van Eyssen fall in love with the same girl (Barbara Payton, star of *Bride of the Gorilla*) they solve their rivalry by making a duplicate of her. But then the lovesick duo face an even worse situation as the identical copy still loves the same man. One of the earliest Hammer movies made prior to their international breakthrough with *The Quatermass Experiment* and *The Curse of Frankenstein*, this slow-moving cautionary tale is methodically helmed by future Hammer in-house director Terence Fisher with little of the flair he would soon be famous for. Reminiscent of *Frankenstein* in a Home Counties setting, this literate curiosity is seen by Hammer fans as a distinct pointer towards the House of Horrors to come.

Barbara Payton Lena/Helen • **Percy Marmont** Sir Walter • **James Hayter** Dr Harvey • **Stephen Murray** Bill • **John Van Eyssen** Robin • **Glynn Dearman** Bill as a child • **Sean Barrett** Robin as a child
Director *Terence Fisher*
Screenplay *Terence Fisher, Paul Tabori, from the novel "Four-Sided Triangle" by William F Temple*

14 Going on 30 ★★ U

1988 US Colour 81mins

This Disney made-for-TV movie just managed to beat the similarly themed *Big* on to the screen in 1988, although the subsequent fame of the latter means it will always been seen as a cash-in. However, it is certainly superior to some of the bigger-budget body-swapping comedies that followed in *Big*'s wake. Gabriel Olds is the young boy besotted with his teacher, who finds that being a grown-up isn't what it's cracked up to be when he takes a secret growth drug. This now familiar tale still boasts a modest charm and the performances are uniformly good.

Steve Eckholdt Danny O'Neil/Mr Forndexter • **Daphne Ashbrook** Miss Noble • **Adam Carl** Lloyd • **Gabriel Olds** Young Danny O'Neil • **Rick Rossovich** Roy Kelton • **Loretta Swit** Miss Horton • **Patrick Duffy** Film Star
Screenplay *Richard Jefferies, from a story by James Orr, Jim Cruickshank*

Frank Herbert's Dune ★★★★ 12

TV 2000 US Colour 360mins

The US Sci-Fi Channel whips up a real desert storm with its engrossing six-hour adaptation of Frank Herbert's epic masterpiece. Written and directed by John Harrison, the mini-series charts Paul Atreides's transformation from banished prince to intergalactic messiah in a manner which is much more coherent than David Lynch's bewildering yet bedazzling film adaptation. William Hurt, Saskia Reeves, Alec Newman and Ian McNeice head an admirable cast, while the mini-series' cinematic production design and photography provide an oasis from its dry patches and variable effects. Ultimately, though, the project's main strength lies with its source material and its adherence to Herbert's unique tale of sci-fi, politics and mysticism. Following the mini-series' record ratings, a sequel is in the works based on *Dune Messiah*.

William Hurt Duke Leto Atreides • **Alec Newman** Paul Atreides/Muad'Dib • **Saskia Reeves** Lady Jessica Atreides • **Ian McNeice** Baron Vladimir Harkonnen • **James Watson** Duncan Idaho • **Jan Vlasak** Thufir Hawak • **Laura Burton** St Alia Atreides • **Julie Cox** Princess Irulan Corrino • **Christopher Lee** Jamis
Director *John Harrison*
Written by *John Harrison, from the novel by Frank Herbert*
Cinematographer *Vittorio Storaro*

Frankenstein ★★★★★ PG

1931 US BW 68mins

"It's Alive!" Shocking in its day and still a genuinely creepy experience, director James Whale's primitive yet enthralling interpretation of Mary Shelley's classic tale of man playing God is the most influential genre movie ever made. Its success kick-started the golden age of horror for Universal Studios and provided inspiration for scores of imitators and successors. Boris Karloff breathes miraculous life into his definitive monster portrayal: the most touching moment is the creature reaching up to grasp a ray of sunlight. A superb cast, imaginative set design and Whale's innovative direction using bizarre camera angles invoke a remarkably tense and melancholy atmosphere, while the creation scene itself is a masterpiece of gothic science gone mad.

Colin Clive Dr Frankenstein • **Boris Karloff** The Monster • **Mae Clarke** Elizabeth • **John Boles** Victor • **Edward Van Sloan** Dr Waldman • **Dwight Frye** Fritz, the dwarf • **Frederick Kerr** Baron • **Lionel Belmore** Burgomaster • **Michael Mark** Ludwig, peasant father • **Marilyn Harris** Maria, the child • **Arletta Duncan** Bridesmaid • **Pauline Moore** Bridesmaid • **Francis Ford** Villager
Director *James Whale*
Screenplay *Garrett Fort, Francis Edwards Faragoh, John L Balderston, Robert Florey, from the novel by Mary Shelley, from the play by Peggy Webling*
Cinematographer *Arthur Edeson* • ***Art director*** *Charles D Hall*

SCI Q

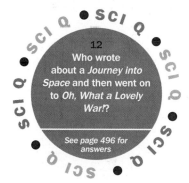

12
Who wrote about a *Journey into Space* and then went on to *Oh, What a Lovely War!*?

See page 496 for answers

Frankenstein ★★

TV 1973 US Colour 130mins

The same year as he directed *Dracula*, Dan Curtis produced and co-wrote this doggedly undistinguished version of the Mary Shelley classic as a two-part, three-hour mini-series. Much of the threadbare padding is thankfully missing in the cut-down video version starring miscast Robert Foxworth as the rebellious baron and gentle giant Bo Svenson as his sympathetic monster. Hammy performances can't disguise the cheapness of the enterprise or the pedestrian direction by Glenn Jordan. Roger Corman starlet Susan Strasberg is the love interest.

Robert Foxworth Dr Frankenstein • **Susan Strasberg** Elisabeth • **Bo Svenson** Creature • **Heidi Vaughan** Agatha • **Philip Bourneuf** Alphonse Frankenstein • **Robert Gentry** Henri Clerval • **Jon Lormer** Charles • **William Hansen** Prof Waldman • **John Karlen** Otto Roget • **Willie Aames**

William Frankenstein
Director Glenn Jordan
Screenplay Sam Hall, Richard Landaur, from the novel by Mary Shelley

Frankenstein ★★★ 15

1992 US/UK Colour 111mins

Made for cable television by David Wickes, the writer/producer/director of the TV mini-series *Jack The Ripper* and *Jekyll & Hyde*, this faithful adaptation of the classic tale is remarkably similar in tone and style to Kenneth Branagh's *Mary Shelley's Frankenstein* (1994), which it beat into European cinema release. Patrick Bergin is good as the Baron who duplicates his own body into the unfinished Randy Quaid, and Sir John Mills plays the blind hermit. Shot in England and Poland, this richly ornate version is told as one long flashback to a ship's captain.

Patrick Bergin Victor Frankenstein • **Randy Quaid** The Monster • **John Mills** Delacey •
Director David Wickes

SCI Q • SCI Q • SCI Q • SCI Q • SCI Q •

13

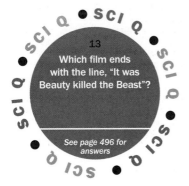

Which film ends with the line, "It was Beauty killed the Beast"?

See page 496 for answers

Frankenstein and the Monster from Hell ★★ 15

1973 UK Colour 90mins

The sixth Hammer *Frankenstein* goes back to the gothic roots of its fifties versions in style, and is a fitting end to both the series and director Terence Fisher's brilliant career. Peter Cushing returns as the obsessed Baron Frankenstein, this time creating a new monster (Dave Prowse) from the lunatic inmates of Carlsbad's asylum for the criminally insane. Hammer protégé Shane Briant engagingly plays his willing disciple, while Madeline Smith stars as a mute girl in this efficiently horrifying exercise, packed with gruesome close-ups and laboratory black humour. Cushing thought his hairpiece made him look like Helen Hayes.

Peter Cushing Baron Frankenstein • **Shane Briant** Dr Simon Helder • **Dave Prowse** Creature • **Madeline Smith** Sarah, the Angel • **Bernard Lee** Tarmut • **Norman Mitchell** Policeman • **Patrick Troughton** Body snatcher • **Charles Lloyd Pack** Professor Durendel • **Sydney Bromley** Muller • **Philip Voss** Ernst • **John Stratton** Asylum Director • **Clifford Mollison** Judge • **Janet Hargreaves** Chatter
Director Terence Fisher
Screenplay John Elder [Anthony Hinds]

Frankenstein Created Woman ★★★ 15

1966 UK Colour 87mins

Considered by Hammer aficionados to be the best Frankenstein made by the House of Horror, veteran director Terence Fisher's off-beat entry finds the good doctor experimenting with soul transference. Re-animating the corpse of a young girl Susan Denberg, once *Playboy's* Miss August, the ever-dependable Peter Cushing (in his fourth outing as the mad doctor) gives it the soul of her boyfriend, who was wrongly guillotined for murder. The chilling result is a vengeful creature luring his/her enemies to remote places promising romance but delivering death. Fisher's neat balance of fairy-tale fear, psychological horror, murky sexuality and engaging lunacy makes this a fine addition to the genre.

Peter Cushing Baron Frankenstein • **Susan Denberg** Christina • **Thorley Walters** Dr Hertz • **Robert Morris** Hans • **Duncan Lamont** Prisoner • **Peter Blythe** Anton • **Barry Warren** Karl • **Derek Fowlds** Johann • **Alan MacNaughtan** Kleve • **Peter Madden** Chief of police • **Ivan Beavis** New landlord • **Colin Jeavons** Priest • **Stuart Middleton** Hans as a boy
Director Terence Fisher

Frankenstein General Hospital ★ 15

1988 US Colour and BW 86mins

Nowhere near as cleverly funny as improv comedian Mark Blankfield's first outing *Jekyll and Hyde… Together Again*, this smut-ridden, toilet-obsessed lampoon is a tedious trawl through Mary Shelley territory. Blankfield stars as Dr Robert Frankenheimer, great-grandson of you-know-who, who builds a body from autopsy leftovers with the help of his assistant Iggy (Leslie Jordan). A flat farce drenched in awful puns with only the subterranean laboratory scenes – shot in black and white – showing any imagination on director Deborah Roberts's part. Bobby "Boris" Pickett of *Monster Mash* fame appears in a cameo.

Mark Blankfield Dr Bob Frankenheimer • **Leslie Jordan** Iggy • **Jonathan Farwell** Dr Frank Reutger • **Lou Cutell** Dr Saperstein • **Kathy Shower** Dr Alice Singleton • **Katie Caple** Nurse Verna • **Irwin Keyes** Monster • **Bobby "Boris" Pickett** Man in elevator
Director Deborah Roberts
Screenplay Michael Kelly, Robert Deel, from the novel by Mary Shelley

Frankenstein Meets the Devil Fish ★★

1964 Jap/US Colour 87mins

One of the more inventive re-workings of the *Frankenstein* myth collapses into a typical Toho monster battle in *Godzilla* director Inoshiro Honda's daffy spectacular. A young kid eats the Hiroshima-infected heart of the Frankenstein monster and grows into a 30-foot tall mutated caveman, who saves Japan's rebuilding programme from the rampaging dinosaur Baragon. Nick Adams is on call as the friendly American scientist in a ridiculous, yet enormously fun, addition to the Japanese monster hall of fame.

Nick Adams Dr James Bowen • **Tadao Takashima** Scientist • **Kumi Mizuno** Woman doctor • **Yoshio Tsuchiya** • **Takashi Shimura** • **Kenchiro Kawaji** • **Seuko Togami**
Director Inoshiro Honda
Screenplay Kaoru Mabuchi, from a synopsis by Jerry Sohl, from a story by Reuben Bercovitch

Frankenstein Meets the Space Monster ★

1965 US BW 76mins

One of the worst movies ever made, this poverty-stricken camp turkey provides loads of unintentional laughs thanks to misplaced rock music and some very obvious stock footage. All this and go-go girls being abducted, too. Shot in Puerto Rico, it actually has nothing whatsoever to do with the Frankenstein legend. Evil space Princess Marcuzan (Marilyn Hanold) and her effeminate gnome assistant Nadir (Lou Cutell) land on earth to capture fresh virgins for their dying planet. Android astronaut Saunders (Robert Reilly) crash lands near them, becomes a crazed killer when short-circuited by their ray gun, and battles their pet monster Mull in an attempt to free the kidnapped go-go girls. It's so crudely made that director Robert Gaffney's juvenile heap actually resembles a home movie, and the startling Freudian terms bandied around by Nadir seem to belong to a different film altogether.

James Karen Dr Adam Steele • **David**

Kernan General Bowers • **Nancy Marshall** Karen Grant • **Marilyn Hanold** Princess Marcuzan • **Lou Cutell** Nadir • **Robert Reilly** Col Frank Saunders/Frankenstein
Director *Robert Gaffney*
Screenplay *George Garrett, from a story by George Garrett, John Rodenbeck*
Cinematographer *Saul Midwall*

Frankenstein Meets the Wolf Man ★★★

1943 US BW 73mins

While not quite the clash of the century as touted by Universal, the fifth feature in its series was the first time two celebrity monsters shared the screen. Picking up where both *The Wolfman* (1941) and *The Ghost of Frankenstein* (1942) left off, this entertaining sequel has werewolf Lon Chaney Jr seeking out the dead Frankenstein's diary, containing the cure for his lycanthropy, and stumbling across the monster (Bela Lugosi in his only appearance as the creature) encased in ice. Not particularly horrific, director Roy William Neill's monster mish-mash is still charming fun because of the skilled acting, cheap thrills and trademark Universal back-lot atmosphere.

Lon Chaney Jr The Wolf Man/Lawrence Talbot • **Ilona Massey** Baroness Elsa Frankenstein • **Patric Knowles** Dr Mannering • **Lionel Atwill** Mayor • **Bela Lugosi** Monster • **Maria Ouspenskaya** Maleva • **Dennis Hoey** Inspector Owen • **Don Barclay** Franzec
Director *Roy William Neill*
Screenplay *Curt Siodmak*
Producer *George Waggner*

Frankenstein Must Be Destroyed ★★★ 18

1969 UK Colour 96mins

The fifth of Hammer's Frankenstein series is graced by an incisive performance from Peter Cushing, up to his old tricks as the Baron performing brain transplants, and a haunting turn by Freddie Jones as the main recipient, an asylum employee whom the Baron has murdered. Jones is astonishing as the anguished victim of the transplant, whose wife fails to recognise him and rejects him, prompting his revenge plan. The gothic gore is once more directed with spirited skill and economy by Terence Fisher (his fourth in the series), although the most memorable Grand Guignol scare has a buried body bursting through the earth because of a broken water pipe. Veronica Carlson wears the diaphanous gowns well.

Peter Cushing Baron Frankenstein • **Simon Ward** Dr Karl Holst • **Veronica Carlson** Anna Spengler • **Freddie Jones** Prof Richter • **Thorley Walters** Insp Frisch • **Maxine Audley** Ella Brandt • **George Pravda** Dr Brandt • **Geoffrey Bayldon** Police doctor • **Harold Goodwin** Burglar
Director *Terence Fisher*
Screenplay *Bert Batt, from a story by Anthony Nelson Keys, Bert Batt*

Frankenstein – 1970 ★

1958 US BW 82mins

Made in the wake of Hammer's successful rejuvenation of the *Frankenstein* franchise, this hugely inept plummet into gothic fakery is significant only in the fact that for the first time in his career Boris Karloff played the Baron and not the creature. Karloff is the grandson of the deceased and disfigured (courtesy of Nazi torturers) Baron Frankenstein, who finds himself so strapped for cash to buy an atomic reactor with which to resuscitate his latest creation that he allows a television crew into the family castle for a touch of *Through the Keyhole* Transylvanian-style. Cue monster goes berserk scenario. A total waste of time, Howard W Koch directs as if in a coma, with Karloff hamming it up as if it were an Olympic event.

Boris Karloff Baron Victor von Frankenstein • **Tom Duggan** Mike Shaw • **Jana Lund** Carolyn Hayes • **Don "Red" Barry [Donald Barry]** Douglas Row • **Charlotte Austin** Judy Stevens • **Irwin Berke** Inspector Raab • **Rudolph Anders** Wilhelm Gottfried
Director *Howard W Koch*
Screenplay *Richard Landau, George Worthing Yates, from a story by Aubrey Schenck, Charles A Moses*

Frankenstein: the College Years ★★ PG

1991 US Colour 88mins

Lightweight but mildly amusing spin on Mary Shelley's venerable horror classic, one which is firmly pitched at a family audience. William Ragsdale, still best known for the horror spoof *Fright Night*, and Christopher Daniel Barnes play a pair of medical students who inadvertently create their own monster, which they name Frank N Stein. It's a long way from the original, but it's attractively played by the two leads, and there is solid support from Larry Miller.

William Ragsdale Mark Chrisman • **Christopher Daniel Barnes** Jay Butterman • **Larry Miller** Albert Loman • **Vincent Hammond** Frank N Stein • **Andrea Elson** Andi Richmond • **De'voreaux White** Kingston Sebuka • **Patrick Richwood** Blaine Muller
Director *Tom Shadyac*
Screenplay *Bryant Christ, John Trevor Wolff*

Frankenstein: the True Story ★★★★

1973 US Colour 122mins

Kenneth Branagh's 1994 version of the classic horror tale made much of its fidelity to Mary Shelley's source novel, but this earlier version (originally made for US television) remains among the most faithful of the *Frankenstein* adaptations. The most striking aspect of the production is the sympathy with which the monster is portrayed by Michael Sarrazin, minus the once obligatory nuts and bolts, and his relationship with his creator (Leonard Whiting) has a tragic resonance. The film is intelligently scripted by Christopher Isherwood and boasts a distinguished cast of supporting players including John Gielgud, Ralph Richardson and a pre-*Doctor Who* Tom Baker.

James Mason Dr Polidori • **Leonard Whiting** Dr Victor Frankenstein • **David McCallum** Henry Clerval • **Jane Seymour** Agatha/Prima • **Michael Sarrazin** The creature • **Nicola Pagett** Elizabeth Fanschawe • **Michael Wilding** Sir Richard Fanschawe • **Clarissa Kaye** Lady Fanschawe • **Agnes Moorehead** Mrs Blair • **Margaret Leighton** Francoise Duval • **Ralph Richardson** Mr Lacey • **John Gielgud** Chief Constable • **Tom Baker** Sea captain • **Dallas Adams** Felix • **Julian Barnes** Young man • **Arnold Diamond** Passenger in coach
Director *Jack Smight*
Screenplay *Christopher Isherwood, Don Bachardy, from the novel by Mary Shelley*
Producer *Hunt Stromberg Jr*

Frankenstein Unbound ★★★ 18

1990 US Colour 82mins

After nearly 20 years in retirement as a director, Roger Corman returned to the job with an engagingly loopy rewriting of the Frankenstein myth. Based on the novel by Brian W Aldiss, this camp confection jumbles time travel, Mary Shelley's circle of friends, her monstrous fictional creation, dream sequences and an apocalyptic future for a mind-boggling baroque soap opera. More fun, and far scarier, than any other recent *Frankenstein* you might care to mention, Corman's endearing reliance on his trademark terror skills means it feels like he's never been away. Contains violence and sex scenes.

John Hurt Dr Joseph Buchanan • **Raul**

Julia Dr Victor Frankenstein • **Bridget Fonda** Mary Godwin Shelley • **Jason Patric** Lord Byron • **Michael Hutchence** Percy Shelley • **Nick Brimble** The Monster • **Catherine Rabett** Elizabeth • **Bruce McGuire** Prosecutor • **Grady Clarkson** Judge • **Catherine Corman** Justine Moritz
Director *Roger Corman*
Screenplay *Roger Corman, FX Feeney, from the novel by Brian W Aldiss*

Frankenstein's Baby ★★★

TV 1990 UK Colour 75mins

In this futuristic feminist black comedy, that's faintly ridiculous but also highly watchable, Nigel Planer plays a very different character from the much loved Neil in seminal British comedy series *The Young Ones*: a man who gets pregnant. As a yuppy businessman, miffed that his career-orientated girlfriend doesn't want to settle down and have kids, Planer falls into the clutches of the slightly unhinged Dr E Frankenstein (what sort of hospital would hire someone called Frankenstein!) and is impregnated with a living embryo. Much of the humour of Planer's performance derives from the growing dread that his swelling tummy doesn't stem from an over-indulgance at too many power lunches. In 1994, *Junior* subjected Arnold Schwarzenegger to a similar predicament.

Nigel Planer Paul Hocking • **Kate Buffery** Jane Bligh • **Yvonne Bryceland** Dr Frankenstein • **William Armstrong** Rick Cole • **Sian Thomas** Judith Cole • **Gillian Raine** Mrs Bligh
Director *Robert Bierman*
Written by *Emma Tennant*
Producer *Ruth Baumgarten*

FreakyLinks ★★

TV 2000-2001 US Colour 9x60mins

Created by *Blair Witch Project* producer Gregg Hale and veteran genre scribe David Goyer (of *Blade* and *Dark City* fame), this much-hyped show promised major thrills, chills and chuckles, but was fighting for survival within weeks of its US debut. The series revolves around a group of friends who run an underground website devoted to unexplained phenomena, and follows their search for answers. Although its concept and cast are quite promising, the show swiftly emerges as an awkward mix of sci-fi comedy and horror, and feels far too derivative to make logging-on really worthwhile. In fact, the only really remarkable thing about the series was its use of the actual *FreakyLinks* website, which provided US viewers with additional clues about plotlines and even offered extra footage from episodes. Pity the show wasn't half as innovative!

Ethan Embry Derek Barnes/Adam Barnes • **Lisa Sheridan** Chloe Tanner • **Karim Prince** Jason Tatus • **Lizette Carrion** Lan Williams • **Dennis Christopher** Vince Elsing
Written by *Ricardo Festiva, Gregg Hale*

Freedom ★★

TV 2000 US Colour 7x 60mins

The premise is fairly basic: renegade military forces take over the US government leaving the future of the country in the hands of a resistance movement. Four people – Holt McCallany, Scarlet Chorvat, Bodhi Elfman and Darius McCrary – are set free after being arrested by the military and must join forces to try to reinstate the legitimate government. The leads generate a great deal of on-screen chemistry, while the series takes its audience seriously. But despite the balletic fight scenes *à la Matrix*, this only survived for seven episodes.

Holt McCallany Owen Decker • **Scarlett Chorvat** Becca Shaw • **Bodhi Elfman** Londo Pearl • **Darius McCrary** James Barrett • **Georg Stanford Brown** Walter Young • **James Morrison** Colonel Tim Devon • **Francoise Yip** Jin
Created by *Hans Tobeason*
Executive producer *Dan Cracchiolo, Joel Silve, Hans Tobeason*

Freejack ★★ 15

1992 US Colour 105mins

Based on an imaginative and surprising novel, this opts instead for sci-fi cliché and obvious thrills as Emilio Estevez is plucked from near-death in a racing accident to house the brain of a future-age Anthony Hopkins. Mick Jagger – appearing in a big-screen dramatic role for the first time since 1970's *Performance* and *Ned Kelly* – suitably interprets his devious mercenary as a cynical yobbo, but it's a sin not to give talent like Rene Russo and Hopkins himself meatier roles. Contains swearing and violence.

Emilio Estevez Alex Furlong • **Rene Russo** Julie Redlund • **Mick Jagger** Vacendak • **Anthony Hopkins** McCandless • **Jonathan Banks** Michelette • **David Johansen** Brad • **Amanda Plummer** Nun • **Grand L Bush** Boone • **John Shea** Morgan • **Frankie Faison** Eagle man • **Esai Morales** Ripper
Director *Geoff Murphy*
Screenplay *Steven Pressfield, Ronald Shusett, Dan Gilroy, from a story by Steven Pressfield, Ronald Shusett, from the novel "Immortality Inc" by Robert Sheckley*

Frequency ★★★★ 15

2000 US Colour 118mins

Changing the past to alter the present is the intriguing premise of this diverting thriller. Via an ancient ham radio set, Jim Caviezel is able to speak to his beloved fireman dad (Dennis Quaid) across 30 years of time, on the day before the latter is due to die in a warehouse blaze. Forewarned by Caviezel, Quaid escapes his fate, but his survival changes history: suddenly, Caviezel's mum (Elizabeth Mitchell) no longer exists! Combining a relationship yarn with a race-against-time bid to hunt down a killer, *Frequency* plays like a big-budget episode of *The Twilight Zone*. Paradoxes appear as the film gets increasingly complex, but our interest is maintained by fine performances from Quaid and Caveziel and by sharp direction from Gregory Hoblit, whose only serious misjudgement is an unforgivably slushy finale.

Dennis Quaid Frank Sullivan • **Jim Caviezel [James Caviezel]** John Sullivan • **André Braugher** Satch DeLeon • **Elizabeth Mitchell** Julia Sullivan • **Noah Emmerich** Gordo Hersch • **Shawn Doyle** Jack Shepard • **Jordan Bridges** Graham Gibson • **Melissa Errico** Samantha Thomas
Director *Gregory Hoblit*
Screenplay *Toby Emmerich*

The Friendly Persuaders ★★

TV 1969 UK BW 90mins

A feature-length ATV play, scripted by Paul Wheeler and directed by John Sichel, on the time-honoured "first contact" theme, in which civil servant Steven Leach (regular UK sci-fi hero Edward Judd) is one of the few humans to distrust the utopian vision of the Taraxians, humanoid aliens from a world where automation has afforded the general population a very 1969 opportunity to drop out, make love and lounge around indulgently. Among the familiar faces caught up in the controversy are Joe Melia, Grant Taylor, Jonathan Newth and Milton Johns.

Edward Judd Stephen Leach • **Grant Taylor** Sir Terence Norrington • **Joe Melia** Michael Donnell • **Julian Curry** Adrian Collingwood • **Jonathan Newth** Bernard Webb • **Libby Glenn** Sue Long • **Milton Johns** John Frisby
Director *John Sichel*
Written by *Paul Wheeler*

Frogs ★★

1972 US Colour 90mins

One of the many ecologically-correct horror films of the seventies and certainly one of the silliest. Ray Milland is the wheelchair-bound Southern patriarch whose birthday celebrations are disrupted by a revolt of the swamp creatures he has tried to eliminate with DDT and various insecticides. The intelligent frog population also enrol snakes, bugs and snapping turtles to leap around attacking the obvious upper-class types on their private island. Those who find such creatures scary will find parts of this dumb chiller likewise. If not, it's about as thrilling as a gardening documentary.

Ray Milland Jason Crockett • **Sam Elliott** Pickett Smith • **Joan Van Ark** Karen Crockett • **Adam Roarke** Clint Crockett • **Judy Pace** Bella Berenson • **Lynn Borden** Jenny Crockett • **Mae Mercer** Maybelle • **David Gilliam** Michael
Director *George McCowan*
Screenplay *Robert Hutchison, Robert Blees, from a story by Robert Hutchison*
Producer *George Edwards, Peter Thomas*

From Beyond ★★ 18

1986 US Colour 81mins [video]

Following his gross-out hit *Re-Animator*, Stuart Gordon reunited leads Jeffrey Combs and Barbara Crampton in another HP Lovecraft-based splatter-fest. This sometimes crude clash of horror and sci-fi elements stars Combs as typically unhinged scientist Crawford Tillinghast, whose experiments with the Resonator spark off the usual orgy of murder and mutilation, turning him into a mutated creature with increasingly rubbery effect. This demented tale is sloppily directed, but once it gets going after a stalled start, you can't fault its energy and audacity. Horror fans will delight in the scare-defusing moments of humour and stomach-churning effects.

Jeffrey Combs Crawford Tillinghast • **Barbara Crampton** Dr Katherine McMichaels • **Ken Foree** Bubba Brownlee • **Ted Sorel** Dr Edward Pretorius • **Carolyn Purdy-Gordon** Dr Bloch • **Bunny Summers** Neighbour lady • **Bruce McGuire** Jordan Fields • **Del Russel** Ambulance driver
Director *Stuart Gordon*
Screenplay *Dennis Paoli, Stuart Gordon, Brian Yuzna, from the story by HP Lovecraft*

From Hell It Came ★★

1957 US BW 70mins

Not a problem which pops up too often in *Gardeners' Question Time* – what exactly *do* you do with a man-eating, walking tree? This is the particular dilemma facing Tod Andrews and Tina Carver when an island paradise becomes haunted by a sapling seeking revenge. The unknowns in the cast do their best to keep a straight face, but this really is one for trash fans.

Tod Andrews Dr William Arnold • **Tina Carver** Dr Terry Mason • **Linda Watkins** Mrs Kilgore • **John McNamara** Dr Howard Clark • **Gregg Palmer** Kimo • **Robert Swan** Witch doctor Tano
Director *Dan Milner*
Screenplay *Richard Bernstein, from a story by Richard Bernstein, Jack Milner*

SCI Q

14

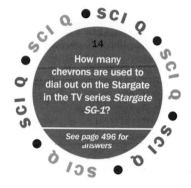

How many chevrons are used to dial out on the Stargate in the TV series *Stargate SG-1*?

See page 496 for answers

From the Earth to the Moon ★★ U

1958 US Colour 99mins [video]

This clunky sci-fi drama can't overcome the miniscule size of its budget, despite the cast of veterans who lurch their way through the material. Made in the wake of the hugely popular *20,000 Leagues under the Sea*, this Jules Verne dramatisation stars Joseph Cotten and George Sanders as the rival scientists with differing views on space travel. Although it's nice to see Debra Paget appearing as the leading lady, the use of ageing stars such as Henry Daniell and Melville Cooper only serve to add to the morbid enjoyment.

Joseph Cotten Victor Barbicane • **George Sanders** Stuyvesant Nicholl • **Debra Paget** Virginia Nicholl • **Don Dubbins** Ben Sharpe • **Patric Knowles** Josef Cartier • **Carl Esmond** JV • **Henry Daniell** Morgana • **Melville Cooper** Bancroft • **Ludwig Stossel** Aldo Von Metz • **Morris Ankrum** US Grant
Director *Byron Haskin*
Screenplay *Robert Blees, James Leicester, from the novel by Jules Verne*

The Frozen Dead ★★

1966 UK Colour and BW 92mins

In this clinically ghoulish, low-budget British shocker, imported American star Dana Andrews plays a latter-day Frankenstein set on reviving 1,500 top Nazi officials who've been in a deep freeze since the war. Although directed with a fatal lack of gusto by Herbert J Leder, the sheer delirium of the premise takes some beating. We have a row of severed arms, all neatly mounted and awaiting use rather like a macabre store aisle of Limbs 'R' Us, and a woman's severed head that lives in a box and which, through the power of mental telepathy, warns others of Andrews' nefarious scheme for jackbooted world domination. It's all bonkers for sure, but also petty dull and the gravitas presence of Andrews lends a credibility that is scarcely merited. Look closely, too, for a young Edward Fox trying desperately hard not to be recognised.

Dana Andrews Dr Norberg • **Anna Palk** Jean Norberg • **Philip Gilbert** Dr Ted Roberts • **Kathleen Breck** Elsa Tenney • **Karel Stepanek** Gen Lubeck • **Basil Henson** Tirpitz • **Alan Tilvern** Karl Essen • **Edward Fox** Prisoner No 3
Director *Herbert J Leder*
Screenplay *Herbert J Leder, from his story*
Cinematographer *Davis Boulton*

Fugitive Mind ★

1999 US Colour

Plagued by nightmares and flashbacks to events he cannot remember, Michael Dudikoff takes much longer than the audience to realise he's not who he thinks he is, and even longer to find out he's the key element of a planned assassination in this *Total Recall* inspired thriller. *Suspect Device* did something similar to this four years earlier (even using one of the same key locations), and at least did it with some zip and crowd-pleasing action. Although director Fred Olen Ray makes this look better than his usual efforts, it's an endless talkfest that becomes as numbing as the many faces that get punched in the course of the movie – which is about as exciting as the action gets.

Michael Dudikoff Robert • **Michele Greene** Robyn • **David Hedison** Davis • **Heather Langenkamp** Suzanne • **Ian Ogilvy** Grace
Director *Fred Olen Ray*

The Fury ★★★★ 18

1978 US Colour 113mins [video]

Brian De Palma finds himself in familiar territory with this follow-up to *Carrie* – an adaptation of John Farris's telekinetic conspiracy thriller. The director adopts a broader suspense canvas than he'd utilised before (the action and slow-motion sequences remain the best he's ever crafted), and turns in a gorgeous horror adventure about two teenagers with psychic powers who become pawns in the machinations of spy factions. Ingeniously plotted, extravagantly staged and beautifully balanced between apocalyptic goriness and full-blooded pyrotechnic imagery, this nail-biting shocker is De Palma's most under-rated movie.

Kirk Douglas Peter Sandza • **John Cassavetes** Childress • **Carrie Snodgress** Hester • **Charles Durning** Dr Jim McKeever • **Amy Irving** Gillian Bellaver • **Fiona Lewis** Dr Susan Charles • **Andrew Stevens** Robin Sandza • **Carol Rossen** Dr Ellen Lindstrom • **Rutanya Alda** Kristen • **Joyce Easton** Katharine Bellaver

Director *Brian De Palma*

Screenplay *John Farris, from his novel*

Future Cop ★★

1976 US Colour 78mins

Veteran policeman Ernest Borgnine is assigned a new partner, who just happens to be an android, in this TV movie. The one-joke premise is that the new cop, Michael Shannon, has a few glitches in his programme and keeps screwing up at the most inopportune times. Borgnine rises to the reasonably funny occasion, Shannon doesn't, and Jud Taylor directs with little panache and feel for the subject matter. A short-lived TV series followed, as well as another forgettable TV movie, the wittily titled *Cops and Robin*.

Ernest Borgnine Joe Cleaver • **Michael Shannon [Michael J Shannon]** John Haven • **John Amos** Sgt Bundy • **John Larch** Forman • **Herbert Nelson** Klausmeier • **Ronnie Claire Edwards** Avery • **James Luisi** Paterno • **Stephen Pearlman** Dorfman • **James Daughton** Young Rookie • **Shirley O'Hara** Grandmother

Director *Jud Taylor*

Screenplay *Anthony Wilson*

Future Hunters ★★ 18

1988 Phil/US Colour 95mins

Veteran British director J Lee Thompson (*Guns of Navarone*, two of the *Planet of the Apes* sequels) had a hand in the script, but this is an otherwise undistinguished straight to video fodder. Robert Patrick, in the days before hitting paydirt with *Terminator 2*, stars in this convoluted fantasy set both in a post-apocalyptic world and modern day Los Angeles. Patrick gives it his best shot, but director Cirio H Santiago never manages to convincingly combine the disparate elements of the story.

Robert Patrick Slade • **Linda Carol** Michelle • **Ed Crick** Fielding • **Bob Schott** Bauer

Director *Cirio H Santiago*

Screenplay *J Lee Thompson, from a story by Anthony Maharaj*

Future Schlock ★

1984 Aus Colour 75mins

Conservative suburbanites imprison non-conformists in a walled-up ghetto after a 21st-century Australian civil war in this blunted political satire. The comedy revs up slightly when rebel prisoners escape to harass their straight-laced captors with vicious pranks. *Mad Max* and *National Lampoon's Animal House* are thrown into this quasi-fantasy blender, but directors Barry Peak and Chris Kiely can't compete with either on the inspiration front, and the title says it all.

Mary-Anne Fahey Sarah • **Michael Bishop** Bear • **Tracey Callander** Ronnie • **Tiriel Mora** Alvin • **Simon Thorpe** Sammy • **Peter Cox** Cap'n Fruitcake • **Keith Walker** Sergeant Tatts • **Evan Zachariah** Skunk • **Gary Adams** Bob • **Deborah Force** Trish

Director/Screenplay *Barry Peak, Chris Kiely*

Futuresport ★★ 15

1998 US Colour 86mins DVD

Made especially for American television consumption, this glossily unimaginative movie borrows so liberally from the far superior *Rollerball* as to appear totally redundant. In the future, a violent game is created in a bid to ease gang tensions, a sort of amalgam of basketball and rugby played on levitating skateboards with an electrified ball. The trio of stars – Dean Cain (*The New Adventures of Superman*), Vanessa L Williams and Wesley Snipes add some much needed lustre to Ernest Dickerson's join-the-dots direction. If you like the more dark, futuristic films such as *Demolition Man*, you may find something satisfying here. Contains swearing and violence, with some sexual references.

Wesley Snipes Obike Fixx • **Dean Cain** Tremaine "Tre" Ramzey • **Vanessa L Williams** Alex Torres • **Bill Smitrovich** Coach Douglas Freeman

Director *Ernest R Dickerson*

Screenplay *Robert Hewitt Wolfe, from a story by Steve Dejarnatt, Robert Hewitt Wolfe*

Executive producer *Wesley Snipes*

Futureworld ★★★ PG

1976 US Colour 102mins

The follow-up to the excellent *Westworld*, this sci-fi thriller is one of the most inventive sequels of the Hollywood blockbuster era. With more than a nod in the direction of Don Siegel's classic *Invasion of the Body Snatchers*, the action concerns the replacement of the world's ruling elite by lookalike robots. A milestone in movie technology, this was the first picture to perfect the use of 3-D computer animation, with the video screen image of Peter Fonda having been produced by computer mapping. Less explosive than its predecessor, this is nevertheless an unnerving watch.

Peter Fonda Chuck Browning • **Blythe Danner** Tracy Ballard • **Arthur Hill** Duffy • **Yul Brynner** Gunslinger • **John Ryan [John P Ryan]** Dr Schneider • **Stuart Margolin** Harry • **Jim Antonio** Ron • **Allen Ludden** Game show host • **Nancy Bell** Erica • **Angela Greene** Mrs Reed • **Robert Cornthwaite** Mr Reed • **Darrell Larson** Eric

Director *Richard T Heffron*

Screenplay *Mayo Simon, George Schenck*

“**This** is Tokyo. Once a city of six million people. What has happened here was caused by a force which up until a few days ago was entirely beyond the scope of man's **imagination.**”

Godzilla 1954

G

Galactica 1980 ★

TV 1980 US Colour 10x60mins

Excruciating sequel to *Battlestar Galactica*, in which the Galacticans finally reach 20th-century Earth, only to discover that its population is not advanced enough to join their fight against the Cylons. As Commander Adama attempts to lead the Cylons away from the planet, Captain Troy and Lieutenant Dillon embark on an undercover mission to secretly speed-up the development of earth's technology. Cancelled after just 10 episodes, the series is unbelievable, unengaging and largely unwatchable sub-kiddie fare. Tellingly, the show's single saving grace is its final instalment, *The Return of Starbuck*, which is set during the original series' run and is quite possibly the entire *Battlestar Galactica*'s franchise's finest hour.

Lorne Greene Cmdr Adama • **Kent McCord** Capt Troy • **Barry Van Dyke** Lt Dillon • **Robyn Douglass** Jamie Hamilton • **James Patrick Stuart** Dr Zee

Created by *Glen A Larson*

Executive producer *Glen A Larson*

Galaxina ★★

1980 US Colour

A late *Star Wars* spoof featuring lowbrow comedy, duff special effects, an awkward *Alien* parody and a central performance by Dorothy Stratten, who was murdered by her estranged husband on the very day it received its American premiere. The doomed starlet is the robot navigator on board a police spaceship, who gets sent on a mission to recover possession of the powerful Blue Star crystal. Few laughs and even fewer thrills are raised thanks to an unfocused script and haphazard direction by Z-movie maestro William Sachs. A sad epitaph for Stratten, whose life story was turned into the acclaimed Bob Fosse movie *Star 80*.

Dorothy Stratten Galaxina • **Stephen Macht** Thor • **Ronald Knight** Ordric • **Lionel Smith** Maurice • **Tad Horino** Sam Wo • **Nancy McCauley** Elexia • **Avery Schreiber** Captain Butt • **Fred D Scott** Commander

Director/Screenplay *William Sachs*

Galaxis ★★★ 15

1995 US Colour 86mins

Statuesque star Brigitte Nielsen can only save her planet from a destructive war by finding a particular magic crystal on Earth in the possession of regular guy John H Brennan. Darth Vader clone Richard Moll follows the armour-plated wonder bra-wearing Wonder Woman to halt her quest. Although nothing more than a cheap imitation of *Star Wars*, director William Mesa (a special effects technician himself) piles on the explosive thrills, computer graphic spills and mindless action adventure so it doesn't matter. Good fun overall, with *EastEnders* star Craig Fairbrass and a cameo by *Evil Dead* director Sam Raimi providing extra entertainment value.

Brigitte Nielsen Ladera • **Richard Moll** Kyla • **John H Brennan** Jed Sanders • **Craig Fairbrass** Tarkin • **Sam Raimi** Nervous official

Director *William Mesa*

Screenplay *Nick Davis*

Not so boldly going: aliens mistake TV for the real thing in the entertaining satire *Galaxy Quest*

Galaxy of Terror ★★ 18

1981 US Colour 78mins [video]

A band of astronauts on a rescue mission to a remote planet come face-to-face with all manner of slimy alien horrors in this inferior, Roger Corman-produced shocker. The no-holds-barred pace and kooky style divert attention from the overall feeling of formula fatigue, but the gore on show is completely repellent, especially a rape sequence involving a giant worm that just about scrapes the genre's well-worn barrel. The motley cast includes Erin Moran from TV's *Happy Days* and Robert Englund, soon to find fame as monster legend Freddy Krueger; future *Titanic* and *Terminator* director James Cameron is the production designer.

Edward Albert Cabren • **Erin Moran** Alluma • **Ray Walston** Kore • **Bernard Behrens** Ilvar • **Zalman King** Baelon • **Robert Englund** Ranger • **Grace Zabriskie** Captain Trantor

Director *B D Clark*

Screenplay *Marc Siegler, BD Clark*

Galaxy Quest ★★★★ PG

1999 US Colour 97mins [video] DVD

In this enormously entertaining send-up of the *Star Trek* universe, a bunch of actors from a cult sci-fi TV show are mistaken for the real thing and recruited to defend a dying alien race. It's an inspired premise, fired into orbit by a fantastic script, sublime visual effects and an absolutely perfect cast, including Tim Allen, Sigourney Weaver and Alan Rickman, hysterical as a grumpy British actor who hates his half-reptilian character. The story is so cleverly executed and the characters so nicely fleshed-out that it not only succeeds as a *Trek* spoof, a satire on the acting profession and a parody of sci-fi fans, but also as an engaging, original space saga in its own right.

Tim Allen Jason Nesmith/Commander Peter Quincy Taggart • **Sigourney Weaver** Gwen DeMarco/Lt Tawny Madison • **Alan Rickman** Alexander Dane/Dr Lazarus • **Tony Shalhoub** Fred Kwan/Tech Sgt Chen • **Sam Rockwell** Guy Fleegman • **Daryl Mitchell** Tommy Webber/Laredo

Director *Dean Parisot*

Screenplay *Robert Gordon, David Howard, from a story by David Howard*

Gamera: Guardian of the Universe ★ PG

1995 Jap Colour 95mins [video]

The giant flying turtle returns for a nineties update. Sadly, the special effects ren't what they could have been and Shinji Higuchi's miniatures are still mired in sixties hokum. Basically Gamera is still a misunderstood monster who just wants to have at his old nemesis Gaos, and the movie is essentially a re-hash of the 1967 flick. One wonders why the film-makers bothered. Japanese language film.

Tsuyoshi Ihara Yoshinari Yonemori • **Akira Onodera** Naoya Kusanagi • **Ayako Fujitani** Asagi Kusanagi • **Shinobu Nakayama** Mayumi Nagamine

Director *Shusuke Kaneko, Matt Greenfield*

Screenplay *Matt Greenfield, Kazunori Ito*

Special Effects *Shinji Higuchi*

Gamera the Invincible ★★

1965 Jap BW 86mins

Created by the Daiei Studio to rival Toho's *Godzilla*, Gamera is a giant prehistoric fire-breathing turtle, which is awakened by an atomic blast and spins its way to Tokyo, destroying everything in its path. As with the original *Godzilla*, American stars Albert Dekker and Brian Donlevy make their appearance, in footage especially shot for the international market, as government officials liaising with the Japanese authorities to trap the super-turtle in a rocket and blast it to Mars. Although competent in every standard Japanese monster movie department, *Gamera* never really caught on outside its home turf despite numerous wacky sequels. Japanese dialogue dubbed into English.

Albert Dekker Secretary of Defense • **Brian Donlevy** General Terry Arnold • **Diane Findlay** WAF A/IC Susan Embers • **John Baragrey** Miles Standish • **Dick O'Neill** General O'Neill • **Ejii Funakoshi** Dr Hidaka • **Harumi Kiritachi** Kyoke • **Yoshiro Uchida** Toshio

Director *Noriyaki Yuasa, Sandy Howard*

Screenplay *Fumi Takahashi, Richard Kraft, from an idea by Yonejiro Saito*

Gamera versus Barugon ★★

1966 Jap Colour 101mins

The second screen adventure for the flying prehistoric turtle, the Japanese Daiei Studio's answer to Toho's box-office winner *Godzilla*. After being shot into space in *Gamera the Invincible*, the child-friendly giant turtle comes back to Earth to fight Barugon, a dinosaur which can project a freezing rainbow energy field through spikes on its back. As Tokyo and Osaka get devastated once more (special effects courtesy of Noriaki Yuasa, the director of almsot all the other movies in the series), the titans go to Lake Biwa for their final battle royal. Standard Japanese monster shenanigans given some stylish visual touches by director Shigeo Tanaka, such as Barugon's blue blood seeping into the lake and Gamera's flaming flying propulsion technique. A Japanese language film.

Kojiro Hongo Keisuke Hirata • **Kyoko Enami** Karen • **Akira Natsuki** Ichiro Hirata • **Koji Fujiyama** Onodera • **Yuzo Hayakawa** Kawajiri • **Ichiro Sugai** Dr Matsushita

Director *Shigeo Tanaka*

Screenplay *Fumi Takahashi*

Special Effects *Noriyaki Yuasa*

Gamera versus Gaos ★

1967 Jap Colour 87mins

The third Gamera adventure pits the flying prehistoric turtle against Gaos, a winged cannibal reptile with laser beam breath, woken up from hibernation by an exploding volcano. A very minor entry in the series with only Kazufumi Fujii's special effects work – in particular the natural disaster footage of earthquakes and flowing lava – its saving grace. Arguably the worst acted *Gamera* movie in history. A Japanese language film.

Kojiro Hongo Shiro Tsutsumi • **Reiko Kasahara** Sumiko Kanamura

Director *Noriyaki Yuasa*

Screenplay *Fumi Takahashi*

Special effects *Kazafumi Fujii, Yuzo Kaneko*

Gamera versus Guiron ★

1969 Jap Colour 88mins

The fifth Gamera adventure finds the flying prehistoric turtle battling the knife-headed Guiron to rescue two children from the clutches of brain-eating beauties from the planet Tera, a world situated on the other side of the sun. The same old monster mash with very little to distinguish it from all the other creatively moribund Japanese creature features from the same period. Two more films featuring Gamera, *Gamera versus Monster X* (1970) and *Gamera versus Zigra* (1971) were produced before 1995's revival movie, *Gamera: Guardian of the Universe*. A Japanese language film.

Nobuhiro Kashima Akio • **Christopher Murphy** Tom • **Miyuki Akiyama** Tomoko • **Yuko Hamada** Kuniko

Director *Noriyaki Yuasa*

Screenplay *Fumi Takahashi*

Special effects *Kazafumi Fujii*

Gamera versus Viras ★

1968 Jap Colour 75mins

The fourth Gamera adventure has the flying prehistoric turtle falling under the control of aliens after attacking their spaceship. Two boy scouts, captured by Gamera for sabotaging a nuclear submarine, release him from the evil force and send him back into outer space to defeat the alien ally Viras, a giant squid with three tentacles and six legs. The intergalactic setting is a colourful bonus in this very juvenile Japanese jape. A Japanese language film.

Kojiro Hongo • **Toru Takatsuka**
Director *Noriyaki Yuasa*
Screenplay *Fumi Takahashi*
Special effects *Kazafumi Fujii, Yuzo Kaneko*

The Gamma People ★★★

1956 UK BW 78mins

An anti-communist fable by director John (*Plague of the Zombies*) Gilling that's a unique oddity in the annals of British sci-fi. Reporter Paul Douglas and photographer Leslie Phillips get jailed as spies in the mythical European country of Gudavia where dictator Walter Rilla has instituted a super-education system. Bombarding schoolchildren with intense gamma radiation, the rays penetrate the brain and create either geniuses or idiots. Unfortunately the Goons (idiots) outweigh the masterminds and that means possible revolution. Peculiar and quaint, with Eva Bartok sporting an outré line in fifties designer outfits, this interesting failure veers between Ealing comedy and *Brave New World* horror with surprisingly engaging awkwardness.

Paul Douglas Mike Wilson • **Eva Bartok** Paula Wendt • **Leslie Phillips** Howard Meade • **Walter Rilla** Boronski • **Philip Leaver** Koerner • **Martin Miller** Lochner
Director *John Gilling*
Screenplay *John Gilling, John Gossage, from a story by Louis Pollock*

Gappa the Trifibian Monster ★★★ U

1967 Jap Colour 78mins

A witty and entertaining send-up of monster movies by Japan's Nikkatsu Corporation (their one and only foray into the genre) takes the Toho and Daiei Studio conventions, as exemplified by *Godzilla* and *Gamera*, and throws them all into the blender for a breakneck fantasy adventure. Actually using the same plot as the British effort *Gorgo*, the giant dinosaur Gappa is captured for display in a Tokyo freak show. Then its even bigger parents stomp through Japan to recover their offspring and teach Gappa how to fly back to their home island. Although full of the expected standard destruction and explosive effects, it's the unexpected playful satirising of the genre that proves more entertaining. A good place to start for the fullest understanding of the whole *Kaiju Eiga* monster genre ethos. A Japanese language film.

Tamio Kawaji • **Yoko Yamamoto** • **Yuji Okada** • **Koji Wada** • **Tatsuya Fuji**
Director *Haruyasu Noguchi*
Screenplay *Ryuzo Nakanishi, Iwao Yamazaki*
Special Effects *Akira Watanabe*

The Garbage Pail Kids Movie ★ PG

1987 US Colour 91mins

The movie spin-off from the Topps Company's bubble gum trading cards series is purposely offensive rubbish. The alien kids, who rejoice in names such as Greaser Greg and Nat Nerd, land on Earth in a dustbin and end up in Anthony Newley's shop. Unfortunately Newley's assistant takes the lid off the dustbin, subjecting us to a bad-taste mix of mean-spirited pranks, grotesque humour and knockabout violence. Director Rod Amateau's lousy movie is supposed to be mindless trash and sadly achieves that aim in the lowest possible common denominator way imaginable. Garbage is putting it mildly.

Anthony Newley Captain Manzini • **MacKenzie Astin** Dodger • **Katie Barberi** Tangerine • **Ron MacLachlan** Juice • **Kevin Thompson** Ali Gator • **Phil Fondacaro** Greaser Greg • **Robert Bell** [Robert N Bell] Foul Phil • **Larry Green** Nat Nerd • **Arturo Gil** Windy Winston • **Sue Rossitto** Messy Tessie
Director *Rod Amateau*
Screenplay *Rod Amateau, Melinda Palmer*
Producer *Rod Amateau*

Gas-s-s-s, or It Became Necessary to Destroy the World in Order to Save It ★★

1970 US Colour 79mins

A nerve gas leak in Alaska kills everyone over 25 in this hopelessly surreal comedy from cult director Roger Corman. However, the expected Utopia doesn't materialise in a free-wheeling romp that features Hell's Angels, Che Guevara, Edgar Allan Poe and Martin Luther King. Talia Shire, Ben Vereen, Bud Cort and Cindy Williams all make appearances in this time-capsule oddity, but Corman takes aim at too many hip targets and doesn't hit any of them successfully. After the film was heavily cut by his usual distributors, AIP, Corman set up his own production company, New World.

Robert Corff Coel • **Elaine Giftos** Cilla • **Pat Patterson** Demeter • **George Armitage** Billy the Kid • **Alex Wilson** Jason • **Alan Braunstein** Dr Drake • **Ben Vereen** Carlos • **Cindy Williams** Marissa • **Bud Cort** Hooper • **Talia Shire** Coralie • **Country Joe and the Fish** FM Radio
Director *Roger Corman*
Screenplay *George Armitage*
Producer *Roger Corman*

Gattaca ★★★★ 15

1997 US Colour 106mins DVD

Before screenplay writer Andrew Niccol stood the science-fiction genre on its end with *The Truman Show*, he had already shaken it up with this superlative futuristic thriller (which he also directed), built around the controversial subject of genetic engineering and how it might lead to a socio-economic class divide. Vincent Freeman (Ethan Hawke) is the imperfect human with ambitions of joining a space mission, who illegally exchanges identities with Jerome (Jude Law), a paraplegic with perfect DNA. How he does this armed with blood and urine samples is ingeniously shown by Niccol, who mints a new genre vocabulary with his utterly absorbing, intelligent and suspenseful story. In Niccol's future society a dustbuster is deadlier than a gun and wearing contact lenses means the choice between life or death. Stunningly designed, Niccol's cautionary tale with a twist is as inspirational as *Blade Runner*, with Hawke, Law and Uma Thurman giving career best performances. Contains swearing and some violence.

Ethan Hawke Jerome/Vincent • **Uma Thurman** Irene • **Jude Law** Eugene/Jerome • **Gore Vidal** Director Josef • **Xander Berkeley** Lamar • **Jayne Brook** Marie • **Elias Koteas** Antonio • **Blair Underwood** Geneticist • **Ernest Borgnine** Caesar • **Tony Shalhoub** German • **Alan Arkin** Detective Hugo
Director/Screenplay *Andrew Niccol*
Producer *Danny DeVito, Michael Shamberg, Stacey Sher*

The Gemini Man ★★

TV 1976 US Colour 1x120m; 11x60m

When NBC's *Invisible Man* series starring David McCallum flunked in the ratings, the studio hurriedly re-worked the formula, this time casting a more all-American hero in the lead. The result was even more of an audience turn-off. Ben Murphy, famous as Kid Curry in *Alias Smith and Jones*, stars as special agent Sam Casey who is rendered invisible after being exposed to radiation. Thanks to a clever watch device he's able to control his invisibility, although there's a time limit to how long he can remain unseen, a device introduced for suspense purposes. Brought to the screen without flair, many *Gemini Man* stories were actually unused *Invisible Man* scripts dusted off and re-jigged to fit the new format. What a cheat! A young Kim Basinger guest stars in one episode. Originally, only five of the 11 episodes made were aired. The series included one feature-length episode.

Ben Murphy Sam Casey • **William Sylvester** Leonard Driscoll • **Katherine Crawford** Abby Lawrence
Screenplay *H G Wells*
Executive producer *Harve Bennett*

Generation X ★★★ 15

1996 US/Can Colour 86mins [video]

Filmed as a pilot for a TV series, this entertaining sci-fi romp was executive produced by Stan Lee, on whose *Marvel* comic characters the action is based. A band of mutant misfits is called in to save the planet after mad scientist Matt Frewer perfects the ability to infiltrate people's dreams. Everyone is clearly enjoying themselves enormously, notably *Staying Alive* star Finola Hughes as "White Queen" Emma Frost. Turning the low budget to his advantage, designer Douglas Higgins has fashioned some wonderfully kitsch sets, although the same constraints render the special effects much less effective.

Matt Frewer Russell Tresh • **Finola Hughes** Emma "White Queen" Frost • **Jeremy Ratchford** Sean "Banshee" Cassidy • **Agustin Rodriguez** Angelo "Skin" Espinosa • **Heather McComb** Jubilation "Jubilee" Lee • **Randall Slavin** Kurt "Refrax" Pastorious
Director *Jack Sholder*
Screenplay *Eric Blakeney, Scott Lobdell, from the comic book by Chris Bachalo*
Executive producer *Eric Blakeney*

SFacts

The helmet used to infiltrate dreams reappeared again, later in the same year, in the TV-movie, *Doctor Who*.

Genesis II ★★

1973 US Colour 74mins

Creator of *Star Trek* Gene Roddenberry failed to strike similar gold with this contrived tale involving Alex Cord as the lone survivor of a post-millennium holocaust, watching as the Earth is re-created by two opposing factions a tale not to be taken as seriously as it takes itself and clearly owing more to *Flash Gordon* than *Star Trek*. British director John Llewellyn Moxey does what he can here in his own second incarnation, as director of formulaic American fare after a career in low-budget chillers in the UK. Nothing featuring Mariette Hartley is completely unwatchable, however.

Alex Cord Dylan Hunt • **Mariette Hartley** Lyra-a • **Ted Cassidy** Isiah • **Percy Rodrigues** Dr Isaac Kimbridge • **Harvey Jason** Singh • **Titos Vandis** Yuloff • **Bill Striglos** Dr Kellum • **Lynne Marta** Harper-Smythe
Director *John Llewellyn Moxey*
Screenplay *Gene Roddenberry*

Ghidrah, the Three-Headed Monster ★★★

1965 Jap Colour 73mins

Ghidrah (or Ghidorah as Japanese movie-goers correctly know and love him) is a three-headed, fire-breathing, dragon which lands on Earth to cause the usual global destruction. Godzilla (in his first adventure as a good monster) defends the planet, with help from Mothra and Rodan, Toho Studios' other big earners, defeating Ghidrah in a spectacular battle on Mount Fuji (again!). With bigger production values and better visual effects than normal, this engaging behemoth bash established the use of various monsters in combat combinations that would increase in goofiness over successive years. Japanese dialogue dubbed into English.

Yosuke Natsuki Shindo • **Yuriko Hoshi** Naoko • **Hiroshi Koizumi** Professor Murai • **Takashi Shimura** Dr Tsukamoto • **Emi Ito** One of "The Peanuts", twin sisters • **Yumi Ito** One of "The Peanuts", twin sisters • **Akiko Wakabayashi** Princess Salno • **Hisaya Ito** Malness
Director *Ishiro Honda [Inoshiro Honda]*
Screenplay *Shinichi Sekizawa*

Ghost in the Machine ★★★ 18

1993 US Colour 91mins [video]

A byte-sized horror thriller from Rachel Talalay, director of *Freddy's Dead* and *Tank Girl*, about a serial killer whose death during a freak electrical storm transforms him into a computer virus. His evil spirit then murderously stalks through Cleveland's communication networks using Karen Allen's lost address book. Engaging and fast-paced, it's a very contemporary tale, laced with inventive mayhem (the room-turned-microwave oven is great fun) and cool wit (the clever crematorium nightmare), augmented by well-executed digital special effects. Contains swearing and violence.

Karen Allen Terry Munroe • **Chris Mulkey** Bram • **Ted Marcoux** Karl • **Wil Horneff** Josh Munroe • **Jessica Walter** Elaine • **Brandon Quintin Adams [Brandon Adams]** Frazer • **Rick Ducommun** Phil • **Nancy Fish** Karl's landlord • **Jack Laufer** Elliott • **Shevonne Durkin** Carol
Director *Rachel Talalay*
Screenplay *William Davis, William Osborne*

Ghost in the Shell ★★★★ 15

1995 Jap/UK Colour 82mins [video] DVD

A hypnotic, animated fusion of thrilling, highly cinematic action sequences and philosophical soul-searching. Dynamic use of traditional cel techniques and computer-aided artwork, a vivid *Blade Runner*-esque landscape and a curvy cyborg heroine make this even more of a visual feast than the previous *manga* benchmark *Akira*. The fluid elegance of the animation is matched by Kenji Kawai's haunting music and, although the script occasionally gets bogged down in its own artfulness, there's moody atmosphere here to match any Ridley Scott movie. An animé to convert the unconverted. Japanese dialogue dubbed into English.

Richard George Bateau • **Mimi Woods** Kusanagi • **William Frederick** Aramaki • **Abe Lasser** Puppet master • **Christopher Joyce** Togusa • **Mike Sorich** Ishikawa
Director *Mamoru Oshii*
Screenplay *Kazunori Ito, from the graphic novel "Kokaku Kidotai" by Shirow Masamune*

The Ghost of Frankenstein ★★

1942 US BW 67mins [video]

Technically and artistically second-rate, the fourth episode in Universal's *Frankenstein* series sees Bela Lugosi back for a second stint as the vengeful Ygor. His brain gets transplanted by mistake into Lon Chaney Jr's creature by Dr Frankensein's second son, Cedric Hardwicke. Sloppy sequel continuity means that characters who died in the previous *Son of Frankenstein* suddenly appear without explanation. The running time is bolstered by scenes from the original 1931 classic. Creaky more than creepy.

Lon Chaney Jr Monster • **Sir Cedric Hardwicke [Cedric Hardwicke]** Frankenstein • **Ralph Bellamy** Erik • **Lionel Atwill** Dr Bohmer • **Bela Lugosi** Ygor • **Evelyn Ankers** Elsa • **Janet Ann Gallow** Cloestine • **Barton Yarborough** Dr Kettering • **Doris Lloyd** Martha
Director *Erle C Kenton*
Screenplay *Scott Darling, from the story by Eric Taylor*

Ghost Patrol ★★ U

1936 US BW 55mins

Taking a break from his circus stint with the Ringling Brothers, Tim McCoy headlined this sci-fi western for the indie outfit Puritan Pictures. A suspicious run of mail plane crashes over the Shiloh Mountains puts McCoy on the case as an all-action government agent who soon discovers that the mastermind behind the misdemeanours is gangleader Walter Miller, armed with kidnapped scientist Lloyd Ingraham's motor-zapping laser. Like so many good B-heroines, Claudia Dell proves more of a hindrance than a help, but she doesn't distract from the expressionist magnificence of Kenneth Strickfadden's laboratory sets. A curio, but nothing more.

Tim McCoy Tim Caverly/Tim Toomey • **Claudia Dell** Natalie Brent • **Walter Miller** Ted Dawson • **Wheeler Oakman** Kincaid • **Jimmy Burtis [James P Burtis]** Henry Brownlee • **Lloyd Ingraham** Professor Brent • **Dick Curtis** Charlie
Director *Sam Newfield*
Screenplay *Wyndham Gittens, from his story*
Cinematographer *Jack Greenhalgh*

Ghostbusters ★★★★ PG

1984 US Colour 100mins DVD

The often dazzling, special effects-driven slapstick tends to overshadow the fact that there are some slyer, more sophisticated laughs on offer in this blockbusting family comedy. Bill Murray is terrifically deadpan and sleazy as the dubious leader of a troupe of ghostbusters (writers Dan Aykroyd and Harold Ramis, plus Ernie Hudson) who are called into action when ancient spirits are let loose in New York. Sigourney Weaver shows an admirably light touch as a possessed cellist, and Rick Moranis also scores in his breakthrough movie. Director Ivan Reitman stages some spectacular set pieces, including an enjoyably daft finale with a giant marshmallow man. The concept was so successful that the film spawned a cartoon series and almost the entire team reunited for a sequel. Contains swearing.

Bill Murray Dr Peter Venkman • **Dan Aykroyd** Dr Raymond Stantz • **Sigourney Weaver** Dana Barrett • **Harold Ramis** Dr Egon Spengler • **Rick Moranis** Louis Tully • **Annie Potts** Janine Melnitz • **Ernie Hudson** Winston Zeddemore • **William Atherton** Walter Peck • **David Margulies** Mayor • **Jordan Charney** Dean Yeager • **Michael Ensign** Hotel manager • **Slavitza Jovan** Gozer • **Alice Drummond** Librarian • **Ruth Oliver** Library ghost • **Kathryn Janssen** Mrs Van Hoffman • **Cheryl Birchfield** Annette
Director *Ivan Reitman*
Screenplay *Dan Aykroyd, Harold Ramis*

Ghostbusters II ★★★ PG

1989 US Colour 103mins DVD

Having reassembled virtually the entire team behind the first blockbuster, director Ivan Reitman was not prepared to mess with a successful formula. This time the self-styled ghostbusters – Bill Murray, Dan Aykroyd, Harold Ramis and Ernie Hudson – are called back into service when evil emanating from a painting Sigourney Weaver's boss Peter MacNicol has been restoring awakens spirits around New York. The effects are bigger and more spectacular than before, Murray once again shines as the shyster scientist and there is an expanded role for Rick Moranis. But Ramis and Aykroyd's script fails to sparkle and there is very little new to show for all the big-budget endeavour. Contains swearing.

Bill Murray Dr Peter Venkman • **Dan Aykroyd** Dr Raymond Stantz • **Sigourney Weaver** Dana Barrett • **Harold Ramis** Dr Egon Spengler • **Rick Moranis** Louis Tully • **Ernie Hudson** Winston Zeddemore • **Annie Potts** Janine Melnitz • **Peter MacNicol** Janosz Poha • **Harris Yulin** Judge • **David Margulies** Mayor • **Kurt Fuller** Hardemeyer • **Janet Margolin** Prosecutor
Director *Ivan Reitman*
Screenplay *Dan Aykroyd, Harold Ramis*

The Giant Behemoth ★★★

1959 UK BW 71mins

Director Eugène Lourié cannibalised his own *The Beast from 20,000 Fathoms* and added sterling special effects by *King Kong* creator Willis O'Brien for another classic fifties giant-monster-on-the-loose fantasy. This time a prehistoric dinosaur is revived by an atomic explosion and travels to London to wreak radioactive havoc. Gene Evans saves the city by shooting the creature down with a radium-filled torpedo – but not before London Bridge is destroyed in the exciting climax. Lourié builds suspense and mood through evocative lighting and excellent use of O'Brien's stop-motion puppet. The director recycled the same story again for *Gorgo*.

Gene Evans Steve Karnes • **André Morell** Professor James Bickford • **John Turner** Ian Duncan • **Leigh Madison** Jeanie MacDougall • **Jack MacGowran** Dr Sampson • **Maurice Kaufmann** Submarine officer • **Henry Vidon** Tom • **Leonard Sachs** Scientist
Director *Eugène Lourié, Douglas Hickox*
Screenplay *Eugène Lourié, Daniel James (uncredited), from a story by Robert Abel, Allen Adler*

The Giant Claw ★ U

1957 US BW 71mins

One of the most inept monster movies ever made featuring atrocious special effects, laugh-out-loud dialogue, and incompetence on both sides of the camera lens. A giant alien bird from outer space arrives on Earth to hatch an egg. But no-one believes Jeff Morrow's sighting tale until the clumsy creature (woodenly manipulated by obvious wires) carries off a toy train set and attacks model planes. As scientists work on a ray gun to penetrate its invisible force field, the humungous vulture builds a nest on top of the Empire State Building. Tawdry, tacky and totally stupid, this really is one giant turkey in both senses.

Jeff Morrow Mitch MacAfee • **Mara Corday** Sally Caldwell • **Morris Ankrum** Lt Gen Edward Lewis • **Lou Merrill [Louis Merrill]** Pierre Broussard • **Edgar Barrier** Dr Noyman
Director *Fred F Sears*
Screenplay *Paul Gangelin, Samuel Newman*

The Giant Gila Monster ★★

1959 US BW 74mins

A badly rear-projected giant lizard stomps through model Texan towns and terrorises the local teens, who always seem to be having hot-rod races or rock 'n' roll dance hall parties. The creature is eventually beaten by one brave lad who drives a hot rod packed with explosives into the beast's belly. Unintentionally amusing rather than scary, this is directed by Ray Kellogg, who also made the hilarious *The Killer Shrews*.

Don Sullivan Chace Winstead • **Lisa Simone** Lisa • **Shug Fisher** Mr Harris • **Jerry Cortwright** Bob • **Beverly Thurman** Gay • **Don Flournoy** Gordy • **Clarke Browne** Chuck • **Pat Simmons** Sherry
Director *Ray Kellogg*
Screenplay *Jay Sims, Ray Kellogg, from a story by Ray Kellogg*

The Giant Spider Invasion ★

1975 US Colour 75mins

A rash of outsize spider sightings are traced to Wisconsin, but greedy farmer Robert Easton, thinking the radioactive spiders' eggs from another dimension are jewels, won't let the authorities investigate until it's too late. This shoddily-made trash from schlock maestro Bill Rebane has bottom-of-the-barrel special effects, including a Volkswagen in hairy drag masquerading as the largest spider of all. It is irredeemable dreck, with the star cast wasted in pointless roles.

Barbara Hale Dr Jenny Langer • **Steve Brodie** Dr Vance • **Leslie Parrish** Ev Kester • **Alan Hale Jr** Sheriff • **Robert Easton** Kester • **Kevin Brodie** Dave Perkins • **Christiane Schmidtmer** Helga • **Bill Williams** Dutch
Director *Bill Rebane, Richard L Huff*
Screenplay *Richard L Huff, Robert Easton*

The Gibson ★★★

Radio 1992 UK 6x30mins

This time-hopping thriller unravels a network of "pre-ordained accidents" to reveal the real reason for the building of Stonehenge, the founding of Bath and the importance of pigs... Sharon Duce and Robert Glenister are the bemused parents who can't understand why their toddler refuses to go to playgroup, insisting there is something "bad, old" about the Gibson Room where it is held. Meanwhile, Glenister aspires to become the "Poet of Bath" ignorant of the mysterious link between him and a scribe from the year 999. The script is sharp and well-written, the cast strong and the music (by Thomas Johnson, realised by Robin Lever) particularly effective.

Robert Glenister Saul Judd • **Sharon Duce** Elise Judd • **Freddie Jones** Scribe • **Kate Binchy** Scribe's wife / Thomas • **Constance Chapman** Haensel Sethria • **Timothy West** Selwyn Fist • **John Telfer** Prince Bladud
Written by *Bruce Bedford*
Producer *Andy Jordan*
Music *Thomas Johnson*

The Girl from Mars ★★★

1991 Can/NZ Colour

A warm-hearted tale for all the family about an outwardly normal teenager caught up in a conservation battle, who claims she comes from the red planet. It's a lightweight yet engaging affair, made for cable, and director Neill Fearnley elicits a bubbly performance from Sarah Sawatsky in only her second movie role. There's also reliable support from Edward Albert, as Sawatsky's politically ambitious father, as well as his real-life father Eddie, who plays an environmental scientist.

Edward Albert Dan • **Eddie Albert** Charles • **Sarah Sawatsky** Deedee • **Gwynyth Walsh** Stacey • **Christianne Hirt** Liane • **Gary Day** Virgil • **Leslie Carlson** Mr Sharbut • **Kaj-Erik Erikson** Ricky • **Lochlyn Munro** Earl West • **Jeremy Radick** Wayne West
Director *Neill Fearnley*
Screenplay *Brian Alan Lane*

The Girl from Tomorrow ★★★

TV 1990-1991 Aus Colour 24x25mins

Katharine Cullen is plays a teenager from the distant future, who is dragged back to early nineties Australia by a time-hopping villain. She's lucky to make friends with wannabe punk Jenny (Melissa Marshall) and her know-it-all little brother Petey (James Findley), and to have every girl's ideal accessory, a transducer, which gives her telekinetic powers. The pair find themselves up against a pleasingly wicked baddie, played with gusto by John Howard, in an effort to return Cullen to her own time. The serial, and its sequel *Tomorrow's End* both rattle along with a solid mix of thrills, humour and drama.

Katharine Cullen Alana • **Melissa Marshall** Jenny Kelly • **John Howard** Silverthorn • **James Findley** Petey Kelly • **Helen O'Connor** Irene Kelly
Director *Kathy Mueller, Noel Price*
Screenplay *Mark Shirrefs, John J Thomson*

The Girl Who Loved Robots ★★★

TV 1965 UK BW 75mins

A rare venture into sci-fi from the BBC's staid *Wednesday Play*, with a murder investigation and political satire thrown in. Victory du Cann (Isobel Black), a nightclub hostess and space programme groupie, is murdered; plodding Inspector Antrobus (Dudley Foster) identifies a heroic astronaut as the culprit, only to have the crime covered up by bureacrats concerned with a forthcoming moon mission. A typically strong cast includes Norman Rodway, Michael Gough and (as a character named "Vonnegut") Kevin Stoney.

Dudley Foster Antrobus • **Isobel Black** Victory du Cann • **Norman Rodway** Cage • **George Bettton** Toms • **David Dodimead** Cafritz • **John Bryans** Lederman • **Geoffrey Hinsliff** Gogol • **Kevin Stoney** Vonnegut
Director *Brian Parker*
Written by *Peter Everett*
Producer *James MacTaggart*

Give Us the Moon ★★★ U

1944 UK BW 95mins

Made during the Second World War but set in a postwar future, this unusual British comedy is based on a Caryl Brahms and SJ Simon novel about a Soho club founded by a group of idlers who refuse to work. The satire is slight, but co-screenwriter/director Val Guest keeps it moving along nicely, and there's terrific work from stars Margaret Lockwood, Vic Oliver and Peter Graves. There's also a wonderfully brash performance from 14-year-old Jean Simmons as Lockwood's sister, demonstrating her future star quality even at that tender age. Other familiar faces include Max Bacon, Irene Handl and a young Harry Fowler.

Margaret Lockwood Nina • **Vic Oliver** Sascha • **Peter Graves** Peter Pyke • **Roland Culver** Ferdinand • **Max Bacon** Jacobus • **Frank Cellier** Pyke • **Jean Simmons** Heidi • **Eliot Makeham** Dumka • **Iris Lang** Tania • **George Relph** Otto • **Gibb McLaughlin** Marcel • **Irene Handl** Miss Haddock
Director *Val Guest*
Screenplay *Val Guest, Howard Irving Young, Caryl Brahms, SJ Simon, from the novel "The Elephant Is White" by Caryl Brahms, SJ Simon*

The Gladiator ★★★ U

1938 US BW 72mins

Joe E Brown will always be remembered for *Some Like It Hot*. But did you know the character he essays in this mischievous adaptation of Philip Wylie's novel was, allegedly, the inspiration for Superman? However, instead of being a repressed mutant, Brown plays Hugo Kipp, a college weakling who allows himself to be injected with Lucien Littlefield's strength serum in order to become a football hero and subsequently impress both co-ed June Travis and his scathingly macho pa. As befits Buster Keaton's regular collaborator, Edward Sedgwick handles the slapstick with apolomb, although there's a pronounced cornball aspect to the proceedings.

Joe E Brown Hugo Kipp • **Man Mountain Dean** • **June Travis** Iris Bennett • **Dickie Moore** Bobby • **Lucien Littlefield** Prof Abner Danner • **Robert Kent** Tom Dixon • **Ethel Wales** Mrs Matilda Danner
Director *Edward Sedgwick*
Screenplay*George Marion, Charlie Melson, James Mulhauser, Arthur Sheekman, Earle Snell, from a novel by Philip Wylie*
Cinematographer *George Schneiderman*

Glen and Randa ★★★

1971 US Colour 94mins

Forty years after the A bomb has devastated Earth, nomadic Glen (Stephen Curry) and Randa (Shelley Plimpton) leave their isolated tribe to go in search of the city of Metropolis which they've read about in a faded *Wonder Woman* comic. On their innocent quest through the Idaho wilderness they learn lessons about existence from the relics of mankind's past. Very much a product of the hippie "Flower Power" era, director Jim McBride's semi-pretentious cult movie is a mostly effective mix of biblical earnestness and pop culture satire. Although episodic and slow moving, this esoteric apocalyptic fable – shot in 16mm and blown up to 35mm – is a gently evocative fantasy using drama-documentary style for extra resonance. McBride eventually entered the

Hollywood mainstream with *The Big Easy* and a remake of *A Bout de Souffle*.

Steve Curry Glen • **Shelley Plimpton** Randa • **Woodrow Chambliss** Sidney Miller • **Garry Goodrow** Magician
Director *Jim McBride*
Screenplay *Lorenzo Mans, Jim McBride, Rudy Wurlitzer*

The Glitterball ★★★ U

1977 UK Colour 53mins

When two boys, Max and Pete, find a small alien (the glitterball) that has become separated from its mother ship, they try to help it get home. You might get the feeling this children's film just took the plot of *ET the Extra-Terrestrial* and made a good low-budget version, until you notice that it came out five years before the Spielberg classic.

Ben Buckton Max • **Keith Jayne** Pete • **Ron Pember** Filthy • **Marjorie Yates** Mrs Fielding • **Barry Jackson** Mr Fielding • **Andrew Jackson** Corporal
Director *Harley Cockliss*
Screenplay *Howard Thompson, from a story by Harley Cockliss, Howard Thompson*

The Glove ★★

1978 US Colour 90mins

Convict Roosevelt "Rosey" Grier has a custom-built steel glove that can smash through people and solid metal. When he's not causing damage with his lethal appendage, Grier shows his philanthropic side to underprivileged kids. Ex-cop turned bounty hunter John Saxon is offered $20,000 for his recapture. This is an odd before-its-time combination of sci-fiction, action and social issues that fails to make its mark in each area it tries to embrace. Written and produced by Julian Roffman, director of 3-D exploiter *The Mask*, and directed by former B-movie actor Ross Hagen, this bizarre effort is entertaining by default. US football star Grier shows his versatility by playing the guitar as well.

John Saxon Sam Kellough • **Roosevelt Grier [Rosey Grier]** Victor Hale • **Joanna Cassidy** Sheila Michaels • **Joan Blondell** Mrs Fitzgerald • **Jack Carter** Walter Stratton • **Keenan Wynn** Bill Schwartz
Director *Ross Hagen*
Screenplay *Hubert Smith, Julian Roffman*
Producer *Julian Roffman*

GoBots: Battle of the Rocklords ★ U

1986 US Colour 70mins

Yet another kid's animation movie that is little more than an extended commercial for a new line of toys. Hanna-Barbera, home of *Yogi Bear* and *The Flintstones*, provides the less-than-inspired animation, while the Tonka corporation provides the product – a range of robots that can be transformed into vehicles and spaceships. The plot is yet another tired *Star Wars* rehash, set in a futuristic world in which the GoBots and the beleaguered Rock People (living mineral creatures that can change from human form into stone) join forces to defeat an evil overlord. A host of familiar guest voices, including Telly Savalas and Roddy McDowall, add a certain stellar something to what amounts to little more than an arcade game.

Margot Kidder Solitaire • **Roddy McDowall** Nuggit • **Michael Nouri** Boulder • **Telly Savalas** Magmar • **Ike Eisenmann** Nick • **Bernard Erhard** Cy-Kill • **Marilyn Lightstone** Crasher • **Morgan Paull** Matt
Director *Don Lusk, Alan Zaslove, Ray Patterson*
Screenplay *Jeff Segal*

God Told Me to ★★

1976 US Colour 91mins

The title is a sniper's justification for climbing to the top of a water tower in New York, loading up a high velocity rifle and casually popping innocent people in the street. Initially telling a story similar to that of Peter Bogdanovich's *Targets*, Larry Cohen's thriller (also known as *Demon*) spirals off into a weird world of sexual fantasy, religious fanaticism and even alien invasion. Lovers of movie schlock might well find their lusts satisfied, although audiences who value more prosaic things, such as decent photography, a script that makes sense and convincing performances, might find it lacking.

Tony LoBianco Peter Nicholas • **Deborah Raffin** Casey Forster • **Sandy Dennis** Martha Nicholas • **Sylvia Sidney** Elizabeth Mullin • **Sam Levene** Everett Lukas • **Robert Drivas** David Morten
Director/Screenplay *Larry Cohen*
Producer *Larry Cohen*

Godzilla ★★★

1954 Jap/US BW 80mins

A gigantic dinosaur with radioactive breath is awakened by atomic testing and goes on a rampage to destroy Tokyo. The first, and best, of the long-running monster franchise from Toho Studios is sombre science fiction (rather than the children-friendly sequels) that incorporates award-winning special effects by Eiji Tsuburaya into its nuclear age allegory. Additional footage, directed by Terry Morse, featuring reporter Raymond Burr commenting on the manic mayhem, was spliced into a cut-down dubbed version of the longer Japanese original, called *Gojira* for world markets. Director Inoshiro Honda's original 98-minute masterpiece makes a plea for peace and no more A-bomb testing. The 80-minute Americanised version doesn't. Japanese dialogue dubbed into English.

Raymond Burr Steve Martin • **Takashi Shimura** Dr Yamane • **Momoko Kochi** Emiko • **Akira Takarada** Ogata • **Akihiko Hirata** Dr Serizawa • **Sachio Sakai** Hagiwara • **Fuyuki Murakami** Dr Tabata
Director *Terry Morse, Inoshiro Honda*
Screenplay *Takeo Murata, Inoshiro Honda, from the story "Godzilla, King of the Monsters" by Shigeru Kayama*
Special Effects *Eiji Tsuburaya*

Godzilla ★★ PG

1984 Jap Colour 87mins

After a decade-long hibernation from the screen, the King of the Monsters returned as the villain again to cause an international Cold War incident after trashing a Soviet submarine. Russia and America want the outsized nuisance destroyed and almost trigger a nuclear holocaust because Godzilla is out to punish mankind for its careless atomic experiments. Oh, and Tokyo is nearly razed to the ground for the umpteenth time. Raymond Burr pops up as an intrepid reporter, just as he did in the original 1954 movie (and flashback clips from that are included), in footage added for western markets. Elsewhere, it's also business as usual – thin plot, inane dialogue, daft dubbing and cheap, but fun, special effects. In Japanese with English subtitles.

Raymond Burr Steve Martin • **Keiju Kobayashi** Prime Minister Mitamura • **Ken Tanaka** Goro Maki • **Yasuko Sawaguchi** Naoko Okumura • **Shin Takuma** Hiroshi Okumura • **Eitaro Ozawa** Finance Minister Kanzaki
Director *Kohji Hashimoto, R J Kizer*
Screenplay *Shuichi Nagahara, Lisa Tomei, from a story by Tomoyuki Tanaka*

Godzilla ★★ PG

1997 US Colour 132mins DVD

In this dreary American overhaul from *Independence Day* director Roland Emmerich, Japan's favourite giant lizard crawls out of radioactive waters in the South Pacific and heads for New York. Resembling an over-produced version of *The Beast from 20,000 Fathoms*, Emmerich's blockbuster behemoth replaces man-in-suit special effects with dodgy computer digitals and sub-*Jurassic Park* thrills. What it doesn't replicate is the endearing charm the celebrated fire-breather had when he stomped through cardboard skyscrapers. The old Toho Studios' fantasy adventures may have lower budgets, but even the cheapest shows more imagination and flair than this dismal monster mish-mash.

Matthew Broderick Dr Niko Tatopoulos • **Jean Reno** Philippe Roaché • **Maria Pitillo** Audrey Timmonds • **Hank Azaria** Victor "Animal" Palotti • **Kevin Dunn** Colonel Hicks • **Michael Lerner** Mayor Ebert • **Harry Shearer** Charles Caiman • **Arabella Field** Lucy Palotti
Director *Roland Emmerich*
Screenplay *Dean Devlin, Roland Emmerich, from a story by Ted Elliott, Terry Rossio, Dean Devlin, Roland Emmerich, from the character created by Toho Co Ltd*

Godzilla Raids Again ★

1955 Jap/US BW 77mins

The first *Godzilla* sequel finds the giant lizard battling the spiky-backed Angurus before stomping towards Tokyo and trashing Osaka en route. The usual shaky backdrops and hysterical civilian panic footage make less impact this time, and it was eight years before Godzilla met King Kong to triumph again. In Japanese with English subtitles.

Hiroshi Koizumi Shoichi Tsukioka • **Setsuko Wakayama** Hedemi Yamaji • **Minoru Chiaki** Koji Kobayashi
Director *Motoyoshi Oda, Hugo Grimaldi*
Screenplay *Takeo Murata, Sigeaki Hidaka*
Producer *Paul Schreibman, Tomoyuki Tanaka*

Godzilla 2000 ★★★

1999 Jap Colour 97mins

Japan's riposte to Hollywood's mega-budget *Godzilla* in 1998 was to repackage their most durable monster for a new series of glossy movies containing upgraded special effects. Even though Toho Studios couldn't really compete with Hollywood's finesse or professionalism – and die-hard fans didn't really want them to anyway – their first effort is still solid, campy escapist entertainment with the usual silly plot. The prehistoric dinosaur takes on aliens whose spaceship transforms into an ugly monster in director Takao Okawara's enjoyable romp. Naturally, Tokyo is destroyed yet again in the titans' no-holds-barred grudge match. With dubbed character scenes kept to a minimum and the battle sequences impressively mounted by *Godzilla* veteran Okawara, the time-honoured formula proves there's still life yet in the new millennium for the not-so-jolly Green Giant. Japanese dialogue dubbed into English.

Takehiro Murata Yuji Shinoda • **Hiroshi Abe** Mitsuo Katagiri • **Naomi Nishida** Yuki Ichinose • **Shiro Sano** Mayazaki • **Mayu Suzuki** Io Shinoda • **Tsutomu Kitagawa** Gojira
Director *Takao Okawara*
Screenplay *Hiroshi Kashiwabara, Wataru Mimura*
Special effects *Kenzi Suzuki*

Godzilla vs Gigan ★★★ PG

1972 Jap Colour 85mins

More totally bonkers fantasy mayhem from Japan's Toho Studios, as Godzilla makes another appearance to save the planet from intergalactic domination. This time around, alien cockroaches plan to occupy the earth and summon Ghidorah, the three-headed dragon, and Gigan, a crimson-eyed metal bird with a chainsaw chest, to fight the Monster Island duo of Godzilla and Anzilla at a children's amusement park. For the first time, the monsters actually talk to each other, and a note of contemporary relevance is struck as shots of Tokyo depict the aliens' dying world. This is, however, one of the better Godzilla efforts. Japanese dialogue dubbed into English.

Haruo Nakajima Godzilla • **Yukietsu Omiya** Angurus • **Kanta Ina** Ghidorah • **Kengo Nakayama** • **Hiroshi Ichikawa** • **Yuriko Hishimi** • **Tomoko Umeda** • **Minoru Takashima** • **Kunio Murai** • **Toshiaki Nishizawa**
Director *Jun Fukuda*
Screenplay *Takeshi Kimura, Shinichi Skizawa*

Godzilla vs Hedora ★★ PG

1971 Jap Colour 81mins

Godzilla goes psychedelic and gets ecology minded in his 11th adventure, in which he

10 MOST INFLUENTIAL SCIENCE FICTION MOVIES

• *Metropolis* (1926) Its vision of the urban hell wrought by science clearly influenced films such as *Blade Runner* – as did its use of a "replicant" robot villain

• *Frankenstein* (1931) Cinema's first great mad-scientist movie has at its heart a tale of human experimentation and medical horror that remains uncannily relevant

• *Flash Gordon* (1936) *Star Wars* finds its roots in the wild invention, epic narrative and ray-gun-wielding heroics of this hugely popular movie series

• *Invasion of the Body Snatchers* (1956) The first great psychological sci-fi movie, this laces its tale of body horror with a chilling cocktail of cynicism and paranoia

• *Forbidden Planet* (1956) Sci-fi takes on Shakespeare (via Freud) in a brilliantly realised adaptation of *The Tempest* that produced cinema's first robot star, Robbie.

• *2001: a Space Odyssey* (1968) The first – and still just about the only – film that dared revel in the grace and stillness of space, Stanley Kubrick's ambitious fusion of science and spirituality is still being interpreted

• *Star Wars* (1977) George Lucas rode the wave of a technological revolution to produce this exhilarating space opera, which cleaned up at the box office and set the scene for the current dominance of the effects-fuelled blockbuster.

• *Alien* (1979) Made more than 20 years ago, such is the influence of Ridley Scott's space-bound thriller that all spaceships still look like the Nostromo and all evil aliens still resemble HR Giger's monstrous bio-mechanical creation

• *Blade Runner* (1982) Ridley Scott rewrote the design manual once more with this definitive portrait of the overcrowded future city, while source writer Philip K Dick's concern with identity has become one of the signatures of the genre.

• *The Terminator* (1984) Working closely with producer (and then-wife) Gale Anne Hurd, writer/director James Cameron combined sci-fi and action genres to thrilling effect and created the cinema's greatest cyborg – plus there's an ingenious time-travel paradox thrown in for good measure

battles an animated pile of industrial waste, complete with deadly crimson laser eyes, called Hedora (the Japanese for pollution). Cute kid Hiroyuki Kawase teams up with Godzilla to get rid of the Smog Monster with the help of giant electric generators. Aimed at a young audience – hence the knockabout comedy, explanatory cartoon segments and mind-boggling pop songs such as *Save the Earth* – this is a slapdash and slow addition to the Godzilla series. The usual silly special effects refuse to work their charm in such a loopy context, although Hedora, with its ability to turn itself into a flying saucer, is a striking creation. Japanese dialogue dubbed into English.

Akira Yamauchi Dr Yano • **Hiroyuki Kawase** Ken Yano • **Toshie Kimura** Mrs Yano • **Toshio Shibaki** Yukio Keuchi • **Keiko Mari** Miki Fujimiya
Director *Yoshimitsu Banno*
Screenplay *Yoshimitsu Banno, Kaoru Mabuchi*

Godzilla vs King Ghidorah ★★★ PG

1991 Jap Colour 102mins

One of the best of the entire 22-strong Japanese *Godzilla* series, this also boasts one of the saga's most complex plots. It involves time travellers from the future intervening in the 1944 nuclear events causing the monster lizard's birth and creating his three-headed flying nemesis Ghidorah instead to defeat Japan and stop it becoming a future world power. The time warp elements do cause some confusion, but are easy to forgive in such an imaginative story – one that also neatly fills in details of Godzilla's humble beginnings. All the monster battles are epic, exciting and fast-paced, and, overall, this enormous Asian box-office hit is more fun than the new American blockbuster take on the Godzilla myth. Japanese dialogue dubbed into English.

Anna Nakagawa Emmy Kano • **Kosuke Toyohara** Kenichiro Terasawa • **Megumi Odaka** Miki Saegusa • **Kiwako Harada** Chiaki Moriyuma • **Shoji Kobayashi** Yuzo Tsuchiashi • **Chuck Wilson** • **Richard Berger** Grenchiko • **Robert Scottfield** Android M-11 • **Tokuma Nishioka** Takehito Fujio
Director/Screenplay *Kazuki Omori*

Godzilla vs Megalon ★★★ PG

1973 Jap Colour 78mins

Megalon, a giant insect monster with drills for arms plus a death ray head, and Gigan are teamed by the Seatopians to conquer the world in revenge for inflicting nuclear damage under the oceans. That's the cue to call Godzilla in to fight the monster menace and save Japan once more. Here Godzilla joins the brightly coloured Jet Jaguar robot (a clear Power Rangers inspiration) for the barren desert battles, meaning part of the fun in watching cardboard model cities topple is missing from this popcorn extravaganza. But hilariously risible dubbed dialogue, along the lines of "those damned Seatopians", more than makes up for the lack of stupid spectacle and the plot is interspersed with a rather sobering anti-pollution theme.Japanese dialogue dubbed into English.

Katsuhiko Sasaki Professor Goro Ibuki • **Hiroyuki Kawase** Rokuro Ibuki
Director *Jun Fukuda*
Screenplay *Jun Fukuda, Shinichi Sekizawa, Takeshi Kimura*

Godzilla vs Mothra ★★★ PG

1964 Jap Colour 102mins

Godzilla's fourth screen appearance, and Mothra's second, makes for an enjoyable romp through the odd conventions of Japanese monster moviedom. Mothra's giant egg is washed ashore by a hurricane and found by carnival promoters. When tiny twin guardians arrive to ask for its return to the giant moth's island home, the authorities beg for their help to get Mothra to fight Godzilla, who's once more embarking on a Tokyo attack. But the ageing Mothra isn't up to the battle royal, so the two hatching larvae move into silky-webbed action instead in a funny – both intentionally and otherwise – and reasonably exciting slice of zany mayhem. In Japanese with English subtitles.

Akira Takarada News reporter • **Yuriko Hoshi** Girl photographer • **Hiroshi Koisumi** Scientist • **Yu Fujiki** Second reporter • **Emi Ito** One of twin girls • **Yumi Ito** One of twin girls • **Yoshifumi Jajima** Kumayama • **Kenji Sahara** Banzo Torahata • **Jun Tazaki** Newspaper editor
Director *Inoshiro Honda*
Screenplay *Shinichi Sekizawa*

Godzilla vs Mothra ★★★ PG

1992 Jap Colour 102mins

Nearly 30 years after Toho first introduced Mothra to Godzilla, the studio virtually remade the same story in their attempt to modernise their monster dinosaur series for a new generation. It worked and this was a huge hit in Japan. Two tiny women, known as the Cosmos, summon up the creature Mothra to fight the evil Battra, who has been sent to destroy Earth. However, Godzilla appears and a three-way battle occurs in a fiery finale set in Tokyo. Good, colourful fun with Megumi Odaka making a third return appearance in the rejuvenated *Godzilla* franchise as a psychic sidekick. Japanese dialogue dubbed into English.

Tetsuya Bessho Takuya Fujita • **Akiji Kobayashi** Ryuzo Dobashi • **Satomi Kobayashi** Masako Tezuka • **Takehiro Murata** Kenji Ando • **Megumi Odaka** Miki Saegusa
Director *Takao Okawara*
Screenplay *Kazuki Omori*
Executive Producer *Tomoyuki Tanaka* •
Producer *Shogo Tomiyama*

Godzilla vs the Cosmic Monster ★★

1974 Jap Colour 79mins

You can't keep a good monster down, and for his 20th anniversary (and 14th film), Japan's Toho Studios created a worthy adversary for its money-making prehistoric lizard – a cyborg version of Godzilla himself! In this average entry in the variable series, Mechagodzilla is the secret weapon of a race of ape-like aliens who are seeking world domination. Plenty of sparks fly in the extended cardboard battle scenes, and there are a couple of daft new creatures to smirk at, but it's pretty much children's comic book stuff. In Japanese with English subtitles.

Masaaki Daimon Keisuke Shimizu • **Kazuya Aoyama** Masahiko Shimizu • **Akihiko Hirata** • **Hiroshi Koizumi** • **Masao Imafaku** • **Beru-Bera Lin** • **Mori Kishida** • **Kenji Sahara** • **Barbara Lynn**
Director *Jun Fukuda*
Screenplay *Hiroyasu Yamamura, Jun Fukuda*

Godzilla's Revenge ★

1969 Jap Colour 70mins

A bullied schoolboy realises his dream of going to Monster Island where he meets Godzilla and his son, Minya, who teach him how to be brave. Stripped of the serious A-bomb underpinnings that made early entries in the Toho series so irony-rich, the tenth *Godzilla* movie is a very sad affair indeed. Insult is added to injury by the inclusion of battle scenes from earlier adventures such as *Son of Godzilla* and *Ebirah, Terror of the Deep* to save money on expensive special effects. This is pure kids' stuff. In Japanese with English subtitles.

Kenji Sahara Kenkichi Miki • **Tomonori Yazaki** Ichiro Miki • **Machiko Naka** Mrs Miki • **Sachio Sakai** Senbayashi • **Chotaro Togin** Assistant detective • **Yoshibumi Tajima** Policeman
Director *Ishiro Honda [Inoshiro Honda]*
Screenplay *Shinichi Sekizawa*
Executive producer *Tomyuki Tanaka*

Gog ★★★

1954 US Colour 82mins

Don't let the Z-grade title put you off – this is actually a decent little sci-fi techno shocker that predates *2001: a Space Odyssey* by more than a decade in its depiction of a computer programmed to kill. It's produced by Ivan Tors, famous for TV shows such as *Daktari*. Richard Egan leads an undistinguished cast, with people being bumped off by two malevolent robots let loose in a subterranean laboratory in New Mexico. Originally released in 3-D, this combines great Saturday matinee thrills with Cold War tension and topical fears about all-powerful machines.

Richard Egan David Sheppard • **Constance Dowling** Joanna Merritt • **Herbert Marshall** Dr Van Ness • **John Wengraf** Dr Zeltman • **Philip Van Zandt** Dr Elzevir • **Valerie Vernon** Madame Elzevir • **Stephen Roberts** Major Howard • **Byron Kane** Dr Carter
Director *Herbert L Strock*
Screenplay *Tom Taggart, Richard G Taylor, from a story by Ivan Tors*
Producer *Ivan Tors*

Goke, Bodysnatcher from Hell ★★★ 15

1968 Jap Colour 78mins [video]

One of the goriest and most lurid movies to come from the Japanese sci-fi horror industry, director Hajime Sato's pulp shocker is a vague *Invasion of the Body Snatchers* remake, complete with the same twist ending. After an aeroplane passes through a strange cloud and crashes, Hideo Ko becomes a blood-sucking maniac and turns most of the other passengers into space vampires. Once again, it's all down to aliens planning to invade Earth. Grisly and inventive make-up effects (oozing slime entering smashed noses) make this a livelier effort than usual. A Japanese language film.

Hideo Ko Hijacker • **Teruo Yoshida** Sugisaka • **Tomomi Sato** Kuzumi • **Eizo Kitamura** Mano • **Masaya Takahashi** Sagai
Director *Hajime Sato*
Screenplay *Kyuzo Kobayashi, Susumu Takaku*

Gold ★★★

1934 Ger BW 120mins

Deriving from the days when simultaneous foreign-language versions were made of potential hits, Karl Hartl's futuristic fable was reworked by Serge de Poligny, with Louis Gauthier and Pierre Blanchar standing in for Friedrich Kayssler and Hans Albers. Only Brigitte Helm appeared in both takes on this idealistic tale, in which a pair of scientists destroy their atomic alchemising apparatus (which was so realistic some suspected Germany had perfected a genuine reactor) for fear it will be misappropriated by the forces of capitalism. Swathes of lab footage (co-shot by *Metropolis* photographer Günther Rittau) resurfaced in the 1953 Hollywood B-movie, *The Magnetic Monster*. A German language film.

Hans Albers Werner Holk • **Helm Brigitte** Florence Wills • **Lien Deyers** Margit Moller • **Michael Bohnen** John Wills • **Friedrich Kayssler** Prof Achenbach • **Eberhard Leithoff** Harris • **Ernst Karchow** Willi Luders allas Charlie Jenkins
Director *Karl Hartl*
Screenplay *Rolf E Vanloo*
Cinematographer *Otto Baecker, Werner Bohne, Günther Rittau*

Golden Years ★★ 15

TV 1991 US Colour 236mins [video]

Written specifically for the small screen by Stephen King, this mini-series sees an elderly janitor facing an age-old dilemma. After accidentally uncovering a top-secret regeneration experiment in a military installation, Harlan Williams discovers that he has started to age backwards. When the authorities learn of his condition, the increasingly youthful Harlan soon finds himself running for his life. Although the mini-series' central premise raises some intriguing ideas about genetic manipulation and the very nature of human existence, they generally take a back seat to unimaginative *Fugitive*-style action antics. Keith Szarabajka convincingly dons a variety of prosthetic guises to portray Harlan's changing appearance, and portrays his character's predicament well. But nothing can regenerate the immature plotting or undeveloped ending.

Keith Szarabajka Harlan Williams • **Felicity Huffman** Terry Spann • **Ed Lauter** General Louis Crewes • **RD Call** Jude Andrews • **Bill Raymond** Dr Richard X Toddhunter • **Frances Sternhagen** Gina Williams
Director *Allen Coulter, Kenneth Fink, Michael Gornick, Stephen Tolkin*
Written by *Stephen King*

The Golem ★★★

1979 Pol Sepia Colour 92mins

Having forged his reputation with a series of inventive shorts, Piotr Szulkin made his feature debut with this post-apocalyptic revision of the classic Mitteleuropean myth. It's as though Maria from *Metropolis* had been set loose in a Stepford sort of society, as Pernat (Marek Walczewski) and his android doppleganger stand together against a humanity artificially programmed to conform by a master race of sinister scientists. Shot predominantly in sepia, this is clearly a Kafkaesque parable about politico-media manipulation. But it's given a human core by Krystyna Janda's outstanding performance as Pernat's unconventional ally. Visually striking, but occasionally it's impenetrably symbolic. Polish language film.

Marek Walczewski Pernat • **Krystyna Janda** Rozyna • **Joanna Zolkowska** Miriam
Screenplay *Tadeusz Sobolewski, Piotr Szulkin, from the novel "The Golem" by Gustav Meyrink*

Goliath Awaits ★★★

TV 1981 US Colour 200mins

An unusual two-part mini-series, in which oceanographer Mark Harmon investigates the wreck of the *Goliath*, a luxury liner sunk in the early days of the Second World War, and discovers a community of survivors in the airtight vessel, living under the apparently benign but actually fascist rule of Captain McKenzie (Christopher Lee). It's an underwater elaboration of the *On Thursday We Leave for Home* episode of *The Twilight Zone*, about the consequences of rescue on a long-standing group of maroonees and the inability of the leader who has got his people through the crisis to cope with the end of his rule. To fill out the whole thing to double-feature length, the crew and passengers all have soap opera-style subplots and comedy bits. Director Kevin Connor marshals a large cast, including John Carradine as a swashbuckling thirties movie star, Emma Samms as the captain's lovely daughter (raised all her life in the sunken ship) and Frank Gorshin as Mckenzie's chief enforcer.

Mark Harmon Peter Cabot • **Christopher Lee** John McKenzie • **Emma Samms** Lea McKenzie • **Eddie Albert** Admiral Sloan • **John Carradine** Ronald Bentley • **Frank Gorshin** Dan Wesker • **Jean Marsh** Dr Goldman • **John Ratzenberger** Bill Sweeney • **Duncan Regehr** Paul Ryker
Director *Kevin Connor*
Written by *Richard M Bluel, Pat Fielder*

Gonks Go Beat ★ U

1965 UK BW 87mins

An endearing yet still tedious slice of sixties nonsense, starring Kenneth Connor as the Martian mediator in the war between Beatland and Balladisle – we all know rockin' hepcats and lounge lizards are mortal enemies, right? With the threat of exile to the planet Gonk hanging over the proceedings, a *Romeo and Juliet*-style romance between the factions is arranged, providing the excuse for a seemingly endless parade of forgettable songs. Lulu and Ginger Baker are among the misguided musicians doing their best in this daft flop.

Kenneth Connor Wilco Roger • **Frank Thornton** Mister A&R • **Barbara Brown** Helen • **Ian Gregory** Steve • **Terry Scott** PM • **Lulu** Lulu
Director *Robert Hartford-Davis*
Screenplay *Jimmy Watson*

Goodnight Sweetheart ★★★ PG

TV 1993-1999 UK Colour 58x30mins

It may be that this gentle, sometimes barbed comedy works as well as it does because it isn't weighted down by sci-fi gobbledegook. The premise is that a mildly harassed TV repairman Nicholas Lyndhurst discovers that Duckett's Alley leads from the present to the forties (although only for him) and begins to live a double life, partnered in the nineties by nagging wife Michelle Holmes (later Emma Amos) and in the past by unhappily-married barmaid Dervla Kirwan (later Elizabeth Carling). Creators Laurence Marks and Maurice Gran seem to have decided to come up with a mainstream take on the Dennis Potter world of *Pennies from Heaven* and *The Singing Detective*, and title episodes after popular songs of the war era.

Nicholas Lyndhurst Gary Sparrow • **Dervla Kirwan** Phoebe Bamford • **Elizabeth Carling** Pheobe (Series 4-6) • **Michelle Holmes** Yvonne Sparrow • **Emma Amos** Yvonne Sparrow (Series 4-6) • **David Ryall** Eric • **Victor McGuire** Ron Wheatcroft • **Christopher Ettridge** PC Reg Deadman
Created by *Laurence Marks, Maurice Gran*
Producer *John Bartlett*

Gorath ★★★

1962 Jap Colour 83mins

A little known space fantasy directed by Inoshiro (*Godzilla*) Honda that develops one of his most interesting concepts. In 1980 a huge red-hot celestial body, Gorath, is hurtling through space on a collision course with Earth. Quick-thinking Japanese scientists install giant rockets at the South Pole to shift Earth out of orbit long enough to allow Gorath to pass by with minimal tidal waves and high-temperature damage. In the Japanese version, the rocket explosions wake up a giant walrus which causes last-minute complications, but these scenes were deleted from the American print. Beginning with a stodgy lecture about constellation astronomy, Honda's nifty fantasy (featuring the first movie space walk) soon settles down to become a suspenseful adventure with some great special effects. A Japanese language film.

Ryo Ikebe • **Akihiko Hirata** • **Jun Tazaki** • **Yumi Shirakawa** • **Takashi Shimura** • **Kumi Mizuno**
Director *Inoshiro Honda*
Screenplay *Takeshi Kimura*
Special effects *Eiji Tsuburaya* •
Cinematographer *Hajime Koizumi*

Gorgo ★★★ PG

1961 UK Colour 73mins

Seven years after making *The Beast from 20,000 Fathoms*, Eugène Lourié came to Britain for what turned out to be his swansong. This highly derivative film has borrowed from so many other monster movies that it is almost as much fun spotting the swipes (mostly from *King Kong* and the *Godzilla* series) as it is watching the picture itself. Special effects boffin Tom Howard's creatures are the sweetest rampaging dinosaurs you will ever see, and the model London landmarks trampled by Mrs Gorgo are risible. Bill Travers and William Sylvester manage to keep admirably straight-faced as this eminently enjoyable tosh unfolds around them.

Bill Travers Joe Ryan • **William Sylvester** Sam Slade • **Vincent Winter** Sean • **Bruce Seton** Professor Flaherty • **Joseph O'Conor** Professor Hendricks • **Martin Benson** Dorkin • **Barry Keegan** First Mate • **Christopher Rhodes** McCartin • **Basil Dignam** Admiral Brooks • **Maurice Kauffman** Radio reporter
Director *Eugène Lourié*
Screenplay *John Loring [Robert L Richards], Daniel Hyatt [Daniel James], from their story*

The Greatest American Hero ★★★ PG

TV 1981-1983 US Colour 45x60mins

A light-hearted superhero show from writer/producer Stephen J Cannell (*The Rockford Files*), this stars William Katt as nice guy teacher Ralph Hinkley, who is given a costume ("the magic red jammies") by alien visitors. The suit makes the wearer super-powered, but Katt loses the instruction book, and so has to struggle with his unpredictable abilities (flight, invisibility, super-speed, size-changing, telepathy) as he fights evil with the aid of FBI Agent Bill Maxwell (Robert Culp) and lawyer Pam Davidson (Connie Sellecca). The wind-up episode was *The Greatest American Heroine*, a potential spin-off pilot in which Hinckley's secret identity is blown and the aliens hand the costume to Holly Hathaway (Mary Ellen Stuart). Good-humoured, with amiable leads, the show mostly pit the fantastical hero against ordinary villains like drug dealers, arsonists, kidnappers, biker gangs and mad bombers, although there was a bogus dinosaur in the Bermuda Triangle.

William Katt Ralph Hinkley • **Connie Sellecca** Pam Davidson • **Robert Culp** Bill Maxwell • **Michael Paré** Tony Villicana • **Faye Grant** Rhonda Blake
Created by *Stephen J Cannell*
Producer *Stephen J Cannell, Alex Beaton, Jo Swerling Jr*

SFacts

Ralph Hinkley briefly became Ralph Hanley during the first series, after President Reagan was shot by the real-life John Hinkley. By the second series, however, the character had reverted back to his original surname.

The Green Hornet ★★★

Radio 1936-1952 US

Writer Fran Striker created the Green Hornet in 1936 for a US radio show in which millionaire playboy/publisher Britt Reid adopted his wildlife-themed masked identity and fought big city crime from his gadget-filled, streamlined car with the aid of a faithful sidekick, three years before Bruce Wayne began his similar crusade. Actually, the Hornet was conceived as a modernised Lone Ranger, with the car Black Beauty updating the horse Silver, Japanese chauffeur Kato (who became simply oriental during the War) replacing Indian tagalong Tonto and Rimsky-Korsakov's *Flight of the Bumble Bee* instead of the Ranger's famous *William Tell Overture*. Striker made Britt Reid the great-nephew of John Reid, the Lone Ranger, and an emotional episode dealt with the hero's realisation that he was carrying on the good work of the western masked man, "bringing to justice those he would fight if he were here today". The hero was played by Al

Hodge (1936-43), Donovan Fause (1943), Bob Hall (1943-46, and a 1964 revival) and Jack McCarthy (1946-52). The hero appeared in comics, film serials (*The Green Hornet*, 1939; *The Green Hornet Strikes Again*, 1944) and a 1966 TV series.

Al Hodge Britt Reid/The Green Hornet (1936-43) • **Donovan Faust** Britt Reid/The Green Hornet (1943) • **Bob Hall** Britt Reid/The Green Hornet (1943-46) • **Jack McCarthy** Britt Reid/The Green Hornet (1946-52) • **Raymond Hayashi** Kato • **Rollon Parker** Kato • **Mickey Tolan** Kato • **Lee Allman** Lenore Case

Screenplay *George W Trendle, Fran Striker*
Producer *James Jewell*

The Green Hornet ★★ U PG

TV 1966-1967 US Colour 26x30mins

Having struck camp gold with the *Batman* TV series, producer William Dozier tried to get another masked hero franchise going with this short-lived version of the vintage radio hero, casting bland Van Williams as Britt Reid (the Green Hornet) and future legend Bruce Lee as sidekick Kato. The retro-look show carried over the Rimsky-Korsakov theme from radio, and mostly pits the hero against slouch-hatted bootleggers, extortionists and mobsters handling the villainy as if the forties were still running – although John Carradine put in a value-for-money appearance as a Jack the Ripper-type in *Alias the Scarf* and the final two-parter featured a bogus *Invasion from Outer Space*. Although the Black Beauty car, emerging from a secret garage beneath Reid's luxury apartment, was a sleek, Dinky toy-worthy vehicle and glimpses of Lee's kung fu stylings enlivened the scrappy fights, the show had very little personality. A bunch of episodes were scrambled together to make pretend TV movies, *Green Hornet 1: Kato and the Green Hornet* and *Green Hornet II: Fury of the Dragon*.

Van Williams Britt Reid/The Green Hornet • **Bruce Lee** Kato • **Wende Wagner** Lenore "Casey" Case • **Lloyd Gough** Mike Axford • **Walter Brooke** District Attorney FP Scanlon

Source *from the radio series by George W Trendle*
Producer *Richard Bluel* • ***Executive producer*** *William Dozier*

The Green Slime ★★

1968 US/Jap Colour 90mins

The first official Japanese/American co-production mixes the worst of both industries in this blah monster confection. After successfully thwarting an earthbound asteroid, astronauts unknowingly take on board a cargo of native green cells. On commander Richard Jaeckel's Gamma III space station, the slimy amoebas proliferate into one-eyed triffids with stiff tentacles that multiply further when shot. Will Jaeckel and rocket pilot Robert Horton ever stop fighting over mini-skirted Luciana Paluzzi long enough to notice the growing alien threat? While initially intriguing in a space opera context, all interest evaporates once the silly protoplasmic squids become visible. Vivid colour photography can't make up for the inadequacies, either.

Robert Horton Jack Rankin • **Richard Jaeckel** Vince Elliot • **Luciana Paluzzi** Lisa Benson • **Bud Widom** Jonathan Thompson • **Ted Gunther** Dr Halvorsen • **Robert Dunham** Captain Martin • **David Yorston** Lt Curtis • **William Ross** Ferguson

Director *Kinji Fukasaku*
Screenplay *Charles Sinclair, William Finger, Tom Rowe, from a story by Ivan Reiner*
Cinematographer *Yoshikazu Yamasawa*

Gremlins ★★★★ 15

1984 US Colour 101mins DVD

Although Steven Spielberg ensures (as executive producer) that things don't get too nasty, this remains a wonderfully anarchic affair that is probably one of Hollywood's blackest mainstream hits. Zach Galligan is the teenager who is given a cuddly exotic pet mogwai called Gizmo, but through carelessness unwittingly unleashes a viciously murderous swarm of little gremlins. There's no doubt whose side director Joe Dante is on and he gleefully trashes the view of small-town America portrayed by feel-good movies such as *It's a Wonderful Life* (which is being screened on TV throughout the tale). Film buffs will delight in all the in-jokes and the long list of cameos, ranging from Roger Corman veteran Dick Miller to Spielberg himself. And Phoebe Cates's admirably straight-faced Christmas speech should be compulsory viewing during the festive season. Contains violence and swearing.

Zach Galligan Billy Peltzer • **Phoebe Cates** Kate • **Hoyt Axton** Rand Peltzer • **Frances Lee McCain** Lynn Peltzer • **Polly Holliday** Mrs Deagle • **Keye Luke** Grandfather • **John Louie** Chinese boy • **Dick Miller** Mr Futterman • **Jackie Joseph** Mrs Futterman • **Scott Brady** Sheriff Frank • **Harry Carey Jr** Mr Anderson • **Don Steele** Rockin' Ricky Rialto • **Corey Feldman** Pete • **Arnie Moore** Pete's father • **Glynn Turman** Roy Hanson • **Belinda Balaski** Mrs Harris • **Judge Reinhold** Gerald

Director *Joe Dante*
Screenplay *Chris Columbus*

Gremlins 2: the New Batch ★★★ 15

1990 US Colour 102mins

With Steven Spielberg's influence seemingly absent this time around, Joe Dante's anarchic view of life is given full rein in this chaotic but cracking sequel. The action is transplanted to a skyscraper in New York where mad scientist Christopher Lee inadvertently lets the evil gremlins loose to take over the entire building. As with the original, Dante bombards the screen with a never-ending stream of movie spoofs, slapstick violence and sly little treats for film buffs. Stars Phoebe Cates and Zach Galligan are back again, but most of the laughs come from the supporting players: Lee, John Glover, Robert Prosky and Roger Corman veteran Dick Miller. Treat it as a live-action cartoon and strap yourself in for a roller-coaster ride. Contains swearing.

Zach Galligan Billy Peltzer • **Phoebe Cates** Kate Beringer • **John Glover** Daniel Clamp • **Robert Prosky** Grandpa Fred • **Howie Mandel** Gizmo • **Tony Randall** "Brain" Gremlin • **Robert Picardo** Forster • **Christopher Lee** Dr Catheter • **Haviland Morris** Marla Bloodstone • **Dick Miller** Murray Futterman • **Jackie Joseph** Sheila Futterman • **Keye Luke** Mr Wing • **Gedde Watanabe** Katsuji • **Kathleen Freeman** Microwave Marge • **Leonard Maltin** • **Hulk Hogan**

Director *Joe Dante*
Screenplay *Charlie Haas, from characters created by Chris Columbus*
Executive Producer *Steven Spielberg • Kathleen Kennedy, Frank Marshall*

Gremloids ★★★ PG

1990 US Colour 86mins

In this reasonably successful low-budget *Star Wars* spoof, a navigation mistake lands cosmic bad guy Buckethead on Earth instead of in a galaxy far, far away. He's in hot pursuit of a princess who's run off with some secret radio transmissions. Buckethead (and indeed he does have a bucket on his head!) is the Darth Vader of director Todd Durham's refreshing piece, which doesn't set its satirical sights too high and hits more targets dead on as a result. Far more innovative and surreal than Mel Brooks's similar *Spaceballs*, this ragged-around-the-edges lampoon achieves much with very little.

Paula Poundstone Karen • **Chris Elliott** Hopper • **Alan Marx** Max

Director/Screenplay *Todd Durham*

Grid Runners ★★ 18

1996 US Colour 86mins

This future shocker mixes martial arts action with virtual reality. The premise may have worked better as a graphic novel; on screen, though, it is leadenly executed. Don "the Dragon" Wilson is the requisitely muscled hero getting to grips with an evil cyberspace kickboxer Dante (Michael Bernardo), who goes on the rampage after escaping from inside a computer game. Luckless and plodding – even the action scenes are disappointingly dull – the script is worsened by the inclusion of a cast of no-hopers, save for the presence of sixties siren Stella Stevens, whose son Andrew handles the directorial chores with a none-too-steady hand.

Don "the Dragon" Wilson David Quarry • **Michael Bernardo** Dante • **Stella Stevens** Mary • **Athena Massey** Liana

Director/Screenplay *Andrew Stevens*

The Groundstar Conspiracy ★★

1972 Can Colour 95mins

This thriller about spies in the space programme was severely cut on its original UK release, but now shows in its full (although still slightly incomprehensible) version. It's really one of those high-gloss features that Universal made to show off and use up its contract players – in this case George Peppard and Michael Sarrazin. Director Lamont Johnson handles the suspense well enough, but his talent never really found an outlet in grade A features. The scripting could have been tighter and the leading lady (Christine Belford) more distinguished – and perhaps not excised from the plot quite so harshly – but the Vancouver locations look splendid.

George Peppard Tuxan • **Michael Sarrazin** Welles • **Christine Belford** Nicole • **Cliff Potts** Mosely • **James Olson** Stanton • **Tim O'Connor** Gossage • **James McEachin** Bender • **Alan Oppenheimer** Hackett • **Roger Dressler** Kitchen • **Ty Haller** Henshaw

Director *Lamont Johnson*

Screenplay *Matthew Howard, from the novel "The Alien" by LP Davies*

The Guardians ★★★

TV 1971 UK Colour 13x60mins

This plausible and imaginatively presented political thriller from co-writer Rex Firkin (the man behind *The Power Game*), paints a forlorn picture of a future Britain ruled by a government reduced to hiring a quasi-military and political police force, known as "The Guardians", to maintain law and order. Of course this view of Britain under the boot of totalitarian rule was broached by George Orwell in his novel *Nineteen Eighty-Four*, but this marked the first occasion a television serial had tackled the subject. It wouldn't be the last time either. One episode was directed by Mike Newell who famously went on to make *Four Weddings and a Funeral*. Watch out also for a pre-*Poldark* Robin Ellis as one of the agitators determined to overthrow the repressive regime.

Cyril Luckham Sir Timothy Hobson • **John Collin** Tom Weston • **Gwynneth Powell** Clare Weston • **Edward Petherbridge** Christopher Hobson • **David Burke** Dr Benedict • **Derek Smith** Norman • **Lynn Farleigh** Eleanor

Created by *Rex Firkin, Vincent Tilsley*

Producer *Andrew Brown*

Gunhed ★★★ 12

1989 Jap Colour 100mins

In 2025, the super computer Kyron-5 began hostilities with mankind. By 2083, fearless techno-bounty hunters assault the computer's Pacific Island HQ, initiating the great Robot War. The only hope for man's future lies in the fabled fighting machine Unit 507, the last of the Gunheds. Can this adaptable bio-droid penetrate the island's dizzying battle levels for victory over the machine? A smash hit in Japan, director Masato Harada's dark vision of a hardware driven future may play like *Aliens* remodelled as a computer game, but it's an exciting helter-skelter action adventure, with few pauses for breath. A Japanese and English language film.

Landy Leyes Gunhed • **Masahiro Takashima** Brooklyn • **Brenda Bakke** Sergeant Nim • **Yujin Harada** Steven • **Kaori Mizushima** Eleven • **Aya Enyoji** Bebe • **Mickey Curtis** Bancho • **James B Thompson** Balba

Director *Masato Harada*

Screenplay *Masato Harada, James Bannon*

The Guyver ★★

1992 US Colour 92mins

One day you're saving the universe as Luke Skywalker in *Star Wars*, the next you're playing a CIA agent who turns into a cockroach. Such is the fate of Mark Hamill in this often unintentionally hilarious movie based on a popular Japanese comic book. Co-directors Steve Wang and Joji Tani handle the action well in this tale of a college student who becomes an armour-plated superhero, courtesy of the titular device, and takes on monster-changing bad guys. Unfortunately, characterisation and dialogue play second-fiddle to a series of hilariously rubbery monsters. Asian star Vivian Wu co-stars. Be warned: somewhere out there is an even worse sequel.

Mark Hamill Max • **Vivian Wu** Mizky • **Jack Armstrong** Sean • **David Gale** Balcus • **Michael Berryman** Lisker • **Jimmie Walker** Striker • **Spice Williams** Weber • **Peter Spellos** Ramsey

Director *Steve Wang, Screaming Mad George [Joji Tani]*

Screenplay *Jon Purdy, from characters created by Yoshiki Takaya*

Guyver 2: Dark Hero ★★★ 15

1994 US Colour 95mins

The same mix of science fiction, genetic tampering, martial arts and weird creatures as the Japanese comic book-inspired original, director Steve Wang's rousing sequel is even more lunatic and action-packed. David Hayter takes over from Jack Armstrong as the armour-plated hero. This time he's after the Zoanoid aliens responsible for double-crossing archaeologist Kathy Christopherson as she unearths a cave-bound spaceship. Lots of fun acrobatic monster-bashing ensues with just enough eye-opening plot between each bout to keep the mind similarly amused.

David Hayter Sean Barker • **Kathy Christopherson** Cori • **Christopher Michael** Atkins • **Bruno Giannotta** Crane • **Stuart Weiss** Marcus

Director *Steve Wang*

Screenplay *Nathan Long, from a story by Steve Wang, from characters created by Yoshiki Takaya*

H

"**If** there's anything more important than my ego, I want it caught and shot **now.**" Zaphod Beeblebrox

The Hitch-Hiker's Guide to the Galaxy, TV series 1981

The H-Man ★★★

1954 Jap Colour 78mins

Taking time-out from his *Godzilla/Rodan* industry, director Inoshiro Honda came up with one of his best movies. His Japanese answer to *The Blob* has men turned into oozing green slime after being exposed to a nuclear test zone. Rain washes some of the gelatinous residue into the Tokyo sewers where it proliferates to attack the population. Flame throwers set the city sewage system alight in a spectacular climax to an engaging fantasy chock-full of hallucinatory images and impressive visual effects. Honda's semi-sequel *The Human Vapor* (1964) failed to match the same extraordinary weirdness. Japanese dialogue dubbed into English.

Yumi Shirakawa Girl • **Kenji Sahara** Detective • **Akihiko Hirata** Scientist • **Eitaro Ozawa** Inspector Tominaga • **Koreya Senda** Dr Maki • **Mitsuru Sato** Uchida
Director *Inoshiro Honda*
Screenplay *Takeshi Kimura, Hideo Kaijo*

Habitat ★★

1997 Can/Neth Colour 103mins

Basically a teen-thriller with an eco-twist, Rene Daalder's feature is set in a future in which pollution has destroyed the ozone layer, and unfiltered sunlight can be lethal. Son Balthazar Getty runs into the usual high-school angst, while scientist Dad (Tcheky Karyo) transforms into lush vegetation, with Mum (Alice Krige) supporting her tendrilly spouse. Despite some genuinely creepy moments and good special effects this neve r really fulfills the promise of the potentially interesting premise. Contains violence, nudity and swearing.

Balthazar Getty Andreas Symes • **Tcheky Karyo** Hank Symes • **Alice Krige** Clarissa Symes • **Kenneth Welsh** Coach Marlowe • **Laura Harris** Deborah Marlowe • **Christopher Heyerdahl** Eric • **Brad Austin** Blaine
Director/Screenplay *Rene Daalder*

Halfway across the Galaxy and Turn Left ★★★ [U]

TV 1994 Aus Colour 28x30mins

A lively children's series from Australia, based on the novel by Robin Klein. After a scandal involving a state lottery, a family from the planet Zyrgon flee across the universe and wind up in the Australian town of Bellwood, where they blend in by pretending to be from Peru. The basic joke is that on Zyrgon children are responsible and mature but become more juvenile as they get older, so that daughter X (Lauren Hewett) has to cope with the antics of her father (Bruce Myles) and mother (Jan Freidl). X's siblings are Dovis (Silva Seidel, voiced by Amanda Douge) and Qwrk (Jeffrey Walker), while Zyrgon's Chief is played by Bruce Spence, the familiar tall character actor from the *Mad Max* sequels. The first half of the 28-episode run is based closely on the novel, but the remainder carry on and conclude the story.

Lauren Hewett X/Charlotte • **Jeffrey Walker** Qwrk/George • **Silvia Seidel** Dovis/Astrella • **Bruce Myles** Father/Mortimer • **Jan Friedl** Mother/Renee • **Amanda Douge** Voice of Dovis • **Bruce Spence** Chief
Director *Rod Hardy, Paul Maloney, Brendan Maher*
Written by *John Reeves, Michael Harvey, from the novel by Robin Klein*
Executive producer *Terry Ohlsson* • ***Producer*** *Jan Marnell*

The Handmaid's Tale ★★★ [18]

1990 US Colour 103mins

As a portrait of a depraved new world, this lacks the conviction to put the frighteners on us. Adapted from a Margaret Atwood bestseller, its heroine, Kate (Natasha Richardson), lives in a born-again America run on puritanical lines in a polluted future. As one of the few fertile women around, she's ordered to bear Commander Robert Duvall a child for wife Faye Dunaway. The republic's religious rites and oppression of women echo some of today's theocratic fanaticisms, but it's a scary story that never gets its act or its acting together, although Duvall is a formidable male presence in this feminist protest. The script is by Harold Pinter, but not so you'd notice. Contains violence, swearing and sex scenes.

Natasha Richardson Kate • **Faye Dunaway** Serena Joy • **Aidan Quinn** Nick • **Elizabeth McGovern** Moira • **Victoria Tennant** Aunt Lydia • **Robert Duvall** Commander • **Blanche Baker** Ofglen • **Traci Lind** Ofwarren/Janine • **Zoey Wilson** Aunt Helena • **Kathryn Doby** Aunt Elizabeth • **Reiner Schoene** Luke • **Lucia Hartpeng** Cora • **Karma Ibsen Riley** Aunt Sara • **Lucile McIntyre** Rita
Director *Volker Schlöndorff*
Screenplay *Harold Pinter, from the novel by Margaret Atwood*

The Handmaid's Tale ★★★★

Radio 2000 UK/US 180mins

This Radio 4 two-part dramatisation of Margaret Atwood's 1985 dystopian novel is a far more satisfactory adaptation than the disappointing cinema film. Set in a near-

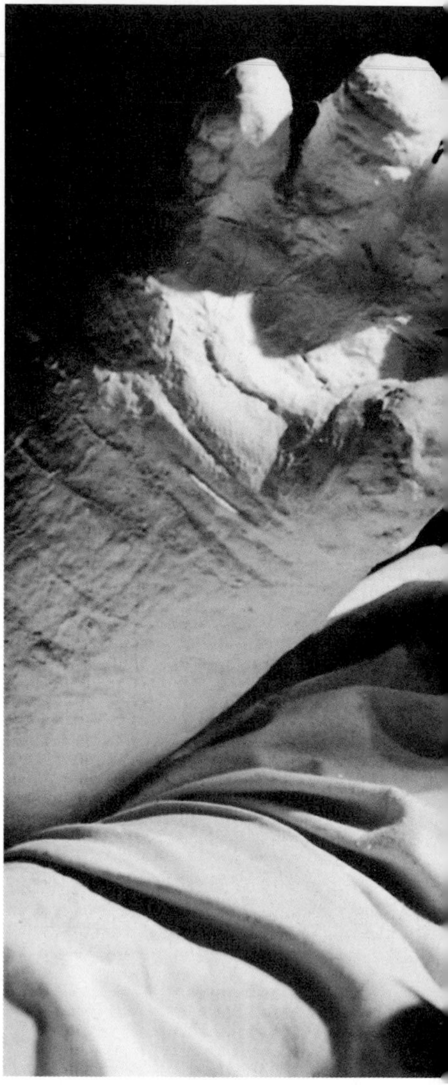

future America ruled on Biblical lines by the religious right, who act as a Christian version of the Taliban militia, it follows the sufferings of Marsha Dietlein, who is captured at the Canadian border as she attempts to flee with her husband and child. Since childbirth is rare in this polluted future, fertile women are re-educated to serve as handmaids, legitimised concubines in the homes of the powerful. The first part is mostly concerned with the increments by which the old freedoms were lost and the retraining process implemented, as run by a former Weight Watchers organiser known as Aunt Lydia (Marian Seldes); the second part deals with Dietlein's troubles in the home of the "Commander" (Earl Hindman), a hypocritical church zealot, and his wife

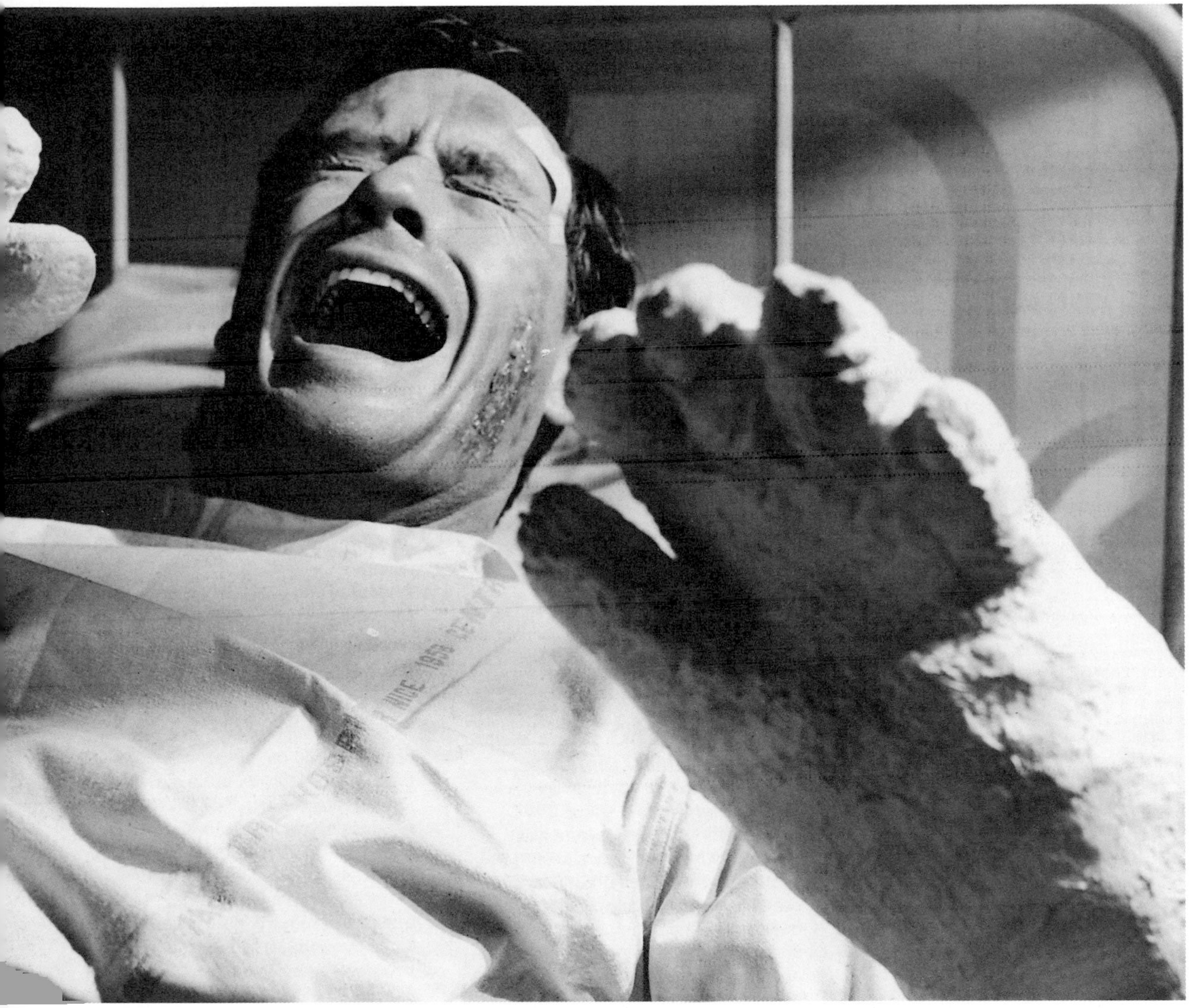

Hands of a murderer: Mel Ferrer is the tormented musician in *The Hands of Orlac* (1960)

Leslie Hendrix. The details are chilling – with community stonings, brainwashed converts and persuasive oppressors – and the audio medium delivers them with maximum impact. Taped in the United States, with an all-American cast. Available on audio-cassette.

Marsha Dietlein Offred • **Leslie Hendrix** Serena Joy • **Marian Seldes** Aunt Lydia • **Tasha Lawrence** Moira • **Emma Roberts** Janine • **Mireille Enos** Ofglen • **Christopher Burns** Luke • **Peggity Price** Aunt Elizabeth • **Earl Hindman** Commander
Director *Jane Quill*
Dramatised by *John Dryden, from the novel by Margaret Atwood*
Producer *John Dryden*

Hands of Orlac ★★★

1924 A BW 90mins

Made five years after his seminal horror outing, *The Cabinet of Dr Caligari*, Robert Wiene's adaptation of Maurice Renard's sensationalist novel suffers from an uncertainty of tone. For the most part, the action is staged in a realistic manner, thus making the moments of expressionist stylisation all the more incongruous. However, Conrad Veidt is mesmerising as the concert pianist living on his nerves after his shattered hands are replaced with those of a murderer. Equally compelling is Fritz Kortner's blackmailer, but not even he's prepared for the final twist. Remade as *Mad Love* in 1935, and also under the original title in 1960.

Conrad Veidt Orlac • **Fritz Kortner** Nera • **Carmen Cartellieri** Regine • **Paul Adkonas** Diener
Director *Robert Wiene*
Screenplay *Louis Nerz, from the novel by Maurice Renard*

The Hands of Orlac ★★★★

1960 UK/Fr BW 101mins

Filmed twice before (most notably as *Mad Love* in 1935), this elegant version of Maurice Renard's psychological case study of murderous obsession still exerts a morbid fascination. Mel Ferrer is a little lightweight as the pianist transplanted with a convicted strangler's hands after a plane crash. But Christopher Lee is a remorseless revelation as the sadistic magician tormenting him, ensuring the palpably chilling tension is maintained right up until the final surprise twist.

Mel Ferrer Steven Orlac • **Christopher Lee** Nero • **Dany Carrel** Li-Lang • **Felix Aylmer** Dr Cochrane • **Basil Sydney** Siedelman • **Lucile Saint-Simon** Louise Cochrane • **Donald Wolfit** Prof Volcheff • **Anita Sharp Bolster [Anita Bolster]** Volcheff's Assistant • **Mireille Perrey** Madame Aliberti • **Donald Pleasence** Coates
Director *Edmond T Gréville*
Screenplay *John Baines, Donald Taylor, Edmond T Gréville, from the novel by Maurice Renard*

Hangar 18 ★ PG

1980 US Colour 96mins

Two space shuttle astronauts witness a collision with a UFO which crash-lands in Texas. When the White House hides the wreck in a remote air base hangar, astronaut Gary Collins tries to uncover the conspiracy over the accident for which he is being blamed. Any resemblance to *Close Encounters* and the Roswell Incident are purely intentional in another sluggish and slapdash slice of sci-fi from the notorious Sunn Classics outfit who exclusively made drive-in exploitation fare.

Darren McGavin Harry Forbes • **Robert Vaughn** Gordon Cain • **Gary Collins** Steve Bancroft • **Joseph Campanella** Frank Lafferty • **Pamela Bellwood** Sarah Michaels • **James Hampton** Lew Price
Director *James L Conway*
Screenplay *Steven Thornley, James L Conway, Tom Chapman, from a novel by Robert Weverka, Charles E Sellier*

The Happiness Cage ★★

1972 US Colour 92mins

In this slow-moving drama, army scientists use controversial shock therapy on overly aggressive soldiers who find it difficult to conform to army life. Ronny Cox and a pre-stardom Christopher Walken play two victims who respond to the pleasure-centre brain treatment in differing ways. Despite powerful moments, the movie never fully conquers its stage play origins although it manages to put across the psychological trauma of the experimental euphoria.

Christopher Walken Private James Reese • **Joss Ackland** Dr Frederick • **Ralph Meeker** Major • **Ronny Cox** Miles • **Marco St John** Orderly
Director *Bernard Girard*
Screenplay *Ron Whyte, from the play by Dennis Reardon*

Hardware ★★★★ 18

1990 UK Colour 89mins

Sex, drugs and rock 'n' roll are the components greasing the splatter-punk engine of director Richard Stanley's impressive debut. His *Terminator*-style shocker with attitude is an amusing, gore-drenched thrill ride. Twenty-first century soldier of fortune Dylan McDermott gives his estranged sculptress girlfriend, Stacey Travis, a junked robot so she can weld the spare parts into surreal artwork. Neither know that the cyborg is really a scrapped prototype developed for future military warfare to kill without mercy – until it reconstructs itself and goes on the bloody rampage. A purposely trashy shock to the system, Stanley's nuts and bolts science-fiction slasher is meant to disturb, and does so without apology.

Dylan McDermott Mo • **Stacey Travis** Jill • **John Lynch** Shades • **William Hootkins** Lincoln • **Iggy Pop** Angry Bob • **Mark Northover** Alvy
Director *Richard Stanley*
Screenplay *Richard Stanley, Mike Fallon, from the story "Shok!" from the comic book "Fleetway Comics 2000 AD" by Steve McManus, Kevin O'Neill*

Harrison Bergeron ★★★

1995 Can Colour 99mins

Based on a short story by Kurt Vonnegut, this Canadian TV movie is set in 2053, some time after the Second American Revolution when intelligence is controlled by electronic headbands that make everyone equally mediocre. But no sooner has director Bruce Pittman established this arresting situation, than we dash headlong into the familiar territory already covered by such films as *Logan's Run* and *THX 1138*. As the eponymous rebel, Sean Astin just about holds the action together, and there's typically strong support from Christopher Plummer. Contains violence and swearing.

Sean Astin Harrison Bergeron • **Miranda de Pencier** Phillipa • **ChristopherPlummer** Klaxon • **Buck Henry** Havlicek • **Eugene Levy** President McKloskey • **Howie Mandel** Charlie • **Andrea Martin** Heather Hoffman
Director *Bruce Pittman*
Screenplay *Arthur Crimm, from the short story by Kurt Vonnegut*

Harsh Realm ★★

TV 1999-2000 Can/US Colour 9x60mins

Following the cancellation of *Millennium*, *X Files* creator Chris Carter once again failed to prove that he wasn't a one-hit wonder with this short-lived virtual reality drama. Famously scrapped after just three episodes had aired in the US (although another six episodes were screened on the FX network), the series follows Scott Bairstow's attempts to escape from an experimental military-built, computer-generated world and overthrow its self-imposed leader, Santiago (Terry O'Quinn). In its brief run, Carter's game of life and death struggles to offer any surprises or much variety of storytelling, and isn't helped by its obvious similarities to the infinitely superior Keanu Reeves vehicle, *The Matrix*. Fortunately, the thrilling visuals and some sterling interplay between Scott Bairstow, DB Sweeny and Terry O'Quinn give the show's final score a much-needed boost.

Scott Bairstow Lt Thomas Hobbes • **DB Sweeney** Mike Pinnochio • **Terry O'Quinn** Omar Santiago • **Samantha Mathis** Sophie Green • **Max Martini** Lt Mel Waters • **Rachel Hayward** Florence • **Sarah-Jane Redmond** Inga Fossa
Created by *Chris Carter*
Executive producer *Chris Carter*

Have Rocket, Will Travel ★★ U

1959 US BW 76mins

As their movie contract with Columbia came to an end, the Three Stooges thought their careers were over, but this juvenile romp in outer space put them back on top as firm family favourites. The trio, with new Stooge Joe De Rita, play cleaners at a rocket base who accidentally send themselves to Venus where they encounter a talking unicorn, a brain machine, a flame-throwing giant spider and doppelgangers of themselves. Silly, aimless fun substituting painful sight gags and assorted weird sound effects for any shred of wit or inventive routines.

Moe Howard Moe • **Larry Fine** Larry • **Joe De Rita** Curley Joe • **Jerome Cowan** JP Morse • **Anna-Lisa** Dr Ingrid Naarveg • **Bob Colbert [Robert Colbert]** Dr Ted Benson • **Don Lamond** Narrator
Director *David Lowell Rich*
Screenplay *Raphael Hayes*

The Head ★★★

1959 W Ger BW 95mins

This *Grand Guignol*-ish lab chiller is proof (if it were needed) that impeccable credentials can't guarantee quality. Hermann Warm, one of the production team behind *The Cabinet of Dr Caligari*, designed the sets; Russian émigré, Victor Trivas (who'd directed the pacifist curio, *Hell on Earth*) called the shots; and the inimitable Michel Simon plays the scientist whose severed head is kept alive thanks to his miraculous Serum X. Yet, curiously, the story of his eccentric assistant, Horst Frank's bid to transplant the head of hunchbacked nurse Karin Kernke on to stripper Christiane Maybach's voluptuous torso never really gels. A German language film.

Horst Frank Dr Ood • **Michel Simon** Prof Abel • **Paul Dahlke** Crime commissioner • **Karin Kernke** Irene • **Helmut Schmid** Bert • **Christiane Maybach** Lilly
Director/Screenplay *Victor Trivas*

Heartbeeps ★★★ U

1981 US Colour 74mins

Love means never having to say you're soldered in an under-rated sci-fi comedy featuring a rare screen performance from cult *Taxi* star Andy Kaufman (immortalised recently by Jim Carrey in *Man in the Moon*) and a welcome movie outing for Broadway diva Bernadette Peters. Set in 1995, they play servant robots who meet in a factory, fall in love, run away and hide out in a junkyard where they have a robot baby. Full of charming details – an entertainment robot programmed to tell jokes – and honest sentiment, Stan Winston's mechanical makeovers were deservedly Oscar-nominated.

Andy Kaufman Val • **Bernadette Peters** Aqua • **Randy Quaid** Charlie • **Kenneth McMillan** Max • **Melanie Mayron** Susan • **Christopher Guest** Calvin • **Dick Miller** Watchman
Director *Allan Arkush*
Screenplay *John Hill*
Music *John Williams*
Make-up *Stan Winston*

Heatseeker ★ 18

1995 US Colour 87mins

Human boxer Keith Cooke is forced to fight an android adversary in the low-tech (by this film's poverty-stricken standards) world of 2019 in this cyber-killer drivel. A vague William Gibson-style cyber-punk ethos is attempted – countries are referred to as New Manila and New America – but that route soon peters out along with any viewer interest. Quite why Albert Pyun is so prolific in the sci-fi movie industry is a mystery because he consistently manages to display little ability or talent in any area.

Norbert Weisser Tung • **Keith Cooke** Chance O'Brien • **Gary E Daniels [Gary Daniels]** Xao
Director *Albert Pyun*
Screenplay *Albert Pyun, Christopher Borkgren, from a story by Albert Pyun*

Heavy Metal ★★ 15

1981 US Colour 86mins DVD

This cult favourite from the eighties, based on an American comic book, now looks a tad dated. A mix of mythical imagery and X-rated animation, this compendium of stories was eagerly lapped up by American teens, but it pales in comparison to the amoral savagery of nineties Japanese *anime*, while the AOR rock soundtrack now seems quaint rather than subversive. Nevertheless, the animation is still striking and a talented cast of American comics provide voices.

Richard Romanus Harry Canyon • **Susan Roman** Girl/Satellite • **John Candy** Desk sergeant • **Marilyn Lightstone** Queen/Whore • **Jackie Burroughs** Katherine • **George Touliatos** Pilot • **Don Francks** Co-pilot • **Eugene Levy** Male reporter/Edsel • **Roger Bumpass** Dr Anrak • **Alice Playten** Gloria • **Harold Ramis** Zeke • **August Schellenberg** Taarak • **John Candy** Dan/Den • **John Candy** Robot • **George Touliatos** Barbarian
Screenplay *Dan Goldberg, Len Blum, from the comic magazine by Richard Corben, Angus McKie, Dan O'Bannon, Thomas Warkentin, Berni Wrightson*
Producer *Ivan Reitman*
Music *Elmer Bernstein*

SCI Q • SCI Q • SCI Q • SCI Q

15

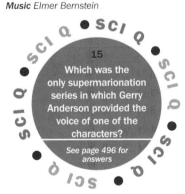

Which was the only supermarionation series in which Gerry Anderson provided the voice of one of the characters?

See page 496 for answers

Hell Comes to Frogtown ★ 15

1988 US Colour 82mins

The ultimate in dumb movie plotlines. Professional wrestler "Rowdy" Roddy Piper stars as Sam Hell, the last potent man alive, who is chosen to rescue and impregnate various buxom maidens held captive by mutant frogfolk. The directors never allow anything as trivial as common sense to get in the way of the fun, with most of the *Carry On*-style jokes focusing on Piper's "below the belt" equipment. Bad enough to be beyond criticism: how can you hate a movie which includes such immortal lines as "Eat lead, froggies!"

Roddy Piper Sam Hell • **Sandahl Bergman** Spangle • **Cec Verrell** Centinella • **William Smith** Captain Devlin/Count Sodom • **Rory Calhoun** Looney Tunes • **Nicholas Worth** Bull • **Kristi Somers** Arabella
Director *R J Kizer, Donald G Jackson*
Screenplay *Randall Frakes, from a story by Donald G Jackson, Randall Frakes*

Hello Down There ★★ U

1969 US Colour 97mins

This would-be comedy comes across as a sort of underwater *Swiss Family Robinson*, with Tony Randall as the designer of a submersible house who agrees to test it out on his wife and children, who just happen to be in a pop group. The plethora of generation gap jokes soon grates on the nerves, as do the bratty adolescent cast members, including a young Richard Dreyfuss, but there's no denying an ingenious premise that should dazzle the youngsters. Director Jack Arnold was reunited with his *Creature from the Black Lagoon* colleague Ricou Browning, who helped co-ordinate the diving sequences.

Tony Randall Fred Miller • **Janet Leigh** Vivian Miller • **Jim Backus** TR Hollister • **Roddy McDowall** Nate Ashbury • **Merv Griffin** • **Ken Berry** Mel Cheever • **Kay Cole** Lorrie Miller • **Richard Dreyfuss** Harold Webster • **Harvey Lembeck** Sonarman
Director *Jack Arnold, Ricou Browning*
Screenplay *Frank Telford, John McGreevey, from a story by Ivan Tors, Art Arthur*

Hemoglobin ★★★ 18

1997 US/Can Colour 88mins

Troubled John Strauss (Roy Dupuis) and his wife visit a remote North American island in an attempt to find descendants of his twin ancestors who had lived there hundreds of years before. There they meet a clan of strange mutants with rather unsavoury eating habits. This is a slick and sick story of hereditary horror from Dan O'Bannon and Ron Shusett, the scriptwriters of *Alien*. Romance, vampirism and incest are all touched on in this bizarre stomach-churner with ubiquitous video star Rutger Hauer's performance keeping a tight rein on the scare tactics and gory horror. Contains graphic violence and sex scenes.

Rutger Hauer Dr Marlowe • **Roy Dupuis** John Strauss • **Kristin Lehman** Kathleen Strauss • **Jackie Burroughs** Lexie Krongold • **Joanna Noyes** Byrde • **Felicia Shulman** Yolanda
Director *Peter Svatek*
Screenplay *Charles Adair, Dan O'Bannon, Ronald Shusett*

The Hidden ★★★★ 18

1987 US Colour 92mins

A rip-roaring buddy movie with an extra-terrestrial twist. LAPD cop Michael Nouri and his alien partner Kyle MacLachlan investigate a series of weird crimes, and find the culprit responsible is a renegade slug-like creature from MacLachlan's home planet which invades earthly bodies and makes them commit nasty mayhem. Beginning in frantic top gear, director Jack Sholder keeps the high-energy proceedings rattling along, yet still manages to find time for sharp and meaningful character interplay between the fun-packed slimy gross-out special effects. A minor gem.

Michael Nouri Tom Beck • **Kyle MacLachlan** Lloyd Gallagher • **Ed O'Ross** Cliff Willis • **William Boyett** Jonathan Miller • **Clu Gulager** Lieutenant Ed Flynn • **Claudia Christian** Brenda Lee Van Buren • **Clarence Felder** Lieutenant John Masterson • **Richard Brooks** Sanchez
Director *Jack Sholder*
Screenplay *Bob Hunt*

The Hidden II ★★ 18

1994 US Colour 89mins

This hopelessly second-rate sequel to the brilliant 1987 original, set 15 years later, finds Raphael Sbarge taking on the Kyle MacLachlan benevolent alien role. This time he searches out the daughter (Kate Hodge) of the Michael Nouri character to help him defeat the shape-shifting slug-like alien menace organising a mass spawning at a warehouse rave. Very talky, ineptly comic and shamelessly using the best footage from the first film, this soon falls into formula chase theatrics.

Raphael Sbarge MacLachlan • **Kate Hodge** Juliet • **Michael Nouri** Detective Beck
Director/Screenplay *Seth Pinsker*
Producer *Michael Meltzer*

Hideous Sun Demon ★ PG

1955 US BW 71mins

Scientist Robert Clarke is exposed to nuclear radiation and turns into a scaly lizard-like monster when exposed to the sun's rays. Wordy dialogue, hopeless acting, wonky photography and a soundtrack that later turned up in *Night of the Living Dead* have made this farcical science-fiction fantasy a cult hit in the *Plan 9 from Outer Space* so-bad-it's-funny tradition.

Robert Clarke Dr Gilbert McKenna/Pitnik • **Patricia Manning** Ann Russell Polly • **Nan Peterson** Trudy Osborne Bunny • **Patrick Whyte** Dr Frederick Buckell/Major • **Fred LaPorta** Dr Jacob Hoffman • **Bill Hampton** Police Lieutenant • **Donna Conkling** Mother • **Xandra Conkling** Little Girl • **Del Courtney** Radio Announcer • **Cameron Clarke** College kid
Director *Robert Clarke, Thomas Boutross, Craig Mitchell*
Screenplay *ES Seeley Jr, Doane Hoag, Craig Mitchell, Robert Clarke, Phil Hiner*

The High Crusade ★★ 15

1994 US/Ger Colour 86mins

Before making American blockbusters such as *Independence Day*, director Roland Emmerich produced this lame combination of *Star Wars* and *Monty Python and the Holy Grail*. During the Crusades, a spaceship lands outside the castle of knight Rick Overton. When his trusty army defeats the laser gun-wielding aliens, he decides to use the craft to get to the Holy Land quickly and save the day. Unfortunately events take an even more bizarre turn as the slapstick and anachronistic humour stubbornly refuse to gel with the cheap science-fiction elements. Although the plot is unique, and John Rhys-Davies elicits the most sniggers by playing it straight as the monk convinced the aliens are demons, the scattershot style and hyperkinetic insanity become old remarkably quickly.

Rick Overton Sir Roger • **John Rhys-Davies** Brother Parvus • **Patrick Brymer** Red John • **Debbie Lee Carrington** Branithar • **Michael Des Barres** Monsieur du Lac
Director *Holger Neuhäuser, Klaus Knoesel*
Screenplay *Robert G Brown, from a novel by Poul Anderson, Jürgen Egger*
Producer *Ute Emmerich, Thomas Woebke, Roland Emmerich*

High Desert Kill ★★★ 15

1989 US Colour 88mins

An intriguing sci-fi chiller in which a group of hunters falls prey to a sinister alien force in the New Mexican desert. Craggy Chuck Connors (in one of his last roles) and Marc Singer are among the threatened marksmen and director Harry Falk makes great use of the desolate landscape. The superior screenplay is from TS Cook, who co-wrote the Oscar-nominated script for 1979's acclaimed *The China Syndrome*. Contains some violence.

Anthony Geary Dr Jim Cole • **Marc Singer** Brad Mueller • **Chuck Connors** Stan Brown • **Micah Grant** Ray Bettencamp • **Vaughn Armstrong** Paul Bettencamp • **Lori Birdsong** Terry • **Deborah Anne Mansy** Kathleen
Director *Harry Falk*
Screenplay *TS Cook*

High Treason ★

1929 UK BW 95mins

Based on a Noel Pemberton-Billing play that tanked in the West End, this mockery of a movie was considered the height of futuristic sophistication by many critics on its release. However, there is a sticky-backed plastic feel to the world of 1940 created by director Michael Elvey on Gaumont's Shepherd's Bush soundstage, while the plot demonstrates a singular ignorance of political reality. For the record, United Europe and United America are set for Armageddon unless the Peace League (which is dominated by mini-skirted women) can broker a truce which its leader, Humberston Wright, will stop at nothing to secure. Yikes!

Jameson Thomas Michael Deane • **Benita Hume** Evelyn Seymour • **Basil Gill** President Stephen Deane • **Humberston Wright** Vicar-General Seymour • **Henry Vibart** Lord Sycamore • **James Carew** Lord Rowleigh • **Hayford Hobbs** Charles Falloway • **Raymond Massey** Man
Director *Maurice Elvey*
Screenplay *L'Estrange Fawcett*
Cinematographer *Percy Strong [Percival Strong]*

Highlander II: the Quickening ★★ 15

1990 US Colour 85mins

Despite some absurdly silly casting (Christopher Lambert as a Scotsman?), the first *Highlander* went on to become a worldwide smash and was a hoot into the bargain. Director Russell Mulcahy was on board again for this second instalment, with a sci-fi element added to the fantasy, but this time around it just doesn't click, even though both stars – Lambert and Sean Connery – also return from the original. Set in 2034, this finds our intrepid time warrior (Lambert) up against an evil new threat in the shape of Michael Ironside and getting mixed up with a gang of ecological radicals led by Virginia Madsen. The two leads once again exude charisma, if not credible accents, and Ironside is splendid as the baddie, while Mulcahy gleefully unleashes an impressive array of visual tricks. However, there's not enough flash to cover the lack of substance. Contains swearing and violence.

Christopher Lambert Connor MacLeod • **Sean Connery** Juan Villa-Lobos Ramirez • **Virginia Madsen** Louise Marcus • **Michael Ironside** General Katana • **Allan Rich** Alan Neyman • **John C McGinley** Blake • **Phil Brock** Cabbie • **Rusty Schwimmer** Drunk • **Ed Trucco** Jimmy • **Stephen Grives** Hamlet

• **Jimmy Murray** Horatio • **Peter Antico** Corda • **Peter Bucossi** Reno • **Peter Bromilow** Joe • **Jeff Altman** Doctor • **Diana Rossi** Virginia • **Randall Newsome** Max Guard • **Karin Drexler** Brenda • **Max Berliner** Charlie • **Eduardo Sapac** Holt
Director *Russell Mulcahy*
Screenplay *Peter Bellwood, from a story by Brian Clemens, William N Panzer, from characters created by Gregory Widen*

The Hitch-Hiker's Guide to the Galaxy: the Primary Phase ★★★★★

Radio 1978 UK 6x30mins

This Radio 4 comedy series was the first incarnation of a story the late Douglas Adams and various collaborators remade as a play, an album, a series of books, a TV show, a long in-development film script, a computer game, a tea-towel, etc. Ironically, this is a case where the property was right the first time and all subsequent retreads, including a sequel radio series, are far less effective. The serial opens with representative Earthman Simon Jones protesting a motorway that has been planned to run through his house, only for the Earth to discover that the Vogons, an officious alien race, have scheduled the whole planet for demolition. Jones is further shocked to learn that his friend Geoffrey McGivern is an alien with the job of revising the eponymous handbook, which offers dollops of information, editorial and comedy in the inimitable voice of Peter Jones. Traipsing through an absurd universe, the heroes hook up with two-headed renegade Mark Wing-Davey, leftover Earthwoman Susan Sheridan and the Eeyore-like Marvin the Paranoid Android (Stephen Moore). Adams's amazingly packed scripts (with John Lloyd joining him as co-writer of the last two episodes) throw out more ideas and jokes than would seem possible as the plot straggles through such weighty matters as the meaning of "life, the universe and everything" and the search for the Ultimate Question to which the answer is "42" and zooms from the Restaurant at the End of the Universe to Earth's prehistory where we discover that mankind is descended not from hominids but a stranded group of societally useless aliens conned into leaving their homeworld. Available on audio-cassette and CD.

Peter Jones The Book • **Simon Jones** Arthur Dent • **Geoffrey McGivern** Ford Prefect/Deep Thought • **Richard Vernon** Slartibarfast • **Anthony Sharp** Garkbit/Zarquon • **Roy Hudd** Compére • **David Jason** Captain of the B Ark • **Jonathan Cecil** Number One of the B Ark • **Bill Wallis** Prosser/Vogon captain • **Jo Kendall** Lady Cynthia Fitzmelon
Written by *Douglas Adams*
Producer *Geoffrey Perkins*

The Hitch-Hiker's Guide to the Galaxy: Secondary Phase ★★★

Radio 1978-1980 UK 6x30mins

Though Douglas Adams keeps up the level of invention in the footnotes and editorialising (delivered mostly by Peter Jones), this six-part sequel to the original Radio 4 serial is a far less satisfying work because it lacks the overall (albeit absurd) plot arc that made the first story work so well. The main plot strands involve Simon Jones and cloned archaeologist Rula Lenska attempting to survive on a world whose economy has been wrecked by the rise of a shoe-based civilisation, while Mark Wing-Davey and Geoffrey McGovern attempt to keep an appointment with visionary publisher Jonathan Pryce. The "infinite improbability" device which was so inspired in keeping the plot of the first serial on the move is overused here to yank in sketch-like tid-bits while Adams vaguely copes with the question of who really rules the universe. Too many of the old characters just reprise their old catch-phrases, while few of the new ones are as memorable, despite a starry guest cast. The first episode was broadcast as a Christmas special in 1978, but the next five didn't come along until 1980. Available on audio-cassette and CD.

Peter Jones The Book • **Simon Jones** Arthur Dent • **Geoffrey McGivern** Ford Prefect/Frogstar robot • **Mark Wing-Davey** Zaphod Beeblebrox • **Alan Ford** Roosta • **David Tate** Eddie/Captain/Commentator/et al • **Bill Paterson** Assistant Arcturian Pilot • **Valentine Dyall** Gargravarr
Written by *Douglas Adams*
Producer *Geoffrey Perkins*

The Hitch-Hiker's Guide to the Galaxy ★★★★

TV 1981 UK Colour 6x30mins

Douglas Adams's extraordinarily inventive and hilarious satire, which manages to poke fun at sci-fi concepts and conventions without alienating true fans of the genre, is a prime candidate for best TV fantasy series of the eighties. Based on a successful radio production, it centres around the boring and oh so very English Arthur Dent (Simon Jones) who learns that not only is his friend Ford Prefect (David Dixon) an alien but that the earth is due for demolition in order to make way for a hyperspace bypass. Talk about a bad day. Using an intergalactic guide book, whose pages are shown by computer graphics and narrated with dead-pan panache by Peter Jones, the duo thumb their way around the galaxy hooking up with a two-headed space pirate and a paranoid android called Marvin, in a vain and ultimately pointless search for the meaning of life, the universe and everything.

Simon Jones Arthur Dent • **Peter Jones** Book • **David Dixon** Ford Prefect • **Joe Melia** Mr Prosser • **Martin Benson** Vogon captain • **Sandra Dickinson** Trillian • **Mark Wing-Davey** Zaphod Beeblebrox • **Richard Vernon** Slartibartfast
Adapted by *Douglas Adams, from his radio series*
Producer *Alan J W Bell*
Animated sequences *Rod Lord*

SFacts

When the series finally came to television, *Radio Times* promoted it with the headline, "At last, the first intergalactic, multi-media epic – cheap, too." According to Douglas Adams, the plot was always incidental to the comedy and detail, so "setting the production on too large a scale would inflate it. We've tried to be realistic." Alien planet sequences were filmed in a clay-pit.

A Hitch in Time ★★★ U

1978 UK Colour 56mins

A fast-paced offering from the Children's Film Foundation, this is *Back to the Future* before its time, although without the budget. Patrick Troughton, Doctor Who mark 2, plays the proverbial scatty scientist who sends a pair of children back in time to meet their ancestors.

Michael McVey Paul Gibson • **Pheona McLellan** Fiona Hatton-Jones • **Patrick Troughton** Professor Wagstaff • **Jeff Rawle** "Sniffy" Kemp • **Sorcha Cusack** Miss Campbell
Director *Jan Darnley-Smith*
Screenplay *TEB Clarke*

Hollow Man ★★ 18

2000 US/Ger Colour 107mins [video] DVD

RoboCop director Paul Verhoeven's nasty streak comes to the fore in this updating of the *Invisible Man* tale. Arrogant scientist Kevin Bacon makes himself invisible and promptly embarks on prattish schoolboy pranks, graduating to sexual assault and murder when he becomes peeved by his inability to become visible again. Challenged for much of a story, the film resorts to turning Bacon's laboratory into a haunted house, from where the see-through psychopath traps his colleagues to dispose of them one by one. Unlikely scientist Elisabeth Shue leads the fight back in an exceptionally unambitious sci-fi thriller, whose predictability is alleviated only by some impressive and interesting special effects.

Elisabeth Shue Linda McKay • **Kevin Bacon** Sebastian Caine • **Josh Brolin** Matthew Kensington • **Kim Dickens** Sarah Kennedy • **Glen Grunberg** Carter Abbey • **Joey Slotnick** Frank Chase • **Mary Randle** Janice Walton • **William Devane** Doctor Kramer

Director *Paul Verhoeven*

Screenplay *Andrew W Marlowe, from a story by Gary Scott Thompson, Andrew W Marlowe*

SFacts

The man who played Isabelle the Gorilla, Tom Woodruff Jr, Also played the lead Alien in *Alien 3* and *Alien Resurrection*.

Holmes and Yoyo ★★

TV 1976-1977 US Colour 13x30mins

The old one about the human cop and his robot partner, done seriously in *The Caves of Steel*, was here spun off into a fairly desperate half season's worth of sit-com. Alexander Holmes (Richard B Shull), ribbed on the force because he's not as perspicacious as Sherlock, is unpartnered because his last couple of sidekicks wound up invalided off the beat, so Dr Babcock (Larry Hovin) lands him with Gregory "Yoyo" Yoyonovich (John Schuck), a prototype robot which still has a few bugs to work out. Besides the usual plodding cases, episodes featured "comic" hijinks as Officer Maxine Moon (Andrea Howard), not in on the secret, tries to seduce the human-shaped gadget. Creator Leonard Stern had done many of the robot gags with the Yoyo-like character of Hymie on *Get Smart*.

Richard B Shull Alexander Holmes • **John Schuck** Gregory "Yo-Yo" Yoyonovich • **Bruce Kirby** Capt Harry Sedford • **Andrea Howard** Officer Maxine Moon • **Larry Hovin** Dr Babcock

Created by *Leonard B Stern*

Executive producer *Leonard B Stern*

Producer *Arne Sultan*

Holocaust 2000 ★★★

1977 It/UK Colour 101mins

The coming of the Antichrist is the theme of Alberto De Martino's spaghetti horror film – even the score is by Ennio Morricone – in which Kirk Douglas flexes his sense of morality and does battle with the Devil. Meanwhile his cherub-faced son Simon Ward (who's called Angel) is committing obnoxious acts that are anything but angelic. Derivative of supernatural successes such as *The Omen*, its special effects only spark distaste, although its acts of Revelation send the goose pimples flying. Enjoyably appalling and appallingly enjoyable.

Kirk Douglas Robert Caine • **Agostina Belli** Sara Golan • **Simon Ward** Angel Caine • **Anthony Quayle** Professor Griffith • **Virginia McKenna** Eva Caine • **Alexander Knox** Meyer • **Romolo Valli** Monsignor Charrier • **Massimo Foschi** Assassin

Director *Alberto De Martino*

Screenplay *Sergio Donati, Alberto De Martino, Michael Robson, from a story by Sergio Donati, Alberto De Martino*

Producer *Edmondo Amati*

Music *Ennio Morricone*

Homeboys in Outer Space ★

TV 1996-1997 US Colour 21x30mins

Sci-fi comedy boldly goes where no one has been stupid enough to go before in this short-lived and short-on-laughs series. Set in the 23rd century, the show follows the exploits of two space-faring "homeboys", Ty and Morris, and their zany encounters with assorted aliens, artificial lifeforms and "space babes". At best, the show is a lame and derivative affair, propelled by routine scenarios and obvious jokes. At worst, its stereotypical, seemingly blaxploitation-inspired characterisation makes for offensive viewing. Not even some amusing cameos from the likes of *Star Trek*'s James Doohan and George Takei, *Species* star Natasha Henstridge and *CHiPs*'s Erik Estrada can get this show off the ground. Stick with *Red Dwarf*.

Flex Tyberius Walker • **Darryl M Bell** Morris Clay • **Rhona Bennett** Loquatia • **Kevin Michael Richardshon** Vashti • **Paulette Braxton** Amma • **Michael Colyar** Milky Ray • **Peter Mackenzie** Andrew Lloyd Wellington III

Homewrecker ★★ PG

1992 US Colour 83mins

Despite the intriguing concept, this is safe-as-houses, formulaic TV fare. Robby Benson is the boffin who develops a female personality for his prized computer, only to discover that he has unwittingly programmed a violent jealous streak towards his estranged wife into the device. The performances are bland, as is the direction of Fred Walton, who made the similarly insipid *Stepford Husbands*. However, Kate Jackson is perfectly cast as the voice of the machine.

Robby Benson Dr David Whitson • **Sydney Walsh** Jane Whitson • **Sarah Rose Karr** Dana Whitson • **Kate Jackson** Voice of Lucy

Director *Fred Walton*

Screenplay *Eric Harlacher, Fred Walton, from a story by Eric Harlacher*

Honey I Blew Up the Kid

★★★ U

1992 US Colour 85mins

After nerdy scientist Rick Moranis accidentally pumps up his son into a 50ft giant, this film is reduced to a one-note romp that almost creaks to a halt. However, until that occurs, there is a well-sustained spirit of infectious enthusiasm, bug-eyed innocence and wild lunacy that harks back to the glory days (the fifties) of the "creature features". The central idea of a normally harmless child running amok in the adult world is strong, the special effects have their own power and magic, and Moranis himself is reliably goofy.

Rick Moranis Wayne Szalinski • **Marcia Strassman** Diane Szalinski • **Robert Oliveri** Nick Szalinski • **Daniel Shalikar** Adam Szalinski • **Joshua Shalikar** Adam Szalinski • **Lloyd Bridges** Clifford Sterling • **John Shea** Hendrickson • **Keri Russell** Mandy • **Ron Canada** Marshall Brooks • **Amy O'Neill** Amy Szalinski • **Michael Milhoan** Captain Ed Myerson • **Gregory Sierra** Terence Wheeler • **Leslie Neale** Constance Winters • **John Paragon** Lab technician • **Ken Tobey** Smitty • **Alex Daniels** Uncle Yanosh • **John Hora** Helicopter observer

Director *Randal Kleiser*

Screenplay *Thom Eberhardt, Peter Elbling, Garry Goodrow, from a story by Garry Goodrow, from characters created by Stuart Gordon, Brian Yuzna, Ed Naha*

Honey, I Shrunk the Kids

★★★★ U

1989 US Colour 89mins DVD

The Absent-Minded Professor meets *The Incredible Shrinking Man* in a joyous, innocuous and thrilling Walt Disney adventure that will appeal to both young and old. Rick Moranis makes you laugh long and loud, as the wacky inventor whose molecular reducer shrinks his two kids, and the children next door, to the size of Tom Thumb's thumb. How they cope with giant insects and water sprinklers in their hazardous garden-turned-jungle makes for epic fantasy chills and spills, doubling as a neat eco-learning quest in the best Disney tradition.

Rick Moranis Wayne Szalinski • **Matt Frewer** Big Russ Thompson • **Marcia Strassman** Diane Szalinski • **Kristine Sutherland** Mae Thompson • **Thomas Brown [Thomas Wilson Brown]** Little Russ Thompson • **Jared Rushton** Ron Thompson • **Amy O'Neill** Amy Szalinski • **Robert Oliveri** Nick Szalinski • **Carl Steven** Tommy Pervis • **Mark L Taylor** Don Forrester
Director *Joe Johnston*
Screenplay *Ed Naha, Tom Schulman, from a story by Stuart Gordon, Brian Yuzna, Ed Naha*

Honey, I Shrunk the Kids ★★★

TV 1997-2000 US Colour 66x60mins

Disney's small-screen spin-off from the 1989 comedy-fantasy movie sees Peter Scolari assuming the role of madcap scientist Wayne Szalinski and unleashing more wacky inventions on an unsuspecting world. Not content with miniaturising his children, Wayne leads his family through a series of adventures involving everything from time travel and aliens to super villains, clones and sentient technology. While the movie's production values are inevitably shrunk to fit the small screen, the Szalinski family's TV exploits remain enormous fun for kids of all ages. Scolari amiably leads a delightful cast, and the show's clever scripting and amusing dialogue give even the most small-time plotline a major boost.

Peter Scolari Wayne Szalinski • **Barbara Alyn** Diane Szalinski • **Hillary Tuck** Amy Szalinski • **Thomas Dekker** Nick Szalinski • **Bruce Jarchow** Mr Jennings
Executive producer *Leslie Belzberg, John Landis*

Honey, We Shrunk Ourselves

★★ PG

1997 US Colour 71mins DVD

Despite the presence of original star Rick Moranis, the concept was clearly running out of steam by the time Disney made this straight-to-video second sequel to *Honey, I Shrunk the Kids*. This time it's the adults who get downsized as Moranis, together with his wife, brother and sister-in-law, are miniaturised by his shrinking machine. The effects are fine, and director Dean Cundey (cinematographer on *Jurrasic Park*), keeps the action bustling along. For all that, it still feels a little old hat.

Rick Moranis Wayne Szalinski • **Eve Gordon** Diane Szalinski • **Robin Bartlett** Patty Szalinski • **Allison Mack** Jenny Szalinski • **Jake Richardson** Gordon Szalinski • **Bug Hall** Adam Szalinski
Director *Dean Cundey*
Screenplay *Karey Kirkpatrick, Nell Scovell, Joel Hodgson, from characters created by Stuart Gordon, Brian Yuzna, Ed Naha*
Producer *Barry Bernardi*

SCI Q SCI Q SCI Q SCI Q

16

Planet of the Apes **was adapted from Pierre Boule's novel *Monkey Planet* – but which was the novel that won Boule an Oscar?**

See page 496 for answers

Horror Express ★★★ 15

1972 UK/Sp Colour 83mins

A rattlingly good chiller set on the Trans-Siberian railway at the turn of the century, where what is believed to be a frozen Missing Link starts to revive in the presence of classic horror movie stars Peter Cushing and Christopher Lee, here playing rival anthropologists. The suspense is kept to a maximum by the clever and beautifully timed editing of Robert Dearberg, who deserves better movies: just study the opening sequence and guess how little material he had to work with. As in the previous year's *Pancho Villa*, director Eugenio (Gene) Martin is unable to control Telly Savalas, who this time chews the scenery as the leader of a group of Cossacks. Shame.

Christopher Lee Prof Alexander Saxton • **Peter Cushing** Dr Wells • **Telly Savalas** Kazan • **Silvia Tortosa** Irina
Director *Eugenio Martin*
Screenplay *Armand D'Usseau, Julian Halevey [Julian Zimet], from a story by Eugenio Martin*

Horror Hospital ★★ 18

1973 US Colour 88mins

Combining audience preoccupations with medicine and terror, director Antony Balch attempts to spoof the usual horror contents by taking them so far over the edge that they self-destruct. There's a Rolls-Royce with scythes, belligerent bikers and a burns-scarred mad scientist, plus Robin Askwith (*Confessions of a Window Cleaner*) as an aspiring rock musician seeking a rest cure. Unfortunately, the result is an almost unwatchable mess, but try to stay the course – the psychological subtext is fascinating. Contains some swearing.

Michael Gough Dr Storm • **Robin Askwith** Jason Jones • **Vanessa Shaw** Judy Peters • **Ellen Pollock** Aunt Harris • **Skip Martin** Frederick • **Dennis Price** Mr Pollack
Director *Antony Balch*
Screenplay *Antony Balch, Alan Watson*

The Horror of Frankenstein

★★ 15

1970 UK Colour 91mins

Ralph Bates is no substitute for Peter Cushing in Hammer's feeble attempt to remake its classic *Curse of Frankenstein*. He overplays the good/bad doctor as ridiculously evil in this throwaway comic variation on the well-worn theme. David Prowse (the Green Cross Code man and Darth Vader's body in the first *Star Wars* trilogy) is a poor replacement for sympathetic Christopher Lee as the Monster. Writer/director Jimmy Sangster displays little subtlety, accenting instead the black humour in a very lowbrow entry, even considering the poor quality of Hammer's seventies output. Sangster wrote many early Hammer classics and the big shock here is his apparent lack of feeling for the genre.

Ralph Bates Victor Frankenstein • **Kate O'Mara** Alys • **Graham James** Wilhelm • **Veronica Carlson** Elizabeth • **Bernard Archard** Elizabeth's father • **Dennis Price** Grave robber • **Joan Rice** Grave robber's wife • **David Prowse [Dave Prowse]** Monster
Director *Jimmy Sangster*
Screenplay *Jimmy Sangster, Jeremy Burnham, from characters created by Mary Shelley*

Horror of the Blood Monsters ★

1970 US/Phil Colour and Tinted 85mins

A preposterous paste-up job from exploitation king Al Adamson (director of such terrible trash as *Blood of Dracula's Castle*) using footage from *One Million BC* (1940), *Unknown Island* (1948) and a mystery Filipino feature. This black-and-white stock footage was tinted (a process hyped as "Spectrum X") and cut into newly-filmed sequences showing John Carradine, Robert Dix and Vicki Volante rocketing to an unknown planet to save Earth from an alien vampire invasion. Snake men, bat demons and claw creatures must also be dispensed with in the course of the dire action. Incredibly, Oscar-winning (*Close Encounters*) cinematographer Vilmos Zsigmond shot this celluloid atrocity.

John Carradine Dr Rynning • **Robert Dix**

Col Manning • **Vicki Volante** Valerie • **Joey Benson** Willy • **Jennifer Bishop** Lian Malian • **Bruce Powers** Bryce • **Fred Meyers** Capt Bob Scott • **Britt Semand** Linda • **Theodore [Theodore Gottlieb]** Narrator
Director *Al Adamson*
Screenplay *Sue McNair*
Cinematographer *William Zsigmond [Vilmos Zsigmond], William Troiano*

House of Dracula ★★

1945 US BW 67mins

Not to be confused with *House of Frankenstein*, this sequel stars Glenn Strange as Frankenstein's monster, Lon Chaney Jr as the Wolf Man and, most impressively, the elegant John Carradine as Count Dracula. Needless to add, they are all splendid to watch under the famously copyrighted Universal make-up. It's the plot that's tiresome, as Onslow Stevens tries to "cure" the monsters of their evil qualities by resorting to science. Erle C Kenton's direction keeps things suitably murky, however, and that Universal house style always adds pleasure to the experience.

Lon Chaney Jr Lawrence Talbot • **John Carradine** Count Dracula • **Martha O'Driscoll** Miliza Morell • **Lionel Atwill** Inspector Holtz • **Jane Adams** Nina • **Onslow Stevens** Dr Edelman • **Ludwig Stossel** Ziegfried • **Glenn Strange** The Monster • **Skelton Knaggs** Steinmuhl • **Joseph E Bernard [Joseph Bernard]** Brahms • **Dick Dickinson** Villager • **Harry Lamont** Villager • **Fred Cordova** Gendarme • **Carey Harrison** Gendarme • **Gregory Muradian** Johannes
Director *Erle C Kenton*
Screenplay *Edward T Lowe*

House of Frankenstein ★★★

1944 US BW 70mins

The sequel to *Frankenstein Meets the Wolfman* adds John Carradine as Dracula into the engaging Universal monster mix. Mad doctor Boris Karloff escapes from prison after the building is struck by lightning and, with hunchback J Carrol Naish, seeks revenge on those who put him there. For this he enlists the help of the trio of vintage horror characters: Dracula, Frankenstein's monster and the Wolf Man. Glenn Strange plays the monster and Lon Chaney Jr returns as the Wolf Man in a bumper bundle of laughs, thrills and nostalgic suspense.

Boris Karloff Dr Gustav Niemann • **Lon Chaney Jr** Lawrence Stewart Talbot • **J Carrol Naish** Daniel • **John Carradine** Count Dracula • **Anne Gwynne** Rita Hussman • **Peter Coe** Carl Hussman • **Lionel Atwill** Inspector Arnz • **George Zucco** Prof Bruno Lampini • **Elena Verdugo** Ilonka • **Glenn Strange** The Monster
Director *Erle C Kenton*
Screenplay *Edward T Lowe, from the story "The Devil's Brood" by Curt Siodmak*
Producer *Paul Malvern*

How to Make a Monster ★★ PG

1958 US BW and Colour 73mins

When a Hollywood make-up effects man is told horror is passé, he applies special drugged cosmetics to the actors playing Frankenstein's creature and the Werewolf on his last movie so they'll think they really are monsters and murder the meddlesome moguls. Cue the re-use of old fright masks, props and veteran stars from AIP successes such as *I Was a Teenage Werewolf*, *Invasion of the Saucer Men* and *The She Creature*, affectionately mocking the genre in which the film's real-life co-writer Herman Cohen originally found fame as a producer. A must for fifties schlock fans, despite the plodding script and weak Herbert L Strock direction. The final scenes were shot in colour.

Robert H Harris Pete Dummond • **Paul Brinegar** Rivero • **Gary Conway** Tony Mantell • **Gary Clarke** Larry Drake
Director *Herbert L Strock*
Screenplay *Kenneth Langtry, Herman Cohen*

Howard, a New Breed of Hero ★★ PG

1986 US Colour 105mins

Marvel Comics meets George Lucas's Industrial Light and Magic, and an uneasy, bland alliance it is, too, with Howard T Duck – a series of anonymous actors camping it up in yellow suits – transported to mid-eighties punkland. Howard takes to the dreadful music of the time and feisty chanteuse Lea Thompson, but fails to ignite any form of discernible plot line or audience response. The movie remains a tedious mess until the final few reels, when Mr Lucas's boys remember they are good at special effects and throw some highly dynamic ones into the burbling pot. This wakes everyone up with a severe jolt, but, too late, alas, to save a pretty execrable movie. Contains mild swearing.

Lea Thompson Beverly Switzler • **Tim Robbins** Phil Blumburtt • **Jeffrey Jones** Dr Jenning • **Paul Guilfoyle** Lieutenant Welker • **Liz Sagal** Ronette • **Dominique Davalos** Cal • **Holly Robinson** KC • **Tommy Swerdlow** Ginger Moss • **Richard Edson** Ritchie • **Miles Chapin** Carter • **Ed Gale** Howard T Duck

BLACK HOLE OF OBLIVION I

These potential TV series never got past the pilot stage

Agent for HARM (1966) Starring Mark (who?) Richman as a special agent trying to keep the Russians from getting their hands on a deadly space spore, this poor man's UNCLE never got his own series.

The Annihilator (1986) Newspaper editor Mark Lindsay Chapman discovers that his girlfriend has been possessed by killer humanoids, but the network killed off any possibility of a series.

City beneath the Sea (1971) Irwin Allen's would-be series about a vast submerged 21st-century metropolis called Pacifica sank beneath the waves.

Humanoid Defender (1985) The public didn't take to JOE (J-type Omega Elemental), genetically engineered to be the ultimate soldier, but would-be do-gooder instead.

Generation X (1996) An entertaining sci-fi romp executive produced by Stan Lee, on whose Marvel comic characters the action is based. Sadly, the band of mutant misfits called in after mad scientist Matt Frewer perfects the ability to infiltrate people's dreams never got the chance to save the planet.

Journey to the Center of the Earth (1993) When it says "based on the novel by Jules Verne", it means based in the loosest possible sense.

The Mysterious Two (1982) *Dynasty*'s John Forsythe and Priscilla Pointer are extra-terrestrials He and She posing as religious leaders. They had a devious plan to conquer the world, but they couldn't conquer the ratings.

Steel Justice (Robosaurus) 1992) The action centres on a cop who follows the advice of a time traveller and transforms his son's toy robot into a fire-breathing, villain-crunching dinosaur. More Roboflop than *RoboCop*.

Director Willard Huyck
Screenplay Willard Huyck, Gloria Katz, from a character created by Steve Gerber

Hu-Man ★★★

1975 Fr Colour 105mins

Documentarist Jerome Laperrousaz seems to have done a little jaunting of his own in preparing for this sombre treatise on time and memory, as its entire central premise derives from Alain Resnais's 1967 drama, *Je T'Aime, Je T'Aime*. However, there are a couple of interesting twists. In addition to incorporating a welter of trippy time-travel visuals, Laperrousaz also casts Terence Stamp as an ageing actor called Terence Stamp and sends him back and forth through the temporal continuum so that Jeanne Moreau's mysterious scientist can harness his shifting emotions. Stamp's reunions with deceased wife Agnès Stevenin turn out to be, however, surprisingly moving. French language film.

Terence Stamp • Jeanne Moreau • Agnès Stevenin • Frederick Van Pallandt

Director Jerome Laperrousaz
Screenplay Francis Guilbert, Guillaume Laperrousaz, Jerome Laperrousaz

The Human Duplicators ★

1965 US Colour 82mins

Electronics expert George Macready finds his mansion taken over by an alien plan to create a race of androids who will control Washington. Richard "Jaws" Kiel (of seventies Bond fame) leads the invasion, which entails cloning humans for nasty operations. Hero George Nader and perennial dumb blonde Barbara Nichols lead the resistance fighters and, with a laser beam, succeed in destroying Kiel and his robot minions. Atrociously acted by Nader, Keie and Nichols as if they already were automatons, director Hugo Grimaldi's howler is a real chore to sit through despite some camp laughs.

George Nader Glenn Martin • **Barbara Nichols** Gale Wilson • **George Macready** Prof Dornheimer • **Dolores Faith** Lisa • **Richard Kiel** Kolos • **Richard Arlen** National Intelligence Agency head • **Hugh Beaumont** Austin Welles • **Ted Durant** Voice from outer space
Director Hugo Grimaldi
Screenplay Arthur C Pierce, from his story

The Human Vapour ★★

1960 Jap Colour 79mins

Convict Mizuno (Yoshio Tsuchiya) is experimented on in prison and becomes capable of transforming himself into a cloudy mist. Able to waft under doors and through keyholes, he embarks on a crime spree in order to buy the affections of dancer Fujichiyo (Kaoru Yachigusa). Inoshiro (*Godzilla*) Honda's direction doesn't match the eccentric delirium he brought to *The H-Man* (his best transformation movie), but expert special effects (by veteran Eiji Tsuburaya) bolster the dodgy narrative sufficiently for medium exploitation enjoyment. A Japanese language film.

Yoshio Tsuchiya Mizuno/The Vapour Man • **Kaoru Yachigusa** Fujichiyo, the dancer • **Tatsuya Mihashi** Okamoto, the detective • **Keiko Sata** Kyoko, the reporter
Director Inoshiro Honda
Screenplay Takeshi Kimura
Special effects Eiji Tsuburaya

BLACK HOLE OF OBLIVION II

Beyond the TV pilot, but not far...

Automan (1983) A half-season Glen A Larson superhero series of no particular distinction: police computer expert Desi Arnaz Jr creates a crime-fighting hologram called Automan (Chuck Wagner), which partners him in the battle against crime.

FreakyLinks (2000) This much-hyped series created by *Blair Witch Project* producer Gregg Hale was fighting for survival within weeks of its US debut. The series revolves around a group of friends who run an underground website devoted to unexplained phenomena, and follows their search for answers. Of the 13 episodes made, only nine were screened.

Harsh Realm (2000-2001) Chris Carter's *Matrix*-inspired effort about a military-controlled, computer-generated world was cancelled after only three episodes, although nine in total were made.

Hypernauts (1996) The final five episodes of the 13 made in this Saturday morning kids' show were never screened. The adventures of a teenage starship crew had spectacular computer-generated effect sequences and impressive alien creations. Unfortunately, the show's superior visuals were not enough to save it from being cancelled midway through its opening season.

Mann & Machine (1992) A state-of-the-art female android is partnered with a streetwise detective, but the robot was canned after just nine episodes.

Otherworld (1985) The series about the adventures of the Sterling family, who stumble through a dimensional gateway in an Egyptian pyramid and find themselves on an alien planet, was cancelled after eight feeble episodes.

Probe (1988) A writers' strike crossed off this potentially good series (Isaac Asimov was one of the creative consultants). Starring Parker Stevenson as an eccentric scientist solving baffling cases, it only lasted seven episodes.

Quark (1978) The few fans who saw the nine episodes of this spoof sitcom featuring Richard Benjamin as the captain of an intergalactic garbage ship thought it was brilliant. The network didn't agree and scuppered the scow.

The Humanoid ★★ PG

1979 It Colour 95mins [video]

A trio of Bond stars – Richard Kiel ("Jaws"), Corrine Clery (*Moonraker*) and Barbara Bach (*The Spy Who Loved Me*) – are insipidly called into action for this Italian *Star Wars* variant directed by gore-maestro Aldo Lado. Mad scientist Arthur Kennedy and his girlfriend Bach want to conquer the universe, but invincible humanoid Kiel prevents him with the help of dwarf guru Marco Yeh and a robot dog. Lado's leaden direction fluffs any outrageous pantomime enjoyment that could have been gleaned. Ennio Morricone's avant-garde electronic score is one of his most unusual.

Richard Kiel Golob • **Corinne Clery** Barbara Gibson • **Leonard Mann** Nick • **Barbara Bach** Lady Agatha • **Arthur Kennedy** Kraspin • **Marco Yeh** Tom-Tom
Director Aldo Lado
Screenplay Adriano Bolzoni, Aldo Lado
Music Ennio Morricone

Humanoid Defender ★★ PG

1985 US Colour 89mins [video]

A routine sci-fi adventure, squarely in the comic-strip mould, about a renegade scientist who creates the perfect super-soldier thanks to a process called molecular recombination. Named J.O.E. – J-type Omega Elemental – the hunky humanoid is designed to handle dangerous assignments, but becomes the target when he refuses to comply with his sinister government taskmasters. The empathy between the scientist and his creation is unusual, but a solitary intriguing touch is insufficient to raise this failed pilot for a TV series above the hundreds of other similarly-themed movies cluttering the video-store shelves.

Terence Knox Michael Rourke • **Gary Kasper** Joe • **William Lucking** Colonel Fleming • **Gail Edwards** Dr Lena Grant
Director *Ron Satlof*
Screenplay *Nicholas Corea*

Humanoid Woman ★★★ PG

1981 USSR Colour 90mins

The doyen of Soviet sci-fi in the detente era, Richard Viktorov was no stranger to epic narratives, as he proved with his 1974 teen take on *2001: a Space Odyssey*, *Moscow-Cassiopeia* and its sequel *Teenagers in Space*. He closed his career with this sprawling two-parter, which begins as an alien-on-earth story as Elena Metelkina learns about human endeavour after being rescued from an abandoned spaceship. However, the action passes into a planet-in-peril phase, as she leads a mission to her homeland, Dessu, to combat both its pollution problem and its evil ruler. Steadily paced, gently humorous and subtly subversive. A Russian language film.

Elena Metelkina Niya • **Nadezhda Sementsova** Nadezhda • **Vaclav Dvorzhetsky** Piotr • **Alexander Lazarev** Klimov • **Vadim Ledogorov** Rakan
Director *Richard Viktorov*
Screenplay *Richard Viktorov, Kir Bulychov*

Hybrid ★★ 18

1997 US Colour 78mins

The ever-prolific Fred Olen Ray sticks faithfully to his no-budget, no-talent formula with this silly sci-fi adventure. After the world has been destroyed – very handy, because that takes care of the sets – a group of military boffin types teams up with a mysterious stranger to fight off a mutant creature at a secret facility. Cult fans will get a kick out of B-movie babe Brinke Stevens's casting as a doctor, while trivia buffs should keep an eye out for John Blyth Barrymore, half-brother of Drew. By the way, Ray's son Christopher is the monster of the title.

Tim Abell McQueen • **JJ North** Carla Ferguson • **Brinke Stevens** Dr Leslie Morgan • **John Blyth Barrymore** Dr Paul Hamilton • **Ted Monte** Milo Tyrel • **Nikki Fritz** Susan • **Christopher Ray** Hybrid
Director *Fred Olen Ray*
Screenplay *Sean O'Bannon*

SFacts

John Blyth Barrymore offers his own version of *Invasion of the Body Snatchers* on his website. It is, he writes, the true story about how he and his father (John Barrymore Jr) stole his grandfather's remains from the Barrymore mausoleum in Los Angeles for cremation (as had been the senior Barrymore's wish).

Hyper Sapien: People from Another Star ★★ U

1986 US/Can Colour 92mins

Cheesily heart-warming family fare suitable only for the most junior space truckers. The story follows a trio of nice aliens who find a welcoming new home when they are befriended by a youngster on an isolated ranch. This syrupy confection is directed by Britain's Peter Hunt, best known for the Bond movie *On Her Majesty's Secret Service*; Talia Shire, who executive produces, pops up in a cameo.

Ricky Paull Goldin Robert Edward "Dirt" McAlpin • **Sydney Penny** Robyn • **Keenan Wynn** Jasper McAlpin • **Rosie Marcel** Tavy • **Gail Strickland** Senator Myrna King • **Dennis Holahan** Aric • **Talia Shire** Dr Tedra Rosen
Director *Peter Hunt*
Screenplay *Christopher Adcock, Christopher Blue, Marnie Paige, from a story by Christopher Blue*

Hypernauts

TV 1996 US Colour 13x30mins

Made by the special effects team and producers behind *Babylon 5*'s first three seasons, this Saturday morning kids' show is an unpretentious hybrid of *Thunderbirds*, *Lost in Space* and *Star Wars*. While on a deep space mission, a teenage starship crew encounter a brutal race of alien conquerors known as the Triad. With the help of a friendly alien, Kulai, the cadets escape the Triad's clutches and attempt to return to earth to warn humanity about the alien invaders. The plots are nothing to subspace home about and the characterisation is pure kids' stuff, but *Hypernauts* still makes a thrilling space race, due largely to its spectacular computer-generated effect sequences and impressive alien creations. Unfortunately, the show's superior visuals were not enough to save it from being cancelled midway through its opening season.

Marc Brandon Daniel Ricardo "Sharkey" Alvarez • **Glen Herman** Russell "Ace" Antonov • **Heidi Lucas** Noriko "Max" Matsuda • **Lewis Arquette** Voice of Horton • **Ron Campbell** Paiyin • **Carrie Dobro** Kulai
Executive story editor *Christy Marx*
Executive producer *Ron Thornton*

I
"Suddenly I realised the power I held. The power to rule. To make the world grovel at my feet."
The Invisible Man 1933

I Love You I Kill You ★★

1971 W Ger Colour 94mins

Debuting director Uwe Brandner seeks to expose the fatal flaws of the German character here by taking a genre from the past, dousing it with contemporary political polemic and setting it sometime in the near future. Initially, there is something chilling about his starkly shot Stepford-like subversion of the *Heimatfilm* (an upbeat style of rural melodrama that had sustained the national cinema since before the Nazi era). But, as his then fashionable anarchist sensibilities take over and a gay teacher and a despised gamekeeper emerge as the prime threats to the tyrannical rule of a smug oligarchy, it loses impetus. A German language film.

Rolf Becker Hunter • **Hannes Fuchs** Teacher • **Helmut Basch** Mayor • **Thomas Eckelmann** Policeman • **Nikolaus Dutsch** Policeman
Director/Screenplay *Uwe Brandner*

I Married a Monster ★ 12

1998 US Colour 86mins

In this unnecessary remake of the 1958 semi-classic *I Married a Monster from Outer Space*, a groom becomes possessed by a monstrous extra-terrestrial entity intent on procreating its dying race through humans. After the wedding, his new bride realises there's something otherworldly about her husband. When other men begin behaving like him, it's up to her to fight the beast that's taking over the town. Lacking the black-and-white eerieness of the original, this is for die-hard sci-fi fans only. Contains some violence and swearing.

Richard Burgi Nick Farrell • **Susan Walters** Kelly Farrell • **Barbara Niven** Linda • **Tim Ryan** Steve • **Richard Herd** Uncle Paul
Director *Nancy Malone*
Screenplay *Duane Poole, from the film "I Married a Monster from Outer Space" by Louis Vittes*

I Married a Monster from Outer Space ★★★

1958 US BW 77mins

Soon-to-be-wed Tom Tryon has his body taken over by a rhubarb-faced alien in Gene Fowler Jr's smartly directed fifties paranoia classic: substitute Gloria Talbott's UFO-duplicated husband for a red in her bed and the true anti-Communist undercurrent becomes apparent. Fowler worked as an editor for Fritz Lang and the German expressionist influence is evident in the use of shadows and weird angles to heighten the atmospheric tension. Despite its outrageously exploitative title, this is good solid science fiction, which is intelligently and intriguingly well packaged.

Tom Tryon Bill Farrell • **Gloria Talbott** Marge Farrell • **Peter Baldwin** Swanson • **Robert Ivers** Harry • **Chuck Wassil** Ted • **Valerie Allen** B Girl • **Ty Hungerford** Mac • **Ken Lynch** Dr Wayne • **John Eldredge** Collins • **Alan Dexter** Sam Benson
Director *Gene Fowler Jr*
Screenplay *Louis Vittes*
Producer *Gene Fowler Jr*

I, Monster ★★ 12

1971 UK Colour 77mins

Dr Jekyll and Mr Hyde become Dr Marlowe and Mr Blake in a vapid attempt to give a Freudian psychological interpretation to Robert Louis Stevenson's oft-told tale. Christopher Lee is convincing as the doctor meddling with a schizophrenic formula, and the Victorian London atmosphere is well captured, but director Stephen Weeks's inexperience means that any complex themes are quickly abandoned, and the end result is flatter than you might expect.

Christopher Lee Dr Marlowe/Mr Blake • **Peter Cushing** Utterson • **Mike Raven** Enfield • **Richard Hurndall** Lanyan • **George Merritt** Poole • **Kenneth J Warren** Dean • **Susan Jameson** Diane
Director *Stephen Weeks*
Screenplay *Milton Subotsky*

I Was a Teenage Frankenstein ★★★ 15

1957 US BW and Colour 73mins

If *I Was a Teenage Werewolf* has one of the most famous exploitation titles of all time, this quickie sequel contains some of the best remembered dialogue: "Answer me, you have a civil tongue in your head. I know, I sewed it in there." As the resident evil scientist, horror dependable Whit Bissell swaps lucrative lycanthropy for ugly monster-making using car-crash cadavers. Immensely idiotic, naturally, but sometimes incredibly effective (especially the lively, colour climax), this lurid hokum has an unexpectedly neat line in self-parody.

Whit Bissell Professor Frankenstein • **Phyllis Coates** Margaret • **Robert Burton** Dr Karlton • **Gary Conway** Teenage Monster • **George Lynn** Sergeant Burns • **John Cliff** Sergeant McAffee • **Marshall Bradford** Dr Randolph
Director *Herbert L Strock*
Screenplay *Kenneth Langtry*

I Was a Teenage Werewolf ★★ 15

1957 US BW 75mins

Rebel without a Cause meets *The Wolf Man* in a trend-setting cult classic, complete with rock 'n' roll, rumbles and teen traumas. Michael Landon (yes, Little Joe Cartwright from *Bonanza* himself) is the troubled student who tears his classmates to shreds after therapy administered by mad scientist Whit Bissell regresses him to his primal past. The suspense is minimal, the production values low, and the time-lapse special effects are hokey, but, even if this seminal shocker now only scrapes by on quaint nostalgia, its title will always be a part of horror history.

Michael Landon Tony • **Yvonne Lime** Arlene • **Whit Bissell** Dr Alfred Brandon • **Tony Marshall** Jimmy • **Dawn Richard** Theresa • **Barney Phillips** Detective Donovan • **Ken Miller** Vic
Director *Gene Fowler Jr*
Screenplay *Ralph Thornton*

The Ice Pirates ★★★ 15

1984 US Colour 89mins

Although little more than an Errol Flynn-type intergalactic swashbuckler, this slight space opera is good inventive fun, even if it does err on the crudely silly side. Space pirate Robert Urich searches the universe for the prized commodity of water, gets captured, falls in love with princess Mary Crosby and escapes with her to search for her father on a mysterious planet covered in water. Great art direction and neat special effects – the clever time-warp birth sequence, the castration device and the robot pimp – augment the constant stream of smart-aleck remarks and sexual innuendo. Off-the-wall and amusing enough even if it is more *Carry On* than *Star Wars*.

Robert Urich Jason • **Mary Crosby** Princess Karina • **Anjelica Huston** Maida • **Michael D Roberts** Roscoe • **John Matuszak** Killjoy • **Ron Perlman** Zeno • **John Carradine** Supreme Commander • **Natalie Core** Nanny • **Jeremy West** Zorn • **Bruce Vilanch** Wendon • **Alan Caillou** Count Paisley • **Marcia Lewis** Frog lady
Director *Stewart Raffill*
Screenplay *Stewart Raffill, Stanford Sherman*

Iceman ★★★★ PG

1984 US Colour 96mins

Two of Universal's most successful pictures are recalled in this fascinating sci-fi outing. With an opening that echoes *Frankenstein* and a plotline reminiscent of *ET*, Fred Schepisi's film couldn't have much better role models. While its subject matter is hardly new, the approach is refreshingly intelligent. John Lone gives a remarkable performance as the primitive man rescued from a 40,000-year incarceration in a block of ice, registering fear, bewilderment, trust and curiosity with shifts of expression so subtle they cannot fail to convince. As the scientists monitoring his progress, Timothy Hutton and Lindsay Crouse also underplay to good effect. Contains violence and swearing.

Timothy Hutton Dr Stanley Shephard • **Lindsay Crouse** Dr Diane Brady • **John Lone** Charlie • **Josef Sommer** Whitman • **David Strathairn** Dr Singe • **Philip Akin** Dr Vermeil • **Danny Glover** Loomis • **Amelia Hall** Mabel • **Richard Monette** Hogan • **James Tolkan** Maynard
Director *Fred Schepisi*
Screenplay *Chip Proser, John Drimmer, from a story by John Drimmer*

Idaho Transfer ★

1973 US Colour 87mins

Director Peter Fonda was still in hippy *Easy Rider* message mode with this well-intentioned but ridiculous sci-fi parable. Some present day kids take part in an experiment with a time machine that "teleports" them to Idaho in 2044, where they plan to start a new civilisation. None of them are emotionally equipped for the job, and anarchy soon rears its head as they become savages without leadership. Bleak, boring and unfocused, Fonda clearly can't direct the bland cast or give any dramatic edge to the rambling plot.

Kelley Bohanan Karen • **Kevin Hearst** Ronald • **Caroline Hildebrand** Isa • **Keith Carradine** Arthur • **Dale Hopkins** Leslie
Director *Peter Fonda*
Screenplay *Thomas Matthiesen*
Producer *William Hayward*

The Illustrated Man ★★★★ 15

1969 US Colour 98mins

Despite Rod Steiger inventing dialogue as he goes along, and the original author, Ray Bradbury, being angered by the producers' refusal to let him in on the filming, this fantasy fable from director Jack Smight works surprisingly well. Steiger is in moody mode as an Everyman whose futuristic adventures are depicted in tattoos over a large part of his body. Claire Bloom, then Steiger's real-life wife, shares the drama if not the star billing, which Steiger deserved if only for the daily make-up routine in which he underwent four hours of painful application. Contains violence and nudity.

Rod Steiger Carl • **Claire Bloom** Felicia • **Robert Drivas** Willie • **Don Dubbins** Pickard • **Jason Evers** Simmons • **Tim Weldon** John • **Christie Matchett** Anna
Director *Jack Smight*
Screenplay *Howard B Kreitsek, from the book by Ray Bradbury*

The Immortal ★★

TV 1970-1971 US Colour 15x60mins

An unsuccessful one-season spin-off from a 1970 TV movie, which was based on a novel by James Gunn, with Christopher George as a young-looking, middle-aged test driver Ben Richards who discovers that his rare blood type retards ageing and fends off all diseases. Like many other fringe sci-fi shows, it adopts the template of *The Fugitive* (some writers even dusted off old *Fugitive* scripts), with Don Knight as the pursuer, chasing drifter George in order to drain his blood as a youth serum for infirm tycoon David Brian. The social and scientific issues of the pilot were dropped in favour of a lot of chase sequences, with George helping out the downtrodden-of-the-week and hustling on to the next episode. Among the guest cast names is include Carol Lynley, a hold-over from the TV movie.

Christopher George Ben Richards • **Don Knight** Fletcher • **David Brian** Arthur Maitland • **Carol Lynley** Sylvia Cartwright
Source *from the novel "The Immortals" by James Gunn*
Producer *Richard Caffey, Howie Horwitz, Lou Morheim*

The Incredible Hulk ★★★ PG

1977 US Colour 87mins

Based on the Marvel Comics cartoon, this pilot feature (released theatrically in the UK) spawned a successful series. The show itself borrowed its formula from *The Fugitive*, but this TV movie is more of a sci-fi affair, with scientist Bill Bixby channelling the grief caused by his wife's death into an exploration of the link between stress, strength and gamma radiation. Former Mr Universe Lou Ferrigno became a cult figure as Bixby's hulking green alter ego, but the same can't be said of Jack Colvin, whose performance as the persistent *National Register* reporter is highly resistible. Another TV movie, *The Return of the Incredible Hulk* was screened shortly after this launch feature. Contains violence.

Bill Bixby Dr David Bruce Banner • **Susan Sullivan** Dr Elaina Marks • **Jack Colvin** Jack McGee • **Lou Ferrigno** The Hulk • **Susan Batson** Mrs Maier • **Charles Siebert** Ben • **Mario Gallo** Mr Bram • **Eric Server** Policeman
Director *Kenneth Johnson*
Screenplay *Kenneth Johnson, Thomas E Szollosi, Richard Christian Matheson, from the comic books by Stan Lee, Jack Kirby*

SFacts

Arnold Schwarzenneger was allegedly considered too short to play the part of the Hulk, so the role went to Ferrigno instead. Ang Lee is to direct a new feature film of *The Incredible Hulk* for a release.

The Incredible Hulk ★★★ U PG

TV 1978-1982 US Colour 85x60mins

A mostly bland series, hammering Marvel Comics's long-running Jekyll-and-Hyde character into yet another redo of *The Fugitive*. Bill Bixby is scientist David Banner (Bruce Banner in the comics), whose experiments with gamma radiation alter his genetic structue so that when he gets angry he transforms briefly into green-skinned, inarticulate giant the Hulk (Lou Ferrigno). The two pilots, *The Incredible Hulk* (1977) and *The Return of the Incredible Hulk* (1977) were fairly serious, if lacking in the fantastical material of the comics, but the show was the usual business with the wandering hero helping out different characters each week, sometimes in stories written around stock footage (*Never Give a Trucker an Even Break* uses most of the stunts from Steven Spielberg's TV movie *Duel*). The "hulk-out" sequences offer a memorable set of images – Bixby wearing contact lenses, muscles splitting shirt-seams (but never trousers), green shaggy hair – but quickly became monotonous, although full points for when Bixby conscientuously tries to telephone the emergency services and is prompted to turn into the Hulk by an infuriating phone company runaround. The show's Lieutenant Gerard was muckraking reporter Jack McGee (Jack Colvin), who blamed the Hulk for Banner's supposed death. Over four seasons, guest stars included Loni Anderson, Jeremy Brett, Mariette Hartley (who won an Emmy for a *Love Story* haircut, in *Married*, in which Bixby marries a terminally-ill psychiatrist) and Ray Walston (Bixby's co-star from *My Favorite Martian*, in an episode entitled *My Favorite Magician*).

Bill Bixby Dr David Banner • **Jack Colvin** Jack McGee • **Lou Ferrigno** Hulk
Consultant *Stan Lee*
Executive producer *Kenneth Johnson*

The Incredible Hulk Returns
★★ PG

1988 US Colour 93mins

Bursting from the pages of Marvel Comics on to our TV screens in 1978, the *Incredible Hulk* was, briefly, essential viewing for teenagers everywhere. But, by the time this TV movie appeared a decade later, audiences had grown out of his superheroic exploits, in much the same way that Bill Bixby grew out of his clothes (and turned into snarling Lou Ferrigno) every time he had a temper tantrum. Convinced that mere mortals were no longer a match for the far-from-jolly green giant, the producers brought in another Marvel regular, the mighty Thor, to provide the villainy. The plot is as tatty as Bixby's ripped shirt, but it's undemanding fun. Contains some violence and swearing.

Bill Bixby David Banner • **Lou Ferrigno** The Incredible Hulk • **Lee Purcell** Maggie Shaw • **Tim Thomerson** Le Beau • **Steve Levitt** Donald Blake • **Eric Kramer [Eric Allan Kramer]** Thor • **Jack Colvin** Jack McGee
Director/Screenplay *Nicholas Corea*

The Incredible Invasion ★

1971 Mex/US Colour 90mins

This is last film horror superstar Boris Karloff ever appeared in, and his scenes were shot in Los Angeles in 1968 when he was at his most frail – the reason why he is always shown sitting down or leaning for support. He plays Professor John Mayer whose radioactive death ray invention attracts the interest of the military as a potential weapon and two aliens from outer space worried about its global misuse. Body snatching and the time-honoured storming of Mayer's house by fearful villagers in true *Frankenstein* tradition are also thrown into this cobbled together Mexican mix. A very sad end to Karloff's illustrious career, this inept disaster was allegedly co-directed by Jack Hill and Juan Ibanez.

Boris Karloff Prof John Mayer • **Enrique Guzman** Paul • **Christa Linder** Laura • **Maura Monti** Isabel • **Yerye Beirute** Convict
Director *Jack Hill, Juan Ibanez*
Screenplay *Karl Schanzer, Enrique Vergara*
Special effects *Jack Tannenbaum*

The Incredible Melting Man
★★ 18

1977 US Colour 82mins

Astronaut Alex Rebar returns from Saturn a changed man. His flesh is decomposing and he finds he's developed a taste for human flesh. A deliberate throwback to such cheap fifties' frights as *The First Man into Space*, hack writer/director William Sachs does little of interest within the tried and tested old school format apart from showcasing Oscar winner (*An American Werewolf In London*) Rick Baker's slimy and putrefying make-up to stunning effect.

Alex Rebar Melting Man • **Burr DeBenning** Dr Ted Nelson • **Myron Healey** General Perry • **Michael Alldredge** Sheriff Blake • **Ann Sweeny** Judy Nelson • **Lisle Wilson** Dr Loring • **Rainbeaux Smith [Cheryl Smith]** The model • **Julie Drazen** Carol • **Stuart Edmond Rodgers** Little boy • **Chris Whitney** Little boy • **Jonathan Demme** Matt
Director/Screenplay *William Sachs*
Make-up special effects *Rick Baker*

The Incredible Shrinking Man
★★★★★

1957 US BW 91mins

A must-see classic, directed by the master of fifties' science fiction, Jack Arnold, and derived from the thought-provoking novel by genre luminary Richard Matheson. Grant Williams slowly shrinks after passing through a radioactive cloud and, on the way down, sees his marriage disintegrate and is terrorised by the pet cat and a basement spider. A cogent comment on the plight of the "little man" in today's high-tech world, Arnold's superlative thriller still retains its irony, shock and power. Williams gives a sensitive portrayal of a man hounded by the media and consigned to a freak's world, whose descent into being and nothingness provides a memorable climax.

Grant Williams Scott Carey • **Randy Stuart** Louise Carey • **April Kent** Clarice • **Paul Langton** Charlie Carey • **Raymond Bailey** Dr Thomas Silver • **William Schallert** Dr Arthur Bramson • **Frank Scannell** Barker
Director *Jack Arnold*
Screenplay *Richard Matheson, from his novel "The Shrinking Man"*

The Incredible Shrinking Woman ★★★

1981 US Colour 88mins

A very odd spoof on the wonderful *The Incredible Shrinking Man*, brought bang up to date with some neat special effects, but lacking the shock value of the original. Lily Tomlin is very funny as the housewife accidentally sprayed with a new perfume and ending up the size of the germs she tries so hard to eradicate in her home. This is a pleasing little jaunt through by now highly-familiar territory, directed with flair and a light touch by Joel Schumacher. But nothing comes close to the astounding originality of the 1957 classic. Contains swearing.

Lily Tomlin Pat Kramer/Judith Beasley • **Charles Grodin** Vance Kramer • **Ned Beatty** Dan Beame • **Henry Gibson** Dr Eugene Nortz • **Elizabeth Wilson** Dr Ruth Ruth • **Mark Blankfield** Rob • **Maria Smith** Concepcion • **Pamela Bellwood** Sandra Dyson • **John Glover** Tom Keller • **Nicholas Hormann** Logan Carver • **Mike Douglas** Mike Douglas
Director *Joel Schumacher*
Screenplay *Jane Wagner, from the novel "The Shrinking Man" by Richard Matheson*

The Incredible Two-Headed Transplant ★

1971 US Colour 87mins

This low-budget nonsense is so laughably bad as to have garnered a minor cult reputation among trash horror movie fans. Bruce Dern is perfectly cast as a deranged scientist who grafts the head of a murderer on to the body of a retarded giant who – predictably – goes on a Frankenstein-style rampage. Well, it seemed like a good idea at the time. Anthony M Lanza, unsurprisingly, never directed another film again. Cheesy seventies fashion and diabolical dialogue manage to raise a few unintentional laughs. Acclaimed make-up effects artist Rick Baker was responsible for the gorilla suit.

Bruce Dern Roger • **Pat Priest** Linda • **Casey Kasem** Ken • **Albert Cole** Cass • **John Bloom** Danny
Director *Anthony M Lanza*
Screenplay *James Gordon White, John Lawrence*
Producer *John Lawrence*

The Incredibly Strange Creatures Who Stopped Living and Became Mixed-Up Zombies ★★

1963 US Colour 82mins

This legendary turkey was billed as "The First Monster Musical" and features such awful production numbers as *The Mixed-Up Zombie Stomp*, complete with tacky striptease routines. Cash Flagg (director Ray Dennis Steckler's alter ego) falls under the sinister spell of a sideshow fortune-teller who throws acid in her patron's faces and then confines them to cages where they become rabid zombies ready to break loose when the rock songs begin. A heady mix of carnival freaks, beatniks, voodoo and knife-murders, this unbelievably messy romp has something for every follower of trash. Originally shown in

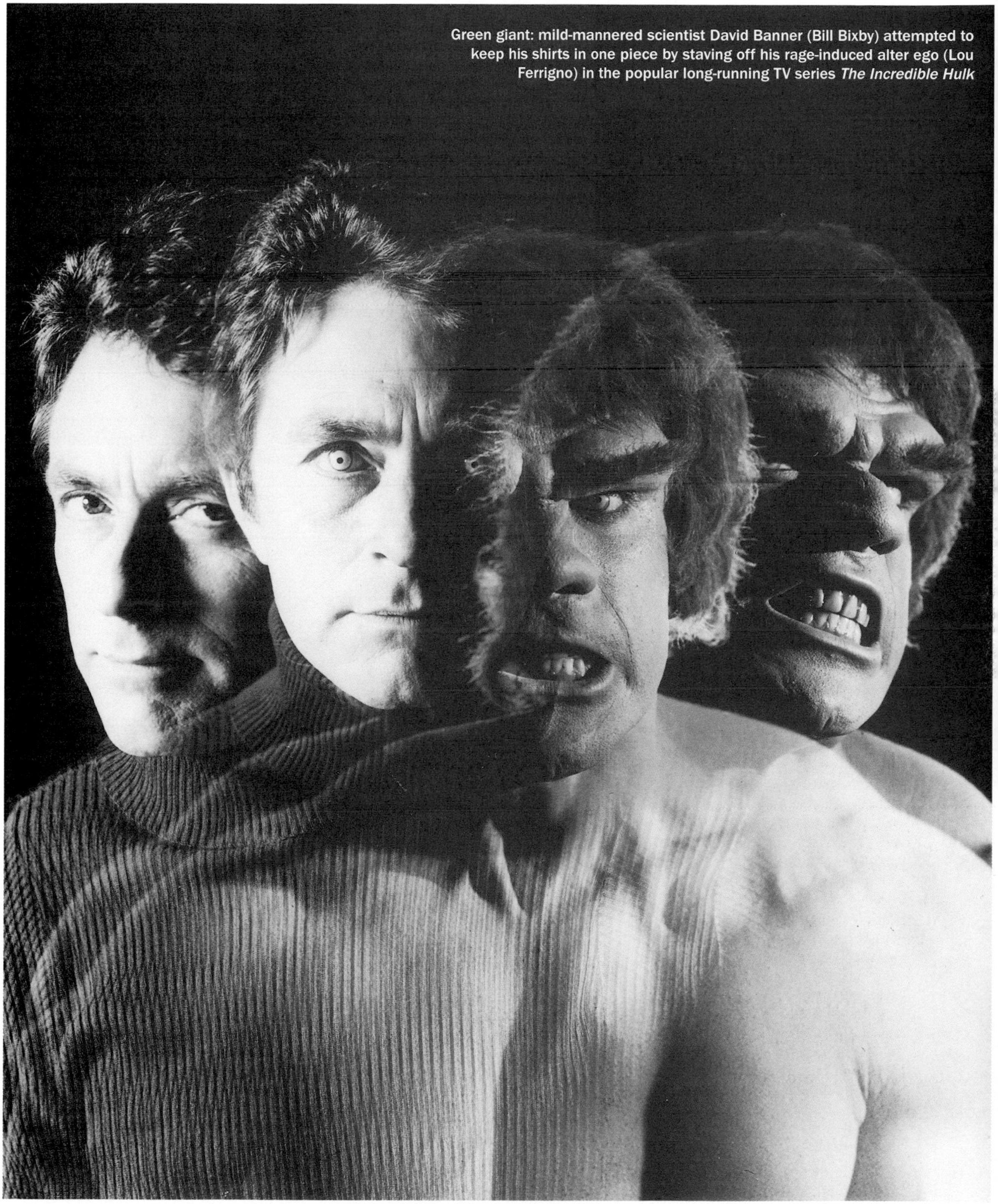

Green giant: mild-mannered scientist David Banner (Bill Bixby) attempted to keep his shirts in one piece by staving off his rage-induced alter ego (Lou Ferrigno) in the popular long-running TV series *The Incredible Hulk*

"Hallucinogenic Hypnovision" – whatever that means.

Cash Flagg [Ray Dennis Steckler] Jerry • **Carolyn Brandt** Marge Neilson • **Brett O'Hara** Madame Estrella • **Atlas King** Harold • **Sharon Walsh** Angela • **Madison Clarke** Madison • **Erina Enyo** Carmelita • **Jack Brady** Ortega
Director *Ray Dennis Steckler*
Screenplay *Gene Pollock, Robert Silliphant, from a story by EM Kevke*
Producer *Ray Dennis Steckler*

Independence Day ★★★★ 12

1996 US Colour 138mins

Alien invasion has long fascinated movie audiences, but no film has presented the destruction of the Earth on such an epic scale before this preposterously successful smash-hit movie, directed by Roland Emmerich, came along and blitzed everything before it at the box office. Of course, when we say the Earth, we really mean the United States. Aside from a few brief, silly appearances from foreign TV news presenters – including one from Sky News – the rest of the globe barely gets a look in; this is about how the good old US of A saves the world again. The story is simple: gigantic alien spacecraft hover above major cities and set about destroying everything below. Those plucky Yanks, however, won't go down without a fight. There are subplots focusing on the fate of ordinary folk, but most of the effort goes on the mind-boggling set pieces of mass destruction. Such scenes of digital mayhem are now becoming commonplace – think *Armageddon, Deep Impact* and Emmerich's subsequent *Godzilla* – but this really provided the template, and scenes such as the levelling of Washington still take the breath away. So what of the actors? Well, Will Smith, playing the wisecracking fighter pilot, was the big winner, with his charismatic performance in this, the following year's *Men in Black* and even the critically hammered *Wild Wild West* making him one of the biggest box-office draws in the western world. Jeff Goldblum delivers a variation of his boffin role in *Jurassic Park*, while Bill Pullman manfully keeps a straight face as the initially ineffectual American president. Of the females, Vivica A Fox fares the best, although the likes of Mary McDonnell and Margaret Colin are largely wasted in supporting roles. But this is, after all, a special effects, not an acting, showcase, and a darn entertaining one at that. Contains violence.

Will Smith Captain Steve Hiller • **Bill Pullman** President Thomas J Whitmore • **Jeff Goldblum** David Levinson • **Mary McDonnell** Marilyn Whitmore • **Judd Hirsch** Julius Levinson • **Robert Loggia** General William Grey • **Randy Quaid** Russell Casse • **Margaret Colin** Constance Spano • **James Rebhorn** Albert Nimziki • **Harvey Fierstein** Marty Gilbert • **Adam Baldwin** Major Mitchell • **Brent Spiner** Dr Brakish Okun • **James Duval** Miguel • **Vivica A Fox** Jasmine Dubrow
Director *Roland Emmerich*
Screenplay *Dean Devlin, Roland Emmerich*

Independence Day UK ★★★

Radio 1996 UK 60mins

"When this is all over and we've defeated these monsters, the Yanks'll take the credit for it, you wait and see." An unusual co-production between BBC Radio 1 and 20th Century Fox, this hour-long special from writer/producer/director Dirk Maggs borrows a few licks from the Orson Welles *War of the Worlds* broadcast while delivering a tie-in with the Roland Emmerich-Dean Devlin blockbuster movie, recounting the story of what happened in Britain offscreen during the film but, considering that it was transmitted while the movie was still in theatres, not giving away the ending. It starts as a "Radio 1 UFO-watch special", with DJ Nicky Campbell and Mark Goodyer and celebrity eccentric astronomer Patrick Moore as themselves reporting on the arrival of an alien invasion fleet and the destruction of London.Colin Baker and Toyah Wilcox play stiff-upper-lip RAF pilots who take a rather less emotional approach to the catastrophe than the characters in the film. The events chronicled include the escape of the Royal Family via Radio 1 traffic helicopter and Patrick Moore's fist-to-tentacle fight with an alien.

Nicky Cambell • **Patrick Moore** • **Toyah Wilcox** • **Colin Baker** • **Simon Treves** • **Mark Goodier** • **Toby Longworth** • **Peter Serafinowicz** • **Mark Courtney**
Director/Written by *Dirk Maggs*

Indestructible Man ★★ PG

1956 US BW 70mins

Lacking the class of its uncredited source (the Karloff-Curtiz collaboration, *The Walking Dead*), this revenge B-movie is saved by another patented display of dolour from Lon Chaney Jr. As in *Man Made Monster*, he's transformed into a Frankensteinian lug by a jolt of electricity, this time applied to his executed cadavre by cancer specialist Robert Shayne. Thenceforth it's stalk 'n' slash fifties-style, as Chaney seeks to prevent crooked lawyer Ross Elliott from locating loot stashed in the LA sewer system. Thankfully, the flamethrower-bazooka denouement provides a sensationalist touch that atones for the soppiness of the gratuitous romance between a stripper and a cop.

Lon Chaney Jr The Butcher • **Marian Carr** Eva Martin • **Robert Shayne** Prof Bradshaw • **Ross Elliott** Paul Lowe • **Ken Terrell** Joe Marcella • **Marvin Ellis** Squeamy Ellis
Director *Jack Pollexfen*
Screenplay *Sue Bradford, Vi Russell*

Infra-Man ★★

1976 HK Colour 92mins

Horror, martial arts, magic, Chinese folklore and science-fiction are all served up in this haphazard Hong Kong version of *Superman*. An evil ruler of a subterranean kingdom wants to extend her powers to the surface. So a kung-fu fighter is scientifically transformed into an invincible superhero to halt her world domination plans that include unleashing earthquakes, erupting volcanoes and tidal waves to beat mankind into submission. Typically lunatic fare from the Shaw Brothers Studio factory, this genre hodgepodge suffers from Hua Shan's episodic direction. Cantonese dialogue dubbed into English.

Wang Hsieh • **Terry Liu** • **Lin Wen-Wei**
Director *Hua Shan*

Innerspace ★★★ PG

1987 US Colour 114mins

This botched attempt to update *Fantastic Voyage* – or "Honey, I Shrunk the Test Pilot" – is probably director Joe Dante's worst movie, but it's still a notch above the usual Hollywood fodder. Dennis Quaid is the hot-shot military man who is miniaturised and mistakenly pumped into the body of lowly supermarket clerk Martin Short. The effects are excellent and Dante's sly humour shines through occasionally, but it lacks the anarchy of his best work and Short's hysterics eventually begin to grate. Meg Ryan pops up as the love interest and there are good supporting turns from Kevin McCarthy and Henry Gibson. Dante regular Dick Miller, once a fixture in Roger Corman's movies, has a cameo as a cab driver. Contains some swearing.

Dennis Quaid Lt Tuck Pendelton • **Martin Short** Jack Putter • **Meg Ryan** Lydia Maxwell • **Kevin McCarthy** Victor Scrimshaw • **Fiona Lewis** Dr Margaret Canker • **Vernon Wells** Mr Igoe • **Robert Picardo** The cowboy • **Wendy Schaal** Wendy • **Harold Sylvester** Pete Blanchard • **William Schallert** Dr Greenbush • **Henry**

Gibson Mr Wormwood
Director *Joe Dante*
Screenplay *Jeffrey Boam, Chip Proser, from a story by Chip Proser*

Inseminoid ★★★ 18

1981 UK Colour 89mins

The basic concepts of *Alien* are taken to the sleaziest and goriest extremes in director Norman J Warren's lively addition to the murderous space-creature genre. Shot entirely in Chiselhurst caves, it stars Judy Geeson and Stephanie Beacham as two members of an interstellar archaeological mission. Geeson is impregnated by a nasty ET and mutates into a killer, horrifically murdering anyone who threatens her impending motherhood. The pace is fast enough to cover the film's more ridiculous aspects – chainsaws in space, really! – and the endlessly screaming Geeson gives a first-rate performance that's far above the call of duty. Easily the best film in Warren's exploitation canon, which includes *Satan's Slave* and *Terror*.

Judy Geeson Sandy • **Robin Clarke** Mark • **Jennifer Ashley** Holly • **Stephanie Beacham** Kate • **Steven Grives** Gary • **Barrie Houghton** Karl • **Rosalind Lloyd** Gail • **Victoria Tennant** Barbra
Director *Norman J Warren*
Screenplay *Nick Maley, Gloria Maley*

Intruders ★★ 15

TV 1992 US 161mins

An 1992 update of *The UFO Incident* that skews somewhere between the blandness of *Project UFO* and the paranoia of *The X Files*. Partly based by writers Barry Oringer and Tracy Tormé on a non-fiction book by Bud Hopkins, this two-part miniseries marked a return to the fantastic for producer/director Dan Curtis (*The Night Stalker*, *Dark Shadows*) after his successes with the *Winds of War* miniseries. Fatherly doctor Richard Crenna treats two women (Daphne Ashbrook, Mare Winningham) who have repressed memories of alien abduction experiences, which extend to cranial implants and impregnation. The familiar story is strung out to tiresome length, with the traditional sub-plot about government cover-up and a final revelation that the advanced aliens, while unaware of the concept of medical ethics, are benevolent.

Richard Crenna • **Mare Winningham** • **Susan Blakely** • **Daphne Ashbrook** • **Alan Autry** • **Ben Vereen** • **Steven Berkoff**
Director *Dan Curtis*
Written by *Tracy Tormé, from a story by Barry Oringer, from a book by Budd Hopkins*

Invader ★★ 15

1991 US Colour 91mins

A bargain-basement but quietly ambitious sci-fi thriller that should keep conspiracy theorists happy with its tale of an alien artificial intelligence system taking over a US air-force base and plotting Armageddon. Scandal sheet reporter Hans Bachmann (never heard of before or since) discovers what's going on and, with the Pentagon understandably sceptical, teams up with defence department agent A Thomas Smith to kick some UFO butt. Explosions for the sake of them and bouts of weak humour – there's some rather obvious ribbing of military stereotypes – dampen the best efforts of director Philip J Cook. Still, the imaginative use of special effects on such an obviously cramped budget is certainly impressive.

Hans Bachmann Frank McCall • **A Thomas Smith** Captain Harry Anders • **Rick Foucheux** Colonel Faraday • **John Cooke** General Anheiser
Director/Screenplay *Philip J Cook*

The Invader ★★ 15

1997 US Colour 92mins

Pregnant school teacher Sean Young is carrying the "Eve" infant of a threatened alien race. As good alien Ben Cross tries to protect her, bad alien Nick Mancuso cons cop Daniel Baldwin (also Young's boyfriend) into helping him find Cross. Mancuso's intentions are strictly murderous. Although rather pointless and silly, with director Mark Rosman playing down the action side of things and focusing on the unconvincing alien love triangle aspect, this fast-moving science-fiction thriller plays down the *Terminator* references in favour of fish-out-of-water comedy. Acting beyond the call of duty ensures the one-dimensional characters register effectively. Contains some violence.

Sean Young Annie • **Ben Cross** Renn • **Daniel Baldwin** Jack • **Nick Mancuso** Willard • **Lynda Boyd** Gail • **Tim Henry** Older cop • **Ken Tremblett** Davidson • **Robert Andre** McNeil
Director/Screenplay *Mark Rosman*

The Invaders ★★★★ PG

TV 1967-1968 US Colour 43x60mins

This Quinn Martin show combines the premises of his influential series *The Fugitive* and the film *Invasion of the Body Snatchers* (1956) as architect David Vincent (Roy Thinnes) stumbles over an invasion plot and runs about from episode to episode, getting involved with strangers in soap-style trouble and thwarting whatever the aliens were plotting that week. Created by Larry Cohen, the show started well with the unsettling *Beach Head* (directed by Joseph Sargent), in which Vincent's life falls apart after he has witnessed the arrival of a flying saucer and learned that human-seeming aliens (some of whom can't bend their little fingers – an absurd but creepy detail) are working among us to take over the planet ("and make it their world"). As announced by the usual Quinn Martin stentorian narrator, "tonight's guest stars" were often good value: Suzanne Pleshette (as an alien dissident in *The Mutation*), Jack Lord, Michael Rennie, Roddy McDowall, James Whitmore, Ed Begley, Peter Graves, Burgess Meredith, Ralph Bellamy, Anne Francis, Gene Hackman, Sally Kellerman, Karen Black and Barbara Hershey. However, repetition swiftly set in and, despite a slight rejig of the format for the second season (in which Kent Smith became another regular cast member, head of a group known as "The Believers") the show was cancelled without any resolution. A 1995 two-part revival mini-series revealed that Vincent (Thinnes again) was still out there fighting the invaders and introduced Scott Bakula as a new alien-buster, but this fine effort didn't lead to a continuing show.

Roy Thinnes David Vincent • **Kent Smith** Edgar Scoville
Created by *Larry Cohen*
Executive producer *Quinn Martin*

SFacts

YOU KNOW YOU'RE AN ALIEN IF:
- You have no heartbeat
- You have a deformed fourth finger
- You don't bleed
- You don't like pure oxygen
- You could be described as sub-zero on the emotional scale

The Invaders ★★ 15

TV 1995 US 170mins

A spin-off from the sixties' sci-fi show, this four-hour mini-series stars *Quantum Leap*'s Scott Bakula as Nolan Wood, an ex-con who resumes the legendary David Vincent's one-man battle against secret alien forces on earth. Bakula's real enemy here, though, is a slow-moving and uninspired script, which provides the basis of an occasionally good but mostly mundane adventure. The mini-series isn't helped by Elizabeth Pena's grating female lead, or its inexcusable failure to make better use of the original show's star, Roy Thinnes, who is reduced to a cameo role. Although Bakula delivers a predictably good central performance and gives the mini-series a much-needed edge, it remains a disappointing encore.

Scott Bakula Nolan Wood • **Elizabeth Pena** Ellen Garza • **Richard Thomas** Jerry Thayer • **Roy Thinnes** David Vincent
Director *Paul Shapiro*
Written by *James Dott, from the TV series created by Larry Cohen*

Invaders from Mars ★★★★ PG

1953 US Colour 77mins

William Cameron Menzies helped to design *Gone with the Wind* and directed *Things to Come*, and his Martian menace fairy tale has achieved cult status because of its distorted sets and abstract surrealism. Yes, you can see the zippers on the aliens' suits, and, yes, the paranoia scares are strictly kids' stuff, but that's precisely why this pulp science-fiction nightmare has built up a following. It perfectly depicts, from a child's point of view, the ultimate horror of having no one to trust and nowhere to turn – a fear that will strike a chord of recognition in anyone who's ever trembled behind the living-room sofa.

Helena Carter Dr Pat Blake • **Arthur Franz** Dr Stuart Kelston • **Jimmy Hunt** David MacLean • **Leif Erickson** George MacLean • **Hillary Brooke** Mary MacLean • **Morris Ankrum** Colonel Fielding • **Max Wagner** Sergeant Rinaldi • **Janine Perreau** Kathy Wilson • **Milburn Stone** Captain Roth • **Walter Sande** Sergeant Finley • **John Eldredge** Mr Turner • **Robert Shayne** Dr Wilson • **Luce Potter** Martian leader
Director *William Cameron Menzies*
Screenplay *William Cameron Menzies, Richard Blake, John Tucker Battle, from a story by John Tucker Battle*

Invaders from Mars ★★★ PG

1986 US Colour 94mins

Director Tobe Hooper, best known for *Texas Chainsaw Massacre*, skirts a fine line between kitsch and spoof in his big-budget remake of the 1953 B-movie. Clinging closely to the original primal paranoia story of a young boy's neighbourhood suddenly being overrun by aliens, Hooper's deadpan sci-fi comedy provides good scares, great visual design and Stan Winston's wonderfully wild Martian monster special effects. High points are the expedition into the blob-like Martians' subterranean lair, Oscar-winner Louise Fletcher snacking on live frogs, and Hunter Carson and his real-life mother Karen Black working well together as a team.

Karen Black Linda • **Hunter Carson** David Gardner • **Timothy Bottoms** George Gardner • **Laraine Newman** Ellen Gardner • **James Karen** General Wilson • **Louise Fletcher** Mrs McKeltch • **Bud Cort** Mark Weinstein • **Jimmy Hunt** Police chief
Director *Tobe Hooper*
Screenplay *Dan O'Bannon, Don Jakoby, Richard Blake*
Producer *Yoram Globus, Menahem Golan* • ***Associate Producer*** *Edward L Alperson Jr, Wade H Williams III*

Invasion ★★ PG

1965 UK BW 77mins

Aliens put an invisible force field around a secluded country hospital in this daffy British oddity, which must feature the cheapest alien takeover in history. Edward Judd is the hero scientist battling the extraterrestrial Oriental women in spacesuits, in an efficiently made and, yes, mildly exciting slice of cut-price science fiction. Director Alan Bridges imbues the Home Counties atmosphere with an ambience that's astonishingly heady, too.

Edward Judd Dr Vernon • **Yoko Tani** Lystrian leader • **Valerie Gearon** Dr Claire Harlan • **Lyndon Brook** Brian Carter
Director *Alan Bridges*
Screenplay *Roger Marshall, from a story by Robert Holmes*

Invasion: Earth ★★ PG 12

TV 1998 UK/US Colour 6x50mins

Earth looks destined to become the site of a long-awaited conflict between two alien races, and humanity's only hope of survival lies with a small band of soldiers in Britain's answer to *Independence Day*. There are some intriguing ideas at the centre of this six-episode offering, but after a promising start, it gradually degenerates into a run-of-the-mill alien invasion saga. The mini-series' limited production values struggle to capture accurately the storyline's epic scope and its sluggish pacing culminates in a sorely unsatisfying ending. Still, the Anglo-American cast do their best to offer a believable response to an alien encounter and, when given the opportunity, deliver some moving moments.

Vincent Regan Flt Lt Chris Drake • **Maggie O'Neill** Dr Amanda Tucker • **Fred Ward** Maj Gen David Reece • **Phyllis Logan** Sqn Ldr Helen Knox • **Anton Lesser** Lt Charles Terrell • **Paul J Medford** Nick Shay • **Jo Dow** Flt Lt Jim Radcliffe • **Gerard Rooney** Sergeant Tuffley • **Chris Fairbank** Wing Cmdr Friday
Director *Patrick Lau, Richard Laxton*
Written by *Jed Mercurio*
Producer *Jed Mercurio, Chrissy Skinns*

SFacts

The BBC's biggest sci-fi programme to date: a reported £750,000 was spent on each of the six episodes, including 85 custom-built sets and state-of-the-art computer graphics. "If you want to deal with this kind of subject matter, and have dodgy special effects, people would switch off after ten minutes," said writer and co-producer Jed Mercurio. "You have to follow the audience's sophistication."

Invasion Earth: the Aliens Are Here! ★

1987 US Colour and BW 83mins

As a compilation of clips from fifties and sixties science-fiction movies, this might have been worth a look. Unfortunately, the film-makers here have added an overlong and redundant framing story, in which a cinema hosting a sci-fi festival – hence the clips – is taken over by mind-controlling aliens, leaving it up to the few unaffected audience members to stage a fight-back. It's a neat idea, but every human character in the movie is so obnoxiously stupid that you'll be cheering for the insect-like invaders by the time the film crawls to its needlessly drawn-out conclusion. Rent the originals instead.

Janice Fabian Joanie • **Christian Lee** Billy • **Larry Bagby III** Tim • **Dana Young** Mike • **Mel Welles** Mr Davar
Director *George Maitland [Robert Skotak]*
Screenplay *Miller Drake*

Invasion of the Animal People ★★

1960 Swe/US BW 73mins

Your verdict on this rampaging creature feature will very much depend on which version you see. Virgil Vogel's original is by no means a masterpiece. But an uneasy atmosphere hangs over the story of a ferocious monster that goes on a murderous spree around Lapland before its alien handlers manage to recapture it. In Jerry Warren's ham-fisted American revision, however, the critter becomes part of an extraterrestrial invasion force, which is confounded by geologist John Carradine and his niece, Barbara Wilson. One thing these alternative tellings do have in common, however, are Bertil Jernberg's other-worldly snowscapes.

John Carradine Dr Wilson (US version) • **Robert Burton** Dr Frederick Wilson/Eric Engstrom (US version) • **Barbara Wilson**

Diane Wilson • **Stan Gester** Erik
Director *Virgil Vogel, Jerry Warren (additional scenes)*
Screenplay *Arthur C Pierce, from his story (additional US scenes by Jerry Warren)*

Invasion of the Astro-Monster

★★ U

1965 Jap Colour 90mins

More commonly known as *Monster Zero*, this marked Godzilla's fifth film appearance and his change of status from Japan's evil enemy to much-loved national institution. The incomprehensible plot is something about Godzilla and Rodan being shipped off in space bubbles to Planet X so they can defeat three-headed Ghidrah. But don't bother trying to work out the alien double-cross, just lie back, relax and enjoy the usual cheesy special effects, atrocious dubbing and Nick Adams (re-creating his astronaut role from *Frankenstein Conquers the World*) trying to look as if his scenes weren't shot separately in the States.

Nick Adams Glenn • **Akira Takarada** Fuji • **Kumi Mizuno** Namikawa • **Keiko Sawai**
Director *Inoshiro Honda*
Screenplay *Shinichi Sekizawa*
Special Effects *Eiji Tsuburaya*

Invasion of the Bee Girls ★★★

1973 US Colour 85mins

A drive-in classic scripted by future *Star Trek* movie director Nicholas Meyer. William Smith (*Hells Angels* movie stalwart) arrives in a small town to investigate deaths attributed to sexual exhaustion. He discovers that a group of suburban housewives (including Queen Bee Victoria Vetri from *When Dinosaurs Ruled the Earth*) have the ability to metamorphose into bees and are busily sapping red-blooded males of their bodily fluids. Naturally, it's all part of an insidious alien takeover plot. Shot in fluorescent colours at stilted angles by director Denis Sanders, this is a witty, titillating and slime-encrusted send-up of the swinger-party seventies.

William Smith Neil Agar • **Anitra Ford** Dr Susan Harris • **Victoria Vetri** Julie Zorn
Director *Denis Sanders*
Screenplay *Nicholas Meyer*

Invasion of the Body Snatchers

★★★★★ PG

1956 US BW 80mins DVD

Pods from outer space land in a small Californian town and start replicating the inhabitants, turning them into brainwashed slaves, in director Don Siegel's chilling science-fiction tale. This classic of the genre (co-scripted by an uncredited Sam Peckinpah from the novel by Jack Finney) reflects the blacklisting hysteria of the McCarthy era, as Siegel tersely piles on the nightmare with pulse-pounding briskness. Although expertly remade twice (in 1978 and 1993), the original is still the most striking, with a justly famous scalp-freezing ending.

Kevin McCarthy Miles Bennell • **Dana Wynter** Becky Driscoll • **Larry Gates** Danny • **King Donovan** Jack • **Carolyn Jones** Theodora • **Jean Willes** Sally • **Ralph Dumke** Nick • **Virginia Christine** Wilma
Director *Don Siegel*
Screenplay *Daniel Mainwaring, Sam Peckinpah (uncredited), from the novel "The Body Snatchers" by Jack Finney*

Invasion of the Body Snatchers

★★★ 15

1978 US Colour 110mins

It was always going to be hard to better Don Siegel's fifties classic, and if director Philip Kaufman doesn't quite succeed, he does manage to summon up an equally chilling air of paranoia in this remake, set in a coldly impersonal San Francisco. Donald Sutherland stars as the health inspector who begins to worry that people are acting weirdly normal and there is solid support from Brooke Adams and a young Jeff Goldblum, plus a creepy turn from Leonard Nimoy. Kaufman also throws in some neat in-jokes in the form of cameos from Siegel and the star of the original, Kevin McCarthy. Contains some swearing.

Donald Sutherland Matthew Bennell • **Brooke Adams** Elizabeth Driscoll • **Leonard Nimoy** Dr David Kibner • **Veronica Cartwright** Nancy Bellicec • **Jeff Goldblum** Jack Bellicec • **Art Hindle** Geoffrey • **Lelia Goldoni** Katherine • **Kevin McCarthy** Running man • **Robert Duvall** Priest on swing • **Don Siegel** Taxi driver
Director *Philip Kaufman*
Screenplay *WD Richter, from the novel "The Body Snatchers" by Jack Finney*

Invasion of the Saucer Men ★

1957 US BW 69mins

A "so-bad-it's-almost-good" sci-fi quickie where aliens with hypo-hands inject Hicksville teens with alcohol so they'll be arrested for drink driving. Well, it's one way to take over the world, but won't it take rather a long time? Fifties monster enthusiasts will salivate over the giant-headed "hell creatures" with bug-eyes and exposed brains, while fans of the sixties TV series *Batman* will recognise Frank Gorshin (the Riddler) as the con man planning to keep a dead alien in his ice box. They really don't come any worse, or as unintentionally funny as this Martian mash, incredibly remade as *The Eye Creatures* in 1965.

Steven Terrell Johnny • **Gloria Castillo** Joan • **Frank Gorshin** Joe • **Raymond Hatton** Larkin • **Lyn Osborn** Art
Director *Edward L Cahn*
Screenplay *Robert J Gurney Jr, Al Martin, from a story by Paul Fairman*

Invasion of the Star Creatures

★ U

1962 US BW 70mins

A lamentably awful spoof of alien invasion movies written by Jonathan Haze, star of numerous Roger Corman-directed programmers and whose prior experience at the Z-movie frontline should have sharpened up his target range. Two army imbeciles (Bob Ball and Frankie Ray) meet up with a pair of outer-space Amazon beauties (in ill-fitting two-piece swimsuits) and their vegetable-headed alien slaves. When the two jerks give the two statuesque babes their first ever kiss, love blossoms and they cancel their Earth invasion plans. Endless chase scenes and minimal thrills make director Bruno Ve Sota's comedy by default a painful experience.

Robert Bail Philbrick • **Frankie Ray** Penn • **Gloria Victor** Dr Tanga • **Dolores Reed** Professor Puna • **Mark Ferris** Colonel Rank
Director *Bruno Ve Sota*
Screenplay *Jonathan Haze, from the story "Monsters from Nicholson Mesa" by Jonathan Haze*
Cinematographer *Basil Bradbury*

Invasion USA ★★

1952 US BW 73 mins

Patrons in a New York bar are hypnotised by a weird stranger (Dan O'Herlihy) into believing America has been attacked by communist nuclear weapons. The customers react accordingly, some taking their own lives. The reason for this theme? To prove the nation must always be prepared for such an event. A laughable slice of nostalgic Cold War hysteria, ineptly handled by director Alfred E Green, with cheap special effects and a reliance on newsreel footage.

Gerald Mohr Vince • **Peggie Castle** Carla • **Dan O'Herlihy** Mr Ohman • **Robert Bice** George Sylvester • **Tom Kennedy** Bartender • **Wade Crosby** Congressman • **Erik Blythe** Ed Mulvory • **Phyllis Coates** Mrs Mulvory
Director *Alfred E Green*
Screenplay *Robert Smith, from the story by Robert Smith, Franz Spencer*

Invention of Destruction ★★★★

1958 Cz BW 95mins

Adapted from a Jules Verne novel, this ingenious fantasy (with its pirates, volcanoes, submarines, underwater cycles, hidden laboratories and rocket cannon) also borrows liberally from *20,000 Leagues under the Sea* and *The Mysterious Island*. There's also a hint of Méliès in Karel Zeman's audacious blend of animation, puppetry, models, glass shots and live-action, which miraculously evokes the glorious 19th-century illustrations of the novel. The story of villainous aristocrat Miroslav Holub's attempt to steal the explosive developed by professor Arnost Navratil and his intrepid assistant, Lubor Tokos, is action-packed. But it's also a thoughtful treatise on the misappropriation of science. In Czech with English subtitles.

Arnost Navratil Prof Roche • **Lubor Tokos** Simon Hart • **Miroslav Holub** Argitas • **Frantisek Slegr** Pirate captain • **Vaclav Kyzlink** Serke • **Jana Zatloukalova** Jana • **Hugh Downs** Narrator
Director *Karel Zeman*
Screenplay *Karel Zeman, from the novel "Face au Drapeau" by Jules Verne*

Invisible Adversaries ★★

1978 W Ger Colour 109mins

Austrian avant-garde artist Valie Export made her feature debut with this feminist take on the "body snatcher" theme. Susanne Widl plays a Viennese photographer, who becomes convinced that a long-vanished Egyptian tribe called the Hyksos are beaming white noise from outer space in order to subjugate Earth. But no one, including her abusive boyfriend, Peter Weibel (who made several experimental shorts with Export in the late sixties), believes her. Outspoken in its views on the way men perceive women, the marginalisation of art and the covert return of fascism, this aggregation of uncompromisingly ambiguous images is challenging in the extreme. In German with English subtitles.

Susanne Widl Anna • **Peter Weibel** Anna's boyfriend
Director *Valie Export*
Screenplay *Peter Weibel*

The Invisible Agent ★★★ U

1942 US BW 81mins

In the same year he produced Alfred Hitchcock's *Saboteur*, Frank Lloyd (who twice won the Best Director Oscar) found himself supervising this tenuously connected response to the 1933 Claude Rains classic. Once again the emphasis is on flagwaving escapism, with Jon Hall inheriting the evaporating talents of grandfather Rains, this time behind enemy lines in an attempt to confound the Axis. John P Fulton's Oscar-nominated special effects steal the show, but there are also some sterling supporting performances, notably from Peter Lorre (inverting his Moto impersonation to play a scheming Japanese spy) and J Edward Bromberg and Cedric Hardwicke as the Gestapo officers who terrorise Hall and his plucky accomplice, Ilona Massey.

Ilona Massey Maria Sorenson/Maria Goodrich • **Jon Hall** Frank Raymond/Frank Griffin • **Peter Lorre** Baron Ikito • **Sir Cedric Hardwicke [Cedric Hardwicke]** Conrad Stauffer • **J Edward Bromberg** Karl Heiser • **Albert Basserman** Dr Arnold Schmidt • **John Litel** John Gardiner • **Holmes Herbert** Sir Alfred Spencer • **Keye Luke** Surgeon
Director *Edwin L Marin*
Screenplay *Curtis Siodmak [Curt Siodmak], H G Wells*
Special effects *John P Fulton*

The Invisible Boy ★★★ U

1957 US BW 90mins

Edmund Cooper's original short story made no mention of a robot. But, following the success of *Forbidden Planet*, producer Nicholas Nayfack persuaded Cyril Hume to rework it as a vehicle for Robby the Robot. The parallel between young Richard Eyer being groomed for greatness by his scientist father (Philip Abbott), and Robby's rebellion against a megalomanic supercomputer (was HAL a microchip off this block?) is neatly drawn. But younger viewers will be more interested in Robby and Eyer's invisible antics (designed to teach his folks a lesson) than any cornball moralising. A must for anyone who enjoyed *The Iron Giant*.

Richard Eyer Timmie Merrinoe • **Philip Abbott** Dr Merrinoe • **Diane Brewster** Mary Merrinoe • **Harold J Stone** General Swayne • **Robert H Harris** Professor Allerton • **Dennis McCarthy** Colonel Macklin
Director *Herman Hoffman*
Screenplay *Cyril Hume, from a story by Edmund Cooper*

Invisible Invaders ★★

1959 US BW 67mins

A space age horror with a theme startlingly close to the one used by director George Romero in his landmark *Night of the Living Dead*. Invisible aliens arrive on Earth from the moon in an invisible spaceship to take possession of corpses and turn them into an invincible army of cadaverous soldiers. Scientist John Agar saves the day with high-frequency sound. Veteran horror star John Carradine plays a dead nuclear physicist brought back to life to lead the hordes of white-faced zombies with blackened eyes. No great shakes as science fiction, but hugely entertaining thanks to the continuously misplaced accent on riotously bad acting, shoddy special effects and mismatching stock footage by director Edward L Cahn.

John Agar Maj Bruce Jay • **Jean Byron** Phyllis Penner • **Robert Hutton** Dr John Lamont • **John Carradine** Dr Karol Noymann • **Philip Tonge** Dr Adam Penner • **Hal Torey** The Farmer
Director *Edward L Cahn*
Screenplay *Samuel Newman*

The Invisible Kid ★ 15

1988 US Colour 92mins

Weird Science meets *Porky's* as nerd student Grover (Jay Underwood) stumbles on to an invisibility formula and uses it to wander into the girls' locker rooms and cause havoc. A juvenile fantasy laden with dumb jock gags and inane sexist humour that would be offensive if it weren't so laboured and pathetic. Karen Black, queen of the B-movie cameo, wastes her talents once more playing Grover's air-head mother, who's obsessed with cable television trash. Stuff similar to this, in fact.

Jay Underwood Grover Dunn • **Karen Black** Mom • **Wally Ward [Wallace Langham]** Milton McClane • **Chynna Phillips** Cindy Moore • **Brother Theodore** Dr Theodore • **Mike Genovese** Officer Chuck Malone • **Jan King** Singer • **Andre De Toth** Donny Zanders
Director/Screenplay *Avery Crounse*

The Invisible Man ★★★★★ PG

1933 US BW 68mins

Claude Rains is one of the most undervalued stars of Hollywood's Golden Age. It's ironic that a familiar face that few could put a name to should have made his name in a film in which he spends most of the action swathed in bandages or invisible. In truth, the success of this superb adaptation of HG Wells's novel is down to John P Fulton and John Mescall's pioneering special effects and the eerie atmosphere conjured up by horror master James Whale. When playful pranks give way to megalomania and murder, the hidden dangers of Rains's miraculous concoction begin to take effect. A classic.

Claude Rains Jack Griffin, the Invisible Man • **Gloria Stuart** Flora Cranley • **William Harrigan** Dr Kemp • **Henry Travers** Dr Cranley • **Una O'Connor** Mrs Hall • **Dudley Digges** Chief of Detectives • **Forrester Harvey** Mr Hall • **Holmes Herbert** Chief of Police • **EE Clive** Jaffers • **Harry Stubbs** Insp Bird • **Donald Stuart** Insp Lane • **Merle Tottenham** Milly
Director *James Whale*
Screenplay *RC Sherriff, Philip Wylie (uncredited), from the novel by HG Wells*

The Invisible Man ★★

1958 Mex BW 95mins

Approaching the end of his 25-year career, Arturo De Cordova embarked on his fifth and final collaboration with one of Mexico's most prolific B-hivers, Alfredo B Crevenna. Having more in common with a Lon Chaney Jr vehicle than HG Wells's novel, the story concerns De Cordova's gradual descent into murderous madness after his scientist brother, Augusto Benedico, injects him with an invisibility serum to aid his escape from prison. Although Ana Luisa Peluffo plays an increasingly prominent part in proceedings as her lover embraces anarchy, it's De Cordova's personality that carries the film – even when you can't see him. A Spanish language film.

Arturo De Cordova • **Ana Luisa Peluffo** • **Augusto Benedico**
Director *Alfredo B Crevenna*
Screenplay *Julio Alejandro, from the novel by HG Wells*

The Invisible Man ★★★

TV 1958-1959 UK BW 26x30mins

This British series owes very little to its supposed inspiration, though his heroic activities might be in imitation of the wartime Universal sequel *The Invisible Agent*. Dr Peter Brady, a researcher, becomes invisible after a lab accident, but rather than go mad and try to rule the world, he patriotically dedicates himself to thwarting criminals and spies. No actor was credited in the role of Brady, and controversy remains as to the identity of the disembodied voice (Robert Beatty and Tim Turner seem to have shared the work), but Lisa Daniely and future *Doctor Who* assistant Deborah Watling were billed as Brady's sidekick sister and niece. The half-hour shows were tidy, predictable little Cold War cases.

Lisa Daniely Diane, "Dee" • **Deborah Watling** Sally • **Ernest Clark** Sir Charles Anderson
Created by *Ralph Smart, from the novel by HG Wells*
Producer *Ralph Smart*

The Invisible Man ★★

TV 1975-76 US Colour 1x120m; 12x60m

Like the series of the same name from the fifties and the new millenium, this evokes HG Wells but uses only the premise of scientific invisibility from his novel. Dr Daniel Westin (David McCallum) becomes an invisible secret agent after a lab accident, using clothes and a mask to disguise his condition, working with his wife Kate (Melinda Fee) and executive Walter Carlson (Craig Stevens). The show was cancelled after 13 episodes, in which Westin tackled the same boring kidnappers and bank robbers Steve Austin was hammering over on *The Six Million Dollar Man*. The same production crew rejigged the premise as *The Gemini Man*, in which Ben Murphy goes see-through only for brief periods, but that did equally badly.

David McCallum Dr Daniel Westin • **Melinda Fee** Dr Kate Westin • **Craig Stevens** Walter Carlson
Developed for TV by *Harve Bennett, Steven Bochco, from the novel by H G Wells*

The Invisible Man ★★★★

TV 1984 UK Colour 6x30mins

The BBC gave this adaptation of the HG Wells classic an attractive period gloss and an authenticity that makes it perhaps the most successful of the small-screen attempts at the tale. Whereas the 1975 David McCallum version only used the premise of invisibility as a starting point for a short-lived series of adventures, here Pip Donaghy's scientist fully succumbs to the dark horrific side of his nature that the power of invisibility unleashes. Donaghy is given strong support by Frank Middlemass, David Gwillim and Ron Pember.

Pip Donaghy Griffin, the Invisible Man • **Michael Sheard** Rev Bunting • **Frank Middlemass** Thomas Marvel • **David Gwillim** Dr Samuel Kem • **Gerald James** Dr Cuss • **Jonathan Adams** Teddy Henfrey • **Ron Pember** Mr Hall • **Lila Kaye** Mrs Hall • **Roy Holder** Sandy Wadgers • **Anna Wing** Mrs Roberts
Director *Brian Lighthill*
Written by *James Andrew Hall, from the novel by H G Wells*
Producer *Barry Letts*

The Invisible Man ★★★★

TV 2000 – US Colour

A small-time crook pulls the ultimate vanishing act in the US Sci-Fi Channel's vibrant and refreshing reworking of HG Wells's classic tale. Faced with a life sentence, good-hearted thief Darien Fawkes agrees to have an invisibility-rendering Quicksilver Gland implanted into his brain by a government agency. Now dependent on a serum that counteracts the gland's effects and saves him from "Quicksilver Madness", Fawkes is forced to embark on a series of top-secret invisible missions. A fast-moving and witty sci-fi drama, the series clearly provides a great vehicle for Vincent Ventresca, who visibly – and invisibly – establishes Fawkes as a likeable hero with a dangerous edge. The series' eye-popping special effects are also an unmissable treat.

Vincent Ventresca Darien Fawkes • **Paul Ben-Victor** Bobby Hobbes • **Shannon Kenny** The Keeper • **Eddie Jones** The Official • **Brandy Ledford** Agent Alex Monroe • **Michael McCafferty** Albert Eberts
Source *the novel by HG Wells*
Executive producer *Jonathan Glassner, Matt Greenberg, David Levinson*

An Invisible Man Goes through the City ★★★

1933 Ger BW

Although he'd directed a sci-fi comedy, *The Big Bet* back in 1915, it's Harry Piel's long stint in serials that's most readily apparent in this hectic morality tale. Once his taxi driver realises that the helmet and booster pack he finds in the back of his cab can render him invisible, he hurtles around town on a series of adventures that involve him getting rich, acquiring a gold-digging girlfriend in Lissy Arna and tracking his best pal, Fritz Odemar, who has begun putting the apparatus to criminal use. There's even an airship pursuit. But the "dream" ending is a let down. In German with English subtitles.

Harry Piel Harry • **Lissy Arna** Lissy Verhagen • **Fritz Odemar** Fritz • **Annemarie Sörensen** Annie Bergmann • **Olga Limburg** Frau Bergmann • **Gerhard Dammann** Maxe • **Walter Steinbeck**
Director *Harry Piel*
Screenplay *Hans Rameau*

The Invisible Man Returns ★★★

1940 US BW 81mins

The first sequel to the Claude Rains classic, while more modestly scaled than its predecessor, still receives a first-class treatment from director Joe May and, in many instances, surpasses the visual magic of the original. Vincent Price replaces Rains and gets his first starring role as a man condemned to hang for a murder he didn't commit. He persuades the brother of the man who created the invisible serum to give him a dose so he can find the real killer. Price's rich theatrical voice assures his invisible man has a credible presence in a diverting tale filled with comedy, drama and eerie moments.

Sir Cedric Hardwicke [Cedric Hardwicke] Richard Cobb • **Vincent Price** Geoffrey Radcliffe • **Nan Grey** Helen Manson • **John Sutton** Dr Frank Griffin • **Cecil Kellaway** Inspector Sampson • **Alan Napier** Willie Spears • **Forrester Harvey** Ben Jenkins • **Frances Robinson** Nurse
Director *Joe May*
Screenplay *Curt Siodmak, Lester Cole, Cecil Belfrage, from a story by Curt Siodmak, Joe May*
Producer *Ken Goldsmith*

The Invisible Man's Revenge ★★ PG

1944 US BW 74mins

Special effects maestro John P Fulton is (yet again) the saviour of this Universal programmer, which puts an invisible spin on the 1936 Boris Karloff revenge thriller *The Walking Dead*. Jon Hall (who'd headlined *The Invisible Agent* two years earlier) also returns, this time seeking retribution for his abandonment on a diamond-seeking safari by the aristocratic Lester Matthews and Gale Sondergaard. Scream queen Evelyn Ankers plays their daughter, whom Hall plans to seduce despite her romantic ties to newspaper reporter Alan Curtis. The inimitable John Carradine makes the most of his limited time as a reclusive, eccentric scientist while Leon Errol provides the comic relief as a cockney cobbler.

Jon Hall Robert Griffin/Martin Field • **Leon Errol** Herbert Higgins • **John Carradine** Dr Peter Drury • **Alan Curtis** Mark Foster • **Evelyn Ankers** Julie Herrick • **Gale Sondergaard** Lady Irene Herrick • **Lester Matthews** Sir Jasper Herrick • **Halliwell Hobbes** Cleghorn • **Leland Hodgson** Sir Frederick Travers • **Doris Lloyd** Maud
Director *Ford Beebe*
Screenplay *Bertram Millhauser, from the novel "The Invisible Man" by HG Wells*
Producer *Ford Beebe*
Cinematographer *Milton Krasner* • ***Special effects*** *John P Fulton*

Invisible Mom ★★★

1995 US Colour 82 mins.

Dee Wallace's scientist husband accidentally makes her invisible in this fun family comedy. Similar in style to *Honey, I Shrunk the Kids*, it has more than a few laughs as Wallace Stone tries to carry on running the household while her husband desperately seeks an antidote. Directed by B-movie specialist Fred Olen Ray (*Bad Girls from Mars, Dinosaur Island, Scalps*), this chirpy comedy was followed by a disappointing sequel, uninspiringly called *Invisible Dad* in 1997, and even more uninspired was *Invisible Mom II* in 1999.

Dee Wallace Stone Laura Griffin • **Barry Livingston** Karl Griffin • **Trenton Knight** Josh Griffin • **Russ Tamblyn** Dr Woorter • **Christopher Stone** Colonel Cutter • **Phillip Van Dyke** Skeeter • **Stella Stevens** Mrs Pringle • **Brinke Stevens** Dr Price
Director *Fred Olen Ray*
Screenplay *Rennie Piccolo*
Producer *Fred Olen Ray*

The Invisible Ray ★★

1920 US BW

A silent 15-chapter serial revolving around the discovery of a lethal radioactive substance by mineralogist Sidney Bracey and the criminal gang who want it for use in deadly weapons. Bracey disappears, presumed dead, leaving his daughter Ruth Clifford in an orphanage with a sample of the mineral. She eventually meets and falls in love with Jack Sherrill, the son of the professor possessing another lethal sample. Considered average in its day, this fast-paced lavish production from minor director Harry Pollard has since been re-evaluated as a prime example of the cliffhanger genre.

Ruth Clifford Mystery • **Sidney Bracey** Jean Deaux • **Edward Davis** John Haldene • **Jack Sherrill** Jack Stone
Director *Harry Pollard*
Screenplay *Guy McConnell*

The Invisible Ray ★★★

1936 US BW 82mins

The film that introduced Boris Karloff to a role he would visit throughout his career – that of a sympathetic scientist whose remarkable discovery makes him a threat to society. Here, as Dr Janos Rukh, he becomes contaminated by a radioactive meteor found in Africa and learns his touch means death. When he suspects Dr Benet (Bela Lugosi) of trying to take the credit for his discovery, the "Radium X" substance within the meteor causes him to go insane and seek vengeance. A lively, early science-fiction horror tale, with innovative special effects for its era and the ever-dependable "gruesome twosome" supplying the thrills.

Boris Karloff Dr Janos Rukh • **Bela Lugosi** Dr Felix Benet • **Frances Drake** Diane Rukh • **Frank Lawton** Ronald Drake • **Walter Kingsford** Sir Francis Stevens • **Beulah Bondi** Lady Arabella Stevens
Director *Lambert Hillyer*
Screenplay *John Colton, from a story by Howard Higgin, Douglas Hodges*

The Invisible Woman ★★

1940 US BW 72mins

It's hard to see how John P Fulton's special effects merited an Oscar nomination when the titular Virginia Bruce's shadow is often clearly visible, but that sums up this sloppy lampoon, which was co-written by the director of *The Invisible Man Returns*, Joe May. Much merriment is to be had at Bruce's encounters with her abusive boss Charles Lane and hoodlum Oscar Homolka, while Margaret Hamilton and Charles Ruggles provide amusement as a couple of scandalised domestics. But the primary reason for catching this hackneyed comedy is John Barrymore's performance as the eccentric scientist, which is a dead-on impersonation of his elder brother Lionel.

John Barrymore Prof Gibbs • **Virginia Bruce** Kitty Carroll • **John Howard** Richard Russell • **Charlie Ruggles [Charles Ruggles]** George • **Oscar Homolka** Blackie • **Edward Brophy** Bill • **Donald MacBride** Foghorn • **Margaret Hamilton** Mrs Jackson • **Shemp Howard** Frankie • **Anne Nagel** Jean • **Charles Lane** Grawley
Director *A Edward Sutherland*
Screenplay *Robert Lees, Gertrude Purcell, Fred Rinaldo [Frederic I Rinaldo], from a story by Kurt Siodmak [Curt Siodmak], Joe May*
Special effects *John Fulton [John P Fulton]*

The Iron Giant ★★★★★ U

1999 US Colour 83mins DVD

It might not have the Disney stamp, but this wonderful Warner Bros version of Ted Hughes's children's fable, *The Iron Man*, is a first-class achievement in cartoon virtuosity that liberally borrows images from fifties comic-book art and science-fiction movies to stunning effect. To a soundtrack of *American Graffiti*-style hits, this heavy metal *ET* tells the riveting tale of nine-year-old Hogarth Hughes and the giant alien robot he saves from self destruction when it attempts to munch its way through a power station. The fiercely protective relationship that develops between these two characters is both emotionally rewarding and rather funny. But the real thrills begin when a Communist-hating FBI agent becomes suspicious of the strange occurrences taking place in Rockwell, Maine. Convinced that the walking Meccano set is a dangerous weapon that poses a serious Cold War threat, he summons the military. With political allegory and clever nostalgia for the adults, and dazzling

Best friend: Hogarth Hughes is enthralled by his new mechanical mate in Warner Bros' *The Iron Giant*

visuals and excitement galore for the kids, this poignant fairy tale is outstanding on every artistic level.

Jennifer Aniston Annie Hughes • **Harry Connick Jr** Dean McCoppin • **Vin Diesel** The Iron Giant • **James Gammon** Marv Loach/Floyd Turbeaux • **Cloris Leachman** Mrs Tensedge • **Christopher McDonald** Kent Mansley • **John Mahoney** General Rogard • **Eli Marienthal** Hogarth Hughes • **M Emmet Walsh** Earl Stutz
Director *Brad Bird*
Screenplay *Tim McCanlies, Andy Brent Forrester [Brent Forrester], from a story by Brad Bird, from the novel by Ted Hughes*
Executive producer *Pete Townshend*

The Island at the Top of the World ★★★ U

1974 US Colour 89mins

You'd be forgiven for thinking this Disney adventure's source was Jules Verne (it is, in fact, based on a novel called *The Lost Ones* by Ian Cameron), but there's no question that this offering falls below the studio's usual high standards. However, the film is certainly not the unmitigated disaster that many critics considered it to be. Donald Sinden holds things together as an Edwardian explorer who sets out to rescue his son's Arctic expedition. Sinden's clash with a long lost Viking tribe stretches credibility to breaking point, but the effects are pretty fair for their day, with the voyage by airship nicely done.

Donald Sinden Sir Anthony Ross • **David Hartman** Professor Ivarsson • **Jacques Marin** Captain Brieux • **Mako** Oomiak • **David Gwillim** Donald Ross • **Agneta Eckemyr** Freyja • **Gunnar Ohlund** The Godi
Director *Robert Stevenson*
Screenplay *John Whedon, from the novel "The Lost Ones" by Ian Cameron*

The Island of Dr Moreau ★★★ 15

1977 US Colour 94mins

HG Wells's story about a mad scientist living on a remote island was filmed in 1932 with Charles Laughton as *Island of Lost Souls* and in 1996 with Marlon Brando. This first remake stars Burt Lancaster as the lunatic who thinks he's sane, conducting genetic experiments for the sake of mankind. Michael York shows up, unwisely, as does Barbara Carrera and Lancaster's acrobatic sidekick from the fifties, Nick Cravat. While never trying to be a classic, it's still a ripping yarn with a moral gloss, and Lancaster's taciturn evil is often frightening. Pretty Virgin Islands locations impersonate the South Pacific. Contains brief nudity.

Burt Lancaster Dr Moreau • **Michael York** Andrew Braddock • **Nigel Davenport** Montgomery • **Barbara Carrera** Maria • **Richard Basehart** Sayer of the law • **Nick Cravat** M'ling • **The Great John "L"** Boarman • **John Gillespie** Tigerman • **David Cass** Bearman
Director *Don Taylor*
Screenplay *John Herman Shaner, Al Ramrus, from the novel by HG Wells*

The Island of Dr Moreau ★ 12

1996 US Colour 91mins

The third, and worst, version of HG Wells's classic fantasy about mad Doctor Moreau (here played by Marlon Brando), who genetically reshapes the animal kingdom to form a new species of man in a remote tropical paradise. Badly miscast – David Thewlis, Val Kilmer and Brando give lousy performances – and hopelessly directed by John Frankenheimer (who stepped in four days after writer Richard Stanley was fired), this jungle jumble is a horrible miscalculation from start to finish. Brando's Popemobile-style entrance and Stan Winston's hokey creature effects (from the *Cats* school of make-up) are just two of the laughter-inducing embarrassments in this pretentious terror turkey. Contains violence and swearing.

Marlon Brando Dr Moreau • **Val Kilmer** Montgomery • **David Thewlis** Edward Douglas • **Fairuza Balk** Aissa Moreau • **Temuera Morrison** Azazello • **Daniel Rigney** Hyena-Swine • **Nelson De La Rosa** Majai • **Peter Elliott** Assassimon
Director *John Frankenheimer*
Screenplay *Richard Stanley, Ron Hutchinson, from the novel by HG Wells*

Island of Lost Souls ★★★★★ 12

1932 US BW 67mins

Banned in Britain for 21 years, the first, and best, version of HG Wells's provocative fantasy *The Island of Dr Moreau* is one of the best chillers ever made. Few horror films have as many terrifying facets or the harsh maturity of director Erle C Kenton. It's the uncompromising tale of doctor Charles Laughton grafting animals on to men in his tropical House of Pain to change evolution. Shot on beautiful sets, adding enormous atmospheric gloominess to the quite shocking and repellent imagery, Laughton turns in a memorably sadistic performance as the scarily mad scientist. Equally unforgettable is Bela Lugosi as the Sayer of the Law: "What is the law – are we not men!".

Robert Kortman Hogan • **Alan Ladd** Ape man • **Randolph Scott** Ape man • **Larry "Buster" Crabbe** Ape man • **Joe Bonomo** Ape man • **Charles Laughton** Dr Moreau • **Richard Arlen** Edward Parker • **Leila Hyams** Ruth Walker • **Bela Lugosi** Sayer of the Law • **Kathleen Burke** Lota, the panther woman • **Arthur Hohl** Montgomery • **Stanley Fields** Captain Davies • **Paul Hurst** Capt Donahue • **Hans Steinke** Ouran
Director *Erle C Kenton*
Screenplay *Philip Wylie, Waldemar Young, from the novel "The Island of Dr Moreau" by HG Wells*
Cinematographer *Karl Struss*

Island of Terror ★★ PG

1966 UK Colour 83mins

Bone marrow-sucking monsters are the by-product of cancer-cure research in this chiller cheapie directed by the ever-efficient Terence Fisher (on a busman's holiday from Hammer Studios) that's long on logic, but high on hysteria. Making the most of the isolated Irish setting and infusing the colourful carnage with a neat line in macabre humour (scientist Peter Cushing mutilating his own body to save himself, for instance), it's a reasonably tense offering, with the tentacled silicate creatures more fun than most of their B-feature sci-fi ilk.

Peter Cushing Dr Stanley • **Edward Judd** Dr David West • **Carole Gray** Toni Merrill • **Eddie Byrne** Dr Landers • **Sam Kydd** Constable Harris • **Niall MacGinnis** Mr Campbell
Director *Terence Fisher*
Screenplay *Edward Andrew Mann, Alan Ramsen*

Island of the Fish Men ★★★

1978 It BW 91mins

Quaint, unusual and ambitious, this science-fiction fantasy from director Sergio Martino, one of the foremost proponents of the Italian *giallo* thriller, is an eccentric Jules Verne-skewed mixture of mutant sea life, mad scientists, voodoo rites and the lost continent of Atlantis. Claudio Cassinelli is shipwrecked on an uncharted Caribbean Island in 1891, only to be menaced by aquatic Atlantis descendents addicted to a chemical manufactured by evil doctor Richard Johnson. Former Bond girl Barbara Bach becomes Cassinelli's love interest as Martino mixes gory pulp horror and swashbuckling escapism in one heady exploitative concoction. (Extensively cut for international distribution with prologue scenes starring Mel Ferrer and Cameron Mitchell added by director by Joe Dante, using the alias Miller Drake, and released under the US title *Screamers*.) A forgettable sequel *The Fish-Men and Their Queen* followed in 1995.

Barbara Bach Amanda • **Claudio Cassinelli** Claude • **Richard Johnson** Edmund • **Joseph Cotten** Prof Marvin • **Beryl Cunningham** Shakira • **Mel Ferrer** Radcliffe • **Cameron Mitchell** Decker
Director *Sergio Martino, Miller Drake [Joe Dante]*
Screenplay *Sergio Donati, Cesare Frugoni, Sergio Martino*

It! ★★

1966 UK Colour 95mins

Director Herbert J Leder made this dismal attempt to resurrect the legend of the Golem monster – most famously filmed in 1920 by Paul Wegener – for Swinging Sixties audiences. Roddy McDowall is an assistant museum curator, living with the mummified corpse of his mother (*Psycho* has a lot to answer for), who revives the original Golem to do his psychopathic bidding. A confused mix of black humour and horror, this is distinctly lacking in style, invention or (crucially) budget, as evidenced in the monster's less than awesome destruction of a London bridge. At least the Golem itself is well realised and lives to fight another day surviving, of all things, an atomic blast!

Roddy McDowall Arthur Pimm • **Jill Haworth** Ellen Grove • **Paul Maxwell** Jim Perkins • **Aubrey Richards** Professor Weal • **Ernest Clark** Harold Grove • **Oliver Johnston** Trimingham • **Noel Trevarthen** Inspector White
Director/Screenplay *Herbert J Leder*
Producer *Herbert J Leder*

It Came from beneath the Sea ★★★ U

1955 US BW 75mins

Careless atomic testing spawns a giant octopus in this classic monster flick, which includes stop-motion special effects from the great Ray Harryhausen. But radiation wasn't the cause of the suction-cup horror

ALIEN BOOK OF RECORDS

CHEAPEST **B-movie maestro Roger Corman set new standards of economy with his alien disguise for 1956's *Not of This Earth* – all it took was a pair of sunglasses**

LEAFIEST **Trying to make plants scary is usually a big mistake, yet 1990's *Seedpeople* compounds the problem with no less than three different varieties of vegetable villain**

GROOVIEST **Planet Gonk is the place to be if you want to swing to the sounds of Lulu and the Graham Bond Organisation in *Gonks Go Beat* (1965)**

CHEEKIEST **Russia's *Battle beyond the Sun* (1959) wins the censor-baiting award for its stylised confrontation between aliens resembling male and female genitalia**

CHEESIEST **variously described as "flying pizza" and "carnivorous flapjacks", the alien projectiles of *Without Warning* (1980) are guaranteed to leave a bad aftertaste**

STUPIDEST **When a desert town is menaced by a shuffling rug from outer space in *The Creeping Terror* (1964), credibility is the first thing to be swept under the carpet**

SLEAZIEST **shamelessly addicting its human hosts to it secretions, the slimy parasite protagonist of *Brain Damage* (1986) is a drug-pusher with a difference – it eats brains, too**

LUCKIEST **the nocturnal predators of *Pitch Black* (2000) only get out to hunt during an eclipse once every 22 years – the very day a spaceship-load of succulent humans crashlands on their planet.**

having a shortage of titanic tentacles the ridiculously low budget saw to that! As the "killer calamari" rampages through San Francisco to destroy the Golden Gate Bridge, B-movie star Kenneth Tobey still finds time to battle biologist Donald Curtis for vampy Faith Domergue's charms. Predictable tosh, but good fifties fun.

Kenneth Tobey Pete Mathews • **Faith Domergue** Lesley Joyce • **Ian Keith** Admiral Burns • **Donald Curtis** John Carter • **Dean Maddox Jr** Adam Norman • **Lieutenant C Griffiths** Griff • **Harry Lauter** Bill Nash • **Captain R Peterson** Captain Stacy • **Del Courtney** Robert Chase • **Tol Avery** Navy intern • **Rudy Puteska** Hall

Director *Robert Gordon*

Screenplay *George Worthing Yates, Hal Smith, from a story by George Worthing Yates*

It Came from Hollywood ★★ 15

1982 US Colour and BW 76mins [video]

It must have seemed like a good idea at the time to rope in some well-known comedians to introduce clips from a batch of Z-grade sci-fi and horror "classics". Sadly, the end result is as tepid and exploitative as the films it purports to poke fun at. The usual suspects are all present and correct: *Attack of the Killer Tomatoes*, *Plan 9 from Outer Space*, *Robot Monster*, and so on. But while the clips themselves are often amusing, the comedians – including Dan Aykroyd, Cheech and Chong, and John Candy – struggle to deliver the required wit. Directors Malcolm Leo and Andrew Solt are best known for their music documentary *This Is Elvis*: Solt also made *Gimme Some Truth*, which charts the recording of John Lennon's *Imagine* album.

Dan Aykroyd • **John Candy** • **Richard "Cheech" Marin** • **Tommy Chong** • **Gilda Radner**

Director *Andrew Solt, Malcolm Leo*

Screenplay *Dana Olsen*

It Came from Outer Space ★★★★ PG

1953 US BW 76mins [video]

Based on Ray Bradbury's story *The Meteor*, this early 3-D classic was the first of many brilliant sci-fi films from director Jack Arnold, who went on to make *Tarantula* and *The Incredible Shrinking Man*. An alien spaceship lands in the Arizona desert, and its giant-eyed occupants adopt human identities while they repair their vessel. Amateur astronomer Richard Carlson sees it happen, but no one believes him. While top heavy on eerie atmosphere, Arnold's film incorporates a neat plea for inter-racial tolerance and stylish flourishes – including a fish-eye lens to simulate the aliens' point-of-view. The result is an entertaining B movie that's as good as fifties science fiction gets.

Richard Carlson John Putnam • **Barbara Rush** Ellen Fields • **Charles Drake** Sheriff Matt Warren • **Russell Johnson** George • **Kathleen Hughes** Jane • **Joe Sawyer** Frank Daylon • **Dave Willock** Pete Davis • **Alan Dexter** Dave Loring

Director *Jack Arnold*

Screenplay *Harry Essex, from the short story "The Meteor" by Ray Bradbury*

Producer *William Alland*

It Came from Outer Space II ★ PG

1996 US Colour 84mins [video]

This lacklustre update of Jack Arnold's 1953 classic has Brian Kerwin witnessing the arrival of the aliens while on a desert photo assignment. It 's not too long before the blue rocks scattered from the spacecraft are causing havoc in the local community, where the townsfolk are being replicated by aliens. Just to add to the fun, the temperatures are soaring and the water supply is disappearing. Proof positive that 40 years of technical advances can't compensate for poor production values, boring characters and a complete lack of thrills. File this under "don't bother".

Brian Kerwin Jack Putnam • **Elizabeth Pena** Ellen Fields • **Jonathan Carrasco** Stevie Fields • **Bill McKinney** Roy Minter • **Adrian Sparks** Alan Paxson

Director *Roger Duchowny*

Screenplay *Jim Wheat, Ken Wheat, from the film "It Came from Outer Space" by Harry Essex, from the short story "The Meteor" by Ray Bradbury*

It Conquered the World ★ PG

1956 US BW 68mins [video]

Monster flicks rarely come dafter than this. Get ready to scream with laughter as a gravitationally challenged, fanged carrot from Venus crawls around the Los Angeles countryside like a snail on valium. It clearly couldn't conquer the world even if It tried! Hence It prepares to turn us dumb earthlings into zombie slaves with the aid of what are supposed to be electronic bat-mites, but which more closely resemble drunken boomerangs. One of director Roger Corman's all-time worst films, yet cult fans will enjoy it for exactly that reason.

Peter Graves Paul Nelson • **Beverly Garland** Claire Anderson • **Lee Van Cleef** Tom Anderson • **Sally Fraser** Joan Nelson

Director *Roger Corman*

Screenplay *Lou Rusoff*

It Happens Every Spring ★★★ U

1949 US BW 81mins

It's the time of year when every American's fancy turns to baseball, and this is an original (if blinkered) little comedy about chemistry professor Ray Milland inventing a substance that causes baseballs to veer away from the bats. Quite obviously, he then gives up the distinguished groves of Academe to become a star pitcher. This daffy nonsense is endearingly played, particularly by Milland and co-stars Jean Peters and Paul Douglas. The inventive screenplay is by Valentine Davies, who had just won an Oscar for his original story *Miracle on 34th Street*, a tale of whimsy with more international appeal than this.

Ray Milland Vernon Simpson • **Jean Peters** Deborah Greenleaf • **Paul Douglas** Monk Lanigan • **Ed Begley** Stone • **Ted De Corsia** Dolan • **Ray Collins** Professor Greenleaf • **Jessie Royce Landis** Mrs Greenleaf • **Alan Hale Jr** Schmidt

Director *Lloyd Bacon*

Screenplay *Valentine Davies, from a story by Valentine Davies, from the short story "The Sprightly Adventures of Instructor Simpson" by Shirley W Smith*

It Lives Again ★★★ 15

1978 US Colour 86mins [video]

Director Larry Cohen's sequel to his own cult classic *It's Alive* doesn't quite hit the same subversive targets, but as a gory action thriller it certainly delivers. Frederic Forrest and Kathleen Lloyd are the expectant parents who get a shock when their offspring turns out to be a fanged and clawed mutant. The mayhem takes an even weirder turn when the infant joins up with two other pint-sized, baby-faced killers to wreak murderous havoc after their hide-out is discovered. Hardly subtle, but played with a winning conviction well above the call of duty. Contains violence and swearing.

Frederic Forrest Eugene Scott • **Kathleen Lloyd** Jody Scott • **John P Ryan** Frank Davis • **John Marley** Mallory • **Andrew Duggan** Dr Perry • **Eddie Constantine** Dr Forrest • **James Dixon** Detective Perkins

Director/Screenplay *Larry Cohen*

Producer *Larry Cohen*

It! The Terror from beyond Space ★★★

1958 US BW 69mins

A rocket-ship crew returning from an interplanetary mission is menaced by a blood-drinking reptilian stowaway in this low-budget classic from science fiction's golden age. If the plot sounds familiar, it's because Edward L Cahn's briskly directed shocker is frequently cited as the blueprint for Ridley Scott's *Alien*. Ray "Crash" Corrigan wears the scaly rubber suit as the Martian monster, ably menacing Marshall Thompson and his fellow astronauts in a relic from the fifties that still manages to deliver some decent scares.

Marshall Thompson Colonel Carruthers • **Shawn Smith** Ann Anderson • **Kim Spalding** Colonel Van Heusen • **Ann Doran** Mary Royce • **Dabbs Greer** Eric Royce • **Paul Langton** Calder • **Robert Bice** Purdue • **Ray Corrigan** "It"
Director *Edward L Cahn*
Screenplay *Jerome Bixby*

It's about Time ★

TV 1966-1967 US BW 26x30mins

Famously witless US sit-com, often paired with *My Mother the Car* as examples of the vast wasteland of sixties TV programming, this was conceived by Sherwood Schwartz (*Gilligan's Island, The Brady Bunch*), who realised it wasn't working halfway through the first and only season and reconceived it with a different, no more successful format. Astronauts Mac (Frank Aletter) and Hector (Jack Mullaney) pass through a timewarp and land on prehistoric Earth, where they pal around with cave family Shad (Imogene Coca), Gronk (Joe E "ooh ooh" Ross), Mlor (Mary Grace) and Breer (Pat Cardi), who live in a tribe run by the Boss (Cliff Norton) and his wife (Kathleen Freeman). After bumbling about with Flintstones gags (typical episode, *Mark Your Bullets*, in which the astronauts persuade the cave people to try democracy), the show pre-empted *Escape from the Planet of the Apes* by having the whole regular cast warped back to the 20th century where they fumble with primitives-puzzled-by-mod-cons gags. It had a catchy theme tune, though. The pilot (*And Then I Wrote Happy Birthday to You*) was directed by Richard Donner, and an equally overqualified Jack Arnold handled the *Me Caveman – You Woman* episode.

Frank Aletter Mac • **Jack Mullaney** Hector • **Imogene Coca** Shad • **Joe E Ross** Gronk • **Cliff Norton** Boss • **Kathleen Freeman** Mrs Boss • **Mary Grace** Mlor
Created by *Sherwood Schwartz*
Producer *Sherwood Schwartz*

It's Alive ★

1968 US BW 80mins

Not to be confused with Larry Cohen's 1974 mutant baby shocker, this disagreeably cheap man-in-a-monster suit nonsense from *Mars Wants Women* director Larry Buchanan qualifies as one of those films that is actually psychically painful to endure. You know you're in B-movie hell when the opening five minutes consists of nothing but silent views of the Texan countryside shot from a handheld camera out of a car window. Help!!! Regular Buchanan player Bill Thurman plays a crazed backwoods farmer who discovers a lizard man on his land and proceeds to feed it with unwary tourists. Enter dinosaur expert Tommy Kirk who is captured and must escape the creature's clutches before the dinner gong sounds. Apparently inspired by the Richard (*Incredible Shrinking Man*) Matheson novel *Being*.

Tommy Kirk Wayne Thomas • **Shirley Bonne** Leila Sterns • **Bill Thurman** Greely • **Corveth Ousterhouse** Norman Sterns
Director *Larry Buchanan*
Screenplay *Larry Buchanan, from the novel "Being" by Richard Matheson*

It's Alive ★★★ 18

1974 US Colour 87mins

This breakthrough "mutant baby" movie marked the first time director Larry Cohen employed shock horror tactics to deal with serious social issues. Unsafe fertility drugs are blamed when Sharon Farrell's hideous newborn offspring, complete with claws and fangs, slaughters all the medics in the delivery room and embarks on a murder spree, leaving its still protective parents to face the publicity, and the shame. Cohen's absorbing, grisly and cleverly written brainchild provides food for thought while still delivering the chilling and often repugnant goods. Oscar-winning make-up man Rick Baker designs the baby, and the movie features one of Bernard Herrmann's last scores. Followed by *It Lives Again* and a second sequel.

John Ryan [John P Ryan] Frank Davies • **Sharon Farrell** Lenore Davies • **Andrew Duggan** Professor • **Guy Stockwell** Clayton • **James Dixon** Lieutenant Perkins • **Michael Ansara** Captain • **Robert Emhardt** Executive • **William Wellman Jr** Charlie
Director/Screenplay *Larry Cohen*
Producer *Larry Cohen*
Music *Bernard Herrmann*

It's Alive III: Island of the Alive ★★★ 18

1987 US Colour 91mins

Topical issues, socially conscious humour and a great performance by Michael Moriarty (one of director Larry Cohen's rep company regulars) make this a worthy successor to the previous two killer mutant baby shockers. Moriarty plays a third-rate actor who deals with his mixed-up feelings about fathering one of the vicious tots by going to court to stop them being destroyed and getting them quarantined to a Florida island. But when cynical media exploitation still dogs their existence, he joins an expedition to the island to help them, only to find they've grown collectively stronger, bigger and more eager to take revenge on an uncaring society. A lively, absorbing and scary indictment crafted with Cohen's usual care and attention.

Michael Moriarty Steve Jarvis • **Karen Black** Ellen Jarvis • **Laurene Landon** Sally • **Gerritt Graham** Ralston • **James Dixon** Dr Perkins • **Neal Israel** Dr Brewster • **Art Lund** Swenson • **Ann Dane** Miss Morrell • **Macdonald Carey** Judge Watson
Director/Screenplay *Larry Cohen*
Music *Laurie Johnson, Bernard Herrmann* • ***Special Effects*** *Steve Neill, Rick Baker, William Hedge*

It's Great to Be Alive ★★★

1933 US BW 68mins

This is a musical remake of John G Blystone's 1923 comedy *The Last Man on Earth*. The plot finds heartbroken playboy Raul Roulien becoming the sole survivor of an epidemic called "masculitis", which has decimated the entire male population. Rescued from a desert island, he becomes the target of both gangster Dorothy Burgess and ex-fiancée Gloria Stuart. But much more intriguing are such futuristic details as the division of labour within the ruling matriarchy (unsurprisingly, the prettier girls get all the breaks) and scientist Edna May Oliver's attempts to construct a synthetic man. Flopping on release, it's creaky, but quirky.

Raul Roulien Carlos Martin • **Gloria Stuart** Dorothy Wilton • **Edna May Oliver** Dr Prodwell • **Herbert Mundin** Brooks • **Joan Marsh** Toots • **Dorothy Burgess** Al Moran • **Emma Dunn** Mrs Wilton • **Edward Van Sloan** Dr Wilton
Director *Alfred Werker*
Screenplay *Arthur Kober, Paul Perez, from the novelette "The Last Man on Earth" by John D Swain*
Cinematographer *Robert Planck*

J

John Hammond: "**All** major theme parks have delays. When they opened Disneyland in 1956 nothing worked."

Ian Malcolm: "But John, if the Pirates of the Caribbean breaks down, the pirates don't eat the **tourists**."

Jurassic Park 1993

Jason of Star Command ★★

TV 1979-1981 US Colour 16x15/12x30mins

Not quite a spin-off from *Space Academy*, this series reuses many sets, costumes, effects and stunts from that show and was, in fact, set in a space academy. A throwback to the *Captain Video* era, this serial-like program was originally screened among cartoons on the *Tarzan and the Super 7* Saturday morning show. Jason (Craig Littler), a blow-dried, spacefaring good guy with no especial character, working for Cmdr Canarvin (James "Scotty" Doohan) in the first season, with John Russell stepping in as Commander Stone the next year. The other regulars were eccentric inventor professor Charlie Dell, a couple of allegedly comic robots (Wiki and Peepo) and the villainous one-eyed, pockmarked Sid Haig. *Femme* interest was provided in successive seasons by computer expert Susan O'Hanlon and alien Tamara Dobson. It is one of the few sci-fi series ever to have been dubbed into Welsh, as *Guran, Gwarchodwry Gofod*.

Craig Littler Jason • **Charlie Dell** Prof EJ Parsafoot • **Sid Haig** Dragos • **Susan O'Hanlon** Capt Nicole Davidoff • **James Doohan** Cmdr Canarvin • **Tamara Dobson** Samantha • **John Russell** Cmdr Stone
Director *Arthur H Nadel*

Je T'Aime, Je T'Aime ★★★

1968 Fr Colour 94mins

Returning to the subjects of lapsing time and unreliable memory that had informed all his earlier features, Alain Resnais harnessed that old sci-fi standby, the time machine, to bring an extra dimension to this intriguing study of lost happiness, despair and death. But, as the suicide survivor dispatched to retrace his past, Claude Rich struggles to make an impact amid the fragmentary recollections of his affair with Olga Georges-Picot, for whose demise he may be responsible. There may be a fantastical poetry about the enterprise, but it's also a searching investigation into the helpless insignificance of human existence. In French with English subtitles.

Claude Rich Claude Ridder • **Olga Georges-Picot** Catrine • **Anouk Ferjac** Wiana Lust • **Marie-Blanche Vergnes** Young woman
Director *Alain Resnais*
Screenplay *Jacques Sternberg, Alain Resnais*

Jekyll and Hyde ★★ 15

1989 UK/US Colour 94mins

The much-filmed horror classic gets an unconvincing TV movie makeover, with Michael Caine going through the motions as Victorian gentleman Dr Jekyll and his evil counterpart Mr Hyde. There's a sterling supporting cast that includes Joss Ackland, Ronald Pickup and Lionel Jeffries, but Cheryl Ladd is out of her depth as Jekyll's concerned girlfriend, Sara Crawford. David Wickes's direction is uninspired, and the surfeit of all-enveloping fog and "gorblimey, guv" chirpy cockneys soon becomes wearying. Wickes and Caine had already worked together on another Victorian-set horror tale, 1988's TV-movie version of *Jack the Ripper*, with similarly bland results. Contains some violence and swearing.

Michael Caine Dr Henry Jekyll/Mr Edward Hyde • **Cheryl Ladd** Sara Crawford • **Joss Ackland** Dr Lanyon • **Ronald Pickup** Jeffrey Utterson • **Kim Thomson** Lucy • **Kevin McNally** Sergeant Hornby • **David Schofield** Ted Snape • **Lee Montague** Inspector Palmer • **Miriam Karlin** Mrs Schneider • **Lionel Jeffries** Mr Jekyll • **Joan Heal** Mrs Clark • **Frank Barrie** Poole • **Martyn Jacobs** Young man • **Gary Shail** Sailor • **Diane Keen** Annabel • **Lance Percival** Beresford Mount • **Jill Pearson** Nurse • **Kiran Shah** Sara's son
Director *David Wickes*
Screenplay *David Wickes, from the novel "The Strange Case of Dr Jekyll and Mr Hyde" by Robert Louis Stevenson*

Jekyll and Hyde . . . Together Again ★★ 18

1982 US Colour 83mins

Satirical comedy show *Saturday Night Live* was famous for spawning a number of careers and a host of film spin-offs. It also gave rise to a number of imitators, arguably the best of which was *Fridays*, a similarly trendy late-night mix of jokes and sketches. That show in turn gave rise to this spin-off, a movie designed to cash in on the popularity of Mark Blankfield's drug-crazed pharmacist. Here he plays a surgeon who changes personalities whenever he sniffs a strange powder. The transformation from small screen to big, however, wasn't so successful.

Mark Blankfield Jekyll/Hyde • **Bess Armstrong** Mary • **Krista Errickson** Ivy • **Tim Thomerson** Dr Lanyon • **Michael McGuire** Dr Carew
Director *Jerry Belson*
Screenplay *Monica Johnson, Harvey Miller, Jerry Belson, Michael Leeson*

Jesse James Meets Frankenstein's Daughter ★★ PG

1966 US Colour 79mins

Poorly made exploitation quickie and the last ever feature from prolific B-movie director William Beaudine, who began his career working for DW Griffith and made over 200 films. Boasting the production values of an episode of TV's *Bonanza*, it profiles Frankenstein's *grand*daughter (Narda Onyx), who carries on in the family tradition by transplanting a synthetic brain into Jesse James's musclebound sidekick. Will our hero be forced to shoot his pal? Can we stay awake long enough to find out? The film's singular highlight is the over-ripe performance from Onyx; it's certainly refreshing to see a female having fun playing the role of a mad scientist. Like its same-year companion piece *Billy the Kid vs Dracula*, this has since achieved mind-boggling cult status.

John Lupton Jesse James • **Cal Bolder** Hank Tracy/Igor • **Narda Onyx** Maria Frankenstein • **Steven Geray** Rudolph Frankenstein • **Felipe Turich** Manuel
Director *William Beaudine*
Screenplay *Carl K Hittleman, from a story by Carl K Hittleman*

La Jetée ★★★★★ PG

1962 Fr BW 26mins

Composed almost exclusively of still photographs, Chris Marker's classic of post-apocalyptic sci-fi makes for unforgettable viewing. Beginning with the childhood memory of a woman's face, the film traces Davos Hanich's efforts to uncover the meaning of this haunting image. Exploring many of the themes found in the *ciné-romans* of Alain Resnais, Marker uses photomontage to dazzling and disturbing effect, but even more devastating is the one simple but indelible live-action sequence. This exploration of time, memory and vision provided the inspiration for Terry Gilliam's *Twelve Monkeys*. In French with English subtitles.

Hélène Chatelain The woman • **Davos Hanich** The man • **Jacques Ledoux** The experimenter • **Jean Négroni** Narrator
Director/Screenplay *Chris Marker*
Editor *Jean Ravel* • ***Music*** *Trevor Duncan*

Jetsons: the Movie ★★★ U

1990 US Colour 78mins

Hanna-Barbera's less successful flipside of *The Flintstones* were the Space Age equivalent. Atom-powered ovens, robot vacuum cleaners, jet-propelled cars and flying saucer-shaped houses, the Jetson family has it all. What the film doesn't have is a strong story, just a thinly-disguised environmental tract about furry space creatures losing their homes due to an asteroid mining operation. This could have been a rather charmless exercise – the songs are instantly forgettable, the ecology issue is no substitute for the original sixties'-themed whimsy – but, fortunately, the animation is colourful and inventive enough to amuse the kids.

George O'Hanlon George Jetson • **Mel Blanc** Mr Spacely • **Penny Singleton** Jane Jetson • **Tiffany** Judy Jetson • **Patric Zimmerman** Elroy Jetson • **Don Messick** Astro • **Jean Vanderpyl** Rosie the Robot
Director *William Hanna, Joseph Barbera*
Screenplay *Dennis Marks, additional dialogue Carl Sautter*

Joe 90 ★★★ U

TV 1968-1969 UK Colour 30x25mins

This was Gerry Anderson's puppet pastiche of the James Bond phenomenon, the joke being that the special agent here is a nine-year-old schoolboy. Thanks to his father's invention BIG RAT (Brain Impulse Galvanoscope Record and Transfer) Joe McClaine is able to absorb specialist adult brain patterns, of a fighter pilot for example, thus making him the perfect agent for WIN (World Intelligence Network), a sort of United Nations with clout. He even has his own 007-style gadget-laden briefcase containing code books, a two-way radio communicator, a pistol and most importantly of all special glasses that trigger all the information our pint-sized hero needs to carry out his missions. Not nearly as visually interesting or technically proficient as *Thunderbirds*, but entertaining enough and keenly remembered by adults of a certain age.

Len Jones Joe McClaine • **Rupert Davies** Prof Ian "Mac" McClaine • **Keith Alexander** Sam Loover • **David Healy** Shane Weston
Created by *Gerry Anderson*
Executive Producer *Reg Hill* • ***Producer*** *David Lane, Gerry Anderson*

Johnny Mnemonic ★ 15

1995 Can/US Colour 92mins

Director Robert Longo's turgid sci-fi thriller, based on William Gibson's cyberpunk short story, is cyber junk. Keanu Reeves sleepwalks through the title role as a 21st-century high-tech messenger who carries top-secret information thanks to a computer chip in his brain allied to bio-enhanced memory cells. Unfortunately, his latest employers have overloaded his cranial capacity to such an extent that his head will explode unless he downloads fast. Empty, flashy and incredibly dull, Longo's unpleasant movie fails to generate any suspense and, worse still, is lamely tarted up with incomprehensible surf-cowboy jargon, gratuitous violence and second-rate special effects. Software lacking any byte. Contains swearing, violence and nudity.

Keanu Reeves Johnny Mnemonic • **Dina Meyer** Jane • **Ice-T** J-Bone • **Takeshi Kitano** Takahashi • **Denis Akiyama** Shinji • **Dolph Lundgren** Street Preacher • **Henry Rollins** Spider • **Barbara Sukowa** Anna K • **Udo Kier** Ralfi • **Tracy Tweed** Pretty
Director *Robert Longo*
Screenplay *William Gibson, from his short story*

Johnny 2.0 ★★

1998 US Colour

How much Jeff Fahey is too much? In this low-budget sci-fi film, Fahey plays Johnny Dalton, a brilliant biochemist who has invented the technology that will allow humans to make perfect clones of themselves. Surprise, surprise, the inventor clones himself and years later, his doppelgänger is sent to find him at the behest of an all-powerful corporation. It all boils down to a bunch of dumb action scenes in a grungy future and Jeff Fahey wearing a silly grey wig to simulate his older self. At least classic genre bad guy Michael Ironside is on hand to provide some bite.

Jeff Fahey Johnny Dalton • **Tahnee Welch** Nikki Holland • **Michael Ironside** Frank • **John Neville** Bosch • **Michael Rhoades** Taylor • **Von Flores** Carlos • **Cliff Saunders** Dan-O
Director *Neill Fearnley*
Screenplay *Wynne McLaughlin*

Josh Kirby . . . Time Warrior ★★

1995 US Colour

Not to be confused with the artist behind the British covers of bestselling author Terry Pratchett's novels, *Josh Kirby... Time Warrior!* is the series title for a series of six movies starring Corbin Allred as the eponymous Kirby. The 14-year-old becomes caught up in the battles between two scientists (Barrie Ingham and Derek Webster) in the 25th century. Both are after a super-weapon called the Nullifier, which can destroy past, present and future. The weapon has been broken into six parts by Barrie and the parts scattered throughout time. He and Allred, together with warrior Jennifer Burns and a creature called Prism, set off to try to prevent Webster from finding and assembling the Nullifier. The series was not helped by shoddy effects and a lack of control in the scripting leading to abrupt endings. Watch out for a bit-part appearance by Charisma Carpenter, later to find fame as Cordelia in *Buffy, the Vampire Slayer* and *Angel*.

Corbin Allred Josh Kirby • **Jennifer Burns** Azbeth Siege • **Derek Webster** Dr Zoetrope • **Barrie Ingham** Irwin 1138 • **Charisma Carpenter** Beth Sullivan
Written by *Paul Callisi, Ethan Reiff, Cyrus Voris, Nick Paine*

Journey into Space: Operation Luna ★★★

Radio 1953-1954 UK 18x30mins

Writer/producer Charles Chilton created *Journey into Space* for BBC Radio in 1953, with a serial entitled *A Tale of the Future*, soon followed by *The Red Planet* and *The World in Peril*. All of these were broadcast on the Light Programme and lost, but slightly rewritten versions were recorded for overseas sale in 1957, and these have been released commercially. In the surviving version of their first adventure, retitled *Operation Luna*, space pilot Jet Morgan (played by future MP Andrew Faulds) set off for the moon in 1965, with crewmen Guy Kingsley Pointer, David Williams and comedy engineer Alfie Bass, who serves much the same purpose as Dan Dare's sidekick Digby in speaking up for the ordinary, tea-drinking bloke among the sometimes overly high-flown or science-minded geniuses that compose the rest of the crew. A serial, complete with cliffhangers, it has space for some lighter moments between the big concepts, and the effective incidental music is by Van Phillips. Available on audio-cassette.

Andrew Faulds Captain Jet Morgan • **Alfie Bass** Lemmy Barnet • **Guy Kingsley Poynter** Doc Matthews • **David Williams** Stephen "Mitch" Mitchell
Written by *Charles Chilton*
Producer *Charles Chilton*
Music *Van Phillips*

Journey into Space: The Red Planet ★★★

Radio 1954-1955 UK 20x30mins

The second of writer-producer Charles Chilton's Light Programme space operas, this picks up the story in 1971, when man has established a base on the moon after the events of the first serial and is mounting a manned expedition via a fleet of spaceships to visit Mars. Along the way, they discover that several of the crew are brainwashed zombies in the thrall of Martians and, upon arrival, most of the crew succumb to the illusion that they are on Earth, in an Australian desert where everyone (including a community of human abductees from the last hundred years) accepts that dogs are six-legged giant beetle-like creatures. It turns out that the Martians have been planning a Wellsian invasion of Earth and are recruiting humans as a fifth column, but good old Andrew Faulds – not to mention his stalwart pals David Kossoff, Bruce Beeby and Guy Kingsley Pointer – resists the alien influence and escapes from the Red Planet to bring the Earth a warning of the space war that would form the plot of the third serial. Available on audio-cassette.

Andrew Faulds Captain Jet Morgan • **David Kossoff** Lemmy Barnet • **Guy Kingsley Poynter** Doc Matthews • **Bruce Beeby** Stephen "Mitch" Mitchell
Written by *Charles Chilton*
Producer *Charles Chilton*

Journey into Space: The Return from Mars ★★★

Radio 1981 UK 90mins

A feature-length 1981 sequel to writer/producer Charles Chilton's fifties BBC Radio space operas, this opens in the 21st century with the good ship *Discovery* returning to Earth after a generation in space and commander John Pullen – plus his crew Anthony Hall, Nigel Graham and Ed Bishop – being debriefed. It turns out that the spacemen think they've been away for only seven years, but they've actually been through (another) timewarp and had an adventure vaguely inspired by *Lost Horizon* in which the hitherto celibate Faulds finally gets some love interest, Elizabeth Proud, who turns out to be 150 years old and unhappy with her perfect society. A pleasing re-creation of the style of fifties wireless, this makes some modest attempts to update the format and delivers nostalgic thrills. The BBC audio release also includes a 1999 documentary on the original series. Available on audio-cassette.

John Pullen Captain Jet Morgan • **Anthony Hall** Lemmy Barnet • **Ed Bishop** Doc Matthews • **Nigel Graham** Stephen "Mitch" Mitchell
Director *Glyn Dearman*
Written by *Charles Chilton*

Journey into Space: The World in Peril ★★★

Radio 1955-1956 UK 20x30mins

The wind-up of writer/producer Charles Chilton's wireless sci-fi trilogy, at least until the one-off 1981 revival *The Return from Mars*, this picks up where *The Red Planet* left off, with Andrew Faulds and his crew returning to warn the Earth of a long-planned Martian invasion, and discovering that the aliens already have mind-controlled minions working among us. With his trusty crew, Faulds returns to Mars to discover more about the Martian plans and learns – in a twist that suggests how radio professionals felt about an impertinent new medium in 1956 – that they intend to use television to hypnotise humanity into accepting a utopian but oppressive society. The latter stages of the story are surprisingly complex morally, as the unwarlike but manipulative Martians argue that their rule would be better for humanity. A strange frill is *The Green Hills of Earth*, a Martian rebel song belted out by a male voice choir at any opportunity. Available on audio-cassette.

Andrew Faulds Captain Jet Morgan • **Alfie Bass** Lemmy Barnet • **Guy Kingsley Poynter** Doc Matthews • **Don Sharp** Stephen "Mitch" Mitchell
Written by *Charles Chilton*
Producer *Charles Chilton*

Journey to the Center of the Earth ★★★★ U

1959 US Colour 129mins

A lavish, well-crafted adaptation of Jules Verne's classic tale, with James Mason leading an expedition into a volcano shaft and finding large mushrooms, giant lizards, an underground ocean and the lost city of Atlantis. Bernard Herrmann's fabulous music sets the mood for the spirited adventure, with the accent firmly on wholesome light-heartedness rather than vivid Verne danger. Singer Pat Boone adds his own brand of fantasy swashbuckling to the colourful proceedings, played out against some staggeringly imaginative subterranean sets.

Pat Boone Alec McEwen • **James Mason** Professor Oliver Lindenbrook • **Arlene Dahl** Carla • **Diane Baker** Jenny • **Thayer David** Count Saknussemm • **Peter Ronson** Hans • **Robert Adler** Groom • **Alan Napier** Dean • **Alex Finlayson** Professor Bayle
Director *Henry Levin*
Screenplay *Walter Reisch, Charles Brackett, from the novel "Voyage au Centre de la Terre" by Jules Verne*

Journey to the Center of the Earth ★★ PG

1989 US Colour 76mins

Bearing only a passing resemblance to the Jules Verne classic, this harmless family adventure relocates the action to Hawaii as a group of teens stumble upon an alternative world while out exploring caves. The eclectic cast includes Nicola Cowper (*Dreamchild*), Kathy Ireland and wacky American stand-up comic Emo Philips and although Verne purists will be disgusted, it makes for blandly enjoyable entertainment

Paul Carafotes Richard • **Nicola Cowper** Chrystina • **Ilan Mitchell-Smith** Bryan • **Janie DuPlessis** General Rykov/Shank • **Jeff Weston** Tola • **Jaclyn Bernstein** Sara • **Kathy Ireland** Wanda
Director *Rusty Lemorande, Albert Pyun*
Screenplay *Rusty Lemorande, Debra Ricci, Regina Davis, Kitty Chalmers, from the novel "Voyage au Centre de la Terre" by Jules Verne*

Journey to the Center of the Earth ★ U

1993 US Colour 91mins

Once you're over the disappointment that this isn't the 1959 version starring James Mason, you'd better prepare yourself for some more bad news. This was the pilot for a TV series that never saw the light of day and when it says "based on the novel by Jules Verne", it means based in the loosest possible sense. Having directed *Bigfoot and the Hendersons*, William Dear should have spotted that the script left a lot to be desired, but maybe he couldn't resist the chance to work with F Murray Abraham, an Oscar winner for *Amadeus*. Sam Raimi, the *Evil Dead* director who pops up in a cameo.

David Dundara Tony • **Farrah Forke** Margo • **Kim Miyori** Tesue • **John Neville** Chalmers • **Jeffrey Nordling** Chris • **Tim Russ** Briggs • **Carel Struycken** Dallas • **Fabiana Udenio** Sandy • **Justina Vail** Devin • **F Murray Abraham** Professor Harlech
Director *William Dear*
Screenplay *David Mickey Evans, Robert Gunter, from the novel "Voyage au Centre de la Terre" by Jules Verne*

Journey to the Center of Time ★★

1967 US Colour 82mins

Mediocre sci-fi fare, made with little money and even less imagination. Scott Brady leads a group of scientists who, facing eviction from their time research lab, stage a hasty demonstration of their unfinished experiments and are hurtled back and forth in time encountering aliens and prehistoric monsters (in reality a photographically-enlarged lizard). Any ambition director David L Hewitt might have had are hopelessly defeated by the non-existent budget. It's all talk and not enough action, with the actors expounding sheet-loads of technobabble dialogue, while the time travel process is signified by spinning the camera around really fast. Take my advice,

Fantastic voyage: 1959's lavish production of *Journey to the Center of the Earth*

watch an episode of *Time Tunnel* instead.

Scott Brady Stanton Jr • **Anthony Eisley** Mark Manning • **Gigi Perreau** Karen White • **Abraham Sofaer** Dr von Steiner
Director *David L Hewitt*
Screenplay *David Prentiss*

Journey to the Far Side of the Sun ★★★

1969 UK Colour 100mins

On the other side of the sun, astronaut Roy Thinnes finds a hidden planet mirroring Earth in every exact detail. Writer/producers Gerry and Sylvia Anderson, who created the cult puppet shows *Thunderbirds* and *Captain Scarlet*, as well as the live action series *UFO* and *Space 1999*, combine a clever concept with solid special effects. Add commendable direction from Robert Parrish and a memorable twist ending, and the result is a minor science-fiction gem.

Ian Hendry John Kane • **Roy Thinnes** Col Glenn Ross • **Patrick Wymark** Jason Webb • **Lynn Loring** Sharon Ross • **Loni von Friedl** Lise • **Herbert Lom** Dr Hassler • **George Sewell** Mark Newman • **Franco Derosa** Paulo • **Edward Bishop** David Poulson
Director *Robert Parrish*
Screenplay *Gerry Anderson, Sylvia Anderson, Donald James*

Journey to the Seventh Planet ★★ U

1961 US/Den Colour 73mins

When an exploratory spaceship lands on Uranus in 2001, its five-man crew must do battle with a giant-eye, telepathic alien intelligence that plays on their fears and memories. The men not only encounter women from their past lives, but start hallucinating from the depths of their subconciousness (resulting in Cyclopean dinosaurs, giant spiders, etc). Co-written by Ib (*Planet of the Vampires*) Melchior and shot in Denmark with practically the same cast as producer Sidney Pink's monster disaster *Reptilicus*, this poor man's *Forbidden Planet* is directed in Pink's lackadaisical style.

John Agar Don • **Greta Thyssen** Greta • **Ann Smyrner** Ingrid • **Mimi Heinrich** Ursula • **Carl Ottosen** Eric • **Ove Sprogoe** Barry
Director *Sidney Pink, Ib Melchior*
Screenplay *Ib Melchior, Sidney Pink, from a story by Sidney Pink*

Judge Dredd ★★★ 15

1995 US Colour 91mins DVD

Star Wars meets *Ben-Hur* in director Danny Cannon's imaginatively over-the-top science-fiction rendering of the celebrated *2000 AD* comic-strip hero. In the future, the world has formed into densely populated Mega Cities with the Cursed Earth being the uninhabitable region lying between them. Law and order is maintained by a fleet of elite officers who are judge, jury and executioner all rolled into one, and Judge Dredd (Sylvester Stallone) is the most prolific of the brigade. This is how fans like their Stallone served up best – without subtlety, monosyllabic, biceps bulging and in constant action. Diane Lane as Judge Hershey, the romantic judge with a conscience, has some excellent moments, and Armand Assante puts in a fine performance of manic evil as a villain with a secret. Cannon accents the spark and humour of the comic, while ensuring the visuals are always spectacular. Contains swearing and violence.

Sylvester Stallone Judge Dredd • **Armand Assante** Rico • **Rob Schneider** Fergie • **Jürgen Prochnow** Judge Griffin • **Max von Sydow** Judge Fargo • **Diane Lane** Judge Hershey • **Joanna Miles** McGruder • **Joan Chen** Ilsa • **Balthazar Getty** Olmeyer • **Mitchell Ryan** Hammond • **Ian Dury** Geiger • **Chris Adamson** Mean Machine
Director *Danny Cannon*
Screenplay *William Wisher, Steven E de Souza, from a story by William Wisher, Michael DeLuca, from characters created by John Wagner, Carlos Ezquerra*

SFacts

In 1995, Radio 1 broadcast an 80-episode serial based on the Judge Dredd character and stories, starring Gary Martin.

Judgment Day ★★★ 18

1999 US Colour 85mins

This sci-fi thriller from director John Terlesky rises above its bargain-basement special effects, but suffers instead from a palpable lack of tension. As a giant meteor heads straight for Earth, FBI agent Suzy Amis and convict Ice-T go in search of academic Linden Ashby, who alone can prevent annihilation. Trouble is, he's been kidnapped by cult leader Mario Van Peebles, who believes the impending doom is God's will. Willing performances and sly humour place this just above the direct-to-video average. Contains swearing, drug abuse and violence.

Ice-T Reese • **Suzy Amis** Tyrell • **Mario Van Peebles** Payne • **Coolio** Luther • **Linden Ashby** Corbett • **Tom "Tiny" Lister Jr** Clarence • **Max Gail** Meech • **Mark Deakins** McNally

Director *John Terlesky*

Screenplay *William Carson*

Jules Verne's Rocket to the Moon ★★ U

1967 UK Colour 88mins DVD

No prizes for guessing where the inspiration for the alternative title to this film, *Those Fantastic Flying Fools*, came from. But beware! These not-so-magnificent men in their rocketship to the moon provide strictly routine science fantasy. A fabulous cast (including ex-Bond villain Gert Frobe and fifties' teen idol Troy Donahue) breathes life into an insipid Jules Verne concoction that has Burl Ives (as Phineas T Barnum) sending circus performers into Victorian orbit only to have them crash-land in tsarist Russia.

Burl Ives Phineas T Barnum • **Troy Donahue** Gaylord Sullivan • **Gert Frobe** Professor von Bulow • **Hermione Gingold** Angelica • **Lionel Jeffries** Sir Charles Dillworthy • **Daliah Lavi** Madelaine • **Dennis Price** Duke of Barset • **Dennis Price** Duke of Barset • **Dennis Price** Duke of Barset • **Stratford Johns** Warrant Officer • **Graham Stark** Grundle • **Terry-Thomas** Captain Sir Harry Washington-Smythe

Director *Don Sharp*

Screenplay *Dave Freeman, from a story by Peter Welbeck [Harry Alan Towers], from the writings of Jules Verne*

Jules Verne's Strange Holiday ★★

1969 Aus Colour 75mins

This is a disappointingly tame attempt to film Jules Verne's adventure of boys marooned on an island, who find themselves with unwanted visitors. The enthusiastic performances show plenty of youthful zest, but it's not a pleasant story, further let down by stale scripting.

Jaeme Hamilton Briant • **Mark Healey** Doniphan • **Jaime Messang** Moco • **Van Alexander** Gordon • **Carmen Duncan** Kate

Director *Mende Brown*

Screenplay *Mende Brown, from the novel "Deux Ans en Vacance" by Jules Verne*

Junior ★★★ PG

1994 US Colour 105mins DVD

A case of "we'll be back", as Arnold Schwarzenegger reunites with the *Twins* team of Danny DeVito and director Ivan Reitman for another comedy romp designed to show the lighter side of the muscle-bound superstar. Schwarzenegger and DeVito play struggling medical researchers working on a new fertility drug. When they lose their grant, in desperation Schwarzenegger injects himself with the experimental solution and, lo and behold, ends up pregnant. It's pretty much a one-joke concept, but Reitman milks it for all it's worth, and DeVito and Schwarzenegger look like they're having a ball. Only Emma Thompson as a fellow scientist and love interest looks out of place. Contains some strong language.

Arnold Schwarzenegger Dr Alexander Hesse • **Danny DeVito** Dr Larry Arbogast • **Emma Thompson** Dr Diana Reddin • **Frank Langella** Noah Banes • **Pamela Reed** Angela • **Judy Collins** Naomi • **James Eckhouse** Ned Sneller

Director *Ivan Reitman*

Screenplay *Kevin Wade, Chris Conrad*

Jupiter Moon ★

TV 1990-1991 UK 150x30mins

Billed as a blend of believable science fiction and powerful soap drama, British Satellite Broadcasting's short-lived space station saga ultimately delivers the worst of both galaxies. The series combines juvenile soap antics with tedious sci-fi chestnuts, in a manner than will leave few viewers feeling over the moon. Set in the year 2050, the show focuses on the lives and loves of the young students aboard the Ilea space station, which is realised with no-frills production values. Most of the show's European cast spacewalk through their two-dimensional roles, although the presence of several familiar faces – including Anna Chancellor and a pre-*EastEnders* Lucy Benjamin – does at least give the series some curiosity value.

Lucy Benjamin Fiona McBride • **Andy Rashleigh** Eliot Creasy • **Richard Derrington** Charles Brelan • **Phil Willmott** Finbow Lewis • **Suzy Cooper** Melody Shaw • **Karen Murden** Sarah Robbins • **Anna Chancellor** Mercedes Page • **Jason Durr** Alex Hartman • **Dominic Arnold** Piers Gilpin

Created by *William Smethurst*

Producer *William Smethurst*

Jurassic Park ★★★★★ PG

1993 US Colour 121mins

Steven Spielberg soared to new heights with this massively successful, electrifying adventure taken from Michael Crichton's bestseller. The world's ultimate theme park, featuring genetically re-created dinosaurs, is about to open and owner Richard Attenborough decides to give a sneak preview to a select few, including scientists Sam Neill and Laura Dern. However, all is not well in this new Garden of Eden. T-Rex and his chums are the undoubted stars of the show and the mix of computer animation and models is truly inspiring. Spielberg orchestrates the action with effortless verve and, although it's a little too long and full of loose ends, only the most Scrooge-like viewer will fail to be transfixed by the thrilling action and the sheer scale of the director's vision. Contains strong language, and includes scenes that may be disturbing for children.

Sam Neill Dr Alan Grant • **Laura Dern** Dr Ellie Sattler • **Jeff Goldblum** Ian Malcolm • **Richard Attenborough** John Hammond • **Bob Peck** Robert Muldoon • **Martin Ferrero** Donald Gennaro • **B D Wong** Dr Wu • **Joseph Mazzello** Tim • **Ariana Richards** Lex • **Samuel L Jackson** Arnold • **Wayne Knight** Nedry • **Jerry Molen** Harding

Director *Steven Spielberg*

Screenplay *Michael Crichton, David Koepp, from the novel by Michael Crichton*

Cinematographer *Dean Cundey* • ***Editor*** *Michael Kahn* • ***Music*** *John Williams* • ***Visual effects*** *Michael Lantieri, Dennis Muren, Phil Tippet, Stan Winston*

Just Imagine ★★ U

1930 US BW 104mins

Buoyed by *Sunny Side Up*, songwriters Ray Henderson, Buddy De Sylva and Lew Brown reteamed with director David Butler for this misfiring sci-fi musical. It matters not that the songs are awful or that El Brendel is struck by lightning and projected to the New York of 1980, where he helps John Garrick wed Maureen O'Sullivan by his heroics on Mars. What is significant is the splendour of the Oscar-nominated cityscape and the accuracy of so many of the technological predictions (including test-tube babies and image phones).

El Brendel Single O • **Maureen O'Sullivan** LN-18 • **John Garrick** J-21 • **Marjorie White** D-6 • **Frank Albertson** RT-42 • **Hobart Bosworth** Z-4 • **Kenneth Thomson** MT-3 • **Wilfred Lucas** X-10 • **Mischa Auer** B-36 • **Joseph Girard** Commander • **Joyzelle** Loo Loo/Boo Boo • **Ivan Linow** Loko/Boko

Director *David Butler*

Screenplay *Lew Brown, David Butler, BG De Sylva, Ray Henderson*

Cinematographer *Ernest Palmer* • ***Art director*** *Stephen Goosson, Ralph Hammeras*

K

"He was a king and a god in the world he knew, but now he comes to civilisation merely a captive – on show to gratify your curiosity. Ladies and gentlemen, look at Kong, the Eighth Wonder of the World!"

King Kong 1933

Kamikaze ★★★ 15

1986 Fr Colour 88mins

Produced and co-written by Luc Besson (*Subway, The Big Blue*), this is a classic example of the style of French films dubbed *cinéma du look* on account of their flashy visuals and throwaway narratives. Directed by Besson's former assistant Didier Grousset, it boasts a wonderfully over-the-top central performance from Michel Galabru, as a mad scientist who invents a death ray that can zap anyone he takes a dislike to while watching TV, without leaving a single clue as to the killer's identity. Great idea, but in all honesty there is really only enough material in this satire on couch-potato culture for a razor-sharp sketch. In French with English subtitles.

Richard Bohringer Detective Romain • **Michel Galabru** Albert • **Dominique Lavanant** Laure Frontenac • **Riton Leibman** Olive • **Kim Massee** Léa • **Harry Cleven** Patrick • **Romane Bohringer** Julie
Director *Didier Grousset*
Screenplay *Luc Besson, Didier Grousset, Michèle Halberstadt*
Producer *Luc Besson*

Katilon Ke Katil ★★★

1981 Ind Colour

Anyone still labouring under the misapprehension that Indian movies are all about goddesses, poverty and arranged marriages should take a look at this frantic Hindi hybrid that takes ingredients from just about every available genre to serve up a spicy cinematic feast. The subcontinent's favourite villain, Amjad Khan, stars as a criminal mastermind called the Black Cobra, but there's also a space-age monster for Dharmendra and Rishi Kapoor to contend with. Low on artistic merit, but packed with songs, fights and exotic locations, this all-action masala even has a case of mistaken identity to keep the mixture simmering. In Hindi with English subtitles.

Director *Arjun Hingorani*
Cinematographer *Zeenat Aman*

Killdozer ★★

1974 US Colour 74mins

Here's a daft thriller about a bulldozer that becomes possessed by mysterious forces and becomes a wieldy death machine. Clint Walker is the leader of the construction gang under threat and the sharp-eyed will spot a youthful Robert Urich as well as the more distinctive features of top screen heavy, Neville Brand. However, in the suspense stakes, it's a long way from *Duel*.

Clint Walker Lloyd Kelly • **Carl Betz** Dennis Holvig • **Neville Brand** Chub Foster • **James Wainwright** Jules "Dutch" Krasner • **James A Watson Jr** Al Beltran • **Robert Urich** Mack McCarthy
Director *Jerry London*
Screenplay *Theodore Sturgeon, Ed Mackillop, from the novel by Theodore Sturgeon*

Killer Ape ★ U

1953 US BW 68mins

The twelfth (of 16) Jungle Jim adventures based on Alex Raymond's cartoon strip featuring Johnny Weissmuller after he got too old to effectively wear his trademark Tarzan loincloth. In this micro-budget production – the killer ape's ludicrous fur waistcoat outfit sets an all-time low standard for such exotic fare – mad scientist Nestor Paiva is testing out a pacifying drug on apes provided by the Waculi tribe for future use by warring nations. Jungle Jim comes to the rescue of mankind after one caveman-ape guinea pig goes berserk and kills Paiva.

Johnny Weissmuller Jungle Jim • **Carol Thurston** Shari • **Max Palmer** Man-Ape • **Burt Wenland** Ramada • **Nestor Paiva** Andrews • **Paul Marion** Mahara
Director *Spencer Gordon Bennet*
Screenplay *Arthur Hoerl, Carroll Young, from a story by Carroll Young, from a comic strip by Alex Raymond*

Killer Klowns from Outer Space ★★★ 15

1988 US Colour 82mins

Combining inspired amateur brashness, delightful *Loony Tunes* design and a winningly bizarre unreality, this engagingly cheap affair from effects wizards Stephen and Charles Chiodo is an infantile and vicious delight. Alien clowns invade Earth in a spacecraft masquerading as a circus tent and intend to cocoon the local population in candy floss and suck out their life juices, unless two teens and a cop can stop them. Cleverly paying homage to fifties schlock, with its acid custard pies, homicidal Jack in the Boxes and malevolent Punch and Judy shows, this is definitely not for children.

Grant Cramer Mike • **Suzanne Snyder** Debbie • **John Allen Nelson** Officer Dave Hanson • **Royal Dano** Farmer Green
Director *Stephen Chiodo*
Screenplay *Stephen Chiodo, Charles Chiodo*

The Killer Shrews ★ PG

1959 US BW 68mins

Surely one of the all-time movie howlers. For sheer nerve the makers ought to have grabbed an Oscar for attempting to demonise an animal not much bigger than a mouse. But these are not ordinary shrews, but the rampaging and flesh-eating side effects of genetic research carried out by scientist Baruch Lumet (father of director Sidney Lumet). Lacklustre to say the least, the film boasts inept special effects – the mutated shrews are in reality greyhounds sporting shaggy coats and plastic fangs – and bargain basement production values, all factors which have contributed to its status today as a cult bad movie. Watch and enjoy, for all the wrong reasons.

James Best Thorne Sherman • **Ingrid Goude** Ann Craigis • **Baruch Lumet** Dr Craigis • **Ken Curtis** Jerry Lacer
Director *Ray Kellogg*
Screenplay *Jay Simms*

SCI Q

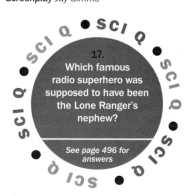

17. Which famous radio superhero was supposed to have been the Lone Ranger's nephew?

See page 496 for answers

Killer Tongue ★ 18

1996 Sp/UK Colour 94mins

This sloppy made-in-Spain venture is a mixture of horror and humour posing as camp genre pastiche. Following her close encounter with an alien meteorite, amoral bank robber Melinda Clarke inexplicably grows an 18ft-long tongue which commits all manner of stupidly gory crimes on nuns, escaped prisoners and other lust-crazed victims. Oh, and her pet poodles turn into bitchy transvestites, too! Everything from Russ Meyer to Russ Abbot is dragged screaming into this purposely tacky collage of hammy performances (take a bow, horror icons Robert Englund and Doug Bradley) and shaky special effects. Spainful!

Melinda Clarke Candy • **Jason Durr** Johnny • **Mapi Galán** Rita • **Mabel Karr** Old nun • **Robert Englund** Chief screw • **Alicia Borrachero** Reporter • **Doug Bradley** Wig
Director/Screenplay *Alberto Sciamma*

Killers from Space ★ U

1954 US BW 71mins

Ping-pong-ball-eyed aliens in hooded sweatshirts and mittens from the planet Astron Delta intend to invade Earth by using fuzzy rear screen projected stock footage of lizards and insects. Plane crash survivor Peter Graves stsumbles on their plan and, after being disbelieved by everyone, short circuits the aliens' atomic equipment and saves the world. Cheaply-made boredom with astonishingly bad special effects produced and directed by W Lee Wilder, Billy (*Some Like It Hot*) Wilder's far less successful brother.

Peter Graves • **James Seay** • **Frank Gerstle**
Screenplay *William Raynor, from a story by Myles Wilder*

The Killings at Outpost Zeta ★

1980 US Colour 92mins

Cheap science fiction gets scraped from the bottom of a very deep barrel in this unwatchable feature. Inhabitants of the planet Zeta are being found dead in the tinsel-and-plastic universe of 2002. Astronauts Gordon Devol and Jacqueline Ray discover the murders are caused by a blood-drinking rock creature. Even TV's *Lost in Space* didn't look this bad or show such lousy acting and not-so-special effects.

Gordon Devol • **Jacqueline Ray**
Director *Robert Emenegger, Allan Sandler*
Screenplay *Peter Dawson*

The Kindred ★ 18

1986 US Colour 88mins [video]

Once hailed as one of America's greatest actors, Rod Steiger suffered a career breakdown in the mid-eighties appearing in straight-to-video horror trash, of which this is fairly typical. The man who shared screen time with Brando in *On the Waterfront* is here reduced to hamming it up as a mad scientist in a fright wig whose experiments result in the inevitable things in the cellar. Totally uninvolving from start to finish, with characters so unappealing you rather hope they do mutate into something dreadful. Let's hope Steiger sacked his agent after this.

David Allen Brooks John Hollins • **Amanda Pays** Melissa Leftridge • **Talia Balsam** Sharon Raymond • **Kim Hunter** Amanda Hollins • **Rod Steiger** Dr Phillip Lloyd
Director *Jeffrey Obrow, Stephen Carpenter*
Screenplay *Stephen Carpenter, Jeffrey Obrow, John Penney, Earl Ghaffari, Joseph Stefano*

King Cobra ★ 15

1999 US Colour 89mins [video]

Scientists genetically create a giant snake in order to test a formula that will increase aggression without causing harmful side effects. It goes without saying that the snake escapes from the lab, re-appearing in a small town just before its annual beer festival is about to begin. The collection of very familiar characters – the mayor who won't cancel the festival, the concerned scientist, the maverick animal hunter – may not have immediately doomed the film, but the scenes involving the snake do. The animatronic creation is so unconvincing that it's hardly surprising the snake does most of its business off-screen or in quick, blurry movements.

Pat Morita Nick Hashimoto • **Scott Brandon [Scott Hillenbrand]** Dr Brad Kagan • **Kasey Fallo** Deputy Jo Biddle • **Hoyt Axton** Mayor Ed Biddle • **Joseph Ruskin** Dr Irwin Burns • **Courtney Gains** Dr IMcConnell • **Eric Lawson** Sheriff Ben Lowry • **Erik Estrada** Bernie Alvarez
Director/Screenplay *David Hillenbrand, Scott Hillenbrand*

King Dinosaur ★

1955 US BW 59mins

The first effort from legendary skid-row producer/director Bert I Gordon clearly set the low standard for all his subsequent genre offerings. Astronaut Bill Bryant leads an expedition to the planet Nova where they are menaced by giant "prehistoric" creatures courtesy of that all-purpose saviour of bargain basement productions – stock footage from *One Million BC* (1940). An exploding atom bomb – more documentary material – ends the explorers' terror. Allegedly shot over a weekend. We believe it.

Bill Bryant [William Bryant] Dr Richard Gordon • **Wanda Curtis** Dr Patricia Bennett • **Douglas Henderson** Dr Ralph Martin • **Patti Gallagher** Nora Pierce
Director *Bert I Gordon*
Screenplay *Tom Gries, from a story by Bert I Gordon, Al Zimbalist*

King Kong ★★★★★ PG

1933 US BW 100mins [video]

In this timeless *Beauty and the Beast* classic, Willis O'Brien's amazing ape animation has lost little of its ability to startle, while Fay Wray's screams from the top of the Empire State Building remain etched in the memory. This is one of the very few movies that will live for ever, and you cannot call yourself a fantasy fan unless you've seen it at least three times. Made by a team of documentary film-makers who patterned fast-talking adventurer Carl Denham (Robert Armstrong) after themselves, this is as good as mythic monster movies get.

Fay Wray Ann Darrow • **Robert Armstrong** Carl Denham • **Bruce Cabot** John Driscoll • **Frank Reicher** Capt Englehorn • **Sam Hardy** Charles Weston • **Noble Johnson** Native chief • **James Flavin** Second mate • **Steve Clemento** Witch king • **Victor Wong** Lumpy • **Merian C Cooper** Flight commander • **Ernest B Schoedsack** Chief observer
Director *Merian C Cooper, Ernest B Schoedsack*
Screenplay *James Creelman, Ruth Rose, from an idea by Merian C Cooper, Edgar Wallace*
Producer *Merian C Cooper, Ernest B Schoedsack*
Cinematographer *Eddie Linden, Vernon Walker, JO Taylor* • ***Music*** *Max Steiner* • ***Special effects*** *Willis O'Brien*

King Kong ★ PG

1976 US Colour 128mins [video]

This leaden and over-budgeted remake of the classic simian *Beauty and the Beast* fantasy abandons all the exotic mystery of the 1933 masterpiece in favour of glossy high camp and atrocious satire. A man in a monkey suit and pathetic giant models replace the wonderful stop-motion techniques pioneered by Willis O'Brien for the original, and the result is this epic bomb. How Jessica Lange's career survived her debut in such a turkey – "Put me down, you male chauvinist ape!" – is a cinematic miracle. Another version has been talked about, but it couldn't possibly be as bad as this misbegotten stinker. Younger children may find it frightening.

Jessica Lange Dwan • **Jeff Bridges** Jack Prescott • **Charles Grodin** Fred Wilson • **John Randolph** Captain Ross • **René Auberjonois** Bagley • **Ed Lauter** Carnahan • **Mario Gallo** Timmons • **Jorge Moreno** Garcia • **Jack O'Halloran** Joe Perko • **Julius Harris** Boan • **Rick Baker** King Kong
Director *John Guillermin*
Screenplay *Lorenzo Semple Jr, from the 1933 film*
Producer *Dino De Laurentiis*

King Kong Escapes ★

1967 Jap Colour 95mins

A few laughs and some low-rent toy model excitement are the only saving graces of director Inoshiro Honda's return *King Kong* engagement, Japanese-style. After battling Godzilla in 1962, the giant ape takes on Mechani-Kong, a robot version of himself and the invention of mad scientist Eisei Amamaoto. He needs the real Kong to continue mining radioactive minerals once his android version goes haywire in this vulgar continuation of the Kong myth, relying on over-familiar battles and typical Tokyo devastation. *You Only Live Twice* Bond Girl Mie Hama appears as Madame Piranha, while Rhodes Reason and Linda Miller feature in the specially directed American footage.

Rhodes Reason Cmdr Nelson • **Mie Hama** Madame Piranha • **Linda G Miller [Linda Miller]** Susan • **Akira Takarada** Lt Jiro Nomura • **Eisei Amamoto** Dr Who
Director *Inoshiro Honda, Arthur Rankin Jr*
Screenplay *William J Keenan, Kaoru Mabuchi*

King Kong Lives ★ PG

1986 US Colour 100mins

As if the 1976 remake of *King Kong* wasn't bad enough, director John Guillermin sinks to even more ludicrous depths with this awful sequel. The giant ape didn't die when he fell off the World Trade Centre ten years earlier, and now Linda Hamilton leads a surgical team attempting to revive him with a giant artificial heart. Meanwhile, back in the jungle, Indiana Jones-style adventurer Brian Kerwin has discovered a female Kong – with breasts! Although there is some demented fun to be had – the transplant operation uses laughably over-sized props – this couldn't be worse if it tried.

Brian Kerwin Hank Mitchell • **Linda Hamilton** Amy Franklin • **Peter Elliot** King Kong • **George Yiasoumi** Lady Kong • **John Ashton** Colonel Nevitt • **Peter Michael Goetz** Dr Ingersoll • **Frank Maraden** Dr Benson Hughes
Director *John Guillermin*
Screenplay *Steven Pressfield, Ronald Shusett, from characters created by Merian C Cooper, Edgar Wallace*

King Kong vs Godzilla ★★★ PG

1962 Jap Colour 87mins

Based on an early draft script by *King Kong* creator Willis O'Brien, and completely rewritten by the Japanese as a co-starring vehicle for their own monster hero Godzilla, director Inoshiro Honda's clash of the pop culture titans works more as an engagingly silly comedy more than a fully-fledged fantasy. After defeating a giant octopus threatening Japanese fishermen, Kong is drugged with narcotic berries and flown to Tokyo. Meanwhile Godzilla is woken up from frozen hibernation by an atomic sub and heads for the capital, where he battles Kong at Mount Fuji. Honda's allegory of Japanese-American political rivalries falls fast from that lofty perch and indulges in what Asian monster movies do best – loud body-bashing and epic landmark destruction. Additional footage, starring Michael Keith and others, was directed by Thomas Montgomery for the American market. A Japanese language film.

Michael Keith Eric Carter • **James Yagi** Yataka Omura • **Tadao Takashima** O Sakurai • **Mie Hama** Fumiko Sakurai • **Yu Fujiki** Kinzaburo Furue
Director *Inoshiro Honda, Thomas Montgomery*
Screenplay *Bruce Howard, Paul Mason, Shinichi Sekizawa, from a story by Willis O'Brien*

King of the Rocket Men ★★

1949 US BW

The serial was entering its twilight zone when this hackneyed 12-part Republic chapterplay was released. There are some deliciously camp touches – Mae Clarke's magazine is called *Miracle Science* and Tristram Coffin's other-worldly rocket suit has switches labelled "On", "Up" and "Fast". But not even the prospect of seeing the maniacal Dr Vulcan use James Craven's stolen Decimator to inflict an earthquake and a tidal wave upon New York will entice you towards the edge of your seat. The flying sequences and the disaster effects are adequate, but the spot-the-villain contest is a non-starter.

Tristram Coffin Jeff King • **Mae Clarke** Glenda Thomas • **Don Haggerty** Tony Dirken • **I Stanford Jolley** Prof Bryant/Dr Vulcan • **James Craven** Prof Millard • **House Peters Jr** Burt Winslow • **Douglas Evans** Chairman
Director *Fred C Brannon*
Screenplay *Royal Cole, William Lively, Sol Shor*

Kingdom of the Spiders ★★★ PG

1977 US Colour 90mins

Angered by pesticides, swarms of tarantulas attack an Arizona town in this neat low-budget chiller, directed by dependable B-movie veteran John "Bud" Cardos. William Shatner, in one of his better non-*Star Trek* roles, plays a veterinarian who joins forces with insect expert Tiffany Bolling to ascertain why nature has once more run amok in the grand tradition of *The Birds*. The creepiness is made credible by an above-average script and some admirable staging. Arachnophobes, beware!

William Shatner Rack Hansen • **Tiffany Bolling** Diane Ashley • **Woody Strode** Walter Colby • **Lieux Dressler** Emma Washburn • **David McLean** Sheriff Gene Smith • **Natasha Ryan** Linda Hansen •
Director *John "Bud" Cardos*
Screenplay *Richard Robinson, Alan Caillou, from a story by Jeffrey M Sneller, Stephen Lodge*

Kinvig ★★★

TV 1981 UK Colour 7x30mins

An odd sit-com from Nigel Kneale, which slightly alienated its potential audience by confusing UFO conspiracy nuts with science-fiction fans, but did get some strange laughs from the situation of Tony Haygarth, a put-upon electrical engineer who escapes from his nagging wife Patsy Rowlands by obsessing over alien-themed paranoid theories with his tag-along friend Colin Jeavons. Into Haygarth's life comes Prunella Gee, a customer whom he imagines to be a dominatrix from Mercury and who whirls him off to adventures among the stars, eventually thwarting an invasion by the insectile Xux. Kinvig, like Kneale's Quatermass, has an unusual Manx name, and much of the show's humour comes from the uncomfortable possibility that he's having a breakdown and is as cracked as his wife thinks he is.

Tony Haygarth Des Kinvig • **Prunella Gee** Miss Griffin • **Patsy Rowlands** Netta Kinvig • **Colin Jeavons** Jim Piper • **Patrick Newell** Mr Horsley • **Simon Williams** Buddo • **Danny Schiller** Sagga • **Stephen Bent** Loon • **Alan Bodenham** Bat
Director *Les Chatfield, Brian Simmons*
Written by *Nigel Kneale*
Producer *Les Chatfield*

The Kirlian Witness ★★

1978 US Colour 91mins

A very odd fantasy thriller made by one-time workers in the hard-core pornography industry. A plant is the sole witness to a murder and Nancy Snyder, the victim's sister, uses her telepathic powers and sensitivity to flora to unmask the killer. Kirlian photography, capturing the aura around a living object, is used to solve the case. Slow, moody and just plain weird.

Nancy Snyder Rilla • **Ted Laplat** Dusty • **Joel Colodner** Robert • **Nancy Boykin** Laurie • **Lawrence Tierney** Detective • **Maia Danziger** Claire
Director *Jonathan Sarno*
Screenplay *Jonathan Sarno, Lamar Sanders, from a story by Jonathan Sarno*
Producer *Jonathan Sarno*

Knight Rider 2000 ★★

1991 US Colour 91mins

Viewers tuning into this feature-length spin-off from the popular eighties TV series will split their sides at this nineties version and its depiction of the year 2000 (yes, David Hasselhoff is still something of a fashion victim), which finds Michael Knight being called out of retirement in a suspiciously crime-free Los Angeles. There is only one problem – his beloved KITT car is now scrap metal. As well as Hasselhoff, Edward Mulhare and the voice of William Daniels (as KITT) have transferred from the series, so fans of the original will be delighted. And the writers also got something

Costume drama: despite an other-wordly space suit and some interesting special effects, *King of the Rocket Men* failed to ignite the screens

right: the plot predates the very similarly themed *Demolition Man*.

David Hasselhoff Michael Knight • **Edward Mulhare** Devon • **Susan Norman** Shawn • **Eugene Clark** Kurt • **Megan Butler** Marla Hedges • **Carmen Argenziano** Russell Maddock • **Lou Beatty Jr** Harold Abbey • **Robert F Cawley** Prison guard
Director *Alan J Levi*
Screenplay *Rob Hedden, from characters created by Glen A Larson*

Knight Rider 2010 ★★ PG

1994 US Colour 86mins

Even now, somewhere in the world, there is undoubtedly someone watching a rerun of the series that featured David Hasselhoff and his smart aleck car. Such improbable global success has resulted in a fair few attempts to breathe new life into the concept. This unremarkable adventure, set in a post-apocalypse world where vehicles are in short supply, bears only a passing resemblance to the original and the absence of Hasselhoff is a blessing in disguise.

Richard Joseph Paul Jake McQueen • **Heidi Leick [Hudson Leick]** Hannah • **Brion James** Jared • **Michael Beach** Will McQueen
Director *Sam Pillsbury*
Screenplay *John Leekley*

Knights ★★ 15

1993 US Colour 90mins

Former world kick-boxing champion Kathy Long has probably been seen by more people as a stunt double for the likes of Michelle Pfeiffer in *Batman Returns*; here, however, she gets to take centre stage in this futuristic thriller about the battle between humans and vampiric cyborgs. She throws long punches, grapples and kicks her little socks off, while Kris Kristofferson and Lance Henricksen provide a bit of class as good and bad robots, respectively.

Kris Kristofferson Gabriel • **Lance Henriksen** Job • **Kathy Long** Nea • **Scott Paulin** Simon • **Gary Daniels** David • **Nicholas Guest** Farmer • **Clare Hoak** Mother
Director/Screenplay *Albert Pyun*

Kolchak: The Night Stalker ★★★★

TV 1974-1975 US 20x60mins

Quite simply one of the best TV fantasy shows produced in America in the seventies, and almost the precursor to *The X Files*. The format was simple: crime reporter Carl Kolchak, played with bemused charm by Darren McGavin, encounters each week some monster or supernatural presence from werewolves to zombies, Jack the Ripper to UFOs. Naturally he has trouble convincing the police or his boss of their existence so must combat them alone. Cleverly the "monsters" were largely kept in the shadows, an enforced necessity due to budget restrictions and network concerns that they may prove too intense for audiences. Born out of two highly successful TV movies, *The Night Stalker* (1971) and *The Night Strangler* (1973), the series – surprisingly – did badly and was cancelled after just one season.

Darren McGavin Carl Kolchak • **Simon Oakland** Tony Vincenzo • **Ruth McDevitt** Emily Cowles • **Jack Grinnage** Ron Updike
Created by *Jeff Rice*

Konga ★★ PG

1960 UK Colour 85mins

Michael Gough as a botanist inventing a growth serum, a ratty zip-up gorilla suit, Margo Johns as a comely housekeeper, a miniature cardboard Big Ben and pop star Jess Conrad! What more could you want in a cheap and cheerful British *King Kong* imitation originally titled *I Was a Teenage Gorilla*? With its crude horror always verging on the farcical, the entertainment value in this hilarious monkey business stems from the sheer incompetence on full view. Enjoyably terrible and filmed on location in Croydon High Street.

Michael Gough Dr Charles Decker • **Margo Johns** Margaret • **Jess Conrad** Bob Kenton • **Claire Gordon** Sandra Banks • **Austin Trevor** Dean Foster
Director *John Lemont*
Screenplay *Herman Cohen, Aben Kandel*

The Kraken Wakes ★★★

Radio 1998 UK 90mins

A good, feature-length adaptation of John Wyndham's 1953 novel of alien invasion, this combines light satire with surreal despair. The aliens (Xenobathites) land in the deeps of the world's oceans and set about sinking shipping, "shrimping" for human specimens from coastal areas (an especially gruesome sequence, with tentacular sound effects) and raising the sea level to drown humanity. The story is told from the viewpoint of a flirtatious pair of married reporters, Jonathan Cake and Saira Todd, whose circle of friends allow for various frivolous or paranoid approaches to the alien attack, which is dismissed as a Russian offensive or a silly season news story until it's too late.
Available on audio-cassette.

Jonathan Cake Mike • **Saira Todd** Phyl • **David Fleeshman** Freddie • **Russell Dixon** Dr Bocker • **William Oxborrow** Captain Winters • **Malcolm Hebden** Mallarby • **John Branwell** Bennell • **Kathryn Hunt** Tuny
Director *Susan Roberts*

The Krofft Supershow ★★

TV 1976-1978 US Colour

From the stables of Sid and Marty Krofft, creators of *HR Pufnstuf*, came this seventies musical variety series. In much the same way as *The Banana Splits*, the programme combined linking material with insert episodes of other shows. Hosts for the series were Kaptain Kool (Michael Lembeck) and the Kongs. The first season featured inserts of *Electra Woman and DynaGirl* (Deidre Hall and Judy Strangis fighting crime as the leotard-and-tights-clad superheroines who pose as magazine writers by day), *Dr Shrinker* (Jay Robinson is the traditionally evil scientist), and repeats of *The Lost Saucer*. In 1978 the show moved to NBC and pop group the Bay City Rollers were brought in to host it, but it was cancelled four months later.

Michael Lembeck Kaptain Kool • **Deirdre Hall** Lori/ElectraWoman in *ElectraWoman and DynaGirl* • **Judy Strangis** Judy/DynaGirl in *ElectraWoman and DynaGirl* • **Norman Alden** Prof Frank Heflin in *ElectraWoman and DynaGirl* • **Jay Robinson** Dr Shrinker in *Dr Shrinker* • **Jeff McKay** Gordie in *Dr Shrinker* • **Susan Lawrence** BJ in *Dr Shrinker* • **Ted Eccles** Brad in *Dr Shrinker* • **Billy Barty** Hugo in *Dr Shrinker*
Producer *Sid Krofft, Marty Krofft*

Kronos ★★★

1957 US BW 78mins

An enormous alien robot lands off the California coast and tramples on everything in sight as it advances towards Los Angeles on an energy-sucking spree. Despite its reliance on stock footage, cost-cutting special effects (mainly large-size props) and average direction – by *The Fly's* Kurt Neumann – this unusually slanted invasion thriller is a perfect example of engagingly deranged fifties B movie-making. A minor classic with the cube-like heavy metal conqueror relieving the occasional bouts of tedium where arch scientists Jeff Morrow and Barbara Lawrence race to save the Earth from total destruction.

Jeff Morrow Dr Leslie Gaskell • **Barbara Lawrence** Vera Hunter • **John Emery** Dr Eliot • **George O'Hanlon** Dr Arnie Culver • **Morris Ankrum** Dr Albert R Stern •
Director *Kurt Neumann*
Screenplay *Lawrence Louis Goldman, from a story by Irving Block*

L

Danger! Danger! The Space Family Robinson

Lost in Space 1965-1968

Laboratory ★

1980 US Colour

More science-fiction junk from the specialist shoestring-budget duo of directors Allan Sandler and Robert Emenegger. On a sleep-inducing par with their epic *The Killings on Outpost Zeta*, this obscurity finds humanoid aliens abducting assorted earthlings and placing them under observation in a desert research facility. And then... nothing happens! Excruciating low-grade trash.

Camille Mitchell • **Corinne Michaels** • **Garnett Smith**
Director *Allan Sandler, Robert Emenegger*

Ladron de Cadaveres ★★★★

1956 Mex BW 80mins

The Mexican fantasy film industry is largely unknown internationally aside from the cult horror wrestler series featuring Santo. But one of Mexico's most popular masked wrestler stars, Wolf Ruvinskis, whose Neutron character became a national hero, made his name in this visually-rich mix of classic monster themes and literary references directed with flamboyant verve by Fernando Mendez. Mad doctor Carlos Riqueleme is transplanting animal brains into fresh corpses and when he puts an ape's one into Ruvinskis's body it makes the tortured wrestler search for his lover Columba Dominguez before losing all memory of her. Packed with *grand guignol* incident, bizarre horror and unforgettable Gothic images, all given a Latin twist, this impressively expressionistic romance is one of the best Mexican fantasy films. A Spanish language film,

Columba Dominguez Lucia • **Crox Alvarado** Captain Carlos Robles • **Wolf Ruvinskis** Guillermo Santana • **Carlos Riquelme** Don Panchito • **Arturo Martinez** Felipe Dorantes
Director *Fernando Mendez*
Screenplay *Fernando Mendez, Americo Verbitzky*

The Lady and the Monster ★★

1944 US BW 86mins

The first of several adaptations of Curt Siodmak's cult novel *Donovan's Brain* was brought to the screen by Republic boss Herbert Yates as a change of pace for Vera Hruba Ralston, the Czech figure skater he would eventually marry. However, the only memorable thing about this laboured lobotomy romp is John Alton's disconcerting expressionist images and Erich von Stroheim's gleefully deranged showboating as the scientist detailed to keep alive the criminal brain of a ruthless millionaire. Sadly, Ralston's approximation of terror, as her lover Richard Arlen is possessed by the brain's malignant spirit and goes on a vengeful killing spree, is remembered only for its ineptitude.

Vera Hruba Ralston [Vera Ralston] Janice Farrell • **Richard Arlen** Patrick Cory • **Erich von Stroheim** Prof Franz Mueller • **Helen Vinson** Chloe Donovan • **Mary Nash** Mrs Fame • **Sidney Blackmer** Eugene Fulton • **Janet Martin** Café singer
Director *George Sherman*
Screenplay *Frederick Kohner, Dane Lussier, from the novel "Donovan's Brain" by Curt Siodmak*

Land of the Giants ★★★

TV 1968-1970 US Colour 51x60mins

Last of the run of sci-fi shows Irwin Allen produced before becoming the big screen's disaster specialist in the early seventies, this offered impressive effects and props, a silly premise and bland storylines for two seasons. In the near future (1983), the spaceliner *Spindrift* passes through "a space warp" and strands a small group of earthlings on an Earth-like planet where they are the size of mice. They are of some interest to the giant human beings who live under an oppressive totalitarian regime much like those intended to represent eastern block states in *Mission: Impossible* (giants had non-specific foreigner character names like "Thorg", "Krenko" and "Gorn"). Yet another *Fugitive* variant, this used secret policeman Kobick (Kevin Hagen) as an occasional pursuer figure, but also played whiny businessman Alexander Fitzhugh (Kurt Kasznar) as the Dr Smith character whose scheming ineptitude got the straighter heroes – Gary Conway, Don Marshall, Heather Young, Don Matheson and Deanna Lund – into trouble.

Gary Conway Capt Steve Burton • **Don Matheson** Mark Wilson • **Don Marshall** Dan Erickson • **Stefan Arngrim** Barry Lockridge • **Deanna Lund** Valerie Scott • **Heather Young** Betty Hamilton • **Kurt Kasznar** Alexander Fitzhugh • **Kevin Hagen** Inspector Kobick
Producer *Irwin Allen*

Land of the Lost ★★★

TV 1974-1976 US Colour 43x30mins

In the seventies, producers Sid and Marty Krofft (*HR Pufnstuf*) took over from Irwin Allen as the prime source of juvenile sci-fi and fantasy – although their work was explicitly confined to the ghetto of Saturday morning kidvid. This was their magnum opus, a kind of *Lost in Time* answer to *Lost in Space* (with elements of *Gilligan's Island* and *The Flintstones*) in which the Marshall family – father Spencer Milligan, kids Wesley Eure and Kathy Coleman, with uncle Ron Harper replacing Dad for the third and last season – fall through a crack in time while on a camping trip along the Colorado river and find themselves in a prehistoric world that owes more to Edgar Rice Burroughs than paleontology. Besides the dinosaurs (some done in impressive stop-motion supervivsed by Gene Warren Jr), the family tangled with the Pakuni, a tribe of shaggy missing links, and the Sleestaks, a race of lizard-men, not to mention Grumpy the T-Rex (a semi-comic foil always failing to eat them) and Dopey the baby brontosaurus (a pet). In Season Two, Enik (Walker Edmiston), an intelligent time-travelling Sleestak, shows up to explain in surprisingly complex sci-fi terms that the Lost Land was a pocket universe created by his own people. Among the well-known writers recruited to script segments (mostly in the first two seasons before the show deteriorated into self-parodic cheapness) were Norman Spinrad, Larry Niven, Ben Bova, Theodore Sturgeon, Donald F Glut, DC Fontana and David Gerrold, although Walter ("Chekhov") Koenig also wrote an episode. Even the children who were the main audience wondered how come the Marshalls' trusty Bic lighter never ran short of fuel.

Spencer Milligan Rick Marshall • **Wesley Eure** Will Marshall • **Kathy Coleman** Holly Marshall • **Ron Harper** Uncle Jack • **Phillip Paley** Cha-Ka • **Walker Edmiston** Enik
Producer *Sid Krofft, Marty Krofft*

Land of the Lost ★★ U

TV 1991-1992 US Colour 26x30mins

A revival of the seventies Sid and Marty Krofft show, with a new lost family, the Porters – Dad Timothy Bottoms, kids Jennifer Drugan and Robert Guam. As before, they slipped through time into a fantastical prehistoric world where dinosaurs co-exist with cavemen and humanoid reptiles. A new addition, reflecting an appeal to slightly older boys, was Shannon Day, as a Sheena-like jungle girl in the regulation fur bikini, and more regulars included Tasha, a baby dinosaur (Ed Gale in a suit, voiced by Danny Mann) and Stink (Bobby Porter), a caveman. Less ambitious scientifically than the earlier incarnation, this ambled through two seasons of unexceptional episodes (some directed by effects man John Carl Buechler) before cancellation. While the original family clung to their prized Bic lighter, the Porters had more high-tech survival gear, including a video camera.

Timothy Bottoms Tom Porter • **Jennifer Drugan** Annie Porter • **Robert Guam** Kevin • **Shannon Day** Christa • **Ed Gale** Tasha • **Bobby Porter** Stink • **Danny Mann** Voice of Tasha
Story editor *Len Janson*
Producer *Marty Kroff, Sid Krofft, Len Janson, Chuck Menville*

SCI Q • SCI Q • SCI Q • SCI Q •

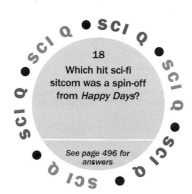

18
Which hit sci-fi sitcom was a spin-off from *Happy Days*?

See page 496 for answers

The Land That Time Forgot ★★ PG

1974 UK Colour 86mins

The first, and worst, of the trilogy of Edgar Rice Burroughs lost world adventures produced by Amicus, despite the fact that it was co-scripted by sci-fi giant Michael Moorcock. A First World War submarine discovers an uncharted South American haven for dinosaurs, cavemen and volcanoes in director Kevin Connor's excessively fake and slipshod saga. Doug McClure is out of his depth as the heroic lead, and the puppet monsters – a phoney amalgam of prop heads and men in rubber suits dangling on wires – are just as weak.

Doug McClure Bowen Tyler • **John McEnery** Captain Von Schoenvorts • **Susan Penhaligon** Lisa Clayton • **Keith Barron** Bradley • **Anthony Ainley** Dietz • **Godfrey James** Borg • **Bobby Farr** Ahm • **Declan Mulholland** Olson • **Colin Farrell** Whiteley • **Ben Howard** Benson • **Roy Holder** Plesser • **Andrew McCulloch** Sinclair
Director *Kevin Connor*
Screenplay *James Cawthorn, Michael Moorcock, from the novel by Edgar Rice Burroughs*

The Land Unknown ★★

1957 US BW 78mins

A really cheesy sci-fi drama with Jock Mahoney, a TV star and one-time Tarzan, down in the frozen wastes of Antarctica where dinosaurs frolic around a hot water oasis, apparently discovered in 1947. This is *The Lost World* on ice, with an entire menagerie of monsters, including the pantomime villain T-Rex as well as the flying pterodactyl, which brings down our hero's helicopter in the opening scenes. Shawn Smith adds some romantic interest as a newshound whose clothes become more sparse, while Henry Brandon is the man who's been this way before and clearly left his marbles behind.

Jock Mahoney Commander Hal Roberts • **Shawn Smith** Margaret Hathaway • **William Reynolds** Lieutenant Jack Carmen • **Henry Brandon** Hunter • **Phil Harvey** Steve Miller • **Douglas Kennedy** Captain Burnham
Director *Virgil Vogel*
Screenplay *Laszlo Gorog, from a story by Charles Palmer*

The Langoliers ★★ 15

TV 1995 US Colour 179mins

Ten airline passengers awaken from a mid-flight sleep to find that everyone else aboard their plane has gone missing. As the "survivors" attempt to work out what happened, they become increasingly convinced that they are being pursued by a strange force. Based on a Stephen King novella, Tom Holland's mini-series takes off on an extremely promising note, but its slow plotting soon becomes tedious and its final touchdown lacks any real impact. Still, there are plenty of genuinely chilling moments along the way, and the cast offer a suitably scared and sympathetic response to their characters' dilemmas.

Patricia Wettig Laurel Stevenson • **Dean Stockwell** Bob Jenkins • **David Morse** Brian Engle • **Mark Lindsay Chapman** Nick Hopewell • **Frankie Faison** Don Gaffney • **Baxter Harris** Rudy Warwick • **Kimber Riddle** Bethany Simms • **Christopher Collet** Albert Kaussner • **Kate Maberly** Dinah Bellman • **Bronson Pinchot** Craig Toomy • **Tom Holland** Harker
Director *Tom Holland*
Teleplay *Tom Holland, from the novella "From Four Past Midnight" by Stephen King*

Laserblast ★

1978 US Colour 80mins

This low-budget sci-fi drama appears to have been shot in director Michael Rae's back garden and living room. When teenager Kim Milford finds a laser gun left behind by visiting aliens he decides to wreak vengeance on those who have been making his life a misery. The action seems to consist mainly of cars being blown up, leading one to surmise that Rae must have had a deal going on with a local second-hand car dealer. This isn't as interesting as it sounds and is executed with little imagination or feeling for the genre, although the stop-motion effects are fun and Roddy McDowall makes a pleasing guest appearance. There's also a nice moment when a billboard poster for *Star Wars* bites the dust.

Kim Milford Billy Duncan • **Cheryl Smith** Kathy Farley • **Gianni Russo** Tony Craig • **Ron Masak** Sheriff • **Dennis Burkley** Pete Ungar • **Barry Cutler** Jesse Jeep • **Keenan Wynn** Colonel Farley • **Roddy McDowall** Dr Mellon
Director *Michael Rae*
Screenplay *Franne Schacht, Frank Ray Perilli*
Producer *Charles Band*

The Laserman ★★★

1988 US/HK Colour 92mins

Mixing sci-fi spoof with a sermon about the proliferation of weapons, this is a hit-and-miss affair from writer/director Peter Wang, who is best known for his gentle comedy drama *A Great Wall*. Wang also appears as a New York cop, whose scientist friend Marc Hayashi gets embroiled in a sinister plot involving his laser gun project. There are some neat cultural insights and, fittingly, as Wang is on Woody Allen's Manhattan stomping ground, there is an interfering Jewish mother who makes Allen's mama from *New York Stories* look like a beginner. Notably, the associate producer is the celebrated Hong Kong director Tsui Hark. Contains brief nudity and strong language.

Marc Hayashi Arthur Weiss • **Maryann Urbano** Jane Cosby • **Tony Kar-Fai Leung [Tony Leung]** Joey Chung • **Peter Wang** Lieutenant Lu • **Joan Copeland** Ruth Weiss • **George Bartenieff** Hanson
Director/Screenplay *Peter Wang*
Producer *Peter Wang* • ***Associate producer*** *Tsui Hark*

The Last Battle ★★★★ 15

1983 Fr BW 92mins

With his first feature – an arresting poetic vision of post-apocalyptic Paris after an unspecified cataclysm has reduced the earth to a desolate wasteland – director Luc Besson laid the groundwork for *The Fifth Element* and began his long relationship with actor Jean Reno. Four survivors battle for the future of mankind in this stark alternative to *Mad Max*, which conveys its raw emotions in carefully orchestrated, black-and-white visuals without any dialogue (poisonous gases having rendered the characters' vocal chords useless). It's a remarkable achievement that deals with hackneyed holocaust clichés on a compelling, humanistic and touching plane.

Pierre Jolivet Young man • **Jean Bouise** Old doctor • **Fritz Wepper** Gang leader • **Jean Reno** Swordsman
Director *Luc Besson*
Screenplay *Luc Besson, Pierre Jolivet*

The Last Chase ★★

1981 US Colour 101mins

A hymn to that most American of institutions: the car. Set in the near future, this reactionary riposte to the green movement has Lee Majors achieving heroic status when he defies the authorities by driving his banned gas-guzzler across the country. Burgess Meredith is the wily pilot detailed to stop him. Hugely funny, although for all the wrong reasons.

Lee Majors Frank Hart • **Burgess Meredith** Captain Williams • **Chris Makepeace** Ring • **Alexandra Stewart** Eudora • **George Touliatos** Hawkings
Director *Martyn Burke*
Screenplay *C R O'Christopher, Taylor Sutherland, Martyn Burke, from the story by CR O'Christopher*

Last Days of Planet Earth ★★★

1974 Jap Colour 90mins

Michel de Nostradamus's prediction about the world ending in July 1999 has proved to be wide of the mark. But with warnings about global warning continuing to go unheeded, there's an eerie prescience about Toshio Masuda's catastrophic vision. With giant slugs turning the seas red, vegetation mutating and monsters roaming the desolate wilderness, this can either be viewed as a dire portent of biospheric and civil meltdown or as a camp classic. A vaguely similar scenario informs *Nostradamus: Fearful Prediction* (1995), which was sponsored by a religious cult and was, unusually for a Japanese film, directed by a woman, Yumiko Awaya. Japanese dialogue dubbed into English.

Tetsuro Tamba Dr Nishiyama • **Toshio Kurosawa** Akira • **So Yamamura** Prime Minister • **Kaoru Yumi** Mariko Nishiyama
Director *Toshio Masuda*
Screenplay *Toshio Yasumi*

Last Lives ★ 18

1997 US Colour 91mins

Billy Wirth, a convict living in a parallel universe, emerges from that dimension to search for Jennifer Rubin, the earthbound soul mate to whom he is psychically connected. When he whisks her away on her wedding day, would-be groom C Thomas Howell goes in hot pursuit armed with an endless supply of life-saving magical wristbands. A poorly scripted sci-fi letdown, it sports lousy special effects and career-worst performances from practically everyone. A virtually unwatchable disaster that reaches lunatic heights with Howell mangled, burnt, blown to bits, dropped from a great height, shot and repeatedly killed so many times it becomes a bad joke.

C Thomas Howell Aaron • **Jennifer Rubin** Adrienne • **Billy Wirth** Malakai • **Judge Reinhold** Merkhan • **Robert Pentz** Khafar • **David Lenthall** Denza • **J C Quinn** Lieutenant Denny Parks • **Richard Fullerton** Roma • **Rick Wagner** Dad • **Talmadge Ragan** Tess
Director *Worth Keeter*
Screenplay *Dan Duling*

The Last Man ★★

1968 Fr BW 82mins

Writer/director Charles Bitsch clearly has little hope for humanity judging by this unpersuasive combination of morality tale and bawdy satire. Emerging from a caving expedition to find himself in a post-apocalyptic wilderness, Jean-Claude Bouillon immediately reverts to stereotype by cheating on his pregnant wife, Sofia Torkeli, with her pretty companion, Corinne Brill. Had Bitsch spent more time exploring the rat-infested ruins of civilisation, this may have been more challenging. But, instead, he's content to string together a checklistof platitudes that reveal little about either the battle of the sexes or man's inability to resist his basest instincts. A French language film.

Jean-Claude Bouillon The husband • **Sophia Torkeli** The wife • **Corinne Brill** The friend
Director/Screenplay *Charles Bitsch*
Cinematographer *Pierre Lhomme*

The Last Man on Earth ★★

1923 US BW

Every post-pubescent male has been wiped out by a mysterious illness and only mountain hermit Earle Foxe has survived. Not surprisingly, his services are required by the rulers of the new matriarchy. But while Congress and the President squabble over his value, the childhood sweetheart who spurned his advances, Derelys Perdue, has realised the error of her ways. Depicting women as either flighty gals or muddle-headed dears, John G Blystone's patronising oddity (which would form the blueprint for the 1933 musical *It's Great to Be Alive*) is of prime interest for the brief appearance of 1910s serial queen Grace Cunard.

Earle Foxe Elmer Smith • **Grace Cunard** Gertie • **Gladys Tennyson** Frisco Kate • **Derelys Perdue** Hattie • **Marion Aye** Red Sal • **Clarissa Selwynne** Dr Prodwell • **Pauline French** Furlong • **Marie Astaire** Paula Prodwell
Director *J G Blystone [John G Blystone]*
Screenplay *Donald W Lee, from the story "Last Man on Earth" published in "Munsey's Magazine" by John D Swain*
Cinematographer *Allan Davey*

SFacts

When presented in the UK for classification in 1924, this pre-Hays Code film was considered too much for the British public and was rejected by the censors.

The Last Man on Earth ★★★

1964 It/US BW 85mins

Based on Richard Matheson's classic horror novel *I Am Legend* (as was the weaker *The Omega Man* in 1971), directors Ubaldo Ragona (Italian version) and Sidney Salkow's (US version) atmospheric shocker marks one of the few times in his macabre movie career that Vincent Price was pitted against a traditional "monster" – in this instance people infected with a mysterious plague that has turned them into vampires. Robert Morgan (Price) is apparently the only living creature immune to the disease, and spends his entire existence rebuffing and killing the undead. But some of the bloodsuckers have found a way of chemically surviving without losing their humanity, and they must erase Morgan, who can't differentiate between the two species. Shot on stark Rome locations (standing in for Los Angeles), Price delivers one of his more restrained performances in this engrossing, superior slice of futuristic horror.

Vincent Price Robert Morgan • **Franca Bettoja** Ruth • **Emma Danieli** Virginia • **Giacomo Rossi-Stuart [Giacomo Rossi Stuart]** Ben Cortman
Director *Ubaldo Ragona, Sidney Salkow*
Screenplay *William P Leicester, Logan Swanson, from the novel "I Am Legend" by Richard Matheson*
Cinematographer *Franco Delli Colli*

The Last Man on Planet Earth ★★ PG

1999 US Colour 85mins

Years after a weapon called the Y-Bomb has wiped out the world's male population, scientist Julie Bowen genetically engineers a (supposedly) violence-free man – but he's not exactly welcome in a land run by man-hating women. This made-for-TV effort has occasional fun with its outlandish premise, but by-and-large it's still far too glum for its own good. Most disappointingly, the movie fails to illustrate how an all-female population might change society, an idea that could have been interesting in the hands of more gifted film-makers.

Julie Bowen Hope Chayse • **Paul Francis** Adam • **L Scott Caldwell** Esther Gray • **Tamlyn Tomita** Agent Kara Hastings • **Nancy Hower** Agent Green • **Veronica Cartwright** Director Elizabeth Riggs
Director *Les Landau*
Screenplay *Kenneth Biller*

The Last Starfighter ★★★★ PG

1984 US Colour 96mins

Lance Guest's prowess at video games is monitored by emissaries from the Star League of the future, who recruit him to defend the universe from evil invaders in this glossy, space-age fairy tale. While highly derivative *Star Trek*-like aliens mix with *Star Wars*-inspired dog-fights against a computer-graphic backdrop, the sensitive love story between Guest and Catherine Mary Stewart cuts through the cuteness and gives the intergalactic adventures a major boost. Children will love it, especially the fun moments with Guest's android double. Contains some strong language.

Lance Guest Alex Rogan • **Dan O'Herlihy** Grig • **Catherine Mary Stewart** Maggie Gordon • **Barbara Bosson** Jane Rogan • **Norman Snow** Xur • **Robert Preston** Centauri • **Kay E Kuter** Enduran • **Chris Hebert** Louis Rogan • **Dan Mason** Lord Kril • **John O'Leary** Rylan Bursar • **Charlene Nelson** Rylan technician
Director *Nick Castle*
Screenplay *Jonathan Betuel*

The Last Train ★★

TV 1999 UK Colour 6x60mins

Called *Cruel Earth* in the United States, this six-part series starred Nicola Walker, Amita Dhiri, Steve Huison, James Hazeldine, Zoe Telford, Chris Fulford, Treva Etienne and Janet Dale as passengers on a train headed from London to Sheffield. As the train goes through a tunnel, a massive meteorite hits the Earth almost destroying it. When the passengers eventually emerge from the tunnel they are faced with the perils of contaminated water, acid rain, no food and feral dogs. As drama, *The Last Train* treads the same territory as *Survivors* and quickly falls into the same mistakes: life is very boring in post-holocaust England, and once you get past the standard tropes, there seems little left on which to hang successive episodes.

Nicola Walker Harriet Ambrose • **Amita Dhiri** Jandra Nixon • **James Hazeldine** Austin Danforth • **Christopher Fulford** Ian Hart • **Treva Etienne** Mick Sizer • **Zoe Telford** Roe Germaine • **Dinita Gohil** Anita Nixon • **Sacha Dhawan** Leo Nixon • **Janet Dale** Jean Wilson • **Steve Huison** Colin Wallis • **Caroline Carver** Hild
Director *Stuart Orme, Alex Pillai*
Written by *Matthew Graham*
Producer *Sita Williams*

The Last Woman on Earth ★

1960 US Colour 64mins

Crooks Anthony Carbone and Ed Wain fight over Betsy Jones-Moreland when they turn out to be the only survivors of a nuclear war in Puerto Rico. Not one of cult director Roger Corman's best efforts, this sci-fi *ménage à trois* tale is cheap, dull and unappealing. "Ed Wain" is the pseudonym of future Oscar-winning screenwriter Robert Towne, who hadn't finished the script (his first) in time and was brought along to complete it on location. Ever the cost-cutter, Corman then had Towne play the second lead, even though he'd never acted before.

Antony Carbone Harold • **Betsy Jones-Moreland** Evelyn • **Edward Wain [Robert Towne]** Martin
Director *Roger Corman*
Screenplay *Edward Wain [Robert Towne]*
Producer *Roger Corman*

SCI Q • SCI Q • SCI Q • SCI Q • SCI Q •

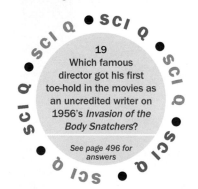

19
Which famous director got his first toe-hold in the movies as an uncredited writer on 1956's *Invasion of the Body Snatchers*?

See page 496 for answers

Late for Dinner ★★ PG

1991 US Colour 88mins

After directing the under-rated action film *The Adventures of Buckeroo Banzai across the Eighth Dimension* and co-writing the explosive spoof *Big Trouble in Little China*, this is something of a comedown for director WD Richter. Brian Wimmer and Peter Berg show why they are fully paid-up members of the "straight-to-video club" as two fugitives who emerge from a 29-year suspended animation experiment to find that (you'll never guess it) the world has moved on since 1962 and they are more than slightly out of place. It takes a while to warm up, but at least it predates Mel Gibson's defrost drama *Forever Young*.

Brian Wimmer Willie Husband • **Peter Berg** Frank Lovegren • **Marcia Gay Harden** Joy Husband • **Colleen Flynn** Jessica Husband • **Kyle Secor** Leland Shakes • **Michael Beach** Dr David Arrington • **Bo Brundin** Dr Dan Chilblains • **Peter Gallagher** Bob Freeman • **Cassy Friel** Little Jessica Husband • **Ross Malinger** Little Donald Freeman • **Steven Schwartz-Hartley** Dwane Gardener
Director *W D Richter*
Screenplay *Mark Andrus*

The Lathe of Heaven ★★★

1979 US Colour 105mins

Bruce Davison's dreams have the power to change reality in a classy adaptation of Ursula K LeGuin's popular novel. Can psychologist Kevin Conway manipulate him into dreaming a better world? Taking on lofty Kafka-esque subtexts, and using Texas landscapes to suggest the future, this subtle fantasy raises pertinent questions about individualism and the march of progress at any cost. Recommended.

Bruce Davison George Orr • **Kevin Conway** Dr William Haber • **Margaret Avery** Heather LeLache • **Peyton Park** Mannie Ahrens • **Niki Flacks** Penny Crouch • **Vandi Clark** Aunth Ethel
Director *David Loxton, Fred Barzyk*
Screenplay *Roger E Swaybill, Diane English, from the novel by Ursula K LeGuin*
Producer *Fred Barzyk*

Latitude Zero ★★★

1969 Jap/US Colour 104mins

The *Godzilla* team of director Inoshiro Honda and special effects genius Eiji Tsuburaya inhabit Jules Verne territory in this absurdly enjoyable underwater fantasy mixing monsters and morality. Submarine commander Joseph Cotton ferries scientists to the underwater city of Latitude Zero, where radiation-immunisation research is being carried out. Cesar Romero is the evil genius who experiments with human brain transplants in animals and whose mission it is to destroy the undersea complex because of its good works. Giant rats, batmen and, weirdest of all, a winged lion with the brain of woman Romero has spurned, are a few of the charms in this delightfully campy combo of Captain Nemo and *The Island of Dr Moreau*.

Joseph Cotten Capt Craig McKenzie • **Cesar Romero** Malic • **Richard Jaeckel** Perry Lawton • **Patricia Medina** Lucretia • **Linda Haynes** Dr Anne Barton • **Akira Takarada** Dr Ken Tashiro • **Masumi Okada** Dr Jules Masson • **Hikaru Kuroki** Kroiga • **Mari Nakayama** "Tsuroko" Okada
Director *Ishiro Honda [Inoshiro Honda]*
Screenplay *Shinichi Sekizawa, Ted Sherdeman, from stories by Ted Sherdeman*
Special effects *Eiji Tsuburaya*
Set decoration *Takeo Kita*

The Lawnmower Man ★★★ 15

1992 UK/US Colour 103mins DVD

Eye-popping special effects are the star of this science-fiction tale, vaguely based on a Stephen King short story, but otherwise notable only for crossing a variation on the Frankenstein theme with a more original attempt to probe the cinematic opportunities offered by "virtual reality". Pierce Brosnan plays a misguided scientist – is there any other kind? – who selects his simple-minded gardener as a guinea pig for his experiments with high-tech teaching aids and intelligence-boosting drugs. The film offers shades of everything from *My Fair Lady* to *Carrie*, but, unlike either, also boasts cinema's first known cybersex scene. Contains violence and swearing.

Jeff Fahey Jobe Smith • **Pierce Brosnan** Dr Lawrence Angelo • **Jenny Wright** Marnie Burke • **Mark Bringleson** Sebastian Timms • **Geoffrey Lewis** Terry McKeen • **Jeremy Slate** Father McKeen • **Dean Norris** Director • **Colleen Coffey** Caroline Angelo
Director *Brett Leonard*
Screenplay *Brett Leonard, Gimel Everett, from the short story by Stephen King*

Lawnmower Man 2: Beyond Cyberspace ★ 12

1995 US Colour 89mins

Stephen King's name is nowhere to be seen and his original concept from the first hit film has also vanished. What's left behind is a tedious slice of confusing science fiction as Matt Frewer (Max Headroom himself) attempts to take over the world through cyberspace in director Farhad Mann's virtual unreality jumble. Scientist Patrick Bergin must stop him, aided by three computer whizkids, with only a barrage of special effects to call on for help. But the flashiest digital technology in the world couldn't disguise this incoherent plot or make up for the fact that not one of the main players comes across with any believability. Contains violence and swearing.

Patrick Bergin Dr Benjamin Trace • **Matt Frewer** Jobe • **Austin O'Brien** Peter
Director *Farhad Mann*
Screenplay *Farhad Mann, from a story by Michael Miner, Farhad Mann, from the film "The Lawnmower Man" by Brett Leonard, Gimel Envett*

The Leech Woman ★★

1960 US BW 77mins

Scientist Coleen Gray goes to Africa in search of eternal youth and learns from a strange tribe that the ageing process can be reversed by drinking secretions from the pineal gland of sacrificial male victims. Her husband is the first dupe to provide the youth serum, but when it wears off she resorts to further murder to top up her supply. This is a workman-like pot-boiler, taking most of its inspiration from other modish chillers of

Virtual reality: incredible special effects helped turn *The Lawnmower Man* into a surprise hit

the day although its faint feminist slant adds an extra touch.

Phillip Terry Dr Paul Talbott • **Coleen Gray** June • **Grant Williams** Neil Foster • **Gloria Talbott** Sally
Director *Edward Dein*
Screenplay *David Duncan, from a story by Ben Pivar, Francis Rosenwald*

Legend of Death ★★★

TV 1965 UK BW 5x25mins

This BBC2 serial provided a fringe sci-fi update of the story of Theseus and the Minotaur, with a father-son-mad scientist conflict reminiscent of *Metropolis*. Industrialist Edward Gargan (John Phillips), sponsor of the Icarus III nuclear-powered aeroplane, is agonised because the project has proved to have an enormous cost in human lives. Instead of a labyrinth, the show focuses on a nuclear power plant on the island of Mitremos, which has been swallowing up 14 volunteers a year. Theodore (David Andrews), Gargan's illegitimate son, joins the latest batch of doomed sacrifices, and discovers that the Minotaur is Dr Minolti (John Hollis), an insane researcher who is exposing victims to radiation to see what happens. The good cast also includes Sarah Lawson, Gerald Sim, Andrew Sachs and Brian Cant. Scripted by Brian Hayles, whose credits range from *Doctor Who* to *The Archers*.

David Andrews Theodore • **John Phillips** Edward Gargan • **Victor Brooks** Finn • **Sarah Lawson** Myra Gargan • **Gerald Sim** Edgarsund • **Andrew Sachs** Dr Zemouron • **Felicity Mason** Yvonne • **James Cossins** Irwin • **Brian Cant** Arnold • **Sheila Hammond** Francesca • **John Hollis** Dr Minolti
Director *Gerald Blake*
Written by *Brian Hayles*
Producer *Alan Bromly*

Legion ★ 18

1998 US Colour 93mins [video]

Ten military prisoners sent to destroy a weapons base come up against a shape-shifting alien who exploits their weaknesses in this lamentable sci-fi appropriation of Agatha Christie's *Ten Little Indians. Deep Space Nine* babe Terry Farrell, erstwhile Brat Packer Corey Feldman and pop star Rick Springfield do their best to spark some life into the clichéd mess, but it's an uphill battle. This sub-standard mixture of *Predator* and *Event Horizon* can't even cover its threadbare plot in gore thanks to its TV movie status. Contains swearing and violence.

Parker Stevenson Aldrich • **Terry Farrell** Major Agatha Doyle • **Corey Feldman** Siegal • **Rick Springfield** Ryan • **Troy Donahue** Flemming • **Audie England** Dr Jones • **Gretchen Palmer** Karlson
Director *Jon Hess*
Screenplay *Evan Spiliotopoulos*

Legion of Fire: Killer Ants! ★★

1998 US Colour

Watching this in the wake of hits such as *Antz* and *A Bug's Life*, it's even harder to keep a straight face through what is already a pretty laughable concept. Eric Lutes and *X Files* regular Mitch Pileggi are among those trying to stop the march of some nasty South American killer ants which are threatening a small town in Alaska. The direction is plodding, the performances from the anonymous cast are pretty dull, and, unless you have a phobia about ants, it's not remotely scary. Contains violence and swearing.

Eric Lutes Dr Jim Conrad • **Julia Campbell** Laura Sills • **Mitch Pileggi** Sheriff Jeff Croy • **Jeremy Foley** Chad Croy • **Dallen Gettling** Bob Hazzard
Director *Jim Charleston*
Screenplay *Linda Palmer, Wink Roberts*

Legion of Iron ★ 18

1990 US Colour 85mins [video]

The story takes place deep under the surface of the earth – where the negative of this clumsy and appallingly cheap movie should be hidden. It promises ample sex and violence – male athletes are kidnapped and forced to fight gladiator-style in a secret underground arena, with sexual rewards for the victors – but fails to deliver. The director misses every opportunity to exploit the material or even place a sense of fun; one big orgy sequence takes place with all its participants hidden under the covers.

Kevin T Walsh Billy Hamilton • **Erika Nann** Diana • **Camille Carrigan** Allison • **Reggie De Morton** Lyle Wagner • **Nelson Anderson** Lopez
Director *Yakov Bentsvi*
Screenplay *Rueben Gordon, Steven Schoenberg, from a story by Edward Hunt*

Lensman ★★ PG

1984 Jap Colour 107mins [video]

Edward E "Doc" Smith's pulp sci-fi novels were among the inspirations behind *Star Wars*. This tale, set in the 25th century, features a young "lensman" who is endowed with mysterious powers to aid him in the fight against the forces of evil. Unfortunately, it's an uninspired amalgam of sci-fi clichés, redeemed only by the animation, which combines traditional hand-drawn artwork with state-of-the-art computer graphics. A real letdown after the brilliant cyber-punk energy of *Akira* did so much to put Japanese *anime* and *manga* on the international map. The American dubbed version was released in 1991. Japanese dialogue dubbed into English.

Edie Mirman Clarisse • **Gregory Snegoff** Admiral Haynes • **Tom Weiner** Zwilk
Director *Yoshiaki Kawajiri, Kazuyuki Hirokawa*
Screenplay *Soji Yoshikawa, from a novel by Edward E "Doc" Smith*
Producer *Tadami Watanabe*

Level 9 ★★

TV 2000-2001 US Colour 12x60mins

This was cancelled before it even got off the starting blocks. The idea was that an *A-Team*-like elite group of investigators probes crimes which take place in Cyberspace. The PR for the show promised *Level 9* would do for the internet what James Cameron did for the *Titanic* and highlighted the endless parade of cyber-criminals that the show, starring a cast of newcomers, would feature. Predictably and somewhat ironically, after the series was cancelled, there sprung up on the internet numerous campaigns to save it.

Kate Hodge Annie Price • **Fabrizio Filippo** Roland Travis • **Kim Murphy** Sosh • **Esteban Powell** Jargon • **Romany Malco** Jerry Hooten • **Susie Park** Joss Nakano • **Michael Kelley** Tibbs • **Max Martini** Jack Wiley
Producer *Jane Bartelme*
Executive producer *Michael Connelly*

Leviathan ★★★ 18

1989 US/It Colour 93mins [video]

As trashy and outstandingly stupid as this underwater *Alien* is, director George Pan Cosmatos does a great job of disguising its huge credibility gaps with a diverting fast pace and superior production design. A team of deep-sea miners discover a Russian shipwreck containing a stash of vodka laced with a genetically-mutated virus which progressively turns them into tentacled half-man, half-fish aqua-Draculas. Every shock twist from *The Fly* to *Jaws* is plumbed by Cosmatos for this enjoyable, if standard, monster scare work-out. You may laugh at the sight of the rubber humanoids from the deep and cringe at Amanda Pays as the Sigourney Weaver clone, but this waterlogged action adventure is adept at milking predictable suspense clichés.

Peter Weller Beck • **Richard Crenna** Doc • **Amanda Pays** Willie • **Daniel Stern**

Sixpack • **Ernie Hudson** Jones • **Michael Carmine** DeJesus • **Lisa Eilbacher** Bowman • **Hector Elizondo** Cobb
Director *George Pan Cosmatos*
Screenplay *David Webb Peoples, Jeb Stuart, from a story by David Webb Peoples*
Producer *Luigi DeLaurentiis, Aurelio DeLaurentiis*

Lexx ★★★ PG 12 15 18

TV 1997 – Can/Ger Colour

Billed as "*Star Trek*'s evil twin" and also known as *Tales from a Parallel Universe*, this is certainly the boldest, darkest and most crass sci-fi comedy-adventure series yet. Its opening four feature length telemovies (1997) and subsequent series revolve around the wacky voyages of the titular *Lexx*, a phallic-shaped living space ship crewed by a lowly security guard, a half-lizard sex slave, a dead assassin and a disembodied robot head. Brian Downey, Michael McManus and Eva Havermann (followed by Xenia Seeberg) do their best in this low-budget and extremely hit-and-miss series, which is absolutely hilarious and insanely imaginatively at times but offensive and downright dull in other places. To its credit, though, the show always strives to present a refreshingly different take on the genre. Fans of the cult series were pleased when a fourth batch of 24 episodes went into production.

Brian Downey Stanley H Tweedle • **Eva Habermann** Zev Bellringer • **Xenia Seeberg** Xev Bellinger • **Michael McManus** Kai • **Jeffrey Hirschfield** Voice of 790 • **Tom Gallant** Voice of the Lexx
Executive producer *Paul Donovan, Wolfram Tichy*

Lifeforce ★ 18

1985 US Colour 97mins

It's hard to believe that Tobe Hooper, director of the influential *The Texas Chain Saw Massacre*, came up with this laughably bad adaptation of Colin Wilson's *The Space Vampires*. Steve Railsback stars as the surviving astronaut from a team that discovers parasitic energy suckers on an invasion course for Earth when they investigate a strange craft lurking in the tail of Halley's Comet. A few interesting special effects help mask the appalling dialogue in the script by Dan O'Bannon, who co-wrote *Alien*, and Don Jakoby, who were clearly having an off day. Rather than the homage to vintage Hammer horror that Hooper wanted to make, the daft result is more a cruel parody; it's not sci-fi as we know it, yet as sheer camp, *Lifeforce* is a "Lifefarce". Contains violence, swearing and nudity.

Steve Railsback Colonel Tom Carlsen • **Peter Firth** Colonel Colin Caine • **Frank Finlay** Dr Hans Fallada • **Mathilda May** Space Girl • **Patrick Stewart** Dr Armstrong • **Michael Gothard** Bukovsky • **Nicholas Ball** Derebridge • **Aubrey Morris** Sir Percy • **Nancy Paul** Ellen • **John Hallam** Lamson
Director *Tobe Hooper*
Screenplay *Dan O'Bannon, Don Jakoby, from the novel "The Space Vampires" by Colin Wilson*

Lifeform ★★

1996 US Colour 90mins

A low-budget science-fiction movie that has its rewards, but falls just short of being a good movie. The emphasis here is not on the special effects, but an intriguing script that doesn't telegraph the plot twists. Essentially, the movie is a take on *Alien*, with an alien loose in a military compound, and the scientists and soldiers on the base trying to stop the menace. The scientists are intelligent and, for once, the military are portrayed in a sympathetic light. Much fun comes with unexpected situations forcing the viewer to reassess what he has just seen. Overall cheap production values, and a truly bad ending stop this from reaching sleeper status.

Cotter Smith Case Montgomery • **Deirdre O'Connell** Dr Gracia Scott • **Robert Wisdom** Col Jesse Pratt • **Ryan Phillippe** Private Ryan • **Raoul O'Connell** Private Jeffers • **Leland Orser** Michael Perkett
Director/Screenplay *Mark H Baker*

Lifepod ★★★ 15

1993 US Colour 84mins

Inspired by Alfred Hitchcock's *Lifeboat*, and co-scripted by Pen Densham, who worked on *Robin Hood: Prince of Thieves*, actor-turned-director Ron Silver's "stranded in space" saga is a great example of stylish, economical film-making. Silver uses claustrophobic tricks to great advantage to tell the tale of survivors escaping aboard an emergency spacepod when their Venusian cruiser explodes. Exciting, fast-moving and containing many memorable twists, this is a neat mix of Agatha Christie whodunit and *Alien* paranoia. Silver also stars, and has given himself a strong supporting cast . Contains violence.

Ron Silver Miles Terman • **Robert Loggia** Daniel Banks • **Adam Storke** Kane • **Jessica Tuck** Clair • **Ed Gale** Q-Three • **Kelli Williams** Rena • **Stan Shaw** Parker • **C C H Pounder** Lieutenant Janna Mayvene
Director *Ron Silver*
Screenplay *M Jay Roach, Pen Densham, from a story by Jo Swerling, from the film "Lifeboat"*

Lifespan ★★★ 18

1975 US/Neth Colour 77mins

Stitching together elements from the Faust and Frankenstein stories, this shoestring thriller posits an intriguing contrast between humanitarian hopes for the elimination of disease and the sinister medical experimentation undertaken by the Nazis. Representing enlightened science is Hiram Keller, who discovers that a dead colleague may have concocted an elixir for eternal life, while the forces of darkness summon up Klaus Kinski, as the deranged industrialist sponsoring the unnatural project. Writer/director Alexander Whitelaw makes atmospheric use of both his Amsterdam locations and the antiseptic interiors that contrast so tellingly with the gloriously Gothic labs of expressionist horror.

Hiram Keller Dr Ben Land • **Tina Aumont** Anna • **Klaus Kinski** Nicholas Ulrich • **Fons Rademakers** Professor Van Arp
Director *Alexander Whitelaw*
Screenplay *Alexander Whitelaw, Judith Rascoe, Alva Ruben*

The Lift ★★★ 15

1983 Neth Colour 94mins

A lift with a mind of its own is the baffling culprit in a series of bizarre office block "accidents" in this rare example of Dutch horror exploitation. Maintenance man Huub Stapel can't find any mechanical fault and, in between soap opera interludes of domestic strife, which greatly diffuse the claustrophobic suspense, eventually uncovers the alarming – if silly – truth. But writer/director Dick Maas does extract every ounce of fear and menace in the final confrontation between man and machine, as the blackened shaft area comes into its own as a credibly frightening setting and the early longueurs are forgotten. Appalling dubbing aside, and the lame double act who pass themselves off as policemen, Maas does manage to shock without a single drop of blood being spilt. Dutch dialogue dubbed into English.

Huub Stapel Felix Adelbaar • **Willeke Van Ammelrooy** Mieke de Beer • **Josine Van Dalsum** Saskia Adelaar • **Piet Romer** Manager • **Gerard Thoolen** 1st Watchman • **Hans Veerman** "Rising Sun" researcher • **Manfred DeGraaf** Estate agent • **Onno Molenkamp** Blind man • **Siem Vroom** Police Inspector
Director/Screenplay *Dick Maas*

Light Years ★★

1988 Fr Colour 83mins

This long-awaited space fantasy from French director René Laloux, creator of the 1973 cult classic *Fantastic Planet*, is a disappointingly weak attempt to blend adult science-fiction with children's fables. The *Heavy Metal* magazine-inspired animation is highly stylised and imaginative, but this tale of a young hero defending a Utopian land from destruction is often too static and laboriously talky to engage young adults fully. Taken up by Harvey Weinstein's Miramax, this American version of the French original was scripted by none other than sci-fi literature alumnus Isaac Asimov and features such stellar voices as Christopher Plummer and Glenn Close.

Glenn Close Ambisextra • **Christopher Plummer** Metamorphis • **Earl Hammond** Blaminhor • **Jennifer Grey** Airelle • **John Shea** Sylvain • **Alexander Marshall** Apod/Man of Metal • **Penn Jillette** Chief of the Deformed • **Bridget Fonda** Historian/Head • **Earl Hyman** Maxum
Director *Harvey Weinstein, René Laloux*
Screenplay *Raphael Cluzel, Isaac Asimov (American version), from the novel "Robots Against Gandahar" by Jean-Pierre Andrevan, adapted by René Laloux*

Light Years Away ★★★

1981 Swi Colour 106mins

With its evocative Irish landscapes and its essentially two-handed approach to the drama, there's a touch of Samuel Beckett about Alain Tanner's reworking of the Daedalus/Icarus myth. Garage owner Trevor Howard takes on the mantle of the ancient Athenian whose son perished while flying too close to the sun, while Mick Ford plays the drifter who becomes his apprentice in the hope of learning the reality of Howard's closely guarded dream. Although it centres on the notion of manned flight, this is more a study of eccentricity and ambition than science fiction. However, Jean-François Robin's photography lends an element of fantasy.

Trevor Howard Yoshka • **Mick Ford** Jonas • **Bernice Stegers** Betty • **Henri Virlojeux** Lawyer • **Odile Schmitt** Dancer • **Louis Samier** Trucker • **Joe Pilkington** Thomas
Director *Alain Tanner*
Screenplay *Alain Tanner, from the novel "La Voie Sauvage" by Daniel Odier*

Link ★ [15]

1986 UK Colour 99mins

Ever wondered what a horror movie would look like made as PG Tips commercial? The answer lies here in this oddity, in which American zoologist Elisabeth Shue arrives at professor Terence Stamp's remote house-cum laboratory to work on his revolutionary simian theories. On the brink of a major breakthrough, he mysteriously disappears, and Shue is left in charge of three gifted chimpanzees. Not hard to guess what's going on as Shue's three wards gradually revert to instinctive laws of the jungle and start a campaign of ludicrous menace. A stab at something different that ends up being highly off-putting monkey business from Hitchcock student Richard Franklin, director of *Psycho II* and *Patrick*.

Terence Stamp Dr Steven Phillip • **Elisabeth Shue** Jane Chase • **Steven Pinner** David • **Richard Garnett** Dennis • **David O'Hara** Tom • **Kevin Lloyd** Bailey
Director *Richard Franklin*
Screenplay *Everett DeRoche, from the story by Lee Zlotoff, Tom Ackerman*
Executive producer *Verity Lambert* •
Producer *Richard Franklin*

Liquid Dreams ★★★ [18]

1992 US Colour 88mins

Set in the not-too-distant future, this is a surprisingly stylish slice of steamy sci-fi, which has a bit more substance than most straight-to-video erotic thrillers. Candice Daly plays a young woman investigating the death of her sister who uncovers a sinister conspiracy behind an adult entertainment complex. Although it veers towards the softcore, it's well acted by the largely unknown cast (but with cameos from Paul Bartel and Mink Stole, among others) and director Mark Manos fashions some disturbing imagery.

Richard Steinmetz Rodino • **Candice Daly** Eve Black • **Juan Fernandez** Juno • **Tracey Walter** Cecil • **Frankie Thorn** Paula • **Paul Bartel** Angel • **James Oseland** Maurice • **Mink Stole** Felix
Director *Mark Manos*
Screenplay *Mark Manos, Zack Davis*

Liquid Sky ★★ [18]

1982 US Colour 107mins

A dirty, funny, perverse and pretentiously over-long look at New York's punk-chic drug culture. An alien spacecraft lands on a Manhattan skyscraper and its inhabitants quickly get hooked on the powdered and sexual thrills indulged in by everyone populating the sordid landscape. Anne Carlisle, playing both male and female leads (don't ask, it's art!), then uses the aliens to vaporise her enemies at the height of their drug-fuelled passions. Indulgent and stylistically over the top to a distracting degree, this self-important put-on is more a fashion extravaganza than a science-fiction movie. The soundtrack is a poseur's delight, too.

Anne Carlisle Margaret/Jimmy • **Paula Sheppard** Adrian • **Bob Brady** Owen • **Susan Doukas** Sylvia • **Otto von Wernherr** Johann • **Elaine C Grove** Katherine
Director *Slava Tsukerman*
Screenplay *Slava Tsukerman, Nina V Kerova, Anne Carlisle*

Little Shop of Horrors ★★★ [PG]

1960 US BW 71mins

One of cult director Roger Corman's best-loved productions, this riotous no-budget comedy horror romp was shot in three-days on a leftover set, according to Hollywood legend. Jonathan Haze is the browbeaten florist's apprentice breeding a carnivorous plant which starts decimating the neighbourhood in Corman's off-beat sick joke. Look out for Jack Nicholson, hilarious as Wilbur Force, the masochistic dental patient reading *Pain* magazine in the waiting room. A hit stage musical followed, as did a glorious remake in 1986.

Jonathan Haze Seymour Krelboined • **Jackie Joseph** Audrey Fulguard • **Mel Welles** Gravis Mushnik • **Myrtle Vail** Winifred Krelboined • **Leola Wendorff** Mrs Shiva • **Jack Nicholson** Wilbur Force
Director *Roger Corman*
Screenplay *Charles B Griffith*
Producer *Roger Corman*

SCI Q

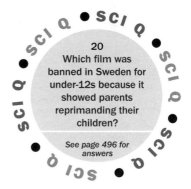

20
Which film was banned in Sweden for under-12s because it showed parents reprimanding their children?

See page 496 for answers

Little Shop of Horrors ★★★★ [PG]

1986 US Colour 89mins DVD

Phil Spector cross-pollinates with Roger Corman (who directed the 1960 version). This rockery horror show is packed with great doo-wop songs, a killer line-up of stars and clever horticultural special effects that underline, but never swamp, the charming theatricality of the stylised whole. The Four Tops' Levi Stubbs voices the alien Venus People-Trap that causes deliciously nerdy Rick Moranis to hack up victims for plant

Seed of change: Jonathan Haze cultivates his own special revenge in the 1960 comedy horror classic *Little Shop of Horrors*

food and impress his Monroe-inspired lover Ellen Greene, who reprises her award-winning off-Broadway role. A memorably weird musical in the grand old Hollywood tradition. Contains violence and swearing.

Rick Moranis Seymour Krelborn • **Ellen Greene** Audrey • **Vincent Gardenia** Mushnik • **Steve Martin** Orin Scrivello, DDS • **Tichina Arnold** Crystal • **Tisha Campbell** Chiffon • **Michelle Weeks** Ronette • **James Belushi** Patrick Martin • **John Candy** Wink Wilkinson • **Christopher Guest** First customer • **Bill Murray** Arthur Denton • **Levi Stubbs** Audrey II

Director *Frank Oz*

Screenplay *Howard Ashman, from the play by Howard Ashman, from the film by Charles B Griffith*

The Living Dead at the Manchester Morgue ★★★

1974 Sp/It Colour 88mins

Night of the Living Dead gets an extreme gore makeover in this high-level Spanish shocker from splatter-maestro Jorge Grau. An experimental pesticide developed by the government not only succeeds in killing bugs, but also raising the corpses in a nearby Manchester hospital. Wooden Ray Lovelock is the hippie hero who tries to stop the flesh-eating hordes after they consume his girlfriend Christine Galbo. Although nauseatingly graphic – bowels ripped open and emptied – Grau's cannibal holocaust is stylishly presented and effectively orchestrated by Giuliano Sorgini's chilling score. One of the most vilified Video Nasty titles of the early eighties.

Raymond Lovelock George • **Christina Galbo** Edna • **Arthur Kennedy** Inpector McCormick • **Jeanine Mestre** Katie • **Jose Lifante** Martin

Director *Jorge Grau*

Screenplay *Sandro Continenza, Marcello Coscia*

Lobster Man from Mars ★★ PG

1989 US Colour 78mins

Borrowing liberally from Mel Brooks's classic *The Producers*, this good-natured spoof of all those drive-in monster movies of the fifties is just about tacky and smart enough to be intermittently enjoyable. Tony Curtis stars as movie mogul JP Shelldrake who, upon being told he needs a flop for tax purposes, sets out to make the biggest howler in Hollywood history. The performances are enthusiastic and suitably ripe, but director Stanley Sheff fails to maintain the high level of inspirational parody that made *Airplane!* and *The Naked Gun* into such comedy classics.

Tony Curtis JP Shelldrake • **Deborah Foreman** Mary • **Patrick Macnee** Professor Plocostomos • **Billy Barty** Throckmorton • **Anthony Hickox** John • **Tommy Sledge** • **Dean Jacobson** Stevie Horowitz • **Fred Holiday** Colonel Ankrum • **Bobby Pickett** King of Mars, the Astrologer

Director *Stanley Sheff*

Screenplay *Bob Greenberg*

Logan's Run ★★★ PG

1976 US Colour 113mins

Michael York and Jenny Agutter star in this tale adapted by David Zelag Goodman from the novel by William F Nolan and George Clayton Johnson that earnestly depicts a society that dooms those over the age of 30

Food for thought: Audrey II makes a real song and dance about feeding time in the 1986 musical version of *Little Shop of Horrors*

to the myth of "renewal". Made 20 years after his *Around the World in 80 Days*, director Michael Anderson takes almost as long to make his point here, but puts on a real spurt when the runners head for the outside, only to find a wrinkled Peter Ustinov living in the ruins of what was Washington DC. Dale Hennesy and Robert De Vestel's Oscar-nominated designs were some compensation for the rather cumbersome plot. Contains some violence and brief nudity.

Michael York Logan • **Jenny Agutter** Jessica • **Richard Jordan** Francis • **Roscoe Lee Browne** Box • **Farrah Fawcett-majors [Farrah Fawcett]** Holly • **Peter Ustinov** Old man
Director *Michael Anderson*
Screenplay *David Zelag Goodman, from the novel by William F Nolan, George Clayton Johnson*

Logan's Run ★★

TV 1977-1978 US Colour 14x60mins

Based on the 1975 Michael York/Jenny Agutter film, this was lauded at the time as being one of the most expensive TV shows ever made, with each episode costing around $400,000. Set in a Utopian future where life is terminated at 30, Logan is a police officer convinced that the law is wrong. He escapes with Jessica, a young rebel girl intent on finding a safe haven, but is pursued by his former partner. Brought to the screen by Ivan Goff, the man behind *Charlie's Angels*, this played like a plodding sci-fi version of *The Fugitive* with Logan and Jessica encountering burgeoning communities, helping them out, only to be forced back on the run to avoid capture. In the end Logan was never caught: TV executives terminated him without prejudice.

Gregory Harrison Logan • **Heather Menzies** Jessica • **Donald Moffat** Rem • **Randy Powell** Francis
Executive producer *Ivan Goff, Ben Roberts*

Lois and Clark: the New Adventures of Superman

★★★★ U PG

TV 1993-97 US Col 1x120m; 86x60m [video]

The Superman legend soared to new heights at the start of this romantic drama series, which its makers accurately dubbed "*Moonlighting* in a cape". A clever reworking on the familiar comic-strip mythos, the show skilfully balances the Man of Steel's super heroics with Clark Kent's attempts to lead a normal life and capture the heart Lois Lane. The show is unbeatable in its flawless first year, which combines surprisingly sophisticated scripting with rich characterisation and outstanding performances from a uniformly strong cast. Unfortunately, its subsequent three seasons are undermined by an emphasis on campy villains and an all-too-apparent failure to sustain the romantic tension between its central characters. Throughout everything, though, Dean Cain makes a suitably super lead, and is beautifully supported by the captivating Teri Hatcher.

Dean Cain Clark Kent/Superman • **Teri Hatcher** Lois Lane • **Lane Smith** Perry White • **Eddie Jones** Joanthan Kent • **K Callan** Martha Kent • **Michael Landes** Jimmy Olsen (series 1) • **Justin Whalin** Jimmy Olsen • **John Shea** Lex Luthor
Developed for TV by *Deborah Joy LeVine,*

from the characters created by Jerry Siegel, Joe Shuster
***Executive Producer** Deborah Joy LeVine, Robert Singer, Randall Zisk*

The Lone Gunmen ★★★

TV 2001 US Colour 12x60mins

The first *X Files* spin-off series reveals what the franchise's resident paranoid computer hackers get up to in-between aiding Mulder and Scully. Best described as *Mission: Impossible* meets *The Three Stooges*, the show follows Byers, Frohike and Langly's comical investigations into the covert conspiracies featured in their underground newspaper, *The Lone Gunman*. Although its blend of high-tech hijinks and crazy comedy isn't as sharp-shooting as it could be, the series remains an entertaining and frequently hilarious piece of frivolous fun. Bruce Harwood, Tom Braidwood and Dean Haglund ensure that the Gunmen's familiar schtick hits the target, while Zuleikha Robinson and Stephen Snedden add some spice to proceedings.

Bruce Harwood John Fitzgerald Byers • **Tom Braidwood** Melvin Frohike • **Dean Haglund** Richard "Ringo" Langly • **Stephen Snedden** Jimmy Bond • **Zuleikha Robinson** Yves Adele Harlow
***Created by** Chris Carter, Vince Gilligan, John Shiban, Frank Spotnitz*
***Executive producer** Chris Carter*

Lone Wolf ★★ 18

1988 US Colour 94mins

Standard horror fare about high school computer hackers and a struggling rock band tracking down a killer terrorising Denver, Colorado, which the police think is a wild dog. The teenagers are convinced the killings are due to a werewolf, while the police force bumble around getting nowhere. A quite gory, but minor, entry in *The Howling*-inspired sweepstakes.

Kevin Hart Joel • **Dyann Brown** Julie Martin • **Jamie Newcomb** Eddie • **Ann Douglas** Deirdre • **Tom Henry** The Wolf
***Director** John Callas*
***Screenplay** Michael Krueger, John Callas, Nancy M Gallanis*

Long Live Life ★★

1984 Fr Colour

According to Claude Lelouch, the idea for this film came to him in a dream on the day that *Edith and Marcel* opened to disastrous reviews. Critics and public alike were exhorted not to reveal the twist ending, only to deprive this psychological sci-fi puzzle of its sole talking point. The nub of the story concerns the claims of businessman Michel Piccoli and actress Evelyne Bouix that they were kidnapped by aliens and sent back to Earth to preach anti-nuclear pacifism. Piccoli's wife, Charlotte Rampling and teacher Jean-Louis Trintignant are among the sceptics bemused by the hokum. In French with English subtitles.

Charlotte Rampling Catherine Perrin • **Michel Piccoli** Michel Perrin • **Jean-Louis Trintignant** Francois Gaucher • **Evelyne Bouix** Sarah Gaucher • **Anouk Aimée** Anouk • **Charles Aznavour** Eduoard
***Director** Claude Lelouch*
***Screenplay** Claude Lelouch*

Looker ★★★★

1981 US Colour 93mins

Way before he cloned dinosaurs in *Jurassic Park*, writer/director Michael Crichton played with similar themes for this under-rated blend of techno horror and suspense. It's a slick sci-fi outing about subliminal advertising, in which plastic surgeon Albert Finney joins pin-up Susan Dey to investigate the deaths of his model clients and their association with advertising agency chief James Coburn. Although it's confusing at times, the design is fabulous, the time-continuum blaster gizmo is a brilliant device allowing Crichton to indulge in some great visual effects and the acting, from Finney especially, is outstanding. Contains nudity.

Albert Finney Dr Larry Roberts • **James Coburn** John Reston • **Susan Dey** Cindy • **Leigh Taylor-Young** Jennifer Long • **Dorian Harewood** Lieutenant Masters
***Director/Screenplay** Michael Crichton*

Lorca and the Outlaws ★★ PG

1985 UK Colour 86mins

One might have expected something a bit more visually arresting from *Alien* art director Roger Christian. Instead what we have is another dreary *Star Wars* clone with a bit of *Mad Max* thrown in about a miner's strike on a remote desert world put down by militaristic police. Despite killer robots and numerous fights and chases, the whole affair is a chaotic bore.

John Tarrant Lorca • **Donogh Rees** Abbie • **Deep Roy** Kid • **Cassandra Webb** Suzi • **Ralph Cotterill** Jowitt
***Director** Roger Christian*
***Screenplay** Roger Christian, Matthew Jacobs*

Lords of the Deep ★ PG

1989 US Colour 74mins

Producer Roger Corman rushed out this cheapie in order to take advantage of the late eighties underwater movie trend, and it makes *DeepStar Six* look as lavish and compelling as *The Abyss*. Once again, we have an underwater crew of a multinational company encountering strange creatures in the brine. Although some of the underwater special effects aren't bad, everything else – the sets, dialogue, and characters – are right out of one of Corman's fifties quickies.

Bradford Dillman Dobler • **Priscilla Barnes** Claire • **Melody Ryane** Barbara • **Daryl Haney** O'Neill • **Eb Lottimer** Seaver
***Director** Mary Ann Fisher*

The Lost City ★★★

1935 US Colour

It's bad enough having to tackle a Ligurian wizard, whose plan to conquer the world involves an army of braindead giants. But when members of your own rescue party turn traitor and try to exploit a kidnapped scientist and his daughter, then a hero's got to play rough. Fortunately, Kane Richmond is able to marshal his wits during the endless turns of Harry Revier's 12-parter and confound the devilish William "Stage" Boyd. It's preposterous fun, although the machine capable of whitening the skin of a tribe of pygmy spidermen is decidedly distasteful.

Kane Richmond Bruce Gordon • **William "Stage" Boyd [William Boyd]** Zolok • **Claudia Dell** Natacha • **Gabby Hayes [George "Gabby" Hayes]** Butterfield
***Director** Harry Revier*
***Screenplay** Perley P Sheehan, Eddie Graneman, Leon D'Usseau*

Lost Continent ★★★ U

1951 US BW Tinted 79mins

Recycling footage from *Rocketship X-M*, producer Sigmund Neufeld and director-brother Sam Newfield (who anglicised his surname) take their time getting down to the nitty gritty of this prototype space-dinosaur hybrid. But once Cesar Romero's rescue party discovers the rocket downed in the depths of an island jungle, the action becomes shrouded in an eerie green tint and the stop-motion brontosaurus and a couple of angry triceratops are called upon to strut their stuff. Although much of the model work is seen in long shot, it's still more than acceptable for such a tightly-costed flick. Well worth the wait.

Cesar Romero Maj Joe Nolan • **Hillary Brooke** Maria Stevens • **Chick Chandler** Lt Danny Wilson • **John Hoyt** Michael Rostov • **Acquanetta** Native girl • **Sid Melton** Sgt Willie Tatlow • **Whit Bissell** Stanley Briggs
***Director** Sam Newfield*
***Screenplay** Richard Landau, from a story by Carroll Young*

The Lost Continent ★★

1968 US Colour 103mins

Director Leslie Norman probably heaved a huge sigh of relief when he parted company with this Hammer stinker just a few days into production. Michael Carreras took over and immediately ran the project on to the cinematic rocks. The story (written by Carreras under the pseudonym Michael Nash) is wonderfully bizarre, with Eric Porter and his crew setting foot on an island ruled by the Spanish Inquisition. But it's the monsters that will have you shrieking with laughter, though, not terror. One of the effects wizards, Robert A Mattey had the last laugh, as he went on to design *Jaws*.

Eric Porter Captain Lansen • **Hildegarde Neff** Eva • **Suzanna Leigh** Unity • **Tony Beckley** Harry Tyler • **Nigel Stock** Dr Webster • **Neil McCallum** First Officer Hemmings
Director *Michael Carreras*
Screenplay *Michael Nash [Michael Carreras], from the novel "Uncharted Seas" by Dennis Wheatley*

Lost in Space ★★★★ U

TV 1965-68 US BW/Colour 83x60mins

In its first (black and white) season, this Irwin Allen-produced sci-fi series was an outer space version of *The Swiss Family Robinson* (its working title was *Space Family Robinson*, following the crew of the *Jupiter 2* – professor Guy Williams, his wife June Lockhart, son Billy Mumy, daughters Angela Cartwright and Marta Kristen and pilot Mark Goddard – after their 1997 colonial expedition to Alpha Centauri goes off course thanks to sabotage and strands them on an inhospitable (if much-visited by guest creatures) planet. However, the show was usurped by camp, with snippy, treacherous stowaway Dr Zachary Smith (Jonathan Harris) and a lumbering robot (voiced by Dick Tufeld) becoming the stars. When the show went to colour in its second outrageous premises became dominant. The memorable theme tune is by John Williams.

Guy Williams Professor John Robinson • **June Lockhart** Maureen Robinson • **Mark Goddard** Don West • **Marta Kristen** Judy Robinson • **Bill Mumy** Will Robinson • **Angela Cartwright** Penny Robinson • **Jonathan Harris** Dr Zachary Smith
Producer *Irwin Allen*

SFacts

Robot was never given a name, although some fans took to calling him Robby (the name of the much-loved robot in *Forbidden Planet*. Both robots, however, were designed by the same man, Robert Kinoshita.

Lost in Space ★★ PG

1997 US Colour 124mins DVD

This big-budget screen version of Irwin Allen's cult sixties TV series is a charmless flash, bang, wallop affair under the too-straightforward direction of Stephen Hopkins. The Robinson family's Earth migration experiment is sabotaged by evil Doctor Smith (Gary Oldman) and they are forced to land on a mysterious planet where time becomes distorted and they encounter mutated monster spiders. Trying to be all things to all audiences results in the children's stuff (the loveable space monkey) annoying adults, while the "family values" sermons bore the kids rigid. The special effects, the nostalgia, the varying tone and the acting (although Matt LeBlanc is an honorary exception) never jell into an enjoyable whole in what is basically a cynical marketing exercise.

William Hurt John Robinson • **Mimi Rogers** Maureen Robinson • **Heather Graham** Judy Robinson • **Lacey Chabert** Penny Robinson • **Jack Johnson** Will Robinson • **Gary Oldman** Dr Smith/Spider Smith • **Matt LeBlanc** Don West • **Jared Harris** Older Will
Director *Stephen Hopkins*
Screenplay *Akiva Goldsman, from the TV series*

The Lost Missile ★

1958 US BW 70mins

"There may be no tomorrow. There maybe no this afternoon". So goes the narration for this lacklustre Cold War fantasy spawned by the nuclear jitters of the fifties. A missile launched somewhere in Eastern Europe circles Earth and, after destroying Ottawa with the heat generated by its 5000-mph speed, homes in on New York. Scientist Robert Loggia invents an atomic missile to destroy it but a battle against time begins when delinquents steal its vital warhead. Perfunctorily directed by William Berke.

Robert Loggia David Loring • **Ellen Parker** Joan Woods • **Larry Kerr** Gen Barr • **Phillip Pine** Joe Freed
Director *William Berke*
Screenplay *Jerome Bixby, John McPartland, from a story by Lester William Berke [William Berke]*

The Lost Planet ★★★ U

1953 US BW 15x16mins

This has the distinction of being the last Hollywood serial to be released in theatres. Essentially, it's a tale of two metals – cosmonium (which the ruler of Planet Ergro, Michael Fox, needs to rule the universe) and dornite (which renders journalist Judd Holdren invisible in times of crisis). As for the rest, it's a standard story about a kidnapped professor, his plucky daughter and various solar-thermo lasers, which only serves to confirm that even the most clued-in villain could never get decent henchmen, as an escaping Dr Grood's cosmojet robot sets his course for infinity instead of deep space.

Judd Holdren Rex Barrow • **Vivian Mason** Ella Dorn • **Gene Roth** Reckow • **Michael Fox** Dr Grood • **Ted Thorpe** Tim Johnson
Director *Spencer Gordon Bennet*
Screenplay *George H Plympton, Arthur Hoerl*

The Lost Planet ★★

TV 1954 UK BW 6x30mins

Angus MacVicar originally scripted this children's hour space opera for BBC Radio in 1952, but it was remade two years later in six fortnightly episodes for TV. The premise was that a group of boffins and hangers-on were cooped up inside an atomic-powered spaceship, en route to the lost planet of Hesikos. The child identification figure was Peter Kerr, tag-along nephew of Scots scientist John Stuart. The crew also had room for stereotypical competent males (Geoffrey Lumsden, John Springett) and equally stereotypical servile females, Mary Law and Joan Allen (not to be confused with the star of *The Contender*).

Peter Kerr Jeremy Grant • **Mary Law** Janet Campbell • **John Stuart** Dr Lachlan McKinnon • **Geoffrey Lumsden** Prof Lars Bergman • **John Springett** Spike Stranahan • **John Pincombe** Kurt Oppenheimer • **Joan Allan** Madge Smith • **Van Boolen** Hermanoff • **Woolfe Morris** Andrieff
Written by *Angus MacVicar, from his radio serial*
Producer *Kevin Sheldon*
Special effects *Reginald Jeffryes*

The Lost Saucer ★★

TV 1975-1976 US Colour 16x30mins

Jim Nabors stars in this ABC series which featured title graphics almost directly lifted from *Lost in Space*. It was therefore not surprising that it was very similar to the Irwin Allen serial. Two androids, Fum and Fee (Nabors and Ruth Buzzi), who hail from the year 2369 land their saucer in modern day Chicago. There they meet young Jarrod Johnson and his babysitter Alice Playten and whisk them off on adventures, never succeeding to find their way home.

Jim Nabors Fum • **Ruth Buzzi** Fi • **Alice Playten** Alice
Producer *Sid Krofft, Marty Krofft*

The Lost World ★★★ U

1925 US BW 107mins

Of great historical interest, this film of Arthur Conan Doyle's novel was a smash hit in 1925 because of its sensational representation of prehistoric creatures by the special effects team headed by Willis O'Brien, who later perfected his skills on *King Kong*. Wallace Beery stars as Professor Challenger, leading an expedition to a South American plateau where an abundance of wild life previously thought extinct still lives. The spectacular finale has a huge brontosaurus, brought back to London, breaking loose and rampaging through the streets. O'Brien combined live action and stop-action animation (in which models are moved fractionally between frame exposures) to fairly convincing effect for the first time. His contribution certainly has a lot more life in it than the hackneyed work of the actors.

Bessie Love Paula White • **Lloyd Hughes** Edward J Malone • **Lewis Stone** Sir John Roxton • **Wallace Beery** Prof Challenger • **Arthur Hoyt** Prof Summerlee
Director *Harry O Hoyt, Earl Hudson*
Screenplay *Marion Fairfax, from the novel by Sir Arthur Conan Doyle*
Cinematographer *Arthur Edeson*
Special effects *Willis H O'Brien*

The Lost World ★★

1960 US Colour 94mins

Long before Steven Spielberg and Michael Crichton got there, the "master of disaster" Irwin Allen had already transported audiences to a lost world author Sir Arthur Conan Doyle's South American plateau forgotten by time. In one of his later roles, Claude Rains leads the cast of lesser stars on an Amazon expedition where they confront a host of magnified pet-shop lizards with plastic fins in a glossy, if conventionally plotted, *Boys' Own* adventure with intermittent thrills. Clips from this would be a mainstay of Allen's TV fantasy series for years to come.

Michael Rennie Lord Roxton • **Jill St John** Jennifer Holmes • **David Hedison** Ed Malone • **Claude Rains** Professor Challenger • **Fernando Lamas** Gomez • **Richard Haydn** Professor Summerlee
Director *Irwin Allen*
Screenplay *Irwin Allen, Charles Bennett, from the novel by Sir Arthur Conan Doyle*

The Lost World ★★

1992 US/Can Colour 99mins

There are so many things wrong with this third cinematic adaptation of Sir Arthur Conan Doyle's novel. It's unbelievably politically correct, the shot-in-Zimbabwe locations make Africa look like southern California, and half the movie goes by before the adventurers even get to the title location. Worst of all, the few dinosaurs we actually get to see have a remarkable rubbery appearance. Yet despite these and many more problems, the movie remains strangely watchable. Much of this credit is thanks to the likable and talented cast, especially the superb John Rhys-Davis, who just may be the best Professor Challenger to date. Followed by *Return to the Lost World*, which was filmed simultaneously.

John Rhys-Davies Prof Challenger • **David Warner** Summerlee • **Eric McCormack** Edward Malone • **Nathania Stanford** Malu
Director *Timothy Bond*
Screenplay *Harry Alan Towers, from the novel by Arthur Conan Doyle*

The Lost World ★★

TV 1999 – US/Can Colour

Definitely not to be confused with Spielberg's *Jurassic Park* sequel, this limp-wristed TV pilot is quite the worst screen interpretation of Sir Arthur Conan Doyle's classic dinosaur novel. Peter McCauley plays Edwardian adventurer Professor Challenger, whose expedition up the Amazon encounters ape-men, man-eating plants and, of course, prehistoric monsters. The family-audience-friendly approach is reminiscent of seventies creature-feature *At the Earth's Core*, only minus the charm. Incredibly, this dud has gone on to spawn a TV series, no doubt thanks in part to the clout of *Blues Brothers* director John Landis in the executive producer's chair.

Peter McCauley Professor Challenger • **Rachel Blakely** Marguerite Krux • **Will Snow** Lord John Roxton • **Jennifer O'Dell** Veronica • **David Orth** Ned Malone
Executive producer *John Landis*

The Lost World: Jurassic Park ★★★ PG

1997 US Colour 123mins DVD

There's another island full of genetically created dinosaurs in director Stephen Spielberg's exuberantly calculated sequel to his own *Jurassic Park*. But while the cloned package does elicit a nagging sense of *déjà vu*, such feelings never get in the way of the overpowering excitement and spectacular special effects, which are served up in deliciously scary dollops. With Richard Attenborough and Jeff Goldblum on hand once more to test the balance of nature off the coast of Costa Rica, Spielberg ensures his epic thrill-ride runs smoothly along well-oiled tracks. Even though the final third of the movie, where the T-Rex rampages through San Diego, seems slightly tacked on, events move at such a breakneck pace there's barely time to think about anything other than screaming in amazement.

Jeff Goldblum Dr Ian Malcolm • **Julianne Moore** Dr Sarah Harding • **Pete Postlethwaite** Roland Tembo • **Arliss Howard** Peter Ludlow • **Richard Attenborough** John Hammond • **Vince Vaughn** Nick Van Owen • **Vanessa Lee Chester** Kelly Curtis • **Peter Stormare** Dieter Stark
Director *Steven Spielberg*
Screenplay *David Koepp, from the novel by Michael Crichton*
Producer *Gerald R Molen, Colin Wilson*

The Lucifer Complex ★

1978 US Colour 87mins

Not so much a movie as an interesting editing exercise. A mountain hiker finds a secret cave containing a super-computer database of mankind's history. After he watches an endless reel of warfare/disaster stock footage with his own morally indignant thoughts as narration, a completely different film begins (apparently an unsold TV series pilot) detailing secret agent Robert Vaughn uncovering a neo-Nazi plot in future 1986 to clone Adolf Hitler and other key figures from the past political world stage. Making no sense whatsoever, and ending with more plot questions than could even be answered by the two directors involved – David L Hewitt and Kenneth Hartford – this cobbled together poor excuse for a proper movie is by dint of its genesis a negligible item.

Robert Vaughn Glenn Manning • **Keenan Wynn** Chief • **Merrie Lynn Ross** April • **Aldo Ray** Karl
Director *David L Hewitt, Kenneth Hartford*

M

NEO: "What are you trying to tell me? That I can dodge bullets?"

MORPHEUS: "No, Neo. I'm trying to tell you that when you're ready, you won't have to."

The Matrix 1999

MacGyver: Lost Treasure of Atlantis ★★

1994 US Colour 96mins

Richard Dean Anderson had 141 cases to solve in the TV series *MacGyver* that screened from 1985–92. However, drug barons, Soviet spies and terrorists were small beer compared to finding the treasure buried in the fabled underwater city of Atlantis. Accompanying the Phoenix Foundation's top agent are Brian Blessed's eccentric archaeologist and a spirited female scholar, played by Sophie Ward, but all eyes are on the man from Mission City, as you'd expect in a film produced by Anderson's own company. Incidentally, Henry "Fonzie" Winkler had a hand in the production.

Richard Dean Anderson MacGyver • **Brian Blessed** Atticus • **Sophie Ward** Kelly Carson • **Christian Burgess** Lord Cyril Cleeve • **Oliver Ford Davies** Professor Simon Carson • **Tim Woodward** Colonel Petrovic • **Kevork Malikyan** Zavros
Director *Michael Vejar*
Screenplay *John Sheppard*

The Machine ★★★ 18

1994 Fr/Ger Colour 91mins

There are strange echoes here of *The Return of Martin Guerre*, in which Nathalie Baye wasn't quite sure if Gérard Depardieu was her husband. In this psychological thriller, Depardieu is Marc, a psychologist with a particular fascination for the criminal mind. He develops a machine that enables him to swap brains with Dider Bourdon, a man convicted of stabbing three women to death. Unfortunately, the experiment becomes permanent: Bourdon's brain is in Depardieu's body. But does his wife, Baye, still recognise him? Grafting bits of *Frankenstein* and *The Island of Dr Moreau* on to *Dr Jekyll and Mr Hyde*, this exercise in schlock provides some effective jolts as Depardieu surfs someone else's brainwaves. A French language film.

Gérard Depardieu Marc • **Nathalie Baye** Marie • **Didier Bourdon** Zyto • **Natalia Woerner** Marianne • **Erwan Baynaud** Leonard
Director *Francois Dupeyron*
Screenplay *Francois Dupeyron, from a novel by René Belletto*

Mad Love ★★★★

1935 US BW 67mins

Peter Lorre made his American debut in this, one of the all-time classic horror stories, the first sound remake of the 1925 silent shocker *The Hands of Orlac*. Colin Clive is the concert pianist given the hands of an executed killer when his own are lost in an accident. Lorre brilliantly conveys twisted compassion and obsessive madness as the surgeon who performs the operation because he loves the pianist's actress wife. A real chiller about psychological fear, made even more effective by Karl Freund's hard-edged poetic direction, way ahead of its time for haunting atmosphere, eerie visuals and imaginative camera technique.

Peter Lorre Doctor Gogol • **Frances Drake** Yvonne Orlac • **Colin Clive** Stephen Orlac • **Ted Healy** Reagan • **Sara Haden** Marie • **Edward Brophy** Rollo • **Henry Kolker** Prefect Rosset • **May Beatty** Francoise • **Keye Luke** Dr Wong • **Isabel Jewell** Marianne
Director *Karl Freund*
Screenplay *Guy Endore, PJ Wolfson, John L Balderston, from the novel "Les Mains d'Orlac " by Maurice Renard*
Cinematographer *Gregg Toland, Chester Lyons* • ***Music*** *Dmitri Tiomkin*

Mad Max ★★★★★ 18

1979 Aus Colour 88mins

It's ironic that *Waterworld* Kevin Costner's post-apocalyptic sci-fi extravaganza turned out to be one of the most expensive movies of all time, given that *Mad Max*, the film everyone said it resembles, was a supremely low-budget affair. Irrespective of the money that was spent, Australian director George Miller's debut feature is a highly inventive, violent action picture, which became an international hit, made a star of Mel Gibson and has spawned two sequels. Gibson is at his mean and moody best as a heroic cop, one of the few who are left trying to hold together a disintegrating society in a bleak and desolate future. Perhaps the reason this vigilante fantasy cost so little was that Gibson was being paid by the word, since he, like the rest of the cast, hardly utters a syllable. What the film lacks in repartee, it makes up for in rip-roaring spectacle, marvellous chase sequences, terrific stunts and natty leather costumes, setting an early example of grunge chic. Throughout, Miller exhibits a striking visual style and his use of fender-level cameras helps crank up the excitement. This is as entertaining as it is simple, and greatly influenced subsequent eighties action fare: the genre was never the same again after Miller's landmark classic. However, the American distributors (AIP) didn't quite know what to make of the dialogue so they dubbed what little Australian speech there was, using American actors. The sequel that followed in 1981 called *The Road Warriors* in the USA used a similar formula with equally sparse dialogue and breathtaking stunts. Miller and Gibson teamed up again for the third instalment *Beyond Thunderdome* in 1985, featuring singer Tina Turner in a leading role.
Interesting facts: 1) Director George Miller started life as a top Australian dentist. He is not to be confused with the other Australian George Miller, director of *The Man from Snowy River* and *The Neverending Story II*.
2) Miller was compelled to make the movie because he lost three of his closest friends in car accidents.
3) Because they ran out of money, the film was edited in Miller's bedroom.
4) Rumours persist that *Mad Max 4* is being considered by Warner Bros and Gibson. Contains violence and swearing.

Mel Gibson Max Rockatansky • **Joanne Samuel** Jessie • **Hugh Keays-Byrne** Toecutter • **Steve Bisley** Jim Goose • **Tim Burns** Johnny the Boy • **Roger Ward** Fifi Macaffee • **Vince Gil** Nightrider • **GeoffParry** Bubba Zanetti • **Paul Johnstone** Cundalini • **John Ley** Charlie • **David Bracks** Mudguts
Director *George Miller*
Screenplay *George Miller, James McCausland, from a story by George Miller, Byron Kennedy*
Producer *Byron Kennedy*

Mad Max 2 ★★★★ 18

1981 Aus Colour 91mins DVD

After the low-budget nihilism of the original movie, director George Miller moved up a gear and the result was this violent, slick and exhilarating action thriller that further launched Mel Gibson into superstardom. His police days now well behind him, Mel the road warrior comes to the aid of a peace-loving group that owns a valuable source of fuel and is being threatened by the voracious gangs that patrol the highways of the future. Gibson is charismatic as the introspective hero and Bruce Spence shines in a supporting role. And, although the quirky details of the original are missed, Miller doesn't take his foot off the accelerator for a second. The ingeniously designed and staged road action is stunning. Contains violence and swearing.

Mel Gibson Max Rockatansky • **Bruce Spence** Gyro captain • **Vernon Wells** Wez • **Emil Minty** Feral Kid • **Mike Preston** Pappagallo • **Kjell Nilsson** Humungus • **Virginia Hey** Warrior woman • **Syd Heylen** Curmudgeon • **Moira Claux** Big Rebecca
Director *George Miller*
Screenplay *Terry Hayes, George Miller, Brian Hannant*

Mad Max beyond Thunderdome

★★★ 15

1985 Aus Colour 102mins DVD

The third in Mel Gibson's sci-fi series is the weakest, but it remains a hugely entertaining futuristic spectacular. This time around Gibson finds himself a reluctant surrogate father to a lost tribe of youngsters, as well as getting mixed up with gladiatorial battles in the thunderdome of the wild city of Bartertown, ruled over by the extraordinary Tina Turner. Directors George Miller and George Ogilvie stage some exhilarating set pieces and keep the action bustling along nicely, even if there are also some daft dollops of new ageism that tend to hold up the proceedings. Gibson is effortlessly charismatic in the lead role, but you can't escape the feeling that, at this late stage in the saga, he just isn't mad enough any more. Contains violence and swearing.

Mel Gibson Mad Max • **Tina Turner** Aunty Entity • **Bruce Spence** Jedediah • **Adam Cockburn** Jedediah Jr • **Frank Thring** The collector • **Angelo Rossitto** The master • **Paul Larsson** The blaster • **Angry Anderson** Ironbar • **Robert Grubb** Pigkiller • **George Spartels** Blackfinger • **Edwin Hodgeman** Dr Dealgood • **Bob Hornery** Waterseller • **Andrew Oh** Ton Ton Tattoo • **Helen Buday** Savannah Nix • **Mark Spain** Mr Skyfish • **Mark Kounnas** Gekko

Director *George Miller, George Ogilvie*

Screenplay *Terry Hayes, George Miller*

Music *Maurice Jarre*

SCI Q • SCI Q • SCI Q • SCI Q •

21

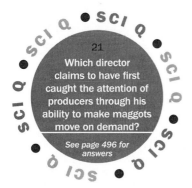

Which director claims to have first caught the attention of producers through his ability to make maggots move on demand?

See page 496 for answers

The Magnetic Monster ★★★

1953 US Colour 75mins

An excellent, low-budget slice of science-fiction about a new radioactive element, created by scientists' unauthorised experiments, that doubles its size every 12 hours by converting surrounding energy into matter. Confidently directed by Curt Siodmak with an accent on approximate authenticity, and incorporating stock footage from the 1934 German classic *Gold* to good effect, this cosmic *Frankenstein* makes full use of its offbeat tone and interesting cast.

Richard Carlson Dr Jeffrey Stewart • **King Donovan** Dr Dan Forbes • **Jean Byron** Connie Stewart • **Harry Ellerbe** Dr Allard • **Leo Britt** Dr Benton • **Leonard Mudie** Dr Denker • **Byron Foulger** Simon • **Michael Fox** Dr Serny

Director *Curt Siodmak*

Screenplay *Curt Siodmak, Ivan Tors*

Making Mr Right ★★★ 15

1987 US Colour 94mins

Quirky satire that was Susan Seidelman's next movie after her big hit, *Desperately Seeking Susan*. John Malkovich plays both an inventor and the android he has created, while Ann Magnuson is a wacky PR whiz hired to promote the robot, but soon, wouldn't you know it, falling in love with it. Worse still, it reciprocates. It's all zany stuff, combining shades of vintage B movies with punk hairstyles and post-modern sensibilities. Yes, plenty of invention, in every sense, but ultimately less than the sum of its rather too diverse parts.

John Malkovich Dr Jeff Peters/Ulysses • **Ann Magnuson** Frankie Stone • **Glenne Headly** Trish • **Ben Masters** Congressman Steve Marcus • **Laurie Metcalf** Sandy • **Polly Bergen** Estelle Stone • **Harsh Nayyar** Dr Ravi Ramdas • **Susan Berman** Ivy Stone • **Polly Draper** Suzy Duncan • **Hart Bochner** Don

Director *Susan Seidelman*

Screenplay *Floyd Byars, Laurie Frank*

Malevil ★★

1981 Fr/W Ger Colour 119mins

Based on the novel by Robert Merle, Christian de Chalonge's post-nuclear fable opens effectively enough with the residents of a country chateau emerging to inspect the consequences of conflagration. As Jean Penzer's camera roves across the devastated landscape, it's easy to see why Max Douy's production design won a César. But once Michel Serrault and his fellow survivors resume contact with the outside world (in the form of Jean-Louis Trintignant's fascistic forest outlaws), the action descends into predictable melodramatics, which culminate in three of the band breaking out of a government concentration camp to return to their ravaged Utopia. A French language film.

Michel Serrault Emmanuel • **Jacques Dutronc** Colin • **Robert Dhéry** Peyssou • **Jacques Villeret** Momo • **Hanns Zischler** Veterinarian • **Jean-Louis Trintignant** Fulbert

Director *Christian de Chalonge*

Screenplay *Christian de Chalonge, Pierre Dumayet, from the novel by Robert Merle*

The Man from Atlantis ★★★ U

TV 1977-1978 US Colour 13x60mins

With Marvel Comics' Spider-Man and the Hulk in their own series in the late seventies, this show did its best to be an unauthorised take on their stable-mate, Prince Namor the Sub-Mariner. Patrick Duffy is a human amphibian amnesiac washed ashore in the pilot, and taken into care by Belinda Montgomery, who believes him to be a survivor of the lost underwater kingdom of Atlantis. Duffy is a Spock-like innocent among venal men, and resembles a web-fingered surfie in too-tight trunks. His frequent nemesis, a more comic-like villain than anyone who turned up on *The Incredible Hulk* and *The Amazing Spider-Man*, was the megalomaniac but whimsical scientist Mr Schubert (Victor Buono). Time travel zapped the hero into the plot of Romeo and Juliet (*The Naked Montague*) and the Wild West (*Shoot out at Land's End*), and other stories featured a giant jellyfish (*Man o' War*) and a personality-changing enzyme (*CW Hyde*). The series consisted of four TV movies and half a season's worth of hour-long episodes.

Patrick Duffy Mark Harris • **Belinda Montgomery** Dr Elizabeth Merrill • **Victor Buono** Mr Schubert • **Alan Fudge** CW Crawford

Executive producer *Herbert F Solow*

The Man from Planet X ★★★

1951 US BW 70mins

Shot in six days by B-movie maven Edgar G Ulmer on crumbling *Joan of Arc* sets, this mini-classic was one of the first sci-fi movies to accent sombre and serious issues above gung-ho fantasy. A lonely alien seeking assistance from Earth to help his freezing planet finds a similar coldness in humanity when he lands his spaceship on the Scottish moors. Ulmer's odd camera angles create a real sense of unease in this decent cosmic fable, while the alien – a bubble-headed midget with immobile white face and chest-plate speaker/translator – is one of sci-fi's most haunting creations.

Robert Clarke Lawrence • **Margaret Field** Enid Elliot • **Raymond Bond** Prof Elliot • **William Schallert** Mears • **Roy Engel** Constable • **Charles Davis** Geordie

Director *Edgar G Ulmer*

Screenplay *Aubrey Wisberg, Jack Pollexfen*

Man in the Moon ★★ U

1960 UK BW 98mins

Apart from an amiable performance by Kenneth More as the test pilot whose A1 fitness makes him the ideal candidate to become Britain's first astronaut, this British spoof on the Nasa space programme never leaves the launch pad. Seemingly stuck for ideas, writers Michael Relph and Bryan Forbes fall back on that old plot stand-by, the rival with his nose out of joint, to enliven the scenes of More's training with a few acts of unfunny sabotage while the ultimate destination proves to be anything but the final frontier. Mildly amusing, but hardly out of this world.

Kenneth More William Blood • **Shirley Anne Field** Polly • **Norman Bird** Herbert • **Michael Hordern** Dr Davidson • **John Glyn-Jones** Dr Wilmot • **John Phillips** Professor Stephens • **Charles Gray** Leo • **Bernard Horsfall** Rex
Director *Basil Dearden*
Screenplay *Michael Relph, Bryan Forbes*

The Man in the White Suit ★★★★★ U

1951 UK BW 81mins

Telling the story of a scientist who is undone by the seeming perfection of his own invention, Alexander Mackendrick's astute film is the only Ealing comedy truly to bare its teeth. Capitalist greed, professional jealousy, the spectre of unemployment and a fear of progress are just some of the provocative themes explored in this razor-sharp satire that spurns the studio's customary whimsy. Alec Guinness is wonderfully unworldly as the boffin whose indestructible cloth unites the textile industry against him, while Joan Greenwood is perhaps even more impressive as the spirited daughter of mill owner Cecil Parker.

Alec Guinness Sidney Stratton • **Joan Greenwood** Daphne Birnley • **Cecil Parker** Alan Birnley • **Michael Gough** Michael Corland • **Ernest Thesiger** Sir John Kierlaw • **Vida Hope** Bertha • **Howard Marion-Crawford** Cranford • **Duncan Lamont** Harry • **Henry Mollison** Hoskins
Director *Alexander Mackendrick*
Screenplay *Roger Macdougall, John Dighton, Alexander Mackendrick, from the play by Roger Macdougall*

Man Made Monster ★★★

1941 US BW 56mins

Lon Chaney Jr made his horror acting debut in this above-average Universal B-movie, which lacks the verve and gusto of the studio's earlier genre hits. Chaney is circus sideshow performer "Dynamo Dan, the Electric Man", and ever-reliable Lionel Atwill the mad doctor who wants to turn up his voltage and convert him into a prototype zombie killer with a shocking lethal touch. *Frankenstein* make-up genius Jack Pierce provided Chaney's fiendish look as the natty rubber-suited "atomic monster" (the film's re-release title). A vintage classic of its kind.

Lionel Atwill Dr Paul Rigas • **Lon Chaney Jr** Dan McCormick • **Anne Nagel** June Lawrence • **Frank Albertson** Mark Adams • **Samuel S Hinds** Dr Lawrence • **William Davidson** District Attorney • **Ben Taggart** Detective Sergeant • **Connie Bergen** Nurse
Director *George Waggner*
Screenplay *Joseph West [George Waggner], from the short story "The Electric Man" by H J Essex, Sid Schwartz, Len Golos*
Special effects *John P Fulton* • ***Make-up*** *Jack P Pierce*

The Man They Could Not Hang ★★★

1939 US BW 64mins

While not exactly the "holocaust of horror" promised at the time, this incredibly prophetic sci-fi thriller is laced with enough sinister menace to get by. British bogeyman Boris Karloff plays a crazed scientist dabbling in heart transplant surgery who is sentenced to death by the medical authorities. After his execution, his own technology is used to turn him into a vengeful maniac with a mechanical ticker. As usual, kindly Karloff elevates standard fear fare with wit, grace and presence.

Boris Karloff Dr Henryk Savaard • **Lorna Gray [Adrian Booth]** Janet Saavard • **Robert Wilcox** Scoop Foley • **Roger Pryor** District Attorney Drake • **Don Beddoe** Lt Shane • **Ann Doran** Betty Crawford
Director *Nick Grinde*
Screenplay *Karl Brown, from a story by Leslie T White, George W Sayre*

The Man Who Changed His Mind ★★★

1936 UK BW 61mins

Boris Karloff is up to his brain transference tricks again in this seldom-seen British chiller. As Dr Laurience, he's in love with lab assistant Anna Lee. Unfortunately, she's planning to marry John Loder. So Karloff plans to switch brains with him using the usual strange scientific apparatus so popular in thirties borderline sci-fi melodrama. Stereotypically cast, as so often happened, Karloff nevertheless gives one of his best performances in the matchlessly amusing leading role.

Boris Karloff Dr Laurience • **Anna Lee** Dr Claire Wyatt • **John Loder** Dick Haslewood • **Frank Cellier** Lord Haslewood • **Donald Calthrop** Clayton • **Cecil Parker** Dr Gratton • **Lyn Harding** Professor Holloway
Director *Robert Stevenson*
Screenplay *L DuGarde Peach, Sidney Gilliat, John L Balderston*

The Man Who Fell to Earth ★★★★ 18

1976 UK Colour 133mins

Director Nicolas Roeg's typically eccentric and multi-dimensional movie transforms Walter Tevis's novel into an enigmatic and chilling mosaic of corporate satire and effective science-fiction. In his feature debut, David Bowie is exactly right as the Swiftian starman who becomes fabulously wealthy from his intergalactic inventions, but soon gets corrupted by such earthbound vices as alcohol, television and sex. Already an established sci-fi classic, this is a fascinating new age fairy tale, with Bowie's "fall" open to numerous allegorical interpretations.

David Bowie Thomas Jerome Newton • **Rip Torn** Nathan Bryce • **Candy Clark** Mary-Lou • **Buck Henry** Oliver Farnsworth • **Bernie Casey** Peters • **Jackson D Kane** Professor Canutti • **Rick Riccardo** Trevor • **Tony Mascia** Arthur • **Linda Hutton** Elaine • **Captain James Lovell** Captain James Lovell
Director *Nicolas Roeg*
Screenplay *Paul Mayersburg, from the novel by Walter Tevis*

The Man Who Fell to Earth ★★ PG

1986 US Colour 93mins

No, not Nicolas Roeg's sci-fi film of 1976 with David Bowie, but a made-for-TV remake starring Lewis Smith as the weird alien and Beverly D'Angelo as the earthling who tends to his every comfort while he absorbs our capitalist culture and looks for a way to export water to his arid planet. Intended to herald a TV series based on Walter Tevis's source novel, this inevitably pales in comparison with Roeg's visually dazzling adaptation. Contains swearing.

Lewis Smith John Dory • **Beverly D'Angelo** Eva Milton • **James Laurenson** Felix Hawthorne • **Robert Picardo** Richard Morse • **Bruce McGill** Vernon Gage • **Wil Wheaton** Billy Milton • **Annie Potts** Louise • **Chris Derose** Record Clerk
Director *Robert J Roth*
Screenplay *Richard Kletter, from the novel by Walter Tevis*

The Man Who Thought Life ★★

1969 Den BW 96mins

Sci-fi has never been a priority on the Danish cinematic agenda, indeed, this was only the second such feature of the sound era (the first being, Sidney Pink's amateurish 1961 prehistoric adventure, *Reptilicus*). John Price stars as a scientist with the power to materialise objects simply by brain power. However, when his surgeon buddy, Preben Neergaard, refuses to co-operate in the construction of a "thought" being, he loses control and creates a doppleganger who slowly begins to assume his sidekick's identity. The premise has possibilities, but a combination of budgetary restraint and Jens Ravn's unimaginative direction kills it stone dead. A Danish language film.

Preben Neergaard Max Holst • **John Price** Steinmetz • **Lotte Tarp** Susanne
Director *Jens Ravn*
Screenplay *Jens Ravn, Henrik Stangerup*

The Man Who Turned to Stone ★

1957 US BW 74mins

Dismal junk from the sadly all-too ubiquitous Sam Katzman, the *Jungle Jim* producer. Alchemist Victor Jory has lived for two centuries, thanks to learning the secret of eternal youth, which involves putting women in tubs of chemicals and sapping their life force, but psychiatrist William Hudson discovers what's going on, burns the facility down and Jory, without the human energy to survive, turns to stone. Rather like the faces of anyone unfortunate enough to have to sit through director Leslie Kardos's mind number.

Victor Jory Dr Murdock • **William Hudson** Dr Jess Rogers • **Ann Doran** Mrs Ford • **Charlotte Austin** Carol Adams • **Paul Cavanagh** Cooper • **Tina Carver** Big Marge • **Jean Willes** Tracy
Director *Leslie Kardos*
Screenplay *Raymond T Marcus [Bernard Gordon]*
Producer *Sam Katzman*

The Man with the Power ★★★

1977 US Colour

Unmomentous but diverting TV movie about a man who inherits psychokinetic powers from his father, a native of a distant planet. He is forced to call on them when he is assigned the task of guarding a beautiful Bengali princess. Persis Khambatta, a former Miss India, is suitably decorative as the princess in peril, while Vic Morrow, who played the heavy in countless movies down the years, turns up as a kidnapper.

Bob Neill Eric Smith • **Tim O'Connor** Agent Walter Bloom • **Vic Morrow** Paul • **Persis Khambatta** Princess Siri • **Roger Perry** Farnsworth • **Rene Assa** Major Sajid
Director *Nicholas Sgarro*
Screenplay *Allan Balter*

The Man with the Transplanted Brain ★★

1972 Fr/W Ger BW 72mins

Adapted from the novel by Victor Vicas and Alain Franck, this is more about philosophy than Frankenstein. Director Jacques Doniol-Valcroze quickly loses interest in the scientific ramifications of ailing surgeon Jean-Pierre Aumont transplanting his brain into the otherwise healthy body of tumour-afflicted racing driver, Mathieu Carrière, in order to concentrate on the incestual dilemma that arises when Aumont discovers that his daughter, Nicoletta Machiavelli, is Carrière's lover. Although stylishly filmed by Etienne Becker, it's a disappointing piece, all the more so considering it was made by one of the co-founders of that arbiter of French filmic taste, *Cahiers du Cinéma*. A French language film.

Mathieu Carrière Franz • **Jean-Pierre Aumont** Marcilly • **Nicoletta Machiavelli** Helena • **Michel Duchaussoy** Degagnac
Director *Jacques Doniol-Valcroze*
Screenplay *Jacques Doniol-Valcroze, from the novel by Alain Franck, Victor Vicas*

The Man with the X-Ray Eyes ★★★★ PG

1963 US Colour 75mins [video]

Ray Milland plays one of his best remembered roles in Roger Corman's pocket-sized, yet highly potent, sci-fi shocker. He stars as scientist Dr Xavier, who experiments on himself and gains the power to see through solid materials. However, as his sight gets stronger, so do the side-effects – Corman's cue to move from playful sideshow terror to mystical allegory, with plenty of engaging surreal imagery along the way. The Bible provides the inspiration for this cult classic, something clearly evident in the unforgettable revival-meeting climax.

Ray Milland Dr James Xavier • **Diana Van Der Vlis** Dr Diane Fairfax • **Harold J Stone** Dr Sam Brant • **John Hoyt** Dr Willard Benson • **Don Rickles** Crane • **Lorie Summers** Carnival owner/party dancer
Director *Roger Corman*
Screenplay *Robert Dillon, Ray Russell, from the story by Ray Russell*

The Man with Two Brains ★★★★★ 15

1983 US Colour 85mins [video]

There have been more accomplished Steve Martin films – *Roxanne, LA Story* – but this remains his finest moment: a dazzlingly inventive comedy that contains more laughs than his last half-dozen movies put together. Martin is Doctor Hfuhruhurr, the brilliant brain surgeon who marries black widow Kathleen Turner, but falls for a disembodied brain, voiced by Sissy Spacek. Martin gets to read his favourite poem ("Pointy Birds"), carry out a citizen's divorce and endure the world's toughest drink-driving test; and Turner hilariously sends up the *femme fatale* persona she established in *Body Heat*. David Warner is a fellow mad scientist, and there is also a surprise cameo in the form of the Elevator Killer. Sublime.

Steve Martin Dr Michael Hfuhruhurr • **Kathleen Turner** Dolores Benedict • **David Warner** Dr Necessiter • **Paul Benedict** Butler • **Richard Brestoff** Dr Pasteur • **James Cromwell** Realtor • **George Furth** Timon • **Peter Hobbs** Dr Brandon • **Earl Boen** Dr Conrad • **Frank McCarthy** Olsen • **William Traylor** Inspector • **Randi Brooks** Fran • **Bernard Behrens** Gladstone • **Russell Orozco** Juan • **Natividad Vacio** Ramon • **Sissy Spacek** Anne Uumellmahaye
Director *Carl Reiner*
Screenplay *Steve Martin, Carl Reiner, George Gipe*

The Man without a Body ★

1957 UK BW 80mins

Rock-bottom British shocker with an almost wilfully stupid story about a surgeon who revives Nostradamus's head and later grafts it on to someone else's body – don't ask why. The only interesting thing is that both directors had more famous siblings: W Lee Wilder was Billy's brother, while Charles Saunders is the brother of *Mousetrap* producer Peter. Some of the same team went on to produce the similarly maniacal *Woman Eater*.

Robert Hutton Dr Phil Merritt • **George Coulouris** Karl Brussard • **Julia Arnall** Jean Kramer • **Nadja Regin** Odette Vernet • **Sheldon Lawrence** Dr Lew Waldenhaus
Director *W Lee Wilder, Charles Saunders*
Screenplay *William Grote*
Producer *W Lee Wilder, Guido Coen*

Mandroid ★★ 15

1993 US Colour 77mins [video]

Sci-fi B-movie producer Charles Band here oversees a rehash of ideas from his own vastly more entertaining *Eliminators*, which also featured a character called

Head case: President Jack Nicholson leads a stellar cast in Tim Burton's alien invasion comedy *Mars Attacks!*

Mandroid. This Romania-set tale still makes for cheap and cheerful viewing, as scientists from East and West fight for control of a secret formula. The usual intrigues are spiced up by the presence of a lethal robot that can be controlled by thought alone. The largely unknown cast has the good sense not to take it seriously and director Jack Ersgard keeps the action rattling along.

Brian Cousins Dr Wade Franklin • **Jane Caldwell** Zanna • **Michael Dellafemina** Benjamin Knight • **Curt Lowens** Dr Ivan Drago • **Patrick Ersgard** Joe Smith
Director *Jack Ersgard*
Screenplay *Earl Kenton, Jackson Barr, from an idea by Charles Band*

Manhunt of Mystery Island ★★

1945 US BW

Despite a splendid suspension bridge sequence (directed by master stuntman and second unit director Yakima Canutt), this turns out to be a less than enthralling 15-part serial. Plodding around a tiny Pacific island, criminologist Richard Bailey and kidnapped scientist's daughter (is there any other kind?) Linda Stirling take an eternity to uncover the identity of Mephisto, a legendary cutthroat who materialises each time our mysterious villain uses a Transformation Chair to alter the molecular structure of his blood. Roy Barcroft is enthusiastically piratical, but professor Forrest Taylor's top-secret radiatomic power transmitter is little more than what Alfred Hitchcock used to call a McGuffin.

Richard Bailey Lance Reardon • **Linda Stirling** Claire Forrest • **Roy Barcroft** Captain Mephisto • **Kenne Duncan** Brand • **Forrest Taylor** Prof Forrest
Director *Spencer Gordon Bennet, Yakima Canutt, Wallace A Grissell*
Screenplay *Albert DeMond, Basil Dickey, Jesse A Duffy, Alan James, Grant Nelson, Joseph Franklin Poland*

Manimal ★

TV 1983 US Colour 1x90mins; 8x60mins

Glen A Larson's short-lived blend of crime-fighting drama and animal antics stars Simon MacCorkindale as Jonathan Chase, a British professor who can transform himself into any animal at will. Teaming up with an American police detective, MacCorkindale uses his shape-shifting powers to solve crimes and defeat villains. Although the show's premise is certainly intriguing, its beastly execution makes for unbelievable and unrewarding viewing. Amid a zoo of clichéd plots and cardboard characters, the series' only memorable moments are provided by MacCorkindale's weekly transformations into various creatures. Unsurprisingly, that wasn't enough to save the show from cancellation after just nine episodes.

Simon MacCorkindale Jonathan Chase • **Melody Anderson** Brooke McKenzie • **Michael D Roberts** Ty • **Reni Santoni** Lt Rivera
Created by *Glen A Larson*
Producer *Glen A Larson*

Mann & Machine ★

TV 1992 US Colour 9x60mins

In the near future, streetwise detective Bobby Mann is assigned an extremely unusual new partner – a state-of-the-art female android, dubbed Sergeant Eve Edison. Together, the mismatched cops tackle the usual assortment of criminals while learning to accept each other's obvious differences. As its premise suggests, this sci-fi cop show is a nuts 'n' bolts cross between *RoboCop* and *Lethal Weapon*, which proves to be a bit too mechanical for its own good. While Yancy Butler is clearly programmed to thrill male viewers as the voluptuous Eve, the show remains largely devoid of any real human interest. No wonder this robot was canned after just nine episodes.

David Andrews Detective Bobby Mann • **Yancy Butler** Sergeant Eve Edison • **S Epatha Merkerson** Captain Margaret Claghorn
Executive producer *Robert De Laurentiis, Dick Wolf*

Man's Best Friend ★★ 15

1993 US Colour 83mins

Those who thought Stephen King's *Cujo* had the last word on mad dogs should watch this sci-fi thriller. Ally Sheedy stars as a reporter who rescues a large canine from a laboratory, only to discover that there's a reason why scientist Lance Henriksen keeps it in a cage. The initially loveable pooch has been genetically mutated and is now a furry killer! It may be enjoyable for genre fans, who will spend the entire movie groaning at how the characters walk into dark rooms, open things they shouldn't open and so on, as if they've never seen a horror movie in their lives.

Ally Sheedy Lori Tanner • **Lance Henriksen** Dr Jarret • **Robert Costanzo** Detective Kovacs • **Fredric Lehne** Perry • **John Cassini** Detective Bendetti • **J D Daniels** Rudy • **William Sanderson** Ray
Director/Screenplay *John Lafia*

The Manster ★

1959 Jap/US BW 72mins

Inaugurating a theme that would become prevalent in the early seventies (*The Incredible Two-Headed Transplant* and *The Thing with Two Heads*), this loopy obscurity is a genuine guilty pleasure. While on assignment in Japan, snoopy reporter Peter Dyneley is given a strange injection by a mad doctor causing him to grow a second, albeit obviously fake rubber, head. To make matters worse, the head is homicidal and forces him to kill people until it finally grows its own body and splits into an ape man. A funny and sometimes scary redefinition of the classic Jekyll and Hyde fable that carries its insane premise beyond fantasy by having two heads at the helm – co-directors George Breakston and Kenneth Crane.

Peter Dyneley Larry Stanford • **Jane Hylton** Linda Stanford • **Tetsu Nakamura** Dr Suzuki • **Terri Zimmern** Tara
Director *Kenneth Crane, George Breakston*
Screenplay *Walter J Sheldon, from the story "Nightmare" by George Breakston*

M.A.N.T.I.S. ★ PG

TV 1994-1995 Colour 22x60mins [video]

A wheelchair-bound black scientist dons a revolutionary exoskeleton and becomes the powerful, insect-like crime-fighter M.A.N.T.I.S. in this unusual superhero caper. Former *Cagney and Lacey* sidekick Carl Lumbly takes centre stage as Dr Miles Hawkins, the believably grouchy disabled do-gooder beneath the Mechanically Augmented Neuro Transmitter Interception System, while Roger Rees provides some solid support as his dry-witted partner, John Stonebrake. Their politically correct adventures initially combine the requisite comic-strip thrills and spills with some refreshingly quirky characterisation and plotlines, but become increasingly sanitised and run-of-the-mill during the course of the show's one-year run. The series' included a feature-length pilot that made its UK debut on video.

Carl Lumbly Dr Miles Hawkins/Mantis • **Roger Rees** John Stonebrake • **Galyn Gorg** Lt Leora Maxwell • **Christopher Gartin** Taylor Savidge
Executive producer *Sam Raimi, Sam Hamm, Rob Taper, James McAdams*

Marching out of Time ★★

1993 US Colour

One of those films where the pitch was probably more interesting than the finished result. Here, it's *Home Alone* meets *Hogan's Heroes*, with a dash of *Back to the Future* thrown in and, yes, this is about as misguided as that concept sounds. Frederick Andersen is the brattish Californian teen who finds himself drawn into the Second World War when Nazis appear in the neighbourhood, courtesy of a misfiring time machine. Will he be able to stop them changing the course of history? Who cares? The cast is instantly forgettable and the script and direction aren't much better.

Frederick Andersen • **Matthew Henerson** • **Heinrich James** • **Jeff Rector** • **Robert Z'Dar**
Director/Screenplay *Anton Vassil*

Marooned ★★★ U

1969 US Colour 123mins [video]

Winner of the Oscar for best special visual effects, this astute blend of science fact and fiction eerily anticipated the kind of lost-in-space crisis that would actually occur during the *Apollo 13* mission just one year later. Gene Hackman, Richard Crenna and James Franciscus successfully combine public confidence with private misgivings as the stranded crew, while Gregory Peck heads the Nasa operation with typical reserve. But although he makes the most of his space hardware, director John Sturges never gets the domestic drama off the ground, with Lee Grant and the other wives being reduced to mere cardboard cut-outs.

Gregory Peck Charles Keith • **Richard Crenna** Jim Pruett • **David Janssen** Ted Dougherty • **James Franciscus** Clayton Stone • **Gene Hackman** Buzz Lloyd • **Lee Grant** Celia Pruett • **Nancy Kovack** Teresa Stone • **Mariette Hartley** Betty Lloyd • **Scott Brady** Public affairs officer • **Craig Huebing** Flight director
Director *John Sturges*
Screenplay *Mayo Simon, from the novel by Martin Caidin*
Special effects *Lawrence Butler Donald C Glouner, Robie Robinson*

Mars ★ 18

1996 US Colour 86mins [video]

Another grungy future, another nameless corporation running everything… didn't we cover this in *Blade Runner*? This time around, Olivier Gruner is a police officer (called a "keeper") who's investigating the death of his brother on Mars. It's tough to stay interested in the film: Gruner, who could be described as overly reserved in even his best film roles, is not being paid enough here to change facial expression, or even use his own voice. The sloppily edited fights hardly make up for the paint-by-numbers script and wooden acting. Contains sex scenes, violence and some swearing.

Olivier Gruner Caution Templar • **Shari Belafonte** Doc Halliday • **Gabriel Dell Jr [Gabriel Dell]** Buckskin Greenberg • **Alex Hyde-White** Phillip Clement • **Scott Valentine** Pete the Hermit • **Lindsey Lee Ginter** Ike Ringo
Director *Jon Hess*
Screenplay *Patrick Highsmith, Steven Hartov, from a story by Patrick Highsmith*

Mars Attacks! ★★★★ 12

1996 US Colour 101mins [video] DVD

Director Tim Burton's unintended lampoon of *Independence Day* is a total mess but an absolutely glorious one. Little green men from the angry red planet launch a flying saucer attack on Earth in this uneven space oddity based on a bubblegum card storyline from the sixties. While assuring the US government that they come in peace, the Martians consistently ray-gun humans down to steaming multi-coloured skeletons. What's President Jack Nicholson to do? Listen to advisor Pierce Brosnan who thinks the visitors must be benign because they are so technologically advanced? Or take heed of General Rod Steiger and blast the bulbous headed varmints out of the sky? Eventually the fate of the world rests in Grandma Sylvia Sidney's Country and Western record collection. Both paying tribute to and spoofing fifties B-movies, Burton stumbles as many times as he succeeds in playing with the entire back catalogue of lurid pulp sci-fi references. But once the computer-generated bug-eyed Martians strut their evil stuff, this daffy and sweetly subversive Ray Harryhausen-meets-*War of the Worlds* satire comes alive. The sequence where the glittering aliens inhale the best of America's nuclear deterrent and give their trademark Three Stooges laugh in response is a major highlight. Among the amazing roster of stars, including Annette Bening, Sarah Jessica Parker, Natalie Portman and singer Tom Jones, Burton's muse Lisa Marie stands out in a weirdly creepy turn as a disguised alien temptress.

Jack Nicholson President James Dale/Art Land • **Glenn Close** Marsha Dale • **Annette Bening** Barbara Land • **Pierce Brosnan** Donald Kessler • **Danny DeVito** Rude gambler • **Martin Short** Jerry Ross • **Sarah Jessica Parker** Nathalie Lake • **Michael J Fox** Jason Stone • **Rod Steiger** General Decker • **Tom Jones** • **Lukas Haas** Richie Norris • **Natalie Portman** Taffy Dale • **Jim Brown** Byron Williams • **Lisa Marie** Martian girl • **Sylvia Sidney** Grandma Norris • **Paul Winfield** General Casey • **Pam Grier** Louise Williams • **Joe Don Baker** Glenn Norris • **Christina Applegate** Sharona
Director *Tim Burton*
Screenplay *Jonathan Gems, from his story, from the illustrated card series by the Topps Company*
Producer *Tim Burton, Larry Franco*

Facts

The Topps trading cards on which the film was based were considered so violent at the time (1962) that concerned parents mounted a successful campaign to have them withdrawn.

Mars Needs Women ★

1966 US Colour 80mins

Made for fast TV play-off by genre exploitation factory AIP, this terminally stupid travesty is directed by Larry Buchanan, the supreme schlock-meister behind such brain-freezing offerings as *Zontar, the Thing from Venus*. Disney teen star Tommy Kirk plays Dop, who lands on Earth to kidnap beautiful chicks for the men of his planet. Repopulation is all that's on the Martian agenda, but the military see their arrival as a future invasion threat. Further complications occur when Dop falls in love with go-go scientist Yvonne "Batgirl" Craig. Hopelessly below standard in every area this has been called the worst movie ever made.

Tommy Kirk Dop • **Yvonne Craig** Dr Marjorie Bolen • **Byron Lord** Colonel Page
Director/Screenplay *Larry Buchanan*

The Martian Chronicles ★★ PG

TV 1979 US Colour 3x95mins

Ray Bradbury's classic novel celebrating mankind's colonisation of Mars and his first contact with alien beings became one of the most anticipated events of the sci-fi calendar in 1979. Alas, the end result was a positive disappointment, rather like discovering that wonderfully wrapped Christmas present is just another pair of socks. Bradbury himself was the most disillusioned, complaining that all the poetry of his writing had been lost in its translation to the small screen. A real surprise, given that it was handled by one of the genre's top writers, Richard Matheson. It's certainly ambitious, but Rock Hudson lacks the necessary charisma to hold such a lengthy saga together and Michael Anderson's direction is too lumbering and vapid. It could and should have been so much better. The effects are pretty kitsch, too.

Rock Hudson Colonel John Wilder • **Gayle Hunnicutt** Ruth Wilder • **Bernie Casey** Jeff Spender • **Darren McGavin** Sam Parkhill • **Nicholas Hammond** Captain Black • **Robert Beatty** General Halstead • **Fritz Weaver** Fr Peregrine • **Roddy McDowall** Fr Stone • **Maria Schell** Anna Lustig • **Nyree Dawn Porter** Alice Hathaway
Director *Michael Anderson*
Teleplay by *Richard Matheson, from the novel by Ray Bradbury*

Martians Go Home ★★ 15

1990 US Colour 82mins

Alien invasion is played strictly for laughs in this sporadically entertaining sci-fi comedy. Randy Quaid is the musician whose sci-fi movie theme unwittingly encourages hordes of Martian wiseguys to make a complete nuisances of themselves on Earth. Quaid is as good as ever and there is solid support from the likes of Ronny Cox and Anita Morris. Although much of the humour is hit-and-miss, this is still a refreshingly bonkers take on a familiar sci-fi theme.

Randy Quaid Mark Devereaux • **Margaret Colin** Sara Brody • **Anita Morris** Dr Jane Buchanan • **Vic Dunlop** Martian • **Barry Sobel** Martian • **John Philbin** Donny • **Ronny Cox** President
Director *David Odell*
Screenplay *Charles S Haas, from a novel by Fredrick Brown*

Mary Reilly ★★★ 15

1995 US Colour 103mins DVD

A clever twist on that evergreen tale *Dr Jekyll and Mr Hyde*, as seen through the eyes of his housemaid, played by a totally miscast but oddly touching Julia Roberts. As the famous split personality, John Malkovich gives a typically complex and powerful performance. Director Stephen Frears's lavish, black-bricked and gaslit production is satisfying both as a meditation on a literary classic and as an old-fashioned Victorian horror story, complete with a suggestive eel, dead babies and oceans of blood cascading down the stairs. But this was a jinxed movie, subject to much re-shooting and ridicule and virtually disowned by the studio that financed it.

Julia Roberts Mary Reilly • **John Malkovich** Dr Jekyll/Mr Hyde • **George Cole** Mr Poole • **Michael Gambon** Mary's father • **Kathy Staff** Mrs Kent • **Glenn Close** Mrs Farraday • **Michael Sheen** Bradshaw • **Bronagh Gallagher** Annie • **Linda Bassett** Mary's mother • **Henry Goodman** Haffinger
Director *Stephen Frears*
Screenplay *Christopher Hampton, from the novel by Valerie Martin, from the novel "The Strange Case of Dr Jekyll and Mr Hyde" by Robert Louis Stevenson*

Mary Shelley's Frankenstein
★★ 15

1994 US Colour 118mins DVD

Kenneth Branagh's version of the much-filmed story is as pompous as it is perverse in the way it wastes not only his own talents (as Victor Frankenstein), but also those of Robert De Niro (who boasts a few moving moments as the man-made monster) and Helena Bonham Carter. The creation of the creature is undoubtedly spectacular, but the rest of the movie is not a fraction as frightening or funny as the 1931 classic with Boris Karloff. In attempting to keep faith with the original novel, Branagh concentrates too much on design and content, and loses the heart and soul of the story in the process. Contains violence, sex scenes and nudity.

Robert De Niro Creature/Sharp-featured man • **Kenneth Branagh** Victor Frankenstein • **Tom Hulce** Henry • **Helena Bonham Carter** Elizabeth • **Aidan Quinn** Captain Walton • **Ian Holm** Victor's father • **Richard Briers** Grandfather • **John Cleese** Professor Waldman • **Robert Hardy** Professor Krempe • **Cherie Lunghi** Victor's mother
Director *Kenneth Branagh*
Screenplay *Steph Lady, Frank Darabont, from the novel by Mary Shelley*

The Master ★★★

TV 1966 UK BW 6x25mins

Adapted by Rosemary Hill from the novel by TH (*The Once and Future King*) White, this spirited children's serial is essentially *Swallows and Amazons* vs Fu Manchu. Paul Guess and Adrienne Posta discover on the barren island of Rockall a super-scientific base commanded by the

150-year-old telepathic megalomaniac the Master (Olaf Pooley), who is working on the typical super-villain gambit of taking over the world with laserbeams, aided by the sinister Terence Soall and the mad Scots scientist John Laurie. The kids wrestle with moral problems and are aided by a dashing military older brother figure, squadron leader George Baker, but it was the melodrama that appealed to the audiences. It may not be a coincidence that *Doctor Who*, which was considered to have been bested on its own turf, later introduced their own superfiend called the Master.

Olaf Pooley The Master • **Terence Soall** Chinaman • **Paul Guess** Nicky • **Adrienne Posta** Judy • **John Laurie** Dr McTurk • **George Baker** Squadron Leader Frinton
Written by *Rosemary Hill, from a novel by TH White*
Producer *John Braybon*

Master of the World ★★

1934 Ger BW 109mins

Some 20 years after he entered the genre, Harry Piel made his fourth and last sci-fi picture. Considering the rise of Hitler was still being greeted with considerable enthusiasm, the story of a mad scientist who seeks to assemble an army of subservient robots was both radical and courageous. However, Piel's borrowings from both *Metropolis* and *Dr Mabuse* never quite gel, and he's let down by the blandness of heroic mining engineer Sigfried Schürenberg and Sybille Schmitz as the widow of scientist Arlbert Wäschler, who becomes the first victim of Walter Janssen's death-ray-toting troopers when he tries to sabotage the lab. In German with English subtitles.

Walter Janssen Dr Heller • **Sybille Schmitz** Vilma, his wife • **Walter Franck** Prof Wolf • **Aribert Wäscher** • **Siegfried Schürenberg** Werner Baumann, mining engineer • **Willi Schur** Karl • **Otto Wernicke**
Director *Harry Piel*
Screenplay *Georg Muühlen-Schulte*
Cinematographer *Ewald Daub*

Master of the World ★★ U

1961 US Colour 98mins

An uneven mixture of two Jules Verne novels to make one highly moralistic anti-war fable. Vincent Price plays a 19th-century inventor planning to destroy all of mankind's weapons from a flying airship with his usual suave and sinister panache. Spiced up with stock battle footage taken from other costume epics (the reason why the Globe theatre suddenly appears in Victorian London), it's a cheap and cheerful fantasy, reuniting Charles Bronson with Price for the first time since *House of Wax*.

Vincent Price Robur • **Charles Bronson** Strock • **Henry Hull** Prudent • **Mary Webster** Dorothy • **David Frankham** Philip • **Richard Harrison** Alistair • **Vito Scotti** Topage • **Wally Campo** Turner • **Steve Masino** Weaver • **Ken Terrell** Shanks • **Peter Besbas** Wilson
Director *William Witney*
Screenplay *Richard Matheson, from the novels "Master of the World" and "Robur, the Conqueror" by Jules Verne*

Masters of the Universe ★★ PG

1987 US Colour 101mins

It is exceedingly difficult to make convincing live-action versions of cult cartoon strips, and this big-screen version of the momentarily popular TV series is one of the least successful attempts. Dolph Lundgren has the necessary physique for He-Man and Frank Langella has been splendidly made-up for the role of Skeletor. But the story – about a cosmic key that will enable its holder to become master of the universe – is uninspired, while the special effects look painfully cheap.

Dolph Lundgren He-Man • **Frank Langella** Skeletor • **Meg Foster** Evil-Lyn • **Billy Barty** Gwildor • **Courteney Cox** Julie Winston • **Robert Duncan McNeill** Kevin • **Jon Cypher** Man-at-Arms • **Chelsea Field** Teela • **James Tolkan** Detective Lubic • **Christina Pickles** Sorceress • **Tony Carroll** Beastman • **Pons Maar** Saurod • **Anthony DeLongis** Blade • **Robert Towers** Karg
Director *Gary Goddard*
Screenplay *David Odell*

Matango ★★ 15

1963 Jap BW 72mins

Japanese tourists on a luxury, get-away-from-it-all yachting holiday are shipwrecked on a mysterious Pacific island where they eat narcotic mushrooms and turn into walking phallic-shaped fungi. Told in flashback by a padded-cell survivor, director Inoshiro (*Godzilla*) Honda's drug allegory-cum-monster movie is an insanely illogical romp suffused with dream logic and startling sexual imagery. A Japanese language film.

Akira Kubo Kenji Murai • **Kenji Sahara** Senzo Koyama • **Yoshio Tsuchiya** Fumio Kasai • **Hiroshi Koizumi** Naoyuki Sakeda • **Kumi Mizuno** Mami Sekiguchi
Director *Inoshiro Honda*
Screenplay *Takeshi Kimura*
Special effects *Eiji Tsuburaya*

The Matrix ★★★★★ 15

1999 US Colour 136mins DVD

Keanu Reeves reclaims his action hero crown in the Wachowski brothers' super-smart science-fiction action adventure set across two dimensions. Thematically complex, yet intelligently integrating Eastern philosophy, Lewis Carroll, Christianity and ancient mysticism, this slick postmodern thriller posits an intriguing notion – what if the world you think is "real" is actually being fed into your brain by a computer master race that took control of mankind after a future war with machines left Earth a ravaged hellhole? Well, that's *The Matrix*, a Big Brother super-highway that keeps the human population passive by plugging them at birth into a virtual reality universe resembling the late-20th century. The fashion-plate remodelled and pumped-up Reeves plays Neo, a reclusive computer hacker who may be able to save humanity from the evils of cyberspace slavery. Taking a quantum leap beyond anything the fantasy sensation seeker has seen before (it rightly stole the special effects Oscar from *Star Wars Episode I: the Phantom Menace*), Andy and Larry Wachowski's masterpiece mixes ultra-cool visuals, vertigo-inducing kung-fu and a deliciously paranoid scenario for an adrenalin-pumping roller-coaster ride of extraordinary vision and astounding power. This eye-popping genre milestone pushes the boundaries of imagination and digital effects technology further than ever before from its riveting opening right up to its "gasp-out loud" climax. With two sequels currently in production, now is the time to catch up with the original or revisit it to be astonished once more. Contains violence.

Keanu Reeves Neo • **Carrie-Anne Moss** Trinity • **Laurence Fishburne** Morpheus • **Hugo Weaving** Agent Smith • **Joe Pantoliano** Cypher • **Gloria Foster** Oracle • **Marcus Chong** Tank
Director/Screenplay *Larry Wachowski, Andy Wachowski*

Max Headroom ★★★★ PG 15

TV 1987 UK/US 1x 70mins; 14x60

Originally devised as a groundbreaking pop video host, Max Headroom swiftly inspired a British telemovie, which led to this fully-fledged American TV series. The show features the same cast as the original telemovie, and begins by retelling how reporter Edison Carter's investigation into a sinister conspiracy involving a TV network leads to the birth of his computer-generated alter ego, Max Headroom. Just like the original movie, the series' 14 episodes offer an ahead-of-its-time blend of intelligent sci-fi, provocative satire, taut drama and stunning imagery. In a bravura central performance, Matt Frewer deftly shifts between his dual roles and ensures that Max Headroom is a completely convincing "computer-generated" character without the use of any CGI.

Matt Frewer Max Headroom • **Amanda Pays** Theora Jones • **George Coe** Ben Cheviot • **Chris Young** Bryce Lynch • **William Morgan Sheppard** Blank Reg • **Jeffrey Tambor** Murray
Executive Producer *Philip DeGuere, Peter Wagg*

Maximum Overdrive ★★ 18

1986 US Colour 93mins

... but minimum credibility, as horror maestro Stephen King decided his neon-lit prose needed his equally neon-lit direction. He makes a courageous debut with this story about machinery in a North Carolina small town coming to lethal life and besieging a group headed by Emilio Estevez and Pat Hingle. The trouble is that writer King should have explained to director King that you must not outpace your audience's interest, however well you manage the action. Then again, when you're a mega-bestselling author, you forget the little things. But those little things grow into bigger ones that devour any good intentions King might have started out with. Contains violence and swearing.

Emilio Estevez Bill Robinson • **Pat Hingle** Hendershot • **Laura Harrington** Brett • **Yeardley Smith** Connie • **John Short** Curt • **Ellen McElduff** Wanda June • **J C Quinn** Duncan • **Christopher Murney** Camp Loman • **Holter Graham** Deke • **Frankie Faison** Handy
Director *Stephen King*
Screenplay *Stephen King, from his story*

Maybe ★★

1999 Fr Colour 109mins

Cédric Klapisch's sci-fi comedy begins with a workable (if hardly original) premise. It's Millennium Eve and Romain Duris's refusal to start a family with girlfriend Geraldine Pailhas causes a portal to open in time that allows his son, Jean-Paul Belmondo, to return from the future to beg for his existence. The sight of 2070 Paris being Eiffel-high in Saharan sand is also a sly touch. But once Duris's descendants commence their temporal jauntings, the action becomes as contrivedly trite as a Hollywood concept movie. Belmondo shines over an energetic supporting cast, but the ideas and the gags just aren't there. In French with English subtitles.

Romain Duris Arthur • **Jean-Paul Belmondo** Ako • **Geraldine Pailhas** Lucie • **Vincent Elbaz** Philippe • **Riton Liebman** Mathieu • **Julie Depardieu** Nathalie
Director *Cédric Klapisch*
Screenplay *Cédric Klapisch, Santiago Amigorena, Alexis Galmot*

Medicine Man ★★★ PG

1992 US Colour 100mins

An eco movie that would have been swiftly forgotten if not for an effortlessly charismatic performance from Sean Connery, who not only manages to overcome an unfocused script from *Dead Poets Society* writer Tom Schulman and Sally Robinson, but also an even worse ponytail. He plays a grumpy scientist who has discovered a cure for cancer deep in the heart of the South American rainforest, but is now unable to reproduce it. He also has to cope with the twin threats of rampant developers out to destroy the forest and Lorraine Bracco (badly miscast and truly irritating), who has been sent from head office to supervise him. *Die Hard* director John McTiernan makes the most of the spectacular setting, but looks a little lost away from his trademark action and explosions.

Sean Connery Dr Robert Campbell • **Lorraine Bracco** Dr Rae Crane • **José Wilker** Dr Miguel Ornega • **Rodolfo De Alexandre** Tanaki • **Francisco Tsirene Tsere Rereme** Jahausa • **Elias Monteiro Da Silva** Palala • **Edinei Maria Serrio Dos Santos** Kalana • **Bec-kana-re Dos Santos Kaiapo** Imana • **Angelo Barra Moreira** Medicine man • **Jose Lavat** Government man
Director *John McTiernan*
Screenplay *Tom Schulman, Sally Robinson*

Meego ★★

TV 1997 US Colour 13x30mins

Cult comedy actor Bronson Pinchot falls to Earth with a thud in this tepid sci-fi sitcom. The series revolves around Pinchot's shape-shifting 9,000-year-old alien alter ego, Meego, and his bumbling attempts at playing nanny to the three children of a busy doctor. Pinchot's alien antics are generally more irritating than amusing, and the show's tired plotlines will only appeal to truly spaced-out viewers. Fortunately, however, the series is lifted enormously by its strong supporting cast, which includes the ever-dependable Ed Begley Jr, Jonathan Lipnicki (of *Jerry Maguire* and *Stuart Little* fame) and *Buffy*'s Michelle Trachtenberg. All three quickly went on to better things following the completion of *Meego*'s 13th and final episode.

Bronson Pinchot Meego • **Ed Begley Jr** Dr Edward Parker • **Michelle Trachtenberg** Maggie Parker • **Will Estes** Trip Parker • **Jonathan Lipnicki** Alex Parker
Created by *Ross Brown*
Producer *Karen K Miller*

Megaforce ★ PG

1982 US Colour 94mins

Former Hollywood stunt man Hal Needham made a bad name for himself with a succession of Redneck road movies with pal Burt Reynolds (*Smokey and the Bandit, Cannonball Run et al*) but he destroys any shred of credibility remaining with this motorised turkey about a high-tech secret army led by Barry Bostwick that comes to the aid of beleaguered nations. But Needham bypasses plot for hardware, modified dirt bikes, dune buggies and so on, all lovingly photographed as if this were some porno flick for lonely spark plugs. As usual Henry Silva is cast as the villain. it serves him right for looking like a Latin Jack Palance. Turgid rot.

Barry Bostwick Ace Hunter • **Persis Khambatta** Zara • **Michael Beck** Dallas • **Edward Mulhare** Byrne-White • **George Furth** Professor Eggstrum • **Henry Silva** Guerera
Director *Hal Needham*
Screenplay *Andre Morgan, Hal Needham, Albert S Ruddy, James Whittaker, from a story by Robert Kachler*

Memoirs of a Survivor ★★ 18

1981 UK Colour 110mins

This heavy going and structurally murky fantasy, derived from a 1974 novel by Doris Lessing, was typical of the kind of esoteric films Julie Christie was being drawn to at this stage in her career, but even her luminous star quality can't save it from coming across as a pretentious bore. Set in the near future, Christie plays a woman struggling to come to terms with the urban decay and anarchy outside her apartment block window, escaping periodically into an alternative world of plush Victorian splendour. She must also look after a precocious teenager Emily, a standout debut performance from Leonie Mellinger. Made for a modest £800,000, this proved to be the one and only directorial assignment by distinguished editor

David Gladwell, a statistic one is not altogether surprised by.

Julie Christie "D" • **Christopher Guard** Gerald • **Leonie Mellinger** Emily Mary Cartwright • **Debbie Hutchings** June • **Nigel Hawthorne** Victorian father • **Pat Keen** Victorian mother
Director *David Gladwell*
Screenplay *Kerry Crabbe, David Gladwell, from a novel by Doris Lessing*

Memoirs of an Invisible Man ★★★ PG

1992 US Colour 94mins [video]

Director John Carpenter returned to the Hollywood mainstream after a couple of quirky independent horror films – *Prince of Darkness, They Live* – for this flawed thriller. While Carpenter ensures that the action whips along at a cracking pace and the effects are stunning, the main problem is the uncertainty of tone. Chevy Chase, the innocent man who inadvertently becomes invisible, looks at home with the comic elements but is less convincing as a straightforward action hero, and it's left to Sam Neill, as the scheming spy who wants Chase's invisibility kept secret, and Stephen Tobolowsky to take the acting honours.

Chevy Chase Nick Halloway • **Daryl Hannah** Alice Monroe • **Sam Neill** David Jenkins • **Michael McKean** George Talbot • **Stephen Tobolowsky** Warren Singleton • **Jim Norton** Dr Bernard Wachs • **Pat Skipper** Morrissey • **Paul Perri** Gomez • **Richard Epcar** Tyler • **Steven Barr** Clellan • **Gregory Paul Martin** Richard
Director *John Carpenter*
Screenplay *Robert Collector, Dana Olsen, William Goldman, from the novel by HF Saint*

Memory Run ★★ 18

1995 US Colour 89mins [video]

An unnecessarily complicated slice of sci-fi which sees Karen Duffy going on the run from an evil corporate empire after she discovers that its executives have been literally playing with her mind. Saul Rubinek, Matt McCoy and Chris Makepeace add a further smidgen of respectability, but this one is really for genre fans only. Released as *Synapse* in the United States.

Karen Duffy Celeste/Josette • **Saul Rubinek** Dr Munger • **Matt McCoy** Gabriel • **Chris Makepeace** Andre Fuller
Director *Allan A Goldstein*
Screenplay *David Gottlieb, Dale Hildebrand, from the novel "Season of the Witch" by Hank Stine*

Men in Black ★★★★ PG

1997 US Colour 93mins [video]

The smash-hit science-fiction comedy based on a short-lived eighties comic strip, with secret agent Tommy Lee Jones and new recruit Will Smith as part of a top secret agency responsible for regulating all alien activity on Earth. While investigating an alien sighting the pair become involved in the search for a missing galaxy to appease an interstellar force and avert the Earth's destruction. Great special effects, inventive alien designs and Smith and Jones's hip, hilarious double act make director Barry Sonnenfeld's bug-eyed *Lethal Weapon*-style buddy picture a fast-paced pleasure.

Tommy Lee Jones K • **Will Smith** J • **Linda Fiorentino** Laurel • **Vincent D'Onofrio** Edgar • **Rip Torn** Zed • **Tony Shalhoub** Jeebs • **Siobhan Fallon** Beatrice • **Mike Nussbaum** Gentle Rosenberg • **Jon Gries [Jonathan Gries]** Van driver • **Sergio Calderon** Jose • **Carel Struycken** Arquillian • **Fredric Lane** INS Agent Janus
Director *Barry Sonnenfeld*
Screenplay *Ed Solomon, from the comic book by Lowell Cunningham*
Executive producer *Steven Spielberg*

Men into Space ★★★

TV 1959-1960 US BW 38x30mins

Made in the wake of Sputnik and Gagarin, this topical series imagined a near future when America had retaken the lead in the space race. William Lundigan is the commander of America's first moon mission, and the series followed his progress in getting out of earth's atmosphere and onto the moon, then establishing a base on our satellite and investigating various mysteries that arise. Alhough there were encounters with alien artefacts or fossils, the show concentrated mostly on more science- or politics-related problems, with the Yankee heroes having to rescue inept Soviet or British astronauts. Perhaps expecting more lively, monster-filled stuff, audiences didn't much care for the series, which boasted of obtaining "the cooperation of the Department of Defense and especially the United States Air Force" in creating credible space scenes and also used astronomical artist Chesley Bonestell (*Destination Moon*) as advisor.

William Lundigan Col Edward McCauley • **Joyce Taylor** Mary McCauley
Story editor *Robert Warnes Leach*
Producer *Sol Dolgin, Lewis J Rachmil*
Space concepts creator *Chesley Bonestell* • ***Music*** *David Rose*

Menno's Mind ★

1996 US Colour 90mins

A minor futuristic non-thriller about a computer programmer (Bill Campbell) at a virtual-reality resort who is forced into helping a a group of rebels stop a corrupt politician (Corbin Bernsen) from being elected. Because it's that sort of film, the plan involves the mind of the murdered rebel leader (*The Evil Dead*'s Bruce Campbell) being downloaded into the programmer's cranium. Failing resolutely to explore the implications of having someone else's memories as well as one's own, this lacklustre made-for-TV bore musters a few cheesy computer graphics as it lumbers towards its predictable outcome.

William Campbell [Bill Campbell] Menno • **Stephanie Romanov** Loria • **Corbin Bernsen** Felix Medina • **Michael Dorn** Simon • **Robert Picardo** Senator Taylor • **Robert Vaughn** Zachary Powell • **Bruce Campbell** Mick Dourif
Director *Jon Kroll*
Screenplay *Mark Valenti*

Mercy Point ★

TV 1998-1999 US Colour 8x60mins

An assortment of humans, aliens and androids play doctors and nurses aboard a 23rd-century space station, with less than life-affirming results. Although promisingly billed as *Star Trek* meets *ER*, this sci-fi medical drama sorely lacks all the style, innovation and narrative drive of its illustrious precursors and instead emerges as a low-key and lacklustre offering. *Terminator 2*'s Joe Morton earnestly struggles with the pedestrian plotlines and ill-conceived aliens, but there's no disguising his ailing patient. Unsurprisingly, the series failed to get a clean bill of health from apathetic US viewers and was cancelled after just eight episodes had been shot.

Joe Morton Dr Grote Maxwell • **Maria Del Mar** Dr Haylen Breslauer • **Alexandra Wilson** Dr Dru Breslauer • **Brian McNamara** Dr Caleb "CJ" Jurado • **Julia Pennington** ANI, Android Nursing Interface • **Gay Thomas-Wilson** Dr Rema Cook • **Jordan Lund** Dr Batung
Created by *Trey Callaway*
Executive producer *Lee David Zlotoff, Joe Voci, Trey Callaway*

Mesa of Lost Women ★ PG

1953 US BW 67mins [video]

Mad scientist Dr Aranya (Jackie Coogan in a patently obvious fake beard) is creating a race of superwomen using the venom of tarantula spiders. Hero Richard Travis is led by Aranya's lobotomised ex-partner Harmon Stevens back to the mysterious Mexican mesa and engineers the explosive climax. Incredibly cheesy Grade-Z trash featuring a bevy of fifties starlets as the bikini-clad women, depressing not-so-special effects and unintentional hilarity from start to finish. A must-see camp classic or to be avoided at all costs, depending on one's point of view. The same flamenco jazz score was reused for Ed Wood's *Jailbait*.

Jacke Coogan Dr Aranya • **Richard Travis** Dan Mulcahey • **Allan Nixon** Doc Tucker • **Mary Hill** Doreen • **Robert Knapp** Grant Phillips • **Tandra Quinn** Tarantella • **Harmon Stevens** Masterson
Director *Ron Ormond, Herbert Tevos*
Screenplay *Herbert Tevos*

Message from Space ★★★

1978 Jap Colour 105mins

Seven samurai plus one are needed by inhabitants of the planet Jiluca to stave off an attack by the Gavanas Empire in this undistinguished Japanese *Star Wars* effort. Borrowing as much from past Asian martial arts adventures as from George Lucas iconography – cute robots, spaceship chases through narrow canyons, a feisty heroine and cantina loads of space creatures – director Kinji Fukasaku's pale imitation still has enough intergalactic action and spectacular special effects to satisfy undemanding Skywalkers. Headliner Vic Morrow has virtually nothing to do, while kung fu expert Sonny Chiba (playing Hans!) shines brightest out of the star Asian cast. Japanese dialogue dubbed into English.

Vic Morrow General Garuda • **Philip Casnoff** Aaron • **Sonny Chiba** Hans • **Peggy Lee Brennan** Meia • **Mikio Narita** Rocksaia XII • **Sue Shiomi [Etsuko Shihomi]** Esmeralida • **Tetsuro Tamba** Noguchi
Director *Kinji Fukasaku*
Screenplay *Hiroo Matsuda, from a story by Kinji Fukasaku, Shotaro Ishinomori, Masahiro Noda*

Metal Beast ★★ 18

1995 US Colour 83mins

A daft monster movie that tries ringing a few changes on the werewolf myth with little success. A werewolf is discovered in seventies Hungary by deranged agent Barry Bostwick, who uses its blood for top secret government experiments and then puts it in suspended animation. Twenty years later, biology expert Kim Delaney defrosts it to carry on synthetic skin tests and turns the lycanthrope into something resembling a mutated gorilla before it goes on the rampage through the research facility. Bad special make-up effects and laughable genre riffs – the rocket launcher armed with silver shells being the prime example – fail to promote interest in the limp *Predator/Alien*-styled suspense. Contains violence and swearing.

Kim Delaney Anne De Carlo • **John Marzilli** Donald Butler • **Barry Bostwick** Pete Miller • **Musetta Vander** Debbie
Director *Alessandro DeGaetano*
Screenplay *Alessandro DeGaetano, Timothy E Sabo*

Metal Mickey ★★

TV 1980-1983 UK Colour 39x30mins

This fondly remembered, but hardly accomplished, long-running sitcom featured a young boy who invents a robot to help with the family chores at home but brings chaos instead. It was perhaps best known at the time for being the brainchild of Mickey Dolenz of the pop group The Monkees. An instant hit with audiences, the five-foot high robot, a sort of bargain-bucket R2D2 which generally out-acted the human performers and later developed magical powers enabling it to travel through time and the like, became a household celebrity with kids in playgrounds across the country mimicking his war cry of "Boogie Boogie". The walking dustbin even received a kidnap threat during the shooting of one episode and was given its own bodyguard. Fame indeed.

Michael Stainton Father • **Georgina Melville** Mother • **Gary Shail** Steve • **Ashley Knight** Ken • **Lucinda Bateson** Haley • **Lola Young** Janey • **Irene Handl** Granny
Written by *Colin Bostock-Smith*
Producer *Michael Dolenz*

Metalstorm: the Destruction of Jared-Syn ★ PG

1983 US Colour 80mins

Most notable for the fact it was originally released in 3-D, this misconceived, messy sci-fi epic got a big thumbs-down on its first release and hasn't aged particularly well since. An early effort from B-movie maestro Charles Band, it has hard-bitten Jeffrey Bryon coming to the aid of a miner's daughter (the future Mrs John Travolta, Kelly Preston) who has been kidnapped by intergalactic bad guy Michael Preston. Genre fans will spot Tim Thomerson in a supporting role – he and Band hit paydirt with *Trancers* in 1985.

Jeffrey Byron Dogen • **Michael Preston** Jared-Syn • **Tim Thomerson** Rhodes • **Kelly Preston** Dhyana • **Richard Moll** Hurok • **R David Smith** Baal
Director *Charles Band*
Screenplay *Alan J Adler*

Metamorphosis ★★ 18

1987 It Colour 81mins

The Fly meets *Altered States* in this bizarre oddity, written and directed by GL Eastman – in reality Luigi Montefiore, Italian restaurateur and star of such schlock-horror "classics" as *Antropophagus* and *Porno Holocaust*. Attempting to reverse the aging process, genetic scientist Gene LeBrock injects himself in the eye with a DNA serum, mutates into a murderous reptile monster, then goes further back on the evolutionary scale to become a living fossil. Despite the so-so effects and barely adequate acting (*Black Emmanuelle* star Laura Gemser also designed the costumes), this has a quirky atmosphere that's quite unusual.

Gene LeBrock Dr Peter Houseman • **Catherine Baranov** Sally Donnelly • **Harry Cason** Mike • **David Wicker** Willy • **Laura Gemser** Prostitute
Director *GL Eastman [Luigi Montefiori]*
Screenplay *GL Eastman [Luigi Montefiori]*

Metamorphosis: the Alien Factor ★★★ 18

1993 US Colour 81mins

An unexpectedly atmospheric revisiting of the desperately nondescript *Metamorphosis*, this finds a missing nightwatchman's teenage daughters trying to solve the mystery of their dad's disappearance, only to tangle with a ravening mutant or two at his corporate employer's sinister lab. While the cast can do little with the derivative script, the standard of the gruesome monster effects is well above the low-budget norm and writer/director Glenn Takakjian delivers a few well-aimed jolts of horror amid the carnage. Destined for minor cult status.

Tara Leigh Sherry Griffen • **Tony Gigante** Mitchell • **Dianna Flaherty** Kim Griffen • **Katherine Romaine** Nancy Kane • **Marcus Powell** Doctor Viallini • **Allen Lewis Rickman** Doctor Elliot Stein
Director/Screenplay *Glenn Takakjian*

Meteor ★★ PG

1979 US Colour 102mins

Wrapping up the spate of seventies blockbuster disaster movies such as *The Towering Inferno* and *The Swarm*, director

Urban planning: Fritz Lang's futuristic masterpiece from the silent era received a spectacular overhaul in 1984 with Oscar-winning composer Giorgio Moroder's updated score

Ronald Neame here places the planet on a hopeless, star-studded collision course with a gigantic asteroid. Spectacle has never looked cheaper or more pathetic than the tidal waves, avalanches and mud-slides on view in this celluloid catastrophe. Reaching an apex of absurdity when America (in the person of Sean Connery) and Russia (Natalie Wood) bury the hatchet to nuke the big rock, this mega-flop was initiated, amazingly, by Anthony Burgess.

Sean Connery Dr Paul Bradley • **Natalie Wood** Tatiana Donskaya • **Karl Malden** Harry Sherwood • **Brian Keith** Dr Dubov • **Martin Landau** General Adlon • **Trevor Howard** Sir Michael Hughes • **Richard Dysart** Secretary of Defense • **Henry Fonda** President • **Roger Robinson** Hunter

Director *Ronald Neame*

Screenplay *Stanley Mann, Edmund H North, from a story by Edmund H North*

Meteorites! ★ PG

1998 US Colour 85mins

Tom Wopat (*The Dukes of Hazzard*) and Roxanne Hart (*Chicago Hope*) struggle under the debris of this derivative disaster TV movie. When a meteorite shower wreaks havoc, the people of an Arizona desert town must band together to survive in a lame dog from space that leaves a vast, empty crater where the drama should be. Contains some swearing and violence.

Tom Wopat Tom Johnson • **Roxanne Hart** Cath Johnson • **Pato Hoffmann** John Whitehorse • **Amiel Daemion** Crystal Cassidy • **Darrin Klimek** Mac Johnson • **Leo Taylor** Filbo

Director *Chris Thomson*

Screenplay *Bart Baker*

Metropolis ★★★★★ PG

1926 Ger/US BW 138mins DVD

Fritz Lang's futuristic landmark of the silent era got an overhaul in 1984 when Oscar-winning composer Giorgio Moroder added an electronic score and songs by Freddie Mercury, Bonnie Tyler and Adam Ant. Re-edited with some forgotten footage, colour-tinted and with the special effects segments optically enhanced, the result is a fabulous reminder of how truly great this twenties *Star Wars* is. A contrived and simplistic parable in retrospect, it still contains unforgettable images of the 21st century that have been mercilessly plagiarised ever since. Purists may moan, but Moroder's achievement was to make this masterpiece of German expressionism live again for a new generation.

Alfred Abel John Fredersen • **Gustav Frolich** Freder • **Rudolf Klein-Rogge** Rotwang • **Brigitte Helm** Maria/Robot • **Fritz Rasp** Slim • **Theodor Loos** Josaphat/ Joseph • **Erwin Biswanger** Georg, No 11811 • **Heinrich George** Grot, foreman • **Olaf Storm** Jan • **Hans Leo Reich** Marinus • **Heinrich Gotho** Master of ceremonies • **Margarete Lanner** Woman in car

Director *Fritz Lang*

Screenplay *Fritz Lang, Thea von Harbou, from the novel by Thea von Harbou*

Cinematographer *Karl Freund, Günther Rittau*

Midnight Movie Massacre ★

1987 US Colour 86mins

An alien monster closes in on a movie theatre packed with fifties teens watching a sci-fi double bill, in this cobbled-together mess of lame nostalgia, nerd humour, and bad re-creations of black-and-white serials that use unreleased footage from shelved projects. The idea of hack producer Wade Williams, who shoehorns his uncompleted production of *Space Patrol* into director Mark Stock's *Animal House*-style antics, the result is a gory but completely nonsensical farrago.

Ann Robinson Dr Van Buren • **Robert Clarke** Colonel Carlyle

Director/Screenplay *Mark Stock*

Mighty Morphin Power Rangers ★ U PG

TV 1993-1996 US/Fr/Jap Colour

During the mid-nineties, the Mighty Morphin Power Rangers successfully fought off critics and all common sense to become the stars of the decade's most inexplicably popular TV phenomenon. A curious blend of original material and footage culled from Japanese action epics (primarily the *Sentai/Star Rangers* saga), the series follows the Rangers' repetitive battles against a variety of intergalactic monsters. While the show is a cheap, tacky and largely pathetic affair, its energetic action sequences, lively cast and irritatingly catchy theme tune tend to be appealing to primary school viewers. The series spawned two movies and a handful of short-lived TV spin-offs, including *Power Rangers in Space* and *Power Rangers Lightspeed Rescue*. A staggering 156 half-hour episodes were made.

David Yost Billy Cranston/Blue Ranger • **Amy Jo Johnson** Kimberly Hart/Pink Ranger • **Austin St John** Jason Lee Scott/Red Ranger • **Thuy Trang** Trini Kwan/Yellow Ranger • **Walter Jones** Zack Taylor/Black Ranger • **Jason David Frank** Tommy Oliver/Green Ranger • **David Fielding** Zordon

Executive producer *Shuki Levy, Haim Saban*

Mighty Morphin Power Rangers: the Movie ★★★ PG

1995 US Colour 91mins

Remember them? A few years ago these superheroes in vinyl tights were the hottest thing around. Now the tie-in toys are about as fashionable as Cabbage Patch dolls. Here the Power Rangers battle their old enemy Rita Repulsa, fight off slime creatures and squash the world domination plans of evil Ivan Ooze. If your children are feeling nostalgic, then this colourful junk will while away a couple of very mindless hours. Go, go, Power Rangers. And they did!

Karan Ashley Aisha/Yellow Ranger • **Johnny Yong Bosch** Adam/Black Ranger • **Stephen Antonio Cardenas** Rocky/Red Ranger • **Jason David Frank** Tommy/White Ranger • **Amy Jo Johnson** Kimberly/Pink Ranger • **David Harold Yost** Billy/Blue Ranger • **Paul Schrier** Bulk • **Jason Narvy** Skull • **Paul Freeman** Ivan Ooze • **Julia Cortez** Rita Repulsa

Director *Bryan Spicer*

Screenplay *Arne Olsen, from a story by John Kamps, Arne Olsen*

Mike & Angelo ★★★

TV 1989-2000 UK Colour

A surprisingly long-running ITV kids' show, veering between fantasy sit-com and teen drama, following the adventures of Mike King, an American boy living in England, and Angelo, a miraculous being discovered in the wardrobe of the new King house in London. Creators Lee Pressman and Grant Cathro made Angelo an actual angel in the first season, but then decided he was an alien – tapping into the *Mork & Mindy/ALF* business as more and more was revealed of his background. The show lasted long enough to recast both leads: when Tim Whitnall took over from Tyler Butterworth as Angelo it was explained that the alien had the Doctor Who-like power of assuming a new form, but when Steven Geller took over from Michael Benz who took over from Matt Wright as Mike it was a straight "new Darrin" shift.

Matt Wright Mike • **Michael Benz** Mike • **Steven Geller** Mike • **Tyler Butterworth** Angelo • **Tim Whitnall** Angelo

Created by *Lee Pressman, Grant Cathro*

Millenium ★★★

TV 1996-1999 US Colour 67x60mins

One of the most eagerly-awaited TV launches of the last millennium, Chris Carter's follow-up to *The X Files* instantly divided critics and fought an uphill struggle to stay on the air throughout its three-year run. Veteran movie actor Lance Henriksen stars as Frank Black, a former FBI profiler whose gift for seeing into villains' minds brings him into contact – and eventually conflict – with the mysterious Millennium Group. The series is arguably at its best in its chilling *Se7en/Manhunter*-inspired first season, while season two awkwardly ups the sci-fi/apocalyptic ante and season three turns the show into a conventional FBI thriller series. But through everything, Henriksen is utterly compelling, and the show always matches *The X Files*'s famed production values. Following the series' demise, Henriksen reprised the role of Frank Black in *The X Files*'s seventh season episode, *Millennium*.

Lance Henriksen Frank Black • **Megan Gallagher** Catherine Black • **Terry O'Quinn** Peter Watts • **Brittany Tiplady** Jordan Black • **Klea Scott** Emma Hollis
Created by *Chris Carter*
Executive producer *Chris Carter, Glen Morgan, James Wong*

Millennium ★★ PG

1989 US Colour 101mins [video]

Although based upon an interesting short story called *Air Raid* by John Varley, who also wrote the script, this doesn't have enough meat on it for a feature and it turns out to be quite a struggle to stay watching to the end. Kris Kristofferson is the investigator trying to work out what happened after an air disaster, who discovers that the passengers were whisked off by time traveller Cheryl Ladd before the crash, her intention being to take the survivors to a disease-ridden planet of the future and save the human race. Unfortunately, a promising premise gets lost among the clichés and B-movie performances. For hardened sci-fi fans only.

Kris Kristofferson Bill Smith • **Cheryl Ladd** Louise Baltimore • **Daniel J Travanti** Arnold Mayer • **Robert Joy** Sherman • **Lloyd Bochner** Walters • **Brent Carver** Coventry • **David McIlwraith** Tom Stanley • **Maury Chaykin** Roger Keane
Director *Michael Anderson*
Screenplay *John Varley, from the short story "Air Raid" by John Varley*

The Million Dollar Duck ★★★ U

1971 US Colour 92mins [video]

Disney's unofficial remake of the Douglas Fairbanks Jr vehicle, *Mr Drake's Duck*, provides yet another twist on the nutty professor story. Dean Jones, the original driver of *The Love Bug*, stars as a scientist whose experiments on the behaviour of ducks go haywire when his prize specimen, Charley, dips his beak into some radioactive apple sauce and begins laying golden eggs. From then on, it's the familiar tale of bungling baddies and government agents seeking to snatch the remarkable bird from the prof and his young friends. Youngsters will probably think it's all quackers.

Dean Jones Professor Albert Dooley • **Sandy Duncan** Katie Dooley • **Joe Flynn** Finley Hooper • **Tony Roberts** Fred Hines • **James Gregory** Rutledge • **Lee Harcourt Montgomery [Lee Montgomery]** Jimmy Dooley • **Jack Kruschen** Dr Gottlieb • **Virginia Vincent** Eunice Hooper
Director *Vincent McEveety*
Screenplay *Roswell Rogers, from a story by Ted Key*

Mimic ★★★ 15

1997 US Colour 101mins [video]

In the same vein as *The Relic* and all those other movies about creepy-crawlies that go crunch in the night, this horror movie stars Mira Sorvino as an entomologist determined to find out exactly what has invaded the New York subway system. It's preposterous stuff, but the tale of oversized insects (a genetically-enhanced species bred to eradicate an epidemic-spreading breed of cockroaches) is suitably gruesome thanks to *Cronos* director Guillermo del Toro's dark direction. Sorvino is believably tough, too, and smartly supported by Jeremy Northam, Charles S Dutton and Josh Brolin as potential monster munchies. Yummy. Contains violence and swearing.

Mira Sorvino Dr Susan Tyler • **Jeremy Northam** Dr Peter Mann • **Josh Brolin** Josh Maslow • **Giancarlo Giannini** Manny • **Alexander Goodwin** Chuy • **Alix Koromzay** Remy • **F Murray Abraham** Doctor Gates • **Charles S Dutton** Leo
Director *Guillermo Del Toro*
Screenplay *Matthew Robbins, Guillermo Del Toro, from a story by Matthew Robbins, Guillermo Del Toro, Donald A Wollheim*

The Mind Benders ★★

1963 UK BW 113mins

Ahead of its time in 1963 and now hopelessly dated, this melodrama about spying, brainwashing and Oxford dons was ill-fated from the start. Dirk Bogarde is just one of the scientists who spends a few hours in an isolation tank and ends up even more unpleasant than he was before. The film boasts some fine performances – not to mention the screen debut of Edward Fox – but Basil Dearden's direction is far too straightforward for such a bizarre story. It cries out for a Michael Powell or a Hitchcock.

Dirk Bogarde Dr Henry Longman • **Mary Ure** Oonagh Longman • **John Clements** Major Hall • **Michael Bryant** Dr Tate • **Wendy Craig** Annabelle • **Harold Goldblatt** Professor Sharpey • **Geoffrey Keen** Calder • **Terry Palmer** Norman • **Edward Fox** Stewart
Director *Basil Dearden*
Screenplay *James Kennaway*
Cinematographer *Denys Coop*

Mind Breakers ★

1996 US Colour 92mins

Cult director-turned-producer Roger Corman ruthlessly plunders his extensive back catalogue for a cobbled-together tale about dying aliens looking to mankind for ways to sustain their race. This incredibly cheap trash takes its special effects scenes from *Battle beyond the Stars* and other Corman classics, and criminally wastes the talents of actors such as Adam Baldwin and Robert Englund in nonsensical roles. A real stinker.

Adam Baldwin Lee • **Robert Englund** Father O'Neill • **Kate Rodger** Susan • **Duane Davis** Charles • **Gretchen Palmer** Carrie • **Jeannie Millar** Jana • **Jerry Trimble** Trit
Director/Screenplay *Fred Gallo*

The Mind of Mr Soames ★★★★

1970 UK Colour 97mins

An unusually thought-provoking psychological study of human behaviour, director Alan Cooke's sensitive work signalled an exciting new direction for Amicus, Hammer's nearest British rival, as they entered the horror-swamped seventies. Based on Charles Eric Maine's best-selling 1961 novel, and quite similar to *Charly* from two years earlier, Terence Stamp is brought out of a 30-year coma by neurosurgeon Robert Vaughn and, following a crash course in the ways of society, is sent into the terrifying outside world. Unfortunately the film can't cope with a childish simpleton in a man's body and a downbeat violent climax is assured. In one of his finest roles, Stamp is outstanding; his subtle character shadings ooze a captivating truth. Exploitation by the mass media is also broached in this intelligent science-fiction thriller that is something of an overlooked classic.

Terence Stamp John Soames • **Robert Vaughn** Dr Michael Bergen • **Nigel**

Davenport Dr Maitland • **Donal Donnelly** Dr Joe Allen • **Christian Roberts** Thomas Fleming • **Vickery Turner** Naomi • **Scott Forbes** Richard Bannerman • **Judy Parfitt** Jenny Bannerman
Director *Alan Cooke*
Screenplay *John Hale, Edward Simpson, from the novel by Charles Eric Maine*
Cinematographer *Billy Williams*

Mindwarp ★★ 18

1992 US Colour 91mins

Marta Alicia is a young woman in a society where everybody spends their lives hooked into virtual reality fantasies. But when she shows the ability to leap into other people's fantasies, she is banished to the real world: a post-apocalyptic wasteland crawling with cannibals and violent, fanatical despots. Despite the presence of B-movie stalwart Bruce Campbell, *Mindwarp* is too slow, grimy and serious to be fun.

Bruce Campbell Stover • **Marta Alicia** Judy • **Elizabeth Kent** Cornelia • **Angus Scrimm** Seer • **Wendy Sandow** Claude • **Mary Becker** Mom
Director *Steve Barnett*
Screenplay *Henry Dominic, Michael Ferris*

Miracle Mile ★★★ 15

1989 US Colour 83mins

A thoughtful and much under-rated apocalyptic drama that puts a human face on the threat of global holocaust. Anthony Edwards plays a musician who accidentally intercepts a phone call in which a man reveals to his father that a nuclear Armageddon is on its way, with an hour to go before the world's destruction. Writer/director Steve De Jarnatt, who also made the cult favourite *Cherry 2000*, specifically zeroes in on Edwards to capture the impact of the bad news. The man is caught between his moral responsibilities and his desire to see his new love (Mare Winningham) one last time. But will it be that? De Jarnatt keeps you guessing right up to the end.

Anthony Edwards Harry Washello • **Mare Winningham** Julie Peters • **John Agar** Ivan Peters • **Lou Hancock** Lucy Peters • **Mykel T Williamson [Mykelti Williamson]** Wilson • **Kelly Minter [Kelly Jo Minter]** Charlotta • **Kurt Fuller** Gerstead • **Denise Crosby** Landa
Director/Screenplay *Steve De Jarnatt*

The Misadventures of Merlin Jones ★★

1964 US Colour 88mins

A pleasant, undemanding Disney comedy from the reliable director of *The Absent-Minded Professor*. A college genius accidentally develops a means of reading minds. Turning this new ability to good use – in contrast to the way some of us might be tempted to exploit it – he tries to solve crimes, but he winds up in court himself. The characters were stretched a little too far for a 1965 sequel, *The Monkey's Uncle*.

Tommy Kirk Merlin Jones • **Annette Funicello** Jennifer • **Leon Ames** Judge Holmby • **Stuart Erwin** Police Capt Loomis • **Alan Hewitt** Prof Shattuck • **Connie Gilchrist** Mrs Gossett
Director *Robert Stevenson*
Screenplay *Tom August [Alfred Lewis Levitt], Helen August [Helen Levitt], from a story by Bill Walsh*

Misfits of Science ★★ PG

TV 1985-1986 US Colour 17x60mins

A group of mutants team up to form a crime-fighting band of superheroes and unleash a tongue-in-cheek superhero series firmly in the *X-Men* and *Fantastic Four* mould. Dean Paul Martin stars as the leader of the 'Misfits', whose eccentric troupe consists of incredible shrinking man Kevin Peter Hall, walking electricity conductor Mark Thomas Miller and a teenage telekinetic played by a pre-*Friends* Courtney Cox. Together, the likeable band of mismatched mutants take all on manner of quirky villains in a season's worth of modestly diverting but instantly forgettable superhero capers.

Dean Paul Martin Dr Billy Hayes • **Kevin Peter Hall** Dr Elvin "El" Lincoln • **Mark Thomas Miller** Johnny "Johnny B" Bukowski • **Courteney Cox** Gloria Dinallo • **Jennifer Holmes** Jane Miller • **Max Wright** Dick Stetmeyer • **Diane Civita** Miss Nance
Created by *James D Parriott*
Executive Producer *James D Parriott*

Missile to the Moon ★

1958 US BW 78mins

Cat-Women of the Moon was bad enough, but this uncredited remake is even more stupid, shoddy and pathetic. Astronaut Richard Travis leads an expedition to the moon with two escaped juvenile delinquents on board who encounter a lost civilisation of Amazons (all winners of a tie-in beauty contest) who are terrified by a giant hairy spider (the same puppet from *Cat-Women* reprising its original role). After more cardboard mayhem, poverty row thrills and rock creature hijinks, they blast off back to Earth. An absolute stinker.

Richard Travis Arnold Dayton • **Gary Clarke** Lon • **Tommy Cook** Gene Fennell • **Cathy Down** June Saxton • **KT Stevens** Queen Lido • **Laurie Mitchell** Lambda • **Michael Whalen** Dirk Green • **Nina Bara** Alpha
Director *Richard E Cunha*
Screenplay *HE Barrie, Vincent Fotre*

Mission Eureka ★★

TV 1990 Ger/UK/Fr Colour 1x105m; 6x55m

This was a rather dull series produced by Michael Rohrig and the aptly named Helmut Krapp, which originated in Europe and was partially dubbed for its UK transmissions. The plot revolved around a mission control centre which loses a satellite named Pallido in space and subsequently launches a shuttle to rescue it. With far too much talk and not enough action the show died a death partly because Channel 4 scheduled it in a late night slot but mostly because it just wasn't very good. Some dialogue dubbed into English.

Peter Bongartz Altenburg • **Delia Boccardo** Giovanna • **Patrick Fierry** Lefebre • **Agnes Dunneisen** Meike • **Michael Degen** Waldegs • **James Aubrey** Swann • **Elisabeth Rath** Marianne Altenburg
Director *Klaus Emmerich*
Written by *Ian Curteis, Terence Feely, from an idea by Peter Marthesheimer*

Mission Mars ★★

1968 US Colour 78mins

Barely adequate sci-fi programmer about the first American astronauts to land on Mars, only to face a challenge from a sun-activated, mechanical object called a polarite. Interplanetary explorers Darren McGavin and Nick Adams also encounter a frozen Russian cosmonaut, who returns to life and joins them in their war with the polarite. Restricted by a glaringly low budget – witness the shoddy model effects and the over-reliance on Nasa stock footage – famed director of cult turkey *Santa Claus Conquers the Martians* Nick Webster does manage at least to keep the drama on course. The soundtrack is pure dated hippy, with songs by the Forum Quorum. Actor Adams died of a drug overdose before the film was released.

Darren McGavin Mike Blaiswick • **Nick Adams** Nick Grant • **George De Vries** Duncan • **Heather Hewitt** Edith Blaiswick • **Michael De Beausset** Cliff Lawson • **Shirley Parker** Alice Grant • **Bill E Kelly** Russian astronaut • **Chuck Zink** Chuck
Director *Nicholas Webster*
Screenplay *Michael St Clair, from a story by Aubrey Wisberg*

Mission Stardust ★★

1968 W Ger/It/Sp Colour 95mins

One of only two movies based on the popular *Perry Rhodan* German pulp sci-fi novels written by Walter Ernsting under the alias Clark Darlton, this combined space opera and exotic adventure stars Lang Jeffries and Essy Persson, the Danish sex star of *I, a Woman*. Chief astronaut Rhodan (Lang) goes to the moon and discovers two super-intelligent space-wrecked aliens (Persson and John Karlsen). Karlsen has developed leukaemia so Rhodan secretly ferries them back to East Africa, where a famous blood specialist sets out to cure the disease. Enter renegade scientists who want to capture the creatures for their advanced technological know-how. Enjoyable enough juvenile hokum with a zany script that fails to ignite under Primo Zeglio's remote direction.

Lang Jeffires Maj Perry Rhodan • **Essy Persson** Thora • **Gianni Rizzo** Criminal leader • **John Karlsen** Kress • **Pinkas Braun** Rotkin • **Luis Davila** Capt Bull

Director *Primo Zeglio*

Screenplay *Federico de Urrutia, Sergio Donati, Karlheinz Scheer, Karlheinz Vogelmann, Primo Zeglio, from a story by Karlheinz Vogelmann, from the "Perry Rhodan" novels by Clark Darlton [Walter Ernsting]*

Cinematographer *Riccardo Pallottini*

Mission to Mars ★★★ PG

1999 US Colour 108mins [video] DVD

Brian De Palma slums it with his first science-fiction melodrama, which comes loaded with sentiment, camp moments and risible dialogue. However, while there's nothing new in this red planet space opera (mostly lifted from *2001: a Space Odyssey* and *Close Encounters of the Third Kind*) the *Carrie* director covers its drawbacks with pristine craftsmanship, trademark suspense sequences and a full quota of sharp computer visuals. The age-old question "Is there life on Mars?" is answered by Nasa astronauts Gary Sinise and Tim Robbins when they embark on a rescue mission to the planet and make an extraordinary discovery. It may be an overbaked *Mission: Improbable*, but De Palma's outer space adventure is still a highly affecting warp drive.

Gary Sinise Jim McConnell • **Don Cheadle** Mission Commander Luke Graham • **Connie Nielsen** Mars Rescue Mission specialist Dr Terri Fisher • **Tim Robbins** Commander Woody Blake • **Jerry O'Connell** Mission Specialist Phil Ohlmyer • **Kim Delaney** Maggie McConnell • **Elise Neal** Debra Graham • **Peter Outerbridge** Mars One Cosmonaut Sergei Kirov • **Armin Mueller-Stahl** Ray Beck

Director *Brian De Palma*

Screenplay *John Thomas, Jim Thomas, Graham Yost, from a story by John Thomas, Jim Thomas, Lowell Cannon*

Music *Ennio Morricone*

Cinematographer *Stephen H Burum*

Mr Drake's Duck ★★★ U

1950 UK BW 85mins

A bright, breezy comedy from British writer/director Val Guest (from his own script, based on a radio play) about a duck that lays uranium eggs, filmed in an innocent postwar era when the long-term effects of radiation poisoning were still unknown. Mrs Guest, the blonde and perky Yolande Donlan, plays Mrs Drake, who's married to suave Douglas Fairbanks Jr and who, together with her husband, breeds ducks on their Sussex farm, one of which turns out to be a source of possible riches. Very enjoyable, and deservedly very popular in its day, this is still a charming and overlooked British comedy.

Douglas Fairbanks Jr Don Drake • **Yolande Donlan** Penny Drake • **Howard Marion-Crawford** Major Travers • **Reginald Beckwith** Mr Boothby • **Wilfrid Hyde White** Mr May • **John Boxer** Sergeant • **Jon Pertwee** Reuben • **Peter Butterworth** Higgins

Director *Val Guest*

Screenplay *Val Guest, from the play by Ian Messiter*

SCI Q • SCI Q • SCI Q • SCI Q • SCI Q •

22

Who did The Believers believe?

See page 496 for answers

Mr Murder ★★ 15

1998 US/Ger/Neth Colour 126mins [video]

Although based on a book by horror maestro Dean R Koontz, this thriller places the emphasis on action rather than chills. Stephen Baldwin plays a writer of bizarre murder mysteries who becomes embroiled in a deadly real-life game, when a mix-up involving blood samples during a shady genetics experiment results in the creation of Baldwin's evil clone. The supporting cast – including Julie Warner and James Coburn – adds a touch of class and the end result is enjoyable, if a tad unbelievable. Contains violence, swearing and nudity.

Stephen Baldwin Marty Stillwater/Alfie • **Julie Warner** Paige Stillwater • **Bill Smitrovich** Lieutenant Lowbock • **Don McManus** Clocker • **James Coburn** Drew Oslett Sr • **Thomas Haden Church** Drew Oslett Jr • **Dan Lauria** General Aames • **Kaley Cuoco** Charlotte Stillwater • **Brittney Lee Harvey** Emily Stillwater • **Don Hood** James Stillwater

Director *Dick Lowry*

Screenplay *Stephen Tolkin, from a novel by Dean R Koontz*

Mr Smith ★

TV 1983-1984 US Colour 13x30mins

A supposedly surefire sit-com, especially with Ronald (*Bedtime for Bonzo*) Reagan in the White House, this eighties show was a famous flop. Mr Smith, a chimp played by CJ (Clyde from *Every Which Way but Loose*), is subjected to an experimental enzyme and develops a vast IQ (and speech, voiced by Ed Weinberger), becoming a government consultant on everything (the two-part opening story was inevitably called *Mr Smith Goes to Washington*). They must have laughed a lot in the development meetings, but the show debuted to hollow silence.

Tim Dunigan Tommy Atwood • **Leonard Frey** Raymond Holyoke • **Terri Garber** Dr Judy Tyson • **Laura Jacoby** Ellie Atwood • **Stuart Margolin** Dr Klein • **Ed Weinberger** Voice of Cha Cha/Mr Smith

Mr Superinvisible ★ U

1970 It/Sp/W Ger Colour 92mins

A stab at the Disney juvenile market by cult horror director Antonio Margheriti, this strained comedy thriller is a dismal Euro-pudding of the worst order. Disney star Dean Jones is a scientist conducting experiments to discover a cure for the common cold who instead finds a formula for invisibility. Sexy villain Amalia de Isaura attempts to steal it with the usual knockabout results. Lacking anything remotely entertaining or ersatz Disney in the gloss and charm departments, Margheriti's atrociously dubbed superhero wannabe is a total bust. Italian dialgue dubbed into English.

Dean Jones • **Gastone Moschin** • **Ingeborg Schoener** • **Amalia de Isaura** • **Philippe Leroy**

Director *Antonio Margheriti*

Screenplay *Mary Eller [Maria Laura Rocca], Luis Marquina, from a novel by Mary Eller [Maria Laura Rocca]*

Mistress of the World ★★

1959 Fr/It/W Ger BW 107mins

William Dieterle closed a glorious career with his longest and least distinguished film. Based on a silent German serial, this rambling two-parter centres on the efforts of superspy Micheline Presle to seize an energy-giving gravity device patented by Swedish scientist, Gino Cervi. However, standing in her way are government agents Lino Ventura and Carlos Thompson. A cursory glance at the cast list should clue you in that this is one of those fabled Euro-puddings, with parts commensurate with the generosity of the subscribing nations – which perhaps explains why Sabu, as Cervi's nefarious assistant, is so marginalised.

Martha Hyer Karin Johansson • **Carlos Thompson** Peter Lundstrom • **Micheline Presle** Madame Latour • **Gino Cervi** Prof Johansson • **Lino Ventura** Biamonte • **Sabu** Dr Lin-Chor • **Wolfgang Preiss** Brandes
Director *William Dieterle*
Screenplay *Jo Eisinger, Harald G Petersson*

Modern Problems ★

1981 US Colour 90mins

Stressed-out air traffic controller Chevy Chase is driving along the freeway when a truck carrying nuclear waste springs a leak, drenching our hero in radioactive slime. Instead of making him grow an extra head or simply killing him, the incident causes Chase to develop telekinetic powers. These help him sort out the problems in his life and enable him to take sweet revenge on his enemies. Mostly this involves sub-Stephen King stuff and some flying vomit *à la The Exorcist*. An idea that might have occupied a five-minute sketch on a TV show is stretched to full feature-film length here and shows that, without the Griswold clan, Chase can't carry a picture.

Chevy Chase Max • **Patti D'Arbanville [Patti D'Arbanville-Quinn]** Darcy • **Mary Kay Place** Lorraine • **Nell Carter** Dorita • **Brian Doyle-Murray** Brian • **Dabney Coleman** Mark • **Mitch Kreindel** Barry
Director *Ken Shapiro*
Screenplay *Ken Shapiro, Tom Sherohman, Arthur Sellers*

The Mole People ★★

1956 US BW 77mins

Anthropologists John Agar and Hugh Beaumont fall into a deep cave in Asia, discover a lost Sumerian city, and get captured by albino natives who have Mole Men as slaves. Armed with only flashlights to keep the sunlight-hating race at bay, they make their escape when the Mole Men stage a revolt against their masters. Nonsensical pulp made lots more fun thanks to the weird rubber Mole suits, Agar and Beaumont making a hilarious hero team and a few fanciful directorial glimmers by Virgil Vogel. Could be a minor cult classic.

John Agar Dr Roger Bentley • **Cynthia Patrick** Adad Gizelle • **Hugh Beaumont** Dr Jud Bellamin • **Alan Napier** Elinu High Priest • **Nestor Paiva** Prof Etienne Lafarge • **Phil Chambers** Dr Paul Stuart • **Rodd Redwing** Nazer
Director *Virgil Vogel*
Screenplay *Laszlo Gorog*
Special effects *Clifford Stine*

Mom and Dad Save the World ★ PG

1992 US Colour 86mins

This infantile comedy, which pokes broad fun at those creaky old *Flash Gordon* serials, hails from the same writers as the *Bill and Ted* movies – and don't it show! When middle-class parents Teri Garr and the wonderful Jeffrey Jones are spirited away to a far distant planet whose ruler intends making Garr his bride, Jones is forced into warrior mode to oust the tyrant and put rightful heir Eric Idle on to the throne. With its tasteless sets and rubber-suited monsters, the film's modest budget is flaunted as if it were a selling point. Yet director Greg Beeman can't disguise the lamentable script which, despite the best efforts of a likeable and willing cast, falls flat. Best viewed with your finger permanently pressed on fast forward.

Teri Garr Marge Nelson • **Jeffrey Jones** Dick Nelson • **Jon Lovitz** Tod Spengo • **Dwier Brown** Sirk • **Kathy Ireland** Semage • **Thalmus Rasulala** General Afir • **Wallace Shawn** Sibor • **Eric Idle** Raff
Director *Greg Beeman*
Screenplay *Ed Solomon, Chris Matheson*

Le Monde Tremblera ★★★

1939 Fr BW 108mins

Predication is an underpopulated sci-fi sub-genre, which is a pity, as, following Alfred Hitchcock's rules for suspense, it might have been profitably exploited. Richard Pottier's melodrama stars Armand Bernard as a scientist who patents a device that infallibly indicates the precise moment of a person's demise. When news of the invention leaks, the populace revolts and Bernard is killed exactly as the machine prophesied. Madeleine Sologne and Erich von Stroheim lend class, while Leon Barsacq's sets add atmosphere to an already pronounced sense of foreboding. A French language film.

Madeleine Sologne • **Mady Berry** • **Armand Bernard** • **Erich von Stroheim** • **Claude Dauphin** • **Roger Duchesne**
Director *Richard Pottier*
Screenplay *Henri-Georges Clouzot, J Villard, from the novel "La Machine à Prédire la Mort" by CR Dumas, RF Didelot*
Set designer *Leon Barsacq*

Monolith ★★ 18

1993 US Colour 90mins

Police detectives Bill Paxton and Lindsay Frost stumble onto a secret government plot to exploit an ancient and evil alien creature, while John Hurt sounds like he's fighting a case of laryngitis in his role as the conspiracy's wispy-voiced mastermind. Snappy patter and competent acting makes up for some rough editing, but the film-makers have a tough time deciding whether they're making a police procedural or a sci-fi thriller.

Bill Paxton Tucker • **Lindsay Frost** Terri Flynn • **John Hurt** Villano • **Louis Gossett Jr** Capt MacCandless • **Paul Ganus** Connor • **Musetta Vander** Katya
Director *John Eyres*
Screenplay *Steven Lister*

The Monolith Monsters ★★★

1957 US Colour 77mins

Meteor fragments land on earth, absorb moisture and grow to epic proportions. After a rainstorm, they start covering the world like living skyscrapers. An effective minor entry from sci-fi's golden era, based on a story by fifties icon Jack Arnold (*The Incredible Shrinking Man, Creature from the Black Lagoon*) and set in his favourite small-town desert locale. A simple story, well told with terrific special effects.

Grant Williams Dave Miller • **Lola Albright** Cathy Barrett • **Les Tremayne** Martin Cochrane • **Trevor Bardette** Arthur Flanders • **Phil Harvey** Ben Gilbert • **William Flaherty** Police Chief Dan Corey
Director *John Sherwood*
Screenplay *Norman Jolley, Robert M Fresco, from a story by Jack Arnold, Robert M Fresco*

The Monster ★★★

1925 US BW 71mins

One of Lon Chaney's more tongue-in-cheek horror films, this is a delight, if less memorable than *The Unholy Three* and *The Phantom of the Opera*, released in the same year. Here he's without elaborate make-up as the dapper Dr Ziska, a mad surgeon who arranges car accidents on a lonely road, thereby obtaining subjects for his experiments to discover the secret of life. Director Roland West, best known for *The Bat Whispers*, handles the story with considerable humour and visual flair.

Lon Chaney Dr Ziska • **Johnny Arthur** Under clerk • **Gertrude Olmsted** Betty Watson • **Hallam Cooley** Watson's head clerk • **Charles A Sellon [Charles Sellon]** Constable
Director *Roland West*
Screenplay *Willard Mack, Albert Kenyon, from a play by Crane Wilbur*

Monster ★★★ 18

1980 US Colour 80mins [video]

Pollution-spawned creatures go on a carnal rampage in a lively update of the concepts Roger Corman adeptly used for his own cult films of the fifties. Director Barbara Peeters complained producer Corman spliced in the sensationalised rape scenes after she had finished with the project, but they only add to the lurid, lip-smacking sleaze of the whole enjoyably tacky enterprise. Doug McClure and Ann Turkel finish off the sex-mad bimbo hunters after they've torn a carnival apart in a zestful guilty pleasure that has not a single dull moment. Also known as *Humanoids from the Deep*.

Doug McClure Jim Hill • **Ann Turkel** Dr Susan Drake • **Vic Morrow** Hank Slattery • **Cindy Weintraub** Carol Hill • **Anthony Penya** Johnny Eagle • **Denise Galik** Linda Beale • **Lynn Theel** Peggy Larson • **Meegan King** Jerry Potter • **Breck Costin** Tommy Hill
Director *Barbara Peeters*
Screenplay *Frederick James, from a story by Frank Arnold, Martin B Cohen*

Monster a Go-Go! ★

1965 US BW 70mins

Infamous gore guru Herschell Gordon Lewis (director of *Blood Feast*) bought the unfinished *Terror at Halfday* from director Bill (later *The Giant Spider Invasion*) Rebane, shot a few transitional scenes and inserts, added an absurd narration and released the whole boring mess as *Monster a Go-Go!* under the Sheldon Seymour alias. An astronaut returns from deep space and is transformed into a ten-foot high monster that then runs amok. Henry "Horace" Hite, the tallest man in the world, played the mutated pilot.

Phil Morton • **June Travis** • **George Perry** • **Lois Brooks** • **Henry Hite** Monster
Director *Sheldon Seymour [Herschell Gordon Lewis], Bill Rebane*
Screenplay *Sheldon Seymour [Herschell Gordon Lewis], Bill Rebane, Jeff Smith, Don Stanford*

SFacts

A poster campaign in the American Deep South (the only place this ever played theatrically) said it all: "You've never seen a picture like this – thank goodness!"

The Monster and the Ape ★★

1945 US BW

B-western fans will recognise several names on the call sheet of this 15-part derivative serial. Howard Bretherton, for example, directed numerous Hopalong Cassidy adventures, while Ray "Crash" Corrigan (who plays Thor the evil ape) made his name in the *Three Mesquiteers* series. As for the story, enemy agent George Macready poses as a scientist to steal Ralph Morgan's Metalogen Man and the valuable element that powers him. However, company executive Robert Lowery (who would go on to play Batman in the Columbia chapterplays) is having none of it. Only a last-reel plane smash and an embankment tussle are worthy of attention.

Robert Lowery Ken Morgan • **George Macready** Prof Ernst • **Ralph Morgan** Prof Arnold • **Carole Mathews** Babs Arnold • **Ray Corrigan** Ape
Director *Howard Bretherton*
Screenplay *Royal K Cole, Sherman Lowe*

Monster from Green Hell ★★ PG

1958 US BW 67mins [video]

Future *Dallas* star Jim Davis leads an expedition of scientists through the African jungle, courtesy of stock footage from *Stanley and Livingstone* (1939) and some cheap backlot trimmings. He's looking for a crashed space probe and its cargo of radioacatively enlarged wasps, but he needn't have bothered: after going on a weakly-rendered trail of destruction, the inept wasps eventually stumble into an erupting volcano. Although just as ridiculous as producer Al Zimbalist's infamous clinker *Robot Monster*, this thick-witted trek through fifties clichés is by far the more enjoyable bet.

Jim Davis Quent Brady • **Robert E Griffin [Robert Griffin]** Dan Morgan • **Barbara Turner** Lorna Lorentz • **Eduardo Ciannelli** Mahri • **Vladimir Sokoloff** Dr Lorentz • **Joel Fluellen** Arobi
Director *Kenneth Crane*
Screenplay *Louis Vittes, Endre Boehm*

Monster from the Ocean Floor ★ U

1954 US BW 51mins

Cult director Roger Corman's first production effort was written overnight, shot in six days and cost $12,000. A giant puppet octopus with a light bulb eye is terrorising a Mexican fishing village. Marine biologist Stuart Wade eventually rams it in the eye with a mini-sub when it tries to attack damsel in distress Anne Kimbell. A dull sea-going saga that sinks like a stone thanks to snail-paced direction, lifeless performances and post-synch dubbing giving all the voices a sleep-inducing disembodied tone.

Stuart Wade Steve Dunning • **Anne Kimbell** Julie Blair • **Richard Pinner** Dr Baldwin • **Jack Hayes [Jonathan Haze]** Joe • **Wyott Ordung** Pablo
Director *Wyott Ordung*
Screenplay *William Danch*
Producer *Roger Corman*

The Monster Maker ★

1944 US BW 62mins

This repellent horror movie – more closely allied to surgical fiction than imaginative fantasy – casts J Carrol Naish (later to play Charlie Chan on TV) as a mad scientist who infects his enemies with distorting bacteria. Directed by Sam Newfield and co-starring Ralph Morgan and Wanda McKay, it has little to recommend it apart from its freak-show novelty and an audience-pulling title.

J Carrol Naish Dr Igor Markoff • **Ralph Morgan** Lawrence • **Tala Birell** Maxine • **Wanda McKay** Patricia Lawrence • **Terry Frost** Blake • **Glenn Strange** Giant
Director *Sam Newfield*
Screenplay *Pierre Gendron, Martin Mooney, from a story by Lawrence Williams*

Monster on the Campus ★★

1958 US BW 76mins

This typically wacky fifties monster movie might have scared the pants off teen audiences back in the days of drive-ins, but will probably send today's youngsters straight to sleep. Still, there's much to enjoy in this corny tale of a fossilised fish whose blood transforms everything it touches into snarling monsters. A dog becomes a sabre-toothed beast, while poor old professor Arthur Franz turns into a Neanderthal apeman with a bad attitude. The effects are quaint, but the stilted script makes this perhaps the least interesting of Jack Arnold's genre efforts. (It proved to be his last excursion in the realms of monster movie-making.) Leading lady Joanna Moore later married Ryan O'Neal and is mother to Tatum.

Arthur Franz Donald Blake • **Joanna Moore** Madeline Howard • **Judson Pratt** Mike Stevens • **Nancy Walters** Sylvia Lockwood • **Troy Donahue** Jimmy Flanders • **Phil Harvey** Sergeant Powell • **Helen Westcott** Molly Riordan
Director *Jack Arnold*
Screenplay *David Duncan*

The Monster That Challenged the World ★★★

1957 US BW 84mins

A fun, low-budget sci-fi horror movie, in which the eggs of an extinct sea monster are released during an earthquake and hatch as giant snail-like creatures that kill humans for their blood and water. Tim Holt, former cowboy star and occasional actor of note (*The Magnificent Ambersons, The Treasure of the Sierra Madre*), came out of retirement to play the naval officer teaming up with Hans Conried's boffin to prevent the monsters breeding and spreading. An effective piece of film-making results from the good script by Pat Fielder (based on a story by David Duncan), suspenseful direction by Arnold Laven, a menacing score by Heinz Roemheld and convincing monsters created by Augie Lohman.

Tim Holt Lieutenant Commander John Twillinger • **Audrey Dalton** Gail MacKenzie • **Hans Conried** Dr Jess Rogers • **Harlan Warde** Lieutenant Bob Clemens • **Casey Adams [Max Showalter]** Tad Johns
Director *Arnold Laven*
Screenplay *Pat Fielder, from a story by David Duncan*

The Monsters ★★★

TV 1962 UK BW 1x45mins/3x50mins

A four-part BBC1 serial from writers Evelyn Frazer and Vincent Tilsley, directed by Mervyn Pinfield – who carried over his skill with studio-bound special effects to the William Hartnell seasons of *Doctor Who*. Honeymooning scientist William Greene and his wife Elizabeth Weaver search for a Loch Ness-style monster in a mysterious lake in the north of England, and discover foreign villain Robert Harris and his infiltrating force of miniature submarines. The monsters also show up, and the serial takes an ecological tack with a threat to the survival of humanity.

Robert Harris Professor Cato • **William Greene** John Brent • **Elizabeth Weaver** Felicity Brent • **Alan Gifford** Van Halloren • **Mark Dignam** Hopkins • **Helen Lindsay** Esmee Pulford
Director *Mervyn Pinfield*
Written by *Evelyn Frazer, Vincent Tilsley*
Producer *George R Foa*

SFacts

***The Monster*'s two writers worked out their story over lunch at London's BBC Television Centre the day after watching a *Panorama* report on the Loch Ness monster.**

Monstrosity ★

1963 US BW 70mins

Joseph V Mascelli, the cinematographer behind *The Incredibly Strange Creatures Who Stopped Living and Became Mixed-Up Zombies*, turned director with this formula mad-scientist saga and proved he could make a science-fiction cheapie every bit as brainlessly as his former directing colleague Ray Dennis Steckler. A wealthy old widow hires a nutty professor to transfer her brain into the body of a gorgeous girl, but the three candidates become zombies when the evil doctor and his mutant assistant foul up the experiments.

Frank Gerstle Doctor • **Erika Peters** Nina • **Judy Bamber** Bee • **Marjorie Eaton** Hazel • **Frank Fowler** Victor • **Margie Fisco** Zombie
Director *Joseph V Mascelli*
Screenplay *Vi Russell, Sue Dwiggins, Dean Dillman, Jack Pollexfen*

Moon 44 ★★ 15

1990 W Ger/US Colour 95mins

Before his Hollywood success with *Universal Soldier, Independence Day* and *Godzilla*, Roland Emmerich directed this German-financed sci-fi thriller about a cop (Michael Paré) going undercover as a convict on an industrial planet to investigate ongoing sabotage. Over-plotted, cliché-ridden and highly derivative, this mining mess certainly benefits from Emmerich's talent for getting every dollar on screen, and both the effects and production values belie its origins. But so little of it makes any sense – particularly an unpleasant rape subplot. Emmerich's ambitious approach deserves praise, but Dean Heyde and Oliver Eberle's muddled script doesn't do him any favours.

Michael Paré Felix Stone • **Lisa Eichhorn** Terry Morgan • **Dean Devlin** Tyler • **Malcolm McDowell** Major Lee • **Brian Thompson** Jake O'Neal • **Stephen Geoffreys** Cookie
Director *Roland Emmerich*
Screenplay *Dean Heyde, Oliver Eberle, from a story by Dean Heyde, Eberle, Roland Emmerich, PJ Mitchell*

Moon Pilot ★★★ U

1962 US Colour 98mins

One of the better Disney live-action pictures, in which Tom Tryon is selected to become the first man in space by a test-flight chimpanzee. The unwilling Tryon's resolve to remain on Earth is reinforced when he falls for Dany Saval, but when he discovers that she is a visitor from another planet, his feelings about outer space quickly change. Solidly supported by Brian Keith and Edmond O'Brien, Tryon and Saval make an engaging couple, and there are plenty of smart jokes at the expense of Nasa and the US obsession with conquering the final frontier.

Tom Tryon Captain Richmond Talbot • **Brian Keith** Major General John Vanneman • **Edmond O'Brien** McClosky • **Dany Saval** Lyrae • **Tommy Kirk** Walter Talbot • **Bob Sweeney** Senator McGuire
Director *James Neilson*
Screenplay *Maurice Tombragel, from a story by Robert Buckner*

Moon Zero Two ★★ U

1969 UK Colour 100mins

In an effort to diversify, Hammer attempted this "U" certificate space western, in which James Olson and Ori Levy do battle with the bad guys for prospecting rights on a somewhat bleak-looking moon. It's exactly what you might expect from a western set on the moon: shoot-outs, ambushes and dancing girls. The plot and dialogue are terrible, but look out for Monty Python's Carol Cleveland as a hostess, while Chrissie Shrimpton (sister of supermodel Jean) pops up in a boutique.

James Olson Bill Kemp • **Catherina von Schell [Catherine Schell]** Clementine Taplin • **Warren Mitchell** JJ Hubbard • **Adrienne Corri** Liz Murphy • **Ori Levy** Karminski • **Dudley Foster** Whitsun • **Bernard Bresslaw** Harry • **Carol Cleveland** Hostess • **Chrissie Shrimpton** Boutique attendant
Director *Roy Ward Baker*
Screenplay *Michael Carreras, from a story by Gavin Lyall, Frank Hardman, Martin Davison*

Moonbase 3 ★★★

TV 1973 UK Colour 6x50mins

Set early in the 21st century, this was the BBC's attempt at a realistic drama about what life might be like on the moon. It starred David Caulder as the commander of a scientific community based on the lunar surface jointly established by Britain and the European community. Despite the involvement of a trio of *Doctor Who* collaborators, producer Barry Letts, director Christopher Barry and script editor Terrance Dicks, there isn't a bug-eyed monster in sight; instead the focus is on human relationships and conflicts. (This prompted one callous critic to compare the show to an orbital *Crossroads*.) Consistent with many BBC sci-fi shows, the effects and model work on display have a beguiling amateurish charm about them.

David Caulder Donald Houston • **Barry Lowe** Tom Hill • **Ralph Bates** Michel Lebrun • **Fiona Gaunt** Helen Smith • **Christine Bradwell** Ingrid • **Tom Kempinski** Stephen Partness • **John Hallam** Peter Conway • **Jurgen Andersen** Per Bengtson
Director *Ken Hannam, Christopher Barry*
Script editor *Terrance Dicks*
Producer *Barry Letts*

SFacts

Old tricks: To prevent the visors steaming up during filming, dresser Leslie Hallam says: "I had to go back to my wartime experience. We used to rub soap inside our gas masks, so I used washing-up liquid. It works well, but in a long take it can start to bubble."

Moonbeam Mask ★★

1958 Jap BW 102mins

Constructed from a couple of serials, this is a Good *v* Evil confrontation, with the sinister Skull Mask battling superhero Moonbeam Mask for possession of a top-secret nuclear device known as the Ho-Joe Bomb. Fumitake Omura is the undercover cop who assumes the titular identity, while there's no prizes for guessing his nemesis is really corrupt lab assistant, Junya Usami. A string of cut 'n' paste sequels followed – *Moonbeam Mask II: Satan Nails* (1958), *Monster Kong, Ghost Gang's Counter-Attack* and *Last of the Devil* (all 1959) – while Yukihiro Sawada made an updated version in 1981. A Japanese language film.

Fumitake Omura • **Junya Usami** • **Hiroko Mine** • **Mitsue Komiya**
Director *Tsuneo Kobayashi*
Screenplay *Yarunori Kawauchi*

Moonraker ★★ PG

1979 UK Colour 121mins [video]

The 11th Bond movie jettisons Ian Fleming's marvellous novel and sends 007 into space. Weighed down by its often clunky special effects and non-existent plotting, the movie seems to be merely an attempt to update Bond in the wake of *Star Wars*. Roger Moore smirks throughout, Michael Lonsdale makes a lacklustre master criminal and Jaws, the towering sub-villain from *The Spy Who Loved Me*, makes a return appearance. Venice and Rio are also part of the package, but too much of the budget was wasted in overblown spectacle, without enough attention being given to the basics.

Roger Moore James Bond • **Lois Chiles** Holly Goodhead • **Michael Lonsdale [Michel Lonsdale]** Hugo Drax • **Richard Kiel** Jaws • **Corinne Cléry** Corinne Dufour • **Bernard Lee** "M" • **Geoffrey Keen** Frederick Gray • **Desmond Llewelyn** "Q" • **Lois Maxwell** Miss Moneypenny • **Emily Bolton** Manuela • **Toshiro Suga** Chang
Director *Lewis Gilbert*
Screenplay *Christopher Wood, from the novel by Ian Fleming*

Moontrap ★★ PG

1989 US Colour 84mins [video]

If you've ever wanted to see Chekov from *Star Trek* swearing or locked in a steamy clinch, this is the film for you. There are several more equally silly moments in this lively sci-fi adventure, although since a few of them were clearly intended to be funny, it's hard to say just how serious a movie the film-makers were trying to make. Whatever the case, it must be admitted that the story – concerning astronauts Walter Koenig and Bruce Campbell searching the moon for the remains of an ancient cybernetic civilisation – rattles along nicely, while the film actually boasts some pleasing special effects.

Walter Koenig Colonel Jason Grant • **Bruce Campbell** Ray Tanner • **Leigh Lombardi** Mera • **Robert Kurcz** Koreman • **John J Saunders** Barnes • **Reavis Graham** Haskell
Director *Robert Dyke*
Screenplay *Tex Ragsdale*

Mork & Mindy ★★★★

TV 1978-1982 US Colour 95x30mins

This was a spin off from an episode of *Happy Days* first transmitted in February 1978 which featured Williams in a cameo role as an Orkan alien. Williams made such an impact that he was given his own series.

Williams' interpretation of Mork was an incredible and often surreal performance fully utilising all of Williams' own madcap lunacy and verbal dexterity. He would drink through his index finger (which would then 'burp'), wear suits back to front, and generally get everything upside down and topsy turvy. The show gained incredible success during its first few seasons, and introduced several catch phrases, most popular being "na noo, na noo", meaning "goodbye", and "shazbut!" being an Orkan swear word. As with all the best comedy, the show also explored more serious elements of human life, with Williams bringing his Orkan point of view to bear in delivering pathos and emotion as well as madcap physical comedy and impressions. One of the most enjoyable and consistently entertaining shows on television.

Robin Williams Mork • **Pam Dawber** Mindy O'Connell • **Robert Donner** Exidor • **Ralph James** Orson
Created by *Garry Marshall*
Executive producer *Garry Marshall, James O'Keefe*

Morons from Outer Space ★ PG

1985 UK Colour 86mins [video]

Moronic isn't the word! Mel Smith and Griff Rhys Jones's lamentable lampoon is a shambling spoof of *2001*, *Star Wars* and *Close Encounters*, with little wit or wisdom on display. Directed by Mike Hodges, who really should have known better, the pathetic story concerns aliens from the planet Blob crash-landing on Earth and forming a glam-rock band. But the end result wouldn't have made the grade during the Oxbridge duo's student rag week. If sneezing in an astronaut suit, aliens mistaking a dustbin for a human and a spaceship trailing a caravan sound funny, then you may find this miserable farce on the cheap and cheerful side. Otherwise, alas Smith and Jones indeed. Contains some swearing.

Mel Smith Bernard • **Griff Rhys Jones** Graham Sweetley • **James B Sikking** Col Laribee • **Dinsdale Landen** Cdr Matteson • **Jimmy Nail** Desmond • **Joanne Pearce** Sandra • **Paul Bown** Julian
Director *Mike Hodges*
Screenplay *Mel Smith, Griff Rhys Jones, Bob Mercer*

Mortal Kombat ★★★ 15

1995 US Colour 97mins [video] DVD

At the time this film was made, *Mortal Kombat* was the world's biggest-selling game franchise, so it was a natural choice for a Hollywood makeover. And, unlike other games-inspired turkeys (*Super Mario Bros*, *Street Fighter*), this one actually works, thanks mainly to director Paul Anderson's single-minded dedication to nonstop, expertly choreographed martial-arts action, all set to a thumping techno beat. Christopher Lambert is the nominal star, but the best work comes from Cary-Hiroyuki Tagawa, who steals the show with a typically charismatic performance. Contains violence and some swearing.

Christopher Lambert Lord Rayden • **Bridgette Wilson** Sonya Blade • **Linden Ashby** Johnny Cage • **Talisa Soto** Princess Kitana • **Cary-Hiroyuki Tagawa** Shang Tsung • **Trevor Goddard** Kano • **Robin Shou** Liu Kang
Director *Paul Anderson*
Screenplay *Kevin Droney, from the video game by Ed Boon, John Tobias*

Mosquito ★★

1995 US Colour 92mins

If you ever wondered what Leatherface, the killing machine from *The Texas Chain Saw Massacre*, really looked like behind that mask, then here's your chance, as Gunnar Hansen does battle with a swarm of pesky mozzies that have mutated into insects the size of a Spitfire. A throwback to such fifties sci-fi B movies as *Them!*, Gary Jones's bargain-basement schlocker is clearly aimed at the seven-pints-and-a-takeaway market, and has enough gore, cheap effects and wincingly bad dialogue to amuse down to the last mouthful. Seekers of truth and beauty should look elsewhere. Contains violence and swearing.

Gunnar Hansen Earl • **Ron Asheton** Hendricks • **Steve Dixon** Parks
Director *Gary Jones*
Screenplay *Steve Hodge, Tom Chaney, Gary Jones, from a story by Gary Jones*

The Most Dangerous Man Alive ★

1961 US Colour 80mins

Escaped convict Ron Randell is accidentally exposed to radiation by a cobalt bomb explosion and becomes an unstoppable superman, hell-bent on revenge against the gangsters who framed him. The last film directed by silent pioneer Allan Dwan is an over-familiar, poverty-row mix of science-fiction thriller and mob melodrama, with only the halting exploration of Randell's post-holocaust sex life adding any unusual spin to the proceedings.

Ron Randell Eddie Candell • **Debra Paget** Linda Marlow • **Elaine Stewart** Carla Angelo • **Anthony Caruso** Andy Darmon • **Gregg Palmer** Lt Fisher
Director *Allan Dwan*
Screenplay *James Leicester, Phillip Rock, from the story "The Steel Monster" by Michael Pate, Phillip Rock*

Mothra ★★★

1962 Jap Colour 90mins

This introduction to one of Japan's most famous radioactive monsters was one of Toho Studios' best efforts, boasting colourful photography, a more ambitious story and good special effects. Surprisingly, Mothra here stays in egg or caterpillar form for most of the movie before finally growing wings, leaving less time than usual for monster mayhem. Much of the movie instead concerns Mothra's guardians – two tiny twin girls – and the greedy businessman who covets them. This is cute, although a sober reminder of the increased campiness that would later give the genre a bad name. Japanese dialogue dubbed into English.

Frankie Sakai Reporter • **Hiroshi Koizumi** Photographer • **Kyoko Kagawa** Showman • **Emi Ito** Twin • **Yumi Ito** Twin
Director *Inoshiro Honda*
Screenplay *Shinichi Sekizawa, Robert Myerson (English dialogue), from a story by Shinichiro Nakamura, Takehiko Fukunaga, Yoshie Hotta*

The Mouse on the Moon ★★ U

1963 UK Colour 86mins

The combination of a witty Michael Pertwee script, the exuberant direction of Richard Lester and the unique talents of Margaret Rutherford would normally have been enough to guarantee comic gold. But, perhaps because Peter Sellers in a triple role was a hard act to follow, this sequel to *The Mouse That Roared* never really gets off the ground – a not inconsiderable handicap since its topic is the space race. Once again, the tiny duchy of Grand Fenwick takes on the superpowers, this time using a rocket fuelled by the local wine. Although fitfully amusing, it wastes a rather splendid supporting cast.

Margaret Rutherford The Grand Duchess Gloriana • **Ron Moody** Mountjoy • **Bernard Cribbins** Vincent • **David Kossoff** Kokintz • **Terry-Thomas** Spender • **June Ritchie** Cynthia • **John Le Mesurier** British delegate • **John Phillips** Bracewell
Director *Richard Lester*
Screenplay *Michael Pertwee, from the novel by Leonard Wibberley*

Multiplicity ★★★ 12

1996 US Colour 112mins DVD

Michael Keaton finds his time stretched to the limit between his wife, career and family, until he meets a scientist who offers to clone him, in director Harold Ramis's inventive comedy. Of course, one clone ends up not being enough and soon he has an attic full of them – all played by Keaton and each with a different personality – while his unsuspecting wife (Andie MacDowell) wonders what on earth is going on. Not as eye-wateringly funny as Ramis's *Groundhog Day*, this is nonetheless a sprightly romp that benefits from superb, very funny performances by Keaton.

Michael Keaton Doug Kinney • **Andie MacDowell** Laura Kinney • **Zack Duhame** Zack Kinney • **Katie Schlossberg** Jennifer Kinney • **Harris Yulin** Dr Leeds • **Richard Masur** Del King • **Eugene Levy** Vic • **Ann Cusack** Noreen
Director *Harold Ramis*
Screenplay *Chris Miller, Mary Hale, Lowell Ganz, Babaloo Mandel, from a short story by Chris Miller*

Munchies ★ PG

1987 US Colour 78mins

What's worse than a rip-off of *Gremlins*? A rip-off of *Gremlins* with Harvey Korman in multiple roles, of course. Alien-hunter Korman thinks he's found definitive proof in the form of Arnold, a cute little creature who eats junk food. His evil brother (Korman again) gets hold of the little guy and, before you know it, there are scads of them, causing trouble for everyone. This is so imitative it's hard to believe it didn't prompt a lawsuit.

Harvey Korman Cecil/Simon Waterman • **Charles Stratton** Paul • **Nadine Van Der Velde** Cindy • **Alix Elias** Melvis • **Charlie Phillips** Eddie • **Hardy Rawls** Big Ed • **Jon Stafford** Dude • **Robert Picardo** Bob Marvelle
Director *Bettina Hirsch*
Screenplay *Lance Smith*

Muppets from Space ★★★★ U

1999 UK/US Colour 85mins DVD

Although more earthbound than the title suggests, this is one of the better Muppet movies, with a relatively coherent storyline and gags that achieve a high chuckle factor. Nasally challenged Gonzo believes his long-lost family are aliens and that they're coming to take him home. Aspiring TV reporter Miss Piggy and assorted government agents, led by Jeffrey Tambor, want to abduct him for their own ends. Fozzie Bear still doesn't get the starring role he deserves, but movies from *Close Encounters* to *The Shawshank Redemption* are wickedly parodied and guest stars F Murray Abraham, Ray Liotta and Andie MacDowell seem to be having a great time.

Frank Oz Miss Piggy/Fozzie Bear Animal/Sam Eagle • **Dave Goelz** Gonzo/Bunsen Honeydew/Waldorf/The Birdman • **Steve Whitmire** Kermit the Frog /Rizzo the Rat/Beaker/Cosmic Fish No 1 • **Bill Barretta** Pepe the Prawn/Bobo as Rentro/Bubba the Rat/Johnny Fiama/Cosmic Fish No 2 • **Jerry Nelson** Robin/Statler/Ubergonzo • **Brian Henson** Dr Phil Van Neuter/Sal Minella • **Kevin Clash** Clifford • **Jeffrey Tambor** K Edgar Singer • **F Murray Abraham** Noah • **Rob Schneider** TV producer • **Josh Charles** Agent Barker • **Ray Liotta** Gate guard • **David Arquette** Dr Tucker • **Andie MacDowell** Shelley Snipes • **Kathy Griffin** Female armed guard • **Pat Hingle** General Luft • **Hollywood Hogan [Hulk Hogan]** Man in black
Director *Tim Hill*
Screenplay *Jerry Juhl, Joseph Mazzarino, Ken Kaufman*

Murder by Phone ★★ 15

1982 Can Colour 89mins [video]

If you answer the phone in this picture you end up dead. The killer has devised a system that sends an electric pulse down the line, which sends the brain into immediate meltdown. The room you are in also gets a makeover. Richard Chamberlain is the science lecturer investigating the death of a student, John Houseman is a glorified telephone engineer and Sara Botsford an artist who taps into phone company files to trap the killer. Whodunit? It's veteran British action director Michael Anderson's job to keep us guessing.

Richard Chamberlain Nat Bridger • **John Houseman** Dr Stanley Markowitz • **Sara Botsford** Ridley Taylor • **Robin Gammell** Noah Clayton • **Gary Reineke** Detective Meara • **Barry Morse** Fred Waits
Director *Michael Anderson*
Screenplay *Michael Butler, Dennis Shryack, John Kent Harrison*

Murder in My Mind ★ 15

1997 US Colour 87mins [video]

The TV-movie spoiler for John Dahl's *Unforgettable* was this lacklustre science-fiction tinged thriller with a sleepwalking cast to match. Soap opera icon Nicollette Sheridan is the sexy FBI agent assigned to an apparently unsolvable case of a serial killer who preys on beautiful blondes. Her scientist husband is experimenting with memory transplants among rats and, in an attempt to break the investigative deadlock, she ill-advisedly decides to take on the memory of one of the killer's victims who is in a coma. Bad idea. In fact, make that bad movie all round. Contains violence and some swearing.

Nicollette Sheridan Agent Callain Peterson • **Stacy Keach** Agent Cargill • **Peter Outerbridge** Jack Bolinas • **Peter Coyote** Dr Arthur Lefcourt
Director *Robert Iscove*
Screenplay *Tom Swale*

Murder on the Moon ★★

TV 1989 UK/US Colour 94mins

Made by LWT, this lavish co-production was a mixed success. A Cold War-style thriller, the moon is divided into sectors along national lines. When a murder occurs at an American mine located in the Soviet sector, Russian military policeman Julien Sands is sent to investigate. He comes up against Brigitte Nielsen, an agent from Nasa. The success of the piece depends on the supposed sexual chemistry between the pair which, sadly, never ignites. As for the plot, ludicrous twists don't make up for the paucity of dramatic tension.

Brigitte Nielsen Lieutenant Maggie Bartok • **Julian Sands** Major Stefan Kirilenko • **Gerald McRaney** Dennis Huff • **Jane Lapotaire** Louise Mackey • **Michael J Shannon** Vincent Ivanov • **Brian Cox** Voronov • **Celia Imrie** Patsy Diehl
Director *Michael Lindsay-Hogg*
Screenplay *Carla Jean Wagner*

Murders in the Rue Morgue ★★★

1932 US BW 60mins [video]

Vintage *Grand Guignol* as director Robert Florey plunders German expressionism and atmospheric shocks while allowing plenty of room for Bela Lugosi to enjoy his Dr Caligari-esque mad scientist role. As Dr Mirakle, Lugosi runs an offbeat carnival attraction featuring a giant gorilla by day. By night, however, he's engaged in diabolical blood transfusion experiments involving apes and beautiful virgins. Although far removed from its Edgar Allan Poe inspiration, the lurid overtones of the pulp plot are handled with surprising candour.

Bela Lugosi Dr Mirakle • **Sidney Fox** Camille • **Leon Waycoff [Leon Ames]** Pierre Dupin • **Bert Roach** Paul • **Brandon Hurst** Prefect of Police • **Noble Johnson** Janos
Director *Robert Florey*
Screenplay *Tom Reed, Dale Van Every, John Huston, from the story by Edgar Allan Poe*

Mutant ★★ 18

1984 US Colour 95mins [video]

A small midwestern town is menaced by zombie mutants who have been

10 TOP MAD SCIENTISTS

● **Dr Victor Frankenstein** The original God-defying genius epitomised by Colin Clive in the 1931 film suffers from a flaw in his mad scientist credentials – he is not killed by his own creation

● **Dr Henry Jekyll** Cinema's ultimate split personality is also the only Oscar-winning mad scientist – actor Fredric March took the statue in 1932

● **Dr Jack Griffin** Trainee mad scientists take note – the original Invisible Man, as portrayed by Claude Rains in 1933, is the model of spiralling dementia and god-like delusion leading to death

● **Dr Moreau** Portrayed on film three times, but only once memorably (by Charles Laughton in 1932's *Island of Lost Souls*), Moreau's battle to take control of evolution has chilling resonances for contemporary science

● **Dr Strangelove** His gloved hand may have been borrowed from *Metropolis*'s Rotwang, but otherwise Peter Sellers's Nazi-genius-turned-presidential-advisor is a wholly original comic creation

● **Dr Seth Brundle** Jeff Goldblum's 1986 interpretation of a scientist-turned-mutant-insect in the *The Fly* is a masterpiece of gory pathos. Now, where did I put those nail-clippers?

● **Dr Thorkel** Better known as *Dr Cyclops* (1940), this jungle-bound genius wasn't afraid of shrinking anyone who threatened his radium supply

● **Dr Krank** Perfector of a process that steals the dreams of children, the creepy genius of *The City of Lost Children* is surely one of the movies' strangest scientists

● **Dr Emmett Brown** They're not all bad guys: witness the daffy inventor of the time-travelling DeLorean in the *Back to the Future* movies

● **Dr Janos Rukh** Exposure to *The Invisible Ray* (1936) turns boffin Boris Karloff into a memorably malevolent villain with the power to kill by touch – until his mother destroys the antidote

contaminated by a toxic waste spill. As usual, the local corporation is trying to cover up the scandal that has endangered the whole community. Although the zombies do little more than lunge at people with outstretched arms, the movie is well-paced and makes some attempt at characterisation. Yet it lacks the tension and relentless suspense of the *Living Dead* landmarks director John "Bud" Cardos is so clearly trying to copy. Nowhere near as entertaining as Cardos's best offering, *Kingdom of the Spiders*.

Wings Hauser Josh Cameron • **Bo Hopkins** Sheriff Will Stewart • **Jody Medford** Holly Pierce • **Lee Montgomery** Mike Cameron • **Marc Clement** Albert • **Cary Guffey** Billy • **Jennifer Warren** Dr Myra Tate • **Danny Nelson** Jack
Director *John "Bud" Cardos*
Screenplay *Peter Orton, Michael Jones, from a story by John Kruize*

Mutant Hunt ★ 18

1987 US Colour 76mins

An utterly pointless futuristic thriller in which a scientist seeks the help of a soldier of fortune when an evil businessman turns his cyborg inventions into crazed killers intent on a murder spree. This is one for Z-movie buffs only: the effects are risible and suspense is virtually non-existent., while the performances are uniformly unimpressive. Leading man Rick Gianisi has since carved out a micro-niche in the schlock-movie genre as Troma Films's infamous *Sgt Kabukiman*.

Rick Gianasi Matt Riker • **Mary-Anne Fahey** Darla Haynes • **Ron Reynaldi** Johnny Felix • **Taunie Vrenon** Elaine Eliot • **Bill Peterson** Z • **Mark Umile** Paul Haynes
Director/Screenplay *Tim Kincaid*

Mutant on the Bounty ★★ 15

1989 US Colour 88mins

Great title – but sadly that's about the only thing going for this otherwise predictable slice of sci-fi spoofery. The plot revolves around a spacecraft that finds itself with an unwelcome hitchhiker in the form of mutated musician Kyle T Heffner. Little thought or effort seems to have gone into even the most basic genre elements – sets, design and effects are all poor. The performances are pretty anonymous, too.

Kyle T Heffner Max Gordon • **John Roarke** Carlson • **Deborah Benson** Justine • **John Furey** Dag • **Victoria Catlin** Babette • **John Fleck** Lizardo
Director *Robert Torrance*
Screenplay *Martin Lopez*

The Mutations ★★

1973 UK Colour 92mins

Frankenstein meets *Freaks* in veteran cinematographer-turned-director Jack Cardiff's mind-boggling mad scientist extravaganza, which triumphantly embraces bad taste to provide queasy frissons rarely witnessed in British horror. Demented biologist Donald Pleasence (in one of his few latter-day roles not leavened with over-acted irony) crosses humans with plants and sends his gruesome failures to Michael Dunn, a dwarf who runs a circus sideshow. His most successful hybrid is a man-sized Venus fly trap (Scott Antony) who ingests a tramp before traumatising perennial Brit-screamer Jill Haworth and former Miss Norway Julie Ege. Mixing genuinely deformed performers with made-up actors, the discomfiting template may be that of *Freaks* (the party scene is a direct lift from Tod Browning's 1932 classic) but its prurient atmosphere is most definitely rooted in seventies British sleaze.

Donald Pleasence Dr Nolter • **Tom Baker** Lynch • **Brad Harris** Brian • **Julie Ege** Hedi • **Michael Dunn** Burns • **Scott Antony** Tony • **Jill Haworth** Lauren
Director *Jack Cardiff*
Screenplay *Robert D Weinbach, Edward Mann*

Producer *Robert D Weinbach*

Mutator ★★★

1991 US Colour 89mins

When a group of animal rights activists break into a top-secret research facility they release a lot more than rabbits, in a genre entry that's strong on thrills, if a bit predictable of plot. Brion James plays a former researcher who takes a job as a security guard at the lab in the hope of controlling the threat he has helped create. *Mutator* manages to rise above its low budget by creating fully-rounded, believable characters and using the claustrophobic atmosphere of the laboratory and its subterranean passages to great effect – the monsters themselves, when revealed, are actually the least scary thing about the film.

Brion James David Allen • **Carolyn Clark** Ann Taylor • **Milton Raphael Murrill** Travers • **Neil McCarthy** Adam • **Brian O'Shaughnessy** Axelrod • **Embeth Davidtz** Jennifer • **Lindsay Orbach** Tina • **Greg Latter** Murphy
Director *John R Bowey*
Screenplay *Lynn Rose Higgins, from a story by Lynn Rose Higgins, Gerald A Rose*

Mutiny in Outer Space ★

1965 US BW 80mins

Astronaut William Leslie returns from a moon mission with a deadly alien fungus that thrives on heat. After it takes over an orbiting space station, and sets it sights on invading Earth, Leslie and company destroy it with frozen ice particles. Slight suspense and deft photography by Arch Dalzell do little to raise director Hugo (*The Human Duplicators*) Grimaldi's slow effort above the routine.

William Leslie Major Towers • **Dolores Faith** Faith Montaine • **Pamela Curran** Connie • **Richard Garland** Col Cromwell
Director *Hugo Grimaldi*
Screenplay *Arthur C Pierce*

My Favorite Martian ★★★★

TV 1963-1966 US BW/Colour 107x30mins

The archetypal fantasy sit-com, this featured an odd couple in reporter Bill Bixby and his "Uncle Martin" Ray Walston, a crash-landed Martian who is holing up in Bixby's apartment while he repairs his saucer and gets the pair into and out of scrapes by using his frankly magical alien powers. Pamela Britton, the landlady, is curious about the strange relationship, especially because the "uncle's" presence means the eligible bachelor is less interested in her. The covert joke, of course, was that the secret kept by Walston, suavely snide with retractable antennae, and Bixby, aggressively macho but given to falling over, was that they were gay. The show ran for three seasons from 1963, was revived from 1973 as a cartoon *My Favorite Martians* (with Jonathan Harris as the voice of Martin) and ended up as a dire theatrical film, in which Walston had a cameo.

Ray Walston Uncle Martin • **Bill Bixby** Tim O'Hara • **Pamela Britton** Mrs Lorelei Brown • **Alan Hewitt** Det Bill Brennan • **Roy Engel** Police chief • **Ann Marshall** Angela Brown
Created by *John L Greene*
Executive producer *Jack Chertok*

My Favorite Martian ★ PG

1999 US Colour 93mins DVD

Another cult sixties TV show gets a commercially crass, leaden make-over. A numbing headache in movie disguise, this special-effects farce is a pointless farrago that's nowhere near as fun as the show that inspired it, despite an in-joke appearance by original Martian Ray Walston. Unemployed TV news producer Jeff Daniels hides crash-landed alien Christopher Lloyd in his car as the manic

Relative values: Ray Walston and Bill Bixby learn to live together in *My Favorite Martian*

shape-shifter searches for spaceship spare parts. A highly talented cast – yes, even Elizabeth Hurley – drown in a mass of bad quips, slapstick pratfalls and shameless mugging clearly tailored as a youngster's *Men in Black*. Worse than *Flubber*!

Jeff Daniels Tim O'Hara • **Christopher Lloyd** Uncle Martin • **Elizabeth Hurley** Brace Channing • **Daryl Hannah** Lizzie • **Christine Ebersole** Mrs Lorelei Brown • **Wallace Shawn** Coleye • **Michael Lerner** Mr Channing • **Jeremy Hotz** Billy • **Ray Walston**
Director *Donald Petrie*
Screenplay *Deanna Oliver, Sherri Stoner, from the TV series by John L Greene*

My Hero ★★

TV 2000-2001 UK Colour 13x30mins

Father Ted star Ardal O'Hanlon slips easily into the comic role of shy health-food shop owner, trying to lead a normal life and wooing nurse Emily Joyce in the London suburb of Northolt. But in his spare time, he's really an alien super-hero called Thermoman. What could have been an interesting premise resorts too often to nursery-level humour, but O'Hanlon's charm is compensation. Enough people enjoyed the first series to justify a second round of episodes.

Ardal O'Hanlon George Sunday/ Thermoman • **Emily Joyce** Janet Dawkins • **Geraldine McNulty** Mrs Ravens • **Hugh Dennis** Piers • **Lou Hirsch** Arnie • **Lill Roughley** Ella Dawkins
Written by *Paul Mendelson, Paul Mayhew-Archer*
Producer *Marcus Mortimer, John Stroud*

My Living Doll ★★★

TV 1964-1965 US BW 26x30mins

With shows on air about regular guys living with Martians, genies, witches, talking horses and talking cars, it was inevitable that some network (CBS) would greenlight a sit-com in which a man, psychiatrist Bob Cummings is living with a robot, AAF709/Rhonda Miller (Julie Newmar), whom he is supposed to teach about human behaviour although she often reacts with literalisms and gaffes. As with *I Dream of Jeannie*, the implication was that the hero had a super-powered sex slave, but the show went out of its way to seem innocent, although the statuesque Newmar made this hard to take seriously. Behind-the-scenes conflicts meant that Cummings bowed out of the last four episodes and lovestruck neighbour Jack Mullaney found out Rhoda was a gadget not a gidget and became the leading man.

Robert Cummings Dr Bob McDonald • **Julie Newmar** Rhoda Miller (Robot AF709) • **Jack Mullaney** Dr Peter Robinson • **Doris Dowling** Irene McDonald
Executive producer *Jack Chertok*

SFacts

It's reported that Julie Newmar's co-star was to have been Jerry van Dyke, who opted instead to wait for a better sitcom opportunity, which turned out to be... *My Mother the Car.* Newmar was nominated for a Golden Globe as best TV actress for her role as the endearing robot AF709.

My Science Project ★★ 15

1985 US Colour 90mins [video]

This laugh-free comedy typifies the problems that the Disney studios have always had in producing films for kids who've outgrown their cartoons. The plot is OK: high school students get their hands on an extra-terrestrial gizmo that lets them summon up objects from the past and future. But its development, especially the emphasis on clumsily portrayed and badly integrated adolescent sex, leaves a nasty taste in the mouth. You'll spot some familiar faces in the cast (Fisher Stevens, Richard Masur, Barry Corbin), while Dennis Hopper is truly funny as an ageing hippy science teacher.

John Stockwell Michael Harlan • **Danielle Von Zerneck** Ellie Sawyer • **Fisher Stevens** Vince Latello • **Raphael Sbarge** Sherman • **Dennis Hopper** Bob Roberts • **Barry Corbin** Lew Harlan • **Richard Masur** Detective Isadore Nulty
Director/Screenplay *Jonathan Betuel*

My Secret Identity ★★

TV 1988-1991 Can Colour 72x30mins

A Canadian series that puts a *Spider-Man*-like teenage spin on the sit-com superheroics of *Mr Terrific*, *Captain Nice* and *My Hero*. Young Jerry O'Connell (later of *Sliders*), a comics fan, is exposed to gamma radiation in the laboratory of his eccentric neighbour Derek McGrath and gains super-powers (flight, invulnerability, super-speed). O'Connell decided to call himself Ultraman (not to be confused with the Japanese one) and to fight crime, but mostly dealt with regular schoolyard problems.

Jerry O'Connell Andrew Clements • **Derek McGrath** Dr Benjamin Jeffcoate, "Dr J" • **Christopher Bolton** Kirk Stevens • **Wanda Cannon** Stephanie Clements • **Marsha Moreau** Erin Clements

My Stepmother Is an Alien ★★★ 15

1988 US Colour 103mins

"Barbarella Goes Shopping" is the premise of this clunky cosmic satire, saved by Kim Basinger's untapped flair for light comedy. She plays a gorgeous ET who shacks up with scientist slob Dan Aykroyd to save her planet from destruction. Forget the plot, just settle down and watch a series of goofy culture-clash sketches revolving around Basinger coping with suburban life on Earth armed only with her talking alien handbag. Fine moments of inspired lunacy jostle with predictably slight comic relief, but Basinger's eager-to-please freshness and verve make this intergalactic muddle impossible to dislike. Contains swearing.

Dan Aykroyd Dr Steven Mills • **Kim Basinger** Celeste Martin • **Jon Lovitz** Ron Mills • **Alyson Hannigan** Jessie Mills • **Joseph Maher** Dr Lucas Budlong • **Seth Green** Fred Glass • **Wesley Mann** Grady • **Adrian Sparks** Dr Morosini
Director *Richard Benjamin*
Screenplay *Jerico Weingrod, Herschel Weingrod, Timothy Harris, Jonathan Reynolds*

My Uncle the Alien ★★

1996 US Colour 90mins

There aren't any American princesses to have *Roman Holiday*-style adventures, so it's up to the President's young daughter to slip her secret service minders and go walkabout in downtown Los Angeles. But, in trying to raise some money for a struggling shelter for the homeless, Kelly Sullivan (played by Hayley Foster) doesn't have to rely solely on her own devices, as she's joined on her mission by guardian alien Joshua Paddock. With lashings of yuletide sentimentality coating the already sugary asides on patriotism and the duties of the privileged, this corny fantasy comedy should amuse youngsters, but will leave grown-ups feeling slightly sickly.

Hayley Foster Kelly Sullivan • **Joshua Paddock [Josh Paddock]** Zig • **Ace Ross** Ratt • **Wendi Westbrook** Lois Sullivan • **Dink O'Neal** President Patrick J Sullivan
Director *Henry Charr [Henri Charr]*
Screenplay *Robert Newcastle, from a story by Henry Charr [Henri Charr], Jess Mancilla*

The Mysterians ★★★

1957 Jap Colour 87mins

Lively direction by Insohiro (*Godzilla*) Honda and luridly imaginative special effects lift this Japanese space invasion opus from its B-movie doldrums. Horny aliens from the planet Mysteroid arrive on Earth following the destruction of their home by Strontium-90. They use giant, robotic, bird-like tanks and lethal death rays to force the earthlings to marry into their race. Short on plot, high in visually arresting destruction – the cockroach-headed ET's take off their sunglasses to shoot blue flames from their eyes – veteran Toho effects genius Eiji Tsuburaya outdoes his *Godzilla* accomplishments here in this fun, stylish, and colourful juvenile extravaganza. A Japanese language film.

Kenji Sahara Joji Atsumi • **Yumi Shirakawa** Etsuko Shiraishi • **Momoko Kochi** Hiroko • **Akihiko Hirata** Ryoichi Shiraishi • **Takashi Shimura** Dr Adachi • **Susumu Fujita** Gen Morita • **Hisaya Ito** Capt Seki
Director *Inoshiro Honda*
Screenplay *Takeshi Kimura, Shigeru Kayama, Jojiro Okami*

The Mysterious Dr Satan ★★★ U

1940 US BW 15x16mins

Wearing the metallic mask that helped his father evade crooked lawmen in the Old West, Robert Wilcox – as Copperhead – is the indestructible hero of this fondly remembered serial. But while his frequent brushes with death keep the entertainment levels high, it's the army of robots (which resemble silver post boxes on legs) controlled by the demonic Eduardo Ciannelli that brought in the punters. Ciannelli also raises the ante as the debonair criminal mastermind whose plans for global domination depend on acquiring Professor C Montague Shaw's remote control device. Indeed, for once, there's a temptation to cheer on the bad guys.

Eduardo Ciannelli Dr Satan • **Robert Wilcox** Bob Wayne/Copperhead • **William Newell** Speed Martin • **Ella Neal** Lois Scott • **Dorothy Herbert** Alice Brent • **Montague Shaw [C Montague Shaw]** Prof Scott • **Charles Trowbridge** Governor Bronson
Director *William Witney, John English*
Screenplay *Franklin Adreon, Ronald Davidson, Norman S Hall, Joseph F Poland, Sol Shor*

The Mysterious House of Dr C ★★

1976 US/Sp Colour 88mins

After almost a decade in the wilderness and having failed, five years earlier, to mount a long-cherished biopic of Isabella of Castile, über-producer Samuel Bronston (who had specialised in lavish costume epics) bowed out of movies with this mediocre sequel to Doctor Coppelius. Working from his own stage play, which was itself based on the Délibes ballet, director Ted Kneeland creates an adequate sense of wonderment, as eccentric inventor Walter Slezak once again animates a clockwork doll. American prima ballerina Claudia Corday also reprises her earlier role of Swanilda, while Swedish star Caj Selling returns as the lovesick Franz.

Walter Slezak Dr Coppelius • **Claudia Corday** Swanilda/Coppelia • **Caj Selling** Franz • **Eileen Elliott** Brigitta • **Terry-Thomas** Voice of the Bull
Director *Ted Kneeland*
Screenplay *Ted Kneeland*

The Mysterious Island ★★★

1929 US Colour and BW 95mins

Three years in the making, shot mostly in brilliant two-strip Technicolour and featuring wonderfully elaborate sets, miniature work and special effects, this is the first of five adaptations of Jules Verne's sequel to *20,000 Leagues under the Sea*. Using only basic plot elements from the novel and minimal dialogue, Lionel Barrymore (in one of his best roles) plays Count Dakkar, scientist ruler of the mythical kingdom of Hetvia, who invents a submarine to search the oceans for sea monsters. He finds an undersea world populated by fish-men and, after winning their gratitude by slaying a water dragon, takes on the evil Falon (Montagu Love) who wants to depose him. More battles later, with a giant octopus and revolting fish-men, Dakkar goes to a willing watery death. Director Lucien Hubbard took over the troubled production from Maurice Tourneur and Benjamin Chistensen when storms wrecked the sets, and he finds exactly the right melodramatic tenor for the fantastical elements that keep both tension and interest at an unusually high level for transitional silent films of this period.

Lionel Barrymore Count Dakkar • **Lloyd Hughes** Nicolai • **Jane Daly** Sonia • **Montagu Love** Falon • **Harry Gribbon** Mikhail • **Snitz Edwards** Anton • **Gibson Gowland** Dmitry • **Dolores Brinkman** Teresa
Director *Lucien Hubbard, Benjamin Christensen, Maurice Tourneur*
Screenplay *Lucien Hubbard, from the novel by Jules Verne*

Mysterious Island ★★

1941 USSR BW 75mins

With the exception of Tinseltown's serial-makers, science fiction was low on most people's agenda during the Second World War. So this Soviet offering is something of a curio, particularly as it doesn't have any discernable propaganda value. Much more faithful to the Jules Verne novel than the 1929 Hollywood version, it chronicles the further adventures of Captain Nemo and his nemesis, Ayrton. Filmed at the Gorky studios in Moscow (which later became synonymous with children's and fantasy features), it's an efficient rather than an effective picture, with Mikhail Karyukov's special effects falling on the amateurish side of quaint. A Russian language film.

N V Komissarov • **A S Krasnapolski** • **P I Klansky** • **R Ross** • **A A Andrienkov**
Director *B M Chelintsev, E A Penzlin*
Screenplay *BM Chelintsev, MP Kalinin, from the novel by Jules Verne*

Mysterious Island ★★★ U

1961 UK/US Colour 96mins [video]

Based on Jules Verne's sequel to *20,000 Leagues under the Sea*, this enjoyable British production blends Sinbad-style giant monster thrills, pirates, volcanic eruptions and, of course, Captain Nemo (not James Mason this time, but Herbert Lom). As ever, stop-frame animation maestro Ray Harryhausen's monstrous menagerie provides most of the film's highlights, as oversized bees and colossal crabs threaten the health of Michael Craig, Joan Greenwood and their companions. Although the rather colourless cast doesn't do much to raise excitement levels, Harryhausen's fine work and Bernard Herrman's atmospheric score make this fantasy island worth an excursion.

Michael Craig Captain Cyrus Harding • **Joan Greenwood** Lady Mary Fairchild • **Michael Callan** Herbert Brown • **Gary Merrill** Gideon Spilett • **Herbert Lom** Captain Nemo • **Beth Rogan** Elena • **Percy Herbert** Sergeant Pencroft • **Dan Jackson** Neb • **Nigel Green** Tom
Director *Cy Endfield*
Screenplay *John Prebble, Daniel Ullman, Crane Wilbur, from the novel "L'Ile Mysterieuse" by Jules Verne*
Special effects *Ray Harryhausen* • ***Music*** *Bernard Herrmann*

SCI Q • SCI Q • SCI Q • SCI Q •

23

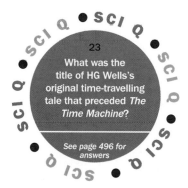

What was the title of HG Wells's original time-travelling tale that preceded *The Time Machine*?

See page 496 for answers

Mysterious Island ★★

TV 1995 Can/NZ Colour 22x60mins

Loosely based on Jules Verne's classic novel, Captain Nemo's landlocked voyage of discovery takes place on his exotic island hide-away. When Nemo's secret base is accidentally discovered by a group of escapees from the Confederate Army, they soon become involved in his world of daring experiments, tribal natives and sea-faring monsters. A buoyant but rarely captivating affair, Nemo and company's small-screen exploits primarily coast along on the strength of the show's timeless premise. *Seven Days*'s Alan Scarfe and *Andromeda*'s Gordon Michael Woolvett are among the series' assured ensemble of performers, while their island home is beautifully visualised by some impressive photography of New Zealand. By the end of its first season, however, nothing could stop the series from sinking without a trace.

Alan Scarfe Captain Cyrus Harding • **Colette Stevenson** Joanna Pencroft • **John Bach** Captain Nemo • **C David Johnson** Jack Pencroft • **Stephen Lovatt** Gideon Spilett • **Gordon Michael Woolvett** Herbert Pencroft • **Andy Marshall** Neb Brown •
Executive story editor *Glenn Norman*
Source *from the novel by Jules Verne*

The Mysterious Satellite ★★★

1956 Jap Colour 87mins

Friendly aliens from the planet Paira, looking like giant one-eyed starfish, arrive on Earth to warn mankind about the dangers of the atom bomb. After getting their message across by adopting human guise, they join forces with humanity to destroy a fiery planet that will soon collide with Earth. Far more serious in intention than the usual Japanese monster rally – although the formula disaster footage is very much in evidence courtesy of special effects man Kemmei Yuasa – director Koji Shima's thoughtful fantasy is a far more mature addition to the genre than would at first seem apparent. A Japanese language film.

Toyomi Karita Ginko • **Keizo Kawasaki** Toru • **Isao Yamagata** Dr Matsuda
Director *Koji Shima*
Screenplay *Hideo Oguni, from the novel "Uchujin Tokyo ni Arawaru" by Gentaro Nakajima*
Special effects *Kenmai Yuasa*

The Mysterious Two ★★

1982 US Colour 100mins

Shot in 1979 as *Follow Me If You Dare*, and inspired by the Jonestown Massacre of 1978, this TV movie pilot for a proposed series is another typically quirky and weird offering from director Gary (*Death Line, Dead & Buried*) Sherman. *Dynasty* star John Forsythe and Priscilla (*Carrie*) Pointer are He and She, two alien emissaries from another dimension, posing as Evangelists who promise their growing sect of devoted acolytes that if they follow their divine ways they will reach blissful nirvana. In reality it's a devious plan to take over Earth. Saddled with an inconclusive ending that was clearly going to be continued in the anticipated series, Sherman's oddball mix of religion and sci-fi is could almost be a continuation of Larry Cohen's *God Told Me To* (1976).

John Forsythe He • **Priscilla Pointer** She • **James Stephens** Tim Armstrong • **Robert Pine** Arnold Brown • **Vic Tayback** Ted Randall • **Noah Beery Jr** Virgil Molloy • **Robert Englund**
Director/Screenplay *Gary Sherman*

Mysterious Ways ★★★

TV 2000 – Can/US Colour

Adrian Pasdar stars as an anthopologist obsessed with finding absolute proof that miracles happen, and Rae Dawn Chong as a skeptical psychiatrist. If this sounds a little like *The X Files* then take heart because, like all good spins on tried and trusted ideas, *Mysterious Ways* differs in that it leaves the mysteries unresolved. Its opening episode achieved the rare distinction of knocking the voyeristic *Big Brother* show off the top spot in America, achieving over eight million viewers. Another selling point touted by the series is that it is family entertainment, so there is no sex, no bad language and no "dark themes".

Adrian Pasar Declan Dunn • **Rae Dawn Chong** Peggy Fowler • **Alisen Down** Miranda
Created by *Carl Binder*
Executive producer *Carl Binder, Frank Giustra, Peter O'Fallon, Harold Tichenor, Jonathan Goodwill*

Mystery Science Theatre 3000 ★★★

TV 1988-1999 US Colour and BW

Heckling becomes an art form in this low-budget sci-fi comedy show. Set aboard a deep space vessel, the series sees a group of humans and robots viewing, booing and relentlessly mocking the Z-grade B-movies they are forced to watch by an evil scientist who is determined to drive them insane. Its jokes are obvious and extremely variable, and the success of its episodes largely hinges on how awful the featured movies are, but *MS3K* (as it's affectionately known to regular viewers) generally makes a thoroughly entertaining cosmic caper. The show's central premise is simple and is ably realised by the cast's merciless and frequently magnificent film commentaries. Towards the end of its long run, the series spawned a disappointing spin-off movie. A total of 198 two-hour episodes were made.

Joel Hodgson Joel/Robinson • **Michael J Nelson** Mike • **Trace Beaulieu** Crow T Robot/Dr Clayton Forrester • **Kevin Murphy** Tom Servo
Head writer *Michael J Nelson*
Executive producer *Joel Hodgson* • ***Producer*** *Jim Mallon, Kevin Murphy*

Mystery Science Theater 3000: the Movie ★★★ PG

1996 US Colour 70mins

In this big-screen version of the long-running American cable TV series, we watch Mike Nelson (Michael J Nelson) and his two robot friends (voiced by Trace Beaulieu and Kevin Murphy) watch the fifties sci-fi movie *This Island Earth*. Mike and the droids are adept at poking fun at the bad movies they're forced to watch by evil scientist Dr Forrester (also played by Beaulieu), though *This Island Earth* is cut above the vast majority of films featured on the original TV show.

Trace Beaulieu Dr Clayton Forrester/Crow T Robot • **Michael J Nelson** Mike Nelson • **Jim Mallon** Gypsy • **Kevin Murphy** Tom Servo • **John Brady** Benkitnorf
Director *Jim Mallon*
Screenplay *Michael J Nelson, Trace Beaulieu, Jim Mallon, Kevin Wagner Murphy [Kevin Murphy], Mary Jo Pehl, Paul Chaplin, Bridget Jones, from the TV series by Joel Hodgson*

N

"**From** the age of Big Brother, from the age of the Thought Police, from a dead man... **greetings.**"

Nineteen Eighty-Four 1984

Naked Souls ★ 18

1995 US Colour 81mins DVD

Pamela Anderson's main assets unsurprisingly play a prominent role in this daft erotic science-fiction thriller. The pneumatic former *Baywatch* babe portrays an artist – don't laugh – whose geeky scientist boyfriend (Brian Krause) gets into trouble when he starts playing around with the memories of dead serial killers and messing with sinister rival David Warner. As Anderson's art consists of pouring gloop over naked female models, the nudity is fairly evenly shared, which will no doubt please the lads. Be warned: this makes *Barb Wire* look like a classic. Contains violence, swearing, sex scenes and nudity.

Pamela Anderson Lee [Pamela Anderson] Britanny "Brit" Clark • **Brian Krause** Edward Adams • **David Warner** Everett Longstreet • **Clayton Rohner** Jerry • **Justina Vail** Amelia • **Dean Stockwell** Duncan Ellis
Director *Lyndon Chubbuck*
Screenplay *Frank Dietz*

National Lampoon's Men in White ★★★ PG

1998 US Colour 83mins

This National Lampoon send-up of sci-fi smash *Men in Black* is more in the tradition of *The Naked Gun* and *Airplane!* than the more usual misadventures of the Griswold family. Karim Prince and Thomas F Wilson (*Back to the Future*) play a pair of klutzy dustmen whose lives are changed when they are abducted by aliens. Back on this planet, they turn their dustcart into a space-going attack vehicle to tackle a menace from another galaxy. The sight gags come thick and fast.

Tom Wilson [Thomas F Wilson] Ed Klingbottom • **Karim Prince** Roy DuBro • **Barry Bostwick** President Robert "Bud" Smith • **Donna D'Errico** Press Secretary Blansfield • **M Emmet Walsh** Stanley • **Wigald Boning** Dr Strange
Director *Scott Levy*
Screenplay *Rob Kerchner, Scott Sandin*

Natural Selection ★★★ 15

1994 US Colour 87mins

Perhaps it was Philadelphia-born director Jack Sholder's experience of living in Edinburgh (where he studied philosophy and English) that enabled him to make small budgets go so far. This is one of his most accomplished offerings to date, an unsettling sci-fi thriller in which computer expert C Thomas Howell's life is turned upside down when he discovers he's really the end result of a high-tech cloning experiment, and that his dead ringer brother is planning to eradicate, then replace him. Sholder resourcefully tweaks the deliberate mistaken identity ploys to great cumulative effect.

C Thomas Howell Ben Braden/Alex Connelly • **Lisa Zane** Elizabeth Braden • **Cameron Dye** Craig • **Jenna Cole** Carol • **Ethan Phillips** Henry • **Miko Hughes** Nick • **Joanna Miles** Claudia • **Brenda Varda** Donna • **John Mahon** Coach Dickler • **JP Bumstead** Manager
Director *Jack Sholder*
Screenplay *Todd Slavkin, Darren Swimmer*
Executive producer *Kiefer Sutherland*

The Navy vs the Night Monsters ★★ 12

1966 US Colour 85mins

Antarctic vegetable samples replanted on an island naval base grow into acid-bleeding, walking trees and terrorise the inhabitants of a South Seas navy base. But most of the cast are too busy ogling fifties blonde bombshell Mamie Van Doren to even notice, in this kiddie version of *The Day of the Triffids*. A terrible script (based on the novel *The Monster from Earth's End* by Murray Leinster, author of the equally dreadful *The Wailing Asteroid*, made into *The Terrornauts* in 1967), awful direction and ham acting from an eclectic bunch of Z-movie celebrities make this mind-boggling misfire a camp must-see.

Mamie Van Doren Lt Nora Hall • **Anthony Eisley** Lt Charles Brown • **Pamela Mason** Maria, a scientist • **Billy Gray** Petty Officer Fred Twining • **Bobby Van** Ens Rutherford Chandler • **Walter Sande** Dr Arthur Beecham • **Phillip Terry** Spalding
Director *Michael A Hoey*
Screenplay *Michael A Hoey, from the novel "The Monster from Earth's End" by Murray Leinster*

The Neanderthal Man ★

1953 US BW 78mins

Well-meaning scientist Robert Shayne turns his pet cat into a sabre-tooth tiger, his housekeeper into an ape-woman and himself into a beast man during a batch of serum experiments gone astray. A prehysterical Jekyll and Hyde affair with Shayne sporting a terrible rubber mask and directed by one-time German film critic EA Dupont.

Robert Shayne Dr Cliff Groves • **Richard Crane** Dr Ross Harkness • **Doris Merrick** Ruth Marshall • **Joyce Terry** Jan • **Robert Long** Jim • **Dick Rich** Sheriff Andrews
Director *EA Dupont*
Screenplay *Jack Pollexfen, Aubrey Wisberg*

Necronomicon ★★ 18

1993 US Colour 92mins

Pacts with sea devils, mad scientists searching for eternal life and alien sacrifices are the themes of this Brian Yuzna, Christophe Gans and Shu Kaneko-directed trilogy of terror based on the works of HP Lovecraft. Nothing too remarkable is on offer here, although the gothic lyricism of Gans's episode *The Drowned* is noteworthy and the gruesome Edgar Allan Poe poetry of Kaneko's *The Cold* gets a lift from the manic performance of David Warner. Yuzna's *Whispers* is the goriest and daftest of the three horrors, which are held together by Jeffrey Combs, of *Re-Animator* fame, who plays Lovecraft himself, reading the tales in a library. The anthology format is a good old staple because no story ever lingers too long to become irredeemably boring, but the idea is stretched to the limit here.

Jeffrey Combs HP Lovecraft • **Tony Azito** Librarian • **Brian Yuzna** Cabbie • **Bruce Payne** Edward de la Poer • **Richard Lynch** Jethro de la Poer • **Belinda Bauer** Nancy Gallmore • **David Warner** Dr Madden
Director *Christophe Gans, Shu Kaneko [Shusuke Kaneko], Brian Yuzna*
Screenplay *Brent V Friedman, Christophe Gans, Kazunori Ito, from stories by HP Lovecraft*

Nemesis ★ 18

1993 US Colour 91mins DVD

Cyborg ex-cop Olivier Gruner is forced by police chief Tim Thomerson into stopping a band of techno-terrorists planning to disrupt a summit meeting. If he refuses, he'll die from a bomb implanted in his body. Pyun has had a long fascination with futuristic stories involving cyborgs, but this effort is just as threadbare and unconvincing as his other attempts. The action sequences make it marginally better than its sequels, however, while Gruner's stiff delivery is at least appropriate for his character.

Olivier Gruner Alex Rain • **Tim Thomerson** Farnsworth • **Deborah Shelton** Julian • **Marjorie Monaghan** Jared • **Merle Kennedy** Max Impact • **Cary-Hiroyuki Tagawa** Angie Liv • **Nicholas Guest** Germaine
Director *Albert Pyun*
Screenplay *Rebecca Charles*

Nemesis 2 – Nebula ★ 15

1995 US Colour 81mins

The *Nemesis* series's emulation of *The Terminator* is most blatant in this entry, with a future world enslaved by cyborgs sending one back in time to terminate Sue Price, a genetically enhanced woman warrior living in the African desert who is the hope for mankind. Director Albert Pyun makes this entry more action-oriented than the original, but the strident, frenzied tone numbs the viewer as much as the desolate landscape (actually filmed in the American southwest). It all makes one wish for the more restrained original, believe it or not. This was shot back to back with *Nemesis 3*.

Sue Price Alex • **Chad Staholaki** Nebula • **Tina Cote** Emily • **Earl White** Po • **Jahi JJ Zuri** Zumi
Director/Screenplay *Albert Pyun*

SCI Q

24

Which robot had the catchphrase "Boogie boogie"?

See page 496 for answers

Nemesis 3 – Time Lapse ★ 18

1996 US Colour 90mins

The third entry in the *Nemesis* series plays less like a rip-off than the previous two entries, though that's mainly because of a storyline that's both incoherent and unfinished, leaving the viewer hanging for *Nemesis 4*? Assuming viewers have seen the first two parts, the story starts shortly after the previous film, with Sue Price waking up with amnesia and trying to retrace her steps in the midst of very familiar danger. Tim Thomerson returns from the first movie, but to no avail.

Sue Price Alex • **Norbert Weisser** Edson • **Xavier Declie** Johnny
Director/Screenplay *Albert Pyun*

Neon City ★★ 15

1992 Can Colour 103mins

In 2053, the Earth has been decimated by an environmental disaster that has destroyed the ozone layer. Bounty hunter Michael Ironside and his prisoner (rock-chick-turned-actress Vanity) are among the motley group of passengers aboard an armoured transport vehicle that's heading toward the city of the title. This futuristic take on *Stagecoach* woefully lacks that film's colourful characteristions – even the usually reliable Ironside is underwhelming. However, the portrayal of a dying world is first rate, blending superior production design with eye-catching locations to make the post-apocalypse setting a surprisingly believable one.

Michael Ironside Harry Stark • **Vanity** Reno • **Lyle Alzado** Bulk • **Nick Klar** Tom • **Richard Sanders** Dickie Devine • **Valerie Wildman** Sandy • **Juliet Landau** Twink • **Arsenio "Sonny" Trinidad** Wing
Director *Monte Markham*
Screenplay *Jeff Begun, Buck Finch, Monte Markham*

The Neptune Factor ★ U

1973 Can Colour 98mins

In this feeble slice of aquatic sci-fi, Ben Gazzara and Ernest Borgnine are in charge of a mini-submarine, which offers the only chance of rescuing the crew of a sea-lab trapped by an earthquake on the ocean floor. Daniel Petrie brings zero excitement to a talky first half largely set in the cramped confines of the sub, while the sea monsters the crew later encounter are a huge let-down. Photographically enhanced goldfish, they give the impression of the whole enterprise having been filmed in somebody's fish tank.

Ben Gazzara Commander Adrian Blake • **Yvette Mimieux** Leah Jansen • **Walter Pidgeon** Dr Samuel Andrews • **Ernest Borgnine** "Mack" MacKay • **Chris Wiggins** Captain Williams
Director *Daniel Petrie*
Screenplay *Jack DeWitt*

The Nest ★★ 18

1988 US Colour 83mins

A somewhat revolting sci-fi splatter movie from director Terence H Winkless (who co-wrote *The Howling* with John Sayles), this gleefully relates how a small community is decimated by ravenous mutant bugs after scientists who should have known better start tampering with nature. It's more entertaining than most entries in the genre, but there are still moments of wince-inducing clumsiness in most departments. US TV veteran Robert Lansing stars; the script is by Robert King, who has gone on to pen blockbusters such as *Cutthroat Island* and *Vertical Limit*.

Robert Lansing Elias Johnson • **Lisa Langlois** Elizabeth Johnson • **Franc Luz** Richard Tarbell • **Terri Treas** Dr Morgan Hubbard • **Stephen Davies** Homer • **Diana Bellamy** Mrs Pennington • **Jack Colins** Shakey Jake • **Nancy Morgan** Lillian • **Jeff Winkless** Church
Screenplay *Robert King, from a novel by Eli Cantor*

The New Avengers ★★★ PG 12

TV 1976-1977 UK Colour 26x60mins

This seventies makeover of a sixties TV institution is something of a damp squib by comparison, but still yards better than most British fantasy serials being made at the time, or since for that matter. Patrick Macnee resumed his role of John Steed, ably assisted this time by the glamorous Purdey, famously played by Joanna Lumley who was chosen out of 300 girls, and Gareth Hunt's Gambit, brought in to handle the rough stuff Macnee, with a touch of arthritis, could no longer manage. Both Lumley and Hunt underwent a Commando training course to toughen them up for their roles. Not as fantastical as its predecessor, with a larger proportion of poor stories, too, there were, however, some cracking episodes including a plot by neo-Nazis to re-vive their Führer (guest-starring Peter Cushing), a power mad computer and the return of the cybernauts, the killer robots from the Diana Rigg era.

Patrick Macnee John Steed • **Joanna Lumley** Purdey • **Gareth Hunt** Mike Gambit
Producer *Albert Fennell, Brian Clemens*

New Eden ★★ PG

1994 US Colour 85mins

It's not really Mel Gibson's fault, but we'll blame him anyway. Yes, it's *Mad Max* time again, although without the style or black humour. Stephen Baldwin and Michael Bowen are among a group of convicts dumped on a barren, futuristic prison planet who are not expected to live long enough to apply for parole. While Bowen looks for supremacy among the criminals of the desert, Baldwin fights off the bad guys while helping struggling Lisa Bonet and her tribe. Turgidly directed by Alan Metzger, this will sorely test the patience of even the most dedicated fan of post-apocalypse adventures, though the action scenes are well staged. Contains violence, swearing and nudity.

Stephen Baldwin Adams • **Lisa Bonet** Lily • **Michael Bowen** Kyne • **Tobin Bell** Ares • **Janet Hubert-Whitten** Queen Ashtarte • **M C Gainey** Thor • **Abraham Verduzco** Luke
Director *Alan Metzger*
Screenplay *Dan Gordon*

The New People ★★

TV 1969-1970 US Colour 17x45mins

Created by Aaron Spelling and Larry Gordon, this near-future adventure series would have liked to be an optimistic *Lord of the Flies* but (inevitably?) devolved into a hippie era *Gilligan's Island*. Forty American students are marooned on the island of Bomano, once used for atomic testing, and move into a makeshift abandoned city, where they have to create their own society and learn to cope with all manner of crises without the help or hindrance of adult influence. Episodes dealt with race issues, unwed pregnancy, marijuana growing, gun control, hot-rodding and other subjects of interest to teenagers. The guest stars included Richard Kiley, Richard Dreyfuss, Tim O'Kelly, Aron Kincaid, Billy Dee Williams and Tyne Daly.

Peter Ratray George Potter • **Tiffany Bolling** Susan Bradley • **David Moses** Gene Washington • **Zooey Hall** Bob Lee
Created by *Aaron Spelling, Larry Gordon*
Producer *Harold Gast, Aaron Spelling*

SFacts

The series was developed for television by the legendary Rod Serling, who wrote the pilot but removed his name from the credits. He is reported to have commented, "It may work, but not for me."

New Rose Hotel ★

1998 US Colour 92mins

Based on a William Gibson short story, cult director Abel Ferrara's cyberpunk *Pygmalion* is an incomprehensible mess. It's an arrogantly arty sci-fi reverie about Willem Dafoe's life unravelling as the dirty deals he's involved in finally catch up with him and he anguishes over the true meaning of love. Throughout the murkily-shot action which recycles the same images over and over, Dafoe and Christopher Walken give creditable performances as the two retro Cold War pawns in a geo-political chess game. But Asia Argento sensually shimmering across the screen makes the biggest impact with her amusing and amoral turn as the malleable hooker who comes between them. Otherwise Ferrara's pretentious drone is a boring insult to the intelligence.

Christopher Walken Fox • **Willem Dafoe** X • **Asia Argento** Sandii • **Yoshitaka Amano** Hiroshi • **Annabella Sciorra** Madame Rosa
Director *Abel Ferrara*
Screenplay *Christi Zois, Abel Ferrara, from a short story by William Gibson*

Next One ★

1984 US Colour 105mins

This is a tedious fantasy with quasi-religious overtones from Greek hack director Nico Mastorakis, producer of *The Greek Tycoon*. Adrienne Barbeau and her son Jeremy Licht are living on the island of Mykonos when stranger Kier Dullea washes ashore. It turns out he's a Jesus Christ figure from the future. As well as being totally ludicrous, this is slow-paced from the start. Pathetic, dull, hopeless.

Keir Dullea Glenn/The Next One • **Adrienne Barbeau** Andrea Johnson • **Jeremy Licht** Timmy • **Peter Hobbs** Dr Barnaby
Director/Screenplay *Nico Mastorakis*

A Nice Plate of Spinach ★★★

1976 Cz Colour 90mins

Released the same year he made the children's fable, *The Best Way to Wake Princesses*, Vaclav Vorlicek's sci-fi comedy owes much to the inspiration of his frequent collaborator (and this time co-director), Milos Makourek. There's a pronounced element of social satire in the story of a beautician who steals a rejuvenating machine, only to discover it has a tendency to miniaturise on a whim. Moreover, it works twice as well if the client has recently consumed spinach. Vorlicek regular Jiri Sovak is joined by Vladimir Mensik and Josef Somr, who expertly milk the abundance of knockabout gags. A Czech language film.

Vladimir Mensik • **Jiri Sovak** • **Josef Somr** • **Peter Kostka** • **Eva Treytnorova** TBC
Director *Vaclav Vorlicek*
Screenplay *Milos Makourek, Vaclav Vorlicek*

The Night Caller ★★

1965 UK BW 83mins

You are an alien sent to Earth to find women to help re-populate your planet. How would you go about recruiting them? A wanted advert in *Bikini Girl* magazine, of course. That is the premise behind this cheerful piece of nonsense from cheapie specialist John Gilling. Playing along with it are John Saxon as the earnest American scientist who is called in to investigate the arrival of a mysterious pod, and Alfred Burke as the copper unable to explain a spate of disappearances of young women. The undoubted highlight is the TV interview spoof in which Warren Mitchell plays an parent discussing the generation gap.

John Saxon Jack Costain • **Maurice Denham** Professor Morley • **Patricia Haines** Ann Barlow • **Alfred Burke** Superintendent Hartley • **Jack Carson** Major • **Jack Watson** Sergeant Hawkins • **Warren Mitchell** Lilburn • **Ballard Berkeley** Commander Savage • **Anthony Wager** Private Higgins • **Robert Crewdson** Medra
Director *John Gilling*
Screenplay *Jim O'Connolly, from the novel "The Night Callers" by Frank Crisp*

The Night Is Young ★★★ 15

1986 Fr Colour 114mins

For all his visual flair, director Léos Carax's storytelling skills leave a lot to be desired. There's a carelessly pulpy quality about this futuristic thriller, in which Denis Lavant's commitment to the theft of a serum that cures a fatal disease afflicting only the romantically insincere is diminished by his growing obsession with Juliette Binoche, the mistress of fellow gang member, Michel Piccoli. Away from the plot's comic-book sensibilities, however, the compositions irresistibly recall the pictorial genius of film-makers as different as Fritz Lang and Jean-Luc Godard. A fascinating yet frustrating experience. In French with English subtitles.

Denis Lavant Alex • **Juliette Binoche** Anna • **Michel Piccoli** Marc • **Hans Meyer** Hans • **Julie Delpy** Lise • **Carroll Brooks** The American • **Hugo Pratt** Boris • **Serge Reggiani** Charlie • **Mireille Perrier** Young mother
Director/Screenplay *Léos Carax*

The Night of the Big Heat ★★★

TV 1960 UK BW 90mins

A feature-length Associated-Rediffusion drama, adapted by Giles Cooper from John Lymington's sub-John Wyndham novel, that plays up the claustrophobia in an inarguably British variant of the alien invasion in which the main setting is a pub on Salisbury Plain and the topic of endless talk is the weather. Alien maggots raise the temperature in winter, prompting a lot of sweatiness in the cast, which includes civilians Lee Montague, Melissa Stribling, Karel Stepanek, Bernard Archard and June Ellis, and military men Bernard Cribbins, Patrick Holt and Nicholas Selby. The novel was done again as a 1967 film, with Christopher Lee and Peter Cushing.

Lee Montague Richard • **Melissa Stribling** Patricia • **Sally Bazely** Frankie • **Bernard Cribbins** Corporal Pearce • **Bernard Archard** Sir James Murray • **Karel Stepanek** Dr Harsen • **June Ellis** Brenda • **Patrick Holt** Squadron Leader Grieves • **Nicholas Selby** Group Captain Griffiths
Director *Cyril Coke*
Written by *Giles Cooper, from the novel by John Lymington*

Night of the Big Heat ★★

1967 UK Colour 92mins

The ever-reliable team of Peter Cushing and Christopher Lee put a crisp British cast through its horror-struck paces as mystified islanders are plagued by a winter heatwave caused by energy-starved protoplasmic aliens. Most of the action takes place at a local inn, where the helpless survivors get on each other's nerves. However, the final arrival of the monsters signals a few tepid thrills, even if they do resemble badly fried eggs with tinned spaghetti innards. Otherwise, the film, unlike most of its characters, rarely catches fire. Contains some violence.

Christopher Lee Hanson • **Peter Cushing** Dr Stone • **Patrick Allen** Jeff Callum • **Sarah Lawson** Frankie Callum • **Jane Merrow** Angela Roberts • **William Lucas** Ken Stanley • **Kenneth Cope** Tinker Mason • **Jack Bligh** Ben Siddle • **Thomas Heathcote** Bob Hayward
Director *Terence Fisher*
Screenplay *Ronald Liles, Pip Baker, Jane Baker, from the novel by John Lymington*

Night of the Bloody Apes ★★ 18

1968 Mex Colour 76mins [video]

A gruesome Frankenstein monster-cum-wrestler horror nasty from maverick Mexican schlock director Rene (*Survive*) Cardona. Jose Elias Moreno transplants a gorilla's heart into his dying son, Armando Silvestre, who then transforms into a muscle-bound ape-man with a taste for rape and grisly murder. Norma Lazareno is the cat-suited wrestler heroine who takes as many gratuitous shower scenes as she does prisoners. Fleshed out with eye-gouging gore and surgical splatter – real open-heart operation footage is spliced in for extra nausea-inducing value – this is offensively stupid and tasteless trash which many critics cite as one of the most sickening movies ever made. Classic line of dubbed dialogue: "Maybe you have been watching on your television too many pictures of terror!" Spanish dialogue dubbed into English.

Jose Elias Moreno Dr Krallman • **Carlos Lopez Moctezuma** Goyo • **Armando Silvestre** Dr Arturo Martinez • **Norma Lazareno** Lucy Ossorio
Director *Rene Cardona*
Screenplay *Rene Cardona, Rene Cardona Jr*

Night of the Comet ★★★ 15

1984 US Colour 94mins [video]

Full of fun scares, gleeful unease, cheap – but effective – special effects and touching warmth, director Thom Eberhardt's tongue-in-cheek cult item pastes together numerous ideas from other science-fiction flicks and takes them the full distance. The same comet that wiped out the dinosaurs reappears to make most of mankind extinct this time. Catherine Mary Stewart and Kelli Maroney are two tough talking Valley girls who survive to take on the remaining flesh-eating zombies, marauding punks and sinister scientists in this upbeat, funky and ultimately uplifting metaphor for maturity.

Catherine Mary Stewart Regina • **Robert Beltran** Hector • **Kelli Maroney** Samantha • **Geoffrey Lewis** Carter • **Mary Woronov** Audrey • **John Achorn** Oscar • **Sharon Farrell** Doris • **Michael Bowen** Larry • **Ivan Roth** Willy • **Raymond Lynch** Chuck • **Janice Kawaye** Sarah • **Chance Boyer** Brian • **Bob Perlow** News reporter
Director/Screenplay *Thom Eberhardt*

Night of the Lepus ★

1972 US Colour 88mins

When a laboratory rabbit, injected with an experimental pest control serum, escapes into the Arizona desert and starts breeding with the local wild bunny population you either have the potential for an eco-thriller of the stature of *Them!* or you have the ingredients of a Monty Python sketch. Alas for stars Stuart Whitman, Janet Leigh and *Star Trek*'s De Forest Kelley this giant killer bunny flick is as unintentionally hilarious as anything Cleese and Co could have dreamt up. The problem for director William F Claxton, best known for his low budget westerns, is that even with close-ups of slavering blood-red jaws fluffy bunnies just aren't frightening. A total bloody shambles. Poor old Janet Leigh probably wishes she was back in the Bates motel shower.

Stuart Whitman Roy Bennett • **Janet Leigh** Gerry Bennett • **Rory Calhoun** Cole Hillman • **DeForest Kelley** Dr Elgin Clark • **Paul Fix** Sheriff Cody • **Melanie Fullerton** Amanda Bennett • **Chris Morrell** Jackie Hillman
Director *William F Claxton*
Screenplay *Don Holliday, Gene Kearney, from the novel "The Year of the Angry Rabbit" by Russell Braddon*

Night of the Living Dead ★★★★★ 18

1968 US BW 95mins [video] DVD

Director George Romero's seminal classic redefined the meaning of horror for fear-sated audiences in the sixties. It starts suddenly, without rhyme or reason, with a jolting attack in a cemetery (radioactive fallout from a space rocket brings the corpses to life) and relentlessly continues on a downward spiral of frantic despair as terrified people take fragile shelter in a secluded house to fight off an army of cannibalistic zombies. Conveying visceral terror through an unrelieved black-and-white documentary atmosphere, Romero's graphic cult chiller no longer scares the daylights out of viewers because of its countless imitations. But the director's radical style, lethal wit and political themes still impress.

Judith O'Dea Barbara • **Russell Streiner** Johnny • **Duane Jones** Ben • **Karl Hardman** Harry Cooper • **Keith Wayne** Tom • **Judith Ridley** Judy • **Marilyn Eastman** Helen Cooper • **Kyra Schon** Karen
Director *George A Romero*
Screenplay *John A Russo, from a story by George A Romero*

Night of the Living Dead ★★★★ 18

1990 US Colour 84mins [video] DVD

Familiarity breeds content, not the expected contempt, in gore-meister director Tom Savini's highly acceptable remake of George A Romero's 1968 zombie classic. Staying close to the ingrained terror events of the original while keeping the viewer off-guard with fresh slants is Romero (who wrote the script) and Savini's joint masterstroke. A group of people are trapped inside a farmhouse by a gang of flesh-eating zombies. Shot in atmospheric muted colours and well-acted by Patricia Tallman and Tom Towles in particular, Savini's sure hand underscores the flair, intelligence and imagination with which he's tackled such a thankless task. Laced with great zombie effects and gripping suspense, this is one remake that's better than anyone had a right to expect.

Tony Todd Ben • **Patricia Tallman** Barbara • **Tom Towles** Harry • **McKee Anderson** Helen • **William Butler** Tom • **Katie Finneran** Judy Rose • **Bill Mosley [Bill Moseley]** Johnnie
Director *Tom Savini*
Screenplay *George A Romero, from the 1968 film*

The Night That Panicked America ★★★

1975 US Colour 100mins

On October 30 1938, Orson Welles and his company broadcast a version of HG Wells's *The War Of The Worlds* on the radio – and millions took it seriously as a warning of alien invasion. Director Joseph Sargent's made-for-TV docudrama shows how some people fled to the hills, while others prayed in the streets; it was as near to a state of emergency as America has ever seen.

Paul Shenar Orson Welles • **Vic Morrow** Hank Muldoon • **Cliff De Young** Stefan Grubowski • **Michael Constantine** Jess

Wingate • **Walter McGinn** Paul Stewart • **Eileen Brennan** Ann Muldoon • **Meredith Baxter** Linda Davis • **Tom Bosley** Norman Smith • **Will Geer** Reverend Davis • **John Ritter** Walter Wingate
Director *Joseph Sargent*
Screenplay *Nicholas Meyer, Anthony Wilson*

The Night the World Exploded

★★ U

1957 US BW 63mins

This pedestrian addition to the list of apocalyptic disaster movies has seismologist William Leslie predicting that the earth is doomed thanks to an unstable subterranean element that explodes when exposed to the air. It's an intriguing idea but the denouement is poorly conceived and the disaster itself is rendered unconvincing by the over-use of stock footage of fires and floods. The weak cast and unengaging characters don't help this disappointing effort from director Fred F Sears, who had scored the previous year with *Earth vs the Flying Saucers*.

Kathryn Grant Laura Hutchinson • **William Leslie** Dr David Conway • **Tristram Coffin** Dr Ellis Morton • **Raymond Greenleaf** Governor Cheney
Director *Fred F Sears*
Screenplay *Jack Natteford, Luci Ward*

Night Visitors ★ 15

1996 US Colour 90mins

Graduate student Faith Ford is pursued by secret agents after her brother is killed for stealing a box containing alien remains. With the help of journalist boyfriend Thomas Gibson, she struggles to survive and expose the conspiracy. This is a race to see who is the dumbest: the crash-prone aliens, the inept spies or the spunky but clueless heroine. The grand prize, however, goes to the makers of this derivative TV movie, who should have known better than to inflict this kind of rubbish on an unsuspecting planet.

Faith Ford Kelly Wells • **Thomas Gibson** Ross Williams • **Stephen Tobolowsky** Taylor • **Todd Allen** David Wells • **Eric McCormack** Andy Robinson • **Charles S Dutton** Dr Eldon James
Director *Jorge Montesi*
Screenplay *D Brent Mote*

Nightbreed ★★★ 18

1990 US Colour 97mins

Hellraiser established Clive Barker as a major force in modern horror, but nothing he's done since has ever quite matched its unique visceral power. The trump up Barker's sleeve this time is the casting of cult horror director David Cronenberg as a malevolent shrink. He dupes a patient into believing that he's a serial killer and then tracks him down to the netherworld of Midian, a secret sanctuary for mutants and freaks. While this is certainly self-indulgent – Barker directs and adapted the screenplay from his own novel *Cabal* – the imagination on view certainly impresses. A veritable truck-load of monsters are brought vividly to life by masterful make-up, although most are seen too briefly to establish proper identities. Plenty of gore and a suitably apocalyptic finale should ensure horror seekers are satisfied.

Craig Sheffer Boone • **Charles Haid** Captain Eigerman • **David Cronenberg** Dr Decker • **Anne Bobby** Lori • **Hugh Quarshie** Detective Joyce
Director *Clive Barker*
Screenplay *Clive Barker, from his novel "Cabal"*

Nightflyers ★ 18

1987 US Colour 85mins

Adapted from a novella by George RR Martin, this futuristic tale had potential, but lacked the budget and the expertise to capitalise on it. (The production had a troubled history, while a major re-edit by the producers made director Robert Collector opt for the pseudonym "TC Blake".) The fog machine works overtime to hide the substandard sets as the motley crew of a decrepit spaceship goes in search of an alien race. The cast includes Catherine Mary Stewart and Michael Des Barres; they've both done better work elsewhere.

Catherine Mary Stewart Miranda • **John Standing** D'Branin • **Michael Praed** Royd • **Lisa Blount** Audrey • **Michael Des Barres** Jon Winderman
Director *TC Blake [Robert Collector]*
Screenplay *Robert Jaffe, from a novella by George RR Martin*

NightMan ★

TV 1997-99 Can/US Colour 1x120m, 42x60m

Based on a little-known comic strip, Glen A Larson's low-frills and low-on-thrills superhero series is a bit of a NightMare. Former stuntman Matt McColm stars (well, technically at least) as Johnny Domino, a saxophonist with the telepathic ability to sense the evil thoughts of those around him. Donning some state-of-the-art military equipment, Domino fights crime as the bullet-proof and high-flying superhero, NightMan. Take that silly premise, add some dull characters, unconvincing special effects, tedious musical interludes and a series of plotlines which range from routine to ridiculous, and you have *NightMan*'s live-action capers. Ironically, the show's guest stars include Simon MacCorkindale, who reprises his role as Professor Jonathan Chase from another of Larson's weakest offerings, *Manimal*.

Matt McColm Johnny Domino/NightMan • **Derek Webster** Raleigh Jordan • **Derwin Jordan** Raleigh Jordan • **Earl Holliman** Frank Dominus • **Felecia M Bell** Jessica Rodgers • **Jayne Heitmeyer** Lieutenant Briony Branca
Source *comic strip created by Steve Englehart*
Executive producer *Scott Mitchell Rosenberg, Harold Tichenor, Glen A Larson*

The Nightmare Man ★★

TV 1981 UK Colour 4x30mins

Broadcast on BBC 1, this four-part adaptation of David Wiltshire's negligible novel *Child of Vodyanoi* has the feel of a grown-up(ish) *Doctor Who*, with *Who* director Douglas Camfield and regular monster Pat Gorman on board. The first episode is a straight horror-thriller as a subjective camera heavy-breather prowls the Scots island of Inverdee committing murders, but forensics reveal that the killer has inhuman teeth, mysterious militiary men led by a bogus Brit (Jonathan Newth) turn up to take over and there's much talk of radioactivity and a crashed flying saucer. The culprit, rather disappointingly Gorman in a wet-suit and a gas-mask, turns out to be the bio-altered pilot of a Soviet bioweapons plane, driven mad by the crash.

James Warwick Michael Gaffikin • **Celia Imrie** Fiona Patterson • **Jonathan Newth** Colonel Howard • **James Cosmo** Sergeant Carch • **Tom Watson** Dr Goudry • **Maurice Roëves** Inspector Inskip • **Pat Gorman** Killer
Director *Douglas Camfield*
Dramatised by *Robert Holmes, from the novel "Child of Vodyanoi" by David Wiltshire*
Producer *Ron Craddock*

Nightmares ★★ 15

1983 US Colour 94mins

Originally the pilot for an intended TV series in *The Twilight Zone* tradition, this uneven four-part anthology is more miss than hit. A housewife under murderous threat, a deadly video game obsessing Emilio Estevez, a priest losing faith on the eve of battling a possessed truck, and a giant rat terrorising a suburban family jostle for attention in a workmanlike collection accenting substandard eerieness and few scares. While the first two tales are OK, the other two are dire.

Emilio Estevez JJ Cooney • **Cristina Raines** Lisa • **Joe Lambie** Phil • **Anthony James** Clerk • **Clare Nono** Newswoman • **Raleigh Bond** Neighbour • **Robert Phelps** Newsman • **Lee James Jude [Lee Ving]** William Henry Glazier
Director *Joseph Sargent*
Screenplay *Christopher Crowe, Jeffrey Bloom*

Nineteen Eighty-Four ★★★★

TV 1954 UK BW 120mins

Nigel Kneale's careful, spirited adaptation of George Orwell's classic dystopian novel was actually broadcast three times – two live outings in the same week in 1954, produced (which means also directed) by Rudolph Cartier, with Peter Cushing as the ultimately crushed dissenter Winston Smith, Yvonne Mitchell as rebel heroine Julia, André Morell as secret policeman O'Brien and Donald Pleasence as the toady Syme; and a less-effective remake in 1965, directed by Christopher Morahan, with David Buck, Jane Merrow, Joseph O'Conor and Cyril Shaps. The controversial 1954 production survives in a kinescope of the Thursday repeat, and is more effective than either of the cinema versions of the novel. The cramped live studio feel effectively conveys the grey, gloomy totalitarian future Britain of Big Brother, a notional figurehead for a blankly malevolent state. Vivid performances, especially from the nervous Cushing and the smooth Morell in the famous "Room 101" torture-by-rats sequence, make Orwell's terrifying political fable work as a horror story as well as an awful warning.

Peter Cushing Winston Smith • **André Morell** O'Brien • **Yvonne Mitchell** Julia • **Donald Pleasence** Syme • **Arnold Diamond** Emmanuel Goldstein • **Campbell Gray** Parsons • **Hilda Fenemore** Mrs Parsons
Adapted by *Nigel Kneale, from the novel "Nineteen Eighty-Four" by George Orwell*
Producer *Rudolph Cartier*
Designer *Barry Learoyd*

1984 ★★★

1955 UK BW 89mins

The 1955 version of George Orwell's dystopian novel is set in a futuristic 1984, while the 1984 version of *1984* was set in the grim, postwar era in which Orwell lived and wrote. All of which proves that Orwell's book was at once timely and timeless. Michael Anderson's adaptation is reasonably faithful to its source, concentrating on the possibility of love and humanity in a totalitarian state ruled by a powerful bureaucratic elite, a world of "Big Brother", "Thought Police" and "Doublethink".

Edmond O'Brien Winston Smith • **Michael Redgrave** O'Connor • **Jan Sterling** Julia • **David Kossoff** Charrington • **Mervyn Johns** Jones • **Donald Pleasence** Parsons
Director *Michael Anderson*
Screenplay *William P Templeton, Ralph Bettinson, from the novel by George Orwell*

Nineteen Eighty-Four ★★★★ 15

1984 UK Colour 108mins [video]

Inspired less by Soviet tyranny than the paranoia induced by British wartime censorship and propaganda, George Orwell's study of a dystopian future has lost none of its pessimism and dread. Much bleaker than the 1955 version, Michael Radford's superbly designed return to Oceania holds out little hope that the human spirit will be able to withstand the onset of totalitarianism. John Hurt is perfectly cast as the government cog who enters into a relationship with co-worker Suzanna Hamilton as an act of rebellion. But it's his encounter with Richard Burton, as the personification of the omnipresence of "Big Brother" that provides the dramatic highlight.

John Hurt Winston Smith • **Richard Burton** O'Brien • **Suzanna Hamilton** Julia • **Cyril Cusack** Charrington • **Gregor Fisher** Parsons • **James Walker** Syme • **Andrew Wilde** Tillotson • **David Trevena** Tillotson's friend • **David Cann** Martin • **Anthony Benson** Jones • **Phyllis Logan** Telescreen announcer • **Roger Lloyd Pack** Waiter
Director *Michael Radford*
Screenplay *Michael Radford, Jonathan Gems, from the novel by George Orwell*

SFacts

Michael Radford carefully followed the locations and dates set out in Orwell's novel. Several scenes were filmed on the actual day they were meant to be taking place, such as the scene in which Winston writes in his diary on 4 April 1984 which was filmed on that day.

1990 ★★★

TV 1977 UK Colour 16x55mins

Either as *Callan* or *The Equalizer*, depending on what generation of coach potato you are, Edward Woodward convinces whatever the part. In yet another gloomy take on *Nineteen Eighty-Four* – this one set six years on from Orwell's book – Woodward plays Jim Kyle, a subversive journalist out to smash a totalitarian system top heavy with administrators who control the population's every move through the implementation of ID cards, rationing and electronic surveillance. Operating an underground press and smuggling out dissidents puts Woodward on a collision course with Robert Lang, tyrannical head of the new power in Britain, the PCD (the Department of Public Control). Despite maintaining a high level of suspense throughout and never pulling its punches, *1990* inevitably suffers in comparison with Orwell, who after all said this kind of stuff first and much more profoundly, too.

Edward Woodward Jim Kyle • **Robert Lang** Herbert Skardon • **Tony Doyle** Dave Brett • **Barbara Kellermann** Delly Lomas • **George Murcell** Greaves • **Clifton Jones** Henry Tasker • **Lisa Harrow** Lynn Blake • **Yvonne Mitchell** Kate Smith • **David McKail** Inspector Macrae
Devised by *Wilfred Greatorex*
Producer *Prudence Fitzgerald*

Nirvana ★★★★★

1996 It/Fr Colour 112mins

A stunning cyber-fantasy, rich in design and innovative ideas, that engages the mind while always remaining enjoyable on the purest pulp levels. Superstar video game inventor Christopher Lambert creates a new game called *Nirvana*, then realises his virtual reality hero (Italian matinée idol Diego Abatantuono) has a human consciousness. How he tries to erase the game before its mass-market Christmas release, which would condemn Abantantuono to a never-ending existence, pits Lambert against a ruthless multi-national corporation and takes him through the seedy underworlds of a future metropolis known as the Northern Agglomerate. Directed by Gabriele Salvatores (*Mediterraneo*) with one eye on meaningful psychodrama and the other on giving his existential *Blade Runner* a unique look, this epic plea for Utopian harmony is one of the best science-fiction films ever made. Yet few people outside Italy have seen it. An Italian language film.

Christopher Lambert Jimi • **Diego Abatantuono** Solo • **Sergio Rubini** Joystick • **Emmanuelle Seigner** Lisa • **Stefania Rocca** Naima • **Amanda Sandrelli** Maria
Director *Gabriele Salvatores*
Screenplay *Gabriele Salvatores, Gloria Corica, Pino Cacucci*

No Blade of Grass ★★★ 15

1970 UK Colour 91mins [video]

This bleak but affecting eco-message drama from forties B-movie swashbuckler-turned-director Cornel Wilde casts Nigel Davenport and, in her last film, Jean

Wallace (Wilde's real-life wife) as parents leading their family (which includes a young Lynne Frederick, who would become the last bride of Peter Sellers) across a British countryside devastated by environmental pollution and blighted by anarchy. Making a point that's arguably more relevant now than it was back in the seventies, Wilde's rough-edged handling of the material oddly gives it a semi-documentary feel that's intermittently effective, although the marauding bikers who terrorise the family do look as if they're on their way to a Led Zeppelin gig. A sober, well-meaning film that is well worth catching.

Nigel Davenport John Custance • **Jean Wallace** Ann Custance • **John Hamill** Roger Burnham • **Lynne Frederick** Mary Custance • **Patrick Holt** David Custance • **Anthony May** Andrew Pirrie • **Wendy Richard** Clara

Director *Cornel Wilde*

Screenplay *Sean Forestal, Jefferson Pascal, from the novel "The Death of Grass" by John Christopher*

No Escape ★★★ 15

1994 US Colour 118mins

Try as he might, Ray Liotta is never going to make a hero. Nevertheless, he gives it his best shot in this cheerfully trashy futuristic thriller from British director Martin Campbell. In the 21st century, Liotta finds himself imprisoned on an isolated island where the convicts have split, *Lord of the Flies*-style, into caring hippies and warmongering tribesmen, and he has to choose between them. Lance Henriksen and Stuart Wilson ham it up as the leaders of the rival factions and, although his direction is a little erratic, Campbell delivers some satisfying action set pieces. Contains swearing and violence.

Ray Liotta Robbins • **Lance Henriksen** The Father • **Stuart Wilson** Marek • **Kevin Dillon** Casey • **Kevin J O'Connor** Stephano • **Don Henderson** Killian • **Ian McNeice** King • **Jack Shepherd** Dysart • **Michael Lerner** Warden • **Ernie Hudson** Hawkins • **Russell Kiefel** Iceman • **Brian M Logan** Scab • **Chan Cheuk-Fai** Skull • **Machs Colombani** Ratman • **David Argue** Cellmate • **Stephen Shanahan** Screaming inmate

Director *Martin Campbell*

Screenplay *Michael Gaylin, Joel Gross, from the novel "The Penal Colony" by Richard Herley*

No Survivors Please ★★

1963 W Ger BW and Colour 91mins

1963 was something of a banner year for Steve Sekely, the Hungarian-born director who had handled a baker's dozen features during his Hollywood stint in the forties. Not only did he co-script this pacifist Cold War parable, but he also directed a lavish adaptation of John Wyndham's *The Day of the Triffids*. But, considering the proximity of the Cuban Missile Crisis, the depiction of politicians and brass hats as unrepentant warmongers (notwithstanding the fact they're aliens plotting to conquer Earth by letting humanity obliterate itself) is pretty provocative. A German language film.

Maria Perschy Ginny Desmond • **Robert Cunningham** John Fransworth • **Uwe Friedrichsen** Howard Moore • **Karen Blanguernon** Very Svenson • **Gustavo Rojo** Armand De Guedez

Director *Peter Berneis, Hans Albin*

Screenplay *Istvan Szekely [Steve Sekely], Peter Berneis*

Not of This Earth ★★★

1956 US BW 67mins

Cult director Roger Corman mixes science-fiction, horror and humour in his classic alien invasion quickie with vampiric overtones. Paul Birch is a visitor from the planet Davanna on the trail of human blood because his own race is facing extinction from nuclear anaemia. Death rays are generated whenever he removes his black sunglasses. Corman's elegantly styled, fast-paced gem was the first of his prolific output to successfully lace comedy with suspense, inspiring him to continue in the same vein. The flying, head-crushing bat monster is a fine example of pure fifties pulp sci-fi.

Paul Birch Paul Johnson • **Beverly Garland** Nadine Story • **Morgan Jones** Harry Sherbourne • **William Roerick** Dr Rochelle • **Jonathan Haze** Jeremy Perrin • **Richard Miller [Dick Miller]** Joe Piper • **Anne Carroll** Davanna woman

Director *Roger Corman*

Screenplay *Charles Griffith, Mark Hanna*

Producer *Roger Corman*

Not of This Earth ★ 18

1988 US Colour 77mins

Ex-porn queen Traci Lords tried to go respectable in this dire remake of Roger Corman's 1956 cult favourite. After opening, for no apparent reason, with numerous clips from the New World Pictures back catalogue – *Piranha*, *Galaxy of Terror* and *Humanoids from the Deep*, a segment of which is also intercut into the main narrative – director Jim Wynorski's laughably cheap effort tells exactly the same story as the original (a vampire from outer space checks out earthlings' blood types for possible invasion purposes). Trash with no flash, dash or cash.

Traci Lords Nadine Story • **Arthur Roberts** Mr Johnson • **Lenny Juliano** Jeremy • **Ace Mask** Dr Rochelle • **Roger Lodge** Harry • **Michael Delano** Vacuum cleaner salesman • **Rebecca Perle** Davanna Girl

Director *Jim Wynorski*

Screenplay *Jim Wynorski, RJ Robertson, from the 1956 film*

Not of This Earth ★★

1995 US Colour 90mins

Not satisfied with the dismal 1988 remake, Roger Corman himself oversaw a 1995 update of his cult favourite, produced for the *Roger Corman Presents* cable series. Michael York (what was he thinking?) took over the role of the blood-seeking alien Johnson from the planet Davanna.Not worth the effort, but still an improvement on than the Jim Wynorski version.

Michael York Paul Johnson • **Parker Stevenson** Jack Sherbourne • **Elizabeth Barondes** Amanda Sayles • **Mason Adams** Dr Rochelle • **Richard Belzer** Jeremy

Director *Terence H Winkless*

Screenplay *Charles B Griffith, Mark Hanna, Charles Philip Moore*

Executive producer *Roger Corman*

Not of This World ★★ 15

1991 US Colour 89mins

An alien blob that thrives on electricity and fancies a trip to the local nuclear power plant terrorises a small town in this bland but good-looking made-for-TV salute to the B-movie creature-features of the fifties. The solid cast of familiar television faces – including Lisa Hartman, Pat Hingle and A Martinez – gets in the spirit of the occasion and the effects are occasionally impressive. However, it lacks the edge and humour fifties pulp favourites such as the similarly named *Not of This Earth*.

Lisa Hartman Linda Fletcher • **A Martinez** Sheriff Tom Conway • **Pat Hingle** Doc Avery • **Luke Edwards** Billy Fletcher • **Michael Greene** Walt Tressie

Director *Jon Daniel Hess*

Screenplay *Robert Glass, from a story by Les Alexander, Don Enright, Jonathan Brauer, Robert Glass*

Not Quite Human ★ U

1987 US Colour 87mins

Not quite funny or entertaining either. A super-intelligent android is programmed never to tell a lie, leading to a series of "embarrassing" situations in this dire Disney comedy. Probably the most embarrassing thing is the script, which lacks both originality and humour, as well as a decent plot. But the most horrible thing to contemplate is the fact that there was actually a sequel made two years later, in which the android gets to attend college.

Alan Thicke Dr Jonas Carson • **Jay Underwood** Chip Carson • **Robyn Lively** Becky Carson • **Joseph Bologna** Gordon Vogel
Director *Steven Hilliard Stern*
Screenplay *Alan Ormsby, from characters created by Seth McAvoy*

Not Quite Human II ★ U

1989 US Colour 91mins [video]

This comedy repeats the theme of the 1987 original, with teenage humans and androids having lots of predictable "fun" as the android continues his education. It contains eccentric, stupid or horrified adults, one or two near-villains and a complete lack of dramatic tension. Nearer the bottom of the Disney pile than the top. A second sequel, *Still Not Quite Human*, followed in 1992.

Alan Thicke Dr Jonas Carson • **Jay Underwood** Chip Carson • **Robyn Lively** Becky Carson • **Greg Mullavey** Dr Phil Masters • **Dey Young** Prof Victoria Gray
Director *Eric Luke*
Screenplay *Eric Luke, from characters created by Seth McAvoy*

Now and Again ★★★★

TV 1999-2000 US Colour 22x60mins

Michael Wiseman is a middle-aged family man and insurance executive (played in the opening episode by an uncredited John Goodman) who is involved in a fatal accident, after which he "wakes up" in the care of the US government. Seems they have an magnificent, lab-created super-body that just happens to need a brain. Eric Close is thus re-born, on the condition he never reveal who he really is to anyone from his past, including his much loved wife and daughter. The characters are superbly realised by the strong cast, the dialogue sparkles – especially the sharp repartee between Close and his "creator" Dennis Haysbert – so naturally it was abruptly cancelled, despite winning several television awards. The show was created by Glenn Gordon Caron who was also behind the hugely popular Bruce Willis/Cybill Shepherd show *Moonlighting*, and *Now and Again* follows the pattern of concentrating on the lives and relationships of the characters rather than the sci-fi or action/adventure elements.

Eric Close Michael Wiseman • **Dennis Haysbert** Dr Theodore Morris • **Margaret Colin** Lisa Wiseman • **Gerrit Graham** Roger Bender • **Heather Matazarro** Heather Wiseman • **John Goodman** Michael Wiseman (uncredited) • **Christine Baranski** Voice of Ruth Bender (uncredited)
Created by *Glenn Gordon Caron*
Executive producer *Glenn Gordon Caron, Ronald L Schwary*

Nowhere Man ★★★★

TV 1995-1996 US 25x60mins

The initial success of *The X Files* quickly spawned a wave of short-lived imitators, but none were as memorable as *Nowhere Man*. An occasionally surreal and deliciously paranoid drama with clear shades of *The Prisoner*, the show revolves around Thomas Veil, a photojournalist whose identity is "erased" by forces unknown. Now a stranger to even his own family, Veil embarks on a personal quest to discover who destroyed his life and how they did it. Although the series only lasted for a year, this one-season wonder remains a brilliantly written and extremely stylish take on a classic idea. The series' star is the sensational Bruce Greenwood, who brings a welcome degree of edginess and despair to its enormously sympathetic central character.

Bruce Greenwood Thomas Veil
Written by *Jane Espenson*
Executive producer *Lawrence Hertzog, Stan Rogow*

Nude on the Moon ★

1961 US Colour 83mins

"You're acting like a schoolboy. Don't forget we're rocket scientists," says an ageing doctor to a multi-millionaire playboy as they lift off in this weird space oddity from bargain-basement cult director Doris Wishman. Their journey ends, as the title suggests, with the discovery of topless models on the Moon. This pitiful production contains Nasa stock footage and is decorated with toy spaceships, funny-coloured tights and star-covered astronaut boots. It also features the songs *Moon Doll* and *I'm Mooning over You*. Wishman went on to give the world Chesty Morgan and her 73-inch bust in *Deadly Weapons*. Absolutely awful.

Marietta Cathy/Moon Goddess
Director/Screenplay *Doris Wishman*

Nukie ★ U

1992 S Afr Colour 95mins [video]

This has got to be the worst *ET* rip-off ever made, and that's against some stiff competition (*Mac and Me*, **batteries not included*). Nukie, who looks like a char-broiled Tinky Winky, lands in Africa and befriends two twins from a rural village. He enlists their help to find his brother, who is the subject of cruel tests by the "Space Foundation" in Florida. Incoherent and frustrating, you have to wonder why anyone bothered.

Glynis Johns Sister Anne • **Steve Railsback** Dr Eric Harvey • **Ronald France** • **Fats Dibeco** • **Michael McCabe** • **Kurtis Kent** • **Janice Honeyman**
Director *Sias Odendal*
Screenplay *Benjamin Taylor, from a story by Sias Odendal*

The Nutty Professor ★★★★ PG

1963 US Colour 102mins [video]

In spite of almost universal criticism, this immensely accomplished comedy remains actor/co-writer/director Jerry Lewis's best and funniest screen work. It's really "Doctor Jerry and Mister Love" (the film's French title translated), as Lewis plays nerdish chemistry professor Julius Kelp who is hooked on lovely student Stella Stevens. Lewis makes and takes a potion that turns him into Buddy Love, singing lounge lizard *par excellence*. The witty design and the use of fabulously rich Paramount Technicolor are major bonuses, and this clever movie remains extremely funny. Eat your heart out, Jim Carrey.

Jerry Lewis Professor Julius Kelp/Buddy Love • **Stella Stevens** Stella Purdy • **Del Moore** Dr Hamius R Warfield • **Kathleen Freeman** Millie Lemmon • **Med Flory** Football player • **Norman Alden** Football player • **Skip Ward** Football player • **Elvia Allman** Mother Kelp • **Howard Morris** Father Kelp • **Milton Frome** Dr Leevee • **Buddy Lester** Bartender • **Marvin Kaplan** English boy
Director *Jerry Lewis*
Screenplay *Jerry Lewis, Bill Richmond, from a story by Jerry Lewis*

The Nutty Professor ★★★★ 12

1996 US Colour 91mins [video] DVD

A reworking of the 1963 Jerry Lewis comedy, this has Eddie Murphy back on form after some so-so films (*Beverly Hills Cop III*, *Vampire in Brooklyn*) as Sherman Klump, a quiet and sweet obese science whiz who perfects a potion that turns him into a sexy, skinny lurve machine who looks like, well, Eddie Murphy. Of course, the potion wears off at the most unfortunate of times, which affects his attempts at romance with attractive teaching assistant Jada Pinkett (now best known as Mrs Will

Smith). Murphy plays the prof to poignant perfection, and also (thanks to the genius of the Oscar-winning make-up and computer graphics departments) portrays three generations of his family at the same dinner table. Snappily directed by Tom Shadyac (who made *Liar Liar* and *Ace Ventura: Pet Detective* with Jim Carrey) and featuring superb supporting performances from a cast which includes James Coburn, this isn't quite as eye-wateringly daft as the mad, much-loved-by-the-French original. It is, nonetheless, a thoroughly enjoyable and well-played laugh-fest, providing plenty of rib-tickling moments for the audience.

Eddie Murphy Sherman Klump/Buddy Love • **Jada Pinkett [Jada Pinkett Smith]** Carla Purty • **James Coburn** Harlan Hartley • **Larry Miller** Dean Richmond • **Dave Chappelle** Reggie Warrington • **John Ales** Jason • **Patricia Wilson** Dean's secretary • **Jamal Mixon** Ernie Clump Jr • **Nichole McAuley** Fit woman • **Hamilton Von Watts** Health instructor
Director *Tom Shadyac*
Screenplay *David Sheffield, Barry W Blaustein, Tom Shadyac, Steve Oedederk, from the 1963 film*

Nutty Professor 2: the Klumps ★★★ 12

2000 US Colour 106mins DVD

In this sequel to Eddie Murphy's 1996 success (itself a remake of the 1963 Jerry Lewis comedy), Murphy gets to play rotund scientist Sherman Klump and his entire corpulent family (bar one, his little brother), including his father at two different ages. His performance is an amazing tour de force, which could be compared to the best work of Alec Guinness and Peter Sellers if it weren't for the fact that half the time he's unintelligible. The basis of the new story is an amusing variation on *The Fly*: Klump is desperate to rid himself of his slim, supercool alter ego, Buddy Love, but only manages to regenerate (and mutate) him. Janet Jackson is sweetly effective, playing it straight as Klump's girlfriend, while the writers also manage to include the Fountain of Youth and a giant, sex-mad hamster in the mix. This, and a lot of scatological humour, forms the very silly premise, yet children (and adults with an juvenile sense of fun) will adore it.

Eddie Murphy Professor Sherman Klump/Cletus "Papa" Klump/Young Cletus Klump/Anna "Mama" Klump/Ernie Klump /Grandma Klump/Buddy Love/Lance Perkins • **Janet Jackson** Professor Denise Gaines • **Larry Miller** Dean Richmond • **John Ales** Jason • **Richard Gant** Denise's father • **Anna Maria Horsford** Denise's mother • **Melinda McGraw** Leanne Guilford • **Jamal Mixon** Ernie Klump Jr • **Freda Payne** Claudine
Director *Peter Segal*
Screenplay *Barry W Blaustein, David Sheffield, Paul Weitz, Chris Weitz, from a story by Steve Oedekerk, Barry W Blaustein, David Sheffield, from characters created by Jerry Lewis, Bill Richmond*
Make-up *Nena Smarz* • ***Make-up special effects*** *Rick Baker*

A Nymphoid Barbarian in Dinosaur Hell ★★ 18

1991 US Colour 81mins

Even the guys from Troma, who produced this sci-fi fantasy, would be the first to admit it isn't one of their finest hours. But who could resist sneaking a peak at a movie that sells itself with the immortal line "The prehistoric and the prepubescent, together at last"? The plot outline is as scanty as Linda Corwin's costume, as she endures the nightmare of being the last female alive following a nuclear conflagration. Moreover, it's hard to dispute the claim that the whole lot cost a mere $5,000 to shoot somewhere in Massachusetts and New Hampshire, though the hilarious stop-motion Tromasaurus and the one-eyed "D'ya-think-e-saurus" almost save the day. Contains violence and nudity.

Linda Corwin Lea • **Paul Guzzi** Marn • **Mark Deshaies** Man with No Face
Director/Screenplay *Brett Piper*

O

"**You** are about to experience the awe and mystery which reaches from the inner mind to the **Outer Limits.**"

The Outer Limits 1963-1965

Oblivion ★★

1993 US Colour 94mins

Some critics called *Star Wars* a western in space. That probably inspired low-budget guru Charles Band to try setting a literal western on an alien planet. The cast of characters are amusingly eccentric, including reluctant sheriff Richard Joseph Paul (who, as an empathic psychic, feels the pain of anybody he kills), saloon owner Julie Newmar and George Takei as Doc Valentine, who speaks in *Star Trek* puns. It probably looked a lot funnier on paper – the script is by popular comic book writer Peter David – but the resulting film is rather flat.

Richard Joseph Paul Zack Stone • **Jackie Swanson** Mattie Chase • **Andrew Divoff** Redeye • **Meg Foster** Stell Barr • **Jimmie Skaggs [Jimmie F Skaggs]** Buteo • **George Takei** Doc Valentine • **Julie Newmar** Miss Kitty • **Isaac Hayes** Buster
Director *Sam Irvin*
Screenplay *Peter David, from a story by Charles Band*
Executive producer *Charles Band*

Ocean Girl ★★

TV 1994-1998 Aus Colour 78x30mins

An Australian teen-themed drama, starring Marzena Godecki as Neri, a strange young girl who can live underwater and talk to whales. It seemed for a while that she would be a Pacific Rim version of *The Man from Atlantis*, but the second season revealed that she was an alien from a waterworld stranded on Earth, and that she had a less boringly virtuous sister Mera (Lauren Hewett), who was troubled after bad experiences in a foster home, to take some of the dramatic strain. The show is also known as *Ocean Odyssey*.

Marzena Godecki Neri • **David Hoflin** Jason Bates • **Jeffrey Walker** Brett Bates • **Alex Pinder** Dr Winston Seth • **Lauren Hewett** Mera • **Nina Landis** Voice of HELEN
Executive producer *Jennifer Clevers, Jonathan M Shiff*

Octaman ★

1971 US/Mex Colour 90mins

Kerwin (*Sinbad*) Matthews, Jeff (*This Island Earth*) Morrow and Pier (*Sodom and Gomorrah*) Angeli were all dragged out of retirement for this lumbering Mexican-shot disaster written and directed by Harry Essex, the scripter of *Creature from the Black Lagoon*. The rubber humanoid octopus (an early creation by Oscar-winning make-up artist Rick Baker), a "Horror Heap from the Nuclear Trash" as the poster so eloquently put it, causes absurd mayhem and boring love triangle problems before being despatched back to the contaminated waters from whence it came.

Kerwin Mathews • **Pier Angeli** • **Jeff Morrow** • **Jerome Guardino** • **Norman Fields** • **Robert Warner** • **David Essex**
Director *Harry Essex*
Screenplay *Lawrence Morse, Harry Essex*
Make-up special effects *Rick Baker*

SFacts

One-time James Dean girlfriend Pier Angeli died of a drug overdose during filming. She was only of 39.

Official Denial ★★ PG

1993 US Colour 83mins

Erin Gray made her name as Buck Rogers's sidekick in the TV series of the same name. Here she is grounded on Earth in this better than average sci-fi chiller about the possibilies of alien life. Parker Stevenson is the victim of an alien kidnapping who is pressed into service by the military when they capture their own ET. Despite the bland TV faces – the cast includes another sci-fi veteran, *Battlestar Galatica's* Dirk Benedict – it is directed with some intelligence and perception by Brian Trenchard-Smith.

Parker Stevenson Paul Corliss • **Chad Everett** General Kenneth Spalding • **Dirk Benedict** Lt Col Dan Lerner • **Erin Gray** Annie Corliss • **Michael Pate** Wisdomkeeper • **Christopher Pate** Sam Fools Crow • **Robert Mammone** Michael Novado • **Natalie McCurry** Janine • **Holly Brisley** DOS A • **Serena Dean** DOS B • **Justin Monjo** Franklin Kolbe • **Michael Edwards-Stevens** Savage • **Maegan-Freyja Mason** DOS number one • **Jason Chong** Jeff Iwasaki • **Don Halbert** Sergeant Bridges • **Peter Curtin** Jonathan Applegate
Director *Brian Trenchard-Smith*
Screenplay *Bryce Zabel*

The Offshore Island ★★★

TV 1959 UK BW 90mins

A BBC play, scripted by Marghanita Laski, this was one of many TV contributions to the nuclear debates of the fifties and sixties. Eight years after World War III, a fluke that had taken place in *The Day the World Ended* and would be repeated in *Z Is for Zachariah* means that an isolated valley remains uncontaminated. Ann Todd and her children, Tim Seely and Diane Clare, survive on a farm, but are devastated to learn that the war is still going and that the Americans and the Russians have agreed that the area should be irradiated to finish off the new Battle of Britain. Passionate if hardly convincing, it has a despairing end as the family choose to be under the Bomb rather than relocated to a camp in America.

Ann Todd Rachel Verney • **Phil Brown** Captain Charles • **Robert Brown** Martin • **George Pravda** Captain Baltinsky • **Tim Seely** James Verney • **Diane Clare** Mary Verney
Written by *Marghanita Laski*
Producer *Dennis Vance*

Oktober ★★★

TV 1998 UK Colour 3x60mins

Scripted and directed by Stephen Gallagher from his own 1988 novel, this thriller stars Stephen Tompkinson as teacher Jim Harper, who discovers that he has been used by an evil drugs company for unethical experiments and that he can shift his consciousness into a blue-lit limbo that turns out to be where souls come from and go to. It's mostly a familiar paranoid thriller, in which an ordinary man finds that everyone he knows is in a conspiracy against him – an eerie moment has a whole convivial party fall silent and exchange knowing looks as Tompkinson steps out for a moment – and that he is being pursued by sadistic corporate minions and a cool blonde mad scientist (Lydzia Englert). The plot zigzags from Chechnya to Scotland via the Frankensteinian shores of Lake Geneva, and never quite gells – though there are good performances and a lot of effectively creepy moments.

Stephen Tompkinson Jim Harper • **Lydzia Englert** Rochelle • **Maria Lennon** Linda • **James McCarthy** Viveros • **James Duke** Daniel • **Michael Bertenshaw** Dr Franks • **Richard Leaf** Bruno • **Lisa Jacobs** Dr Bauer • **Stephen Jenn** Russian
Director *Stephen Gallagher*
Written by *Stephen Gallagher, from his novel*
Producer *Brian Eastman*

Omega Doom ★ 15

1996 US Colour 80mins

Those familiar with director Albert Pyun's movies will not be surprised by the quality of this, or the fact it reworks the premise of a better-known film. This time, Pyun borrows from *Yojimbo*/*A Fistful of Dollars*, updating the basic story to a post-apocalypse future. Rutger Hauer sleepwalks through his role as a mysterious robot who arrives in a ruined amusement park occupied by two robot groups and plays both sides against each other. Dark and dreary, the movie's action sequences are both sporadic and so poorly directed as to be incomprehensible. But its biggest mistake is making every character a robot, as with no human element, no emotion whatsoever is generated. Contains violence.

Rutger Hauer Omega Doom • **Shannon Whirry** Zed • **Tina Cote** Blackheart • **Anna Katarina** Bartender • **Norbert Weisser** The Head • **Jill Pierce** Zinc • **Simon Pollard** Zed Too • **Cynthia Ireland** Ironface
Director *Albert Pyun*
Screenplay *Albert Pyun, Ed Naha, from a story by Albert Pyun*

The Omega Factor ★★★

TV 1979 UK Colour 10x50mins

Despite sounding like an episode of *Doctor Who*, this was an intelligent and intriguing mixture of espionage and the paranormal made by BBC Scotland, a sort of "Mc X-Files". James Hazeldine, later to achieve household fame in *London's Burning*, plays journalist Tom Crane who, during the course of tracking down a dangerous occultist, discovers he has psychic powers himself. He is recruited by Department 7, a secret government run team of parapsychology investigators based in Edinburgh who look into reports of paranormal phenomena. Louise Jameson, fresh from her stint as *Doctor Who* companion Leela, plays his skeptical partner. Curiously, in real life it was Jameson who admitted to a belief in the paranormal, extending to palm reading, and Hazeldine who was the skeptic.

James Hazeldine Tom Crane • **Louise Jameson** Anne Reynolds • **John Carlisle** Ray Martindale
Written by *Jack Gerson*
Producer *George Gallaccio*

The Omega Man ★★★★ PG

1971 US Colour 93mins

If you're hooked on sci-fi, this is for you – a weirdly engrossing futuristic tale about the world after a viral apocalypse. The conflict between "normals" (led by Charlton Heston) and light-sensitive mutants (led by Anthony Zerbe) is one of science against superstition, and, while lacking the vampiristic teeth of Richard Matheson's novel, it still has an eerie topicality. One of two great science-fiction allegories starring Heston, the other being Richard Fleischer's thriller set in the 21st century, *Soylent Green*. Contains violence, swearing and brief nudity.

Charlton Heston Robert Neville • **Anthony Zerbe** Matthias • **Rosalind Cash** Lisa • **Paul Koslo** Dutch • **Lincoln Kilpatrick** Zachary • **Eric Laneuville** Richie • **Jill Giraldi** Little girl • **Anna Aries** Woman in cemetery crypt • **Brian Tochi** Tommy
Director *Boris Sagal*
Screenplay *John William Corrington, Joyce H Corrington, from the novel "I Am Legend" by Richard Matheson*

Omicron ★★★

1963 It BW 102mins

An invisible being from another world, an Omicron, enters the dead body of factory worker Renato Salvatori, learns how to function like a human and soon becomes a national phenomenon because of its rapid and tireless ability to work machinery. An earthy comedy, very much in the broad Italian style, that quickly runs out of chuckle-some steam in the latter half when director/writer Ugo Gregoretti piles on the political allegory about mankind becoming slaves to the industrial world. Salvatori rises to the rib-tickling occasion as the flesh puppet attempting to learn human behaviour and the reanimation special effects are extremely effective. But Gregoretti ultimately tries to do too much and the resulting confusion sadly negates all its early brilliant moments. An Italian language film.

Renato Salvatori Omicron/Angelo • **Rosemarie Dexter** Lucia • **Gaetano Quartaro** Midollo • **Mara Carisi** Mrs Midollo • **Ida Serasini** Widow Piattino • **Calisto Calisti** Torchio
Director/Screenplay *Ugo Gregoretti*

On the Beach ★★★

1959 US BW 134mins

An atomic submarine boldly goes where no atomic sub has gone before: to survey a nuclear-wasted Earth, captained by Gregory Peck. Meanwhile, in Australia, survivors await the radioactive fall-out that will eventually kill them. However, it is a case of contamination by cliché, a sickness of conversational banality. Stanley Kramer's film of Nevil Shute's bestseller means well, and Peck, Ava Gardner, Anthony Perkins and a Fred Astaire (as a car-racing scientist) certainly try their best, but it lacks any apocalyptic excitement to go with its appalling premise. Dreary solemnity may well be the way it might happen in real life. However, as it's fiction, let's go out with a bang, not a whimper. The film was nominated for two Oscars, including best score, and made *Waltzing Matilda* a hit in the States.

Gregory Peck Dwight Towers • **Ava Gardner** Moira Davidson • **Fred Astaire** Julian Osborn • **Anthony Perkins** Peter Holmes • **Donna Anderson** Mary Holmes • **John Tate** Admiral Bridie • **Lola Brooks** Lieutenant Hosgood • **John Meillon** Swain • **Lou Vernon** Davidson • **Guy Doleman** Farrel
Director *Stanley Kramer*
Screenplay *John Paxton, James Lee Barrett, from the novel by Nevil Shute*
Producer *Stanley Kramer*
Cinematographer *Giuseppe Rotunno, Daniel L Fapp* • ***Music*** *Ernest Gold*

On the Comet ★★★

1970 Cz Colour 88mins

Adapted from the novel Hector Servadac, this is Karel Zeman's fourth and final foray into the realms of Jules Verne and it's infinitely superior to the 1961 American version, *Valley of the Dragons*. Skilfully combining a human cast with stop-motion creatures and fantastical engraved backdrops, Zeman creates a magical universe through which a comet-severed piece of Earth passes, while its stranded inhabitants come to recognize the futility of nationalism and co-operate to survive. The sequences with the dinosaurs and a giant sea serpent may not be Zeman's most inventive, but the marvellously facetious twist in the tale more than compensates. A Czech language film

Emil Horvath Hecktor Servadec • **Magda Vasaryova** Angelika • **Frantisek Filipovsky** Captain
Director *Karel Zeman*
Screenplay *Jan Prochazka, Karel Zeman, from the novel "Hector Servadac" by Jules Verne*
Cinematographer *Rudolf Stahl*

Once upon a Spy ★★★ PG

1980 US Colour 91mins

Christopher Lee chews the scenery again as a paralysed mad scientist who invents a shrinking machine in a whimsical spy spoof that hits the 007 targets dead on, especially in the Bond theme department. But what else would you expect from producer Jay Daniel, who was co-producer of *Moonlighting*? Jimmy Sangster, another Hammer veteran, scripted this glitzy tale of unbelievable derring-do or rather don't, in star Ted Danson's case which moves along at a bright and breezy pace, thanks to some engagingly quirky humour.

Ted Danson Jack Chenault • **Mary Louise Weller** Paige Tannehill • **Christopher Lee** Marcus Velorium • **Eleanor Parker** The Lady • **Leonard Stone** Dr Charlie Webster
Director *Ivan Nagy*
Screenplay *Jimmy Sangster, from a story by Jimmy Sangster, Lemuel Pitkin*

One ★★★

TV 1956 UK BW 90mins

Evidently an Associated-Rediffusion attempt to imitate the BBC's 1954 adaptation of *Nineteen Eighty-Four*, this feature-length 1956 drama was based by John Letts on the 1953 novel by David Karp, set in a gently oppressive future Britain (the novel has an American background), with Donald Pleasence (who had been in *Nineteen Eighty-Four*) as Burden, a Cambridge don and lackey of the Ministry of Internal Security who is denounced as a subversive on flimsy grounds, in explicit parallel of the situation in America during McCarthyism. He is brainwashed (like Winston Smith) and turned into a weak-willed civil servant, but (like Alex in *A Clockwork Orange*) his original personality isn't quite erased.

Jack May Conger • **Ruth Trouncer** Miss Allam • **Kenneth Hyde** Wright • **Donald Pleasence** Burden • **Jonathan Meddings** Wilkin

Director *Peter Graham Scott*

Written by *John Letts, from the novel by David Karp*

One Step Beyond ★★★ U PG

TV 1959-1961 US BW 96x30mins

With the success of such documentary-style cop shows as *Dragnet* and *Highway Patrol*, it was only a matter of time before someone applied the approach to the more controversial area of psychic and supernatural phenomena. This show, hosted and directed by John Newland, pales in comparison with its contemporary, *The Twilight Zone*, precisely because it was trying to sell its anecdotes as true stories – they were all supposed to be based on authenticated cases – and therefore too often neglects the melodramatic or creepy possibilities. Each episode is hung on ESP, premonition, firestarting, apparitions or some such pre-*X Files* business. Unusually, a clutch of episodes were shot in Britain, taking advantage of some upscale acting talent. Newland reprised the premise, and remade a few episodes, in *The Next Step Beyond* (1978).

John Newland Host

Director *John Newland*

Producer *Collier Young*

The Only Way Out Is Dead ★★ U

1970 Can Colour 88mins

Sandy Dennis and Stuart Whitman play surgeons who suddenly discover that their secret medical research facility is, in fact, an unending source of heart donors for their benefactor (Burl Ives), a bedridden billionaire who craves immortality like a villain in a Bond movie. This cleverly plotted but rather flashily directed drama was made three years after the world's first heart transplant operation, giving it a topicality unusual for the sci-fiction genre.

Stuart Whitman McCarter Purvis • **Sandy Dennis** Enid • **Burl Ives** T M Trask • **Tom Harvey** McBride • **Robert Goodier** Morton

Director *John Trent*

Screenplay *Henry Denker*

Operation Ganymed ★★★

1977 W Ger Colour 126mins

TV director Rainer Erler makes an impressive transition to the big screen with this doomed mission adventure. Years overdue from a multi-ship trip to Jupiter, Dieter Laser and his four-man crew crash land in the Mexican desert. Whether Earth has succumbed to a nuclear conflagration is never made clear (but surely some attempt at contact with the craft would otherwise have been made?). However, it's clear that Erler is driving at some such point, as the unit that had co-operated so well in interstellar isolation begins bickering – even resorting to cannibalism before the sole survivor reaches a semblance of civilisation. German dialogue dubbed into English.

Horst Frank • **Dieter Laser** • **Uwe Friedrichsen** • **Jürgen Prochnow** • **Claus Theo Gaestner** • **Vicky Roskilly**

Director/Screenplay *Rainer Erler*

SCI Q • SCI Q • SCI Q • SCI Q

25

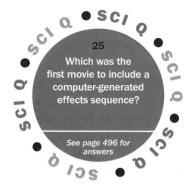

Which was the first movie to include a computer-generated effects sequence?

See page 496 for answers

Orbit ★★ 15

1996 US Colour 79mins

An ambitious but unnecessarily complicated conspiracy thriller, which centres on an abortive attempt to sabotage a US shuttle mission via a virus in the computer system. Unfolded in flashback at a subsequent court case, the story stirs in right-wing American terrorists and even alien life forms into an already overheated brew and for all the intriguing ideas on show, budgetary restraints means it's largely a static, earth-bound affair. Look out for an early screen role for future *Starship Trooper* Casper Van Dien. Contains swearing.

Casper Van Dien • **Bentley Mitchum** • **Kelly Ann Sweeney** • **Joe Estevez** • **Carrie Mitchum** • **Nick Wilder** • **Jan-Michael Vincent** • **Chris Mitchum [Christopher Mitchum]** • **Ulli Lommel**

Director *Mario Van Cleef [Ulli Lommel]*

Screenplay *Budd Garrison*

Orlak, the Hell of Frankenstein ★★★★

1960 Mex BW 103mins

Frankenstein, Mexican-style with a side order of refried Universal Studio horror clichés. Convict Joaquin Cordero springs mad doctor Andres Soler from jail and is introduced to his creation Orlak (Cordero again), a remote-controlled, blood-drinking monster wearing a steel box on its head to hide disfigurement scars. Cordero then uses the creature to murder those who put him in prison and take revenge on his unfaithful lover, cabaret singer Rosa de Castilla. Directed by ex-forties matinée idol Rafael Baledon with a distinct eye on rich Gothic atmosphere and scintillating romantic imagery, this Latino shocker is an impressive masterwork.
A Spanish language film.

Joaquin Cordero Jaime/Orlak • **Andres Soler** Dr Frankenstein • **Rosa de Castilla** Estela • **Irma Dorantes** Elvira

Director *Rafael Baledon*

Screenplay *Alfredo Ruanova, Carlos Enrique Taboada*

Otherworld ★

TV 1985 US Colour 8x60mins

The Sterling family, in hideous mid-eighties clothes and hairstyles, stumbles through a dimensional gateway in an Egyptian pyramid, and find themselves on an alien planet composed of the sort of freak-society-of-the-week provinces found in *The Fantastic Journey* and *Logan's Run* (and later *Sliders*), with Kommander Nuveen Kroll (Jonathan Banks) and his Zone Troopers pursuing them in the inevitable manner of *The Fugitive*. This set out to be mildly satirical (*I Am Woman Hear Me Roar* is set in a province where men are sex slaves) but was mostly the usual pap about romantic robots, immortality serums, drug-dealing bikers and the like. It was cancelled after eight feeble episodes.

Sam Groom Hal Sterling • **Gretchen Corbett** June Sterling • **Tony O'Dell** Trace

Sterling • **Jonna Lee** Gina Sterling • **Brandon Crane** Smith Sterling • **Chris Hebert** Smith Sterling • **Jonathan Banks** Kommander Nuveen Kroll
Written by *Bruce A Taylor*
Executive producer *Roderick Taylor*

Out of the Unknown ★★★★

TV 1965-1971 UK BW and Colour 49x50m

This distinguished anthology series was Britain's answer to *The Twilight Zone*, intelligent adult-themed stories from such masters of the genre as Ray Bradbury, John Wyndham, Nigel (*Quatermass*) Kneale, Terry Nation (creator of the Daleks and later *Blake's 7*) and Troy Kennedy Martin, who'd go on to conceive the best ever cop show, *The Sweeney*. Avoiding the cliché conventions of science fiction (there were no bug-eyed monsters), the series managed to attract top-drawer actors (David Hemmings, Rachel Roberts) while also embracing a wide variety of themes and scenarios despite a restrictive budget. In 1969 the series was revived, this time in colour, after a two-year hiatus, but its emphasis switched from sci-fi to more horror and suspense. Future *Alien* director Ridley Scott worked on some episodes as production designer.

Script editor *Roger Parkes*
Producer *Irene Shubik, Alan Bromly*
Music *Norman Kay*

Out of This World ★★★

TV 1962 UK BW 13x60mins

Made by ABC television, basking in the success of their *Armchair Theatre* collection of single dramas, this was Britain's first attempt at a science-fiction anthology series. Under the competent stewardship of Leonard White, one of the men responsible for *The Avengers*, it featured consistently strong dramatisations of stories by world-class genre writers such as Isaac Asimov, John Wyndham and Philip K Dick (whose most famous novel *Do Androids Dream of Electric Sheep?* was filmed as *Blade Runner*). Hosted by an out-of-place Boris Karloff, *sans* bandages and neck bolts, the pilot episode was shown as part of *Armchair Theatre* in the hope of enticing that audience to stay for the rest of the series. It worked to a degree, but the anthology format was much more successfully exploited by the BBC three years later with their *Out of the Unknown*.

Boris Karloff Host
Producer *Leonard White*

Out of This World ★★

TV 1987-1991 US Colour 96x30mins

A sit-com about an adolescent girl, Maureen Flannigan, who discovers from her mother Donna Pescow that her absent father (voiced by an uncredited Burt Reynolds) is an alien from Antares. On her 13th birthday, the teenager develops all manner of plot-generating special powers that seem more like magic than anything an alien might actually do, from the ability to stop time to transmutate objects. Like Samantha Stevens and many other sit-com magical beings, Evie is torn between revelling In her powers (which often go wrong) and concealing them from a world that would be threatened.

Maureen Flannigan Evie Ethel Garland • **Donna Pescow** Donna Garland • **Doug McClure** Mayor Kyle Applegate • **Joe Alaskey** Beano Froelich • **Christina Nigra** Lindsey Selkirk • **Burt Reynolds** Voice of Troy Garland of Anterias

Out There ★★★

1995 US Colour 98mins

Bill Campbell (*The Rocketeer*) headlines this irreverent, at times tongue-in-cheek, sci-fi TV movie. Trouble ensues when a down-on-his-luck Pulitzer Prize-winning photographer buys an old Brownie camera with still undeveloped film inside. When he develops the prints, he sees what appear to be snapshots of the alien abduction of two deer hunters. When he is dismissed by the military as a phoney, he searches for the truth, aided by the daughter (Wendy Schaal) of one of the victims. Fresh direction by Sam Irvin makes the unconventional subject matter amusingly believable. Comic turns by June Lockhart (*Lost in Space*), Bobcat Goldthwait and Rod Steiger all add to the sci-fi silliness that will surely appeal to fans of the genre.

Bill Campbell Delbert Mosley • **Wendy Schaal** Paige Davis • **Rod Steiger** Colonel Buck Gunner • **Jill St John** Bunny Wells • **Bill Cobbs** Lyman Weeks • **Paul Dooley** Emmett Davis • **Bobcat Goldthwait** Cobb • **Billy Bob Thornton** Biker • **June Lockhart** Donna
Director *Sam Irvin*
Screenplay *Thomas Strelich, Alison Nigh*

Outbreak ★★★★ 15

1995 US Colour 122mins [video] DVD

An exciting eco-thriller, with army medic Dustin Hoffman trying to save the world from a lethal virus imported into America from Africa. You could read this as an Aids allegory, but it also works well as a regular against-the-clock jeopardy thriller with almost mandatory conspiracy cover-up overtones. Director Wolfgang Petersen marshals the effects superbly and there's terrific support from the likes of Morgan Freeman, Kevin Spacey and a particularly nasty Donald Sutherland. While Hoffman may lack the requisite heroic quality needed for the lead, you certainly feel you could put your trust in him. Contains violence and swearing.

Dustin Hoffman Col Sam Daniels • **Rene Russo** Dr Roberta "Robby" Keough • **Morgan Freeman** General Billy Ford • **Cuba Gooding Jr** Major Salt • **Kevin Spacey** Major Casey Schuler • **Patrick Dempsey** Jimbo Scott • **Donald Sutherland** General Donald McClintock • **Zakes Mokae** Dr Benjamin Iwabi • **Malick Bowens** Dr Raswani • **Susan Lee Hoffman** Dr Lisa Aronson • **Benito Martinez** Dr Julio Ruiz • **Bruce Jarchow** Dr Mascelli • **Leland Hayward III** Henry Seward • **Daniel Chodos** Rudy Alvarez • **Dale Dye** Colonel Briggs
Director *Wolfgang Petersen*
Screenplay *Laurence Dworet, Robert Roy Pool*

The Outer Limits ★★★★★ PG 12

TV 1963-1965 US BW 49x60mins [video]

"There is nothing wrong with your television set. Do not attempt to adjust the picture. We are controlling transmission..." With these immortal words, a TV legend was born. Produced in the wake of *The Twilight Zone*, Leslie Stevens's sci-fi anthology series shifts the emphasis away from Serling-esque twists and whimsy, and instead successfully focuses on human reactions to extraordinary phenomena. Although the show is famed for its terrifying monsters, its rich characterisation and thought-provoking drama are the real keys to its success. The series features the likes of William Shatner, Leonard Nimoy, Adam West, Sam Wanamaker, David McCallum, Robert Culp and Martin Landau, while its obvious highlights include the Hugo Award-winning *Demon with a Glass Hand*, *I, Robot* and *Soldier*, an early forerunner to *The Terminator*.

Vic Perrin Control voice
Executive producer *Leslie Stevens*

The Outer Limits ★★★★ U PG 12 15 18

TV 1995 – Can/US Colour [video]

Three decades after the original series began terrifying successive generations of viewers, this glossy revival show took control of the transmission. As suggested by its opening sequence, the series strives to be a faithful update of its illustrious predecessor and offers more studies of human responses to the unknown and unexpected. After overcoming an unfortunate early penchant for superficial, titillation-driven plotlines, the series soon emerges as a worthy follow-up to an all-time classic. Although the new *Outer Limits* storylines tend to be less mind-bending and provocative than those of the original series, they are always consistently well written and confidently produced. The show's guest list reads like a "Who's Who" of American TV, and even features an Emmy Award-winning turn from Amanda Plummer in *A Stitch in Time*.

Kevin Conway Control voice
Story editor *Chris Dickie*
Executive producer *Jonathan Glassner, Richard B Lewis, Pen Densham, John Watson*

Outland ★★ 15

1981 UK Colour 104mins DVD

It's *High Noon* in outer space as mining colony marshal Sean Connery confronts the pushers peddling lethal drugs to Jupiter moon workers so they'll produce more ore. This bleak dramatisation of final frontier contamination comes complete with *Alien*-inspired decor and smooth direction by Peter Hyams. But eschewing the cleverness of his *Capricorn One* for a doggedly one-dimensional approach to both plot and character, Hyams sinks this far-flung fantasy with cheap scare tactics, illogical science and B-movie western-style gun battles that scupper credibility. And why does Connery never call for back up? Contains violence and swearing.

Sean Connery O'Niel • **Peter Boyle** Sheppard • **Frances Sternhagen** Lazarus • **James B Sikking** Montone • **Kika Markham** Carol • **Clarke Peters** Ballard • **Steven Berkoff** Sagan • **John Ratzenberger** Tarlow • **Nicholas Barnes** Paul O'Niel • **Manning Redwood** Lowell • **Pat Starr** Mrs Spector • **Hal Galili** Nelson • **Angus MacInnes** Hughes • **Stuart Milligan** Walters • **Eugene Lipinski** Cane • **Norman Chancer** Slater • **Ron Travis** Fanning • **Gary Olsen** Worker • **Sharon Duce** Prostitute
Director/Screenplay *Peter Hyams*

The Outsider ★★ 15

1997 US Colour 87mins

Westworld is poorly revisited in director David Bishop's workmanlike fantasy saddled with an ersatz Raymond Chandler narration to suggest it's supposed to be futuristic *noir*. In a high-tech theme park, tourists interact with robot actors in mafia scenarios unleashing their pent up violence on the gangster androids and their sexual desires on the cyborg molls. When a new character is mysteriously created, called the Outsider, it begins to target and hunt down one of the top computer programmers. Variable action plugs the plot holes in this carelessly cast and put together TV movie but as director Michael Crichton created and used the clever situation so much better in his 1973 original, what was the point? Contains violence, swearing and brief nudity.

Xavier DeClie Outsider • **Gabriel Dell** Garland Widmark • **Bridget Flannery** Lita Hayworth • **David Leisure** Dr Greenstreet • **Julia Dahl** Claire Arden
Director *David Bishop*
Screenplay *Patrick Highsmith, Evan Spiliotopoulos*

P

"You know what they say. Human see, human do."

Planet of the Apes 1968

Pajama Party ★ U

1964 US Colour 84mins

One of those terribly kitsch movies so rooted in sixties Californian beach parties, that it erupts into hilarious entertainment. This is part of a teen culture series which began with *Beach Party* and was slowly strangled to death by awful scripts. In this one, "star" Tommy Kirk plays a Martian who drops in on the hijinks with suitably nonplussed results. It is meant to be gently amusing but is unintentionally gut-wrenchingly funny, despite the presence of such greats as Buster Keaton and Dorothy Lamour.

Tommy Kirk Go-Go • **Annette Funicello** Connie • **Elsa Lanchester** Aunt Wendy • **Harvey Lembeck** Eric Von Zipper • **Jesse White** J Sinister Hulk • **Buster Keaton** Chief Rotten Eagle • **Dorothy Lamour** Head saleslady • **Don Rickles** • **Frankie Avalon**
Director *Don Weis*
Screenplay *Louis M Heyward*

Panic in Year Zero ★★★★

1962 US BW 91mins

Ray Milland directs and stars in this story about a nuclear war and the breakdown of society that follows. Milland's direction is plain, even nondescript, which sometimes makes the film even more chilling as survivors take the law into their own hands and head for the hills, through a traffic jam of surreal proportions. It's as if *Fail-Safe* had been grafted on to Marlon Brando's biker movie *The Wild One*, with Milland as the boring, everyday Joe who holds up a store, takes his wife and family to live in a cave and kills the thugs who threaten them. There's a lot going on in this movie, with much to think about, and there's Frankie Avalon, too!

Ray Milland Harry Baldwin • **Jean Hagen** Ann Baldwin • **Frankie Avalon** Rick Baldwin • **Mary Mitchell** Karen Baldwin • **Joan Freeman** Marilyn Hayes • **Richard Garland** Mr Johnson
Director *Ray Milland*
Screenplay *Jay Simms, John Morton, from a story by Jay Simms*

Paradis pour Tous ★★★

1982 Fr Colour 110mins

There's a cruel irony in the fact that Patrick Dewaere, who plays a suicidal insurance salesman in this sinister satire, shot himself shortly after its completion. With one foot in the mad scientist camp and another in Stepford-body snatcher territory, it's as witty as it's dark, as inventive as it's derivative. Jacques Dutronc co-stars as the scientist whose technique of "flashing" makes Dewaere so sanguine that he irritates the life out of everyone around him – that is, until he allies with fellow converts in a misguided bid to eradicate stress forever. Fanny Cottençon and Stéphane Audran provide practised support. A French language film.

Patrick Dewaere Alain Durieux • **Jacques Dutronc** Pierre Valois • **Fanny Cottençon** Jeanne Durieux • **Stéphane Audran** Edith • **Philippe Léotard** Marc Lebel
Director *Alain Jessua*
Screenplay *Alain Jessua, André Ruelian*

Parasite ★ 18

1982 US Colour 84mins

In a post-holocaust future, where paramilitary forces and mutant punks clash continuously, scientist Robert Glaudini creates a parasitic monster that burrows into its victims and eats them from the inside. This is a crummy *Alien* meets *Mad Max* exploitation movie, directed by straight-to-video maven Charles Band, which wastes the talents of musical star Vivian Blaine, ex-Runaways singer Cherie Currie and fledgling superstar Demi Moore. Its one feature of note is that it cashed in on the early eighties 3-D revival frenzy and so cinema audiences got to experience the slimy creature leaping out of abdomens at them with eye-straining effect. Without that gimmick, it's a nothing piece of junk.

Robert Glaudini Dr Paul Dean • **Demi Moore** Patricia Welles • **Luca Bercovici** Ricus • **James Davidson** Merchant • **Al Fann** Collins • **Tom Villard** Zeke • **Cherie Currie** Dana
Director *Charles Band*
Screenplay *Michael Shoob, Frank Levering, Alan Adler [Alan J Adler]*

Paris Qui Dort ★★

1923 Fr BW 61mins

René Clair's first feature, completed in three weeks, reflected some of the anarchic preoccupations of the surrealist and Dadaist artists with whom Clair associated at the time. The story, which he wrote in one night, tells of a crazed inventor who creates a "sleep ray" that suspends animation throughout Paris. Although the film is full of comic invention and absurdity, it is sometimes too self-consciously in love with its own cleverness, and some of the cinematic tricks begin to pall.

Henri Rollan Albert • **Madeleine Rodrigue** Woman passenger • **Marcel Vallée** Thief • **Albert Préjean** Pilot
Director/Screenplay *René Clair*

Pathfinders ★★★

TV 1960-1961 UK BW 21x30mins

A sequel to *Target Luna*, this was three stories: *Pathfinders in Space*, *Pathfinders to Mars* and *Pathfinders to Venus*. The first follows the exploits of professor Peter Williams and journalist Gerald Flood as Williams plans to visit the Moon at the same time as his children are visiting during their school holidays. Things go awry and the children (Stewart Guidotti, Richard Dean, Gillian Ferguson), end up joining the expedition. *Pathfinders to Mars* has sabotaur George Colouris causing a further lunar mission to end up on Mars. In the third part of the saga , the team ends up on Venus where they encounter dinosaurs and Cro-Magnon man! As usual with television of this period, production errors were rife (microphones in shot, voices heard from other sets in studio and so on) however the scripts were ambitious, and some of the effects managed live in the studio are still remembered today by those who saw them.

Stewart Guidotti Geoffrey Wedgwood • **Gerald Flood** Conway Henderson • **Peter Williams** Prof Wedgwood • **Gillian Ferguson** Valerie Wedgwood • **Richard Dean** Jimmy Wedgwood • **Pamela Barney** Mary Meadows • **George Coulouris** Harcourt Brown
Created by *Malcolm Hulke, Eric Paice*
Producer *Sydney Newman*

Patlabor: the Mobile Police ★★★ PG

1989 Jap Colour 98mins

With *manga* movies, the emphasis is usually on ultra-violence and stunning design, but this is a more cerebral affair. The plot revolves around an attempt by the Tokyo police, assisted by advanced robots (Labors) to track down a gang of criminals planning to bring down the city, and in many ways this works as a pure detective story. There are still the trademark scenes of explosive action, but director Mamoru Oshii takes a more measured approach to the tale, which may upset die-hard fans but is more digestible to those new to the genre. In Japanese with English subtitles.

Director *Mamoru Oshii*
Screenplay *Kazunori Ito, from a story by Masami Yuuki*

The Peace Game ★★★

1969 Swe Colour 91mins

Made four years after the BBC banned his Oscar-winning holocaust masterpiece, *The War Game*, Peter Watkins sought to wreak revenge on the Establishment by holding it up to ridicule in this futuristic satire. Comfortably predating both *Rollerball* and the millennial vogue for actuality TV, the premise posits that warfare has been outlawed and that the global hierarchy is now decided by a cynical updating of the ancient gladiatorial games, which are more a means of mass repression than a celebration of national prowess. Peter Suschitzky achieves some memorable images, but Watkins's message is lost in the imprecision of his protest.

Arthur Pentelow British general • **Frederick Danner** British staff officer • **Hans Bendrik** Capt Davidsson • **Daniel Harle** French officer • **Hans Berger** West German officer • **Rosario Gianetti** American officer
Director *Peter Watkins*
Screenplay *Nicholas Gosling, Peter Watkins*
Cinematographer *Peter Suschitzky*

Peacemaker ★★★ 18

1990 US Colour 87mins [video]

Despite an at times quite noticeable low budget this exhilarating sci-fi thriller really delivers the goods for action fans. A well-worn theme for sure – alien cop tracking down alien villain – but the twist comes when they crash-land on Earth and both claim to be the good guy. Cue a virtual non-stop montage of chases, explosions and shoot-outs. Kevin S Tenney, with 56 stunt performers at his disposal, keeps you easily engrossed, while Robert Forster and Lance Edwards as the humanoid and virtually indestructible aliens make it fun guessing who's who.

Robert Forster Yates • **Lance Edwards** Townsend • **Hilary Shepard** Dori Caisson • **Robert Davi** Sergeant Frank Ramos • **Bert Remsen** Doc • **John Denos** Reeger • **Wally Taylor** Moses
Director/Screenplay *Kevin S Tenney*

The People That Time Forgot ★★ U

1977 UK Colour 86mins [video]

An okay sequel to *The Land That Time Forgot* in which missing explorer Doug McClure is traced to an exotic prison on the lost island of Caprona. Not as trashy as the original Edgar Rice Burroughs adventure, but director Kevin Connor's constipated confection still features silly dinosaurs (ludicrous mechanised mock-ups) and hopeless acting from an interesting cast (John Wayne's son Patrick, David Bowie protégée Dana Gillespie and the Green Cross Code man himself, David Prowse). A few shots, composed around celebrated fantasy illustrations, compensate for all the film's shortcomings.

Patrick Wayne Major Ben McBride • **Doug McClure** Bowen Tyler • **Sarah Douglas** Lady Charlotte "Charly" • **Dana Gillespie** Ajor • **Thorley Walters** Dr Edward Norfolk • **Shane Rimmer** Hogan • **Tony Britton** Captain Lawton • **John Hallam** Chang-Sha • **David Prowse [Dave Prowse]** Executioner • **Milton Reid** Sabbala • **Kiran Shah** Bolum • **Richard Parmentier** Lieutenant Whitby • **Jimmy Ray** Lieutenant Graham • **Tony Hale** Telegraphist
Director *Kevin Connor*
Screenplay *Patrick Tilley, from the novel by Edgar Rice Burroughs*

Perfect Assassins ★★ 18

1998 US Colour 94mins [video]

A passable variation on *The Manchurian Candidate*, which has Andrew McCarthy as the FBI agent on the trail of a team of ruthless, emotionless assassins. It turns out they are the creation of a mad scientist (Nick Mancuso) and that McCarthy may have more in common with him than he thinks. McCarthy does pretty well, even though he is never really going to convince as a hard-nosed action hero, while Portia de Rossi provides the glamour. Director H Gordon Boos seems more comfortable with the action sequences than the psychological insights, but at least the pace never slackens. Contains swearing and violence.

Andrew McCarthy Ben Carroway • **Robert Patrick** Leo Benita • **Nick Mancuso** Dr Samuel Greely • **Portia de Rossi** Lana Collins • **Matthew Laurance** Special Agent Clark • **Aaron Lohr** Billy Collins • **Lisa Jane Persky** Janice Franklin
Director *H Gordon Boos*
Screenplay *John Penney*

The Perfect Woman ★★★ U

1949 UK BW 83mins [video]

Patricia Roc, one of the most capable British second leads of the forties, was rarely given the chance to show what she could do in starring roles. When she did get her name above the title, she was invariably given a raw deal when it came to dialogue. This frantic comedy of errors is a case in point, for while she handles the dual role of a scientist's social-climbing niece and a beautiful robot with considerable ease, the choicest lines land in the laps of co-stars Stanley Holloway and Nigel Patrick.

Patricia Roc Penelope • **Stanley Holloway** Ramshead • **Nigel Patrick** Roger Cavendish • **Miles Malleson** Professor Belmond • **Irene Handl** Mrs Butter • **Pamela Devis** Olga, the robot • **Fred Berger** Farini • **David Hurst** Wolfgang Winkel • **Anita Sharp-Bolster** Lady Diana • **Phillipa Gill** Lady Mary
Director *Bernard Knowles*
Screenplay *Bernard Knowles, JB Boothroyd, George Black, from the play by Wallace Geoffrey, Basil John Mitchell*

Perversions of Science ★★

TV 1997 US 10x30mins

The makers of *Tales from the Crypt* shift their attention from comedy-horror to bizarre science-fiction drama, and deliver this weird but seldom wonderful half-hour anthology series. Produced by HBO, the show certainly isn't afraid of pushing the boundaries, with stories that combine familiar sci-fi chestnuts such as time travel with less commonplace plot twists – a sex change leading to the ultimate case of self-loving! Unfortunately, the series' unusual plots never deliver more than lightweight viewing, and their half-hour running time further restricts their dramatic impact. The show's varied guest list encompasses the likes of William Shatner, Chris Sarandon and horror B-movie veteran Jeffrey Combs, while Tobe Hooper, Walter Hill and Russell Mulcahy are among its directors.

Maureen Teefy Voice of Chrome
Source *several stories from William M Gaines's "Weird Science" magazine*
Executive producer *Robert Zemeckis* •
Producer *Joel Silver*

Phantasm ★★★ 18

1978 US Colour 84mins [video]

In director Don Coscarelli's fantasy horror with a science-fiction twist, Angus Scrimm impresses as the demon who sends human victims into another dimension where they become slave dwarves. Don't even ask! As wildly imaginative as it's totally illogical, this film's main concern is to shock you senseless. With its unforgettable flying sphere that drills out brains, a macabre fun-house mortuary, severed fingers and cemetery romance, Coscarelli's lurid chiller easily fulfils that lofty aim.

A Michael Baldwin Mike • **Bill Thornbury** Jody • **Angus Scrimm** Tall Man • **Reggie Bannister** Reggie • **Kathy Lester** Lady in lavender • **Terrie Kalbus** Fortune teller's granddaughter • **Ken Jones** Caretaker • **Susan Harper** Girlfriend • **Lynn Eastman** Sally
Director/Screenplay *Don Coscarelli*

The Phantom Creeps ★★

1939 US BW 67mins

Universal never missed an opportunity to show off its invisibility effects. In this 12-

part chapterplay demented scientist Bela Lugosi (in his serial swansong) gets to pass undetected thanks to his "divisualiser belt". Not that that's the only weapon in his armoury. He also has a gigantic robot and a meteorite with the power to cause suspended animation. But Dr Zorka wasn't always bad; the death of his wife has turned him into a megalomaniac with ambitions of world domination. But his plans are thwarted by government agent Robert Kent and plucky reporter Dorothy Arnold.

Bela Lugosi Dr Alex Zorka • **Robert Kent** Capt Bob West • **Edward Van Sloan** Chief Jarvis • **Regis Toomey** Jim Daly • **Dorothy Arnold** Jean Drew • **Edward Stanley** Dr Mallory
Director *Ford Beebe, Saul A Goodkind*
Screenplay *George Plympton, Basil Dickey, Mildred Barish*

Phantom Empire ★★ U

1935 US BW 12x19mins

Despite its many failings, this ranks among the most influential serials ever made – as from its frustratingly staccato episodes emerged the B-movie's most distinctive hero: the singing cowboy. A late choice for the lead, Gene Autry plays the dude rancher and radio star who, in a struggle with crooks wanting his radium-laden real estate, plunges 20,000 feet beneath the prairie to the advanced metallic metropolis of Murania. He may be confronted with giant robots at the height of a civil war, but Gene's never too busy for a tune. A feature-length version, *Men with Steel Faces*, appeared in 1940. Fred Olen Ray directed an obscure re-make in 1988.

Gene Autry Gene • **Frankie Darro** Frankie Baxter • **Lester "Smiley" Burnette [Smiley Burnette]** Oscar • **Betsy King Ross** Betsy • **Dorothy Christie** Queen Tika • **Wheeler Oakman** Argo
Director *Otto Brower, Breezy Eason [B Reeves Eason]*
Screenplay *Wallace McDonald, Gerald Geraghty, H Freedman*

Phantom from Space ★★ U

1953 US BW 72mins

More terminal nonsense from *Killers from Space* producer/director W Lee Wilder, Hollywood legend Billy Wilder's brother. An invisible alien crash-lands on Earth, terrorises some Santa Monica beach picnickers and is tracked to the Griffith Park Observatory in Los Angeles by communications expert Ted Cooper and cop Harry Landers. Earth's atmosphere kills the ET eventually and, as it becomes visible, a man in shorts with a bulbous head is revealed to the world. Shot in semi-documentary style (it opens without titles) and with clear gung-ho enthusiasm on the actors' parts, Wilder's undemanding direction results in workmanlike suspense.

Ted Cooper Lt Hazen • **Rudolph Anders** Dr Wyatt • **Noreen Nash** Barbara Randall • **James Seay** Maj Andrews • **Harry Landers** Lt Bowers • **Jack Daly** Wakeman • **Dick Sands** Phantom
Director *W Lee Wilder*
Screenplay *William Raynor, Myles Wilder*

Phantom from 10,000 Leagues ★

1956 US BW 80mins

Drive-in dreck from Hollywood trash producers Dan and Jack Milner, Bert I Gordon's nearest rivals in the lowest grade teen exploitation market. Oceanographer Kent Taylor investigates beach deaths and discovers a mutant sea monster resulting from radiation exposure experiments carried out by loony professor Michael Whalen. The laughable puppet monster fails to generate any thrills and Dan Milner's amateur direction matches it in motionlessness.

Kent Taylor Ted • **Cathy Downs** Lois • **Michael Whalen** King • **Helene Stanton** Wanda • **Phillip Pine** George • **Rodney Bell** Bill • **Pierce Lyden** Andy
Director *Dan Milner*
Screenplay *Lou Rusoff, from a story by Doris Lukather*
Producer *Dan Milner, Jack Milner*

The Phantom Planet ★

1961 US BW 82mins

In future 1980 astronaut Dean Fredericks, investigating the disappearance of a second Pegasus rocket, lands on the asteroid Rehton, only to discover a race of slow-moving Lilliputian people. After breathing the air, the space age Gulliver shrinks to their size but wins their hearts when he helps them to repulse their enemy, the fast-moving cannibalistic giant Richard "Jaws" Kiel, leader of the dog-faced Solarites. Cut-rate special effects and plodding direction by William Marshall do not help this already convoluted space opera that is barely literate and deadly dull to boot.

Dean Fredericks Capt Frank Chapman • **Coleen Gray** Liara • **Anthony Dexter** Herron • **Dolores Faith** Zetha • **Frances X Bushman** Seson • **Richard Weber** Lt Makonnen • **Al Jarvis** Judge Eden • **Richard Kiel** Solarite
Director *William Marshall*
Screenplay *Fred de Gortner, Fred Gebhardt, William Telaak*

Phantoms ★★ 18

1998 US Colour 82mins

A curiously clunky mix of sci-fi and horror from Miramax offshoot Dimension Films, a company that has revitalised the teen horror market with movies such as *Scream* and *The Faculty*. Rose McGowan and Joanna Going play sisters who return to their isolated hometown and discover that virtually everyone has vanished. Ben Affleck is the puzzled local cop, while Peter O'Toole hams it up as a dotty scientist who holds the key to the mystery. However, despite the presence of *Scream* alumni McGowan and Liev Schreiber and a script from horror maestro Dean R Koontz (adapting his own novel), this fails in the fright department, with too much talk and not enough gore. Contains violence and swearing.

Peter O'Toole Timothy Flyte • **Joanna Going** Dr Jennifer Pailey • **Rose McGowan** Lisa Pailey • **Ben Affleck** Sheriff Bryce Hammond • **Liev Schreiber** Deputy Stu Wargle • **Clifton Powell** General Leland Copperfield • **Nicky Katt** Deputy Steve Shanning • **Michael DeLorenzo** Soldier Velazquez • **Rick Otto** Scientist Lockland
Director *Joe Chappelle*
Screenplay *Dean R Koontz, from his novel*

Phase IV ★★ PG

1973 UK/US Colour 79mins

This messy eco-upheaval picture was the first feature directed by title sequence maestro Saul Bass, whose work is notable for its animation and stylised use of colour and caption. Yet here, when he has a fuller range of visual techniques to experiment with, he fails to conjure up any sense of suspense. The special effects don't improve matters much, nor do the lacklustre performances of Nigel Davenport and Michael Murphy as scientists who discover that a desert ant colony is preparing to take over the planet before humans destroy it.

Nigel Davenport Ernest Hubbs • **Michael Murphy** James Lesko • **Lynne Frederick** Kendra • **Alan Gifford** Eldridge • **Robert Henderson** Clete • **Helen Horton** Mrs Eldridge
Director *Saul Bass*
Screenplay *Mayo Simon*

Phenomenon ★★★ PG

1996 US Colour 118mins DVD

A strange light in the sky gives small-town mechanic John Travolta paranormal powers in director Jon Turteltaub's feel-good sci-fi fable. As scientists attempt to evaluate his sudden escalation to genius,

Travolta battles against an obvious script to focus all his energies on wooing divorced single mother Kyra Sedgwick. Hidden among the waves of sentiment are some genuinely funny moments, but, for all its well-meaning tear-jerking, this tribute to human potential is less than phenomenal.

John Travolta George Malley • **Kyra Sedgwick** Lace Pennemin • **Forest Whitaker** Nate Pope • **Robert Duvall** Doc • **David Gallagher** Al • **Ashley Buccille** Glory • **Tony Genaro** Tito • **Sean O'Bryan** Banes
Director *Jon Turteltaub*
Screenplay *Gerald DiPego*

The Philadelphia Experiment
★★★ PG

1984 US Colour 101mins

What might have worked better as an episode of *The Twilight Zone* is given the big-screen treatment and almost comes off. Michael Paré and Bobby DiCicco play a couple of American sailors from 1943 who are yanked into 1984 when an experiment to render ships invisible to radar backfires. They team up with gung ho Nancy Allen (whose character is named after the actress in *Attack of the 50 Ft Woman*) in a bid to get home. Enjoyably intriguing slice of sci-fi hokum, with the cast delivering their lines with deadpan élan. The project had been kicking around Hollywood since the late seventies; by the time it got rolling, Stewart Raffill had replaced original director John Carpenter, who instead installed himself as executive producer. A strained sequel followed in 1993.

Michael Paré David Herdeg • **Nancy Allen** Allison Hayes • **Eric Christmas** Dr James Longstreet • **Bobby DiCicco** Jim Parker • **Kene Holliday** Major Clark • **Joe Dorsey** Sheriff Bates
Director *Stewart Raffill*
Screenplay *William Gray, Michael Janover, from a story by Don Jakoby, Wallace Bennett, from the book by William I Moore, Charles Berlitz*
Executive producer *John Carpenter*

The Philadelphia Experiment 2
★★ 18

1993 US Colour 94mins

Brad Johnson steps into the time-travelling shoes vacated by Michael Paré and gets propelled to an alternate 1993 where America has become a military state thanks to Hitler winning the Second World War. Then it's back to Germany, 1943, to set history straight. If you can follow the sometimes bewildering plot, this is a reasonably taut action fantasy, relying perhaps a little too heavily on slow-motion battles, black-and-white newsreel footage and wacky hallucination scenes. Contains some violence and mild swearing.

Brad Johnson David Herdeg • **Marjean Holden** Jess • **Gerrit Graham** Mailer/Mahler • **John Christian Graas** Benjamin • **Cyril O'Reilly** Decker • **Geoffrey Blake** Logan • **David Wells** Ainstripes • **Larry Cedar** Hank the controller • **Al Pugilese** Coach
Director *Stephen Cornwell*
Screenplay *Kevin Rock, Nick Paine*

SCI Q SCI Q SCI Q SCI Q

26

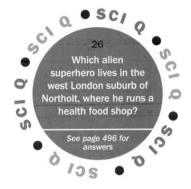

Which alien superhero lives in the west London suburb of Northolt, where he runs a health food shop?

See page 496 for answers

Pi ★★★ 15

1997 US BW 80mins DVD

An original, fascinating thriller about reclusive maths genius Sean Gullette, who becomes obsessed with the notion that everything in the universe can be broken down into mathematics and therefore follows a predictable pattern. This acclaimed black-and-white feature debut from Darren Aronofsky is filled with complex issues (can Gullette's "gift" be used to decipher the true name of God?) and makes arresting use of disorientating camerawork to depict Max's distorted view of the world. But, despite its many virtues, *Pi* becomes increasingly hard to follow because of an overload of intricate idea. Contains swearing and some violence.

Sean Gullette Maximillian Cohen • **Mark Margolis** Sol Robeson • **Ben Shenkman** Lenny Meyer • **Pamela Hart** Marcy Dawson • **Stephen Pearlman** Rabbi Cohen • **Samia Shoaib** Devi
Director *Darren Aronofsky*
Screenplay *Darren Aronofsky, from a story by Sean Gullette, Eric Watson, Darren Aronofsky*
Cinematographer *Matthew Libatique*

Piranha ★★★ 18

1978 US Colour 90mins

A sly, witty cash-in on *Jaws*, with director Joe Dante (*Gremlins*, *The Burbs*) and writer John Sayles (*Alligator*, *Matewan*) dreaming up a deliriously silly tale about a shoal of killer fish, bred by the army for use in Vietnam, which escapes and munches its way through the waterways of America. Bradford Dillman keeps an admirably straight face as the hero and there are neat supporting turns from Kevin McCarthy, Keenan Wynn, Dick Miller and Barbara Steele. Even at this early stage of his career, Dante embellishes the film with an array of references to other movies, and the laughs and blood flow in equal measure. Contains violence, swearing and brief nudity.

Bradford Dillman Paul Grogan • **Heather Menzies** Maggie McKeown • **Kevin McCarthy** Dr Robert Hoak • **Keenan Wynn** Jack • **Dick Miller** Buck Gardner • **Barbara Steele** Dr Mengers • **Belinda Balaski** Betsy • **Melody Thomas** Laura • **Bruce Gordon** Colonel Waxman • **Barry Brown** Trooper
Director *Joe Dante*
Screenplay *John Sayles, from a story by Richard Robinson, John Sayles*

Piranha ★★

1996 US Colour 90 mins

Not the Joe Dante *Jaws* parody, but a TV movie based on the same John Sayles script. Scientists William Katt and Alexandra Paul accidentally let loose some genetically modified snappers into the tributary running through the holiday resort of Lost River. Scott Levy's horror movie remake is devoid of the knowing references that always make Dante's films so much fun. It takes the premise far too seriously and is overly preoccupied with blood-letting special effects at the expense of character development and suspense. Contains swearing, violence and nudity.

William Katt Paul Grogan • **Alexandra Paul** Maggie MacNamara • **Mila Kunis** Susie Grogan • **Soliel Moon Frye** Laura • **Kehli O'Byrne** Gina • **Monte Markham** J R Randolph • **Darleen Carr** Dr Leticia Baines • **Leland Orser** Terry Wechsler
Director *Scott Levy*
Screenplay *Alex Simon, from the 1978 film*

Pitch Black ★★★★ 15

1999 Aus/US Colour 110mins DVD

It might start out resembling another assembly-line sci-fi saga, but David N Twohy's visually stunning adventure soon becomes as thrilling as it is imaginatively striking. The setting is a world with three suns, where a tri-solar eclipse allows screeching, flesh-hungry creatures to emerge from underground. The motley crew that must traverse this nightmare landscape is led by tough guy Vin Diesel, whose charismatic performance is pitched somewhere between (Mad) Max and the T-1000 from *Terminator 2*. With the first half sporting a brilliant desert surrealism and the second loaded with stylised gore, Twohy's futuristic frightener is a vivid and unique achievement.

Radha Mitchell Fry • **Vin Diesel** Riddick • **Cole Hauser** Johns • **Keith David** Imam • **Lewis Fitz-Gerald** Paris • **Claudia Black** Shazza • **Rhiana Griffith** Jack • **John Moore** Zeke • **Simon Burke** Owens
Director *David N Twohy*
Screenplay *Jim Wheat, Ken Wheat, David N Twohy, from a story by Jim Wheat, Ken Wheat*
Cinematographer *David Eggby* • ***Production designer*** *Graham Walker*

Plan 9 from Outer Space ★ PG

1959 US BW 75mins

Camp aliens attempt to take over the world by reviving the dead in Ed Wood Jr's science-fiction opus, built around a few minutes of footage Bela Lugosi shot days before he died and often cited as the worst movie ever made. While there is some unintentional humour to be had from the way Wood desperately incorporates his shots of Lugosi (and a fake body double) into a mess of stock footage, amateur acting, crude special effects (hub-caps as flying saucers) and wobbly sets, it's a tediously depressing experience. Tim Burton re-created many of its scenes in his entertaining biography, *Ed Wood*.

Gregory Walcott Jeff Trent • **Bela Lugosi** Ghoul man • **Mona McKinnon** Paula Trent • **Duke Moore** Lieutenant Harper • **Richard Powers** Colonel Tom Edwards • **Vampira** Vampire girl • **Lyle Talbot** General Roberts
Director/Screenplay *Edward D Wood Jr*

Plan 10 from Outer Space ★★

1995 US Colour 82mins

Why Salt Lake City film-maker Trent Harris would purposely want to invoke the memory of the worst movie ever made is not the only cause of wonderment in this science-fiction spoof. While researching a book about local Mormon history, Stefene Russell finds a plaque which reveals faith founder Brigham Young married an alien queen from the planet Kolob (Karen Black) who's currently plotting a revenge attack on Utah. The chuckles may be few and far between, but good special effects and Black's over-the-top performance add to the eye-rolling bemusement.

Stefene Russell Lucinda Hall • **Karen Black** Nehor • **Karen Nielson**
Director/Screenplay *Trent Harris*

Planet Earth ★★ PG

1974 US Colour 70mins

Gene Roddenberry may have struck gold with *Star Trek*, but his subsequent sci-fi creations have aged less well. Working from a similar blueprint to Roddenberry's *Genesis II* (filmed the previous year), this is once again set in a post-apocalyptic future, with scientist John Saxon waking up after a deep sleep to find that women rule the roost. However, it's all a little po-faced compared to the racy fun of Kirk and Co, and the cast (which includes Janet Margolin, Ted Cassidy and Diana Muldaur) struggles to breathe life into the concept. The sets, too, look suspiciously creaky when viewed today.

John Saxon Dylan Hunt • **Janet Margolin** Harper-Smythe • **Ted Cassidy** Isiah • **Diana Muldaur** Marg • **Majel Barrett** Yuloff • **Christopher Cary** Baylok
Director *Marc Daniels*
Screenplay *Gene Roddenberry, Juanita Bartlett, from a story by Gene Roddenberry*

Planet of Blood ★★

1966 US Colour 81mins

This largely unmemorable space opera from the Roger Corman stable is distinguished by an eclectic cast (John Saxon, Basil Rathbone, Dennis Hopper) and may be viewed today as a precursor to *Alien* with its tale of a US manned space probe rescuing an alien craft that has ditched on the surface of Mars. Unfortunately, the green-skinned female occupant (Florence Marly) turns out to be a galactic vampire. Filmed in a week for just $65,000, the crude plot was concocted by writer/director Curtis Harrington to fit around cannibalised footage from a big-budget Russian sci-fi movie. To his credit, Harrington creates a feeling of eeriness and delivers an off-the-wall ending.

Basil Rathbone Dr Farraday • **John Saxon** Allan • **Dennis Hopper** Paul • **Judi Meredith** Laura • **Florence Marly** Alien queen
Director/Screenplay *Curtis Harrington*
Executive producer *Roger Corman*

Planet of the Apes ★★★★ PG

1968 US Colour 107mins

In this celebrated sci-fi allegory, Charlton Heston is the leader of a team of astronauts who crash on a desolate planet that remains suspiciously reminiscent of Earth, but where apes rule and the humans are the dumb animals. Heston is appropriately square-jawed as the rebellious human and Roddy McDowall and Kim Hunter shine through the marvellous ape make-up from John Chambers, who received an honorary Oscar for his work. Rod Serling and Michael Wilson provide a sly, clever script and the twist at the end still delights. A smash hit that was followed by a number of increasingly inferior sequels, plus a rather mundane TV series. Tim Burton's long-awaited remake (opening summer 2001) stars Mark Wahlberg and Helena Bonham Carter. Contains violence.

Charlton Heston George Taylor • **Roddy McDowall** Cornelius • **Kim Hunter** Dr Zira • **Maurice Evans** Dr Zaius • **James Whitmore** President of the assembly • **James Daly** Honorius • **Linda Harrison** Nova • **Robert Gunner** Landon • **Lou Wagner** Lucius • **Woodrow Parfrey** Maximus • **Jeff Burton** Dodge • **Buck Kartalian** Julius
Director *Franklin J Schaffner*
Screenplay *Michael Wilson, Rod Serling, from the novel "Monkey Planet" by Pierre Boulle*
Cinematographer *Leon Shamroy* • ***Music*** *Jerry Goldsmith* • ***Make-up*** *John Chambers*

Planet of the Apes ★★

TV 1974 US Colour 14x60mins

After a classic opening instalment and four increasingly lacklustre sequels, the *Planet of the Apes* franchise goes back to basics for its TV debut. Set before events in the original film, the series propels contemporary astronauts Graeme Harper and James Naughton over a thousand years into the future, where they discover that the Earth is ruled by intelligent apes. Much like all the franchise's spin-offs, their ongoing flight from their simian pursuers has nothing new to add to the saga, and soon becomes repetitive and predictable. But the show's early instalments do at least have some modest allegorical value, and veteran *Ape* star Roddy McDowall provides some monkey magic as Galen. Although the series was cancelled after 14 episodes, it has subsequently been re-cut and re-released as a series of telemovies under the *Back to the Planet of the Apes* banner.

Roddy McDowall Galen • **Ron Harper** Alan Virdon • **James Naughton** Peter Burke • **Booth Colman** Zaius • **Mark Lenard** Urko
Executive producer *Herbert Hirschman* • ***Producer*** *Stanley Hough*

Planet of the Vampires ★★★ 15

1965 It/Sp/US Colour 83mins

Italian horror maestro Mario Bava's only pure science-fiction movie – co-scripted by Ib (*The Angry Red Planet*) Melchior – melds the supernatural to space opera with

Accidental art or the worst film ever made? Edward D Wood Jr's film is famous for its awfulness and is considered the worst film, of any genre, ever made. Wood's original title for the movie was *Grave Robbers from Outer Space*

haunting results. Barry Sullivan and Norma Bengell (a former Miss Brazil) investigate the mysterious planet Aura and discover that its ancient inhabitants are disembodied spirits who await visitors in order to possess them as a means of escaping their dying planet. A superb example of how Bava's impressive visual sensibilities disguised a very low budget to depict a convincing alien environment and atmosphere – so much so that Ridley Scott paid homage to it in *Alien* 14 years later. The vampirised astronauts rising from shallow graves in slow motion still carries a potent charge today, and is a testament to Bava's visionary influence on the fantasy genre.

Barry Sullivan Capt Mark Markary • **Norma Bengell** Sanya • **Angel Aranda** Wess • **Evi Marandi** Tiona • **Fernando Villena** Karan • **Stelio Candelli** Mud • **Massimo Righi** Nordeg
Director *Mario Bava*
Screenplay *Mario Bava, Alberto Bevilacqua, Callisto Cosulich, Antonio Roman, Rafael J Salvia, Louis M Heyward, Ib Melchior, from a story by Ib Melchior, Renato Pestriniero*
Cinematographer *Antonio Rinaldi*

Planeta Burg ★★★★

1962 USSR BW 74mins

It's likely you've seen this Soviet space odyssey without realising it. Roger Corman acquired the rights and hacked off huge chunks for his own B-movies, Curtis Harrington's *Voyage to the Prehistoric Planet* (1965) and *Voyage to the Planet of Prehistoric Women* (1966), which was directed by Peter Bogdanovich under the pseudonym, Derek Thomas. Pavel Klushantsev's film, however, is an original and highly entertaining piece of work, chronicling a mission to Venus and the encounters of cosmonaut Gennadi Vernov with both the treacherous landscape and various hostile life forms. Colourfully designed and wittily directed, in short, a minor classic. A Russian language film..

Gennadi Vernov Aloysha • **Vladimir Temelianov** Ilya Vershinin • **Yuri Sarantsev** Scherba • **Georgi Zhonov** Bobrov • **Kyunna Ignatova** Masha • **Georgi Teikh** Kern
Director *Pavel Klushantsev*
Screenplay *Alexander Kazantsev, Pavel Klushantsev*

El Planeta de las Mujeres Invasoras ★★★

1965 Mex Colour 85mins

A sexy south of the border space opera in which astronauts Guillermo Murray and Adriana Roel discover the all-women planet Sibila ruled by good twin Lorena Velazquez and evil twin Elizabeth Campbell. They want to invade Earth but, because their deformed lungs are not up to the demands of air absorption, are carrying out experiments on humans to adapt their breathing organs. After halting their plan to kidnap children for further surgical tests, the duo, along with boxer Rogelio Guerra and his comic-relief manager Jose Angel Espinosa Ferrusquilla, destroy the twins. This is an entertaining comic book affair spiced up with Latino vim and vigour by the engaging cast and Alfredo B Crevenna's atmospheric direction. A Spanish language film..

Lorena Velazquez Adastrea / Alburnia • **Elizabeth Campbell** Martesia • **Maura Monti** Eritrea • **Guillermo Murray** Daniel Wolf • **Adriana Roel** Silvia • **Rogelio Guerra** Marcos Godoy • **Jose Angel Espinosa Ferrusquilla** Taquito King
Director *Alfredo B Crevenna*
Screenplay *Alfredo Ruanova*

The Planets against Us ★★★

1961 It/Fr BW 85mins

Stalwart French B-movie actor Michel Lemoine is a runaway humanoid from a galaxy far, far way who has hypnotic eyes and a radioactive touch of death that turns humans to dust. With the Italian army's help, a spaceship load of alien hunters eventually exterminate him with ray guns. Surprising special effects – Jany Clair melts when she kisses Lemoine – and director Romano Ferrara's keen visual sensibility keeps this French/Italian co-production firing on all imaginative cylinders. Dubbed into English.

Michel Lemoine • **Maria Pia Luzi** • **Jany Clair** • **Marco Guglielmi** • **Otello Toso** • **Peter Dane**
Director *Romano Ferrara*
Screenplay *Romano Ferrara, Piero Pierotti*
Cinematographer *Pier Ludovico Pavoni*

Los Platillos Voladores ★★

1955 Mex BW 95mins

Inventor Adalberto Martinez Resortes enters a motor race with a car customised with an aeroplane engine so he can win the prize money and finally get married to his fiancée Evangelina Elizondo. When they breakdown in a small village, the superstitious inhabitants believe they are Martians and subject them to innumerable tests. Eventually they come clean but leave the villagers with a new sense of community pride. Then they meet real Martian... A light musical comedy sugar-coating its blatant peacekeeping message with sharply observed humour and political satire. An early work by director Julian Soler who would make a long-lasting impression on the Mexican genre with the *Santo* wrestler movies. A Spanish language film.

Adalberto Martinez Resortes Marciano • **Evangelina Elizondo** Saturnina • **Andres Soler** Professor Saldana • **Famie Kaufman Vitolo** Saldana's daughter
Director *Julian Soler*
Screenplay *Carlos Leon*

Plughead Rewired: Circuitry Man II ★

1994 US Colour 97mins

It's distressing to see Dennis Christopher (*Breaking Away*) wasted in a witless sequel that makes his character look even more foolish and aimless than he was in the original. The film feels like a collection of out-takes from the first *Circuitry Man*, even recycling some of its effects. The incomprehensible plot has something to do with Plughead (Vernon Wells) again setting his sights on capturing Danner (Jim Metzler).

Vernon Wells Plughead • **Deborah Shelton** Kyle • **Jim Metzler** Danner • **Dennis Christopher** Leech • **Nicholas Worth** Rock • **Traci Lords** Norma
Director/Screenplay *Steven Lovy, Robert Lovy*

Plymouth ★★

1991 US/It Colour 96mins

Plymouth (named after the rock that the Pilgrim Fathers allegedly landed on in 1620) is the first city on the Moon in this ho-hum TV movie that doesn't have the budget to properly do justice to its eventual disaster theme. Doctor Cindy Pickett tries keeping her pregnancy a secret from space hubby Dale Midkiff as a solar flare threatens to wipe out the lunar population. Aside from the few plot points raised – the most interesting being a baby born on the Moon can't survive on Earth – it's a basic low-rent rescue mission adventure.

Cindy Pickett Addy Mathewson • **Dale Midkiff** Gil Eaton • **Richard Hamilton** Wendell Mackenzies • **Jerry Hardin** Lowell • **Perrey Reeves** Hannah • **Matthew Brown** Jed • **Lindsay Price** April • **John Thornton** Eugene • **Brent Fraser** Nathan • **James R Rebhorn** Ezra • **Anne Haney** Emily • **Carlos Gomez** Jimmy • **Eugene Clark** Larry • **Ron Vawter** Percy • **Robin Frates** Donna
Director/Screenplay *Lee David Zlotoff*

The Poisoned Earth ★★

TV 1961 UK BW 90mins

A chatty, issue-heavy ATV network play, transmitted in 1961, foreshadowing the development of battlefield nuclear weapons and the neutron bomb as the government is about to test an atomic device which will only blast a target area of one square mile and thus be suitable for deployment in conventional wars. A group of Aldermaston-style protestors try to occupy the test area, hoping to be blasted and make a point, and come into conflict not only with the boffins and the secret state but the many locals – from shopkeepers to tarts – who benefit from the wealth-producing test range and associated scientific base.

Michael Gough Rev Claude Bell • **Frederick Bartman** James Whittier • **Joseph Furst** Dr Brockmeyer • **Stratford Johns** Insp Matthews • **Barry Keegan** Len Beckett • **Jack May** Barratt

Director *Casper Wrede*

Written by *Arden Winch*

Poltergeist: the Legacy ★★

TV 1996-1999 Can/US Colour 88x60mins

A loose spin-off from the big-screen supernatural shockers, this sci-fi/horror series pits the San Francisco-based Legacy Group against the assorted demons, monsters and evil forces which threaten mankind. It's hardly cutting-edge or spellbinding stuff, but the Legacy Group's weekly endeavours are watchable, and usually deliver the requisite thrills and chills. Derek de Lint and Helen Shaver head an eclectic mix of central characters, all of whom gallantly struggle with the show's familiar line-up of supernatural villains and their equally commonplace evil plots. The series' dark tone and sterling special effects will also possess regular viewers.

Derek de Lint Derek Rayne • **Helen Shaver** Rachel Corrigan • **Martin Cummins** Nick Boyle • **Robbi Chong** Alexandra "Alex" Moreau • **Patrick Fitzgerald** Father Philip Callaghan • **Kristin Lehman** Kristin Adams

Created by *Grant Rosenberg*

Popdown ★★

1968 UK Colour 54mins

Two aliens observe life in Swinging London and become fascinated by youth culture and Flower Power rock music, One of the innumerable fantasy-based exploitation quickies made to cash-in on the British Invasion, like *Gonks Go Beat* and *The Ghost Goes Gear* before it, the genre element is merely a thin excuse to string an endless catalogue of current chart-toppers and pop-fillers together. The eclectic list here includes Julie Driscoll and the Brian Auger Trinity (*This Wheel's on Fire*), busker Don Partridge (*Rosie*), Idle Race, Dantalion's Chariot and the Blossom Toes. Zoot Money plays the character Sagittarius in this pop time capsule gaining in retrospective interest as the years go by.

Diane Keen Miss 1970 • **Jane Bates** Aries • **Zoot Money** Sagittarius • **Carol Rachell** Miss Withit • **Debbie Slater** Girl • **Bill Aron** Host

Director/Screenplay *Fred Marshall*

The Postman ★ 15

1997 US Colour 170mins [video] DVD

There's more than a touch of vanity about Kevin Costner's overlong futuristic epic, which will surely test the patience of his most ardent fans. Costing over $100 million and grossing less than $20 million in America, this retread of *Waterworld* on solid ground has gone down as one of Hollywood's biggest flops. It's a slightly barmy allegory about the need for communication, in which Costner drifts across a post-apocalypse America claiming to be a postman with 15-year-old mail. As director, Costner ensures that every shot shows him in a flattering light, even when mouthing unintentionally hilarious dialogue. A complete dud. Contains violence and a sex scene.

Kevin Costner The Postman • **Will Patton** Bethlehem • **Larenz Tate** Ford • **Olivia Williams** Abby • **James Russo** Idaho • **Tom Petty** Bridge City mayor • **Daniel Von Bargen** Sheriff Briscoe • **Giovanni Ribisi** Bandit 20

Director *Kevin Costner*

Screenplay *Eric Roth, Brian Helgeland, from the novel by David Brin*

Powder ★★★★ 12

1995 US Colour 107mins [video]

This extremely moving fantasy drama tells the tale of a teenager whose mother was struck by lightning during labour, giving him a ghostly white appearance, an extraordinary intellect and miraculous powers. Sean Patrick Flanery (completely shorn of body hair) delivers a wonderfully sympathetic central performance as the young misfit whose unique abilities generate feelings of hostility from the small-minded townsfolk. There's fine support from Jeff Goldblum, Mary Steenburgen and an unusually expressive Lance Henriksen. Victor Salva's intelligent script and assured direction take some fairly familiar themes to some quite unexpected places – and the scene where Flanery transfers the feelings of a dying deer to its heartless hunter is unforgettable.

Mary Steenburgen Jessie Caldwell • **Sean Patrick Flanery** Powder • **Lance Henriksen** Sheriff Barnum • **Jeff Goldblum** Donald Ripley • **Brandon Smith** Duncan • **Bradford Tatum** John Box • **Susan Tyrrell** Maxine

Director/Screenplay *Victor Salva*

The Power ★★

1968 US Colour 109mins

A number of B-league players (George Hamilton, Suzanne Pleshette, Michael Rennie) can't invest much conviction or authority in this science-fiction tale about a group of scientists who discover that one of them can kill by willpower alone. Director Byron Haskin adds some clever touches of menace, but authenticity is sorely lacking.

George Hamilton Jim Tanner • **Suzanne Pleshette** Margery Lansing • **Richard Carlson** N E Van Zandt • **Yvonne De Carlo** Sally Hallson • **Earl Holliman** Talbot Scott • **Gary Merrill** Mark Corlane • **Michael Rennie** Arthur Nordlund

Director *Byron Haskin*

Screenplay *John Gay, from the novel by Frank M Robinson*

Music *Miklos Rozsa*

SCI Q • SCI Q • SCI Q • SCI Q

27

Which renowned horror actor is said to have been the inspiration for a famous comic book creation?

See page 496 for answers

The Powers of Matthew Star ★★

TV 1982-1983 US 22x60mins

A *Superboy* ripoff with Peter Barton as Matthew Star, a mullet-haired 16-year-old alien prince (from the planet Quadris) hiding out on earth with his teacher Louis Gossett Jr, attending school and avoiding assassins. Matthew's superhero suit was a daft disco/fencing outfit, and he could communicate with dolphins. Spun off from a pilot called *Starr Knight* (1981), in which Gerard S O'Loughlin played the teacher and the premise is slightly different, the show managed a season's worth of feeble episodes before the prince was wiped out, not by his alien enemies but low ratings. Amy Steel plays Matthew's blonde girlfriend, and there are appearances from Julie Newmar, Don Stroud, John Vernon, Martine Beswick and Maxwell Caulfield. Among the episode's directors were Gossett and Leonard Nimoy; Richard Matheson wrote a few shows, but nothing memorable made it to the air.

Peter Barton Matthew Star • **Louis Gossett Jr** Walter Shephard • **Amy Steel** Pamela Elliot
Producer *Harve Bennett*

Prayer of the Rollerboys ★★ 15

1990 US/Jap Colour 90mins

In a future where the American economy has failed, Los Angeles is run by a group of rollerblading junior fascists known as the Rollerboys. Standing against them is Griffin (Corey Haim), a pizza delivery boy who used to be a friend of the Rollerboys' leader, Gary Lee (Christopher Collet). Patricia Arquette plays Haim's love interest, and the action scenes are sometimes exciting. As dark futures go, though, it's rather silly.

Corey Haim Griffin • **Patricia Arquette** Casey • **Christopher Collet** Gary Lee • **J C Quinn** Jaworski • **Julius Harris** Speedbagger • **Devin Clark** Miltie • **Mark Pellegrino** Bingo
Director *Rick King*
Screenplay *W Peter Iliff*

Precious Find ★ 15

1996 US Colour 86mins

Space prospector Rutger Hauer scours the asteroids for precious metal in this dismal science-fiction remake of *The Treasure of the Sierra Madre*. Australian director Philippe Mora (who made two of the *Howling* sequels) blatantly lifts key scenes from John Huston's 1948 masterpiece and places them against an unremarkable intergalactic backdrop to minimal effect. Hauer has starred in some trash in his later career, but this badly produced and illogical effort marks a new low, despite the presence of the watchable Joan Chen.

Rutger Hauer Armond Crile • **Joan Chen** Camilla Jones • **Harold Pruett** Ben • **Brion James** Sam Horton • **Morgan Hunter** Salomon
Director *Philippe Mora*
Screenplay *Lenny Britton*

Predator ★★★★ 18

1987 US Colour 106mins DVD

It may not seem much of a compliment, but this is one of Arnold Schwarzenegger's most efficient movies: a stripped-down thriller that cheerfully sacrifices characterisation on the altar of exhilarating action and special effects. Schwarzenegger is the leader of an elite special forces team whose jungle mission is thrown into chaos when they are tracked by a lethal alien game-hunter. As with *Aliens*, much of the fun derives from watching a bunch of macho soldiers crack under pressure. Director John McTiernan ensures the tension is kept at snapping point, helped no end by the sci-fi gimmick of a "cloaking" device that keeps the predator hidden from view. This smash hit propelled McTiernan on to the Hollywood A-list, a position he consolidated with 1988's *Die Hard*. Contains violence and swearing.

Arnold Schwarzenegger Major Alan "Dutch" Schaeffer • **Carl Weathers** Dillon • **Elpidia Carrillo** Anna • **Bill Duke** Mac • **Jesse Ventura** Sergeant Blain • **Sonny Landham** Billy • **Richard Chaves** Pancho • **RG Armstrong** General Phillips • **Shane Black** Hawkins • **Kevin Peter Hall** Predator
Director *John McTiernan*
Screenplay *Jim Thomas, John Thomas*

Predator 2 ★★★ 18

1990 US Colour 107mins DVD

After playing straight man to Mel Gibson in *Lethal Weapon*, Danny Glover seized this opportunity to play a loose cannon, an unorthodox cop who is always turning his nose up at authority. The setting is Los Angeles in 1997, and Glover can't work out who or what is murdering the city's gangsters, or why sinister government official Gary Busey is so interested. However, it's not long before he realises that the culprit is far from human. The action sequences are ably staged by *Blown Away* director Stephen Hopkins, but it lacks the sweaty, claustrophobic tension of the Arnold Schwarzenegger original. Contains swearing and violence.

Danny Glover Detective Mike Harrigan • **Gary Busey** Peter Keyes • **Rubén Blades** Danny Archuletta • **Maria Conchita Alonso** Leona Cantrell • **Kevin Peter Hall** Predator • **Bill Paxton** Jerry Lambert
Director *Stephen Hopkins*
Screenplay *Jim Thomas, John Thomas*

The Pretender ★★★

TV 1996-2000 US Colour 82x60m; 4x120m

Michael T Weiss becomes the ultimate impostor in the sci-fi drama series that gives *The Fugitive* a *Quantum Leap*-style twist. After spending 30 years as a test subject in a secret research project, Weiss escapes from his captors and embarks on a quest to find both his true identity and his family. While pursued by the mysterious Andrea Parker, Weiss fights injustice and evil using his unique ability to instantly become an expert at any profession. Its format may owe a lot to the adventures of Richard Kimble and Sam Beckett, but the series remains an extremely gripping and thrilling affair. Weiss' exotic good looks are perfect suited to the enigmatic Pretender, and the actor also imbues Jarod with an intriguing dark edge. After four seasons, the saga ended, but TNT produced a TV movie one-off in 2001.

Michael T Weiss Jarod • **Andrea Parker** Miss Parker • **Patrick Bauchau** Sydney • **Jon Gries** Broots
Written by *Javier Grillo-Marxuach, Joel Metzger*
Executive producer *Steven Long Mitchell, Craig W Van Sickle*

Prey ★★

TV 1998 US Colour 13x60mins

A new species of "super" humans has evolved, and its members are intent on conquering the world. On uncovering their secret, bio-anthropologist Debra Messing enlists the help of one such "homo superior", the enigmatic Adam Storke, to stop the strong from preying on the weak. Taking its cue from both *The X Files* and Charles Darwin's theories of evolution, *Prey* pursues a superior central concept with a modest degree of success. Although the show frequently lacks pace and its central leads tend to take things a bit too solemnly for their own good, the series generally remains provocative and engaging viewing. There's no telling how the series would ultimately have evolved, though, as it was cancelled after its cliffhanging 13th episode.

Debra Messing Dr Sloan Parker • **Adam Storke** Tom Daniels • **Vincent Ventresca** Dr Ed Tate • **Frankie Faison** Ray Peterson • **Larry Drake** Dr Walter Attwood
Created by *William Schmidt*
Executive producer *Charles Grant Craig, William Schmidt*

Primal Impulse ★★

1974 It Colour

A talky and arty slice of science-fiction pretension directed with starchy precision by Luigi Bazzoni but beautifully photographed by Vittorio Storaro. Interpreter Florinda Bolkan is having strange dreams and identity problems. Seems like the phases of the moon, and in particular abandoned astronaut Peter

McEnery and scientist Klaus Kinski, have a lot to do with her mood swings and general demeanour. What's it all about? Even the cast, also including Lila Kedrova and Nicoletta (*The Beyond*) Elmi, can't seem to fathom it out. A strained and irritatingly weird avant-garde confection.

Florinda Bolkan Alice Campos • **Peter McEnery** Henry • **Nicoletta Elmi** Little Paola • **John Karlsen** Alfredo Rovelli • **Evelyn Stewart** Mary • **Lila Kedrova** Signora Ilse • **Klaus Kinski** Blackmann
Director *Luigi Bazzoni*
Screenplay *Mario Fenelli, Luigi Bazzoni*
Cinematographer *Vittorio Storaro*

Primal Species ★ 15

1996 US Colour 77mins VIDEO DVD

About the best one can say about this third entry in Roger Corman's *Carnosaur* series is that it isn't as terrible as the original, and it doesn't rip off *Aliens* as blatantly as the second one did. Otherwise, everything else is as cheap and uninspired as ever, including the recycled animatronics. Scott Valentine is an odd choice to play the leader of an anti-terrorist squad that sets out to recover a shipment of stolen dinosaurs. Most of the first half takes place in one warehouse, with endless stalking down crumbling hallways. Things pick up slightly when the action moves on to a ship, though it's here that the influence of *Aliens* becomes ever more apparent. Contains violence and some swearing.

Scott Valentine Rance • **Janet Gunn** Dr Hodges • **Rick Dean** Polchek • **Rodger Halston** Sanders • **Anthony Peck** Gen Mercer • **Terri J Vaughn** BT Coolidge
Director *Jonathan Winfrey*
Screenplay *Scott Sandin*

Prince of Darkness ★★ 18

1987 US Colour 101mins VIDEO

Virtually a supernatural remake of his own *Assault on Precinct 13*, director John Carpenter takes one of his sporadic delves into Nigel Kneale sci-fi/horror territory (he even wrote the script as Martin Quatermass!) with tedious results. It's old superstitions versus the computer age in an awkward yarn about a weird container full of green liquid in an LA church that contains pure evil. Zombies, squirt-gun vomit theatrics, gore galore and metaphysical ramblings are overused to keep a mechanical plot moving relentlessly. Contains violence and swearing.

Donald Pleasence Priest • **Jameson Parker** Brian • **Victor Wong** Professor Birack • **Lisa Blount** Catherine • **Dennis Dun** Walter • **Susan Blanchard** Kelly • **Anne Howard** Susan Cabot • **Ann Yen** Lisa • **Alice Cooper** Street people leader • **Ken Wright** Lomax • **Dirk Blocker** Mullins
Director *John Carpenter*
Screenplay *Martin Quatermass [John Carpenter]*

The Prisoner ★★★★★ PG

TV 1968-69 UK Colour 17x60m VIDEO DVD

Arguably the most surreal and allegorical TV show ever made, this was the brainchild of Patrick McGoohan, one of the faces of British cult television in the sixties and the highest paid TV actor of his generation. Intended as a plea by McGoohan for the liberty of the individual, since its controversial first run *The Prisoner* has acquired a mammoth cult following – even university courses have been set up to study the series' "hidden" messages. Shot at the beautiful resort of Portmerion in north Wales McGoohan, who wrote and directed several of the stories, is a secret agent (*Danger Man*'s John Drake?) who resigning from a government ministry is kidnapped and sent to a remote village, a sort of cross between Butlins and MI5, from which there is no escape. The series grew more bizarre each week and out-weirded itself with the last baffling episode, complete with gun battles choreographed to the strains of The Beatles' *All You Need Is Love*, which left more questions than answers and TV switchboards were flooded with angry callers. In the press backlash that followed, the intensely private McGoohan left the country.

Patrick McGoohan Number 6 • **Angelo Muscat** The butler • **Peter Swanwick** The supervisor
Created by *Patrick McGoohan, George Markstein*
Executive producer *Patrick McGoohan* • ***Producer*** *David Tomblin*

SFacts

The bald-headed man sitting behind the desk in the opening credits of the early episodes is George Markstein, the series script editor, who is sometimes credited with being the co-creator with McGoohan. The two men did not part friends; in one of his rare interviews, Markstein said he left the series "when egomania took over".

Prisoners of the Lost Universe ★ PG

1983 UK Colour 90mins VIDEO

Arguably the best of the three cut-rate fantasy efforts (*Hawk the Slayer*, *Jane and the Lost City*) from the British duo of director Terry Marcel and horror film composer-turned producer Harry Robertson, this South African shot action adventure only sporadically sparks into life. TV celebrity Kay Lenz and electrician Richard Hatch, transported into another dimension by scientist Kenneth Hendel's matter transmitter, land on the alternate medieval world of Planet Vonya ruled by evil warrior John Saxon. They're captured and escape, captured and escape etc, throughout the rest of this unimaginative comic-strip pot boiler.

Richard Hatch Dan Roebuck • **Kay Lenz** Carrie Madison • **John Saxon** Kleel • **Peter O'Farrell** Malachi • **Ray Charleson** Greenman • **Kenneth Hendel** Dr Hartmann
Director *Terry Marcel*
Screenplay *Terry Marcel, Harry Robertson*

Probe ★★★★

TV 1988 US Colour 1x120mins, 6x60mins

Co-created by renowned science fiction author Isaac Asimov, this innovative series is an obvious forerunner of *The X Files*. Parker Stevenson is perfectly cast as Austin James, an eccentric but brilliant scientist who uses his legendary deductive powers to investigate the world's most baffling crimes. In his quest for truth and justice, Stevenson is helped – and unintentionally hindered – by his plucky secretary, Ashley Crowe. Much like Mulder and Scully's subsequent adventures, Austin's weekly exploits are driven by believable science, smart scripts and a subtle sense of fun. Disappointingly, the series was curtailed by the 1998 writers' strike and wrapped after a mere seven episodes.

Parker Stevenson Austin James • **Ashley Crow** Michelle "Mickey" Castle
Created by *Isaac Asimov, Michael I Wagner*
Executive producer *Alan J Levi, Michael I Wagner* • ***Producer*** *Stephen Caldwell, Michael Piller*
Science advisor *Isaac Asimov*

Progeny ★★★ 18

1998 US Colour 91mins VIDEO DVD

A interesting change of pace for splatter specialist Brian Yuzna (*Society*, *Bride of Re-Animator*) in this *Outer Limits*-style tale of a pregnancy that might not be of this world. Although the alien abduction angle has been tackled more convincingly in films like *Communion*, Yuzna creates some unsettling imagery. Arnold Vosloo (*The Mummy*) isn't exactly leading man material, but he does convey an escalating sense of paranoia with some gusto, while

Lindsay Crouse and Brad Dourif provide solid support. Although Yuzna does occasionally betray his roots with dollops of gore and nudity, this is a far more restrained and atmospheric tale than you might expect. Contains violence, nudity and some swearing.

Arnold Vosloo Dr Craig Burton • **Jillian McWhirter** Sherry Burton • **Brad Dourif** Dr Bert Clavell • **Lindsay Crouse** Dr Susan Lamarche
Director *Brian Yuzna*
Screenplay *Aubrey Solomon, from a story by Stuart Gordon, Aubrey Solomon*

Project ALF ★★

1996 US/Ger Colour 95mins

Spun off from an eighties American television series, director Dick Lowry's unassuming sci-fi comedy about an orange, furry and funny extraterrestial – ALF stands for Alien Life Form – is amiable family fare. Here the wisecracking ET has close encounters with the military, who have taken him to a top secret base for analysis; but others at the establishment wish to see him destroyed. Miguel Ferrer, Ed Begley Jr and Martin Sheen are the well known faces in the cast.

Miguel Ferrer Moyers • **William O'Leary** Captain Rick Mulligan • **Jensen Daggett** Major Melissa Hill • **Scott Michael Campbell** Lieutenant Reese • **Ed Begley Jr** Dr Warner • **Martin Sheen** Colonel Milfoil
Director *Dick Lowry*
Screenplay *Tom Patchett, Paul Fusco*

Project: Alien ★ 15

1990 US/Aus/Yug Colour 88mins

Michael Nouri plays journalist Milker, who investigates a plane crash and other mysterious events including a meteor shower and unexplained illness among a group of geologists. He enlists the help of renowned bush pilot Darlanne Fluegel but the authorities, including Charles Durnin, want everything to be hushed up. The convoluted plot will probably have lost your attention long before our hero gets to the bottom of the mystery. Even the flight sequences manage to be boring.

Michael Nouri Jeff Milker • **Charles Durning** Colonel Clancy • **Maxwell Caulfield** George Abbott • **Darlanne Fluegel** Bird McNamara
Director *Frank Shields*
Screenplay *David Peoples*

Project Moonbase ★

1953 US BW 63mins

Science-fiction icon Robert Heinlein co-wrote the script for this talky space odyssey about man conquering the moon (in 1970, nearly right!). The highlights are communists sabotaging all chances of a return to Earth and the first lunar marriage, which is given a female president's blessing. A pseudo-scientific bore cobbled together from an unsold TV series with mind-boggling space outfit designs.

Donna Martell Col Britels • **Hayden Rorke** Gen Greene • **Ross Ford** Maj Moore • **Larry Johns** Dr Wernher • **Ernestine Barrier** Mme President
Director *Richard Talmadge*
Screenplay *Robert A Heinlein, Jack Seaman*
Producer *Jack Seaman*

Project: Shadowchaser ★ 15

1992 UK/Can Colour 94mins

Mercenaries led by robot Romulus (Frank Zagarino) take over a hospital, holding the President's daughter (Meg Foster) to ransom. A convicted murderer (Martin Kove) is mistakenly brought in as the only person in the building who can save the hostages. Yes, it's *The Terminator* meets *Die Hard*, but even by cheap rip-off standards this movie is slavishly devoted to its models. Even the music bears a close resemblance to Danny Elfman's score to *Batman*. The only new wrinkle is that the daughter clashes romantically with our hero, like something out of *Moonlighting*. Save yourself the time and watch the originals.

Martin Kove DaSilva • **Meg Foster** Sarah • **Frank Zagarino** Romulus • **Paul Koslo** Trevanian • **Joss Ackland** "Kinderman"
Director *John Eyres*
Screenplay *Steven Lister*

Project UFO ★★

TV 1978-1979 US Colour 26x60mins

Jumping on the UFO bandwagon started the previous year by Steven Spielberg's mega-hit *Close Encounters of the Third Kind* producer Jack Webb, most famous for TV's police series *Dragnet*, was quick to seize on the potential of a docu-drama based on the American Air Force's own investigations into flying saucer sightings – Project Blue Book. The format was simple: a UFO appears, two Air Force investigators arrive on the scene, played by William Jordan and Caskey Swaim, to collect evidence, interview witnesses and then finally reveal their conclusions. The big problem was that after all the build up most of the cases turned out to be anti-climactic, logically explained away as natural phenomena or hoaxes, thus robbing the viewer of any sense of wonderment about the possibility of visitors from the stars. As a result the series never really took off.

William Jordan Major Jake Gatlin • **Edward Winter** Captain Ben Ryan • **Caskey Swaim** Staff Sergeant Harry Fitz • **Aldine King** Libby Virdon
Written by *Dirk Wayne Summers*
Producer *William T Coleman* • ***Executive producer*** *Jack Webb*

SFacts

Producer William T Coleman was a retired USAF colonel who in the early sixties was the public liaison for Project Blue Book. For 21 years the project reviewed almost 13,000 cases, of which, claims Coleman, "Just over a hundred were what we'd consider worrisome, or suggestive of a technology we don't know about. High strangeness."

Project X ★★★

1968 US Colour 96mins

As Hollywood's foremost hustler of horror, William Castle was a legend in his own spook-time. He had cinema seats installed with "tinglers" and promised insurance if you died of fright during one of his movies. He directed this science-fiction film after producing *Rosemary's Baby*, but its story of Christopher George, from the next century, time-trapped in the present to discover a humankind destructor, is unlike Castle's usual scary stuff. A low-budget, low-key affair, it's imaginatively thought through, with enough data to convince. What's sadly missing, though, is the kind of gusto he brought to his other work. Ironically, he was a better salesman of trash than he was of quality a more persuasive dealer in fool's gold than the real thing.

Christopher George Hagen Arnold • **Greta Baldwin** Karen Summers • **Henry Jones** Dr Crowther • **Monte Markham** Gregory Gallea • **Harold Gould** Colonel Holt • **Phillip E Pine [Phillip Pine]** Lee Craig
Director *William Castle*
Screenplay *Edmund Morris, from two novels by Leslie P Davies*

The Projected Man ★★ PG

1966 UK Colour 86mins

A mid-sixties B-feature, with special effects that have the distinct look of wobbly cardboard about them, especially when viewed from a post-*Star Wars* vantage point. The story is hardly original either, with a dotty scientist getting his sums wrong in a teleportation experiment and ending up hideously disfigured. However, for all its shortcomings, this still manages to pack a minor punch, largely due to the sense of menace engendered by Ian Curteis's direction, and some passable acting by the likes of Ronald Allen and Derek Farr. The kids will snort with derision, though.

Bryant Halliday Professor Paul Steiner • **Mary Peach** Dr Pat Hill • **Ronald Allen** Dr Mitchell • **Norman Wooland** Dr Blanchard • **Derek Farr** Inspector Davis
Director *Ian Curteis*
Screenplay *John C Cooper, Peter Bryan, from a story by Frank Quattrocchi*

Prophecy ★★ 15

1979 US Colour 97mins

One of the earliest of the eco-shockers, this demonstrates the decline of director John Frankenheimer (*The Manchurian Candidate*). Doctor Robert Foxworth and his pregnant classical musician wife, Talia Shire, go to investigate a report of mercury poisoning in the Maine backwoods and find themselves battling giant biological mutants. If only the direction had been as fluid as the mercury.

Talia Shire Maggie • **Robert Foxworth** Rob Vern • **Armand Assante** John Hawks • **Richard Dysart** Isley • **Victoria Racimo** Ramona • **George Clutesi** M'Rai
Director *John Frankenheimer*
Screenplay *David Seltzer*

Proteus ★★★ 18

1995 UK Colour 92mins DVD

This typical monsters-on-the-loose movie is creepy all the way, floundering only slightly in its pacing and acting. A group of inept yuppies-turned-amateur drug-runners stumble upon a seemingly abandoned research rig in mid-ocean. The few people left seem terrified of something, but they never stick around long enough to say what. Have no fear, our heroes will discover what's plaguing the rig and fight it off – they hope. The dark industrial setting makes for good atmosphere, but it's still just a monster movie with much owed to earlier flicks like *Alien*. Director Bob Keen is probably better known for make-up and special effects work on the *Hellraiser* films. Contains swearing and violence.

Craig Fairbrass Alex • **Toni Barry** Linda • **William Marsh** Mark • **Jennifer Calvert** Rachel • **Robert Firth** Paul • **Margot Steinberg** Christine
Director *Bob Keen*
Screenplay *John Brosnan, from the novel "Slimer" by Harry Adam Knight [John Brosnan]*

Prototype ★★★ U

1983 US Colour 95mins

The veteran scriptwriting team of Richard Levinson and William Link also took on executive producing duties for this superior TV movie. Although the premise the US government is the real monster may be a little obvious, this is still a tidy reworking of the Frankenstein story. Christopher Plummer clearly revels in the role of the scientist out to recover the android he has created before the military can turn it into a killing machine, while David Morse is a credible robotic human. Director David Greene keeps things nice and tense.

Christopher Plummer Dr Carl Forrester • **David Morse** Michael • **Frances Sternhagen** Dorothy Forrester • **James Sutorius** Dr Gene Pressman • **Stephen Elliott** Dr Arthur Jarrett • **Doran Clark** Chris
Director *David Greene*
Screenplay *Richard Levinson, William Link*

Prototype X29A ★ 18

1992 US Colour 93mins

During the post-holocaust 21st century, feeling that humanity is in danger, the government systematically wipes out all cyborgs. Learning years later that one cyborg female still exists, scientists resurrect the cyborg-killing Prototype – a *RoboCop*-like creation – using her former lover in the device. All of this takes about 15 minutes; in the rest of the 90-minute-plus running time, nothing of any real consequence happens. Though there are signs the film-makers were trying very hard to present most things onscreen in the most imaginative way possible, it seems they were very limited by the fact that most of the budget seems to have gone into the construction of the Prototype suit. Only insomniacs need apply.

Lane Lenhart Chandra Kerkorian • **Robert Tossberg** Hawkins Cosslow • **Brenda Swanson** Dr Alexis Zelazny • **Paul Coulj** Dr Laurence Roberts • **Mitchell Cox** Ariel • **Sebastian Scandiuzzi** Sebastian
Director *Phillip Roth [Phillip J Roth]*
Screenplay *Phillip Roth [Phillip J Roth], from a story by Gian-Carlo Scandiuzzi, Phillip Roth [Phillip J Roth]*

Psi Factor: Chronicles of the Paranormal ★★

TV 1996-2000 Can Colour 88x60mins

One of the more unusual shows inspired by the *X Files* bandwagon, this low-budget exploration of unexplained phenomena takes time to find its way, but ultimately becomes a modestly engaging sci-fi drama series. Supposedly inspired by the real-life case files of the Office of Scientific Investigation and Research (OSIR), the show follows the exploits of various OSIR agents as they study paranormal, extraterrestrial and supernatural activity. Afer featuring half-hour storylines and an alternating cast in season one, the show wisely adopts one-hour plotlines and a regular character line-up usually led by *Max Headroom*'s Matt Frewer for the rest of its run. While its episodes are extremely hit and miss, the series generally makes for intriguing, atmospheric and satisfying viewing. The show is hosted by former *Ghostbuster* Dan Akyroyd, whose brother was one of its original producers.

Dan Aykroyd Host • **Colin Fox** Dr Anton Hendricks • **Nancy Anne Sakovich** Lindsay Donner • **Barclay Hope** Peter Axon • **Joanne Vannicola** Mia Stone • **Matt Frewer** Matt Praeger • **Soo Garay** Claire Davison • **Nigel Bennett** Frank Elsinger
Executive producer *James Nadler, Seaton McLean, Peter Aykroyd* • ***Producer*** *David N Rosen*

Pulse ★★★ 18

1988 US Colour 86mins

A quirky little horror tale that makes up for what it lacks in blood and gore with a neat line in suspense. A mysterious, intelligent form of electricity pulses through the neighbourhood, with Cliff De Young as the puzzled suburbanite who can't work out why all the appliances in the house are beginning to turn on their owners. Writer/director Paul Golding pokes some fun at life in the 'burbs, and makes ingenious use of the rogue machines.

Cliff De Young Bill • **Roxanne Hart** Ellen • **Joey Lawrence** David • **Matthew Lawrence** Stevie • **Charles Tyner** Old Man
Director/Screenplay *Paul Golding*

The Puma Man ★

1979 It Colour 96mins

An Aztec legend claims aliens appeared on Earth at the dawn of time and gave super-powers to a race of men. A descendant of one of the Puma man-gods is museum paleontologist Walter George Alton who is told of his lineage by South American Indian Miguel Angel Fuentes. Soon Alton is wearing a cape, walking through walls and battling deranged monk Donald Pleasence who has stolen a gold Aztec mask enabling him to hypnotise people into taking on the superhero. A badly acted, flimsy fantasy perfunctorily directed by Alberto De Martiino and featuring some of the worst special effects ever committed to film.

Walter George Alton Tony Farmes • **Donald Pleasence** Kobras • **Miguel Angel Fuentes** Vadinho • **Sydne Rome** Jane Dawson • **Silvano Tranquilli** Dawson
Director *Alberto De Martino*
Screenplay *Massimo De Rita*

Punishment Park ★★★★

1971 US Colour 88mins

The best of the socio-political fantasies made by documentary film-maker Peter Watkins whose *Privilege* and *The War Game* also interpreted present ills through reconstructions of the future. Draft dodgers who oppose America's Indo-China war are put in detention camps where they must chose between a three-day ordeal in "Punishment Park" to win their freedom or a long jail sentence. Watkins plays the leader of a British documentary film unit observing one group of dissenters as they take the former option and run for their lives across a desert and face fascist terror tactics. Powerful and depressing, this virtual restaging of the Vietnam War in America's heartland is an outstanding indictment of repression and insidious state bullyboy tactics.

Jim Bohan Captain, Sheriff's Department • **Van Daniels** County Sheriff • **Frederick Franklyn** Professor Daly • **Carmen Argenziano** Jay Kaufman • **Stan Armsted** Charles Robbins • **Gladys Golden** Mrs Jergens • **Sanford Golden** Sen Harris • **Patrick Boland** Defendant • **Peter Watkins** Documentarist

Director/Screenplay *Peter Watkins*

The Puppet Masters ★★ 15

1994 US Colour 104mins

A dumb incarnation of Robert Heinlein's excellent short science-fiction novel, with Donald Sutherland in the lead role. Far from remaining faithful to the book, the film takes liberties with the story in such a way that Heinlein might have objected. If you've seen Sutherland's similarly-themed *Invasion of the Body Snatchers*, you've already got a pretty good idea of what's in store here. While technically competent, this offers little in the way of a plot.

Donald Sutherland Andrew Nivens • **Eric Thal** Sam Nivens • **Julie Warner** Mary • **Yaphet Kotto** Ressler • **Keith David** Holland • **Will Patton** Graves • **Richard Belzer** Jarvis • **Tom Mason** President Douglas

Director *Stuart Orme*

Screenplay *David S Goyer, Ted Elliot, Terry Rossio, from the novel by Robert A Heinlein*

The Purple Monster Strikes ★★★ U

1945 US BW 15x13mins

Undoubtedly inspired by wartime paranoia, this was the first serial to consider the prospect of alien invasion. It's also one of the chapterplay's finest hours, with shape-shifting Martian Roy Barcroft and his sidekick Mary Moore duping gangster Bud Geary into helping them build James Craven's top secret spaceship. The need to collect various devices to fulfil the mission (including special fuel and an electroannihilator) anticipates videogaming. But the way in which lawyer Dennis Moore constantly has to rescue Craven's niece, Linda Stirling, dates back to the Pearl White era.

Dennis Moore Craig Foster • **Linda Stirling** Sheila Layton • **Roy Barcroft** Purple monster • **James Craven** Dr Cyrus Layton • **Bud Geary** Hodge Garrett • **John Davidson** Emperor of Mars • **Mary Moore** Marcia

Director *Spencer Gordon Bennet, Fred C Brannon*

Screenplay *Royal K Cole, Albert DeMond, Basil Dickey, Barney Sarecky, Lynn Perkins, Joseph Poland*

The Purple People Eater ★★★

1988 US Colour 91mins

Thirty years after Sheb Wooley had a hit with the song of the title in 1958, this daft little movie attempted to rekindle the spirit of a time when aliens were synonymous with communists and rock 'n' roll was considered the Devil's music. Parts of the plot bear more than a passing resemblance to **batteries not included*, but there's something irresistible about seeing Ned Beatty and Shelley Winters playing helpless pensioners. Neil Patrick Harris (of *Doogie Howser, MD* fame) co-stars as the lad who brings the eponymous alien to Earth by playing Wooley's hit, and there are fascinating cameos from Little Richard and Chubby Checker.

Ned Beatty Grandpa • **Neil Patrick Harris** Billy Johnson • **Shelley Winters** Rita • **Peggy Lipton** Mom • **James Houghton** Dad • **Thora Birch** Molly Johnson • **John Brumfield** Mr Noodle • **Little Richard** Mayor • **Chubby Checker** Singer

Director *Linda Shayne*

Screenplay *Linda Shayne, from the song by Sheb Wooley*

Q

"We're all Martians!"

Quatermass and the Pit 1958-1959

QED ★★★

TV 1982 US/UK Colour 6x60mins

Definitely not to be confused with the BBC's long-running strand of scientific documentaries, the initials QED here stand for Quentin E Deverill, played by *The Killing Fields* Sam Waterston, an eccentric professor from Harvard University whose scientific ideas are mocked by his peers so he journeys to Edwardian England to solve mysteries and do battle with power-crazed geniuses bent on global conquest. Borrowing liberally from both TV's *Wild Wild West*, with its crackpot futuristic inventions, and James Bond, plots that revolve around rockets aimed at London, its tongue-in-cheek approach was exploited with playful earnestness by directors Don Sharp and Roy Ward Baker, veterans of many a Hammer horror. Produced in Britain on a high budget with a host of home-grown supporting players, this series sadly never caught on.

Sam Waterston Quentin E Deverill • **George Innes** Phipps • **A C Weary** Charlie Andrews • **Julian Glover** Dr Stefan Kilkiss • **Caroline Langrishe** Jenny Martin

Director *Don Sharp, Roy Ward Baker, Henry Herbert*

Executive producer *John Hawkesworth* • ***Producer*** *Christopher Neame*

Quantum Leap ★★★★ PG

TV 1989-93 US Colour 1x120m; 95x60m

When a time travel experiment goes "a little ca-ca", American scientist Dr Sam Beckett finds himself temporarily "becoming" various people at critical moments of their pasts. With the help of his holographic guide Al, Sam attempts to "change history for the better", while always hoping that his next leap will take him back to his own life. A unique blend of drama, action, comedy, time travel and body-swapping, *Quantum Leap* largely eschews high-concept sci-fi adventure in favour of telling nostalgic everyday tales about everyday people. While its storylines tend to very predictable, the show still invariably manages to hit its emotional target. The versatile Scott Bakula (soon to be seen as Captain Jonathan Archer in the new *Star Trek: Enterprise*) shines in even the most inane – and insane – episode, and is well supported by the supremely charismatic Dean Stockwell.

Scott Bakula Dr Sam Beckett • **Dean Stockwell** Rear Admiral Albert "Al" Calavicci • **Deborah Pratt** Narrator/Voice of Ziggy

Created by *Donald P Bellisario*

Producer *Donald P Bellisario*

Quarantine ★ 15

1989 Can Colour 91mins

Schlock Canadian horror, made in the creative mould of David Cronenberg's *Shivers* and *Rabid*, in which a deadly disease leads to the overthrow of democracy and the installation of a dictatorship that confines everyone to death camps. Cheap and shoddy, with subplots glued on, the film fires off metaphors and allegories and makes no sense at all. Contains swearing and violence.

Beatrice Boepple Ivan Joad honest! • **Garwin Sanford** Spencer Crown • **Jerry Wasserman** Senator Ford • **Michelle Goodger** Berlin Ford • **Kaj-Erik Erikson** • **Tom McBeath** • **Charles Wilkinson**

Director/Screenplay *Charles Wilkinson*

SCI Q • SCI Q • SCI Q • SCI Q

28

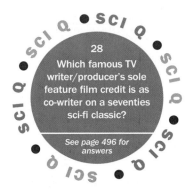

Which famous TV writer/producer's sole feature film credit is as co-writer on a seventies sci-fi classic?

See page 496 for answers

Quark ★★★★

TV 1978 US Colour 9x30mins

Devised as a parody of such popular films as *Star Wars*, this short-lived sitcom starred Richard Benjamin as Adam Quark, commander of a space garbage scow in the service of the United Galaxy Sanitation Patrol. The sharp scripts were a mixture of sex, intelligent jokes and slapstick comedy. Benjamin's crew include a robot (Bobby Porter), a half-man, half-vegetable named Ficus (Richard Kelton) and Betty I (Tricia Barnstable) and Betty II (Cyb Barnstable), one of which is a clone but which one? The few fans who did manage to catch one of the episodes claim it was perhaps the wittiest send-up of science fiction ever to appear on television.

Richard Benjamin Adam Quark • **Richard Kelton** Ficus • **Tim Thomerson** Gene/Jean • **Bobby Porter** Andy the Androis • **Alan Caillou** Head • **Conrad Janis** Otto Palindrome • **Patricia Barnstable** Betty I • **Cyb Barnstable** Betty II

Created by *Buck Henry*

Executive producer *David Gerber, Mace Neufeld*

Quatermass ★★★★ 15

TV 1979 UK Colour 4x60mins

Written originally for the BBC in 1972 Nigel Kneale's fourth and final Quatermass story was rejected due to budgetary concerns and picked up instead by Euston Films, the company responsible for *The Sweeney*. With more than a passing nod to its immediate predecessor *Quatermass and the Pit*, dealing as it does with ancient mythology, superstition and malignant alien influences over mankind, this makes for compellingly bleak viewing. With society on the brink of collapse Quatermass, washed up as a rocket scientist after seeing his research exploited for military purposes, finds himself drawn to the plight of gangs of young new-age travellers who congregate at ancient monuments to be transported into space to what they believe is a better life on other worlds. But Quatermass suspects a far more sinister purpose: that aliens are culling the earth's population. Made for a modest £1.5 million, full marks go to director Piers Haggard for giving his production the look and feel of something far more expensive. And John Mills is first class as Kneale's world-weary hero. A cut-down version (renamed *The Quatermass Conclusion*) was released later as a feature in cinemas abroad and on video in the UK.

John Mills Quatermass • **Simon MacCorkindale** Joe Kapp • **Ralph Arliss** Kickalong • **Rebecca Saire** Hettie • **Barbara Kellerman** Clare Kapp • **Neil Stacy** Toby Gough • **Margaret Tyzack** Annie Morgan • **Brewster Mason** Gurov • **Paul Rosebury** Caraway • **Brenda Fricker** Alison

Director *Piers Haggard*

Written by *Nigel Kneale*

Executive producer *Verity Lambert* • ***Producer*** *Ted Childs*

Quatermass and the Pit ★★★★★ PG

TV 1958-1959 UK BW 6x35mins

This is revered by many as the best of the Quatermass stories, with a startlingly original script by Nigel Kneale that mixes sci-fi, black magic and ancient history to devastating effect. The costliest TV drama then undertaken by the BBC, the story begins when workmen unearth a strange object thought by the MOD to be an unexploded bomb. Again Quatermass is called for, this time played by André Morell, who discovers inside the object dead insect-like creatures he is convinced are aliens that visited the earth millions of years earlier and still hold a supernatural power over mankind. Such was the impact of this story, the BBC estimated that 29 per cent of the adult population tuned in to the final nerve-shredding episode, that weeks later both Tony Hancock and The Goons satirised it on their radio shows. It also made the news when a woman who was watching while ironing suddenly dropped dead. Next day the *Daily Express* headline read – "Woman killed by Quatermass and the Pit".

André Morell Professor Quatermass • **Cec Linder** Dr Matthew Roney • **Anthony Bushell** Colonel Breen • **John Stratton** Captain Potter • **Christine Finn** Barbara Judd • **Michael Ripper** Sergeant • **Harold Goodwin** Corporal Gibson • **John Walker** Private West • **Brian Worth** James Fullalove
Written by *Nigel Kneale*
Producer *Rudolph Cartier*

Quatermass and the Pit

★★★★ PG

1967 UK Colour 178mins [video]

This remains the most popular of the movies taken from Nigel Kneale's acclaimed BBC TV serial. Although the Deluxe Color dissipates some of the atmosphere and mystery, the story of the Martian spaceship uncovered in a London tube station retains much of its intrigue and sense of disquiet thanks to Roy Ward Baker's careful direction and special effects that never attempt to exceed their technical or budgetary limitations. As well as providing a generous helping of shocks, Kneale's script gives his complex themes and theories plenty of space, and both action and argument are neatly judged by Andrew Keir, James Donald and Hammer favourite Barbara Shelley.

James Donald Dr Matthew Roney • **Andrew Keir** Professor Bernard Quatermass • **Barbara Shelley** Barbara Judd • **Julian Glover** Colonel Breen • **Duncan Lamont** Sladden • **Bryan Marshall** Captain Potter • **Peter Copley** Howell
Director *Roy Ward Baker*
Screenplay *Nigel Kneale, from his TV serial*

The Quatermass Experiment

★★★★★

TV 1953 UK BW 6x30mins

Amazingly this landmark production, whose influence on British television science fiction is immeasurable, did not find favour with critics of the day. The real judges were the public who tuned in in record breaking numbers each week to be scared half to death as ill-fated astronaut Victor Carroon mutated into something decidedly nasty. This was the era of early manned flights into space and writer Nigel Kneale brilliantly exploited a public fear that some nasty germ (or worse) might be picked up in space and brought back to earth in his grisly tale about British government rocket scientist Quatermass (Reginald Tate), sending a man to the stars who returns contaminated and slowing transforms into a walking vegetable patch with attitude. Made on a shoestring budget and with no effects department at the BBC the climactic giant "gunge" monster was actually both made and performed by Kneale himself on live television! A highly successful movie version quickly followed made by Hammer.

Reginald Tate Professor Bernard Quatermass • **Isabel Dean** Judith Carroon • **Duncan Lamont** Victor Carroon • **Oliver Johnston** News editor of "Daily Gazette" • **Paul Whitsun-Jones** James Fullalove • **Hugh Kelly** John Paterson • **Christopher Rhodes** Dr Ludwig Reichenheim • **Peter Bathurst** Charles Greene • **Moray Watson** Peter Marsh • **W Thorp Devereux** Blaker • **Van Boolen** Len Matthews • **Iris Ballard** Mrs Matthews • **Neil Wilson** Policeman • **Katie Johnson** Miss Wilde • **Enid Lindsay** Louisa Greene
Written by *Nigel Kneale*
Producer *Rudolph Cartier*
Settings *Richard R Greenough, Stewart Marshall*

The Quatermass Experiment

★★★

1955 UK BW 81mins

Hammer's film of Nigel Kneale's groundbreaking television serial was a huge success, encouraging the studio to concentrate on the production of horror films; in that regard, it can truly be said to have changed the course of British film history. The story, of an astronaut who returns to earth only to gradually mutate into a vegetable, was subsequently much emulated. Veteran director Val Guest detested the casting of American actor Brian Donlevy, though his portrayal of Quatermass was generally well-received at the time; while Jack Warner, PC George Dixon in *The Blue Lamp* and the long-running TV series *Dixon of Dock Green*, plays the inspector who helps the professor destroy the terror from outer space.

Brian Donlevy Professor Bernard Quatermass • **Jack Warner** Inspector Lomax • **Margia Dean** Judith Carroon • **Richard Wordsworth** Victor Carroon • **David King-Wood** Dr Gordon Briscoe • **Thora Hird** Rosie • **Gordon Jackson** TV producer • **Harold Lang** Christie • **Lionel Jeffries** Blake
Director *Val Guest*
Screenplay *Val Guest, Richard Landau, from the TV serial by Nigel Kneale*

The Quatermass Memoirs ★★★★

Radio 1996 UK 5x20mins

Broadcast in five parts on BBC Radio 3 in 1996, this isn't quite a new Quatermass adventure, but it does provide a wonderful, thoughtful overview of the character's entire career. It mixes new material, as an interviewer tracks down the Professor in Scotland just before the events of 1979's *Quatermass* and persuades him to give an interview about his exploits, with flashbacks to the three original BBC TV serials and brilliantly-selected archive news recordings that put the stories in a fifties context. Written by Nigel Kneale (who also contributes sound-bites about his work), produced by Paul Quinn, and starring Andrew Keir, reprising his role from the *Quatermass and the Pit* film (interacting with actors from the TV versions) and getting a lot of heart into the old character.

Andrew Keir Quatermass • **Emma Gregory** Mandy • **Zulema Dene** Maire
Written by *Nigel Kneale*
Producer *Paul Quinn*

SFacts

Nigel Kneale (whose received £250 in 1953 for *The Quatermass Experiment*, his first BBC commission), is scathing of current-day television sci-fi. Interviewed by *Radio Times* in 1996, he opined that *Star Trek* "is for small children and feeble-minded fans who can't appreciate style or quality. It really is rubbish."

Quatermass II ★★★★★

TV 1955 UK BW 6x30mins

If anything Nigel Kneale's wonderfully subversive sequel to his 1953 shocker is even more disturbing than its predecessor with its plot of brainwashed politicians and alien invaders kept alive in government-run secret "domes" reflecting contemporary concerns about scientific progress in a burgeoning nuclear-powered world. Set to reprise his role as Quatermass Reginald Tate died shortly before shooting began and was replaced at short notice by the less effective John Robinson. The acting overall has a typical fifties BBC feel to it and the effects are naturally primitive, but Rudolph Cartier's expert direction ensures this has lost none of its dramatic power or ability to shock, notably the image of a man emerging out of a vat of burning alien goo to die screaming at Quatermass's feet. Look out too for a young Roger Delgado playing a reporter. Delgado would later find TV immortality as Doctor Who's greatest foe – the Master.

John Robinson Professor Bernard Quatermass • **Monica Grey** Paula Quatermass • **Hugh Griffith** Dr Leo Pugh • **John Stone** Captain John Dillon • **Rupert Davies** Vincent Broadhead • **Austin Trevor** Fowler • **John Miller** Stenning • **Roger Delgado** Reporter
Written by *Nigel Kneale*
Producer *Rudolph Cartier*

SFacts

A number of highly effective scenes were shot out on location at the huge Shellhaven oil refinery on the Essex coast, permission given provided the crew didn't strike any matches

Quatermass II ★★★

1957 UK BW 84mins

The second in Hammer's *Quatermass* trilogy is a potent, low-budget roller coaster ride through government conspiracies and alien invasions, set against the chilling backdrop of postwar new town paranoia. Great writing by Nigel Kneale (based on his original BBC TV serial), superb direction by Val Guest and Gerald Gibbs's stark black-and-white photography make this British classic one of the best science-fiction allegories of the fifties.

Brian Donlevy Quatermass • **John Longden** Inspector Lomax • **Sidney James** Jimmy Hall • **Bryan Forbes** Marsh • **William Franklyn** Brand • **Vera Day** Sheila • **Charles Lloyd Pack** Dawson • **Michael Ripper** Ernie
Director *Val Guest*
Screenplay *Val Guest, Nigel Kneale, from the TV serial by Nigel Kneale*
Cinematographer *Gerald Gibbs*

Queen of Outer Space ★ U

1958 US Colour 79mins

A serious contender for the worst film ever made list, this idiotic would-be sexy sci-fi movie was actually based on an original story by Ben Hecht. The titular monarch is Laurie Mitchell (who?), but top-billed is Zsa Zsa Gabor, who succeeds in rescuing our astronaut heroes in trouble, headed by *Rawhide's* Eric Fleming, who should have known better than to land on Venus, anyway. The skimpy costumes are interesting – Anne Francis's complete *Forbidden Planet* wardrobe is recycled here. The colour gives the film an illusion of expense, but most British prints have faded to pink. Pink or restored, this one's for deadheads.

Zsa Zsa Gabor Talleah • **Eric Fleming** Patterson • **Laurie Mitchell** Queen Yllana • **Paul Birch** Professor Konrad • **Barbara Darrow** Kaeel • **Dave Willock** Cruze • **Lisa Davis** Motiya • **Patrick Waltz** Larry Turner
Director *Edward Bernds*
Screenplay *Charles Beaumont, from a story by Ben Hecht*

Quest for Love ★★★ PG

1971 UK Colour 87mins

Before *Dynasty*, Joan Collins made a bid for stardom in a series of British features, including this beguiling British science-fiction outing from *Carry On* producer Peter Rogers and *Doctor in the House* director Ralph Thomas. Tom Bell co-stars as a physicist who, after an explosion, finds himself in an alternative universe where his girlfriend Collins is dying. A supporting cast of the usual British stalwarts – including Denholm Elliott, Laurence Naismith and Ray McAnally – puts in a decent effort, while Bell is believably bemused.

Joan Collins Ottilie • **Tom Bell** Colin Trafford • **Denholm Elliott** Tom Lewis • **Laurence Naismith** Sir Henry Lanstein • **Lyn Ashley** Jennifer • **Juliet Harmer** Geraldine Lambert • **Ray McAnally** Jack Kahn • **Neil McCallum** Jimmy Rand • **Trudy Van Dorn** Sylvia • **John Hallam** Jonathan Keane
Director *Ralph Thomas*
Screenplay *Terence Feely, from the short story "Random Quest" by John Wyndham*

The Quiet Earth ★★★ 15

1985 NZ Colour 87mins

A scientist awakes one morning only to realise he may be the only person left alive on earth after an experiment goes wrong. It's an intriguing if not altogether original concept. *The World, the Flesh and the Devil* and Charlton Heston's cult *The Omega Man* were there first. Bruno Lawrence gives a beguiling central performance as someone who is suddenly able to live out his fantasies, to enjoy the empty city without guilt or interference. Shot against stunning Auckland backdrops by Geoff Murphy, the acclaimed New Zealand director of the Maori historical drama *Utu*, the early section develops a strong sense of mystery, but after Lawrence discovers two other survivors, one male, one female, the script follows an all too predictable path.

Bruno Lawrence Zac Hobson • **Alison Routledge** Joanne • **Peter Smith** Api • **Anzac Wallace** Api's mate • **Norman Fletcher** Perrin • **Tom Hyde** Scientist
Director *Geoff Murphy*
Screenplay *Bill Baer, Bruno Lawrence, Sam Pillsbury*

Quintet ★★ 15

1979 US Colour 113mins

One of Robert Altman's more forgettable films, made during a spell when he was out of favour with critics and audiences alike (see also *Popeye*). An uncomfortable looking Paul Newman heads a largely European cast (Bibi Andersson, Vittorio Gassman) in a slow-moving and pretentious piece of post-apocalyptic sci-fi, about a deadly survival game played out in a deep-frozen future city. Everyone looks cold and watching it will have a similar effect on the viewer. Music trivia fans might like to note the presence in the cast of Nina Van Pallandt, formerly one half of the chart-topping Nina & Frederik folk duo.

Paul Newman Essex • **Vittorio Gassman** St Christopher • **Fernando Rey** Grigor • **Bibi Andersson** Ambrosia • **Brigitte Fossey** Vivia • **Nina Van Pallandt** Deuca • **David Langton** Goldstar
Director *Robert Altman*
Screenplay *Robert Altman, Frank Barhydt, Patricia Resnick, from a story by Lionel Chetwynd, Robert Altman, Patricia Resnick*

R

IVANHOE
Oh, what a kn
Radio Times
11–17 January 1997 72p
They're back!
02
9 770961 886050
Red Dwarf, Friday BBC2

Rabid ★★★★ 18

1976 Can Colour 90mins

Another formative exercise in fear and loathing of the human body from director David Cronenberg, which takes up the themes of his first "mainstream" (in the loosest sense of the word) success *Shivers*. This time a plague spreads after accident victim Marilyn Chambers (a porn star in a rare, er, straight role) becomes the unwitting carrier of a rabid disease that turns people into bloodsuckers. This disturbing film lacks the stomach-churning claustrophobia of *Shivers*, but is an altogether slicker affair, and the spiralling, random violence still shocks.

Marilyn Chambers Rose • **Frank Moore** Hart Read • **Joe Silver** Murray Cypher • **Howard Ryshpan** Dr Dan Keloid • **Patricia Gage** Dr Roxanne Keloid • **Susan Roman** Mindy Kent • **J Roger Periard** Lloyd Walsh • **Lynne Deragon** Nurse Louise • **Terry Schonblum** Judy Glasberg • **Victor Désy** Claude Lapointe • **Julie Anna** Rita • **Gary McKeehan** Smooth Eddy • **Jerome Tiberghien** Dr Carl • **John Gilbert** Dr Royce Gentry • **Una Kay** Jackie
Director/Screenplay *David Cronenberg*

Radar Men from the Moon ★★★

1951 US BW 12x13mins

The suit worn by Tristram Coffin in *King of the Rocket Men* (1949) was dusted down for this Republic chapterplay, which also contains countless snippets from the B-hiver's archive. George Wallace essays the flying hero, who jets into outer space to discover the source of the mysterious atomic element "lunarium" and, thus, prevent the tyrannical Roy Barcroft from launching an invasion. The presence of gravity on the Moon betrays the fact the science is wholly fictional. But the volcanic eruptions, laser shootouts and spaceship chases make for rattling entertainment. A feature version, *Retik, the Moon Menace*, was released in 1966.

George Wallace Jeff King/Commando Cody • **Aline Towne** Joan Gilbert • **Roy Barcroft** Retik • **William Bakewell** Ted Richards
Director *Fred C Brannon*
Screenplay *Ronald Davidson*

Radioactive Dreams ★★ 18

1986 US/Mex Colour 94mins

The warning sign of this movie – Albert Pyun was the writer and director – won't stop a number of viewers, because of the nutty but very promising premise. Two little boys are taken into a bomb shelter just as World War III breaks out and grow up reading the works of Raymond Chandler. As adults (Michael Dudikoff and John Stockwell), they rename themselves after Phillip Marlowe, take on the personality of the hero of Chandler's novels and set out on a journey across the wastelands. However, Pyun quickly forgets the private eye angle, and settles for a routine story concerning the heroes trying to stop some goofy *Mad Max*-type villains from getting their hands on a remaining nuclear bomb. Somewhat lively and much better than Pyun's subsequent works, but unforgivable for pretty much ignoring its potential.

John Stockwell Phillip • **Michael Dudikoff** Marlowe • **Lisa Blount** Miles • **George Kennedy** Spade Chandler • **Don Murray** Dash Hammer • **Michele Little** Rusty Mars • **Norbert Weisser** Sternwood
Director/Screenplay *Albert Pyun*

The Rat Saviour ★★★

1977 Yug Colour 87mins

Best known for his documentary shorts and the Stalinist parable, *Handcuffs* (1968), Kristo Papic based this body snatcher allegory on a novel by the Soviet writer, Alexander Greene, who perished in one of the dictator's many purges. Considerably more graphic than the majority of Iron Curtain shockers, the action follows Ivica Vidovic's bid to exterminate a race of mutant rats, who have the ability to assume the shape of their victims. However, he, ultimately, has to subject his own lover, Mirjana Majurec, to Fabijan Sovagovic's deadly serum. Somewhat muddled in its political thinking, this still makes for uneasy viewing. A Serbo-Croatian language film.

Ivica Vidovic • **Mirjana Majurec** • **Relja Basic** • **Fabijan Sovagovic** • **Ilija Ivezic**
Director *Krsto Papic*
Screenplay *Ivo Brexan, Krsto Papic, from a story by Alexander Greene*

Ratataplan ★★★

1979 It Colour 100mins

Former mime artist and animator-turned-comedy actor Maurizio Nichetti made his directing debut with this nonsense comedy filled with inventive sketches, macabre slapstick and pop culture references of the Disco Generation day. He plays a timid Milanese engineer who builds himself a robot double to achieve longed-for social success. But it blows up during a crucial romantic moment with Edy Angelillo, the girl downstairs he adores from afar. Played at a frantic pitch, and hitting as many targets as it misses, this surreal fable lurches between self-indulgence and heightened weirdness for a winning oddball pay-off where the lovers inhabit a fantasy world of their own making. Raffaella Carra, the Italian Cilla Black, sings the title hit song. An Italian language film.

Maurizio Nichetti Colombo • **Angela Finocchiaro** Unpretty girl • **Edy Angelillo** Ballerina girl • **Lidia Biondi** Pregnant woman • **Roland Topor** Boss • **Giorgio White** Boss's assistant
Director/Screenplay *Maurizio Nichetti*

Rats Night of Terror ★★★

1983 It Colour 92mins

Easily the best work from Italian hack director Bruno (*Zombie Creeping Flesh*) Mattei, this Biblically-toned apocalyptic horror fantasy is set in 225 AB (After the Bomb) where the world either lives underground or roams the *Mad Max*-style surface looking for sustenance. Biker Richard Raymond's Hells Angel pack find a food cache in the desert but must battle hordes of flesh-eating mutant rats for its ownership. Gory special effects (the rats devour victims from within) and above-average stunts, twists and surprise turns make all the inspired stupidity a worthwhile endeavour for Italo-splatterati lovers. Italian dialogue dubbed into English.

Richard Raymond Kurt • **Richard Cross** Videogame • **Janna Ryan** Chocolate • **Alex McBride [Massimo Vanni]** Taurus • **Ann Gisel Glass** Myrna
Director *Vincent Dawn [Bruno Mattei]*
Screenplay *Claudio Fragasso, Hervé Piccini*
Cinematographer *Franco Delli Colli*

Ravager ★★★ 15

1997 US Colour 88mins

Outbreak meets *Alien* in a competently made and acted science-fiction thriller. In the near future, a space cruiser commanded by straight-to-video action hero Bruce Payne crash-lands in an uncharted area – actually a dumping ground for biological weapons. While exploring the seemingly uninhabited site, one of the crew is infected by something nasty, known as "ravager" – a highly contagious disease which drives people insane after endowing them with super-human strength. Can Payne and crew escape from the insidious terror? Nothing new on the story front but a reasonable time-waster all the same. Contains violence and some swearing.

Bruce Payne Cooper • **Yancy Butler** Avedon • **Salvator Xuereb** Lazarus • **Juliet Landau** Sarra • **Robin Sachs** Shepard
Director *James D Deck*
Screenplay *Donald J Loperfido, James D Deck*

Ravagers ★★ 15

1979 US Colour 87mins

The phrase "a good cast wasted" is perhaps the most overused in film criticism, but it certainly applies to this woeful post-apocalyptic turkey about warring gangs that somehow managed to lure names like Richard Harris, Art Carney and Ernest Borgnine. Shot in Alabama, some of the images of desolated towns and poisoned countryside are visually arresting, but the disagreeably violent tone is no surprise coming as it does from Richard Compton, director of the red neck *Macon County* vigilante films. This film also coincided with a drastic slide in Richard Harris's box office fortunes which lay dormant for just over a decade until his professional rehabilitation in *The Field*.

Richard Harris Falk • **Ann Turkel** Faina • **Art Carney** Sergeant • **Ernest Borgnine** Rann • **Anthony James** Leader • **Woody Strode** Brown

Director *Richard Compton*

Screenplay *Donald S Sanford, from the novel "Path to Savagery" by Robert Edmond Alter*

The Ray Bradbury Theatre ★★

TV 1985-1992 Can Colour 65x30mins

Uniquely, this surprisingly long-running Canadian anthology show drew only on the work of one author, Ray Bradbury (even *Tales of the Unexpected* abandoned Roald Dahl after two seasons) – which meant that some episodes were de facto remakes of *The Twilight Zone*, *Alfred Hitchcock Presents* or chunks of *The Martian Chronicles* and *The Illustrated Man*. The first two seasons, of three episodes apiece, was quite impressive, with starry turns from Leslie Nielsen, William Shatner, Nick Mancuso, Jeff Goldblum, Drew Barrymore and Peter O'Toole. The next four seasons were larger clumps, with thinner resources and were further handicapped by the fact that Bradbury, a master of poetic prose, remains an especially clod-hopping scriptwriter, often wringing his own terrific material into pompous, dull and plodding little TV half-hours.

Ray Bradbury Host

Written by *Ray Bradbury*

Executive producer *Ray Bradbury, Larry Wilcox*

Re-Animator ★★★★ 18

1985 US Colour 83mins DVD

A groundbreaking horror/black comedy that reintroduced HP Lovecraft to a new generation, and set a new level as to how far on-screen outrageousness could go. It also introduced cult star Jeffrey Combs, excellent as the funny and scary borderline-mad Herbert West, a young medical student working on a formula that brings the dead back to life. However, the dead don't come back in either tip-top or co-operative shape, leading to a number of wildly escalating problems. First-time director Stuart Gordon never lets up from the start, constantly pushing the limits with the gory antics, but also showing an absurd side to such sequences. Contains violence and sex scenes.

Jeffrey Combs Herbert West • **Bruce Abbott** Dan Cain • **Barbara Crampton** Megan Halsey • **Robert Sampson** Dean Halsey • **David Gale** Dr Carl Hill • **Gerry Black** Mace • **Carolyn Purdy-Gordon** Dr Harrod • **Peter Kent** Melvin, the Re-animated

Director *Stuart Gordon*

Screenplay *Dennis Paoli, William J Norris, Stuart Gordon, from the story "Herbert West – the Re-Animator" by HP Lovecraft*

Red Dwarf ★★★★★ PG 12 15

TV 1988-1999 UK Colour 52x30mins

Not only one of the funniest sci-fi shows ever made, this also ranks among the very best of British sit-coms. Created by Doug Naylor and written by Naylor together with Rob Grant, who in the mid-eighties worked on *Spitting Image*, *Red Dwarf* first appeared in 1988 and is still going strong with a series of spin-off books, fan conventions and a movie version set for release in 2002. Famous for its wacky and ingenious storylines, the core of its appeal lies in the interaction between the marvelously observed main characters – Lister (Craig Charles), the only human survivor of a radiation leak aboard the mining ship *Red Dwarf*, Rimmer (Chris Barrie), a hologram of his former ship-mate, a mutated cat/human (Danny John-Jules) and the android Kryten (Robert Llewellyn).

Chris Barrie Arnold Rimmer • **Craig Charles** Dave Lister • **Danny John-Jules** Cat • **Robert Llewellyn** Kryten • **Hattie Hayridge** Holly • **Norman Lovett** Holly (series 1 and 2)

Written by *Rob Grant, Doug Naylor*

SFacts

In 1992 a US network tried to mould the show for American sensibilities and totally "smegged" it up. Of the original cast only Llewellyn was kept with Holly, the ship's computer played by a pre-*Frasier* Jane Leeves, but the project never got past the pilot stage.

Red Planet ★★ 12

2000 US/Aus Colour 102mins DVD

The second of 2000's Mars-based science-fiction adventures makes Brian De Palma's under-rated *Mission to Mars* look like *2001: a Space Odyssey*. It's 2050, and a team including Val Kilmer, Tom Sizemore, Carrie-Anne Moss and a hammier-than-ever Terence Stamp is sent to investigate when long-range efforts to make Mars habitable run into problems. Vital equipment is damaged in a crash-landing and the survivors are forced to depend on one another to fend off man-eating alien bugs and their own malfunctioning exploration robot while surviving the inhospitable terrain. Director Antony Hoffman's feel-bad fantasy can't be faulted technically: it looks great, and features some nifty space gadgets and nice special effects. But the plot lacks dramatic drive and the supposedly realistic depiction of interplanetary travel is markedly unengaging. The spectres of other, far better, sci-fi epics haunt the whole misbegotten patchwork: *Alien*, *Starship Troopers*, *Short Circuit* – you name it, it's in here somewhere. Aside from the ever-cool Sizemore, none of the actors registers as anything more than easily expendable ciphers, and the whole damp squib ensures Mars won't be a Hollywood travel destination for many moons to come. Contains some violence, swearing and brief nudity.

Val Kilmer Gallagher • **Tom Sizemore** Burchenal • **Carrie-Anne Moss** Kate Bowman • **Benjamin Bratt** Santen • **Simon Baker** Pettengil • **Terence Stamp** Chantilas

Director *Antony Hoffman*

Screenplay *Chuck Pfarrer, Jonathan Lemkin, from a story by Chuck Pfarrer*

Cinematographer *Peter Suschitzky*

Red Planet Mars ★★ U

1952 US BW 87mins

One of the oddest science-fiction movies ever made and worth sitting through every unwatchable preachy moment and ludicrous plot twist just to feel your jaw drop at various junctures. Could utopian Mars really be ruled by God? That's what TV contact via "hydrogen valve" reveals. But it's only a Nazi plot, controlled by Soviet agents, to destroy the world's economy. What can Earth do? Easy. Draft religious revolutionaries into Russia to overthrow the Communist government and replace them with a priestly monarchy. Possibly Billy Graham's favourite movie? Based on a play, hence the talky crusading, this simple-minded slice of po-faced seriousness is sci-fi's most explicit anti-Communist tract in disguise.

Peter Graves (1) Chris Cronyn • **Andrea King** Linda Cronyn • **Orley Lindgren** Steward Cronyn • **Bayard Vellier** Roger Cronyn • **Walter Sande** Admiral Carey • **Marvin Miller** Arjenian • **Herbert Berghof** Franz Calder • **Willis Bouchey** President
Director *Harry Horner*
Screenplay *Anthony Veiller, John L Balderson, from the play "Red Planet" by John L Balderson, John Hoare*

Redline ★★★ 18

1997 Can/Neth Colour 94mins

Cheekily renamed *Armageddon* for its rental release – it hit the shelves a good six months before the Bruce Willis blockbuster arrived on these shores – this is actually a rather nifty thriller set in the near future. Rutger Hauer stars as an American smuggler who is brought back from the dead after being betrayed by his partner in crime Mark Dacascos. The charismatic Hauer can do this sort of thing in his sleep, though martial-arts star Dacascos steals the show as a very nasty villain. Director Tibor Takacs makes the most of the striking eastern European locations and stages the action sequences with some style.

Rutger Hauer John Anderson Wade • **Mark Dacascos** Merrick • **Yvonne Scio** Marina K/Katya • **Patrick Dreikauss** Mishka • **Randall William Cook** Vanya the Special Prosecutor • **Michael Mehlmann** Serge • **Ildiko Szucs** Antonia • **Istvan Kanizsay** Assistant Prosecutor
Director *Tibor Takacs*
Screenplay *Tibor Takacs, Brian Irving*

Redneck Zombies ★★

1988 US Colour 83mins

Troma didn't actually make this *Night of the Living Dead* spoof (though the cult company did distribute it), but it could easily be mistaken for one of Troma's in-house productions. Shot on videotape, it concerns a drum of radioactive waste lost during a military transport through redneck country. Some locals find the drum and use it to repair their broken still, contaminating their moonshine. As a result, the area's residents become flesh-eating zombies. There are plentiful (and extremely graphic) gore sequences, but the production values hit a new low and the script grabs every opportunity to use stereotypes and juvenile humour. Fans of movies such as this will find it offers some laughs thanks to the enthusiasm of the cast and crew, but others should avoid it. Contains violence.

Lisa DeHaven Lisa Dubois • **WE Benson** Jed "Pa" Clemson • **William W Decker** • **James Housely** Wilbur
Director/Screenplay *Pericles Lewnes*

The Rejuvenator ★★★ 18

1988 US Colour 84mins

An offbeat and serious perversity pervades this oddly affecting gore fantasy version of *Sunset Boulevard*. Ageing actress Jessica Dublin is financing demented doctor John Mackay's experiments in eternal youth. When he finally creates a serum from human brains to make her young again, she pretends to be her actress niece in order to revive her film career. But sex makes her mutate into a giant-headed monster with huge claws, which she uses to decapitate victims before eating their brains. Well made by co-writer/director Brian Thomas Jones, this is oppressively creepy until it degenerates into over-done gooey silliness towards the end.

Vivian Lanko Elizabeth Warren/Monster • **John MacKay** Dr Gregory Ashton • **James Hogue** Wilhelm • **Katell Pleven** Dr Stella Stone • **Marcus Powell** Dr Germaine • **Jessica Dublin** Ruth Warren • **Roy MacArthur** Hunter • **Louis F Homyak** Tony
Director *Brian Thomas Jones*
Screenplay *Simon Nuchtern, Brian Thomas Jones, from a story by Simon Nuchtern*

The Reluctant Astronaut ★★ U

1967 US Colour 101mins

Don Knotts gets shot into space in this one – a happy thought for the comedian's many detractors. Knotts's gormless comic style always polarised audiences, with some lapping it up and others unable to bear him. Here he plays Roy Fleming, a timid chap afraid of heights who is bullied by his father into going for a job at the Nasa space centre. He ends up working as a trainee janitor. But as the Russians prepare to launch a man into space, US scientists bring forward their plans and urgently need a volunteer. Enter Roy. Simplistic comedy for serious Knotts fans only.

Don Knotts Roy Fleming • **Arthur O'Connell** Buck Fleming • **Jeanette Nolan** Mrs Fleming • **Leslie Nielsen** Major Fred Gifford • **Joan Freeman** Ellie Jackson • **Jesse White** Donelli
Director *Edward J Montagne*
Screenplay *Jim Fritzell, Everett Greenbaum, from a story by Don Knotts*

Remote Control ★★ 15

1988 US Colour and BW 84mins

Kevin Dillon is good as a video-store clerk who stumbles into an alien conspiracy involving a video release of a cheesy fifties movie called *Remote Control*. Viewers of the tape are hypnotised into committing violent psychotic acts, leading Dillon and girlfriend Deborah Goodrich not just to gather and destroy the tapes, but also to try and take on the aliens. The black-and-white movie-within-a-movie is amusing, but although this is ostensibly a science-fiction comedy, the entire enterprise is frequently stuck awkwardly between being funny and being serious.

Kevin Dillon Cosmo • **Deborah Goodrich** Belinda • **Jennifer Tilly** Allegra • **Christopher Wynne** Georgie • **Frank Beddor** Victor • **Kaaren Lee** Patricia • **Bert Remsen** Bill Denver
Director/Screenplay *Jeff Lieberman*

Replikator ★★ 18

1994 Can Colour 96mins

A cyberpunk technological thriller about the race to create a machine that can reproduce human tissue, this is, unfortunately, low on thrills, focusing mainly on dark sets punctuated with neon lights and lots of talking heads. The future presented here has all the flashy toys you might expect, but shouldn't the television reception be better? Eventually a human is replicated and the results are unpleasant, of course. It could have been worse – they could have replicated Ned Beatty, who puts in a token appearance.

Michael St Gerard Ludo Ludovic • **Brigitte Bako** Kathy Moskow • **Ned Beatty** Inspector Valiant • **Cicciolina** Stripper
Director *G Philip Jackson*
Screenplay *Michelle Bellerose, Tony Johnston, John Dawson*

Repo Man ★★★★ 18

1984 US Colour 88mins

Despite poor reviews on its initial release, Alex Cox's darkly satirical swipe at American urban low life mutated into one of the eighties' greatest cult movies. Emilio Estevez, who's never been in a better movie since, plays a novice car repossession man in Los Angeles, learning the tricks of the trade from veteran Harry Dean Stanton, while coming into contact with aliens and drug pushers. The film is a winning blend of sci-fi, social commentary and *film noir*, with lots of quotable dialogue. Estevez's new-wave punk and his friends are portrayed as characters existing on the fringes of society (note the names taken from beers – Bud, Miller and Lite) and it's a world that's beautifully captured by Wim Wenders's regular cinematographer Robby Müller. This film marked out Cox as a director to watch in the future, but alas nothing he's made since has ever been equally worth watching. This deserves multiple viewings.

Emilio Estevez Otto • **Harry Dean Stanton** Bud • **Tracey Walter** Miller • **Olivia Barash** Leila • **Sy Richardson** Lite • **Susan Barnes** Agent Rogersz • **Fox Harris** J Frank Parnell • **Tom Finnegan** Oly • **Del Zamora** Lagarto • **Eddie Velez** Napo • **Zander Schloss** Kevin • **Jennifer Balgobin** Debbi • **Dick Rude** Duke • **The Circle Jerks** Nightclub band
Director/Screenplay *Alex Cox*
Cinematographer *Robby Müller*

Reptilicus ★

1961 Den/US Colour 76mins

Producer Sidney (*The Angry Red Planet*) Pink's sluggish clone of Japanese monster movies revolves around the regenerative tail of a prehistoric beast found by a Copenhagen-based oil expedition. When the fossil thaws out it grows into the eponymous monster and escapes from its museum confines to knock over the usual array of papier-mâché buildings and Danish landmarks. The cast and crew from Pink's *Jouney to the Seventh Planet* go through the same arch motions in this horrendously bad *Godzilla* copy, co-written by Ib (*Planet of the Vampires*) Melchior. A Danish/English language film.

Carl Ottosen Mark Grayson • **Ann Smyrner** Lise Martens • **Mimi Heinrich** Karen Martens • **Asbjorn Andersen** Prof Martens • **Marla Behrens** Connie Miller
Director *Sidney Pink, Poul Bang*
Screenplay *Ib Melchior, Sidney Pink, Poul Bang, Bob Ramsing, from a story by Sidney Pink*
Producer *Sidney Pink*

Resistance ★★

1992 Aus Colour 112mins

In the not-to-distant future Down Under, life is not good for the poor. Lack of readies condemns one to a life of near slavery, toiling for nasty giant corporations. Of course, the workers fight back, and lots of action ensues. This is the only film to date directed by actor Hugh Keays-Byrne (occasional character Grunchlk in *Farscape*).

Lorna Lesley Jean Skilling • **Jennifer Claire** Ruby • **Bobby Noble** Jackal • **Allan Penney** Cy • **Mirabelle Peart** Loretta • **Helen Jones** Natalie • **Arianthe Galani** Mother • **Maya Sheridan** Sister • **Stephen Leeder** Colonel Webber
Director *Paul Elliott, Hugh Keays-Byrne*
Screenplay *Paul Elliott, Christina Ferguson, Hugh Keays-Byrne, Stephen Leeder, Peter Mitchell, Pauline Rosenberg, Robyn Wells*

FUTUREVISIONS

METROPOLIS (1926) Set in the year 2000, the world of towering skyscrapers, skies crowded with planes and cars driving on elevated freeways has in many ways come to pass, but the film's malevolent female robot is still a flight of sci-fi fancy, however.

JUST IMAGINE (1930) Test-tube babies, videophones and automatic doors are all on display in this fanciful vision of 1930, as is the classic sci-fi device of pills instead of meals – a prophecy of the vitamin supplement revolution, perhaps?

DESTINATION MOON (1950) Many details of spaceflight hit the mark – weightlessness is countered with magnetised boots, for example – as does the plot line involving a millionaire backer who also comes along for the ride. Shades of Dennis Tito, anyone?

1984 (1956) Written in 1948 and made into a movie in 1956, Orwell's nightmare vision of 24-hour surveillance has certainly proved a reality – only now Big Brother is synonymous with big ratings rather than big government. The art of "Newspeak" has also acquired modern-day adherents in the form of spin-doctors.

2001: A SPACE ODYSSEY (1968) Still ahead of the game when it comes to moonbases and space hotels, but some technological details – phone cards, TVs on the back of airplane seat headrests – are spot on, as is the portrayal of computers as central to future of technology. And at the turn of the millenium, the world was gripped with the fear that our PCs would go as loopy as HAL does!

THE YEAR OF THE SEX OLYMPICS (1968) Nigel Kneale's eerily prescient play for BBC predicted a near future world where "reality TV" would be the television norm, and among the gameshows on the box is one in which families try to survive on an island beyond the comforts of automated society. Big Brother is watching *Castaway* and *Surviving the Iron Age* perhaps?

The Resurrection of Zachary Wheeler ★★

1971 US Colour 100mins

Blending elements from John Frankenheimer's *Seconds* and Michael Crichton's *Coma*, this is an efficiently mounted thriller, shot on videotape. A playboy presidential hopeful (Bradford Dillman) is brought back from the dead thanks to organ transplants from synthetic zombies (called "somas"), which have been bred for the purpose by mad doctor James Daly. Reporter Leslie Nielsen uncovers the grisly manufacturing plant in Almogordo, New Mexico and is about to suppress the story – thinking it's in America's best interests – when he learns Daly's next patient is a prominent Asian leader whose change in politics is to be the price of his rebirth. This suffers from too much Cold War philosophy and stodgy chase footage of Nielsen, which ultimately get in the way of the intriguing plot.

Leslie Nielsen Harry Walsh • **Bradford Dillman** Senator Zachary Wheeler • **James Daly** Dr Redding • **Angie Dickinson** Dr Layle Johnson • **Robert J Wilke** Hugh Fielding • **Jack Carter** Dwight Childs • **Don Haggerty** Jake
Director *Robert Wynn*
Screenplay *Jay Simms, Tom Rolf*

The Retaliator ★★ 18

1987 US Colour 87mins [video]

Warrior babe Sandahl Bergman follows in the footsteps of her *Conan the Barbarian* co-star Arnold Schwarzenegger for this silly and derivative slice of futuristic action. She plays a ruthless Middle Eastern terrorist who is transformed by CIA scientists into a ruthless robotic assassin, only for her to set her sights on her nemesis, agent Robert Ginty, when her wiring goes wonky. The direction is uninspired and Bergman carries out her terminating duties with a singular lack of charisma, while one-time *Exterminator* Ginty sleepwalks through his role.

Robert Ginty Eric Mathews • **Sandahl Bergman** Samira • **Louise Caire Clark** Sharon • **Alex Courtney** Blake • **James Booth** Broxk • **Paul W Walker [Paul Walker]** Jason
Director *Allan Holzman*
Screenplay *Robert Short*

Retroactive ★★ 18

1997 US Colour 87mins

Although this major studio production was sent direct to video, it does have satisfying moments for more patient viewers who are in the mood for quirkiness. James Belushi is miscast as a lowlife involved in dirty deals in the desert, but Shannon Whirry compensates with an excellent, subtle performance as Belushi's abused wife. When they are unknowingly caught in a time loop caused by a nearby experiment, passer-by Kylie Travis repeatedly tries to "do the right thing" to prevent disasters, though she never succeeds. It's fun and energetic, but the plot is full of holes. Contains violence and some swearing.

James Belushi Frank Lloyd • **Kylie Travis** Karen • **Shannon Whirry** Rayanne • **Frank Whaley** Brian • **M Emmet Walsh** Sam
Director *Louis Morneau*
Screenplay *Michael Hamilton-Wright, Robert Strauss*

Return from Witch Mountain ★★★★ U

1978 US Colour 89mins

Of course, it had to be Bette Davis who could disprove the old warning about scene-sharing with children – few others would have the nerve or the talent. She, however, is in her element, giving a scene-stealing performance as henchwoman to Christopher Lee's mad scientist. Lee is seeking world domination by gaining control of two extraterrestrial kids, who possess all kinds of strange powers (telekinesis, anti-gravity, cute expressions). A sequel to *Escape to Witch Mountain*, it's a Disney fantasy in which the usual milk-shake blandness has been spiked with an interesting touch of colour, courtesy of the film's legendary star.

Bette Davis Letha Wedge • **Christopher Lee** Dr Victor Gannon • **Kim Richards** Tia Malone • **Ike Eisenmann** Tony Malone • **Jack Soo** Mr Yokomoto • **Anthony James** Sickle • **Dick Bakalyan [Richard Bakalyan]** Eddie • **Ward Costello** Mr Clearcole • **Christian Juttner** Dazzler • **Poindexter** Crusher • **Brad Savage** Muscles • **Jeffrey Jacquet** Rocky • **Stu Gilliam** Dolan
Director *John Hough*
Screenplay *Malcolm Marmorstein, from characters created by Alexander Key*

The Return of Captain Invincible ★★ PG

1983 Aus Colour 87mins

Intermittently enjoyable comic book spoof starring Alan Arkin as a down-and-out, alcoholic superhero dragged from his dazed retirement to save the world one last time. Christopher Lee rises to the occasion as the evil megalomaniac Mr Midnight in a cheaply-made Australian comedy fantasy, peppered with songs by *Rocky Horror Show* creator Richard O'Brien. Director Philippe Mora tries hard to combine all genres, but the film doesn't quite come off.

Alan Arkin Captain Invincible • **Christopher Lee** Mr Midnight • **Michael Pate** US President • **Graham Kennedy** Australian PM • **Kate Fitzpatrick** Patty Patria
Director *Philippe Mora*
Screenplay *Steven de Souza, Andrew Gaty*
Music/lyrics *Richard O'Brien*

The Return of Dr X ★★

1939 US BW 62mins

With Humphrey Bogart in a clichéd role as a murderous monster, brought back to life when he's given an injection of a rare type of blood. This is a conventional account of a vampire terrorising a city. An attempt by Warner Bros to appeal to horror fans, it's notable for the inclusion of many members of the studio's acting B-league, including Dennis Morgan and Rosemary Lane. Only two years later, Bogart became a major star – and wisely steered clear of horror films for the rest of his career.

Humphrey Bogart Marshall Quesne/Dr Maurice J Xavier • **Rosemary Lane** Joan Vance • **Wayne Morris** Walter Barnett • **Dennis Morgan** Michael Rhodes • **John Litel** Dr Francis Flegg • **Lya Lys** Angela Merrova • **Huntz Hall** Pinky
Director *Vincent Sherman*
Screenplay *Lee Katz, from the story "The Doctor's Secret" by William J Makin*

The Return of Swamp Thing ★★ 15

1989 US Colour 83mins

"Where do you come from?" asks a hillbilly saved from a mutant leech attack by the original (D C Comics) Swampy. "The bog", replies our leaf-in-cheek Jolly Green Giant. No comment! Louis Jourdan also returns as evil genius Dr Arcane, back in melodramatic Dr Moreau mode, and still gene-splitting to halt the ageing process. Soap queen Heather Locklear is his stepdaughter searching for the truth behind her mother's death, but how and why she falls for Swampy in this bayou Garden of Eden fable has to be seen to be believed. It's a moss-eaten slice of splat-stick packed with laboured in-jokes – Jourdan's pet parrot is called "Gigi" – and daffy heroics.

Louis Jourdan Dr Anton Arcane • **Heather Locklear** Abby Arcane • **Sarah Douglas** Dr Lana Zurrell • **Dick Durock** Swamp Thing • **Ace Mask** Dr Rochelle • **Joey Sagal** Gunn
Director *Jim Wynorski*
Screenplay *Derek Spencer, Grant Morris, from the DC Comics character*

Return of the Ape Man ★

1944 US BW 60mins

A typical Monogram quickie produced by infamous junk purveyor Sam Katzman with no connection to the previous year's Bela Lugosi headliner *The Ape Man*. Lugosi defrosts and revives a prehistoric man and gives it the brain of his assistant John Carradine. Formulaic rampage results in this sloppy, slow moving, hammed up old-fashioned relic. Look for the underwear under the ape man's animal skins! The ape man was played either by boxer Frank Moran or George Zucco at different times, although some sources say the third-billed Zucco became ill before filming and never actually appeared.

Bela Lugosi Prof Dexter • **John Carradine** Prof John Gilmore • **George Zucco** Ape man • **Frank Moran** Ape man • **Judith Gibson** Anne • **Michael Ames [Tod Andrews]** Steve Rogers • **Mary Currier** Mrs Hilda Gilmore • **Ed Chandler [Eddy Chandler]** Sergeant
Director *Philip Rosen [Phil Rosen]*
Screenplay *Robert Charles, from a story by Robert Charles*
Cinematographer *Marcel LePicard* •
Special effects *Ray Mercer*

Return of the Fly ★★ 15

1959 US BW 76mins

The sequel to the original 1958 horror hit is a more standard black-and-white B-movie retelling of the same story, with Brett Halsey playing Al Hedison's son, repeating his father's teleportation tinkering with similarly disastrous results. Thankfully Vincent Price is back, again playing the concerned uncle, and goes a long way towards keeping things buzzing along. But, aside from a few horrific moments in a mortuary and the sick guinea pig experiment, director Edward Bernds (best known for his *Three Stooges* work) sadly stresses plot gimmicks at the expense of an involving story. Price himself always joked that he wanted this inevitable follow-up to be called "The Zipper".

Vincent Price François Delambre • **Brett Halsey** Phillipe Delambre • **David Frankham** Alan Hinds • **John Sutton** Inspector Charas • **Dan Seymour** Max Berthold • **Danielle de Metz** Cecile

Bonnard • **Janine Graudel** Madame Bonnard
Director *Edward Bernds*
Screenplay *Edward Bernds, from a story by George Langelaan*

Return of the Killer Tomatoes

★ 15

1988 US Colour 94mins

As *Attack of the Killer Tomatoes* was a big video rental (solely because of its catchy title), a belated sequel was commissioned and it is even worse than the original. Professor Gangrene (John Astin) turns a tomato into a sexy babe by playing music at it and plans to take over the world wlth a bevy of similarly exposed red fruits. Stupid send-ups of popular TV commercials and movies (two Spielbergs get satirised – *1941* and *ET*) mix uneasily with broad science-fiction farce in director John DeBello's charmless wonder, which is only notable for an early appearance by future heart-throb George Clooney.

Anthony Starke Chad • **Karen Mistal** Tara • **George Clooney** Matt • **Steve Lundquist** Igor • **John Astin** Professor Gangrene
Director *John DeBello*
Screenplay *Constantine Dillon, John DeBello, John Stephen Peace [Steve Peace]*

Return of the Living Dead

★★★ 18

1985 US Colour 86mins

This enjoyable horror comedy marked the directorial debut of long-time sci-fi scribe Dan O'Bannon, of *Dark Star* and *Alien* fame. This semi-sequel to George A Romero's 1968 cult classic *Night of the Living Dead* is like an DC comic come alive, in that it'll make you laugh and squirm – often at the same time. "They're back. They're hungry. And they're not vegetarian," blared the poster. O'Bannon cleverly makes the zombies – rather than the actors – the real stars of this movie and, unlike the Romero variety, these can speak, though they're mostly limited to spouting, "Brains, more brains!" The brain-eaters are the result of two bumbling workers who spill a missing army shipment of top-secret gas, which then contaminates the local cemetery where a gang of punks are holding a party. Later, after munching on some policemen, a zombie calls the local precinct and orders them to, "Send more cops!". A must for horror fans, this was followed by two sequels of varying quality.

Clu Gulager Burt • **James Karen** Frank • **Don Calfa** Ernie • **Thom Matthews** Freddy • **Beverly Randolph** Tina • **John Philbin** Chuck • **Jewel Shepard** Casey • **Miguel A Nunez Jr** Spider
Director *Dan O'Bannon*
Screenplay *Dan O'Bannon, from a story by Judy Ricci, John Russo, Russell Streiner*

Return to the Lost Planet ★★

TV 1955 UK BW 6x30mins

A sequel to 1954's *The Lost Planet*, also adapted for television by Angus MacVicar from his Scots-in-Space BBC wireless serial. Lachlan McKinnon (John Stuart) is stranded on Hesikos, the lost planet, but makes contact with the friendly, telepathic Hesikosians. Wolfe Morris and Van Boolen are back as the dastardly foreign baddies. Oddly, the BBC never did a TV remake of their most successful radio space opera franchise, *Journey into Space*.

Peter Kerr Jeremy Grant • **John Stuart** Dr Lachlan McKinnon • **Joan Allan** Madge Smith • **Wolfe Morris** Andrieff • **Greta Watson** Janet Campbell • **Derek Benfield** Prof Bergman • **Van Boolen** Prof Hermanoff • **Michael Alexander** Spike Stranahan
Written by *Angus McVicar, from his radio serial*
Producer *Kevin Sheldon*

SCI Q

29

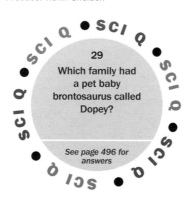

Which family had a pet baby brontosaurus called Dopey?

See page 496 for answers

The Return to the Lost World

★★ PG

1994 US Colour 93mins

Having nothing remotely to do with the Spielberg blockbuster, this is a little-seen sequel to a little-seen version of Sir Arthur Conan Doyle's *The Lost World* tale, which starred David Warner, John Rhys-Davies and Eric McCormack as scientists exploring a lost land where dinosaurs still roam. All three return for this follow-up, in which the lost land faces the twin threats of a greedy oil exploiter and an active volcano. The laughably low-budget dinosaurs are still sights for sore eyes. But otherwise this is entertaining hokum for grown-ups and older dino-mites.

John Rhys-Davies Challenger • **David Warner** Summerlee • **Eric McCormack** Edward Malone
Director *Timothy Bond*
Screenplay *Peter Welbeck [Harry Alan Towers], from the novel "The Lost World" by Sir Arthur Conan Doyle*

The Revenge of Frankenstein

★★★ 15

1958 UK Colour 86mins

Hammer's first sequel to *The Curse of Frankenstein* has the baron (Peter Cushing) rescued from execution, changing his name to Dr Stein and continuing his body-part experiments in a charity hospital. The usual first-rate performances, excellent production values and gothic atmosphere are permeated by a macabre sense of humour in this superior spine-chiller that's crisply directed, as ever, by studio regular Terence Fisher. The unexpectedly light-hearted moments neatly counterpoint the more horrific elements, including hints of cannibalism.

Peter Cushing Dr Victor Stein • **Francis Matthews** Dr Hans Kleve • **Eunice Gayson** Margaret • **Michael Gwynn** Karl • **John Welsh** Bergman • **Lionel Jeffries** Fritz • **Oscar Quitak** Karl • **Richard Wordsworth** Patient • **Charles Lloyd Pack** President
Director *Terence Fisher*
Screenplay *Jimmy Sangster, H Hurford Janes, from characters created by Mary Shelley*

Revenge of the Radioactive Reporter ★ 18

1990 Can Colour 80mins

This Canadian attempt to emulate the kind of movies the Troma studio is famous for has none of the mayhem, outrageousness and cynicism for which Troma movies are famous. In fact, it frequently takes itself quite seriously, completely missing the point of its premise. Also, it somehow manages to look cheaper and cruder than Troma's ultra low-budget efforts, with little merit except for a few amusing one-liners and some comic rock songs. Like *The Toxic Avenger*, the plot concerns an unlucky hero forced into toxic waste by his enemies, then later coming back in a hideously mutated form for revenge.

David Scammell Mike R Wave • **Kathryn Boese** Richelle Darlington • **Derrick Strange** Richard Swell • **Randy Pearlstein** Joe Wave Junior
Director *Craig Pryce*
Screenplay *Craig Pryce, David Wiechorek*

Revenge of the Stepford Wives ★★

1980 US Colour 95mins

Unwarranted and ill-judged, this sort-of-sequel is an insult to the Ira Levin source novel and the original movie, which was one of the most ambitious sci-fi thrillers of the mid-seventies. Arriving in Stepford to do a story on the town's remarkably low crime and divorce rates, a TV reporter discovers the womenfolk are being "programmed" to act as perfect domestic automatons for their husbands. A dud and yet, incredibly, this was followed by two more inferior made-for-TV affairs. Among the cast are television superstars-in-waiting Don Johnson and Sharon Gless.

Sharon Gless Kay Foster • **Julie Kavner** Megan Brady • **Audra Lindley** Barbara Parkinson • **Don Johnson** Andy Brady • **Mason Adams** Wally • **Arthur Hill** Dale "Diz" Corbett • **Ellen Weston** Kitten • **Thomas Hill** Dr Edgar Trent
Director *Robert Fuest*
Screenplay *David Wiltse, from the characters created by Ira Levin*

Revenge of the Teenage Vixens from Outer Space ★★ 15

1986 US Colour 83mins

As is to be expected with such a title, this low-budget movie is deliberately campy. Female alien teenagers come to Earth and turn their human boyfriends into ping-pong eyed vegetables when they are not satisfied by their sexual performances. Though there are plenty of ludicrous situations, the performers generally play it straight, giving the movie more amusement and credibility than it would ordinarily have had. There's also a sweet affection for the characters, giving them time to develop personalities. The numerous cheesy effects throughout also add to the mirth.

Lisa Schwedop Carla • **Howard Scott** Paul Morelli • **Amy Crumpacker** Stephanie • **Sterling Ramberg** Danny • **Julian Schembri** Jack Morelli • **Peter Guss** John • **Anne Lilly** Mary Jo • **Lisa McGregor** Vixen • **Kim Wickenburg** Vixen
Director *Jeff Farrell*
Screenplay *Michelle Lichter, Jeff Farrell*

Riders to the Stars ★ U

1954 US Colour 80mins

More science fact than fiction, this detailed textbook account of how to handle future problems in space follows astronauts on a meteor hunt to discover why their cosmic rays cause crumbling steel crystalisation in rocketships. Methodical direction by Richard Carlson, also starring as a space pilot on the recovery mission, and Curt (*Donovan's Brain*) Siodmak's script, revolving around dry scientific analysis, stops the action stone dead and neither the slick production mounting nor William Lundigan's well-played central scientist role helps it over the utterly worthy hurdle.

William Lundigan Richard Stanton • **Herbert Marshall** Dr Donald Stanton • **Richard Carlson** Jerry Lockwood • **Martha Hyer** Jane Flynn • **Dawn Addams** Susan Manners • **Robert Karnes** Walter Gordon
Director *Richard Carlson*
Screenplay *Curt Siodmak*
Cinematographer *Stanley Cortez*

Rising Storm ★ 18

1989 US Colour 95mins

A lot of effort was put in the set design and photography of this post-apocalypse adventure-comedy (which was shot in South Africa), resulting in a constantly strong visual look. Unfortunately, no effort was put into writing a script with likable characters or an engaging plot. Brothers Zach Galligan and Wayne Crawford find themselves conned into helping rebels find the lost lair of a legendary 20th century DJ, which has the key to overthrowing the country's religious fascist government run by a Billy Graham lookalike named Jimmy Joe II. It's just as stupid as it sounds, and it gets even worse as it goes along.

Zach Galligan Artie Gage • **Wayne Crawford** Joe Gage • **June Chadwick** Mila Hart • **John Rhys-Davies** Don Waldo • **Elizabeth Keifer** Blaise Hart • **Graham Clark [Graham Clarke]** Lt Ulmer • **Rod McCary** Jimmy Joe II • **William Katt** DJ
Director *Francis Schaeffer*
Screenplay *Gary Rosen, William Fay*

The Road to Hong Kong ★★ U

1962 US/UK BW 102mins

Bing Crosby and Bob Hope reteamed ten years after *Road to Bali*, for the seventh and last in a once fabulously funny series. Sadly, by now the spark had gone from the relationship and the English locations and parsimonious filming in black and white make the movie look shabby. Worse is the graceless demoting of Dorothy Lamour to "guest star", with the co-starring role being taken by an ill-suited Joan Collins. The silly plot has the pair blasted off to the planet Plutonium after Hope develops a photographic memory thanks to a miracle drug and inadvertantly memorises the secret formula of s super rocket fuel. The film's not without interest, of course, and there's super work from some distinguished supporting players – especially Peter Sellers – but on the whole this is neither funny nor attractive.

Bing Crosby Harry Turner • **Bob Hope** Chester Babcock • **Joan Collins** Diane • **Dorothy Lamour** • **Robert Morley** The Leader • **Walter Gotell** Dr Zorbb • **Roger Delgado** Jhinnah • **Felix Aylmer** Grand Lama • **Peter Madden** Lama • **Robert Gifford** American official • **Alan Ayres** American official • **Robin Hughes** American official • **Peter Sellers** • **Frank Sinatra** • **Dean Martin** • **David Niven** • **Zsa Zsa Gabor**
Director *Norman Panama*
Screenplay *Norman Panama, Melvin Frank*

Robin Cook's Formula for Death ★★★ 15

1995 US Colour 89mins

If we tell you that this TV movie is also known as *Virus* and was taken from a Robin Cook novel entitled *Outbreak*, you'll have a pretty shrewd idea what it's all about. And, although not on a par with the film of Cook's best-known book, *Coma*, this is still quite a decent little thriller, even though the audience has twigged who was responsible for the spread of a supposedly extinct plague, long before ace medical researcher, Nicollette Sheridan manages to do so. But, as Alfred Hitchcock knew so well, feeling superior to the characters accounts for a good deal of the viewer's pleasure. No nail-biter, then, but a well-told tale nonetheless. Contains some violence and sexual references.

Nicollette Sheridan Dr Marissa Blumenthal • **William Devane** Dr Ralph Harbuck • **William Atherton** Dr Reginald Holloway • **Stephen Caffrey** Tad Shockley • **Dakin Matthews** Cyrill Dubcheck • **Barry Corbin** Dr Jack Clayman • **Jim Minjares** Dr Newman
Director *Armand Mastroianni*
Screenplay *Roger Young, from the novel "Outbreak" by Robin Cook*

Robin Cook's Invasion

TV 1997 US Colour 130mins

Straying slightly from his customary hospital turf, *Coma* author Robin Cook here inflicts an interstellar virus upon the Earth in a slickly made adventure first shown as a two-part mini-series. A re-tread of *Invasion of the Body Snatchers* spiced up with a modern medical slant, it boasts an ominous atmosphere and some decent special effects. However, the cast of TV stalwarts – including Luke Perry and *Sex and the City*'s Kim Cattrall – gets little chance to shine. Adapter Rockne S

O'Bannon's would have more success two years later with the TV series, *Farscape*.

Luke Perry Beau Stark • **Kim Cattrall** Dr Moran • **Rebecca Gayheart** Cassy Winslow • **Christopher Orr** Pitt • **Neal McDonough** North • **Rosanna DeSoto** Nancy
Director *Armand Mastroianni*
Teleplay *Rockne S O'Bannon, from the novel "Invasion" by Robin Cook*

Robinson Crusoe on Mars

★★★★ U

1964 US Colour 105mins

Once you get passed the ridiculous title this is a wholly satisfactory and intelligent slice of pulp sci-fi from Byron Haskin, director of *The War of the Worlds*. Shot in the bleak hostility of California's Death Valley, this is an innovative retelling of the classic Defoe tale, centering on astronaut Paul Mantee's survival challenges following a crash-landing that leaves him stranded on the red planet. Haskin wisely bypasses flashy effects to concentrate on the human element, notably the growing relationship between Mantee and the alien he rescues from a slave ship, although the harsh planet landscape, with its craters and hovering fire balls, offers a visual feast. By the way, that's Adam West – TV's Batman – as Mantee's doomed astronaut companion.

Paul Mantee Cmdr Christopher "Kit" Draper • **Vic Lundin** Friday • **Adam West** Col Dan McReady
Director *Byron Haskin*
Screenplay *John C Higgins, Ib Melchior, inspired by the novel "The Life and Strange Surprising Adventures of Robinson Crusoe" by Daniel Defoe*
Cinematographer *William C Hoch*
Special effects *Lawrence W Butler*

Robo Warriors ★★ 15

1996 US/Phil Colour 89mins

Glum, joyless sci-fi tale of a legendary resistance leader (a thoroughly miserable James Remar), who emerges from hiding to pilot a robot-fighting machine against the Teridaxx aliens, who have declared martial law on Earth. *Predator*, *Jurassic Park* and *Terminator 2* are among the influences evident in this slow-moving and thoroughly unlikely tale – the fascistic villains agree to leave Earth peaceably if they lose the climactic robot fracas. Even the occasional action sequences are sunk by static, unexciting direction and mundane effects work. A sense of humour might have helped. Contains violence, swearing.

Kyle Howard • **James Lew** • **James Remar**
Director *Ian Barry*
Screenplay *Michael Berlin, from a character created by Stuart Gordon*

RoboCop ★★★★★ 18

1987 US Colour 98mins

High-tech meets *High Noon* in Dutch director Paul Verhoeven's deft science-fiction masterpiece, which delivers on both violent action and satirical fronts. Peter Weller gives a great mime performance as the Detroit cop of the near future, resurrected as a cyborg, who goes head-hunting the sadistic gang responsible for his plight as his human memory begins to return. But it's Verhoeven's scabrous dissection of American social issues, trashy sitcom culture and corporate greed that makes this comic-book opus a subversive and thought-provoking edge-of-

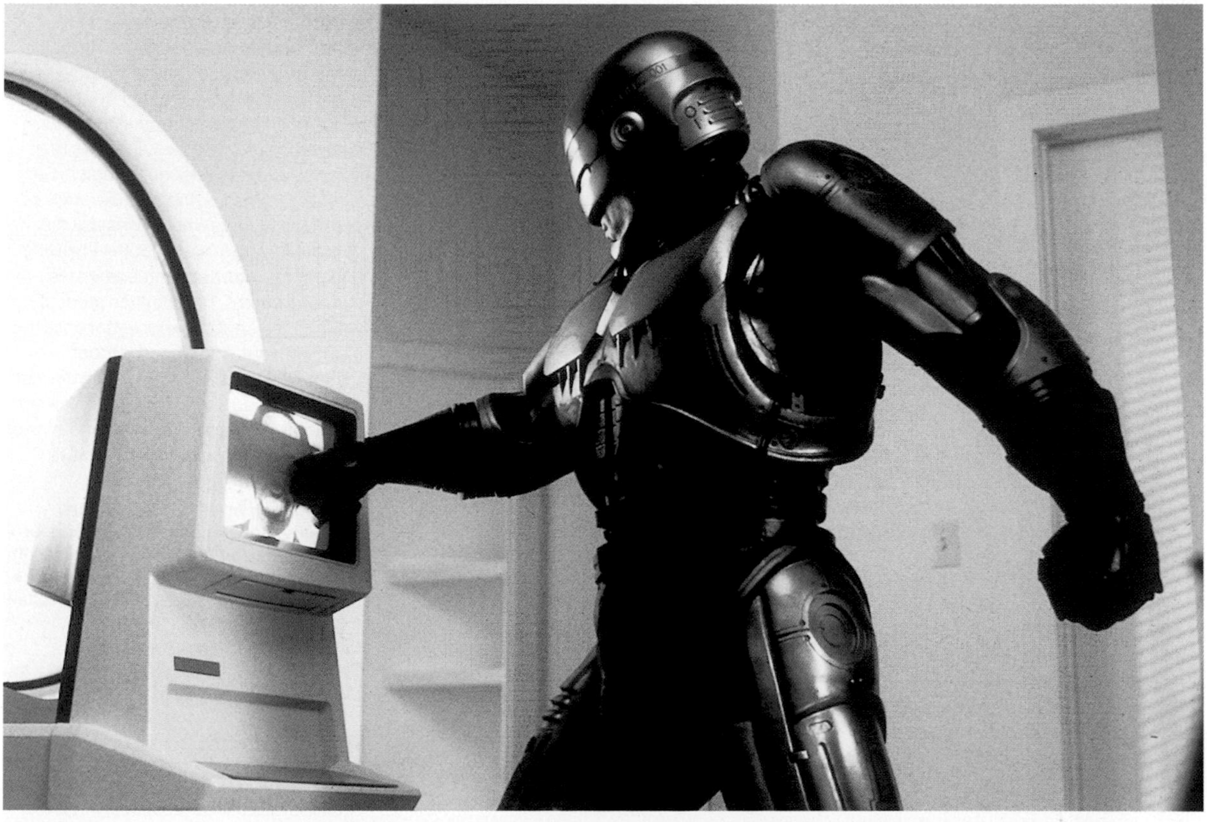

Part man, part machine, all cop – the future of law enforcement: Peter Weller is the cyborg in Paul Verhoeven's *RoboCop*

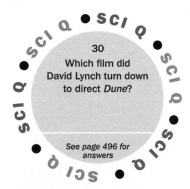

the-seat treat. Contains violence, swearing, drug abuse, brief nudity.

Peter Weller Murphy/RoboCop • **Nanc Allen** Officer Anne Lewis • **Daniel O'Herlihy [Dan O'Herlihy]** Old man • **Ronny Cox** Dick Jones • **Kurtwood Smith** Clarence Boddicker • **Miguel Ferrer** Robert Morton • **Robert DoQui** Sergeant Reed • **Ray Wise** Leon • **Felton Perry** Johnson • **Paul McCrane** Emil

Director *Paul Verhoeven*

Screenplay *Edward Neumeier, Michael Miner*

Cinematographer *Jost Vacano*

RoboCop 2 ★★★ 18

1990 US Colour 111mins ▭

An efficient, but rather empty retread of the original, with Peter Weller returning as the cyborg policeman patrolling the mean streets of Detroit. Daniel O'Herlihy, ostensibly the good tycoon from the first film, becomes the bad guy this time around, teaming up with psycho Tom Noonan to destroy his company's creation. It's once again a spectacularly violent affair and the satirical news items still provide a chuckle or two, but, sadly, it lacks the gloriously black excess of Paul Verhoeven's original. Nevertheless, it has proved to be a very serviceable franchise; a second sequel, a children's animated series and a live action TV spin-off followed. Contains swearing, strong violence.

Peter Weller Robocop • **Nancy Allen** Officer Anne Lewis • **Belinda Bauer** Dr Juliette Faxx • **Daniel O'Herlihy [Dan O'Herlihy]** Old man • **Tom Noonan** Cain • **Gabriel Damon** Hob • **Willard Pugh** Mayor Kuzak • **Stephen Lee** Duffy • **Felton Perry** Donald Johnson • **Patricia Charbonneau** Dr Garcia

Director *Irvin Kershner*

Screenplay *Frank Miller, Walon Green, from a story by Frank Miller, from characters created by Edward Neumeier, Michael Miner*

RoboCop 3 ★★★ 15

1993 US Colour 100mins ▭ DVD

Robert Burke, who made a big impression in the title role of British horror thriller, *Dust Devil*, replaces Peter Weller as the unstoppable cyborg cop in director, Fred Dekker's more comedy driven, and far less violent, futuristic fantasy, which returns the series to the central themes of Verhoeven's original "Christian fairy tale". The mechanised flatfoot this time defends the downtrodden homeless when an amoral Japanese magnate decides to clean up downtown Detroit, to build a luxury apartment complex. Complete with "splatterpunk" villains, cyborg samurai and Burke flying to trouble spots using a jet pack, Dekker's fun sequel is well directed and written with a firm eye on the family TV series the concept eventually became. Contains violence.

Robert John Burke [Robert Burke] Robocop/Alex J Murphy • **Nancy Allen** Officer Anne Lewis • **Rip Torn** Merrit W Morton, CEO • **John Castle** Paul McDaggett • **Jill Hennessy** Dr Marie Lazarus • **CCH Pounder** Bertha • **Mako** Kanemitsu • **Robert Do'Qui [Robert DoQui]** Sergeant Reed • **Remi Ryan [Remy Ryan]** Nikko • **Bruce Locke** Otomo • **Stanley Anderson** Zack • **Stephen Root** Coontz • **Daniel Von Bargen** Moreno • **Felton Perry** Johnson • **Bradley Whitford** Fleck • **Mario Machado** Casey Wong

Director *Fred Dekker*

Screenplay *Frank Miller, Fred Dekker, from a story by Frank Miller, from the characters created by Edward Neumeier, Michael Miner*

SCI Q • SCI Q • SCI Q • SCI Q • SCI Q •

30

Which film did David Lynch turn down to direct *Dune*?

See page 496 for answers

Robocop: the Series U PG 12

TV 1994 Can/US Colour 85mins ▭

Taking its cue from *RoboCop 3*, Officer Alex Murphy's TV debut completely eradicates the franchise's hard-hitting violence and biting satire to target a family audience. Richard Eden becomes the third actor to don Murphy's RoboSuit, and tackles an array of comic-strip villains and their equally silly schemes. Completely lacking the emotional resonance and sophisticated scripting which made the original film a sci-fi classic, RoboCop's small screen tour of duty makes for a by-the-numbers high-tech crime-fighting caper. Still, younger members of the audience will probably love the show's resident cute kid, Gadget, while older male viewers can take solace in lovely Yvette Nipar's feisty portrayal of Robo's latest partner, Detective Madigan. A four-part mini-series, *RoboCop: Prime Directives* followed in early 2001, starring Page Fletcher.

Richard Eden Alex Murphy/Robocop • **Yvette Nipar** Det Lisa Madigan • **Blu Mankuma** Sgt Stanley Parks • **Sarah Campbell** Gadget • **Andrea Ruth** Diana Powers/NeuroBrain

Executive producer *Kevin Gillis, Brian K Ross*

A Robot Called Golddigger ★★ PG

1993 US Colour 85mins ▭

Even the canniest character actors seem occasionally to like the idea of taking star billing. And that can be the only explanation for the appearance of Joe Pantoliano in this dire *Short Circuit* rip-off. As the kindly inventor who builds a robot to save his family from financial ruin, Pantoliano can do nothing with the juvenile script and unimaginative direction. Talented performers Amy Wright and John Rhys-Davies are also left stranded.

Joe Pantoliano Jack Shamir • **Amy Wright** Kristina Shamir • **John Rhys-Davies** Eli Taki

Director *Mark Richardson, Jack Shaoul*

Screenplay *Jack Shaoul*

Robot Jox ★★ 15

1989 US Colour 80mins ▭

In a post-nuclear world of banished warfare, nations settle scores with one another via televised games, in which representative heroes battle it out while inside hulking, transformer-like robots. A fascinating premise sadly let down by a scrawny budget and script to match. Gary Graham, from TV's *Alien Nation*, stars as one of the fighters who, having quit the game following a fatal accident involving spectators, returns to battle when his girlfriend enlists. This plagued production was actually shut down for a year once the money ran out. And while the robot miniature work is highly effective, the rest of the film has a shoddy, cheap look. A sort high-tech *Rollerball*, this was something of a departure for horror director Stuart Gordon, known for *Re-Animator*.

Gary Graham Achilles • **Anne-Marie Johnson** Athena • **Paul Koslo** Alexander • **Robert Sampson** Commissioner Jameson • **Danny Kamekona** Doctor Matsumoto • **Hilary Mason** Professor Laplace • **Michael Alldredge** Tex Conway

Director *Stuart Gordon*

Screenplay *Joe Haldeman, from a story by Stuart Gordon*

Robot Monster ★ U

1953 US BW 62mins

After *Plan 9 from Outer Space*, this is the best known bad movie in the science-fiction genre. The last six human survivors in existence struggle against the dreaded Ro-Man (a man dressed in a gorilla suit and a plastic diving helmet), whose race has destroyed the planet with their "calcinator ray" to stop Earthlings going into space and causing intergalactic friction. Made for next-to-nothing in four days, and padded out with bizarre stock footage montages (from *One Million BC* and *Flight to Mars*), this legendary trash masterpiece is hilariously banal, naive and threadbare. And it was all originally presented in 3-D!

George Nader Roy • **Claudia Barrett** Alice • **Selena Royle** Mother • **Gregory Moffett** Johnny • **John Mylong** Professor • **Pamela Paulson** Carla • **George Barrows** Ro-Man • **John Brown**
Director *Phil Tucker*
Screenplay *Wyott Ordung*
Producer *Phil Tucker*
Music *Elmer Bernstein*

The Robot vs the Aztec Mummy ★★★

1957 Mex BW 65mins

Mad scientist Dr Krupp (Luis Aceves Castanada) irks the Aztec Mummy when, after trying to steal the scared jewels it guards, he builds a half metal-half human robot to break into the tomb for him. The third, last, and most popular of the three variable Mexican Aztec Mummy movies (*The Aztec Mummy, The Curse of the Aztec Mummy*), director Rafael Portillo's half-cocked zombie/Egyptian/Frankenstein hybrid filters its endless genre clichés through a deranged Latino sensibility for fun entertainment returns. The human-faced tin-can robot with light bulb ears is an extraordinarily zany creation and a cult favourite. A Spanish language film.

Ramon Gay Dr Eduardo Almadan • **Rosita Arenas** Flora Almadan / Princess Xochi • **Crox Alvarado** Pincate • **Luis Aceves Castaneda** Dr Krupp
Director *Rafael Portillo*
Screenplay *Alfredo Salazar, William C Stell, from a story by Alfredo Salazar*

Robot Wars ★ PG

1993 US Colour 69mins [video]

This dire, futuristic tale from cheapo father and son director/producer team, Albert and Charles Band, may be set in 2041, but it's got the production values of 1970. The stop-frame animation of the giant robot vehicles is passable, but the acting and dialogue ("You're way too negative. You're a walking minus sign.") is beyond bad. Although *Re-Animator's* (1985) Barbara Crampton adds a little feistiness to the heroine, Don Michael Paul's, Han Solo-esque robot pilot, barely has a pulse. Chuck in a co-pilot called Stumpy and some of the shoddiest back projection work ever seen and you have a film of considerable awfulness.

Don Michael Paul Captain Drake • **Barbara Crampton** Dr Leda Fannon • **James Staley** Stumpy • **Lisa Rinna** Annie
Director *Albert Band*
Screenplay *Jackson Barr, from an idea by Charles Band*
Producer *Charles Band*

The Rocket Man ★ U

1954 US Colour 79mins

For a film written by the celebrated and notorious satirist Lenny Bruce, and featuring the same Klaatu robot costume from *The Day the Earth Stood Still*, this is nothing more than a minor message comedy. A spaceman gives orphan George Winslow a ray gun which, when fired at human targets, makes them tell the truth. Justice of the Peace Spring Byington adopts him as honesty sweeps through the community eventually leading to villain Emory Parnell halting all plans of taking over the local orphanage. More directorial verve on Oscar Rudolph's part and more lethal Bruce wit could have given extra bite to this moribund gentle feel-good fantasy.

Charles Coburn Mayor Ed Johnson • **Spring Byington** Justice Amelia Brown • **George Winslow** Timmy • **Anne Francis** June Brown • **John Agar** Tom Baxter • **Emory Parnell** Big Bill Watkins • **Stanley Clements** Bob
Director *Oscar Rudolph*
Screenplay *Lenny Bruce, Jack Henley, from a story by George W George, George F Slavin*

The Rocketeer ★★★★ PG

1991 US Colour 104mins [video] DVD

Director Joe Johnston (*Honey, I Shrunk the Kids*) clearly had fun making this vastly entertaining swashbuckler that will jet-propel you back to your most cherished childhood fantasies. Based on a cult graphic novel blending Second World War adventure and superhero thrills, this brilliant ode to those corny thirties movie serials has an added Art Deco sheen that enhances the sophisticated nostalgia. It also benefits from Timothy Dalton's hissably slimy Nazi agent, masquerading as a devil-may-care, Errol Flynn-inspired matinée idol. A treat.

Bill Campbell Cliff Secord • **Jennifer Connelly** Jenny • **Alan Arkin** Peevy • **Timothy Dalton** Neville Sinclair • **Paul Sorvino** Eddie Valentine • **Terry O'Quinn** Howard Hughes • **Ed Lauter** Fitch • **James Handy** Wooly • **Tiny Ron** Lothar • **Robert Guy Miranda** Spanish Johnny • **Nada Despotovich** Irma • **Margo Martindale** Millie
Director *Joe Johnston*
Screenplay *Danny Bilson, Paul DeMeo, from a story by Danny Bilson, Paul DeMeo, William Dear, from the graphic novel by Dave Stevens*

Rocketman ★★★ PG

1997 US Colour 89mins [video]

When a computer genius finally gets his chance to be an astronaut, he turns out to be too eccentric for his Nasa colleagues, who are treated to a touch more slapstick chaos than they'd bargained for. This goofy comedy, aimed primarily at children, will succeed mostly with those younger viewers predisposed to humour of the flatulent variety. *Rocketman* is really a vehicle for the antics of Harland Williams as the misguided computer whiz, but credit must be given to William Sadler as Mission Commander "Wild Bill" Overbeck, who does a slow burn while Williams inadvertently spoils his dreams. Contains strong language.

Harland Williams Fred Z Randall • **Jessica Lundy** Mission Specialist Julie Ford • **William Sadler** Comdr "Wild Bill" Overbeck • **Jeffrey DeMunn** Chief Flight Director Paul Wick • **James Pickens Jr** Ben Stevens • **Beau Bridges** Bud Nesbitt • **Peter Onorati** Gary Hackman • **Shelley Duvall** Mrs Randall
Director *Stuart Gillard*
Screenplay *Craig Mazin, Greg Erb, from a story by Oren Aviv*

Rocketship X-M ★★★ U

1950 US BW 77mins [video]

Made by the Robert Lippert quickie company to cash in on the publicity engendered by producer George Pal's *Destination Moon*, this pulp space opera was released before it and by default claims the honour of being the first "serious" post-Second World War science-fiction movie. The first manned space expedition to the moon veers off course and lands on Mars, where the crew discover a hostile race of mutants blinded by radiation from an atomic catastrophe. Unlike most fifties sci-fi that would follow it, pioneer director Kurt Neumann's surprisingly effective thriller ends with a downbeat shock. In the mid-seventies director Wade Williams shot new special effects scenes in colour and, along with long-shot extra footage using actors

TIN MEN

Mechanical men, automatons, androids, robots, cyborgs – whether companion, servant or destroyer, these technical marvels have long been part of our dream – or nightmare – of the future.

▼ **Drones** Nicknamed after Donald Duck's nephews, drones Huey, Dewey and Louie (in reality operated by multiple amputee actors) are the unusually vulnerable robot protagonists treated like children by wayward astronaut Bruce Dern in 1971's *Silent Running*.

▼ **Robot** Known to its admirers as **B9**, the robot from TV's *Lost in Space* was designed by Robert Kinoshita, the man behind Robby the Robot. Voiced by Dick Tufeld, its warning cry, "Danger, Danger", would become a TV catchphrase.

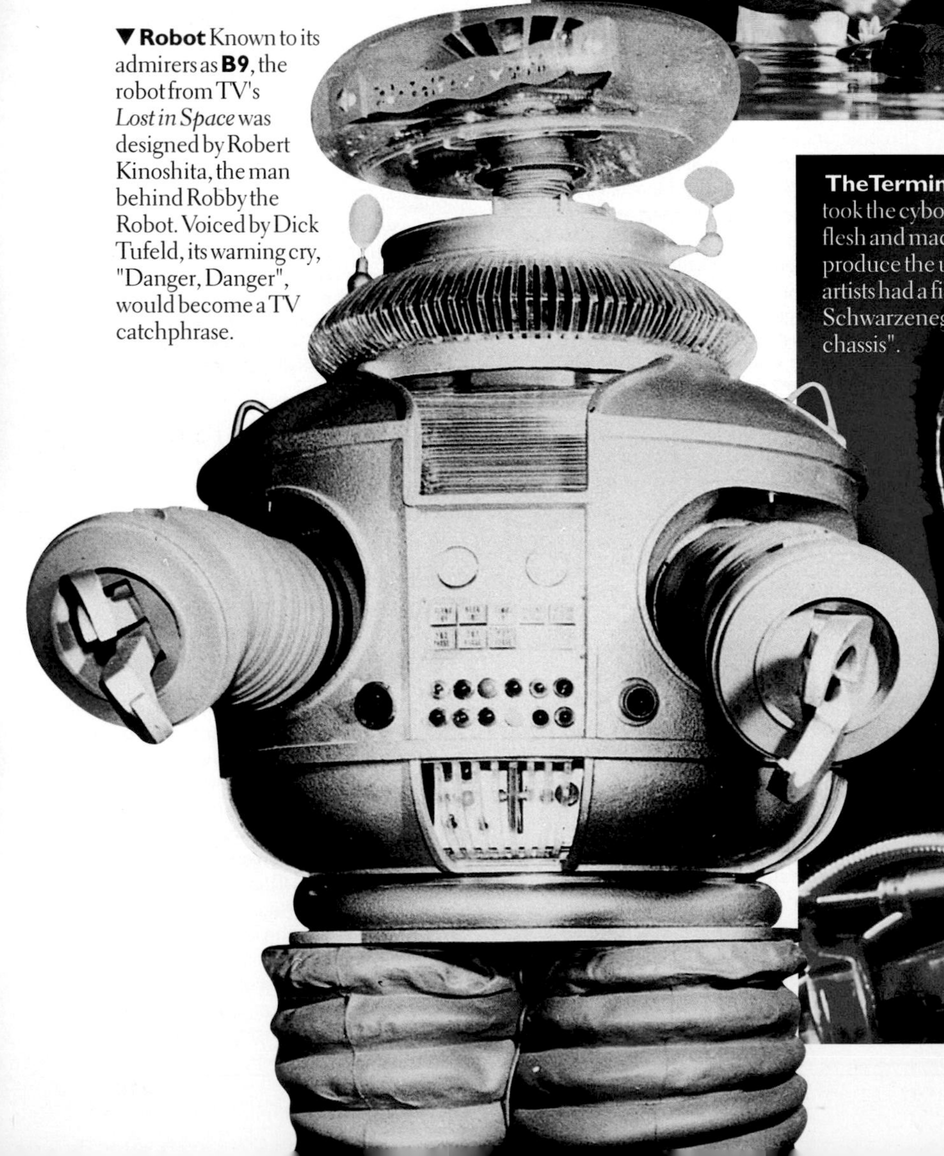

The Terminator James Cameron's Terminator took the cyborg concept to its logical conclusion as flesh and machinery were married together to produce the ultimate fighting machine - make-up artists had a field day stripping organic Arnold Schwarzenegger back to his metallic "combat chassis".

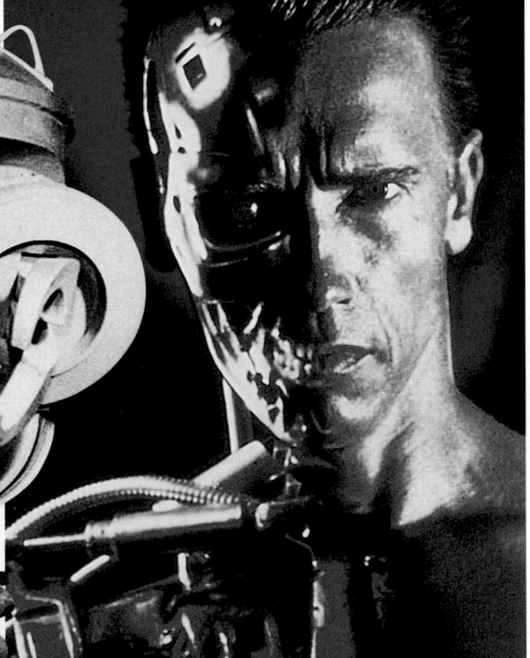

▼ Robby the Robot With his impeccable manners, mastery of languages and miraculous ability to manufacture food and drink, the dome-headed robot servant of *Forbidden Planet* caught the imagination of the fifties audiences to such an extent that he was given his own starring vehicle, 1957's *The Invisible Boy*.

Number Five Its wide-eyed stare bore an uncanny resemblence to ET, as did its childlike curiosity for the world, but *Short Circuit*'s malfunctioning military robot Number Five also had the capacity for destruction, lending its character unexpected pathos.

▶ Twiki (*Buck Rogers in the 25th Century*) Buck Rogers's gruff robot sidekick, Twiki, was voiced by Mr Bugs Bunny himself, Mel Blanc, which might account for the Road Runner-like "meep, meep" noises he made. With mega-brain Dr Theopolis around his neck, Twiki was a medallion man with a difference - let's hear it for the little guy.

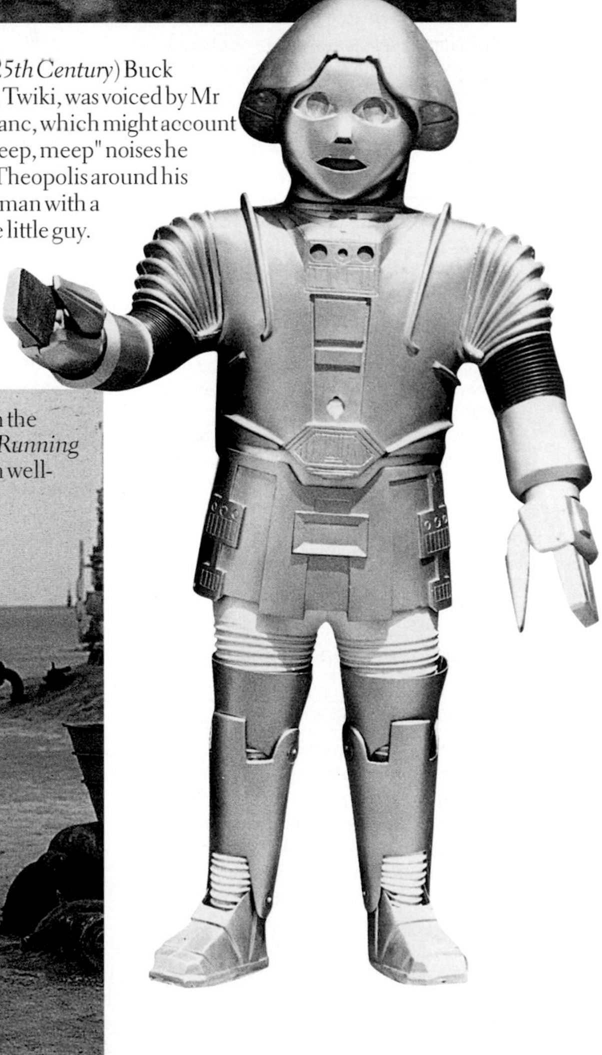

R2-D2 and C-3PO The charming robot buddies from the *Star Wars* saga both had clear design influences - *Silent Running* and *Metropolis* (1926) respectively - but benefitted from well-defined characterisation and comic interplay.

dressed as the original cast, spliced them into a restored original print.

Lloyd Bridges Col Floyd Oldham • **Osa Massen** Dr Lisa Van Horn • **John Emery** Dr Karl Eckstrom • **Noah Beery Jr** Maj William Corrigan • **Hugh O'Brian** Harry Chamberlin • **Morris Ankrum** Dr Fleming
Director *Kurt Neumann, Clarence Marks*
Screenplay *Kurt Neumann, Orville Hampton*
Cinematographer *Karl Struss* • ***Special effects*** *Don Stewart, Jack Rabin*

The Rocky Horror Picture Show
★★★★ 15

1975 UK Colour 95mins DVD

The Queen Mother of cult movies is a campy, vampy, kinky musical send-up of old horror flicks that's surprisingly witty and wickedly naughty. Telling what happens when strait-laced Brad and Janet get stranded at the weird castle of Frank N Furter – Tim Curry wringing every ounce of deranged humour from his glam-rock role in a landmark performance – this frantic diversion cleverly satirises *Frankenstein*, haunted house mysteries, science-fiction clichés and *Carry On* sexual identity confusion. The score is justifiably famous – stand-out songs are *Touch-a Touch-a Touch Me*, and *Sweet Transvestite* – and if you've never seen it give yourself a treat. If you have, then let's do *The Time Warp* again! Contains swearing, brief nudity.

Tim Curry Frank N Furter • **Susan Sarandon** Janet Weiss • **Barry Bostwick** Brad Majors • **Richard O'Brien** Riff Raff • **Jonathan Adams** Dr Everett Scott • **Nell Campbell** Columbia • **Peter Hinwood** Rocky Horror • **Patricia Quinn** Magenta • **Meat Loaf** Eddie • **Charles Gray** Criminologist • **Jeremy Newson** Ralph Hapschatt • **Hilary Labow** Betty Munroe
Director *Jim Sharman*
Screenplay *Jim Sharman, Richard O'Brien, from the musical by Richard O'Brien*
Music director *Richard Hartley* • ***Costume designer*** *Richard Pointing, Gillian Dods* • ***Costume consultant*** *Sue Blane*

Rocky Jones, Space Ranger
★★★ U

TV 1954 US BW 39x30mins

The most elaborately-made of the many *Captain Video* imitations of the fifties, this half-hour TV show was shot on film rather than telecast live and consisted mostly of three-episode serials which could also be edited into 78-minute features for television or theatrical release. Rocky Jones (Richard Crane) was a Space Ranger for the United Worlds of the Solar System, one of the many cosmos-spanning political systems modelled on fifties America (cf: *Star Trek*'s Federation), and his arch-enemies are Patsy Parsons, "suzerain of Ophicius", and "fallen ranger" Leonard Penn, who act like a cross between Soviet, fascist and Biblical tyrants.

Richard Crane Rocky Jones • **Sally Mansfield** Vena Ray • **Robert Lyden** Bobby • **Maurice Cass** Professor Newton • **Charles Meredith** Secretary Drake •
Director *Hollingsworth Morse*
Created by *Roland D Reed*
Producer *Roland D Reed, Guy V Thayer Jr*

SCI Q • SCI Q • SCI Q • SCI Q • SCI Q •

31

In which film did Jim Carrey join Jeff Goldblum and Damon Wayans to make a furry alien trio?

See page 496 for answers

Rod Brown of the Rocket Rangers ★★

TV 1953-1954 US BW 58x30mins

Having produced *Tom Corbett, Space Cadet* in 1950, CBS droped the show, which was picked up by ABC, who made a hit of it. CBS reacted by cloning their original premise (itself derivative of *Captain Video*) as *Rod Brown of the Rocket Rangers*, with a pre-stardom Cliff Robertson, who ranged in a rocket (the good ship *Beta*) from Omega Base in the 22nd century. The requisite gang included a crusty commander (John Boruff), sidekick Bruce Hall and comedy relief Jack Weston. The show offered self-contained half-hour stories rather than serials, and ran for two mostly undistinguished seasons.

Cliff Robertson Rod Brown • **Bruce Hall** Frank Boyle • **Jack Weston** Wilbur "Wormsey" Worsmer • **John Boruff** Commander Swift
Director/Screenplay *George Gould*

Rodan ★★★

1956 Jap Colour 70mins

Two years after Inoshiro Honda launched the "creature feature" with *Godzilla*, he moved into colour production with this all-action tale of the Cretaceous pterodactyl, which was hatched in a coal mine and gained its powers from consuming giant dragonflies. The atomic theme is once more to the fore, with the seismic shocks created by Rodan's supersonic speeds capable of reducing cities to rubble. But there's also a tragic element, as Rodan seeks to protect its brooding mate from prying scientists. The monster may be a man may be a suit, but the urban decimation and volcanic explosion are effectively staged. Japanese dialogue dubbed into English.

Kenji Sahara Shigeru • **Yumi Shirakawa** Kiyo • **David Duncan** Narrator
Director *Ishiro Honda [Inoshiro Honda]*
Screenplay *Takeshi Kimura, Takeo Murata, from a story by Takashi Kuronuma*
Special effects *Eiji Tsuburaya*

Rollerball ★★★ 15

1975 US Colour 119mins

Director Norman Jewison's futuristic drama is set at a time when the only violence that remains is channelled through the corporate-controlled sport of rollerball. The sets look suitably striking thanks to John Box's production design, while James Caan and John Beck make a pair of convincing athletes. They are backed by the thespian muscle of Ralph Richardson and John Houseman, but for all these pluses the film somehow remains as soulless as the world it depicts. Even the action scenes barely have enough tension to keep you on the edge of your seat.

James Caan Jonathan E • **John Houseman** Bartholomew • **Maud Adams** Ella • **John Beck** Moonpie • **Moses Gunn** Cletus • **Pamela Hensley** Mackie • **Barbara Trentham** Daphne • **Ralph Richardson** Librarian
Director *Norman Jewison*
Screenplay *William Harrison, from his story "Rollerball Murders"*
Cinematographer *Douglas Slocombe* • ***Production designer*** *John Box*

Roswell ★★★★ 12

1994 US Colour and BW 87mins

The year is 1947, and Kyle MacLachlan is the military intelligence officer who begins investigating what appears to be the crash-landing of a flying saucer and starts to suspect a cover-up. MacLachlan is convincing as the questioning officer, there are neat supporting turns from Martin Sheen and country singer Dwight Yoakam, and director Jeremy Kagan summons up an air of paranoia that Mulder and Scully would have felt quite at home with. The film is based on a true story that has long intrigued those investigating extraterrestrial phenomena, and, only a couple of years ago, a video was released allegedly containing documentary proof that autopsies were carried out on aliens following the incident. Contains swearing.

Kyle MacLachlan Major Jesse Marcel • **Martin Sheen** Townsend • **Dwight Yoakam** Mac Brazel • **Xander Berkeley** Sherman Carson • **Bob Gunton** Frank Joyce • **Kim Greist** Vy Marcel • **Peter MacNicol** Lewis Rickett • **John M Jackson** Colonel Butch Blanchard • **Charles Martin Smith** Sheriff George Wilcox

Director *Jeremy Kagan [Jeremy Paul Kagan]*
Screenplay *Arthur Kopit, from a story by Paul Davids, Jeremy Kagan, from the book "UFO Crash at Roswell" by Donald R Schmitt, Steven Poster*

Roswell ★★★

TV 1999 – US Colour

Dawson's Creek meets *The X Files* in UFO-obsessed New Mexico, with enjoyable if hardly groundbreaking results. This youth-orientated series revolves around the lives and loves of four aliens who are posing as ordinary angst-ridden teenagers. Liz Appleby and Jason Behr head an attractive cast, and the show's scripting and direction are far superior to most teen dramas. Season one successfully focuses on the slow-burning Romeo and Juliet-style romance between its two leads, while the show's second year shifts the emphasis towards high-concept sci-fi action.

Shiri Appleby Liz Parker • **Jason Behr** Max Evans • **Katherine Heigl** Isabel Evans • **Majandra Delfino** Maria DeLuca • **Brendan Fehr** Michael Guerin • **Colin Hanks** Alex Charles Whitman • **Nick Wechsler** Kyle Valenti • **William Sadler** Sheriff Jim Valenti • **Emilie de Ravin** Tess

Created by *Jason Katims, David Nutter, from the "Roswell High" books by Melinda Metz*
Executive producer *Jonathan Frakes, Kevin Kelly Brown, Lisa J Olin*

SFacts

Roswell is hot: when fans heard back in February 2000 that the show might be cancelled, they inundated studio bosses at WB Television with letters and 6,000 bottles of Tabasco sauce (the aliens' favourite condiment). Their campaign succeeded, but had to be repeated the following year, this time with 12,000 bottles of hot sauce sent to UPN; a third season has been confirmed.

Roswell: the Aliens Attack ★★ PG

1999 Can Colour 84mins

A far-fetched tale reporting the "truth" about what really happened at Roswell in 1947: supposedly the crashed vehicle was carrying alien agents intent on detonating a nuclear device at the local military base. This made-for-TV effort does have acceptable production values and a capable cast, but the invasion process itself has never been so unexciting. Barely related to the historical evidence, the main reason for the Roswell setting seems to have been so that fortles naivety can excuse the questionable plot turns.

Steven Flynn John Dearman • **Kate Greenhouse** Kate Harras • **Brent Stait** Phillips • **Heather Hanson** Eve • **Sean McCann** Woodburn

Director *Brad Turner*
Screenplay *Jim Makichuk*

R.O.T.O.R ★★ 15

1988 US Colour 86mins

RoboCop inspired a number of low-budget cash-ins, none of which got anywhere near the blackly satiric wit of Paul Verhoeven's original. The initials in the title of this Z-grade attempt stand for Robotic Officer Tactical Operation Research, but this rewired cop of the future looks as if it was made in someone's back garage. Nevertheless, it still manages to wreak plenty of mayhem when it breaks out of a boffin's lab. The less said about the anonymous cast the better. Contains violence and swearing.

Richard Gesswein Coldyron • **Margaret Trigg** Sony • **Jayne Smith** Dr Steele • **James Cole** Greg Hutchins • **Clark Moore** Houghtaling • **Carroll Baker** R.O.T.O.R.

Director *Cullen Blaine*
Screenplay *Budd Lewis*

Roujin Z ★★★★ 15

1991 Jap Colour 80mins

Written by Katsuhiro Otomo, who made perhaps the best-known *manga* movie, *Akira*, this animated feature concentrates more on character than on the futuristic concepts and designer violence that tend to dominate the genre. Translating roughly as "Old Man Z", this is primarily a "people versus the powers that be" picture, with a student nurse named Haruko siding with the elderly Takazawa when they discover that a luxury bed experiment is the front for more sinister activities. However, it's also a mischievously romantic ghost story and an ironic study of male-female hegemony, while for action fans there's a storming robot battle finale. In Japanese with English subtitles.

Director *Hiroyuki Kitakubo*
Screenplay *Katsuhiro Otomo, from his story*

Runaway ★★ 15

1984 US Colour 95mins

Although Tom Selleck was unable to break free of his *Magnum, PI* contract to make *Raiders of the Lost Ark*, he did abscond for this silly futuristic thriller, written and directed by *Jurassic Park* creator Michael Crichton. Selleck is a cop who suffers from vertigo (sound familiar?) and the villain is Gene Simmons, leader of the rock group Kiss, who has an army of deadly spider-like robots at his command the aspect of the plot that presumably interested Crichton most. Apart from some amusing romantic banter between Selleck and his police partner Cynthia Rhodes, and a fairly exciting climax that predictably plays on the vertigo idea, it's routinely made. Contains swearing and violence.

Tom Selleck Jack Ramsay • **Cynthia Rhodes** Karen Thompson • **Gene Simmons** Dr Charles Luther • **Kirstie Alley** Jackie Rogers • **Stan Shaw** Marvin • **GW Bailey** Chief • **Joey Cramer** Bobby Ramsay • **Chris Mulkey** Johnson

Director/Screenplay *Michael Crichton*

Running against Time ★★★ U

1990 US Colour 88mins

Yet another time-travelling movie, but this time a surprisingly good one. *Airplane!'s* Robert Hays discovers a time machine and uses it to go back to that fateful day in American history, 22 November 1963, to try and prevent John F Kennedy's assassination in Dallas. Of course, things don't go quite as planned, but that's part of the fun in this often highly entertaining and enjoyable tale, which also stars Catherine Hicks and Sam Wanamaker.

Robert Hays David Rhodes • **Catherine Hicks** Laura Whittaker • **Sam Wanamaker** Dr Koopman • **James Distefano** Lee Harvey Oswald • **Brian Smiar** President Lyndon Johnson • **Tracy Fraim** Teddy

Director *Bruce Seth Green*
Screenplay *Robert Glass, Stanley Shapiro, from the book "A Time to Remember " by Stanley Shapiro*

Running Delilah ★

1992 US Colour 92mins

Only serving to remind the audience of her less-than-grand contribution to *Porky's* and *Police Academy*, Kim Cattrall is here saddled with several miles of dialogue, all of which is unintentionally hilarious. Clearly unaware that the James Bond genre has already reached self-parody, director Richard Franklin (whose mentor was, gasp, Alfred Hitchcock) bungles his female 007 plot, featuring a dead Cattrall who becomes a vengeance-seeking cyborg. Ludicrous hardly begins to describe later events.

Kim Cattrall Delilah • **François Guetary** Kercharian • **Billy Zane** Paul
Director *Richard Franklin*
Screenplay *Robert Avrech, from a story by Ron Koslow, Robert Avrech*

The Running Man ★★★ 18

1987 US Colour 96mins

Given TV's increasingly desperate search for new programme formats, this futuristic blockbuster about a game show where a pumped-up audience bays for the blood of convicts on a lethal combat course isn't so far-fetched. Arnold Schwarzenegger, busy consolidating his position as the number one action star of the eighties, is the former police helicopter pilot who is forced into the game of death when he rebels against his totalitarian superiors. While it's a long way from the original Stephen King (writing as Richard Bachman) novel, Schwarzenegger gets to do what he does best – destroying baddies with a quip – and director Paul Michael Glaser – fondly remembered for his role in *Starsky and Hutch* – handles the action sequences with some panache. Maria Conchita Alonso is Arnie's reluctant partner, while Richard Dawson steals the acting honours as the game-show host. Contains swearing and violence.

Arnold Schwarzenegger Ben Richards • **Maria Conchita Alonso** Amber Mendez • **Yaphet Kotto** Laughlin • **Jim Brown** Fireball • **Jesse Ventura** Captain Freedom • **Erland Van Lidth** Dynamo • **Marvin J McIntyre** Weiss • **Gus Rethwisch** Buzzsaw • **Professor Toru Tanaka** Professor Subzero • **Mick Fleetwood** Mic • **Dweezil Zappa** Stevie • **Richard Dawson** Damon Killian
Director *Paul Michael Glaser*
Screenplay *Steven E DeSouza, from the novel "The Running Man" by Richard Bachman [Stephen King]*

SFacts

The film was originally conceived as a starring vehicle for Superman Christopher Reeve. Richard Dawson, who plays evil gameshow host Damon Killian, was once married to Diana Dors. He was a regular character in the sixties TV show *Hogan's Heroes*, and hosted his own gameshow *Family Feud*, in the seventies and eighties.

S

"For more than a thousand generations the Jedi were the guardians of peace and justice in the galaxy. Before the dark times. Before the Empire."

Star Wars Episode IV: a New Hope 1977

SOS Coastguard ★★ U

1937 US BW

Ralph Byrd exchanged Dick Tracy's raincoat for a naval uniform in this middling Republic serial. His adversary is no less than Bela Lugosi, who camps it up as a maniacal inventor whose plans to develop a fiendish disinterating gas. As ever, there's plenty of chasing about, most of it involving Byrd wrestling with Lugosi's henchman Richard Alexander. The sequence in which the gas reduces a room to atoms is splendid, but it's easy to lose patience with the constant shifting between ships, caves and kelp factories.

Ralph Byrd Lt Terry Kent • **Bela Lugosi** Boroff • **Maxine Doyle** Jean Norman • **Richard Alexander** Thorg • **Lee Ford** Snapper McGee • **John Picorri** Rackerby • **Herbert Rawlinson** Cmdr Boyle
Director *William Witney, Alan James*
Screenplay *Barry Shipman, Franklyn Adreon [Franklin Adreon], from a story by Morgan Cox, Ronald Davidson*

The Salute of the Jugger ★★

1989 US/Aus Colour 102mins

Mad Max meets *Rollerball* in this lame post-apocalyptic action adventure. Rutger Hauer stars as a veteran player of a savage future sport that combines rugby, basketball and gratuitous violence, who's reduced to leading a ragbag outfit of semi-pros from village to village to take on all comers. That is, until ambitious apprentice Joan Chen spurs him towards a return to the big city and a showdown with the elite teams. Sounds interesting on paper, but in execution it's both trite and dull. Though the two leads bring intensity to their roles, it was a definite career low for David Webb Peoples, the writer of such masterpieces as *Blade Runner* and *Unforgiven*, who made his directorial debut here. Contains violence, swearing and nudity.

Rutger Hauer Sallow • **Joan Chen** Kidda • **Vincent Phillip D'Onofrio [Vincent D'Onofrio]** Young Gar • **Delroy Lindo** Mbulu • **Anna Katarina** Big Cimber • **Gandhi MacIntyre** Gandhi • **Justin Monju** Dog Boy • **Max Fairchild** Gonzo • **Hugh Keays-Byrne** Lord Vile
Director/Screenplay *David Peoples [David Webb Peoples]*

Salvage 1 ★★

TV 1979 US Colour 1x120m; 18x60m

This off-beat adventure series was inspired by a newspaper article about all the valuable equipment left on the moon by Nasa. Andy Griffith, famous as Matlock in the eighties TV series, plays a junkman who, together with an ex-astronaut pal builds his own rocket ship, christened *The Vulture*, and flies out to the moon to bring all that Apollo junk back and sell it for scrap – the ultimate example of free enterprise. After their successful lunar mission Griffith and his crew find themselves undertaking other hazardous salvage operations. But despite the show's infectious sense of fun and positive outlook (even normal joes can do extraordinary things) whatever Griffith and Co did next couldn't possibly top going to the moon and so the series ultimately ran out of steam.

Andy Griffith Harry Broderick • **Joel Higgins** Skip Carmichael • **Trish Stewart** Melanie Slozar • **Richard Jaeckel** Agent Jack Klinger • **J Jay Saunders** Mack • **Heather McAdam** Michelle Ryan
Created by *Mike Lloyd Ross*
Executive producer *Harve Bennett, Harris Katleman*
Science advisor *Isaac Asimov*

Santa Claus Conquers the Martians ★ U

1964 US Colour 77mins

One of the all-time great movie titles is, surprise, surprise, also one of cinema's great howlers. Preparing for another busy Christmas our Santa (a suitably festive John Call) is kidnapped by green and atenna-topped Martians who want to exploit Santa's happiness in order to lift the spirits of their planet's listless, automated youth. Directed on schmaltz overload by Nicholas Webster and further enhanced by amateurish production values and acting, it has garnered unworthy cult status among bad-movie lovers over the years and, amazingly, was remade in 2000.

John Call Santa Claus • **Leonard Hicks** Kimar • **Vincent Beck** Voldar • **Victor Stiles** Billy • **Donna Conforti** Betty • **Bill McCutcheon** Dropo • **Christopher Month** Bomar • **Pia Zadora** Girmar
Director *Nicholas Webster*
Screenplay *Glenville Mareth, from an idea by Paul L Jacobson*
Cinematographer *David Quaid*

Sapphire & Steel ★★★★ PG

TV 1979-1982 UK Colour 34x30mins

This off-beat blend of sci-fi and detective thriller which on a low budget succeeded in creating a chilling atmosphere, almost of ghost story quality, was the creation of former *Z Cars* writer PJ Hammond who penned 28 out of the 34 episodes. Joanna Lumley and David McCallum are otherworldly beings with special powers, including telepathy, sent to Earth to repair or prevent ruptures in the fabric of time. Irritatingly the origin of their characters was never sufficiently explained; Hammond himself termed them as "supernatural do-gooders", but the stories themselves were pleasingly imaginative, even esoteric, requiring the viewer to think a little harder than is usual with such fare. The final episode saw the duo trapped in a time bubble, a predicament from which they were to escape in a future series that sadly never materialised.

Joanna Lumley Sapphire • **David McCallum** Steel
Created by *PJ Hammond*
Executive Producer *David Reid* • ***Producer*** *Shaun O'Riordan*

SFacts

David (*Poirot*) Suchet provides the uncredited narration for the title sequence to the stories: "All irregularities will be handled by the forces controlling each dimension. Transuranic, heavy elements may not be used where there is life. Medium atomic weights are available: Gold, Lead, Copper, Jet, Diamond, Radium, Sapphire, Silver and Steel. Sapphire and Steel have been assigned."

The Satan Bug ★★★ PG

1965 US Colour 109mins

Compared to the more straightforward heroics of other Alistair MacLean hits such as *The Guns of Navarone* and *Where Eagles Dare*, this is an altogether more subtle affair, with George Maharis searching for the madman who is threatening to unleash a deadly virus. There's a solid supporting cast in the shape of Richard Basehart, Anne Francis, Ed Asner and Dana Andrews, and director John Sturges never lets the suspense slip for a minute. Contains some violence and strong language.

George Maharis Lee Barrett • **Richard Basehart** Dr Hoffman/Ainsley • **Anne Francis** Ann • **Dana Andrews** The General • **Edward Asner [Ed Asner]** Veretti • **Frank Sutton** Donald • **John Larkin** Michaelson
Director *John Sturges*
Screenplay *James Clavell, Edward Anhalt, from the novel by Ian Stuart [Alistair MacLean]*

Satellite in the Sky ★★ U

1956 UK Colour 84mins

Did Stanley Kubrick derive *Dr Strangelove*'s missile-riding finale from this full-throttled, but hopelessly inadequate space opera? Whether he did or not, he was obviously sufficiently impressed with

Wally Veevers's special effects work to hire him for *2001: a Space Odyssey*. However, there's little else to recommend documentarist Paul Dickson's move into features. Kieron Moore barely passes muster as the commander of an orbital mission to test a tritonium bomb, while Lois Maxwell displays none of Miss Moneypenny's sang-froid as a stowed-away pacifist reporter. But no one stands a chance of making much impression alongside Donald Wolfit's risibly bombastic inventor.

Kieron Moore Cmdr Michael Haydon • **Lois Maxwell** Kim Hamilton • **Donald Wolfit** Prof Merrity • **Bryan Forbes** Jimmy Wheeler • **Jimmy Hanley** Larry • **Thea Gregory** Barbara Noble • **Barry Keegan** "Lefty" Blake
Director *Paul Dickson*
Screenplay *Edith Dell, John Mather, JT McIntosh*
Special Effects *Wally Veevers*
Cinematographer *Georges Périnal, Jimmy Wilson [James Wilson]*

Saturday the 14th ★ 15

1981 US Colour 72mins [video]

Despite its title, this childish parody is more a monster-movie spoof than a send-up of slasher movies such as *Friday the 13th*. Real-life husband and wife Richard Benjamin and Paula Prentiss move into a haunted house where their son Kevin Brando opens an ancient *Book of Evil* and a horde of monsters, aliens and vampires pop out eager to take up residence. There are some flashes of humour – a *Creature from the Black Lagoon* in the bubble bath and nothing but *Twilight Zone* episodes on the TV set – but for the most part this juvenile affair is a crudely produced rag-bag of half-baked sketches. Some of the aliens are merely leftover rubber suits from the movie *Galaxina*.

Richard Benjamin John • **Paula Prentiss** Mary • **Severn Darden** Van Helsing • **Jeffrey Tambor** Waldemar • **Kari Michaelsen** Debbie • **Kevin Brando** Billy • **Rosemary De Camp** Aunt Lucille
Director *Howard R Cohen*
Screenplay *Howard R Cohen, from a story by Jeff Begun*

Saturn 3 ★★ 15

1980 UK Colour 83mins [video] DVD

Kirk Douglas and Farrah Fawcett live an idyllic Adam and Eve existence in a synthetic food-making factory on Titan, the third moon of Saturn. Then along comes snake Harvey Keitel, a psychopath on the run from Earth, with his equally disturbed robot Hector. Great sets and futuristic hardware paper over the black holes in an, at times, ridiculous space shocker directed, for two weeks anyhow, by *Star Wars/Superman* production designer John Barry. Stanley Donen took over, but was unable to improve the mass of contrivance and plot confusion (scripted by Martin Amis, no less). Note Keitel's dubbed English accent.

Farrah Fawcett Alex • **Kirk Douglas** Adam • **Harvey Keitel** Benson • **Douglas Lambert** Captain James • **Ed Bishop** Harding • **Christopher Muncke** Second crewman
Director *Stanley Donen*
Screenplay *Martin Amis, from a story by John Barry*
Producer *Stanley Donen*

Savage ★ 18

1995 US Colour 98mins [video]

The same writer, director, and star of *Automatic* and *The Mercenary* teamed up again for this science-fiction movie, but the end result here is underwhelming. Most of the blame goes to Patrick Highsmith and Peter Sagal's script, which does not properly explain the mysterious alien force that awakens shooting victim Olivier Gruner from his stupor, and subsequently drives him to destroy an evil corporation headed by Kario Salem. Other questions brought up later in the movie are also unexplained. While director Avi Nesher usually brings a sharp look and high impact action, Gruner's martial arts sequences are cramped and generic, and the visual quality is frequently dark, with blurry effects. Contains swearing, violence and a sex scene.

Olivier Gruner Alex Verne/Savage • **Jennifer Grant** Nicky Carter • **Kario Salem** Reese Burroughs • **Sam McMurray** Edgar Wallace • **Kristin Minter** Marie
Director *Avi Nesher*
Screenplay *Patrick Highsmith, Peter Sagal, from a story by Patrick Highsmith*

Scanner Cop ★★★ 18

1994 US Colour 90mins [video]

The fourth entry in the *Scanners* series gets a boost with its change in locale (moving from Canada to LA), and introduces a new psychic hero, who happens to be a police officer. The irresistible set-up has scanner cop Daniel Quinn on the trail of bad guy Richard Lynch, a scientist with a grudge against policemen. Lynch is fun as usual, hypnotising innocent people into killing cops in his usual hammy fashion, and the whole movie is executed with a healthy amount of zip. However some violent scenes, especially the climax, seem to have been trimmed in order to get a more accessible rating.

Daniel Quinn Samuel Staziak • **Darlanne Fluegel** Dr Joan Alden • **Richard Lynch** Glock • **Hilary Shepard** Zena • **Richard Grove** Commander Peter Harrigan
Director *Pierre David*
Screenplay *George Saunders, John Bryant*

Scanners ★★★★ 18

1980 Can Colour 102mins [video] DVD

Evil Michael Ironside and derelict Stephen Lack are the leaders of two rival groups of telepaths – or "scanners" – in David Cronenberg's modern horror classic. The Canadian director seamlessly blends science fiction and conspiracy thriller into an exhilarating ride and, while the stunning (and occasionally stomach-churning) set pieces such as the exploding heads and the final apocalyptic battle will delight genre fans, it's Cronenberg's fascination with the horrors lurking within the human body and our inability to control them that provide the interest in this landmark movie.

Stephen Lack Cameron Vale • **Jennifer O'Neill** Kim Obrist • **Patrick McGoohan** Dr Paul Ruth • **Lawrence Dane** Braedon Keller • **Charles Shamata [Chuck Shamata]** Gaudi • **Adam Ludwig** Arno Crostic • **Michael Ironside** Darryl Revok • **Victor Desy** Dr Gatineau • **Mavor Moore** Trevellyan • **Robert Silverman** Benjamin Pierce
Director/Screenplay *David Cronenberg*

Scanners II: the New Order ★★ 18

1991 Can Colour 99mins [video]

This first sequel lacks the intriguing and thought-provoking script of Cronenberg's original *Scanners*, opting for a more conventional and exploitable story. David Hewlett is the naive "scanner" recruited by police chief John Forrester (Yvan Ponton) on the pretext of helping out the city. In fact Forrester plans to use Hewlett's telepathic powers to pursue his own political agenda. Whatever his budgetary restrictions, director Christian Duguay (in his movie debut) brings more style and a much slicker look to the movie, and never allows the pacing to falter for long. Splatter fans will particularly enjoy both the quality and the quantity of the exploding head sequences, which are wisely given centre stage.

David Hewlett David Kellum • **Deborah Raffin** Julie Vale • **Yvan Ponton** Commander John Forrester • **Isabelle**

Mejias Alice Leonardo • **Tom Butler** Doctor Morse • **Raoul Trujillo** Drak • **Vlasta Vrana** Lieutenant Gelson
Director *Christian Duguay*
Screenplay *BJ Nelson, from characters created by David Cronenberg*

Scared to Death ★★ 18

1980 US Colour 87mins

In this earthbound *Alien* rip-off, top secret genetic experiments produce a lethal killing machine organism that stalks the sewers of Los Angeles. John Stinson stars as a tough cop turned best-selling author whose job it is to hunt it down. "If you're frightened by the unknown – wait until you face reality" declared the poster. This substandard debut feature from William Malone, who went on to direct the disappointing 1999 remake *House on Haunted Hill* offers nothing fresh to the actor-in-a-rubber-suit genre save the usual high body count and gruesome gore. The creature sucks out human spinal fluid to feed to its offspring. Yuck! An unofficial sequel entitled *Syngenor* followed in 1990.

John Stinson Ted Lonergan • **Diana Davidson** Jennifer Stanton • **Jonathan David Moses** Lou Capell • **Toni Jannotta** Sherry Carpenter • **Kermit Eller** Syngenor
Director/Screenplay *William Malone*
Cinematographer *Patrick Prince*

Schlock ★

1971 US Colour 77mins

Before achieving fame with *The Blues Brothers* and *National Lampoon's Animal House*, director John Landis donned an ape suit in his debut as a director. This sci-fi horror spoof sees the monkey-suited title character – a thawed prehistoric missing link – running amok in a small town, and leaving a trail of banana skins in his murderous wake. Nothing more than a poor excuse to lampoon Kubrick's *2001*, this was advertised with the spoof tag-line "No One Will Be Admitted into the Cinema to See This Film". Unfortunately they were, and all they saw was a game, but lame, student effort featuring cameos by the usual fanzine suspects Forrest J Ackerman, Don Glut and producer Jack Harris. Future Oscar winner Rick Baker designed the hairy costume.

John Landis The Schlockthropus • **Saul Kahan** Detective/Sgt Wino • **Joseph Piantadosi** Prof Shlibovitz • **Eliza Garrett** Mindy Binerman • **Eric Allison** Joe Puzman • **Enrica Blankey** Mrs Binerman
Director/Screenplay *John Landis*
Make-up special effects *Rick Baker*

Sci-Fighters ★★ 18

1996 Can Colour 90mins

Roddy Piper stars in this pathetic rip-off of *Blade Runner*. But instead of an android, Piper is hunting a seemingly deceased rapist (Billy Drago) who has somehow developed the ability to infect people with a disgusting alien virus. The movie is generally drab (we are told that in 2009 the sun never comes out because of volcanic ash in the atmosphere), and the actors seem to have taken their cue from their surroundings. Do yourself a favour and rent the real thing.

Roddy Piper Cameron Grayson • **Jayne Heitmeyer** Dr Kirbie Younger • **Billy Drago** Adrian Dunn • **Tyrone Benskin** Gene Washington • **Richard Raybourne** Casper • **Donna Sarrasin** Tricia Rollins
Director *Peter Svatek*
Screenplay *Mark Sevi*

Science Fiction Theatre ★★

TV 1955-1957 US BW 78x30mins

An anthology show with an aesthetic that looks back to *Dragnet* rather than forward to *The Twilight Zone*, this tries to get away from the monsters and rockets associated with juvenile science-fiction programmes but too often gets bogged down in illustrated science lectures and an approach typical of producer/writer Ivan Tors (*The Magnetic Monster*, *The Man and the Challenge*) whereby the extraordinary is made to seem matter-of-fact. Though *Time Is Just a Place* is an adaptation of a Jack (*Invasion of the Body Snatchers*) Finney story, this mostly came up with trite little originals, many from the prolific but plodding Tors (Steven Spielberg repeated the mistake on *Amazing Stories* in the eighties). The show – in an era when established film players were reluctant to do television – managed to land solid guest stars such as William Lundigan, Otto Kruger, Richard Arlen, Basil Rathbone, Adolphe Menjou, Beverly Garland, William Schallert, Vincent Price, Kenneth Tobey, Whit Bissell, Victor Jory and June Lockhart.

Truman Bradley Host and narrator
Producer *Ivan Tors, Maurice Ziv*

Scream and Scream Again ★★★ 18

1969 UK Colour 90mins

A highly regarded, but confusing, sci-fi horror tale tinged with political allegory. Vincent Price (in one of the few present-day pictures he made) is a scientist creating an artificial super-race via gruesome transplant surgery for a foreign fascist power. Peter Cushing is an ex-Nazi and Christopher Lee a British agent in veteran genre director Gordon Hessler's imaginative blood-curdler, but the three leads' highly publicised (at the time) teaming is a cheat, as they have virtually no scenes together. Giving a more straightforward performance than normal, Price lends dignity and class to some credible chills. Contains violence, swearing and some nudity.

Vincent Price Dr Browning • **Christopher Lee** Fremont • **Peter Cushing** Major Benedek Heinrich • **Judy Huxtable** Sylvia • **Alfred Marks** Superintendent Bellaver • **Anthony Newlands** Ludwig • **Peter Sallis** Schweitz • **David Lodge** Det Insp Strickland
Director *Gordon Hessler*
Screenplay *Christopher Wicking, from the novel "The Disorientated Man" by Peter Saxon*

Screamers ★★ 18

1995 Can/US/Jap Colour 103m DVD

Resembling a less atmospheric hybrid of *Alien* and *The Thing*, this dingy adaptation of Philip K Dick's short story *Second Variety* is only a moderate success. Peter Weller (*RoboCop*) plays the soldier brokering peace with his futuristic enemies, who comes up against the eponymous deadly defence units, which have evolved into increasingly sophisticated adversaries. Although there are decently mounted action sequences and the post-nuclear production design is nicely realised, there are far too many lulls in the story, and crucially, with the exception of Weller, it's difficult to care whether these under-developed characters live or die.

Peter Weller Colonel Hendricksson • **Andy Lauer [Andrew Lauer]** Ace • **Roy Dupuis** Becker • **Charles Powell** Ross • **Jennifer Rubin** Jessica • **Ron White** Elbarak
Director *Christian Duguay*
Screenplay *Dan O'Bannon, Miguel Tejada-Flores, from the short story "Second Variety" by Philip K Dick*

The Sea Serpent ★

1984 Sp Colour 92mins

Moby Dick meets the Loch Ness Monster in this Spanish produced throwback to the bad old fifties creature days. Ex-alcoholic sea captain Timothy Bottoms discovers an (obvious puppet) sea serpent that's been awakened by atom bomb tests, but the only person believing him is heroine Taryn Power, who joins him for a dangerous voyage after taking portentous advice from professor Ray Milland (in his very last big screen role). A worthless and boring aquatic adventure.

Timothy Bottoms Captain Pedro Barrios • **Taryn Power** Margaret Roberts • **Ray Milland** Prof Timothy Wallace • **Jared Martin** Lenares • **Carol James** Jill

Director *Gregory Greens [Amando de Ossorio]*

Screenplay *Gordon A Osburn [Amando de Ossorio]*

seaQuest DSV ★★

TV 1993-96 US Colour 1x120m; 57x60m

Produced by Steven Spielberg, this big-budget, star-studded undersea odyssey set sail on a tidal wave of hype, but swiftly failed to emerge – or submerge – as an underwater *Star Trek*. Despite its tendency towards unremarkable storylines, though, the adventures of the *seaQuest DSV* (Deep Submergence Vessel) still makes for a reasonably diverting voyage. Distinguished film actor Roy Scheider assuredly leads the show's capable cast, while further buoyancy is provided by the series' big-name guest stars (including Charlton Heston, William Shatner and *Star Wars* icon Mark Hamill), superior production values and cutting-edge special effects. The show's first year is dominated by earnest but dull "science fact" plotlines, while season two's emphasis is on high-concept and often unbelievable sci-fi adventure. In its third and final season, the series is successfully reborn as the action-packed war saga *seaQuest 2032*, which sees Scheider taking a back seat to new super-sub captain Michael Ironside.

Roy Scheider Captain Nathan Bridger • **Stephanie Beacham** Dr Kirstin Wesphalen • **Don Franklin** Cmdr Jonathan Ford • **Stacy Haiduk** Lt Cmdr Katherine Hitchcock • **Royce D Applegate** Manilow Crocker • **Ted Raimi** Lt Mack O'Neill • **Jonathan Brandis** Lucas Wolenczak • **Michael Ironside** Captain Oliver Hudson

Created by *Rockne S O'Bannon*

Executive producer *Steven Spielberg, Tommy Thompson*

The Second Hundred Years ★

TV 1967-1968 US Colour 26x30mins

Another entry in the freak sit-com boom of the mid-sixties, this was the one about Luke Carpenter (Monte Markham), a prospector frozen inside an Alaskan glacier since 1900, who is thawed out and reunited with his now elderly son Edwin (Arthur O'Connell) and lookalike grandson Ken (also Markam). As usual, and for no real reason, Luke has to keep his origins a secret and passes himself off as Ken's twin, allowing for purportedly humorous confusion. It didn't even make it to its second 26 episodes.

Arthur O'Connell Edwin Carpenter • **Monte Markham** Luke Carpenter/Ken Carpenter • **Karen Black** Marcia

Seconds ★★★★

1966 US BW 105mins

Dealing with the uncomfortable subject of spiritual rebirth, this brilliant social science-fiction movie from seminal sixties director John Frankenheimer is years ahead of its time in both theme and style. X-rated on its original release, the frightening premise is intensified by cameraman James Wong Howe's use of stark black-and-white photography and distorting fish-eye lenses. Under-rated star Rock Hudson gives one of his best performances as the deeply disturbed recipient of life-changing plastic surgery.

Rock Hudson Antiochus "Tony" Wilson • **Salome Jens** Nora Marcus • **John Randolph** Arthur Hamilton • **Will Geer** Old man • **Jeff Corey** Mr Ruby • **Richard Anderson** Dr Innes

Director *John Frankenheimer*

Screenplay *Lewis John Carlino, from the novel by David Ely*

Cinematographer *James Wong Howe*

Music *Jerry Goldsmith*

SCI Q • SCI Q • SCI Q • SCI Q

32

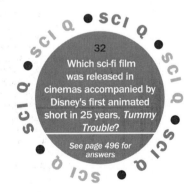

Which sci-fi film was released in cinemas accompanied by Disney's first animated short in 25 years, *Tummy Trouble*?

See page 496 for answers

The Secret Adventures of Jules Verne ★★★★

TV 1999 Can Colour 22x60mins

What if Jules Verne's visionary sci-fi stories were semi-autobiographical? That question is at the heart of this imaginative adventure-drama series. Set in a Victorian era which is just starting to exploit industrial technology, the show sees Chris Demetral's twentysomething Jules Verne teaming up with embittered scoundrel Phileas Fogg (Michael Praed) to battle the evil League of Darkness. A great idea provides the basis of a very entertaining series, which combines many of the best elements of *The Wild Wild West* and *The Young Indiana Jones Chronicles*. Young Jules Verne's covert exploits make full use of the show's inventive scripts and epic (if sometimes overly-ambitious) computer-generated effects, while Demetral, Praed and the rest of the show's regular cast form a highly engaging group of adventurers.

Chris Demetral Jules Verne • **Michael Praed** Phileas Fogg • **Francesca Hunt** Rebecca Fogg • **Michel Courtemanche** Passepartout

Created by *Gavin Scott, inspired by the novels of Jules Verne*

Producer *Neil Zeiger*

The Secret Empire ★★

TV 1979 US BW and Colour 12x20mins

A segment of the short-lived *Cliffhangers!*, which also included the semi-horror *The Curse of Dracula* and the adventure *Stop Susan Williams*, this was a western/sci-fi hybrid intended to hark back to the old Gene Autry serial, *Phantom Empire* (1935). In the Wild West, Marshal Jim Donner (Geoffrey Scott) discovers a subterranean city called Chimera, where evil Emperor Thorval (Mark Lenard) rules through a mind control device that needs gold to work – hence the Emperor's involvement with aboveground stagecoach robbers. It began with an "episode three", in mid-plot, and was cancelled after "episode twelve", which ended with a cliffhanger, though two concluding episodes were made. In *Wizard of Oz* style, the aboveground stuff was in black and white while the underground empire was in colour.

Geoffrey Scott Marshal Jim Donner • **Carlene Watkins** Millie Thomas • **Tiger Williams** Billy Thomas • **David Opatoshu** Hator • **Mark Lenard** Emperor Thorval

The Secret of the Telegian ★★★

1960 Jap Colour 85mins

Rarely seen outside Japan, director Jun Fukuda's creepy *noir* fantasy is of equal stature to the Toho studio's more famous transformation movies (eg *Matango*). A soldier left for dead in a cave at the end of the Second World War teams up with a scientist who has invented a teleportation device. After having all the blood in his body replaced by electricity, the revenge-driven corporal uses the glass machine to kill his double-crossing friends in different locations and returns to base unnoticed. Great visual tricks by effects master Eiji (*Godzilla*) Tsuburaya once again round off a nifty fantasy package. A Japanese language film.

Koji Tsuruta • **Yumi Shirakawa** • **Akihiko Hirata** • **Tadao Nakamaru** • **Seizaburo Kawazu** • **Yoshio Tsuchiya** • **Sachio Sakai**
Director *Jun Fukuda*
Screenplay *Shinichi Sekizawa*
Special effects *Eiji Tsuburaya* •
Cinematographer *Kazuo Yamada*

The Secret World of Alex Mack ★★★

TV 1994-1998 US Colour 79x30mins

A teenage girl gains superpowers in Nickelodeon's youth-orientated sci-fi sitcom. Larisa Oleynik stars as Alexandra "Alex" Mack, an ordinary high-school student whose close encounter with a secret chemical leaves her with a range of shape-shifting and telekinetic powers. Much like *Sabrina the Teenage Witch*, Alex secretly uses her gifts to get through the trials and traumas of teen life. While Alex's unchallenging exploits are strictly kids' stuff, they provide an excellent showcase for Oleynik, whose winning central performance really keeps the *World* turning. The special effects are surprisingly good, too. viewers will also appreciate the opportunity to see TV's *Dark Angel* Jessica Alba in an early role.

Larisa Oleynik Alexandra "Alex" Mack • **Darris Love** Raymond Alvarado • **Meredith Bishop** Annie Mack • **Michael Blakley** George Mack • **Dorian Lopinto** Barbara Mack • **Louan Gideon** Danielle Atron • **Jessica Alba** Jessica
Created by *Thomas W Lynch, Ken Lipman*

Secrets of the Phantom Caverns ★★ 15

1984 UK Colour 87mins

Robert Powell's presence is so negligible as to be negative in this British lost-world fantasy, which should never have been found. Director Don Sharp, who could usually turn out high action from low budgets, never got to grips with this story of a whiter-than-white albino tribe discovered in South American caves. With the quality of acting from Lisa Blount and Richard Johnson, besides the pathetic Powell, a stranglehold wouldn't have been enough. Undemanding teenagers might like it

Robert Powell Wolfson • **Timothy Bottoms** Major Stevens • **Lisa Blount** Leslie Peterson • **Richard Johnson** Ben Gannon • **Anne Heywood** Frida Shelley • **Jackson Bostwick** Hunter
Director *Don Sharp*
Screenplay *Christy Marx, Robert Vincent O'Neil, from a story by Ken Barnett*

The Seed of Man ★★★★★

1969 It Colour 101mins

Director Marco Ferreri, dubbed the "Italian Master of Bad Taste" by critics for such shocking male fantasies as *La Grande Bouffe* and *L'Ultima Donna*, brilliantly adapted his coolly sardonic gender-specific observations to the sci-fi genre in this outstanding work. After global warfare, plagues and catastrophes have virtually wiped out mankind, Marco Margine and Anne Wiazemsky (then married to Jean-Luc Godard) survive together on a deserted beach. But the post-nuclear Adam and Eve can't agree on having kids; he wants a son but she doesn't want to repopulate the self-destructive planet. Ferreri's engrossing fable, heightend by stunningly surreal art direction and sunny photography, ends suitably bleakly. Politically, morally and allegorically incorrect *à la* Ferreri, this poignant evocation of masculinity's last stand in the face of encroaching feminism is a provocative and compelling sexual apocalypse. An Italian language film.

Marco Margine Ciro • **Anne Wiazemsky** Dora • **Annie Girardot** Anna • **Milva Frosini [Deanna Frosini]** • **Rada Rassimov** • **Maria Teresa Piaggio** • **Angela Pagano**
Director *Marco Ferreri*
Screenplay *Sergio Bazzini, Marco Ferreri*
Cinematographer *Mario Vulpiani*

Seedpeople ★ 15

1992 US Colour 78mins

This has the gall to state it's "based on an original idea by Charles Band" when it's clearly derived from *Invasion of the Body Snatchers*, right down to the story being told in flashback, as the inhabitants of a small town are possessed by aliens grown from seeds sent through space. It's very badly written, with indistinguishable characters that are poorly acted by the amateur cast. Even die-hard horror fans will be utterly bored by the slow-moving story and the very sporadic appearances of some truly dreadful monster creations.

Sam Hennings Tom Baines • **Andrea Roth** Heidi Tucker • **Dane Witherspoon** Brad Yates • **David Dunard** Ed • **Holly Fields** Kim Tucker • **Bernard Kates** Doc Roller • **John Mooney** Frank Tucker
Director *Peter Manoogian*
Screenplay *Jackson Barr, from a story by Charles Band*

The Sender ★★★ 18

1982 UK Colour 87mins

Former art director Roger Christian's directorial debut was this piece of metaphysical sci-fi, in which psychiatrist Kathryn Harrold pieces together the bizarre circumstances of amnesiac Zeljko Ivanek's condition. At times extremely disturbing, and regularly punctuated by set pieces highlighting Nick Allder's special effects, this mystery keeps one constantly alert and on the edge of one's seat. The scene in which an entire hospital is convulsed by Ivanek's shock treatment is electrifying. Too bad about the many loose ends.

Kathryn Harrold Gail Farmer • **Zeljko Ivanek** Sender • **Shirley Knight** Jerolyn • **Paul Freeman** Dr Denman • **Sean Hewitt** Messiah • **Harry Ditson** Dr Hirsch • **Olivier Pierre** Dr Erskine • **Tracey Harper** Young girl • **Al Matthews** Vietnam veteran • **Marsha A Hunt** Nurse Jo
Director *Roger Christian*
Screenplay *Thomas Baum*
Cinematographer *Roger Pratt*
Special effects *Nick Allder*

The Sender ★

1997 US Colour 98mins

Like its other recent efforts, PM Entertainment appears to have spent a lot of time and money on this sci-fi action movie, but this time they fell far short. A listless Michael Madsen is Dallas Grayson, a naval officer endowed with a mysterious power that makes him a target for the government. There are superior special effects, and large-scale action sequences, but everything seems wrong, from the position of the camera to how the action moves on the screen. The closing credits list a number of assistant directors, suggesting that there were some problems during the production. Cult favorites R Lee Ermey and Robert Vaughn liven things up during their brief appearances.

Michael Madsen Dallas Grayson • **Robert Vaughn** Fairfax • **Dyan Cannon** Gina Fairfax • **R Lee Ermey** Rosewater • **Shelli Lether** Angel • **Brian Bloom** Jack Greyson
Director *Richard Pepin*
Screenplay *Richard Preston Jr, Nathan Long*

Sergeant Deadhead ★★ U

1965 US Colour 88mins

One-time pop star Frankie Avalon plays a dual role in this watchable, if rowdy, musical comedy. Sergeant OK Deadhead is the kind of nervous, Jerry Lewis-style klutz the US Air Force doesn't need when it's about to launch a top secret rocket. Deadhead is accidentally blasted off into space with a chimpanzee and, on his return, temporarily becomes a crazed rebel. So his commander substitutes Deadhead with his double. Buster Keaton, in one of his final movies, supplies some quieter visual humour as a mad electrician.

Frankie Avalon Sgt OK Deadhead/Sgt Donovan • **Deborah Walley** Col Lucy Turner • **Fred Clark** Gen Rufus Fogg • **Cesar Romero** Adm Stoneham • **Gale Gordon** Capt Weiskopf • **Harvey Lembeck** Pvt McEvoy • **John Ashley** Pvt Filroy • **Buster Keaton** Pvt Blinken • **Eve Arden** Lt Kinsley
Director *Norman Taurog*
Screenplay *Louis M Heyward*

Sgt Kabukiman NYPD ★★★ 18

1991 US/Jap Colour 100mins

Gleefully disregarding trifles such as quality and taste, Troma has produced some of the most delirious B-movies of recent times. However, none can rival the silliness of this comic-book caper. Doltish cop Rick Gianasi is possessed by the spirit of a kabuki actor and masters the heat-seeking chopsticks and suffocating sushi rolls that will prevent The Evil One from taking over the world. Mercilessly – and with large dollops of political incorrectness – mocking the superhero tradition, directors Michael Herz and Lloyd Kaufman resort too readily to stereotypes and socko slapstick. But, somehow, the manic mixture gets laughs.

Rick Gianasi Harry Griswold / Sergeant Kabukiman • **Susan Byun** Lotus • **Bill Weeden** Reginald Stuart • **Thomas Crnkovich** Rembrandt • **Larry Robinson** Reverend Snipes • **Noble Lee Lester** Captain Bender • **Brick Bronsky** Jughead • **Pamela Alster** Connie LaRosa
Director *Lloyd Kaufman, Michael Herz*
Screenplay *Lloyd Kaufman, Andrew Osborne, Jeffrey W Sass*

Seven Days ★★★

TV 1998-2001 US Colour 1x120m; 64x60m

A time travel series firmly in the *Quantum Leap* and *Time Tunnel* mould, *Seven Days* revolves around an experimental government project which allows an ex-CIA operative to travel exactly one week into the past. Jonathan LaPaglia stars as Frank Parker, a troubled hero who uses the Backstep device to prevent various disasters and tragedies on a weekly basis. While LaPaglia's exploits tend to be predictable, repetitive and highly derivative, the series remains a reasonably satisfying blast through the immediate past. The star skilfully drives the action, drama and comedy, and the show's supporting cast and production values are well up to par.

Jonathan LaPaglia Lt Frank Porter • **Don Franklin** Capt Craig Donovan • **Justina Vail** Dr Olga Vukavitch • **Nick Searcy** Nathan Ramsey • **Alan Scarfe** Dr Bradley Talmadge
Created by *Christopher Crowe*
Executive Producer *Christopher Crowe* •
Producer *John McPherson, Ron Binkowski*

Seven Days to Noon ★★★★

1950 UK BW 96mins

Doomsday movies were everywhere in the early fifties as the Cold War chill began to bite. This is the finest British contribution to that sub-genre, indeed, a pretty convincing case could be made for its nomination as one of this country's best science-fiction films. Although the threat of an atomic explosion in London makes for compelling viewing, the true power of the picture comes from a magnificent performance by Barry Jones as the professor driven to suicidal despair by the misappropriation of his work. Thanks to Jones and cinematographer Gilbert Taylor's eerie images of the capital, the Boulting brothers maintain an unbearable tension.

Barry Jones Professor Willingdon • **Olive Sloane** Goldie • **André Morell** Superintendent Folland • **Sheila Manahan** Ann Willingdon • **Hugh Cross** Stephen Lane • **Joan Hickson** Mrs Peckett • **Ronald Adam** Prime Minister
Director *John Boulting*
Screenplay *Roy Boulting, Frank Harvey, from a story by Paul Dehn, James Bernard*
Cinematographer *Gilbert Taylor*

The Sex Mission ★★★ 15

1984 Pol Colour 121mins

The cinematic supremacy of genre confirms that films gain acceptance from being pigeon-holed. But, occasionally, an unholy alliance of artistic ambiguity and cultural perversity precludes definitive classification. Containing elements of political parable, feminist satire and sex comedy, Juliusz Machulski's futuristic fable is a case in point, as no single strain dominates and the resulting mismatch proves both the film's fascination and its failing. The study of social strictures and gynocentric revisionism within the all-female civilisation is amusing and acute. But the way in which cryogenic returnees Olgierd Lukaszewicz and Jerzy Stuhr seek to reimpose chauvinist ideals is bawdy in the extreme. A Polish language film.

Olgierd Lukaszewicz Albert • **Jerzy Stuhr** Maks • **Bozena Stryikowna** Lamia
Director *Juliusz Machulski*
Screenplay *Pavel Hajny, Jolanta Jartwig, Juliusz Machulski*

The Shadow ★★★ 12

1994 US Colour 102mins

"Who knows what evil lurks in the hearts of men?" Alec Baldwin does, here playing both wealthy socialite Lamont Cranston and his mysterious alter ego, the Shadow, who uses psychic powers to render himself invisible at will. The famous thirties' pulp crime-fighter takes on a descendant of Genghis Khan who's out to conquer the world with a pre-Second World War nuclear device in *Highlander* director Russell Mulcahy's flight of comic-strip fantasy. It's stuffed with fun clichés of the genre, and the spectacle of the exquisite design easily matches the visual punch of the special effects. Unfortunately, the flashy production values rather overshadow the performances of Baldwin and the star-studded supporting cast, while the plot rarely grips. Contains swearing and violence.

Alec Baldwin Lamont Cranston/The Shadow • **John Lone** Shiwan Khan • **Penelope Ann Miller** Margo Lane • **Peter Boyle** Moe Shrevnitz • **Ian McKellen** Reinhardt Lane • **Tim Curry** Farley Claymore • **Jonathan Winters** Wainwright Barth • **Sab Shimono** Dr Tam • **Andre Gregory** Burbank • **Brady Tsurutani** Tulku • **James Hong** Li Peng • **Arsenio "Sonny" Trinidad** Wu • **Joseph Maher** Isaac Newboldt • **John Kapelos** Duke Rollins • **Max Wright** Berger
Director *Russell Mulcahy*
Screenplay *David Koepp, from the characters created by Walter Gibson*
Producer *Joseph Nemec III*
Cinematographer *Stephen H Burum*
Music *Jerry Goldsmith*

SFacts

The Shadow, who made his radio debut in 1931, had his own show from 1937 to 1955, initially starring Orson Welles as Lamont Cranston, before he went on to stun the nation with his *War of the Worlds*.

The Shadow Men ★★ 12

1997 US Colour 90mins

This was the original *Men in Black*, but these dark-suited characters are a far cry from Will Smith and Tommy Lee Jones. The Shadow Men here are a sinister force out to silence Eric Roberts and Sherilyn Fenn, who have inadvertently witnessed extraterrestrial activity. It's *The X Files* on the cheap, but this made-for-TV result is entertaining enough, and Dean Stockwell adds a touch of class in a supporting role.

Eric Roberts Bob Wilson • **Sherilyn Fenn** Dez Wilson • **Dean Stockwell** Stan Mills •

Brendon Ryan Barrett Andy Wilson • **Andrew Prine** First man in black • **Chris McCarty** Second man in black • **Tom Poster** Third man in black • **Valerie Swift** Jane
Director *Timothy Bond*
Screenplay *Eric Miller, Justin Stanley*

Shadowman ★★★★★

1973 Fr/It Colour 87mins

This movie spin-off from Georges Franju's TV serial *Nuits Rouges* was inspired by the novels of Pierre Souvestre and Marcel Allain. One of these, *Fantomas*, was brought to the screen by silent maestro Louis Feuillade, whose visual style is evident in almost every frame and whose grandson Jacques Champreux plays the anti-heroic lead attempting to track down the outlawed Knights Templar in order to steal their golden horde. With every street secreting a hidden passage, each character a perfectly observed archetype and no opportunity missed to glory in a futuristic gadget or gimmick, this is comic book with class. In French with English subtitles.

Jacques Champreux The Man • **Gayle Hunnicut** The Woman • **Gert Fröbe [Gert Frobe]** Sorbier • **Josephine Chaplin** Martine • **Ugo Pagliani** Paul • **Patrick Préjean** Seraphin • **Clément Harari** Dutreuil • **Henry Lincoln** Prof Petri
Director *Georges Franju*
Screenplay *Jacques Champreux*

Shadowzone ★★★ 18

1990 US Colour 84mins

In this intriguing and competent low-budget shocker, a team of scientists working in an isolated underground complex investigate the mysteries of dreams and long-term sleep but accidentally unleash a shape-shifting monster from another dimension. One of literally countless *Alien* rip-offs, but director/writer JS Cardone displays considerable flair by heightening the sense of foreboding inherent within the claustrophobic set design and pumping up the suspense. Although, like so many of these movies, the unveiling of the monster is a big let-down. Louise Fletcher is excellent in the lead which begs the question why her career never hit the heights it deserved to after winning that Oscar for *One Flew Over the Cuckoo's Nest*.

Louise Fletcher Dr Erhardt • **Miguel A Nunez Jr** Wiley • **David Beecroft** Captain Hickock • **Lu Leonard** Mrs Cutter • **James Hong** Dr Van Fleet • **Shawn Weatherly** Dr Kidwell • **Frederick Flynn** Tommy Shivers
Director/Screenplay *JS Cardone*
Executive producer *Charles Band*

The Shape of Things to Come ★ PG

1979 Can Colour 94mins

This shoestring TV-movie version of the HG Wells novel that inspired the 1936 classic *Things to Come* is a sorry endeavour, indeed. Clearly director George McCowan didn't have the resources to create a credible lunar colony. But in excusing the fact that the space storm has homemade stamped all over it and that the robotic army is limited to around four animated tin cans, it's difficult to see how he could have made a worse job of marshalling his cast, with the erratic Jack Palance disappointing as he attempts to impose his authority on a band of post-apocalyptic exiles.

Jack Palance Omus • **Carol Lynley** Niki • **Barry Morse** Dr John Caball • **John Ireland** Senator Smedley • **Nicholas Campbell** Jason Caball • **Eddie Benton [Anne-Marie Martin]** Kim Smedley • **Bill Lake** Astronaut
Director *George McCowan*
Screenplay *Martin Lager, Mike Cheda, Joseph Glazner, from the novel by HG Wells*
Cinematographer *Reginald Morris* •
Special effects *Bill Wood, Wally Gentleman*

She ★ 18

1982 It Colour 100mins

This tacky, post-apocalyptyic take on H Rider Haggard's story bears little resemblance to other versions of the tale – apart from the scene that has lead actress Sandahl Bergman bathing nude in a fountain of eternal youth. Otherwise, Israeli writer/director Avi Nesher throws everything into the mix – vampires, mutants, armour-plated heroes, cloned comedians, levitation – in a lame attempt at parodying sci-fi and television culture. Sixties sword-and-sandal regular Gordon Mitchell plays the ugly villain; bizarrely, the soundtrack is supplied by Justin Heyward, Rick Wakeman and Motörhead.

Sandahl Bergman She • **David Goss** Tom • **Quin Kessler** Shanda • **Harrison Muller** Dick • **Elena Wiedermann** Hari • **Gordon Mitchell** Hector • **Laurie Sherman** Taphir • **Andrew McLeay** Tark
Director *Avi Nesher*
Screenplay *Avi Nesher, from the novel by H Rider Haggard*

The She-Creature ★★

1956 US BW 80mins

The Great Lombardi hypnotises sexy Marla English back to prehistoric times, and has her reptilian alter ego materialise in the present to help him and money-grabbing promoter Tom Conway con the police. He predicts a murder and the scaly, large-breasted amphibian carries it out. One of those bonkers fifties sci-fi quickies that are so awful they become irresistibly compelling. Incidentally, the monster itself is quite an impressive work of trash art.

Chester Morris Carlo Lombardi • **Marla English** Andrea • **Tom Conway** Timothy Chappel • **Cathy Downs** Dorothy • **Lance Fuller** Ted Erickson • **Ron Randell** Lieutenant James • **Frieda Inescort** Mrs Chappel • **Frank Jenks** Police sergeant
Director *Edward L Cahn*
Screenplay *Lou Rusoff, from his play*

She Devil ★

1957 US BW 77mins

A suspense-free, over-talkative bust from Kurt Neumann, director of the far more impressive fifties landmarks *Rocketship X-M*, *Kronos* and *The Fly*. Dying Mari Blanchard's hair colour changes from blonde to brunette when she's given an experimental tuberculosis serum, distilled from fruit flies by scientist Jack Kelly, causing her to develop Jekyll-and-Hyde-type murderous tendencies. Neumann's poor version of John Jessel's short story *The Adaptive Ultimate* is pretty wretched on all artistic levels, although fifties sexpot Blanchard does add a certain erotic aura to her chameleon character.

Albert Dekker Dr Bach • **Jack Kelly** Dr Daniel Scott • **Mari Blanchard** Kyra Zelas • **Marie Blake** Hannah • **John Archer** Kendall • **Fay Baker** Mrs Kendall • **Paul Cavanagh** Sugar Daddy
Director *Kurt Neumann*
Screenplay *Kurt Neumann, Carroll Young, from the story "The Adaptive Ultimate" by John Jessel*
Cinematographer *Karl Struss*

Shirley Thompson versus the Aliens ★★

1968 Aus Colour and BW 104mins

Seven years before directing the queen of cult movies *The Rocky Horror Picture Show*, Jim Sharman brought, with far less success, one of his own Australian stage musicals to the screen. Fifties suburban teen rebel Shirley (Jane Harders) gets lost in Sydney's Luna Park and meets up with aliens in drag as Hells Angels. She then spends the next ten years trying to convey her discovery to friends and the authorities, while slowly going mad in the process. Flashy, annoyingly experimental and over-indulgent, Sharman's self-described "psycho thriller cum fifties rock musical science fiction fantasy'" is an intermittently engaging failure. Ron Haddrick plays a wax model of the Duke of Edinburgh, the spokesperson for the alien visitors.

Jane Harders Shirley Thompson • **John Likoxitch** Bruce • **Tim Eliott** George • **June Collins** • **Marion Johns** Rita • **John Llewellyn** Reg • **Ron Haddrick** Duke of Edinburgh • **Helmut Bakaitis** Harold
Director *Jim Sharman*
Screenplay *Jim Sharman, Helmut Bakaitis*

Shivers ★★★★ 18

1975 Can Colour 84mins

David Cronenberg's first important horror film may now look a little crude, but the obsessions that would colour his later works are already apparent. The story is centred around a vaguely futuristic apartment complex where a parasite is gradually working its way through the occupants, transforming them into sex-obsessed zombies. It's not exactly subtle, but Cronenberg delights in some stomach-churning imagery and the stark, chilling design would later be revisited in films such as *Dead Ringers* and *The Fly*. There are no big names in the cast, although horror aficionados will be pleased to see the presence of Hammer stalwart Barbara Steele. Contains swearing and violence.

Paul Hampton Roger St Luc • **Joe Silver** Rollo Linsky • **Lynn Lowry** Forsythe • **Alan Migicovsky** Nicholas Tudor • **Susan Petrie** Janine Tudor • **Barbara Steele** Betts • **Ronald Mlodzik** Merrick
Director/Screenplay *David Cronenberg*

Shock Waves ★★★ 15

1975 US Colour 84mins

Survivors of a shipwreck are washed up on a tropical island where fugitive Gestapo officer Peter Cushing is busy re-animating drowned Nazi soldiers to form a zombie army. Relying more on atmosphere and tension than gore or jolts, Ken Wiederhorn's directorial debut is a genuinely eerie cult favourite featuring a fine performance from Cushing as evil personified. The sub-aqueous undead marching along the ocean floor in jackboots is one of the creepiest sequences in this Florida-shot independent, which also stars John Carradine, the king of B-movie horror, as the doomed sea captain. A surprisingly effective shocker that's well worth a look.

Peter Cushing Scar, SS Commander • **John Carradine** Captain Ben • **Brooke Adams** Rose • **Fred Buch** Chuck • **Jack Davidson** Norman • **Luke Halpin** Keith • **D J Sidney** Beverly • **Don Stout** Dobbs
Director *Ken Wiederhorn*
Screenplay *John Harrison, Ken Wiederhorn*

Shocker ★ 18

1989 US Colour 104mins

A bit like *Nightmare on Elm Street*, *Prison* and *Carrie* but with all the wrong bits, this dud from Wes Craven charts the murderous exploits of an electrocuted maniac TV repair man who can appear wherever someone switches on a set. Sci-fi TV fans will recognise the television bogeyman Horace Pinker as Mitch Pileggi, who went on to play Director Skinner in *The X Files*. Confusing, tedious, far too long and decidedly unshocking, it's a shame such a neat concept was wasted by Craven in his worst movie.

Michael Murphy Lt Don Parker • **Peter Berg** Jonathan Parker • **Mitch Pileggi** Horace Pinker • **Cami Cooper [Camille Cooper]** Alison
Director/Screenplay *Wes Craven*

SCI Q

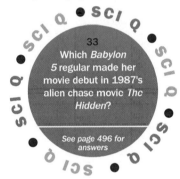

33
Which *Babylon 5* regular made her movie debut in 1987's alien chase movie *The Hidden*?

See page 496 for answers

Short Circuit ★★★ PG

1986 US Colour 94mins

A government robot gets struck by lightning, goes Awol, takes on hilarious human characteristics and befriends vegetarian animal lover Ally Sheedy. Meanwhile, the machine's goofy inventor, Steve Guttenberg, must locate his missing Number Five model. Cue madcap misadventures, during which our cute cyborg mimics John Wayne, the Three Stooges and John Travolta. Youngsters will especially love this hip spoof on hardware movies, neatly directed with the lightest of touches by John Badham. Others may find Number Five's incessant whine of "Stephanie" a little grating and start reaching for a handy screwdriver. Contains some swearing.

Ally Sheedy Stephanie Speck • **Steve Guttenberg** Newton Crosby • **Fisher Stevens** Ben Jabituya • **Austin Pendleton** Howard Marner • **GW Bailey** Skroeder • **Brian McNamara** Frank • **Tim Blaney** Number Five
Director *John Badham*
Screenplay *SS Wilson, Brent Maddock*

Short Circuit 2 ★★ PG

1988 US Colour 105mins

This sequel about the former military robot Number Five, now Johnny Five, has several moments of humour (becoming involved with a bank robbery, for example), but too many minutes of tedium as it wonders whether to be social satire or pratfall parody. Fisher Stevens returns as the Indian co-inventor of the robot, and again his clichéd character is infuriating, representing the kind of prejudice Johnny Five is supposed to be against. Contains swearing.

Fisher Stevens Ben Jahrvi • **Michael McKean** Fred Ritter • **Cynthia Gibb** Sandy Banatoni • **Jack Weston** Oscar Baldwin • **Dee McCafferty** Saunders • **David Hemblen** Jones • **Don Lake** Manic Mike • **Damon D'Oliveira** Bones • **Tito Nunez** Zorro • **Tim Blaney** Johnny Five • **Jason Kuriloff** Lil Man • **Robert LaSardo** Spooky • **Lili Francks** Officer Mendez • **Wayne Best** Officer O'Malley • **Gerry Parkes** Priest • **Adam Ludwig** Hans de Ruyter • **Rex Hagon** Dartmoor • **Rummy Bishop** Newsvendor • **Richard Comar** Mr Slater
Director *Kenneth Johnson*
Screenplay *SS WIlson, Brent Maddock*

Sierra Nine ★★★

TV 1963 UK BW 13x30mins

This 13-part Associated Rediffusion UK series featured a special organision, S9, set up to keep a watching eye on anything which may threaten life on Earth, whether that be a miniature atomic warhead, telepathic hypnosis, potions which confer eternal life and, of course, the obligatory death ray. Preceeding *Doctor Who* and its Unit organisation by some five years, *Sierra Nine* starred Max Kirby as Sir Willoughby Dodd, David Sumner as Doctor Peter Chance and Deborah Stanford as Anna Parsons. The guest cast featured in the four individual stories were impressive: David Garth, Norman Mitchell, Jack May, Peter Halliday, Rodney Bewes and Ivor Salter.

Max Kirby Sir Willoughby Dodd • **David Sumner** Dr Peter Chance • **Deborah Stanford** Anna Parsons
Written by *Peter Hayes*

The Silence of Dr Evans ★★★

1973 USSR BW 90mins

An inspired piece of casting sheds new light on this Soviet parable. Half a century after he appeared in *The Extraordinary Adventures of Mr West in the Land of the Bolsheviks* (in which a sceptical American comes to embrace communism), Leonid

Obolensky co-starred in this subtle inversion, in which a trio of aliens arrive on Earth to discover it's a planet utterly unprepared to receive the wisdom of their civilisation. The scientist whom they befriend (played by the great director Sergei Bondarchuk) reaches a similar conclusion and abandons his research around longevity. It's often unbearably preachy, but a bold venture nevertheless. A Russian language film.

Sergei Bondarchuk Dr Evans • **Zhanna Bolotova** • **I Kuznetsov** • **Leonid Obolensky** • **Irina Skobtseva**
Director/Screenplay *Budimir Metalnikov*

The Silencers ★★ 18

1995 US Colour 96mins

This isn't the spy spoof that launched Dean Martin's Matt Helm series, and don't be fooled by the fact that there are several close encounters with "Men in Black". This is sci-fi, but strictly of the third-rate kind. Director Richard Pepin clearly hoped to overcome his budgetary restrictions by recalling the alien invasion pictures of the fifties. But neither undercover agent Jack Scalia's discovery of a plot involving government officials and an army of shape-changing ETs nor his alliance with Dennis Christopher's intergalactic troubleshooter is going to hook anyone but genre fanatics.

Jack Scalia Chuck Rafferty • **Dennis Christopher** Comdor
Director *Richard Pepin*
Screenplay *Joseph John Barmettler, from a story by Joseph John Barmettler, Richard Preston Jr, William Applegate Jr*

Silent Rage ★ 18

1982 US Colour 95mins

Chuck Norris doesn't say much in his movies, which is just as well given scripts like this one. As a former karate champion turned actor he lets his feet do the talking. Here we discover him in one of those small Texas towns that seem to have sheriffs like Chuck – especially when an axe killer he's already dealt with is back in town. But now he's been genetically engineered by an insane scientist, so the psychopath is not just mad and bad but indestructible (well, nearly) as well. Norris looks bemused, as well as he might, in a preposterously silly film which is less fun than it should be.

Chuck Norris Dan Stevens • **Ron Silver** Dr Tom Halman • **Steven Keats** Dr Philip Spires • **Toni Kalem** Alison Halman • **William Finley** Dr Paul Vaughn • **Brian Libby** John Kirby • **Stephen Furst** Charlie
Director *Michael Miller*
Screenplay *Joseph Fraley*

Silent Running ★★★★ U

1971 US Colour 85mins

Special-effects ace Douglas Trumbull (of *2001* fame) turned director with this ecologically based science-fiction thriller about the last of Earth's plant-life preserved on the *Valley Forge* spaceship, lovingly cared for by space ranger Bruce Dern and his three cute "drone" robots. Dern mutinies when orders arrive to destroy the precious cargo. Although the film may seem rather hippy-influenced now – those syrupy Joan Baez ballads! – Trumbull's gentle direction highlights a sensitive performance by Dern, and there are some spectacular images of the spacecraft floating between planets, exploding suns and solar storms. Imaginative and much admired.

Bruce Dern Freeman Lowell • **Cliff Potts** Wolf • **Ron Rifkin** Barker • **Jesse Vint** Keenan • **Mark Persons** Drone • **Steven Brown** Drone • **Cheryl Sparks** Drone • **Larry Whisenhunt** Drone
Director *Douglas Trumbull*
Screenplay *Deric Washburn, Mike Cimino, Steve Bocho*

SFacts

John Dykstra, later to find fame as a special effects wizard on films such as *Star Wars Episode IV: a New Hope* and *Star Trek: the Motion Picture*, was a college student when Douglas Trumball hired him to work on this film, along with other students, which helped keep the costs down.

Silver Dust ★★★

1953 USSR BW 102mins

Having frequently fallen foul of the Kremlin with films positing the notion of socio-economic equality, Abram Room plumped for the safer option of knocking the enemy in this unsubtle but undeniably perspicacious piece of Cold War propaganda. Exploitative business practices, racial intolerance, lynch mob justice and irresponsible science are just some of the charges lodged against the States as boffin M Bolduman is courted by rival tycoons (complete with fascistic henchmen) for possession of his radioactive powder. Angered at having the mirror held so close to their faces, certain sections of the American media whipped up a storm of protest. A Russian language film.

M Bolduman • **Valentina Ushakova** • **Vladimir Larionov** • **A Chanov**
Director *Abram Room*
Screenplay *Aleksandr Filimonov, August Jakobson*
Cinematographer *Edouard Tissé* • ***Special effects*** *P Malaniksev*

Simon ★★ PG

1980 US Colour 93mins

This half-baked satirical comedy from Woody Allen associate Marshall Brickman (the pair shared *Annie Hall's* best screenplay Oscar) is too clever by half. In truth, it's not funny where it's meant to be, and tiresome long before it reaches its conclusion. But there's some compensation in Alan Arkin's strong central performance as a professor of psychology who's brainwashed into thinking he's an alien, and clever support from a cast clearly hand-picked for their eccentricity: bucktoothed Austin Pendleton, sexy Madeline Kahn, Fred Gwynne from *The Munsters* and the great, slack-jawed Adolph Green, co-author of *Singin' in the Rain* and *The Band Wagon*. Contains swearing.

Alan Arkin Simon Mendelssohn • **Madeline Kahn** Cynthia • **Austin Pendleton** Becker • **Judy Graubart** Lisa • **William Finley** Fichandler • **Jayant** Barundi • **Wallace Shawn** Van Dongen • **Max Wright** Hundertwasser • **Fred Gwynne** Korey • **Adolph Green** Commune leader
Director/Screenplay *Marshall Brickman*

Sinners in Silk ★★★

1924 US BW

What with *Black Oxen* and *Vanity's Price* appearing about the same time, eternal youth was clearly a hot topic in 1924. Louis B Mayer personally produced this high-society melodrama, which was given a whisper of sensationalism by its incestuous undertone. Little attention is paid to the scientific process by which Jean Hersholt relieves ageing roué Adolphe Menjou of 20 years. Instead, director Hobart Henley concentrates on the fact that Menjou and his dashing son, Conrad Nagel, are in competition for the affections of the ravishing Eleanor Boardman. The sudden resolution leaves all sorts of unsatisfactory loose ends, but it's expertly performed.

Adolphe Menjou Arthur Merrill • **Eleanor Boardman** Penelope Stevens • **Conrad Nagel** Brock Farley • **Jean Hersholt** Dr Eustace • **Edward Connelly** Bates • **Jerome Patrick** Jerry Hall • **Hedda Hopper** Mrs Stevens
Director *Hobart Henley*
Screenplay *Carey Wilson, from a story by Benjamin Glazer*
Cinematographer *John Arnold*

Sir, You Are a Widower ★★★

1971 Cz BW 90mins

Vlastimil Brodsky might have performed organ transplants in the Pavel Hobl's Czech farce *The Lost Face* (1965), but that film can't hold a candle to this offering from Vaclav Vorlicek and co-scenarist Milos Macourek, two masters of the macabre medical comedy. Star of the show is undoubtedly Iva Janzurova, who takes on a trio of roles – an actress, a killer and a respectable housewife who is made completely of spare body parts. However, subplots involving a king who can't salute his subjects and an incompetent psychic also offer juicy parts for Vorlicek regulars Jiri Sovak and Olga Schoberova. A Czech language film.

Iva Janzurova Evelyna Kelettiova • **Olga Schoberova** Molly Adamsova • **Eduard Cupak** Col Steiner • **Jiri Sovak** King Josef IV • **Frantisek Filipovsky** King Oskar XV • **Jan Libicek** Bobo • **Jiri Hrzan** Stuart Hample

Director *Vaclav Vorlicek*

Screenplay *Milos Macourek, Vaclav Vorlicek, from their story*

Cinematographer *Vaclav Hanus*

SCI Q • SCI Q • SCI Q • SCI Q •

34

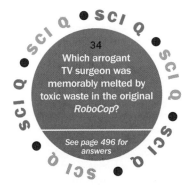

Which arrogant TV surgeon was memorably melted by toxic waste in the original *RoboCop*?

See page 496 for answers

Siren of Atlantis ★★

1948 US BW 75mins

Only camp followers of sultry forties star Maria Montez will put up with this inept fantasy showing the "Cobra Woman" posturing, pouting and slinking her way through a cobbled-together slice of exotica. La Montez stars as Queen Antinea, cruel ruler of the lost kingdom of Atlantis, found by French Legionnaires Jean-Pierre Aumont (Montez's husband) and Dennis O'Keefe when they stumble on a secret passage in the desert. Shot by three directors, including Arthur Ripley and John Brahm, and beset by Production Code difficulties over an 18-month period, the resulting film was shoddy stuff even compared to Montez's other daft encounters with lost civilisations. The actress was found drowned in a bathtub three years after the completion of this throwaway programme-filler.

Maria Montez Queen Antinea • **Jean-Pierre Aumont** Andre St Avit • **Dennis O'Keefe** Jean Morhange • **Morris Carnovsky** Le Mesge • **Henry Daniell** Blades • **Alexis Minotis** Cortot • **John Shelton** French officer

Director *Gregg G Tallas [Gregg Tallas]*

Screenplay *Rowland Leigh, Robert Lax, Thomas Job, from the novel "L'Atlantide" by Pierre Benoit*

Cinematographer *Karl Struss*

Special effects *Rocky Cline*

6 Hours to Live ★★

1932 US BW 80mins

What would you do if you were placed in the titular scenario? Assassinated diplomat Warner Baxter certainly manages to pack plenty into his unexpected span after he's miraculously revived in William Dieterle's preposterous melodrama. In addition to preventing his native Sylvaria from signing up to a ruinous trade agreement with an exploitative neighbour, he also manages to persuade his heartbroken lover Miriam Jordan that John Boles is her new Mr Right. George F Marion's cranky scientist might have resuscitated Baxter, but not even the stylish Dieterle (making the fourth of his six 1932 features) could breathe life into this stillborn hokum.

Warner Baxter Paul Onslow • **Miriam Jordan** Valerie von Sturm • **John Boles** Karl Kranz • **George Marion Sr [George F Marion]** Prof Otto Bauer • **Halliwell Hobbes** Baron Emil von Sturm • **Irene Ware** The woman • **Beryl Mercer** The widow • **Edward McWade** Ivan

Director *William Dieterle*

Screenplay *Bradley King, from the story "Auf Wiedersehen" by Gordon Morris, Morton Barteaux*

Cinematographer *John Seitz*

The Six Million Dollar Man ★★★★ U PG

TV 1974-78 US Colour 3x90m; 100x60m [video]

"We can rebuild him, we have the technology." When astronaut and Nasa test pilot Colonel Steve Austin (former football player Lee Majors) is injured in a plane crash his shattered limbs are replaced with bionic ones, bestowing on him superhuman strength. Recruited by spy master Oscar Goldman (Richard Anderson), Steve Austin becomes a top government agent fighting aliens, terrorists, even Bigfoot. Following on from three pilots screened in 1973, what turned out to be one of the most popular series of the seventies was almost cancelled early in its second season. To boost ratings a love element was introduced in the form of Steve Austin's high school sweetheart Jaime Sommers, played by Lindsay Wagner, who critically injured in a parachuting accident becomes the Bionic Woman and got her own equally successful spin-off series. The series's enduring appeal resulted in two reunion TV movies in the eighties and another in 1994 in which Austin and Sommers finally married.

Lee Majors Colonel Steve Austin • **Richard Anderson** Oscar Goldman • **Jennifer Darling** Peggy Callahan • **Martin E Brooks** Dr Rudy Wells • **Lindsay Wagner** Jaime Sommers • **Alan Oppenheimer** Dr Rudy Wells (Series 1)

Source *from the novel "Cyborg" by Martin Caidin*

Executive producer *Harve Bennett*

The 6th Day ★★★★ 15

2000 US/Can Colour 123mins [video] DVD

Easily the most satisfying slice of science fiction Arnold Schwarzenegger has appeared in since *Terminator 2*, director Roger Spottiswoode's futuristic thriller is fast-paced fare. Exploring similar themes to *Total Recall*, it depicts the moral hell mankind could unleash if DNA tampering isn't properly regulated. When ex-fighter pilot Schwarzenegger discovers he has been illegally cloned, he embarks on a turbo-charged mission to get his identity back and expose the corrupt organisation behind the experiment. Even if the plot doesn't bear close scrutiny, the movie packs some surprise twists and builds to a chilling climax. Schwarzenegger looks a little too old and tired for the kick-ass lead, and his stiffly delivered, trademark one-liners often get in the way of the serious issues raised, but the strong supporting cast compensates. This is what science-fiction film-making should be about – dark speculation, a sense of wonder and ace special effects. Contains violence and swearing.

Arnold Schwarzenegger Adam Gibson • **Michael Rapaport** Hank Morgan • **Tony Goldwyn** Michael Drucker • **Michael Rooker** Robert Marshall • **Sarah Wynter** Talia Elsworth • **Rod Rowland [Rodney Rowland]** Wiley • **Terry Crews** Vincent • **Ken Pogue** Speaker Day • **Colin Cunningham** Tripp • **Robert Duvall** Dr Griffin Weir • **Don S Davis** Cardinal de la Jolla

Director *Roger Spottiswoode*

Screenplay *Cormac Wibberley, Marianne Wibberley*

Skeeter ★ 15

1993 US Colour 91mins

It's the old story about radiation mutating insects into bigger and deadlier versions of themselves, but a slower and sometimes even shoddier retelling. It all takes place in the desert, which conveniently doesn't require many sets or complicated shots to arrange. An evil industrialist dumps toxic waste in an abandoned mine, which gets into a water supply full of mosquito eggs, and very low-budget havoc erupts. The only lifts in the doldrums come when cult stars Charles Napier and Michael J Pollard appear.

Jim Youngs Boone • **Tracy Griffith** Sarah • **Michael J Pollard** Hopper • **Charles Napier** Sheriff Buckle • **Jay Robinson** Drake • **William Sanderson** Gordon Perry
Director *Clark Brandon*
Screenplay *Clark Brandon, Lanny Horn, from an idea by Joe Rubin*

Sky ★★

TV 1976 UK Colour 7x30mins

Created for children, but a series that captured the imagination of their parents as well, *Sky* was about a visiting alien (Mark Harrison) on a mysterious mission who is aided by three teenagers (Richart Speight, Stuart Lock and Cherrald Butterfield). While the occasionally confusing mysticism sometimes bogged down the plotline, the series – written by *Doctor Who* alumni Bob Baker and Dave Martin – presented powerful themes for a younger audience.

Mark Harrison Sky • **Richard Speight** Roy Briggs • **Stuart Locke** Arby Vennor • **Cherrald Butterfield** Jane Vennor
Director *Derek Clark*
Written by *Bob Baker, Dave Martin*
Executive producer *Patrick Dromgoole* •
Producer *Leonard White*

Sky Pirates ★★ PG

1986 Aus Colour 83mins

John Hargreaves does his best as the pilot flying into a time warp, in this Australian attempt to recapture the excitement and adventure of the old Saturday morning serials. But, whereas Spielberg and Lucas showed in their *Indiana Jones* escapades that the secret of remaking old B-movies for modern audiences is to apply A-movie polish and production values, this effort struggles at points to rise above C-movie standards of either writing or effects.

John Hargreaves Flight Lieutenant Harris • **Meredith Phillips** Melanie Mitchell • **Max Phipps** Squadron Leader Savage • **Bill Hunter** O'Reilly • **Simon Chilvers** Reverend Kenneth Mitchell • **Alex Scott** General Hackett
Director *Colin Eggleston*
Screenplay *John Lamond*

The Sky Ranger ★★★

1921 US BW

This is the ninth of the 19 chapterplays directed by "Serial King" George B Seitz. He also found himself in front of the camera in this silent 15-part escapade, as the boyfriend of June Caprice, whose father, Frank Redman, has locked horns with fellow inventor Harry Semels (who also happens to be a megalomanic mesmerist). But the key to the battle between Redman's interstellar laser ray and Semels's silent superplane is the latter's daughter, Peggy Shanon, who has more than a few conscience-*v*-loyalty issues. The opening sequences featuring Seitz and a mystic are downright peculiar. But the remainder is top-notch escapism.

June Caprice June Elliot • **George B Seitz** George Rockwell • **Harry Semels** Dr Santro • **Peggy Shanon** Peggy Santro • **Frank Redman** Mr Elliot
Director *George B Seitz*

Slapstick of Another Kind ★★

1982 US Colour 87mins

The handful of attempts made to bring the work of cult novelist Kurt Vonnegut to the big screen have all met with less than resounding success. *Slapstick of Another Kind* is no exception. A would-be satirical comedy about the birth of huge, hideously ugly twins (Jerry Lewis and Madeline Kahn) who in reality are super-intelligent beings from another planet, the film widely misses the mark. A strong cast ensure that some good moments survive but it demonstrates the difficulty certain idiosyncratic novelists have with their on-screen adaptations. This was unseen in the US until 1984.

Jerry Lewis Wilbur Swain/Caleb Swain • **Madeline Kahn** Eliza Swain/Letitia Swain • **Marty Feldman** Sylvester • **John Abbott** Dr Frankenstein • **Jim Backus** United States President • **Samuel Fuller** Colonel Sharp • **Merv Griffin** Anchorman • **Pat Morita** Ah Fong • **Orson Welles** Alien Father
Director *Steven Paul*
Screenplay *Steven Paul, from the novel "Slapstick" by Kurt Vonnegut Jr*

Slaughterhouse-Five ★★★★

1972 US Colour 102mins

Kurt Vonnegut's science-fiction masterpiece is done marvellous justice by director George Roy Hill's wildly complex, truly bizarre and poignant commentary on the absurdity of human existence. In this postmodern *Pilgrim's Progress*, Michael Sacks is Billy Pilgrim, a man "unstuck in time" who constantly leaves the present to either return to the past, when he was a prisoner of war in Dresden, or flit to the future, where his existence with half-naked actress Valerie Perrine is viewed under glass by aliens. A wry, intelligent and thought-provoking parable with a haunting surreal quality.

Michael Sacks Billy Pilgrim • **Ron Leibman** Paul Lazzaro • **Eugene Roche** Derby • **Sharon Gans** Valencia • **Valerie Perrine** Montana Wildhack • **Roberts Blossom** Wild Bob Cody • **Sorrell Booke** Lionel Merble • **Kevin Conway** Weary
Director *George Roy Hill*
Screenplay *Stephen Geller, from the novel by Kurt Vonnegut Jr*
Cinematographer *Miroslav Ondricek*

Slave Girls from beyond Infinity ★ 18

1987 US Colour 71mins

An inspired title masks an atrocious jiggle junk remake of that perennial favourite, *The Most Dangerous Game*. Bikini-clad space bimbos Cindy Beal, Elizabeth Cayton and fantasy pin-up icon Brinke Stevens must escape the laser crossbow of a castle-dwelling mad human hunter and his decapitation-programmed androids. High on topless shots but inanely rock bottom in every other department, producer/director Ken Dixon's stage-bound and slow-moving snooze-fest is a typical product from the early straight-to-video days where fun entertainment took a back seat to pandering sexploitation.

Elizabeth Cayton Daria • **Cindy Beal** Tisa • **Brinke Stevens** Shela • **Don Scribner** Zed • **Carl Horner** Rik • **Kirk Graves** Vak
Director/Screenplay *Ken Dixon*

Sleeper ★★★ PG

1973 US Colour 83mins DVD

With this energetic but over-eager tribute to such silent clowns as Charlie Chaplin, Buster Keaton, Harry Langdon and Harold Lloyd, Woody Allen proved once and for all that his talents did not lie in physical comedy. Fun though some of the slapstick is, it's Allen's satirical view of the future and his priceless one-liners that linger longest in the memory. Once more he strikes up an effortless rapport with Diane Keaton, but too many of the other characters fail to register, while the plot too often slows down the comic pace. The costumes were designed by none other than *Batman and Robin* director Joel Schumacher. Contains swearing.

Woody Allen Miles Monroe • **Diane Keaton** Luna Schlosser • **John Beck** Erno Windt • **Marya Small** Dr Nero • **Bartlett Robinson** Dr Orva • **Mary Gregory** Dr Melik • **Chris Forbes** Rainer Krebs
Director *Woody Allen*
Screenplay *Woody Allen, Marshall Brickman*
Costume designer *Joel Schumacher*

SCI Q

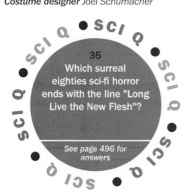

35
Which surreal eighties sci-fi horror ends with the line "Long Live the New Flesh"?

See page 496 for answers

Sleeping Dogs ★★

1997 US/Can Colour 90mins

This doggedly predictable attempt at "*Die Hard* in space" is stuck firmly in the B-movie doldrums. The contrived plot has Scott McNeil rescuing Heather Hanson from villain C Thomas Howell's emerald factory just as a police raid is under way. Hiding in a packing crate, the pair find themselves being shipped to a prison colony along with the imprisoned Howell. When a meteor storm results in Howell being freed from in stasis, he revives his sidekicks – including sexy cyborg Zee 4R – and commandeers the space vessel. Howell rants, raves and shamelessly hams it up in this tepid TV action thriller that wants to duplicate the engaging atmosphere of *Fortress*. Sadly, director Michael Barafo doesn't have the savvy or visual smarts to pull it off.

C Thomas Howell Sanchez Boon • **Scott McNeil** Harry Maxwell • **Heather Hanson** Pandora Grimes • **Ciara Hunter [Kiara Hunter]** Zee 4R • **Paul Jarrett** Willy Boy Pruitt • **Richard Toth** Wallace
Director *Michael Bafaro*
Screenplay *Christopher Hyde*

Sliders ★★★ U PG 12

TV 1995-2000 US Colour 86x60mins

Best described as a cross between *The Time Tunnel* and the *Star Trek* franchise's famed "Mirror Universe" episodes, this dimension-crossing adventure series propels a mismatched group of "Sliders" on a tour of parallel Earths. During their quest to return to their home world, the reluctant travellers not only find themselves in a series of weird and wonderful situations, but also learn how life on Earth can be radically altered by only the slightest changes in history. The show is at its best in its amusing and provocative satire-driven first two seasons and its action-orientated fourth year, which pits the Sliders in an ongoing battle against the dimension-conquering Kromaggs. Season five, on the other hand, successfully propels *Sliders* into oblivion, dues to its uninspired scripts and the painful absence of most of the show's original castmembers, including the ever-engaging Jerry O'Connell and deliriously larger-the-life John Rhys-Davies. (A feature-length episode preceded the series.)

Jerry O'Connell Quinn Mallory • **Sabrina Lloyd** Wade Wells • **John Rhys-Davies** Prof Maximillian Arturo • **Cleavant Derricks** Rembrandt Brown • **Kari Wuhrer** Maggie Beckett • **Charlie O'Connell** Colin Mallory • **Robert Floyd** Quinn Mallory (series 5) • **Tembi Locke** Diana Davis
Created by *Tracy Tormé, Robert K Weiss*
Consulting producer *David Peckinpah*

The Slime People ★★★

1963 US BW 60mins

Forties heart-throb Robert Hutton stars in this hoot-a-minute cheapie about prehistoric subterranean mutants who climb out of Los Angeles sewers in the wake of errant nuclear testing in order to erect a dome over the city to regulate the temperature and control the inhabitants. Hutton also directed this, his sole effort, in a warehouse with a tiny cast barely up to the task of memorising the dumb dialogue, which includes the classic line of romantic banter, "When I'm sitting here with you, I don't even think about Slime People"! Solid laughs from start to finish, with the rubber-slime creatures looking more like perambulating rotting vegetables than scary monsters.

Robert Hutton Tom Gregory, the Aviator • **Robert Burton** Professor • **Susan Hart** Lisa, the professor's daughter • **William Boyce** Marine • **Les Tremayne** Norman Tolliver
Director *Robert Hutton*
Screenplay *Vance Skarstedt*
Cinematographer *Wiliam Troiano*

Slipstream ★★ PG

1989 US/UK Colour 87mins

The forgotten man of *Star Wars*, Mark Hamill, attempted to get his career airborne again with a return to the sci-fi genre. However, this muddled, British-shot affair barely got off the ground itself. The concept – a post-apocalyptic world where the favoured form of transportation is the glider – has potential, but director Steven Lisberger never makes up his mind whether this is an escapist fantasy or a more cerebral affair. Nevertheless, the flight sequences are pretty good and there is an eclectic cast that includes Bob Peck, Bill Paxton, Ben Kingsley, F Murray Abraham and Robbie Coltrane.

Mark Hamill Tasker • **Bob Peck** Byron • **Bill Paxton** Matt Owen • **Kitty Aldridge** Belitski • **Tony Allen** Bartender • **Susan Leong** Abigail • **Rita Wolf** Maya • **Eleanor David** Ariel • **Deborah Leng** Girl on swing • **F Murray Abraham** Cornelius • **Ben Kingsley** Avatar • **Robbie Coltrane** Madeleine
Director *Steven Lisberger*
Screenplay *Tony Kayden, Charles Pogue, Steven Lisberger, from a story by Bill Bauer*

Small Wonder ★

TV 1985-1989 US Colour 96x30mins

An ordinary family plays host to an experimental robot, VICI (Voice Input Child Indenticat), who hides her true nature from the outside world by posing as a hyper-cute 10-year-old girl and calling herself Vicki. Vicki's weekly domestic trials and triumphs repeatedly prove to those around her that she's a "small wonder", but will lead viewers to conclude her show would have been more accurately titled *Small Blunder*. Lacking any of the charm and genuine hilarity of the similarly-themed mid-eighties' sci-fi sitcom, *ALF*, this is a sickly sweet one-joke affair. Tiffany Brisset's robotic central performance is more strange than cute, and the show's well-meaning storylines are painfully mechanical.

Dick Christie Ted Lawson • **Marla Pennington** Joan Lawson • **Jerry Supiran** Jamie Lawson • **Emily Schulman** Harriet Brindle • **Tiffany Brissette** VICI, Vicki the robot
Created by *Howard Leeds*
Executive producer *Howard Leeds*

The Snow Creature ★

1954 US BW 66mins

The most abominable Abominable Snowman movie ever made. More cheap fifties fright fare from producer/director W Lee Wilder, sibling of Billy (*Some Like It Hot*) Wilder. Botanist/explorer Paul Langton captures the yeti after it threatens his wife, and ships it home to Los Angeles. Once there, it escapes its cage, goes on a ho-hum rampage and gets chased into the sewers, where it's killed. The yeti – an indescribable creation of badly stitched together fur pelts – is played by Dick Sands, who in 1953 appeared as the creature in Wilder's *Phantom from Space*. The monster is mostly shown here in shadow because it's so risible.

Paul Langton Dr Frank Parrish • **Leslie Denison** Peter Welles • **Teru Shimada** Subra • **Rollin Moriyama** Leva • **Robert Kino** Inspector Karma • **Dick Sands** The Snow Creature
Director *W Lee Wilder*
Screenplay *Myles Wilder*
Cinematographer *Floyd Crosby*

The Snow Devils ★

1965 It BW 78mins

Space explorers Giacomo Rossi-Stuart and Ombretta Colli discover Abominable Snowmen look-alike aliens on the planet Atyia who intend to disturb the Earth's weather to make it more hospitable for their takeover bid. Pretty feeble in all departments – rudimentary acting, incoherent narrative, banal left-field twists – a very minor work from the haphazard career of exploitation maverick Antonio Margheriti. An Italian language film.

Giacomo Rossi-Stuart [Giacomo Rossi Stuart] Commander Rod • **Ombretta Colli** Lisa Nielson • **Renato Baldini** Capt Frank Pulasky
Director *Antonio Margheriti*
Screenplay *Charles Sinclair, William Finger, Ivan Reiner, Moretti [Renato Moretti], from a story by Aubrey Wisberg*

Solar Crisis ★★ 15

1990 Jap/US Colour 107mins

This expensive US/Japan co-production was filled with production problems, including director Richard C Sarafian opting for a pseudonym when the producers dictated additional shooting after the movie bombed in Japan. Despite the new footage, it's easy to see why the movie went straight to video in North America. Though the story of a 21st-century space station crew working to save the broiling Earth by firing a special bomb into the Sun (while industrialist Peter Boyle attempts to sabotage the mission) has plenty of impressive special effects, the proceedings are bogged down by a lack of tension, awe, and excitement.

Charlton Heston Skeet Kelso • **Peter Boyle** Teague • **Tetsuya Bessho** Ken Minami • **Jack Palance** Travis • **Tim Matheson** Steve Kelso • **Annabel Schofield** Alex • **Corin "Corky" Nemec [Corin Nemec]** Mike Kelso • **Brenda Bakke** Claire
Director *Alan Smithee [Richard C Sarafian]*
Screenplay *Joe Gannon, Crispan Bolt [Ted Sarafian], from a novel by Takeshi Kawata*
Music *Maurice Jarre*

Solar Force ★ 18

1994 US Colour 87mins

At first, this looks like it will be a space action flick, concerning the exploits of moon base cop Michael Paré fighting terrorists on his turf. Then it switches into *Road Warrior* territory, when he's sent down to a now-desert Earth to retrieve a stolen formula, fighting off a very tired looking Billy Drago and his motorcycle cohorts. This is ruined by a poor script filled and a sluggish action-filled midsection that could have been easily edited out with no real consequence to the story. Contains violence and swearing.

Michael Paré Joe Brody • **Billy Drago** Kay • **Walker Brandt** Thora • **Robin Smith** Stopper
Director *Boaz Davidson*
Screenplay *Terence P Paré*

Solaris ★★★ PG

1972 USSR Colour 159mins

For some, director Andrei Tarkovsky's philosophical cult movie is the Soviet equivalent of *2001*; for others, it's an obscure intellectual snore-fest. Based on Polish writer Stanislaw Lem's 1961 novel, the tale involves astronauts on an alien planet who are confronted by illusions from their subconscious memories (usually their morose girlfriends back on earth). Tarkovsky's highly influential and cerebral science-fiction epic is ponderous, very talky and contains minimal special effects, but its remote strangeness exerts a compelling hypnotic power that's often extraordinarily potent. In Russian with English subtitles.

Natalya Bondarchuk Hari • **Donatas Banionis** Kris Kelvin • **Yuri Jarvet** Snow • **Anatoli Solonitsin [Anatoli Solonitsyn]** Sartorius • **Vladislav Dvorjetzki** Burton
Director *Andrei Tarkovsky*
Screenplay *Andrei Tarkovsky, Friedrich Gorenstein, from the novel by Stanislaw Lem*

Solarwarriors ★ 15

1986 US Colour 90mins

This feeble futuristic fantasy about roller-skating orphans, arrived too late to cash in on the teen market of the eighties. The orphans, imprisoned by tyrant Richard Jordan, try to bring moisture to a universe as parched as the Yorkshire Water Board. Other science-fiction films are ripped off without mercy, and the kids aren't even all that likeable. Contains violence.

Jami Gertz Terra • **Jason Patric** Jason • **Lukas Haas** Daniel • **Richard Jordan** Grock • **James LeGros** Metron • **Claude Brooks** Rabbit • **Peter DeLuise** Tug • **Adrian Pasdar** Darstar • **Charles Durning** Warden • **Alexei Sayle** Malice
Director *Alan Johnson*
Screenplay *Walon Green, Douglas Anthony Metrov*

Soldier ★ 18

1998 US Colour 94mins DVD

Shane goes to outer space in director Paul (*Event Horizon*) Anderson's depressingly unoriginal slice of science fiction from David Webb Peoples, the writer of *Blade Runner*. Kurt Russell is the brainwashed army killing machine dumped on a garbage planet when a newer DNA manipulated model is developed. There he finds a forgotten outpost of stranded humans who adopt him as their warrior saviour, when Jason Scott Lee's genetically enhanced battalion arrive for practice manoeuvres. With hardly an original bone in its story body, Anderson trots out familiar clichés against a tired post-apocalyptic backdrop with zero emotional engagement, lots of mindless slam-bang action and heaps of unintentional laughs. A by-the-numbers empty spectacle. Contains violence.

Kurt Russell Todd • **Jason Scott Lee** Caine 607 • **Connie Nielsen** Sandra • **Gary Busey** Captain Church • **Michael Chiklis** Jimmy Pig • **Jason Isaacs** Colonel Mekum • **Sean Pertwee** Mace
Director *Paul Anderson*
Screenplay *David Webb Peoples*

Solo ★★ 18

1996 US/Mex Colour 89mins DVD

A pumped-up Mario Van Peebles plays a cyber-soldier who refuses to kill innocent Latin American villagers and becomes their friend, in this derivative, but amiable sci-fi action thriller. You'll recognise themes, scenes and characters from dozens of other movies but Van Peebles isn't bad as a lower budget Arnie and it displays much less violence and more heart than you would expect. That said, there are a few too many moments of unintentional comedy, caused by the ropey macho dialogue and the hammy performances of bad guys William Sadler and Barry Corbin.

Mario Van Peebles Solo • **Barry Corbin** General Clyde Haynes • **William Sadler** Colonel Madden • **Jaime Gomez** Lorenzo • **Adrian Brody** Bill Stewart • **Damian**

Bechir Rio • **Seidy Lopez** Agela • **Abraham Verduzco** Miguel
Director *Norberto Barba*
Screenplay *David Corley, from the novel "Weapon" by Robert Mason*

Something Is Out There ★★ 15

TV 1988 US Colour 12x60mins

This began as a four-hour 1988 miniseries (set in the US but shot in Australia) in which tough cop Joe Cortese and alien blonde Maryam D'Abo track down a "Xenomorph" alien serial killer (designed by effects genius Rick Baker) in the big city, then turned into a short-lived series on the mismatched cop premise as the team tackled mildly weird cases (CIA telekinetic experiments, alien abduction, a crazed ventriloquist). The original is a solid effort with a good monster, but the weekly version is a bit of a waste of time, with plots that seem recycled from any number of other shows. Plans were afoot to liven things up by bringing back the Xenomorph for a two-parter, but the show as cancelled before they could be carried through.

Joe Cortese Jack Breslin • **Maryam D'Abo** Ta'Ra • **Gregory Sierra** Vic Maldano
Created by *Frank Lupo*
Make-up special effects *Rick Baker*

Son of Flubber ★★★ U

1962 US BW 98mins

You will remember that "flubber" was the flying rubber invented by Fred MacMurray in the fun family comedy *The Absent-Minded Professor*. Disney reassembled many of the same cast two years later, but usually reliable director Robert Stevenson could not repeat the winning formula. Most of the jokes about jumping to unfeasible heights had been used up in the original and somehow dry rain and flubber-gas just don't have the same comic potential. Keenan Wynn enjoys himself as the villain and veterans Leon Ames and Charlie Ruggles demonstrate the value of experienced character support.

Fred MacMurray Professor Ned Brainard • **Nancy Olson** Betsy Brainard • **Keenan Wynn** Alonzo Hawk • **Tommy Kirk** Biff Hawk • **Elliott Reid** Shelby Ashton • **Joanna Moore** Desiree de la Roche • **Leon Ames** President Rufus Daggett • **Ed Wynn** A J Allen • **Ken Murray** Mr Hurley • **Charlie Ruggles [Charles Ruggles]** Judge Murdock • **William Demarest** Mr Hummel • **Paul Lynde** Sportscaster
Director *Robert Stevenson*
Screenplay *Bill Walsh, Don DaGradi, from the story "A Situation of Gravity" by Samuel W Taylor, from novels by Jay Williams, Raymond Abrashkin*

Son of Frankenstein ★★★★

1939 US BW 95mins

The third instalment of Universal's classic series features Boris Karloff's last fling as the Monster and is a superior shocker all round. Basil Rathbone (the Baron), Bela Lugosi (Ygor) and Lionel Atwill (the police chief with a noisy artificial arm) all turn in unforgettably eccentric performances along with the ever-imposing Karloff, in his last feature film appearance as Frankenstein's monster. Add Rowland V Lee's eerie direction and the result is a majestically macabre chiller.

Basil Rathbone Baron Wolf von Frankenstein • **Boris Karloff** The Monster • **Bela Lugosi** Ygor • **Lionel Atwill** Inspector Krogh • **Josephine Hutchinson** Elsa von Frankenstein • **Donnie Dunagan** Peter von Frankenstein • **Emma Dunn** Amelia • **Edgar Norton** Benson
Director *Rowland V Lee*
Screenplay *Willis Cooper, from characters created by Mary Shelley*
Make-up *Jack Pierce*

SFacts

Make-up artist Jack Pierce, who didn't like the then current title of "chief cosmetician", was responsible for transforming Karloff in all three of the films. Up to 62lbs of plaster and other materials went into the process of turning the actor into Frankenstein's monster.

Son of Godzilla ★★ U

1967 Jap Colour 81mins

Intense heat from Japanese weather experiments causes cute Godzilla offspring, Minya, to hatch. Then mother must protect her son from a giant hairy spider, and other insect life enlarged by the atmospheric conditions. The eighth in the Toho monster series is an inept juvenile adventure . Japanese dialogue dubbed into English.

Tadao Takashima Dr Kuzumi • **Akira Kubo** Goro
Director *Jun Fukuda*
Screenplay *Shinichi Sekizawa, Kazue Shiba*

Son of Kong ★★★

1933 US BW 69mins

Rushed out within a year of its predecessor *King Kong*'s release, the official sequel took a more light-hearted approach and was dismissed by critics because of the accent on comedy. From a distance it plays as short, inoffensive and good fun. The ludicrous story has Robert Armstrong returning to Skull Island to hunt for treasure and finding the giant ape's cute, albino offspring stuck in quicksand. As always, Willis O'Brien's stop-motion animation is as endearing as it was ground-breaking.

Robert Armstrong Carl Denham • **Helen Mack** Hilda Peterson • **Frank Reicher** Captain Englehorn • **John Marston** Helstrom • **Victor Wong** charlie • **Lee Kohlmar** Mickey
Director *Ernest B Schoedsack*
Screenplay *Ruth Rose*

The Sorcerers ★★★

1967 UK Colour 85mins

Prior to *Witchfinder General* and his death at the age of 24, Michael Reeves directed this intelligent shocker, working along the same lines as Michael Powell with *Peeping Tom*, by questioning the role of vicarious fantasies in cinema. Boris Karloff invents a mesmeric machine to control the mind of bored, swinging Londoner Ian Ogilvy, which can also absorb and pass on the sensations he experiences. Karloff's wife gets hooked on the voyeuristic thrills, and wills the mod zombie to steal and kill. Cult brilliance on a small budget.

Boris Karloff Professor Monserrat • **Catherine Lacey** Estelle Monserrat • **Ian Ogilvy** Mike • **Elizabeth Ercy** Nicole • **Victor Henry** Alan • **Susan George** Audrey
Director *Michael Reeves*
Screenplay *Michael Reeves, Tom Baker, from a idea by John Burke*

Soylent Green ★★★ 15

1973 US Colour 92mins

Charlton Heston is the lone honest cop in a polluted and over-populated 21st-century New York, investigating a murder at the company responsible for a new synthetic food product. Harry Harrison's sober novel has been rather ploddingly adapted with an eye for the box office by director Richard Fleischer as a curious blend of the private eye genre with grim glimpses of a future consumer society run amok, though the film still manages to retain the book's anti-utopian sentiments. Edward G Robinson, in his final performance, gives a very poignant turn as a citizen past his sell-by date. Contains violence.

Charlton Heston Detective Thorn • **Leigh Taylor-Young** Shirl • **Chuck Connors** Tab Fielding • **Joseph Cotten** William Simonson • **Brock Peters** Hatcher • **Paula Kelly** Martha • **Edward G Robinson** Sol Roth • **Stephen Young** Gilbert • **Mike Henry** Kulozik • **Lincoln Kilpatrick** Priest
Director *Richard Fleischer*
Screenplay *Stanley R Greenberg, from the novel "Make Room! Make Room!" by Harry Harrison*

Space ★★★★

TV 1985 US Colour 780mins

Novelist James A Michener's epic account of the US space programme takes flight as a 13-hour mini-series, with suitably stellar results. The saga spans from the Second World War to the early eighties, and primarily follows America's flight to the stars through the eyes of a diverse group of characters headed by a senator, two astronauts, a reporter and a scientist. Like the real-life space programme, this mini-series is slow-moving and frustrating at times, but ultimately emerges as a consistently riveting and extremely rewarding endeavour. James Garner, Harry Hamlin, Beau Bridges and Michael York lead an accomplished cast through the small screen's answer to *The Right Stuff*, and are well served by the mini-series' compelling plotting and strong production values.

James Garner Senator Norman Grant • **Harry Hamlin** John Pope • **Bruce Dern** Stanley Mott • **Blair Brown** Penny Pope • **Beau Bridges** Randy Claggett • **Martin Balsam** Senator Glancy • **Susan Anspach** Elinor Grant • **Roscoe Lee Brown** Farquar • **Melinda Dillon** Rachel Mott • **Michael York** Dieter Kolff

Director *Lee Philips, Joseph Sargent*
Written by *Richard Berg, Silliphant Stirling, from the novel by James A Michener*

Space: Above and Beyond ★★★★ PG

TV 1995-96 US Col 1x120m; 22x60m

The year is 2063, and humanity is at war with an unknown alien race. Propelled to the front line, a group of mismatched rookie space marines fight "above and beyond the call of duty" to save the Earth. A familiar premise is given a superior reworking by former *X Files* producers Glen Morgan and James Wong, who deliver a hard-hitting and powerful sci-fi war show more akin to *All Quiet on the Western Front* than *Star Wars*. The series' excellent writing is capably realised by a sterling cast, convincing production design and some truly high-flying computer-generated effects. As an added bonus, its guest list features several *X Files* alumni, including Fox Mulder himself, David Duchovny. Disappointingly, however, the show was cancelled at the end of its first season, leaving the fates of several key characters – and, indeed, the whole human race, in limbo.

Morgan Weisser Lt Nathan West • **Kristen Cloke** Capt Shane Vansen • **Rodney Rowland** Lt Cooper Hawkes • **Joel de la Fuente** Lt Paul Wang • **Lanei Chapman** Lt Vanessa Damphousse • **James Morrison** Lt Col Tyrus Cassius "TC" McQueen • **Tucker Smallwood** Commodore Glen Van Ross

Created by *Glen Morgan, James Wong*
Executive Producer *Glen Morgan, James Wong*

Space Academy ★★

TV 1977-1979 US Colour 15x30mins

Short-lived series set more than 1,000 years in the future, this children's adventure series followed the lives of young cadets at an elite space school, run by *Lost in Space*'s Dr Smith, Jonathan Harris. The obligatory cute robot was called Peepo, and the friendly alien was played by Eric Greene. A follow-up series, *Jason of Star Command*, began in 1979.

Jonathan Harris Cmdr Isaac Gampu • **Pamelyn Ferdin** Cadet Laura Gentry • **Ric Carrott** Capt Chris Gentry • **Ty Henderson** Lt Paul Jerome • **Maggie Cooper** Cadet Adrian • **Brian Tochi** Tee "Teegar" Garsoom • **Eric Greene** Loki

Director *Arthur H Nadel, Jeffrey Hayden, Ezra Stone, George Tyne*

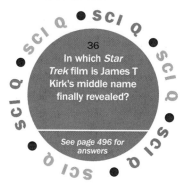

SCI Q • SCI Q • SCI Q • SCI Q

36
In which *Star Trek* film is James T Kirk's middle name finally revealed?

See page 496 for answers

The Space Amoeba ★

1970 Jap Colour 84mins

An unmanned space probe aimed at Jupiter is invaded by an evil, intelligent and invisible force that returns to Earth near a small island south of Japan and starts mutating and controlling the local wildlife including crabs, bats, turtles and squids. Industrial spy Kenji Sahara is also taken over by the alien blue mist and is engulfed by an erupting volcano along with the other giant mutants. The penultimate movie directed by Inoshiro (*Godzilla*) Honda is not up to his usual standard and neither are the pitiful special effects by Sadamasa Arikawa. A Japanese language film.

Akira Kubo Taro Kudo • **Atsuko Takahashi** Ayako Hoshino • **Yoshio Tsuchiya** Kyoichi Miya • **Kenji Sahara** Makoto Obata • **Noritake Saito** Rico • **Yukiko Kobayashi** Saki

Director *Inoshiro Honda*
Screenplay *Ei Ogawa*
Cinematographer *Taiichi Kankura*
Special effects *Sadamasa Arikawa*

Space Cases ★★★

TV 1996-1997 US Colour 26x30mins

Five young cadets from the Starcadamy find themselves lost in an alien galaxy with just two adults and a robot for company in Nickelodeon's short-lived but amiable sci-fi kids' show. Created by popular sci-fi author Peter David and *Lost in Space*/*Babylon 5* star Bill Mumy, the series propels its young cast through 26 lightweight starship-based adventures, which are written and performed firmly with the young at heart in mind. Despite the obvious restraints of its very lean budget, *Space Cases* makes for a delightfully good-natured cosmic caper. The show is also packed with sci-fi in-jokes, and includes guest turns from the likes of *Star Wars*' Mark Hamill, *Star Trek*'s George Takei and Mumy himself.

Walter Emanuel Jones Harland Band • **Kristian Ayre** Radu • **Anik Matern** Thelma • **Rahi Azizi** Bova • **Paige Christina** Rosie Ianni • **Cary Lawrence** TJ Davenport • **Paul Boretski** Commander Seth Goddard

Created by *Peter David, Bill Mumy*

The Space Children ★★★ U

1958 US BW 69mins

Twenty years after serving as Orson Welles's co-director on the legendary *War of the Worlds* radio broadcast, William Alland found himself producing Jack Arnold's very different alien invasion story. Going against the hawkish tone of many contemporary Cold War movies, it centres on the concerted efforts of a giant extraterrestrial brain to convince the kids from a nearby military facility to sabotage their parents' current mission – the launch of a hydrogen bomb into space. With sets by 23-times nominated art director Hal Pereira and some evocative landscapes from Ernest Laszlo, this is a B with pedigree.

Adam Williams Dave Brewster • **Peggy Webber** Anne Brewster • **Michel Ray** Bud Brewster • **John Crawford** Ken Brewster • **Jackie Coogan** Hank Johnson • **Sandy Descher** Eadie Johnson

Director *Jack Arnold*
Screenplay *Bernard C Schoenfeld, from a story by Tom Filer*
Producer *William Alland*
Cinematographer *Ernest Laszlo* • ***Production designer*** *Hal Pereira, Roland Anderson* • ***Special effects*** *John P Fulton*

Space Command ★★

TV 1953-1954 Can BW 33x30mins

Space Command follows the adventures of a young astronaut in the space corps and featured Bob Barclay, Aileen Taylor and a young James Doohan, who was to find fame in *Star Trek* some 13 years later. The show was produced live in Canada and information is sketchy. Among the actors who guested were William Shatner and Barry Morse (*Space: 1999*).

Bob Barclay Frank Anderson • **Aileen Taylor** Ilene Morris • **Andrew Anthony** Dr Joseph Edwards • **James Doohan** Phil Mitchell • **Austin Willis** Dr Fleming
Written by *Alfred Harris*
Producer *Murray Chercover*

Space Cowboys ★★★ PG

2000 US/Aus Colour 125mins [video]

Clint Eastwood's self-deprecating and winningly indulgent cosmic adventure is a complete macho-fuelled fantasy set in the ultra-realistic world of Nasa operations today. With an irresistible premise – four geriatric astronauts finally get the chance to go into orbit 40 years after being sidelined by a monkey – this slice of gung-ho wish-fulfilment is an entertaining feel-good pleasure. Team Daedalus is called back into service because no other has the obsolete knowledge to prevent a Cold-War era Russian telecommunications satellite from crashing to Earth. There's absolutely no point in taking anything seriously in this high-tech fable, but Eastwood and his space-aged company shine as the ageing astronauts wheezing through basic training, navigating past feuds and becoming all-American heroes as co-stars Tommy Lee Jones, Donald Sutherland and James Garner also reveal the right stuff as well as the true meaning of star charisma. Contains some swearing.

Clint Eastwood Frank D Corvin • **Tommy Lee Jones** Hawk Hawkins • **Donald Sutherland** Jerry O'Neill • **James Garner** Tank Sullivan • **James Cromwell** Bob Gerson • **Marcia Gay Harden** Sara Holland • **William Devane** Eugene Davis • **Loren Dean** Ethan Glance • **Courtney B Vance** Roger Hlnes
Director *Clint Eastwood*
Screenplay *Ken Kaufman, Howard Klausner*

SFacts

The space-set climax was constructed by *Star Wars* supremo George Lucas's Industrial Light and Magic company from actual photographs and space shuttle footage, combined with miniatures and digital animation.

Space Island One ★★

TV 1998 UK/US Colour 26x60mins

Boldly billed as a realistic look at how people can survive living and working on the world's first space station, Sky One's sci-fi drama certainly has an unusually strong ring of authenticity to it. Unfortunately, the down-to-Earth space-farers' day-to-day activities make for slow-moving and largely unexciting television. Judy Loe, Angus MacInnes and Indra Ové head the eclectic but not particularly interesting occupants of the Space Station *Unity*, while the show's setting is realised through a combination of believably low-key sets and passable special effects. After a few episodes, though, most viewers will be longing for outlandish aliens and ludicrous time travel plots!

Judy Loe Commander Kathryn McTiernan • **Angus MacInnes** Lt Cmdr Walter Shannon • **Bruno Eyron** Dusan Kashkavian • **Kourosh Asad** Dr Kaveh Homayuni • **William Oliver** Chief Science Officer Lyle Campbell • **Indra Ové** Paula Hernandez • **Julia Bremermann** "Harry" Eschenbach
Created by *Andrew Maclear*
Executive producer *Andrew Maclear*

Space Jam ★★★ U

1997 US Colour 83mins [video] DVD

American basketball star Michael Jordan makes a charismatic big screen acting debut, as he teams up with the entire Warner Bros cartoon catalogue, in this part-animated, part live-action adventure with a sci-fi twist. Aliens from the failing intergalactic theme park Moron Mountain are under orders to get Bugs Bunny, Daffy Duck, Tweety, Elmer Fudd, Porky Pig *et al* to be their new attraction. So, in a desperate attempt to keep their freedom, the animated brigade challenge their would-be captors to a basketball game and up their chances by kidnapping Jordan. The humour cleverly mixes typical Looney Tunes gags with references to *Reservoir Dogs*, comic jibes at their sports star's new choice of career (baseball) and some hilarious moments provided by Bill Murray. And Jordan is joined in the film by other basketball luminaries including Charles Barclay and Larry Bird. Children will love the energy of both the live and animated characters, and there's plenty to keep adults amused, too.

Michael Jordan • **Wayne Knight** Stan Podolak • **Danny DeVito** Swackhammer • **Theresa Randle** Juanita Jordan • **Eric Gordon** Marcus Jordan • **Penny Bae Bridges** Jasmine Jordan • **Bill Murray**
Director *Joe Pytka*
Screenplay *Leo Benvenuti, Steve Rudnick, Timothy Harris, Herschel Weingrod*

Space Marines ★★ 18

1996 US Colour 89mins [video] DVD

For all its technology and futuristic settings, this is actually a throwback to the gritty war movies of the fifties. Here a hard-bitten crew of interstellar GIs lines up against an extravagantly evil gang of space terrorists who have kidnapped an important diplomat. Billy Wirth and Edward Albert manage to keep straight faces throughout, and the special effects are actually pretty decent, but no amount of explosions and gunplay can compensate for the resolutely formulaic plotting.

Billy Wirth Zake Delano • **Cady Huffman** Dar Mullins • **John Pyper-Ferguson** Colonel Fraser • **Edward Albert** Captain Gray • **Meg Foster** Commodore Lasser
Director *John Weidner*
Screenplay *Robert Moreland*

Space Master X 7 ★★

1958 US BW 70mins

Treat this *Blob/Quatermass* derivative as farce and you'll have a good time. For thought-provoking science fiction, look elsewhere. Fungus from a space probe mixes with human blood and turns deadly, in this prime example of a fifties' copycat chiller. Told in routine, and extremely padded out, semi-documentary style, the presence of Three Stooges funnyman Moe Howard (playing a cab driver), suggests director Edward Bernds thought it was a comedy, too. Unfortunately, the other actors take it all very seriously which only adds to the hilarity.

Bill Williams John Hand • **Lyn Thomas** Lora Greeling • **Robert Ellis** Radigan • **Paul Frees** Charles Palmer • **Joan Nixon Barry** Miss Meyers • **Thomas Browne Henry** Professor West • **Fred Sherman** Morse • **Rhoda Williams** Miss Archer
Director *Edward Bernds*
Screenplay *George Worthing Yates, Daniel Mainwaring*

Space Men ★ U

1960 It BW 74mins

Antonio Margheriti's first feature as a director is one of the worst in his variable career. A malfunctioning computer aboard the *Alfa II* space probe sets it on a collision course for Earth. Reporter Rik Von Nutter is part of the orbiting space station crew who try to stop it while arguing with other mission members over the charms of

Gabriella Farinon. The half-baked plot comes a poor second to the striking visual design and Margheriti is clearly out of his directorial depth with this dramatic non-starter. An Italian language film.

Rik Von Nutter [Rik Van Nutter] Ray Peterson • **Gabriella Farinon** Lucy • **Archie Savage** Al • **Dave Montresor** George • **Alain Dijon** Commander • **Jack Wallace** Narrator
Director *Anthony Daisies [Antonio Margheriti]*
Screenplay *Vassily Petrov*
Cinematographer *Marcello Masciocchi*
Special effects *Joseph Von Stroheimx Caesar Peace*

Space Mutiny ★★ 15

1988 US Colour 87mins

The fact that this has featured on the American TV show *Mystery Science Theater* – a programme that sends up tacky sci-fi movies – gives a clue to this filmfis particular merits. The story revolves around a spacecraft heading for a brave new world, but hampered by enemies both on-board and in space. However, forget about the detail and marvel instead at the hammy performances and cheapo effects.

Reb Brown Dave Ryder • **John Phillip Law** Kalgan • **James Ryan** MacPhearson • **Cameron Mitchell** Alex Jansen • **Cissy Cameron** Lea Jansen • **Graham Clark [Graham Clarke]** Scott Dyers
Director *David Winters, Neal Sundstrom*
Screenplay *Maria Dante*

Space: 1999 ★★★★ U PG

TV 1975-77 UK/US Colour 48x60m DVD

Gerry Anderson's second live action series, after *UFO*, was clearly intended to attract a prime-time American audience, not least in the casting of Martin Landau and Barbara Bain, the husband-and-wife team from *Mission: Impossible*. Moonbase Alpha is a scientific research colony, blasted out of Earth's orbit after a massive explosion, that hurtles alone through the universe encountering hostile aliens, discovering new worlds and bumping into the odd guest star such as Joan Collins and Christopher Lee. For its time, the effects and production design were of a superior standard (the show was made at Pinewood, the UK's premier film studio and home to the 007 movies), but what began as an intriguing, thought-provoking series ultimately degenerated to the level of a comic strip. Still, splendid entertainment and a real cult item today. Though Landau and Co were keen to return and ratings were good showbiz tycoon Lord Lew Grade cancelled the show to offset losses he'd suffered on films such as *Raise the Titanic*.

Martin Landau Commander John Koenig • **Barbara Bain** Dr Helena Russell • **Nick Tate** Captain Alan Carter • **Zienia Merton** Sandra Benes • **Barry Morse** Professor Victor Bergman
Created by *Gerry Anderson, Sylvia Anderson*
Executive producer *Gerry Anderson*

Space Patrol ★★★

TV 1950-1955 US BW

Yet another futuristic cop show for kids, this is set a thousand years after the fifties, when Commander Buzz Corry (Edward Kemmer) keeps the United Planets safe from the usual space pirates and tyrants, with the aid of comedy sidekick Cadet Happy (Lyn Osborn), whose Noo Yawk-accented catchphrase is "smokin' rockets!" Carol Karlyle (Virginia Hewitt), daughter of the Secretary General, has a crush on Buzz, but slinky villainess Tonga (Nina Bara) was more exciting and eventually reforms to be a semi-goodie. At first a 15-minute daily serial, the show (which also went out on radio with the same cast) became a half-hour effort for its final two seasons. To cash in on Sputnik, the show was repeated in 1957 under the title *Satellite Police*.

Ed Kemmer Commander Buzz Corry • **Lyn Osborn** Cadet Happy • **Virginia Hewitt** Carol Karlyle • **Nina Bara** Tonga • **Ken Mayer** Major Robbie Robertson • **Norman Jolley** Agent X
Created by *Mike Moser*

SFacts

This was the first television series to broadcast an episode in 3D. Viewers could get the special specs by buying selected breakfast cereal packets.

Space Patrol ★★

TV 1963-1964 UK BW 39x30mins

Created by Roberta Leigh, who had written for Gerry Anderson's *The Adventures of Twizzle* and *Torchy the Battery Boy*, this primitive, black-and-white puppet show was something of a knock-off of Anderson's *Fireball XL5*. In 2100, the Space Patrol's finest flying saucer is crewed by intrepid Earthman Larry Dart (Dick Vosburgh), a rare sixties space hero with a beard and long-ish hair, plus his buddies Husky the Martian (squat, food-loving) and Slim the Venusian (very fey). Their chief was gruff Colonel Raeburn (Murray Kash), and there was an Irish inventor Professor Haggerty and his daughter Cassiopea, Venusian secretary Marla and an annoying alien parrot called the Gabblerdictum. All the supporting characters were played by Ronnie Stevens and Libby Morris. Among the odder merchandising items associated with *Space Patrol* were the now unthinkable Sweet Cigarettes, fag-shaped tubes of sugary stuff that presumably trained children to be smokers when they grew up.

Dick Vosburgh Space Captain Larry Dart • **Ronnie Stevens** Husky/Slim/Prof Haggerty • **Murray Kash** Colonel Raeburn • **Libby Morris** Marla/Cassiopeia/Gabblerdictim
Created by *Roberta Leigh*
Producer *Roberta Leigh*

Space Precinct ★★

TV 1994-95 UK/US Colour 24x60m DVD

Gerry Anderson's first live action series since *Space: 1999* evolved from an earlier discarded idea about a human cop working with an alien partner. Although a pilot of that show was made (*Space Police*) it was never broadcast, but Anderson reworked the basic premise and came up with *Space Precinct*, set in the middle of the 21st century on a distant planet where law and order is kept in check by a high-tech, multi-alien police force. Ted Shackelford, best known as Gary Ewing from the US soap *Knot's Landing*, plays Lieutenant Patrick Brogan, a former New York cop now operating in space. Shackelford was one of two American lead actors, betraying the show's eagerness to appeal to the US market. Despite one of the biggest price tags ever for a British TV series this didn't translate to the screen with the effects and make-up being scarcely out of this world.

Ted Shackelford Lt Patrick Brogan • **Nancy Paul** Sally Brogan • **Megan Olive** Liz Brogan • **Nic Klein** Matt Brogan • **Jerome Willis** Captain Podly • **Simone Bendix** Officer Jane Castle • **Mary Woodvine** Officer Took • **Rob Youngblood** Officer Jack Haldane
Created by *Gerry Anderson*

Space Rage ★★ 18

1986 US Colour 74mins

Conrad Palmisano is a past president of the Stuntman Association, so maybe that was how he managed to coax stunt-man-turned-actor Richard Farnsworth to take a part in his botched sci-fi western. He gives a typically accomplished performance as a space tracker on the trail of nasty escaped convict (a cast-against-type Michael Paré). However, even the two leads can't compensate for the pedestrian plotting and unimaginative direction.

Richard Farnsworth The Colonel • **Michael Paré** Grange • **John Laughlin** Walker • **Lee Purcell** Maggie • **William Windom** Governor Tovah • **Lewis Van Bergen** Drago
Director *Peter McCarthy, Conrad E Palmisano*
Screenplay *Jim Lenahan, from a story by Morton Reed*

Space Raiders ★★ PG

1983 US Colour 79mins [video]

This Roger Corman recycle job is typical of the *Star Wars* rip-offs that infected late seventies and early eighties cinema like zits on a teenager. Writer/director Howard R Cohen seems to have concocted his tale of a boy who stows away on a ship belonging to a motley band of space mercenaries, merely to fit around special effects footage lifted from Corman's own *Battle beyond the Stars*. Even the score by the celebrated James Horner is the same. Still, undemanding kids may find some enjoyment in its strictly limited thrills and cheap gags, such as the pastiche of the famous *Star Wars* cantina scene.

David Mendenhall Peter Tracton • **Vince Edwards** Hawk • **George Dickerson** Arthur Tracton • **Thom Christopher** Flightplan • **Drew Snyder** Alderbarian • **Patsy Pease** Amanda • **Ray Stewart** Zariatin
Director/Screenplay *Howard R Cohen*

Space Rangers ★★

TV 1993 US Colour 6x60mins

After taking a shot at one of the 12th century's greatest legends, *Robin Hood: Princes of Thieves* co-writer Pen Densham turned his attention to a thousand years in the future and produced this futuristic sci-fi western series. A fast-moving but completely mindless comic-strip romp, the show revolves around the crime-fighting exploits of the titular Space Rangers stationed on a remote deep space outpost known as Fort Hope. Bland rent-a-lead Jeff Kaake heads a mismatched cast, which includes Academy Award-winner Linda Hunt (who presumably needed the money), B-movie veteran Clint Howard, Gottfried John and the show-stealing Marjorie Monaghan. Despite their best efforts, though, the series was cancelled after just six episodes had been shot.

Jeff Kaake Captain John Boon • **Marjorie Monaghan** JoJo Thorson • **Cary-Hiroyuki Tagawa** Zylyn • **Jack McGee** Doc Kruger • **Clint Howard** Mimmer • **Danny Quinn** Daniel Kincaid • **Gottfried John** Colonel Weiss • **Linda Hunt** Cmdr Chennault
Created by *Pen Densham*

Space School ★★

TV 1956 UK BW 4x30mins

Four half hour episodes on the BBC following the adventures of three children (Michael Maguire, Winifred Ann Cooke and Meurig Jones) living on a space satellite. John Stuart, who also starred as the dignified Space Commodore Sir Hugh Sterling popped up in numerous sci-fi films, including *Quatermass 2*, *Village of the Damned* and *Superman* (1978).

John Stuart Space Commodore Sir Hugh Sterling • **Matthew Lane** Space Captain Michael O'Rorke • **Donald McCorkindale** Space Engineer Tubby Thompson • **Nell McCallum** Sam Scroop • **Julie Webb** Miss Osborne • **Michael Maguire** Wallace Winter • **Meurig Jones** Wilfred Winter • **Ann Cooke** Winnie Winter • **David Drummond** Humphrey Soames
Written by *Gordon Ford*
Producer *Kevin Sheldon*
Designer *Gordon Roland*

The Space Ship ★★★

1935 USSR BW 70mins

This was the Soviet's first sci-fi talkie. Considering that one of the rockets is named after Stalin and that the bulk of the action conforms to the prescribed socialist realist style, the open criticism of the (albeit fictional) Moscow Institute for Interplanetary Travel's reluctance to accelerate a space programme is surprisingly bold. Indeed, Ukrainian director Vasili Zhuravlev also ignores the party line by opting for a single, recognisable hero in Sergei Komarov, the zealous scientist who heads for the moon in his homemade spacecraft. The artwork may not be as ambitious as that in *Aelita*, but it's still pretty impressive. A Russian language film.

Sergei Komarov • **Vasili Kovrigin** • **Nicolai Feokistov** • **Vassili Gaponenko** • **K Maskalenko**
Director *Vasili Zhuravlev*
Screenplay *A Filimonov [Aleksandr Filimonov]*
Cinematographer *A Galperin*

Space Truckers ★★★ 12

1996 US/Ire Colour 92mins [video]

A better than expected cast has an intergalactic brush with killer robots, pirates and motorised body parts in this off-the-wall sci-fi romp from *Re-Animator* director Stuart Gordon. Dennis Hopper, Stephen Dorff and Debi Mazar are among those on the receiving end, while Charles Dance's bio-mechanical adversary even out-camps his pantomime *Last Action Hero* villain. At a time when sci-fi seems to have lost its sense of fun, this is a colourful, unpretentious slice of entertaining nonsense.

Dennis Hopper John Canyon • **Stephen Dorff** Mike Pucci • **Debi Mazar** Cindy • **George Wendt** Mr Keller • **Barbara Crampton** Carol • **Charles Dance** Nabel / Macanudo • **Shane Rimmer** E J Saggs
Director *Stuart Gordon*
Screenplay *Ted Mann, from a story by Stuart Gordon, Ted Mann*

Spaceballs ★★ PG

1987 US Colour 92mins [video]

Mel Brooks seems to think that just by appearing on screen, assembling assorted clowns (Rick Moranis and John Candy chief among them) and substituting noise for wit, hilarity will somehow ensue. Unfortunately, as you think back longingly to the imaginative wildness and barbed humour of *The Producers*, you see how Brooks has descended to a pick 'n' mix approach to comedy. In this limp spoof of *Star Wars* (where the obvious is never avoided), visual and verbal gags leap across the screen with manic abandon. At least a handful of decent jokes and japes do brighten the mundane proceedings. Contains strong language.

Mel Brooks President Skroob/Yogurt • **John Candy** Barf the Mawg • **Rick Moranis** Lord Dark Helmet • **Bill Pullman** Lone Starr • **Daphne Zuniga** Princess Vespa • **Dick Van Patten** King Roland • **George Wyner** Colonel Sandurz • **Michael Winslow** Radar technician • **Joan Rivers** Voice of Dot Matrix • **Lorene Yarnell** Dot Matrix • **John Hurt** • **Dom DeLuise** Pizza the Hutt
Director *Mel Brooks*
Screenplay *Mel Brooks, Thomas Meehan, Ronny Graham*

SpaceCamp ★ PG

1986 US Colour 106mins [video]

This space opera for youngsters brought Kate Capshaw (later to become Mrs Steven Spielberg) down to earth with something of a bump from the heady heights of *Indiana Jones and the Temple of Doom*. Younger teenagers might well relish the idea of a group of aspiring astronauts who accidentally blast off into orbit, but they will be less forgiving about the cut-price special effects. Several of the cast notably Lea Thompson, Kelly Preston and Tate Donovan went on to better things, altough, bearing in mind their dim-witted performances here, it's not easy to see why.

Lea Thompson Kathryn • **Tate Donovan** Kevin • **Kelly Preston** Tish • **Larry B Scott** Rudy • **Leaf Phoenix [Joaquin Phoenix]**

Max • **Kate Capshaw** Andie Bergstrom • **Tom Skerritt** Zach Bergstrom • **Barry Primus** Brennan • **Terry O'Quinn** Launch Director • **Mitchell Anderson** Banning
Director *Harry Winer*
Screenplay *WW Wicket, Casey T Mitchell, from a story by Patrick Bailey, Larry B Williams*

Spaced Invaders ★ U

1990 US Colour 95mins

This painfully juvenile endurance test degenerates rapidly into a muddled slapstick mess as the mini *Bill and Ted* speaking leftovers from the *Star Wars* cantina race to Earth to join up with invaders about to conquer the planet. But the invasion alert is really only the 50th anniversary radio re-broadcasting of the classic Orson Welles *War of the Worlds* programme – the movie's one great idea. Remaining undetected among Halloween revellers, the stupid aliens are finally sent on their way to the real intergalactic battlefield by redneck citizens. A mind-numbing vacuum of Darth Vader-voiced villains, Farm Aid consciousness-raising, a Jack Nicholson alien mimic and the "Donut of Destruction", ex-special effects man-turned director Patrick Read Johnson's mishmash of comical mishaps and mistaken identities is high-concept sparseness on depressing over-drive.

Douglas Barr Sheriff Sam Hoxly • **Royal Dano** Old Man Wrenchmuller • **Ariana Richards** Kathy Hoxly • **JJ Anderson** Brian "Duck" • **Gregg Berger** Steve W Klembecker • **Wayne Alexander** Vern • **Fred Applegate** Russell Pillsbury • **Patrika Darbo** Mrs Vanderspool
Director *Patrick Read Johnson*
Screenplay *Scott Lawrence Alexander, Patrick Read Johnson*

Spacehunter: Adventures in the Forbidden Zone ★★ 15

1983 US Colour 86mins

Galactic adventurer Peter Strauss aims to rescue cosmic travellers held prisoner by an evil man-machine on the plague-ridden planet of Terra Eleven, in this messy jump on the science-fiction bandwagon. Directed with a weary eye by Lamont Johnson, the feeble script gives Strauss's bratty sidekick Molly Ringwald nothing to do, and only the sheer force of Michael Ironside's personality, proving he can be good in anything, turns the mutant cyborg Overdog into a decently hissable villain.

Peter Strauss Wolff • **Molly Ringwald** Niki • **Ernie Hudson** Washington • **Andrea Marcovicci** Chalmers • **Michael Ironside** Overdog McNabb • **Beeson Carroll** Grandma Patterson • **Hrant Alianak** Chemist • **Deborah Pratt** Meagan
Director *Lamont Johnson*
Screenplay *David Preston, Edith Rey, Dan Goldberg, Len Blum, from a story by Stewart Harding, Jean LaFleur*

The Spaceman and King Arthur ★★★ U

1979 US/UK Colour 89mins

Also known, with delightful Disney whimsy, as *Unidentified Flying Oddball*, this reworking of Mark Twain's *A Connecticut Yankee in King Arthur's Court* has a frantic charm and provides a chance to see the desperately amiable Jim Dale as a baddie. The tale follows Nasa technician Dennis Dugan and his lookalike astronaut android as they're caught in a time warp and find themselves in King Arthur's kingdom. There, Kenneth More as the engagingly elderly king and John Le Mesurier as a hesitant Sir Gawain – a peer position that would have made *Dad's Army*'s Captain Mainwaring fume – seem to find nothing unusual in these cultures clashing. Lots of science "friction" and jolly japes make this a worthwhile tale, especially for younger viewers.

Dennis Dugan Tom Trimble • **Jim Dale** Sir Mordred • **Ron Moody** Merlin • **Kenneth More** King Arthur • **John Le Mesurier** Sir Gawain • **Rodney Bewes** Clarence • **Sheila White** Alisande • **Robert Beatty** Senator Milburn
Director *Russ Mayberry*
Screenplay *Don Tait, from the novel "A Connecticut Yankee in King Arthur's Court" by Mark Twain*

The Spacemen of St Tropez ★★

1978 Fr Colour

The last entry in the comedy cop series to be completed by writer/director Jean Girault (who died while shooting *The Gendarme Wore Skirts*) borrows its premise from *Invasion of the Body Snatchers* in order to both exploit and satirise the vogue for all things interstellar in the wake of *Star Wars*. However, the action is utterly reliant on broad slapstick, as the bungling Louis De Funès assaults the cream of St Tropez in a bid to expose some oil-swilling aliens with a gift for impersonation who seem set to take over the Riviera. The script is weak, but the cast is willing. French and Italian dialogue dubbed into English.

Michel Galabru Insp Gerber • **Maurice Risch** Beaupied • **Maria Mauban** Josepha • **Guy Crasso** Tricard • **Jean-Pierre Rambal** Taupin • **Louis De Funès** Ludovic Cruchot
Director/Screenplay *Jean Girault*

Spaceways ★ U

1953 UK BW 77mins

This big-screen version of Charles Eric Maine's space-age whodunit leaves the viewer with one burning question: why did anybody who read the radio play think it was worth doing anything with it other than hurl it across the room? The plot has leads Howard Duff and Eva Bartok blasting off in pursuit of a satellite to prove Duff's innocence following an accusation of double murder. Sci-fi was never the strong suit of Hammer horror specialist Terence Fisher, and his funereal pace kills this cheaply-made picture stone dead.

Howard Duff Stephen Mitchell • **Eva Bartok** Lisa Frank • **Alan Wheatley** Smith • **Philip Leaver** Dr Keppler • **Michael Medwin** Toby Andrews
Director *Terence Fisher*
Screenplay *Paul Tabori, Richard Landau, from a radio play by Charles Eric Maine*

Spawn ★★ 12

1997 US Colour 92mins DVD

A live-action comic book spin-off that promised to duplicate the grim and extremely violent images that are the bestselling comic's hallmarks, but ended up being distributed in an edited "12" certificate version and then an 18-rated video "director's cut". Michael Jai White plays Al Simmons, a special forces assassin betrayed by boss Martin Sheen and left to fry in a burning chemical factory. Somehow passing beyond death, he is revived as Spawn, scarred costumed henchman to the demonic Malebolgia who is also bent on revenge against Sheen. Dark in tone and crammed with computer-generated effects, it found a cult popularity and spawned a follow-up animated series.

Michael Jai White Al Simmons/Spawn • **Martin Sheen** Jason Wynn • **John Leguizamo** Clown • **Theresa Randle** Wanda • **Nicol Williamson** Cogliostro • **Melinda Clarke** Jessica Priest • **DB Sweeney** Terry Fitzgerald
Director *Mark AZ Dippé*
Screenplay *Alan McElroy, from a story by Mark AZ Dippé, Alan McElroy, from the comic book by Todd McFarlane*

Special Report: Journey to Mars ★★ U

1996 US Colour 86mins

In the year 2015 an international TV audience watches the first manned space mission to Mars as it suffers a computer malfunction, possibly due to sabotage, endangering the crew and the entire mission. This formulaic TV movie is anything but special, which American audiences obviously knew ahead of time: the film has the dubious distinction of being the lowest-rated primetime network movie in TV history. A surprisingly capable group of actors collectively lowered their usual standards for this predictable "what-if" sci-fi scenario, including Keith Carradine and Alfre Woodard. There's nothing fresh or distinctive enough to necessitate sitting through this one.

Keith Carradine Captain Eugene Slader • **Judge Reinhold** Ryan West • **Alfre Woodard** Tamara O'Neil • **Philip Casnoff** Nick Van Pelt • **Rosalind Chao** Dr Lin Yo Yu • **Elizabeth Wilson** President Richardson • **Michael Murphy** Dean Rumplemeyer • **Dean Jones** Dr Scott Berlin
Director *Robert Mandel*
Screenplay *Augustus Taylor*

Species ★★★ 18

1995 US Colour 103mins VIDEO DVD

Natasha Henstridge is the dangerous spawn of combined alien and human DNA in director Roger Donaldson's sexy sci-fi shocker. Ben Kingsley, Michael Madsen and Alfred Molina are among the inept government scientists speaking daft dialogue as they attempt to track down the genetic engineering experiment gone awry, before she devours half the male population of LA. Nifty designs by surrealist HR Giger (who gave the extraterrestrial in *Alien* its incredible look) and some engaging, tongue-in-cheek thrills go part way to disguising the fact that this is essentially clichéd B-movie stuff, albeit delivered with a pleasingly glossy sheen. Contains violence, swearing, sex scenes and nudity.

Ben Kingsley Fitch • **Michael Madsen** Press • **Alfred Molina** Arden • **Forest Whitaker** Dan • **Marg Helgenberger** Laura • **Natasha Henstridge** Sil • **Michelle Williams** Young Sil • **Jordan Lund** Aide • **Don Fischer** Aide
Director *Roger Donaldson*
Screenplay *Dennis Feldman*
Producer *Frank Mancuso Jr, Dennis Feldman*

SFacts

Creature designer HR Giger stumped up $100,000 of his own money to shoot the film's train-bound transformation sequence when producers threatened to cut the scene for budgetary reasons

Species II ★★★ 18

1998 US Colour 89mins VIDEO DVD

Head explosions, torso-bursting and computer-generated aliens in heat: it's all here in Peter Medak's science-fiction howler which continues the half-human/half-alien DNA experiment as a sex rampage saga. Far gorier and camper than the original film, this lascivious popcorn treat is a spectacularly lunatic shocker revelling in soft-core sleaze and grisly death. Piling up the unintentional laughs alongside the bloodied victims, the actors coast through the mayhem as if they couldn't be bothered bringing an iota of credibility to this terminally daft scenario. An absolute hoot. Contains sex scenes, swearing and violence.

Michael Madsen Press Lennox • **Natasha Henstridge** Eve • **Marg Helgenberger** Doctor Laura Baker • **Mykel T Williamson** Dennis Gamble • **George Dzundza** Colonel Carter Burgess Jr • **James Cromwell** Senator Ross • **Myriam Cyr** Anne Sampas
Director *Peter Medak*
Screenplay *Chris Brancato, from characters created by Dennis Feldman*

Specimen ★★ 15

1996 Can Colour 81mins VIDEO

There are some intriguing ideas bubbling around in this otherwise standard piece of straight-to-video fodder. Mark-Paul Gosselaar, better known as Zach from the saccharine high-school comedy series *Saved By the Bell*, is the confused young man wondering who his real father is and why he seems to have inherited an ability to spark fires whenever he gets in a bit of a temper. It soon transpires that his immediate family may not be of this Earth – and they havenfit got a happy reunion in mind. Director John Bradshaw never quite gets to grips with the material but there are some thoughtful moments.

Mark-Paul Gosselaar Mark Hillary • **Doug O'Keeffe** Eleven • **Ingrid Kavelaars** Jessica • **David Herman** Sheriff Masterson • **Andrew Jackson** Sixty-Six • **Michelle Johnson** Sarah
Director *John Bradshaw*
Screenplay *Sheldon Inkol, Lauren McLaughlin, from a story by John Bradshaw, Damian Lee*

Spectreman ★★

TV 1971-1972 Jap Colour

This Japanese live action series featured themes in the great tradition of *kaiju eiga* splicing pollution-spawned monsters and environmental messages with superhero antics, and laid the groundwork for the later *Power Rangers* series. Japanese dialogue dubbed into English.

Tetsuo Narikawa Joji "George" Gamou • **Toru Ohira** Chief Kurata • **Takanobu Toya** Dr Gori
Created by *Shoji Ushio*
Producer *Tomio Sagisu*

Sphere ★★★ 12

1998 US Colour 128mins VIDEO DVD

A submerged spacecraft from the future containing a golden sphere that has the ability to physically manifest the darkest fears of anyone who enters its enigmatic interior is at the centre of director Barry Levinson's cerebral adaptation of Michael Crichton's bestselling novel. Alternating between being genuinely creepy (the aquanauts' phobias are all unseen) and overly tame through the deliberate under-use of shock effects, this underwater *Solaris* relies on moody dread rather than cheap thrills to weave its spell. A wittily scripted science-fiction chamber piece that focuses on characters thrust into an extraordinary situation rather than the situation itself.

Dustin Hoffman Dr Norman Goodman • **Sharon Stone** Dr Beth Halperin • **Samuel L Jackson** Harry Adams • **Peter Coyote** Harold C Barnes • **Liev Schreiber** Dr Ted Fielding • **Queen Latifah** Fletcher
Director *Barry Levinson*
Screenplay *Stephen Hauser, Paul Attanasio, from the novel by Michael Crichton*
Production designer *Norman Reynolds*

Spies ★★★★

1928 Ger BW 86mins

Perhaps the most underrated of Fritz Lang's silent spectacles, this tale of master criminality has all the visceral thrill and visual atmospherics of one of Louis Feuillade's *Fantomas* serials. Many of the *Metropolis* alumni were reunited for the picture, with Karl Vollbrecht and Otto Hunte creating the Expressionist sets which added menace to the dastardly deeds laid at the door of the Mabuse-like Rudolf Klein-Rogge by Lang and Thea von Harbou's breathless script. However, once again, this is very much Lang's own vision, as he abandons political allegory to place the emphasis firmly on escapism and his genius for the awe-inspiring set piece.

Rudolf Klein-Rogge Haghi • **Gerda Maurus** Sonia Barranikova • **Willy Fritsch** Number 326
Director *Fritz Lang*
Screenplay *Fritz Lang, Thea von Harbou, from their story*
Art director *Otto Hunte, Karl Vollbrecht*

Split Second ★★ 18

1991 UK Colour 86mins

Rutger Hauer mugs shamelessly in a nonsensical science-fiction effort from Tony Maylam, the director of *The Burning*. Hauer's an on-edge cop in the flooded London of 2008, in search of a monstrous heart-ripping serial killer with Satanic origins with whom he shares a psychic link. Sidekick Neil Duncan and love interest Kim Cattrall take their places for the daft battle royal denouement in Cannon Street tube station. Cartoon gore, noisy violence, plot strands left hanging in the air and a few fleeting glimpses of a black rubber creature aren't enough to satisfy anyone but the most undiscriminating trash addict.

Rutger Hauer Harley Stone • **Kim Cattrall** Michelle • **Neil Duncan** Dick Durkin • **Michael J Pollard** The Rat Catcher • **Pete Postlethwaite** Paulsen • **Ian Dury** Jay Jay • **Roberta Eaton** Robin • **Alun Armstrong** Thrasher

Director *Tony Maylam*

Screenplay *Gary Scott Thompson*

Spoiler ★★ 18

1998 US Colour 90mins

If one considers its low budget ($500,000) and 18-day shooting schedule, then this movie can be considered more of an accomplishment that it otherwise is. Martial arts actor Gary Daniels is miscast as a prisoner in the future, whose frequent attempts to escape see him recaptured, frozen for several years and put through various hells. The underlying weakness of the story is that Daniels's stubborn and seemingly illogical behavior is never properly explained, making one wonder if he deserves his fate after all. The sets and most of the special effects are appallingly cheap, though one always senses the director squeezed every last penny of the budget to construct and present them the best way possible. Various B-movie stars make cameos throughout. Contains swearing and violence.

Jeffrey Combs Captain • **Gary Daniels** Roger Mason • **Jean Speegle Howard** Jennifer

Director *Michael Kalesniko*

Spy in Your Eye ★★ U

1965 It Colour 88mins

While hardly in the James Bond league, director Vittorio Sala's espionage adventure is one of the better Italian attempts to recreate the 007 ambience. Partially blinded American agent Brett Halsey has a miniature camera secretly implanted in his false eye when Russians operate on him to supposedly cure him of sight problems. What they really want is for him to find a death ray formula developed by a scientist who, before dying, had it tattooed it on his daughter Pier Angeli's scalp. Sala gets some clever mileage out of the voyeuristic concept and the usual glamorous foreign locations (eg Beirut) provide some visual interest, but routine direction and minimal action ultimately get the upper hand. Italian dialogue dubbed into English.

Brett Halsey Bert Morris • **Pier Angeli** Paula Krauss • **Dana Andrews** Col Lancaster • **Gastone Moschin** Boris • **Tania Beryl**

Director *Vittorio Sala*

Screenplay *Romano Ferrara, Adriano Baracco, Adriano Bolzoni, from a story by Lucio Marcuzzo*

SPYkids ★★★★ U

2001 US Colour 87mins

A junior-league "James Bond" that'll seem like heaven to the over-sevens, and that's rollicking entertainment for accompanying adults, too. After all, how many kids' films can *you* name that boast a director of the calibre of Robert Rodriguez (*Desperado*, *From Dusk till Dawn*) and that star such luminaries as Antonio Banderas, Robert Patrick and a cameoing George Clooney? Banderas and Carla Gugino play married spies who get captured by a megalomaniac kids' TV presenter (Alan Cumming) who's seeking world domination by replacing the children of people in high places with runt-size lookalike robots. To the rescue come the couple's pleasingly non-precocious kids (one boy, one girl), aided and abetted by a cool array of gizmoes that range from rocket-packs to electromagnetic chewing gum. Smartly and sassily directed by Rodriguez (who quite rightly pitches the film at youngsters, not down to them) and sporting some nifty special effects, *SPYkids* is family cinema as it should be.

Antonio Banderas Gregorio Cortez • **Carla Gugino** Ingrid Cortez • **Alexa Vega** Carmen Cortez • **Daryl Sabara** Juni Cortez • **Alan Cumming** Fegan Floop • **Tony Shalhoub** Alexander Minion • **Teri Hatcher** Ms Gradenko • **Cheech Martin [Richard "Cheech" Marin]** Felix Gumm • **Danny Trejo** Machete • **Robert Patrick** Mr Lisp • **George Clooney** Devlin

Director/Screenplay *Robert Rodriguez*

Squirm ★★★ 18

1976 US Colour 92mins

In this cheap but cheerfully repellent horror film, one of several during the seventies in which all creatures great and small became monsters, the worm turns. A pylon, struck by lightning, electrifies the earth in typical small town, USA, and the worms go on the offensive. Writer/director Jeff Lieberman, making the most of a limited budget, builds the tension expertly, and limits the shock effects, giving full value to the scenes (created by master of the art Rick Baker) in which worms crawl through human flesh. This black comedy is seen by some as a satire of American small town values. Far better than many of its ilk.

Don Scardino Mick • **Patricia Pearcy** Geri • **R A Dow** Roger • **Jean Sullivan** Naomi • **Peter MacLean** Sheriff • **Fran Higgins** Alma • **William Newman** Quigley

Director/Screenplay *Jeff Lieberman*

Make-up special effects *Rick Baker*

Ssssss ★★★

1973 US Colour 99mins

The marvellously villainous Strother Martin – in a rare leading role – is a mad doctor, who wants to turn men into snakes in this outrageous but often nightmarish horror. Playing cleverly on the audience's fear of snakes, it sustains a strange and suspenseful atmosphere virtually throughout, aided by the excellent make-up work of John Chambers, who had won an Oscar for *Planet of the Apes*. It is only towards the end that the temperature falls as the contrivances pile up and the special effects show their age. Nevertheless this is still a very effective shocker.

Strother Martin Dr Carl Stoner • **Dirk Benedict** David Blake • **Heather Menzies** Kristine Stoner • **Richard B Shull** Dr Ken Daniels • **Jack Ging** Sheriff Dale Hardison • **Tim O' Connor** Kogen

Director *Bernard L Kowalski*

Screenplay *Hal Dresner, from a story by Dan Striepeke*

Make-up special effects *John Chambers*

Stalker ★★★★ PG

1979 USSR Colour and BW 154mins

The son of a poet, Andrei Tarkovsky could always be relied upon for visual lyricism. But the terrain traversed during this gruelling trek is anything but picturesque. Chillingly shot in muted colour by Aleksandr Knyazhinsky, the Zone is an area of the forbidding post-meteoric wilderness, that can only be crossed by "stalkers" like Aleksandr Kaidanovsky He has been hired to guide writer Anatoli Solonitsyn and professor Nikolai Grinko to the Room, a place in which truth and innermost desire can be attained. The metaphysical discussion feels somewhat mundane after what has gone before, but it still leaves you questioning your own beliefs and values. In Russian with English subtitles.

Alexander Kaidanovsky Stalker • **Anatoly Solonitsin [Anatoli Solonitsyn]** Writer • **Nikolai Grinko** Professor • **Alisa Freindlikh** Stalker's wife • **Natasha Abramova** Stalker's daughter

Director *Andrei Tarkovsky*

Screenplay *Arkady Strugatsky, Boris Strugatsky, from the book "Picnic by the Roadside" by Arkady Strugatsky*

The Stand ★★★★ 15

TV 1994 US Colour 345mins

The forces of good take a post-apocalyptic stand against evil in Stephen King's four-part, eight-hour adaptation of his own 1,150-page über-novel. Set after the world has been decimated by a military-created "super-flu" virus, the mini-series follows the epidemic's survivors as they struggle to cope with the collapse of civilisation. While some are drawn to the mysterious Mother Abigail (Ruby Dee) and her hopeful view of humanity's future, others seek out the demonic Randall Flagg (Jamey Sheridan). Gary Sinise, Rob Lowe and Laura San Giacomo head a star-studded cast, who successfully deliver an eclectic mix of fine performances. King's screenplay is consistently scary, surprising and enthralling, and director Mick Garris makes the most of the project's extensive location photography and no-expense-spared production values. Despite its occasional lulls and strangely low-key climax, this remains an out-Stand-ing offering

Gary Sinise Stu Redman • **Molly Ringwald** Frannie Goldsmith • **Jamey Sheridan** Randall Flagg • **Laura San Giacomo** Nadine Cross • **Ruby Dee** Mother Abigail • **Ossie Davis** Judge Farris • **Miguel Ferrer** Lloyd Henreid • **Corin Nemec** Harold Lauder • **Matt Frewer** Trashcan Man • **Adam Storke** Larry Underwood • **Ray Walston** Glen Bateman • **Rob Lowe** Nick Andros

Director *Mark Garris*

Teleplay *Stephen King, from his own novel*

Star Cops ★★★

TV 1987 UK Colour 9x55mins

Originally conceived for radio, this detective show with a difference was created by Chris Boucher, who'd written for *Doctor Who* and *Blake's 7*, and is set in the near future where mankind has begun colonising space. To battle interstellar crime a special police force is set up and non-conformist cop Nathan Spring (David Calder) is reluctantly put in charge. Expect no alien invasions or slimy green blobs here, the investigations revolve around such mundane matters as murder and industrial espionage, indeed typical whodunit plots that could form part of any cop show but given a new twist by virtue of taking place in space. The series only ran for nine episodes – a shame as the characters were well developed and the plots nicely thought out, if a little bit too plodding in its desire for total realism over fantasy.

David Calder Nathan Spring • **Erick Ray Evans** David Theroux • **Trevor Cooper** Colin Devis • **Linda Newton** Pal Kenzy • **Jonathan Adams** Alexander Krivenko • **Sayo Inaba** Anna Shoun

Devised by *Chris Boucher*

Producer *Evgeny Gridneff*

Star Kid ★★★ PG

1997 US Colour 96mins

This is clearly aimed at the pre-pubescent crowd, but it will manage to touch the child in older viewers as well. Joseph Mazzello gives an engaging performance as an ignored and bullied child who isn't having much luck with girls either. In a scrap yard he comes across a combat-enhancement suit (with its own intelligence) from an alien race. After using it to get revenge against the school bully, he is confronted by a much more formidable enemy, in the form of an alien determined to capture the suit. Cyborsuit's intelligence – taking everything Mazzello says literally – provides much amusement, and the rest of the movie serves up enough action to satisfy the kids. Contains some strong language.

Joseph Mazzello Spencer Griffith • **Richard Gilliland** Roland Griffith • **Corinne Bohrer** Janet Holloway • **Alex Daniels** Cyborsuit • **Joey Simmrin** Turbo Bruntley • **Ashlee Levitch** Stacey Griffith • **Jack McGee** Hank Bruntley • **Lauren Eckstrom** Michelle

Director/Screenplay *Manny Coto*

Star Knight ★★★ PG

1985 Sp Colour 87mins

One of the last movies cult actor Klaus Kinski made before his death is this very weird Spanish-produced mixture of medieval adventure and science fiction. Kinski is a benevolent alchemist who introduces a telepathic alien to the king's daughter, Maria Lamor. When she falls in love with the extraterrestrial hunk and decides to accompany him back home to the stars, priest Fernando Rey encourages knight Harvey Keitel to stop battling dragons and turn his attention towards felling the spaceship. As peculiar as it sounds, with an oddball sense of humour permeating every frame, director/producer Fernando Colomo's impressively mounted sword and sorcery saga with a sci-fi edge has real curiosity value.

Klaus Kinski Boetius • **Harvey Keitel** Clever • **Fernando Rey** Fray Lupo • **Maria Lamor** Alba • **Miguel Bose** Ix

Director *Fernando Colomo*

Screenplay *Andreu Martin, Miguel Angel Nieto, Fernando Colomo*

Star Maidens ★★

TV 1976 UK/W Ger Colour 13x30mins

Two men, Adam (Pierre Brice) and Shem (Gareth Thomas, later to find fame as the titular character in *Blake's 7*) escape from the woman-ruled planet of Mendusa to Earth only to find themselves hunted down by female security officers including Judy Geeson as Grand Councillor Fulvia and Christiane Kruger as Security Controller Octavia. Effects were patchy with models for the futuristic Menusan cities clearly being constructed from egg boxes and cotton reels while the acting and casting clearly showed that Mendusa was populated entirely by beautiful, scantily clad women and their humble men-servants. Although the writing was generally of a high standard, the show is remembered more for its overt sexist role-reversal tricks and it's restrictively low budget. Unfortunately it will allways be regarded as a poor cousin to *Space: 1999.*

Pierre Brice Adam • **Gareth Thomas** Shem • **Judy Geeson** Fulvia • **Christiane Kruger** Octavia • **Lisa Harrow** Liz Becker • **Dawn Addams** President

Star Trek ★★★★★ U PG

TV 1966-1969 US Colour 79x60mins

Without doubt the most popular and influential TV sci-fi series of all-time, Gene Roddenberry's 23rd-century "wagon train to the stars" offers a groundbreaking blend of space adventure, drama, comedy and allegory. The series revolves around the legendary deep space exploits of Captain James T Kirk and the crew of the original Starship *Enterprise*, and successfully combines an enormously enjoyable tour of the "final frontier" with a feel-good look at human potential. While cynics may mock its dated visuals and occasionally ridiculous plotlines, the show's imaginative concepts, uplifting tone and endearing performances remain timeless in their appeal, and have left successive generations of viewers beaming with joy. Followed by nine movies and three TV

Classic *Trek*: with an impact beyond its time, *Star Trek* featured US TV's first inter-racial kiss among other memorable moments

series, the franchise still going strong. A new series, *Star Trek: Enterprise*, is scheduled to launch in Autumn 2001, with *Quantum Leap*'s Scott Bakula going where no man has gone before...

William Shatner Capt James T Kirk • **Leonard Nimoy** Mr Spock • **DeForest Kelley** Dr Leonard "Bones" McCoy • **James Doohan** Chief Engineer Montgomery "Scotty" Scott • **George Takei** Lt Sulu • **Nichelle Nicholls** Lt Uhuru • **Majel Barrett** Nurse Christine Chapel
Created by *Gene Roddenberry*
Producer *Gene Roddenberry*

SFacts

Gene Roddenberry's first pilot for the series, *The Cage*, was rejected by network executives. Not transmitted until September 1988, the episode was screened during the run of *Star Trek: the Next Generation*, to fill a gap created by a writers' strike. However, footage from the episode popped up in the two-parter, *The Menagerie*, featuring Jeffrey Hunter as Captain Christopher Pike, who was to have been the original commander of the starship *Enterprise*.

Star Trek: the Motion Picture

★★★ U

1979 US Colour 138mins

Dubbed "The Motionless Picture" when it was first released it is rather talky and the *Enterprise* crew does stand around looking awestruck a lot yet the long-delayed big-screen debut of the cult TV series hits epic heights fans can't fail to be moved by. Robert Wise, director of the classic *The Day the Earth Stood Still*, purposely went for *2001* grandeur rather than *Star Wars* mock heroics in an effort to give the beloved characters an enduring film career above their TV repeats. And it worked, as time has shown, despite the plot merely combining *The Changeling* and *The Doomsday Machine* episodes in one glorious space glob.

William Shatner Captain James T Kirk • **Leonard Nimoy** Mr Spock • **DeForest Kelley** Dr Leonard "Bones" McCoy • **Stephen Collins** Commander Willard Decker • **Persis Khambatta** Ilia • **James Doohan** Scotty • **George Takei** Sulu • **Nichelle Nichols** Uhura • **Walter Koenig** Chekov • **Majel Barrett** Dr Christine Chapel
Director *Robert Wise*
Screenplay *Harold Livingston, Gene Roddenberry, from a story by Alan Dean Foster, from the TV series created by Gene Roddenberry*
Music *Jerry Goldsmith*

Star Trek II: the Wrath of Khan

★★★★ 15

1982 US Colour 108mins

The big screen sequel to the 1967 TV episode *Space Seed* is truer in spirit to the beloved space opera than the first feature and a firm favourite with some fans. Nicholas Meyer – who also directed *Star Trek VI* – stresses the narrative values that made the original series so compelling and vibrantly weaves the thematic motifs of life, loss and adventure together as he expertly continues the saga of genetic superman Ricardo Montalban wreaking vengeance against the *Enterprise* crew for sending him to a prison colony. Leonard Nimoy has rarely been so moving.

William Shatner Admiral James T Kirk • **Leonard Nimoy** Spock • **DeForest Kelley** Dr Leonard "Bones" McCoy • **James Doohan** Scotty • **Walter Koenig** Chekov • **George Takei** Sulu • **Nichelle Nichols** Commander Uhura • **Bibi Besch** Dr Carol Marcus • **Merritt Butrick** David • **Paul Winfield** Captain Terrell • **Kirstie Alley** Saavik • **Ricardo Montalban** Khan
Director *Nicholas Meyer*
Screenplay *Jack B Sowards, from a story by Harve Bennett, Jack B Sowards, from the TV series created by Gene Roddenberry*

Star Trek III: the Search for Spock ★★★ PG

1984 US Colour 100mins

There are no real surprises in this ponderous journey to the final frontier, in which Admiral Kirk hijacks the starship *Enterprise* to help in the rejuvenation of the deceased Spock on the planet Genesis. It's a good character-driven story, marred by Leonard Nimoy's workmanlike direction, a pseudo-mystical ending and an all-pervasive funereal tone that permeates every frame. Amazing special effects supply the wonder and emotional charge missing from what is, in essence, nothing more than a bloated TV episode.

William Shatner Admiral James T Kirk • **DeForest Kelley** Dr Leonard "Bones" McCoy • **James Doohan** Scotty • **George Takei** Sulu • **Walter Koenig** Chekov • **Nichelle Nichols** Uhura • **Christopher Lloyd** Kruge • **Robin Curtis** Lieutenant Saavik • **Merritt Butrick** David Marcus • **James B Sikking** Captain Styles • **Mark Lenard** Ambassador Sarek
Director *Leonard Nimoy*
Screenplay *Harve Bennett, from the TV series created by Gene Roddenberry*

Star Trek IV: the Voyage Home ★★★★ PG

1986 US Colour 117mins DVD

While the anorak Trekker brigade may have grumbled, this Leonard Nimoy-directed instalment is easily one of the most entertaining of the spin-offs from the cult TV series. After three impressive but rather po-faced adventures, the *Enterprise* regulars got the chance to let their hair (what was left of it) down a little for this hugely enjoyable trek. This time around, the chaps have to travel back to eighties San Francisco to free a couple of whales that can save the Earth from a destructive space probe. William Shatner gets to romance whale expert Catherine Hicks, although his comic double act with Nimoy is a lot more fun, and, while there is little in the way of traditional sci-fi spectacle, the crew clearly relish the opportunity to poke fun at the idiosyncrasies of modern-day California. Contains swearing.

William Shatner Captain James T Kirk • **Leonard Nimoy** Spock • **Catherine Hicks** Dr Gillian Taylor • **DeForest Kelley** Dr Leonard "Bones" McCoy • **James Doohan** Scotty • **George Takei** Sulu • **Walter Koenig** Chekov • **Nichelle Nichols** Commander Uhura • **Majel Barrett** Dr Christine Chapel • **Jane Wyatt** Amanda, Spock's mother • **Mark Lenard** Sarek • **Robin Curtis** Lieutenant Saavik
Director *Leonard Nimoy*
Screenplay *Harve Bennett, Steve Meerson, Peter Krikes, Nicholas Meyer, from a story by Leonard Nimoy, Harve Bennett, from the TV series created by Gene Roddenberry*

Star Trek V: the Final Frontier ★★★ PG

1989 US Colour 102mins DVD

It was only fair that William Shatner should get the chance to take the controls following Leonard Nimoy's stint in the director's chair for the preceding two adventures, and, while this lacks the wit and panache of number four, it still makes for an enjoyable romp. The story this time revolves around a messianic figure (Laurence Luckinbill) who is holding a distant planet hostage but, in reality, wants to lay his hands on the ageing *Enterprise* and its even creakier crew. Shatner, who also had a hand in the script, seems to be aiming for a more mystical plane than usual, but the plot is embarrassingly trite at times. In the end it just about gets by, thanks to the delightful interplay between Shatner, Nimoy and DeForest Kelley, and a typically action-packed finale. Contains swearing.

William Shatner Captain James T Kirk • **Leonard Nimoy** Mr Spock • **DeForest Kelley** Dr Leonard "Bones" McCoy • **James Doohan** Scotty • **Walter Koenig** Chekov • **Nichelle Nichols** Lieutenant Uhura • **George Takei** Sulu • **Laurence Luckinbill** Sybok • **David Warner** St John Talbot
Director *William Shatner*
Screenplay *David Loughery, from a story by William Shatner, Harve Bennett, David Loughery, from the TV series created by Gene Roddenberry*

Star Trek VI: the Undiscovered Country ★★★★ PG

1991 US Colour 108mins DVD

The *Star Trek* movie series goes supernova with an outstanding episode directed by Nicholas Meyer, who also gave the first sequel, *The Wrath of Khan*, massive hit-and-myth credibility. Mirroring world news events of the time (the Soviet Union's dissolution), Meyer crafts a near perfect blend of humanistic messages, affectionate lampooning, epic visuals and fairy-tale imagination as the classic *Enterprise* crew encounters treachery during prospective peace negotiations with the Klingons. Clever Shakespearean touches also heighten the drama.

William Shatner Captain James T Kirk • **Leonard Nimoy** Spock • **DeForest Kelley** Dr Leonard "Bones" McCoy • **James Doohan** Montgomery "Scotty" Scott • **Walter Koenig** Pavel Chekov • **Nichelle Nichols** Nytoba Uhuru • **George Takei** Captain Hikaru Sulu • **Kim Cattrall** Lieutenant Valeris • **Mark Lenard** Sarek • **Christopher Plummer** General Chang • **Iman** Martia • **Grace Lee Whitney** *Excelsior* communications officer • **Brock Peters** Admiral Cartwright • **Leon Russom** Chief in Command • **Kurtwood Smith** Federation President • **David Warner** Chancellor Gorkon • **Rosana Desoto** Azetbur • **Christian Slater** *Excelsior* crew-man
Director *Nicholas Meyer*
Screenplay *Nicholas Meyer, Denny Martin Flinn, from a story by Leonard Nimoy, Lawrence Konner, Mark Rosenthal, from the TV series created by Gene Roddenberry*

Star Trek: Generations ★★★★ PG

1994 US Colour 113mins

A clever story in which some of the old *Star Trek* cast, led by William Shatner, unite with the *Next Generation* crew, commanded by Patrick Stewart, to stop mad scientist Malcolm McDowell tapping into an intergalactic energy source that can bring one's most desired fantasies to life. Non-fans may get a little confused, but if you can stay with the multi-layered, character-heavy and self-referential plot, this fun science-fiction saga builds up to warp speed for an exciting climax. Similar in tone to the *Next Generation* TV series (it was produced, written and directed by the same team), this special-effects laden adventure shamelessly trades in fan sentiment and nostalgia as the movie baton is passed from one *Enterprise* crew to the other, and the two-much loved generations of space folk heroes merge into one space/time continuum. Stewart brings all his dignity to bear as the commander of the famous starship and almost single-handedly makes *The Next Generation's* transition from small to big screen an effective and winning one. There's great work, too, from McDowell on snarlingly good villainous

The Next Generation: frequent trips to the holodeck and excursions to alternate universes characterised many of the episodes

form, and Brent Spiner as Data, coping well with the wonders of human emotions courtesy of a new silicon chip.

Patrick Stewart Captain Jean-Luc Picard • **Jonathan Frakes** Commander William T Riker • **Brent Spiner** Lt Commander Data • **Levar Burton** Lt Commander Geordi La Forge • **Michael Dorn** Lt Worf • **Gates McFadden** Dr Beverly Crusher • **Marina Sirtis** Counselor Deanna Troi • **Malcolm McDowell** Soran • **James Doohan** Scotty • **Walter Koenig** Chekov • **William Shatner** Captain James T Kirk • **Whoopi Goldberg** Guinan

Director *David Carson*

Screenplay *Ronald D Moore, Brannon Braga, from a story by Brannon Braga, Ronald D Moore, Rick Berman, from characters created by Gene Roddenberry*

Star Trek: First Contact

★★★★★ 12

1996 US Colour 106mins DVD

The eighth instalment in the long-running series marks the first time *The Next Generation* crew carry an entire adventure on their capable shoulders and the result is a first-rate intergalactic cracker. Determined to assimilate mankind into their own race, the Borg travel back in time to sabotage that pivotal moment in Earth's destiny when zany scientist James Cromwell invented Warp Drive, allowing humanity to make contact with aliens for the first time. Because he almost became one of the half organic/half machine Borg himself in the distant past, what else can Patrick Stewart do except follow his nemesis and sort things out? Epic in scope, grandiose in emotional sweep and featuring orgasmic special effects – especially the Borg, redesigned from the television series for extra chills – *First Contact* is captivating science fiction packed with subversive thrills, tense action and Trekker in-jokes. Expertly marshalled by first-time director Jonathan Frakes with a keen visual eye and an inherent understanding of the history and importance of the series, this is one movie that satisfies both Trek fanatics and general audiences alike. Stewart turns in his usual commanding performance and Alice Krige (*Ghost Story*) is sensational as the insidious Borg Queen, who brilliantly veers between villainy, mystery and sensuality.

Patrick Stewart Captain Jean-Luc Picard • **Jonathan Frakes** Commander William Riker • **Brent Spiner** Lt Commander Data • **LeVar Burton** Lt Commander Geordi La Forge • **Michael Dorn** Lt Commander Worf • **Gates McFadden** Dr Beverly Crusher • **Marina Sirtis** Counselor Deanna Troi • **Alice Krige** Borg Queen • **James Cromwell** Zefram Cochrane • **Alfre Woodard** Lily Sloane • **Dwight Schultz** Lt Barclay • **Robert Picardo** Holographic doctor

Director *Jonathan Frakes*

Screenplay *Brannon Braga, Ronald D Moore, from a story by Rick Berman, Brannon Braga, Ronald D Moore, from the TV series created by Gene Roddenberry*

Star Trek: Insurrection ★★★ PG

1998 US Colour 98mins DVD

Ethnic cleansing gets the *Star Trek* treatment in the ninth feature aimed squarely at fans of the long-running series and its feature-film spin-offs. But even they will have seen plenty of episodes of *The Next Generation* that are better, richer and deeper than this. Going comfortably where *Star Trek* has boldly gone before, this light-hearted tale concerns a Fountain of Youth planet and the two races who are struggling for the right to use it. There's nothing new in this proficient cocktail of predictable space heroics and *Lost Horizon* homages with its push-button script that allows each member of the crew a moment of glory, especially Brent Spinder's Data. Visually impressive (marking the first use of computer digitals for the spaceship sequences), the film also features F Murray Abraham as a neat villain, while Broadway star Donna Murphy is affecting as Captain Picard's love interest.

Patrick Stewart Captain Jean-Luc Picard • **Jonathan Frakes** Riker • **Brent Spiner** Lt Commander Data • **LeVar Burton** Lt Commander Geordi La Forge • **Michael Dorn** Lt Commander Worf • **Gates McFadden** Beverly Crusher • **Marina Sirtis** Troi • **F Murray Abraham** Ru'afo • **Donna Murphy** Anij • **Anthony Zerbe** Dougherty • **Gregg Henry** Gallatin

Director *Jonathan Frakes*

Screenplay *Michael Piller, from a story by Rick Berman, Michael Piller, from the TV series created by Gene Roddenberry*

Star Trek: Deep Space Nine

★★★★ U PG 12

TV 1993-1999 US Colour 176x60mins

Widely dubbed as "*Star Trek*'s problem child", the franchise's controversial third small-screen incarnation, offers a darker, edgier and altogether more challenging look at humanity's future. Set aboard a Federation-controlled space station which becomes the focal point of an epic interstellar power struggle, the first post-Roddenberry *Trek* ups the political, pseudo-religious and militaristic content, and boldly introduces an element of moral ambiguity into the mix. Avery Brooks's underwhelming portrayal of Captain Sisko awkwardly heads a rich ensemble of strong and distinctive characters, all of whom are well served by a diverse range of fascinating storylines. While the resulting series doesn't always feel like *Star Trek*, it still makes for a rewarding, memorable and visually impressive sci-fi saga.

Avery Brooks Captain Benjamin Sisko • **Rene Auberjonois** Odo • **Nana Visitor** Kira Nerys • **El Fadil Siddig** Dr Julian Bashir • **Colm Meaney** Chief Miles O'Brian • **Armin Shimerman** Quark • **Terry Farrell** Jadzia Dax • **Cirroc Lofton** Jake Sisko • **Michael Dorn** Lt Cmdr Worf

Created by *Rick Berman, Michael Piller*

Star Trek: the Next Generation

★★★★★ U PG

TV 1987-1994 US Colour 178x60mins

Almost a century after the original *Star Trek*, Captain Jean-Luc Picard and the crew of the fifth Starship *Enterprise* continue humanity's mission to boldly go where no one has gone before. Essentially a big-budget update of its illustrious predecessor, *Star Trek*'s first spin-off series delivers more of the superlative sci-fi adventure, inspiring social commentary and warm character interplay that is at heart of the franchise's success. This new enterprise also benefits enormously from an infusion of movie-quality special effects and a truly commanding central performance from Royal Shakespeare Company veteran Patrick Stewart. Despite a bumpy opening two seasons and the occasional wrong turn, this seven-year voyage comfortably emerges as both a worthy successor to *Star Trek* and a classic science-fiction series in its own right.

Patrick Stewart Captain Jean-Luc Picard • **Jonathan Frakes** Commander William T Riker • **Gates McFadden** Dr Beverly Crusher • **Brent Spiner** Lieutenant Commander Data • **Marina Sirtis** Lt Cmdr Deanna Troi • **LeVar Burton** Lt Geordie LaForge • **Michael Dorn** Lt Worf • **Wil Wheaton** Wesley Crusher

Created by *Gene Roddeberry*

Executive producer *Gene Roddenberry, Rick Berman, Michael Pille, Jeri Taylor*

The emissary: Avery Brooks as Capt Sisko, beleaguered leader of *Deep Space Nine*

Welcome to the Delta quadrant, *Voyager*: Kate Mulgrew leads the journey home

Star Trek: Voyager ★★★ U PG 12

TV 1995-2001 US Colour 172x60mins

The *Star Trek* franchise goes back-to-basics with its fourth series, which propels the Starship *Voyager* into the deep reaches of the Delta Quadrant and follows its epic journey back to Earth. Despite being set in an unchartered alien galaxy, *Voyager* struggles to go anywhere *Star Trek* has not gone before, and seems laden with storylines and characters that have come straight out of *The Next Generation*. But even as a "greatest hits" package, the series isn't short of crowd-pleasing sci-fi adventure, stunning effects or feel-good human drama. Kate Mulgrew confidently leads the voyage home (having replaced first choice star Geneviève Bujold), while Robert Picardo's Doctor and Jeri Ryan's irresistible Borg bombshell Seven of Nine have no trouble filling the show's laughter and lust quotas respectively.

Kate Mulgrew Captain Kathryn Janeway • **Robert Beltran** Cmdr Chakotay • **Tim Russ** Lt Cmdr Tuvok • **Robert Duncan McNeill** Lt Tom Paris • **Roxann Dawson** Chief Engineer Lt B'Elanna Torres • **Robert Picardo** The Doctor • **Ethan Phillips** Neelix • **Garrett Wang** Ensign Harry Kim • **Jeri Ryan** Seven of Nine • **Jennifer Lien** Kes

Created by *Rick Berman, Michael Piller, Jeri Taylor*

Executive producer *Rick Berman, Kenneth Biller, Brannon Bragga*

Star Wars Episode IV: a New Hope ★★★★★ U

1977 US Colour 115mins

Endlessly imitated but never rivalled, this first instalment of George Lucas's space opera dresses up the timeless tale of good versus evil with ground-breaking special effects and a dazzling array of intergalactic characters. Mark Hamill plays Luke Skywalker, whose dull life on a remote planet is thrown into chaos when he intercepts a distress call from beleaguered Princess Leia (Carrie Fisher). With robots R2D2 and C3PO in tow, Luke teams up with an ageing Jedi warrior (Alec Guinness) and a cynical space rogue (a star-making turn from Harrison Ford) to rescue Leia from the clutches of the evil Darth Vader. Breathless action collides with sci-fi theatrics and more than a hint of mysticism to create a new style of cinema that remains unmatched for sheer entertainment value.

Mark Hamill Luke Skywalker • **Harrison Ford** Han Solo • **Carrie Fisher** Princess Leia Organa • **Peter Cushing** Grand Moff Tarkin • **Alec Guinness** Ben (Obi-Wan) Kenobi • **Anthony Daniels** See Threepio (C3PO) • **Kenny Baker (1)** Artoo-Detoo (R2D2) • **Peter Mayhew** Chewbacca • **Dave Prowse** Darth Vader • **James Earl Jones** Darth Vader • **Phil Brown** Uncle Owen Lars • **Shelagh Fraser** Aunt Beru Lars

Director/Screenplay *George Lucas*

Producer *Gary Kurtz*

Cinematographer *Gilbert Taylor* • ***Music*** *John Williams* • ***Art director*** *John Barry (2)*

Star Wars Episode V: the Empire Strikes Back ★★★★★ U

1980 US Colour 124mins

In the second part of George Lucas's first *Star Wars* trilogy, Darth Vader sends Imperial troops to crush the rebels on the ice planet Hoth, while Luke Skywalker searches out Jedi master Yoda for further instruction in the mysterious ways of "the Force". Irvin Kershner takes over the directing reins and splendidly continues the space saga, darkening the imagery of Lucas's vibrant, futuristic fairy tale and deepening its narrative with provocative plot strands. The much-loved characters are developed in intriguing ways, events take place all over the universe, and there's a cynical, harder edge that lifts this sequel above the serial roots of its predecessor. Kershner's imaginative supervision of Lucas's brainchild gives it a truly epic dimension, adding a mature, philosophical aspect to the nonstop barrage of brilliant special effects.

Mark Hamill Luke Skywalker • **Harrison Ford** Han Solo • **Carrie Fisher** Princess Leia • **Billy Dee Williams** Lando Calrissian • **Anthony Daniels** C-3PO • **David Prowse [Dave Prowse]** Darth Vader • **James Earl Jones** Voice of Darth Vader • **Peter Mayhew** Chewbacca • **Kenny Baker (1)** R2-D2 • **Frank Oz** Yoda • **Julian Glover** General Veers • **Jeremy Bulloch** Boba Fett • **Kenneth Colley** Admiral Piett • **Alec Guinness** Ben Kenobi
Director *Irvin Kershner*
Screenplay *Leigh Brackett, Lawrence Kasdan, from a story by George Lucas*
Executive producer *George Lucas*
Music *John Williams* • ***Art Director*** *Norman Reynold*

Star Wars Episode VI: Return of the Jedi ★★★★ U

1983 US Colour 131mins

Sequels are usually a case of diminishing returns, but this third instalment of the *Star Wars* saga is still essential viewing. Director Richard Marquand jumps straight in where the *The Empire Strikes Back* finished off with a stunning sequence involving the monstrous Jabba the Hutt, and the pace rarely falters from then on, even if the plot is a dash stop-start at times. Mark Hamill still looks more like an enthusiastic schoolboy than an intergalactic hero, but his climactic scenes with Darth Vader work a treat, and, while adults will probably cringe at the cutesy Ewoks, their presence makes this a particular favourite with younger viewers. The massive success of the series' relaunch on video and the first of the new trilogy demonstrated that *Star Wars*'s popularity has not waned.

Mark Hamill Luke Skywalker • **Harrison Ford** Han Solo • **Carrie Fisher** Princess Leia • **Billy Dee Williams** Lando Calrissian • **Anthony Daniels** C-3PO • **Peter Mayhew** Chewbacca • **Sebastian Shaw** Anakin Skywalker • **Ian McDiarmid** Emperor Palpatine • **Frank Oz** Yoda • **David Prowse [Dave Prowse]** Darth Vader • **James Earl Jones** Voice of Darth Vader • **Alec Guinness** Obi-Wan "Ben" Kenobi • **Kenny Baker (1)** R2-D2 • **Michael Pennington** Moff Jerjerrod • **Kenneth Colley** Admiral Piett
Director *Richard Marquand*
Screenplay *Lawrence Kasdan, George Lucas, from a story by George Lucas*

Star Wars Episode I: the Phantom Menace ★★★ U

1999 US Colour 132mins DVD

The second coming of director George Lucas's mythic brainchild is finally here. Was it worth the wait? No. Does it disappoint? Yes. No matter how hard he's tried to recapture the magic of the original *Star Wars*, that vital sense of wonder is missing from *The Phantom Menace*. Instead, Lucas provides a welter of incident, cosmic dilemmas, cryptic forebodings and idiotic dialogue; absolutely phenomenal on the visual front, the film is completely mindless in the story department as characters are placed in position to explain what we already know from his middle trilogy. Forget the overworked plot about Queen Amidala (Natalie Portman) trying to stop the Trade Federation invading her peaceful planet with help from Jedi Knights Qui-Gon Jinn (Liam Neeson) and Obi-Wan Kenobi (Ewan McGregor). Especially forget Portman's overelaborate costumes, McGregor's clipped English accent (throw away those Alec Guinness diction tapes immediately, Ewan) and Jake Lloyd's reading of the child who grows up to be Darth Vader as if he were an extra in a TV commercial. Thrill instead at the state-of-the-art technical wizardry and just enough fizzing action (the truly exciting pod race) to keep nostalgic wistfulness at bay. With virtually nothing on show to touch the heart, only Neeson gives this schematic ever-vending space opera – sadly trapped by its own legacy – what little emotional gravitas it contains.

Liam Neeson Qui-Gon Jinn • **Ewan McGregor** Obi-Wan Kenobi • **Natalie Portman** Queen Amidala/Padmé • **Jake Lloyd** Anakin Skywalker • **Ian McDiarmid** Senator Palpatine • **Pernilla August** Shmi Skywalker • **Oliver Ford Davies** Sio Bibble • **Frank Oz** Yoda • **Anthony Daniels** C-3PO • **Kenny Baker (1)** R2-D2 • **Terence Stamp** Chancellor Valorum • **Brian Blessed** Boss Nass • **Ray Park** Darth Maul • **Celia Imrie** Fighter Pilot Bravo 5 • **Samuel L Jackson** Jedi Knight Mace Windu • **Sofia Coppola** Saché • **Greg Proops** Fode • **Scott Capurro** Beed • **Lindsay Duncan** TC-14
Director/Screenplay *George Lucas*
Music *John Williams*

SFacts

Thanks to digital technology, the sets only had to be built high enough to reach the tops of the casts' heads At 6'4", it was estimated that Liam Neeson necessitated an extra $150,000 in construction costs

Starchaser: the Legend of Orin ★★ PG

1985 S Kor/US Colour 95mins

Notable chiefly for being the first animated 3D film, this is now showing its age but is engaging enough fare. The Orin of the title is a young boy (voiced by Joe Colligan) with hidden powers who finds himself the unlikely saviour of a human race when he discovers a sword with magical powers. The striking animation and design helps distract attention from a plot, which shameless helps itself to elements of both *Star Wars* and the legend of King Arthur. Worth checking out if you're an animé fan.

Joe Colligan Orin • **Carmen Argenziano** Dagg • **Noelle North** Elan / Aviana • **Anthony De Longis** Zygon • **Les Tremayne** Arthur
Director *Steven Hahn*
Screenplay *Jeffrey Scott*

Starcrash ★★ PG

1979 It/US Colour 92mins

Arguably the best directed chocolate box fantasy from Italian hack Luigi Cozzi, co-writer of Dario Argento's *Four Flies on Grey Velvet*. *Star Wars* meets *Barbarella* when space hoodlum Zarth Arn (*Maniac* director Joe Spinell) has delusions of intergalactic grandeur and attacks Christopher Plummer's peaceful empire. So black leather bikini-clad Stella Star (Hammer Scream Queen Caroline Munro) is sent to stop him aided by robot Judd Hamilton (Munro's then husband) and super-powered alien (ex-evangelist) Marjoe Gortner. A truly bad movie that's quite easy to like because of its self-conscious arrogance, garish special effects, almost psychedelic look and Munro's outlandish outfits.

Marjoe Gortner Akton • **Caroline Munro** Stella Star • **Christopher Plummer** Emperor • **David Hasselhoff** Simon • **Robert Tessier** Thor • **Joe Spinell** Count Zarth Arn • **Nadia Cassini** Queen of the Amazon • **Judd Hamilton** Elle
Director *Lewis Coates [Luigi Cozzi]*
Screenplay *Lewis Coates [Luigi Cozzi], Nat Wachsberger*
Production designer *Aurelio Crugnola*

Starflight One ★★★ U

1983 US Colour 109mins

Jerry Jameson specialised in this type of jeopardy movie in the seventies and eighties, directing such made-for-TV gems as *Terror on the 40th Floor* and *The Deadly Tower*, and usually managing to crank up the suspense – often with the most unpromising material. Here, Lee *The Six Million Dollar Man* Majors deals with a new-fangled jetliner in crisis, having been inadvertently chucked into outer space on its maiden flight. Naturally there's a sturdy cast of watchables on board, including Ray Milland and Marlon's acting sister, Jocelyn

(*The Big Heat*) Brando. Keep your eyes peeled for *A Nightmare on Elm Street's* Robert Englund, minus the Freddy Krueger make-up. The special effects, by the way, are courtesy of *Star Wars* wizard John Dykstra, former head of Industrial Light & Magic.

Lee Majors Capt Cody Briggs • **Hal Linden** Josh Gilliam • **Ray Milland** QT Thornwell • **Gail Strickland** Nancy Gilliam • **Lauren Hutton** Erika Hansen • **George DiCenzo** Bowdish • **Robert Englund**
Director *Jerry Jameson*
Screenplay *Robert Malcolm Young, from a story by Gene Warren, Peter R Brooke*
Special effects *John Dykstra*

Stargate ★★★★ PG

1994 US/Fr Colour 115mins DVD

Aliens colonised ancient Egypt through a space-time portal, according to this derivative yet hugely enjoyable cosmic adventure. A shameless marriage between Indiana Jones and the ideas of Erich Von Daniken, its clunkier plot details are neatly disguised by director Roland Emmerich's flair for epic action. James Spader is terrific as the code-cracking archaeologist who accompanies soldier Kurt Russell across the universe to fight galactic tyrant Jaye Davidson, who's clearly wearing the frocks *The Crying Game* couldn't afford. *Stargate* is simple in execution, yet classic in the nostalgic way it evokes the feel of vintage forties serials, with Emmerich doing an outstanding job combining plot strands from literature and other films of the genre with some imaginative special effects and impressive visuals. One of the film's best achievements in this area is its depiction of what it might actually feel and look like being hurtled across the universe at the speed of light. An action-packed, science-fiction rollercoaster ride, it's fabulous fun. Contains swearing and violence.

Kurt Russell Col Jonathan "Jack" O'Neil • **James Spader** Dr Daniel Jackson • **Jaye Davidson** Ra • **Viveca Lindfors** Catherine • **Alexis Cruz** Skaara • **Mili Avital** Sha'uri • **Leon Rippy** General WO West • **John Diehl** Lieutenant Kawalsky • **Carlos Lauchu** Anubis • **Djimon** Horus
Director *Roland Emmerich*
Screenplay *Roland Emmerich, Dean Devlin*
Cinematographer *Karl Walter, Lindenlaub*
Production designer *Holger Gross*

Stargate SG1 ★★★★ U PG

TV 1997– Can/US Colour DVD

A superior spin-off from Roland Emmerich's 1994 sci-fi spectacular, this smash-hit series continues humanity's gate-crashing exploration of the cosmos. Former *MacGuyver* star Richard Dean Anderson leads the SG1 team's tour of alien worlds and civilisations, where they encounter an agreeably eclectic range of aliens and storylines. Although hardly groundbreaking, *Stargate SG1* is consistently well written and successfully veers from undemanding action-packed adventures to thoughtful tales and even comedic romps. In a further parallel to the original *Star Trek*, the show also benefits enormously from the warm interplay between its compelling central characters, with Anderson assuredly heading an extremely likeable cast. Some excellent visuals and a rousing score complete the winning package.

Richard Dean Anderson Colonel Jack O'Neill • **Michael Shanks** Dr Daniel Jackson • **Amanda Tapping** Samantha Carter • **Christopher Judge** Teal'c • **Don S David** General George Hammond
Created by *Brad Wright, Jonathan Glassner*
Executive producer *Brad Wright, Michael Greenburg, Richard Dean Anderson, Jonathan Glassner*
Production designer *Richard Hudolin*

Stargazy on Zummerdown ★★

TV 1978 UK Colour 80mins

A BBC2 *Play of the Week*, written by John Fletcher, this is set in the 23rd Century and tells the story of an annual festival held between the two halfs of England: a high-technology faction and a rural faction (called Albion). A strong cast features Stephen Murray, Roy Dotrice and the future Inspector Dalgliesh, Roy Marsden. In an interesting bit of scheduling, this sci-fi-meets-New Age gentle drama was screened in March 1978, the same week as the 500th edition of *Tomorrow's World*

Stephen Murray Fr John Cuchlain • **Roy Dotrice** Israel Tonge • **Peggy Mount** Opinionated Alice • **Toni Arthur** Ruth Baxter • **Roy Marsden** Sidney Frederick Hayes • **John Hartley** Contrary Harry • **John Ringham** Alf Smith
Director *Michael Ferguson*
Written by *John Fletcher*
Producer *David Rose*
Music *David Fanshawe*

The Starlost ★

TV 1973-1974 Can Colour 16x60mins

Produced by *2001*'s special effects wizard Douglas Trumbull and starring the same film's leading man, Keir Dullea, as a post-apocalyptic space traveller aboard the space ship *Ark*, this had the potential to be something special. The first sign of serious trouble was when creator Harlan Ellison, unhappy with the way his concept was being developed, insisted that his name be removed from the credits (to be replaced with the pseudonym Cordwainer Bird). The bargain-basement production values were the nail in the coffin of this series that died after only 16 episodes, although some of the episodes were re-edited into TV movies.

Keir Dullea Devon • **William Osler** Computer voice/host • **Gay Rowan** Rachel • **Robin Ward** Garth
Created by *Cordwainer Bird [Harlan Ellison]*
Producer *Douglas Trumbull*

Starman ★★★★ PG

1984 US Colour 110mins

A curious alien responds to the *Voyager II* spacecraft's invitation to visit Earth, lands in Wisconsin and takes the form of Karen Allen's late husband in a romantic road movie with a cosmic twist. John Carpenter's religious science-fiction parable has as much heart and emotion as it does special effects, and gives Jeff Bridges a real chance to stretch his acting talent as the extraterrestrial eager to learn about the pleasures and pain of human existence. (Bridges was nominated for a best actor Oscar but lost out to F Murray Abraham.) As the widow Jenny, Karen Allen never had a better role. Funny, suspenseful and moving – have those tissues ready for the heart-rending climax – this engaging space odyssey is one of Carpenter's best efforts. Contains swearing and violence.

Jeff Bridges Starman • **Karen Allen** Jenny Hayden • **Charles Martin Smith** Mark Shermin • **Richard Jaeckel** George Fox • **Robert Phalen** Major Bell • **Tony Edwards** Sergeant Lemon • **John Walter Davis** Brad Heinmuller • **Ted White** Deer hunter • **Dirk Blocker** Cop • **MC Gainey** Cop • **Sean Faro** Hot rodder
Director *John Carpenter*
Screenplay *Bruce A Evans, Raynold Gideon*

Starman ★★★

TV 1986-1987 US Colour 22x60mins

Fourteen years after events in his movie debut, the "Starman" returns to Earth and continues his exploration of human life on the small screen. Assuming the form of *Airplane!* star Robert Hays, the benevolent alien befriends his now-teenage human son and attempts to reunite him with his missing mother, Jenny. While an alien-hunting government agent provides the Starman's quest with a *Fugitive*-style vibe, his TV exploits are actually driven by a touching exploration of everyday human relationships and human problems. Hays's sensitive central performance is captivating, as is his warm rapport with his screen son, a pre-*Brady Bunch Movie* Christopher Daniel Barnes. Their emotionally-charged but admittedly slow-moving adventures were brought to a halt after just one season.

Robert Hays Paul "Starman" Foster • **CD Barnes [Christopher Daniel Barnes]** Scott Hayden • **Michael Cavanaugh** George Fox • **Patrick Culliton** Agent Wylie
Source *the film by Bruce A Evans, Raynold Gideon*
Executive producer *Michael Douglas, James S Henerson, James G Hirsch*

Starship Invasions ★★ 15

1977 Can Colour 83mins [video]

It's hard to say whether this homage to all those cliffhanging serials of the thirties and forties which, like *Star Wars*, decks out its heroes in white and villains in black, is being deliberately cheesy or is just plain bad. Let's give it the benefit of the doubt shall we, or then again, let's not. The calibre of acting is pretty good, with ever-reliable Robert Vaughn as a UFO expert who teams up with a group of earthbound good guy aliens to defeat an invasion by Martian rebels led by Christopher Lee, who only agreed to appear in the film because of Vaughn's participation. This was shot by unheralded B-movie maestro Ed Hunt, who also wrote the script, in Canada to save money, as demonstrated by the retrograde flying saucer effects and dodgy costumes.

Robert Vaughn Prof Duncan • **Christopher Lee** Capt Rameses • **Daniel Pilon** Anaxi • **Tiiu Leek** Phi • **Helen Shaver** Betty
Director/Screenplay *Ed Hunt*

Starship Troopers ★★★★ 18

1997 US Colour 129mins [video] DVD

Director Paul Verhoeven's ultra-violent adaptation of science-fiction writer Robert A Heinlein's classic 1959 novel – a right-wing saga about Earth versus alien bugs – is popcorn exploitation at its lip-smacking, blood-spattered best. Verhoeven opens his delirious extravaganza with a recruitment commercial for the Intergalactic Mobile Infantry and a teaser TV transmission from the distant planet of Klendathu. From there, a race of giant insects wages war against Earth, where society is now run along militaristic lines. Flashback to one year earlier, when poor little rich boy Casper Van Dien enlists in the Infantry to be near his girlfriend Denise Richards (a girl with Fleet Academy pilot ambitions). But he faces stiff competition from handsome Patrick Muldoon. Forget the corny romantic subplots, and thrill instead to the chilling spectacle of millions of giant arachnids swarming over the planet slicing open soldiers with their pincer mouths and impaling them on their razor-sharp legs. The outstanding digitally created effects include a stunning scene in which a starship is scythed in two, revealing multi-deck loads of disaster. Only when Verhoeven tries to elicit sympathy over the deaths of some of his cardboard leads does this sensational cartoon carnage come unstuck. Fortunately the dull bits are never long enough to spoil the sheer, visceral enjoyment of Verhoeven's absurdly apocalyptic, gore-drenched satire. Contains violence and some swearing.

Casper Van Dien Johnny Rico • **Dina Meyer** Dizzy Flores • **Denise Richards** Carmen Ibanez • **Jake Busey** Ace Levy • **Neil Patrick Harris** Carl Jenkins • **Clancy Brown** Sergeant Zim • **Seth Gilliam** Sugar Watkins • **Patrick Muldoon** Zander Barcalow • **Michael Ironside** Jean Rasczak
Director *Paul Verhoeven*
Screenplay *Edward Neumeier, from the novel by Robert A Heinlein*

Steel and Lace ★★★ 18

1990 US Colour 89mins [video]

When his pianist sister Clare Wren commits suicide after being raped, her mad scientist brother Bruce Davison reconstructs her as a cyborg and sends her out to take gory revenge on the five gangster businessmen responsible for her death. Courtroom artist Stacy Haiduk and her cop boyfriend David (*An American Werewolf in London*) Naughton go on Davison's trail. The over-familiar murderous android plot gains enormous shock value thanks to the range of splatter effects used in the death scenes including torso drilling, decapitation and castration. Ex-special effects man Ernest Farino (responsible for animating the Pillsbury Doughboy) keeps things moving at a fair clip with stylish direction and a good eye for suspense building.

Clare Wren Gaily Morton • **Bruce Davison** Albert • **Stacy Haiduk** Alison • **David Naughton** Detective Clifford Dunn • **Michael Cerveris** Daniel Emerson • **Scott Burkholder** Tobby • **Paul Lieber** Oscar
Director *Ernest D Farino*
Screenplay *Joseph Dougherty, Dave Edison*

Steel Frontier ★★ 18

1994 US Colour 101mins [video]

There's nothing wrong with genre splicing, but this lazy post-apocalyptic western is a numbingly predictable affair. Directors Paul G Volk and Jacobson Hart are content to pile up the clichés as Joe Lara, a mysterious gunslinger, comes to the aid of a nice little community which is being terrorised by a gang of futuristic bikers. Brion James is his usual over-the-top self, but you will have seen it all before.

Joe Lara Yuma • **Bo Svenson** Roy Ackett • **Stacie Foster** Sarah • **Billy L Sullivan** Luke • **Brion James** General JW Quantrell • **James C Victor** Julius Quantrell • **Sandra Ellis Lafferty** Ada
Director *Paul G Volk, Jacobsen Hart*
Screenplay *Jacobsen Hart*

Steel Justice ★ PG

1992 US Colour 86mins [video]

This TV movie predated *Jurassic Park* by a year, but it had nowhere near the same impact. Set some time in the next century, the action centres on a cop who follows the advice of a time traveller and transforms his son's toy robot into a fire-breathing, villain-crunching dinosaur. More "Roboflop" than *RoboCop*, this might have worked had it been played for laughs, but this pilot for a TV series that never took off is directed with no sense of its own ludicrousness by Christopher Crowe.

Robert Taylor (2) Lieutenant David Nash • **JA Preston** Jeremiah Jonas • **Joan Chen** Nicole Robbins • **Season Hubley** Gina Morelli • **John Finn** Lt Aaron Somes • **Roy Brocksmith** Colonel Roland Duggins • **Maxwell Crowe** David Nash Jr • **Jacob Vargas** Arturo Gomez • **Neil Giuntoli** Jerrod • **John Toles-Bey** Detective Steve Totten
Director *Christopher Crowe*
Screenplay *John Hill, Christopher Crowe*

The Stepford Children ★★ 15

1987 US Colour 95mins [video]

A dull sequel to Bryan Forbes's genuinely creepy *The Stepford Wives*, with the focus this time on the robotic offspring. Familiar TV faces Barbara Eden and Don Murray are the new family in town who begin to worry that the atmosphere in Stepford is just too good to be true in particular how worryingly responsible the teenagers are. It's an interesting premise but director Alan J Levi singularly fails to find any black humour in the entire piece and the result is a suspense chiller devoid of both suspense and chills.

Don Murray Steven Harding • **Barbara Eden** Laura Harding • **Randall Batinkoff** David Harding • **Tammy Lauren** Mary Harding • **Richard Anderson** Lawrence Danton • **Dick Butkus** Tim Wilcox
Director *Alan J Levi*
Screenplay *William Bleich*

The Stepford Husbands ★★

1996 US Colour

In a desperate attempt to breathe new life into a now predictable concept, this second made-for-TV sequel to 1975's *The Stepford Wives* finds women very much in control of the sinister Connecticut town. Donna Mills is the long-suffering wife trying to make a new start with her petulant husband Michael Ontkean, a novelist with writer's block. He quickly becomes suspicious of the locals' apparent contentment; Mills, meanwhile, starts to wonder if there may be something in the town's revolutionary psychiatric scheme for stroppy males.

Donna Mills Jodi Davison • **Michael Ontkean** Mick Davison • **Sarah Douglas** Dr Frances Borzage • **Louise Fletcher** Mariam Benton • **Cindy Williams** Caroline Knox • **Joe Inscoe** Dennis Knox • **Jeffrey Pillars** Gordon Hayes • **Caitlin Clarke** Lisa Hayes • **Christopher Mallon** Scotty • **Paul Sincoff** Doctor • **Terry Loughlin** Cameron Wallace

Director *Fred Walton*

Screenplay *Ken Wheat, Jim Wheat*

The Stepford Wives ★★★ 15

1975 US Colour 114mins

Intelligent scripting and thoughtful direction by Bryan Forbes turn Ira Levin's bestseller about surburban housewives becoming obedient robots into an intriguing frightener highlighting society's increasing obsession with perfection. It unfolds at a measured pace so the suspenseful mystery can exert a chilling grip before it ultimately appals, and Katharine Ross and Paula Prentiss shine as the two nonconformist women fighting their animatronic-like fate. You'll be looking at those Nanette Newman washing-up liquid commercials in a different light after this. Contains swearing and some violence.

Katharine Ross Joanna • **Paula Prentiss** Bobby • **Peter Masterson** Walter • **Nanette Newman** Carol • **Patrick O'Neal** Dale Coba • **Tina Louise** Charmaine • **Carol Rosson** Dr Fancher • **William Prince** Artist

Director *Bryan Forbes*

Screenplay *William Goldman, from the novel by Ira Levin*

Cinematographer *Owen Roizman*

Make-up *Dick Smith*

Stereo ★★

1969 Can BW 65mins

In the near future, experiments in telepathic exchange are being conducted by the Canadian Academy for Erotic Inquiry. The idea is to remove a group of volunteers' power of speech, increase their latent telepathic powers, give them aphrodisiac drugs and ultimately expose sexuality for its "polymorphous perversity". The tests result in antagonism and violence. This was David Cronenberg's directorial debut and it's a confused, distanced, but quietly disturbing cautionary tale, which introduced some of the major themes of his more mature work.

Ronald Mlodzik • **Iain Ewing** • **Jack Messinger** • **Clara Mayer** • **Paul Mulholland** • **Arlene Mlodzik** • **Glenn McCauley**

Director/Screenplay *David Cronenberg*

The Sticky Fingers of Time ★★ 15

1997 US Colour and BW 82mins

The basic premise of Hilary Brougher's first feature is intriguing enough, with fifties sci-fi novelist Terumi Matthews finding her work taking her in an unexpected direction – 40 years into the future. There she meets fellow writer Nicole Zaray, who shares her mysterious time-travelling abilities and some other disturbing symptoms. However, Brougher's recurring shifts between monochrome and colour, an excess of expository chat and the introduction of other (malevolent) time-travellers make it almost impossible to maintain a grip on the plot. Clearly the intention is profundity, but the overall impression is one of pretension.

Terumi Matthews Tucker • **Nicole Zaray** Drew • **Belinda Becker** Ofelia • **James Urbaniak** Isaac • **Amanda Vogel** Girl in window • **Leo Marks** Dex • **Samantha Buck** Gorge

Director/Screenplay *Hilary Brougher*

Still Not Quite Human ★★

1992 US Colour 90mins

This is the third instalment of a low-tech Disney trilogy about a scientist father (Alan Thicke) and his android son. In this chapter, the son must join forces with other androids to free his eccentric father from an evil industrialist who has kidnapped him. Although there's nothing particularly memorable here, , there's probably enough solid light entertainment to amuse an adolescent audience.

Alan Thicke Dr Jonas Carson/Bonus • **Jay Underwood** Chip • **Betsy Palmer** Aunt Mildred • **Christopher Neame** Dr Frederick Berrigon • **Sheelah Megill** Miss Prism • **Rosa Nevin** Officer Kate Morgan

Director/Screenplay *Eric Luke*

Stingray ★★★ U

TV 1964-65 UK Colour 39x25m DVD

One of the most fondly remembered of all Gerry Anderson puppet shows. *Stingray* is an atomic powered super sub working for WASP (World Aquanaut Security Patrol) in their 2065 war against Titan, despotic ruler of an undersea army intent on dry land supremacy. Piloted by Troy Tempest, whose puppet was modelled on Hollywood actor James Garner, and his trusty second mate Phones, *Stingray*'s nautical adventures also involved Marina, a mermaid with a difference, she has legs!! Marina was rival for Tempest's affections with Atlanta, daughter of WASP's commander in chief, voiced by Lois Maxwell, famous as Miss Moneypenny in the James Bond films, in what must have been the puppet world's first love triangle!

Don Mason Captain Troy Tempest • **Robert Easton** Lt George "Phones" Sheridan/X20 • **Lois Maxwell** Lt Atlanta Shore • **Ray Barrett** Cmdr Sam Shore/It Fisher/Titan

Created by *Gerry Anderson*

Producer *Gerry Anderson* • ***Associate producer*** *Reg Hill*

Facts

Although *Stingray* was the first British television series to be filmed in colour, it was originally broadcast in black and white, as colour television wasn't launched in the UK until 1967.

The Stolen Dirigible ★★★

1966 Cz Colour 88mins

Two years after disappointing with *Insane Chronicle*, Karel Zeman edged back towards form with this Jules Verne-inspired fantasy. Opening at the Paris Exhibition of 1889, the action soon shifts to the transatlantic voyage made by a quintet of mischievous children aboard Cestmir Randa's airship. This culminates in an encounter with the legendary submariner, Captain Nemo. But the highlights are the stop-motion vehicular parades, one of dirigibles – including one crewed by can-can dancers and another that is rowed (Noggin the Nog-style) with gigantic oars – the other of cars (one of which has horse's legs instead of wheels). A Czech language film.

Cestmir Randa Prof Findejs • **Michal Pospisil** Jakoubek • **Hanus Bor** Tomas • **Jan Malat** Pavel • **Jitka Zelenohorska** Katya • **Josef Hauvic** Petr

Director *Karel Zeman*

Screenplay *Radovan Kraty, Karel Zeman*

Cinematographer *Josef Novotny, Bohuslav Pikhart*

The Stone Tape ★★★★★

TV 1972 UK Colour 90mins

Commissioned as "a ghost story for Christmas", this Nigel Kneale script is one of the masterpieces of genre television, a genuine alliance of mind-stretching sci-fi concepts with the suspense mechanics of horror. An electronics company buys up a derelict country house as a research centre to develop new recording media, and the project co-ordinator (Michael Bryant) discovers that a particular room needed for computer storage has not been made ready because the workmen refuse to go into it. A sensitive computer programmer (Jane Asher) sees the ghost of a terrified 19th-century servant girl, and Bryant decides to treat the haunting as a set of data which can be analysed with all the scientific equipment at the company's disposal. As the rational scientists dissect the phenomena, the instinctive Asher decides that something more frightening and much older lies beneath the Victorian spook and is drawn into a tragic finish. Intensely acted, this carries over the themes of Kneale's work on *Quatermass and the Pit*, pitting science against the supernatural and discovering that an explanation doesn't always mean an end to the terror.

Michael Bryant Peter Brock • **Jane Asher** Jill • **Iain Cuthbertson** Collinson • **Michael Bates** Eddie • **Reginald Marsh** Crawshaw

Director *Peter Sasdy*

Written by *Nigel Kneale*

Producer *Innes Lloyd*

Stranded ★★ 15

1987 US Colour 77mins [video]

Friendly aliens crash-land and establish contact with an old woman and her granddaughter in a rural area, but the usual movie misunderstandings occur and the local authorities rush in to make a mess of things. Add an alien assassin and some feisty locals into the mix and you've got 80 minutes of science-fiction fun starring Joe Morton as the Sheriff. It looks pretty good and Maureen O'Sullivan adds a nice touch as a grandma, but it takes a long time to go anywhere.

Ione Skye Deirdre • **Joe Morton** Sheriff McMahon • **Maureen O'Sullivan** Grace Clark • **Susan Barnes** Helen Anderson • **Cameron Dye** Lieutenant Scott • **Michael Greene** Vernon Burdett • **Brendan Hughes** Prince • **Gary Swanson** Sergeant • **Jester** Flea • **Warrior** Spice Williams

Director *Tex Fuller*

Screenplay *Alan Castle*

The Strange Case of the Man and the Beast ★★★

1951 Arg BW 80mins

Considering this was something of a one-man show, it's ironic that it was inspired by Robert Louis Stevenson's classic tale of latent schizophrenia, *Dr Jekyll and Mr Hyde*. But while Mario Soffici co-wrote, directed and headlined this horror fantasy, it was a major departure for an artist whose social-folkloric dramas (owing much to the style of John Ford) had made him a feared critic of the Establishment. Perhaps this explains why, despite the title, the alter ego looks nothing like a beast and seems to spend as much time contemplating the piteousness of his state than commiting acts of unspeakable evil. A Spanish language film.

Mario Soffici • **Olga Zubarry** • **José Cibrian** • **Rafael Frontura**

Director *Mario Soffici*

Screenplay *Ulises Petit de Murat, Carlos Marin, Mario Soffici, from the novel "Dr Jekyll and Mr Hyde" by Robert Louis Stevenson*

Strange Days ★★★★ 18

1995 US Colour 139mins [video]

Ralph Fiennes is a dealer in virtual reality clips that replicate sensory perceptions in director Kathryn Bigelow's dazzling sci-fi thriller. As New Year's Eve 1999 approaches, he tries to track down a killer recording his crimes for the ultimate "snuff" experience in a fascinating look at the dangers of advanced technology and their moral implications. Controversial, highly imaginative and inventively staged, using galvanising subjective camerawork to place the viewer in the voyeuristic frame, Bigelow cleverly reinvents *film noir* for audiences raised on *Terminator 2* while presenting a dark vision on where cinema for pure sensation's sake could be heading. An unsettling and masterpiece. Contains violence and swearing.

Ralph Fiennes Lenny Nero • **Angela Bassett** Lornette "Mace" Mason • **Juliette Lewis** Faith Justin • **Tom Sizemore** Max Peltier • **Michael Wincott** Philo Gant • **Vincent D'Onofrio** Burton Steckler • **Glenn Plummer** Jeriko One

Director *Kathryn Bigelow*

Screenplay *James Cameron, Jay Cocks, from a story by James Cameron*

Strange Holiday ★

1942 US BW 61mins

One of the more bizarre artefacts to have survived from the Second World War, this propaganda piece was financed by General Motors and stars Claude Rains, who returns from a holiday in the backwoods to find America transformed into a Nazi dictatorship. Not quite an American version of *It Happened Here*, it was made in 1942 and shelved until 1945 when Rains himself arranged its limited release. Writer/director Arch Oboler was a maverick talent who started on radio and was best known for the 3-D feature *Bwana Devil*.

Claude Rains John Stevenson • **Bobbie Stebbins** John Jr • **Barbara Bates** Peggy Lee • **Paul Hilton** Woodrow Jr • **Gloria Holden** Mrs Jean Stevenson • **Milton Kibbee** Sam Morgan

Director/Screenplay *Arch Oboler*

Strange Invaders ★★★★ 12

1983 US Colour 89mins [video]

An affectionate parody of fifties' alien invasion B-movies, this film's deceptively simple premise evokes memories of *It Came from Outer Space*, with co-writer/director Michael Laughlin bringing the genre bang up to date courtesy of the marvellous special effects, warmly comic overtones and a sharply observed script. Positively aglow with references to the past, this recaptures exactly the heady atmosphere and demented imagery of its major inspirations. The second in a loose trilogy that began with *Strange Behaviour* but was never completed, this is an almost flawless piece of science-fiction fun. Contains some swearing.

Paul LeMat Charles Bigelow • **Nancy Allen** Betty Walker • **Diana Scarwid** Margaret • **Michael Lerner** Willie Collins • **Louise Fletcher** Mrs Benjamin • **Wallace Shawn** Earl • **Fiona Lewis** Waitress/Avon Lady • **Kenneth Tobey** Arthur Newman • **June Lockhart** Mrs Bigelow • **Charles Lane (1)** Professor Hollister

Director *Michael Laughlin*

Screenplay *William Condon, Michael Laughlin*

The Strange World of Planet X ★★

TV 1956 UK BW 7x30mins

A seven-part ATV serial from 1956, this was among the first attempts at getting in on the *Quatermass* band-wagon. Scripted by René Ray, who also wrote it up as a novel, the story dealt with a couple of scientists, William Lucas and David Garth, who use "Formula Magnetic Field X" to open up a dimensional gateway to Planet X, an otherworldly place where nothing much happens. Director Quentin Lawrence had another stab at the genre with *The*

Trollenberg Terror, surprisingly, both serials were snapped up and remade as relishably silly British sci-fi films with Forrest Tucker.

William Lucas David Graham • **David Garth** Gavin Laird • **Helen Cherry** Fenella Laird • **Paul Hardtmuth** Professor Kollheim • **Maudie Edwards** Pollie Boulter
Director *Quentin Lawrence*
Written by *René Ray*

The Strange World of Planet X ★★

1957 UK BW 78mins

Perhaps because the hysterical levels of fifties Cold War paranoia that swept America never reached the same heights here, Britain never really went for big insect movies. However, the odd ones did slip out and here Forrest Tucker is the obligatory square-jawed imported American out to stop irradiated bugs taking over the world. Cheap and cheerful fun.

Forrest Tucker Gil Graham • **Gaby André** Michele Dupont • **Martin Benson** Smith • **Hugh Latimer** Jimmy Murray • **Wyndham Goldie** Brigadier Cartwright • **Alec Mango** Dr Laird
Director *Gilbert Gunn*
Screenplay *Paul Ryder, Joe Ambor, from the TV serial by René Ray*

The Stranger ★★

TV 1964-1965 Aus BW 12x30mins

An Australian production in two six-part episode blocks telling the story of an alien (Ron Haddrich) who becomes stranded on Earth and befriends three children, played by Bill Levis, Janice Dinnen and Michael Thomas. Eventually the children make a trip back to the alien's home planet of Soshuniss and meet Varossa (Reginald Livermore), the alien's mate. The second six-part story takes on political overtones with a clash between the aliens, the media and Australian politicians.

John Faassen Mr Walsh • **Jessica Noad** Mrs Walsh • **Bill Levis** Bernard Walsh • **Janice Dinnen** Jean Walsh • **Michael Thomas** Peter Cannon • **Ron Haddrick** The Stranger • **Reginald Livermore** Varossa
Written by *GK Saunders*

Stranger from Venus ★ U

1954 UK BW 74mins

A low budget British remake (although uncredited) of *The Day the Earth Stood Still* and starring the same lead Patricia Neal, this is directed by Burt Balaban, who adds a mere hint of American zip to the stiff upper lip atmosphere and limited public house setting. After crashing her car, Neal meets mysterious Helmut Dantine who has travelled from Venus to persuade mankind to abandon their nuclear power experiments. A spaceship arrives to increase the pressure, but the dying Dantine sends it away as he disappears in a puff of smoke.

Patricia Neal Susan North • **Helmut Dantine** The Stranger • **Derek Bond** Arthur Walker • **Cyril Luckham** Dr Meinard • **Willoughby Gray** Tom • **Marigold Russell** Gretchen • **Arthur Young** Scientist • **Kenneth Edwards** Charles Dixon
Director *Burt Balaban*
Screenplay *Hans Jacoby, from a story by Desmond Leslie*
Producer *Burt Balaban, Gene Martel*

The Strangerers ★★

TV 2000 UK Colour 10x30mins

Red Dwarf co-creator Rob Grant once again sets phasers on fun with this Sky One-produced sci-fi comedy. The series follows the bumbling exploits of three aliens who come to Earth on a secret mission and try to pass themselves off as ordinary human beings, much to the bemusement of everyone they encounter. While the aliens' quirky use of language and B-movie-inspired behaviour are initially intriguing, it soon becomes more grating than amusing, and their run-of-the-mill weekly adventures prove increasingly tiresome. Mark Williams, Jack Doherty and a decapitated Milton Jones try hard as the show's eponymous visitors, and Sarah Alexander fills Rina's slinky outfit beautifully. But neither they nor some funny guest turns from former *Blake's 7* stars Paul Darrow and Gareth Thomas can give this offbeat series any lasting impact.

Mark Williams Cadet Flynn • **Jack Docherty** Cadet Niven • **Sarah Alexander** Rina • **Mark Heap** Harry • **Milton Jones** Supervisor • **Morwenna Banks** Supersupervisor
Written by *Rob Grant*

Stronger Than the Sun ★★★

TV 1977 UK Colour 95mins

A typically starry mid-seventies BBC play, combining the powerhouse talents of director by Michael (*Gorillas in the Mist*, *Nell*), writer Stephen (*Shooting the Past*, *Close My Eyes*) Poliakoff and star Francesca (*Dune*) Annis. Annis's performance ia a worker at a nuclear plant who steals some plutonium to make an environmental point, only to find no one really cares, drew wide praise.

Francesca Annis Kate • **Tom Bell** Alan • **Clive Merrison** Gregory • **John Proctor** Edwards • **Gerald James** Higby • **Albert Welling** Bruce • **Bridget Ashburn** Joan
Director *Michael Apted*
Written by *Stephen Poliakoff*

Facts

While directing this *Play for Today*, Michael Apted told his *Radio Times* interviewer: "When this article is read I'll either be in the middle of directing a feature film, or out of work." In fact, Apted went on to direct *The Squeeze*, starring Stacy Keach and Freddie Star, followed by *Agatha* (1978), starring Dustin Hoffman and Vancessa Redgrave.

Stryker ★ 18

1983 US Colour 80mins

What would the exploitation industry have done without *Mad Max*? Here's another quickie clone, directed by the all-too-prolific Filipino schlock merchant Cirio H Santiago. Cowboy-hatted Steve Sandor is the road warrior battling over water with weirdly dressed tribes, including an army of midgets, in this corny futuristic mess. Nothing looks real, everything seems daft and Sandor engenders zero sympathy in a poorly constructed apocalyptic fantasy failure. Contains violence, swearing and nudity.

Steve Sandor Stryker • **Andria Savio** Delha • **William Ostrander** Bandit • **Michael Lane [Mike Lane]** Kardis • **Julie Gray** Laurenz • **Monique St Pierre** Cerce
Director *Cirio H Santiago*
Screenplay *Howard R Cohen, from a story by Leonard Hermes*

Suburban Commando ★★★ PG

1991 US Colour 86mins

The appeal of Hulk Hogan may seem bewildering unless you enjoy seeing chaps pretending to throw each other around a wrestling ring, but at least he is well aware of his limitations when it comes to films. This is one of his more enjoyable efforts, in which Hogan is the alien warrior who lands on Earth and struggles to blend in with Christopher Lloyd's puzzled family. Hogan makes Arnold Schwarzenegger look like an actor of great subtlety, but there are some nice one-liners and *Support Your Local Sheriff!* director Burt Kennedy ropes in a classy supporting cast, which includes Shelley Duvall, Larry Miller and western veteran Jack Elam. Contains swearing and violence.

Hulk Hogan Shep Ramsey • **Christopher Lloyd** Charlie Wilcox • **Shelley Duvall** Jenny Wilcox • **Larry Miller** Adrian Beltz • **William Ball** General Suitor • **JoAnn**

Dearing Margie Tanen • **Jack Elam** Colonel Dustin "Dusty" McHowell • **Roy Dotrice** Zanuck • **Michael Faustino** Mark Wilcox • **Tony Longo** Knuckles • **Mark Calloway** Hutch • **Laura Mooney** Theresa Wilcox • **Dennis Burkley** Deak
Director *Burt Kennedy*
Screenplay *Frank Cappello*

Sunset Heights ★★ 15

1996 UK/Ire Colour 91mins [video]

Set in the near future, this flawed but intriguing thriller presents a nightmare vision of life in Northern Ireland. Two ruthless gangs now police their communities using fear and violence. Caught between the two is Toby Stephens, whose child is believed to be latest victim of a serial killer known as the Preacher. The gangs believe they have found the killer – but is he really guilty? The plotting is confused but there are strong performances from the cast, and director Colm Villa displays some stylish visual touches. Contains violence.

Toby Stephens Luke • **Jim Norton** Sam Magee • **Patrick O'Kane** Friday Knight • **Joe Rea** Victor • **James Cosmo** MacDonald • **Peter Ballance**
Director/Screenplay *Colm Villa*

Super Force ★★

TV 1990-1992 US Colour 48x30mins

Super Force enjoyed two seasons following the exploits of former astronaut Zach Stone (Ken Olandt) in the year 2020. Stone is given a prototype spacesuit and numerous neat gadgets with which to fight crime, and later in the series he also develops psychic powers as the result of a near-death experience. This *RoboCop* clone also featured Patrick Macnee as the computer personality of the late EB Hungerford and Larry B Scott as FX Spinner. The show was apparently sold to the network on the basis of a seven-minute "teaser" featuring the hero on a super-bike rescuing a woman.

Ken Olandt Zach Stone • **Larry B Scott** FX Spinner • **Patrick Macnee** Voice of EB Hungerford • **Lisa Niemi** Carla Frost
Created by *Bruce A Taylor*

Super Mario Bros ★★ PG

1993 US Colour 99mins [video]

How do you turn a popular interactive video game into an equally engaging and exciting movie? Not like this, you don't! More a derivative hotch-potch of *Batman*, *Teenage Mutant Ninja Turtles* and *Blade Runner*, this awkward fantasy contains few trace elements from the "Super Mario Land" games themselves, thereby instantly betraying the very audience it was made for. Bob Hoskins and John Leguizamo try their best as the two plumbers adrift in a parallel dinosaur dimension, but it isn't super, amusing or thrilling by any stretch of the imagination. And yours will be stretched to breaking point. Contains swearing and violence.

Bob Hoskins Mario Mario • **Dennis Hopper** King Koopa • **John Leguizamo** Luigi Mario • **Samantha Mathis** Daisy • **Fisher Stevens** Iggy • **Richard Edson** Spike • **Fiona Shaw** Lena • **Dana Kaminski** Daniella • **Mojo Nixon** Toad • **Gianni Russo** Scapelli • **Francesca Roberts** Bertha • **Lance Henriksen** The King • **John Fifer** Goomba Toad
Director *Rocky Morton, Annabel Jankel*
Screenplay *Parker Bennett, Terry Runté, Ed Solomon, from the characters created by Shigeru Miyamoto, Takashi Tezuka*

Superboy ★★

TV 1988-1992 US Colour 100x30mins

The makers of the *Superman* movies turn their attention to Clark Kent's college days, and deliver a small-screen spin-off which proves that a boy can fly. Despite some strong aerial effects, though, the Boy of Steel's fight against the forces of evil fails to reach the glorious heights of the magnificent big-screen franchise. Instead, the show is a lightweight and eminently disposable flight of feel-good fantasy, propelled by familiar plotlines and straightforward comic-book characters. John Haymes Newton plays the title role in season one before handing the cape and tights to Gerard Christopher, although both are eclipsed by a pre-*seaQuest DSV* Stacy Haiduk as the adorable Lana Lang. In a bid to maintain viewer interest, the series became increasingly sci-fi-orientated during its four-year flight, and was retitled *The Adventures of Superboy* at the start of its third season.

Gerard Christopher Superboy/Clark Kent • **John Haymes Newton** Superboy/Clark Kent (series 1) • **Stacy Haiduk** Lana Lang • **Sherman Howard** Lex Luthor • **Scott James Wells** Lex Luthor (series 1)
Created by *Alexander Salkind, Ilya Salkind*

Supercar ★★ U

TV 1961-1962 UK BW 39x25mins [video]

Although juvenile in the extreme and utilising primitive effects techniques, this nevertheless was a breakthrough series for Gerry Anderson, being his first stab at science fiction, a genre that dominated his later work. The series also coined the word "supermarionation" to describe the particular style of puppetry pioneered by Anderson as well as seeing the introduction of Derek Meddings to the effects team, who later worked on many of the James Bond films and won an Oscar for *Superman*. The star of the show is a vehicle that is car, plane and submarine all rolled into one. Driven by test pilot Mike Mercury and assisted by various boffins and a talking chimp called Mitch, they fight evildoers intent on stealing the supercar for nefarious ends.

Graydon Gould Mike Mercury • **George Murcell** Prof Rudolph Popkiss • **David Graham** Dr Horatio Beaker/Mitch • **Sylvia Thamm [Sylvia Anderson]** Jimmy Gibson
Created by *Gerry Anderson*
Producer *Gerry Anderson*

Supergirl ★★ PG

1984 UK Colour 111mins [video]

A disastrous attempt to extend the *Superman* series by bringing the Man of Steel's comic book cousin (played here by Helen Slater) to Earth to retrieve a vital power source that has fallen into the hands of the evil Faye Dunaway. The story is pretty daft, the special effects merely ordinary and Slater is a rather weak superheroine. Dunaway attempts to get into the spirit of things with a wildly over-the-top performance, but British actors Peter O'Toole and Peter Cook simply look embarrassed.

Helen Slater Kara, Supergirl/Linda Lee • **Faye Dunaway** Selena • **Peter O'Toole** Zaltar • **Mia Farrow** Alura • **Brenda Vaccaro** Bianca • **Peter Cook** Nigel • **Simon Ward** Zor-El • **Marc McClure** Jimmy Olsen • **Hart Bochner** Ethan • **Maureen Teefy** Lucy Lane • **David Healy** Mr Danvers • **Robyn Mandell** Myra • **Jenifer Landor** Muffy • **Diana Ricardo** Mrs Murray
Director *Jeannot Szwarc*
Screenplay *David Odell*

Superhuman Samurai Syber-Squad ★★

TV 1994-1995 US/Jap Colour 52x30mins

Hot on the heels of the success of *Power Rangers*, came a slew of copycat shows, and perhaps the one with the daftest name was 1994's *Superhuman Samurai Syber-Squad*. The 52 episode series starred Matthew Lawrence who is quoted as saying, when the show is mentioned in interviews, "Oh God, that's horrible". Collins would turn into a costumed super-hero by getting sucked into his television when he strummed on his guitar. The arch enemy was a giant robot called Kilokahn, in reality one of Lawrence's classmates, Glen

Beaudin. Amazingly, Tim Curry provided the voice of Kilokahn, just going to show how low he could go.

Matthew Lawrence Sam "Servo" Collins • **Glen Beaudin** Malcolm Frink • **Troy Slaten** Amp • **Kevin Castro** Tanker • **Robin Mary Florence** Sydney "Syd" Forrester • **Jayme Betcher** Jennifer Doyle • **John Wesley** Principal Pratchert • **Tim Curry** Voice of Kilokahn • **Diana Bellamy** Mrs Starkey
Executive producer *Noboru Tsuburaya*

Superman ★★★ U

1948 US BW 15x16mins

Eleven years after he acquired the rights to Jerry Siegel and Joe Schuster's action comic strip, producer Sam Katzman finally brought Superman to the screen. The opening segment deals with the infant superhero's flight from Krypton. But the remainder focuses on his duel with Carol Forman's Spider Lady as she seeks to destroy her flying foe with a kryptonite laser. It's a laughably cheap affair. Yet such was the appeal of the crimebuster who transformed himself from mild-mannered reporter Clark Kent into the Man of Steel that not even ex-dancer Kirk Alyn's unprepossessing performance could prevent it turning a huge profit.

Kirk Alyn Clark Kent/Superman • **Noel Neill** Lois Lane • **Tommy Bond** Jimmy Olsen • **Carol Forman** Spider Lady • **George Meeker** Driller • **Jack Ingram** Anton
Director *Spencer Gordon Bennet, Thomas Carr*
Screenplay *Arthur Hoerl, Lewis Clay, Royal K Cole, from the comic strip by Jerry Siegel, Joe Shuster*

Superman ★★★★★ PG

1978 US Colour 137mins

This big-budget, epic scale version of the Man of Steel legend is irresistible, fabulous entertainment. The elegiac opening – from the destruction of Krypton to Clark Kent's arrival at the *Daily Planet* in Metropolis – turns more traditional comic book when Clark falls for Lois Lane, before a bright and breezy confrontation with comedic criminal Lex Luthor. The deliberate clash of styles generates much excitement and, yes, you'll believe a man can fly. Christopher Reeve is perfectly cast (though Dean Cain fans may now disagree) and as a spectacle it's a highly satisfying confection.

Christopher Reeve Clark Kent/Superman • **Gene Hackman** Lex Luthor • **Margot Kidder** Lois Lane • **Marlon Brando** Jor-El • **Ned Beatty** Otis • **Jackie Cooper** Perry White • **Glenn Ford** Pa Kent • **Trevor Howard** First Elder • **Valerie Perrine** Eve Teschmacher • **Terence Stamp** General Zod • **Sarah Douglas** Ursa • **Jack O'Halloran** Non • **Marc McClure** Jimmy Olsen • **Phyllis Thaxter** Martha Kent • **Susannah York** Lara • **Jeff East** Young Clark Kent • **Larry Hagman** Major
Director *Richard Donner*
Screenplay *Mario Puzo, David Newman, Leslie Newman, Robert Benton, from the story by Mario Puzo, from the comic strip by Jerry Siegel, Joe Shuster*
Cinematographer *Geoffrey Unsworth* • ***Music*** *John Williams* • ***Production designer*** *John Barry (2)*

Superman II ★★★★ PG

1980 UK/US Colour 127mins

Purists may not agree, but this is probably the best segment of the *Superman* saga in terms of plot, free from the occasionally po-faced seriousness of the first and the rampant silliness of the remaining two. Director Richard Lester delivers a knowing, knockabout cartoon with Superman (Christopher Reeve) finding out that he is no longer the toughest guy around when three baddies (underpants on the inside) are exiled from his home planet and arrive on Earth. The effects are equal to the first film and there's a strong supporting cast, including an irascible Gene Hackman and the excellent Terence Stamp in what, at the time, was something of a comeback role.

Christopher Reeve Clark Kent/Superman • **Gene Hackman** Lex Luthor • **Margot Kidder** Lois Lane • **Terence Stamp** General Zod • **Ned Beatty** Otis • **Sarah Douglas** Ursa • **Jack O'Halloran** Non • **Valerie Perrine** Eve Teschmacher • **Susannah York** Lara • **Jackie Cooper** Perry White • **Marc McClure** Jimmy Olsen • **Clifton James** Sheriff • **EG Marshall** President
Director *Richard Lester*
Screenplay *Mario Puzo, David Newman, Leslie Newman, from the story by Mario Puzo, from the characters created by Jerry Siegel, Joe Shuster*

Superman III ★★ PG

1983 US Colour 119mins

Director Richard Lester injected a much needed irreverence into *Superman II*, but he lost his way badly with this third instalment of "the man from Krypton" saga. There are a few neat touches, such as when Christopher Reeve turns nasty, but this proved to be the beginning of the end for the series. The attempt to up the laughter quotient by introducing Richard Pryor doesn't work, and neither he nor Robert Vaughn proves to be an adequate replacement for Gene Hackman's Lex Luthor. Margot Kidder wanted little to do with this sequel and must have been thankful only to get a look-in as Lois Lane, and Pamela Stephenson would probably rather forget her role as Vaughn's dumb girlfriend. Still, for die-hard fans of the superhero, this is adequate entertainment.

Christopher Reeve Superman/Clark Kent • **Richard Pryor** Gus Gorman • **Jackie Cooper** Perry White • **Margot Kidder** Lois Lane • **Annette O'Toole** Lana Lang • **Annie Ross** Vera Webster • **Pamela Stephenson** Lorelei Ambrosia • **Robert Vaughn** Ross Webster • **Marc McClure** Jimmy Olsen
Director *Richard Lester*
Screenplay *David Newman, Leslie Newman, from the characters created by Jerry Siegel, Joe Shuster*

Superman IV: the Quest for Peace ★★ PG

1987 US Colour 92mins

Despite the return of Gene Hackman as the evil Lex Luthor, this creaky, tired third sequel sounded the final death knell for the *Superman* saga. In this one, Christopher Reeve's man in tights has finally brought about peace in our time, but soon finds himself up against Luthor (now a budding arms baron), his irritating nephew (Jon Cryer) and a powerful new foe called Nuclear Man, while his bespectacled alter ego Clark Kent has to fight off predatory publisher's daughter Mariel Hemingway. However, the enthusiastic hamming can't hide the clunking direction by Sidney J Furie and the poor special effects. Stick to the television series.

Christopher Reeve Superman/Clark Kent • **Gene Hackman** Lex Luthor • **Jackie Cooper** Perry White • **Marc McClure** Jimmy Olsen • **Jon Cryer** Lenny • **Sam Wanamaker** David Warfield • **Mark Pillow** Nuclear Man • **Mariel Hemingway** Lacy Warfield • **Margot Kidder** Lois Lane • **Damian McLawhorn** Jeremy
Director *Sidney J Furie*
Screenplay *Lawrence Konner, Mark Rosenthal, from a story by Christopher Reeve, Lawrence Konner, Mark Rosenthal, from characters created by Jerry Siegel, Joe Shuster*

Superman and the Mole Men ★ U

1951 US BW 67mins

Exploitation producer Sam Katzman strikes again with this tawdry quickie made solely to promote the arrival of George Reeves (taking over the Superman role from Kirk Alyn) in the fifties TV series, *The Adventures of Superman*. Sent to cover a story about drilling the world's deepest oil well, reporter Clark Kent soon becomes the Man of Steel when the excavation forces luminous mole men to the surface and the local townspeople take an immediate dislike to their visitors. A thinly disguised plea for racial tolerance, director Lee Sholem's poorly produced comic strip relies on talky dialogue rather than special effects. As the mole men are dwarves in fur pyjamas toting vacuum cleaner ray guns perhaps that's more a blessing in disguise than a minus point! This routine jape featuring pathetic super stunts was eventually cut in half and aired as two episodes in the TV series.

George Reeves Clark Kent/Superman • **Phyllis Coates** Lois Lane • **Jeff Corey** Luke Benson • **Walter Reed** Bill Corrigan • **J Farrell MacDonald** Pop Shannon • **Stanley Andrews** Sheriff
Director *Lee Sholem*
Screenplay *Robert Maxwell, from characters created by Jerry Siegel, Joe Shuster*
Cinematographer *Clark Ramsey* • ***Special effects*** *Ray Mercer*

Supernova ★ 15

2000 US Colour 90mins [video]

Begun by *Romper Stomper* director Geoffrey Wright, finished by *48 HRS* director Walter Hill, re-edited against his wishes by Francis Ford Coppola and then partly re-shot by *The Hidden* director Jack Sholder. It's no wonder this drag of a science-fiction adventure is an incomprehensible mess. Credited to a bogus name – Thomas Lee, the new century's friendlier-sounding Alan Smithee replacement – this relentlessly mediocre *Alien* rip-off at least looks good, as it shambles through the familiar conventions of the genre. A medical crew in deep space answer a distress call and take on board the only survivor of a mysterious mining accident. The stranger (Peter Facinelli) has discovered an alien artefact from the ninth dimension (looking rather like a large glowing lava lamp!) with the power to destroy all life in the universe and start over from scratch. James Spader and Angela Bassett try in vain to soften the ridiculous impact of such clumsy space-opera theatrics, while the rest of the cast do little but disrobe. Alas, the lack of fresh ideas keep this suspenseless, badly edited and overcooked melodrama from rising above even the most routine B-movie throwaway.

James Spader Nick Vanzant • **Angela Bassett** Kaela Evers • **Robert Forster** A J Marley • **Lou Diamond Phillips** Yerzy Penalosa • **Peter Facinelli** Karl Larson • **Robin Tunney** Danika Lund • **Wilson Cruz** Benj Sotomejor • **Eddy Rice Jr** Flyboy
Director *Thomas Lee [Walter Hill]*
Screenplay *David Campbell Wilson, from a story by William Malone*

Supersnooper ★ PG

1981 It Colour 101mins [video]

Sergio Corbucci, one of the most influential directors of Spaghetti westerns such as *Django*, tried to revive the moribund career of comedy cowboy star Terence Hill (Mario Girotti), who with Bud Spencer (Carlo Pedersoli) made the popular *Trinity* series, with this dreadful cops 'n' robbers fantasy caper. Rookie patrolman Dave Speed (Hill) is sent by sergeant Willy Dunlop (Ernest Borgnine) to a remote Indian village to collect a parking ticket. But the area is being used for testing nuclear bombs and the irradiated Speed winds up with super powers that help him fight Miami gangster Marc Lawrence. Terrible special effects, fluffed gags mainly revolving around bodily functions and surprisingly pedestrian direction from Corbucci put this sheer disaster in the top of the flops file.

Terence Hill Dave Speed • **Ernest Borgnine** Willy Dunlop • **Joanne Dru** Rosy Labouche • **Marc Lawrence** Torpedo • **Julie Gordon** Evelyn • **Lee Sandman** Chief McEnroy
Director *Sergio Corbucci*
Screenplay *Sabatino Ciuffini, Sergio Corbucci*

Supersonic Man ★

1979 Sp Colour 85mins

Is it a bird? Is it a plane? No it's another worthless dud from Spain. A desperate attempt to invade *Superman* territory by Hispanic grad-Z director Juan Piquer Simon, this superhero rip-off is an uneasy mix of non-existent plot, flat comic relief and cardboard special effects. With the words "May the force of the galaxies be with me", private detective Michael Coby turns into the Lurex-knickered Kronos sent to Earth to investigate experiments using stolen shipments of radioactive Iridium. Dire in every possible respect.

Michael Coby Kronos • **Cameron Mitchell** Dr Gulk • **Diana Polakov** • **Richard Yesteran** • **Frank Brana** • **Javier de Campos**
Director *Juan Piquer Simon*
Screenplay *Tonino Moi, Juan Piquer Simon*

Surf Nazis Must Die ★ 18

1987 US Colour 78mins [video]

This is a notoriously titled movie even by Troma's standards, taking its place alongside such B-features as *Rabid Grannies* and *The Toxic Avenger* and featuring the usual bad acting and ludicrous plotline. It's set in a future California, where a devastating earthquake has left millions homeless and the beaches have turned into battlegrounds, as rival surf gangs vie for control. The surf Nazis are the most feared, but when they kill a black child, his mother loads up with guns and grenades to wage a one-woman vigilante war. Lovers of trash movies be warned: this is not as much fun as it sounds. It takes itself far too seriously and doesn't even have the "so bad it's good" label to commend it.

Barry Brenner Adolf • **Gail Neely** Mama Washington • **Michael Sonye** Mengele • **Dawn Wildsmith** Eva • **Bobbie Bresee** Smeg's mom • **Jon Ayre** Narrator
Director *Peter George*
Screenplay *Jon Ayre*

Survivor ★★ 18

1987 US/UK Colour 87mins [video]

Another post-apocalypse adventure inspired by *Mad Max*, boosted by imagination and atmosphere that partially compensates for its painfully low budget. Chip Mayer plays the title figure, an astronaut who returns to a nuked world, and searches for a rumoured underground city. What he finds is danger, lead by the city's crazed leader (Richard Moll). The movie's stunning landscapes – including deserts, a rusted-out wreck of a ship, and the underground city – are breathtaking to look at, and the movie succesfully conveys the despair and hopelessness the characters experience. You genuinely feel that this is a dying world, but the excessive voice-over narration is distracting, and there is a distinct lack of action and tightness in the story.

Chip Mayer Survivor • **Richard Moll** Kragg • **Sue Kiel** Woman • **John Carson** Engineer councillor • **Rex Garner** Surgeon councillor • **Sandra Duncan** Biologist councillor • **Richard Haddon Haines** Russian councillor
Director *Michael Shackleton*
Screenplay *Bima Stagg*

Survivors ★★★★ U PG

TV 1975-1977 UK Colour 38x50mins [video]

Scientists are much maligned in science fiction, if they're not playing God with genetics they're responsible for 10ft tall radiation-mutated bunny rabbits. Dalek and *Blake's 7* creator Terry Nation pleasingly casts them again as the bad guys, responsible for a deadly virus escaping from a lab that quickly spreads across the globe killing practically every

Four faces of the Man of Steel (clockwise from top left): Kirk Alyn was a low-key Superman but audiences loved him; George Reeves donned the “S” next for the fifties television series, *The Adventures of Superman*; heartthrob Dean Cain starred with Teri Hatcher in the stylish nineties take on the superhero in TV’s *Lois and Clark: the New Adventures of Superman*; Christopher Reeve flew like no superhero before him in four feature films from 1978 to 1987

living thing it touches. Nation's doomsday saga focuses on one particular group of survivors, mainly of the stiff-upper-lip, middle-class variety, as they come to terms with what's happened and begin to rebuild society. Falling back on primitive skills in order to live and forge a new future, Nation is applauding the strength and endurance of the human spirit. The series, now cult sci-fi viewing, was shot mainly on location amid the quiet beauty of Herefordshire, ably standing in for plague-riddled Blighty.

Carolyn Seymour Abby Grant • **Ian McCulloch** Greg Preston • **Lucy Fleming** Jenny Richards • **Talfryn Thomas** Tom Price • **Denis Lill** Charles • **John Abineri** Hubert • **Celia Gregory** Ruth • **Lorna Lewis** Pet Simpson • **Stephen Dudley** John

Created by *Terry Nation*

Producer *Terence Dudley*

Suspect Device ★ 18

1995 US Colour 90mins

King of the drive-ins Roger Corman was behind this sci-fi tale of bullets, bodies and bombs. Committed fans of the genre will adore the fast-paced action, but those looking for in-depth character development and a plausible plot will be disappointed. The story revolves around US intelligence employee Dan Jericho, adequately portrayed by C Thomas Howell, who inadvertently opens a top-secret file and instantly becomes a wanted man hunted by assassins. Fleeing to New Mexico he learns he's a cyborg marked for elimination. The bottom line is this *Terminator* wannabe doesn't have a big bomb in it for nothing: it serves as both a special effect and a film rating!

C Thomas Howell Dan Jericho • **Stacey Travis** Jessica • **Jed Allen** Artemus • **John Beck** CIA director

Director *Rick Jacobson*

Screenplay *Alex Simon, from a story by Rob Kerchner*

Swamp Thing ★★ 15

1982 US Colour 84mins

Wes Craven's terminally campy adaptation of the eco-friendly DC comic book character is a trivial pursuit into juvenile territory for the hard-core horror director. Dr Alec Holland (Ray Wise) is transformed into the half-man/half-slime creature after an accident with a plant growth stimulant and battles evil genius Arcane (Louis Jourdan), who sees the formula as a way to gain world domination. Adrienne Barbeau goes way beyond the call of duty as the vague heroine valiantly getting knocked around, falling in dirty swamp water and losing her clothes. Elsewhere the tacky special effects, cheap budget and banal dialogue doom this *Incredible Hulk* meets *Southern Comfort* affair completely.

Louis Jourdan Arcane • **Adrienne Barbeau** Alice Cable • **Ray Wise** Dr Alec Holland • **David Hess** Ferret • **Nicholas Worth** Bruno • **Don Knight** Ritter • **Al Ruban** Charlie • **Dick Durock** Swamp Thing

Director/Screenplay *Wes Craven*

Swamp Thing ★★ 15

TV 1990-1993 US Colour 72x30mins

Fresh from starring in two less than overwhelming movies, DC Comics's ecologically friendly marsh-dwelling hero resurfaces in his own TV series. Dick Durock once again plays the eponymous scientist-turned-slimy superhero, while Mark Lindsay Chapman pursues all manner of brilliant and barmy global domination plots as Swampy's evil nemesis, Dr Anton Arcane. The show works hard to make its central character an endearing and quirky eco-warrior, but Swamp Thing's weekly exploits are bogged down by some recycled scripts and extremely variable performances, especially from the scenery-chewing Chapman. Fortunately, the eye-catching presence of a pre-*Sliders* Kari Wuhrer gives proceedings a welcome lift.

Mark Lindsay Chapman Dr Anton Arcane • **Dick Durock** Swamp Thing • **Scott Garrison** Will Kipp • **Carrell Myers** Tressa Kipp • **Kari Wuhrer** Abigail • **Kevin Quigley** Graham

Producer *Steven Sears*

A Switch in Time ★ 15

1988 Can/US Colour 86mins

Also known as *Norman's Awesome Experience*, this tedious time-travel tale is a long way from the cheery dumbness of *Bill and Ted's Excellent Adventure*. The story concerns a scientist, a model and a photographer – all equally annoying – who find themselves accidentally transported back to the height of the Roman Empire. Though it's ostensibly a comedy, there are precious few laughs here. What's more, the movie keeps forgetting its sense of humour, allowing some unexpectedly grim moments that leave a sour aftertaste.

Tom McCamus Norman • **Laurie Paton** Erika • **Jacques Lussier** Umberto • **Lee Broker** Titanus • **David Hemblen** Fabius • **Marcus Woinski** Serpicus • **Gabriela Salas** Felix

Director/Screenplay *Paul Donovan*

Syngenor ★★ 18

1989 US Colour 98mins

A sequel of sorts to the equally unimpressive *Scared to Death*, this is a lurid, cheapo slice of mutant mayhem. The syngenors of the titles are genetically engineered creatures, programmed to kill anyone who crosses their path and who go on to create havoc when they escape from a mad boffinfis lab. Horror fans will appreciate another deranged turn from *Re-Animator*'s David Gale and fans of the *Alien Nation* television series will recognise Jeff Doucette.

Starr Andreeff Susan • **Mitchell Laurance** Nick • **David Gale** Carter Brown • **Charles Lucia** Stan • **Riva Spier** Paula

Director *George Elanjian Jr*

Screenplay *Brent V Friedman, from a story by Michael Carmody*

T

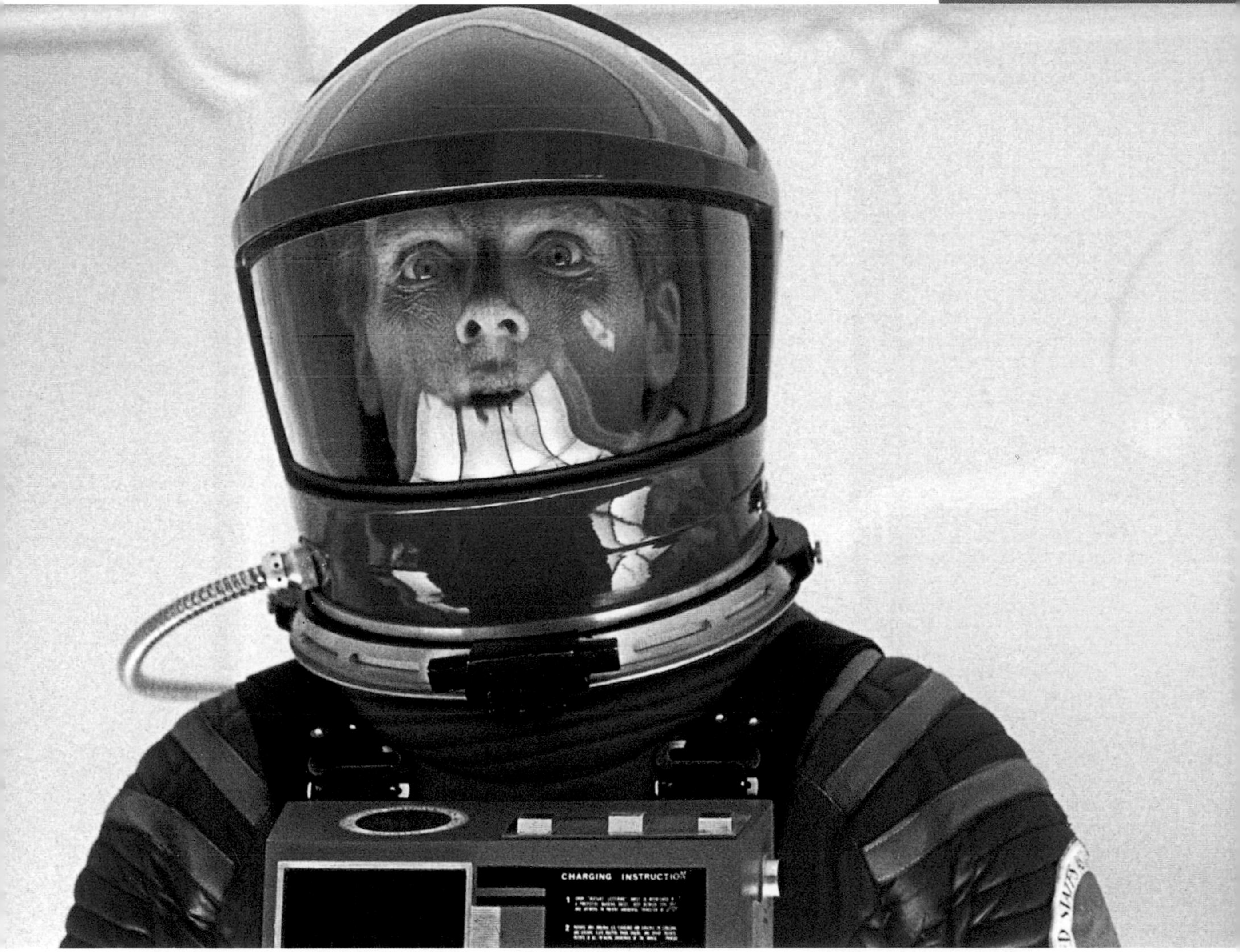

HAL: "**Look**, Dave, I can see you're really upset about this. I honestly think you ought to sit down calmly, take a stress pill, and think things over. I know I've made some very poor decisions recently, but I can give you my complete assurance that my work will be back to normal. I've still got the greatest enthusiasm and confidence in the mission and I want to help **you**."

2001: a Space Odyssey, 1968

TC 2000 ★ 18

1993 US Colour 90mins

In the future, a depleted ozone layer has made living on the surface of the earth almost impossible; the rich have retreated to an underground city, while the less fortunate stay on the surface fighting among themselves and trying to get in. Billy Blanks plays one of the defenders of the city, soon finding himself on the surface and allying with Bolo Yeung when he stumbles onto the inevitable conspiracy. Attempts to pass off run-down locations as part of the futuristic city and other high-tech locations aren't convincing.

Billy Blanks Jason Storm • **Bobbie Phillips** Zoey Kinsella • **Bolo Yeung** Sumai • **Jalal Merhi** Niki Picasso • **Matthias Hues** Bigalow
Director *TJ Scott*
Screenplay *TJ Scott, from a story by J Stephen Maunder*

T-Force ★ 18

1995 US Colour 89mins

The T-Force of the title is the Termination Force, an anti-terrorist squad composed entirely of a form of android called cybernauts. (Didn't they fight the Avengers?) This may excuse the lamentable acting by the main characters, but even the human characters are atrociously played. Really long action sequences are broken up only by half-brained ponderings on whether or not robots are truly sentient beings.

Jack Scalia Jack • **Erin Gray** Mayor Pendleton • **Vernon Wells** Samuel Washington • **Bobby Johnston** Cain • **Evan Lurie** Adam
Director *Richard Pepin*
Screenplay *Jacobsen Hart*

THX 1138 ★★★★ 15

1971 US Colour 82mins

The debut feature from *Star Wars* maestro George Lucas is a bleak, claustrophobic affair which is light years away from the straightforward heroics of Luke Skywalker and Co. The always excellent Robert Duvall takes the title role as a man quietly rebelling against a repressive world where everyone has to have Yul Brynner haircuts, and the police are as frighteningly bland as a McDonald's assistant. The obtuse script doesn't help, but it looks wonderful and Lucas conjures up a genuinely chilling air. Executive producer is none other than Francis Ford Coppola, made under the banner of his Zoetrope production company.

Robert Duvall THX 1138 • **Donald Pleasence** SEN 5241 • **Don Pedro Colley** SRT • **Maggie McOmie** LUH 3417 • **Ian Wolfe** PTO • **Sid Haig** NCH • **Marshall Efron** TWA • **John Pearce** DWY • **Johnny Weissmuller Jr** Chrome Robot
Director *George Lucas*
Screenplay *George Lucas, Walter Murch, from a story by George Lucas*
Executive producer *Francis Ford Coppola*
Music *Lalo Schifrin*

Tales of Tomorrow ★★★

TV 1951-1953 US BW 85x30mins

An anthology show with considerably more ambition than such kidvid rivals as *Captain Video* and *Buck Rogers*, this was produced in co-operation with something called the Science Fiction League of America. It took its material seriously, but was severely hindered by the limitations of live studio broadcasting and often ridiculed, even in an era when on-screen flubbed lines and knocked-over scenery was the norm. The series offered cramped adaptations of famous stories such as *Frankenstein* (with a drunken Lon Chaney Jr as the Monster, failing to smash props under the impression that the live telecast was a rehearsal), but unusually also drew on contemporary sci-fi stories from the magazines. The second season abandoned this quality material and relied on hack TV writers, though Ray Bradbury's *Homecoming* did pop up. Good-ish casts included Cloris Leachman, Lee J. Cobb, Bruce Cabot, Leslie Nielsen (almost a regular, returning several times), Boris Karloff, Franchot Tone, Veronica Lake, Sylvia Sidney, Raymond Burr, Joan Blondell, Darren McGavin, plus unknowns Rod Steiger, Lee Grant, Joanne Woodward and James Dean.

Producer *George F Foley Jr*

Tank Girl ★★ 15

1995 US Colour 99mins DVD

On its release, this was denounced as a travesty, a terrible Hollywoodisation of the cult comic on which it's based. And, yes, this gets nowhere near the sassy black spark of the original, yet those unfamiliar with its source will find it goofy, undemanding fare. Lori Petty is the Tank Girl of the title, demonstrating an early manifestation of "girl power" as she takes on evil Malcolm McDowell in a water-starved post-apocalyptic world. Director Rachel Talalay never quite gets a handle on the mix of comedy and futuristic action, but Petty is surprisingly credible in the lead and McDowell is suitably over the top as the villain. However, the most fun comes from watching hip rapper Ice-T playing a poetry-loving half-man/half-kangaroo. Contains violence and swearing.

Lori Petty Rebecca Buck/Tank Girl • **Ice T [Ice-T]** T-Saint • **Malcolm McDowell** Kesslee • **Naomi Watts** Jet Girl • **Don Harvey** Sergeant Small • **Jeff Kober** Booga • **Reg E Cathey** DeeTee • **Scott Coffey** Donner • **Stacy Linn Ramsower** Sam • **Ann Cusack** Sub Girl
Director *Rachel Talalay*
Screenplay *Tedi Sarafian, from the comic strip by Alan Martin, Jamie Hewlett*

SFacts

British actresss Emily Lloyd was reportedly originally offered the part, but lost out when she refused to shave her head.

Tarantula ★★★

1955 US BW 80mins

Director Jack Arnold's big bug shocker has excellent special effects and makes potent use of haunting desert locations. Scientist Leo G Carroll is working in an isolated laboratory trying to solve world famine and injects a spider with special nutrients that cause it to grow to enormous size. The giant arachnid eventually escapes, first to decimate cattle and then to eat people as it crawls towards a fiery climax. The stillness of the desert allows Arnold to impeccably mount the tension in between the compelling spectacle of a spider on the rampage. Clint Eastwood has a bit part as a jet pilot in this model creature feature.

John Agar Dr Matt Hastings • **Mara Corday** Stephanie Clayton • **Leo G Carroll** Prof Gerald Deemer • **Nestor Paiva** Sheriff Jack Andrews • **Ross Elliott** Joe Burch • **Edwin Rand** Lt John Nolan • **Raymond Bailey** Townsend • **Hank Patterson** Josh • **Clint Eastwood** First pilot
Director *Jack Arnold*
Screenplay *Robert M Fresco, Martin Berkeley, from a story by Jack Arnold, Robert M Fresco*
Special effects *Clifford Stine, David S Horsley*

Target Earth ★

1954 US BW 74mins

A group of misfits stranded in Chicago uneasily band together after robots from Venus launch an invasion attack in director Sherman A Rose's below par programme-filler. Spirited acting by good guys Richard Denning and Kathleen Crowley can't shake off the tedium engendered by an over-reliance on talk rather than action. The lumbering robots with Death Ray eyes are the usual fifties tin cans created by raiding the kitchen appliance draw. An unimaginative pot-boiler.

Richard Denning Frank • **Kathleen Crowley** Nora • **Virginia Grey** Vicki • **Richard Reeves** Jim • **Robert Roark** Davis • **Mort Marshall** Otis
Director *Sherman A Rose*
Screenplay *William Raynor, from the novella "Deadly City" by Ivar Jorgenson [Paul W Fairman]*

Target Earth ★★

1998 US Colour

Extraterrestrials are up to their usual tricks in this made-for-TV sci-fi adventure. When a man goes insane and a little girl is kidnapped, a small-town Illinois cop realises something is terribly wrong. Soon, he finds himself battling insidious aliens who have implanted devices to control the minds of humans, from local citizens to government agents. Writer Michael Vickerman and director Peter Markle have taken every fifties space-invader cliché and fed them into a blender, producing this silly, banal, painting-by-numbers tale.

Christopher Meloni Sam Adams • **Marcia Cross** Karen • **John C McGinley** Agent Naples
Director *Peter Markle*
Screenplay *Michael Vickerman*

Target Luna ★★★

TV 1960 UK BW 6x30mins

Target Luna was the first of four children's shows to air in the early sixties. Written by Malcolm Hulke and Eric Paice, the story resembled André Norton's *The Lost Planet*: three children arrive to stay with their father at his rocket station on a Scottish island. A storm cuts the island off and before long one of the boys (Michael Hammond) takes the place of an astronaut when the rocket heads off to orbit the Moon. Michael Craze went on to star in *Doctor Who* as companion Ben. Three sequels followed: *Pathfinders in Space, Pathfinders to Mars* and *Pathfinders to Venus*.

David Markham Professor Wedgewood • **Michael Hammond** Jimmy • **Sylvia Davies** Valerie • **Michael Craze** Geoffrey • **Annette Kerr** Mrs Wedgewood
Written by *Malcolm Hulke, Eric Paice*
Producer *Sydney Newman*

Tattooed Teenage Alien Fighters from Beverly Hills ★★

TV 1994-1995 US Colour

A deliberately silly spoof of the already-quite-silly-enough *Mighty Morphin Power Rangers*, with licks from *Teenage Mutant Ninja Turtles* and *Beverly Hills 90210* thrown in, this holds the minor distinction of not borrowing its superhero/monster/martial arts scenes from a Japanese show but is otherwise the mixture as usual, with added jokes. The emperor of the planet Molecula (voiced by Ed Gilbert) is sending an army of monsters to make trouble on Earth, and his arch-enemy (Glenn Shadix) rallies four California teenagers, with whom he communicates through special light-up tattoos, to fight for the safety of the planet. The heroes are Leslie Danon, a shallow beauty, Richard Nason, a brainy rich kid, K Jill Sorgen, a liberal vegetarian, and Rugg Williams, a genius nerd. The heroes split their time between kicking alien monster butt and learning life lessons at school; after a single season, they just split.

Richard Nason Gordon Henley/Taurus • **Leslie Danon** Laurie Foster/Scorpio • **K Jill Sorgen** Drew Vincent/Centaur • **Rugg Williams** Swinton Sawyer • **Glenn Shadix** Nimbar • **Ed Gilbert** Emperor Gorganus
Created by *Jim Fisher, Jim Staahl*

Teenage Caveman ★★ U

1958 US BW 65mins

Cult director Roger Corman's prehistoric *Rebel without a Cause* is justly famous for its catchpenny title, cheap dinosaurs (borrowed from the very silly and cheap *One Million BC* made by Hal Roach in 1940), the "stuffed deer" scene and lead actor Robert Vaughn in his pre-*Man from UNCLE* days. He's the titular boy who breaks tribal rules and ventures into the "forbidden land", where he learns his violent society is really a post-apocalyptic one. Vaughn calls this "one of the best-worst films of all time": he's right, but its tackiness is engaging and Corman imbues it with a naive charm.

Robert Vaughn Boy • **Leslie Bradley** Symbol Maker • **Darrah Marshall** Maiden • **Frank De Kova** Villain
Director *Roger Corman*
Screenplay *R Wright Campbell*

Teenage Monster ★ PG

1958 US BW 65mins

This ho-hum science-fiction horror movie was originally titled *Meteor Monster* until the success of *I Was a Teenage Werewolf* caused every horror film to jump on the same bandwagon. In a plot that drags western clichés into its juvenile delinquent mix, teenager Gilbert Perkins is infected by rays from a weird meteor and slowly (very slowly!) turns into a rampaging murderous hairy monster. His protective mother, Anne Gwynne, does her best to hide him in the cellar, but it's not too long before the local sheriff becomes suspicious.

Anne Gwynne Ruth Cannon • **Gloria Castillo** Kathy North • **Stuart Wade** Sheriff Bob • **Gilbert Perkins** Charles Cannon • **Charles Courtney** Marv Howell
Director *Jacques Marquette*
Screenplay *Ray Buffum*

Teenage Mutant Ninja Turtles ★★★ PG

1990 US Colour 87mins

Those kickboxing Teletubbies of yesteryear made their feature debut in this uneven comic-strip fantasy directed by pop-video whiz kid Steve Barron. The story is strictly inane, and what little whiz there is comes from the Henson Creature Shop's nifty turtle effects. In case you'd forgotten, the awesome foursome are pizza-munching, kung-fu fighting, sewer-dwelling super-reptiles who, in this mindless adventure, help perky TV reporter Judith Hoag solve a Manhattan crime spree masterminded by the Shredder, a Darth Vader-voiced rogue ninja master. Elias Koteas scores as a mock turtle vigilante, but little else in this garish affair hits the target, despite Barron covering the cracks with fast editing and cartoon violence. Contains violence.

Judith Hoag April O'Neil • **Elias Koteas** Casey Jones • **Josh Pais** Raphael • **Michelan Sisti** Michaelangelo • **Leif Tilden** Donatello • **David Forman** Leonardo • **Michael Turney** Danny Pennington • **Jay Patterson** Charles Pennington
Director *Steve Barron*
Screenplay *Todd W Langen, Bobby Herbeck, from a story by Bobby Herbeck, from characters created by Kevin Eastman, Peter Laird*

Teenage Mutant Ninja Turtles II: the Secret of the Ooze ★★ PG

1991 US Colour 84mins

Nothing to do with Ivan Ooze (who posed a few problems for the Power Rangers), but the nasty stuff that caused our heroes to live underground, shout "cowabunga" and gorge themselves on bizarre flavoured pizzas in the first place. Seeking once more to stamp out the Foot clan, the turtles team up with reporter Paige Turco and gormless delivery boy Ernie Reyes Jr. The human characters (even scientist David Warner) are pretty pointless, however, as this is all about the latex quartet and monsters like Rahzar and Tokka. Less abrasive than its predecessor and considerably less successful at the box office.

Paige Turco April O'Neil • **David Warner** Professor Jordan Perry • **Michelan Sisti**

Michaelangelo • **Leif Tilden** Donatello • **Kenn Troum** Raphael • **Mark Caso** Leonardo • **Kevin Clash** Splinter • **Ernie Reyes Jr** Keno • **François Chau** Shredder • **Toshishiro Obata** Tatsu
Director *Michael Pressman*
Screenplay *Todd W Langen, from characters created by Kevin Eastman, Peter Laird*

Teenage Mutant Ninja Turtles III ★★ PG

1992 US Colour 91mins

A second sequel, but, by this stage, a largely irrelevant one, as the equally irritating Power Rangers had overtaken the Pizza-loving amphibians in the children's popularity stakes. Writer/director Stuart Gillard tries to inject some life into the project by including some tongue-in-cheek scenes in 17th-century Japan, but it quickly degenerates into half-hearted cartoonish action. Contains some violence.

Elias Koteas Casey Jones/Whit Whitley • **Paige Turco** April O'Neil • **Stuart Wilson** Captain Dirk Walker • **Sab Shimono** Lord Norinaga • **Vivian Wu** Princess Mitsu • **Mark Caso** Leonardo • **Matt Hill** Raphael • **Jim Raposa** Donatello • **David Fraser** Michaelangelo • **James Murray** Splinter
Director *Stuart Gillard*
Screenplay *Stuart Gillard, from characters created by Kevin Eastman, Peter Laird*

Teenagers from Outer Space ★★

1959 US BW 86mins

An all-time good/bad classic featuring one of the most infamous special effects ever put on film – the shadow of a live lobster! When Earth is selected as a breeding ground for herds of giant clawed cannibal Gargons by an intergalactic race, sensitive teen alien David Love arrives on the planet to warn mankind. Pursued by unearthly hit man Bryan Grant and a Gargon that starts decimating the rock 'n' roll population, Love falls for prom queen Dawn Anderson and makes the ultimate sacrifice so Earth can survive. A one-man-show by Tom Graeff, who oversaw every creative department in his $20,000 wonder, this is hilarious trash worth watching for the daft ray-gunning of victims down to plastic skeletons alone.

David Love Derek • **Dawn Anderson [Dawn Bender]** Betty Morgan • **Harvey B Dunn** Grandpa Morgan • **Bryan Grant** Thor • **Tom Lockyear** Joe Rogers
Director/Screenplay *Tom Graeff*

TekWar ★★★ PG 12

TV 1994-96 US/Can Colour 18x60m

Based on the series of "cyberpunk lite" novels penned by *Star Trek* icon William Shatner, the four *TekWar* TV movies (*TekWar, TekLords, TekLab* and *TekJustice*) and short-lived spin-off show follow disgraced cop-turned-private eye Jake Cardigan as he attempts to rid the world of the virtual reality drug known as Tek. Despite being little more than a high-tech cops 'n' robbers caper, the *TekWar* saga makes for a surprisingly addictive slice of fast-moving sci-fi action. Greg Evigan acquits himself well in the undemanding leading role, while Shatner offers a wonderfully OTT performances as his mysterious boss, Walter Bascom. The show's all-important action sequences are deftly mounted and, best of all, production designer Stephen Roloff offers an intriguing and visually fascinating look at tomorrow's cyber-world.

Greg Evigan Jake Corrigan • **William Shatner** Walter H Bascom • **Eugene Clark** Sid Gomez • **Maria Del Mar** Sam Houston • **Natalie Radford** Nika • **Torri Higginson** Beth Kitteridge
Source *the "TekWar" novels by William Shatner*

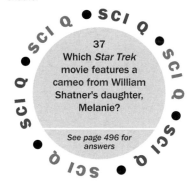

SCI Q • SCI Q • SCI Q • SCI Q • SCI Q •

37
Which *Star Trek* movie features a cameo from William Shatner's daughter, Melanie?

See page 496 for answers

The Tenth Victim ★★★

1965 It Colour 92mins

Famous now as one of the inspirations for *Austin Powers: International Man of Mystery* (Ursula Andress wore the first bullet-firing bra as sported by the "fembots"), director Elio Petri's erratically engrossing science-fiction thriller has a fabulous sixties pop art look. In the 21st century, war has been outlawed and replaced with a legalised game in which the participants are licensed-to-kill assassins, and anyone reaching the score of ten victims hits the financial jackpot. Andress is assigned to kill a cropped blond Marcello Mastroianni, but he makes the mistake of falling in love with his huntress in this convincing futuristic satire that still pleases the eye even when it habitually falls through cracks in the weak script. Italian dialogue dubbed into English.

Ursula Andress Caroline Meredith • **Marcello Mastroianni** Marcello Polletti • **Elsa Martinelli** Olga • **Salvo Randone** Professor • **Massimo Serato** Lawyer • **Evi Rigano** Victim
Director *Elio Petri*
Screenplay *Elio Petri, Tonino Guerra, Giorgio Salvioni, Ennio Flaiano, from the novel "The Seventh Victim" by Robert Sheckley*

Terminal Island ★

1973 US Colour 87mins

A crummy exploitation pic – terminal in all departments – about a future offshore prison colony where California's killers are sent because the death penalty has been abolished. The arrival of women prisoners results in their being treated as sex slaves. No prizes for guessing the extent to which this "Calcatraz" becomes a scene of mayhem and violence. The sole point of interest is an early screen appearance by Tom Selleck, in pre-*Magnum PI* days. In fact, the film was reissued in the early eighties to cash in on Selleck's stardom.

Phyllis Davis Joy Lang • **Don Marshall** AJ Thomas • **Ena Hartman** Carmen Sims • **Marta Kristen** Lee Phillips • **Tom Selleck** Dr Milford
Director *Stephanie Rothman*
Screenplay *Jim Barnett, Charles S Swartz, Stephanie Rothman*

Terminal Justice ★★ 18

1996 US Colour 90mins

Mildly entertaining futuristic nonsense featuring Lorenzo Lamas as a digitally-enhanced cop on the trail of Chris Sarandon's ambitious crime king. Cheap 'n' cheesy, but more creative than many of its ilk, with a plot that somehow takes in virtual reality sex, self-cloning and a deadly miniature helicopter. It would be a more enjoyable movie without Chippendale lookalike Lamas, whose acting talents don't even extend to a convincing swagger.

Peter Coyote Vivyan • **Lorenzo Lamas** Bobby Chase • **Chris Sarandon** Matthews • **Kari Salin [Kari Wuhrer]** Pamela Travis • **Barry Yourgrau** Brady
Director *Rick King*
Screenplay *Wynne McLaughlin, Frederick Bailey*

The Terminal Man ★★★★ 15

1974 US Colour 99mins

An extraordinarily intense performance from the usually laid-back George Segal nicely matches the desolation of this futuristic thriller, in which a scientist has a computer implant connected to his brain and becomes addicted to its killer vibes. Adapted from a novel on the *Frankenstein* theme by Michael Crichton (before Crichton's *Jurassic Park* was a twinkle in Steven Spielberg's eye), writer/director Mike Hodges brilliantly creates a high-tech parable in which meddling scientists get a moral comeuppance. The film was only patchily shown in cinemas on its original release, but deserved better: its implications are as thought-provoking as they are scary. Contains some violence.

George Segal Harry Benson • **Joan Hackett** Dr Janet Ross • **Richard A Dysart [Richard Dysart]** Dr John Ellis • **Jill Clayburgh** Angela Black • **Donald Moffat** Dr Arthur Mcpherson • **Matt Clark** Gerhard • **Michael C Gwynne** Dr Robert Morris • **Normann Burton [Norman Burton]** Detective Captain Anders • **William Hansen** Dr Ezra Manon • **James Sikking [James B Sikking]** Ralph Friedman
Director *Mike Hodges*
Screenplay *Mike Hodges, from the novel by Michael Crichton*

Terminal Virus ★★

1995 US/Phil Colour 74mins

A vaguely distasteful slice of soft porn wrapped up in the flimsiest of sci-fi plots. It's set in a clichéd post-apocalyptic world where a deadly disease makes sexual intercourse a definite no-no. A couple of intrepid chaps come up with a possible cure, but of course they need some consenting couples to try it out. James Brolin is the only recognisable face in the cast, and he should have known better. Contains violence and sex scenes.

Bryan Genesse Joe Knight • **James Brolin** McCabe • **Richard Lynch** Calloway • **Craig Judd** Rieger • **Kehli O'Byrne** Shara
Director *Dan Golden*
Screenplay *Joe Sprosty, Jeff Pulce, Daniella Purcell*

Terminal Voyage ★★★

1994 US Colour

This is the closest we've been to an Agatha Christie mystery in space. Echoes of *Ten Little Indians* abound in this slickly produced TV-movie thriller, as a team of astronauts awakens from a century of cryogenic slumber to discover that one of them is a killer. Ex-*Dynasty* star Emma Samms is a standout as the government agent with a hidden agenda, and there's admirable support from Steven Bauer and Wen Ming-Na (who voiced the lead in Disney's *Mulan*). Contains violence, swearing and drug abuse.

Emma Samms Becker • **Steven Bauer** Reese • **Gregory McKinney** Major Hollis • **Alan Rachins** Lieutenant Jammad • **Brenda Bakke** Zinovitz • **Cliff De Young** Granier • **Wen Ming-Na** Han
Director *Rick Jacobson*
Screenplay *Mark Evan Schwartz*

The Terminator ★★★★★ 18

1984 US Colour 102mins [video] DVD

Arnold Schwarzenegger said "I'll be back," and he was, seven years later. But the success of the sequel should not undermine the powerhouse strengths of James Cameron's original high-tech nightmare, with violent cyborg Arnie time-warped from the future to alter the nuclear war-torn course of history. Generating maximum excitement from the first frame, the dynamic thrills are maintained right up to the nerve-jangling climax. Wittily written with a nice eye for sharp detail, it's hard sci-fi action all the way, and Linda Hamilton shines as the bewildered waitress who will unwittingly become the saviour of the human race. Contains swearing, violence, a sex scene and nudity.

Arnold Schwarzenegger Terminator • **Michael Biehn** Kyle Reese • **Linda Hamilton** Sarah Connor • **Paul Winfield** Traxler • **Lance Henriksen** Vukovich • **Rick Rossovich** Matt • **Bess Motta** Ginger • **Earl Boen** Silberman • **Dick Miller** Pawn shop clerk • **Shawn Schepps** Nancy • **Bruce M Kerner** Desk sergeant • **Franco Columbu** Future Terminator • **Bill Paxton** Punk leader
Director *James Cameron*
Screenplay *James Cameron, Gale Anne Hurd, William Wisher Jr*

Terminator 2: Judgment Day ★★★★★ 15

1991 US Colour 145mins [video] DVD

James Cameron's extraordinary sequel piles on the gutsy grit, hard-edged humour and roller-coaster action. The story picks up with future human saviour Edward Furlong in foster care because his mother, Linda Hamilton, has been institutionalised for insisting events in the first film were true. Thwarted in their earlier attempt to kill Hamilton and prevent the boy's birth, the machines ruling the devastated Earth of 2029 send super-improved Terminator model Robert Patrick back in time to finish the job. Meanwhile, antiquated android Arnold Schwarzenegger (who returned for a fee as large as the entire budget of the original film) is dispatched by resistance fighters to protect their future leader's life from the relentless pursuer. Aside from the astounding visual excitement and Cameron's brilliant direction that milks every ounce of nail-biting suspense from the rock-solid premise, the realisation of the T-1000 super cyborg with its liquid metal shape-changing abilities set a new cinematic standard for stunning computer graphic special effects. While Schwarzenegger is perfectly suited to his robot role, both physically and acting-wise, the real thesping muscle comes from Hamilton who turns in another marvellous performance as the fiercely committed heroine and she alone puts a necessary human face on the high-decibel mayhem and pyro-technical bravura. Hasta la vista, baby! Contains swearing and violence.

Arnold Schwarzenegger The Terminator • **Linda Hamilton** Sarah Connor • **Edward Furlong** John Connor • **Robert Patrick** T-1000 • **Earl Boen** Dr Silberman • **Joe Morton** Miles Dyson • **S Epatha Merkerson** Tarissa Dyson • **Michael Biehn** Kyle Reese
Director *James Cameron*
Screenplay *James Cameron, William Wisher*

SFacts

Rather than a digital effect, Linda Hamilton's identical twin sister Leslie was employed for the scene at the finale when the the shape-shifting T-1000 takes on the form of Sarah Connor

Terrahawks ★ U

TV 1983-1986 UK Colour 39x30mins [video]

Gerry Anderson's only major TV series during the eighties is a major disappointment, embarrassingly childish and sloppily produced, but most severely of all lacking any of that sense of wonder and awe that characterised his entire sixties output. Set in the year 2020, the Terrahawks are an elite international fighting force. Operating from a secret South American base, their mission is to protect the earth from invasion by a race of androids from the planet Guk, led by a witch-like queen. Significantly this was the first Gerry Anderson series made without the involvement of his wife Sylvia and also the first not to come with strings attached. "Supermarionation" gave way to "supermacromation", a lacklustre Muppet-style puppetry technique.

Jeremy Hitchin Dr "Tiger" Ninestein/Lt Hiro /Col Johnson • **Denise Bryer** Captain Mary Falconer/Zelda • **Windsor Davies** Sergeant Major Zero • **Anne Ridler** Captain Kate Kestrel/Cy-Star • **Ben Stevens** Lt Hawkeye/Yung-Star/Stew Dapples/Dix-Huit
Created by *Gerry Anderson*
Producer *Gerry Anderson, Christopher Burr*

Terror beneath the Sea ★★

1966 Jap Colour 95mins

A waterlogged Japanese effort concerning a mad, world domination fixated scientist in an underwater city inventing a machine using atomic waste that turns humans into water-breathing androids. Shinichi Chiba (who would later change his name to Sonny Chiba and become a martial arts star) is the hero who turns the tide in mankind's favour. A wonky blend of Captain Nemo, *The Creature from the Black Lagoon* and home-grown Japanese monster movies, director Hajime Sato's colourful comic strip romp has odd flashes of imagination but not enough to separate it from the more energetically rendered pack.

Shinichi Chiba [Sonny Chiba] • **Peggy Neal** • **Franz Gruber** • **Gunther Braun** • **Andrew Hughes** • **Erik Nielson**
Director *Terence Ford [Hajime Sato]*
Special effects *Nobuo Yajima*

Terror from the Year 5,000 ★

1958 US Colour 66mins

This unbelievable claptrap features a hideously deformed sex kitten who materialises through a time machine to mate and save the future of mankind. The mutant cat with four eyes is a laugh, but not much else is in this brazenly clumsy cheapie, which, amazingly, does have something of a cult following. More famous to horror film buffs these days because part of the soundtrack was later used in the classic *Night of the Living Dead*.

Ward Costello Robert Hedges • **Joyce Holden** Claire Erling • **John Stratton** Victor • **Frederic Downs** Professor Erling • **Fred Herrick** Angelo • **Beatrice Furdeaux** Miss Blake • **Salome Jens** AD 5000 woman
Director/Screenplay *Robert J Gurney Jr*

Terror Is a Man ★★

1959 US/Phil BW 76mins

This commendable rehash of *Island of Lost Souls* (1932) was shot in the Philippines on a low budget, that could only extend to one "manimal" mutant instead of the usual pack. Francis Lederer is the mad doctor conducting experiments on a remote island, enabling him to turn a jungle cat into something resembling a human. His horrified wife Greta Thyssen confides in shipwreck victim Richard Derr, until the monster kidnaps her and sets in motion the tragic cliff-top finale. Originally an on-screen buzzer was the warning signal for the faint-hearted to look away from the gruesome operation footage.

Francis Lederer Dr Charles Girard • **Greta Thyssen** Frances Girard • **Richard Derr** William Fitzgerald • **Peyton Keesee** Tiago • **Oscar Keesee** Walter • **Flory Carlos** Beast-Man
Director *Gerry DeLeon*
Screenplay *Harry Paul Harber*

Terror Island ★★

1920 US BW 5 reels

The third and most expensive major movie flop to star world-famous escapologist Harry Houdini borrows heavily from Jules Verne's underwater fantasy novels. As the inventor of a submarine device used for salvaging First World War craft from previously unattainable depths, he is asked to rescue Lila Lee's hostage father from cannibals on a South Sea island. The natives want a sacred, skull-shaped pearl in Lee's possession in exchange for his release. Nothing more than an excuse to put Houdini in extreme situations – bound and gagged in a flaming shack, nailed into a chest and thrown overboard. The escapes are expectantly amazing, but the only real sci-fi element in director James Cruze's vaudeville adventure is the *Nautilus*-inspired submersible design.

Houdini [Harry Houdini] Harry Harper • **Jack Brammall** Starkey • **Lila Lee** Beverly West • **Wilton Taylor** Job Mourdant • **Eugene Pallette** Guy Mourdant • **Edward Brady** Captain Black
Director *James Cruze*
Screenplay *Walter Woods, from a story by Arthur B Reeve, John W Grey*

Terror of Mechagodzilla ★★★ 15

1975 Jap Colour 79mins

Practically all of Godzilla's enemies from Ghidorah to Rodan are assembled in this 20th anniversary production. So what else could alien powers do in yet another world domination scheme, except build a nasty robot version of the loveable T-Rex? But the old fire-snorter hits back and bangs his tail in suitable disdain at this outrageous ploy to upstage him with a pile of shiny junk. Veteran *Godzilla* creator Inoshiro Honda directs this monster mishmash with a lurid comic-strip style replete with engagingly daffy visual spectacle. Japanese dialogue dubbed into English.

Tomoko Ai • **Akihito Hirata**
Director *Inoshiro Honda*
Screenplay *Katsuhiko Sasaki*

The Terror Within ★ 18

1988 US Colour 84mins

One of producer Roger Corman's countless imitations of *Alien*, this particular effort is no better and no worse than usual – which still means it's pretty terrible. The futuristic setting is not a spaceship, but an underground lab, where Andrew Stevens and George Kennedy are among the few survivors of a holocaust that has left the planet virtually uninhabitable. Trouble arrives when a pregnant woman gives birth to a monster. The rubber-suited mutant is an embarrassment to watch, but looks good compared to the set design that seems to recycle the same hallway and room for all parts of the underground complex.

George Kennedy Hal • **Andrew Stevens** David • **Starr Andreeff** Sue • **Terri Treas** Linda • **John Lafayette** Andre • **Tommy Hinchley** Neil • **Yvonne Saa** Karen
Director *Thierry Notz*
Screenplay *Thomas M Cleaver*
Producer *Roger Corman*

TerrorVision ★★ 15

1986 US Colour 81mins

This supposed satire on the media-obsessed, suburban middle classes is in fact, a toe-curlingly embarrassing *Poltergeist* rip-off featuring a cartoonishly dysfunctional family. A new satellite dish accidentally beams an alien into the Putterman's living room. Unfortunately he turns out to be voracious rather than cute, gobbling up everyone in his path. Writer/director Ted Nicolaou intentionally parodies those Z-grade monster movies of the fifties, but ironically has produced something of which Ed Wood would be proud. If you enjoy crummy special effects, corny one-liners and ripe overacting, this is the movie for you!

Diane Franklin Suzy Putterman • **Gerrit Graham** Stanley Putterman • **Mary Woronov** Raquel Putterman • **Chad Allen** Sherman Putterman • **Jonathan Gries** O D • **Jennifer Richards** Medusa • **Alejandro Rey** Spiro • **Bert Remsen** Grampa
Director/Screenplay *Ted Nicolaou*

The Test of Pilot Pirx ★★★

1978 Pol/USSR Colour 104mins

Although Polish novelist Stanislaw Lem wrote several books about the intrepid Pirx, this marked his maiden screen outing. Unfortunately, director Marek Piestrak didn't have the budget to do justice to an ingenious scenario. Consequently, special effects shots are repeated ad nauseam, as a Saturn probe (crewed by a mix of mortals and robots) is forced into a crisis by Machiavellian manufacturers seeking to prove the superhuman capability of their "finite non-linear" model. It's as if the

 U = SUITABLE FOR ALL Uc = SUITABLE FOR ALL, ESPECIALLY YOUNG CHILDREN (VIDEO ONLY) PG = PARENTAL GUIDANCE

opening of *Alien* had been crossed with the climax of *2001: a Space Odyssey* in order to put an interstellar spin on *The Caine Mutiny*. A Polish language film.

Sergiusz Desnitsky • **Boleslaw Abart** • **Vladimir Ivashov** • **Aleksandr Kaidanovsky**
Director *Marek Piestrak*
Screenplay *Marek Piestrak, Vladimir Valutski, from the story "Inquiry" by Stanislaw Lem*
Cinematographer *Janusz Pavlovski*

Testament ★★★★★ PG

1983 US Colour 85mins

A sobering and moving movie detailing with chilling accuracy how a typical family copes after an unspecified nuclear attack devastates America. There are no fancy special effects, just a shocking interruption during *Sesame Street*, followed by a blinding flash. In the aftermath, Jane Alexander (giving a stunning performance) must cope with situations she has always dreaded – mourning her missing husband, burying her children and coming to terms with the stark reality that she too will eventually die of radiation sickness. But although she tries, she can't commit suicide – and that is her testament in the life-affirmation stakes. Director Lynne Littman accomplishes so much without hammering home the points, becoming preachy or glamorising events. This is one of the best movies ever made about the futility of nuclear war. You'll cry buckets, but don't miss.

Jane Alexander Carol Wetherly • **William Devane** Tom Wetherly • **Ross Harris [Rossie Harris]** Brad Wetherly • **Roxana Zal** Mary Liz Wetherly • **Lukas Haas** Scottie Wetherly • **Philip Anglim** Hollis • **Lilia Skala** Fania • **Leon Ames** Henry Abhart • **Rebecca De Mornay** Cathy Pitkin • **Kevin Costner** Phil Pitkin
Director *Lynne Littman*
Screenplay *John Sacret Young, from the story "The Last Testament" by Carol Amen*

Tetsuo ★★ 18

1989 Jap BW 67mins

This is one of those movies that leaves you feeling unsure what it was about. The basic plot of a Japanese businessman, apparently involved in a road accident, who suddenly finds himself turning into a metallic mutant monster, is merely an excuse for cult Japanese director Shinya Tsukamoto to bombard the viewer with surreal and nightmarish images of violence and sex. Tsukamoto, who not only directed but also wrote, filmed and played one of the leads, has obviously read too many adult comic books and rented *Eraserhead* more times than is healthy. Employing grainy black-and-white photography, minimal dialogue and a pounding techno soundtrack, this short feature will be seen either as pretentious rubbish or a classy art movie. A sequel followed in 1991. In Japanese with English subtitles.

Tomoroh Taguchi Salaryman • **Kei Fujiwara** Salaryman's girlfriend • **Nobu Kanaoka** Woman in glasses • **Shinya Tsukamoto** Young metals fetishist • **Naomasa Musaka** Doctor • **Renji Ishibashi** Tramp
Director/Screenplay *Shinya Tsukamoto*

Tetsuo II: Body Hammer ★★★ 18

1991 Jap Colour 78mins

Not so much a sequel to Shinya Tsukamoto's cult movie *Tetsuo*, as a radical reworking of that "body horror" study in mutant machine madness. Don't try and make sense of the story bizarre experiments turn people into weapons – just savour the shiny images as Tsukamoto highlights "the beauty in destruction", in retina-scorching metallic hues. The central body-machine melding a frenzy of post-modern *Alien* and David Lynch industrial design is well worth waiting for in this homo- and sado-erotic avant-garde abstraction. In Japanese with English subtitles.

Tomoroh Taguchi Taniguchi • **Nobu Kanaoka** Kana • **Shinya Tsukamoto** Yatsu • **Keinosuke Tomioka** Minori
Director/Screenplay *Shinya Tsukamoto*

Them! ★★★★★ PG

1954 US BW 88mins

This taut, atmospheric and totally convincing science-fiction classic is the best giant bug movie of the fifties. Director Gordon Douglas's shocker is laden with clever visual and verbal puns as mutant ants spawned by atomic radiation arrive in Los Angeles from the New Mexico desert and infest the sewer system. Terrific special effects, noble humanitarian sentiments, involving performances – Edmund Gwenn makes the most of his archetypal scientist – and a first-class script make for monster thrills and fantastic suspense.

James Whitmore Sgt Ben Peterson • **Edmund Gwenn** Dr Harold Medford • **Joan Weldon** Dr Patricia Medford • **James Arness** Robert Graham • **Onslow Stevens** Brig Gen O'Brien • **Sean McClory** Major Kibbee • **Leonard Nimoy** Sergeant
Director *Gordon Douglas*
Screenplay *Ted Sherdeman, Russell Hughes, from a story by George Worthing Yates*

Them ★★

1996 US Colour

Not a remake of the fifties' sci-fi B-movie about massive mutant ants, but an even lower-key affair about the strange goings-on in a town at the foot of the Sierra Nevada mountains. The prologue, in which scientist Scott Patterson claims to have witnessed the arrival of aliens, sets the scene for yet another reworking of the *Body Snatchers* scenario; folk disappearing, others behaving like zombies and everyone else a potential suspect. Hindered by some indifferent special effects, this was the TV pilot for a proposed series, and it's not hard to see why the option wasn't picked up. Contains violence.

Scott Patterson Simon Trent • **Tony Todd** Berlin • **Clare Carey** Kelly Black • **Dustin Voigt** Jake Trent • **Scott Bellis** Matt Verlane • **Lochlyn Munro** Cole
Director *Bill L Norton*
Screenplay *Charles Grant Craig, from an idea by Charles Grant Craig, Patrick Gilmore*

Theodore Rex ★★ PG

1995 US Colour 87mins

Only the threat of litigation kept Whoopi Goldberg on board this turkey and it is to her credit that she does her best to make it fly. But she clearly didn't regard being teamed with a doltish detective (who just happens to be a tyrannosaurus) as one of the highlights of her career. Writer/director Jonathan Betuel has problems making us believe in a world in which dinosaurs have been revived, and he needs someone more menacing than mad scientist Armin Mueller-Stahl to distract us from the woeful special effects. Children might enjoy it, but grown-ups should ensure that they are busy elsewhere when it's on. Contains violence and swearing.

Whoopi Goldberg Katie Coltrane • **Armin Mueller-Stahl** Dr Edgar Kane • **Juliet Landau** Dr Shade • **Bud Cort** Spinner • **Stephen McHattie** Edge • **Richard Roundtree** Commissioner Lynch • **Peter Mackenzie** Alex Summers • **Peter Kwong** Toymaker • **George Newbern** Theodore Rex • **Carol Kane** Molly Rex
Director/Screenplay *Jonathan Betuel*

They Came from beyond Space ★★

1967 UK Colour 85mins

A pallid attempt by Hammer rivals Amicus, to rehash some of the thematic lines from the *Quatermass* series. Astral invaders take over a Cornish factory to enslave earthlings so they'll repair a spaceship that has crashed on the moon. Fortunately, astrophysicist Robert (*The Slime People*) Hutton has a metal plate in his head, which makes him immune from alien control, and he single-handedly combats the evil extraterrestrials, led by stalwart genre icon Michael Gough.

Robert Hutton Dr Curtis Temple • **Jennifer Jayne** Lee Mason • **Michael Gough** Monj • **Zia Mohyeddin** Dr Farge • **Geoffrey Wallace** Alan Mullane • **Bernard Kay** Richard Arden • **John Harvey** Bill Trethowan • **Diana King** Mrs Trethowan
Director *Freddie Francis*
Screenplay *Milton Subotsky, from the novel "The Gods Hate Kansas" by Joseph Millard*

They Came from Outer Space ★★ PG

TV 1990-1991 US Colour 20x60mins

A one-season made-for-cable sit-com cross-breeding *Bill and Ted* with *Earth Girls Are Easy*, this stars Dean Cameron and Stuart Fratkin as nerdish sex-crazed teenagers from the planet Crouton. Marooned on Earth, they cruise around like refugees from *Route 66*, getting involved in scrapes every week, pursued in *Fugitive*-style by Allan Royal and occasionally instructed *Mork and Mindy*-style by their parents (Victor Brandt, Rosalee Mayeux). The two-part *Sex, Lies and UFOs* story was released on video in the UK as *They Came from Outer Space*.

Dean Cameron Bo • **Stuart Fratkin** Dean • **Allan Royal** Col Tom Baker • **Christopher Carroll** Lt Pat "Monkey" Wilson

They Live ★★★ 18

1988 US Colour 93mins

A return to his B-movie roots for John Carpenter, this is a cheerful knockabout salute to the alien invasion sci-fi movies of the fifties. Wrestler-turned-actor Roddy Piper is the working-class hero who, on finding a special pair of sunglasses, discovers that alien-like creatures appear to have taken over Los Angeles and are controlling the remaining human residents with subliminal advertising. There's a nicely relaxed feel to Carpenter's direction and he keeps the action roaring along, stopping only to take a few satirical swipes at yuppy life. Piper handles the action scenes better than he deals with dialogue, but he is well supported by Keith David and Meg Foster. Contains violence, swearing.

Roddy Piper Nada • **Keith David** Frank • **Meg Foster** Holly Thompson • **George "Buck" Flower** Drifter • **Peter Jason** Gilbert • **Raymond St Jacques** Street preacher • **Jason Robards III** Family man • **John Lawrence** Bearded man • **Sy Richardson** Brown-haired woman • **Susan Barnes** Black revolutionary
Director *John Carpenter*
Screenplay *Frank Armitage [John Carpenter], from the short story "Eight O'Clock in the Morning" by Ray Nelson*

The Thing ★★★★ 18

1982 US Colour 103mins DVD

John Carpenter's remake of Howard Hawks and Christian Nyby's influential 1951 creature feature, is a special-effects extravaganza of the highest order. In fact, the updated screenplay by Bill Lancaster (son of Burt) sticks more closely to the plot of the classic John W Campbell short story that inspired the original movie, as the occupants of a polar research station are menaced by an alien with the ability to change its shape and impersonate its enemies. Carpenter stresses the slimy ET at the expense of characterisation, mood and practically everything else, yet it's precisely this one grisly facet that makes it such compelling science fiction. Even *Alien* can't hold a candle to the nightmarish images on offer here, so be warned. Contains violence and swearing.

Kurt Russell MacReady • **Wilford Brimley** Blair • **TK Carter** Nauls • **David Clennon** Palmer • **Keith David** Childs • **Richard Dysart** Dr Cooper • **Charles Hallahan** Norris • **Peter Maloney** Bennings • **Richard Masur** Clark • **Donald Moffat** Garry
Director *John Carpenter*
Screenplay *Bill Lancaster, from the story "Who Goes There?" by John W Campbell Jr*
Cinematographer *Dean Cundey* • ***Music*** *Ennio Morricone*

The Thing from Another World ★★★★ 12

1951 US BW 82mins

A pioneering science-fiction outing emphasising suspense and atmosphere, rather than the shock special effects of John Carpenter's 1982 remake, in a tense story of Arctic scientists trying to cope with the first of Hollywood's Cold War aliens. Credited as being only produced by Howard Hawks, it's suspiciously full of his signature flourishes (camaraderie in the face of ambush, for instance) and director Christian Nyby never made anything half as good again.

Kenneth Tobey Captain Patrick Hendry • **Margaret Sheridan** Nikki • **Robert Cornthwaite** Dr Carrington • **Douglas Spencer** Scotty • **James Young** Lt Eddie Dykes • **Dewey Martin** Crew Chief • **James Arness** The "Thing" • **Robert Nichols** Ken Erickson • **William Self** Sgt Barnes • **Eduard Franz** Dr Stern • **John Dierkes** Dr Chapman • **Sally Creighton** Mrs Chapman
Director *Christian Nyby*
Screenplay *Charles Lederer, from the story "Who Goes There?" by John Wood Campbell Jr*
Producer *Howard Hawks*

The Thing with Two Heads ★★

1972 US Colour 87mins

Probably the most lunatic blaxploitation horror film ever made, and also the genre's biggest missed opportunity to say something profound. Bigoted brain surgeon Ray Milland learns he's dying of cancer, so needs to transplant his head on to a healthy body. Unfortunately, racist Milland wakes to find his head next to that of condemned black-killer Rosey Grier, who is intent on clearing his name. With each head trying to seek control of Grier's body, the jokes should have been funnier, the racist allegory more up-front and the pacing more breakneck to cover the absolute idiocy of the premise. It's hard to figure out what's the dumbest stunt of all – the dummy heads substituted for action shots, or the two actors' necks unconvincingly bandaged together.

Ray Milland Dr Maxwell Kirshner • **Rosey Grier** Jack Moss • **Don Marshall** Dr Fred Williams • **Roger Perry** Dr Philip Desmond • **Chelsea Brown** Lila • **Kathy Baumann [Katherine Baumann]** Patricia • **John Dullaghan** Thomas • **John Bliss** Donald
Director *Lee Frost*
Screenplay *Lee Frost, James Gordon White, Wes Bishop*

Things to Come ★★★★ PG

1936 UK BW 89mins

Although a classic slice of British science-fiction, Alexander Korda's elaborate production of HG Wells's prophetic novel is weakened by the prevailing air of over-theatricality, naivety and preachiness. Spanning almost 100 years from 1940 to 2036, it begins during a world war and goes through plague and a technological revolution, ending with everyone living in an enormous Art Deco underground city run by Raymond Massey. Awesome sets and magnificent design make this hugely ambitious antique vision of the future, Britain's answer to *Metropolis*. Amazingly, Wells actually visited the studio while it was being made.

Raymond Massey John Cabal/Oswald Cabal • **Edward Chapman** Pippa Passworthy/Raymond Passworthy • **Ralph Richardson** The Boss • **Margaretta Scott**

Watch the skies! What emerges from under the ice is the scientists' worst nightmare in the classic *The Thing from Another World*

Roxana/Rowena • **Cedric Hardwicke** Theotocopulos • **Maurice Braddell** Dr Harding • **Sophie Stewart** Mrs Cabal • **Derrick de Marney** Richard Gordon • **Ann Todd** Mary Gordon • **George Sanders** Pilot
Director *William Cameron Menzies*
Screenplay *HG Wells, Lajos Biro, from the book "The Shape of Things to Come" by HG Wells*
Cinematographer *Georges Périnal*
Production designer *Vincent Korda*

3rd Rock from the Sun

★★★★ PG 12

TV 1996- US Colour [video]

A group of aliens try to learn about life on Earth by posing as an ordinary American family in Bonnie and Terry Turner's surprisingly successful sci-fi sitcom. John Lithgow leads the group's exploration of human existence as alien commander-turned-college professor Dick Solomon, while his team members Sally, Tommy and Harry pose as a gorgeous young woman, a schoolboy and an ill-adjusted oddball respectively. It's not new, it's not subtle and it's certainly not clever, but *3rd Rock from the Sun* is an enormous amount of fun. The show's scripts are frenetically paced and littered with wonderful one-liners and great sight gags, while the show's main cast – especially larger-than-life Lithgow and the stunning Kristen Johnson – are universally hilarious and completely irresistible.

John Lithgow Dick Solomon • **Kristen Johnston** Sally Solomon • **French Stewart** Harry Solomon • **Joseph Gordon-Levitt** Tommy Solomon • **Jane Curtin** Dr Mary Albright • **Simbi Khali** Nina
Created by *Bonnie Turner, Terry Turner*
Producer *Marcy Carsey, Tom Werner* •
Executive producer *Caryn Mandabach, Bonnie Turner, Terry Turner*
Music *Ben Vaughan*

SFacts

A proverbial galaxy of guest stars have appeared on this multi-award-winning, runaway hit: Roseanne, Mark Hamill (as himself), Elvis Costello, Kathy Bates, Cindy Crawford, Jonathan Frakes, John Cleese (playing Dr Liam Neesom) and William Shatner as the Big Giant Head.

The Thirteenth Floor ★★ 18

1999 US Colour 86mins [video] DVD

Computer technician Craig Bierko finds himself the main suspect when his boss – the mastermind behind a computer simulation of 1937 Los Angeles populated with programmed inhabitants who are oblivious to their actual origin – is found murdered. Though Bierko's subsequent investigation uncovers plenty of twists and turns, most viewers will have a pretty good idea of the final explanation after the first third of the movie is over. Predictable as it is, this still retains some interest. The computer simulation of the thirties world perfectly recreates the era, the performances are acceptable.

Craig Bierko Douglas Hall • **Armin Mueller-Stahl** Hannon Fuller • **Gretchen Mol** Jane Fuller • **Vincent D'Onofrio** Whitney /Ashton • **Dennis Haysbert** Detective Larry McBain • **Steven Schub** Zev Bernstein
Director *Josef Rusnak*
Screenplay *Josef Rusnak, Ravel Centeno-Rodriguez, from the novel "Simulacron 3" by Daniel Galouye*

The 30 Foot Bride of Candy Rock ★ U

1959 US BW 73mins

After he split from his long-time partner Bud Abbott, comedian Lou Costello made this one solo movie, released just after he died. Costello is a meek inventor whose girlfriend Dorothy Provine is enlarged by scientist Jimmy Conlin. Turning to his own invention to reverse the process, it instead sends him back to a prehistoric era and the Civil War and also allows him to fly. Costello is less zany than he was with Abbott, but he still relies on corny slapstick to plug the yawning gaps in this poorly paced sci-fi spoof.

Lou Costello Artie Pinsetter • **Dorothy Provine** Emmy Lou Raven • **Gale Gordon** Raven • **Jimmy Conlin** Magruder • **Charles Lane** Standard Bates

Director *Sidney Miller*

Screenplay *Rowland Barber, Arthur Ross, from a story by Lawrence L Goldman, from an idea by Jack Rabin, Irving Block*

This Island Earth ★★★★ PG

1955 US Colour 82mins

This intelligent slice of fifties sci-fi – two and a half years in the making proclaimed the poster proudly – ranks among the best and most cleverly conceived of the genre. Really it's a film of two parts. A talky earthbound section finds brainy boffins being recruited by the marvellously otherworldly Jeff Morrow to save his distant homeland from destruction by interplanetary warfare. That's followed by a full-blooded space opera featuring astounding surrealistic landscapes on the planet Metaluna and fearsome insect-like mutations. Hokey at times, but its message is clear: the more advanced the technology, the greater the scope for destruction.

Jeff Morrow Exeter • **Faith Domergue** Dr Ruth Adams • **Rex Reason** Dr Cal Meacham • **Lance Fuller** Brack • **Russell Johnson** Steve Carlson • **Richard Nichols** Joe Wilson • **Karl Lindt** Engelborg • **Douglas Spencer** Monitor

Director *Joseph M Newman*

Screenplay *Franklin Coen, Edward G O'Callaghan, from the novel "The Alien Machine" by Raymond F Jones*

Threads ★★★★

TV 1984 UK Colour 115mins

Hideously plausible when first broadcast in 1984, this BBC docu-drama now seems like a terrifying might-have-been though a great deal of what it says about the probable aftermath of a nuclear attack remains horribly pertinent. Scripted by Barry Hines (*Kes*) and directed by Mick Jackson (who later went Hollywood with *The Bodyguard* and *Volcano*), it's an answer to the American TV movie *The Day After*, showing the effects of World War III on the United Kingdom by concentrating on two Sheffield families. Grim in a particularly eighties way, this is a compulsive if uncomfortable watch and accomplishes a great deal without the distraction of spectacle, picking through all the melted milk bottles and firing squad traffic wardens to find the human horror at the heart of it.

Karen Meagher Ruth Beckett • **Reece Dinsdale** Jimmy Kemp • **June Broughton** Mrs Beckett • **Henry Moxon** Mr Beckett • **Sylvia Stoker** Granny Beckett • **David Brierley** Mr Kemp • **Rita May** Mrs Kemp • **Nicholas Lane** Michael Kemp • **Jane Hazlegrove** Alison Kemp • **Harry Beety** Clive Sutton

Director *Mike Jackson*

Written by *Barry Hines*

Producer *Mike Jackson*

The Three Stooges in Orbit ★★ U

1962 US BW 87mins

After many, many years of tweaking, thumping, poking and brawling, the Stooges were moving into weirder and weirder areas. Recent films had seen them meeting Snow White and Hercules, and now they're battling a pair of Martian invaders Ogg (George N Neise) and Zogg (Rayford Barnes) who are plotting to steal the secret plans of a super-vehicle invented by the eccentric Professor Danforth (Emil Sitka). Not one of the boys' best efforts, but there's plenty of the usual flesh-slapping antics once so beloved of small boys and a not insignificant number of their fathers.

Moe Howard • **Larry Fine** • **Joe De Rita** • **Carol Christensen** Carol • **Edson Stroll** Capt Tom Andrews • **Emil Sitka** Prof Danforth • **George N Neise** Ogg • **Rayford Barnes** Zogg

Director *Edward Bernds*

Screenplay *Elwood Ullman, from a story by Norman Maurer*

Threshold ★★★ PG

1981 Can Colour 92mins

American distributors ignored this dramatically persuasive fictional Canadian story of the world's first artificial-heart transplant for two years – until speculative fiction became headline fact. One of the side effects of the publicity that accompanied the real-life operation was an airing for this surprisingly low-key account

Thunderbirds: Gerry Anderson's classic series has two generations of fans

of the effect on people of such revolutionary surgery. It's a pity that some commanding performances – Donald Sutherland as the surgeon, Jeff Goldblum as the artificial heart's inventor and Mare Winningham as the worried recipient – were left in the dark for so long.

Donald Sutherland Dr Thomas Vrain • **Jeff Goldblum** Dr Aldo Gehring • **Allan Nicholls** Dr Basil Rents • **Sharon Acker** Tilla Vrain • **Jana Stinson** Sally Vrain • **Jessica Steen** Tracy Vrain • **Michael Lerner** Henry De Vici • **John Marley** Edgar Fine • **Mare Winningham** Carol Severance • **Mavor Moore** Usher • **Lally Cadeau** Anita

Director *Richard Pearce*

Screenplay *James Salter*

Thrill Seekers ★★★

1999 US Colour 88mins

Revisiting the same territory as 1991's *Timescape* starring Jeff Daniels, this made-for-cable thriller also features time-

travellers from the future who get their holiday jollies from witnessing great disasters of the past. Casper Van Dien plays a sharp-eyed reporter who notices that the same person was present at the crash of the *Hindenberg* and the sinking of the *Titanic*. Another disaster is looming: can it – and should it – be prevented? Director Mario Azzopardi, a TV sci-fi stalwart, keeps the tension mounting in what is a better-than-average effort.

Casper Van Dien Tom Merrick • **Catherine Bell** Elizabeth Wintern • **Martin Sheen** Grifasi • **Julian Richings** Murray Trevor • **Catherine Oxenberg** Thrill Seekers spokesperson
Director *Mario Azzopardi*
Screenplay *Kurt Inderbitzin, Gay Walch*

Thunderbird 6 ★★ U

1968 UK/US Colour 85mins [video]

The second and last big-screen outing for the International Rescue crew is a step down from its predecessor but still diverting entertainment for children and fans of the series with its abundance of high-tech gimmickry. This time Lady Penelope and chauffeur Parker take centre stage as they embark on the round-the-world maiden voyage of *Skyship One*, a new luxury aircraft. While the effects are as impressive as ever the film suffers a similar fate to the first feature: at 90 minutes a bunch of puppets aren't enough to hold the viewer's attention and it was box office dud.

Peter Dyneley Jeff Tracy • **Shane Rimmer** Scott Tracy • **Sylvia Anderson** Lady Penelope • **Jeremy Wilkin** Virgil Tracy/Hogarth • **Matt Zimmerman** Alan Tracy/Carter • **David Graham** Gordon Tracy/Brains/Parker • **Christine Finn** Tin-Tin • **Keith Alexander** John Tracy
Director *David Lane*
Screenplay *Gerry Anderson, Sylvia Anderson*

Thunderbirds ★★★★★ U

TV 1965-66 UK Colour 32x50m [video] DVD

At the time the most expensive children's programme ever made, costing £22,000 per episode (that's around £800,000 in today's money), this remains Gerry Anderson's greatest achievement and one of the most popular TV shows of all time. Inspired by the popular western serial *Bonanza* with Lorne Green playing a father who had three sons, Anderson decided to make his fictitious International Rescue a family affair, too. Set in the 21st century Jeff Tracy, a former astronaut and multi-millionaire creates a top secret team dedicated to saving anyone in mortal danger. Operating from a Pacific island base the five extraordinary Thunderbird machines are operated by his five sons. Arguably the most popular characters were the show's British contingent, Lady Penelope and Parker, whose famous voice ("Yes, m'lady") was based on a 60-year-old Cockney waiter at a pub Anderson frequented.

Peter Dyneley Jeff Tracy • **Ray Barrett** John Tracy • **Shane Rimmer** Scott Tracy • **Matt Zimmerman** Alan Tracy • **David Holliday** Virgil Tracy (series 1) • **Jeremy Wilkin** Virgil Tracy • **David Graham** Gordon Tracy / Brains / Parker • **Sylvia Anderson** Lady Penelope • **Christine Finn** Tin-Tin / Grandma
Created by *Gerry Anderson*
Producer *Gerry Anderson*

SFacts

Although made in colour, when originally screened in the UK the series was shown in black and white. The five Tracy sons were named in tribute to the American astronauts Scott Malcolm Carpenter, Virgil Grissom, John Glenn, Gordon Cooper and Alan B Shepard, while Anderson got the name for the series from an airfield in Mesa, Arizona.

Thunderbirds Are Go! ★★★ U

1966 UK/US Colour 89mins [video]

The first and best big screen spin-off from Gerry Anderson's hugely popular series. Directed with efficient briskness by David Lane, who also directed many of the TV episodes and produced *Joe 90*. International Rescue are requested to oversee the launch of Zero X, a manned mission to Mars, but saboteur and arch nemesis the Hood (yes, the bald guy with the glowing eyes) is waiting in the wings. As ever the effects and model work are superb, but while the TV stories just about held one's interest for the full hour the novelty ultimately wears thin here after almost 90 minutes. Still, children and fans of the original show will lap it up. Watch out for a hilariously camp dream sequence featuring performing puppets of Cliff Richard and the Shadows.

Peter Dyneley Jeff Tracy • **Shane Rimmer** Scott Tracy • **Sylvia Anderson** Lady Penelope • **Jeremy Wilkin** Virgil Tracy/Hogarth • **Matt Zimmerman** Alan Tracy/Carter • **David Graham** Gordon Tracy/Brains/Parker • **Christine Finn** Tin-Tin/Grandma • **Ray Barrett** John Tracy/The Hood • **Bob Monkhouse** Swinging Star compère
Director *David Lane*
Screenplay *Gerry Anderson, Sylvia Anderson*

Ticks ★★ 18

1993 US Colour 81mins

This affectionate homage to the big monster movies of the fifties, such as *Them!*, spoofs the typical moments of the genre while adding gore and dark humour for the nineties audience. One of several marijuana farmers in a mountain village concocts a special fertiliser for his plants, but his leaky machine spills it on to some tick eggs, causing massive mutation and mayhem. It's then up to a group of troubled teenagers on a mountain retreat to save the day and escape. Several plot holes and narrative gaps indicate that the movie was shortened from a longer – and presumably more coherent – cut. Ultimately the level of gore and slime is so extreme, it becomes comical instead of disgusting. Contains violence and swearing.

Peter Scolari Charles Danson • **Rosalind Allen** Holly Lambert • **Ami Dolenz** Dee Dee Davenport • **Alfonso Ribeiro** Darrel "Panic" Lumley • **Ray Oriel** Rome Hernandez • **Seth Green** Tyler Burns • **Virginya Keehne** Melissa Danson
Director *Tony Randel*
Screenplay *Brent V Friedman*
Executive producer *Brian Yuzna*

Time after Time ★★★★ 15

1979 US Colour 107mins

In Nicholas Meyer's splendid literary conceit, the novelist HG Wells (Malcolm McDowell) follows Jack the Ripper (David Warner) from Victorian London to contemporary San Francisco in his time machine. It's a sometimes gruesome experience, but it's wittily aware of anachronisms, as the blood-steeped Ripper, warped in nature as well as time, becomes gratefully aware that the present-day has many more killing devices. That's an advancement Wells was always pessimistically aware of when contemplating the future, and it's a point he would have relished being made in a film that never down-markets his genius even though it up-markets the action. Contains violence and swearing.

Malcolm McDowell Herbert G Wells • **David Warner** Dr John Lesley Stevenson • **Mary Steenburgen** Amy Robbins • **Charles Cioffi** Lieutenant Mitchell • **Laurie Main** Inspector Gregson • **Andonia Katsaros** Mrs Turner • **Patti D'Arbanville [Patti D'Arbanville-Quinn]** Shirley • **Keith McConnell** Harding • **Geraldine Baron** Carol • **James Garrett** Edwards
Director *Nicholas Meyer*
Screenplay *Nicholas Meyer, from a story by Karl Alexander, Steve Hayes*

Time Bandits ★★★★ PG

1981 UK Colour 111mins

Before Terry Gilliam found success in the US with *The Fisher King* and *Twelve Monkeys*, he made a series of wondrously inventive fantasies, of which this was one of the best. Produced by British company HandMade Films, its story of a schoolboy accompanying a group of outlaw dwarves on a jolting trip through time has some astonishing sequences, while the marvellous cast includes John Cleese as Robin Hood, Sean Connery as a Greek warrior-king and Ralph Richardson as God. Ex-Python Gilliam is one of the great conjurers of cinema, and this film is proof of his ample and unpredictable talent. Contains some violence and swearing.

John Cleese Robin Hood • **Sean Connery** King Agamemnon • **Craig Warnock** Kevin • **Shelley Duvall** Pansy • **Katherine Helmond** Mrs Ogre • **Ian Holm** Napoleon • **Michael Palin** Vincent • **Ralph Richardson** Supreme Being • **Peter Vaughan** Ogre • **David Warner** Evil genius • **David Rappaport** Randall • **Kenny Baker (1)** Fidget • **Jim Broadbent** Compère
Director *Terry Gilliam*
Screenplay *Michael Palin, Terry Gilliam*

Time Chasers ★★

1994 US Colour

In sci-fi movies, people who get hold of time machines always make a mess of the future. Presumably there'd be no fun if they just arrived, looked round and then returned home without tinkering with the laws of nature or fouling up the space-time continuum. In director David Giancola's made-for-television spin on the theme, the inventor sells his machine to a defence contractor, who proceeds to create havoc with the future. Unfortunately, while film-makers always manage to think of imaginative ways of travelling (in this case it's a plane fitted with a clever gizmo), they seem to be incapable of dreaming up any original adventures for their intrepid heroes, and lead actor Matthew Burch has no chance to shine above the obvious screenplay and low-budget special effects.

Matthew Burch Nick Miller • **Bonnie Pritchard** Lisa Henson • **Peter Harrington** Matthew Paul • **George Woodard** JK Robertson
Director/Screenplay *David Giancola*

Time Flies ★★★ U

1944 UK BW 84mins

The time travel comedy was big in Britain in 1944, for not only did *ITMA* radio series star Tommy Handley take this trip to Elizabethan England, but Tommy Trinder also ventured back to Ancient Rome in *Fiddlers Three*. This is easily the superior picture, with Handley's regular radio writer Ted Kavanagh as part of the team serving up a generous portion of period gags, such as Handley pipping Sir Walter Raleigh to tobacco and a spot of cloak laying, and George Moon singing a music-hall song at the Globe. Some of the jokes have travelled less well and it falls flat in places, but it's a thoroughly entertaining romp.

Tommy Handley Tommy • **Evelyn Dall** Susie Barton • **George Moon** Bill Barton • **Felix Aylmer** Professor • **Moore Marriott** Soothsayer • **Graham Moffatt** Nephew • **John Salew** William Shakespeare • **Leslie Bradley** Walter Raleigh • **Olga Lindo** Queen Elizabeth
Director *Walter Forde*
Screenplay *Howard Irving Young, JOC Orton, Ted Kavanagh*

The Time Guardian ★★★ PG

1987 Aus Colour 83mins

Mad Max and *The Terminator* have been thrown into the blender along with *Star Wars*, for a reasonably exciting fantasy set in Australia. The quite complicated plot begins in the year 4039. Earth has been destroyed by a cyborg master race called the Jen-Diki. Escaping ruler Dean Stockwell sends warriors Fisher and Tom Burlinson back in time to 1988 to engineer another future battle with the killer robots before they become too strong. In the outback, the two culture-clash soldiers meet loner Nikki Coghill, who helps them fight the corrupt Aussie police to ensure the success of their quest. Good special effects, a quick pace and non-stop action disguise plot holes you could fly a spaceship through.

Tom Burlinson Ballard/The Time Guardian • **Nikki Coghill** Annie • **Dean Stockwell** Boss • **Carrie Fisher** Petra • **Peter Merrill** Zuryk • **Tim Robertson** Sergeant McCarthy • **John Clark** • **Jimmy James**
Director *Brian Hannant*
Screenplay *Brian Hannant, John Baxter*

The Time Machine ★★★★ PG

1960 UK/US Colour 98mins [video]

HG Wells's marvellous story is superbly brought to life in this charming and stylish adaptation by *The War of the Worlds* producer George Pal. Leaving his comfortable Victorian life behind, inventor Rod Taylor hops aboard his ingenious time contraption to explore the horrors of the future and speeds through two world wars and atomic destruction (in 1966!) towards eventual enslavement of the human race by subterranean cannibals. A richly speculative science-fiction classic that both stimulates and entertains, this imaginative film deservedly won an Oscar for special effects.

Rod Taylor George • **Alan Young** David Filby/James Filby • **Yvette Mimieux** Weena • **Sebastian Cabot** Dr Philip Hillyer • **Tom Helmore** Anthony Bridewell • **Whit Bissell** Walter Kemp • **Doris Lloyd** Mrs Watchett • **Paul Frees** The history machine • **Bob Barran** Eloi man

Director *George Pal*
Screenplay *David Duncan, from the novel by HG Wells*
Producer *George Pal*
Special effects *Gene Warren, Tim Baer, Wah Chang*

SFacts

Keeping it in the family: Simon Wells, who is directing the blockbuster new feature film version of this classic (starring Yancey Arias and Guy Pearce) is the great-grandson of author HG Wells.

Time of Roses ★★★

1969 Fin BW 90mins

Shades of *1984* and *Vertigo* colour what is, to date, Finland's sole venture into science fiction, which concerns a classless yet totalitarian society set in 2012. Writer/director Risto Jarva's parable foregrounds TV producer Arto Tuominen's remoulding of a dead woman as part of his professional brief to reinvent the past according to current ideology, while it also sets out to demonstrate the ease with which the media can manipulate our perception of reality. The story of Tuominen's growing preoccupation with the female subject of his latest documentary – a onetime stripper-model-actress and drugstore clerk who was killed in a 1976 road crash – is rather clumsily interrupted by a studio-strike sub-plot whose blatant target is wishy-washy liberalism. In Finnish with English subtitles.

Ritva Vespa Saara • **Arto Tuominen** Raimo • **Tarja Markus** Anu

Director *Risto Jarva*
Screenplay *Risto Jarva, Jaakko Pakkasvirta, Peter von Bagh*
Cinematographer *Antti Peippo*

Time Runner ★ 15

1993 Can Colour 92mins [video]

Fans of Mark Hamill will be embarrassed to see their idol miserably failing in an attempt to emulate Michael Biehn's character from *The Terminator*. Hamill's 21st-century character travels back to 1992 in order to warn Earth of a future alien invasion, but the invaders are already secretly in place and are out to stop him. Appallingly cheap and dull, with a time-jumping script and dim-witted characters, this makes no sense. The only interest comes in seeing how the landscape in the interior of British Columbia (where this was filmed) looks strikingly like southern California.

Mark Hamill Michael Raynor • **Rae Dawn Chong** Karen • **Brion James** Neila • **Marc Baur** Colonel Freeman • **Gordon Tipple** Arnie

Director *Michael Mazo*
Screenplay *Greg Derochie, Ron Tarrant, Ian Bray, Christopher Hyde, Michael Mazo, from a story by John A Curtis*

Time Slip ★★★

1981 Jap Colour 139mins

Modern day Japanese soldiers on manoeuvres are transported back to the 16th century where they take on Samurai warriors with their hi-tech artillery. Squadron leader Sonny Chiba (who also choreographed the beautifully staged battles) decides the only way to return to their era is to change the course of history – that way Mother Nature will send them back home in order to maintain the status quo. Although needlessly bogged down in redundant side plots (one has Chiba culling his own men of a renegade faction), director Kosei Saito's *Seven Samurai* meets *The Final Countdown*, complete with a climax reminiscent of *The Wild Bunch*, is an exciting action adventure with plenty of outrageous comic strip bravado. Japanese dialogue dubbed into English.

Sonny Chiba Lieutenant Iba • **Isao Natsuki** Samurai leader • **Miyuki Ono** Village girl • **Nana Okada** Modern girl

Screenplay *Toshio Kaneda, from a story by Ryo Hanmura*

Time Trackers ★★ U

1989 US Colour 81mins [video]

In 2033, evil scientist Lee Bergere commandeers a time tunnel and uses the device to go back in history so he can claim the credit for inventing it. Unfortunately he ends up in medieval England where a Robin Hood-type hero is the nemesis of villains everywhere. Produced on the cheap by Roger Corman, this sci-fi adventure is more successful on the humour front thanks to Ned Beatty's sparkling turn as a contemporary cop in hot pursuit of Bergere through the centuries. Bergere and co-star Kathleen Beller previously appeared together in *Dynasty*.

Ned Beatty Harry • **Wil Shriner** Charles • **Kathleen Beller** RJ • **Bridget Hoffman** Madeline • **Alex Hyde-White** Edgar • **Lee Bergere** Zandor

Director/Screenplay *Howard R Cohen*
Producer *Roger Corman*

The Time Travelers ★★★ PG

1964 US Colour 80mins [video]

Conceived by director Ib Melchior as a sequel of sorts to *The Time Machine*, this is popcorn entertainment in the old-fashioned sense. A group of scientists led by Preston Foster hurtle 107 years into Earth's future, only to discover it in post-nuclear ruins and its human android survivors living underground and hiding from mutants who roam the surface. Given its modest budget, the film's ambition must be admired, though tarnished somewhat by poor acting and stilted dialogue. The glossy look is courtesy of Vilmos Zsigmond, later a leading Hollywood cinematographer who would win an Oscar for *Close Encounters of the Third Kind*. Film buffs should look out for a cameo by horror fan icon Forrest J Ackerman.

Preston Foster Dr Erik von Steiner • **Philip Carey** Steve Connors • **Merry Anders** Carol White • **John Hoyt** Varno • **Dennis Patrick** Councilman Willard • **Joan Woodbury** Gadra • **Steve Franken** Danny McKee • **Forrest J Ackerman** Technician

Director *Ib Melchior*
Screenplay *Ib Melchior, from a story by Ib Melchior, from a story by David L Hewitt*
Cinematographer *William Zsigmond [Vilmos Zsigmond]*
Special effects *David L Hewitt*

Time Trax ★★ PG

TV 1993-1994 US Colour 44x60mins [video]

A 22nd-century police officer pursues a group of time-travelling criminals 200 years into Earth's past, and finds himself at the centre of a derivative and criminally uninspired sci-fi cops 'n' robbers caper. Dale Midkiff leads the undemanding adventure as the hunky but bland Darien Lambert, while Elizabeth Alexander co-stars as the *Quantum Leap*-inspired Selma, a motherly and frequently overbearing holographic representation of Lambert's computer. Together, the pair seem stuck in a time warp of their own, as they essentially face the same locate-and-capture-a-criminal plotline each week. Still, at least, the production values and action sequences are up to scratch. A passable time-waster.

Dale Midkiff Darien Lambert • **Elizabeth Alexander** Selma • **Peter Donat** Dr Mordecai "Mo" Sahmbi
Created by *Grant Rosenberg, Harve Bennett, Jeffrey Hayes*
Executive producer *Grant Rosenberg*

The Time Tunnel ★★★

TV 1966-1967 US BW 30x60mins

The show which paved the way for *Quantum Leap, Sliders* and most other US TV time-travel series, Irwin Allen's follow-up to *Lost in Space* has two scientists getting lost in time. Propelled into the past by a top-secret experimental time-travelling device, Dr Tony Newman and Dr Doug Phillips embark on an uncontrollable trip through major historical events, and even visit a future Earth which is being conquered by aliens. The show's corny storylines involve excursions to such obvious locales as the *Titanic*, Pearl Harbour and Gettysburg, none of which can be convincingly visualised on the production's lean budget. But through the years, Tony and Doug's tour of time has remained a great deal of lightweight, campy fun. Series stars James Darren and Robert Colbert make timeless heroes, and the show's main set design – the eponymous Time Tunnel – was truly ahead of its time.

James Darren Dr Tony Newman • **Robert Colbert** Dr Doug Phillips • **Lee Meriwether** Dr Ann MacGregor • **Whit Bissell** Lt-Gen Heywood Kirk • **John Zaremba** Dr Raymond Swain
Created by *Irwin Allen*
Executive producer *Irwin Allen*

Timecop ★★★ 18

1994 US Colour 98mins DVD

Evening all. What's all this then – two Jean-Claude Van Dammes for the price of one? Yes, the Muscles from Brussels encounters his younger self – and sports a silly hairdo – when he's sent back in time to catch a sinister senator who is trying to change the past for his own monetary ends. If you can follow the time-travel logic, which everyone seems to be making up as they go along, then director Peter Hyams's gleaming comic-strip action adventure is dumb fun, with good old Jean-Claude causing as much futuristic Van Dammage as possible. However, most sci-fi fans will find it desperately outdated. Best exchange – Jean-Claude: "He read my mind." Jean-Claude's wife: "With your English, I'm not surprised." Contains swearing, violence, sex scenes and nudity.

Jean-Claude Van Damme Max Walker • **Mia Sara** Melissa • **Ron Silver** McComb • **Bruce McGill** Matuzak • **Gloria Reuben** Fielding • **Scott Bellis** Ricky • **Jason Schombing** Atwood • **Scott Lawrence** Spota • **Kenneth Welsh** Utley • **Brent Woolsey** Shotgun
Director *Peter Hyams*
Screenplay *Mark Verheiden, from a story by Mark Verheiden, Mark Richardson, from their comic book series*

Timelock ★★ 18

1996 US Colour 92mins

On a distant maximum security – and minimum budget – prison asteroid, some of the galaxy's baddest convicts are planning a mass breakout. But they haven't reckoned on the unlikely alliance between space-transport captain Maryam d'Abo and small-time techno-crook Ayre Gross, in this unambitious slice of sci-fi action from director Robert Munic. Apart from the odd one-liner and a spectacularly camp performance from Jeffrey Meek, this is formulaic fare for die-hard genre fans only. Contains violence, sexual situations and some swearing.

Maryam d'Abo Teegs • **Arye Gross** Riley • **Jeff Speakman** McMasters • **Jeffrey Meek** Villum • **Ricco Ross** Tibuck • **Thomas G Waites** Warden Andrews
Director *Robert Munic*
Screenplay *Joseph Barmettler, J Reifel*

Timemaster ★★ 12

1995 US Colour 95mins

James Glickenhaus made his name with the spectacularly violent *The Exterminator*, one of the first big straight-to-video hits in the UK. However, this time travelling adventure is softer fare, possibly because his own son Jesse has a lead role. The latter plays an orphan who discovers that Earth is being used as a setting for a giant cosmic game being played out by aliens; it's up to him to prevent his world being destroyed when the game is finished. The experienced Glickenhaus makes it look better than it deservesand it's satisfying entertainment.

Jesse Cameron-Glickenhaus Jesse Parker • **Michelle Williams** Annie • **Noriyuki "Pat" Morita [Pat Morita]** Isaiah • **Michael Dorn** Chairman • **Duncan Regehr** Jonathan Parker • **Joanna Pacula** Evelyn Parker • **Veronica Cameron-Glickenhaus** Veronica Parker
Director/Screenplay *James Glickenhaus*

Timerider: the Adventure of Lyle Swann ★★★

1982 US Colour 93mins

Stunt motorcyclist Fred Ward accidentally steers into the path of a time travel experiment being conducted by scientists in the Californian desert. Ending up in the Wild West of the 1880s, he fights outlaw leader Peter Coyote for ownership of his Baja 500 wheels and romances pistol-packing Belinda Bauer. Produced and scored by ex-Monkee Mike Nesmith, director William Dear's engaging B-movie makes up for in roaring action and solid casting what it lacks in story logic and cheap TV-style production. Dear went on to direct *Bigfoot and the Hendersons* for producer Steven Spielberg.

Fred Ward Lyle Swann • **Belinda Bauer** Clair Cygne • **Peter Coyote** Porter Reese • **Ed Lauter** Padre • **Richard Masur** Claude Dorsett • **LQ Jones** Ben Potter
Director *William Dear*
Screenplay *William Dear, Michael Nesmith*
Executive producer *Michael Nesmith*

Timescape ★★★ 15

1991 US Colour 89mins

Jeff Daniels stars here as a widower whose battered guest house becomes a rendezvous for time travellers from the next century. Daniels carries the film with a characteristically engaging performance, veering toward the comically bug-eyed when he discovers that the visitors have in fact turned up to witness an impending disaster. Writer/director David N Twohy brings enough invention to the plot to flesh out the imaginative premise, while the impressive special effects are by Oscar-winner John Dykstra, whose previous work includes *Star Wars*. Contains some swearing.

Jeff Daniels Ben Wilson • **Ariana Richards** Hillary Wilson • **Emilia Crow** Reeve • **Jim Haynie** Oscar • **Nicholas Guest** Spall
Director *David N Twohy*
Screenplay *David N Twohy, from the novella "Vintage Season" by CL Moore, Lawrence O'Donnell Jr*

Timeslip ★★

1955 UK BW 93mins

A quaint British science-fiction oddity about a radiation overdose propelling an atomic scientist seven seconds into the future. Numerous muddled plotlines intertwine, with gangsters and spies trying to exploit his reaction to events before they happen, but nothing too interesting is done with the nifty premise taken from Charles Eric Maine's novel *The Isotope Man*. Ken Hughes who later directed big movies such as *Cromwell* and *Chitty Chitty Bang Bang* slows it down even further with small-scale thrills and utterly conventional direction.

Gene Nelson Mike Delaney • **Faith Domergue** Jill Friday • **Joseph Tomelty** Inspector Cleary • **Donald Gray** Maitland • **Vic Perry** Vasquo • **Peter Arne** Stephen Maitland • **Launce Maraschal** Editor • **Charles Hawtrey** Scruffy
Director *Ken Hughes*
Screenplay *Charles Eric Maine, Ken Hughes, from the novel "The Isotope Man" by Charles Eric Maine*

Timestalkers ★★★ PG

1987 US Colour 90mins

Science fiction comes to the Wild West in this sharply told TV time-travel adventure. College professor William Devane, a collector of Old West artefacts, travels back in time to the American frontier with mysterious Lauren Hutton, to track down evil gunslinger Klaus Kinski, who has appropriated modern technology for his murderous spree. Thanks to an inventive, well-plotted script by Brian Clemens, and Michael Schultz's fast-paced direction, it all makes eminent sense as the action hurtles toward its gripping conclusion.

William Devane Scott McKenzie • **Lauren Hutton** Georgia Crawford • **Klaus Kinski** Dr Joseph Cole • **John Ratzenberger** General Joe Brodsky • **Forrest Tucker** Texas John Cody • **James Avery** Blacksmith
Director *Michael Shultz*
Screenplay *Brian Clemens, from the unpublished novel "The Tintype" by Ray Brown*

The Tingler ★★★★ 15

1959 US BW 78mins

One of the best examples of the work of the great horror producer/director William Castle, the king of gimmick cinema, whose shockers always shouted "Boo!" with lurid style. Here, doctor Vincent Price discovers that fear creates a parasite that grows on the spine unless the victim screams. Price isolates one of the large insect-like creatures and it escapes… Immensely enjoyable hokum originally featuring the legendary stunt "Percepto" – selected cinema seats wired to administer mild electric shocks! A mini-classic, with a ripe Price performance, bizarre chills and goofy psychedelic imagery.

Vincent Price Dr William Chapin • **Judith Evelyn** Mrs Higgins • **Darryl Hickman** David Morris • **Patricia Cutts** Isabel Chapin • **Pamela Lincoln** Lucy Stevens • **Philip Coolidge** Ollie Higgins
Director *William Castle*
Screenplay *Robb White*

SCI Q

38

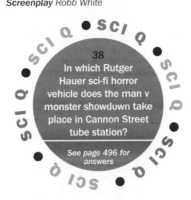

In which Rutger Hauer sci-fi horror vehicle does the man v monster showdown take place in Cannon Street tube station?

See page 496 for answers

Titan AE ★★★★ PG

2000 US Colour mins DVD

Talk about starting with a bang! Don Bluth (*The Land Before Time, An American Tail*) kicks off this animated spectacular with nothing less than the blowing-up of the Earth, forcing survivors Cale (voiced by Matt Damon) and Akima (Drew Barrymore) to put one over on the offending aliens by reactivating a hidden spacecraft, the eponymous *Titan*. Three parts *Star Wars* to one part *Star Trek*, *Titan AE* ("After Earth" in case you were wondering) imaginatively blends top-quality cel and digital animation, resulting in something well beyond mere eye candy for kids. One particularly glorious scene has ephemeral space "angels" riding the bow wake of a starship in the same way that dolphins ride the bow waves of boats.

Matt Damon Cale • **Drew Barrymore** Akima • **Bill Pullman** Korso • **John Leguizamo** Gune • **Nathan Lane** Preed • **Janeane Garofalo** Stith • **Ron Perlman** Prof Sam Tucker • **Alex D Linz** Young Cale • **Tone Loc** Tek • **Jim Breuer** The cook
Director *Don Bluth, Gary Goldman*
Screenplay *Ben Edlund, John August, Joss Whedon, from a story by Hans Bauer, Randall McCormick*
Animation director *Len Simon*

Tobor the Great ★★ U

1954 US BW 77mins

A robot designed by Taylor Holmes to take the place of a human astronaut on a moon flight saves the inventor and his grandson, Billy Chapin, from enemy agents. Tobor also gets its wires crossed and is transformed into a metallic maniac before Chapin saves the day. Lee Sholem directed many episodes of the George Reeves *Superman* television series and that juvenile action slant is very much in operation here. Beginning with a pointless semi-documentary about nuclear war and space travel, Sholem awkwardly marks more time between each Tobor segment with Charles Drake and Karin Booth's limp romantic encounters and broad anti-Communist cloak-and-dagger theatrics. Only clueless viewers who don't cotton on to how Tobor's name was conjured up will be entertained by such kiddie-orientated pap.

Charles Drake Dr Ralph Harrison • **Karin Booth** Janice Roberts • **Billy Chapin** Gadge Roberts • **Taylor Holmes** Professor Nordstrom • **Steven Geray** Man with glasses • **Henry Kulky** Paul • **Franz Roehn** Karl
Director *Lee Sholem*
Screenplay *Richard Goldstone, Philip MacDonald, from a story by Carl Dudley*

Tom Corbett, Space Cadet ★★

TV 1950-1955 US BW

Loosely based on Robert A Heinlein's novel *Space Cadet*, this originated on CBS but ran only three months before being dropped and shifted to ABC, and then to crop up on both NBC and DuMont. Set in the 24th century, the show featured the cadets of Space Academy ("the West Point of the Universe"), especially fresh-faced Frankie Thomas and his pals aboard the good ship *Polaris*, the sometimes-undisciplined Jan Merlin and the Venusian Al Markim. While most similar shows concentrated on the paternal commanders and captains, this essentially dealt with the youths who served as sidekicks on *Captain Video* or *Space Patrol*. Girls weren't allowed, and there were more moral lessons than megalomaniac world-conquerors. Technical advice came from German rocketry expert Willy Ley.

Frankie Thomas Tom Corbett • **Al Markim** Astro the Venusian • **Jan Merlin** Roger Manning • **Margaret Garland** Dr Joan Dale • **Jack Grimes** TJ Thistle • **Carter Blake** Commander Arkwright
Source *the character created by Robert Heinlein in his novel "Space Cadet"*
Technical advisor *Willy Ley*

The Tommyknockers ★★ 15

TV 1993 US Colour 169mins

When the population of a small American town suddenly becomes obsessed with strange activities, a local writer starts to uncover the dark forces behind their

The Tomorrow People (from left): John (Nicholas Young), Hsui Tai (Misako Koba), Elizabeth (Elizabeth Adare) and Stephen (Peter Vaughan-Clarke)

behaviour. Jimmy Smits leads the fight against alien possession in this two-part, mini-series, which is based on the Stephen King novel. Although it seems drawn-out at times and has plenty of plot holes, *The Tommyknockers* still possesses a certain appeal. The set-up is pure Stephen King, and director John Power doesn't stint on crowd-pleasing drama or knock-out moments. Power also makes the most of the ever-engaging Smits and his quirky supporting players, who include Marg Helgenberger, Traci Lords, John Ashton and Cliff De Young.

Jimmy Smits Jim Gardner • **Marg Helgenberger** Bobbi Anderson • **John Ashton** Butch Duggan • **Allyce Beasley** Becka Paulson • **Robert Carradine** Bryant Brown • **Joanna Cassidy** Sheriff Ruth • **Annie Corley** Marie Brown • **Cliff De Young** Joe Paulson • **Traci Lords** Nancy Voss • **EG Marshall** Ev Hillman
Director *John Power*
Teleplay *Lawrence D Cohen, from the novel by Stephen King*

The Tomorrow Man ★★★

1995 US Colour 85mins

A shape-shifting android is sent from a decimated 26th century to change the present in order to protect the future, in a poor man's *Terminator 2* crossed with *Quantum Leap*. This feature-length pilot for a proposed TV series is clichéd sci-fi fare, though there's a surprisingly appealing performance from Julian Sands as Kenn, the super cyborg masquerading as a fashion model. Computer expert Giancarlo Esposito offers strong support as his comic foil, friend and mentor, and, despite its predictability, the film is sufficiently upbeat to pass the time as light-hearted entertainment.

Julian Sands Kenn • **Giancarlo Esposito** Jonathan Driscoll • **Craig Wasson** Doctor Galloway • **Obba Babatunde** Ryan Parrish • **Sydney Walsh** Jill Henderson
Director *Bill D'Elia*
Screenplay *Alan Spencer*

The Tomorrow People ★★★★

TV 1973-1979 UK Colour 68x30mins

What started out as a rival to the BBC's *Doctor Who* turned out to be the most successful sci-fi series ever produced by the ITV network. Created by Frank Price, "Tomorrow People" were the next stage in human evolution, teenagers with incredible psychic powers. From their secret base in London and helped by the paternal TIM, part-computer, part-cola dispenser, they defended mankind from power-mad despots and alien invaders, while also finding the time to become Earth's first ambassadors to the galactic empire. Despite special effects that were worse even than in *Doctor Who*, the show worked because it was aimed at kids and acted by kids. The stories reflected this, pitting the Tomorrow People against adult authority figures or child slavers. Future TV icons Keith Chegwin and Nicholas Lyndhurst make suitably embarrassing early appearances.

Nicholas Young John • **Peter Vaughan-Clarke** Stephen • **Elizabeth Adare** Elizabeth • **Dean Lawrence** Tyso • **Misako Koba** Hsui Tai • **Michael Holoway** Mike • **Nigel Rhodes** Andrew • **Philip Gilbert** TIM • **Sammie Winmill** Carol • **Stephen Salmon** Kenny
Created by *Roger Price*

The Tomorrow People ★★ U

TV 1992-95 UK/US Colour 25x30m [video]

Despite being off the air for years in Britain, *The Tomorrow People* found a welcoming home in the mid-eighties on the Nickelodeon cable channel in America. Piped into 28 million homes it proved so popular Nickelodeon part-funded a reworking of the original series, updated to the nineties and starring Kristian Schmid of *Neighbours* fame. Look out, too, for *Red Dwarf*'s Danny John-Jules in the final five-part story. The premise was as before, a group of teenagers with extraordinary powers (literally "homo-superiors") battling against threats to mankind, while also keeping their own powers a secret from those who might exploit them. However this time their base of operations was from inside an alien spaceship on an uncharted island in the Pacific and not London, despite the show being produced in the UK. This short-lived revival proved a pale shadow of the original.

Kristian Schmid Adam • **Christian Tessier** Megabyte • **Kristen Ariza** Liza • **Adam Pearce** Kevin • **Naomie Harris** Ami • **Laurence Bouvard** Lucy • **Jean Marsh** Dr Culex • **Christopher Lee** Sam Rees • **Alexandra Milman** Jade Weston
Created by *Roger Price*
Producer *Roger Price*

Too Much ★ U

1987 US Colour 85mins [video]

A kiddie clone of the previous year's *Short Circuit* that lives up to its title in saccharine sweetness and nauseating cuteness. Lonely little Bridgette Andersen lives in Japan, where she is given a prototype robot to befriend. When the evil Professor Finkel and his stupid henchmen try and steal the experimental cyborg (looking suspiciously like R2-D2 from *Star Wars*), the duo go on the run and have uninvolving juvenile misadventures. A cloying and banal fantasy that even children will find syrupy beyond redemption.

Bridgette Andersen Suzy • **Masato Fukazama** Too Much • **Hiroyuki Watanabe** Tetsuro • **Char Fontana** Professor Finkel • **Uganda** Bernie
Director/Screenplay *Eric Rochat*

Toomorrow ★★

1970 UK Colour 93mins

Anthropologist Roy Dotrice is really an Alphoid alien in disguise whose Earth mission is to track down a "tonaliser" causing good vibrations on his planet. The instrument is the invention of Vic Cooper who, with fellow Chelsea art students Benny Thomas, Karl Chambers and Olivia Newton-John, has set up the pop group Toomorrow to earn money for college expenses. While appearing at a pop festival organised by Dotrice, the group are whisked to his home planet to add soul to their out-of-tune computerised music. A lightweight musical fantasy, the contrived plot is sweetened enormously by some sophisticated humour, extravagant production design (it was co-produced by 007 veteran Harry Saltzman after all) and expert know-how direction by genre doyen Val Guest. Co-producer Don Kirshner had created The Monkees but the same glorious fate did not await the manufactured Toomorrow band although Newton-John would become a global superstar and *Grease* icon.

Olivia Newton-John Olivia • **Benny Thomas [Ben Thomas]** Benny • **Vic Cooper** Vic • **Karl Chambers** Karl • **Roy Dotrice** John Williams • **Roy Marsden** Alpha
Director/Screenplay *Val Guest*
Producer *Don Kirshner, Harry Saltzman*
Music *Hugo Montenegro*

Total Recall ★★★★ 18

1990 US Colour 108mins [video] DVD

This rip-roaring slice of sci-fi excess remains Arnold Schwarzenegger's most satisfying film since his breakthrough hit *The Terminator*. Director Paul Verhoeven, armed with a smart script from Ronald Shusett, Gary Goldman and Dan O'Bannon (itself loosely based on a short story by cult novelist Philip K Dick), cuts loose with a gloriously over-the-top mix of black humour, ultra-violence and spectacular effects. The result was a massive worldwide hit. Schwarzenegger is the dull construction worker on a futuristic Earth, who is drawn into a conspiracy on the planet Mars when a virtual reality holiday awakens long-dormant memories. Ronny Cox, fresh from his bad-guy role in Verhoeven's *Robocop*, delivers another villainous performance, and is ably assisted by Michael Ironside. However, the real find turned out to be Sharon Stone; she had been on the fringes of Hollywood for some time, but it was this performance that led her to her ground-breaking role in Verhoeven's next movie, *Basic Instinct*. Contains violence, swearing and nudity.

Arnold Schwarzenegger Douglas Quaid • **Rachel Ticotin** Melina • **Sharon Stone** Lori Quaid • **Ronny Cox** Cohaagen • **Michael Ironside** Richter • **Marshall Bell** George/Kuato • **Mel Johnson Jr** Benny • **Michael Champion** Helm • **Roy Brocksmith** Dr Edgemar • **Ray Baker** McClane • **Rosemary Dunsmore** Dr Lull • **David Knell** Ernie

Director *Paul Verhoeven*

Screenplay *Ronald Shusett, Dan O'Bannon, Gary Goldman, from a story by Ronald Shusett, Dan O'Bannon, Jon Povill, from the short story "We Can Remember It for You Wholesale" by Philip K Dick*

Total Recall 2070 ★★

TV 1999 Can/Ger/US Colour 22x60mins

Although ostensibly based on the Philip K Dick-inspired 1990 movie, this small-screen incarnation actually owes just as much to Dick's other most famous brainchild, *Blade Runner*. Set in a dark and disturbing future firmly out of the Ridley Scott school of sci-fi, the series focuses on the weekly investigations of old-fashioned human police detective David Hume and his android partner, Ian Farve. Operating in a world of memory-controlling technology and powerful mega-corporations, the mismatched cops strive to uphold both the law and the reality of existence. The show's robust central performances and eye-catching visuals are certainly memorable, and its storylines become increasingly challenging as the saga progresses. But the series' relentlessly oppressive tone makes *2070* a difficult place to visit, and helped ensure its early demise at the end of its opening season.

Michael Easton David Hume • **Karl Pruner** Ian Farve • **Cynthia Preston** Olivia Hume • **Judith Krant** Olan Chang • **Michael Anthony Rawlins** Martin Ehrenthal • **Matthew Bennett** James Calley

Director *Mario Azzopardi*

Created by *Art Monterastelli*

Executive producer *Art Monterastelli* • ***Supervising producer*** *Jeff King*

Toto in the Moon ★

1957 It/Sp BW 90mins

Toto, the stage name of vaudeville comedian Antonio Furst de Curtis-Gagliardi, took his famous slapstick music hall act to the screen in numerous adventures in a variety of genres. This one found clerk Toto and his sci-fi magazine publisher boss, Ugo Tognazzi, being fought over by space race nations because Tognazzi's blood is thin enough to withstand the astronaut pressures of space flight. Meanwhile, aliens create duplicates of them both to sabotage their impending mission so they won't be discovered. Shameless mugging, broad farce and innumerable cultural references make this of no real interest to non-Italians. Director Steno (Stefano Vanzina) made numerous fantasy spoofs including *Uncle Was a Vampire* with Christopher Lee. Steno's son Carlo Vanzina is one of Italy's most popular directors of soap opera romances and action thrillers. An Italian language film.

Toto Toto • **Ugo Tognazzi** Achille • **Sylva Koschina** Lidia

Director *Steno [Stefano Vanzina]*

Screenplay *Sandro Continenza [Alessandro Continenza], Steno [Stefano Vanzina], Ettore Scola, from a story by Lucio Fulci*

Cinematographer *Marco Scarpelli*

The Tower ★ 15

1992 US Colour 86mins

There's a tower block, right? And it's controlled by this state-of-the-art computer. And the owners are dead chuffed with it. But you'll never guess what happens – the computer goes haywire and only one man can stop it? Oh, you've seen it? If not, you've seen countless films like it. This has to be one of the most derivative plotlines ever concocted.

Paul Reiser Tony Minot • **Roger Rees** Mr Littlehill • **Susan Norman** Linda Furillo • **Annabelle Gurwitch** Sally • **Dee Dee Rescher** Gretchen • **Charmaine Cruise** Secretary • **Jennifer Richards** Cammie • **Richard Gant** Wilson • **Dee Gee Wilkinson** CAS • **Carlos Allen** Operator

Director *Richard Kletter*

Screenplay *John Riley, Richard Kletter, from a story by John Riley*

A Town Has Turned to Dust ★★ 18

1998 US Colour 87mins

Based on a Rod Serling script dusted off from his *Twilight Zone* heyday, this cable movie combines thoughtful storytelling with above average acting. Set in a futuristic desert hamlet, ruthless town boss Ron Perlman lynches an innocent native American, setting the scene for a revolt by the murdered teenager's brother, Frankie Avina, and a clash with drunken sheriff, Stephen Lang. The movie's message – that age-old problems such as racism and oppression are timeless – may be a little dated, and some scenes are awkwardly disjointed, but its heart is in the right place even if the special effects aren't up to scratch. Contains violence.

Ron Perlman Jerry Paul • **Stephen Lang** Harvey Denton • **Judy Collins** Ree • **Gabriel Olds** Hannify • **Babara Jane Reams** Maya • **Frankie Avina** Tooth • **Zahn McClarnon** Tommy • **M Scott Wilkinson** Wavy

Director *Rob Nilsson*

Screenplay *Rod Serling*

The Toxic Avenger ★★★ 18

1985 US Colour 75mins DVD

After years of churning out teen comedies that weren't very funny, New York based Troma Films hit the big time with this outrageously tacky superhero spoof that became one of the cult hits of the decade. Weedy janitor Mark Torgl is transformed into good-guy monster the Toxic Avenger (Mitchell Cohen) after being dumped into a barrel of toxic goo by a gang of thugs. Toxie (as he's known to his friends) is very nice to his blind girlfriend but metes out violent punishment to local criminals. Loaded with infantile slapstick, amateurish acting, teen-orientated erotica and extreme gore (trimmed considerably in this country) this is B-movie making at its crudest and purest. Keep your eyes peeled for future Oscar-winner Marisa Tomei as a walk-on extra.

Andree Maranda Sara • **Mitchell Cohen** Toxic Avenger • **Jennifer Baptist** Wanda • **Cindy Manion** Julie • **Robert Prichard** Slug • **Gary Schneider** Bozo • **Pat Ryan Jr** Mayor Belgoody • **Mark Torgl** Melvin • **Marisa Tomei** Health club girl

Director *Michael Herz, Samuel Weil*

Screenplay *Joe Ritter, Lloyd Kaufman, Gay Partington Terry, Stuart Strutin*

The Toxic Avenger, Part II ★★ 18

1988 US Colour 90mins DVD

Fans of Troma Films' most celebrated creation had to wait three years for the inevitable follow-up. In the meantime their hero had achieved near iconic status, but even his most die-hard fans had trouble finding anything to enjoy in this wholesale debacle which sees Toxie, travelling to Japan to save the planet's ecosystem from an evil industrial conglomerate. Shot back-to-back with the even more lamentable *Part III*, this was co-directed by Lloyd Kaufman, the founder of Troma, who have since given the world such masterpieces as *Surf Nazis Must Die* and *Cannibal! The Musical*.

Ron Fazio The Toxic Avenger • **John Altamura** The Toxic Avenger • **Phoebe Legere** Claire • **Rick Collins** Apocalypse Inc Chairman • **Rikiya Yasuoka** Big Mac
Director *Lloyd Kaufman, Michael Herz*
Screenplay *Gay Partington Terry, from a story by Lloyd Kaufman*

Trancers ★★★ 15

1985 US Colour 73mins

Tim Thomerson is a 23rd-century cop who goes back in time to capture his arch-nemesis who is planning to change the past in order to control the future with his psychically controlled zombie henchmen, the trancers of the title. *Blade Runner* French connects with *The Terminator* in a nail-biting quickie from minor cult director Charles Band. Thomerson gives a wonderfully high-flying Dirty Harry-goes-cyber-punk portrayal and 1997 best actress Oscar winner Helen Hunt makes an early appearance as his innocent sidekick in present day LA.

Tim Thomerson Jack Deth/Philip Dethon • **Helen Hunt** Leena • **Michael Stefani** Martin Whistler/Lt Wiesling • **Art LaFleur** McNulty • **Telma Hopkins** Engineer Raines • **Richard Herd** Chairman Spencer • **Anne Seymour** Chairman Ashe • **Miguel Fernandez** Officer Lopez
Director *Charles Band*
Screenplay *Danny Bilson, Paul DeMeo*

Trancers II: The Return of Jack Deth ★★ 15

1991 US Colour 84mins

Tim Thomerson returns as the no-nonsense Jack Deth, a cop from the future stuck in modern day Los Angeles, in Charles Band's belated sequel to his own mid-eighties cult hit. Once again pitted against zombie-like creatures known as trancers, Thomerson's engagingly laconic Deth also has to deal with a convoluted love life – two wives in different centuries. And yes, that's a pre-*As Good As It Gets* Helen Hunt as one of the spouses. Look out also for two-time Bond girl and Hammer starlet Martine Beswick. Not nearly as much fun as its predecessor, which was a sly mix of time travel antics and *film noir*, but that didn't stop the makers from churning out yet more sequels.

Tim Thomerson Jack Deth • **Helen Hunt** Lena Deth • **Megan Ward** Alice Stillwell • **Biff Manard** Hap Ashby • **Martine Beswick** Nurse Trotter • **Jeffrey Combs** Doctor Pyle • **Alyson Croft** McNulty • **Telma Hopkins** Raines
Director *Charles Band*
Screenplay *Jackson Barr, from a story by Charles Band, Jackson Barr*

Transformations ★★ 18

1988 US Colour 77mins

A steamy but occasionally stylish slice of space vampirism, starring Rex Smith as a hapless pilot who is infected by a mysterious alien being and then unwittingly begins spreading the contagion throughout a prison colony he is forced to land on. Director Jay Kamen made his name as a sound editor, but doesnfit quite make such a successful transition to behind the cameras.

Rex Smith Shadduck • **Lisa Langlois** Miranda • **Patrick Macnee** Father Christopher • **Christopher Neame** Calihan
Director *Jay Kamen*
Screenplay *Mitch Brian*

Transformers – the Movie ★ U

1986 US Colour 84mins

The feature-length version of the cartoon TV series is based on the popular toy line of robots that mutate into hi-tech weaponry and vehicles. The fighting cyborgs must save the universe from the planet Unicron – voiced by Orson Welles – and its intergalactic army led by the evil Megatron. Other top voice talent includes Leonard Nimoy, Robert Stack, Judd Nelson and Eric Idle. The usual mind-numbing blitz of cheap graphics, marginally vulgar dialogue and nasty violence means parents with impressionable children should take heed.

Leonard Nimoy Galvatron • **Robert Stack** Ultra Magnus • **Eric Idle** Wreck Gar • **Judd Nelson** Hot Rod/Rodimus Prime • **Lionel Stander** Kup • **John Moschitta** Blurr • **Orson Welles** Planet Unicron • **Corey Burton** Spike/Brawn/Shockwave • **Peter Cullen** Optimus Prime/Ironhide • **Frank Welker** Soundwave/Megatron/ Rumble/Frenzy/Wheelie/Junkion
Director *Nelson Shin*
Screenplay *Ron Friedman*

Trapped in Space ★★★ 15

1994 US Colour 83mins

Based on the Arthur C Clarke short story *Breaking Strain*, this minor science-fiction gem could be described as Hitchcock's *Lifeboat* in space. When a cargo spaceship is hit by a meteor on a routine assignment, the astronauts find themselves condemned to a lingering death in an airless craft. The devastating effect this has on the once-friendly crew members is shown using plenty of nerve-jangling shocks and suspenseful surprise, and there's a completely unexpected resolution. Tautly and teasingly directed by Arthur Allan Seidelman, this efficient no-nonsense exercise in chilling claustrophobia and fragmented fear is a real discovery.

Jack Wagner Chief Engineer McNeil • **Jack Coleman** Second Mate Grant • **Craig Wasson** Bosun Palmer • **Sigrid Thornton** Engineer Cadet Isaacs • **Kay Lenz** Gillings • **Kevin Colson** Captain Howard • **Mark Lee** Tug first officer • **Kevin Copeland** Tug pilot • **Ian Stenlake** Tug medic
Director *Arthur Allan Seidelman*
Screenplay *Arlington Hughes, Melinda M Snodgrass, from the short story "Breaking Strain" by Arthur C Clarke*

Tremors ★★★★★ 15

1989 US Colour 91mins

The spirit of the "Killer Bs" is gloriously resurrected in this, the ultimate story of the worm that turned. Kevin Bacon and Fred Ward are a sort of "Simple and Simpler", an endearingly goofy pair of handymen who discover that huge underground worms have broken through the Earth's surface and are now swallowing up everything in their path. Director Ron Underwood keeps both the action and laughs roaring along at a tremendous pace and there's a string of entertaining cameos, most notably from Michael Gross – the father in TV's *Family Ties* – and country star Reba McEntire as an unlikely pair of survivalists. Add to that a refreshingly tough and intelligent female lead (Finn Carter) and the result is the sharpest, funniest monster movie in years. Contains swearing.

Kevin Bacon Valentine McKee • **Fred Ward** Earl Basset • **Finn Carter** Rhonda LeBeck • **Michael Gross** Burt Gummer • **Reba McEntire** Heather Gummer • **Bobby Jacoby** Melvin Plug • **Charlotte Stewart** Nancy • **Tony Genaro** Miguel • **Ariana Richards** Mindy • **Richard Marcus** Nestor • **Victor Wong** Walter Chang • **Sunshine Parker** Edgar • **Michael Dan Wagner** Old Fred • **Conrad Bachmann** Jim • **Bibi Besch** Megan • **John Goodwin** Howard
Director *Ron Underwood*
Screenplay *SS Wilson, Brent Maddock, from a story by SS Wilson, Brent Maddock, Ron Underwood*

Tremors II: Aftershocks ★★★ 12

1995 US Colour 95mins

A surprisingly entertaining made-for-video sequel to Ron Underwood's minor classic

13 TRULY TERRIBLE FILMS OR
CAMP CLASSICS
OUR CRITICS' SELECTION

● The Astro-Zombies (1968)
Director: Ted V Mikels
"one of the all-time worst science-fiction camp classics"

● The Attack of the Killer Tomatoes (1978) Director: John De Bello
"a mind-numbing splatter bore"

● Cat-Women of the Moon (1958)
Director Arthur Hilton
"lunar lunacy of the worst kind"

● Dr Black and Mr Hyde (1975)
Director: William Crain
"the worst blaxploitation horror movie ever made, and with at least something to offend every race"

● The Giant Claw (1957)
Director: Fred F Sears
"tawdry, tacky and totally stupid"

● Fire Maidens from Outer Space (1956)
Director: Cy Roth
"bottom-of-the-barrel lunatic nonsense"

● Frankenstein Meets the Space Monster (1965)
Director: Robert Gaffney
"poverty-stricken camp turkey"

● It Conquered the World (1956)
Director: Roger Corman
"monster flicks rarely come dafter than this"

● Mars Needs Women (1966)
Director: Larry Buchanan
"terminally stupid travesty"

● Plan 9 from Outer Space (1959)
Director: Edward D Wood Jr
"a tediously depressing experience"

● The Puma Man (1979)
Director: Alberto De Martino
"featuring some of the worst special effects ever committed to film"

● Queen of Outer Space (1958)
Director: Edward Bernds
"this one's for deadheads"

● Robot Monster (1953)
Director: Phil Tucker
"hilariously banal, naive and threadbare"

monster movie. The giant worms are munching in Mexico, so Fred Ward is called in as bounty hunter, along with enthusiastic assistant Christopher Gartin. Sharply written and engagingly performed, this stays true to the jokey spirit of the original, while adding a new breed of overground "graboids" to literally chew the scenery. Although it lacks the frantic pace and sprightly camera work of the original, it's smarter and more fun than many cinema follow-ups and Michael Gross is once again hilarious as fearless gun-nut Burt.

Fred Ward Earl Bassett • **Michael Gross** Burt Gummer • **Helen Shaver** Kate • **Marcelo Tubert** Senor Ortega • **Christopher Gartin** Grady Hoover • **Marco Hernandez** Julio • **Jose Rosario** Pedro
Director *SS Wilson*
Screenplay *SS Wilson, Brent Maddock*

The Trial of the Incredible Hulk ★★ PG

1989 US Colour 95mins

Surely after three TV movies and a four-year series, the Hulk would have vented all his anger and stopped going through his supply of shirts so rapidly? Well, no. Bill Bixby steps behind the camera to bring yet another instalment of the comic-book hero's adventures to the screen, and it bears all the hallmarks of an idea that has run out of steam. Undeterred, Bixby went on to direct yet another helping of this tame action fare.

Bill Bixby Doctor David Banner • **Lou Ferrigno** The Hulk • **Rex Smith** Matt Murdoch/Daredevil • **John Rhys-Davies** Wilson Fisk • **Marta DuBois** Ellie Mendez • **Nancy Everhard** Christa Klein • **Nicholas Hormann** Edgar • **Joseph Mascolo** Tendelli • **Richard Cummings Jr** Al Pettiman
Director *Bill Bixby*
Screenplay *Gerald DiPego*

The Tribe ★★★

TV 1998– NZ/UK Colour

The world's adult population is annihilated by an unknown virus, which forces children and teenagers across the globe to form separate tribal groups in a quest for survival. The members of one such tribe, the Mall Rats, dream of building a peaceful new world, but their hopes are constantly threatened by the violent Demon Dogs and Locusts. Essentially *Lord of the Flies* meets *Mad Max*, this teen-orientated series gradually emerges as a surprisingly intriguing and compulsive sci-fi soap opera. At its best, the show's plotlines are exceptionally well written, and skilfully juggle the usual post-apocalyptic scenarios with provocative examinations of contemporary issues. The gifted cast members are strong enough to hold their old against the best adult ensembles, while its innovative designs only add to the production's distinctive appeal.

Dwayne Cameron Bray • **Beth Allen** Amber • **Caleb Ross** Lex • **Amy Morrison** Zandra • **Ryan Runciman** Ryan • **Victoria Spence** Salene • **Ari Boyland** KC
Created by *Raymond Thompson, Harry Duffin*
Music *Simon May*

The Tripods ★★★ PG 12

TV 1984-85 UK/Aus Colour 25x25m

One of the BBC's most ambitious forays into TV fantasy, *The Tripods* was a long cherished project of producer Richard Bates who secured the rights to John Christopher's HG Wells-inspired trilogy of books soon after they were published and battled for almost 15 years to get them on screen. The result is a highly polished and visually arresting drama, but also dull and ponderous. Set in 2089, the Earth is ruled over by ruthless, three-legged machines called Tripods who brainwash the population upon adolescence, stifling any thought of rebellion. Two teenagers about to undergo the process escape and with the help of other outlaws intend to overthrow their mechanoid conquerors. Poor ratings and rising costs led to the series being cancelled two thirds of the way through, leaving viewers stranded and the story forever unresolved. Unless you read the novels, of course.

John Shackley Will Parker • **Jim Baker** Henry Parker • **Ceri Seel** Beanpole
Adapted by *Alick Rowe, Christopher Penfold, from the novels by John Christopher*
Producer *Richard Bates*

Trog ★ 15

1970 UK Colour 87mins

Indescribable nonsense with anthropologist Joan Crawford battling Michael Gough over the fate of a recently discovered prehistoric caveman. Will Joan teach the Missing Link all about life in the 20th century before Gough calls in the army to destroy him? You won't care either way in this painful dud directed by Freddie Francis, the usually reliable veteran horror master. Intercut footage from *The Animal World* serves as Trog's memories in Joan's last feature film. It's not hard to see why.

Joan Crawford Dr Brockton • **Michael Gough** Sam Murdock • **Bernard Kay** Inspector Greenham • **Kim Braden** Anne •

David Griffin Malcolm • **John Hamill** Cliff • **Thorley Walters** Magistrate • **Jack May** Dr Selbourne
Director *Freddie Francis*
Screenplay *Aben Kandel, from a story by Peter Bryan, John Gilling*

The Trollenberg Terror ★★★

TV 1956-1957 UK BW 6x30mins

This six-part ATV network serial by Peter Key was among the better *Quatermass* imitations. A hotel in the Alps is the main location, and a stranded mind-reading duo, the Pilgrim Sisters (Sarah Lawson, Rosemary Miller), join forces with boffin Professor Crevet (Raf de la Torre) to defeat the invading Ixodes – fried-egg brains with tentacles, who wisely lurk in a cloud most of the time. Director Quentin Lawrence unusually reprised the act by making the 1958 big-screen version, which was also known as *The Crawling Eye*, and hauled along original cast members Laurence Payne and Stuart Sanders to repeat their roles.

Raf de la Torre Professor Crevet • **Sarah Lawson** Sarah Pilgrim • **Rosemary Miller** Ann Pilgrim • **Laurence Payne** Philip Truscott • **Stuart Saunders** Dr Dewhurst
Director *Quentin Lawrence*
Written by *Peter Key*

The Trollenberg Terror ★★

1958 UK BW 82mins

A Swiss ski resort is terrorised by tentacled monsters from outer space in an efficiently suspenseful British cheapie marred by awful special effects. Two bits of cotton wool stuck on a mountain photo make do for the cloudy snowscapes in veteran Hammer scriptwriter Jimmy Sangster's screen version of Peter Key's BBC TV series. Forrest Tucker is miscast as the hero, but Janet Munro is affecting as the telepathic heroine the aliens seize as their mouthpiece.

Forrest Tucker Alan Brooks • **Laurence Payne** Philip Truscott • **Janet Munro** Anne Pilgrim • **Jennifer Jayne** Sarah Pilgrim • **Warren Mitchell** Professor Crevett • **Frederick Schiller** Klein
Director *Quentin Lawrence*
Screenplay *Jimmy Sangster, from the BBC television series by Peter Key*

Tron ★★★ PG

1982 US Colour 92mins [video]

The road to *Toy Story* for Disney began with this dazzling electronic fantasy. Once computer genius Jeff Bridges entered cyberspace to prove himself the rightful inventor of stolen game patents, director Steven Lisberger broke cinematic territory by using, and inventing, state-of-the-art digital graphics to depict a bizarre video netherworld. The "light cycle" race – where machines create solid walls of colour behind them as they speed around a grid – is the highlight of a complex, but lighthearted, adventure. It's dated already, but computer-game enthusiasts will love it.

Jeff Bridges Kevin Flynn/Clu • **David Warner** Ed Dillinger/Sark • **Bruce Boxleitner** Alan Bradley/Tron • **Cindy Morgan** Lora/Yori • **Barnard Hughes** Dr Walter Gibbs/Dumont • **Dan Shor** Ram • **Peter Jurasik** Crom • **Tony Stephano** Peter/Sark's lieutenant • **Craig Chudy** Warrior • **Vince Deadrick** Warrior • **Sam Schatz** Expert disk warrior • **Jackson Bostwick** Head guard • **Charles Picerni** Tank commander
Director *Steven Lisberger*
Screenplay *Steven Lisberger, from a story by Steven Lisberger, Bonnie MacBird*

Trouble in Mind ★★★★ 15

1985 US Colour 107mins [video] DVD

An intelligent yet not wholly successful attempt by Alan Rudolph to re-create the kind of futuristic *film noir* pioneered by Jean-Luc Godard in *Alphaville*. Kris Kristofferson stars as an ex-cop just out of jail for murder, whose hopes for a fresh start with diner owner Geneviève Bujold are sidetracked by his involvement with Lori Singer and her violent partner, Keith Carradine, a petty crook whose behaviour and appearance grow increasingly bizarre and violent as he becomes entangled with Rain City crime boss, Divine. It's engrossing stuff and if the romance falls flat, the use of comedy to map Carradine's decline is inspired.

Kris Kristofferson John Hawkins • **Keith Carradine** Coop • **Lori Singer** Georgia • **Geneviève Bujold** Wanda • **Joe Morton** Solo • **Divine** Hilly Blue • **George Kirby** Lieutenant Gunther • **John Considine** Nate Nathanson • **Dirk Blocker** Rambo • **Albert Hall** Leo • **Tracy Kristofferson** Tammy Regis
Director/Screenplay *Alan Rudolph*

Trucks ★★ 18

1997 US/Can Colour 94mins [video]

Killer trucks terrorise a small community. Sounds familiar? Sure enough, this is an unnecessary remake of horrormeister Stephen King's only directorial effort to date, *Maximum Overdrive*, itself no masterpiece. This time, Timothy Busfield, still best known from TV's *thirtysomething*, heads the lacklustre cast of human victims. There are a few thrills, but this lacks the sinister atmosphere of *Duel* – still the cinema's definitive statement on the tyranny of the motor vehicle. Contains violence, swearing and sex scenes.

Timothy Busfield Ray • **Brenda Bakke** Hope • **Aidan Devine** Trucker Bob • **Jay Brazeau** Jack • **Brendan Fletcher** Logan • **Roman Podhora** Thad • **Amy Stewart** Abby • **Jonathan Barrett** Brad
Director *Chris Thomson*
Screenplay *Brian Taggert, from a short story by Stephen King*

15 GREAT TITLES
SHAME ABOUT THE SHOW

- **Bella Lugosi Meets a Brooklyn Gorilla (1952)**
- **Dr Goldfoot and the Bikini Machine (1965)**
- **Gas-s-s-s, or It Became Necessary to Destroy the World in Order to Save It (1970)**
- **Have Rocket, Will Travel (1959)**
- **Hell Comes to Frogtown (1988)**
- **The Incredibly Strange Creatures Who Stopped Living and Became Mixed-Up Zombies (1963)**
- **Jesse James Meets Frankenstein's Daughter (1966)**
- **Lobster Man from Mars (1989)**
- **A Nymphoid Barbarian from Dinosaur Hell (1991)**
- **The Robot vs the Aztec Mummy (1957)**
- **Santa Claus Conquers the Martians (1964)**
- **Superhuman Samurai Syber-Squad (1994)**
- **Surf Nazis Must Die (1987)**
- **Tattooed Teenage Alien Fighters from Beverly Hills (1994)**
- **The 30 Foot Bride from Candy Rock (1955)**

The Truman Show ★★★★★ PG

1998 US Colour 98mins [video]

An ingenious concept, scripted by *Gattaca's* director/screenwriter Andrew Niccol, and flawlessly executed by director Peter Weir. From audacious start to poignant finale, Weir's science-fiction comedy drama is both dazzling and sophisticated. Truman Burbank (Jim Carrey) is the star of the world's most popular television show – only he doesn't know it! Although he thinks he lives in the idyllic island community of Seahaven, it's just an elaborate set housed in a vast studio, and all his family and friends are really actors. How that realisation slowly dawns and spurs him on to find out what's real and what's fake in his emotionally confused universe is the stuff of ambitious cinematic brilliance. With superlative support from Ed Harris (as the programme's creator Christof) and Laura Linney (as Truman's "wife", Meryl), Carrey reveals his dramatic range in this compelling fable about media omnipotence.

Jim Carrey Truman Burbank • **Laura Linney** Meryl • **Noah Emmerich** Marlon • **Natascha McElhone** Lauren/Sylvia • **Holland Taylor** Truman's mother • **Brian Delate** Truman's father • **Ed Harris** Christof
Director *Peter Weir*
Screenplay *Andrew Niccol*
Cinematographer *Peter Biziou* • ***Music*** *Philip Glass, Burkhard Dallwitz*

The Tunnel ★★★

1933 Ger BW 80mins

Nationalist megalomania is the theme of this extraordinary disaster movie. Directed in both German and French by Curtis Bernhardt, the film chronicles a pugnacious engineer's attempt to construct a tunnel between Europe and the States. Yet, while Paul Hartmann and Jean Gabin respectively risk everything to succeed (with wives becoming as disposable as workers), Machiavellian moneyman Gustaf Grüdgens (in each version) seeks to sabotage their efforts. Impressed by the message and such spectacular set pieces as the underground deluge, the British film industry jumped on the jingoistic bandwagon with Maurice Elvey's 1935 remake, although the originals were banned during the war as propaganda. A German/French language film.

Paul Hartmann Mac Allan • **Olly von Flint** Mary Allan • **Gustaf Gründgens** Woolf • **Attila Hörbiger** Hobby • **Max Weydner** Lloyd • **Elga Brink** Ethel Lloyd • **Otto Wernicke** Bärmann, bomb expert • **Richard Revy** Gordon
Director *Kurt Bernhardt [Curtis Bernhardt]*
Screenplay *Kurt Bernhardt [Curtis Bernhardt], Reinhart Steinbicker, from the novel "Der Tunnel" by Bernhard Kellermann*
Cinematographer *Karl Hoffmann*

The Tunnel ★★ U

1935 UK BW 88mins

Michael Balcon produced this Gaumont-British remake of a German film, *The Tunnel*. It was heavily geared towards the American market with Hollywood stars including Richard Dix as the engineering genius behind the scheme for a railway tunnel under the Atlantic, Walter Huston (seen only briefly) as the US President, Helen Vinson as the daughter of an American millionaire backer, and Madge Evans as Dix's anxious wife. Leslie Banks leads the British contingent, while George Arliss matches Huston as Britain's prime minister. The massive drilling operations which bring the team into explosive contact with volcanic lava are far more impressive than the human story.

Richard Dix McAllan • **Leslie Banks** Robbie • **Madge Evans** Ruth McAllan • **Helen Vinson** Varlia • **C Aubrey Smith** Lloyd • **Basil Sydney** Mostyn • **Henry Oscar** Grellier • **Jimmy Hanley** Geoffrey as an adult • **Walter Huston** President of the United States • **George Arliss** Prime Minister
Director *Maurice Elvey*
Screenplay *L Du Garde Peach, Kurt Siodmak [Curt Siodmak], from the novel "Der Tunnel" by Bernhard Kellermann*
Producer *Michael Balcon*

Turbo: a Power Rangers Movie ★ PG

1997 US Colour 99mins

Viewers who have never seen the *Mighty Morphin Power Rangers* TV show will be absolutely lost in this second big-screen adaptation. Painfully bad dialogue and technical incompetence rule here as the Power Rangers face a new alien menace, Divatox. She is so powerful, the Rangers must get new weapons (read: more toys to make and sell to kids) and recruit a new and younger ranger (read: greater appeal to the younger viewers.) At least the previous movie had some ambition to entertain beyond being a toy commercial.

Nakia Burrise Tanya • **Jason David Frank** Tommy • **Catherine Sutherland** Kat • **Johnny Yong Bosch** Adam • **Blake Foster** Justin • **Paul Schrier** Bulk • **Jason Narvy** Skull • **Richard Genelle** Ernie • **Hilary Shepard Turner [Hilary Shepard]** Divatox
Director *David Winning, Shuki Levy*
Screenplay *Shuki Levy, Shell Danielson*

Turkey Shoot ★★★ 18

1981 Aus Colour 83mins

In this gore-drenched futuristic version of *The Most Dangerous Game* set in the Australian outback, social deviants (freedom fighter Steve Railsback, shoplifter Olivia Hussey, prostitutes et al) are sent to barbaric concentration camps, supposedly for re-education. But in reality it's to provide human prey for warden Michael Craig to indulge his sadistic predilection for extreme blood sports. Convincingly mounted and violent (with explosive arrows and machetes put to very nasty use), this cynical political allegory may be transparent exploitation, but it sure does deliver a high shock quotient.

Steve Railsback Paul Anders • **Olivia Hussey** Chris Walters • **Michael Craig** Charles Thatcher • **Carmen Duncan** Jennifer • **Noel Ferrier** Mallory • **Lynda Stoner** Rita Daniels • **Roger Ward** Ritter • **Michael Petrovitch** Tito • **Gus Mercurio** Red
Director *Brian Trenchard-Smith*
Screenplay *Jon George, Neill Hicks, from a story by George Schenck, Robert Williams, David Lawrence*

Twelve Monkeys ★★★★ 15

1995 US/UK Colour 123mins DVD

Inspired by Chris Marker's superior 1962 short, *La Jetée*, this sci-fi thriller was penned by David and Janet Peoples, who were responsible for that other dark odyssey into a despondent future, *Blade Runner*. However, this is very much the work of Terry Gilliam, who imposes his own pseudo-poetic vision on to a world that is doomed to viral annihilation unless a seemingly insane time traveller can track down the environmental terrorists who unwittingly caused the disaster. Although it was Brad Pitt who landed the Oscar nomination for his twitchy performance as the leader of the Army of the Twelve Monkeys, it's Bruce Willis's anguished introvert who holds this hauntingly atmospheric film together. Gilliam told his headliner, "I don't want Bruce Willis the superstar around this film, but Bruce Willis the actor," and he was rewarded with a performance of great restraint that matched the director's own. As in *Brazil*, Gilliam succeeds in presenting us with strikingly imaginative imagery, while also forcing us to confront the fragility of both our planet and ourselves. Contains swearing, violence and nudity.

Bruce Willis James Cole • **Madeleine Stowe** Dr Kathryn Railly • **Brad Pitt** Jeffrey Goines • **Christopher Plummer** Dr Goines • **Joseph Melito** Young Cole • **Jon Seda** Jose • **David Morse** Dr Peters • **Frank Gorshin** Dr Fletcher • **Irma St Paule** Poet • **Joey Perillo** Detective Franki • **Harry O'Toole** Louie/Raspy Voice

U = SUITABLE FOR ALL Uc = SUITABLE FOR ALL, ESPECIALLY YOUNG CHILDREN (VIDEO ONLY) PG = PARENTAL GUIDANCE

Director *Terry Gilliam*
Screenplay *David Peoples, Janet Peoples, from the film "La Jetée" by Chris Marker*
Cinematographer *Roger Pratt* • ***Music*** *Paul Buckmaster*

12:01 ★★★★ 15

1993 US Colour 90mins [video]

Whereas *Groundhog Day* used the idea of living the same day over and over again for laughs, director Jack Sholder takes the same premise (from Richard Lupoff's 1973 novella) and goes for dynamic action to craft a clever thriller. Engaging Jonathan Silverman is the clerk caught in a time-loop involving an associate's murder, who tries to prevent the killing from taking place by changing incidental details each time the same day dawns. A neatly cut and highly polished gem, the tale is never contrived, continuously engrossing and has a gut-wrenching climax.

Jonathan Silverman Barry Thomas • **Helen Slater** Lisa Fredericks • **Martin Landau** Dr Thadius Moxley • **Jeremy Piven** Howard Richter • **Robin Bartlett** Ann Jackson • **Nioholas Surovy [Nicolas Surovy]** Robert Denk • **Constance Marie** Joan Zebo • **Glenn Morshower** Detective Frank Kryles • **Paxton Whitehead** Dr Tiberius Scott • **Ann Shea** Annette • **Jonathan Emerson** Ted Fallow • **Mark Christopher Lawrence** Jack Spays • **Mark Phelan** Guard in science wing • **Joey Andrews** Kyle • **Hosea Sanders** • **Mary Hale** Anchorwoman • **Ed Crick** Detective • **Cheryl Anderson** Supervisor • **Frank Collison** Thin assassin • **Drew Gehl** Night guard • **Will Leskin** Guard on walkie-talkie
Director *Jack Sholder*
Screenplay *Philip Morton, from a short film by Jonathan Heap, Hillary Ripps based on the short story "12:01 PM" by Richard Lupoff*

12 to the Moon ★ U

1960 US BW 74mins

The 12 members of the first multi-national expedition to the lunar surface discover subterranean Moon Men who threaten to freeze Earth unless mankind mends their warring ways. Written by DeWitt Bodeen, writer of the classic *Cat People*, and directed by David Bradley, this tedious minor quickie focuses on the astronauts' personal problems, petty squabbling and juvenile moralising more than any special effects driven drama.

Ken Clark Capt John Anderson • **Michi Kobi** Dr Hideko Murata • **Tom Conway** Dr Feodor Orloff • **Anthony Dexter** Dr Luis Vargas • **John Wengraf** Dr Erich Heinrich • **Anna-Lisa** Dr Sigrid Bromark
Director *David Bradley*
Screenplay *DeWitt Bodeen, from a story by Fred Gebhardt*
Producer *Fred Gebhardt*

24 Hours in London ★★ 18

1999 UK Colour 86mins [video]

It's apt that the illegal trade in body parts features in this descent into the capital's underworld, because it rips the heart out of *The Long Good Friday* and attempts to transplant it into a stubbornly lifeless cadaver. It's not the sight of Gary Olsen as an opera-loving, sword-wielding Mr Big that takes the most swallowing, but the indigestible blend of Hong Kong "heroic bloodshed", laddish comedy and *Lock, Stock* swagger. There are plenty of twists in writer/director Alexander Finbow's verbose screenplay, but they're all clearly signposted by the arch playing of an unconvincing cast. Contains swearing, violence and drug abuse.

Gary Olsen Christian • **Anjela Lauren Smith** Martha • **Sara Stockbridge** Simone • **John Benfield** Inspector Duggan • **Amita Dhiri** Helen Lucas • **Tony London** Leon • **Luke Garrett** Richard
Director/Screenplay *Alexander Finbow*

20 Million Miles to Earth ★★★ PG

1957 US BW 79mins [video]

A spaceship returning from an expedition to Venus crashes near Sicily, releasing a fast-growing reptilian beast that rampages through Rome in one of animation master Ray Harryhausen's best fantasy films, and his own personal favourite. The snake-tailed giant Ymir monster is also one of Harryhausen's finest creations: it has a well-defined personality and manages to evoke sympathy for its bewildered plight. The Ymir's fight with an elephant and the Roman locations – especially the climactic Colosseum battle – add unique touches to this minor classic.

William Hopper Calder • **Joan Taylor** Marisa • **Frank Puglia** Dr Leonardo • **John Zaremba** Dr Judson Uhl • **Thomas B Henry [Thomas Browne Henry]** General AD McIntosh • **Tito Vuolo** Police commissioner
Director *Nathan Juran*
Screenplay *Bob Williams, Christopher Knopf, from a story by Charlott Knight, Ray Harryhausen*

The 27th Day ★★★ U

1957 US BW 75mins

A quite extraordinary anti-communist tract masquerading as naive science fiction. An alien gives five people from five different countries a box of capsules capable of destroying life on their continent if opened. The capsules become harmless after 27 days or on the owner's death. Suicide or destruction is the choice until the Russian emissary is ordered to annihilate the western world. A real Cold War curio with an equally bizarre pay-off despite pedestrian direction by William Asher, who graduated to helming *Beach Party* movies.

Gene Barry Jonathan Clark • **Valerie French** Eve Wingate • **George Voskovec** Professor Klaus Bechner • **Arnold Moss** The Alien • **Stefan Schnabel** Leader • **Ralph Clanton** Mr Ingram • **Friedrich Ledebur** Dr Karl Neuhaus • **Paul Birch** Admiral
Director *William Asher*
Screenplay *John Mantley, from his novel*

20,000 Leagues under the Sea ★★★

1916 US BW [video]

Captain Nemo (Allan Holubar) and his crew of the submarine *Nautilus* journey through the ocean depths to a tropical island to rescue Nemo's daughter, encountering challenges such as a fight with an octopus. Written and directed by Stuart Paton, with elements from both *20,000 Leagues under the Sea* and *The Mysterious Island*, this is an impressive achievement for so early a film. The pioneering Williamson brothers built an underwater camera for the production, which cost Universal founder Carl Laemmle such a fortune that even the film's popularity was unable to yield a profit.

Allan Holubar Captain Nemo/Prince Daaker • **Jane Gail** A child of nature/Princess Daaker • **Dan Hanlon** Professor Aronnax • **Edna Pendleton** Aronnax's daughter • **Curtis Benton** Ned Land • **Matt Moore** Lt Bond • **Howard Crampton** Cyrus Harding
Director *Stuart Paton*
Screenplay *Stuart Paton, from the novel by Jules Verne*

20,000 Leagues under the Sea ★★★★ U

1954 US Colour 121mins [video]

A marvellously designed (Oscars for art direction and special effects) and fabulously cast cinema retelling of Jules Verne's fantasy saga about Captain Nemo and his submarine, *Nautilus*. Kirk Douglas gives a bravura performance as harpoonist Ned Land, even using his own voice for the song *A Whale of a Tale*, but it's James Mason's Nemo that gives the film its strength, as the brilliant visionary who has rejected civilisation. Peter Lorre adds comic relief, while Paul Lukas and especially the under-rated Robert J Wilke bring dignity to the proceedings. Director Richard Fleischer makes the most of the action sequences, notably a sensational battle with a giant squid. A treat for grown-ups and children alike, and one of the best live-action movies Disney ever made.

Kirk Douglas Ned Land • **James Mason** Captain Nemo • **Paul Lukas** Professor Aronnax • **Peter Lorre** Conseil • **Robert J Wilke** Mate on the *Nautilus* • **Carleton Young** John Howard • **Ted De Corsia** Captain Farragut • **Percy Helton** Diver • **Eddie Marr** Shipping agent • **Fred Graham** Casey Moore • **JM Kerrigan** Billy
Director *Richard Fleischer*
Screenplay *Earl Felton, from the novel by Jules Verne*

20,000 Leagues under the Sea ★★

TV 1997 US Colour

The first of two Jules Verne-inspired mini-series to surface on US screens in 1997, Michael Anderson's undersea odyssey has Ben Cross' Captain Nemo at the helm and *Due South*'s Paul Gross setting sail as Ned the Whaler. In a loose adaptation of Verne's classic novel, Nemo's latest voyage combines the requisite moral dilemmas and sea battles with a romantic subplot, as the captain becomes involved in a struggle to capture the heart of Professor Aronnax's daughter, Sophie. Despite some effective moments, Michael Anderson's mini-series ultimately lacks the sense of wonder and adventure that characterises the 1954 movie adaptation.

Richard Crenna Professor Henry Aronnax • **Ben Cross** Captain Nemo • **Julie Cox** Sophie Aronnax • **Michael Jayston** Rear Admiral John E Sellings • **Paul Gross** Ned Land • **Jeff Harding** Captain Michael Farragut • **Nicholas Hammond** Saxon
Director *Michael Anderson*
Teleplay *Joe Wiesenfeld, from the novel by Jules Verne*

20,000 Leagues under the Sea ★★

TV 1997 US Colour

A mere two months after the US debut of Captain Nemo's last small-screen adventure, the legendary submariner took centre stage in Rod Hardy's mini-series adaptation of Jules Verne's novel. Michael Caine becomes the latest actor to take command of the *Nautilus*, and plays Nemo as something of a Utopian visionary. Further changes to the original book are provided by the presence of Nemo's daughter and the mini-series' unusual takes on Ned Land and Aronnax, as played by Bryan Brown and Patrick Dempsey respectively. Caine and his able castmates manage to take it all in their stride, but the mini-series still pales in comparison to the 1954 movie. However the production design and computer-generated imagery are first-rate.

Michael Caine Captain Nemo • **Patrick Dempsey** Pierre Aronnax • **Mia Sara** Mara • **Brian Brown** Ned Land • **Adewale** Cabe Attucks • **Kerry Armstrong** Lydia Rawlings • **Peter McCauley** Admiral McCutcheon
Director *Ron Hardy*
Teleplay *Bryan Nelson, from the novel by Jules Verne*

Twice Told Tales ★★

1963 US Colour 119mins

United Artists borrowed AIP's successful *Tales of Terror* omnibus formula, and its star Vincent Price, for this crudely creepy anthology which failed to give horror writer Nathaniel Hawthorne the same box-office cred already achieved by Edgar Allan Poe. Given the sparse production values and varying degrees of horror and atmosphere, it's not difficult to see why, despite the fine source material. In *Dr Heidegger's Experiment*, Price discovers the elixir of eternal youth, while as a Paduan scientist in *Dr Rappaccini's Daughter*, he tragically injects his beloved offspring with a potion that makes her lethal to the touch. Buried treasures, warlocks and ancestral karma are at the devilish heart of *The House of Seven Gables*. Directed by Sydney Salkow, the film still offers enough lush photography and great ensemble acting to make it work more often than not.

Vincent Price Alex Medbourne/Dr Rappaccini/Gerald Pyncheon • **Sebastian Cabot** Dr Carl Heidegger • **Mari Blanchard** Sylvia Ward • **Brett Halsey** Giovanni Guastconti • **Abraham Sofaer** Prof Pietro Baglioni • **Joyce Taylor** Beatrice Rappaccini • **Beverly Garland** Alice Pyncheon • **Richard Denning** Jonathan Maulle • **Jacqueline de Wit** Hannah
Director *Sidney Salkow*
Screenplay *Robert E Kent, from stories by Nathaniel Hawthorne*

Twice Upon a Time ★★

1969 Fr Colour 90mins

Notions of time, space and memory had been a fixture of French cinema since Alain Resnais's *Last Year at Marienbad*. A variation on that scenario is presented in this over-elaborate sci-fi thriller, which ends up tripping over its own conceit. Having helped Anna Karina after a riding accident, banker Bruno Cremer is amazed to find in her possession a film depicting his demise. However, the killer, Jean Rochefort, is equally perplexed when he views the same footage – as he has no motive for the crime. Cremer's gadget-stuffed retreat is quaintly future chic, but the rest is pseudo-intellectual tosh. A French language film.

Anna Karina Girl • **Bruno Cremer** Max • **Jean Rochefort** Hervé • **Catherine Rich** Wife • **Billy Kearns** Bodyguard • **Daniel Moosman** Aide
Director *André Farwagi*
Screenplay *André Farwagi, Alain Morineau*

The Twilight Zone

★★★★★ U PG

TV 1959-64 US BW 18x60m; 138x30m

Unquestionably the best and most enduring science fiction anthology series ever made, whose influence on future film-makers is immeasurable. One young boy growing up in Arizona was particularly affected by the show, his name Steven Spielberg. The brainchild of multi-Emmy award winning television writer Rod Serling, who penned more than half of the 156 episodes and also acted as host, this was the first adult prime-time fantasy series and a big gamble in an age where western shows ruled US networks. The power of the piece lies in its brilliantly off-beat and thought-provoking scripts centering usually on ordinary folk caught up in bizarre situations. There was also an element of morality fable: it was benevolent souls who got a second chance and the cruel of heart who got their comeuppance. Despite finding critical favour the show was never a mainstream hit, acquiring its legendary cult status during unending re-runs. The show is also famous for giving many future stars – such as William Shatner, Lee Marvin, Charles Bronson and Robert Redford – early breaks in television.

Rod Serling Narrator/Host
Created by *Rod Serling*

The Twilight Zone ★★★

TV 1985-89 US Colour 35x60m; 30x30m

Ten years after the death of its creator, Rod Serling, this clever reworking of his winning format of fantasy tales with a twist ending is a mixture of brand new stories and a few remakes of classic *Twilight Zone* episodes. To compete with a glut of anthology shows then on American television, including Steven Spielberg's own *Twilight Zone*-influenced *Amazing Stories* among others,

Visionary: James Mason gives a charismatic portrayal of Captain Nemo in 1954's *20,000 Leagues under the Sea*

a high calibre creative team were assembled, with directors such as William Friedkin, Wes Craven and Joe Dante. As with the original show there was also a healthy mix of well-known faces and up-and-coming stars, among them Bruce Willis, Elliott Gould and Danny Kaye, in his last acting performance before he died. The stories are a bit hit or miss, but at their best certainly compared favourably with Serling's originals.

Charles Aidman Narrator (1985-1987) • **Robin Ward** Narrator
Created by Rod Serling
Creative consultant Harlan Ellison

SFacts

Charles Aidman, who narrated the series from 1985 to 1987, appeared in the original series in two episodes: *And When the Sky Was Opened* (written by Rod Serling from a short story by Richard Matheson) and *Little Girl Lost* (written by Richard Matheson)

Twilight Zone: Rod Serling's Lost Classics ★★ 12

1994 US Colour 88mins

A bit of a misnomer, this one. A couple of unfilmed scripts (not intended for *The Twilight Zone* TV series) were found by creator Rod Serling's widow, Carol, and turned into a television movie. The first lacklustre segment stars Amy Irving, while the second feature-length story is called *Where the Dead Are*, and stars Patrick Bergin and Jack Palance. Basically a homage to HG Wells, the plot has Bergin as a Boston surgeon who treks to a mysterious island. There he finds mad doctor Palance experimenting with human tissue regeneration. It's more a period horror tale than a weird *Twilight Zone* segment, and the pedestrian direction make this a strictly routine affair, despite screenplay involvement by veteran sci-fi writer Richard Matheson. Contains some swearing.

Amy Irving Melissa Sanders • **Gary Cole** James • **Heidi Swedberg** Joanie • **Patrick Bergin** Dr Benjamin Ramsey • **Jack Palance** Jeremy Wheaton • **Jenna Stern** Susan Wheaton • **Julia Campbell** Maureen • **Peter McRobbie** Dr Ames
Director Robert Markowitz
Screenplay Richard Matheson, Rod Serling

Twilight Zone: the Movie ★★★ 15

1983 US Colour 96mins

Despite the involvement of Hollywood major league directors Steven Spielberg, John Landis and Joe Dante, it was Australian George Miller, responsible for cult hit *Mad Max* and its sequel, who produced the one truly scary section of this feature-length stab at Rod Serling's classic television series. In Miller's tale, paranoid passenger John Lithgow is the only person on a plane who can see a creature gnawing away at the wings. The rest of the stories are a mixed bag: the Spielberg tale of OAPs reliving their childhood is pure slush; Dante's wickedly cruel mixture of animation and live action eventually goes the same way; while Landis's contribution remains overshadowed by the controversial death of star Vic Morrow (father of Jennifer Jason Leigh) when a helicopter crashed during filming, killing Morrow and two child actors. Contains violence and swearing.

Burgess Meredith Narrator • **Dan Aykroyd** Passenger • **Albert Brooks** Driver • **Vic Morrow** Bill • **Doug McGrath** Larry • **Charles Hallahan** Ray • **Bill Quinn** Conroy • **Martin Garner** Weinstein • **Selma Diamond** Mrs Weinstein • **Helen Shaw** Mrs Dempsey • **Murray Matheson** Agee
Director *John Landis, Steven Spielberg, Joe Dante, George Miller (2)*
Screenplay *John Landis, George Clayton Johnson, Josh Rogan, Richard Matheson*

The Two Faces of Dr Jekyll ★★

1960 UK Colour 88mins

Hammer's flop version of the overworked Robert Louis Stevenson classic grafts on Oscar Wilde's *The Picture of Dorian Gray* for extra literacy amid the tired Gothic chills. This time the old and weak Jekyll (Paul Massie) transforms into a dashing playboy with an eye for London's cancan girls. Christopher Lee lends his usual excellent support as the lecherous best friend.

Paul Massie Dr Jekyll/Mr Hyde • **Dawn Addams** Kitty • **Christopher Lee** Paul Allen • **David Kossoff** Litauer • **Francis De Wolff** Inspector • **Norma Marla** Maria • **Magda Miller** Sphinx girl • **Oliver Reed** Beau
Director *Terence Fisher*
Screenplay *Wolf Mankowitz, from the novel by Robert Louis Stevenson*

2004 ★★★

Radio 1995 UK 60mins

An effective and chilling futuristic drama from BBC's World Service. Crime is out of control in Britain, and in desperation, the populace puts its support behind the Peace Party, once on the fringes of politics, but soon to be swept to power on their promise of restoring total peace and security to the land, using unspecified high-tech means. Head of the party is the sinister Jason Kennett who, with his brother Franklin, runs Kennett Electronics. Bill Nighy and Derek Waring star as the newspaper reporter and editor who discover, with devasting effect on their personal lives, the horrifying agenda through which the brothers plan to bring about their Utopian vision. Tightly plotted, as demanded by the short running time, and gripping, leaving the listener wanting more with its intriguing ending.

Bill Nighy Quinley • **Derek Waring** Lisle • **David Collins** Franklin Kennett • **Michael Cochrane** Jason Kennett
Director *David Hitchinson*
Written by *Wally K Daly*

2001: a Space Odyssey

★★★★★ U

1968 UK/US Colour 135mins

Stanley Kubrick's seminal sci-fi work is now considered by many to be less a supreme piece of cinema than an interesting, innovative product of the sixties. But the memorable celluloid images still strongly resonate, such as the giant, vulnerable fetus floating through space and the tribe of apes painfully putting two and two together. It is Kubrick's haunting, stylised combination of music and visuals that gives *2001* its eerie, mesmerising quality, but even its most devoted disciples are hard pressed to tell you what it's actually about, and, as a slice of philosophy on how we all got started and where we ultimately go, the movie has little credence. However, it's a must-see if you never have, even though its visual impact is seriously hampered by the small screen.

Keir Dullea Dave Bowman • **Gary Lockwood** Frank Poole • **William Sylvester** Dr Heywood Floyd • **Daniel Richter** Moonwatcher • **Leonard Rossiter** Smyslov • **Margaret Tyzack** Elena • **Robert Beatty** Halvorsen • **Sean Sullivan** Michaels • **Frank Miller** Mission controller • **Alan Gifford** Poole's father • **Douglas Rain** Voice of HAL • **Penny Brahms** Stewardess • **Edwina Carroll** Stewardess • **Vivian Kubrick** "Squirt", Dr Floyd's daughter • **John Ashley** Astronaut
Director *Stanley Kubrick*
Screenplay *Stanley Kubrick, Arthur C Clarke, from the short story "The Sentinel" by Arthur C Clarke*
Producer *Stanley Kubrick*
Cinematographer *Geoffrey Unsworth, John Alcott* • ***Costume designer*** *Hardy Amies*

Facts

***The Sentinel*, the short story by Arthur C Clarke that formed the basis of *2001: a Space Oydssey*, was originally written in 1948 for a BBC competition. It didn't make the short list.**

2010 ★★★ PG

1984 US Colour 111mins

Based on the novel by Arthur C Clarke, writer/director Peter Hyams's earnest script unites Soviets and Americans to discover why astronaut Bowman vanished. Some spectacular special effects (the space walk transference) are the highlights of this unnecessary sequel to the monumental *2001: a Space Odyssey*, which quickly runs out of rocket fuel after a bright start. The Black Monolith is back, but there is little of Stanley Kubrick's epic sense or masterfully ambiguous myths and mysteries. Instead, director Peter Hyams replaces them with banal over-explicitness and a simplified religious ending.

Roy Scheider Heywood Floyd • **John Lithgow** Walter Curnow • **Helen Mirren** Tanya Kirbuk • **Bob Balaban** R Chandra • **Keir Dullea** Dave Bowman • **Douglas Rain** Voice of Hal 9000 • **Madolyn Smith** Caroline Floyd • **Dana Elcar** Dimitri Moisevitch
Director *Peter Hyams*
Screenplay *Peter Hyams, from the novel "2010: Odyssey Two" by Arthur C Clarke*

The Twonky ★★ U

1953 US BW 72mins

Loosely based on a scathing short story by Lewis Padget (a pseudonym for Henry Kuttner), Arch Oboler's fable reflected the former radio producer's detestation of television. With its dire warnings about the new medium's potential for stunting individuality, the premise is splendid – Janet Warren defies her philosopher husband, Hans Conried, and buys a TV, only for it to be a robotic variety intent on manipulating every waking second of their existence. What prevents it from being a great film, however, is Oboler's lack of wit. But then Ealing's contemporaneous effort at televisual satire, *Meet Mr Lucifer*, was equally disappointing.

Hans Conried Cary • **Janet Warren** Caroline • **Billy Lynn** Coach Trout • **Gloria Blondell** Eloise • **Edwin Max** Ed
Director *Arch Oboler*
Screenplay *Arch Oboler, from the story by Lewis Padget [Henry Kuttner]*

U

"**Will** the evil tyrant Unga Khan and his Black Robes defeat noble Sharad, leader of the White Robes? Will Crash Corrigan rescue the brainwashed Professor Norton before he completes the rocket engines Khan needs for his dastardly plan to rule the world? Don't miss the next chapter in Republic's gripping serial, **Undersea Kingdom!**"

Undersea Kingdom, 1936

UFO ★★★★

TV 1970-1973 UK Colour 26x60mins

This was Gerry Anderson's first attempt at a live action show, but more significantly the first time he broached adult themes such as drug abuse. The TV networks, used to his kids-orientated output, in a quandary as to where to put it in their schedules. As a result *UFO* never found the audience it deserved, although it was a belated hit in America and Japan, and remains a firm cult fave to this day. Set in 1980 SHADO (Supreme Headquarters Alien Defence Organization), led by the methodically determined Ed Bishop is Earth's military solution to invading aliens who kidnap and harvest human beings for their body parts. Despite the odd nod to seventies kitsch, notably the leotard-wearing, purple-wigged Moonbase female operatives, the production values and special effects are outstanding, even by today's standard.

Ed Bishop Cmdr Ed Straker • **George Sewell** Col Alec Freeman • **Michael Billington** Col Paul Foster • **Peter Gordeno** Capt Peter Carlin • **Gabrielle Drake** Lt Gay Ellis • **Wanda Ventham** Col Virginia Lake • **Dolores Mantez** Lt Nina Barry

Created by *Gerry Anderson*

Executive Producer *Gerry Anderson* •

Producer *Reg Hill*

SFacts

After leaving the show Michael Billington, who played Colonel Foster, Straker's right-hand man, screen-tested for the part of James Bond, narrowly missing out to Roger Moore.

UFOria ★★★ PG

1980 US Colour 89mins

Grocery store cashier and born-again Christian Cindy Williams awaits the appearance of a flying saucer, which she believes will bring salvation. Her boyfriend (Fred Ward) works for a phoney evangelist (Harry Dean Stanton) who intends to exploit the "God is an astronaut" phenomenon for all that it's worth. Made in 1980 but shelved until the mid-eighties this is an amiable, oddball movie that, on its eventual release, picked up quite a few admirers. The acting is fine throughout and the piece, while undisciplined in places, has undeniable charm.

Cindy Williams Arlene • **Harry Dean Stanton** Brother Bud • **Fred Ward** Sheldon • **Robert Gray** Emile • **Darrell Larson** Toby • **Harry Carey Jr** George Martin • **Hank Worden** Colonel

Director/Screenplay *John Binder*

The Ultimate Warrior ★★★★ 15

1975 US Colour 89mins

Ecological catastrophes have left New York in ruins and controlled by Max von Sydow's ruthless leadership. Yul Brynner is the "street fighter" who guides his own posse of survivors to a better life away from such post-Armageddon tyranny. This is exciting, intelligent stuff from Robert Clouse, the director of Bruce Lee's *Enter the Dragon*, and strangely prophetic of John Carpenter's 1981 movie *Escape from New York*. Loads of ingenious details and chilling moments make this under-rated science-fiction adventure a cut above the rest, with the final chase out of the city a model of gripping suspense. Contains swearing.

Yul Brynner Carson • **Max von Sydow** The Baron • **Joanna Miles** Melinda • **William Smith** Carrot • **Richard Kelton** Cal • **Stephen McHattie** Robert • **Darrell Zwerling** Silas

Director/Screenplay *Robert Clouse*

Ultraman Great ★★

TV 1990 Jap/Aus Colour 13x30mins

Ultraman is one of the great Japanese franchises which continues to go strong. After introducing the world to Godzilla, Eiji Tsuburaya developed an ultimately unproduced show in 1963 called *Woo*. This led to an action/adventure series called *Ultra Q* in 1966. This was, in turn, followed by a wide variety of series, all based around the *Ultraman* idea. An Ultraman is a coloured giant robot-like humanoid with a life gauge on its chest which shows its available power. Each giant can take on a human form who uses a magic talisman to change appearance, and they fight a wide variety of monsters. *Ultraman Great* is the only series to date to be produced in the English language.

Dore Krause Jack Shindo • **Gia Carides** Jean Echo • **Ralph Cotterill** Arthur Grant • **Grace Parr** Kim Shaomin • **Lloyd Morris** Charles Morgan • **Rick Adams** Lloyd Wilder • **Steve Adams** Ultraman • **Robert Simper** Ultraman

Director *Andrew Prowse*

Written by *Terry Larsen, from a story by Sho Aikawa, Hidenori Miyazawa, Chiaki Konaka, Akinori Endo, Satoshi Suzuki*

Ultraviolet ★★★★★ 15

TV 1998 UK Colour 6x60mins

A contemporary vampire hunt firmly in *The X Files* vein, Channel 4's ultra brilliant six-part mini-series gets the blood rushing from start to finish. Written and directed by Joe Aherne (of *This Life* fame) with an emphasis on believable sci-fi rather than fantasy or horror, it's an exceptionally intelligent, atmospheric and compulsive affair. Jack Davenport heads a superb cast as Detective Mike Colefield, a policeman who is involuntarily enlisted by a top-secret, hi-tech governmental organisation know as the CIB to stop the vampire community's planned destruction of humanity. Colefield's subsequent struggles with both his friends and foes allow Aherne to not only raise some fascinating metaphors, but also infuse proceedings with a provocative sense of moral ambiguity. Incidentally, America's Fox network tried to develop the mini-series into an ongoing TV show, but abandoned their plans after making a pilot episode.

Jack Davenport Michael • **Susannah Harker** Angie • **Idris Elba** Vaughn • **Philip Quast** Pearse • **Stephen Moyer** Jack • **Colette Brown** Kirsty • **Fiona Dolman** Frances

Director/Screenplay *Joe Ahearne*

Producer *Bill Shapter*

SFacts

Jack Davenport later went on to star with Matt Damon, Jude Law and Gwynneth Paltrow in *The Talented Mr Ripley*." Like all good horror it's suggestive rather than explicit, and at the risk of sounding wildly pretentious the vampires are a metaphor for anything that threatens our lives," is how he described *Ultraviolet* to *Radio Times*.

The Unborn ★★ 18

1991 US Colour 80mins

This schlocky killer-foetus film has a young wife convinced that her doctor has inseminated her with mutant sperm. She's proved right when the offspring avoids abortion and slithers off and goes on the rampage. The film earns a second star simply for the earnestness of some of the actors, who must have realised what twaddle they were in, but put a brave face on things anyway. Aptly, the film gave birth to a sequel three years later.

Brooke Adams Virginia Marshall • **Jeff Hayenga** Brad Marshall • **James Karen** Dr Richard Meyerling • **K Callan** Martha • **Jane Cameron** Beth • **Lisa Kudrow** Louisa

Director *Rodman Flender*

Screenplay *Henry Dominic*

The Undead ★★★ 15

1957 US BW 71mins

Cult director Roger Corman's first "real" horror movie – albeit one with sci-fi overtones – was this quickie reincarnation tale that cashed in on the "previous existence" craze of the fifties. Filmed in a derelict supermarket (hence the strangely effective claustrophobic atmosphere), the film has Pamela Duncan as a hapless hooker hypnotised by her psychiatrist back to medieval times where she's condemned as a witch. The super-low budget stretched to rampaging knights in armour, a neat metamorphosis of witch to cat, and even an appearance by the Devil. A textbook example of cut-price Corman.

Pamela Duncan Helene/Diana • **Richard Garland** Pendragon • **Allison Hayes** Livia • **Val Dufour** Quintus • **Mel Welles** Smolkin • **Dorothy Neuman** Meg Maud • **Billy Barty** The Imp
Director *Roger Corman*
Screenplay *Charles Griffith, Mark Hanna*

Undermind ★★

TV 1965 UK BW 11x60mins

Trust no one. Long before *The X Files*, this psychological sci-fi thriller series for the ITV network pointed the finger at people in high places acting strangely. Returning from the Antipodes, hero Jeremy Wilkin finds his brother a changed man. It turns out that those undermining the political and social structure of the country are under the malignant influence of aliens. Created by Robert Banks Stewart, who wrote for the *Callan* series, and went on to create *Bergerac*, among other TV successes.

Jeremy Wilkin Drew Heriot • **Rosemary Nicols** Anne Heriot • **Denis Quilley** Professor Val Randolph
Created by *Robert Banks Stewart*
Producer *Michael Chapman*

Undersea Kingdom ★★★

1936 US BW

The chief pleasure of this fast-moving 12-part serial is the blithe anachronism of an ancient civilisation being armed to the teeth with futuristic gadgetry. And it needs every robot, reflectoplate tranformer, juggernaut and volplane (not to mention chariot and catapult), as the lost city of Atlantis is experiencing a civil war between the tyrannical Unga Khan and his Black Robe guards and the White Robes, led by the high priest Sharad. Into this maelstrom blasts Crash Corrigan in his rocket-powered submarine, so that a brilliant boffin can counter the subterranean quakes that have been incommoding North America. Utterly ludicrous – but compulsive fun.

Ray Corrigan Crash Corrigan • **Monte Blue** Unga Khan • **Lois Wilde** Diana • **William Farnum** Sharad • **Boothe Howard** Ditmar • **C Montague Shaw** Prof Norton • **Smiley Burnett** Briny • **Lon Chaney Jr** Hakur
Director *B Reeves Eason, Joesph Kane*
Screenplay *John Rathmell, Maurice Geraghty, Oliver Drake, from a story by Tracy Knight, John Rathmell*

The Underwater City ★ U

1962 US BW 77mins

The world's first undersea city is built as a research centre, atomic fallout shelter and resort destination for those wanting respite from the surface world. So why was it built so close to a deep abyss? And what will happen when there's an earthquake? Director Frank McDonald fails to breathe suspense or any sense of wonder into this waterlogged effort because the emphasis is less on fantasy and more on the unenthralling personal stories of the inhabitants, in this case honeymooners William Lundigan and Julie (*Creature from the Black Lagoon*) Adams. As dull as ditchwater, and though shot in colour, this was only ever released in black and white because even Columbia Pictures knew a stinker when they saw one.

William Lundigan Bob Gage • **Julie Adams** Dr Monica Powers • **Roy Roberts** Tim Graham • **Carl Benton Reid** Dr Halstead • **Chet Douglas** Chuck "Cowboy" Marlow • **Paul Dubov** George Burnett
Director *Frank McDonald*
Screenplay *Owen Harris, from an idea by Alex Gordon, Ruth Alexander*

The Unearthly ★

1957 US BW 68mins

Mad scientist John Carradine and his research assistant Marilyn Buferd discover a new gland containing the secret of youth and, in their crazed efforts to achieve immortality, end up with a cellar full of grotesque monsters. Poorly scripted, crudely directed and overacted by Carradine to a distracting degree, this cheap fear fodder is somewhat similar to the previous year's *The Black Sleep*. Potential victim Allison Hayes starred in the cult classic *Attack of the 50 Ft Woman* and Tor Johnson, playing the manservant Lobo who turns on Carradine, appeared in the awful *Plan 9 from Outer Space*.

John Carradine Professor Charles Conway • **Allison Hayes** Grace Thomas • **Myron Healey** Mark Houston • **Sally Todd** Natalie • **Marilyn Buferd** Dr Sharon Gilchrist • **Arthur Batanides** Danny Green • **Tor Johnson** Lobo • **Harry Fleer** Harry Jedrow
Director *Brook L Peters*
Screenplay *Geoffrey Dennis [John DF Black], Jane Mann, from a story by Jane Mann*

Unearthly Stranger ★★★

1963 UK Colour 78mins

This under-rated and little known British sci-fi chiller is from the same school of cinematic paranoia as *Invasion of the Body Snatchers*. John Neville stars as a scientist working on a secret space project who discovers his wife (Gabriella Licudi) is an alien – after all, she does sleep with her eyes open and lift hot dishes out of the oven with her bare hands! John Krish directs with the kind of pace and imagination that's sadly lacking in so many of today's multi-million-dollar blockbusters, and the film includes the unforgettable image of the Licudi's tears burning marks down her face like acid. There's sterling support work, too, from a cast that includes Jean Marsh and Warren Mitchell.

John Neville Dr Mark Davidson • **Gabriella Licudi** Julie Davidson • **Philip Stone** Professor John Lancaster • **Patrick Newell** Major Clarke • **Jean Marsh** Miss Ballard • **Warren Mitchell** Munro
Director *John Krish*
Screenplay *Rex Carlton, from a story by Jeffrey Stone*

Unforgettable ★★ 15

1996 US Colour 112mins [video]

In order to find his wife's killer, police medical examiner Ray Liotta injects himself with the secret memory-transfer formula of researcher Linda Fiorentino, together with the brain fluid of his wife, in order to "see" her last memories. Amazingly, this outrageous premise manages never to come across as the least bit goofy, but that's where the problem lies. The film is so solemn and serious that it never gets a chance to be exciting and mysterious, making it into a long slog. Fiorentino is good under the circumstances, but Liotta is not convincing as a man who is supposed to be completely obsessed with solving the case. Contains swearing.

Ray Liotta Dr David Krane • **Linda Fiorentino** Dr Martha Briggs • **Peter Coyote** Don Bresler • **Christopher McDonald** Stewart Gleick • **David Paymer** Curtis Avery • **Duncan Fraser** Michael Stratton • **Caroline Elliott** Cara Krane
Director *John Krish*
Screenplay *Rex Carlton, from a story by Jeffrey Stone*

The Uninvited ★★★ 12

TV 1997 UK Colour 4x60mins [video]

This four-part ITV mystery from 1997, based by writer Peter Bowker on a story by ex-soap star Leslie Grantham, is a return to the style of *Quatermass II*. Photographer hero Douglas Hodge stumbles over a mystery when he witnesses a fatal car crash, only to discover the dead driver (David Allister) alive again the next day. It all leads back to Sweethope, a flooded village, and the revelation that the survivors have been rising to positions of power in the government. Grantham himself plays Chief Superintendant Gates, who becomes a glowing-eyed villain.

Douglas Hodge Steve Blake • **Leslie Grantham** Chief Supt Gates • **David Allister** James Wilson • **Lia Williams** Melissa Gates • **Sylvestra Le Touzel** Joanna Ball
Director *Norman Stone*
Written by *Peter Bowker, from a story by Leslie Grantham*
Producer *Ruth Boswell*

Universal Soldier ★★★ 18

1992 US Colour 99mins

Part *Terminator*, part *Robocop*, all dumb fun: *Independence Day* director Roland Emmerich's earlier sci-fi potboiler is a by-the-numbers affair, with dialogue you'd swear appears in comic balloons. But as no one takes the ultimate warrior premise seriously, either behind or in front of the camera, the unpretentious pandering to the action-plus brigade is a likeable strength, not a jarring weakness. The Muscles from Brussels (Jean-Claude Van Damme) has the edge over the Swedish Meatball (Dolph Lundgren) in every respect, from his showcase kick boxing to his send-up nude scene, in this OTT jeopardy jackpot, where what you see is exactly what you get. Contains violence and swearing.

Jean-Claude Van Damme Luc Devreux • **Dolph Lundgren** Andrew Scott • **Ally Walker** Veronica Roberts • **Ed O'Ross** Colonel Perry • **Jerry Orbach** Dr Gregor • **Leon Rippy** Woodward • **Tico Wells** Garth • **Ralph Moeller** GR76 • **Robert Trebor** Motel owner • **Gene Davis** Lieutenant • **Drew Snyder** Charles
Director *Roland Emmerich*
Screenplay *Richard Rothstein, Christopher Leitch, Dean Devlin*

Universal Soldier – the Return ★ 18

1999 US Colour 83mins DVD

Sequels hit an all-time-low in this insultingly awful big-screen follow-up to the 1992 Jean-Claude Van Damme hit (which has already spawned two straight-to-video tales featuring Matt Battaglia in place of the original star). Van Damme's nice guy terminator is now a technical adviser on the secret government project that turns dead soldiers into killing machines. Naturally, they go on the rampage, leading to much thrill-free punching, kicking and riddling with bullets. Thinly plotted and painfully clichéd even by genre standards, this moronic mess doesn't even have the benefit of crowd-pleasing action sequences. Watching a bunch of dull characters hurtling through a plate glass window about 50 times is neither inventive nor exhilarating, proving perhaps that ex-stunt co-ordinators shouldn't be allowed a stab at feature film directing.
Contains violence.

Jean-Claude Van Damme Luc • **Michael Jai White** SETH • **Heidi Schanz** Erin • **Xander Berkeley** Dylan Cotner • **Justin Lazard** Captain Blackburn • **Kiana Tom** Maggie • **Daniel Von Bargen** General Radford • **James Black** Sergeant Morrow
Director *Mic Rodgers*
Screenplay *William Malone, John Fasano, from the characters created by Richard Rothstein, Christopher Leitch, Dean Devlin*
Producer *Allen Shapiro, Jean-Claude Van Damme*

The Unknown Terror ★

1957 US BW 77mins

Mala Powers looks for her lost brother in the Caribbean "Caves of Death" and meets mad doctor Gerald Milton who is turning human guinea pigs into foam-covered creatures with experimental mould cultures. Completely rudimentary in every department – the phoney jungle foliage, the soap-suds make-up, the flat lighting, the predictable romance between Powers and Paul Richards – director Charles Marquis Warren's pathetic programme-filler isn't remotely scary and the dire script is as mould-encrusted as the hilarious monsters themselves.

John Howard Dan Mathews • **Mala Powers** Gina Mathews • **Paul Richards** Pete Morgan • **May Wynn** Concha • **Gerald Milton** Dr Ramsey • **Duane Grey** Lino • **Charles H Gray [Charles Gray]** Jim Wheatly
Director *Charles Marquis Warren*
Screenplay *Kenneth Higgins*

Unknown World ★ U

1951 US BW 74mins

Scientists bore into the Earth aboard a half tank/half submarine mole ship, dubbed a "cyclotram", to find a subterranean safe haven from atomic war. Unfortunately, the peaceful centre proves harmful to human reproduction in a highly moral sci-fi quickie containing a wordy script, plodding direction, dinky special effects and not even an occasional thrill. Once the contrived premise locks in after a fun start, this low-cal effort will probably bore you, too!

Victor Kilian Dr Jeremiah Morley • **Bruce Kellogg** Wright Thompson • **Otto Waldis** Dr Max A Bauer • **Marilyn Nash** Joan Lindsey • **Jim Bannon** Andy Ostengaard
Director *Terrell O Morse [Terry Morse]*
Screenplay *Millard Kaufman*

Until the End of the World ★★ 15

1991 Ger/Fr/Aus Colour 151mins

This misbegotten epic shows how directors who have achieved an arthouse following can believe they possess the secret of the universe, blow $23 million and emerge with a three-hour film that's less than perfect. Thus Wim Wenders, admired for his bleak thrillers and general coolness in movies including *Paris, Texas* and *Wings of Desire*, took William Hurt, Max von Sydow, Sam Neill and others to eight countries without a script, assuming that sheer genius was enough. All they had was an idea about a nuclear satellite crashing to Earth in 1999 and a cluster of unrelated subplots. Hurt is given a not very interesting love interest and seems bored out of his mind. It's nicely shot, though, partly in the Australian outback, but then, so are car advertisements. Contains violence, swearing and nudity.

William Hurt Trevor McPhee/Sam Farber • **Solveig Dommartin** Claire Tourneur • **Sam Neill** Eugene Fitzpatrick • **Max von Sydow** Henry Farber • **Rüdiger Vogler** Philip Winter • **Ernie Dingo** Burt • **Jeanne Moreau** Edith Farber
Director *Wim Wenders*
Screenplay *Wim Wenders, Peter Carey, from a story by Wim Wenders, Solveig Dommartin*

V

"**Beware** the stare that will paralyse the will of the **world**"

Village of the Damned 1960

V ★★★★ 15

TV 1983-1985 US Colour

V is indeed for victory in Kenneth Johnson's acclaimed four-hour mini-series, which successfully combines top-notch sci-fi entertainment with a powerful allegory. The saga opens with the arrival of a seemingly benevolent alien race, who promise to bring prosperity to Earth. But a small group of humans soon learn that the humanoid "Visitors" are literally not what they appear to be, and form a resistance movement. The resistance's subsequent fight for freedom not only provides the basis of an excellently realised alien invasion drama, but also offers a thinly-veiled commentary on the evils of fascism and the rise of Nazism during the thirties. Ignore the many plot-holes and enjoy. The saga was satisfyingly resolved by the more action-orientated *V: The Final Battle* (1984), and then needlessly continued in the mindless and repetitive season-long shoot-'em-up, *V: The Series* (19 episodes, 1984-1985).

Jane Badler Diana • **Michael Durrell** Robert Maxwell • **Faye Grant** Dr Juliet Parrish • **Peter Nelson** Brian • **David Packer** Daniel Bernstein • **Neva Patterson** Eleanor Dupres • **Tommy Petersen** Josh Brooks • **Marc Singer** Mike Donovan • **Andrew Prine** Steven • **Leonardo Cimino** John • **Blair Tefkin** Robin Maxwell • **Robert Englund** Willie

Director/Screenplay *Kenneth Johnson*

SFacts

The role of Robin Maxwell was originally played by Dominique Dunne (Dana Freeling in *Poltergeist*), who was murdered by her estranged boyfriend in the autumn of 1982 while rehearsing her lines with co-star David Packer. Her scenes were deleted and Blair Tefkin took over the role.

VR.5 ★★

TV 1995 US Colour 13x60mins

A dazzlingly innovative but frequently bewildering virtual reality drama, this short-lived offering revolves around a revolutionary technology which can secretly access people's subconscious minds. When shy telephone engineer Sydney Bloom learns how to use "VR.5", she finds herself under scrutiny from a mysterious organisation known as the Committee, and also uncovers evidence that its designer, her long-last father, is still alive. The series has an obvious tendency to be hard to grasp (or believe), and Lori Singer's cold central performance makes viewing even more of a challenge. But if you can get into the right mindset for *VR.5*, it becomes a refreshing, rewarding and visually incredible download. The show also boasts an exceptionally strong supporting cast, which includes David McCallum, Will Patton, Louise Fletcher and a pre-*Buffy* Anthony Head.

Lori Singer Sydney Bloom • **Michael Easton** Duncan • **Will Patton** Dr Frank Morgan • **Anthony Head** Oliver Sampson • **Tracey Needham** Samantha Bloom • **David McCallum** Dr Joseph Bloom • **Louise Fletcher** Nora Bloom

Created by *Michael Katleman, Thania St John*

VR Troopers ★ PG

TV 1994-1996 US Colour 40x30mins

The makers of *Mighty Morphin Power Rangers* get their scissors out once again and unleash another kiddie-orientated sci-fi beat-'em-up. An awkward combination of original footage and clips from several Japanese action series, the show pits three teens-turned-Virtual Reality Troopers against a virtual reality villain, Grimlord, who is determined to reach the real world and conquer it. Undemanding viewers who embraced the Power Rangers' exploits will be prepared for the *VR Troopers'* two seasons of silly, tacky and formulaic adventures, and certainly won't be disappointed by the series' fast pace, shallow but pretty characters, OTT baddies and hard-hitting martial arts action.

Michael Bacon JB Reese • **Gardner Baldwin** Karl Ziktor / Grimlord • **Sarah Brown** Katlin Star • **Brad Hawkins** Ryan Steele • **Kerrigan Mahan** Voice of Jeb

The Valley of Gwangi ★★ 12

1969 US Colour 91mins

An unsuccessful touring Wild West show encounters a forbidden valley full of prehistoric animals, and captures its massive allosaurus leader. Anything to bring in the punters but, guess what – it escapes to terrorise the cast. A watchable fantasy adventure, though as with other films Ray Harryhausen had a hand in, the stop-motion special effects put the flat characters and routine plot in the shade.

James Franciscus Tuck Kirby • **Gila Golan** TJ Breckenridge • **Richard Carlson** Champ Connors • **Laurence Naismith** Prof Horace Bromley • **Freda Jackson** Tia Zorina • **Gustavo Rojo** Carlos Dos Orsos

Director *James O'Connolly [Jim O'Connolly]*
Screenplay *William E Bast, Julian More, from the story by William E Bast*

Valley of the Dragons ★★

1961 US BW 79mins

Based on a story by Jules Verne, this is the tale of two duelling enemies (Cesare Danova Sean McClory) who find themselves swept by a comet up to the moon. There they continue their rivalry surrounded by strange creatures and damsels, while waiting for the comet to swing back in their direction and return them to Earth. Lacking in the charm and adventure of other Verne adaptations, fans would be advised to seek out the Karel Zeman version, *On the Comet* (1970).

Cesare Danova Hector Servadac • **Sean McClory** Denning • **Joan Staley** Deena • **Danielle de Metz** Nateeta • **Gregg Martell** Od-Loo • **Gil Perkins** Tarn/Doctor • **I Stanford Jolley** Patoo

Director *Edward Bernds*
Screenplay *Edward Bernds, from the novel "Hector Servadac" by Jules Verne*

The Vampire Bat ★ PG

1933 US BW 60mins

A series of small-town murders turn out to be the work of scientist Lionel Atwill who drains his victims of blood in order to nourish a flesh parasite he has created. A standard-issue mad doctor tale disguised as a vampire horror, it was evidently made to cash-in on the success of Universal's *Dracula* with frightened Fay Wray and hero Melvyn Douglas lending limp support to the hopelessly outdated proceedings.

Lionel Atwill Dr Otto von Niemann • **Fay Wray** Ruth Bertin • **Melvyn Douglas** Karl Brettschneider • **Maude Eburne** Gussie Schnappmann • **George E Stone** Kringen • **Dwight Frye** Herman Gleib • **Robert Frazer** Emil Borst

Director *Frank R Strayer*
Screenplay *Edward T Lowe*

Vampire Hunter D ★★★ 15

1985 Jap Colour 80mins

An adventurous *manga* animation melange of JR Tolkien, Sergio Leone, Hammer horror and mainstream science fiction. Far off in the 13th millennium, the taciturn D is hired by village beauty Doris to save her from Count Magnus Lee's clutches. Having sampled her jugular, the ancient giant now wants Doris for his vampire bride and D must infiltrate his mountain fortress in order to halt his demonic plans. Director Toyoo Ashida uses a wildly eclectic palate of styles and astonishing depth to achieve his helter-skelter imagery in one of the best Japanese cartoons in the *Akira* tradition.

Michael McConnohie • **Barbara Goodson** • **Jeff Winkless** • **Edie Mirman** • **Kerrigan Mahan** • **Steve Kramer** • **Steve Bulen** • **Joyce Kurtz** • **Lara Cody** • **Tom Syner** • **Kirk Thornton**
Director *Toyoo Ashida, Carl Macek*
Screenplay *Yasuhi Hirano*

Vampirella ★★

1996 US Colour 90mins

It would be an overstatement to say that wooden Talisa Soto brings Forrest J Ackerman's comic book heroine to life, but she does at least portray Vampirella in three dimensions. The plot has something to do with Vampirella coming to Earth from her home planet of Drakulon in order to kill Dracula. But you'll forget all that when you realise that ageing rocker Roger Daltrey is playing the big vampiric cheese, and that Drac's new persona is a Lestat-like rock star named Jamie Blood. Not as much fun as it ought to be. Contains nudity, violence and swearing.

Talisa Soto Vampirella • **Roger Daltrey** Vlad/Jamie Blood • **Richard Joseph Paul** Adam Van Helsing • **Angus Scrimm** High Elder • **Corrina Harney** Sallah
Director *Jim Wynorski*
Screenplay *Gary Gerani, from a story by Forrest J Ackerman*

The Vanishing Man ★★

TV 1997-1998 UK Colour 6x60mins

ITV's seven-part take on *The Invisible Man* sees – or should that be doesn't see? – Neil Morrissey (*Men Behaving Badly*) trying to avoid disappearing off the face of the Earth. After involuntarily participating in an invisibility experiment, freight pilot Morrissey finds himself forced to embark on a series of undercover missions in return for help with finding a cure to his condition. Although the show's premise shares some superficial similarities with the US Sci-Fi Channel's *Invisible Man*, Morrissey's vanishing act is a far more lightweight and much less engaging offering. Fortunately, the show's familiar blend of comedy and drama invariably makes its mark, while its respectable special effects and the star's easy charm are clear for all to see. A feature-length TV film preceded the series.

Neil Morrissey Nick Cameron • **Lucy Akhurst** Alice • **Mark Womak** Joe Cameron • **John Castle** Moreau • **Sheila Ruskin** Michelle Peters • **Razaaq Adoti** Jacob • **Jill Baker** Ms Jeffries
Director *Rick Stroud, Roger Bamford*
Pilot written by *Anthony Horovitz*
Producer *Linda Agran*

The Vanishing Shadow ★★★

1934 US BW 12x20mins

With chapter titles like *Hurled from the Sky* and *Blazing Bulkheads*, it's easy to dismiss this Universal serial as just another comic-book caper. But with inventor James Durkin acting as "Q" to Onslow Stevens's 007, it's not too outlandish to claim it as a forerunner of the James Bond format. With a laser gun and an invisibility belt in his armoury, Stevens sets out to expose the nefarious dealings of Walter Miller, the corrupt tycoon responsible for his father's death. But that's before he discovers his beloved Ada Ince is Miller's estranged daughter. A minor outing, but an intriguing one nonetheless.

Onslow Stevens Stanley Stanfield • **Ada Ince** Gloria • **William Desmond** MacDonald • **Richard Cramer** Dorgan • **Walter Miller** Ward Barnett • **Sidney Bracey** Denny • **James Durkin** Carl Van Dorn
Director *Louis Friedlander [Lew Landers]*
Screenplay *Het Manheim, Basil Dickey, George Morgan*

SCI Q • SCI Q • SCI Q • SCI Q •

39

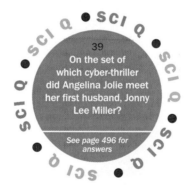

On the set of which cyber-thriller did Angelina Jolie meet her first husband, Jonny Lee Miller?

See page 496 for answers

Vegas in Space ★★ 15

1994 US Colour and BW 86mins

Astronauts, led by Captain Dan Tracy (Doris Fish), take sex-change pills in order to investigate a jewel robbery on the all-female planet Clitoris in this Troma trash cobbled together by San Francisco's drag queen community. Full of glitz, glamour, sexual innuendo and fabulous hairdos, this micro-budget underground home movie is a fitfully amusing spoof of space adventures and gay culture.
Conceived by impresario Phillip R Ford, and co-written with Fish (who died of Aids complications in 1991), this took several years to complete and is a purposely-bad sci-fi musical comedy aimed squarely at the gay community.

Doris Fish Captain Dan Tracy/Tracy Daniels • **Miss X** Vel Croford/Queen Veneer • **Ginger Quest** Empress Nueva Gabor • **Ramona Fischer** Mike/Sheila • **Lori Naslund** Steve/Debbie • **Timmy Spence** Lt Dick Hunter • **Tippi** Princess Angel
Director *Phillip R Ford*
Screenplay *Doris Fish, Phillip R Ford*
Production designer *Doris Fish*

Velocity Trap ★★ 15

1997 US Colour 86mins

Sci-fi sophisticates are going to find little to impress them in this low-budget adventure from director Philip J Roth. It's 2150 and Earth is over-run with computer crime, which means a return to hard cash and more work for the likes of security guard Olivier Gruner. He has to escort millions of dollars through space with pirates aboard, the crew in rebellion and a giant asteroid on a collision course. Essentially, it's an interstellar western, with the spaceship standing in for the wagon train. Negligible, but efficiently done. Contains violence and swearing.

Olivier Gruner Raymond Stokes • **Alicia Coppola** Beth Sheffield • **Ken Olandt** Nick • **Bruce Weitz** Captain Fenner • **Ray Oriel** Cruz • **Jaason Simmons** Simms
Director *Phillip J Roth*

Victor Frankenstein ★★

1977 Ire/Swe Colour 92mins

Elegantly photographed, but a dull viewing experience, this European co-production of Mary Shelley's classic tale of terror directed by American ex-pat Calvin Floyd was promoted as being the most faithful version ever committed to film. Far too melodramatic and psychologically straightforward to qualify as authentic, Per Oscarsson plays the Creature as a juvenile delinquent, brutally railing against his experimental creator, Leon Vitali, and society in general. The complete opposite of the approach Hammer took to the story, this pretentious reading was a festival favourite, but not an audience one.

Leon Vitali Victor Frankenstein • **Per Oscarsson** Monster • **Nicholas Clay** Henry • **Stacy Dorning** Elisabeth • **Jan Ohlsson** William • **Olof Bergstrüm** Father
Director *Calvin Floyd*
Screenplay *Calvin Floyd, Yvonne Floyd, from the novel "Frankenstein" by Mary Shelley*
Cinematographer *Tony Forsberg*

Videodrome ★★★★ 18

1982 Can Colour 84mins

With its subject matter of screen violence, this remains one of David Cronenberg's most personal, complex and disturbing films, even if it doesn't always make a lot of sense. James Woods is the amoral cable programmer who gets drawn to a sickening sadomasochistic channel called "Videodrome", which turns out to have a much more sinister purpose. Cronenberg uses this framework to explore his favourite themes – technology fusing with the human body, voyeurism, the links between sex and violence – and, although the plot begins to unravel, the startling imagery and Woods's fierce performance make for a deeply unsettling experience. The supporting cast includes Blondie singer Debbie Harry as Woods's girlfriend. Contains swearing and graphic and disturbing images.

James Woods Max Renn • **Sonja Smits** Bianca O'Blivion • **Deborah Harry** Nicki Brand • **Peter Dvorsky** Harlan • **Les Carlson** Barry Convex • **Jack Creley** Brian O'Blivion • **Lynne Gorman** Masha • **Julie Khaner** Bridey • **Reiner Schwarz** Moses • **David Bolt** Raphael • **Lally Cadeau** Rena King

***Director/Screenplay** David Cronenberg*

Village of the Damned ★★★★

1960 UK BW 77mins

Twelve women give birth to blond alien offspring after a strange force puts their community into a 24-hour trance in this remarkably faithful adaptation of John Wyndham's novel *The Midwich Cuckoos*. In a film that is compelling, creepy and often unbearably tense, an icy George Sanders becomes their teacher and then tries to halt their world domination plans. Superbly acted, with the human/family side of the horror unusually explored more than the fantasy elements, this British near-classic is a sci-fi treat and remains so, even in the face of John Carpenter's weak remake starring Christopher Reeve, which bypassed cinemas and went straight to video in this country. Contains violence.

George Sanders Gordon Zellaby • **Barbara Shelley** Anthea Zellaby • **Martin Stephens** David • **Michael Gwynn** Major Alan Bernard • **Laurence Naismith** Dr Willers • **Richard Warner** Harrington • **Jenny Laird** Mrs Harrington • **Sarah Long** Evelyn Harrington • **Thomas Heathcote** James Pawle • **Charlotte Mitchell** Janet Pawle

***Director** Wolf Rilla*

***Screenplay** Wolf Rilla, Stirling Silliphant, George Barclay, from the novel "The Midwich Cuckoos" by John Wyndham*

Village of the Damned ★★ 15

1995 US Colour 93mins

Those blond alien youngsters return to wreak havoc in a small town in cult director John Carpenter's pointless update of the 1960 British film. Despite the setting being transferred to California, superior special effects heightening the nastiness (Kirstie Alley's hard-to-watch self-autopsy) and Christopher Reeve giving a nicely heroic performance, the end result forgoes the touches and stylish atmosphere you might expect from Carpenter. This has a bland TV movie-style sheen, relieved only by hints of comedy. Stick with the original. Contains violence.

Christopher Reeve Alan Chaffee • **Kirstie Alley** Dr Susan Verner • **Linda Kozlowski** Jill McGowan • **Michael Paré** Frank McGowan • **Meredith Salenger** Melanie Roberts • **Mark Hamill** Reverend George • **Pippa Pearthree** Mrs Sarah Miller • **Peter Jason** Ben Blum • **Constance Forslund** Callie Blum • **Karen Kahn** Barbara Chaffee • **Thomas Dekker** David • **Lndsey Haun** Mara

***Director** John Carpenter*

***Screenplay** David Himmelstein, from the 1960 film*

SFacts

This remake was released just one month after its star, Christopher (Superman) Reeve was paralysed in a riding accident.

Village of the Giants ★★ PG

1965 US Colour 77mins

Producer Bert I Gordon was a master of crude productions with gimmicky titles, such as *The Amazing Colossal Man* and *Empire of the Ants*, and this improbable but fun tale about a boy genius (Ron Howard) who invents a food that causes growth to gigantic proportions is down to his usual standard. However, it's enjoyable hokum, supposedly based on an HG Wells original, which gets by on pure brio.

Tommy Kirk Mike • **Johnny Crawford** Horsey • **Beau Bridges** Fred • **Ronny Howard [Ron Howard]** Genius • **Joy Harmon** Merrie • **Bob Random** Rick • **Tisha Sterling** Jean

***Director** Bert I Gordon*

***Screenplay** Alan Caillou, by Bert I Gordon, from the novel "The Food of the Gods" by HG Wells*

Viper ★★ PG

TV 1994-1999 US Colour 79x60mins

Not content with unleashing the world's fastest superhero in *The Flash*, Danny Bilson and Paul DeMeo turn their attention to super-fast cars and take viewers on an undemanding drive through *Knight Rider* territory. Set in the near future, the series pursues the high-octane trips of a revolutionary crime-fighting, shape-shifting vehicle, and maps its ongoing battle against organised crime. James McCaffrey's edgy criminal-turned-hero Joe Astor is at the wheel during the show's opening and closing adventures, but is replaced at the start of the revamped second season by former *Space Rangers* star Jeff Kaake as bland Thomas Cole. While its originality tank is clearly empty, the series hits top gear in the action and effects departments, and proves to be a shockingly agreeable comic-strip romp.

James McCaffrey Joe Astor • **Dorian Harewood** Julian Wilkes • **Joe Nipote** Franklin "Frankie" Waters • **Heather Medway** Cameron Westlake • **Jeff Kaake** Thomas Cole • **Dawn Stern** Allie Farrow • **J Downing** Sherman Catlett

***Executive producer** Danny Bilson, Paul DeMeo*

Virtual Girl ★★ 18

1998 US Colour 83mins

A daft erotic thriller about a computer programmer who, while developing a new game, creates the eponymous girl (the alluring Charlie Curtis). Director Richard Gabai (who also stars) made *Assault of the Party Nerds*, *Virgin High* and many more of this ilk, which gives you a good indication of how awful this is. Exclusively for collectors of rarely-seen, straight-to-video trash.

Charlie Curtis Virtuality/Cynthia Lee • **Richard Gabai** Fred Renfield • **Max Dixon** John Lewis • **Warren Draper** Charlie R Poppy

***Director** Richard Gabai*

***Screenplay** Richard Gabai, LA Maddox*

Virtual Obsession ★★

1998 US Colour

The main point of interest here is the appearance of Jake Lloyd, who has since been catapulted to fame as young Anakin Skywalker in *Star Wars Episode I: the Phantom Menace*. His role here is fairly minor, though, with Peter Gallagher taking the lead as a boffin who invents a super computer, only for it to be subverted by his vengeful ex-girlfriend, *I Know What You Did Last Summer*'s Bridgette Wilson. With Robert Vaughn and Mimi Rogers also in the cast, this is a notch above most made-for-TV fare, and director Mick Garris manages to wring a few scares out of what is a rather silly story. Contains violence, swearing and sex scenes.

Peter Gallagher Joe • **Mimi Rogers** Karen • **Jake Lloyd** Jack • **Bridgette Wilson** Juliet Spring • **Robert Vaughn** Adam Spring

Director *Mick Garris*
Screenplay *Mick Garris, Preston Sturges [Preston Sturges Jr], from the novel "Host" by Peter James*

Virtuosity ★★★ 15

1995 US Colour 101mins [video] DVD

If disgraced cop-turned-convict Denzel Washington can eliminate the computer-generated serial killer SID 6.7, he'll be gratefully pardoned in director Brett Leonard's spasmodically entertaining high-tech fantasy adventure. Problem is, SID 6.7 (played by Russell Crowe) has 183 separate homicidal tendencies – including those of Hitler and Charles Manson – to his personality. Cyberspace wizardry covers the yawning gaps in this soulless thriller and the loose ends mount up faster than the body count, despite expert performances by the two commanding leads. Because SID 6.7 can rejuvenate himself out of any predicament (and these sequences are the film's visual highlights), there's basically no suspense generated, and Leonard's film never recovers from this fatal flaw.

Denzel Washington Parker Barnes • **Kelly Lynch** Madison Carter • **Russell Crowe** Sid 6.7 • **Stephen Spinella** Lindenmeyer • **William Forsythe** William Cochran • **Louise Fletcher** Elizabeth Deane • **William Fichtner** Wallace • **Costas Mandylor** John Donovan
Director *Brett Leonard*
Screenplay *Eric Bernt*

Virus ★★ PG

1980 Jap Colour 102mins [video]

One of Japan's biggest budgeted movies, though it seems much of the cash went to the all-star (and mostly American) cast than on the special effects, many of which belong in the cheaper Godzilla movies. Possibly to try to attract a wide audience, the movie is not content to focus on the few survivors of a worldwide plague but packs in everything else under the sun, from forced prostitution to nuclear holocaust. The results don't completely make sense, especially in prints that cut about an hour from the running time. Some striking visuals and seeing all the badly cast stars (including Chuck Connors as a British submarine captain!) provide the main curiosity value.

Sonny Chiba Dr Yamauchi • **Chuck Connors** Captain MacCloud • **Stephanie Faulkner** Sarah Baker • **Glenn Ford** Richardson • **Stuart Gillard** Dr Mayer • **Olivia Hussey** Marit • **George Kennedy** Admiral Conway • **Ken Ogata** Professor Tsuchiya • **Edward James Olmos** Captain Lopez • **Henry Silva** Garland • **Bo Svenson** Major Carter • **Robert Vaughn** Barkley
Director *Kinji Fukasaku*
Screenplay *Koji Takada, Gregory Knapp, Kinji Fukasaku, from a novel by Sakyo Komatsu*

Virus ★★ 18

1998 US Colour 99mins [video]

Oscar-winning visual effects artist/James Cameron protégé John Bruno terminally accents effects over plot in his dreary feature-directing debut and adds insult to injury by making those effects merely tarnished knock-offs of *The Terminator*, *The Abyss* and *Aliens*. A sinking tugboat crew take refuge on a deserted Russian science vessel during a typhoon only to find it harbouring an alien energy force. Derivative of everything from *Leviathan* to *Deep Rising*, Bruno's hybrid mass of genre clichés simply joins the dots and doesn't even entertain on a schlock level. Jamie Lee Curtis, William Baldwin and Donald Sutherland give career-worst performances in this lame-brained terror tripe, with the final robot monster looking more like a mobile junkyard than anything truly scary. Contains strong violence.

Jamie Lee Curtis Kit Foster • **William Baldwin** Steve Baker • **Donald Sutherland** Captain Everton • **Joanna Pacula** Nadia • **Marshall Bell** JW Woods Jr • **Julio Oscar Mechoso** Squeaky • **Sherman Augustus** Richie • **Cliff Curtis** Hiko
Director *John Bruno*
Screenplay *Chuck Pfarrer, Dennis Feldman, from the comic books by Chuck Pfarrer*

Visit to a Small Planet ★★ U

1960 US BW 85mins

Jerry Lewis is Kreton, an unemotional alien visitor who comes to a small Virginian town and encounters the all too emotional inhabitants – including Ellen Spelding (Joan Blackman) who manages to capture Kreton's heart. Based on Gore Vidal's satirical stage play of the same name this was another failed attempt to capture the undoubted genius of Jerry Lewis on screen. Vidal despised the movie and contemporary critics were less than enthusiastic; time has added a certain period charm, though it's still pretty wide of the mark.

Jerry Lewis Kreton • **Joan Blackman** Ellen Spelding • **Earl Holliman** Conrad • **Fred Clark** Major Roger Putnam Spelding • **Lee Patrick** Rheba Spelding • **Gale Gordon** Bob Mayberry • **Ellen Corby** Mrs Mayberry
Director *Norman Taurog*
Screenplay *Edmund Beloin, Henry Garson, from the play by Gore Vidal*

The Visitor ★★

TV 1997-1998 US Colour 13x60mins

Red-hot from the phenomenal success of *Stargate* and *Independence Day*, Roland Emmerich and Dean Devlin failed to score a hat trick with their first foray into TV sci-fi. A well-intentioned but trite cross between *ET*, *The Fugitive* and *Touched by an Angel*, the series follows the adventures of John Corbett, an alien abductee who returns to Earth 50 years after his mysterious disappearance. Now pursued by the authorities, Corbett attempts to help those he encounters during his flight. Largely devoid of the action and spectacle its makers are famed for, the Visitor's glossy exploits make for banal viewing, and not even Corbett's sensitive central performance can break the monotony. The series was cancelled midway through its first year.

John Corbett Adam MacArthur • **Grand L Bush** Agent Douglas Wilcox • **Leon Rippy** Agent Nicholas LaRue • **John Storey** Agent Craig Van Patten • **Steve Railsback** Colonel James Vise
Executive producer *Dean Devlin, Roland Emmerich, John Masius*

Visitors of the Night ★★ 12

1995 US Colour 90mins [video]

Did Markie Post's daughter get abducted by aliens when she disappeared for a few hours one night? Post believes the same thing happened to her when she was a girl, so is history repeating itself? It's an intriguing if fanciful premise, but in fact there's not much to get excited about in this routine TV movie that labours the mystery and menace of the situation to ever-decreasing effect. A lightweight addition to the *Communion* school of science fiction, and equally silly. Contains some violence, strong language.

Markie Post Judith • **Candace Cameron** Katie • **Dale Midkiff** Sheriff Marcus Ashley • **Stephen McHattie** Bryan English • **Pam Hyatt** Judith's mother • **Susan Hogan** Dr Dillard • **Allan Royal** Dr Geary • **Victor A Young** Dr Pandro
Director *Jorge Montesi*
Screenplay *Michael J Murray*

The Voices ★★

TV 1955 UK BW 90mins

A talkative fifties play, performed live on BBC television. Set in the year 2021, when the world is united under one government,

George F Kerr's play focuses on the political wrangling regarding further expansion into space, and power struggles down on Earth. The warnings of a distinguished scientist (Willoughby Goddard) go unheeded, unti voices are heard from millions of miles away. Based on the novel *Hero's Walk* by Robert Crane.

Walter Rilla Dr Werner • **Carl Bernard** Geoffrey Vernon-Cavendish • **Terence Alexander** Neil Harrison • **Willoughby Goddard** Prof Mark Harrison • **Stanley Zevic** Balatov • **Andy Ho** Hsuan • **Ursula Howells** Libby Harrison • **Launce Maraschal** Crandall • **Fred Johnson** Sir Alton Berkeley

***Written by** George F Kerr, from the novel "Hero's Walk" by Robert Crane*

***Producer** Dennis Vance*

The Voodoo Factor ★★

TV 1959-1960 UK BW 6x30mins

A six-part series for ATV. Writer Lewis Griefer went on to write for *The Prisoner* and almost to write for *Doctor Who* (his submission was heavily re-worked by script editor Robert Holmes and became *Pyramids of Mars* by Stephen Harris). The plot concerned a scientist-doctor (Maurice Kaufman) doing battle with a 200-year-old Polynesian spider goddess which releases a Malaria-like virus. Jill Ireland, who plays Renee, went on to appear in many film and television roles, and to marry Charles Bronson.

Maurice Kauffman Dr David Whittaker • **Maxine Audley** Marion Whittaker • **Philip Bond** Dr Tony Wilson • **Charles Carson** Captain Ross • **Jill Ireland** Renee • **Anna May Wong** Malayan girl • **Eric Young** Malayan

***Written by** Lewis Greifer*

***Producer** Quentin Lawrence*

Voodoo Woman ★ PG

1957 US BW 67mins

A cheap and cheerful slice of horror with a mad professor carrying out horrible experiments on a young (and beautiful, of course) woman. The stilted acting and dialogue will probably raise a laugh for some fans of this sort of cult nonsense, but one thing is for sure, no one will be remotely frightened by it.

Marla English Marilyn Blanchard • **Tom Conway** Dr Roland Gerard • **Touch Connors [Mike Connors]** Ted Bronson • **Lance Fuller** Rick/Harry • **Mary Ellen Kaye** Susan • **Paul Dubov** Marcel the Innkeeper

***Director** Edward L Cahn*

***Screenplay** Russell Bender, VI Voss*

Voyage ★★★

Radio 1999 UK 5x30mins

A five-part BBC Radio 4 serial, produced and directed by Dirk Maggs, adapted from Stephen Baxter's novel, which is an alternate history of the US space programme, imagining that as a consequence of John Kennedy surviving an assassination attempt he was able to influence successive administrations in supporting a Nasa Mars mission in 1985. The serial undoes the flashback structure of the book and tells the story straight, beginning with the moon landing and following heroine Laurel Lefkow, a geologist who struggles in the fighter-jock atmosphere of Nasa to become the first woman on Mars, intent on discovering whether or not there's water on the Red Planet. Along the way, there is much debate about means of achieving a Mars landing, with a disastrous nuclear-powered option discarded after an effectively-dramatised space tragedy. A nuts-and-bolts techno-story, with soaring Wilfredo Acosta music, this does what it says in the title and concentrates on the long road to its destination, leaving the question of what happens there and what it means up in the air. Available on audio-cassette.

Laurel Lefkow Natalie York • **Vincent Marzello** Joe Muldoon • **Russell Bentley** Jim Dana • **William Dufris** Mike Conlig • **Michael Roberts** Gregory Dana • **William Roberts** Ben Priest • **Frank Lazarus** Chuck Jones • **Rolf Saxon** Phil Stone • **Mel Taylor** Ralph Gerson

***Director** Dirk Maggs*

***Dramatised by** Dirk Maggs, from the novel by Stephen Baxter*

***Music** Wilfredo Acosta*

Le Voyage dans la Lune ★★★★★

1902 Fr BW 21mins

A cornerstone of narrative cinema – and probably celluloid's first foray into science fiction – Georges Méliès's beautifully designed space adventure about an exploratory trip to the moon comprises 31 scenes – each one a *tableau vivant* shot front on from a stationary camera – whose most famous shot depicts a rocket landing in the Man in the Moon's eye. Drawing from the writings of Jules Verne and HG Wells, this early treasure offers much more in the way of a league of swimsuited beauties waving off the intrepid (and rather aged) members of the Astronomic Club followed by a lunar encounter with the hostile Selenites. Not to be confused with a magician's trick, it's an inspired masterwork from a true visionary of early cinema.

Georges Méliès Professor Barbenfouillis • **Bleuette Bernon** La lune

***Director** Georges Méliès*

***Screenplay** Georges Méliès, from the works of Jules Verne, HG Wells*

***Cinematographer** Lucien Tainguy, Michaut*

Voyage into Prehistory ★★★★

1955 Cz BW 87mins

This was the first feature to boast full-colour stop-motion animation. Unfortunately, much of Karel Zeman's achievement was corrupted by William Clayton's 1966 US reissue, which incorporated thumbnail palentological information to bring an unnecessary educational dimension to the time-travelling adventures of four boys in a cave beneath New York's Central Park. What remains unimpeachable, however, is the scope of Zeman's imagination, the beauty of his stylised backdrops and the ingenuity of his combination of live/animatronic and animated footage. Ranging from woolly rhinos to a battling stegosaurus, the prehistoric menagerie includes more than the predictably rampaging carnivores to truly suggest a lost world. A Czech language film.

Vladimir Bejval Jirka • **Petr Hermann** Tonik/Tony • **Zdenek Hustak** Jenda • **Josef Lukas** Petr • **James Lucas** Doc (US sequences) • **Victor Betral** Joe"Jo-Jo" (US sequences) • **Charles Goldsmith** Ben (US sequences)

***Director** Karel Zeman*

***Screenplay** JA Novotny, Karel Zeman, William Cayton (US version), Fred Ladd (US version)*

SCI Q • SCI Q • SCI Q • SCI Q •

40

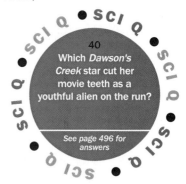

Which *Dawson's Creek* star cut her movie teeth as a youthful alien on the run?

See page 496 for answers

Voyage of the Rock Aliens

★★ 15

1985 US Colour 95mins

The idea of a sci-fi rock musical is camp enough but add Pia Zadora into the mix and the result is a kitsch delight. The bonkers storyline finds an alien rock band arriving on earth to learn about the roots of rock 'n' roll and getting mixed up with a gang of tearaways. The hit-and-miss script is packed with groan-inducing puns and the songs aren't up too much, but it neverthless exudes a cheesy charm. The eclectic cast also includes Michael Jackson's brother Jermaine and screen veteran Ruth Gordon.

Pia Zadora Dee Dee • **Tom Nolan** Absid • **Craig Sheffer** Frankie • **Ruth Gordon** Sheriff • **Michael Berryman** Chainsaw • **Jermaine Jackson** Rain
Director *James Fargo*
Screenplay *S James Guidotti, Edward Gold, Charles Hairston*
Music *Jack White*

Voyage to the Bottom of the Sea ★★★ U

1961 US Colour 100mins [video]

Walter Pidgeon and Joan Fontaine are top billed in this entertaining sci-fi outing, but the real star is the submarine *Seaview*. Accounting for $400,000 of the picture's budget, the glass-fronted nuclear sub went on to star in its own TV series following its exploits here, as admiral Pidgeon fires its missiles into the Van Allen radiation belt and saves Earth from meltdown. Fontaine is totally out of her depth, but Peter Lorre and the rest of the supporting cast are splendid. Co-writer/producer/director Irwin Allen went on to become the king of the disaster movie in the early seventies, as the creative force behind such films as *The Poseidon Adventure* and *The Towering Inferno*.

Walter Pidgeon Admiral Harriman Nelson • **Joan Fontaine** Dr Susan Hiller • **Barbara Eden** Cathy Connors • **Peter Lorre** Commodore Lucius Emery • **Robert Sterling** Capt Lee Crane • **Michael Ansara** Miguel Alvarez • **Frankie Avalon** Chip Romano • **Regis Toomey** Dr Jamieson • **John Litel** Admiral Crawford • **Howard McNear** Congressman Parker • **Henry Daniell** Dr Zucco
Director *Irwin Allen*
Screenplay *Irwin Allen, Charles Bennett, from a story by Irwin Allen*

Voyage to the Bottom of the Sea ★★★

TV 1964-68 US BW/Colour 110x60mins

Spun off from Irwin Allen's colourful but silly 1961 feature, and using plenty of leftover props and effects (like a flying midget sub), this began as a near-future sci-fi/suspense/espionage show following the crew of the high-tech nuclear submarine *Seaview*, but swiftly transformed into an absurd but far more entertaining effort in which the sub was attacked each week by werewolves, mummies, abominable snowmen, aliens, killer plants, puppets, time-travellers, giant mutants, whales, dinosaurs, lobster-men, leprechans and the like. Richard Basehart keeps a straight face as Admiral Harriman Nelson, David Hedison crawls through many ducts as the intrepid Captain Lee Crane and Del Monroe is the more hands-on enlisted man Kowalski (who had to deal with plenty of leaks and sparking equipment), while room was found in various episodes for Jill Ireland, Michael Ansara, Werner Klemperer, June Lockhart, Carroll O'Connor, Viveca Lindfors, Robert Duvall, Leslie Nielsen, George Sanders, Victor Buono, John Cassavetes (!) and Robert Loggia. Earnest nonsense, with many crises on the command deck, this remains somehow more endearing than later, even camper Allen efforts like *Lost in Space* and *Land of the Giants*.

Richard Basehart Admiral Harriman Nelson • **David Hedison** Captain Lee Crane • **Robert Dowdell** Lt Cmdr Chip Morton • **Del Monroe** Kowalski • **Paul Trinka** Patterson • **Richard Bull** Doctor • **Arch Whiting** Sparks
Producer/Created by *Irwin Allen*

Voyage to the End of the Universe ★★ U

1963 Cz BW 70mins

Scripted by Pavel Juracek (who later wrote *The End of August at the Hotel Ozone*) and directed by Jindrich Polak (best known for the kidpic *Rocket to Nowhere*), this is a slow-moving variation on the "lost in space" theme. Set in the 25th century, it follows Zdenek Stepanek's space cruiser around the galaxy as it searches for a planet capable of sustaining life. Encounters with a shipwreck and a star emitting sleep-inducing radiation are the highlights of the mission, although patriotic American viewers will doubtlessly point to the triumphant (if US-tacked on) rediscovery of the Statue of Liberty. Czech dialogue dubbed into English.

Dennis Stephans [Zdenek Stepanek] Expedition Commander Vladimir Abajev • **Francis Smolen [Frantisek Smolik]** Astronomer Anthony Hopkins • **Dana Meredith [Dana Medricka]** Nina Kirova • **Irene Kova [Irena Kacirkova]** Brigit • **Rodney Lucas [Radovan Lukavsky]** MacDonald • **Otto Lack [Otto Lackovic]** Michael
Director *Jack Pollack [Jindrich Polak]*
Screenplay *Pavel Juracek, Jack Pollack [Jindrich Polak]*
Cinematographer *Jan Kalis*

Voyage to the Planet of Prehistoric Women ★

1966 US Colour 78mins

Following *Voyage to the Prehistoric Planet*, this also recycles special effects highlights from the 1962 Russian science-fiction spectacle *Planeta Burg*. A disorientating dog's dinner of a movie with new footage shot by Peter Bogdanovich, it features fifties' sex bomb Mamie Van Doren as the leader of a tribe of bikini-clad alien maidens who lie around a beach and worship a pterodactyl god, while telepathically communicating with lost Earth astronauts. None of the new scenes really match in this tortuously repackaged exploiter.

Mamie Van Doren Moana • **Mary Mark** • **Paige Lee**
Director *Derek Thomas [Peter Bogdanovich]*
Screenplay *Henry Ney*

Voyage to the Prehistoric Planet ★

1965 US Colour 80mins

Another cut-and-paste job from Roger Corman using cannibalised footage from the 1962 Russian space epic *Planeta Burg* and incorporating new material shot by director Curtis Harrington with Basil Rathbone and Faith Domergue on reused sets from his *Planet of Blood*. A spaceship crew crash-land on a planet (Venus in the Soviet picture) and relay their encounters with robot men and dinosaurs (special effects from *Planeta Burg*) to a space platform (Russian footage again) orbiting above them. As was often the case with Corman quickies of the sixties, the story behind the movie is more interesting than the movie itself.

Basil Rathbone Professor Hartman • **Faith Domergue** Marcia
Director/Screenplay *John Sebastian [Curtis Harrington]*

Voyagers! ★★★

TV 1982-1983 US Colour 20x60mins

This light-hearted time-travelling kids show, designed to be both entertaining and educational, mischievously played "what if" with history. What if the Russians and not the Americans landed on the moon first, or if Franklin Roosevelt decided on a career in movies instead of politics? Such time conundrums were solved by Voyagers, time travellers who monitor history and correct it when it goes wrong, notably Phineas Bogg (a name that paid homage to Jules Verne's *Around the World in 80 Days* character Phileas Fogg) who is aided on his adventures by an Earth boy with a thirst for history. Bogg was played by Jon-Erik Hexum, a young actor who was tragically killed by a prop gun on the set of his very next TV show. The *Voyagers* device of meeting famous people who made a mark on history was later echoed in George Lucas' TV epic series *The Young Indiana Jones Chronicles*.

Jon-Erik Hexum Phineas Bogg • **Meeno Peluce** Jeffrey Jones

HG Wells with Orson Welles

"A wave of mass hysteria seized thousands of radio listeners between 8:15 and 9:30 o'clock last night when a broadcast of a dramatization of HG Wells's fantasy, The War of the Worlds, led thousands to believe that an interplanetary conflict had started with invading Martians spreading wide death and destruction in New Jersey and New York.

The broadcast, which disrupted households, interrupted religious services, created traffic jams and clogged communications systems, was made by Orson Welles, who as the radio character, "The Shadow," used to give "the creeps" to countless child listeners. This time at least a score of adults required medical treatment for shock and hysteria." New York Times, 31 October 1938

War of the Worlds 1938

The Walking Dead ★★★

1936 US BW 66mins

Boris Karloff is framed for murder and sent to the electric chair. A mad doctor electronically revives him, however, to wreak vengeance on the gangsters responsible for his fate, in a surprisingly moving and macabre variation on the *Frankenstein* theme. Benefiting enormously from Karloff's first-rate turn as the hollow-eyed zombie with a penchant for the piano, director Michael Curtiz keeps predictability at bay with a slick style and some marvellously expressionistic lighting. A few steps down the poignancy ladder from *Frankenstein*, admittedly, but still a weird Karloff Klassic.

Boris Karloff John Ellman • **Ricardo Cortez** Nolan • **Warren Hull** Jimmy • **Robert Strange** Merritt • **Joseph King** Judge Shaw • **Edmund Gwenn** Dr Evan Beaumont • **Marguerite Churchill** Nancy • **Barton MacLane** Loder • **Henry O'Neill** Warner • **Paul Harvey** Blackstone
Director *Michael Curtiz*
Screenplay *Ewart Adamson, Peter Milne, Robert Andrews, Lillie Hayward, from a story by Ewart Adamson, Joseph Fields*

The War Game ★★★★

1965 UK BW 44mins

Such was the power of *The War Game* that the BBC, which produced it, refused to transmit Peter Watkins's film, leaving it to sit on the shelf, gathering dust and notoriety, before a cinema release in 1966. Watkins uses documentary-style techniques to create an image of England in the moments before a nuclear attack. It's a nightmarish blend of Ealing comedy, *Dad's Army* and those wartime Ministry of Information movies which told you to put a blanket on your window, crawl under a table and pray. View it in the context of 1965 when the Cold War was at its hottest and when the youth of the world awoke each day thinking they would be vaporised at any minute.

Michael Aspel Commentator • **Dick Graham** Commentator
Director *Peter Watkins, Derek Ware*
Screenplay *Peter Watkins*
Cinematographer *Peter Bartlett*

War of the Colossal Beast ★ PG

1958 US BW and Colour 68mins

The Amazing Colossal Man didn't die! He turned up in Mexico with a disfigured face and a gigantic appetite in a sequel from trash-master supremo, Bert I Gordon. The producer/director's initials are the only thing that is BIG about this fourth division science-fiction dud, though. Far funnier than the original, if that counts for anything, some prints of this colossal clunker burst into full colour during the electrifying climax. It doesn't help.

Sally Fraser Joyce Manning • **Dean Parkin [Duncan "Dean" Parkin]** Colonel Glenn Manning • **Roger Pace** Major Baird • **Russ Bender** Dr Carmichael • **Charles Stewart** Captain Harris • **George Becwar** Swanson • **Robert Hernandez** Miguel • **Rico Alaniz** Sgt Luis Murillo • **George Alexander** Army officer
Director *Bert I Gordon*
Screenplay *George Worthing Yates, from a story by Bert I Gordon*

War of the Gargantuas ★★

1970 Jap/US Colour 92mins

Intended as the sequel to *Frankenstein Conquers the World*, the American re-edited version of director Inoshiro Honda's wackily conceived continuation obscures all reference to the original only to emerge as one of the funniest monster extravaganzas ever. No point trying to make sense of the deconstructed plot – scientist Russ Tamblyn blaming himself for an epic battle between a furry brown giant monster and his evil green-hued twin which destroys Tokyo – just thrill along to the spectacular effects (the motorway destruction is particularly well done), a silly giant octopus and the night-club song *The Words Get Stuck in My Throat*.

Russ Tamblyn Dr Paul Stewart • **Kumi Mizuno** His assistant • **Kipp Hamilton** Singer • **Yu Fujiki** Army commander
Director *Inoshiro Honda*
Screenplay *Inoshiro Honda, Kaoru Mabuchi*

War of the Planets ★★

1965 It Colour 99mins

An informal prequel to *The Wild, Wild Planet*, and shot back-to-back with it using virtually the same cast, director Antonio Margheriti's alien invasion saga isn't in the same entertaining league, despite some smart flourishes and cool visual delights. Martians named the Diaphanois, composed mainly of light, attack Earth through its satellite defence system by taking over humans in watered-down *Body Snatchers*-style. Italian dialogue dubbed into English.

Tony Russel • **Franco Nero** • **Michel Lemoine** • **Carlo Giustini** • **Lisa Gastoni**
Director *Anthony M Dawson [Antonio Margheriti]*
Screenplay *Ivan Reiner, Renato Moretti*

War of the Planets ★★

1977 Jap Colour 86mins

Green-skinned Venusians attack Earthlings in the first interplanetary war and Oriental volunteers, in a spaceship looking suspiciously like *Spacecruiser Yamamoto*, speed to the stars where a cosmic battle settles the fate of the universe. Directed by Jun Fukuda as an homage to Inoshiro (*Godzilla*) Honda, this pale imitation *Star Wars* is limp entertainment from its UFO flotilla beginning to its laser-shooting Chewbacca clone ending. A Japanese language film

Kensaku Morita • **Yuke Asano** • **Ryo Ikebe** • **William Ross** • **Masaya Oki**
Director *Jun Fukuda*
Screenplay *Ryuzo Nakanishi*

War of the Satellites ★ U

1958 US BW 66mins

Within months of the first Russian Sputnik being launched into space, cult director Roger Corman had this cash-in released in cinemas. Aliens threaten the destruction of Earth unless the planet's space programme is terminated. Scientist Richard Devon's dead body is taken over by the aliens to sabotage further intergalactic explorations in Corman's excruciatingly dull, over-talkative and rambling exploiter.

Dick Miller Dave Royer • **Susan Cabot** Sybil Carrington • **Richard Devon** Dr Van Pander • **Eric Sinclair** Dr Lazar • **Michael Fox** Akad • **Robert Shayne** Hodgkiss • **Jerry Barclay** John • **Jay Sayer** Jay • **Mitzi McCall** Mitzi • **Roger Corman** Ground control
Director *Roger Corman*
Screenplay *Lawrence Louis Goldman, from the story by Irving Block, Jack Rabin*

War of the Worlds ★★★★★

Radio 1938 US 60mins

The most famous radio sci-fi broadcast of all time, though the familiar stories of a fooled populace and mass panic seem to have been wildly exaggerated (not least by Orson Welles) in the retelling. This 1938 adaptation, by writer Howard W Koch, of HG Wells's 1898 novel was broadcast as a Halloween treat. The story is relocated from the English Home Counties to New Jersey and initially tells the tale as a succession of "we interrupt this broadcast" newscasts reporting on the Martian invasion, with experts and correspondents called in to cover the events. Welles plays a Princeton professor present at the first contact with the alien cylinders, whose audio notes carry through the latter stages of the plot, as New York falls to the Martian war machines, but are brought low by earthly diseases. The first half is especially impressive, simulating a live on-air panic reminiscent of the famous radio coverage of the Hindenberg disaster, and even the stagier second act, which consists mostly of Welles talking to sound effects, retains a certain power to chill.

Orson Welles Professor Pierson • **Paul Stewart** • **Kenneth Delmar** • **William Alland** • **William Herz** • **Ray Collins** • **Howard Smith** • **Stefan Schnabel** • **Frank Readick** • **Carl Frank** • **Richard Wilson**
Director *Orson Welles*
Written by *Howard W Koch, from the novel by HG Wells*
Producer *John Houseman*

The War of the Worlds ★★★★ PG

1953 US Colour 81mins [video]

Although it never comes close to reproducing the panic generated by Orson Welles's famous 1938 radio broadcast, this is a splendid version of HG Wells's sci-fi classic. When the "meteor" that lands in southern California turns out to be the mothership of a Martian invasion, the governments of the world unleash their most potent weapons in a counterproductive attempt to stem the tide of destruction. The miraculous deliverance is clumsily staged, but it scarcely matters. Director Byron Haskin enhances the impact of the Oscar-winning special effects by ensuring that his extras convey a genuine sense of terror as civilisation collapses around them. Contains violence.

Gene Barry Dr Clayton Forrester • **Ann Robinson** Sylvia Van Buren • **Les Tremayne** General Mann • **Robert Cornthwaite** Doctor Pryor • **Sandro Giglio** Doctor Bilderbeck • **Lewis Martin** Pastor Collins • **William Phipps** Wash Perry • **Paul Birch** Alonzo Hogue • **Cedric Hardwicke** Narrator
Director *Byron Haskin*
Screenplay *Barré Lyndon, from the novel by HG Wells*
Producer *George Pal*
Cinematographer *George Barnes*

War of the Worlds ★★★

TV 1988-1990 US Colour 44x60mins [video]

An overlooked and under-rated follow-up to the 1953 movie, the *War of the Worlds* TV series continues humanity's struggle against HG Wells's Martian invaders. Now capable of assuming human form, the Martians embark on an invasion of Earth, and only a small band of freedom fighters led by famed astrophysicist Jared Martin can save the world. In its first season, the series skilfully combines the requisite thrills and chills with unusually smart plotlines, quirky performances and arresting visuals. Season two, however, focuses firmly on cyberpunk action, as Martin's team fight the Martians' colonisation attempts on a post-apocalyptic Earth. Although season two is slightly less impressive than the show's opening year, it does feature a trip back in time to the original 1953 Martian invasion, evocatively shot in black and white.

Jared Martin Dr Harrison Blackwood • **Lynda Mason Green** Dr Suzanne McCullough • **Philip Akin** Norton Drake • **Richard Chaves** Colonel Paul Ironside • **Adrian Paul** John Kincaid • **Rachel Blanchard** Debi McCullough
Created by *Greg Strangis, from the novel by HG Wells*
Executive producer *Greg Strangis*

SCI Q • SCI Q • SCI Q • SCI Q

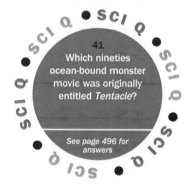

41
Which nineties ocean-bound monster movie was originally entitled *Tentacle*?

See page 496 for answers

The War of the Worlds – Next Century ★★★

1981 Pol Colour 98mins

This compelling Solidarity-era parable examines the way the Polish people had become inured to truth by decades of propaganda and censorship. Neatly inverting the events that ensued on the night of Orson Welles's legendary 1938 radio adaptation of HG Wells's Martian invasion story, director Piotr Szulkin explores the combination of submission and apathy that prevents the populace from reacting to TV journalist Roman Wilhelmi's claim to have witnessed an alien landing. A Polish language film.

Roman Wilhelmi • **Krystyna Janda** • **Mariusz Dmochowski** • **Jerzy Stuhr**
Director/Screenplay *Piotr Szulkin*
Cinematographer *Zygmunt Samosiak*

WarGames ★★★★ PG

1983 US Colour 108mins [video] DVD

Whiz kid Matthew Broderick accidentally hacks into a Pentagon computer and starts playing a game called Global Thermonuclear War, only to discover he's inadvertently pushing the world toward destruction for real. This is an inventive nail-biter that's consistently entertaining and worryingly thought-provoking, laced by director John Badham with just the right amount of humour. Great edge-of-the-seat suspense is generated as defence specialist Dabney Coleman desperately tries to avert the holocaust, while preachy sentiment is kept to a minimum. Said to be one of Ronald Reagan's favourite thrillers. Contains swearing.

Matthew Broderick David Lightman • **Dabney Coleman** John McKittrick • **John Wood** Professor Falken • **Ally Sheedy** Jennifer Mack • **Barry Corbin** General Beringer • **Juanin Clay** Pat Healy • **Dennis Lipscomb** Lyle Watson • **Kent Williams** Arthur Cabot • **Joe Dorsey** Colonel Conley • **Irving Metzman** Richter • **Michael Ensign** Beringer's aide • **William Bogert** Mr Lightman • **Susan Davis** Mrs Lightman • **James Tolkan** Wigan
Director *John Badham*
Screenplay *Lawrence Lasker, Walter F Parkes*

Warlords of Atlantis ★★★ PG

1978 UK Colour 92mins [video]

It may be small beer compared with the monster movies of today's computer age, but this is still a decent romp from director Kevin Connor, and it's far better paced than *The Lost World: Jurassic Park*. Doug McClure is the clean-cut Hollywood hero (who's about as Victorian as skateboards) who discovers the fabled city (ruled, would you believe, by Cyd Charisse and Daniel Massey) and its monstrous menagerie of sundry sea beasties – including a giant octopus. The sets and the creatures are as wobbly as the script and the performances, but that's just part of the charm of this cheesy romp.

Doug McClure Greg Collinson • **Peter Gilmore** Charles Aitken • **Shane Rimmer** Captain Daniels • **Lea Brodie** Delphine Briggs • **Michael Gothard** Atmir • **Hal Galili** Grogan • **John Ratzenberger** Fenn • **Derry Power** Jacko • **Donald Bisset** Professor Aitken • **Ashley Knight** Sandy • **Robert Brown** Captain Briggs • **Cyd Charisse** Atsil • **Daniel Massey** Atraxon
Director *Kevin Connor*
Screenplay *Brian Hayles*

Warning Sign ★★★ 15

1985 US Colour 94mins [video]

Although derivative of a dozen other mind-melt movies, from *The China Syndrome* to *The Andromeda Strain*, Hal Barwood's thriller is engrossing action all the way with its bacterial twists and brain-damaged turns. The excellent acting lifts it above the norm, and mouth-foaming maniac Richard Dysart delivers some stupidly inspired dialogue about rage being beautiful. But you'll be sorry when the curtain finally falls on this exciting, high-tech tale.

Sam Waterston Cal Morse • **Kathleen Quinlan** Joanie Morse • **Yaphet Kotto** Major Connolly • **Jeffrey DeMunn** Dan Fairchild • **Richard Dysart** Dr Nielsen •
Director *Hal Barwood*
Screenplay *Hal Barwood, Matthew Robbins*

Warrior of the Lost World ★★ 18

1983 It Colour 86mins

Robert Ginty was one of the first true video stars, but this loopy Italian-made post-apocalyptic thriller isn't one of his best. He plays a master warrior who comes to the aid of a rebels caught up in a vicious battle against despotic rulers led by Donald Pleasence (hamming it up, unsurprisingly, for all its worth). *Star Trek* fans will be on the look out for Persis Khambatta, who this time gets to keep her head of hair.

Robert Ginty Warrior • **Persis Khambatta** Nastasia • **Donald Pleasence** Prosser • **Fred Williamson** Henchman • **Harrison Muller** Prof McWayne
Director/Screenplay *David Worth*

The Wasp Woman ★★

1959 US BW 62mins

Cosmetics boss Susan Cabot uses wasp enzymes for a rejuvenation formula and turns into a blood-lusting bug-eyed monster in cult director Roger Corman's ironic rip-off of *The Fly*. For a film of barely an hour, it's pretty slow, and more ridiculous than frightening. However, Cabot's coolly professional performance makes up for the cheapness of the production (the first to be made by Corman's own company, Filmgroup) and helps paper over the weak scripting by charactor actor Leo Gordon.

Susan Cabot Janice Starlin • **Fred Eisley [Anthony Eisley]** Bill Lane • **Barboura Morris** Mary Dennison • **Michael Marks** Dr Eric Zinthrop • **William Roerick** Arthur Cooper • **Frank Gerstle** Hellman • **Bruno Ve Sota** Night watchman
Director *Roger Corman*
Screenplay *Leo Gordon*
Producer *Roger Corman*

The Watcher in the Woods ★★★

1982 US/UK Colour 83mins

Disney attempted to shake its kiddie popcorn image with this tale of a composer's family moving into a mysterious cottage owned by sinister Bette Davis. But the psychic alien time-warp plot is too silly for adults and not daft enough to make it a proper children's treat. Director John Hough knows how to use atmosphere, though, and sustains it quite well, despite ex-ice skater Lynn-Holly Johnson's bland central performance. However, his decision to go the soft gothic horror route and then suddenly leave the horror out is a mistake, and the movie never recovers. Disney in fact changed the climax after disastrous test screening. Bette Davis completists won't want to miss it, though.

Bette Davis Mrs Aylwood • **Carroll Baker** Helen Curtis • **David McCallum** Paul Curtis • **Lynn-Holly Johnson** Jan Curtis • **Kyle Richards** Ellie Curtis • **Ian Bannen** John Keller • **Richard Pasco** Tom Colley • **Frances Cuka** Mary Fleming • **Benedict Taylor** Mike Fleming • **Eleanor Summerfield** Mrs Thayer • **Georgina Hale** Young Mrs Aylwood • **Katherine Levy** Karen Aylwood
Director *John Hough, Vincent McEveety*
Screenplay *Brian Clemens, Harry Spalding, Rosemary Anne Sisson, from the novel by Florence Engel Randall*

Watchers ★ 18

1988 Can Colour 86mins

Horror novelist Dean R Koontz was extremely unhappy with this adaptation of his work, though he had plenty of warning with bargain-basement producers Roger Corman and Damian Lee attaching themselves to the project. All hope of redemption disappeared with Corey Haim cast as the teen hero who finds an extremely intelligent dog, not knowing that it is the result of a government experiment that also produced a pursuing Sasquatch-like animal (or is it a guy in a gorilla suit?). Once again Michael Ironside, playing the usual government agent who comes in to try to cover things up, manages to give a stereotyped and poorly written character some menace and personality. Dark, murky and unexciting.

Corey Haim Travis • **Barbara Williams** Nora • **Michael Ironside** Lem • **Lala Sloatman** Tracey • **Duncan Fraser** Sheriff Gaines
Director *Jon Hess*
Screenplay *Bill Freed, Damian Lee, from the novel by Dean R Koontz*

Waterworld ★★★★ 12

1995 US Colour 129mins DVD

Declared dead in the water before it had even been completed owing to horrendous escalating costs, nightmare production problems and clashing egos, *Waterworld* emerged from the wreckage of rumour and speculation as a spectacular and thrilling sci-fi fantasy. In the far future, the polar icecaps have melted, covering the entire planet in water and making dirt the most valuable commodity on Earth. The survivors of the human race live on floating man-made islands – atolls – which are continually being raided by the marauding Smokers under the evil leadership of Dennis Hopper. Only the enigmatic loner Kevin Costner offers a ray of hope to Jeanne Tripplehorn and Tina Majorino, the latest homeless victims of a Smoker sea raid, as he battles the bandits and continues his never-ending search to find the one piece of mythical Dryland. Offering plenty of comic-book heroics and spectacular stunts, director Kevin Reynolds's lavish *Mad Max* on jet-skis often gives new meaning to the term roller-coaster ride. Contains violence and swearing.

Kevin Costner Mariner • **Dennis Hopper** Deacon • **Jeanne Tripplehorn** Helen • **Tina Majorino** Enola • **Michael Jeter** Gregor • **Gerard Murphy** Nord • **RD Call** Enforcer • **Chaim Jeraffi** First drifter • **Kim Coates** Second drifter • **John Fleck** Doctor • **Robert Joy** Ledger guy
Director *Kevin Reynolds*
Screenplay *Peter Rader, David Twohy, Joss Whedon*

SFacts

Commonly regarded as one of the great movie flops, *Waterworld* has in fact made an estimated $255 million at the world box office, a decent enough return on its estimated $175 million outlay

Watt on Earth ★★

TV 1991-1992 UK Colour 24x15mins

This twice-weekly children's series revisits the clichéd territory of alien-visiting-Earth-befriended-by-resourceful-young-fellow. The alien in question, played by Garth Napier-Jones, is 300 years old, but behaves like a child of seven. His long-suffering friend (Tom Brodie) must constantly sort out all the trouble Watt creates. The touch of humour ensured it a modest popularity, however, and it ran for two seasons.

Tom Brodie Sean • **Garth Napier-Jones** Watt • **Jessica Simpson** Zoe
Written by *Pip Baker, Jane Baker*
Producer *Angela Beeching*

Wavelength ★★ 15

1983 US Colour 83mins

The title comes from psychic Cherie Currie being able to mentally "hear" the cries of aliens who were shot down and then imprisoned by the government in a secret desert facility. She enlists the aid of singer Robert Carradine and prospector Keenan Wynn to help her break the visitors out before they're put under the knife. The three actors are very likeable in their roles, and the excellently creepy score by Tangerine Dream generates a decent amount of atmosphere, but it is still somewhat slow.

Robert Carradine Bobby Sinclaire • **Cherie Currie** Iris Longacre • **Keenan Wynn** Dan • **Cal Bowman** General Milton Ward • **James Hess** Colonel James MacGruder
Director/Screenplay *Mike Gray*

Waxwork II: Lost in Time ★★

1992 US Colour and BW 104 mins

A dull and dumber sequel, with a sci-fi spin, reuniting the star and director of an original which wasn't all that great. This picks up directly where the first one left off with Zach Galligan surviving the apocalyptic end of the deadly waxwork museum only to be propelled into various time periods – all recognizable horror settings – to defeat evil. This ploy enables Anthony Hickox to once again prove his uninspired talent for spoofing various genre movies, this time ranging from *Nosferatu* to *The Haunting*. An eclectic cast includes cameos from Drew Barrymore and *Evil Dead*'s Bruce Campbell. Certainly off the wall and enjoyable for horror buffs if they catch it in the right mood.

Zach Galligan Mark Loftmore • **Sophie Ward** Eleanore Pratt • **Patrick Macnee** Sir Wilfred • **Alexander Godunov** Scarabus • **Martin Kemp** Baron Frankenstein • **Monika Schnarre** Sarah • **Bruce Campbell** John Wright • **David Carradine** Beggar • **Marina Sirtis** Gloria • **John Ireland** King Arthur • **Drew Barrymore** Vampire victim
Director/Screenplay *Anthony Hickox*

Way Out ★★★

TV 1961 US BW

A 14-episode TV anthology show, hosted by Roald Dahl, memorable for its gruesome horror comic punchlines, often involving make-up by Dick Smith: in *Soft Focus*, photographer Barry Morse discovers a chemical retouching agent that when applied to photographs affects the subject's real appearance and finally spills some over his own self-portrait, wiping half his face to white nothingness. The series mixed sci-fi (*William and Mary*, a living brain story), suspense, supernatural horror and dark satire.

Roald Dahl Host
Executive producer *David Susskind*

Way... Way Out ★★

1966 US Colour 104mins

When Russian astronomer Anita Ekberg claims she was attacked by a US astronaut on a jointly run moonbase, US Lunar Division chief Robert Morley decrees that in future all US moonbase personnel will be married couples. Consequently Jerry Lewis, next in line to staff the moonbase, hastily has to arrange a wedding to fellow worker Connie Stevens in order to fulfil his mission. This was yet another uncomfortable vehicle for Lewis who was finding it increasingly difficult to find suitable material and collaborators. Thankfully, old pros Morley and Brian Keith provide some amusing substance to the lunatic proceedings.

Jerry Lewis Peter • **Connie Stevens** Eileen • **Robert Morley** Quonset • **Dennis Weaver** Hoffman • **Howard Morris** Schmidlap • **Brian Keith** General Hallenby • **Dick Shawn** Igor • **Anita Ekberg** Anna
Director *Gordon Douglas*
Screenplay *William Bowers, Laslo Vadnay*
Cinematographer *William H Clothier [William Clothier]* • ***Music*** *Lalo Schifrin*

Webmaster ★★

1998 Den Colour 102mins

The race-against-time scenario is almost as old as cinema itself. However, this Danish thriller borrows freely from a film closer to its own genesis, *Johnny Mnemonic*. Lars Bom stars as the computer geek whose world revolves around his palm pilot and a daily cuppa until he's detailed to discover who's been hacking into a web provider's database. And just to focus his mind, he is fitted with a pacemaker that will detonate his heart unless he fulfils his mission within 35 hours. Unfortunately, this contrived sense of urgency only confirms the picture's resemblance to a level one computer game. Danish dialogue dubbed into English.

Lars Bom JB • **Puk Scharbau** Miauv • **Jorgen Kiil** Stoiss • **Karin Rorbeck** Barbie • **Mads Parsum** Dot • **Dorthe Westh Lehrmann** Darling
Director/Screenplay *Thomas Borch Nielsen*

Wedlock ★ 18

1991 US Colour 98mins [video]

Rutger Hauer's presence in this silly sci-fi excursion is understandable – he's been hard up for a decent job for years. But why is Mimi Rogers slumming as a prisoner in a high-tech jail? The inmates wear explosive collars, designed to detonate if ever two matching ones get too far from each other. This supposedly keeps the convicts from escaping, since they don't know who their "deadlock" partner is. But guess which two movie stars figure it out? Why the warden doesn't just set the collars to explode when cons wander too far from the prison itself is a mystery. Contains violence and swearing.

Rutger Hauer Frank Warren • **Mimi Rogers** Tracy Riggs • **Joan Chen** Noelle • **James Remar** Sam • **Stephen Tobolowsky** Warden Holliday
Director *Lewis Teague*
Screenplay *Broderick Miller*

Weird Science ★★ 15

1985 US Colour 89mins [video]

The worst of John Hughes's early comedies, but still a cut above most teen fodder of the time. Hughes regular Anthony Michael Hall and Ilan Mitchell-Smith are the sex-obsessed high-tech anoraks who summon up the computer-generated woman of their dreams (Kelly LeBrock). Hughes remains a sharp observer of teenage woes but this time around there is a crassness to much of the humour and far too much leering. The best performance comes from *Twister's* Bill Paxton as Mitchell-Smith's fascist brother, and look out, too, for an early role for Robert Downey Jr. Contains swearing and brief nudity.

Anthony Michael Hall Gary • **Ilan Mitchell-Smith** Wyatt • **Kelly LeBrock** Lisa • **Bill Paxton** Chet • **Suzanne Snyder** Deb • **Judie Aronson** Hilly • **Robert Downey Jr** Ian • **Robert Rusler** Max • **Vernon Wells** Lord General • **Britt Leach** Al • **Barbara Lang** Lucy • **Ivor Barry** Henry • **Anne Bernadette Coyle** Carmen
Director/Screenplay *John Hughes*

Weird Science ★★★

TV 1994-1998 US Colour 88x30mins

John Hughes's 1985 big-screen sci-fi comedy gets the sitcom treatment and is transformed into a high-tech, teen-orientated *I Dream of Jeannie*. The series follows the adventures of two nerdy teenagers, Michael Manasseri and John Mallory Asher, and their computer-created dream woman, Vanessa Angel, who is able to grant their wishes for a limited period of time. While the trio's weekly exploits prove to be as crass and silly as you'd expect, they're also surprisingly funny, and even demonstrate the occasional flash of inventive brilliance in the scripting department. The show is given a further boost by of its divine star, Vanessa Angel, who conjures up a suitably sexy, smart and irresistible central performance.

Michael Manasseri Wyatt Donnelly • **John**

Mallory Asher Gary Wallace • **Lee Tergesen** Chett Donnelly • **Vanessa Angel** Lisa
Executive producer *John Landis, Leslie Belzberg*

Welcome to Blood City ★★ 15

1977 UK/Can Colour 91mins

A dull Anglo-Canadian production, listlessly directed by Peter Sasdy and owing more than just a little to *Westworld*, as Samantha Eggar monitors the progress of kidnapped Keir Dullea and his fight for survival against "immortal" sheriff Jack Palance in a Wild West town. The film is so badly constructed that caring about Dullea's plight is the last thing on an audience's mind – escape is a primary concern, and not just from Blood City! Talented editor Keith Palmer and composer Roy Budd have little chance to shine. For die-hard Palance fans only.

Jack Palance Frendlander • **Keir Dullea** Lewis • **Samantha Eggar** Katherine • **Barry Morse** Supervisor • **Hollis McLaren** Martine • **Chris Wiggins** Gellor • **Henry Ramer** Chumley • **Allan Royale** Peter • **John Evans** Lyle • **Ken James** Flint • **Larry Reynolds** Bates
Director *Peter Sasdy*
Screenplay *Stephen Schneck, Michael Winder*

Welcome to Paradox ★★★

TV 1998 US Colour 13x60mins

A thoughtful and provoking anthology series? Couldn't last, and it didn't. *Welcome to Paradise* had as its starting point Betaville, a domed city of the near future, where peace and prosperity rule, and disease and crime are a thing of the past, all thanks to technology. The 13 stories may have been derivative, but were well presented and examined mankind's struggle to dominate the technology it has created, from the *Stepford Wives*-inspired tale of a biologically enhanced robot (with Alice Krige) to life in a futuristic "humane" prison, starring Ice-T.

Michael Philip Host
Executive producer *Jeremy Lipp*

Welcome to Planet Earth ★★ 15

1996 US Colour 91mins

It's too cheap for its own good, but this just about passes muster, thanks to a cheerful line in black humour and the always watchable George Wendt, familiar to TV viewers as Norm from *Cheers*. Wendt and former *Colbys* soap icon Shanna Reed play a pair of jolly alien tourists whose idea of a good time is a madcap murder spree among lowlife inhabitants of a squalid neighbourhood. The leads make the most of the few good lines that they are fed but the scripting and direction are haphazard. It was executive produced by Roger Corman, who has done this kind of thing much more effectively elsewhere.

George Wendt Charlie • **Shanna Reed** Rhonda • **Christopher M Brown** Joseph Collins • **Anastasia Sakelaris** Daphne • **Stephen Burrows** Detective Watts • **Dan Martin** Lieutenant Barnes
Director *Lev L Spiro*
Screenplay *Michael James MacDonald*

Welcome II the Terrordome ★★ 18

1994 UK Colour 89mins

A highly controversial film on its release when director Ngozi Onwurah was thought by some to be making a rallying cry for black separatism. This semi-futuristic thriller certainly has more than its fair share of heavy-handed messages to the detriment of any discernible entertainment value. Its starting point, the hounding into the sea of black slaves in 17th-century North Carolina, is powerfully drawn and provides a thumpingly dramatic opening which Onwurah utterly fails to build on. In truth, it's a bit of a yawn. Contains violence.

Suzette Llewellyn Angela McBride/African woman • **Saffron Burrows** Jodie • **Felix Joseph** Black Rad/African leader • **Valentine Nonyela** Spike/African man • **Ben Wynter** Hector/African boy • **Sian Martin** Chrisele/African woman • **Jason Traynor** Jason/Assistant overseer
Director/Screenplay *Ngozi Onwurah*

We're Back! A Dinosaur's Story ★★★ U

1993 US Colour 67mins

Dinosaurs have represented box-office gold for Steven Spielberg over the years, but not in this case. He serves as executive producer on this animated tale that wasn't widely shown in the UK – a shame since it's a jolly enough affair, well designed and featuring a literate script from Oscar-winning writer John Patrick Shanley. The story revolves around four dinosaurs who travel through time to New York and get mixed up in a series of adventures. Children will adore the dino-antics while adults will recognise some familiar voices.

John Goodman Rex • **Blaze Berdahl** Buster • **Rhea Perlman** Mother Bird • **Jay Leno** Vorb • **Rene Levant** Woo • **Felicity Kendal** Elsa • **Charles Fleischer** Dweeb • **Walter Cronkite** Captain Neweyes • **Joe Shea** Louie • **Julia Child** Doctor Bleeb • **Martin Short** Stubbs, the Clown
Director *Dick Zondag, Ralph Zondag, Phil Nibbelink, Simon Wells*
Screenplay *John Patrick Shanley, from the book "We're Back" by Hudson Talbott*

The Werewolf ★★

1956 US BW 79mins

Scientists S John Launer and George Lynn experiment on tormented family man Steven Ritch to find a cure for radiation poisoning and turn him into a werewolf in the process. A competent and timely marriage of horror with science fiction just as the latter form was going out of favour in the fifties. Clever trick photography and Ritch's sympathetic performance take this up a few notches from a routine quickie.

Steven Ritch Duncan Masch/The Werewolf • **Don Megowan** Jack Haines • **Joyce Holden** Amy Standish • **Eleanore Tanin** Helen Marsh • **Harry Lauter** Clovey • **Ken Christy** Dr Gilchrist • **S John Launer** Dr Emery Forrest • **George Lynn** Dr Morgan Chambers
Director *Fred F Sears*
Screenplay *Robert E Kent, James B Gordon*

Wes Craven's Mind Ripper ★★ 18

1995 US Colour 91mins

Everyone loves Wes Craven again following the success of *Scream* and its sequels, but this was from the period when his pictures tended to reside on the six-pack shelf in video stores. He can't take all the blame here, as he only co-executive produced this mutant fifties-style B-movie, which was directed with a refreshing disregard for style or cohesion by Joe Gayton. Lance Henriksen mugs valiantly as he investigates a commotion in the desert, but he's in more danger from the risible dialogue than from the brain-slurping super-soldier he's been ordered to wipe out. Strictly for late-night laughter fans. Contains swearing and violence.

Lance Henriksen James Stockton • **Claire Stansfield** Joanne • **Natasha Gregson Wagner** Wendy
Director *Joe Gayton*
Screenplay *Jonathan Craven, Phil Mittleman*

Westworld ★★★★ 15

1973 US Colour 85mins

The seeds of *Jurassic Park* and its sequel *The Lost World* can easily be recognised in writer/director Michael Crichton's futuristic suspense thriller about a holiday resort where people go to safely live out

Gun-smokin': Yul Brynner is the gunslinger gone haywire in Michael Crichton's cult classic, *Westworld*

their fantasies. But Richard Benjamin and James Brolin's dream cowboy vacation turns into a nightmare when the android population malfunctions and robot gunslinger Yul Brynner pursues them relentlessly. A fun scare flick that puts its clever gimmicks to consistently imaginative and riveting use, with the inspired casting of chilling Brynner, good special effects and an incisive message about the dark side of male fantasies adding extra potent resonance. Contains violence and swearing.

Yul Brynner Gunslinger • **Richard Benjamin** Peter Martin • **James Brolin** John Blane • **Norman Bartold** Medieval knight • **Alan Oppenheimer** Chief supervisor • **Victoria Shaw** Medieval queen • **Dick Van Patten** Banker • **Linda Scott** Arlette • **Steve Franken** Technician • **Michael Mikler** Black knight • **Terry Wilson** Sheriff • **Majel Barrett** Miss Carrie
Director/Screenplay *Michael Crichton*

What Planet Are You From? ★★ 15

2000 US Colour 100mins

When is Greg Kinnear going to tire of playing smarmy love rats? He's at it again in Gary Shandling's hugely disappointing big screen debut, but at least he provides a welcome distraction from the film's only joke – a humming penis. Clearly uneasy with Shandling's screenplay, director Mike Nichols resorts to stuffing the action with cameos from the likes of Ben Kingsley, Linda Fiorentino and John Goodman. But there's just no escaping Shandling's timid alien and his bid to seduce recovering alcoholic Annette Bening in order to repopulate his planet. Crude, crass and utterly devoid of Nichols's usually assured comic touch. Contains some swearing and sex scenes.

Garry Shandling Harold Anderson • **Annette Bening** Susan • **Greg Kinnear** Perry Gordon • **Ben Kingsley** Graydon • **Linda Fiorentino** Helen Gordon • **John Goodman** Roland Jones • **Richard Jenkins** Don Fisk • **Caroline Aaron** Nadine • **Judy Greer** Rebecca
Director *Mike Nichols*
Screenplay *Garry Shandling, Michael Leeson, Ed Solomon, Peter Tolan, from a story by Garry Shandling*

When Time Expires ★★

1997 US Colour 95mins

Why has disgraced alien troubleshooter Richard Grieco been sent back in time to feed a parking meter in a small Nevada town? The answer to that question pits him and his former partner Mark Hamill against a team of sinister assassins determined to stop them fulfilling their puzzling mission. Initially intriguing before becoming increasingly daft, the ideas behind this shaky TV movie were used to far better effect in *Back to the Future* and *The Terminator*. This relies too heavily on Grieco's charisma, while the cavalier treatment of time-travel rules is annoying. However, *Trancers* star Tim Thomerson makes a good show as the baddie. Contains violence, swearing and nudity.

Richard Grieco Travis Beck • **Cynthia Geary** June Kelly • **Mark Hamill** Bill Thermot • **Tim Thomerson** Rifkin Koss • **Ron Masak** TV evangelist • **Pat Corley** TV car salesman • **Chad Everett** Walter Kelly
Director/Screenplay *David Bourla*

When Worlds Collide ★★★ U

1951 US Colour 78mins

From *War of the Worlds* producer George Pal, this paranoid parable about earth's imminent collision with a runaway planet – the only hope of survival being a Noah's Ark expedition to a satellite moon – is a prime example of fifties science-fiction. Compensating for the bland script and generally uninspired cast are the Oscar-winning special effects – especially the destruction of New York – and Rudolph Maté's arresting direction, which exploits the "end of the world" concept to the maximum.

Richard Derr David Randall • **Barbara Rush** Joyce Hendron • **Larry Keating** Dr Cole Hendron • **Peter Hanson** Dr Tony Drake • **John Hoyt** Sydney Stanton • **Stephen Chase** Dean Frye • **Judith Ames** Julie Cummings
Director *Rudolph Maté*
Screenplay *Sydney Boehm, Philip Wylie, from the novel by Edwin Balmer*
Cinematographer *John F Seitz, W Howard Greene*

Where Time Began ★

1977 Sp Colour 90mins

An atrocious Spanish version of Jules Verne's classic novel *Journey to the Centre of the Earth* from Hispanic hack director Juan Piquer Simon of *Supersonic Man* infamy. Kenneth More looks bored and out of place as the expedition leader exploring the bowels of the earth who fights off the usual array of photographically blown-up turtles, men in ape suits and rubber dinosaurs. Sluggish pacing, uninspired direction and deadly dull dialogue make this journey a dreary descent all round.

Kenneth More Prof Lindenbrock • **Pep Munne** Axel • **Ivonne Sentis** Glauben • **Frank Brana** Hans • **Jack Taylor** Olsen • **Lone Fleming** Molly • **Jose-Maria Caffarel** Prof Fridleson • **Emiliano Redondo** Professor Kristoff
Director *Juan Piquer [Juan Piquer Simon]*
Screenplay *Juan Piquer [Juan Piquer Simon], Carlos Puerto, from the novel "Journey to the Centre of the Earth" by Jules Verne*

The Whip Hand ★★★

1951 US BW 82mins

This taut thriller may lack star names, but it is masterfully directed and designed by William Cameron Menzies. Elliott Reid plays the photojournalist on vacation in Wisconsin who stumbles on a village of unfriendly inhabitants, a lake where the fish have vanished, and a mysterious, heavily guarded lodge. The original ending involved Adolf Hitler plotting a comeback (having escaped from his Berlin bunker at the end of the Second World War), but RKO studio boss Howard Hughes, who was virulently anti-communist, opted for a Red threat instead. It is a testament to the skill of Menzies that the film still works despite the disruption of extensive reshooting.

Elliott Reid Matt Corbin • **Raymond Burr** Steve Loomis • **Carla Balenda** Janet Koller • **Edgar Barrier** Dr Edward Koller • **Otto Waldis** Dr Bucholtz • **Michael Steele** Chick • **Lurene Tuttle** Molly Loomis
Director *William Cameron Menzies*
Screenplay *George Bricker, Frank L Moss, from a story by Roy Hamilton*

White Dwarf ★★

1995 US Colour 91mins

Executive produced by Francis Ford Coppola, this futuristic fantasy was a series pilot that failed to lead to further episodes. In the year 3040, a young New York doctor (Neal McDonough) is sent to a war-torn planet circling a white-dwarf star to complete a six-month residency. There he finds a world divided into warring hemispheres, one of perpetual darkness and the other in constant daylight, and gets caught up in quelling sinister forces. Though well acted with stylish special effects, this sci-fi TV film is marred by a murky, slow-moving style.

Paul Winfield Dr Akada • **CCH Pounder** Nurse Shabana • **Neal McDonough** Dr Driscoll Rampart • **Ele Keats** Princess Ariel • **Joey Andrews** Never • **Tara Graham** XaXa • **Beverley Mitchell** XuXu • **Roy Brocksmith** Guv'ner Twist
Director *Peter Markle*
Screenplay *Bruce Wagner*
Executive producer *Francis Ford Coppola*

Who? ★★

1974 UK/W Ger Colour 93mins

An intriguing but not wholly successful sci-fi thriller that attempts to probe somewhat seriously into the nature of identity. The narrative isn't helped by being told in flashback, and Elliott Gould is perhaps a little too laid-back in the lead. There is a stunning performance, however, from third-billed actor Joseph Bova as the scientist Martino, whose face has been restructured following an alleged car crash in Russia, and he alone makes this curious mix of sci-fi and spy drama worth watching. Fans of Trevor Howard should note he only appears in the flashback sequences, and movie buffs ought to be aware that the film's producer Barry Levinson was British-based, and not the distinguished American director of the same name. Contains some swearing and sex scenes.

Elliott Gould Rogers • **Trevor Howard** Azarin • **Joseph Bova** Martino • **Ed Grover** Finchley • **John Lehne** Haller • **James Noble** Deptford • **Lyndon Brook** Barrister • **Michael Lombard** Besser • **Kay Tornborg** Edith • **Joy Garrett** Barbara • **John Stewart** Heywood • **Bruce Boa** Miller
Director *Jack Gold*
Screenplay *John Gould, from the novel by Algis Budrys*

Who Is Julia? ★★ PG

1986 US Colour 90mins [video]

Mare Winningham is stuck in this implausible melodrama as a model who is fatally injured as she is rescuing a child whose mother collapses and dies at the scene. Lucky for all concerned, doctors just "happen" to be working on a remarkable new brain transplant procedure, so our plucky heroine's grey matter is put into the body of the dead mother. Both husbands must struggle with this most unexpected and confusing predicament as everyone walks around asking the burning question, "Who is Julia?" This muddled TV movie is over-plotted and far-fetched; the most you can say is it poses some provocative questions about medical experimentation.

Mare Winningham Mary Frances Beaudine/julia • **Jameson Parker** Don North • **Jeffrey DeMunn** Dr Matt Matthews • **Jonathan Banks** Jack Beaudine • **Bert Remsen** Joseph Dineen • **Mason Adams** Dr Gordon • **James Handy** Greenmeyer • **Philip Baker Hall** Dean May • **Tracy Brooks Swope** Loni • **Judy Ledford** Julia North
Director *Walter Grauman*
Screenplay *James S Sadwith from the novel by Barbara S Harris*

Who Killed Jessie? ★★★★

1965 Cz BW 80mins

Writer/directors Vaclav Vorlicek and Milos Makourek produced some of the zaniest Czech comedies of the Communist era, with *Sir, You Are a Widower* (1971) and *A Nice Plate of Spinach* (1976) also being rooted in science-fiction. There's a comic-book feel to this inventive tale, as scientist Dana Medricka tries out her dream pacifier on husband Jiri Sovak, only to let loose the cartoonish characters from his infantile imaginings – the voluptous Olga Shoberova (who would headline Hammer's *The Vengeance of She* under the alias Olinka Berova), cowboy Karel Effa and pompous superhero, Juraj Visny. Fast, fanciful and very funny. A Czech language film.

Jiri Sovak Professor • **Dana Medricka** Wife • **Olga Schoberova** Jessie • **Karel Effa** Gunman • **Juraj Visny** Superman
Director *Vaclav Vorlicek*
Screenplay *Milos Makourek*

Wicked City ★★★ 18

1992 Jap Colour 80mins [video]

This Japanese animated adaptation of Hideyuki Kikuchi's comic book is coherent enough to pass the typical hurdle of crunching down a *manga* story to 80 minutes. Some details remain murky, but they're almost forgotten because of the eye-catching images of the bizarre and grotesque (violent, and especially sexual) that are constantly paraded. The story concerns Earth's centuries-old relationship with alternate universe the "Black World" and the renewal of a peace treaty. Two agents (one from each world) are assigned to guard a key negotiator from warmongering Black World residents. It's never dull, though the extreme violence and sexual material may be too much for even the most jaded of viewers.

Director *Yoshiaki Kawajiri, Carl Macek*
Screenplay *Kiseo Choo, from his story, from a comic book by Hideyuki Kikuchi*

Wild Palms ★★★★ 15

TV 1993 US Colour 300mins [video]

Wild by name and extremely wild by nature, film director-turned-TV producer Oliver Stone's first small screen offering is a five-hour virtual reality soap opera/thriller with a *Twin Peaks*-style twist. James Belushi stars as Harry Wyckoff, a newly-hired executive of a TV network which is developing revolutionary three-dimensional and "touchable" images for its broadcasts. As the epic story unfolds, Wyckoff becomes embroiled in a deadly conspiracy involving the network's power-mad, immorality-craving owner, Senator Anton Kreutzer (Robert Loggia). Based on Bruce Wagner's comic strip, Harry's mind-bending and frequently hard-to-grasp struggle for survival makes for gripping, intoxicating and disturbingly believable viewing. Belushi is an extremely sympathetic everyman and heads a generally strong cast, although Angie Dickinson's OTT turn is badly misjudged.

James Belushi Harry Wyckoff • **Dana Delany** Grace Wyckoff • **Robert Loggia** Senator Anton Kreutzer • **Kim Cattrall** Paige Katz • **Angie Dickinson** Josie Ito • **Ben Savage** Coty Wyckoff • **Ernie Hudson** Tommy Laszlo • **Bebe Neuwirth** Tabba Schwartzkopf • **Nick Mancuso** Tully Woiwode • **David Warner** Eli Levitt
Director *Peter Hewitt, Keith Gordon, Kathryn Bigelow, Phil Joanou*
Written by *Bruce Wagner, from his comic strip in "Details" magazine*
Executive producer *Oliver Stone, Bruce Wagner*

The Wild, Wild Planet ★★★

1965 It Colour 92mins

Shot back-to-back with *War of the Planets*, this cops-and-robbers-in-outer-space epic from cult Italian journeyman director Antonio Margheriti is a dazzling cocktail of groovy sixties sci-fi, kitschy psychedelia and outrageous special effects. In the 21st century insane scientist Massimo Serato fabricates female androids in order to kidnap VIP space officials, who are miniaturised and transported in special attaché cases. Commander Tony Russel pinpoints the planetoid Delphos, where Serato is experimenting to populate the Earth with perfect specimens. Humans with cat's eyes, four-armed mutants, karate-chopping girls in flimsy chiffon nighties – the wacky zaniness never ends in this wonderfully outlandish romp that *Austin Powers* fans will adore. Italian dialogue dubbed into English.

Tony Russel Cmdr Mike Halstead • **Lisa Gastoni** Connie Gomez • **Massimo Serato** Nels Nurmi • **Franco Nero** Jake • **Charles Justin [Carlo Giustini]** Ken • **Enzo Fiermonte** General
Director *Anthony Dawson [Antonio Margheriti]*
Screenplay *Ivan Reiner, Renato Moretti*
Cinematographer *Richard Pallton [Riccardo Pallottini]*

The Wild Wild West ★★★

TV 1965-69 US BW/Colour 104x60mins

Though its more fantastical episodes are the best-remembered, especially those featuring Michael Dunn as insane dwarf scientist Dr Miguelito Loveless, *The Wild Wild West* was primarily a mix of western and secret service ideas. Robert Conrad, a martial artist in tight toreador pants, and sidekick Ross Martin, a master of disguise, work for President Grant in the (Wild Wild) West, tackling a variety of claim-jumping land-grabbers, would-be emperors and crooked Indian agents fomenting trouble on the Reservation. However, as the show progressed more extreme Jules Verne elements crept in and the bad guys became more flamboyant on the model of the *Batman* series (guest villains included Boris Karloff and Victor Buono). In among the more mundane cases, Conrad and Martin tackled evil doppelgangers, a *Terminator*-style cyborg, bogus alien visitors, time travel and zombies. Two indifferent reunion TV movies – *The Wild Wild West Revisited* (1979), *More Wild Wild West* (1980) – followed, and the concept was dusted off for a spectacular but dull 1999 blockbuster film with Will Smith and Kevin Kline.

Robert Conrad James T West • **Ross Martin** Artemus Gordon • **James Gregory** Ulysses S Grant • **Charles Aidman** Jeremy Pike • **Henry Sharp** Story editor • **Michael Dunn** Dr Miguelito Loveless

Created by *Michael Garrison*

Producer *Fred Freiberger, Bruce Lansbury, John Mantley, Collier Young, Michael Garrison*

The Windows of Time ★★

1969 Hun BW 85mins

Thirty years after he made his first film and almost half-a-century after Hungary's only other venture into science-fiction (Istvan Lazar's *The Mind-Detecting Ray*, 1918), Tamas Fejer explored post-apocalyptic guilt in this Cold War morality tale. Fejer fails to inject any pace into the proceedings; indeed, the decision to cast stars of different nationalities (Polish, Bulgarian, Hungarian, German and Russian) as the quintet who awake from hibernation to confront their culpability for the holocaust that destroyed civilisation is much more imaginative than the leaden screenplay. Miklos Herczenik's photography does warrant mention, however. A Hungarian language film.

Beata Tyszkiewicz Eva • **Ivan Andonov** Avram • **Miklos Gabor** Sini • **Heidemarie Wenzel** Beryl • **Krystyna Mikolajewska** Maguy

Director *Tamas Fejer*

Screenplay *Peter Kuczka*

Cinematographer *Miklos Herczenik*

Wing Commander ★★ PG

1999 US Colour 100mins

It could be argued that 20th Century Fox released this dull space opera in the months before *Star Wars Episode I* just to make the latter film look good. Based on a popular computer game, this movie plays like a pale rip-off of *Star Wars*. Most of the Gen-X actors playing pilots are atrocious and neither the game's space battles, nor its fun feline aliens – who have been drained of all their personality and now look like seals – are transposed well. George Lucas save us! Contains some strong language and sexual references.

Freddie Prinze Jr Christopher "Maverick" Blair • **Matthew Lillard** Todd "Maniac" Marshall • **Saffron Burrows** Jeanette "Angel" Deveraux • **Jürgen Prochnow** Commander Gerald • **Tcheky Karyo** Commander James "Paladin" Taggart • **David Warner** Admiral Geoffrey Tolwyn • **David Suchet** Captain Sansky • **Ginny Holder** Rosie Forbes

Director *Chris Roberts*

Screenplay *Kevin Droney, from characters created by Chris Roberts and the computer game*

SCI Q

42 Which Hollywood action star's tearful farewell to planet Earth drew laughs from the Cannes festival audience in 1998?

See page 496 for answers

The Wings of Honneamise ★★★★ PG

1987 Jap Colour 119mins

Made the year before *Akira* introduced western audiences to the animé movies based on Japanese *manga* comics, this was the most costly example made to date. Yet the budget has clearly been well spent, with a superb Ryuichi Sakamoto score, the feuding nations convincingly futuristic and the camera movements and lighting effects worthy of a Hollywood blockbuster. But, although our hero is a member of the Royal Space Force, his journey is more one of self-discovery than all-conquering bravado. For all his ingenuity, 23-year-old writer/director Hiroyuki Yamaga overdoes the religious symbolism, while revealing a political naivety akin to his hero's. Nevertheless, a classic of its kind. In Japanese with English subtitles.

Director/Screenplay *Hiroyuki Yamaga*

Music *Ryuichi Sakamoto* • ***Art Director*** *Hiromasa Ogura*

Within the Rock ★★★ 18

1995 US Colour 84mins

Mix *Deep Impact* with *Alien* and the result is this surprisingly effective science-fiction shocker. Xander Berkeley and Caroline Barclay head the team mounting a desperate mission to destroy a moon that's on a collision course with Earth, only to find a seemingly dead monster near its core. Naturally, before you can say "Ridley Scott", they find themselves in a life-or-death battle with the flesh-craving beast. An unpretentious and ambitious creature feature providing rock solid entertainment in a variety of cleverly winning ways. Contains swearing and violence.

Xander Berkeley Ryan • **Bradford Tatum** Cody • **Brian Krause** Luke • **Caroline Barclay** Dr Dana Shaw • **Calvin Levels** Banton • **Michael Zelniker** Archer • **Duane Whitaker** Potter • **Barbara Patrick** "Nuke-em"

Director/Screenplay *Gary J Tunnicliffe*

Without Warning ★

1980 US Colour 96mins

An absolute turkey from the director of *Satan's Cheerleaders* is derailed by the outrageous ham acting from two of its all-tarnished-star cast, Jack Palance and Martin Landau. An alien lands in a remote rural area and starts flinging flesh-sucking parasites around in order to decorate his spaceship with human trophies gleaned from hapless campers and redneck locals. Greydon Clark's hopeless direction wastes every opportunity for even the mildest gross-out and quickly overkills the goose laying such golden sci-fi clichés through sheer ineptitude.

Jack Palance Taylor • **Martin Landau** Fred • **Tarah Nutter** Sandy • **Christopher S Nelson** Greg • **Cameron Mitchell** Hunter • **Neville Brand** Leo • **Sue Ann Langdon [Sue Ane Langdon]** Aggie • **Larry Storch** Scoutmaster

Director *Greydon Clark*

Screenplay *Lyn Freeman, Daniel Grodnik, Ben Nett, Steve Mathis*

Without Warning ★★★

1994 US Colour

How would television news deal with the breaking story of huge asteroid fragments crashing into different parts of the world? This well-executed salute to Orson Welles's landmark *War of the Worlds* radio broadcast of the thirties is a fine example of TV imitating itself for potent dramatic effect. This insightful survey transforms into a fascinating offbeat genre item with an amazing climax. The outcome was considered so real in the US that thousands of panicked viewers called in for confirmation it was actually fake.

Sander Vanocur Dr **Jane Kaczmarek** Dr Caroline Jaffe • **Bree Walker Lampley** • **Ernie Anastos** • **Warren Olney** • **Sandy Hill**
Director *Robert Iscove*
Screenplay *Peter Lance, Waon Greene, Jeremy Thorn*

Wizards ★★ PG

1977 US Colour 77mins [video]

This ambitious animated sci-fi tale from the director of *Fritz the Cat* was released the same year as *Star Wars*, both films dealing with a fairy-tale battle between good and evil. But whereas the Lucas epic was set in a galaxy far, far away, Ralph Bakshi has grounded this odd cartoon in Earth's far-flung future where nuclear holocaust has left the world in the hands of elves, fairies, wizards and mutants. Out of this messy miasma come twin wizards – the good Avatar and the evil Blackwolf – who duke it out for survival. Uncertain whether it wants to appeal to children, grown-ups or both – as with *The Lion King* its anti-fascist undertones will be lost on the kids – it's ultimately something of a dull affair.

Bob Holt Avatar • **Jesse Wells** Elinore • **Richard Romanus** Weehawk • **David Proval** Peace • **James Connell** President • **Steve Gravers** Blackwolf • **Mark Hamill** Sean
Director/Screenplay *Ralph Bakshi*

Wolfen ★★★ 18

1981 US Colour 109mins [video]

Eleven years after *Woodstock*, director Michael Wadleigh resurfaced with this classy, thoughtful, gory, but not in the least bit scary horror movie about a mutant breed of killer wolf with super-intelligent tracking abilities running wild in the Bronx. New York cop Albert Finney investigates, and, in a typical Wadleigh eco-addition to Whitley Strieber's so-so supernatural novel, links the plight of the American Indian to the wolves' brutally violent acts; both were deprived of their homeland by nasty white settlers. Subjective camerawork, denoting the wolves' point of view, features extensive optical special effects so the prowling always makes for galvanising viewing, while Finney makes the most of his tart dialogue. Contains violence, swearing and nudity.

Albert Finney Dewey Wilson • **Diane Venora** Rebecca Neff • **Edward James Olmos** Eddie Holt • **Gregory Hines** Whittington • **Tom Noonan** Ferguson • **Dick O'Neill** Warren • **Dehl Berti** Old Indian • **Peter Michael Goetz** Ross • **Sam Gray** Mayor • **Ralph Bell** Commissioner • **Max M Brown** Christopher Vanderveer • **Anne Marie Photamo** Pauline Vanderveer
Director *Michael Wadleigh*
Screenplay *David Eyre, Michael Wadleigh, from the novel by Whitley Strieber*

The Woman Eater ★

1957 UK BW 70mins

Fans of mad scientists and killer vegetables should on no account miss this little-known Z-grade affair, a British studio's successful attempt to match similar trash that was coming out of Hollywood in the late fifties. Boffin George Coulouris propagates a tree that eats young women in the belief that the sap excreted will make him Immortal. Director Charles Saunders began his career with the charming wartime comedy *Tawny Pipit*. Coulouris was in *Citizen Kane*. Their conversations in the studio canteen must have been particularly melancholic.

George Coulouris Dr James Moran • **Vera Day** Sally • **Joy Webster** Judy Ryan • **Peter Wayn** Jack Venner • **Jimmy Vaughan** Tanga • **Sara Leighton** Susan Curtis
Director *Charles Saunders*
Screenplay *Brandon Fleming*

The Woman in the Moon ★★★

1929 Ger BW 107mins

One of the last silent films made in Germany, Fritz Lang's comic-strip fantasy concerns scientist Klaus Pohl who believes the moon is rich in gold and, with the help of rocket designer Willy Fritsch, organises the first flight there. However melodramatic and farcical the plot, the takeoff is portrayed using dramatic montage and camera angles, and there are a few sinister Langian touches. Despite the quaintness of the technology, the Nazis took the film out of distribution because they felt the rocket was too close to one they were creating on the V2 programme at the time.

Gerda Maurus Friede Velten • **Willy Fritsch** Wolf Helius • **Fritz Rasp** Walter Turner • **Gustav von Wangenheim** Hans Windegger • **Klaus Pohl** Prof Georg Manfeldt
Director *Fritz Lang*
Screenplay *Thea von Harbou, Fritz Lang, from a story by Thea von Harbou*

Women of the Prehistoric Planet ★ U

1966 US Colour 93mins

Astronauts John Agar and Wendell Corey from the planet Centaurus land on an unexplored alien planet where one of their fleet has crashed. But a time warp has pushed the clock ahead by 18 years. After battling man-eating plants, giant lizards and a huge spider, they find a sole male survivor – now an adult – who kidnaps rescue ship passenger Irene Tsu. From the safety of space Corey names the planet Earth, while the couple left behind become a neo Adam and Eve. Now that you know the twist ending, there's absolutely no reason to sit through this desperately amateur bomb!

Wendell Corey Adm King • **Keith Larsen** Cmdr Scott • **John Agar** Dr Farrell • **Irene Tsu** Linda • **Paul Gilbert** Lt Bradley • **Merry Anders** Karen
Director/Screenplay *Arthur C Pierce*

Wonder Woman ★★★

TV 1975-1979 US Colour 59x60mins

DC Comics's all-American heroine dons her form-fitting outfit and spins on to the small screen in her first TV series. In its opening season, the show is entitled *The New, Original Wonder Woman* and pits the Amazon princess against the Nazis during the Second World War. Her fight against the forces of evil both on Earth and from space then resumes in the seventies, with *The New Adventures of Wonder Woman*. Its plotlines are silly, its supporting players are unimpressive and its tone is more camp than compelling. But viewed in the right frame of mind, the show is also quite a lot of fun. Lynda Carter's wholesome central portrayal of the Amazon princess is irresistible, as is her costume. The show also boasts an all-time classic theme tune and a steady stream of familiar guest stars, including Debra Winger as Wonder Girl! The series kicked off with a feature-length opener.

Lynda Carter Diana Prince/Wonder Woman • **Lyle Waggoner** Steve Trevor • **Debra Winger** Wonder Girl
Created by *William M Marston, from the character created by Charles Moulton*
Executive producer *Douglas S Cramer*

Facts

Cathy Lee Cosby starred as Wonder Woman in a 1974 TV movie, a pilot for a possibly series. Fans and critics alike rejected her insipid portrayal, and it wasn't until the one-time Miss World Lynda Carter donned the suit that the series took off.

Work Is a Four Letter Word ★★

1968 UK Colour 93mins

In a near future dominated by automation, eccentric David Warner is unemployed, but under pressure from his fiancée, takes a job at the local power station. However, the hot and damp conditions of the plant are ideal for growing his hallucinogenic magic mushrooms which he proceeds to distribute as a protest against a machine-led society. This is one of those films that tells you more about its own decade than the projected futuristic era in which it is set. Nevertheless, it's interesting to see sixties songstress Cilla Black showing her ambition of being more than just a pop star in her role as Warner's girlfriend. A typical Swinging Sixties comedy (Peter Hall's first feature) but never as successful as the surrealistic Henry Livings' stage play (*Eh?*) on which it is based.

David Warner Val Brose • **Cilla Black** Betty Dorrick • **Elizabeth Spriggs** Mrs Murray • **Zia Mohyeddin** Dr Narayana • **Joe Gladwin** Pa Brose • **Julie May** Mrs Dorrick • **Alan Howard** The Reverend Mort

Director *Peter Hall*

Screenplay *Jeremy Brooks, from the play "Eh?" by Henry Livings*

World Gone Wild ★★ 18

1988 US Colour 90mins

Mad Max meets *The Magnificent Seven* in an undistinguished post-holocaust action adventure with a few imaginative riffs along the way to keep interest maintained. It's 2087, water is a precious commodity, and hippy clan leader Bruce Dern is looking for mercenaries to protect the Lost Wells oasis from an attack by power-mad Adam Ant. Unfortunately, he and his choirboy acolytes follow a "bible" based on the wit and wisdom of Charles Manson! Guru Dern acts everybody else off the screen as this lower-bracket sci-fi saga drifts into predictability and flagrant imitation.

Bruce Dern Ethan • **Adam Ant** Derek Abernathy • **Michael Paré** George Landon • **Catherine Mary Stewart** Angie • **Rick Podell** Exline • **Julius J Carry III** Nitro • **Alan Autry** Hank • **Anthony James** Ten Watt

Director *Lee H Katzin*

Screenplay *Jorge Zamacona*

World of Giants ★★

TV 1959-1960 US BW 13x30mins

Often (and embarrassingly) called *W.O.G.*, this is a drab, espionage-themed series whipped together solely because Ziv TV had access to oversized props left over from Jack Arnold's 1957 classic *The Incredible Shrinking Man*. Straight-faced Marshall Thompson is a US secret agent who could take literally a later series hero's claim to be a Man in a Suitcase. The pilot episode, *Look up to a Monster*, is a spin on the film version with Thompson exposed to an exploding rocket while snooping behind the Iron Curtain and then shrinking to a height of six inches, which makes him useful to his spy pal (Arthur Franz) when it comes to infiltration missions – though he was prone to being menaced by dogs and pigeons, or getting lost in the overgrown jungle of a back garden. Despite production input from sci-fi veteran William Alland and direction from (among others) Jack Arnold himself, plus Nathan Juran and Eugene Lourié (experts in gigantism from *Attack of the 50 Ft Woman* and *The Beast from 20,000 Fathoms*), this was an unmemorable, surprisingly undramatic little show, far less lurid than the later *Land of the Giants*.

Marshall Thompson Mel Hunter • **Arthur Franz** Bill Winters • **Marcia Henderson** Miss Brown • **John Gallaudet** Commissioner Hogg

Producer *William Alland, Otto Lang*

The World, the Flesh and the Devil ★★

1959 US BW 94mins

Passionate, earnest and totally daft, this post-holocaust racial allegory takes its inspiration from MP Shiel's novel *The Purple Cloud*. Miner Harry Belafonte lives through an atomic attack and meets two other survivors when he arrives in devastated New York City – gorgeous Inger Stevens and bigoted Mel Ferrer. Can the two men overcome their mutual hatred of each other? And who will get the girl? Aside from a few impressively mounted sequences on the deserted Manhattan streets where the two men stalk each other, this eternal triangle plea for harmony is ultimately condescending and unbelievable.

Harry Belafonte Ralph Burton • **Inger Stevens** Sarah Crandall • **Mel Ferrer** Benson Thacker

Director *Ranald MacDougall*

Screenplay *Ranald MacDougall, from the story "End of the Wall" by Ferdinand Reyher and the novel "The Purple Cloud" by Matthew Phipps Shiel*

The World without a Mask ★★

1934 Ger BW 109mins

One of the notable features of cinema's presentation of pre-boom television is that it never has a good word to say about it. The tube either predisposes viewers to tyrannical manipulation or it presents them with limitless opportunity for mischief. The latter is the case here, as Harry Piel and Kurt Vespermann find themselves pursued by crooks and unscrupulous entrepreneurs once they've invented a set with x-ray capability. The presence of Rudolf Klein-Rogge (who played Rotwang, Dr Mabuse and other notables for Fritz Lang) lends the picture a certain sci-fi legitimacy. But essentially it's a farce – pure and very simple. A German language film.

Harry Piel • **Annie Markart** • **Olga Tschechowa** • **Kurt Vespermann** • **Hubert von Meyerinck** • **Rudolf Klein-Rogge**

Director *Harry Piel*

Screenplay *Hans Rameau*

Cinematographer *Ewald Daub*

World without End ★★

1955 US Colour 80mins

Returning from a Mars mission, an American spaceship enters a time warp and ends up on Earth in the 26th century. Unfortunately, it's after a nuclear war has left the planet's surface inhabited by mutant caveman, giant spiders and a superior, if listless, race forced to live underground. The shocked astronauts, led by Hugh Marlowe, finally inspire the slowly dying survivors to fight back in this colourful and very loose unofficial adaptation of HG Wells' *The Time Machine* – ironically Rod Taylor would star in the actual adaptation five years later. Tacky and fast-paced fun, if a little moralistic, all the sets and props were recycled from other Allied Artist movies and the subterranean fairy-tale-style costumes were designed by famed pin-up artist Vargas.

Hugh Marlowe John Borden • **Nancy Gates** Garnet • **Rod Taylor** Herbert Ellis • **Nelson Leigh** Dr Galbraithe • **Christopher Dark** Henry Jaffe

Director/Screenplay *Edward Bernds*

X

Deep Throat: "I've been a participant in some of the most insidious lies and witness to deeds that no crazed man could imagine. I spent years watching you from my lofty position to know that you were the one I could trust."

Mulder: "Then why did you lie to me?"

Deep Throat: "I needed to divert you. You and Scully are excellent investigators and your motives are just. However, there are still some secrets that should remain secret – some truths that people are just not ready to know."

Mulder: "Who are you to decide that for me?"

Deep Throat: "The world's reaction to such knowledge would be far too dangerous."

Mulder: "Dangerous. You mean in a sense of outrage like the reaction to the Kennedy assassinations or MIAs or radiation experiments on terminal patients, Watergate, Iran-Contra, Roswell, the Tuskegee experiments, where will it end? Oh, I guess it won't end as long as men like you decide what is truth." EBE, series 1, episode 16

The X Files ★★★★★

TV 1993- US/Can Colour DVD

The biggest thing to happen to genre TV since *Star Trek*, Chris Carter's award-winning sci-fi drama series offers an extraordinary exploration of unexplained phenomena on Earth. For the most part, Mulder and Scully's search for the truth behind the government lies and alien conspiracies is incredibly inventive, exhilarating and utterly convincing viewing, with the kind of sterling production values many films can only dream of. The series also provides a unique showcase for David Duchovny's quirky charm and Gillian Anderson's plucky persona. Although the show's lack of answers and confusing mythology becomes increasingly exasperating with each season, Robert Patrick's arrival as Agent John Doggett in season eight helps gives the series a new lease of life, and allows it to maintain its position as one of the finest and most influential TV shows ever made.

David Duchovny Fox Muldaur • **Gillian Anderson** Dana Scully • **Mitch Pileggi** Asst Dir Walter Skinner • **William B Davis** CGB Spender, the cigarette-smoking man • **Nicholas Lea** Krycek • **Bruce Harwood** John Fitzgerald Byers • **Tom Braidwood** Melvin Frohike • **Dean Haglund** Richard "Ringo" Langly • **Robert Patrick** John Jay Doggett • **Annabeth Gish** Monica Reyes • **Robert Patrick** Agent John Doggett
Created by *Chris Carter*
Executive producer *Chris Carter, Frank Spotnitz* • ***Consulting producer*** *Glen Morgan, James Wong*
Creative consultant *Vince Gilligan*

Wind and rain: X-woman Storm (Halle Berry) conjures up some bad weather in *X-Men*

The X Files ★★★ 15

1998 US Colour 117mins DVD

The TV phenomenon of the nineties makes an effortless transition to the big screen, and, while the plot remains firmly grounded in the themes of the series, the uninitiated should not feel put off, as it plays equally well as a classy conspiracy thriller. Here, intrepid FBI duo Mulder and Scully (David Duchovny and Gillian Anderson) investigate an explosion at a federal building and stumble across the biggest alien cover-up in the world's history. Director Rob Bowman (who has also worked on the series) is faithful to the show's paranoiac roots, but gleefully opens the action out to stage some spectacular set pieces. He is well served by his leads and by the likes of Martin Landau, Armin Mueller-Stahl and John Neville. Contains violence, horror, swearing.

David Duchovny Special Agent Fox Mulder • **Gillian Anderson** Special Agent Dana Scully • **John Neville** Well-manicured man • **William B Davis** Cigarette-smoking man • **Martin Landau** Dr Alvin Kurtzweil • **Mitch Pileggi** FBI Assistant Director Walter Skinner • **Armin Mueller-Stahl** Strughold • **Dean Haglund** Lone Gunman Ringo Langley • **Tom Braidwood** Lone Gunman Melvin Frohike • **Bruce Harwood** Lone Gunman John Byers
Director *Rob Bowman*
Screenplay *Chris Carter, from a story by Chris Carter, Frank Spotnitz*

The X from Outer Space ★

1967 Jap Colour 89mins

X doesn't mark the entertainment spot in the first Shochiku Studio entry in the Japanese monster sweepstakes. Guilala, a spear-spitting stegosaurus-cum-chicken creature, grows from a single cell into a behemoth after being brought back from a Moon-to-Mars mission attached to the spaceship hull. Tokyo is destroyed yet again before radiation shrinks it back to amoeba size and the authorities banish it into the galaxy. Hiroshi Ikeda's special effects aren't up to the usual Japanese standard for such moppet-driven fare and Kazui Nihonmatsu's direction borders on the disinterested. A Japanese language film

Eiji Okada Dr Kato • **Toshiya Wazaki** Sano • **Peggy Neal** Liza • **Itoko Harada** Michiko • **Shinichi Yanagisawa** Miyamoto • **Frankus Gruber** Behrman
Director *Kazui Nihonmatsu*
Special Effects *Hiroshi Ikeda*

X-Men ★★★ 12

2000 US Colour 104mins DVD

The first adventure showcasing those Marvel Comic mutant humans sporting *Gladiators*-style names is a qualified success. Directed and co-written by Bryan Singer with a healthy dose of irony, *X-Men* is

the darkest superhero movie since *Batman* and features the coolest special effects this side of *The Matrix*. Though no one, fanatic or novice, will be disappointed by the dazzling display of action derring-do, the story and characters leave a little to be desired. In the not-too-distant future, scared senators insist on legislation to ensure that a new breed of humans with assorted strange powers won't use their special skills against mankind. Meanwhile, professor Patrick Stewart nurtures their talents in a special academy and human magnet Ian McKellen plans total mutant world domination to protect the species. The result is a battle royal, with the good mutants trying to stop the bad. Singer mixes the classic values of good storytelling with liberal amounts of digital magic, but – outside of the theatrically trained Stewart and McKellen – it's star quality that's ultimately missing.

Hugh Jackman Logan/Wolverine • **Patrick Stewart** Professor Charles Xavier • **Ian McKellen** Magneto • **Famke Janssen** Jean Grey • **James Marsden** Scott Summers/Cyclops • **Halle Berry** Aurora/Storm • **Anna Paquin** Marie/Rogue • **Tyler Mane** Sabretooth • **Ray Park** Toad • **Rebecca Romijn-Stamos** Mystique • **Bruce Davison** Senator Robert Frank Kelly
Director *Bryan Singer*
Screenplay *David Hayter, from a story by Tom DeSanto, Bryan Singer, from the characters created by Stan Lee, Jack Kirby*

SFacts

Creator (and executive producer) Stan Lee makes a cameo appearance as the man standing by the hot dog stand when Bruce Davison emerges from the sea.

X Minus One ★★★

Radio 1955-1958 US 110x30mins

"Countdown for blast-off. X minus 5, 4, 3, 2, X minus 1, fire... From the far horizons of the unknown come transcribed tales of new dimensions in time and space" was the introduction to NBC's follow-up to *Dimension X*, which went off air two years earlier. Many of the stories came from *Galaxy* magazine, and leading writers from the fifties, Ray Bradbury, Isaac Asimov and Robert Heinlein among them, contributed tales to the series.

Fred Collins Announcer
Producer *William Welch, Van Woodward*

X the Unknown ★★

1956 UK BW 79mins

Cashing in on the success of the TV drama, *Quatermass*, which Hammer had already made into a feature film, this sc-fi drama deals with a series of baffling deaths at an atomic research establishment in the wilds of Scotland. It could be bog-standard radiation leaks and poisoning but maybe something else is going on, some alien slime on the loose? A typical product of the Cold War, it's all jolly polite as British boffins are led by American import Dean Jagger.

His presence lends box-office appeal and also implies that British defence work has become a branch of American foreign policy.

Dean Jagger Dr Adam Royston • **Edward Chapman** Elliott • **Leo McKern** McGill • **Marianne Brauns** Zena, thenurse • **William Lucas** Peter Elliott • **John Harvey** Major Cartwright • **Peter Hammond** Lieutenant Bannerman
Director *Leslie Norman*
Screenplay *Jimmy Sangster*

Xtro ★ 18

1983 UK Colour 82mins

British family man Philip Sayer is abducted by a UFO. Three years later, he returns to his family, claiming to remember nothing of what happened to him in the intervening years. Soon his wife and son begin to notice some odd behavior, like his penchant for eating snake eggs, and the string of horribly mutilated bodies he leaves in his wake. Released a year after *ET* with the tagline "Not all aliens are friendly", it's only memorable now for its incredibly graphic violence and for Maryam D'Abo's first film role (and her first nude scene).

Philip Sayer Sam Phillips • **Bernice Stegers** Rachel Phillips • **Danny Brainin** Joe Daniels • **Simon Nash** Tony Phillips • **Maryam D'Abo** Analise • **David Cardy** Michael
Director *Harry Bromley Davenport*
Screenplay *Robert Smith, Iain Cassie, Jo Ann Kaplan, from a screenplay by Harry Bromley Davenport, Michel Parry*

Xtro 2: The Second Encounter ★ 18

1990 Can Colour 89mins

Where *Alien* inspired the first *Xtro* movie, this in-name-only sequel is a stone cold rip-off. Scientists at a secret facility discover a way to send people to an alternate dimension, and, after doing so, act really surprised when slimy killer aliens come through from the other side and infest the lab. Familiar scenes of people with guns edging down darkened corridors follow. As if it isn't hard enough to watch yet another *Alien* rip-off, *Xtro II* asks us to believe Jan-Michael Vincent is a maverick scientist. Shocking!

Jan-Michael Vincent Dr Ron Sheperd • **Paul Koslo** Dr Alex Summerfield • **Tara Buckman** Dr Julie Casserly • **Jano Frandsen** McShane • **Nicholas Lea** Baines • **WF Wadden** Jedburg
Director *Harry Bromley Davenport*
Screenplay *John A Curtis, Edward Kovach, Robert Smith, Steven Lister*

DR FRIEDRICH ("IT'S FRONKENSTEEN") VON FRANKENSTEIN:

Igor, would you give me a hand with the **bags?**

IGOR: **Certainly.** You take the blonde and I'll take the one in the **turban.**

Young Frankenstein 1974

The Year of the Sex Olympics ★★★★

TV 1968 UK Colour 105mins

This feature-length satirical look at a dystopian future (influenced by Orwell and Huxley) found Nigel Kneale predicting trends in pornography and reality TV that more or less came to pass by the turn of the century. The mass of the population have become "low-drive" drones with nothing better to do than watch television, which provides a non-stop parade of sexual activity to keep their minds off actually procreating. TV programmer Leonard Rossiter feuds with his ambitious junior Brian Cox as the ratings fall for "sportsex", a show in which copulating couples are awarded points by juries like a crossbreed of *Come Dancing* and *Deep Throat*. Dissident Tony Vogel, having committed the Huxleyan crime of becoming attached to his supposedly temporary mistress (Suzanne Neve), volunteers his family to star in a reality-TV soap as they try to survive on an island beyond the comforts of automated society, only for Cox to beef up the plot by introducing a mad sex-murderer into the mix. Darkly funny, with an invented argot influenced by advertising jargon, and eye-abusingly crass art direction, this turns serious for its grim finale.

Leonard Rossiter Co-ordinator Ugo Priest • **Suzanne Neve** Deanie Webb • **Tony Vogel** Nat Mender • **Vickery Turner** Misch • **Brian Cox** Lasar Opie • **George Murcell** Grels • **Martin Potter** Kin Hodder • **Lesley Roach** Keten Webb
Director *Michael Elliott*
Written by *Nigel Kneale*
Producer *Ronald Travers*

Yellowbacks ★★★

TV 1990 UK Colour 80mins

This drama from BBC Scotland is set in a future where paranoia about a sexually-transmitted plague has led to a sinister, fascist state on overfamiliar dystopian lines. Doctor Janet McTeer and scientist Bill Paterson are interrogated by an unsubtly-named evil government man (Roy Marsden) about the whereabouts of gay virus-carrier-cum-revolutionary (Ciaran Hinds), who is accused of deliberately spreading the infection as a subversive act. Written by Malcolm McKay and directed by Roy Battersby, with a solid supporting cast that includes Tim Roth and Imelda Staunton. Similar thematic material, with virus-positives herded into death camps and secret police enforcing the will of the state, crops up in the American-made TV movie *Daybreak*.

Roy Marsden David Caesar • **Janet McTeer** Dr Juliet Horwitz • **Bill Paterson** Alex McPherson • **Tim Roth** Peter Pike • **Imelda Staunton** Cheryl Newman • **Ciaran Hinds** Martin Pitt • **Luke Hanson** Colin Skye
Director *Roy Battersby*
Written by *Malcolm Mackay*
Executive producer *Bill Bryden*

Yesterday's Target ★ 15

1996 US Colour 76mins

Many viewers will give up on this movie before the first ten incomprehensible minutes are over. Those who stick it out will eventually get a vague idea what the story is – something combining time travel and elements blatantly stolen from *X-Men* comic books – but they'll still be as confused as the movie's three amnesiacs who find themselves hunted by a covert government agency. Even if the movie hadn't been edited down to a ridiculously short running time, the shoddy production values would still sink it. Strange as it may seem, LeVar Burton gives an even hammier performance than Malcolm McDowell.

Daniel Baldwin Paul • **LeVar Burton** Winstrom • **Malcolm McDowell** Holden • **Stacy Haiduk** Jessica • **TK Carter** Carter • **Richard Herd** Aaron Winfield
Director *Barry Samson*
Screenplay *David Bourla*

Yongkari Monster of the Deep ★★

1967 S Kor BW 100mins

Seoul is laid waste by the gas-guzzling lizard unleashed in this allegorical *Godzilla* rip-off. The titular terror goes on the rampage following an earthquake induced by a Chinese bomb test. But, as the populace descends into despair, the fearless, short-trousered brother-in-law of the nation's sole astronaut notes the creature's susceptibility to the ammonia derivative, X2, and suggests an air-raid. The model work is on a par with the scenario. But the socio-political subtext is fascinating. Korean dialogue dubbed into English

Oh Yungil • **Nam Chungim** • **Lee Soonjai** • **Kang Moon** • **Lee Kwang Ho**
Director *Kim Ki-dak*
Screenplay *Suh Yunsung*

Yor, the Hunter from the Future ★ 15

1983 It/Tur Colour 84mins

An inept, cheesy muscleman epic from Italian hack director Antonio Margheriti (Anthony M Dawson). He obviously thought mixing *Conan* with *Star Wars* was a stunningly original idea. An Italian-Turkish production starring one-time Captain America Reb Brown (which says it all, really) this absolute stinker features the blond-wigged hero fighting cardboard dinosaurs and robot hordes (with a touch of the Darth Vaders), accompanied by a tacky disco theme song. Not even fun on a camp level, *Yor* is a bore and absolute hell to sit through.

Reb Brown Yor • **Corinne Cléry** Ka-Laa • **John Steiner** Overlord • **Carole Andre** Ena
Director *Anthony M Dawson [Antonio Margheriti]*
Screenplay *Robert Bailey, Anthony M Dawson [Antonio Margheriti], from the novel "Yor" by Juan Zanotto, Ray Collins*

Young Frankenstein ★★★★ 15

1974 US BW 105mins

One of director Mel Brooks's best comedies, this loopy send-up of classic chiller clichés from Universal's monster heyday is also one of the genre's most thorough and successful fright film parodies. Gene Wilder plays the infamous baron's grandson, who copies his ancestor's experiments only to create the singularly inane Peter Boyle. Filmed in sumptuous black and white, Brooks's ingenious tribute is often hysterically funny and always a scream. Madeleine Kahn's "bride", Gene Hackman's blind hermit, Marty Feldman's hunchbacked Igor and the marvellous *Putting on the Ritz* musical number add to the fun and give this loving homage real staying power.

Gene Wilder Doctor Frederick Frankenstein • **Peter Boyle** Monster • **Marty Feldman** Igor • **Madeline Kahn** Elizabeth • **Cloris Leachman** Frau Blucher • **Teri Garr** Inga • **Kenneth Mars** Inspector Kemp • **Gene Hackman** Blind hermit • **Richard Haydn** Herr Falkstein • **Liam Dunn** Mr Hilltop • **Danny Goldman** Medical student • **Leon Askin** Herr Waldman • **Oscar Beregi** Sadistic jailer
Director *Mel Brooks*
Screenplay *Gene Wilder, Mel Brooks, from characters created by Mary Shelley*

SFacts

This film was shot in the same location, using the same props, as the classic 1931 movie *Frankenstein*.

Into a world of eternal life, he brought the gift of death...

Zardoz 1973

Z

Z for Zachariah ★★★

TV 1984 UK Colour 120mins

Shot entirely on film, this *Play for Today* (one of a glut of nuclear-themed shows from 1984) is a faithful adaptation of Robert C O'Brien's 1974 "young adult" novel, a rare instance of American source material being redone with a British setting rather than the other way about. Borrowing from Roger Corman's *The Day the World Ended* (1956), the setting is a post-World War III Welsh valley with its own climate, protected by mountains from unseen wastelands beyond. In an allegory that works in the novel but seems a little forced in the dramatisation, sensible but glum surviving farmgirl Pippa Hinchley has to cope with incipiently warlike (and radiation-poisoned) scientist Anthony Andrews, who shows up in a clunky decontamination suit and repays her nursing of him by trying to molest and enslave her, demonstrating the adult failings that ended the human race in the first place, finally forcing her to leave her edenic refuge. Well written and directed by Anthony Garner, with good work from unwaiflike junior heroine Hinchley.

Anthony Andrews John Loomis • **Pippa Hinchley** Ann Burden
Director *Anthony Garner*
Written by *Anthony Garner, from the novel by Robert O'Brien*
Producer *Neil Zeiger*

ZPG: Zero Population Growth ★★

1971 US Colour 96mins

There is a story that someone in the audience called out to betray Pia Zadora's hiding place on the opening night of *The Diary of Anne Frank*. This dreary hide-and-seek saga inspires a similar urge. With thought outlawed in *Nineteen Eighty-Four* and age prohibited in *Logan's Run*, it was only a matter of time before reproduction would find itself outside the law. In a smog-bound, overpopulated future a tyrannical regime has launched a line of robot-children and made birth a death penalty offence. Oliver Reed and Geraldine Chaplin play the parents in peril. The Catalonians liked the film, though: they awarded Chaplin the best actress award in the 1972 Catalonian International Film Festival. Contains violence.

Oliver Reed Russ McNeil • **Geraldine Chaplin** Carole McNeil • **Don Gordon** George Borden • **Diane Cilento** Edna Borden • **David Markham** Dr Herrick • **Sheila Reed** Dr Mary Herrick • **Aubrey Woods** Dr Mallory
Director *Michael Campus*
Screenplay *Max Ehrlich, Frank De Felitta*

Zardoz ★★ 15

1973 UK Colour 101mins

Sales of vests plummeted when Clark Gable appeared without one in *It Happened One Night*, but it is unlikely that this naive piece of futuristic hokum from director John Boorman had an equally astounding impact on the fashion of the day by increasing the demand for orange underpants! Poor Sean Connery – Burt Reynolds obviously knew what he was doing when he said no to this film. Yet, thanks to Geoffrey Unsworth's stunning photography, this patently silly story, set in 2293 and telling of a rebellion against sexless intellectualism and soulless technology, has become one of those "risible but unmissable" cult movies, whose main attraction now is the unintentional comedy. The title is a contraction of "Wizard of Oz". Contains swearing and nudity.

Sean Connery Zed • **Charlotte Rampling** Consuella • **Sara Kestelman** May • **Sally Anne Newton** Avalow • **John Alderton** Friend • **Niall Buggy** Zardoz/Arthur Frayn • **Bosco Hogan** George Saden • **Jessica Swift** Apathetic • **Bairbre Dowling** Star • **Christopher Casson** Old scientist • **Reginald Jarman** Death
Director/Screenplay *John Boorman*
Cinematographer *Geoffrey Unsworth*

SCI Q SCI Q SCI Q SCI Q

43
Which thirties nightmare-of-science featured Alan Ladd, Randolph Scott and Buster Crabbe among its deformed extras?

See page 496 for answers

Zenon: Girl of the 21st Century ★★

1999 US Colour 97mins

The antics of a mischievous teenage girl who is sent to Earth as a punishment. While adjusting to life planet-side, after a childhood on a space station, she discovers that only she (naturally) can save mankind from a deadly computer virus. This average sci-fi comedy from director Kenneth Johnson makes for vaguely entertaining family viewing in this average sci-fi comedy.

Kirsten Storms Zenon Kar • **Raven-Symone** Nebula • **Gregory Smith** Greg • **Holly Fulger** Aunt Judy • **Phillip Rhys** Proto Zoa • **Bob Bancroft** Lutz • **Frederick Coffin** Parker Wyndham • **Stuart Pankin** Cmdr Edward Plank
Director *Kenneth Johnson*
Screenplay *Stu Krieger, from the book by Marilyn Sadler, Roger Bollen*

Zeram ★★ 18

1991 Jap Colour 97mins

This mix of animé-style live action and sci-fi thrills has to go down as a missed opportunity, although it is light years ahead of most straight-to-video sci-fi fodder. The story revolves around a bounty tracker (Yuko Moriyama) from another world caught up in a life and death battle with an evil alien (Mizuho Yoshida). Thrown into the fray are two average Earthlings (Yukijiro Hotaru, Kunihiko Iida). It looks good, but unfortunately the pacing is erratic and sometimes it veers a little too close to *Power Rangers* territory for comfort. Japanese dialogue dubbed into English.

Yuko Moriyama • **Yukijiro Hotaru** • **Kunihiko Iida** • **Mizuho Yoshida**
Director *Keita Amemiya*
Screenplay *Keita Amemiya, Hajime Matsumoto, Steve Kramer*

Zeta One ★ 18

1969 UK Colour 82mins

Adapted from a short-lived comic strip this British sexploitation comedy makes the Robin Askwith Confession films look like the works of Sergei Eisenstein. Told in flashback, Robin Hawdon plays the unlikely spy who foils an invasion of the Earth by a race of alien superwomen led by Dawn Addams. Michael Cort directs the yawn-inducing titillation and soft-core romping with all the style of a seventies cinema commercial for a local curry house. The most surprising thing is how he managed to lure comedy legends James Robertson-Justice and Charles Hawtrey into agreeing to appear in such a mess. Put it down as a bad day at the office too for cult horror producer Tony Tenser, responsible for among others the classic *Witchfinder General*.

Robin Hawdon James Word • **Yutte Stensgaard** Ann Olsen • **James Robertson-Justice** Major Bourdon • **Charles Hawtry** Swyne • **Lionel Murton** "W" • **Anna Gael** Clotho • **Dawn Addams** Zeta • **Carol Hawkins** Zara
Director *Michael Cort*
Screenplay *Michael Cort, Alastair McKenzie*
Producer *Tony Tenser, George Maynard*

Zombie Creeping Flesh ★★

1981 It/Sp Colour 99mins

Made at the height of the Italian zombie film frenzy, director Bruno Mattei's schlock gore-fest finds a Swat team in New Guinea trying to control an outbreak of flesh-eating caused by a synthetic food, formulated to ease Third World hunger, awakening cannibalistic urges. Any political lip-service is quickly jettisoned by Mattei in order to supply a splatter spectacle of exploding heads, maggot-infested bodies, gut-munching and grisly intestine waving. Cynical, boring and gruesome all at the same time, this extremely violent and amateurish mess is one for gore hounds only. Italian dialogue dubbed into English

Margit Evelyn Newton • **Franco Giraldi** • **Selan Karay** • **Robert O'Neil** • **Gaby Renom**

Director *Vincent Dawn [Bruno Mattei]*

Screenplay *JM Cunllles, Claudio Fragasso*

Zombie Flesh Eaters ★★★★ 18

1979 It Colour 87mins [video] DVD

Voodoo causes an army of cannibal zombies to leave its tropical island paradise and head for New York in this ultra-gory rip-off of *Dawn of the Dead*, which put Italian director Lucio Fulci on the cult map. Although the movie is extremely silly (a crusty underwater zombie battling a shark) and extremely violent, with several watershed special effects, Fulci often creates a chilling atmosphere amid the hard-core splatter. Tisa Farrow (Mia's sister) had a mini career as a starlet in Italy and heads the cast here, but many will be surprised to see staunch British actor Richard Johnson up to his neck in exploding heads and entrail eating in this landmark fright flick. Contains strong violence and nudity.

Tisa Farrow Anne • **Ian McCulloch** Peter • **Richard Johnson** Dr Menard • **Al Cliver** Brian • **Arnetta Gay** Susan • **Olga Karlatos** Mrs Menard • **Stefania D'Amario** Nurse

Director *Lucio Fulci*

Screenplay *Elsia Briganti*

Zombie High ★★ 15

1987 US Colour 86mins [video]

When female students are admitted to a formerly all-male prep school for the first time they discover their new classmates are walking zombies, the results of experiments carried out by teachers who crave immortal life. The title suggests a kind of camp teen horror flick (the original title *The School That Stole My Brain* was even worse), but what you get plays more like a masculine version of *The Stepford Wives* albeit one that's alternately tedious and unintentionally hilarious. It's a pity as Virginia Madsen's committed central performance deserved a better vehicle than this lacklustre attempt at social satire. Look out, too, among the student population for *Twin Peaks* alumnus Sherilyn Fenn.

Virginia Madsen Andrea • **Richard Cox** Philo • **James Wilder** Barry • **Sherilyn Fenn** Suzi • **Paul Feig** Emerson • **Kay E Kuter** Dean Eisner

Director *Ron Link*

Screenplay *Elizabeth Passerelli, Tim Doyle, Aziz Ghazal*

Zombies of the Stratosphere ★★

1952 US BW 12x13mins

The main reason for watching this 12-part serial from the Fred C Brannon/Franklyn Adreon team is to catch an early glimpse of Leonard Nimoy, playing villain Lane Bradford's sidekick. Other than that questionable highlight, this is pretty standard fare about a devilish Martian plan to blow up Earth so that they can move their own planet into the vacated orbit. Judd Holdren is the hero, donning the same suit that appeared in *King of the Rocket Men* and *Radar Men from the Moon*.

Judd Holdren Larry Martin • **Aline Towne** Sue Davis • **Lane Bradford** Marex • **John Crawford** Roth • **Leonard Nimoy** Narab

Director *Fred C Brannon*

Screenplay *Ronald Davidson*

Producer *Franklyn Adreon [Franklin Adreon]*

Zone Troopers ★★★ 15

1985 US Colour 82mins [video]

Although it was overshadowed a little by the earlier *Trancers* (with which it shares most of the key personnel) this witty, irreverent, time-travelling adventure also deserves cult classic status. The cheerfully bonkers plot surrounds a stranded group of American soldiers who rescue a crashed alien from the Nazis and try to fight their way back to their own lines. The talented cast, headed by *Trancers* star Tim Thomerson and series regulars Art LaFleur and Biff Manard, have a ball with the wisecracking script, while director Danny Bilson (who co-wrote *Trancers* and this with Paul DeMeo) neatly subverts both Second World War and sci-fi conventions.

Tim Thomerson Sgt Patrick "Sarge" Stone • **Timothy Van Patten** Joey Verona • **Art LaFleur** Cpl George "Mittens" Mittinsky • **Biff Manard** Dolan • **William Paulson** The Alien

Director *Danny Bilson*

Screenplay *Danny Bilson, Paul DeMeo*

Zontar, the Thing from Venus ★

1966 US Colour 80mins

Hysterically bad, low-budget time-waster from Larry (*Mars Needs Women*) Buchanan. When a bat-monster from Venus decides to take over the world, it comes up with the convoluted plan of controlling the mind of hapless sci-fi stalwart John Agar, making him turn off all of Earth's sources of power. Some may call it a camp classic, but you should pitch your tent elsewhere.

John Agar Dr Curt Taylor • **Susan Bjurman** Martha Ritchie • **Anthony Houston** Keith Ritchie • **Pat Delaney** Anne Taylor

Director *Larry Buchanan*

Screenplay *Larry Buchanan, Hillman Taylor*

Who's who in science fiction

Be it film or television, these are the people – producers, directors, writers, artists and technicians – who've influenced the way we look at science fiction

By David Parkinson

DOUGLAS ADAMS *(1952-2001)* **UK author** Before The *Hitch-Hiker's Guide to the Galaxy* aired on BBC radio in 1978, the highlight of Douglas Adam's CV was an unoptioned sitcom co-penned with Monty Python's Graham Chapman. However, the intergalactic misadventures of Arthur Dent and his alien companion Ford Prefect soon earned cult status and stage and TV adaptations were followed by a series of novels, including The Restaurant at the End of the Universe (1980) and Life, the Universe and Everything (1982), which sold more than 14 million copies. Later ventures, like the dot.com project, The Digital Village, were less successful.

IRWIN ALLEN *(1916-1991)* **US dir/prod** A former magazine editor and radio producer, Allen began producing movies in 1951. Initially specialising in documentaries, he won an Oscar for *The Sea Around Us* (1953), which he also wrote and directed. But, following the failure of *The Story of Mankind* (1957), he moved into sci-fi with *The Lost World* (1960) and *Voyage to the Bottom of the Sea* (1961). He adapted the latter into a small-screen format in 1964, following it with such popular series as *Lost in Space* (1965-68) and *Land of the Giants* (1968-70). However, his career peaked with the disaster movies *The Poseidon Adventure* (1972) and *The Towering Inferno* (1974).

GERRY ANDERSON *(b 1929)* **UK TV prod** Having directed TV series *The Adventures of Twizzle* (1957-8) and *Torchy* (1960), he embarked on the puppet western show, *Four Feather Falls* (1960). Success came, however, in collaboration with his then-wife Sylvia on a succession of children's classics which exploited "supermarionation" puppetry: *Supercar* (1961-62), *Fireball XL5* (1962-63), *Stingray* (1964-65), *Captain Scarlet and the Mysterons* (1967-68) and *Joe 90* (1968-99). The most popular was *Thunderbirds* (1965-66), but two spin-off movies proved commercial disappointments. He moved into live-action with *UFO* (1970-73), *Space: 1999* (1975-77) and *Space Precinct* (1994-95) before returning to puppetry with *Terrahawks* (1983-86).

MICHAEL ANDERSON *(b 1920)* **UK dir** This onetime Elstree messenger boy began directing alongside Peter Ustinov on *Private Angelo* (1949). He quickly proved himself as assured with comedy (*Will Any Gentleman?*, 1953) and action (*The Dam Busters*, 1954) as he was with drama (*The Shoes of the Fisherman*, 1968) and thrills (*The Quiller Memorandum*, 1966). Following his take on George Orwell's *1984* (1955), he was invited to Hollywood for *Around the World in 80 Days* (1956), an all-star Jules Verne adaptation that won the Oscar for Best Picture. His subsequent science-fiction offerings, included *Doc Savage: Man of Bronze* (1975), *Logan's Run* (1976), *Millennium* (1989) and the TV mini-series, *The Martian Chronicles* (1979).

JACK ARNOLD *(1916-1992)* **US dir** Initially an actor and stage manager on Broadway and in London's West End, he began making films under the great Robert Flaherty, while serving in the US Army Signal Corps. Having made 25 documentaries, he started specialising in exploitation movies, many of which were made in collaboration with producer William Alland. Although he handled westerns, dramas and comedies, his finest achievements were horror and sci-fi Bs, most notably *It Came from Outer Space* (1953), *The Creature from the Black Lagoon* (1954; in 3-D) and *The Incredible Shrinking Man* (1957). His TV credits included *Buck Rogers in the 25th Century*, *Wonder Woman* and *The Bionic Woman*.

FORD BEEBE *(1888-1978)* **US dir** In Hollywood from 1916, Beebe only began directing full time from 1932, churning out westerns and action fodder for Poverty Row outfits like Mascot and Republic. Almost invariably sharing the directorial duties, he became something of a serial specialist, although crime adventures like *Don Winslow of the Coast Guard* (1943) were overshadowed by his numerous sci-fi outings including *Flash Gordon's Trip to Mars* (1938), *Buck Rogers* (1939) and *Flash Gordon Conquers the Universe* (1940). He later co-directed the *Pastoral Symphony* sequence in Disney's *Fantasia* (1940) and handled all 12 entries in the *Bomba the Jungle Boy* series (1949-55)

DONALD P BELLISARIO *(b 1935)* **US TV dir/scr/prod** A former US marine, he resigned as creative director at the famous Bloom Agency to become story editor on the TV series *Baa Baa Black Sheep* (1976). Within a year he had transferred to *Battlestar Galactica*, where he served as writer, director and producer before embarking on his own series, *Magnum PI* (1980-88), starring Tom Selleck. He was to garner even greater acclaim for *Quantum Leap* (1989-93), for which he earned four Emmy nominations and the Edgar Allen Poe writing award.

SPENCER GORDON BENNET *(1893-1987)* US dir Starting out as a stuntman, Bennet collaborated with serial king George B Seitz on *The Perils of Pauline* (1914) and *The Exploits of Elaine* (1915). Having co-directed *Behold the Man* (1921), he went on to make dozens of B-westerns. But he soon returned to his roots and became a serial specialist, making 54 in all to 1956, when Hollywood finally abandoned the format. Known for his ability to generate tension and pace from camera movement and cutting, he handled such sci-fi classics as *Superman* (1948) and *Batman and Robin* (1949), as well as lesser outings like *The Purple Monster Strikes* (1945).

RICK BERMAN *(b 1945)* US prod **& MICHAEL PILLER** *(b 1948)* US scr/prod Having spent a couple of years in programme planning at Paramount, Rick Berman was teamed with Emmy-winning news producer-turned-writer Michael Piller on *Star Trek: the Next Generation* in 1987. Faced with re-inventing Gene Roddenberry's concept without alienating its legion of fans, the pair shifted the emphasis away from gadgetry and alien confrontation and on to character. The new formula proved a hit with Trekkies, who also embraced two further series spin-offs, *Star Trek: Deep Space Nine* (1993-99) and *Star Trek: Voyager* (1995-2001), as well as the movies *StarTrek: Generations* (1994), *Star Trek: First Contact* (1996) and *Star Trek: Insurrection* (1998).

LUC BESSON *(b 1959)* Fr dir/scr/prod Debuting with the short *La P'tite Sirène* (1978), while on military service, Besson worked as an assistant director in France and Hollywood before a series of acclaimed pop promos and commercials enabled him to complete his first feature, the monochromatic post-apocalyptic drama, *The Last Battle* (1982). Cult status arrived with *Subway* (1985), although with it came accusations that he had fostered a *cinéma du look*, in which style mattered more than substance. However, he continued to enjoy mainstream success with *The Big Blue* (1988), *Nikita* (1990) and *Leon* (1994) before making his English-language bow with the futuristic blockbuster, *The Fifth Element* (1997).

CHESLEY BONESTELL *(1888-1986)* US artist/SFX artist Trained as an architect, Chesley Bonestell began as a draughtsman on the Golden Gate Bridge. Relocating to Hollywood, he painted backdrops on such classics as *The Hunchback of Notre Dame* (1939) and *Citizen Kane* (1941). However, some space paintings in *Life* magazine (1944) and his illustrations for Willy Ley's 1949 book, *Conquest of Space*, led to his becoming a major figure in the fifties sci-fi boom. In addition to acting as astronomical art consultant on such key Bs as *Destination Moon* (1950), *When Worlds Collide* (1951) and *The War of the Worlds* (1953), he also helped design TV's *Men into Space* (1959-60).

WALTER R BOOTH *(1869-1938)* UK dir/scr Initially the UK sales rep for Thomas Edison and Georges Méliès, Booth made the first of his countless short films for pioneer producer RW Paul in 1899. Specialising in comedies and trick flicks, he moved into sci-fi with *The ? Motorist* (1905), in which a space-travelling car speeds around Saturn's ring. Shortly after signing to Charles Urban's Warwick Trading Company in 1906, he made Britain's first animated film, *The Hand of the Artist* (1906). However, his lasting achievement was the prototype sci-fi drama, *The Airship Destroyer* (1909), which was relaunched as the wartime propaganda piece, *The Aerial Torpedo*, in 1915.

LARRY BUCHANAN *(b 1924)* US dir/scr/prod Shooting films from the age of 11, this onetime bit-part actor and religious documentarist made his feature debut with the erotic horror, *The Naked Witch* (1960). He is best known for a series of low-budget sci-fi movies commissioned by AIP, including *The Eye Creatures* (1965), *Mars Needs Women* and *Zontar, the Thing from Venus* (all 1966). He also helmed *Beyond the Doors* (1983), in which he claimed the deaths of Jim Morrison, Jimi Hendrix and Janis Joplin were part of a government conspiracy.

TIM BURTON *(b 1960)* US dir/scr/prod A boyhood film-maker, whose career started in the animation department at Disney, Burton cut his directorial teeth on the unconventional short, *Frankenweenie* (1984), and the equally eccentric feature, *Pee-Wee's Big Adventure* (1985). Subsequently, he has juggled Gothic fairy-tales like *Beetle Juice* (1988), *Edward Scissorhands* (1990) and *The Legend of Sleepy Hollow* (1999) with Expressionist comic cuts, *Batman* (1989) and *Batman Returns* (1992), and such homages to fifties science fiction as *Mars Attacks!* (1996) and *Ed Wood* (1994), an affectionate biopic of one of the B-movies least capable practitioners. He returned to the genre in 2001 for a remake of *Planet of the Apes*.

DICK CALKINS *(1895-1962)* US illustrator Calkins cartooned for the *Chicago Examiner* before joining the John F Dille syndicate in 1929. Here, he worked on the *Skyroads* comic strip with Lester J Maitland. But his most important collaboration was with novelist Phil Nowlan on *Buck Rogers in the 25th Century*. A far cry from the camp eighties TV series, the much-imitated original depicted Buck emerging from 500 years suspended animation to team with Dr Huer and Wilma Deering in vanquishing evil warlords. Following Nowlan's death in 1940, Calkins produced the strip alone until a feud with his editors in 1947. He later illustrated the famous Red Ryder western comics.

JAMES CAMERON *(b 1954)* US dir/scr/prod Having started making 16mm films as a teenager, he was signed up by B maestro Roger Corman to work as art director and miniature builder on *Battle beyond the Stars* (1980). Following an inauspicious directorial debut with *Piranha II: the Spawning* (1981), he forged his reputation (and revived Arnold Schwarzenegger's career) with the sleeper smash, *The Terminator* (1984). His aptitude for sci-fi was confirmed with the chilling *Aliens* (1986) and the under-rated underwater epic, *The Abyss* (1989), before he cemented his place on the blockbuster A-list with *Terminator 2: Judgment Day* (1991), the Bond spoof *True Lies* (1994) and a little thing called *Titanic* (1997).

JOHN CARPENTER *(b 1948)* US dir/scr/comp/prod A preteen cinéaste, he published his own movie magazine and began directing with *Revenge of the Colossal Beasts* (1962). He'd already won an Oscar for the short *The Resurrection of Bronco Billy* (1970) before enrolling at the USC Film School, where he embarked on the graduation project he would expanded into the cult classic, *Dark Star* (1974). He impressed with *Assault on Precinct 13* (1976), but it was the seminal teen slasher, *Halloween* (1978), that made his name. Subsequently, he alternated between horror (*The Fog*, 1980; *Christine*, 1983) and sci-fi (*The Thing*, 1982; *Starman*, 1984). A series of costly misfires clipped his creative wings. He always composes his own scores.

CHRIS CARTER *(b 1956)* US scr/prod Formerly of *Surfing* magazine, Californian Carter began screenwriting with the Disney teleplay *B.R.A.T. Patrol* (1986). Initially considered a comedy specialist, he turned producer with the musicomic series *Rags to Riches* (1987). Headhunted by Fox's Peter Roth, he began work on a show based on his childhood favourites, *The Night Stalker* and *The Twilight Zone*. Ultimately, *The X Files* (1993 –) was also to have a touch of *The Avengers* about it, thanks to David Duchovny and Gillian Anderson's unique chemistry. Subsequently, Carter, who is godfather to Anderson's daughter, has executive- produced TV's *Millenium* (1996-99), *Harsh Realm* (1999-2000) and *The Lone Gunmen* (2001).

LARRY COHEN *(b 1938)* US dir/scr/prod Earning his spurs writing TV westerns, Cohen broke into sci-fi with the cult series, *The Invaders* (1967-68). As a feature director, he continued to demonstrate versatility with the race drama *Bone* (1972) and the blaxploitation thriller, *Black Caesar* (1973). But, with *It's Alive!* (1974), he revealed a talent for science-based horror that would resurface in two schlockier sequels. The sci-fi element was stronger, however, in *God Told Me To* (1976). In 1989, he had the dubious distinction of causing Bette Davis to stalk off her last film, *The Wicked Stepmother*, after just one week.

ROGER CORMAN ***(b 1926)*** **US dir/prod** Tired of having his scripts bowdlerised, Corman turned producer with *The Monster from the Ocean Floor* (1954). However, it was at American International Pictures that he became the King of the Bs, churning out dozens of exploitation cheapies, across the generic range, many of which were completed within ten days for under $100,000. Although directorial outings like *Not of This Earth* (1957) and *A Bucket of Blood* (1959) proved his efficient ingenuity, his finest achievement was the series of Edgar Allan Poe adaptations starring Vincent Price. However, he also guided the early careers of such luminaries as Francis Ford Coppola, Martin Scorsese and James Cameron. Having returned to directing after 19-year hiatus, with *Frankenstein Unbound* (1990), he sold his New Horizons company (and its 375+ back catalogue) for $100 million. No wonder he called his autobiography, *How I Made a Hundred Movies in Hollywood and Never Lost a Dime*.

DAVID CRONENBERG ***(b 1943)*** **Can dir/scr** Film-making from his student days, he made his directing debut with *Stereo* (1969). Although the Canadian parliament bemoaned his use of state funding, his unique brand of "body horror" exerted international influence, bringing a visceral element to such cerebral themes as biological experimentation (*The Brood*, 1979), telepathy (*Scanners*, 1981) and media manipulation (*Videodrome*, 1983). Diverting into Stephen King territory for *The Dead Zone* (1983), he returned to sci-fi for *The Fly* (1986) and *Dead Ringers* (1988). However, his adaptations of William Burrough's *The Naked Lunch* (1991) and JG Ballard's *Crash* (1996) split the critics, although *eXistenZ* (1998) proved less divisive.

JOE DANTE ***(b 1946)*** **US dir/scr/prod** A childhood sci-fi fanatic, Dante began editing trailers for Roger Corman, for whom he also reworked Shiro Moritani's *The Submersion of Japan* (1973) as *Tidal Wave* (1975). He made his feature debut, *Hollywood Boulevard* (1976), as a bet to shoot a feature for $50,000 in one week. He had more success with his Jaws parody, *Piranha* (1978), which caught the eye of Steven Spielberg, who hired him for the *It's a Good Life* episode in *Twilight Zone: The Movie* (1983). Unfortunately, since peaking with *Gremlins* (1984) and *Gremlins 2: the New Batch* (1990), only the William Castle tribute, *Matinee* (1993) has matched earlier outings.

JOHN DYKSTRA ***(b 1947)*** **US SFX artist** A stills photographer, he gained film experience as Douglas Trumbull's assistant on *Silent Running* (1971). Having devised a camera kit that facilitated the creation of miniature cityscapes, he won an Oscar for his contribution to *Star Wars Episode IV: a New Hope* (1977) and a special award for the invention of the Dykstraflex camera, a computerised motion control system that allowed George Lucas to shoot moving models with enhanced authenticity. He headed Lucas's Industrial Light & Magic for several years before founding his own Apogee company, which was responsible for the effects of *Batman and Robin* (1997) and *Stuart Little* (1999).

ROLAND EMMERICH ***(b 1955)*** **Ger dir/scr/prod** Debuting with an elongation of his graduation film, *The Noah's Ark Principle* (1984), he misfired with the kidpix, *Joey* (1985) and *Ghost Chase* (1988), before returning to sci-fi with *Moon 44* (1990), which launched his partnership with writer/producer, Dean Devlin. Following *Universal Soldier* (1992), they scored a cult hit with *Stargate* (1994) and a runaway box-office smash with *Independence Day* (1996), "the most expensive B-movie ever made". However, *Godzilla* (1997), the duo's attempt to Hollywoodise the Japanese monster movie, proved a disappointment.

TERENCE FISHER ***(1904-1980)*** **UK dir** A clapper boy-turned-editor, Fisher began directing with *To the Public Danger* (1947). Excepting *So Long at the Fair* (1950), the majority of his early offerings were crime quickies. However, a stint on TV's *Robin Hood* series (1952-56) and a move to Hammer transformed his fortunes, with *The Curse of Frankenstein* (1957) and *Dracula* (1958) forging the company's reputation for horror. Working regularly with Peter Cushing and Christopher Lee, he complemented a fine grasp of period and place with a penchant for violence and gore that revitalised the vampire, werewolf and mad scientist stories that had sustained Universal in its glory days.

RICHARD FLEISCHER ***(b 1916)*** **US dir** The son of cartoon pioneer Max Fleisher, he joined RKO's newsreel department in 1942. Having made his feature debut with *Child of Divorce* (1946), he won an Oscar for his documentary, *Design for Death* (1947). What followed was a prolific and diverse career, which contained such unnerving thrillers as *The Narrow Margin* (1952), the crime biopic *The Boston Strangler* (1968) and expensive failures like *Doctor Doolittle* (1967). His sci-fi output ranged from the submaritime twosome, *20,000 Leagues under the Sea* (1954) and *Fantastic Voyage* (1966) to the disturbing *Soylent Green* (1973) and the camp fantasy, *Conan the Barbarian* (1984).

JUN FUKUDA ***(1924-2000)*** **Jap dir** In 1951, a decade after he arrived from Korea, Fukuda joined the Toho studio, assisting various top-line directors before making his own debut with *Playing with Fire* (1959). Having demonstrated a facility for SFX with *The Secret of the Telegian* (1960), he became a regular contributor to the Godzilla series, with the playful *Son of Godzilla* (1967) standing in stark contrast to the more abrasive *Godzilla vs the Cosmic Monster* (1974). However, he preferred working on crime thrillers, he was lured into outer space for *Kanto 55-Space Adventure* (1969) and *War of the Planets* (1977).

WILLIAM GIBSON ***(b 1948)*** **US novelist** Resident in Canada since 1968,Gibson debuted with *Fragments of a Hologram Rose* (1977). Initially, he concentrated on short stories, one of which, *Johnny Mnemonic* (1981), he adapted for the screen in 1995. By that time, he had coined the term "cyberspace" and become the godfather of cyberpunk thanks to *Neuromancer* (1984), a pulp sci-fi thriller exploring corporate greed and our discomfort with digitised technology. Since completing the cyberpunk cycle with *Count Zero* (1986) and *Mona Lisa Overdrive* (1988), he's published such contrasting books as *The Difference Engine* (1990; with Bruce Sterling), *Virtual Light* (1993) and *All Tomorrow's Parties* (1999).

HR GIGER ***(b 1940)*** **Swi artist** Hans Rudi Giger was already a cult artist and fringe film-maker before he found international fame with *Necronomicon* (1972), a series of images that recalled the grotesques of Breughel and Bosch, yet were inspired by his own horror nightmares. Frustrated in his bid to collaborate with Alejandro Jodorowsky on an adaptation of *Dune*, he moved on to Ridley Scott's *Alien* (1979), for which he won an Best Visual Effects Oscar. A commitment to *Poltergeist II* (1985) prevented his involvement in *Aliens*, but he returned to design David Fincher's *Alien3* (1992). His most recent film commission was for *Species* (1995).

TERRY GILLIAM ***(b 1940)*** **US dir/anim/scr/perf** Long based in London, Gilliam achieved cult status for his surreal animations for *Monty Python's Flying Circus* (1969-76). Having co-directed *Monty Python and the Holy Grail* (1975), he went solo with the kid-friendly fantasies, *Jabberwocky* (1977) and *Time Bandits* (1981). Subsequently, his lavishly ambitious and ceaselessly inventive projects have encountered all manner of difficulties, with Universal interfering in his sub-Orwellian masterpiece, *Brazil* (1985), *The Adventures of Baron Munchausen* (1989) going way over both budget and deadline and *The Man Who Killed Don Quixote* (2000) being abandoned altogether. *The Fisher King* (1991) and *Twelve Monkeys* (1995) were happier ventures.

JEAN GIRAUD *(b 1938)* **Fr artist/designer** Inspired by Gustave Doré and Alex Raymond, he launched his comic career as a teenager with *Frank and Jérémie* (1956), refining his style alongside Joseph "Jije" Gillian on the *Jerry Spring* western strip. Already working under the pseudonyms "Gir" and "Moebius", he introduced his best-known character, Blueberry, in 1963. However, it wasn't until the seventies, when Giraud and his fellow members of Les Humanoides Associés added a more distinctively sci-fi flavour to comics like *Heavy Metal*. He later moved into film, contributing concept designs to Alejandro Jodorowsky's unrealised *Dune*, *Alien* (1979), *Tron* (1982), *Willow* (1988) and *The Fifth Element* (1997).

JEAN-LUC GODARD *(b 1930)* **Fr dir/scr/prod/perf** A naturalised Swiss, JLG wrote for the legendary journal, *Cahiers du Cinéma*, before emerging as one of the driving forces of the *nouvelle vague* with his debut feature, *A Bout de Souffle* (1959). Revelling in his status as the movement's enfant terrible, he brought the same stylistic audacity and political commitment to personal projects and generic revisions like the futuristic *film noir*, *Alphaville* (1965). Constantly experimenting with form, he became increasingly iconoclastic in his Marxist collaborations with Jean-Pierre Gorin and his video experiments with Anne-Marie Miéville. Still active, he's rightly been described as a film critic in disguise.

ROB GRANT & DOUG NAYLOR UK scr Using the pseudonym Grant Naylor with his writing partner Doug Naylor, the pair created BBC2's longest-running sitcom, *Red Dwarf* (1988-99). The duo began contributing sketches to *Spitting Image*, *Alas Smith and Jones* and *Carrott's Lib*, as well as penning the misfiring series, *Pushing Up Daisies* (1984) and *The 10 Percenters* (1993). But with *Red Dwarf* they struck gold, supplementing the shows with several novels, including *Infinity Welcomes Careful Drivers* (1992). They parted ways in the late nineties, with Grant moving on to *Stressed Eric* (1998), *Dark Ages* (1999) and *The Strangerers* (2000), while Naylor began pre-production on *Red Dwarf: the Movie*.

VAL GUEST *(b 1911)* **UK dir/scr** Formerly an assistant to ace journalist Walter Winchell, Guest started out writing comedies for Will Hay and Arthyr Askey. Having directed several escapist vehicles for his wife Yolande Dolan, he gained a reputation for sci-fi with Hammer's big-screen adaptation of the TV classic, *The Quatermass Experiment* (1954). A sequel, *Quatermass II* (1957), and *The Day the Earth Caught Fire* (1961) followed. But he continued to jaunt around the genres, with the horror chiller *The Abominable Snowman* (1957), the 007 spoof *Casino Royale* (1967) and the prehistoric adventure *When Dinosaurs Ruled the Earth* (1970).

RAY HARRYHAUSEN *(b 1920)* **US SFX artist.** Inspired by *King Kong* (1933), he began making stop-motion shorts as a kid. Having served his apprenticeship on George Pal's Puppetoons series, he assisted his hero, Willis O'Brien, on the Oscar-winning SFX for *Mighty Joe Young* (1949). He created his first solo effects for *The Beast from 20,000 Fathoms* (1953) before forging a partnership with producer Charles H Schneer that fostered such sci-fi standards as *It Came from Beneath the Sea* (1955) and *One Million Years BC* (1966). The inventor of the Superdynamation process to blend live-action and stop-motion footage (eg *Jason and the Argonauts*, 1963), he received a special Oscar in 1991.

BYRON HASKIN *(1899-1984)* **US dir/cinematog/SFX artist** A former cartoonist and newsreel cameraman, Haskin began shooting Hollywood features in 1922. Having turned director in 1927, he took over as head of Warners' SFX department in the mid-thirties. Here he won a special Oscar for developing a back projection system, in addition to five other nominations. He resumed his directorial career at Paramount, with the *film noir*, *I Walk Alone* (1947). However, he's best known for his science-fiction output, with *War of the Worlds* (1953) and *Robinson Crusoe on Mars* (1964) held in higher regard than *Conquest of Space* (1955) and *From the Earth to the Moon* (1958).

INOSHIRO HONDA *(1911-1993)* **Jap dir/scr** Fifteen years after he first joined the PLC studio, Ishiro Honda forged a lifelong friendship with master film-maker Akira Kurosawa, while assisting him on *Stray Dog* (1949). Yet their career paths couldn't have been more divergent, once Honda released his post-A-bomb allegory, *Godzilla* (1954). Working in close collaboration with SFX maestro Eiji Tsuburaya and prolific producer Tomoyuki Tanaka (who would amass over 200 feature credits), he would devise all manner of prehistoric, city-crushing critters over the next 30 years. But the star of Toho's 22-strong series would always be the ever-mispronounced Gojira, which translates as half-gorilla, half-whale.

PETER HYAMS *(b 1943)* **US dir/scr/cinematog/ed.** Hyams developed his one-man band approach as a TV news reporter. Surviving a rocky transition to cinema, he hit his stride with the Watergate allegory *Capricorn One* (1978) and *Outland* (1981), an interstellar remake of *High Noon*. The conspiracy thriller, *The Star Chamber* (1983), confirmed his reputation for polished visuals and slickly staged action sequences. But, since his workmanlike take on Arthur C Clarke, *2010* (1984), he's struggled for consistency, with thrillers and black comedies rubbing alongside the Jean-Claude Van Damme vehicles, *Timecop* (1994) and *Sudden Death* (1995), and the horror misfires, *The Relic* (1997) and *End of Days* (1999).

KENNETH JOHNSON *(b 1942)* **US dir/scr/prod** Breaking into TV with *Adam-12* (1968), Johnson found his niche in the mid-1970s. Having served as a producer on *The Six Million Dollar Man* (1974-78), he created its companion show, *The Bionic Woman* (1976-78), before developing the small-screen version of Stan Lee's Marvel comic, *The Incredible Hulk* (1978-82). The miniseries *V* (1983) and its sequel, *V: the Final Battle* (1994), were widely acclaimed, although the ensuing series quickly perished. He's since concentrated on various *Alien Nation* series and teleplays (1989-97), although he has made the odd sortie into cinema, notably *Short Circuit 2* (1988).

JOE JOHNSTON *(b 1950)* **US dir/art dir/prod** This commercial artist entered films as a storyboarder on *Star Wars Episode IV: a New Hope* (1977). Having designed Yoda for *Star Wars Episode V: the Empire Strikes Back* (1980), he shared an Oscar for his SFX work on *Raiders of the Lost Ark* (1981). He made his directorial debut with *Honey, I Shrunk the Kids* (1989) and has since specialised in sci-fi and fantasy subjects. Despite misfiring with *The Rocketeer* (1991) and *The Pagemaster* (1995), for which he did the live-action segments, Johnston bounced back with the kid-pleasing blockbuster, *Jumanji* (1995). Following *October Sky* (1999), he was given another chance to demonstrate his CGI prowess with *Jurassic Park III* (2001).

NATHAN JURAN *(b 1907)* **US dir/art dir** Born in Austria, but in the States as a boy, he trained as an architect. However, he joined the 20th Century-Fox art department in 1937, going on to win an Oscar for *How Green Was My Valley* (1941). After a stint at Universal, he made his directorial debut with *The Black Castle* (1952), initially handling Westerns and action fare. But he'll be best remembered for a trio of sci-fi collaborations with Ray Harryhausen - although movie cultists might point to the 1958 features he made under the pseudonym Nathan Herz: *Attack of the 50ft Woman* and *The Brain from Planet Arous*.

BOB KANE *(1916-98)* **US comic-strip artist** Initially drawing comedy strips like *Peter Pupp*, he teamed up with Bill Finger at DC Comics in 1938. Together they launched *Batman* in May 1939. The result of a weekend's brainstorming, the Dark Knight was inspired by sources as diverse as Leonardo Da Vinci's notebooks, the Scarlet Pimpernel and the 1930 movie, *The Bat Whispers*. Although Kane's artistic role in the Batman myth was essentially supervisory, he retained a copyright interest and came to Hollywood in the mid-sixties to advise on the cult TV series starring Adam West and Burt Ward.

JACK KIRBY ***(1917-94)*** **US comic-strip artist** He'd already worked on *Popeye* cartoons and the first *Captain Marvel* strip by the time he teamed with Joe Simon to create Captain America in 1941. Introducing a cinematic perspective, he also pioneered the cartoon love story with *Young Romance Comics* in 1947. Splitting with Simon in 1956, following a moral backlash against comic-book violence, he bounced back in the early sixties, creating or collaborating on almost all Marvel Comics' best-loved characters, including the Fantastic Four, Spider-Man, Thor, The Hulk, X-Men and Silver Surfer. It's reckoned "the King of Comics" drew some 24,000 pages of art during his career.

NIGEL KNEALE ***(b 1922)*** **UK scr** A Manxman, Kneale found fame with *The Quatermass Experiment* (1953), which, like its sequels, *Quatermass II* (1955) and *Quatermass and the Pit* (1958-59), were filmed by Hammer. He would go on to script *The Abominable Snowman* (1957) and *The First Men in the Moon* (1964), as well as John Osborne's *Look Back in Anger* (1958) and *The Entertainer* (1960). One-off TV dramas included *The Year of the Sex Olympics* (1968) and *The Stone Tape* (1972). He returned to his old stomping ground with *Quatermass* for ITV in 1979.

STANLEY KUBRICK ***(1928-99)*** **US dir/scr** Stills photographer-turned-shorts maker, Kubrick followed his acclaimed crime films, *Killer's Kiss* (1955) and *The Killing* (1956) with the war classic, *Paths of Glory* (1957) and the Roman epic, *Spartacus* (1960). Relocating to Britain, he teamed with Peter Sellers on *Lolita* (1962) and the scathing Cold War satire, *Dr Strangelove* (1964). His place in sci-fi history was cemented with *2001: a Space Odyssey* (1968) and his controversial dystopia drama, *A Clockwork Orange* (1971). He concluded his remarkable career with *Eyes Wide Shut* (1999), while his last project, *AI: Artificial Intelligence*, was filmed by Steven Spielberg in 2001.

VERITY LAMBERT ***(b 1935)*** **UK TV prod** She may have won a Bafta for *W Somerset Maugham* (1969) and overseen such ITV landmarks as *The Naked Civil Servant* (1975), the Emmy-winning *Edward and Mrs Simpson* and *Rumpole of the Bailey* (1978-83). But the jewel of Lambert's legacy is *Doctor Who*, which she commissioned in 1963. Despite being the BBC's youngest producer, she and writer Terry Nation defied the show's creator, Sydney Newman, and transformed it from an educational programme into an instant cult. She remained in time-travelling mode for *Adam Adamant Lives!* (1966-7).

FRITZ LANG ***(1890-1976)*** **Austrian dir/scr** Lang began directing with the sci-fi thriller, *The Spiders* (1919). An inspired phase followed,. as he exploited the unique visual and psychological atmosphere of Expressionism to fashion *Destiny* (1921), *Dr Mabuse, the Gambler* (1922), *Die Nibelingen* (1924) and the peerless *Metropolis* (1926). Such was his grasp of the genre that the countdown he invented for *The Woman in the Moon* (1929) was later adopted for rocket launches. His transition to sound, with *M* (1931) and *The Testament of Dr Mabuse* (1933), was also impressive. But his dictatorial style alienated many in Hollywood and only occasional outings like *Fury* (1936), *Scarlet Street* (1945) and *The Big Heat* (1953) matched past glories.

GLEN A LARSON ***(b 1937)*** **US TV prod** He first found fame as one of The Four Preps pop group in the fifties. But once he sold a story idea to *The Fugitive* his future was in TV. Although he worked as writer and/or director on such westerns as *The Virginian* and *Alias Smith and Jones* and crime shows like *McCloud*, *Quincy* and *Magnum PI*, he's best known for his contribution to such sci-fi staples as *The Six Million Dollar Man*, *Battlestar Galactica* and *Buck Rogers in the 25th Century*. He also pioneered *Knight Rider*, repeating the man-machine formula, with mixed results, in *Manimal*, *Automan* and *The Highwayman*.

STAN LEE ***(b 1922)*** **US comic-book artist** Stanley Lieber got his break because his cousin was married to the owner of Timely Comics. Refining his craft under Jack Kirby, he was appointed editor and chief writer in 1942 and gradually began to change the nature of comic-book heroes, making them less super and more human. By the sixties the re-named Marvel Comics could boast such characters as the Fantastic Four, the Incredible Hulk, Spider-Man, Dr Strange, the X-Men, the Silver Surfer, Iron Man and Daredevil, as well as a resurrected Captain America. Several have featured in movies, while one villain, Doctor Doom, was reportedly the inspiration for Darth Vader.

GEORGE LUCAS ***(b 1944)*** **US dir/scr/prod** Having debuted with a feature version of his dystopian graduation film, *THX-1138* (1971), Lucas virtually invented sixties nostalgia with *American Graffiti* (1973), which bought him the creative independence to make *Star Wars Episode IV: a New Hope* (1977). Costing $10.5 million and intended as the fourth in a nine-part series, it went on to turn $590 million and reinvented film-making, merchandising and movie-going in the process. Yet Lucas opted merely for scripting and producing briefs on its sequels, *The Empire Strikes Back* (1980) and *Return of the Jedi* (1983). He now divided his time between developing new technologies through LucasFilm and Industrial Light & Magic and producing hits like the Indiana Jones trilogy and such flops as *Howard: a New Breed of Hero* (1986). But, in 1999, he ended a 22-year hiatus to direct *Star Wars Episode I: the Phantom Menace* (1999), which will be followed in 2002 by *Star Wars Episode II: Journey of a Sith*. Its yet unnamed sequel will complete the most commercially successful and critically maligned film series of all time. Then what?

DAVID LYNCH ***(b 1946)*** **US dir/scr/prod/perf** Lynch achieved instant cult status with his debut feature, *Eraserhead* (1978), a nightmarish fable that persuaded Mel Brooks to hire him for *The Elephant Man* (1980). This led to an offer to make *Return of the Jedi* (1983), but he opted instead for the ill-fated *Dune* (1984). He bounced back with *Blue Velvet* (1986), confirming his new reputation as the surreal poet of oddball America with *Wild at Heart* (1990), the cult TV series, *Twin Peaks* (1990-91) and its big-screen finale, *Twin Peaks: Fire Walk with Me* (1992), and Lost Highway (1996). He's since made *The Straight Story* (1999) and *Mulholland Drive* (2001).

PATRICK MCGOOHAN ***(b 1928)*** **Ire perf/dir/scr** Rejecting both James Bond and the Saint on moral grounds, McGoohan created two of TV's most famous secret agents - John Drake in *Danger Man* and Number Six in *The Prisoner* (1967-68). This Kafkaesque conundrum was very much a pet project, as he not only devised it, but also wrote one episode under the pseudonym Patrick Fitz and directed two more as Joseph Serf. Yet despite this cult celebrity, he found films harder to crack, despite good showings in *Ice Station Zebra* (1968), *Escape from Alcatraz* (1979) and *Scanners* (1981).

ANTONIO MARGHERITI ***(b 1930)*** **It dir/scr/prod** Frequently credited as Anthony Dawson, Margheriti is a prolific maker of horror, action, sword-and-sandal and sci-fi movies, as well as spaghetti westerns. Yet he began his career as Antony Daisies on *Space Men* (1960), going on to confirm his sci-fi credentials with *Battle of the Worlds* (1961) and *War of the Planets* and its companion *The Wild, Wild Planet* (both 1965). He's also hugely versatile and, in addition to chillers like *Castle of Blood* (1964), he also worked uncredited on Andy Warhol's *Blood for Dracula* and *Flesh for Frankenstein* (both 1974).

SYD MEAD ***(b 1933)*** **US designer/art dir** Gaining experience in an animation department, Mead designed for Ford before forming his own company in 1970. Ranging from vehicles to buildings, installations to digi-sites, his work has earned international acclaim. He moved into films with *Star Trek: the Motion Picture* (1979), going on to provide visual concepts and/or production designs for such sci-fi classics as *Blade*

Runner, Tron (both 1982), *2010* (1984), *Aliens, Short Circuit* (both 1986), *Timecop* (1994) and *Johnny Mnemonic* (1995). He also worked on the Japanese pictures *Crises 2050* (1990) and *Yamato Takeru* (1994), as well as designing the Jules Verne Time Tour at Disneyland Paris.

GEORGES MÉLIÈS ***(1861-1938)*** **Fr dir/perf/prod** Cartoonist and magician Georges Méliès turned film-maker in 1896. He singlehandedly discovered trick cinematography when his camera jammed while shooting a street scene and an omnibus appeared to turn into a hearse. Soon his Star Films company was churning out ingenious féeries and actualités, as well as comedies, dramas, horrors and sci-fi landmarks like *Le Voyage dans La Lune* (1902) and *The Conquest of the Pole* (1912). He pioneered such key visual devices as the dissolve, superimposition and double exposure, as well as the use of SFX models. Yet, by 1915 he was virtually forgotten and wound up running a toy stall on a Paris station.

WILLIAM CAMERON MENZIES ***(1896-1957)*** **US dir/art dir/prod** By the time he won an Oscar for his work on *The Dove* and *Tempest* (both 1928), Menzies had convinced Hollywood that production design was key to the look and feel of a film, a fact that was recognised with a special award for his contribution to *Gone with the Wind* (1939). By then he had already dabbled in direction, following *The Spider* (1931) with a brilliantly stylised adaptation of HG Wells's *Things to Come* (1936). The artwork for *Invaders from Mars* (1953) was so convincing that Tobe Hooper reused it for his 1986 remake.

GEORGE MILLER ***(b 1945)*** **Australian dir/scr/prod** Trained as a doctor, Miller moved into movies with the short, *Violence in the Cinema, Part I* (1972). Collaborating with Byron Kennedy, he launched Mel Gibson on the road to superstardom with *Mad Max* (1979), which they followed with *Mad Max 2* (1981). After Kennedy was killed in a helicopter crash, Miller completed the trilogy with *Mad Max beyond the Thunderdome* (1985), after which he relocated to Hollywood. Here he changed tack with projects like *The Witches of Eastwick* (1987) and *Lorenzo's Oil* (1992), before returning to Oz to co-script/produce the charming sheep-pig pic, *Babe* (1995).

TERRY NATION ***(b 1930)*** **UK scr** Nation was struggling as a stand-up when Spike Milligan invited him to write for *The Goon Show*. After penning some 200 radio scripts, he joined ITV's *Out of This World* (1962), before being head-hunted to write for *Doctor Who*. In the course of 26 years on the show, nothing topped his invention of the Daleks. He scored further sci-fi hits with *Survivors* (1975-7) and *Blake's 7* (1978-81). But he also made significant contributions to such seminal crime shows as *The Avengers, The Saint, The Baron, The Persuaders* and *The Champions*, as well as the US series, *MacGyver*.

DOUG NAYLOR *see* **ROB GRANT**

WILLIS O'BRIEN ***(1886-1962)*** **US SFX artist** Disatisfied with marble-cutting and cartooning, O'Brien, who had made films as a kid, was hired by Edison to produce trick shorts such as *The Dinosaur* and *The Missing Link* (1914). Pioneering the stop-motion technique of animating rubber-based models, he made a splendid job of re-creating Sir Arthur Conan Doyle's *The Lost World* (1925). But his masterpiece would be *King Kong* (1933), for which he fashioned a "gigantic" gorilla out of wire, rubber and rabbit fur. He revisited the "beauty and the beast" scenario in *Son of Kong* (1933) and *Mighty Joe Young* (1949), but later found work harder to come by.

KATSUHIRO OTOMO ***(b 1954)*** **Jap comic-book artist/dir** Hooked on films as a kid, Otomo published his first comics in the early seventies. He emerged as a leading *manga* artist with *Fire Ball* (1979) and *Domu* (1980-82). But it was *Akira* (1982), that brought him fame and fortune, with its 1988 film adaptation sending an animé wave around the world. Subsequently, he scripted *Roujin Z* (1991) and supervised *Perfect Blue* (1997), as well as directing his sole non-animated feature, *World Apartment Horror* (1991). In addition to directing *Memories* (1996) and *Ash* (2000), he also continues to produce comic-books, with recent projects including *Legend of Mother Sara* and *Hunchback*.

GEORGE PAL ***(1908-80)*** **Hun dir/SFX artist** Abandoning studios across Europe, Pal arrived in Hollywood to produce the delightful *Puppetoons* series for Paramount, winning an Oscar in 1943 for his technique of combining live-action and animation. He was to win a further five for his SFX work on *Destination Moon* (1950), *When Worlds Collide* (1951), *War of the Worlds* (1953), *Atlantis, the Lost Continent* and *The Time Machine* (both 1960). He also directed the latter two, as he did *The Wonderful World Of The Brothers Grimm* (1962) and *The 7 Faces of Dr Lao* (1964). Keep an eye out for Woody Woodpecker, who cameos in nearly all his films.

MICHAEL PILLER see **RICK BERMAN**

FRED OLEN RAY ***(b 1954)*** **US dir** Despite shooting movies since his teens, his directorial debut, *The Alien Dead* (1978), was notable only as Buster Crabbe's farewell picture. Yet stars on the skids, like Dick Miller and Huntz Hall, quickly became a feature of his oeuvre, as did such Scream Queens as Michelle Bauer, Linnea Quigley and Brinke Stevens. Rooted firmly in fifties exploitation and packed with in-jokes, *Deep Space* (1987), *Alienator* (1989) and *Dinosaur Island* (1993) are cult items, while *Beverly Hills Vamp* (1988) and *Attack of the 60-Ft Centrefold* (1995) demonstrate his way with titles. He's also a highly perceptive B-movie critic.

ALEX RAYMOND ***(1909-56)*** **US comic-book artist** Lyman and Chic Young played key roles in the development of this comic legend, as he apprenticed on their respective strips, *Tim Tyler's Luck* and *Blondie*, in the early thirties. But it was a call to create a hero to match Buck Rogers that transformed his fortunes. Working in collaboration with Don Moore, he came up with Flash Gordon, whose interstellar exploits were soon holding radio and cinema audiences enthralled. The duo was also responsible for Jungle Jim. Raymond also created Secret Agent X-9 (with crime novelist Dashiell Hammett) and action man Rip Kirby, before his untimely car crash death.

GENE RODDENBERRY ***(1921-91)*** **US TV scr/prod** Decorated for both his wartime and civil aviation exploits, Roddenberry began writing for *Dragnet* in the fifties. He also worked on such tele-classics as *Highway Patrol, Have Gun Will Travel, Dr Kildare* and *The Naked City*. Misfiring with *The Lieutenant* (1965), he looked to have failed with *Star Trek* (1966), too, after its pilots were dismissed as overly cerebral. But it returned to become the first TV series to be preserved in the Smithsonian Institute, which also houses a model of the starship *Enterprise* alongside the Wright Brothers' and Lindbergh's planes. Nasa also named its first space shuttle after Captain Kirk's craft, while Roddenbery became the first writer/producer to receive a star on Hollywood's Walk of Fame. Having made little impact with a couple of pilots and teleplays, he delighted Trekkies with a series of big-screen adaptations before returning to TV with *Star Trek: the Next Generation* (1987)

JOEL SCHUMACHER ***(b 1942)*** **US dir/scr/prod** Quitting the rag trade, he made his mark designing costumes for Woody Allen's *Sleeper* (1973). Ironically, comedy sci-fi also furnished him with his directorial debut, *The Incredible Shrinking Woman* (1981). Having put the Brat Pack through its paces in *St Elmo's Fire* (1986), he bounced back from one of the all-time biggest money losers, *Cousins* (1989), with the out-of-body thriller, *Flatliners* (1990). Subsequently, he's proved himself capable of controversy (*Falling Down*, 1993 and *8MM*, 1998) and commercialism (*The Client*, 1994 and *A Time to Kill*, 1996). But *Batman Forever* (1995) and *Batman and Robin* (1997) suggested blockbusters weren't his style.

RIDLEY SCOTT ***(b 1939)*** **UK dir/prod** Starting out on *Z Cars* in the sixties, he gained a reputation as a commercials director before turning to features with *The Duellists* (1977). Sci-fi looms large in his legend, thanks to *Alien* (1979) and *Blade Runner* (1982). But he's since proved highly versatile, passing from fantasy (*Legend*, 1985) to thriller (*Someone to Watch Over Me*, 1987) to feminist road movie (*Thelma and Louise*, 1991). Not everything has turned out well (think *1492: Conquest of Paradise*, 1992 and *GI Jane*, 1997). But he struck gold with *Gladiator* (2000) and *Hannibal* (2001). In 1994, he and director brother Tony bought Shepperton Studios.

ROD SERLING ***(1924-75)*** **USTV scr/prod** Serling began writing for radio after war service. He moved into television in the early fifties, with the Emmy-winning play *Requiem for a Heavyweight* securing him the clout to launch a series of fantasy mysteries, *The Twilight Zone*, in 1959. In addition to writing 90 shows himself, he also bookended and narrated all 156 episodes. Yet he struggled to adapt after the show's cancellation in 1964, with *The Loner* being ditched at pilot and his draft script for *Planet of the Apes* (1968) being largely rewritten. *Night Gallery* (1969-73) had its moments, but his brand of eerie parable had outlived its era. He had his name removed from the credits of *The New People* (1969-70), the short-lived Aaron Spelling TV series.

DON SHARP ***(b 1922)*** **Aus dir/scr** Born in Tasmania, but in Britain from 1948, this onetime actor/writer began directing with *The Blue Peter* (1954). Following a string of low-budget musicals, he moved into exploitation with *Kiss of the Vampire* (1963) and *Witchcraft* (1965). He was renowned for thrilling action sequences, but *Curse of the Fly* (1965), *Jules Verne's Rocket to the Moon* (1967) and a couple of Christopher Lee's Fu Manchu outings demonstrated a sure touch with sci-fi. He also handled several episodes of *The Avengers* (1965-8) and *The Champions* (1968-69), as well as serviceable remakes of *The Thirty-Nine Steps* and *The Four Feathers* (both 1978).

JEROME SIEGEL ***(1914-1996)*** **& JOE SHUSTER** ***(1914-1992)*** **US comic-book artists** Having published the first-ever sci-fi fanzine, *Cosmic Stories* (1929), Siegel teamed up with schoolmate Shuster on *Science Fiction* (1931). Then, in 1934, they created Superman and his mild-mannered alter ego, Clark Kent. But four years would pass – spent working on *Dr Occult* and *Slam Bradley* – before they found a publisher. Yet, *Superman* was soon syndicated to 300 newspapers and was a radio, cartoon and movie serial star. However, the duo's financial reward was minimal and, in 1946, they unsuccessfully sued Detective Comics to regain the rights to their character. Shuster quit comics altogether, although Siegel struggled on as a jobbing artist until 1964.

CURT SIODMAK ***(1902-2000)*** **Ger novelist/scr/dir** An extra on *Metropolis* (1926), Siodmak quit journalism to co-script *People on Sunday* (1929),which was co-directed by his brother, Robert. His novel, *Secrets of FP1*, was filmed in 1932. But it was only in Hollywood exile that heretumed to screenwriting. In between *Son of Dracula* (1942) and *I Walked with a Zombie* (1944), he penned his best-known book, *Donovan's Brain*,which was adapted under its own title in 1953 and also as *The Monsterand the Lady* (1944) and *The Brain* (1965). However, directorial efforts such as *The Bride of the Gorilla* (1951) and *The Magnetic Monster* (1953)were less memorable.

STEVEN SPIELBERG ***(b 1946)*** **US dir/prod/scr** Spielberg had already been making films for a decade when he signed to Universal, where he directed Joan Crawford in an instalment of *Night Gallery* (1969) and the first-ever episode of *Columbo* (1971). His teleplay debut, *Duel* (1971) was followed by his feature bow, *The Sugarland Express* (1973). But it was *Jaws* (1975) that announced the arrival of cinema's new wünderkind. He drew his first Oscar nomination for *Close Encounters of the Third Kind* (1977) before bouncing back from the calamity of *1941* (1979) with another for *Raiders of the Lost Ark* (1981), the first of three Indiana Jones adventures. Yet another nomination came for *ET the Extraterrestrial* (1982). Yet, despite his commercial success, he craved critical acclaim and began alternating popcorn pictures with serious offerings like *The Color Purple* (1985). The tactic paid off in 1993, when he followed *Jurassic Park* with *Schindler's List*, which finally earned him an Academy Award. Following *The Lost World: Jurassic Park* (1997), he won a second for *Saving Private Ryan* (1998), which was made for his own DreamWorks studio. He returned to sci-fi with *AI: Artificial Intelligence* (2001), which he inherited from Stanley Kubrick.

LESLIE STEVENS ***(1924-1998)*** **US dir/scr** Stevens was just 15 when Orson Welles bought his play *Mechanical Rat* for the Mercury Theater. Having made his screenwriting debut with *The Left-Handed Gun* (1958), he turned director with *Private Property* (1960). But following *Hero's Island* (1962), he was lured into television to work on the rodeo series *Stoney Burke* and *The Outer Limits* (1963-65), the sci-fi anthology show that has since acquired cult status. He returned to cinema with *Incubus* (1966), but the seventies saw him back on the small screen, first with *The Gemini Man* (1976) and then with *Battlestar Galactica* (1978-79) and *Buck Rogers in the 25th Century* (1979-81).

J MICHAEL STRACZYNSKI ***(b 1954)*** **USTV scr/prod** Disillusioned with journalism, this collector of Superman paraphernalia broke into TV on such cartoon series as *He-Man* and *The Masters* (1983) and *She-Ra: Princess of Power* (1985). He moved on to the revival of *The Twilight Zone* (1985-89), penning 11 of its shows. When it folded, JMS worked on *Murder, She Wrote, The Real Ghostbusters* , *Captain Power and the Soldier of the Future* (1987-88). He returned to sc-fi with the *Babylon 5* (1993-9), which so enraged some Trekkies that he received death threats. Subsequently, he's produced *Crusade* (1999) and the radio series, *City of Dreams* (2000).

ANDREI TARKOVSKY ***(1932-86)*** **Russian dir** The son of a prominent Soviet poet, he won the Golden Lion at Venice with his debut feature, *Ivan's Childhood* (1962). But his international reputation was forged with *Andrei Rublev* (1966), a lyrical medieval biopic, in which he experimented with the concept of "sculpted time". However, it was banned until 1971, when it won festival prizes worldwide. He perfected the art of metaphysical sci-fi with *Solaris* (1972), before embarking on the densely personal dramas, *The Mirror* (1975) and *Stalker* (1979). In the early eighties, he accepted exile, shooting his final features, *Nostalgia* (1983) and *The Sacrifice* (1986) in Italy and Sweden.

DOUGLAS TRUMBULL ***(b 1942)*** **US SFX artist/cinematog/dir** He began making films for the US Air Force and Nasa, including *To the Moon and Beyond* (1964), which persuaded Stanley Kubrick to hire him for *2001: a Space Odyssey* (1968). Subsequently, Trumbull landed SFX Oscar nominations for *Close Encounters of the Third Kind* (1976), *Star Trek: the Motion Picture* (1979) and *Blade Runner* (1982). He also directed *Silent Running* (1971) and *Brainstorm* (1983). But his passions lie outside conventional cinema. In addition to patenting the Showscan system and improving IMAX, he also devised a process to enhance the "hurtle" sensation on rides like Back to the Future at Universal Studios.

PAUL VERHOEVEN ***(b 1938)*** **Dutch dir** A onetime documentarist, Verhoeven forged a domestic reputation for the erotic (*Turkish Delight*, 1973 and *The Fourth Man*, 1983) and the violent (*Flesh + Blood*, 1985). The psycho-thriller *Basic Instinct* (1992) and the Vegas bitch-fest *Showgirls* (1995) proved he'd retained a keen interest in these areas. But since arriving in Hollywood, he's emerged as one of sci-fi's most combative and visually audacious adherents. Since achieving critical and commercial success with *RoboCop* (1987), he's reworked Philip K Dick in *Total Recall* (1990) and Robert A Heinlein in *Starship Troopers* (1997), as well as updating the invisible scientist story in *Hollow Man* (2000).

VIRGIL W VOGEL ***(1919-1996)*** **US dir/ed** Vogel's career began at Universal, editing such genre entries as *Mystery Submarine* (1950) and *This Island Earth* (1955). Sci-fi also provided him with his directorial debut, *The Mole People* (1956), which has since become a minor cult classic. Later outings like *The Land Unknown* (1957) and *Invasion of the Animal People* (1960), which each had polar settings, were equally esoteric. But once he moved into television, with the exception of some episodes of *Mission: Impossible*, he became something of a western specialist, directing so many *Wagon Train* and *Bonanza* shows he was inducted into the Cowboy Hall of Fame.

KURT VONNEGUT ***(b 1933)*** **US novelist** As a POW, Vonnegut witnessed the bombing of Dresden that was to inspire his best-known novel, *Slaughterhouse-Five* (1968), which was adapted for the screen in 1972. Launching his writing career with *Report on the Barnhouse Effect* (1950), he tried his hand at numerous jobs before gaining a reputation for such eerily prescient prophecy novels as *Player Piano* (1952) and *Cat's Cradle* (1963) and satirical sci-fi outings like *The Sirens of Titan* (1959), about a thwarted Martian invasion. *Slapstick of Another Kind* and *Harrison Bergeron* were filmed in 1982 and 1995 respectively.

PETER WATKINS ***(b 1935)*** **US dir/scr** Graduating from Cambridge and Rada, Watkins bega making short films while working in advertising. *The Diary of an Unknown Soldier* (1959) and *The Forgotten Face* (1961) so impressed the BBC that he was commissioned to produce *Culloden* (1964). However, such was the controversial nature of his nuclear holocaust documentary, *The War Game* (1965), that it was withheld, even after it won an Oscar in 1966. Disappointed by the reception accorded his morality fable, *Privilege* (1967), he devoted his energies to visually and thematically contentious projects like *The Peace Game* (1968), *Punishment Park* (1971), *The Journey* (1986) and *The Commune* (2000).

ORSON WELLES ***(1915-85)*** **US perf/dir/scr** Orphaned at 12, this precocious talent shocked America to its core on 30 October 1938, when his Mercury Theater radio production of HG Wells's *War of the Worlds* was mistaken for a news bulletin announcing a Martian invasion. Sadly, his subsequent connection with science-fiction would be limited. His screen debut (as both actor and director), *Citizen Kane* (1941), is still hailed as the finest film of all time, while flawed offerings like *The Magnificent Ambersons* (1942) and *Touch of Evil* (1958) are rightly held in critical esteem. Ever the maverick, he later acted in films like *The Third Man* (1949) to fund his personal projects.

JAMES WHALE ***(1896-1957)*** **UK dir** A cartoonist who began acting as a POW, Whale arrived in Hollywood to adapt the classic wartime play, *Journey's End* (1930). As revealed in the biopic, *Gods and Monsters* (1998), he was an unlikely champion of scientific horror. But his affinity for Expressionism was readily evident in Universal's *Frankenstein* (1931), *The Old Dark House* (1932) and *The Bride of Frankenstein* (1935). Moreover, he also possessed a darkly comic streak, as displayed in his SFX-laden take on HG Wells's *The Invisible Man* (1933). However, his fortunes dipped sharply, with only *Show Boat* (1936) and *The Man in the Iron Mask* (1939) finding favour.

JOHN WILLIAMS ***(b 1932)*** **US comp** The son of a film studio musician, Williams began working on TV's *Lost in Space* and *Land of the Giants*. Entering films in 1959, he drew the first of his 38 Oscar nominations for *Valley of the Dolls* (1967). He's converted six to Oscars, most notably on *Jaws* (1975), *Star Wars Episode IV: a New Hope* (1977) and *ET the Extraterrestrial* (1982). His other sci-fi credits include *Superman* (1978) and *Jurassic Park* (1993). But it's not all blockbusters for this prolific composer, as his contributions to *The Big Chill* (1983), *JFK* (1991) and *Angela's Ashes* (1999) prove. His next scores will be for *AI: Artificial Intelligence* and *Harry Potter and the Philosopher's Stone* (both 2001)

ROBERT WISE ***(b 1914)*** **US dir/ed/prod** Joining RKO in the 1930s, he edited *Citizen Kane* (1941) before being afforded the chance to direct by horror maestro, Val Lewton. Eventually, he moved to 20th Century-Fox, where he handled the sci-fi masterpiece, *The Day the Earth Stood Still* (1950). Wise continued to prove his versatility throughout the decade, before sharing an Oscar with Jerome Robbins for *West Side Story* (1961). Having dabbled in the occult with *The Haunting* (1963), he returned to the musical for *The Sound of Music* (1965). However, his later output, which included *The Andromeda Strain* (1971) and *Star Trek: the Motion Picture* (1980), was rather inconsistent.

WILLIAM WITNEY ***(b 1910)*** **US dir** This onetime messenger boy was given a chance to direct when a location western fell seriously behind schedule. The Republic front-office never had cause to regret its decision, as Witney became one of the most prolific serial/B merchants of all time. A student of Busby Berkeley, he brought a choreographed efficiency to his action sequences, which were invariably filmed with an undercranked camera. Frequently collaborating with Spencer Gordon Bennet and John English, he handled three Dick Tracy chapterplays, as well as *Adventures of Captain Marvel* (1941).

EDWARD D WOOD JR ***(1924-1978)*** **US dir/scr** Even Tim Burton's affectionate biopic, *Ed Wood* (1994) had to concede this cross-dressing anti-genius ranks high among the world's worst movie-makers. Obsessed with film as a kid, he seized upon stunt and extra work, while planning his directorial debut. *Glen or Glenda* (1953) featured an ailing Bela Lugosi, whose name alone enable Wood to complete the unmissably awful *Bride of the Monster* (1954) and *Plan 9 from Outer Space* (1957). Scraped together, rather than filmed, *Jail Bait* (1954), *Night of the Ghouls* (1959) and *The Sinister Urge* (1961), were continuity nightmares. But Wood's determination to direct makes him an irresistible character.

KAREL ZEMAN ***(1910-1989)*** **Czech anim/scr/art dir** Zeman worked as a poster artist and window dresser before making puppet films and cartoon shorts. He turned to features with *The Treasure of Bird Island* (1952). Very much an auteur, he used period illustrations, silhouettes and trick photography to fashion the distinctive visual style that made his sci-fi and fantasy films so magical. He was the first to attempt stop-motion animation in colour in *Voyage into Prehistory* (1955), while his *Baron Munchhausen* (1961) rivals Terry Gilliam's for invention. But even more impressive were Jules Verne-inspired trilogy, *The Invention of Destruction* (1958), *The Stolen Dirigible* (1966) and *On the Comet* (1974).

ROBERT ZEMECKIS ***(b 1952)*** **US dir/scr/prod** Zemeckis was working in television when he showed his graduation film, *A Field of Honor* (1973), to Steven Spielberg, who agreed to exec produce his debut feature, *I Wanna Hold Your Hand* (1978). In collaboration with Bob Gale, he scripted his first commercial hit, *Romancing the Stone* (1984). But the *Back to the Future* (1985, 1989, 1990) trilogy and that ingenious blend of live-action and animation, *Who Framed Roger Rabbit?* (1988), propelled him into the blockbuster bracket. However, he was never comfortable with the "movie brat" tag and has since sought to move into more serious film-making with the multi-Oscar winning *Forrest Gump* (1994), *Contact* (1997) and *Cast Away* (2000).

AUTHOR, AUTHOR

see pages 68/69 for the feature on the following authors

ISAAC ASIMOV, RAY BRADBURY, ARTHUR C CLARKE, MICHAEL CRICHTON, PHILIP K DICK, ROBERT A HEINLEIN, RICHARD MATHESON, JULES VERNE, HG WELLS & JOHN WYNDHAM

100 great websites

An eclectic guide to famous, obscure and odd genre websites for research, browsing and fun on the internet

General (film & TV)

www.allscifi.com
All SciFi – discussion site with visitors submitting their own reviews on television, movies and books, plus trivia quizzes

www.cinescape.com
Cinescape Online – "the crossroads of genre entertainment", featuring reviews and news on sci-fi, fantasy, horror and action movies, television, video, comics and books

www.darkhorizons.com
Dark Horizons – Australian-based site for news, pictures, clips and reviews for new films, plus episode guides to cult television in the United States, Australia and the UK

www.eofftv.com/
The Encyclopedia of Fantastic Film and Television – useful database with cast, production credits and plot synopses

http://scifi.ign.com
IGN Sci-Fi – loads of information and reviews about films and TV shows, as well as comics, games, news items, merchandising, plus "Ask the B.E.M" (Bug-Eyed Monster)"

www.imdb.com
Internet Movie Database – IMDB is the godfather of all the online film databases, but also carries similar information and links on television programmes, mini-series and made-for-TV movies

http://sflare.com
Solar Flare – lots of links, books, stories magazines, plus films and TV and interactive reviews, as well as sound and theme tune archives

www.starport.com
Star Port – news and reviews about hard science-fiction films and television; also offers online trivia games and Q&A with science-fiction celebrities

www.stomptokyo.com
Stomp Tokyo - "Illuminating the dark heart of video": not just science-fiction, but lots included. Among the sections are "Attack of the 50 Foot DVD" and the "Bad Movie Report", plus "Diary of a Tuber" has reviews to classic, and not-so-classic, TV shows

www.magicdragon.com/UltimateSF/SF-Index.html
The Ultimate Science Fiction Web Guide – almost 6,000 links to web science-fiction the net

General (film)

www.allmovie.com
All Movie Guide – film database, pus features. Not on the scale of IMDB, but useful nevertheless, with fun "factoids" and links to sister music and games sites

www.radiotimes.com/film
Radio Times Film – access the complete *Radio Times* film database online, plus get news and information on current cinema and video releases, as well as films on television

http://septnet.com/rcramer/scifi.htm
Ronnie Cramer's Cult Film Site – reviews, and many entries with pix and/or film clips. Good site to buy hard-to-find videos

http://scifimovies.about.com/movies/scifimovies/
Science Fiction Movies with Nick Johnson - news, articles, reviews, trivia, screensavers and trailers, plus links to more than 700 sites. The A-Z offers reviews, synopses, sounds and quotes

www.scifimovies.com
SciFi Movies – cast and plot information for lots of classics (and not so classic) golden oldies. Especially good on the old serials and chapterplays, plus usual round-up of video releases etc

http://members.nbci.com/scifimovies/index.html
Sci-Fi Movie Page – more than 200 movies reviews, news on new films, downloadable trailers, articles and pictures

www.tvguide.com/movies
TV Guide Online – access the Cinebooks film database, plus reviews of new releases in the United States

www.unknownmovies.com
The Unknown Movies Page – "the obscure, unknown and little shown": general site, but includes lots of sci-fi movies

www.upcomingmovies.com
Upcomingmovies – clear source of information on new movies, release dates, production schedules and films in development

General (TV)

www.geocities.com/TelevisionCity/7565/index.html
Agent J's Cult Sci-Fi Television – mainly links to well-selected fansites for cult TV series such as *Quark*, *V* and a good selection of UK shows

www.geocities.com/TelevisionCity/5078/AnorakZone.html
The AnorakZone - "Where all the truly sad articles on the internet come to live..." with links to online guides to shows such as *Sapphire & Steel* and *Star Cops*, plus *Doctor Who* and *The X Files*

http://members.aol.com/TampaChatr/index.html
All about TV Shows From the 50s to Today – general TV show database, but includes lots of sci-fi and fantasy. Entries have cast and characters, plus episode titles and original transmission dates

www.ee.surrey.ac.uk/Contrib/SciFi/
Bevis and Duncan's Science Fiction Page – detailed information and extensive guides on a limited number of sci-fi TV shows, plus the best guide to *The Invaders* on the net

www.bbc.co.uk/cult
BBC Online – great site for limited number of shows offering lots on episode and cast information to *Doctor Who*, *Farscape*, *The X Files* and others, plus quizzes and current TV schedules

www.epguides.com
Epguides – episode guides (titles and transmission dates) for more than 1,700 TV shows. Some entries have more detailed episode guides including guest stars and plot synopses

www.geocities.com/Hollywood/Hills/6009/index.htm
Live Action 70s Kid Vid – fan's guide to the Saturday morning shows of the seventies

www.fanderson.org.cuk/fanderson.html
The Official Gerry Anderson Appreciation Society – includes comprehensive guides with cast, crew, background and synopses for all of Gerry Anderson's film and TV productions

www.pazsaz.com
Pazsaz Entertainment Network - good site if you're looking for complete episode lists for TV series, with titles and original transmission. Particularly strong on superheros

www.sadgeezer.com
Sad Geezer – great for people who aren't afraid to admit they'll stay on the couch for sci-fi, any sci-fi, at any time.... Designed for people who like to rant (and obsess) about their favourite TV sci-fi show

http://home.earthlink.net/~joesarno/tvscifi/index.htm
Science Fiction on Television in the 1950s – episode guides and cast lists

http://members.spree.com/sci-fi/prime_1
Sci-Fi Central - TV series include *Farscape*, *Invisible Man*, *MST3K*, *Weird Science*, *Lost in Space*, *Sliders*, *Babylon 5*, *X Files*, with detailed episode guides (some with quotes) plus lots of pix

www.scifi.com/
Sci-Fi Channel's official website, with lots of information and chatrooms regarding past and current shows, plus news amd events

http://freespace.virgin.net/lol.marcus
Television Heaven – classic and modern TV programmes, including science fiction, from the US and the US, with reviews, an A-Z archive, collectibles and an interactive forum

www.tvtome.com
TV Tome – interactive guide to loads of cult TV shows. Browsers can contribute and, with editor privileges, edit selected section of each entry

http://ukculttv.tripod.com/
UK Terrestrial Cult TV – information on 50 television programmes, with episode guides, transmission dates, theme tunes and more. Plus a Cult TV "Babes" section with photos

www.yesterdayland.com/
Yesterdayland – "Your childhood is here": TV shows from the sixties and seventies a speciality, including lots of Saturday morning series not covered elsewhere

General (radio)

www.otrsite.com/radiolog
Jerry's Vintage Radio Logs – useful site if you want transmission dates, episode titles and so on. Audio-clips online in the "preview listening lounge" if you're thinking of buying

www.old-time.com
Old-Time Radio – good source of information about the golden age of radio science fiction, plus a trading post for recordings and books, and The Humongous Old-Time Radio Program Database

www.otrplotspot.com/default.htm
The OTR Plot Spot – another great site for fans of radio, including science fiction – an "audiography" of old-time radio, focusing on plotlines and themes

www.otr.com
Radio Days – celebrating the likes of Buck Rogers and Flash Gordon in the radio days, with audi-clips

www.pe.net/~rnovak/index.html
Radio Tales: Richard's Eclectica – includes the very useful Jack's Killer List of OTR Sites and information of series such as *Dimension X* and *X Minus One*

www.scifiguy.com
The SciFi Guy – site offering an amazing amount of information on English-language scifi and fantasy radio programmes. His mission is "to collect all known recordings of audio science fiction, supernatural/horror and fantasy and also to promote the creation of new production and encourage people to create their own dramas or readings within these genres" – exhaustive, and a great place to trade recordings for enthusiasts

www.thewarpzone.com
The Warp Zone – coming to you from Wichita, Kansas, USA. Lots of links, audio clips and articles celebrating science fiction on the radio. You can even listen to past shows, featuring interviews with people such as Adam *Batman* West, Richard *Apollo* Hatch and *Evil Dead*'s Bruce Campbell and Leonard Nimoy

Special interest

Alien Nation
www.tencton.com
The Alien Nation Homepage – comprehensive fansite of the Alien Nation Appreciation Society, with includes among

other features a guide to the Tenctonese language, as based on the original studio encyclopedia

The Amazing Spider-Man
www.geocities.com/mrathwel/Spidey/index.html
The Amazing Spider-Man Live-Action Television Series Page – fansite with episode guide, audio-clips, picture gallery and biographies

The Avengers
www.davidksmith.com/avengers
The Avengers Forever – a virtual encyclopedia of the cult British televison classic

Babylon 5
http://babylon5.warnerbros.com/
Official Babylon 5 Website – complete episode guide, crew biographies, chat room and audio-visual clips
www.oinc.net/B5/Enc
Babylon 5 Information System – fansite with complete A-Z encyclopedia of the space opera, plus an episode guide with ratings

Batman
www.batmanuk.freeserve.co.uk
Batman UK – fansite covering the comics, animated series and movies, with background on all the villains and the Caped Crusader's allies over the years
www.batman.com
DC Comics – offical website, with information on Batman and all the DC comics creations

Battlestar Galactica
www.kobol.com
Battlestar Galactica – oldest and largest site, including archives, costume and props museum, news, pictures, fan contributions, artwork, games and collectibles

Blade Runner
www.bladezone.com
The Online Blade Runner Fan Club and Museum – comprehensive site with articles, essays, cast and crew biographies and ongoing features including "Lost & Found" (what happened to the props), and an original serial story written by fans
ongoing features including "Lost & Found" (what happened to the props), and an original serial story written by fans

Blake's 7
http://hawks.ha.md.us/blake7
Blake's 7 – not jazzed up, but pages and pages of solid information about the series, including cast and characters, detailed episode guides, a costume index and scripts

Buck Rogers
www.buck-rogers.com
The Buck Rogers Home Page – a complete literary, film and TV biography of the classic space adventurer

Buffy the Vampire Slayer
www.buffy.com
Buffy the Vampire Slayer – official website, with a "full blood-curdling interactive experience" or a simpler option for those with a slower modem
http://buffyguide.com
The Complete Buffy Episode Guide – unofficial site that claims to have the most detailed episode guide available; also offers links, news and memorable quotes

Captain Scarlet and Mysterons
www.geocities.com/Area51/Shire/2010/opening.htm
Captain Scarlet and the Mysterons – fan site background, production, episodes, characters and news

Dark Angel
www.darkangeltheseries.com
Dark Angel – official website for the new James Cameron TV series, with lots of pictures, news, biographies and episode guides

Doctor Who
http://dwas.drwho.org
The Doctor Who Appreciation Society – home page of the longest running organised fan network in the world. Archive of articles and interviews, plus details on conventions, events, publications and merchandise
www.thedoctorwhoproject.freeserve rs.com/main.html
The Doctor Who Project – original fan fiction, based on the premise that the 1996 TV movie starring Paul McGann was never made and the eighth doctor is an unknown stage actor named Jeremy Banks-Walker
http://homepages.which.net/~howe/
Howe's Who – created by *Doctor Who* historian David J Howe which includes news, links, covers from *Doctor Who* books and videos, reviews of merchandise, and archives from *The Frame*, the *Doctor Who* fanzine
www.bbc.co.uk/cult/doctorwho/index.shtml
Doctor Who Homepage – official website for Doctor Who, with new stories, quizzes and games, archives, clips, episode guides, monsters and features

Earth: Final Conflict
www.earthfinalconflict.com
Earth: Final Conflict Official Website – features, news, links, downloads, cast and episodes

Farscape
www.farscape.com
Farscape – official website, with downloads, links and merchandising, as well as character biographies, episode guides and news

Fireball XL5
www.aiai.ed.ac.uk/~bat/GA/fireball-xl5.html
Fireball XL5 Web Site – fan site with background, episode guide, theme song and sound files, flight simulators and 3D computer models

The Green Hornet
www.uvm.edu/~glambert/green.html
The Green Hornet World Wide Web Page – focusing mainly on the TV series, but with background information on the radio series and movie serials

The Incredible Hulk
www.incrediblehulktvseries.com
The Television Series Page – everything you wanted to know about the TV series and TV movies

Lexx
http://fireheart.addr.com/lexx
Two Universes: The Ultimate Guide to Lexx Online – history, episode guides and links to 351 related sites

Lost in Space
http://nbci.com/Zappman/lost-in-space-main.html
The TV Show Web Site – biographies, pictures and an episode guide, together with links, music and sounds

Mork & Mindy
www.sitcomsonline.com/morandmindy.html
Sitcoms Online: Mork & Mindy – background to the show, episode guide, cast biographies and picture galleries, plus trivia

The Outer Limits
www.innermind.com/outerlimits
The Outer Limits – detailed coverage of both the original and nineties TV series, including a picture gallery and sounds

Planet of the Apes
www.movieprop.com/tvandmovie/PlanetoftheApes/
Movieprop.Com's Planet of the Apes Pages – complete guide to all the movies with character profiles, plus details on the TV series (live-action and animated), collectibles and memorabilia, and an outline of primate society

The Prisoner
www.the-prisoner-6.freeserve.co.uk/episode_index.htm
The Prisoner – complete episode guide with background, cast and production details and synopses

Quantum Leap
http://gcalvarez.tripod.com/qul.html
The Quantum Leap Information Kiosk – "the best online source of information about Quantum Leap and Its Stars", plus fan fiction and promotional images from the series

The Six Million Dollar Man
www.sixmilliondollarsite.co.uk
The Six Million Dollar Site – comprehensive site with background, episode guide and plots, plus information on the sister series, *The Bionic Woman*

Sliders
www.brillig.com/sliders/introduction.html
Earth Prime: the Fan's Guide to Sliders – background to all the alternative Earths visited by the Sliders, episode guides, recurring characters and more

Space: Above and Beyond
www.geocities.com/moonflyer.geo/saab/saab.html
MoonFlyer's Space: Above and Beyond Page – includes episode guides, links and MoonFlyer's Chig Recipe Book (101 Ways to Eat a Chig), among other features

Stargate SG1
www.sstargate-sg1.com/home.html
Stargate SG-1 – official website for the TV series, with merchandise, biographies and episode guides
www.sgccheyenne.fsnet.co.uk
Welcome to Cheyenne Mountain: Katana and Friends Stargate SG1 Website – fansite offering wallpaper, pictures, desktop themes, sounds, and an episode guide

Stingray
http://tvcentury21.com/productions/stingray/stingray.html
Stingray – complete guide to credits, episodes, characters and hardware

Star Trek
www.startrek.com
Star Trek – official website, with news on news series and films, plus extensive archives and K'Plett's Klingon Advice Column, among numerous features
www.treknation.com
Trek Nation – fan site, claiming to be the most extensive internet network dedicated to Star Trek. On offer are: Trek Today (www.trektoday.com), a daily updated guide to Trek news; Trek BBS (www.trekbbs.com), 20 forums and discussion groups for the worldwide community of Trekkies; Star Trek Hypertext (www.st-hypertext.com), reviews of all episodes, as well as Gene Roddenberry's *Andromeda*

Star Wars
www.starwars.com
Star Wars – official website, with everything for fans of the first four films, plus news and updates on *Star Wars II*

Superman
www.supermansupersite.com
Superman Super Site – "Everything there is to know about the Man of Steel... and we mean EVERYTHING"

Thunderbirds
www.thunderbirdsonline.com/0401/world_frame.jhtml
Thunderbirds Online – everything you could ever want to know about the classic supermarionation series, including character profiles and Gerry Anderson Q&As

The Twilight Zone
www.thetzsite.com
The Fifth Dimension – complete guide to the classic Twilight Zone series, with "485 pages, 3886 pictures, 62 sounds, 0 ads"

The Wild Wild West
www.wildwildwest.org
The Wildest Page in the West: headquarters of Wildwest2-L – news and complete episode guides, plus links to fan fiction and other related sites

The X Files
www.thexfiles.com
The X Files – official website with a complete archive to episodes, interviews with cast and crew (including video), fan club details and news
http://xtremexfiles.100megspopup.com/index2.html
X-treme X-files – unofficial website with spoilers, desktop goodies, pictures, and detailed episode guides

www.insidethex.co.uk
Inside the X – for those who have to have it all: complete transcripts for every episode of series.

Magazines & misc

www.visimag.com/cultimes/index.htm
Cult Times – specialist guide to cult shows (science fiction, fantasy and horror) on UK television, also including film reviews

www.the11thhour.com
The 11th Hour – web magazine with features devoted to science-fiction and fantasy films, television, plus books and comics

www.otherdimension.com
The Other Dimension – ezine specialising in science fiction and fantasy, includes reviews of new films as well as books

www.mindrobber.com
The Mind Robber Network – ezine with features, reviews, fan fiction and news, plus links to affiliated sites "Canadian Science Fiction & Fantasy Resource Guide" and "The Doctor Who Project"

www.sfsite.com
SF Site – host site that offers Gary Westfahl's Biographical Encyclopedia of Science Fiction Film, ISFDB (Internet Speculative Fiction Database), sci-fi and fantasy magazines such as *Dark Planet*, *Interzone* and *Fantasy and Science Fiction*, plus features and reviews of new books

www.space.com
Space.com – news and features about current and future space missions, tabloid news stories about aliens, plus entertainment and games departments

www.eventhorizon.com/sfzine/index.html
Event Horizon – award-winning webzine on science fiction, fantasy and horror (still online even though active publication is suspended); good stories, features and links

www.mervius.com
Fantastica Daily – webzine devoted to science fiction and fantary, with book and movie reviews, news and a weekly genre crossword puzzle

www.aint-it-cool-news.com
Ain't It Cool News – great gossip, news, spoilers and "epinions", with a genre bias on fantasy, action and sci-fi

http://sf.sig.au.mensa.org
IBN Qirtaiba: Magazine of the SF SIG of Australian Mensa – webzine from Australia includes original fiction and artwork, plus features on film and TV

Directors' index

A

Adamson, Al Dracula vs Frankenstein *1970* • Horror of the Blood Monsters *1970*
Adreon, Franklin Commando Cody: Sky Marshal of the Universe *1953*
Ahearne, Joe Ultraviolet *1998*
Albin, Hans No Survivors Please *1963*
Allen, Irwin The Lost World *1960* • Voyage to the Bottom of the Sea *1961* • City beneath the Sea *1971*
Allen, Woody Sleeper *1973*
Altman, Robert Countdown *1968* • Quintet *1979*
Amateau, Rod The Garbage Pail Kids Movie *1987*
Amemiya, Keita Zeram *1991*
Amici, Vanio *aka* **Collins, Bob** The Bronx Executioner *1989*
Anderson, Lindsay Britannia Hospital *1982*
Anderson, Michael 1984 *1955* • Doc Savage: the Man of Bronze *1975* • Logan's Run *1976* • The Martian Chronicles *1979* • Murder by Phone *1982* • Millennium *1989* • 20,000 Leagues under the Sea *1997*
Anderson, Paul Mortal Kombat *1995* • Event Horizon *1997* • Soldier *1998*
Apted, Michael Stronger Than the Sun *1977*
Argent, Douglas Astronauts *1981/1983*
Arkush, Allan Deathsport *1978* • Heartbeeps *1981*
Arnold, Jack It Came from Outer Space *1953* • Creature from the Black Lagoon *1954* • Tarantula *1955* • The Incredible Shrinking Man *1957* • Monster on the Campus *1958* • The Space Children *1958* • Hello Down There *1969*
Aronofsky, Darren Pi *1997*
Ashcroft, Ronnie The Astounding She-Monster *1958*
Asher, Robert The Bulldog Breed *1960*
Asher, William The 27th Day *1957*
Ashida, Toyoo Vampire Hunter D *1985* • Fist of the North Star *1986*
Azzopardi, Mario Thrill Seekers *1999* • Total Recall 2070 *1999*

B

Bacon, Lloyd It Happens Every Spring *1949*
Badham, John WarGames *1983* • Short Circuit *1986*
Bafaro, Michael Sleeping Dogs *1997*
Baker, Graham Alien Nation *1988*
Baker, Mark H Lifeform *1996*
Baker, Roy Ward Quatermass and the Pit *1967* • Moon Zero Two *1969* • Dr Jekyll and Sister Hyde *1971* • QED *1982*
Bakshi, Ralph Wizards *1977*
Balaban, Burt Stranger from Venus *1954*
Balch, Antony Horror Hospital *1973*
Baledon, Rafael Orlak, the Hell of Frankenstein *1960*
Bamford, Roger The Vanishing Man *1997-1998*
Band, Albert Robot Wars *1993*
Band, Charles Parasite *1982* • Metalstorm: The Destruction of Jared-Syn *1983* • Trancers *1985* • Crash and Burn *1990* • Trancers II: The Return of Jack Deth *1991*
Bang, Poul Reptilicus *1961*
Banno, Yoshimitsu Godzilla vs Hedora *1971*
Baratier, Jacques The Doll *1962*
Barba, Norberto Solo *1996*
Barbera, Joseph Jetsons: the Movie *1990*
Barker, Clive Nightbreed *1990*
Barnett, Steve Mindwarp *1992*
Barr, Douglas Cloned *1997*
Barron, Steve Teenage Mutant Ninja Turtles *1990* • Coneheads *1993*
Barry, Christopher Moonbase 3 *1973*
Barry, Ian The Chain Reaction *1980* • Robo Warriors *1996*
Barry, Wesley E *aka* **Barry, Wesley** The Creation of the Humanoids *1962*
Bartel, Paul Death Race 2000 *1975*
Barton, Charles *aka* **Barton, Charles T** Abbott and Costello Meet Frankenstein *1948*
Barwood, Hal Warning Sign *1985*
Barzyk, Fred The Lathe of Heaven *1979*
Bass, Saul Phase IV *1973*
Battersby, Roy Yellowbacks *1990* • Doomwatch: Winter Angel *1999*
Bava, Mario Caltiki, the Immortal Monster *1959* • Planet of the Vampires *1965* • Dr Goldfoot and the Girl Bombs *1966* • Danger: Diabolik *1967*
Baxley, Craig R Dark Angel *1989* • Deep Red *1994*
Bay, Michael Armageddon *1998*
Bazzoni, Luigi Primal Impulse *1974*
Beaudine, William Bela Lugosi Meets a Brooklyn Gorilla *1952* • Jesse James Meets Frankenstein's Daughter *1966*
Beebe, Ford Flash Gordon's Trip to Mars *1938* • Buck Rogers *1939* • The Phantom Creeps *1939* • Flash Gordon Conquers the Universe *1940* • The Invisible Man's Revenge *1944*
Beeman, Greg Mom and Dad Save the World *1992*
Belson, Jerry Jekyll and Hyde...Together Again *1982*
Benedictus, David Ape and Essence *1966*
Benjamin, Richard My Stepmother Is an Alien *1988*
Bennet, Spencer Gordon *aka* **Bennet, Spencer G** Manhunt of Mystery Island *1945* • The Purple Monster Strikes *1945* • Brick Bradford *1947* • Bruce Gentry – Daredevil of the Skies *1948* • Superman *1948* • Batman and

Robin *1949* • Atom Man vs Superman *1950* • Killer Ape *1953* • The Lost Planet *1953* • The Atomic Submarine *1960*
Bentsvi, Yakov Legion of Iron *1990*
Benveniste, Michael Flesh Gordon *1974*
Bercovici, Luca Convict 762 *1997*
Berke, William The Lost Missile *1958*
Bernds, Edward The Bowery Boys Meet the Monsters *1954* • World without End *1955* • Queen of Outer Space *1958* • Space Master X 7 *1958* • Return of the Fly *1959* • Valley of the Dragons *1961* • The Three Stooges in Orbit *1962*
Berneis, Peter No Survivors Please *1963*
Bernhardt, Curtis *aka* **Bernhardt, Kurt** The Tunnel *1933*
Besson, Luc The Last Battle *1983* • The Fifth Element *1997*
Betuel, Jonathan My Science Project *1985* • Theodore Rex *1995*
Bianchini, Paolo *aka* **Maxwell, Paul** Devilman Story *1967*
Bierman, Robert Frankenstein's Baby *1990*
Bigelow, Kathryn Wild Palms *1993* • Strange Days *1995*
Bilson, Danny Zone Troopers *1985*
Binder, John UFOria *1980*
Bird, Brad The Iron Giant *1999*
Bishop, David The Outsider *1997*
Bitsch, Charles The Last Man *1968*
Bixby, Bill The Trial of the Incredible Hulk *1989* • The Death of the Incredible Hulk *1990*
Blaine, Cullen R.O.T.O.R *1988*
Blake, Gerald Legend of Death *1965*
Bluth, Don Titan AE *2000*
Blystone, John G *aka* **Blystone, J G** The Last Man on Earth *1923*
Bogdanovich, Peter *aka* **Thomas, Derek** Voyage to the Planet of Prehistoric Women *1966*
Boisseau, David The Burning Glass *1960*
Bond, Timothy The Lost World *1992* • The Return to the Lost World *1994* • The Shadow Men *1997*
Boorman, John Zardoz *1973*
Boos, H Gordon Perfect Assassins *1998*
Booth, Walter R The Airship Destroyer *1909*
Borden, Lizzie Born in Flames *1983*
Boulting, John Seven Days to Noon *1950*
Bourla, David When Time Expires *1997*
Boutross, Thomas Hideous Sun Demon *1955*
Bowey, John R Mutator *1991*
Bowman, Rob The X Files *1998*
Boxell, Tim Aberration *1997*
Bradley, David 12 to the Moon *1960*
Bradshaw, John Specimen *1996*
Brambilla, Marco Demolition Man *1993*
Branagh, Kenneth Mary Shelley's Frankenstein *1994*
Brandner, Uwe I Love You I Kill You *1971*
Brandon, Clark Skeeter *1993*
Brannon, Fred C *aka* **Brannon, Fred** The Purple Monster Strikes *1945* • The Crimson Ghost *1946* • King of the Rocket Men *1949* • Flying Disc Man from Mars *1950* • Radar Men from the Moon *1951* • Zombies of the Stratosphere *1952* • Commando Cody: Sky Marshal of the Universe *1953*
Brass, Tinto The Flying Saucer *1964*
Breakston, George The Manster *1959*
Bretherton, Howard The Monster and the Ape *1945*
Brickman, Marshall Simon *1980*
Bridges, Alan Invasion *1965*
Brinckerhoff, Burt Dogs *1976* • Brave New World *1980*
Brooks, Mel Young Frankenstein *1974* • Spaceballs *1987*
Brougher, Hilary The Sticky Fingers of Time *1997*
Brower, Otto Phantom Empire *1935*
Brown, Mende Jules Verne's Strange Holiday *1969*
Browning, Ricou Hello Down There *1969*
Bruno, John Virus *1998*
Buchanan, Larry The Eye Creatures *1965* • Mars Needs Women *1966* • Zontar, the Thing from Venus *1966* • It's Alive *1968*
Burke, Martyn The Last Chase *1981*
Burton, Tim Batman *1989* • Batman Returns *1992* • Mars Attacks! *1996*
Butler, David Just Imagine *1930*
Butler, Robert The Computer Wore Tennis Shoes *1970*

C

Cacoyannis, Michael The Day the Fish Came Out *1967*
Cahn, Edward L Creature with the Atom Brain *1955* • The She-Creature *1956* • Invasion of the Saucer Men *1957* • Voodoo Woman *1957* • It! The Terror from beyond Space *1958* • Invisible Invaders *1959*
Callas, John Lone Wolf *1988*
Cameron, James The Terminator *1984* • Aliens *1986* • The Abyss *1989* • Terminator 2: Judgment Day *1991*
Camfield, Douglas The Nightmare Man *1981*
Cammell, Donald Demon Seed *1977*
Campbell, Martin No Escape *1994*
Campus, Michael ZPG: Zero Population Growth *1971*
Cannon, Danny Judge Dredd *1995*
Cant, Colin Dark Season *1991*
Canutt, Yakima Manhunt of Mystery Island *1945*
Carax, Léos The Night Is Young *1986*
Cardiff, Jack The Mutations *1973*
Cardona, Rene Night of the Bloody Apes *1968*
Cardone, J S Shadowzone *1990*
Cardos, John "Bud" Kingdom of the Spiders *1977* • The Dark *1979* • The Day Time Ended *1980* • Mutant *1984*
Carlson, Richard Riders to the Stars *1954*
Caro, Marc The City of Lost Children *1995*
Carpenter, John Dark Star *1973* • Escape from New York *1981* • The Thing *1982* • Starman *1984* • Prince of Darkness *1987* • They Live *1988* • Memoirs of an Invisible Man *1992* • Village of the Damned *1995* • Escape from LA *1996*
Carpenter, Stephen The Kindred *1986*
Carr, Thomas Bruce Gentry – Daredevil of the Skies *1948* • Superman *1948*
Carreras, Michael The Lost Continent *1968*
Carson, David Star Trek: Generations *1994*
Castle, Nick The Last Starfighter *1984*
Castle, William The Tingler *1959* • Project X *1968*
Chabrol, Claude Dr M *1989*
Chaffey, Don C.H.O.M.P.S. *1979*
Chapman, Michael The Annihilator *1986*
Chappelle, Joe Phantoms *1998*
Charleston, Jim Legion of Fire: Killer Ants! *1998*
Charr, Henri *aka* **Charr, Henry** My Uncle the Alien *1996*
Chatfield, Les Kinvig *1981*
Chayefsky, Paddy *aka* **Aaron, Sidney** Altered States *1980*
Chechik, Jeremiah The Avengers *1998*
Cheek, Douglas CHUD *1984*
Chelintsev, B M Mysterious Island *1941*
Chiodo, Stephen Killer Klowns from Outer Space *1988*
Christensen, Benjamin The Mysterious Island *1929*
Christian, Roger The Sender *1982* • Lorca and the Outlaws *1985* • Battlefield Earth *2000*
Chubbuck, Lyndon Naked Souls *1995*
Clair, René Paris Qui Dort *1923*
Clark, B D Galaxy of Terror *1981*
Clark, Derek Sky *1976*
Clark, Greydon Without Warning *1980*
Clark, Lawrence Gordon Chimera *1991*
Clarke, Phil Doctor Who: The Paradise of Death *1993*
Clarke, Robert Hideous Sun Demon *1955*
Claxton, William F Night of the Lepus *1972*
Clifton, Elmer Captain America *1944*
Clouse, Robert The Ultimate Warrior *1975*
Cockliss, Harley The Glitterball *1977*
Cohen, Howard R Saturday the 14th *1981* • Space Raiders *1983* • Time Trackers *1989*
Cohen, Larry It's Alive *1974* • God Told Me to *1976* • It Lives Again *1978* • It's Alive III: Island of the Alive *1987*
Coke, Cyril The Night of the Big Heat *1960* • Countdown at Woomera *1961*
Cokliss, Harley Battletruck *1982*
Colla, Richard A Something Is Out There *1988*
Collector, Robert *aka* **Blake, T C** Nightflyers *1987*
Colomo, Fernando Star Knight *1985*
Columbus, Chris Bicentennial Man *1999*
Como, Don Aliens from Spaceship Earth *1977*
Compton, Richard Ravagers *1979*
Connor, Kevin The Land That Time Forgot *1974* • At the Earth's Core *1976* • The People That Time Forgot *1977* • Warlords of Atlantis *1978* • Goliath Awaits *1981*
Conrad, Mikel The Flying Saucer *1949*
Conway, James L Hangar 18 *1980* • Earthbound *1981*
Cook, Philip J Invader *1991*
Cooke, Alan The Mind of Mr Soames *1970*
Cookson, Tony And You Thought Your Parents Were Weird *1991*
Cooper, Merian C King Kong *1933*
Corbucci, Sergio Supersnooper *1981*
Corea, Nicholas The Incredible Hulk Returns *1988*
Corman, Roger The Day the World Ended *1956* • It Conquered the World *1956* • Not of This Earth *1956* • Attack of the Crab Monsters *1957* • The Undead *1957* • Teenage Caveman *1958* • War of the Satellites *1958* • The Wasp Woman *1959* • The Last Woman on Earth *1960* • Little Shop of Horrors *1960* • The Man with the X-Ray Eyes *1963* • Gas-s-s-s, or It Became Necessary to Destroy the World in Order to Save It *1970* • Deathsport *1978* • Frankenstein Unbound *1990*
Cornwell, Stephen The Philadelphia Experiment 2 *1993*
Cort, Michael Zeta One *1969*
Coscarelli, Don Phantasm *1978*
Cosmatos, George Pan Leviathan *1989*
Costner, Kevin The Postman *1997*
Coto, Manny Star Kid *1997*
Coulter, Allen Golden Years *1991*
Cox, Alex Repo Man *1984*
Cozzi, Luigi *aka* **Coates, Lewis** Starcrash *1979* • Alien Contamination *1981*
Crabtree, Arthur Fiend without a Face *1957*
Crain, William Dr Black and Mr Hyde *1975*
Crane, Kenneth Monster from Green Hell *1958* • The Manster *1959*
Craven, Wes Swamp Thing *1982* • Deadly Friend *1986* • Shocker *1989*
Crevenna, Alfredo B The Invisible Man *1958* • El Planeta de las Mujeres Invasoras *1965*

D

E

F

G

Gabai, Richard Virtual Girl *1998*
Gaffney, Robert Frankenstein Meets the Space Monster *1965*
Gale, Ricardo Jacques Alien Intruder *1993*
Galeen, Henrik Alraune *1927*
Gallagher, Stephen Oktober *1998*
Gallo, Fred Mind Breakers *1996*
Gance, Abel The End of the World *1930*
Gans, Christophe Necronomicon *1993*
Garner, Anthony Z for Zachariah *1984*
Garris, Mark The Stand *1994*
Garris, Mick Critters 2: the Main Course *1988* • Virtual Obsession *1998*
Gayton, Joe Wes Craven's Mind Ripper *1995*
George, Peter Surf Nazis Must Die *1987*
Giancola, David Time Chasers *1994*
Gibbins, Duncan Eve of Destruction *1991*
Gibson, Alan The Flipside of Dominick Hide *1980* • Another Flip for Dominick *1982*
Gigo, Jorge *aka* **Gigo, Georges** The Devil's Kiss *1971*
Gilbert, Lewis Moonraker *1979*
Gillard, Stuart Teenage Mutant Ninja Turtles III *1992* • Rocketman *1997*
Gilliam, Terry Time Bandits *1981* • Brazil *1985* • The Adventures of Baron Munchausen *1988* • Twelve Monkeys *1995*
Gilling, John The Gamma People *1956* • The Night Caller *1965*
Gilmore, Stuart Captive Women *1952*
Girard, Bernard The Happiness Cage *1972*
Girault, Jean The Spacemen of St Tropez *1978*
Girdler, William Day of the Animals *1977*
Girotti, Ken Captain Power and the Soldiers of the Future *1987-1988*
Gladwell, David Memoirs of a Survivor *1981*
Glaser, Paul Michael The Running Man *1987*
Glickenhaus, James Timemaster *1995*
Glut, Donald F Dinosaur Valley Girls *1996*
Godard, Jean-Luc Alphaville *1965*
Goddard, Gary Masters of the Universe *1987*
Golan, Menahem The Apple *1980*
Gold, Jack Who? *1974*
Golden, Dan Terminal Virus *1995*
Golding, Paul Pulse *1988*
Goldman, Gary Titan AE *2000*
Goldstein, Allan A Memory Run *1995*
Gomer, Steve Barney's Great Adventure *1998*
Goodkind, Saul A Buck Rogers *1939* • The Phantom Creeps *1939*
Gordon, Bert I King Dinosaur *1955* • The Amazing Colossal Man *1957* • Beginning of the End *1957* • The Cyclops *1957* • Attack of the Puppet People *1958* • Earth vs the Spider *1958* • War of the Colossal Beast *1958* • Village of the Giants *1965* • The Food of the Gods *1975* • Empire of the Ants *1977*
Gordon, Keith Wild Palms *1993*
Gordon, Robert It Came from beneath the Sea *1955*
Gordon, Stuart Re-Animator *1985* • From Beyond *1986* • Robot Jox *1989* • Fortress *1992* • Space Truckers *1996*
Gornick, Michael Golden Years *1991*
Gosselin, Bernard The Christmas Martian *1971*
Gottlieb, Carl Amazon Women on the Moon *1987*
Gould, George Rod Brown of the Rocket Rangers *1953-1954*
Graeff, Tom Teenagers from Outer Space *1959*
Graham Scott, Peter One *1956*
Grant, Julian Electra *1995*
Grau, Jorge The Living Dead at the Manchester Morgue *1974*
Grauman, Walter Who Is Julia? *1986*
Gray, Mike Wavelength *1983*
Gréville, Edmond T The Hands of Orlac *1960*
Green, Alfred E Invasion USA *1952*
Green, Bruce Seth Running against Time *1990*
Green, Joseph The Brain That Wouldn't Die *1959*
Greenblatt, William R Doomsday Man *1998*
Greene, David Prototype *1983*
Greene, Herbert The Cosmic Man *1959*
Greenfield, Matt Gamera: Guardian of the Universe *1995*
Gregoretti, Ugo Omicron *1963*
Gries, Tom Earth II *1971*
Griffith, Charles B Dr Heckyl & Mr Hype *1980*
Grimaldi, Hugo Godzilla Raids Again *1955* • The Human Duplicators *1965* • Mutiny in Outer Space *1965*
Grinde, Nick The Man They Could Not Hang *1939* • Before I Hang *1940*
Grinter, Brad F Flesh Feast *1970*
Grissell, Wallace A Manhunt of Mystery Island *1945*
Grousset, Didier Kamikaze *1986*
Guest, Christopher Attack of the 50 Ft Woman *1993*
Guest, Val Give Us the Moon *1944* • Mr Drake's Duck *1950* • The Quatermass Experiment *1955* • Quatermass II *1957* • The Day the Earth Caught Fire *1961* • Toomorrow *1970*
Guillermin, John King Kong *1976* • King Kong Lives *1986*
Gunn, Gilbert The Strange World of Planet X *1957*
Gurney Jr, Robert J Terror from the Year 5,000 *1958*

H

Haber, Mark Alien Cargo *1999*
Hagen, Ross The Glove *1978*
Haggard, Piers Quatermass *1979*
Hagman, Larry Beware! The Blob *1971*
Hahn, Steven Starchaser: the Legend of Orin *1985*
Haines, Richard W Class of Nuke 'Em High *1986* • Alien Space Avenger *1989*
Hall, Peter Work Is a Four Letter Word *1968*
Haller, Daniel Die, Monster, Die! *1965*
Hanna, William Jetsons: the Movie *1990*
Hannam, Ken Moonbase 3 *1973* • The Day of the Triffids *1981*
Hannant, Brian The Time Guardian *1987*
Harada, Masato Gunhed *1989*
Hardy, Rod Halfway across the Galaxy and Turn Left *1994*
Hardy, Ron 20,000 Leagues under the Sea *1997*
Harlin, Renny Deep Blue Sea *1999*
Harrington, Curtis *aka* **Sebastian, John** Voyage to the Prehistoric Planet *1965* • Planet of Blood *1966* • The Dead Don't Die *1975*
Harris, Melanie Chocky *1998*
Harris, Trent Plan 10 from Outer Space *1995*
Harrison, John Frank Herbert's Dune *2000*
Hart, Christopher Eat and Run *1986*
Hart, Harvey The Aliens Are Coming *1979*
Hart, Jacobsen Steel Frontier *1994*
Hartford, Kenneth The Lucifer Complex *1978*
Hartford-Davis, Robert Gonks Go Beat *1965*
Hartl, Karl FP1 *1932* • Gold *1934*
Harvey, Rupert Critters 4 *1992*
Hashimoto, Kohji Godzilla *1984*
Haskin, Byron The War of the Worlds *1953* • Conquest of Space *1955* • From the Earth to the Moon *1958* • Robinson Crusoe on Mars *1964* • The Power *1968*
Hayden, Jeffrey Space Academy *1977-1979*
Hayes, John End of the World *1977*
Heavener, David Deadly Reactor *1989* • Dragon Fury *1995*
Heffron, Richard T Futureworld *1976*
Henenlotter, Frank Brain Damage *1988*
Henley, Hobart Sinners in Silk *1924*
Herbert, Henry QED *1982*
Herek, Stephen Critters *1986* • Bill & Ted's Excellent Adventure *1988*
Herz, Michael The Toxic Avenger *1985* • The Toxic Avenger, Part II *1988* • Sgt Kabukiman NYPD *1991*
Hess, Jon Watchers *1988* • Alligator II: the Mutation *1991* • Mars *1996* • Legion *1998*
Hess, Jon Daniel Not of This World *1991*
Hessler, Gordon Scream and Scream Again *1969*
Heusch, Paolo The Day the Sky Exploded *1958*
Hewitt, David L Journey to the Center of Time *1967* • The Lucifer Complex *1978*
Hewitt, Peter Bill & Ted's Bogus Journey *1991* • Wild Palms *1993*
Hickox, Anthony Waxwork II: Lost in Time *1992*
Hickox, Douglas The Giant Behemoth *1959*
Hidaka, Shigeaki The Final War *1960*
Hill, George Roy Slaughterhouse-Five *1972*
Hill, Jack Alien Terror *1969* • The Incredible Invasion *1971*
Hill, James Captain Nemo and the Underwater City *1969*
Hill, Robert F The Flaming Disk *1920* • Blake of Scotland Yard *1927* • Flash Gordon's Trip to Mars *1938*
Hill, Tim Muppets from Space *1999*
Hill, Walter *aka* **Lee, Thomas** Supernova *2000*
Hillenbrand, David King Cobra *1999*
Hillenbrand, Scott King Cobra *1999*
Hillyer, Lambert The Invisible Ray *1936* • Batman *1943*
Hilton, Arthur Cat-Women of the Moon *1953*
Hindell, Alison A Clockwork Orange *1998*
Hingorani, Arjun Katilon Ke Katil *1981*
Hippolyte, Gregory *aka* **Brown, Gregory** Dead Man Walking *1988*
Hirokawa, Kazuyuki Lensman *1984*
Hirsch, Bettina Munchies *1987*
Hitchcock, Alfred The Birds *1995*
Hitchinson, David 2004 *1963*
Hoblit, Gregory Frequency *2000*
Hodges, Mike The Terminal Man *1974* • Flash Gordon *1980* • Morons from Outer Space *1985*
Hoey, Michael A The Navy vs the Night Monsters *1966*
Hoffman, Antony Red Planet *2000*
Hoffman, Herman The Invisible Boy *1957*
Hogan, David Barb Wire *1995*
Holcomb, Rod Captain America *1979*
Hole Jr, William J Face of Terror *1962*
Holland, Tom The Langoliers *1995*
Holzman, Allan Forbidden World *1982* • The Retaliator *1987*
Honda, Inoshiro *aka* **Honda, Ishiro** Godzilla *1954* • The H-Man *1954* • Rodan *1956* • The Mysterians *1957* • Battle in Outer Space *1959* • The Human Vapour *1960* • Gorath *1962* • King Kong vs Godzilla *1962* • Mothra *1962* • Atragon *1963* • Matango *1963* • Dogora the Space Monster *1964* • Frankenstein Meets the Devil Fish *1964* • Godzilla vs Mothra *1964* • Ghidrah, the Three-Headed Monster *1965* • Invasion of the Astro-Monster *1965* • King Kong Escapes *1967* • Destroy All Monsters *1968* • Godzilla's Revenge *1969* • Latitude Zero *1969* • The Space Amoeba *1970* • War of the Gargantuas *1970* • Terror of Mechagodzilla

M

N

Nadel, Arthur H Space Academy *1977-1979* • Jason of Star Command *1979-1981*
Nagy, Ivan Once upon a Spy *1980*
Napolitano, Joe Earth Angel *1991*
Nassour, Edward The Beast of Hollow Mountain *1956*
Natali, Vincenzo Cube *1997*
Neame, Ronald Meteor *1979*
Needham, Hal Megaforce *1982*
Neill, Roy William Frankenstein Meets the Wolf Man *1943*
Neilson, James Moon Pilot *1962*
Nelson, Art J The Creeping Terror *1964*
Nelson, Gary The Black Hole *1979*
Nelson, Ralph Charly *1968* • Embryo *1976*
Nesher, Avi She *1982* • Savage *1995*
Neuhäuser, Holger The High Crusade *1994*
Neumann, Kurt Rocketship X-M *1950* • Kronos *1957* • She Devil *1957* • The Fly *1958*
Newbrook, Peter The Asphyx *1972*
Newfield, Sam Ghost Patrol *1936* • The Monster Maker *1944* • Lost Continent *1951*
Newland, John One Step Beyond *1959-1961*
Newman, Joseph M This Island Earth *1955*
Nibbelink, Phil We're Back! A Dinosaur's Story *1993*
Niccol, Andrew Gattaca *1997*
Nichetti, Maurizio Ratataplan *1979*
Nichols, Mike The Day of the Dolphin *1973* • What Planet Are You From? *2000*
Nicolaou, Ted TerrorVision *1986* • Bad Channels *1992*
Nielsen, Thomas Borch Webmaster *1998*
Nihonmatsu, Kazui The X from Outer Space *1967*
Nilsson, Rob A Town Has Turned to Dust *1998*
Nimoy, Leonard Star Trek III: the Search for Spock *1984* • Star Trek IV: the Voyage Home *1986*
Noguchi, Haruyasu Gappa the Trifibian Monster *1967*
Norman, Leslie X the Unknown *1956*
Norrington, Stephen Death Machine *1994* • Blade *1998*
Norton, Bill L Them *1996*
Notz, Thierry The Terror Within *1988*
Nutter, David Disturbing Behaviour *1998*
Nyby, Christian The Thing from Another World *1951*

O

O'Bannon, Dan Return of the Living Dead *1984*
O'Connolly, Jim *aka* **O'Connolly, James** The Valley of Gwangi *1969*
Oboler, Arch Strange Holiday *1942* • Five *1951* • The Twonky *1953* • The Bubble *1966*
Obrow, Jeffrey The Kindred *1986*
Oda, Motoyoshi Godzilla Raids Again *1955*
Odell, David Martians Go Home *1990*
Odendal, Sias Nukie *1992*
Ogilvie, George Mad Max beyond Thunderdome *1985*
Okawara, Takao Godzilla vs Mothra *1992* • Godzilla 2000 *1999*
Omori, Kazuki Godzilla vs King Ghidorah *1991*
Onwurah, Ngozi Welcome II the Terrordome *1994*
Ordung, Wyott Monster from the Ocean Floor *1954*
Orme, Stuart The Puppet Masters *1994* • The Last Train *1999*
Ormond, Ron Mesa of Lost Women *1953*
Oshii, Mamoru Patlabor: the Mobile Police *1989* • Ghost in the Shell *1995*
Ossorio, Amando de *aka* **Greens, Gregory** The Sea Serpent *1984*
Oswald, Gerd Agent for H.A.R.M. *1966*
Oswald, Richard Alraune *1930*
Otomo, Katsuhiro Akira *1988*
Oz, Frank Little Shop of Horrors *1986*

P

Pal, George Atlantis, the Lost Continent *1960* • The Time Machine *1960*
Palmisano, Conrad E Space Rage *1986*
Panama, Norman The Road to Hong Kong *1962*
Papic, Krsto The Rat Saviour *1977*
Parisot, Dean Galaxy Quest *1999*
Parker, Brian The Girl Who Loved Robots *1965*
Parrish, Robert Journey to the Far Side of the Sun *1969*
Passer, Ivan Creator *1985*
Paton, Stuart 20,000 Leagues under the Sea *1916*
Patterson, Ray GoBots: Battle of the Rocklords *1986*
Paul, Steven Slapstick of Another Kind *1982*
Peak, Barry Future Schlock *1984* • As Time Goes By *1987*
Pearce, Richard Threshold *1981*
Peeters, Barbara Monster *1980*
Pelletier, Andrée Anchor Zone *1994*
Penzlin, E A Mysterious Island *1941*
Peoples, David Webb *aka* **Peoples, David** The Salute of the Jugger *1989*
Pepin, Richard Firepower *1993* • Cyber-Tracker *1994* • The Silencers *1995* • T-Force *1995* • Darkbreed *1996* • The Sender *1997*
Peters, Brook L The Unearthly *1957*
Petersen, Wolfgang Enemy Mine *1985* • Outbreak *1995*
Peterson, Kristine Critters 3 *1991*
Petri, Elio The Tenth Victim *1965*
Petrie, Daniel The Neptune Factor *1973* • Cocoon: the Return *1988*
Petrie, Donald My Favorite Martian *1999*
Philips, Lee Space *1985*
Pichel, Irving Destination Moon *1950*
Piel, Harry An Invisible Man Goes through the City *1933* • Master of the World *1934* • The World without a Mask *1934*
Pierce, Arthur C Women of the Prehistoric Planet *1966*
Piestrak, Marek The Test of Pilot Pirx *1978*
Pillai, Alex The Last Train *1999*
Pillsbury, Sam Knight Rider 2010 *1994*
Pinfield, Mervyn The Monsters *1962*
Pink, Sidney Journey to the Seventh Planet *1961* • Reptilicus *1961*
Pinsker, Seth The Hidden II *1994*
Piper, Brett A Nymphoid Barbarian in Dinosaur Hell *1991*
Piquer Simon, Juan *aka* **Piquer, Juan** Where Time Began *1977* • Supersonic Man *1979* • Endless Descent *1990*
Pittman, Bruce Harrison Bergeron *1995*
Po, Gilbert Chase Morran *1996*
Polak, Jindrich *aka* **Pollack, Jack** Voyage to the End of the Universe *1963*
Pollard, Harry The Invisible Ray *1920*
Pollexfen, Jack Indestructible Man *1956*
Portillo, Rafael The Robot vs the Aztec Mummy *1957*
Post, Ted Beneath the Planet of the Apes *1969*
Pottier, Richard Le Monde Tremblera *1939*
Powell, Michael The Boy Who Turned Yellow *1972*
Power, John The Tommyknockers *1993*
Pressman, Michael Teenage Mutant Ninja Turtles II: the Secret of the Ooze *1991*
Price, David F Dr Jekyll and Ms Hyde *1995*
Price, Noel The Girl from Tomorrow *1990-1991*
Protazanov, Jakov A Aelita *1924*
Prowse, Andrew Driving Force *1988* • Ultraman Great *1990*
Proyas, Alex Dark City *1998*
Pryce, Craig Revenge of the Radioactive Reporter *1990*
Pytka, Joe Space Jam *1997*
Pyun, Albert Radioactive Dreams *1986* • Alien from LA *1987* • Cyborg *1989* • Deceit *1989* • Journey to the Center of the Earth *1989* • Captain America *1990* • Arcade *1993* • Brain Smasher... a Love Story *1993* • Knights *1993* • Nemesis *1993* • Adrenalin: Fear the Rush *1995* • Heatseeker *1995* • Nemesis 2 – Nebula *1995* • Nemesis 3 – Time Lapse *1996* • Omega Doom *1996*

Q

Quill, Jane The Handmaid's Tale *2000*

R

Rabenalt, Arthur Maria Alraune *1952*
Rader, Peter Escape to Witch Mountain *1995*
Radford, Michael Nineteen Eighty-Four *1984*
Radomski, Eric Batman: Mask of the Phantasm *1993*
Rae, Michael Laserblast *1978*
Raffill, Stewart The Ice Pirates *1984* • The Philadelphia Experiment *1984*
Ragona, Ubaldo The Last Man on Earth *1964*
Raimi, Sam Darkman *1990*
Ramis, Harold Multiplicity *1996*
Randel, Tony Ticks *1993* • Fist of the North Star *1995*
Rankin Jr, Arthur King Kong Escapes *1967*
Rao, Krishna Crossworlds *1996*
Ravich, Rand The Astronaut's Wife *1999*
Ravn, Jens The Man Who Thought Life *1969*
Ray, Fred Olen The Alien Dead *1980* • Biohazard *1984* • Deep Space *1987* • Alienator *1989* • Cyberzone *1995* • Invisible Mom *1995* • Hybrid *1997* • Fugitive Mind *1999*
Razatos, Spiro Class of 1999 II: The Substitute *1993*
Rebane, Bill Monster a Go-Go! *1965* • The Giant Spider Invasion *1975* • The Alpha Incident *1977*
Red, Eric Body Parts *1991*
Reece, Crispin Bliss *1995-1997*
Reed, Peyton The Computer Wore Tennis Shoes *1995*
Reeves, Michael The Sorcerers *1967*
Reid, Alastair Artemis 81 *1981*
Reiner, Carl The Man with Two Brains *1983*
Reitman, Ivan Ghostbusters *1984* • Ghostbusters II *1989* • Junior *1994* • Evolution *2001*
Renoir, Jean Charleston *1927*
Resnais, Alain Je T'Aime, Je T'Aime *1968*
Revier, Harry The Lost City *1935*
Reynolds, Kevin Waterworld *1995*
Rich, David Lowell Have Rocket, Will Travel *1959*
Richardson, Mark A Robot Called Golddigger *1993*
Richter, W D The Adventures of Buckaroo Banzai across the 8th Dimension *1984* • Late for Dinner *1991*

S

T

U

V

W

Y

Z

Actors' index

A

B

Baker, Tom Frankenstein: the True Story *1973* • The Mutations *1973* • Doctor Who: the Fourth Doctor *1974-1981*
Bakewell, William Radar Men from the Moon *1951*
Bakke, Brenda Gunhed *1989* • Solar Crisis *1990* • Terminal Voyage *1994* • Trucks *1997*
Bako, Brigitte Replikator *1994*
Bakula, Scott Quantum Leap *1989-1993* • The Invaders *1995*
Balaban, Bob Close Encounters of the Third Kind *1977* • Altered States *1980* • 2010 *1984*
Balaski, Belinda The Food of the Gods *1975* • Piranha *1978* • Gremlins *1984*
Baldini, Renato The Snow Devils *1965*
Baldwin, A Michael Phantasm *1978*
Baldwin, Adam Digital Man *1994* • Independence Day *1996* • Mind Breakers *1996*
Baldwin, Alec The Shadow *1994*
Baldwin, Daniel Attack of the 50 Ft Woman *1993* • Yesterday's Target *1996* • The Invader *1997*
Baldwin, Gardner VR Troopers *1994-1996*
Baldwin, Greta Project X *1968*
Baldwin, Peter I Married a Monster from Outer Space *1958*
Baldwin, Stephen New Eden *1994* • Mr Murder *1998*
Baldwin, Walter The Devil Commands *1941*
Baldwin, William Flatliners *1990* • Virus *1998*
Balenda, Carla The Whip Hand *1951*
Balfour, Michael Fiend without a Face *1957*
Balgobin, Jennifer Repo Man *1984*
Balk, Fairuza The Island of Dr Moreau *1996*
Ball, Nicholas Lifeforce *1985*
Ball, Robert The Brain Eaters *1958*
Ball, William Suburban Commando *1991*
Ballance, Peter Sunset Heights *1996*
Ballard, Alimi Dark Angel *2000-*
Ballard, Iris The Quatermass Experiment *1953*
Balme, Timothy Braindead *1992*
Balsam, Martin Space *1985*
Balsam, Talia The Kindred *1986*
Bamber, Judy Monstrosity *1963*
Bancroft, Bob Zenon: Girl of the 21st Century *1999*
Banderas, Antonio SPYkids *2001*
Banionis, Donatas Solaris *1972*
Banks, Doug The Brain Eaters *1958*
Banks, Jonathan Otherworld *1985* • Assassin *1986* • Who Is Julia? *1986* • Freejack *1992* • Darkbreed *1996*
Banks, Leslie The Tunnel *1935*
Banks, Morwenna The Strangerers *2000*
Bannen, Ian Doomwatch *1972* • The Watcher in the Woods *1982*
Bannerman, David The Amazing Spider-Man *1995*
Bannister, Reggie Phantasm *1978*
Bannon, Jim Unknown World *1951*
Baptist, Jennifer The Toxic Avenger *1985*
Bara, Nina Space Patrol *1950-1955* • Missile to the Moon *1958*
Baragrey, John The Colossus of New York *1958* • Gamera the Invincible *1965*
Baranov, Catherine Metamorphosis *1987*
Baranski, Christine Now and Again *1999-2000*
Barash, Olivia Repo Man *1984*
Baratto, Luisa Devilman Story *1967*
Barbeau, Adrienne The Darker Side of Terror *1979* • Escape from New York *1981* • Swamp Thing *1982* • Next One *1984*
Barber, Glynis Blake's 7 *1978-1981*
Barberi, Katie The Garbage Pail Kids Movie *1987*
Barbero, Aldo Curious Dr Humpp *1967*
Barbi, Vincent The Astro-Zombies *1968*
Barclay, Bob Space Command *1953-1954*
Barclay, Caroline Within the Rock *1995*
Barclay, Don Frankenstein Meets the Wolf Man *1943*
Barclay, Jerry War of the Satellites *1958*
Barcroft, Roy Manhunt of Mystery Island *1945* • The Purple Monster Strikes *1945* • Radar Men from the Moon *1951*
Bardette, Trevor The Monolith Monsters *1957*
Barker, Tim Dark Season *1991*
Barkin, Ellen The Adventures of Buckaroo Banzai across the 8th Dimension *1984*
Barkley, Lucille Flight to Mars *1951*
Barlow, Reginald Bride of Frankenstein *1935*
Barnes, Barbara The Adventures of Superman *1994*
Barnes, Christopher Daniel *aka* **Barnes, C D** Starman *1986-1987* • Frankenstein: the College Years *1991*
Barnes, Julian Frankenstein: the True Story *1973*
Barnes, Nicholas Outland *1981*
Barnes, Paul Day of the Animals *1977*
Barnes, Priscilla Lords of the Deep *1989*
Barnes, Rayford The Three Stooges in Orbit *1962*
Barnes, Susan Repo Man *1984* • Stranded *1987* • They Live *1988*
Barnes, Theo Brain Damage *1988*
Barnes, Walter Escape to Witch Mountain *1975*
Barney, Pamela Pathfinders *1960-1961*
Barnstable, Cyb Quark *1978*
Barnstable, Patricia Quark *1978*
Baron, Geraldine Time after Time *1979*
Barondes, Elizabeth Adrenalin: Fear the Rush *1995* • Not of This Earth *1995*
Barr, Douglas Spaced Invaders *1990*
Barr, Patrick The Brain Machine *1954* • Countdown at Woomera *1961*
Barr, Steven Memoirs of an Invisible Man *1992*
Barran, Bob The Time Machine *1960*
Barrett, Brendon Ryan The Shadow Men *1997*
Barrett, Claudia Robot Monster *1953*
Barrett, Jonathan Trucks *1997*
Barrett, Majel Star Trek *1966-1969* • Westworld *1973* • Planet Earth *1974* • Star Trek: the Motion Picture *1979* • Star Trek IV: the Voyage Home *1986* • Earth: Final Conflict *1997-*
Barrett, Ray Stingray *1964-1965* • Thunderbirds *1965-1966* • Thunderbirds Are Go! *1966* • As Time Goes By *1987*
Barrett, Sean Four-Sided Triangle *1953*
Barrett, Tim The Deadly Bees *1967*
Barrett, Victoria America 3000 *1986*
Barretta, Bill Muppets from Space *1999*
Barrie, Chris Red Dwarf *1988-1999*
Barrie, Frank Jekyll and Hyde *1989*
Barrier, Edgar The Whip Hand *1951* • The Giant Claw *1957*
Barrier, Ernestine Project Moonbase *1953*
Barron, John Doomwatch *1970-1972*
Barron, Keith The Land That Time Forgot *1974*
Barron, Robert V Bill & Ted's Excellent Adventure *1988*
Barrows, George Robot Monster *1953*
Barry, Donald *aka* **Barry, Don "Red"** Frankenstein – 1970 *1958*
Barry, Gene The War of the Worlds *1953* • The 27th Day *1957*
Barry, Ivor Weird Science *1985*
Barry, Raymond J Flubber *1997*
Barry, Toni Proteus *1995*
Barrymore, Drew Altered States *1980* • ET the Extra-Terrestrial *1982* • Firestarter *1984* • Waxwork II: Lost in Time *1992* • Batman Forever *1995* • Titan AE *2000*
Barrymore, John Dr Jekyll and Mr Hyde *1920* • The Invisible Woman *1940*
Barrymore, John Blyth Hybrid *1997*
Barrymore, Lionel The Mysterious Island *1929*
Bartashevich, K *aka* **Barton, Kirk** Battle beyond the Sun *1959*
Bartel, Paul Liquid Dreams *1992*
Bartenieff, George The Laserman *1988*
Bartlett, Robin 12:01 *1993* • Honey, We Shrunk Ourselves *1997*
Bartman, Frederick The Poisoned Earth *1961*
Bartok, Eva Spaceways *1953* • The Gamma People *1956*
Bartold, Norman Westworld *1973*
Barton, Gary Coma *1977*
Barton, Peter The Powers of Matthew Star *1982-1983*
Barton, Robert ET the Extra-Terrestrial *1982*
Barty, Billy The Undead *1957* • The Krofft Supershow *1976-1978* • Masters of the Universe *1987* • Lobster Man from Mars *1989*
Barzell, Wolfe Atlantis, the Lost Continent *1960*
Basch, Helmut I Love You I Kill You *1971*
Basco, Dante Fist of the North Star *1995*
Basehart, Richard Voyage to the Bottom of the Sea *1964-1968* • The Satan Bug *1965* • City beneath the Sea *1971* • And Millions Will Die! *1973* • The Island of Dr Moreau *1977*
Basham, Tom Colossus: the Forbin Project *1969*
Basic, Relja The Rat Saviour *1977*
Basinger, Kim My Stepmother Is an Alien *1988* • Batman *1989*
Bass, Alfie Journey into Space: Operation Luna *1953-1954* • Journey into Space: The World in Peril *1955-1956*
Basserman, Albert *aka* **Bassermann, Albert** Alraune *1930* • The Invisible Agent *1942*
Bassett, Angela Critters 4 *1992* • Strange Days *1995* • Contact *1997* • Supernova *2000*
Bassett, Linda Mary Reilly *1995*
Bastedo, Alexandra The Champions *1968-1969*
Batanides, Arthur The Unearthly *1957*
Bateman, Tony The Adventures of Don Quick *1970*
Bates, Alan Britannia Hospital *1982* • Dr M *1989*
Bates, Barbara Strange Holiday *1942*
Bates, Jane Popdown *1968*
Bates, Michael A Clockwork Orange *1971* • The Stone Tape *1972*
Bates, Ralph The Horror of Frankenstein *1970* • Dr Jekyll and Sister Hyde *1971* • Moonbase 3 *1973*
Bateson, Lucinda Metal Mickey *1980-1983*
Bathurst, Peter The Quatermass Experiment *1953*
Batinkoff, Randall The Stepford Children *1987*
Batson, Susan The Incredible Hulk *1977*
Bauchau, Patrick The Pretender *1996-2000*
Bauer, Belinda Timerider: the Adventure of Lyle Swann *1982* • RoboCop 2 *1990* • Necronomicon *1993*
Bauer, Steven Terminal Voyage *1994*
Bauleo, Ricardo Curious Dr Humpp *1967*
Baumann, Katherine *aka* **Baumann, Kathy** The Thing with Two Heads *1972*
Baur, Marc Time Runner *1993*
Bavier, Frances The Day the Earth Stood Still *1951*
Baxley, Barbara Countdown *1968*
Baxter, Meredith The Night that Panicked America *1975*
Baxter, Warner 6 Hours to Live *1932*
Baye, Nathalie The Machine *1994*
Bayldon, Geoffrey Frankenstein Must Be Destroyed *1969*

Bolduman, M Silver Dust *1953*
Boles, John Frankenstein *1931* • 6 Hours to Live *1932*
Bolkan, Florinda Primal Impulse *1974*
Bolling, Tiffany The New People *1969-1970* • Kingdom of the Spiders *1977*
Bologna, Joseph Not Quite Human *1987* • Alligator II: the Mutation *1991*
Bolotova, Zhanna The Silence of Dr Evans *1973*
Bolster, Anita *aka* **Bolster, Anita Sharp** The Hands of Orlac *1960*
Bolt , David Videodrome *1982*
Bolton, Christopher My Secret Identity *1988-1991*
Bolton, Emily Moonraker *1979*
Bolton, Heather The Boy from Andromeda *1991*
Bom, Lars Webmaster *1998*
Bonavia, Mike The Alien Dead *1980*
Bond, Derek Stranger from Venus *1954*
Bond, Jilly First Men in the Moon *1996*
Bond, Philip The Voodoo Factor *1959-1960*
Bond, Raleigh Nightmares *1983*
Bond, Raymond The Man from Planet X *1951*
Bond, Tommy Superman *1948* • Atom Man vs Superman *1950*
Bondarchuk, Natalya Solaris *1972*
Bondarchuk, Sergei The Silence of Dr Evans *1973*
Bonet, Lisa New Eden *1994*
Bongartz, Peter Mission Eureka *1990*
Bonham Carter, Helena Mary Shelley's Frankenstein *1994*
Boning, Wigald National Lampoon's Men in White *1998*
Bonne, Shirley It's Alive *1968*
Bono, Sonny Airplane II: the Sequel *1982*
Bonomo, Joe Island of Lost Souls *1932*
Booke, Sorrell Slaughterhouse-Five *1972*
Boolen, Van The Quatermass Experiment *1953* • The Lost Planet *1954* • Return to the Lost Planet *1955*
Boone, Pat Journey to the Center of the Earth *1959*
Booth, Adrian *aka* **Gray, Lorna** The Man They Could Not Hang *1939*
Booth, James The Retaliator *1987*
Booth, Karin Tobor the Great *1954*
Bor, Hanus The Stolen Dirigible *1966*
Borden, Eugene Doctor Renault's Secret *1942* • The Fly *1958*
Borden, Lynn Frogs *1972*
Boreanaz, David Buffy the Vampire Slayer *1997-*
Boretski, Paul Space Cases *1996-1997*
Borg, Brita Invasion of the Animal People *1960*
Borgnine, Ernest The Neptune Factor *1973* • Future Cop *1976* • The Black Hole *1979* • Ravagers *1979* • Escape from New York *1981* • Supersnooper *1981* • Gattaca *1997*
Borland, Carroll Biohazard *1984*
Borneo, Phil Gas-s-s-s, or It Became Necessary to Destroy the World in Order to Save It *1970*
Borrachero, Alicia Killer Tongue *1996*
Boruff, John Rod Brown of the Rocket Rangers *1953-1954*
Bosch, Johnny Yong Mighty Morphin Power Rangers: the Movie *1995* • Turbo: a Power Rangers Adventure *1997*
Bose, Miguel Star Knight *1985*
Bosley, Tom The Night that Panicked America *1975*
Bossell, Simon Aberration *1997*
Bosson, Barbara The Last Starfighter *1984*
Bostwick, Barry Fantastic Planet *1973* • The Rocky Horror Picture Show *1975* • Megaforce *1982* • Metal Beast *1995* • National Lampoon's Men in White *1998*
Bostwick, Jackson Tron *1982* • Secrets of the Phantom Caverns *1984*
Bosworth, Hobart Just Imagine *1930*
Botes, Michelle American Ninja 2: The Confrontation *1987*
Botsford, Sara Murder by Phone *1982*
Bottoms, Joseph The Black Hole *1979*
Bottoms, Timothy The Sea Serpent *1984* • Secrets of the Phantom Caverns *1984* • Invaders from Mars *1986* • Land of the Lost *1991-1992*
Bouchet, Barbara Agent for H.A.R.M. *1966*
Bouchey, Willis Red Planet Mars *1952*
Bouillon, Jean-Claude The Last Man *1968*
Bouise, Jean The Last Battle *1983*
Bouix, Evelyne Long Live Life *1984*
Bourdon, Didier The Machine *1994*
Bourneuf, Philip Frankenstein *1973*
Boushel, Joy The Fly *1986*
Boutsikaris, Dennis *batteries not included *1987*
Bouvard, Laurence The Tomorrow People *1992-1995*
Bova, Joseph Who? *1974*
Bowen, Julie The Last Man on Planet Earth *1999*
Bowen, Michael Night of the Comet *1984* • New Eden *1994*
Bowens, Malick Outbreak *1995*
Bowie, David The Man Who Fell to Earth *1976*
Bowman, Cal Wavelength *1983*
Bown, John Doomwatch *1970-1972*
Bown, Paul Morons from Outer Space *1985*
Boxer, John Mr Drake's Duck *1950*
Boxleitner, Bruce Tron *1982* • Babylon 5 *1993-1999*
Boyce, William The Slime People *1963*
Boyd, Blake Dune Warriors *1991*
Boyd, Lynda The Invader *1997*
Boyd, Stephen Fantastic Voyage *1966*
Boyd, William (II) *aka* **Boyd, William "Stage"** The Lost City *1935*
Boyd-Brent, John The Caves of Steel *1964*
Boyer, Chance Night of the Comet *1984*
Boyett, William The Hidden *1987*
Boykin, Nancy The Kirlian Witness *1978*
Boyland, Ari The Tribe *1998-*
Boyle, Peter Young Frankenstein *1974* • Outland *1981* • Solar Crisis *1990* • The Shadow *1994*
Bracco, Lorraine Medicine Man *1992*
Bracey, Sidney The Invisible Ray *1920* • The Vanishing Shadow *1934* • The Body Disappears *1941*
Bracken, Kathleen Day of the Animals *1977*
Bracket, Sarah Counterstrike *1969*
Bracks, David Mad Max *1979*
Bradbury, Ray The Ray Bradbury Theatre *1985-1992*
Braddell, Maurice Things to Come *1936*
Braden, Bernard The Day the Earth Caught Fire *1961*
Braden, Kim Trog *1970*
Bradford, Lane Zombies of the Stratosphere *1952*
Bradford, Marshall I Was a Teenage Frankenstein *1957*
Bradley (2), David Cyborg Cop *1993* • Cyborg Cop II *1994*
Bradley, Doug Killer Tongue *1996*
Bradley, Leslie Time Flies *1944* • Attack of the Crab Monsters *1957* • Teenage Caveman *1958*
Bradley, Truman Science Fiction Theatre *1955-1957*
Bradstreet, Charles Abbott and Costello Meet Frankenstein *1948*
Bradwell, Christine Moonbase 3 *1973*
Brady, Bob Liquid Sky *1982*
Brady, Edward Terror Island *1920*
Brady, Jack The Incredibly Strange Creatures Who Stopped Living and Became Mixed-up Zombies *1963*
Brady, Janelle Class of Nuke 'Em High *1986*
Brady, John Mystery Science Theater 3000: The Movie *1996*
Brady, Scott Castle of Evil *1966* • Destination Inner Space *1966* • Journey to the Center of Time *1967* • Marooned *1969* • Gremlins *1984*
Braeden, Eric Colossus: the Forbin Project *1969* • Escape from the Planet of the Apes *1971* • The Aliens Are Coming *1979*
Brahms, Penny 2001: a Space Odyssey *1968*
Braidwood, Tom The X Files *1993-* • The X Files *1998* • The Lone Gunmen *2001*
Brainin, Danny Xtro *1983*
Brake, Richard Death Machine *1994*
Brammall, Jack Terror Island *1920*
Brana, Frank Where Time Began *1977* • Supersonic Man *1979*
Branagh, Kenneth Mary Shelley's Frankenstein *1994*
Brand, Neville Killdozer *1974* • Without Warning *1980*
Brandis, Jonathan seaQuest DSV *1993-1996*
Brando, Kevin Saturday the 14th *1981*
Brando, Marlon Superman *1978* • The Island of Dr Moreau *1996*
Brandon, Henry The Land Unknown *1957*
Brandon, Peter Altered States *1980*
Brandt, Carolyn The Incredibly Strange Creatures Who Stopped Living and Became Mixed-up Zombies *1963*
Brandt, Walker Solar Force *1994*
Brandy, Craig T Flesh Gordon *1974*
Bransfield, Marjorie Abraxas *1991*
Brantley, Betsy Dark Angel *1989*
Branwell, John Chocky *1998* • The Kraken Wakes *1998*
Brasseur, Pierre Eyes without a Face *1959*
Bratt, Benjamin Demolition Man *1993* • Red Planet *2000*
Braugher, André Frequency *2000*
Braun, Gunther Terror beneath the Sea *1966*
Braun, Pinkas Mission Stardust *1968*
Braunberger, Pierre Charleston *1927*
Brauns, Marianne X the Unknown *1956*
Braverman, Bart Alligator *1980*
Braxton, Paulette Homeboys in Outer Space *1996-1997*
Brazeau, Jay Trucks *1997*
Breck, Kathleen The Frozen Dead *1966*
Breck, Peter The Crawling Hand *1963*
Breen, Patrick Galaxy Quest *1999*
Breen, Paulette The Clonus Horror *1978*
Brejchova, Jana Baron Munchhausen *1961*
Bremermann, Julia Space Island One *1998*
Brendel, El Just Imagine *1930*
Brendlova, Inka Buttoners *1997*
Brendon, Nicholas Buffy the Vampire Slayer *1997-*
Brennan, Eileen The Night that Panicked America *1975*
Brennan, John H Galaxis *1995* • DNA *1996*
Brennan, Michael Doomwatch *1972*
Brennan, Peggy Lee Message from Space *1978*
Brenner, Barry Surf Nazis Must Die *1987*
Brenner, Dori Altered States *1980*
Brent, Maya Battle of the Worlds *1961*
Brenton, Gilbert Class of Nuke 'Em High *1986*
Bresee, Bobbie Surf Nazis Must Die *1987*
Bresslaw, Bernard Carry On Screaming *1966* • Moon Zero Two *1969*
Brestoff, Richard The Man with Two Brains

C

Corday, Claudia Dr Coppelius *1966* • The Mysterious House of Dr C *1976*
Corday, Mara Tarantula *1955* • The Black Scorpion *1957* • The Giant Claw *1957*
Cordell, Shane Fiend without a Face *1957*
Cordero, Joaquin Orlak, the Hell of Frankenstein *1960*
Cordova, Fred House of Dracula *1945*
Core, Natalie The Ice Pirates *1984*
Corey, Jeff Superman and the Mole Men *1951* • Seconds *1966* • Beneath the Planet of the Apes *1969*
Corey, Wendell Agent for H.A.R.M. *1966* • Women of the Prehistoric Planet *1966* • The Astro-Zombies *1968*
Corff, Robert Gas-s-s-s, or It Became Necessary to Destroy the World in Order to Save It *1970*
Corkill, Danny DARYL *1985*
Corley, Annie The Tommyknockers *1993*
Corley, Pat When Time Expires *1997*
Cormack, Danielle Cleopatra 2525 *2000-2001*
Corman, Catherine Frankenstein Unbound *1990*
Corman, Roger War of the Satellites *1958*
Cornelius, Billy Carry On Screaming *1966*
Cornthwaite, Robert The Thing from Another World *1951* • The War of the Worlds *1953* • Futureworld *1976*
Cornwell, Judy Blake's 7: The Syndeton Experiment *1998*
Corraface, Georges *aka* **Corraface, George** Escape from LA *1996*
Corri, Adrienne Moon Zero Two *1969* • A Clockwork Orange *1971*
Corrigan, Lloyd The Bowery Boys Meet the Monsters *1954*
Corrigan, Ray Undersea Kingdom *1936* • Doctor Renault's Secret *1942* • The Monster and the Ape *1945* • It! The Terror from beyond Space *1958*
Corrigan, Sam Escape to Witch Mountain *1995*
Corseaut, Aneta The Blob *1958*
Cort, Bud Gas-s-s-s, or It Became Necessary to Destroy the World in Order to Save It *1970* • Brave New World *1980* • Invaders from Mars *1986* • Brain Dead *1990* • Theodore Rex *1995*
Cortese, Joe *aka* **Cortese, Joseph** Something Is Out There *1988* • Something Is Out There *1988*
Cortese, Valentina The Adventures of Baron Munchausen *1988*
Cortez, Julia Mighty Morphin Power Rangers: the Movie *1995*
Cortez, Katherine Critters 3 *1991*
Cortez, Ricardo The Walking Dead *1936*
Cortwright, Jerry The Giant Gila Monster *1959*
Corwin, Linda A Nymphoid Barbarian in Dinosaur Hell *1991*
Cosmo, James The Nightmare Man *1981* • Sunset Heights *1996*
Cossins, James Legend of Death *1965* • Death Line *1972*
Costanzo, Paulo Animorphs *1998-2000*
Costanzo, Robert Man's Best Friend *1993*
Costello, Lou Abbott and Costello Meet Frankenstein *1948* • Abbott and Costello Meet the Invisible Man *1951* • Abbott and Costello Go to Mars *1953* • Abbott and Costello Meet Dr Jekyll and Mr Hyde *1953* • The 30 Foot Bride of Candy Rock *1959*
Costello, Ward Terror from the Year 5,000 *1958* • Return from Witch Mountain *1978*
Costin, Breck Monster *1980*
Costner, Kevin Testament *1983* • Waterworld *1995* • The Postman *1997*
Cote, Tina Nemesis 2 -- Nebula *1995* • Omega Doom *1996*
Cotten, Joseph From the Earth to the Moon *1958* • Latitude Zero *1969* • City beneath the Sea *1971* • Soylent Green *1973* • Island of the Fish Men *1978*
Cottençon, Fanny Paradis pour Tous *1982*
Cotterill, Ralph The Chain Reaction *1980* • Lorca and the Outlaws *1985* • Ultraman Great *1990*
Coulj, Paul Prototype X29A *1992*
Coulouris, George The Man without a Body *1957* • The Woman Eater *1957* • Pathfinders *1960-1961* • The Final Programme *1973*
Court, Hazel Devil Girl from Mars *1954* • The Curse of Frankenstein *1957* • Doctor Blood's Coffin *1960*
Courtemanche, Michel The Secret Adventures of Jules Verne *1999*
Courtenay, Tom The Day the Fish Came Out *1967*
Courtleigh, Robert Atom Squad *1953-1954*
Courtney, Alex The Retaliator *1987*
Courtney, Charles Teenage Monster *1958*
Courtney, Del Hideous Sun Demon *1955* • It Came from beneath the Sea *1955*
Courtney, Mark Independence Day UK *1996*
Courtney, Nicholas Doctor Who: the Second Doctor *1966-1969* • Doctor Who: the Third Doctor *1970-1974* • Doctor Who: the Fourth Doctor *1974-1981* • Doctor Who: the Fifth Doctor *1982-1984* • Doctor Who: the Sixth Doctor *1984-1986* • Doctor Who: the Seventh Doctor *1987-1989* • Doctor Who: The Paradise of Death *1993* • Doctor Who: the Ghosts of N-Space *1996*
Cousins, Brian Mandroid *1993*
Covarrubias, Robert Fire in the Sky *1993*
Cowan, Jerome Have Rocket, Will Travel *1959*
Cowl, Darry A Dog, a Mouse and a Sputnik *1958*
Cowper, Nicola Journey to the Center of the Earth *1989*
Cox, Brian The Year of the Sex Olympics *1968* • Murder on the Moon *1989* • The Cloning of Joanna May *1992* • Chain Reaction *1996*
Cox, Courteney Misfits of Science *1985-1986* • Masters of the Universe *1987* • Cocoon: the Return *1988*
Cox, Julie 20,000 Leagues under the Sea *1997* • Frank Herbert's Dune *2000*
Cox, Mitchell Prototype X29A *1992* • A.P.E.X. *1994*
Cox, Peter Future Schlock *1984*
Cox, Richard Zombie High *1987*
Cox, Ronny The Happiness Cage *1972* • RoboCop *1987* • Captain America *1990* • Martians Go Home *1990* • Total Recall *1990*
Coyle, Anne Bernadette Weird Science *1985*
Coyote, Peter ET the Extra-Terrestrial *1982* • Timerider: the Adventure of Lyle Swann *1982* • Terminal Justice *1996* • Unforgettable *1996* • Murder in My Mind *1997* • Sphere *1998*
Crabbe, Larry "Buster" *aka* **Crabbe, Buster** Island of Lost Souls *1932* • Flash Gordon *1936* • Flash Gordon's Trip to Mars *1938* • Buck Rogers *1939* • Flash Gordon Conquers the Universe *1940* • The Alien Dead *1980*
Craig, Edwin Batman *1989*
Craig, James The Cyclops *1957*
Craig, Michael Mysterious Island *1961* • Turkey Shoot *1981*
Craig, Wendy The Mind Benders *1963*
Craig, Yvonne Mars Needs Women *1966* • Batman *1966-1968*
Cramer, Grant Killer Klowns from Outer Space *1988*
Cramer, Joey Runaway *1984* • Flight of the Navigator *1986*
Cramer, Richard The Vanishing Shadow *1934*
Crampton, Barbara Re-Animator *1985* • From Beyond *1986* • Robot Wars *1993* • Space Truckers *1996*
Crampton, Howard 20,000 Leagues under the Sea *1916*
Crane, Brandon Otherworld *1985*
Crane, Chilton The Death of the Incredible Hulk *1990*
Crane, Michael At the Earth's Core *1976*
Crane, Richard Commando Cody: Sky Marshal of the Universe *1953* • The Neanderthal Man *1953* • Rocky Jones, Space Ranger *1954* • The Alligator People *1959*
Cranham, Kenneth Chimera *1991*
Crasso, Guy The Spacemen of St Tropez *1978*
Cravat, Nick The Island of Dr Moreau *1977*
Craven, James Captain Midnight *1942* • The Purple Monster Strikes *1945* • King of the Rocket Men *1949* • Flying Disc Man from Mars *1950*
Crawford, David Dawn of the Dead *1979*
Crawford, Joan Trog *1970*
Crawford, John Zombies of the Stratosphere *1952* • The Space Children *1958*
Crawford, Johnny Village of the Giants *1965*
Crawford, Wayne Rising Storm *1989*
Craze, Michael Target Luna *1960* • Doctor Who: the First Doctor *1963-1966* • Doctor Who: the Second Doctor *1966-1969*
Creed-Miles, Charlie The Fifth Element *1997*
Creighton, Sally The Thing from Another World *1951*
Creley, Jack Videodrome *1982*
Cremer, Bruno Twice Upon a Time *1969*
Crenna, Richard Marooned *1969* • Leviathan *1989* • Intruders *1992* • 20,000 Leagues under the Sea *1997*
Creswell, Jane The Boy from Andromeda *1991*
Crewdson, Robert The Night Caller *1965*
Crews, Terry The 6th Day *2000*
Crewson, Wendy Bicentennial Man *1999*
Cribbins, Bernard The Night of the Big Heat *1960* • The Mouse on the Moon *1963* • Daleks -- Invasion Earth 2150 AD *1966*
Crick, Ed Future Hunters *1988* • 12:01 *1993*
Crider, Missy Alien Cargo *1999*
Crisp, Donald Dr Jekyll and Mr Hyde *1941*
Cristal, Linda The Dead Don't Die *1975*
Cristal, Perla The Awful Dr Orloff *1962*
Critch, Mark Anchor Zone *1994*
Crnkovich, Thomas Sgt Kabukiman NYPD *1991*
Croft, Alyson Trancers II: The Return of Jack Deth *1991*
Croft, Douglas Batman *1943*
Cromwell, James The Man with Two Brains *1983* • Star Trek: First Contact *1996* • Deep Impact *1998* • Species II *1998* • Space Cowboys *2000*
Cronenberg, David The Fly *1986* • Nightbreed *1990*
Cronkite, Walter We're Back! A Dinosaur's Story *1993*
Cronyn, Hume Cocoon *1985* • *batteries not included *1987* • Cocoon: the Return *1988*
Crosby, Bing The Road to Hong Kong *1962*
Crosby, Cathy Lee The Dark *1979*
Crosby, Denise Eliminators *1986* • Miracle Mile *1989*
Crosby, Mary The Ice Pirates *1984*
Crosby, Wade Invasion USA *1952*
Cross, Ben The Invader *1997* • 20,000 Leagues under the Sea *1997*
Cross, Harley The Fly II *1989*
Cross, Hugh Seven Days to Noon *1950*
Cross, Marcia Target Earth *1998*
Cross, Richard Rats Night of Terror *1983*
Cross, Roger R First Wave *1998-*

D

Danner, Frederick The Peace Game *1969*
Danning, Sybil Battle beyond the Stars *1980* • Amazon Women on the Moon *1987*
Dano, Royal Killer Klowns from Outer Space *1988* • Spaced Invaders *1990*
Danon, Leslie Tattooed Teenage Alien Fighters from Beverly Hills *1994-1995*
Danova, Cesare Valley of the Dragons *1961*
Danson, Ted Once upon a Spy *1980*
Dantès, Suzanne Croisières Sidérales *1941*
Dantine, Helmut Stranger from Venus *1954*
Danziger, Cory The Absent-Minded Professor *1988*
Danziger, Maia The Kirlian Witness *1978* • Dr Heckyl & Mr Hype *1980*
Darbo, Patrika Spaced Invaders *1990*
Darden, Severn Conquest of the Planet of the Apes *1972* • Battle for the Planet of the Apes *1973* • The Day of the Dolphin *1973* • Saturday the 14th *1981*
DaRe, Eric Critters 4 *1992*
Darfeuil, Colette The End of the World *1930*
Darien, Frank The Flying Saucer *1949*
Dark, Christopher World without End *1955*
Darling, Jennifer The Six Million Dollar Man *1974-1978*
Darnell, Vicki Brain Damage *1988*
Darrell, Michael ET the Extra-Terrestrial *1982*
Darren, James The Time Tunnel *1966-1967* • City beneath the Sea *1971*
Darro, Frankie Phantom Empire *1935*
Darrow, Barbara Queen of Outer Space *1958*
Darrow, Paul Blake's 7 *1978-1981* • Blake's 7: The Sevenfold Crown *1998* • Blake's 7: The Syndeton Experiment *1998*
Das Gupta, Bandana The Brain *1962*
Daughton, James Future Cop *1976*
Dauphin, Claude Le Monde Tremblera *1939* • Barbarella *1967*
Davalos, Dominique Howard, a New Breed of Hero *1986*
Davenport, Jack A Clockwork Orange *1998* • Ultraviolet *1998*
Davenport, Nigel The Mind of Mr Soames *1970* • No Blade of Grass *1970* • Phase IV *1973* • The Island of Dr Moreau *1977*
Davi, Robert Peacemaker *1990*
David Carson, John The Day of the Dolphin *1973*
David, Chet The Eye Creatures *1965*
David, Clifford Bill & Ted's Excellent Adventure *1988*
David, Don S Stargate SG-1 *1997-*
David, Eleanor Slipstream *1989*
David, Keith The Thing *1982* • They Live *1988* • The Puppet Masters *1994* • Armageddon *1998* • Pitch Black *1999*
David, Thayer Journey to the Center of the Earth *1959*
Davidson, Diana Scared to Death *1980*
Davidson, Jack Shock Waves *1975*
Davidson, James Parasite *1982*
Davidson, Jaye Stargate *1994*
Davidson, John Captain America *1944* • The Purple Monster Strikes *1945*
Davidson, William Man Made Monster *1941*
Davidtz, Embeth Mutator *1991* • Bicentennial Man *1999*
Davies, Rupert Quatermass II *1955* • Joe 90 *1968-1969*
Davies, Stephen The Nest *1988* • Alien Intruder *1993*
Davies, Sylvia Target Luna *1960*
Davies, Windsor Terrahawks *1983-1986*
Davila, Luis Mission Stardust *1968*
Davis, Bette Return from Witch Mountain *1978* • The Watcher in the Woods *1982*
Davis, Buffy The Amazing Spider-Man *1995*
Davis, Charles The Man from Planet X *1951*
Davis, Craig Adrenalin: Fear the Rush *1995*
Davis, Don S *aka* **Davis, Don** Beyond the Stars *1988* • The 6th Day *2000*
Davis, Duane Mind Breakers *1996*
Davis, Edward The Invisible Ray *1920*
Davis, Elaine The Atomic Kid *1954*
Davis, Geena The Fly *1986* • Earth Girls Are Easy *1988*
Davis, Gene Universal Soldier *1992*
Davis, Jim Monster from Green Hell *1958* • Dracula vs Frankenstein *1970* • The Day Time Ended *1980*
Davis, John Walter Starman *1984*
Davis, Lisa Queen of Outer Space *1958*
Davis, Nancy Donovan's Brain *1953*
Davis, Ossie The Stand *1994* • The Android Affair *1995*
Davis, Phyllis Terminal Island *1973*
Davis, Steve Battle beyond the Stars *1980*
Davis, Susan WarGames *1983*
Davis, William B The X Files *1993-* • The X Files *1998*
Davison, Bruce The Lathe of Heaven *1979* • Steel and Lace *1990* • X-Men *2000*
Davison, Peter Doctor Who: the Fifth Doctor *1982-1984*
Dawber, Pam Mork & Mindy *1978-1982*
Dawe, Kathryn Egghead's Robot *1970*
Dawson, George Big Meat Eater *1982*
Dawson, Richard The Running Man *1987*
Dawson, Roxann Star Trek: Voyager *1995-2001*
Day, Gary Crosstalk *1982* • The Girl from Mars *1991*
Day George, Lynda Aliens from Spaceship Earth *1977* • Day of the Animals *1977* • The Amazing Captain Nemo *1978*
Day, Shannon Land of the Lost *1991-1992*
Day, Vera Quatermass II *1957* • The Woman Eater *1957*
Dayton, Howard Dinosaurus! *1960*
Désy, Victor Rabid *1976*
de Alencar, Iracema Brasil Ano 2000 *1969*
De Alexandre, Rodolfo Medicine Man *1992*
De Beausset, Michael Mission Mars *1968*
De Camp, Rosemary Saturday the 14th *1981*
de Campos, Javier Supersonic Man *1979*
De Carlo, Yvonne The Power *1968*
de Castilla, Rosa Orlak, the Hell of Frankenstein *1960*
De Cordoba, Pedro Before I Hang *1940*
De Cordova, Arturo The Invisible Man *1958*
De Corsia, Ted It Happens Every Spring *1949* • 20,000 Leagues under the Sea *1954*
De Funès, Louis The Spacemen of St Tropez *1978*
de Isaura, Amalia Mr Superinvisible *1970*
De Kova, Frank Teenage Caveman *1958*
de la Fuente, Joel Space: Above and Beyond *1995-1996*
De La Paz, Danny City Limits *1985*
De La Rosa, Nelson The Island of Dr Moreau *1996*
de la Torre, Raf The Trollenberg Terror *1956-1957*
de la Tour, Frances Cold Lazarus *1996*
de Lancie, John Deep Red *1994*
de Lint, Derek Poltergeist: the Legacy *1996-1999*
De Longis, Anthony Starchaser: the Legend of Orin *1985*
de Marney, Derrick Things to Come *1936*
De Metz, Danielle Return of the Fly *1959* • Valley of the Dragons *1961*
De Mornay, Rebecca Testament *1983*
De Morton, Reggie Legion of Iron *1990*
De Niro, Robert Brazil *1985* • Mary Shelley's Frankenstein *1994*
de Pencier, Miranda Harrison Bergeron *1995*
de Ravin, Emilie Roswell *1999 -*
De Rita, Joe Have Rocket, Will Travel *1959* • The Three Stooges in Orbit *1962*
de Rossi, Portia Perfect Assassins *1998*
De Toth, Andre The Invisible Kid *1988*
De Vries, George Mission Mars *1968*
de Wit, Jacqueline Twice Told Tales *1963*
De Wolff, Francis The Two Faces of Dr Jekyll *1960*
De Young, Cliff The Night that Panicked America *1975* • Flight of the Navigator *1986* • Pulse *1988* • The Tommyknockers *1993* • Terminal Voyage *1994*
Deacon, Kim Crosstalk *1982*
Deadrick, Vince Tron *1982*
Deakins, Mark Judgment Day *1999*
Dean, Isabel The Quatermass Experiment *1953*
Dean, Ivor Dr Jekyll and Sister Hyde *1971*
Dean, Loren Space Cowboys *2000*
Dean, Man Mountain The Gladiator *1938*
Dean, Margia The Quatermass Experiment *1955*
Dean, Richard Pathfinders *1960-1961*
Dean, Rick Primal Species *1996*
Dean, Serena Official Denial *1993*
Deane, Shirley Flash Gordon Conquers the Universe *1940*
Dearing, JoAnn Suburban Commando *1991*
Dearman, Glynn Four-Sided Triangle *1953*
DeBenning, Burr City beneath the Sea *1971* • The Incredible Melting Man *1977* • The Amazing Captain Nemo *1978*
deBoer, Nicole Cube *1997*
Decker, William W Redneck Zombies *1988*
Declie, Xavier Adrenalin: Fear the Rush *1995* • Nemesis 3 — Time Lapse *1996* • The Outsider *1997*
Dee, Ruby The Stand *1994*
Deebark, Felix The Big Pull *1962*
Defoe, Diane Deceit *1989*
Degen, Michael Dr M *1989* • Mission Eureka *1990*
DeGeneres, Ellen Coneheads *1993*
DeGraaf, Manfred The Lift *1983*
DeHaven, Gloria Bog *1978*
DeHaven, Lisa Redneck Zombies *1988*
Dehelly, Suzanne Croisières Sidérales *1941*
Dehner, John The Bowery Boys Meet the Monsters *1954* • The Day of the Dolphin *1973* • The Boys from Brazil *1978* • Airplane II: the Sequel *1982* • Creator *1985*
Dekker, Albert Dr Cyclops *1940* • She Devil *1957* • Gamera the Invincible *1965*
Dekker, Thomas Village of the Damned *1995* • Honey, I Shrunk the Kids *1997-2000*
DeKova, Frank Atlantis, the Lost Continent *1960*
Del Mar, Maria TekWar *1994-1996* • Mercy Point *1998-1999*
Del Val, Jean Fantastic Voyage *1966*
Delahaye, Michel Alphaville *1965*
DeLancie, John Arcade *1993* • Arcade *1993* • Evolver *1994*
Delaney, Kim Something Is Out There *1988* • Body Parts *1991* • Darkman II: the Return of Durant *1995* • Metal Beast *1995* • Mission to Mars *1999*
Delaney, Pat Zontar, the Thing from Venus *1966*
Delano, Michael Not of This Earth *1988*
Delany, Dana Batman: Mask of the Phantasm *1993* • Wild Palms *1993*
Delate, Brian The Truman Show *1998*
Delbo, Jean-Jacques The Day the Sky Exploded *1958*

E

F

Fierro, Paul The Creature Walks among Us *1956*
Fierry, Patrick Mission Eureka *1990*
Fierstein, Harvey Dr Jekyll and Ms Hyde *1995* • Independence Day *1996*
Fieschi, Jean-André Alphaville *1965*
Fifer, John Super Mario Bros *1993*
Figueroa, Efrain Cosmic Slop *1994*
Filipovsky, Frantisek On the Comet *1970* • Sir, You Are a Widower *1971*
Filippo, Fabrizio Level 9 *2000-2001*
Fillingham, John Lloyd Chocky *1998*
Finch, Jon Counterstrike *1969* • The Final Programme *1973*
Findlay, Diane Gamera the Invincible *1965*
Findley, James The Girl from Tomorrow *1990-1991*
Fine, Larry Have Rocket, Will Travel *1959* • The Three Stooges in Orbit *1962*
Finlay, Frank The Deadly Bees *1967* • Lifeforce *1985*
Finlayson, Alex Journey to the Center of the Earth *1959*
Finley, William Simon *1980* • Silent Rage *1982*
Finn, Catherine The Deadly Bees *1967*
Finn, Christine Quatermass and the Pit *1958-1959* • Thunderbirds *1965-1966* • Thunderbirds Are Go! *1966* • Thunderbird 6 *1968*
Finn, John Steel Justice *1992*
Finnegan, Tom Repo Man *1984*
Finneran, Katie Night of the Living Dead *1990*
Finney, Albert Looker *1981* • Wolfen *1981* • Cold Lazarus *1996*
Finocchiaro, Angela Ratataplan *1979*
Fiorentino, Linda Unforgettable *1996* • Men in Black *1997* • What Planet Are You From? *2000*
First, Joseph And Millions Will Die! *1973*
Firth, Peter The Flipside of Dominick Hide *1980* • Another Flip for Dominick *1982* • Lifeforce *1985*
Firth, Robert Proteus *1995*
Fischer, Don Species *1995*
Fischer, Madeleine The Day the Sky Exploded *1958*
Fischer, Ramona Vegas in Space *1994*
Fisco, Margie Monstrosity *1963*
Fish, Doris Vegas in Space *1994*
Fish, Nancy Ghost in the Machine *1993*
Fishburne, Laurence Event Horizon *1997* • The Matrix *1999*
Fisher, Carrie Star Wars Episode IV: a New Hope *1977* • Star Wars Episode V: the Empire Strikes Back *1980* • Star Wars Episode VI: Return of the Jedi *1983* • Amazon Women on the Moon *1987* • The Time Guardian *1987*
Fisher, Frances Attack of the 50 Ft Woman *1993*
Fisher, Gregor Nineteen Eighty-Four *1984*
Fisher, Shug The Giant Gila Monster *1959*
Fiske, Richard The Devil Commands *1941*
Fiske, Robert Before I Hang *1940*
Fitz, Peter Dr M *1989*
Fitz-Gerald, Lewis Pitch Black *1999*
Fitzgerald, Brendan Fantastic Voyage *1966*
Fitzgerald, Nuala The Brood *1979*
Fitzgerald, Patrick Poltergeist: the Legacy *1996-1999*
Fitzpatrick, Aileen Communion *1989*
Fitzpatrick, Kate The Return of Captain Invincible *1983*
Fitzroy, Kate Counterstrike *1969*
Fix, Paul Dr Cyclops *1940* • Night of the Lepus *1972*
Flacks, Niki The Lathe of Heaven *1979*
Flaherty, Dianna Metamorphosis: The Alien Factor *1993*
Flaherty, Joe Blue Monkey *1987* • Back to the Future Part II *1989*
Flaherty, William The Monolith Monsters *1957*
Flanery, Sean Patrick Powder *1995*
Flannery, Bridget The Outsider *1997*
Flannigan, Maureen Out of This World *1987-1991*
Flavin, James King Kong *1933*
Fleck, John Mutant on the Bounty *1989* • Waterworld *1995*
Fleer, Harry The Unearthly *1957*
Fleeshman, David The Kraken Wakes *1998*
Fleetwood, Mick The Running Man *1987*
Fleischer, Charles Back to the Future Part II *1989* • We're Back! A Dinosaur's Story *1993*
Fleming, Eric Conquest of Space *1955* • Queen of Outer Space *1958*
Fleming, John F Eat and Run *1986*
Fleming, Lone Where Time Began *1977*
Fleming, Lucy Survivors *1975-1977*
Flemyng, Jason Deep Rising *1998*
Flemyng, Robert The Blood Beast Terror *1967* • The Body Stealers *1969*
Fletcher, Brendan Trucks *1997*
Fletcher, Louise Brainstorm *1983* • Strange Invaders *1983* • Firestarter *1984* • Invaders from Mars *1986* • Shadowzone *1990* • VR.5 *1995* • Virtuosity *1995* • The Stepford Husbands *1996*
Fletcher, Norman The Quiet Earth *1985*
Flex Homeboys in Outer Space *1996-1997*
Flint, Olly von The Tunnel *1933*
Flood, Gerald Pathfinders *1960-1961* • City beneath the Sea *1962* • Doctor Who: the Fifth Doctor *1982-1984*
Florek, David The Absent-Minded Professor *1988*
Florence, Robin Mary Superhuman Samurai Syber-Squad *1994-1995*
Flores, Jose Ark II *1976*
Flores, Von Darkman III: Die Darkman Die *1996* • Earth: Final Conflict *1997-* • Johnny 2.0 *1998*
Flory, Med The Nutty Professor *1963*
Flournoy, Don The Giant Gila Monster *1959*
Flower, George "Buck" They Live *1988*
Flowers, Kim Alien: Resurrection *1997*
Floyd, Robert Sliders *1995-2000*
Fluegel, Darlanne Battle beyond the Stars *1980* • Project: Alien *1990* • Scanner Cop *1994* • Darkman III: Die Darkman Die *1996*
Fluellen, Joel Monster from Green Hell *1958*
Flynn, Colleen Late for Dinner *1991*
Flynn, Daniel Biggles *1986*
Flynn, Frederick Shadowzone *1990*
Flynn, Joe The Computer Wore Tennis Shoes *1970* • The Million Dollar Duck *1971*
Flynn, Steven Roswell: the Aliens Attack *1999*
Foley, Dave Blast from the Past *1998*
Foley, Jeremy Legion of Fire: Killer Ants! *1998*
Fonda, Bridget Light Years *1988* • Frankenstein Unbound *1990*
Fonda, Henry Fail-Safe *1964* • Meteor *1979*
Fonda, Jane Barbarella *1967*
Fonda, Peter Futureworld *1976* • Escape from LA *1996*
Fondacaro, Phil The Garbage Pail Kids Movie *1987*
Fong, Benson Conquest of Space *1955*
Fontaine, Joan Voyage to the Bottom of the Sea *1961*
Fontana, Char Too Much *1987*
Foran, Dick The Atomic Submarine *1960*
Forbes, Bryan Satellite in the Sky *1956* • Quatermass II *1957*
Forbes, Chris Sleeper *1973*
Forbes, Michelle Escape from LA *1996*
Forbes, Scott The Mind of Mr Soames *1970*
Force, Deborah Future Schlock *1984* • As Time Goes By *1987*
Ford, Alan The Hitch-hiker's Guide to the Galaxy: Secondary Phase *1978-1980*
Ford, Anitra Invasion of the Bee Girls *1973*
Ford, Carole Ann Doctor Who: the First Doctor *1963-1966*
Ford Davies, Oliver The Cloning of Joanna May *1992* • MacGyver: Lost Treasure of Atlantis *1994* • Star Wars Episode I: the Phantom Menace *1999*
Ford, Faith Night Visitors *1996*
Ford, Francis Frankenstein *1931*
Ford, Glenn Superman *1978* • Virus *1980*
Ford, Harrison Star Wars Episode IV: a New Hope *1977* • Star Wars Episode V: the Empire Strikes Back *1980* • Blade Runner *1982* • Star Wars Episode VI: Return of the Jedi *1983*
Ford, Lee SOS Coastguard *1937*
Ford, Maria Dark Planet *1997*
Ford, Mick Light Years Away *1981*
Ford, Ross Project Moonbase *1953*
Foree, Ken Dawn of the Dead *1979* • From Beyond *1986*
Foreman, Deborah Lobster Man from Mars *1989*
Forester, Wayne A Clockwork Orange *1998*
Forke, Farrah Journey to the Center of the Earth *1993* • Bionic Ever After? *1994*
Forman, Carol Brick Bradford *1947* • Superman *1948*
Forman, David Teenage Mutant Ninja Turtles *1990*
Forman, Joey The Atomic Kid *1954*
Forrest, Frederic It Lives Again *1978*
Forrest, Steve Captain America *1979* • Amazon Women on the Moon *1987*
Forsey, Norman Aberration *1997*
Forslund, Constance Village of the Damned *1995*
Forster, Jill Crosstalk *1982*
Forster, Robert The Black Hole *1979* • The Darker Side of Terror *1979* • Alligator *1980* • Peacemaker *1990* • Supernova *2000*
Forsyth, Brigit Dark Season *1991*
Forsyth, Frank The Brain *1962*
Forsyth, Rosemary City beneath the Sea *1971*
Forsythe, John The Mysterious Two *1982*
Forsythe, William Virtuosity *1995*
Forte, Joe The Crimson Ghost *1946*
Foschi, Massimo Holocaust 2000 *1977*
Fossey, Brigitte Quintet *1979*
Foster, Blake Turbo: a Power Rangers Adventure *1997*
Foster, Dudley The Girl Who Loved Robots *1965* • Moon Zero Two *1969*
Foster, Gloria The Matrix *1999*
Foster, Hayley My Uncle the Alien *1996*
Foster, Jamie First Born *1988*
Foster, Jodie Contact *1997*
Foster, Meg Masters of the Universe *1987* • They Live *1988* • Project: Shadowchaser *1992* • Oblivion *1993* • Space Marines *1996*
Foster, Phil Conquest of Space *1955*
Foster, Preston The Time Travelers *1964*
Foster, Stacie Cyber-Tracker *1994* • Steel Frontier *1994*
Foucheux, Rick Invader *1991*
Foulger, Byron The Magnetic Monster *1953* • Captain Nice *1967*
Fowlds, Derek Frankenstein Created Woman *1966*
Fowler, Frank Monstrosity *1963*
Fowler, Harry Fire Maidens from Outer Space *1956*
Fowley, Douglas Cat-Women of the Moon *1953*
Fox, Allen Dr Cyclops *1940*
Fox, Bernard The Bamboo Saucer *1968*

G

Giraldi, Franco Zombie Creeping Flesh *1981*
Giraldi, Jill The Omega Man *1971*
Girard, Joseph Just Imagine *1930*
Girardot, Annie The Seed of Man *1969*
Gish, Annabeth The X Files *1993-*
Gittins, Paul The Boy from Andromeda *1991*
Giuntoli, Neil The Borrower *1989* • Steel Justice *1992*
Giustini, Carlo *aka* **Justin, Charles** War of the Planets *1965* • The Wild, Wild Planet *1965*
Gladwin, Joe Work Is a Four Letter Word *1968*
Glass, Ann Gisel Rats Night of Terror *1983*
Glass, Ron Deep Space *1987*
Glasser, Isabel Forever Young *1992*
Glaudini, Robert Parasite *1982*
Gleason, Paul Doc Savage: the Man of Bronze *1975* • Digital Man *1994*
Gleeson, Brendan AI *2001*
Gleeson, Redmond Dreamscape *1984*
Glenister, Robert The Gibson *1992*
Glenn, Libby The Friendly Persuaders *1969*
Gless, Sharon Revenge of the Stepford Wives *1980*
Glover, Brian Alien3 *1992*
Glover, Crispin Back to the Future *1985*
Glover, Danny Iceman *1984* • Predator 2 *1990*
Glover, John The Incredible Shrinking Woman *1981* • Doctor Who: Slipback *1985* • Gremlins 2: the New Batch *1990* • Automatic *1994* • Batman and Robin *1997*
Glover, Julian Quatermass and the Pit *1967* • Star Wars Episode V: the Empire Strikes Back *1980* • QED *1982*
Glyn-Jones, John Man in the Moon *1960* • Countdown at Woomera *1961*
Goacher, Dennis City beneath the Sea *1962*
Goddard, Mark Lost in Space *1965-1968* • Blue Sunshine *1976*
Goddard, Paul Farscape *1999-*
Goddard, Trevor Mortal Kombat *1995*
Goddard, Willoughby The Voices *1955*
Godecki, Marzena Ocean Girl *1994-1998*
Godfrey, Peter Dr Jekyll and Mr Hyde *1941*
Godreau, Miguel Altered States *1980*
Godsell, Vanda The Brain Machine *1954* • The Earth Dies Screaming *1964*
Godunov, Alexander Waxwork II: Lost in Time *1992*
Godwin, Christopher Astronauts *1981/1983*
Goelz, Dave Muppets from Space *1999*
Goetz, Peter Michael Wolfen *1981* • King Kong Lives *1986*
Goetzke, Bernhard Alraune *1930*
Goff, John F The Alpha Incident *1977*
Gohil, Dinita The Last Train *1999*
Going, Joanna Phantoms *1998*
Golan, Gila The Valley of Gwangi *1969*
Goldberg, Whoopi Star Trek: Generations *1994* • Theodore Rex *1995*
Goldblatt, Harold The Mind Benders *1963* • Children of the Damned *1964*
Goldblum, Jeff Invasion of the Body Snatchers *1978* • Threshold *1981* • The Adventures of Buckaroo Banzai across the 8th Dimension *1984* • The Fly *1986* • Earth Girls Are Easy *1988* • Jurassic Park *1993* • Powder *1995* • Independence Day *1996* • The Lost World: Jurassic Park *1997*
Golden, Gladys Punishment Park *1971*
Golden, Sanford Punishment Park *1971*
Goldie, Wyndham The Strange World of Planet X *1957*
Goldin, Ricky Paull Hyper Sapien: People from Another Star *1986* • The Blob *1988*
Goldman, Danny Young Frankenstein *1974*
Goldoni, Lelia Invasion of the Body Snatchers *1978*
Goldsmith, Charles Voyage into Prehistory *1955*
Goldstein, Jenette Aliens *1986*
Goldthwait, Bobcat Out There *1995*
Goldwyn, Tony The 6th Day *2000*
Golino, Valeria Escape from LA *1996*
Gomez, Carlos Plymouth *1991* • Asteroid *1997*
Gomez, Jaime Solo *1996*
Gomez, Thomas Beneath the Planet of the Apes *1969*
Goncalves, Enio Brasil Ano 2000 *1969*
Gonzales, Joe Brain Damage *1988*
Gonzalez, Clifton Fortress *1992*
Goode, James Batman: Knightfall *1995*
Gooderson, David Earthsearch II *1982*
Goodger, Michelle Quarantine *1989*
Goodier, Mark Independence Day UK *1996*
Goodier, Robert The Only Way Out Is Dead *1970*
Gooding Jr, Cuba Daybreak *1993* • Outbreak *1995*
Goodliffe, Michael The Day the Earth Caught Fire *1961*
Goodman, Henry Mary Reilly *1995* • Cold Lazarus *1996*
Goodman, John CHUD *1984* • We're Back! A Dinosaur's Story *1993* • Now and Again *1999-2000* • What Planet Are You From? *2000*
Goodrich, Deborah Remote Control *1988*
Goodrow, Garry Glen and Randa *1971*
Goodson, Barbara Vampire Hunter D *1985*
Goodwin, Alexander Mimic *1997*
Goodwin, Bill The Atomic Kid *1954*
Goodwin, Harold Quatermass and the Pit *1958-1959* • Frankenstein Must Be Destroyed *1969*
Goodwin, John Tremors *1989*
Goody, Bob Crime Traveller *1997*
Goorjian, Michael Forever Young *1992*
Gora, Claudio The Doll *1962*
Gorcey, Bernard The Bowery Boys Meet the Monsters *1954*
Gorcey, Leo The Bowery Boys Meet the Monsters *1954*
Gordeno, Peter UFO *1970-1973*
Gordon, Bruce Piranha *1978*
Gordon, Claire Konga *1960*
Gordon, Denni Fortress *1992*
Gordon, Don ZPG: Zero Population Growth *1971* • The Borrower *1989*
Gordon, Eric Space Jam *1997*
Gordon, Eve Honey, We Shrunk Ourselves *1997*
Gordon, Gale The 30 Foot Bride of Candy Rock *1959* • Visit to a Small Planet *1960* • Sergeant Deadhead *1965*
Gordon, Gavin Bride of Frankenstein *1935*
Gordon, Julie Supersnooper *1981*
Gordon, Pam The Borrower *1989*
Gordon, Roy Attack of the 50 Foot Woman *1958*
Gordon, Ruth Voyage of the Rock Aliens *1985*
Gordon-Levitt, Joseph 3rd Rock from the Sun *1996-*
Gorg, Galyn America 3000 *1986* • M.A.N.T.I.S. *1994-1995*
Gori, Gabriele The Bronx Executioner *1989*
Gorman, Lynne Videodrome *1982*
Gorman, Pat The Nightmare Man *1981*
Gorman, Robert Hy Forever Young *1992*
Gorshin, Frank Invasion of the Saucer Men *1957* • Batman *1966* • Goliath Awaits *1981* • Twelve Monkeys *1995*
Gortner, Marjoe The Food of the Gods *1975* • Starcrash *1979*
Goss, David She *1982*
Gosselaar, Mark-Paul Specimen *1996*
Gosselin, François The Christmas Martian *1971*
Gossett Jr, Louis The Powers of Matthew Star *1982-1983* • Enemy Mine *1985* • Monolith *1993*
Gotell, Walter The Damned *1961* • The Road to Hong Kong *1962*
Gothard, Michael Warlords of Atlantis *1978* • Lifeforce *1985*
Gotho, Heinrich Metropolis *1926*
Gottlieb, Theodore *aka* **Theodore** Horror of the Blood Monsters *1970*
Goude, Ingrid The Killer Shrews *1959*
Gough, Lloyd The Green Hornet *1966-1967*
Gough, Michael The Man in the White Suit *1951* • Konga *1960* • The Poisoned Earth *1961* • They Came from beyond Space *1967* • Trog *1970* • Horror Hospital *1973* • The Boys from Brazil *1978* • Batman *1989* • Batman Returns *1992* • Batman Forever *1995* • Batman: Knightfall *1995* • Batman and Robin *1997*
Gould, Elliott Who? *1974* • Capricorn One *1978*
Gould, Graydon Supercar *1961-1962*
Gould, Harold Project X *1968*
Gowland, Gibson The Mysterious Island *1929*
Graas, John Christian The Philadelphia Experiment 2 *1993*
Grace, Mary It's about Time *1966-1967*
Grace, Wayne Fire in the Sky *1993*
Gracen, Elizabeth The Death of the Incredible Hulk *1990*
Graff, Todd The Abyss *1989*
Graham, David Supercar *1961-1962* • Fireball XL5 *1962-1963* • Fireball XL5 *1962-1963* • Thunderbirds *1965-1966* • Thunderbirds Are Go! *1966* • Thunderbird 6 *1968*
Graham, Dick The War Game *1965*
Graham, Fred 20,000 Leagues under the Sea *1954*
Graham, Gary Robot Jox *1989* • Alien Nation *1989-1990*
Graham, Gerrit Demon Seed *1977* • The Creature Wasn't Nice *1981* • TerrorVision *1986* • The Philadelphia Experiment 2 *1993* • Now and Again *1999-2000*
Graham, Gerritt It's Alive III: Island of the Alive *1987*
Graham, Heather Lost in Space *1997*
Graham, Holter Maximum Overdrive *1986*
Graham, Michael Curse of the Fly *1965*
Graham, Nigel Journey into Space: The Return from Mars *1981*
Graham, Reavis Moontrap *1989*
Graham, Tara White Dwarf *1995*
Graham, Tim The Brain from Planet Arous *1958*
Grainger, Holly Chocky *1998*
Granger, Michael Creature with the Atom Brain *1955*
Grant, Bryan Teenagers from Outer Space *1959*
Grant, Cy Captain Scarlet and the Mysterons *1967-1968* • At the Earth's Core *1976*
Grant, David Marshall Forever Young *1992*
Grant, Faye The Greatest American Hero *1981-1983* • V *1983-1985*
Grant, Jennifer Savage *1995*
Grant, Kathryn The Night the World Exploded *1957*
Grant, Lee Marooned *1969*
Grant, Micah High Desert Kill *1989*
Grant, Shelby Fantastic Voyage *1966*
Grantham, Leslie The Uninvited *1997*
Graubart, Judy Simon *1980*
Graudel, Janine Return of the Fly *1959*
Graue, Siegfried The Big Mess *1970*
Gravers, Steve Wizards *1977*
Graves, Kirk Slave Girls from beyond Infinity *1987*
Graves (1), Peter Red Planet Mars *1952* • Killers from Space *1954* • It Conquered the World *1956* • Beginning of the End *1957* • The Clonus Horror *1978* • Airplane II: the Sequel *1982*

H

Haas, Lukas Testament *1983* • Solarwarriors *1986* • Mars Attacks! *1996*
Haas, Victoria Attack of the 50 Ft Woman *1993*
Habermann, Eva Lexx *1997-*
Hackett, Joan The Terminal Man *1974*
Hackman, Gene Marooned *1969* • Young Frankenstein *1974* • Superman *1978* • Superman II *1980* • Superman IV: the Quest for Peace *1987*
Haddon, Dayle Cyborg *1989*
Haddon, Laurence The Aliens Are Coming *1979*
Haddrick, Ron The Stranger *1964-1965* • Shirley Thompson versus the Aliens *1968*
Haden, Sara Mad Love *1935*
Hagan, Ken Dr Frankenstein on Campus *1967*
Hagen, Jean Panic in Year Zero *1962*
Hagen, Kevin Land of the Giants *1968-1970*
Hagen, Ross Alienator *1989*
Hagen, Uta The Boys from Brazil *1978*
Hagerty, Julie Airplane II: the Sequel *1982*
Haggerty, Dan Elves *1989*
Haggerty, Don King of the Rocket Men *1949* • The Resurrection of Zachary Wheeler *1971*
Haglund, Dean The X Files *1993-*
Haglund, Dean The X Files *1998*
Haglund, Dean The Lone Gunmen *2001*
Hagman, Larry Fail-Safe *1964* • Beware! The Blob *1971* • Superman *1978*
Hagon, Garrick The Adventures of Superman *1994* • The Adventures of Superman: Doomsday and Beyond *1995* • The Amazing Spider-Man *1995*
Hagon, Rex Short Circuit 2 *1988*
Hahn, Archie Amazon Women on the Moon *1987*
Hahn, Paul The Angry Red Planet *1959*
Haid, Charles Altered States *1980* • Nightbreed *1990*
Haiduk, Stacy Superboy *1988-1992* • Steel and Lace *1990* • seaQuest DSV *1993-1996* • Yesterday's Target *1996*
Haig, Sid THX 1138 *1971* • Jason of Star Command *1979-1981*
Haim, Corey Watchers *1988* • Prayer of the Rollerboys *1990*
Haines, Patricia The Night Caller *1965*
Haines, Richard Haddon Alien from LA *1987* • Survivor *1987*
Haje, Khrystyne Cyborg 3: The Recycler *1994*
Halbert, Don Official Denial *1993*
Hale Jr, Alan *aka* **Hale, Alan** It Happens Every Spring *1949* • The Crawling Hand *1963* • The Giant Spider Invasion *1975*
Hale, Barbara The Giant Spider Invasion *1975*
Hale, Bernadette The Flight That Disappeared *1961*
Hale, Georgina The Watcher in the Woods *1982*
Hale, Mary 12:01 *1993*
Hale, Nancy The Flight That Disappeared *1961*
Hale, Tony The People That Time Forgot *1977*
Haley, Jackie Earle Damnation Alley *1977*
Hall, Albert Trouble in Mind *1985*
Hall, Amelia Iceman *1984*
Hall, Anthony Journey into Space: The Return from Mars *1981*
Hall, Anthony C Fortress 2: Re-entry *1999*
Hall, Anthony Michael Weird Science *1985*
Hall, Bruce Rod Brown of the Rocket Rangers *1953-1954*
Hall, Bug Honey, We Shrunk Ourselves *1997*
Hall, Deirdre The Krofft Supershow *1976-1978*
Hall, Huntz The Return of Dr X *1939* • The Bowery Boys Meet the Monsters *1954*
Hall, Jerry Batman *1989*
Hall, Jon The Invisible Agent *1942* • The Invisible Man's Revenge *1944*
Hall, Kevin Peter Misfits of Science *1985-1986* • Predator *1987* • Predator 2 *1990*
Hall, Philip Baker Who Is Julia? *1986*
Hall, Zooey The New People *1969-1970*
Hallahan, Charles The Thing *1982* • Twilight Zone: the Movie *1983*
Hallam, John Quest for Love *1971* • Moonbase 3 *1973* • The People That Time Forgot *1977* • Flash Gordon *1980* • Lifeforce *1985*
Haller, Ty Dr Frankenstein on Campus *1967* • The Groundstar Conspiracy *1972*
Hallett, Neil The Brain Machine *1954*
Hallick, Tom The Amazing Captain Nemo *1978*
Halliday, Bryant The Projected Man *1966*
Halliday, Peter A for Andromeda *1961*
Halpin, Luke Shock Waves *1975*
Halsey, Brett Return of the Fly *1959* • The Atomic Submarine *1960* • Twice Told Tales *1963* • Spy in Your Eye *1965* • Expect No Mercy *1995*
Halston, Rodger Primal Species *1996*
Halston, Roger The Alien Within *1995*
Halton, Charles Dr Cyclops *1940*
Hama, Mie King Kong vs Godzilla *1962* • King Kong Escapes *1967*
Hamada, Yuko Gamera versus Guiron *1969*
Hamill, John No Blade of Grass *1970* • Trog *1970*
Hamill, Mark Star Wars Episode IV: a New Hope *1977* • Wizards *1977* • Star Wars Episode V: the Empire Strikes Back *1980* • Star Wars Episode VI: Return of the Jedi *1983* • Slipstream *1989* • Earth Angel *1991* • The Guyver *1992* • Batman: Mask of the Phantasm *1993* • Time Runner *1993* • Village of the Damned *1995* • When Time Expires *1997*
Hamilton, George The Power *1968* • The Dead Don't Die *1975*
Hamilton, Jaeme Jules Verne's Strange Holiday *1969*
Hamilton, John The Adventures of Superman *1952-1958*
Hamilton, Judd Starcrash *1979*
Hamilton, Kipp War of the Gargantuas *1970*
Hamilton, Linda The Terminator *1984* • King Kong Lives *1986* • Terminator 2: Judgment Day *1991*
Hamilton, Margaret The Invisible Woman *1940*
Hamilton, Neil Batman *1966* • Batman *1966-1968*
Hamilton, Richard Plymouth *1991*
Hamilton, Suzanna Nineteen Eighty-Four *1984*
Hamlin, Harry Space *1985*
Hammack, Warren The Eye Creatures *1965*
Hammond, Earl Light Years *1988*
Hammond, Michael Target Luna *1960*
Hammond, Nicholas The Amazing Spider-Man *1978-1979* • The Martian Chronicles *1979* • 20,000 Leagues under the Sea *1997*
Hammond, Peter X the Unknown *1956*
Hammond, Sheila Legend of Death *1965*
Hammond, Vincent Frankenstein: the College Years *1991*
Hampton, Bill Hideous Sun Demon *1955*
Hampton, James The Cat from Outer Space *1978* • Hangar 18 *1980*
Hampton, Paul Shivers *1975*
Hanauer, Terri Communion *1989*
Hancock, Lou Miracle Mile *1989*
Handl, Irene Give Us the Moon *1944* • The Perfect Woman *1949* • Metal Mickey *1980-1983*
Handley, Tommy Time Flies *1944*
Handy, James Who Is Julia? *1986* • The Rocketeer *1991*
Haney, Anne Plymouth *1991*
Haney, Daryl Lords of the Deep *1989*
Hanich, Davos La Jetée *1962*
Hanks, Colin Roswell *1999 -*
Hanley, Jimmy The Tunnel *1935* • Satellite in the Sky *1956*
Hanlon, Dan 20,000 Leagues under the Sea *1916*
Hannah, Daryl Blade Runner *1982* • Memoirs of an Invisible Man *1992* • Attack of the 50 Ft Woman *1993* • My Favorite Martian *1999*
Hannen, Nicholas FP1 *1932*
Hannigan, Alyson My Stepmother Is an Alien *1988* • Buffy the Vampire Slayer *1997-*
Hanold, Marilyn Frankenstein Meets the Space Monster *1965*
Hansen, Gunnar Mosquito *1995*
Hansen, Nicole American Cyborg: Steel Warrior *1993*
Hansen, William Fail-Safe *1964* • Frankenstein *1973* • The Terminal Man *1974*
Hanson, Heather Sleeping Dogs *1997* • Roswell: the Aliens Attack *1999*
Hanson, Kristina Dinosaurus! *1960*
Hanson, Luke Yellowbacks *1990*
Hanson, Peter When Worlds Collide *1951*
Harada, Itoko The X from Outer Space *1967*
Harada, Kiwako Godzilla vs King Ghidorah *1991*
Harada, Yujin Gunhed *1989*
Harari, Clément Shadowman *1973*
Harden, Marcia Gay Late for Dinner *1991* • Flubber *1997* • Space Cowboys *2000*
Harders, Jane Shirley Thompson versus the Aliens *1968*
Hardester, Crofton Android *1982*
Hardie, Russell Fail-Safe *1964*
Hardin, Jerry Plymouth *1991*
Harding, Jeff 20,000 Leagues under the Sea *1997*
Harding, Lyn The Man Who Changed His Mind *1936*
Hardison, Kadeem Drive *1996*
Hardman, Karl Night of the Living Dead *1968*
Hardtmuth, Paul The Strange World of Planet X *1956*
Hardwicke, Cedric *aka* **Hardwicke, Sir Cedric** Things to Come *1936* • The Invisible Man Returns *1940* • The Ghost of Frankenstein *1942* • The Invisible Agent *1942* • The War of the Worlds *1953*
Hardwicke, Edward The Alchemists *1999*
Hardy, Jonathan Farscape *1999-*
Hardy, Robert Mary Shelley's Frankenstein *1994*
Hardy, Sam King Kong *1933*
Harewood, Dorian Looker *1981* • Viper *1994-1999*
Hargreaves, Amy Brainscan *1994*
Hargreaves, Janet Frankenstein and the Monster from Hell *1973*
Hargreaves, John Sky Pirates *1986*
Harker, Susannah Ultraviolet *1998*
Harle, Daniel The Peace Game *1969*
Harmer, Juliet Adam Adamant Lives! *1966-1967* • Quest for Love *1971*
Harmon, Joy Village of the Giants *1965*
Harmon, Mark Goliath Awaits *1981*
Harney, Corrina Vampirella *1996*
Harolde, Ralf Deluge *1933*
Harper, Gerald Adam Adamant Lives! *1966-1967*
Harper, Kate Batman *1989*
Harper, Robert A Clockwork Orange *1998*
Harper, Ron Planet of the Apes *1974* • Land of the Lost *1974-1976*
Harper, Susan Phantasm *1978*
Harper, Tracey The Sender *1982*
Harrigan, William The Invisible Man *1933*

I

J

L

M

Marchat, Jean Croisières Sidérales *1941*
Marco, Paul Bride of the Monster *1955*
Marcoux, Ted Ghost in the Machine *1993*
Marcovicci, Andrea Spacehunter: Adventures in the Forbidden Zone *1983*
Marcus, Richard Enemy Mine *1985* • Deadly Friend *1986* • Tremors *1989*
Margine, Marco The Seed of Man *1969*
Margolin, Janet Planet Earth *1974* • Ghostbusters II *1989*
Margolin, Stuart Futureworld *1976* • Mr Smith *1983-1984*
Margolis, Mark Pi *1997*
Margulies, David Ghostbusters *1984* • Ghostbusters II *1989*
Mari, Fiorella The Day the Sky Exploded *1958*
Mari, Keiko Godzilla vs Hedora *1971*
Marie, Constance 12:01 *1993*
Marie, Lisa Mars Attacks! *1996*
Marienthal, Eli The Iron Giant *1999*
Marietta Nude on the Moon *1961*
Marin, Jacques The Island at the Top of the World *1974*
Marin, Richard "Cheech" *aka* **Martin, Cheech** It Came from Hollywood *1982* • SPYkids *2001*
Marin, Russ Deadly Friend *1986*
Marinaro, Ed Doomsday Rock *1997*
Marinker, Daniel Batman: Knightfall *1995*
Marinker, Peter The Amazing Spider-Man *1995* • Batman: Knightfall *1995*
Marion, George F *aka* **Marion Sr, George** 6 Hours to Live *1932*
Marion, Paul Killer Ape *1953*
Marion-Crawford, Howard Mr Drake's Duck *1950* • The Man in the White Suit *1951*
Mariscal, Alberto Doctor Crimen *1953*
Mark, Mary Voyage to the Planet of Prehistoric Women *1966*
Mark, Michael Frankenstein *1931* • Flash Gordon Conquers the Universe *1940* • Attack of the Puppet People *1958*
Mark Vasquez, Peter Fire in the Sky *1993*
Markart, Annie The World without a Mask *1934*
Markham, David Target Luna *1960* • ZPG: Zero Population Growth *1971*
Markham, Kika Outland *1981*
Markham, Monte The Second Hundred Years *1967-1968* • Project X *1968* • Piranha *1996*
Markham, Petra Ape and Essence *1966* • Ace of Wands *1970-1972*
Markim, Al Tom Corbett, Space Cadet *1950-1955*
Marks, Alfred Scream and Scream Again *1969*
Marks, Leo The Sticky Fingers of Time *1997*
Marks, Michael The Wasp Woman *1959*
Markus, Tarja Time of Roses *1969*
Marla, Norma The Two Faces of Dr Jekyll *1960*
Marleau, Louise *aka* **Monroe, Louise** Alien Contamination *1981*
Marley, John It Lives Again *1978* • Threshold *1981*
Marlowe, Hugh The Day the Earth Stood Still *1951* • World without End *1955* • Earth vs the Flying Saucers *1956* • Castle of Evil *1966*
Marly, Florence Planet of Blood *1966*
Marmont, Percy Four-Sided Triangle *1953*
Maroney, Kelli Night of the Comet *1984*
Marquand, Serge Barbarella *1967*
Marr, Eddie 20,000 Leagues under the Sea *1954*
Marriott, Moore Time Flies *1944*
Mars, Kenneth Young Frankenstein *1974*
Marsden, James Disturbing Behaviour *1998* • X-Men *2000*
Marsden, Roy Toomorrow *1970* • Stargazy on Zummerdown *1978* • Yellowbacks *1990*
Marsh, Jamie Brainscan *1994* • Evolver *1994*
Marsh, Jean Unearthly Stranger *1963* • Goliath Awaits *1981* • The Tomorrow People *1992-1995*
Marsh, Joan It's Great to Be Alive *1933*
Marsh, Keith Daleks -- Invasion Earth 2150 AD *1966*
Marsh, Reginald The Stone Tape *1972*
Marsh, William Proteus *1995*
Marshall, Alexander Light Years *1988*
Marshall, Andy Mysterious Island *1995*
Marshall, Ann My Favorite Martian *1963-1966*
Marshall, Bryan Quatermass and the Pit *1967*
Marshall, Darrah Teenage Caveman *1958*
Marshall, Don Land of the Giants *1968-1970* • The Thing with Two Heads *1972* • Terminal Island *1973*
Marshall, E G The CBS Radio Mystery Theater *1974-1982* • Superman II *1980* • The Tommyknockers *1993*
Marshall, Herbert Gog *1954* • Riders to the Stars *1954* • The Fly *1958*
Marshall, James Doomsday Man *1998*
Marshall, Melissa The Girl from Tomorrow *1990-1991*
Marshall, Mort Target Earth *1954*
Marshall, Nancy Frankenstein Meets the Space Monster *1965*
Marshall, Tony I Was a Teenage Werewolf *1957*
Marshall, William Dinosaur Valley Girls *1996*
Marston, John Son of Kong *1933*
Marta, Lynne Genesis II *1973*
Martel, K C ET the Extra-Terrestrial *1982*
Martell, Chris Flesh Feast *1970*
Martell, Donna Project Moonbase *1953*
Martell, Gregg Dinosaurus! *1960* • Valley of the Dragons *1961*
Marter, Ian Doctor Who: the Fourth Doctor *1974-1981*
Martin, Andrea Harrison Bergeron *1995*
Martin, Anne-Marie *aka* **Benton, Eddie** The Shape of Things to Come *1979*
Martin, Dan Welcome to Planet Earth *1996*
Martin, Daniel The Devil's Kiss *1971*
Martin, Dean The Road to Hong Kong *1962*
Martin, Dean Paul Misfits of Science *1985-1986*
Martin, Dewey The Thing from Another World *1951*
Martin, Gary The Amazing Spider-Man *1995*
Martin, George CHUD *1984*
Martin, Gregory Paul Memoirs of an Invisible Man *1992*
Martin, Janet The Lady and the Monster *1944*
Martin, Jared The Fantastic Journey *1977* • The Sea Serpent *1984* • War of the Worlds *1988-1990*
Martin, Justin Curious Dr Humpp *1967*
Martin, Lewis The War of the Worlds *1953*
Martin, Lock The Day the Earth Stood Still *1951*
Martin, Phelim Anchor Zone *1994*
Martin, Ross Conquest of Space *1955* • The Colossus of New York *1958* • The Wild Wild West *1965-1969*
Martin, Sian Welcome II the Terrordome *1994*
Martin, Skip Horror Hospital *1973*
Martin, Steve The Man with Two Brains *1983* • Little Shop of Horrors *1986*
Martin, Strother Sssssss *1973*
Martin, Todd Crack in the World *1964*
Martindale, Margo The Rocketeer *1991*
Martinelli, Elsa The Tenth Victim *1965*
Martinez, A Not of This World *1991*
Martinez, Arturo Ladron de Cadaveres *1956*
Martinez, Benito Outbreak *1995*
Martinez Solares, Agustin Night of the Bloody Apes *1968*
Martini, Max Harsh Realm *1999-2000* • Level 9 *2000-2001*
Marx, Alan Gremloids *1990*
Marzello, Vincent The Adventures of Superman *1994* • The Adventures of Superman: Doomsday and Beyond *1995* • Batman: Knightfall *1995* • Voyage *1999*
Marzilli, John Metal Beast *1995*
Masak, Ron Laserblast *1978* • When Time Expires *1997*
Mascia, Tony The Man Who Fell to Earth *1976*
Mascolo, Joseph The Trial of the Incredible Hulk *1989*
Mase, Marino *aka* **Mase, Martin** Alien Contamination *1981*
Mashita, Nelson Darkman *1990*
Masino, Steve Master of the World *1961*
Mask, Ace Not of This Earth *1988* • The Return of Swamp Thing *1989*
Maskalenko, K The Space Ship *1935*
Maslow, Walter The Cosmic Man *1959*
Mason, Brewster Quatermass *1979*
Mason, Dan The Last Starfighter *1984*
Mason, Don Stingray *1964-1965*
Mason, Felicity Legend of Death *1965*
Mason, Hilary Robot Jox *1989*
Mason, James 20,000 Leagues under the Sea *1954* • Journey to the Center of the Earth *1959* • Frankenstein: the True Story *1973* • The Boys from Brazil *1978*
Mason, Laura The Bowery Boys Meet the Monsters *1954*
Mason, Lola The Brain That Wouldn't Die *1959*
Mason, Maegan-Freyja Official Denial *1993*
Mason, Pamela The Navy vs the Night Monsters *1966*
Mason, Tom The Aliens Are Coming *1979* • The Puppet Masters *1994*
Mason, Vivian The Lost Planet *1953*
Massee, Kim Kamikaze *1986*
Massen, Osa Rocketship X-M *1950*
Massey, Athena Grid Runners *1996*
Massey, Daniel Warlords of Atlantis *1978*
Massey, Ilona The Invisible Agent *1942* • Frankenstein Meets the Wolf Man *1943*
Massey, Raymond High Treason *1929* • Things to Come *1936*
Massie, Paul The Two Faces of Dr Jekyll *1960*
Masters, Ben Making Mr Right *1987*
Masters, Grant Cold Lazarus *1996*
Masterson, Peter The Stepford Wives *1975*
Mastrantonio, Mary Elizabeth The Abyss *1989*
Mastrogiacomo, Gina Alien Space Avenger *1989*
Mastroianni, Marcello The Tenth Victim *1965*
Masur, Richard The Thing *1982* • Timerider: the Adventure of Lyle Swann *1982* • My Science Project *1985* • California Man *1992* • Multiplicity *1996*
Matazarro, Heather Now and Again *1999-2000*
Matchett, Christie The Illustrated Man *1969*
Matern, Anik Space Cases *1996-1997*
Mathen, Mahdu Children of the Damned *1964*
Matheson, Don Land of the Giants *1968-1970*
Matheson, Murray Twilight Zone: the Movie *1983*
Matheson, Tim Solar Crisis *1990*
Mathews, Carole The Monster and the Ape *1945*
Mathews, Hrothgar Cloned *1997*
Mathews, Kerwin Battle beneath the Earth *1968* • Octaman *1971*
Mathews, Thom Alien from LA *1987*
Mathis, Samantha Super Mario Bros *1993* • Harsh Realm *1999-2000*
Mathot, Olivier The Devil's Kiss *1971*
Matsuo, Reiko August in the Water *1995*
Matthau, Walter Fail-Safe *1964*
Matthews, Al The Sender *1982* • Aliens *1986*

N

Nagel, Bill Fist of the North Star *1995*
Nagel, Conrad Sinners in Silk *1924*
Nagel, Don Bride of the Monster *1955*
Nagy, Bill The Brain Machine *1954* • First Man into Space *1958*
Nail, Jimmy Morons from Outer Space *1985*
Naish, J Carrol Doctor Renault's Secret *1942* • Batman *1943* • House of Frankenstein *1944* • The Monster Maker *1944* • Dracula vs Frankenstein *1970*
Naismith, Laurence Village of the Damned *1960* • The Valley of Gwangi *1969* • Quest for Love *1971*
Najbrt, Marek Buttoners *1997*
Naka, Machiko Godzilla's Revenge *1969*
Nakagawa, Anna Godzilla vs King Ghidorah *1991*
Nakajima, Haruo Godzilla vs Gigan *1972*
Nakamaru, Tadao The Secret of the Telegian *1960*
Nakamura, Nobuo Dogora the Space Monster *1964*
Nakamura, Tetsu The Manster *1959*
Nakayama, Kengo Godzilla vs Gigan *1972*
Nakayama, Mari Latitude Zero *1969*
Nakayama, Shinobu Gamera: Guardian of the Universe *1995*
Naldi, Nita Dr Jekyll and Mr Hyde *1920*
Nam Chungim Yongkari Monster of the Deep *1967*
Nance, Jack Dune *1984* • Chase Morran *1996*
Nann, Erika Legion of Iron *1990*
Napier, Alan The Invisible Man Returns *1940* • The Mole People *1956* • Journey to the Center of the Earth *1959* • Batman *1966* • Batman *1966-1968*
Napier, Charles Deep Space *1987* • Skeeter *1993*
Napier, Russell The Brain Machine *1954* • The Blood Beast Terror *1967*
Napier-Jones, Garth Watt on Earth *1991-1992*
Narelle, Brian Dark Star *1973*
Narikawa, Tetsuo Spectreman *1971-1972*
Narita, Mikio Message from Space *1978*
Narvy, Jason Mighty Morphin Power Rangers: the Movie *1995* • Turbo: a Power Rangers Adventure *1997*
Naschy, Paul Assignment Terror *1970*
Nascimento, Nadia-Leigh Animorphs *1998-2000*
Nash, Joseph *aka* **Nash, Joe** Flash Gordon *1954-1955*
Nash, Marilyn Unknown World *1951*
Nash, Mary The Lady and the Monster *1944*
Nash, Noreen Phantom from Space *1953*
Nash, Simon Xtro *1983*
Naslund, Lori Vegas in Space *1994*
Nasmith, Robert Abraxas *1991*
Nason, Richard Tattooed Teenage Alien Fighters from Beverly Hills *1994-1995*
Nastasi, Frank Eat and Run *1986*
Natsuki, Akira Gamera versus Barugon *1966*
Natsuki, Isao Time Slip *1981*
Natsuki, Yosuke Dogora the Space Monster *1964* • Ghidrah, the Three-Headed Monster *1965*
Naughton, David Steel and Lace *1990*
Naughton, James Planet of the Apes *1974* • The Birds II: Land's End *1994*
Navarro, Carlos Doctor Crimen *1953*
Navarro, Mario The Beast of Hollow Mountain *1956* • The Black Scorpion *1957*
Navratil, Arnost Invention of Destruction *1958*
Nayyar, Harsh Making Mr Right *1987*
Négroni, Jean La Jetée *1962*
Neal, Elise Mission to Mars *1999*
Neal, Ella The Mysterious Dr Satan *1940*
Neal, Patricia The Day the Earth Stood Still *1951* • Stranger from Venus *1954*
Neal, Peggy Terror beneath the Sea *1966* • The X from Outer Space *1967*
Neal, Siri The Cloning of Joanna May *1992*
Neal, Tom Bruce Gentry -- Daredevil of the Skies *1948*
Neale, Leslie Honey I Blew Up the Kid *1992*
Neame, Christopher Transformations *1988* • Still Not Quite Human *1992*
Needham, Tracey VR.5 *1995*
Needles, Nique As Time Goes By *1987*
Neely, Gail Surf Nazis Must Die *1987*
Neergaard, Preben The Man Who Thought Life *1969*
Neeson, Liam Darkman *1990* • Star Wars Episode I: the Phantom Menace *1999*
Neff, Hildegarde Alraune *1952* • The Lost Continent *1968*
Neill, Bob The Man with the Power *1977*
Neill, Noel Superman *1948* • Atom Man vs Superman *1950* • The Adventures of Superman *1952-1958*
Neill, Sam Until the End of the World *1991* • Memoirs of an Invisible Man *1992* • Jurassic Park *1993* • Event Horizon *1997* • Bicentennial Man *1999*
Neilson, Perlita The Day of the Triffids *1981*
Neise, George N The Three Stooges in Orbit *1962*
Nelson, Adam The Abyss *1989*
Nelson, Alberta Dr Goldfoot and the Bikini Machine *1965*
Nelson, Art J *aka* **Savage, Vic** The Creeping Terror *1964*
Nelson, Charlene The Last Starfighter *1984*
Nelson, Christopher S Without Warning *1980*
Nelson, Craig T The Fire Next Time *1992*
Nelson, Danny Mutant *1984*
Nelson, Edwin The Brain Eaters *1958*
Nelson, Gene Timeslip *1955*
Nelson, Herbert Future Cop *1976*
Nelson, Jerry Muppets from Space *1999*
Nelson, Jessica Assassin *1986*
Nelson, John Allen Killer Klowns from Outer Space *1988*
Nelson, Judd Transformers -- The Movie *1986*
Nelson, Lori The Day the World Ended *1956*
Nelson, Michael J Mystery Science Theatre 3000 *1988-1999* • Mystery Science Theater 3000: The Movie *1996*
Nelson, Peter V *1983-1985* • Crime Zone *1989*
Nemec, Corin *aka* **Nemec, Corin "Corky"** Solar Crisis *1990* • The Stand *1994*
Neri, Francesca Captain America *1990*
Nero, Franco War of the Planets *1965* • The Wild, Wild Planet *1965*
Nettleton, Lois The Bamboo Saucer *1968*
Neuman, Dorothy The Undead *1957*
Neuwirth, Bebe Wild Palms *1993*
Neve, Suzanne The Year of the Sex Olympics *1968*
Neville, John Unearthly Stranger *1963* • The Adventures of Baron Munchausen *1988* • Journey to the Center of the Earth *1993* • The Fifth Element *1997* • Johnny 2.0 *1998* • The X Files *1998*
Nevin, Brooke Animorphs *1998-2000*
Nevin, Rosa Still Not Quite Human *1992*
Newark, Derek City under the Sea *1965*
Newberger, Milton Bela Lugosi Meets a Brooklyn Gorilla *1952*
Newbern, George Doorways *1993* • Theodore Rex *1995*
Newcomb, Jamie Lone Wolf *1988*
Newell, Carol Irene The Alpha Incident *1977*
Newell, Patrick Unearthly Stranger *1963* • Kinvig *1981*
Newell, William The Mysterious Dr Satan *1940*
Newland, John One Step Beyond *1959-1961*
Newlands, Anthony The Burning Glass *1960* • Scream and Scream Again *1969*
Newley, Anthony The Garbage Pail Kids Movie *1987*
Newman, Alec Frank Herbert's Dune *2000*
Newman, Laraine Invaders from Mars *1986* • Coneheads *1993*
Newman, Nanette Captain Nemo and the Underwater City *1969* • The Stepford Wives *1975*
Newman, Paul Quintet *1979*
Newman, William Squirm *1976*
Newmar, Julie My Living Doll *1964-1965* • Deep Space *1987* • Oblivion *1993*
Newsome, Randall Highlander II: the Quickening *1990*
Newson, Jeremy The Rocky Horror Picture Show *1975*
Newth, Jonathan The Friendly Persuaders *1969* • The Day of the Triffids *1981* • The Nightmare Man *1981*
Newton, John Haymes Superboy *1988-1992*
Newton, Linda Star Cops *1987*
Newton, Margit Evelyn Zombie Creeping Flesh *1981* • The Bronx Executioner *1989*
Newton, Sally Anne Zardoz *1973*
Newton-John, Olivia Toomorrow *1970*
Nichetti, Maurizio Ratataplan *1979*
Nicholas, Angela Alien Space Avenger *1989*
Nicholls, Allan Threshold *1981*
Nicholls, Anthony The Champions *1968-1969*
Nicholls, Nichelle Star Trek *1966-1969*
Nichols, Barbara The Human Duplicators *1965*
Nichols, Dandy The Bed Sitting Room *1969* • Britannia Hospital *1982*
Nichols, Nichelle Star Trek: the Motion Picture *1979* • Star Trek II: the Wrath of Khan *1982* • Star Trek III: the Search for Spock *1984* • Star Trek IV: the Voyage Home *1986* • Star Trek V: the Final Frontier *1989* • Star Trek VI: the Undiscovered Country *1991*
Nichols, Richard This Island Earth *1955*
Nichols, Robert The Thing from Another World *1951*
Nicholson, Jack Little Shop of Horrors *1960* • Batman *1989* • Mars Attacks! *1996*
Nicholson, Steve The Bionic Boy *1977*
Nick, Bill First Man into Space *1958*
Nickson-Soul, Julia *aka* **Nickson, Julia** Double Dragon *1994*
Nicola, Nassira Evolver *1994*
Nicolaides, Dimitris The Day the Fish Came Out *1967*
Nicols, Rosemary Undermind *1965*
Nielsen, Brigitte Murder on the Moon *1989* • Galaxis *1995*
Nielsen, Connie Soldier *1998* • Mission to Mars *1999*
Nielsen, Leslie Forbidden Planet *1956* • The Reluctant Astronaut *1967* • The Resurrection of Zachary Wheeler *1971* • And Millions Will Die! *1973* • Day of the Animals *1977* • The Creature Wasn't Nice *1981*
Nielson, Erik Terror beneath the Sea *1966*
Nielson, Karen Plan 10 from Outer Space *1995*
Niemi, Lisa Super Force *1990-1992*
Nieto, Jose The Devil's Kiss *1971*
Nighy, Bill 2004 *1995*
Nigra, Christina Out of This World *1987-1991*
Nikaido, Yukiko The Final War *1960*
Niklas, Jan Dr M *1989*
Nikolaev, Valery Aberration *1997*
Nilsson, Kjell Mad Max 2 *1981*
Nimoy, Leonard Zombies of the Stratosphere

O

P

Patrick, Lee Visit to a Small Planet *1960*
Patrick, Nigel The Perfect Woman *1949*
Patrick, Robert Future Hunters *1988* • Terminator 2: Judgment Day *1991* • Fire in the Sky *1993* • The X Files *1993-* • The X Files *1993-* • Double Dragon *1994* • The Faculty *1998* • Perfect Assassins *1998* • SPYkids *2001*
Patterson, Hank Tarantula *1955*
Patterson, Jay Teenage Mutant Ninja Turtles *1990*
Patterson, Neva V *1983-1985*
Patterson, Scott Them *1996*
Patterson, Shirley Batman *1943*
Patton, Will The Puppet Masters *1994* • VR.5 *1995* • The Postman *1997* • Armageddon *1998*
Paul, Adrian War of the Worlds *1988-1990*
Paul, Alexandra Cyber Bandits *1995* • Piranha *1996*
Paul, Don Michael Alien from LA *1987* • Robot Wars *1993*
Paul, John The Blood Beast Terror *1967* • Doomwatch *1970-1972* • Doomwatch *1972*
Paul, Nancy Lifeforce *1985* • Space Precinct *1994-1995*
Paul, Richard Joseph Oblivion *1993* • Knight Rider 2010 *1994* • Vampirella *1996*
Paulin, Scott Forbidden World *1982* • Captain America *1990* • Knights *1993* • Cloned *1997*
Paull, Morgan GoBots: Battle of the Rocklords *1986*
Paulsen, Harald Alraune *1930*
Paulson, Pamela Robot Monster *1953*
Paulson, William Zone Troopers *1985*
Pavlatova, Michaela Buttoners *1997*
Paxton, Bill The Terminator *1984* • Weird Science *1985* • Aliens *1986* • Slipstream *1989* • Brain Dead *1990* • Predator 2 *1990* • Monolith *1993*
Paymer, David The Absent-Minded Professor *1988*
Payne, Bruce Necronomicon *1993* • Ravager *1997*
Payne, Freda Nutty Professor 2: the Klumps *2000*
Payne, Laurence The Trollenberg Terror *1956-1957* • The Trollenberg Terror *1958*
Pays, Amanda The Kindred *1986* • Max Headroom *1987* • Leviathan *1989* • The Flash *1990-1991*
Payton, Barbara Four-Sided Triangle *1953*
Peace, Rock Attack of the Killer Tomatoes *1978*
Peach, Mary The Projected Man *1966*
Pearce, Adam The Tomorrow People *1992-1995*
Pearce, Jacqueline Blake's 7 *1978-1981* • Blake's 7: The Sevenfold Crown *1998* • Blake's 7: The Syndeton Experiment *1998*
Pearce, Joanne Morons from Outer Space *1985*
Pearce, John THX 1138 *1971*
Pearce, Richard Doctor Who: The Paradise of Death *1993* • Doctor Who: the Ghosts of N-Space *1996*
Pearcy, Patricia Squirm *1976*
Pearlman, Stephen Future Cop *1976* • Pi *1997*
Pearlstein, Randy Revenge of the Radioactive Reporter *1990*
Pearson, Drew The Day the Earth Stood Still *1951*
Pearson, Jill Jekyll and Hyde *1989*
Peart, Mirabelle Resistance *1992*
Pearthree, Pippa Village of the Damned *1995*
Pease, Patsy Space Raiders *1983*
Peasgood, Julie First Born *1988*
Peck, Anthony Primal Species *1996*
Peck, Bob Slipstream *1989* • Jurassic Park *1993*
Peck, Cecilia Blue Flame *1995*
Peck, Gregory On the Beach *1959* • Marooned *1969* • The Boys from Brazil *1978*
Peeples, Nia DeepStar Six *1989*
Pellegrino, Mark Prayer of the Rollerboys *1990*
Peluce, Meeno Voyagers! *1982-1983*
Peluffo, Ana Luisa The Invisible Man *1958*
Pember, Ron The Glitterball *1977* • The Invisible Man *1984* • Doctor Who: Slipback *1985*
Pena, Elizabeth *batteries not included *1987* • The Invaders *1995* • It Came from Outer Space II *1996*
Pena, Pascual Garcia The Black Scorpion *1957*
Penalver, Diana Braindead *1992*
Pendleton, Austin Simon *1980* • Short Circuit *1986*
Pendleton, Edna 20,000 Leagues under the Sea *1916*
Pendleton, Sha-Ri The Alien Within *1995*
Penghlis, Thaao Altered States *1980*
Penhaligon, Susan The Land That Time Forgot *1974*
Penn, Christopher *aka* **Penn, Chris** Fist of the North Star *1995*
Penn, Leonard Batman and Robin *1949* • Rocky Jones, Space Ranger *1954*
Pennell, Larry The Borrower *1989*
Penney, Allan Resistance *1992*
Penney, Ralph The Devil Commands *1941*
Pennick, Jack The Beast from 20,000 Fathoms *1953*
Pennington, Julia Mercy Point *1998-1999*
Pennington, Marla Small Wonder *1985-1989*
Pennington, Michael Star Wars Episode VI: Return of the Jedi *1983*
Penny, Sydney Hyper Sapien: People from Another Star *1986*
Pentelow, Arthur The Peace Game *1969*
Pentz, Robert Last Lives *1997*
Penya, Anthony Monster *1980*
Peppard, George The Groundstar Conspiracy *1972* • Damnation Alley *1977* • Battle beyond the Stars *1980*
Pepper, Barry Battlefield Earth *2000*
Percival, Lance Jekyll and Hyde *1989*
Perdue, Derelys The Last Man on Earth *1923*
Perego, Didi *aka* **Sullivan, Didi** Caltiki, the Immortal Monster *1959*
Pereverzev, Ivan *aka* **Perry, Edd** Battle beyond the Sun *1959*
Perez, Tony Alien Nation *1988*
Periard, J Roger Rabid *1976*
Perillo, Joey Twelve Monkeys *1995*
Perkins, Anthony On the Beach *1959* • The Black Hole *1979*
Perkins, Elizabeth Cloned *1997*
Perkins, Gil Valley of the Dragons *1961*
Perkins, Gilbert Teenage Monster *1958*
Perle, Rebecca Not of This Earth *1988*
Perlman, Rhea We're Back! A Dinosaur's Story *1993*
Perlman, Ron The Ice Pirates *1984* • The City of Lost Children *1995* • The Island of Dr Moreau *1996* • Alien: Resurrection *1997* • A Town Has Turned to Dust *1998* • Titan AE *2000*
Perlow, Bob Night of the Comet *1984*
Perreau, Gigi Journey to the Center of Time *1967*
Perreau, Janine Invaders from Mars *1953*
Perrey, Mireille The Hands of Orlac *1960*
Perri, Paul Memoirs of an Invisible Man *1992*
Perrier, Mireille The Night Is Young *1986*
Perrin, Vic The Outer Limits *1963-1965*
Perrine, Valerie Slaughterhouse-Five *1972* • Superman *1978* • Superman II *1980*
Perry, Felton RoboCop *1987* • RoboCop 2 *1990* • RoboCop 3 *1993*
Perry, George Monster a Go-Go! *1965*
Perry, Luke The Fifth Element *1997* • Robin Cook's Invasion *1997*
Perry, Patricia Childhood's End *1997*
Perry, Roger The Thing with Two Heads *1972* • The Man with the Power *1977*
Perry, Vic Timeslip *1955*
Perschy, Maria No Survivors Please *1963*
Persky, Lisa Jane Coneheads *1993* • Perfect Assassins *1998*
Persons, Mark Silent Running *1971*
Persson, Essy Mission Stardust *1968*
Persson, Gene Earth vs the Spider *1958*
Pertwee, Jon Mr Drake's Duck *1950* • Carry On Screaming *1966* • Doctor Who: the Third Doctor *1970-1974* • Doctor Who: The Paradise of Death *1993* • The Adventures of Superman *1994* • Doctor Who: the Ghosts of N-Space *1996*
Pertwee, Sean Event Horizon *1997* • Soldier *1998*
Pescow, Donna Out of This World *1987-1991*
Peters, Bernadette Heartbeeps *1981*
Peters, Brock Soylent Green *1973* • Alligator II: the Mutation *1991* • Star Trek VI: the Undiscovered Country *1991*
Peters, Clarke Outland *1981*
Peters, Erika Monstrosity *1963*
Peters Jr, House King of the Rocket Men *1949*
Peters, Jean It Happens Every Spring *1949*
Peters, Scott Cape Canaveral Monsters *1960*
Peters, Steve Daleks -- Invasion Earth 2150 AD *1966*
Petersen, Tommy V *1983-1985*
Peterson, Amanda Explorers *1985*
Peterson, Bill Mutant Hunt *1987*
Peterson, Captain R It Came from beneath the Sea *1955*
Peterson, Gil The Brain Machine *1972*
Peterson, Haley Cyborg *1989*
Peterson, Lembit The Dead Mountaineer Hotel *1979*
Peterson, Mark Dr Who and the Daleks *1965*
Peterson, Nan Hideous Sun Demon *1955*
Petherbridge, Edward The Guardians *1971*
Petrie, Susan Shivers *1975*
Petrillo, Sammy Bela Lugosi Meets a Brooklyn Gorilla *1952*
Petrovich, Ivan Alraune *1927*
Petrovitch, Michael Turkey Shoot *1981*
Pettitt, Alison Childhood's End *1997*
Petty, Lori Tank Girl *1995*
Petty, Tom The Postman *1997*
Pettyjohn, Angelique Biohazard *1984*
Pfeiffer, Michelle Amazon Women on the Moon *1987* • Batman Returns *1992*
Phalen, Robert Starman *1984*
Phelan, Mark 12:01 *1993*
Phelps, Robert Nightmares *1983*
Philbin, John Return of the Living Dead *1984* • Martians Go Home *1990*
Philbin, Phil Flesh Feast *1970*
Philip, Michael Welcome to Paradox *1998*
Phillippe, Ryan Lifeform *1996*
Phillips, Barney I Was a Teenage Werewolf *1957*
Phillips, Bobbie TC 2000 *1993*
Phillips, Charlie Munchies *1987*
Phillips, Chynna The Invisible Kid *1988*
Phillips, Ethan Critters *1986* • Natural Selection *1994* • Star Trek: Voyager *1995-2001*
Phillips, G Elvis Body Snatchers *1993*
Phillips, Greigh The Brain Eaters *1958*
Phillips, John Man in the Moon *1960* • The Mouse on the Moon *1963* • Legend of Death *1965*
Phillips, Leslie The Gamma People *1956*
Phillips, Lou Diamond Bats *1999* • Supernova *2000*

Phillips, Meredith Sky Pirates *1986*
Phillips, Samantha Deceit *1989*
Phillips, Sian Dune *1984*
Phipps, Max Mad Max 2 *1981* • Sky Pirates *1986*
Phipps, William Five *1951* • Cat-Women of the Moon *1953* • The War of the Worlds *1953*
Phoenix, Joaquin *aka* **Phoenix, Leaf** SpaceCamp *1986*
Phoenix, River Explorers *1985*
Photamo, Anne Marie Wolfen *1981*
Piaggio, Maria Teresa The Seed of Man *1969*
Piantadosi, Joseph Schlock *1971*
Picardo, Robert The Man Who Fell to Earth *1986* • Innerspace *1987* • Munchies *1987* • Gremlins 2: the New Batch *1990* • Star Trek: Voyager *1995-2001* • Menno's Mind *1996* • Star Trek: First Contact *1996*
Piccoli, Michel Danger: Diabolik *1967* • Long Live Life *1984* • The Night Is Young *1986*
Picerni, Charles Tron *1982*
Pickens, Slim Dr Strangelove, or How I learned to Stop Worrying and Love the Bomb *1963*
Pickens Jr, James Rocketman *1997*
Pickett, Blake Dark Universe *1993*
Pickett, Bobby Lobster Man from Mars *1989*
Pickett, Bobby "Boris" Frankenstein General Hospital *1988*
Pickett, Cindy DeepStar Six *1989* • Plymouth *1991* • Evolver *1994*
Pickles, Christina Masters of the Universe *1987*
Pickup, Ronald Jekyll and Hyde *1989*
Picorri, John SOS Coastguard *1937*
Pidgeon, Walter Forbidden Planet *1956* • Voyage to the Bottom of the Sea *1961* • The Neptune Factor *1973*
Piel, Harry An Invisible Man Goes through the City *1933* • The World without a Mask *1934*
Pierce, Bradley Doom Runners *1997*
Pierce, Charles B The Aurora Encounter *1985*
Pierce, Jill Cyborg Cop II *1994* • Omega Doom *1996*
Pierpoint, Eric Alien Nation *1989-1990*
Pierre, Olivier The Sender *1982*
Pigott, Tempe Dr Jekyll and Mr Hyde *1931*
Pilbeam, Nova Counterblast *1948*
Pileggi, Mitch Shocker *1989* • The X Files *1993-* • Legion of Fire: Killer Ants! *1998* • The X Files *1998*
Pilkington, Joe Light Years Away *1981*
Pillars, Jeffrey The Stepford Husbands *1996*
Pillow, Mark Superman IV: the Quest for Peace *1987*
Pilon, Daniel Starship Invasions *1977*
Pinchot, Bronson The Langoliers *1995* • Meego *1997*
Pincombe, John The Lost Planet *1954*
Pinder, Alex Ocean Girl *1994-1998*
Pine, Phillip *aka* **Pine, Phillip E** Phantom from 10,000 Leagues *1956* • The Lost Missile *1958* • Project X *1968*
Pine, Robert The Mysterious Two *1982*
Pinkett Smith, Jada *aka* **Pinkett, Jada** The Nutty Professor *1996*
Pinner, Richard Monster from the Ocean Floor *1954*
Pinner, Steven Link *1986*
Pinon, Dominique The City of Lost Children *1995* • Alien: Resurrection *1997*
Pinsent, Gordon Colossus: the Forbin Project *1969*
Piper, Roddy Hell Comes to Frogtown *1988* • They Live *1988* • Sci-Fighters *1996*
Pitillo, Maria Godzilla *1997*
Pitt, Brad Twelve Monkeys *1995*
Pitt, Ingrid Artemis 81 *1981*
Piven, Jeremy 12:01 *1993* • Dr Jekyll and Ms Hyde *1995*
Place, Mary Kay Modern Problems *1981* • Explorers *1985*
Planer, Nigel Frankenstein's Baby *1990*
Platt, Edward Atlantis, the Lost Continent *1960*
Platt, Howard T The Cat from Outer Space *1978*
Platt, Oliver Flatliners *1990* • Bicentennial Man *1999*
Playten, Alice The Lost Saucer *1975-1976* • Heavy Metal *1981*
Pleasence, Angela The Foundation Trilogy *1973*
Pleasence, Donald Nineteen Eighty-Four *1954* • 1984 *1955* • One *1956* • The Hands of Orlac *1960* • Fantastic Voyage *1966* • THX 1138 *1971* • Death Line *1972* • The Mutations *1973* • Escape to Witch Mountain *1975* • The Puma Man *1979* • Escape from New York *1981* • Warrior of the Lost World *1983* • Prince of Darkness *1987*
Pleshette, Suzanne The Birds *1963* • The Power *1968*
Pleven, Katell The Rejuvenator *1988*
Plimpton, Martha Daybreak *1993*
Plimpton, Shelley Glen and Randa *1971*
Plowright, Joan Britannia Hospital *1982*
Plummer, Amanda Freejack *1992*
Plummer, Christopher Starcrash *1979* • Prototype *1983* • Dreamscape *1984* • Light Years *1988* • Firehead *1991* • Star Trek VI: the Undiscovered Country *1991* • Harrison Bergeron *1995* • Twelve Monkeys *1995*
Plummer, Glenn Strange Days *1995*
Plummer, Terence Batman *1989*
Podell, Rick World Gone Wild *1988*
Podewell, Cathy Earth Angel *1991*
Podhora, Roman Trucks *1997*
Poggi, Daniela Dr M *1989*
Pogo The Illustrated Man *1969*
Pogue, Ken The 6th Day *2000*
Pohl, Klaus The Woman in the Moon *1929*
Poindexter Return from Witch Mountain *1978*
Poindexter, Larry American Ninja 2: The Confrontation *1987*
Pointer, Priscilla The Mysterious Two *1982*
Polakov, Diana Supersonic Man *1979*
Pollard, Michael J Split Second *1991* • Skeeter *1993*
Pollard, Simon Omega Doom *1996*
Polley, Sarah Blue Monkey *1987* • The Adventures of Baron Munchausen *1988* • eXistenZ *1999*
Pollock, Ellen The Escape of RD 7 *1961* • Horror Hospital *1973*
Polo, Teri The Arrival *1996*
Ponti, Sal *aka* **Hall, Anthony** Atlantis, the Lost Continent *1960*
Ponton, Yvan Scanners II: The New Order *1991*
Pooley, Olaf The Master *1966*
Pop, Iggy Hardware *1990*
Popova, A *aka* **Powell, Arla** Battle beyond the Sun *1959*
Porter, Bobby Day of the Animals *1977* • Quark *1978* • Land of the Lost *1991-1992*
Porter, Brett Firehead *1991*
Porter, Eric The Lost Continent *1968*
Porter, Nyree Dawn The Martian Chronicles *1979*
Porter, Todd Earthbound *1981*
Portman, Natalie Mars Attacks! *1996* • Star Wars Episode I: the Phantom Menace *1999*
Posey, Nicole Beach Babes from Beyond *1993*
Pospisil, Michal The Stolen Dirigible *1966*
Post, Markie Visitors of the Night *1995*
Posta, Adrienne The Master *1966*
Poster, Tom The Shadow Men *1997*
Postlethwaite, Pete Split Second *1991* • The Lost World: Jurassic Park *1997*
Postnikow, Michal First Spaceship on Venus *1960*
Pottenger, Marty Born in Flames *1983*
Potter, Luce Invaders from Mars *1953*
Potter, Martin The Year of the Sex Olympics *1968*
Potter, Terry Bad Taste *1987*
Potts, Annie Ghostbusters *1984* • The Man Who Fell to Earth *1986* • Ghostbusters II *1989*
Potts, Cliff Silent Running *1971* • The Groundstar Conspiracy *1972*
Pouget, Ely Death Machine *1994*
Pounder, C C H Lifepod *1993* • RoboCop 3 *1993* • White Dwarf *1995*
Poundstone, Paula Gremloids *1990*
Powell, Charles Screamers *1995*
Powell, Clifton Phantoms *1998*
Powell, Clive Children of the Damned *1964*
Powell, Esteban Level 9 *2000-2001*
Powell, Gwynneth The Guardians *1971*
Powell, Marcus The Rejuvenator *1988* • Metamorphosis: The Alien Factor *1993*
Powell, Randolph Battletruck *1982*
Powell, Randy Logan's Run *1977-1978*
Powell, Robert Doomwatch *1970-1972* • The Asphyx *1972* • Secrets of the Phantom Caverns *1984*
Power, Derry Warlords of Atlantis *1978*
Power, Taryn The Sea Serpent *1984*
Power Jr, Tyrone Cocoon *1985*
Powers, Bruce Horror of the Blood Monsters *1970*
Powers, Mala The Unknown Terror *1957* • The Colossus of New York *1958* • Escape from Planet Earth *1967*
Powers, Richard Plan 9 from Outer Space *1959*
Powers, Tom Destination Moon *1950*
Poyner, Jim Bug *1975*
Poynter, Guy Kingsley Journey into Space: Operation Luna *1953-1954* • Journey into Space: The Red Planet *1954-1955* • Journey into Space: The World in Peril *1955-1956*
Praed, Michael Nightflyers *1987* • The Secret Adventures of Jules Verne *1999*
Prat, Gloria Curious Dr Humpp *1967*
Pratt, Deborah Spacehunter: Adventures in the Forbidden Zone *1983* • Quantum Leap *1989-1993*
Pratt, Hugo The Night Is Young *1986*
Pratt, Judson Monster on the Campus *1958*
Pratt, Kyla Barney's Great Adventure *1998*
Pratt, Peter The Foundation Trilogy *1973*
Pratt, Victoria Cleopatra 2525 *2000-2001*
Pravda, George The Offshore Island *1959* • Frankenstein Must Be Destroyed *1969*
Préjean, Albert Paris Qui Dort *1923*
Préjean, Patrick Shadowman *1973*
Preiss, Wolfgang Mistress of the World *1959* • Dr M *1989*
Prendes, Luis Dr Coppelius *1966* • Alien Predator *1984*
Prentiss, Ann Captain Nice *1967*
Prentiss, Paula The Stepford Wives *1975* • Saturday the 14th *1981*
Prescott, Kerrigan Fiend without a Face *1957*
Presle, Micheline Mistress of the World *1959*
Presson, Jason Explorers *1985*
Preston, Cynthia Total Recall 2070 *1999*
Preston, J A Steel Justice *1992*
Preston, Kelly Metalstorm: The Destruction of Jared-Syn *1983* • SpaceCamp *1986*
Preston, Michael Metalstorm: The Destruction of Jared-Syn *1983*
Preston, Mike Mad Max 2 *1981*
Preston, Robert The Last Starfighter *1984*
Price, Dennis The Earth Dies Screaming *1964* •

Q

R

S

T

Thompson, Jimmy Forbidden Planet *1956*
Thompson, Kevin The Garbage Pail Kids Movie *1987*
Thompson, Lea Back to the Future *1985* • Howard, a New Breed of Hero *1986* • SpaceCamp *1986* • Back to the Future Part II *1989* • Back to the Future Part III *1990*
Thompson, Marshall Fiend without a Face *1957* • First Man into Space *1958* • It! The Terror from beyond Space *1958* • World of Giants *1959-1960* • Around the World under the Sea *1966* • Bog *1978*
Thompson, Ross The Chain Reaction *1980*
Thompson, Shelley The Adventures of Superman *1994*
Thomson, Kenneth Just Imagine *1930*
Thomson, Kim Jekyll and Hyde *1989*
Thoolen, Gerard The Lift *1983*
Thor, Larry The Amazing Colossal Man *1957*
Thorn, Frankie Liquid Dreams *1992*
Thornbury, Bill Phantasm *1978*
Thorne, Stephen Doctor Who: the Ghosts of N-Space *1996*
Thornton, Billy Bob Out There *1995* • Armageddon *1998*
Thornton, Frank Gonks Go Beat *1965* • The Bed Sitting Room *1969*
Thornton, John Plymouth *1991*
Thornton, Kirk Vampire Hunter D *1985*
Thornton, Sigrid Trapped in Space *1994*
Thorpe, Simon Future Schlock *1984*
Thorpe, Ted The Lost Planet *1953*
Thorsen, Sven-Ole Captain Power and the Soldiers of the Future *1987-1988* • Abraxas *1991*
Thorson, Linda The Avengers *1960-1968*
Thourlby, William The Creeping Terror *1964* • Castle of Evil *1966* • Destination Inner Space *1966*
Thring, Frank Mad Max beyond Thunderdome *1985*
Thurman, Beverly The Giant Gila Monster *1959*
Thurman, Bill It's Alive *1968*
Thurman, Uma The Adventures of Baron Munchausen *1988* • Batman and Robin *1997* • Gattaca *1997* • The Avengers *1998*
Thurston, Carol Killer Ape *1953*
Thyssen, Greta Terror Is a Man *1959* • Journey to the Seventh Planet *1961*
Tiberghien, Jerome Rabid *1976*
Tichy, Gerard Face of Terror *1962*
Ticotin, Rachel Total Recall *1990*
Tierney, Lawrence The Kirlian Witness *1978*
Tiffany Jetsons: the Movie *1990*
Tigar, Kenneth Creator *1985*
Tilbury, Peter First Born *1988*
Tilden, Leif Teenage Mutant Ninja Turtles *1990* • Teenage Mutant Ninja Turtles II: the Secret of the Ooze *1991*
Tilly, Jennifer Remote Control *1988*
Tilly, Meg Body Snatchers *1993*
Tilvern, Alan The Frozen Dead *1966*
Tiplady, Brittany Millenium *1996-1999*
Tippi Vegas in Space *1994*
Tipping, Tip Aliens *1986*
Tipple, Gordon Time Runner *1993* • Doctor Who *1996*
Tittle, Bently Dark Universe *1993*
Tobeck, Joel Cleopatra 2525 *2000-2001*
Tobey, Ken Honey I Blew Up the Kid *1992*
Tobey, Kenneth The Thing from Another World *1951* • The Beast from 20,000 Fathoms *1953* • It Came from beneath the Sea *1955* • Strange Invaders *1983*
Tobin, June The Big Pull *1962*
Tobolowsky, Stephen Wedlock *1991* • Memoirs of an Invisible Man *1992* • Dr Jekyll and Ms Hyde *1995* • Night Visitors *1996*
Tochi, Brian The Omega Man *1971* • Space Academy *1977-1979*
Toda, Naho August in the Water *1995*
Todd, Ann Things to Come *1936* • The Offshore Island *1959*
Todd, Saira The Kraken Wakes *1998*
Todd, Sally The Unearthly *1957*
Todd, Tony Night of the Living Dead *1990* • Them *1996*
Togami, Seuko Frankenstein Meets the Devil Fish *1964*
Togin, Chotaro Godzilla's Revenge *1969*
Tognazzi, Ugo Toto in the Moon *1957* • Barbarella *1967*
Tokos, Lubor Invention of Destruction *1958*
Toles Bey, John Endless Descent *1990*
Toles-Bey, John Steel Justice *1992*
Tolkan, James WarGames *1983* • Iceman *1984* • Back to the Future *1985* • Masters of the Universe *1987* • Back to the Future Part II *1989* • Back to the Future Part III *1990*
Tom, Kiana Universal Soldier -- the Return *1999*
Tom, Lauren Escape to Witch Mountain *1995*
Tomei, Marisa The Toxic Avenger *1985*
Tomelty, Joseph Timeslip *1955*
Tomioka, Keinosuke Tetsuo II: Body Hammer *1991*
Tomita, Tamlyn The Burning Zone *1996-1997* • The Last Man on Planet Earth *1999*
Tomlin, Lily The Incredible Shrinking Woman *1981*
Tomlinson, David City under the Sea *1965*
Tomlinson, Ricky Deep Station Emerald *1996*
Tompkins, Angel The Bees *1978*
Tompkins, Darlene Beyond the Time Barrier *1960*
Tompkinson, Stephen Oktober *1998*
Tone Loc Titan AE *2000*
Tonge, Philip Invisible Invaders *1959*
Tonunts, G *aka* **Tonner, Gene** Battle beyond the Sun *1959*
Toomey, Regis The Phantom Creeps *1939* • Voyage to the Bottom of the Sea *1961* • C.H.O.M.P.S. *1979*
Toone, Geoffrey Dr Who and the Daleks *1965*
Topol Flash Gordon *1980*
Topor, Roland Ratataplan *1979*
Torey, Hal Earth vs the Spider *1958* • Invisible Invaders *1959*
Torgl, Mark The Toxic Avenger *1985*
Torkeli, Sophia The Last Man *1968*
Torn, Rip The Man Who Fell to Earth *1976* • Coma *1977* • Airplane II: the Sequel *1982* • RoboCop 3 *1993* • Men in Black *1997*
Tornborg, Kay Who? *1974*
Torre, Joel DNA *1996*
Torres, Gina Cleopatra 2525 *2000-2001*
Tortosa, Silvia Horror Express *1972*
Toso, Otello The Planets against Us *1961*
Tossberg, Robert Prototype X29A *1992*
Toth, Frank ET the Extra-Terrestrial *1982*
Toth, Richard Sleeping Dogs *1997*
Toto Toto in the Moon *1957*
Tottenham, Merle The Invisible Man *1933*
Touliatos, George Firebird 2015 AD *1980* • Heavy Metal *1981* • Heavy Metal *1981* • The Last Chase *1981*
Tovey, Roberta Dr Who and the Daleks *1965* • Daleks -- Invasion Earth 2150 AD *1966*
Towers, Robert Masters of the Universe *1987*
Towles, Tom The Borrower *1989* • Night of the Living Dead *1990* • Fortress *1992*
Towne, Aline Radar Men from the Moon *1951* • Zombies of the Stratosphere *1952* • Commando Cody: Sky Marshal of the Universe *1953*
Towne, Katharine Evolution *2001*
Towne, Robert *aka* **Wain, Edward** The Last Woman on Earth *1960*
Townsend Jr, Vince The Alligator People *1959*
Toya, Takanobu Spectreman *1971-1972*
Toyohara, Kosuke Godzilla vs King Ghidorah *1991*
Trachtenberg, Michelle Meego *1997*
Tracy, Spencer Dr Jekyll and Mr Hyde *1941*
Trang, Thuy Mighty Morphin Power Rangers *1993-1996*
Tranquilli, Silvano The Puma Man *1979*
Travanti, Daniel J Millennium *1989*
Travers, Bill Gorgo *1961*
Travers, Henry The Invisible Man *1933*
Travis, Henry The Brain from Planet Arous *1958*
Travis, June The Gladiator *1938* • Monster a Go-Go! *1965*
Travis, Kylie Retroactive *1997*
Travis, Richard Mesa of Lost Women *1953* • Missile to the Moon *1958*
Travis, Ron Outland *1981*
Travis, Stacey Hardware *1990* • Suspect Device *1995*
Travolta, Joey Amazon Women on the Moon *1987* • Beach Babes from Beyond *1993*
Travolta, John Phenomenon *1996* • Battlefield Earth *2000*
Traylor, William The Man with Two Brains *1983*
Traynor, Jason Welcome II the Terrordome *1994*
Treas, Terri The Nest *1988* • The Terror Within *1988* • Alien Nation *1989-1990*
Trebor, Robert Universal Soldier *1992*
Tredway, Wayne Dinosaurus! *1960*
Trejo, Danny SPYkids *2001*
Tremayne, Les The War of the Worlds *1953* • The Monolith Monsters *1957* • The Angry Red Planet *1959* • The Slime People *1963* • Starchaser: the Legend of Orin *1985*
Tremblett, Ken The Invader *1997*
Tremko, Anne Marie The Computer Wore Tennis Shoes *1995*
Trend, Jean Doomwatch *1970-1972*
Trentham, Barbara Rollerball *1975*
Treva, Etienne The Last Train *1999*
Trevarthen, Noel It! *1966*
Trevena, David Nineteen Eighty-Four *1984*
Treves, Frederick The Big Pull *1962*
Treves, Simon The Amazing Spider-Man *1995* • Independence Day UK *1996*
Trevor, Austin Quatermass II *1955* • Konga *1960* • The Day the Earth Caught Fire *1961*
Treytnorova, Eva A Nice Plate of Spinach *1976*
Tricky The Fifth Element *1997*
Triesault, Ivan The Amazing Transparent Man *1960*
Trigg, Margaret R.O.T.O.R *1988*
Trigger, Sarah Bill & Ted's Bogus Journey *1991*
Trimble, Jerry Mind Breakers *1996*
Trinidad, Arsenio "Sonny" Darkman *1990* • Neon City *1992* • The Shadow *1994*
Trinka, Paul Voyage to the Bottom of the Sea *1964-1968*
Trintignant, Jean-Louis Malevil *1981* • Long Live Life *1984* • The City of Lost Children *1995*
Tripplehorn, Jeanne Waterworld *1995*
Troughton, Patrick Doctor Who: the Second Doctor *1966-1969* • Frankenstein and the Monster from Hell *1973* • A Hitch in Time *1978*
Troum, Kenn Teenage Mutant Ninja Turtles II: the Secret of the Ooze *1991*
Trouncer, Ruth One *1956*
Trowbridge, Charles The Mysterious Dr Satan *1940* • Captain America *1944*
Trucco, Ed Highlander II: the Quickening *1990*
True, Garrison Day of the Animals *1977*
Truffaut, François Close Encounters of the Third

U

V

Man *1987* • Abraxas *1991*
Ventura, Lino Mistress of the World *1959*
Ventura, Viviane Battle beneath the Earth *1968*
Verdon, Gwen Cocoon *1985* • Cocoon: the Return *1988*
Verdugo, Elena House of Frankenstein *1944*
Verduzco, Abraham New Eden *1994* • Solo *1996*
Vereen, Ben Gas-s-s-s, or It Became Necessary to Destroy the World in Order to Save It *1970* • Intruders *1992*
Vergnes, Marie-Blanche Je T'Aime, Je T'Aime *1968*
Vernon, Howard The Awful Dr Orloff *1962* • Alphaville *1965* • Dracula, Prisoner of Frankenstein *1972*
Vernon, James Nugent Class of Nuke 'Em High *1986*
Vernon, John Blue Monkey *1987*
Vernon, Lou On the Beach *1959*
Vernon, Richard The Hitch-Hiker's Guide to the Galaxy: the Primary Phase *1978* • The Hitch-hiker's Guide to the Galaxy *1981*
Vernon, Valerie Gog *1954*
Vernov, Gennadi Planeta Burg *1962*
Verrell, Cec Hell Comes to Frogtown *1988*
Vertinskaya, Anastasia Amphibian Man *1962*
Vespa, Ritva Time of Roses *1969*
Vespermann, Kurt The World without a Mask *1934*
Vetri, Victoria Invasion of the Bee Girls *1973*
Viadas, Juan Acción Mutante *1993*
Vibar, Bon Dune Warriors *1991*
Vibart, Henry High Treason *1929*
Vickers, Yvette Attack of the 50 Foot Woman *1958*
Vickery, John Fist of the North Star *1986*
Victor, Gloria Invasion of the Star Creatures *1962*
Victor, James C Steel Frontier *1994*
Victor, Katherine Cape Canaveral Monsters *1960*
Vidal, Gore Gattaca *1997*
Vidale, Thea Dr Jekyll and Ms Hyde *1995*
Vidler, Steven Encounter at Raven's Gate *1988*
Vidon, Henry The Giant Behemoth *1959*
Vidovic, Ivica The Rat Saviour *1977*
Vigoda, Abe Batman: Mask of the Phantasm *1993*
Vilanch, Bruce The Ice Pirates *1984*
Villard, Tom Parasite *1982*
Villena, Fernando Planet of the Vampires *1965*
Villeret, Jacques Malevil *1981*
Vincent, Jan-Michael Damnation Alley *1977* • Alienator *1989* • Xtro 2: The Second Encounter *1990* • Orbit *1996*
Vincent, Virginia The Million Dollar Duck *1971*
Ving, Lee *aka* **Jude, Lee James** Nightmares *1983*
Vinson, Helen The Tunnel *1935* • The Lady and the Monster *1944*
Vint, Jesse Silent Running *1971* • Bug *1975* • Forbidden World *1982*
Virlojeux, Henri Light Years Away *1981*
Visitor, Nana Star Trek: Deep Space Nine *1993-1999*
Visny, Juraj Who Killed Jessie? *1965*
Vitale, Alex The Bronx Executioner *1989*
Vitali, Leon Victor Frankenstein *1977*
Vitolo, Famie Kaufman Los Platillos Voladores *1955*
Vittet, Judith The City of Lost Children *1995*
Vitti, Monica The Flying Saucer *1964*
Vlasak, Jan Frank Herbert's Dune *2000*
Vogel, Amanda The Sticky Fingers of Time *1997*
Vogel, Tony The Year of the Sex Olympics *1968*
Vogler, Rüdiger Until the End of the World *1991*
Voigt, Dustin Them *1996*
Volante, Vicki Horror of the Blood Monsters *1970*
Von Bargen, Daniel RoboCop 3 *1993* • The Postman *1997* • Universal Soldier -- the Return *1999*
Von Detten, Erik Escape to Witch Mountain *1995*
von Friedl, Loni Journey to the Far Side of the Sun *1969*
von Meyerinck, Hubert The World without a Mask *1934*
Von Palleske, Heidi Falling Fire *1998*
von Stroheim, Erich Le Monde Tremblera *1939* • The Lady and the Monster *1944* • Alraune *1952*
von Sydow, Max The Ultimate Warrior *1975* • Deathwatch *1980* • Flash Gordon *1980* • Dreamscape *1984* • Dune *1984* • Until the End of the World *1991* • Judge Dredd *1995*
Von Teuffen, Hantz The Flying Saucer *1949*
von Trier, Lars The Element of Crime *1984*
von Wangenheim, Gustav The Woman in the Moon *1929*
Von Watts, Hamilton The Nutty Professor *1996*
von Wernherr, Otto Liquid Sky *1982*
Von Zerneck, Danielle My Science Project *1985*
Vorkov, Zandor Dracula vs Frankenstein *1970*
Vosburgh, Dick Space Patrol *1963-1964* • The Adventures of Superman *1994*
Voskovec, George The 27th Day *1957*
Vosloo, Arnold Darkman II: the Return of Durant *1995* • Darkman III: Die Darkman Die *1996* • Progeny *1998*
Voss, Philip Frankenstein and the Monster from Hell *1973* • Childhood's End *1997*
Vrana, Vlasta Scanners II: The New Order *1991* • Brainscan *1994*
Vrenon, Taunie Mutant Hunt *1987*
Vroom, Siem The Lift *1983*
Vuolo, Tito 20 Million Miles to Earth *1957*

W

Wada, Koji Gappa the Trifibian Monster *1967*
Wadden, W F Xtro 2: The Second Encounter *1990*
Wade, Stuart Monster from the Ocean Floor *1954* • Teenage Monster *1958*
Wager, Anthony The Night Caller *1965*
Waggoner, Lyle Journey to the Center of Time *1967* • Wonder Woman *1975-1979*
Wagner, Chuck Automan *1983-1984* • America 3000 *1986*
Wagner, Fernando Doctor Crimen *1953*
Wagner, Jack Trapped in Space *1994*
Wagner, Kristina Malandro Double Dragon *1994*
Wagner, Lindsay The Six Million Dollar Man *1974-1978* • The Bionic Woman *1976-1978* • Bionic Showdown: the Six Million Dollar Man and the Bionic Woman *1989* • Bionic Ever After? *1994*
Wagner, Lou Planet of the Apes *1967* • Beneath the Planet of the Apes *1969* • Conquest of the Planet of the Apes *1972*
Wagner, Max Invaders from Mars *1953*
Wagner, Michael Dan Tremors *1989*
Wagner, Rick Last Lives *1997*
Wagner, Robert City beneath the Sea *1971*
Wagner, Wende Destination Inner Space *1966* • The Green Hornet *1966-1967*
Wainwright, James Killdozer *1974* • Battletruck *1982*
Waite, Ralph Crash and Burn *1990*
Waites, Thomas G Timelock *1996*
Wakabayashi, Akiko Dogora the Space Monster *1964* • Ghidrah, the Three-Headed Monster *1965*
Wakayama, Setsuko Godzilla Raids Again *1955*
Walcott, Gregory Plan 9 from Outer Space *1959*
Walczewski, Marek The Golem *1979*
Walden, Robert Blue Sunshine *1976*
Waldis, Otto Unknown World *1951* • The Whip Hand *1951* • Attack of the 50 Foot Woman *1958*
Waldo, Janet Fantastic Planet *1973*
Wales, Ethel The Gladiator *1938*
Walken, Christopher The Happiness Cage *1972* • Brainstorm *1983* • Communion *1989* • Batman Returns *1992* • Blast from the Past *1998* • New Rose Hotel *1998*
Walker, Ally Universal Soldier *1992*
Walker, Clint Killdozer *1974*
Walker, Erik And You Thought Your Parents Were Weird *1991*
Walker, Fiona The Asphyx *1972*
Walker, James Nineteen Eighty-Four *1984*
Walker, Jeffrey Halfway across the Galaxy and Turn Left *1994* • Ocean Girl *1994-1998*
Walker, Jimmie The Guyver *1992*
Walker, John Quatermass and the Pit *1958-1959*
Walker, Kathryn DARYL *1985*
Walker, Keith Future Schlock *1984*
Walker, Kim Deadly Weapon *1989*
Walker Lampley, Bree Without Warning *1994*
Walker, Mark Rabid *1976*
Walker, Nicola The Last Train *1999*
Walker , Paul *aka* **Walker, Paul W** The Retaliator *1987*
Walker Jr, Robert Beware! The Blob *1971*
Walker, Sullivan Earth 2 *1994-1995*
Wallace, Anzac The Quiet Earth *1985*
Wallace, Geoffrey They Came from beyond Space *1967*
Wallace, George Radar Men from the Moon *1951*
Wallace, George D *aka* **Wallace, George** Forbidden Planet *1956*
Wallace, Jack Space Men *1960*
Wallace, Jean No Blade of Grass *1970*
Wallace, Lee Batman *1989*
Wallace Stone, Dee *aka* **Wallace, Dee** ET the Extra-Terrestrial *1982* • Critters *1986* • Alligator II: the Mutation *1991* • Invisible Mom *1995*
Wallace, William America 3000 *1986*
Walley, Deborah Sergeant Deadhead *1965* • The Bubble *1966*
Wallis, Bill The Hitch-Hiker's Guide to the Galaxy: the Primary Phase *1978*
Walls, Kevin Patrick Blade *1998*
Walsch, John Def-Con 4 *1984*
Walsh, Gwynyth Blue Monkey *1987* • The Girl from Mars *1991*
Walsh, J T Dark Skies *1996-1997*
Walsh, John Body Parts *1991*
Walsh, Kevin T Legion of Iron *1990*
Walsh, M Emmet Blade Runner *1982* • Critters *1986* • Retroactive *1997* • National Lampoon's Men in White *1998* • The Iron Giant *1999*
Walsh, Sharon The Incredibly Strange Creatures Who Stopped Living and Became Mixed-up Zombies *1963*
Walsh, Sydney Homewrecker *1992* • The Tomorrow Man *1995*
Walston, Ray My Favorite Martian *1963-1966* • Galaxy of Terror *1981* • Amazing Stories *1985-1987* • The Stand *1994* • My Favorite Martian *1999*
Walter, Jessica Ghost in the Machine *1993* •

Yamamura, So Last Days of Planet Earth *1974*
Yamauchi, Akira Godzilla vs Hedora *1971*
Yanagisawa, Shinichi The X from Outer Space *1967*
Yap, Johnson The Bionic Boy *1977*
Yarborough, Barton Before I Hang *1940* • The Ghost of Frankenstein *1942*
Yardley, Stephen The Day of the Triffids *1981*
Yarnell, Lorene Spaceballs *1987*
Yasuoka, Rikiya The Toxic Avenger, Part II *1988*
Yates, Marjorie The Glitterball *1977*
Yazaki, Tomonori Godzilla's Revenge *1969*
Yee Jee Tso Doctor Who *1996*
Yeh, Marco The Humanoid *1979*
Yen, Ann Prince of Darkness *1987*
Yesteran, Richard Supersonic Man *1979*
Yeung, Bolo TC 2000 *1993*
Yiasoumi, George King Kong Lives *1986*
Yip, Françoise Freedom *2000*
Yoakam, Dwight Roswell *1994*
York Jr, Duke Flash Gordon *1936*
York, Michael Logan's Run *1976* • The Island of Dr Moreau *1977* • Space *1985* • Not of This Earth *1995* • Dark Planet *1997*
York, Susannah Superman *1978* • Superman II *1980*
Yorston, David The Green Slime *1968*
Yoshida, Mizuho Zeram *1991*
Yoshida, Teruo Goke, Bodysnatcher from Hell *1968*
Yost, David Mighty Morphin Power Rangers *1993-1996*
Yost, David Harold Mighty Morphin Power Rangers: the Movie *1995*
Young, Alan The Time Machine *1960* • The Cat from Outer Space *1978*
Young, Arthur Stranger from Venus *1954*
Young, Carleton The Day the Earth Stood Still *1951* • 20,000 Leagues under the Sea *1954*
Young, Chris Max Headroom *1987*
Young, Dana Invasion Earth: the Aliens Are Here! *1987*
Young, Dey Not Quite Human II *1989*
Young, Eric The Voodoo Factor *1959-1960*
Young, Heather Land of the Giants *1968-1970*
Young, James The Thing from Another World *1951*
Young, Keone Alien Nation *1988*
Young, Lola Metal Mickey *1980-1983*
Young, Nicholas The Tomorrow People *1973-1979*
Young, Ray Blue Sunshine *1976*
Young, Richard Assassin *1986*
Young, Sean Blade Runner *1982* • Dune *1984* • Dr Jekyll and Ms Hyde *1995* • The Invader *1997*
Young, Stephen Soylent Green *1973*
Young, Victor A Visitors of the Night *1995*
Youngblood, Rob Space Precinct *1994-1995*
Younger, Jack Dinosaurus! *1960*
Youngs, Jim Skeeter *1993*
Yourgrau, Barry Terminal Justice *1996*
Yulin, Harris Ghostbusters II *1989* • Multiplicity *1996*
Yumi, Kaoru Last Days of Planet Earth *1974*
Yuzna, Brian Necronomicon *1993*

Z

Z'Dar, Robert Marching out of Time *1993*
Zabriskie, Grace Galaxy of Terror *1981*
Zachariah, Evan Future Schlock *1984*
Zadora, Pia Santa Claus Conquers the Martians *1964* • Voyage of the Rock Aliens *1985*
Zagarino, Frank Project: Shadowchaser *1992* • Convict 762 *1997*
Zahler, Jason The Absent-Minded Professor *1988*
Zajicek, Pavel Buttoners *1997*
Zal, Roxana Testament *1983*
Zamora, Del Repo Man *1984*
Zane, Billy Critters *1986* • Running Delilah *1992*
Zane, Lisa Natural Selection *1994*
Zann, Lenore Def-Con 4 *1984*
Zappa, Dweezil The Running Man *1987*
Zaray, Nicole The Sticky Fingers of Time *1997*
Zaremba, John Earth vs the Flying Saucers *1956* • 20 Million Miles to Earth *1957* • The Time Tunnel *1966-1967*
Zatloukalova, Jana Invention of Destruction *1958*
Zelenohorska, Jitka The Stolen Dirigible *1966*
Zelenovic, Srdjan Flesh for Frankenstein *1974*
Zelniker, Michael Within the Rock *1995*
Zerbe, Anthony The Omega Man *1971* • Star Trek: Insurrection *1998*
Zeretelli, Nikolai M Aelita *1924*
Zevic, Stanley The Voices *1955*
Zhonov, Georgi Planeta Burg *1962*
Ziembinsky Brasil Ano 2000 *1969*
Zimbalist Jr, Efrem Batman: Mask of the Phantasm *1993*
Zimmerman, Joey Earth 2 *1994-1995*
Zimmerman, Matt Thunderbirds *1965-1966* • Thunderbirds Are Go! *1966* • Thunderbird 6 *1968*
Zimmerman, Patric Jetsons: the Movie *1990*
Zimmern, Terri The Manster *1959*
Zink, Chuck Mission Mars *1968*
Zischler, Hanns Malevil *1981* • Dr M *1989*
Znaimer, Moses Abraxas *1991*
Zolkowska, Joanna The Golem *1979*
Zolty, Tania Crimes of the Future *1970*
Zubarry, Olga The Strange Case of the Man and the Beast *1951*
Zucchero, Joe Dune Warriors *1991*
Zucco, George Doctor Renault's Secret *1942* • House of Frankenstein *1944* • Return of the Ape Man *1944*
Zuckert, Bill Captain Nice *1967*
Zuniga, Daphne Spaceballs *1987* • The Fly II *1989*
Zuri, Jahi J J Nemesis 2 -- Nebula *1995*
Zwerling, Darrell Doc Savage: the Man of Bronze *1975* • The Ultimate Warrior *1975*

Writers' index

A

B

Bollen, Roger Zenon: Girl of the 21st Century (book) *1999*
Bolotnick, Troy Cyborg 3: The Recycler *1994*
Bolzoni, Adriano Spy in Your Eye *1965* • The Humanoid *1979*
Bonestell, Chesley Conquest of Space (book) *1955*
Bonicelli, Vittorio Barbarella *1967*
Boon, Ed Mortal Kombat (computer game) *1995*
Boorman, John Zardoz *1973*
Booth, James American Ninja 2: The Confrontation *1987*
Booth, Walter R The Airship Destroyer *1909*
Boothroyd, J B The Perfect Woman *1949*
Borden, Lizzie Born in Flames (story) *1983*
Borkgren, Christopher Heatseeker *1995*
Bortman, Michael Chain Reaction *1996*
Bost, Pierre Croisières Sidérales *1941*
Bostock-Smith, Colin Metal Mickey (creator) *1980-1983*
Boucher, Chris Blake's 7 *1978-1981* • Star Cops (devisor) *1987*
Boulle, Pierre Planet of the Apes (novel) *1967* • Beneath the Planet of the Apes (characters) *1969* • Escape from the Planet of the Apes (characters) *1971* • Conquest of the Planet of the Apes (characters) *1972* • Battle for the Planet of the Apes (characters) *1973*
Boulting, Roy Seven Days to Noon *1950*
Bourla, David Yesterday's Target *1996* • Doomsday Rock *1997* • When Time Expires *1997*
Bowers, William Way... Way Out *1966*
Bowker, Peter The Uninvited *1997*
Brackett, Charles Journey to the Center of the Earth *1959*
Brackett, Leigh Star Wars Episode V: the Empire Strikes Back *1980*
Bradbury, Ray The Beast from 20,000 Fathoms (story) *1953* • It Came from Outer Space (short story) *1953* • Fahrenheit 451 (novel) *1966* • The Illustrated Man (book) *1969* • The Martian Chronicles (novel) *1979* • The Ray Bradbury Theatre *1985-1992* • It Came from Outer Space II (short story) *1996*
Braddon, Russell Night of the Lepus (novel) *1972*
Bradford, Sue Indestructible Man *1956*
Bradley, Elizabeth Cocoon: the Return (story) *1988*
Bradshaw, John Specimen (story) *1996*
Braga, Brannon Star Trek: Generations *1994* • Star Trek: Generations (story) *1994* • Star Trek: First Contact *1996* • Star Trek: First Contact (story) *1996*
Brahms, Caryl Give Us the Moon *1944* • Give Us the Moon (novel) *1944*
Brancato, Chris First Wave (creator)*1998-* • Species II *1998*
Brandner, Uwe I Love You I Kill You *1971*
Brandon, Clark Skeeter *1993*
Brauer, Jonathan Not of This World (story) *1991*
Bray, Ian Time Runner *1993*
Brdecka, Jiri Baron Munchhausen *1961*
Breakston, George The Manster (story) *1959*
Brent, Charles Bliss *1995-1997*
Brexan, Ivo The Rat Saviour *1977*
Brian, Mitch Transformations *1988*
Bricker, George Devil Bat (story) *1940* • The Whip Hand *1951*
Brickman, Marshall Sleeper *1973* • Simon *1980*
Bridges, James Colossus: the Forbin Project *1969*
Briganti, Elsia Zombie Flesh Eaters *1979*
Briley, John Children of the Damned *1964*
Brin, David The Postman (novel) *1997*
Britton, Lenny Precious Find *1996*
Brooke, Peter R Starflight One (story) *1983*
Brooks, Jeremy Work Is a Four Letter Word *1968*
Brooks, Mel Young Frankenstein *1974* • Spaceballs *1987*
Brosnan, John *aka* **Knight, Harry Adam** Proteus (screenplay/novel) *1995*
Brougher, Hilary The Sticky Fingers of Time *1997*
Brown, Fredrick Martians Go Home (novel) *1990*
Brown, Himan The CBS Radio Mystery Theater (creator) *1974-1982*
Brown, Julie Earth Girls Are Easy *1988*
Brown, Karl The Man They Could Not Hang *1939*
Brown, Lew Just Imagine *1930*
Brown, Mende Jules Verne's Strange Holiday *1969*
Brown, Ray Timestalkers (unpublished novel) *1987*
Brown, Robert G The High Crusade *1994*
Brown, Ross Meego (creator) *1997*
Browne, Alan Daybreak (play) *1993*
Bruce, Lenny The Rocket Man *1954*
Bruckner, William Doctor Renault's Secret *1942*
Brulé, Claude Barbarella *1967*
Bryan, Peter The Projected Man *1966* • The Blood Beast Terror *1967* • Trog (story) *1970*
Bryant, John Scanner Cop *1994*
Buchanan, Larry Mars Needs Women *1966* • Zontar, the Thing from Venus *1966* • It's Alive *1968*
Buckner, Robert Moon Pilot (story) *1962*
Budrys, Algis Who? (novel) *1974*
Buffum, Ray The Brain from Planet Arous *1958* • Teenage Monster *1958*
Bulychov, Kir Humanoid Woman *1981*
Bunuel, Joyce Black Moon *1974*
Burdick, Eugene Fail-Safe (novel) *1964*
Burger, Gottfried Baron Munchhausen (novel) *1961*
Burger, Robbyn Asteroid *1997*
Burgess, Anthony A Clockwork Orange (novel) *1971, 1998*
Burke, John The Sorcerers (idea) *1967*
Burke, Martyn The Last Chase *1981*
Burnett, Alan Batman: Mask of the Phantasm (screenplay/story) *1993*
Burney, Robert J The Eye Creatures *1965*
Burnham, Jeremy The Horror of Frankenstein *1970*
Buronson Fist of the North Star (Comic Book) *1995*
Burroughs, Edgar Rice The Land That Time Forgot (novel) *1974* • At the Earth's Core (novel) *1976* • The People That Time Forgot (novel) *1977*
Burton, Michael Flight of the Navigator *1986*
Butcher, Oliver Dr Jekyll and Ms Hyde *1995*
Butler, David Just Imagine *1930*
Butler, Michael Murder by Phone *1982*
Byant, Peter Doctor Who: the Second Doctor *1966-1969*
Byars, Floyd Making Mr Right *1987*
Byrne, John The Adventures of Superman (stories) *1994*
Byrne, Stuart J Escape from Planet Earth *1967*

C

Cacoyannis, Michael The Day the Fish Came Out *1967*
Cacucci, Pino Nirvana *1996*
Caddigan, James L Captain Video and His Video Rangers (creator) *1949-1955*
Caidin, Martin Marooned (novel) *1969* • The Six Million Dollar Man (novel) *1974-1978* • The Bionic Woman (novel) *1976-1978*
Caillou, Alan Village of the Giants *1965* • Kingdom of the Spiders *1977*
Callas, John Lone Wolf *1988*
Callaway, Trey Mercy Point (creator) *1998-1999*
Callisi, Paul Josh Kirby... Time Warrior *1995*
Cameron, Ian The Island at the Top of the World (novel) *1974*
Cameron, James The Terminator *1984* • Aliens (screenplay/story) *1986* • The Abyss *1989* • Terminator 2: Judgment Day *1991* • Strange Days (screenplay/story) *1995*• Dark Angel (creator) *2000–*
Campbell Jr, John Wood *aka* **Stuart, Don A** The Thing from Another World (story) *1951, 1982*
Campbell, R Wright Teenage Caveman *1958* • Captain Nemo and the Underwater City *1969*
Canaan, Christopher Bridge of Time *1997*
Cannell, Stephen J The Greatest American Hero (creator) *1981-1983*
Cannon, Lowell Mission to Mars (story) *1999*
Cantor, Eli The Nest (novel) *1988*
Capek, Karel The Creation of the Humanoids (play) *1962*
Cappello, Frank Suburban Commando *1991*
Carax, Léos The Night Is Young *1986*
Cardella, Richard The Crater Lake Monster *1977*
Cardone, J S Crash and Burn *1990* • Shadowzone *1990*
Cardona, Rene Night of the Bloody Apes *1968*
Cardona Jr, Rene Night of the Bloody Apes *1968*
Caret, Max Devilman Story *1967*
Carey, Peter Dead-End Drive-In (short story) *1986* • Until the End of the World *1991*
Carlino, Lewis John Seconds *1966*
Carlisle, Anne Liquid Sky *1982*
Carlton, Rex The Brain That Wouldn't Die (story) *1959* • Unearthly Stranger *1963*
Carmody, Michael Syngenor (story) *1989*
Caro, Marc The City of Lost Children *1995*
Caron, Glenn Gordon Now and Again (creator) *1999-2000*
Carpenter, John *aka* **Quatermass, Martin** *aka* **Armitage, Frank** Dark Star *1973* • Escape from New York *1981* • Prince of Darkness *1987* • They Live *1988* • Escape from LA (screenplay/characters) *1996*
Carpenter, Stephen The Kindred *1986*
Carreras, Michael *aka* **Nash, Michael** The Lost Continent *1968* • Moon Zero Two *1969*
Carrier, Roch The Christmas Martian *1971*
Carroll, J Larry The Day Time Ended *1980*
Carson, William Judgment Day *1999*
Carter, Chris (creator) The X Files *1993-* • Millenium *1996-1999* • The X Files *1998* • The X Files (story) *1998* • Harsh Realm *1999-2000* • The Lone Gunmen *2001*
Cartmel, Andrew Doctor Who: the Seventh Doctor (script editor) *1987-1989*
Casey, Thomas Flesh Feast *1970*
Cassie, Iain Xtro *1983*
Cast to come 2004 *1995*
Castle, Alan Stranded *1987*
Castle, Nick Escape from New York *1981* • Escape from LA (characters) *1996*
Castle, William Bug *1975*
Cathro, Grant Mike & Angelo *1989-2000*
Catran, Ken The Boy from Andromeda *1991* • Deepwater Black *1997*
Cawthorn, James The Land That Time Forgot

D

E

F

G

Guilbert, Francis Hu-Man *1975*
Gullette, Sean Pi (story) *1997*
Gunn, James The Immortal (novel) *1970-1971*
Gunter, Robert Journey to the Center of the Earth *1993*
Gunzberg, Milton The Devil Commands *1941*
Gurney Jr, Robert J Invasion of the Saucer Men *1957* • Terror from the Year 5,000 *1958*

H

Haas, Charles S *aka* **Haas, Charlie** Gremlins 2: the New Batch *1990* • Martians Go Home *1990*
Haggard, H Rider She (novel) *1982*
Haines, Richard W Class of Nuke 'Em High (screenplay/story)*1986* • Alien Space Avenger *1989*
Hairston, Charles Voyage of the Rock Aliens *1985*
Hajny, Pavel The Sex Mission *1984*
Halberstadt, Michèle Kamikaze *1986*
Haldeman, Joe Robot Jox *1989*
Hale, Gregg FreakyLinks *2000-2001*
Hale, John The Mind of Mr Soames *1970*
Hale, Mary Multiplicity *1996*
Hall, Frank The Astounding She-Monster *1958*
Hall, James Andrew The Invisible Man *1984*
Hall, Norman S Flash Gordon's Trip to Mars *1938* • Buck Rogers *1939* • The Mysterious Dr Satan *1940* • The Adventures of Captain Marvel *1941*
Hall, Parnell CHUD *1984*
Hall, Sam Frankenstein *1973*
Hamilton, Roy The Whip Hand (story) *1951* • Cat-Women of the Moon *1953*
Hamilton-Wright, Michael Retroactive *1997*
Hamm, Sam Batman (screenplay/story) *1989* • Batman Returns (story) *1992*
Hammond, P J Sapphire & Steel (creator) *1979-1982*
Hampton, Christopher Mary Reilly *1995*
Hampton, Orville H Rocketship X-M *1950* • The Alligator People *1959* • The Alligator People (story) *1959* • The Atomic Submarine *1960*
Haney, Daryl Crime Zone *1989* • Lords of the Deep *1989*
Hanmura, Ryo Time Slip (story) *1981*
Hanna, Mark Not of This Earth *1956* • The Amazing Colossal Man *1957* • The Undead *1957* • Attack of the 50 Foot Woman *1958* • Not of This Earth (film) *1988, 1995* • Attack of the 50 Ft Woman (film) *1993*
Hannant, Brian Mad Max 2 *1981* • The Time Guardian *1987*
Hara, Buronson Fist of the North Star (graphic novels) *1986*
Hara, Tetsuo Fist of the North Star (graphic novels) *1986, 1995*
Harada, Masato Gunhed *1989*
Harber, Harry Paul Terror Is a Man *1959*
Harding, Stewart Spacehunter: Adventures in the Forbidden Zone (story) *1983*
Hardman, Frank Moon Zero Two (story) *1969*
Hargreaves, Gerald P Atlantis, the Lost Continent (play) *1960*
Hargreaves, Lance Z First Man into Space *1958* • Battle beneath the Earth *1968*
Harlacher, Eric Homewrecker *1992* • Homewrecker (story) *1992*
Harrington, Curtis *aka* **Sebastian, John** Voyage to the Prehistoric Planet *1965* • Planet of Blood *1966*
Harris, Alfred Space Command *1953-1954*
Harris, Anthony Beware! The Blob *1971* • Beware! The Blob (story) *1971*
Harris, Barbara S Who Is Julia? (novel) *1986*
Harris, Jack H Dinosaurus! (Idea) *1960*
Harris, Owen The Flight That Disappeared *1961* • The Underwater City *1962*
Harris, Timothy My Stepmother Is an Alien *1988* • Space Jam *1997*
Harris, Trent Plan 10 from Outer Space *1995*
Harrison, Harry Soylent Green (novel) *1973*
Harrison, John Shock Waves *1975* • Frank Herbert's Dune *2000*
Harrison, John Kent Murder by Phone *1982*
Harrison, William Rollerball *1975* • Rollerball (story) *1975*
Harryhausen, Ray 20 Million Miles to Earth (story) *1957*
Hart, Christopher Eat and Run *1986*
Hart, Jacobsen Cyber-Tracker *1994* • Steel Frontier *1994* • T-Force *1995*
Hart, James V Contact *1997*
Hart, John Atom Age Vampire *1960*
Hart, Judith The Flight That Disappeared *1961*
Hart, Ralph The Flight That Disappeared *1961*
Hart, Stan Eat and Run *1986*
Hartford, James Dr Goldfoot and the Bikini Machine (story) *1965* • Dr Goldfoot and the Girl Bombs (story) *1966*
Hartov, Steven Mars *1996*
Harvey, Frank Seven Days to Noon *1950*
Harvey, Michael Halfway across the Galaxy and Turn Left *1994*
Harwood, Johanna Don't Play with Martians *1967*
Hasbro Transformers – The Movie (toy range) *1986*
Hashimoto, Izo Akira *1988*
Hatte, T H Anchor Zone *1994*
Hauser, Burford Creepozoids *1987*
Hauser, Stephen Sphere *1998*
Hawks, J G A Blind Bargain *1922*
Hawthorne, Nathaniel Twice Told Tales (short stories/novel) *1963*
Hayes, Carey W Dark Side of the Moon *1990*
Hayes, Chad Dark Side of the Moon *1990*
Hayes, Jeffrey Time Trax *1993-1994*
Hayes, Peter Sierra Nine *1963*
Hayes, Raphael Have Rocket, Will Travel *1959*
Hayes, Steve Time after Time (story) *1979*
Hayes, Terry Mad Max 2 *1981* • Mad Max beyond Thunderdome *1985*
Hayles, Brian Legend of Death *1965* • Warlords of Atlantis *1978*
Hayter, David X-Men *2000*
Hayward, Lillie The Walking Dead *1936*
Haze, Jonathan Invasion of the Star Creatures (screenplay/story) *1962*
Heap, Jonathan 12:01 (short film) *1993*
Heard, H F The Deadly Bees (novel) *1967*
Heath, Arch B The Adventures of Captain Marvel *1941*
Heath, Percy Dr Jekyll and Mr Hyde *1931*
Heavener, David Deadly Reactor *1989* • Dragon Fury *1995*
Hecht, Ben Monkey Business *1952* • Queen of Outer Space (story) *1958*
Hedden, Rob Knight Rider 2000 *1991*
Heinlein, Robert A Destination Moon *1950* • Tom Corbett, Space Cadet (novel) *1950-1955* • Project Moonbase *1953* • The Brain Eaters (novel) *1958* • The Puppet Masters (novel) *1994* • Starship Troopers (novel) *1997*
Helgeland, Brian The Postman *1997*
Heller, Lukas Damnation Alley *1977*
Henderson, Ray Just Imagine *1930*
Henenlotter, Frank Brain Damage *1988*
Henerson, James S The Fire Next Time *1992*
Henley, Jack The Rocket Man *1954*
Henry, Buck Captain Nice *1967* • The Day of the Dolphin *1973* • Quark (creator) *1978*
Hensleigh, Jonathan Armageddon (screenplay/story)
Henstell, Diana Deadly Friend (novel) *1986*
Herbeck, Bobby Teenage Mutant Ninja Turtles *1990* • Teenage Mutant Ninja Turtles (story) *1990*
Herbert, Frank Dune (novel) *1984* • Frank Herbert's Dune (novel) *2000*
Herek, Stephen Critters *1986*
Herley, Richard No Escape (novel) *1994*
Hermes, Leonard Stryker (story) *1983*
Herskovic, Patrica Body Parts (story) *1991*
Hewitt, David L The Time Travelers (story) *1964*
Hewlett, Jamie Tank Girl (Comic Strip) *1995*
Heyde, Dean Moon 44 (screenplay/story)*1990*
Heyward, Louis M Pajama Party *1964* • City under the Sea *1965* • Planet of the Vampires *1965* • Sergeant Deadhead *1965* • Dr Goldfoot and the Girl Bombs *1966*
Hickox, Anthony Waxwork II: Lost in Time *1992*
Hicks, Neill Turkey Shoot *1981*
Hidaka, Sigeaki Godzilla Raids Again *1955*
Higgin, Howard The Invisible Ray (story) *1936*
Higgins, John C The Black Sleep *1956* • Robinson Crusoe on Mars *1964*
Higgins, Kenneth The Unknown Terror *1957*
Higgins, Lynn Rose Mutator (screenplay/story) *1991*
Highsmith, Patrick Automatic *1994* • Savage (screenplay/story) *1995* • Mars (screenplay/story) *1996* • The Outsider *1997*
Hildebrand, Dale Memory Run *1995*
Hill, Debra Escape from LA *1996*
Hill, John Heartbeeps *1981* • Steel Justice *1992*
Hill, Robert The Beast of Hollow Mountain *1956*
Hill, Rosemary The Master *1966*
Hill, Walter Aliens (story) *1986* • Alien3 *1992*
Hillenbrand, David King Cobra *1999*
Hillenbrand, Scott King Cobra *1999*
Hills, Dick Captain Zep – Space Detective *1983-1984*
Himes, Chester Cosmic Slop (short story) *1994*
Himmelstein, David Village of the Damned *1995*
Hindell, Alison A Clockwork Orange *1998*
Hinds, Anthony *aka* **Elder, John** Evil of Frankenstein *1964* • Frankenstein Created Woman *1966* • Frankenstein and the Monster from Hell *1973*
Hiner, Phil Hideous Sun Demon *1955*
Hines, Barry Threads *1984*
Hirano, Yasuhi Vampire Hunter D *1985*
Hirson, Roger O Demon Seed *1977*
Hittleman, Carl K Jesse James Meets Frankenstein's Daughter (screenplay/story) *1966*
Hoag, Doane Hideous Sun Demon *1955*
Hoare, John Red Planet Mars (play) *1952*
Hodge, Steve Mosquito *1995*
Hodges, Douglas The Invisible Ray (story) *1936*
Hodges, Mike The Terminal Man *1974*
Hodgson, Joel Mystery Science Theater 3000: The Movie (TV Series) *1996* • Honey, We Shrunk Ourselves *1997*
Hoerl, Arthur Brick Bradford *1947* • Superman *1948* • Killer Ape *1953* • The Lost Planet *1953*
Hoey, Michael A The Navy vs the Night Monsters *1966*
Hoffenstein, Samuel Dr Jekyll and Mr Hyde *1931*
Holder, Carlton Bridge of Dragons *1999*
Holland, Tom The Langoliers *1995*
Holliday, Don Night of the Lepus *1972*
Holmes, Robert Invasion (story) *1965* • Doctor Who: the Fourth Doctor (script editor) *1974-1981* • The Nightmare Man *1981*

L

M

MacLean, Alistair *aka* **Stuart, Ian** The Satan Bug (novel) *1965*
Maclear, Andrew Space Island One (creator) *1998*
McLeod, Victor Batman *1943*
MacManus, Matt Flight of the Navigator *1986*
McManus, Steve Hardware (story) *1990*
McNair, Sue Horror of the Blood Monsters *1970*
McNally, Terrence *aka* **McNally, Terrence E** Earth Girls Are Easy *1988*
Macourek, Milos Sir, You Are a Widower (screenplay/story) *1971*
McPartland, John The Lost Missile *1958*
MacPherson, Don The Avengers *1998*
McPherson, Stephen Buck Rogers in the 25th Century (executive story consultant) *1979-1981* • Cocoon: the Return (screenplay/story) *1988*
MacVicar, Angus The Lost Planet (teleplay, radio serial) *1954* • Return to the Lost Planet (teleplay/novel) *1955*
Maddock, Brent Short Circuit *1986* • *batteries not included *1987* • Short Circuit 2 *1988* • Tremors (screenplay/story) *1989* • Tremors II: Aftershocks *1995*
Maddox, L A Virtual Girl *1998*
Maetzig, Kurt First Spaceship on Venus *1960*
Maggs, Dirk The Adventures of Superman *1994* • The Adventures of Superman: Doomsday and Beyond *1995* • The Amazing Spider-Man *1995* • Batman: Knightfall *1995* • Voyage *1999*
Maharaj, Anthony Future Hunters (story) *1988*
Maher, John C Devil Girl from Mars (screenplay/play) *1954*
Mahin, John Lee Dr Jekyll and Mr Hyde *1941*
Maine, Charles Eric Spaceways (radio play) *1953* • Timeslip (screenplay/novel) *1955* • Escapement (screenplay/novel) *1958* • The Mind of Mr Soames (novel) *1970*
Mainwaring, Daniel Invasion of the Body Snatchers *1956* • Space Master X 7 *1958* • Atlantis, the Lost Continent *1960*
Maiuri, Dino Doctor Crimen *1953*
Majano, Anton Guilio Atom Age Vampire *1960*
Makichuk, Jim Roswell: the Aliens Attack *1999*
Makin, William J The Return of Dr X (story) *1939*
Makourek, Milos Who Killed Jessie? *1965* • A Nice Plate of Spinach *1976*
Maley, Gloria Inseminoid *1981*
Maley, Nick Inseminoid *1981*
Malle, Louis Black Moon *1974*
Mallon, Jim Mystery Science Theater 3000: The Movie *1996*
Malone, William Scared to Death *1980* • Universal Soldier – the Return *1999* • Supernova (story) *2000*
Mancilla, Jess My Uncle the Alien (story) *1996*
Mandel, Babaloo Multiplicity *1996*
Mandel, Jeff Elves *1989* • Firehead *1991*
Mandel, Loring Countdown *1968*
Mandell, Corey Battlefield Earth *2000*
Manheim, Het The Vanishing Shadow *1934*
Mankowitz, Wolf The Two Faces of Dr Jekyll *1960* • The Day the Earth Caught Fire *1961*
Mann, Edward The Mutations *1973*
Mann, Edward Andrew Island of Terror *1966*
Mann, Farhad Lawnmower Man 2: Beyond Cyberspace (screenplay/story) *1995*
Mann, Jane The Unearthly (screenplay/story) *1957*
Mann, Stanley Meteor *1979* • Firestarter *1984*
Mann, Ted Bionic Showdown: the Six Million Dollar Man and the Bionic Woman *1989* • Space Truckers (screenplay/story) *1996*
Manning, Monroe Face of Terror *1962*
Manos, Mark Liquid Dreams *1992*
Mans, Lorenzo Glen and Randa *1971*
Manson, Graeme Cube *1997*
Mantley, John The 27th Day (screenplay/novel) *1957*
Marcel, Terry Prisoners of the Lost Universe *1983*
Marcus, Peter The Body Stealers *1969*
Marcuzzo, Lucio Spy in Your Eye (story) *1965*
Mareth, Glenville Santa Claus Conquers the Martians *1964*
Margheriti, Antonio *aka* **Dawson, Anthony M** Yor, the Hunter from the Future *1983*
Marin, Carlos The Strange Case of the Man and the Beast *1951*
Marion, George The Gladiator *1938*
Marker, Chris La Jetée *1962* • Twelve Monkeys (film) *1995*
Markham, Monte Neon City *1992*
Marks, Dennis Jetsons: the Movie *1990*
Marks, Laurence Goodnight Sweetheart (creator) *1993-1999*
Markstein, George The Prisoner *1968-1969*
Marlowe, Andrew W Hollow Man (screenplay/story) *2000*
Marmorstein, Malcolm Return from Witch Mountain *1978*
Marquina, Luis Mr Superinvisible *1970*
Marriott, Anthony The Deadly Bees *1967*
Marshall, Bill Dr Frankenstein on Campus *1967*
Marshall, Fred Popdown *1968*
Marshall, Roger Invasion *1965*
Marston, William M Wonder Woman (creator) *1975-1979*
Martell, William C Cyberzone *1995* • Invisible Mom *1995*
Marthesheimer, Peter Mission Eureka (idea) *1990*
Martin, Al Invasion of the Saucer Men *1957* • The Eye Creatures *1965*
Martin, Alan Tank Girl (Comic Strip) *1995*
Martin, Andreu Star Knight *1985*
Martin, Dave Sky *1976*
Martin, Eugenio Horror Express (story) *1972*
Martin, George R R Nightflyers (novella) *1987*
Martin, Steve The Man with Two Brains *1983*
Martin, Valerie Mary Reilly (novel) *1995*
Martino, Sergio Island of the Fish Men *1978*
Marshall, Gary (creator) Mork & Mindy *1978-1982*
Marx, Christy Secrets of the Phantom Caverns *1984* • Hypernauts (executive story editor)*1996*
Marx, Rick Dead Man Walking *1988*
Marxuach, Javier Grillo Dark Skies *1996-1997*
Masamune, Shirow Ghost in the Shell (graphic novel) *1995*
Mason, Paul King Kong vs Godzilla *1962*
Mason, Robert Solo (novel) *1996*
Mastorakis, Nico Next One *1984*
Mather, Berkley Dimension of Fear (story) *1963*
Mather, John Satellite in the Sky *1956*
Matheson, Chris Bill & Ted's Excellent Adventure *1988* • Bill & Ted's Bogus Journey *1991* • Mom and Dad Save the World *1992*
Matheson, Richard The Incredible Shrinking Man (screenplay/novel) *1957* • Master of the World *1961* • The Last Man on Earth (novel) *1964* • It's Alive (novel) *1968* • The Omega Man (novel) *1971* • The Martian Chronicles *1979* • The Incredible Shrinking Woman (novel) *1981* • Twilight Zone: the Movie *1983* • Amazing Stories (creative consultant) *1985-1987* • Twilight Zone: Rod Serling's Lost Classics *1994*
Matheson, Richard Christian The Incredible Hulk *1977*
Mathews, David Atom Man vs Superman *1950*
Mathis, Steve Without Warning *1980*
Mathison, Melissa ET the Extra-Terrestrial *1982*
Matsuda, Hiroo Message from Space *1978*
Matsumoto, Hajime Zeram *1991*
Matthiesen, Thomas Idaho Transfer *1973*
Maunder, J Stephen TC 2000 (story) *1993* • Expect No Mercy *1995*
Maurer, Norman The Three Stooges in Orbit (story) *1962*
Maxwell, Robert Superman and the Mole Men *1951*
May, Joe The Invisible Man Returns (story) *1940* • The Invisible Woman (story) *1940*
Mayersburg, Paul The Man Who Fell to Earth *1976*
Mayhew-Archer, Paul My Hero
Mazin, Craig Rocketman *1997*
Mazo, Michael Time Runner *1993*
Mazzarino, Joseph Muppets from Space *1999*
Méliès, Georges Le Voyage dans la Lune *1902*
Meehan, Thomas Spaceballs *1987*
Meerson, Steve Star Trek IV: the Voyage Home *1986*
Melamed, Ken Digital Man *1994*
Melchior, Ib The Angry Red Planet *1959* • Journey to the Seventh Planet *1961* • Reptilicus *1961* • Robinson Crusoe on Mars *1964* • The Time Travelers (screenplay/story) *1964* • Planet of the Vampires (screenplay/story) *1965* • Death Race 2000 (story) *1975*
Melson, Charlie The Gladiator *1938*
Mendelson, Paul My Hero
Mendez , Fernando Ladron de Cadaveres *1956*
Menzies, William Cameron Invaders from Mars *1953*
Mercurio, Jed Invasion: Earth *1998*
Merle, Robert The Day of the Dolphin (novel) *1973* • Malevil (novel) *1981*
Messina, Phillip Frank Brainstorm *1983*
Messiter, Ian Mr Drake's Duck (play) *1950*
Metalnikov, Budimir The Silence of Dr Evans *1973*
Metrov, Douglas Anthony Solarwarriors *1986*
Metz, Melinda Roswell (novels) *1999 -*
Metzger, Joel The Pretender *1996-2000*
Metzler, Robert *aka* **Metzler, Robert F** Doctor Renault's Secret *1942*
Meyer, Nicholas Invasion of the Bee Girls *1973* • The Night that Panicked America *1975* • Time after Time *1979* • Star Trek IV: the Voyage Home *1986* • Star Trek VI: the Undiscovered Country *1991*
Meyrink, Gustav The Golem (novel) *1979*
Michener, James A Space (novel) *1985*
Mikels, Ted V The Astro-Zombies *1968*
Millard, Joseph They Came from beyond Space (novel) *1967*
Miller, Broderick Wedlock *1991*
Miller, Chris Multiplicity (screenplay/short story) *1996*
Miller, Eric The Shadow Men *1997*
Miller, Frank RoboCop 2 (screenplay/story) *1990* • RoboCop 3 (screenplay/story) *1993*
Miller, Geof DeepStar Six *1989*
Miller (2), George Mad Max (screenplay/story) *1979* • Mad Max 2 *1981* • Mad Max beyond Thunderdome *1985*
Miller, Harvey Jekyll and Hyde... Together Again *1982*
Miller, Jeff Dead & Buried (story) *1981*
Miller, Peter Doctor Blood's Coffin *1960*
Millgate, Irvine H The Blob (Idea) *1958*
Millhauser, Bertram The Invisible Man's Revenge *1944*
Milligan, Spike The Bed Sitting Room (play) *1969*
Milne, Peter The Walking Dead *1936*
Milner, Jack From Hell It Came (story) *1957*
Mimura, Wataru Godzilla 2000 *1999*
Miner, Michael RoboCop *1987* • Deadly

N

O

P

1973-1979 • The Tomorrow People (creator) *1992-1995*
Prochazka, Jan On the Comet *1970*
Proser, Chip Iceman *1984* • Innerspace *1987* • Innerspace (story) *1987*
Protosevich, Mark The Cell *2000*
Proyas, Alex Dark City *1998* • Dark City (story) *1998*
Pryce, Craig Revenge of the Radioactive Reporter *1990*
Puerto, Carlos Where Time Began *1977*
Pugsley, William Dracula vs Frankenstein *1970*
Pulce, Jeff Terminal Virus *1995*
Purcell, Daniella Terminal Virus *1995*
Purcell, Gertrude The Invisible Woman *1940*
Purdy, Jon The Guyver *1992*
Puzo, Mario Superman (screenplay/story) *1978* • Superman II (screenplay/story) *1980*
Pyun, Albert Radioactive Dreams *1986* • Alien from LA *1987* • Brain Smasher... a Love Story *1993* • Knights *1993* • Adrenalin: Fear the Rush *1995* • Heatseeker (screenplay/story) *1995* • Nemesis 2 – Nebula *1995* • Nemesis 3 – Time Lapse *1996* • Omega Doom (screenplay/story) *1996*

Q

Quattrocchi, Frank The Projected Man (story) *1966*

R

Rabin, Jack Cat-Women of the Moon (story) *1953* • War of the Satellites (story) *1958* • The 30 Foot Bride of Candy Rock (idea) *1959*
Rader, Peter Escape to Witch Mountain *1995* • Waterworld *1995*
Radford, Michael Nineteen Eighty-Four *1984*
Raffill, Stewart The Ice Pirates *1984*
Ragsdale, Tex Moontrap *1989*
Raimi, Ivan Darkman *1990*
Raimi, Sam Darkman (screenplay/story) *1990* • Darkman II: the Return of Durant (characters) *1995* • Darkman III: Die Darkman Die (characters) *1996*
Rameau, Hans An Invisible Man Goes through the City *1933* • The World without a Mask *1934*
Ramis, Harold Ghostbusters *1984* • Ghostbusters II *1989*
Ramrus, Al The Island of Dr Moreau *1977* • The Darker Side of Terror *1979*
Ramsen, Alan Island of Terror *1966*
Ramsing, Bob Reptilicus *1961*
Randall, Florence Engel The Watcher in the Woods (novel) *1982*
Randel, Tony Fist of the North Star *1995*
Rao, Krishna Crossworlds *1996*
Rao, Raman Crossworlds *1996*
Rascoe, Judith Lifespan *1975*
Raspe, Rudolph Erich The Adventures of Baron Munchausen (stories) *1988*
Rathmell, John Undersea Kingdom *1936* • Undersea Kingdom (story) *1936*
Rauch, Earl Mac The Adventures of Buckaroo Banzai across the 8th Dimension *1984*
Ravich, Rand The Astronaut's Wife *1999*
Ravn, Jens The Man Who Thought Life *1969*
Ray, Fred Olen The Alien Dead *1980* • Biohazard *1984* • Deep Space *1987*
Ray, René The Strange World of Planet X *1956* • The Strange World of Planet X (TV serial) *1957*
Rayfiel, David Deathwatch *1980*
Raymond, Alex Flash Gordon (comic strip) *1936, 1954-1955, 1980* • Flash Gordon's Trip to Mars (comic strip) *1938* • Flash Gordon Conquers the Universe (comic strip) *1940* • Killer Ape (comic strip) *1953*
Raynor, William Phantom from Space *1953* • Killers from Space *1954* • Target Earth *1954*
Read, Anthony Doctor Who: the Fourth Doctor *1974-1981* • Chocky *1984-1986*
Read, Jan First Men in the Moon *1964*
Reardon, Dennis The Happiness Cage (play) *1972*
Reaves, Michael Batman: Mask of the Phantasm *1993*
Rebane, Bill Monster a Go-Go! *1965*
Recht, Coby The Apple (screenplay/story) *1980*
Recht, Iris The Apple (screenplay/story) *1980*
Red, Eric Body Parts *1991*
Redon, Jean Eyes without a Face (screenplay/novel) *1959*
Reed, Morton Space Rage (story) *1986*
Reed, Roland D Rocky Jones, Space Ranger (creator) *1954*
Reed, Tom Murders in the Rue Morgue *1932*
Reeve, Arthur B Terror Island (story) *1920*
Reeve, Christopher Superman IV: the Quest for Peace (story) *1987*
Reeves, John Halfway across the Galaxy and Turn Left *1994*
Reeves, Michael The Sorcerers *1967*
Regnoli, Piero The Bronx Executioner *1989*
Reifel, J Timelock *1996* • Convict 762 *1997* • Dark Planet *1997*
Reiff, Ethan Josh Kirby... Time Warrior *1995*
Reigle, James Android *1982* • City Limits (story) *1985*
Reiner, Carl The Man with Two Brains *1983*
Reiner, Ivan The Snow Devils *1965* • War of the Planets *1965* • The Wild, Wild Planet *1965* • The Green Slime (story) *1968*
Reisch, Guenther First Spaceship on Venus *1960*
Reisch, Walter FP1 (screenplay/story) *1932* • Journey to the Center of the Earth *1959*
Relph, Michael Man in the Moon *1960*
Renard, Maurice Hands of Orlac (novel) *1924, 1960* • Mad Love (novel) *1935*
Reneau, Robert Demolition Man (screenplay/story) *1993*
Rephun, Hesh Chase Morran *1996*
Resnais, Alain Je T'Aime, Je T'Aime *1968*
Resnick, Patricia Quintet (screenplay/story) *1979*
Rey, Edith Spacehunter: Adventures in the Forbidden Zone *1983*
Reyher, Ferdinand The World, the Flesh and the Devil (story) *1959*
Reynolds, Jonathan My Stepmother Is an Alien *1988*
Rhys Jones, Griff Morons from Outer Space *1985*
Ricci, Debra Alien from LA *1987* • Journey to the Center of the Earth *1989*
Ricci, Judy Return of the Living Dead (story) *1984*
Rice, Jeff Kolchak: The Night Stalker (creator) *1974-1975*
Richard, Jean-Louis Fahrenheit 451 *1966*
Richards, Robert L *aka* **Loring, John** Gorgo *1961*
Richardson, Mark Timecop (story/comic series) *1994*
Richmond, Bill The Nutty Professor *1963* • The Nutty Professor (film) *1996* • Nutty Professor 2: the Klumps (characters) *2000*
Richter, WD Invasion of the Body Snatchers *1978*
Riley, John The Tower (screenplay/story) *1992*
Rilla, Wolf Village of the Damned *1960* • Village of the Damned (film) *1995*
Rinaldo, Frederic I *aka* **Rinaldo, Fred** The Invisible Woman *1940* • Abbott and Costello Meet Frankenstein *1948* • Abbott and Costello Meet the Invisible Man *1951*
Ripps, Hillary 12:01 (short film) *1993*
Ritt, William Brick Bradford (comic strip) *1947*
Ritter, Joe The Toxic Avenger *1985*
Rivera, José Eerie, Indiana *1991-1992*
Roach, M Jay Lifepod *1993*
Robbins, Dick C.H.O.M.P.S. *1979*
Robbins, Matthew Warning Sign *1985* • *batteries not included *1987* • Mimic (screenplay/story) *1997*
Robbins, Paul J Digital Man *1994*
Roberts, Chris Wing Commander (characters) *1999*
Roberts, Wink Legion of Fire: Killer Ants! *1998*
Robertson, Blair Agent for H.A.R.M. *1966*
Robertson, Harry Prisoners of the Lost Universe *1983*
Robertson, R J Forbidden World (story) *1982* • Not of This Earth *1988*
Robeson, Kenneth Doc Savage: the Man of Bronze (novel) *1975*
Robinson, Frank M The Power (novel) *1968*
Robinson, James Cyber Bandits (screenplay/story) *1995*
Robinson, Richard Kingdom of the Spiders *1977* • Piranha (story) *1978*
Robinson, Sally Medicine Man *1992*
Robson, Michael Holocaust 2000 *1977*
Rocca, Maria Laura *aka* **Eller, Mary** Mr Superinvisible (screenplay/novel) *1970*
Rochat, Eric Too Much *1987*
Roche, France Amour de Poche *1957*
Rock, Kevin The Philadelphia Experiment 2 *1993*
Rock, Phillip The Most Dangerous Man Alive (screenplay/story) *1961*
Roddenberry, Gene (creator) Star Trek *1966-1969* • Genesis II *1973* • Planet Earth *1974* • Planet Earth (story) *1974* • Star Trek: the Motion Picture *1979* • Star Trek: the Motion Picture (TV series) *1979* • Star Trek II: the Wrath of Khan *1982* • Star Trek III: the Search for Spock (TV series) *1984* • Star Trek IV: the Voyage Home (TV series) *1986* • Star Trek: The Next Generation *1987-1994* • Star Trek V: the Final Frontier (TV series) *1989* • Star Trek VI: the Undiscovered Country (TV series) *1991* • Star Trek: Generations (Characters) *1994* • Star Trek: First Contact (TV Series) *1996* • Earth: Final Conflict *1997-* • Star Trek: Insurrection (TV series) *1998* • Andromeda *2000-*
Rodenbeck, John Frankenstein Meets the Space Monster (story) *1965*
Rodriguez, Robert SPYkids *2001*
Roellinghoff, Charles Alraune *1930*
Roffman, Julian The Glove *1978*
Rogan, Josh Twilight Zone: the Movie *1983*
Rogers, Roswell The Million Dollar Duck *1971*
Rogers, Wayne *aka* **Rogers, Wayne M** The Astro-Zombies *1968*
Rolf, Tom The Resurrection of Zachary Wheeler *1971*
Rolfe, David Counterstrike *1969*
Roman, Antonio Planet of the Vampires *1965*
Romero, George A Night of the Living Dead (story) *1968* • The Crazies *1973* • Dawn of the Dead *1979* • Night of the Living Dead *1990* • Night of the Living Dead (film) *1990*
Root, Anthony Doctor Who: the Fifth Doctor *1982-1984*
Rose, Gerald A Mutator (story) *1991*
Rose, Ruth King Kong *1933* • Son of Kong *1933* • King Kong (film) *1976*

S

T

Y

Z

Alternative titles

A

A Pied, à Cheval et en Spoutnik A Dog, a Mouse and a Sputnik
The Aberdeen Experiment Scared to Death
Abraxas, Guardian of the Universe Abraxas
The Adventure of Lyle Swann Timerider: the Adventure of Lyle Swann
The Adventures of Stella Star Starcrash
The Adventures of Superboy Superboy
Aelita: Queen of Mars Aelita
Aelita: the Revolt of the Robots Aelita
The Aerial Torpedo The Airship Destroyer
Aerial Warfare The Airship Destroyer
Alien Avengers Welcome to Planet Earth
Alien Encounter Starship Invasions
Alien Force The Aliens Are Coming
Alien Predators Alien Predator
Alien Terror The Incredible Invasion
Alien Warning Without Warning
All Monsters Attack Godzilla's Revenge
Almost Human Shock Waves
The Amazing Dr G Dr Goldfoot and the Girl Bombs
American Inferno The Fire Next Time
Ammutinamento nello Spazio Mutiny in Outer Space
The Amphibious Man Amphibian Man
Andy Warhol's Frankenstein Flesh for Frankenstein
Les Années Lumières Light Years Away
L'Approche finale Final Approach
Armageddon 1975 Escape from Planet Earth
Armageddon Redline
Arrowfeather Gas-s-s-s, or It Became Necessary to Destroy the World in Order to Save It
Assault on Dome 4 Chase Morran
Assignment Outer Space Space Men
Asteroid Falling Fire
Astro Cop Solar Force
The Astronauts First Spaceship on Venus
Ataragon Atragon
Atlantis Siren of Atlantis
The Atomic Brain Monstrosity
Atomic Man Timeslip
The Atomic Man Timeslip
The Atomic Monster Man Made Monster
Atomic Rocketship Flash Gordon
Atoragon, the Flying Supersub Atragon
Attack All Monsters Godzilla's Revenge
Attack from Mars Midnight Movie Massacre
Attack of the Giant Crabs Attack of the Crab Monsters
Attack of the Monsters Gamera versus Guiron
Attack of the Mushroom People Matango
Az Idoe Ablakaj The Windows of Time
The Aztec Mummy vs the Human Robot The Robot vs the Aztec Mummy

B

Baby 2000 Cloned
Babylon 5: Crusade Crusade
Bad Blood The Night Is Young
The Banana Monster Schlock
Baron Prásil Baron Munchhausen
The Batman Batman
Battle beyond the Stars The Green Slime
Battle of the Astros Invasion of the Astro-Monster
Battle of the Clouds The Airship Destroyer
The Beast King Kong
Beautiful Women and the Hydrogen Man The H-Man
Behemoth, the Sea Monster The Giant Behemoth
Bells Murder by Phone
Berlin, Appointment for the Spies Spy in Your Eye
Berlino Appuntamento per le Spie Spy in Your Eye
La Bestia de la Montana The Beast of Hollow Mountain
Betaville Welcome to Paradox
The Big Dust-Up The Big Mess
Big Space Monster Guilala The X from Outer Space
Bijo To Ekitainigen The H-Man
Bionic Breakdown Bionic Ever After?
The Black Widow The Body Disappears
Blast Off Jules Verne's Rocket to the Moon
Bleeders Hemoglobin
Blood Beast from Outer Space The Night Caller
Blood Creature Terror Is a Man
Blood Mad The Glove
Blood Moon Bats
Blood of Frankenstein Dracula vs Frankenstein
The Blood of Heroes The Salute of the Jugger
The Blood Seekers Dracula vs Frankenstein
Bloodstream Daybreak
Body Snatcher from Hell Goke, Bodysnatcher from Hell
The Body Snatchers Ladron de Cadaveres
Boyichi and the Supermonster Gamera versus Gaos
The Boys from Brooklyn Bela Lugosi Meets a Brooklyn Gorilla
The Brainsnatcher The Man Who Changed His Mind
Brazil Year 2000 Brasil Ano 2000
Breakfast at Manchester Morgue The Living Dead at the Manchester Morgue
A Breed Apart Perfect Assassins
Bride of Dragons Bridge of Dragons
Bride of the Atom Bride of the Monster
Bronx Executioners The Bronx Executioner
Die Brut der Nacht Nightbreed
The Brute The Lady and the Monster
Buck Rogers Conquers the Universe Buck Rogers
Buried Alive Doctor Renault's Secret
The Button-Pinchers Buttoners
The Button-Pushers Buttoners
By Rocket to the Moon The Woman in the Moon

C

Oabal Nightbreed
El Caballero del Dragon Star Knight
The Calling Murder by Phone
Cannibal Virus Zombie Creeping Flesh
La Cara del Terror Face of Terror
Carnosaur 3 Primal Species
The Cars That Eat People The Cars That Ate Paris
Catastrophe 1999 Last Days of Planet Earth
Cesta do Praveku Voyage into Prehistory
Charleston Parade Charleston
Der Chef Wunscht Keine Zeugen No Survivors Please
Chelovek Amfibia Amphibian Man
Cherez Ternii k Zvezdam Humanoid Woman
The Chief Wants No Survivors No Survivors Please
Chikyu Boeigun The Mysterians
The Chosen Holocaust 2000
CHUD Cannibalistic Humanoid Underground Dwellers CHUD
Le Cinquième Elément The Fifth Element
La Cité des enfants perdus The City of Lost Children
Cliffhangers: The Secret Empire The Secret Empire
Club Extinction Dr M
Code Name: Trixie The Crazies
Collision Course The Bamboo Saucer
Colonization of the Planet of the Apes Battle for the Planet of the Apes
Colossus 1980 Colossus: the Forbin Project
Coming Down to Earth Doin' Time on Planet Earth
Comme Mars en Carême Don't Play with Martians
Computer Killers Horror Hospital
Contamination Alien Contamination
Contamination: Alien on Earth Alien Contamination
The Corpse Makers Twice Told Tales
The Cosmic Man Appears in Tokyo The Mysterious Satellite
Cosmic Monsters The Strange World of Planet X
Cosmic Shock Doomsday Rock
The Cosmic Voyage The Space Ship
Cosmonauts on Venus Planeta Burg
Cosmos War of the Planets
Cosmos Mortal Alien Predator
Couldn't Possibly Happen Phantom Empire
Counterattack of the Monster Godzilla Raids Again
Coz Takhle Dat si Spenat A Nice Plate of Spinach
The Crawling Eye The Trollenberg Terror
The Crawling Monster The Creeping Terror
The Crazy Ray Paris Qui Dort
Creatures of the Prehistoric Planet Horror of the Blood Monsters
The Creeping Unknown The Quatermass Experiment

Cries in the Night The Awful Dr Orloff
Crimes of the Future eXistenZ
I Criminali della Galassia The Wild, Wild Planet
The Criminals of the Galaxy The Wild, Wild Planet
Cruel Earth The Last Train
Curse of the Golem It!
Curse of the Mushroom People Matango
The Cusp Falling Fire
Cyber Space Lawnmower Man 2: Beyond Cyberspace
Cybertech PD Terminal Justice
Cyborg Soldier Cyborg Cop II
Cyclotrode X The Crimson Ghost

D

D-Day on Mars The Purple Monster Strikes
Dagora the Space Monster Dogora the Space Monster
Dai Sanji Sekai Taisen – Yonju-ichi Jikan no Kyofu The Final War
Daikaiju Gamera Gamera the Invincible
Daikaiju Kuchusen Gamera versus Gaos
Daikoesu Yongkari Yongkari Monster of the Deep
Daikyoju Gappa Gappa the Trifibian Monster
Le Danger Vient de l'Espace The Day the Sky Exploded
Dangerous Charter The Creeping Terror
Dark Breed Darkbreed
Dark Empire Dark City
Dark Fortress A Nymphoid Barbarian in Dinosaur Hell
Dark of the Moon Murder on the Moon
Dark Reflection Natural Selection
Dark World Dark City
Darkman 3 Darkman III: Die Darkman Die
Daughter of Destiny Alraune
Daughter of Evil Alraune
The Day after Tomorrow Strange Holiday
Dead Alive Braindead
A Dead Man Seeks His Murderer The Brain
Deadlock Wedlock
The Deadly Diaphanoids War of the Planets
Deadly Quest Future Hunters
Dean Koontz's Mr Murder Mr Murder
Death Corps Shock Waves
Death from Outer Space The Day the Sky Exploded
Death in Full View Deathwatch
Death Watch Deathwatch
Deathline Redline
La Decima Vittima The Tenth Victim
Demon God Told Me to
The Demon Doctor The Awful Dr Orloff
Denso Ningen The Secret of the Telegian
Le Dernier Combat The Last Battle
Le Dernier Homme The Last Man
Destination Saturn Buck Rogers
Destroy All Planets Gamera versus Viras
The Destruction of Jared-Syn Metalstorm: The Destruction of Jared-Syn
The Devil Men from Space The Snow Devils
The Devil's Man Devilman Story
The Devil's Plot Counterblast
The Diabolic Invention Invention of Destruction
The Diabolical Dr Satan The Awful Dr Orloff
I Diafanoidi Portano la Morte War of the Planets
I Diafanoidi Vengono da Morte War of the Planets
The Diaphanoids Bring Death War of the Planets
I Diavoli della Spazio The Snow Devils
Die Darkman Die Darkman III: Die Darkman Die
Il Disco Volante The Flying Saucer
Disney's Honey, I Shrunk the Kids Honey, I Shrunk the Kids
Docteur M Dr M
Dr Cadmem's Secret The Black Sleep
Dr?? Coppelius!!! Dr Coppelius
Dr G and the Bikini Machine Dr Goldfoot and the Bikini Machine
Dr Iven's Silence The Silence of Dr Evans
Doctor Maniac The Man Who Changed His Mind
Doctor Maniac Who Lived Again The Man Who Changed His Mind
Dr Satan's Robot The Mysterious Dr Satan
Donovan's Brain The Lady and the Monster
Don't Open the Window The Living Dead at the Manchester Morgue
Doomrunners Doom Runners
Doomsday Escape from Planet Earth
The Doomsday Machine Escape from Planet Earth
Doppelgänger Journey to the Far Side of the Sun
Dracula contra Frankenstein Dracula, Prisoner of Frankenstein
Dracula versus Frankenstein Dracula, Prisoner of Frankenstein
Dracula vs Frankenstein Assignment Terror
Dream Breaker Carver's Gate
Dune Frank Herbert's Dune

E

Earth Defence Force The Mysterians
Ecophoria Habitat
Ecotopia Habitat
The Eighth Wonder King Kong
The Electric Man Man Made Monster
The Electronic Monster Escapement
The Empire Strikes Back Star Wars Episode V: the Empire Strikes Back
Encino Man California Man
Enemy from Space Quatermass II
Escape 2000 Turkey Shoot
The Evil Force 4D Man
Expedition Moon Rocketship X-M
El Extrano Caso del Hombre y la Bestia The Strange Case of the Man and the Beast

F

FP1 Antwortet Nicht FP1
FP1 Doesn't Answer FP1
The Fabulous Baron Munchausen Baron Munchhausen
The Fabulous Journey to the Center of the Earth Where Time Began
The Fabulous World of Jules Verne Invention of Destruction
Face of Evil Doctor Blood's Coffin
Face of Fear Face of Terror
The Falling Alien Predator
The Fantastic Invasion of Planet Earth The Bubble
The Fantastic Invention Invention of Destruction
The Fantastic Puppet People Attack of the Puppet People
El Fantiastico Mundo del Dr Coppelius Dr Coppelius
Fatal Sky Project: Alien
Fearsum FreakyLinks
Female Space Invaders Starcrash
The Fifth Season Habitat
Fin de Semana para los Muertos The Living Dead at the Manchester Morgue
La Fin du Monde The End of the World
The Fire Monster Godzilla Raids Again
Five Million Years to Earth Quatermass and the Pit
Flick Dr Frankenstein on Campus
The Flight That Vanished The Flight That Disappeared
Follow Me If You Dare The Mysterious Two
Footprints on the Moon Primal Impulse
The Forbin Project Colossus: the Forbin Project
Forbrydelsens Element The Element of Crime
41 Jikan no Kyofu The Final War
Fragments Murder in My Mind
Frankenstein Mary Shelley's Frankenstein
Frankenstein and the Giant Lizard Frankenstein Meets the Devil Fish
Frankenstein Conquers the World Frankenstein Meets the Devil Fish
Frankenstein Meets the Spacemen Frankenstein Meets the Space Monster
Frankenstein – the Real Story Frankenstein
Frankenstein vs Baragon Frankenstein Meets the Devil Fish
Frankenstein vs the Subterranean Monster Frankenstein Meets the Devil Fish
Frau im Mond The Woman in the Moon
Die Frau im Mond The Woman in the Moon
Frissons Shivers
From Another Star Hyper Sapien: People from Another Star
Fuharankenshutain Tai Baragaon Frankenstein Meets the Devil Fish
Fungus of Terror Matango
Future Cop Trancers

G

Galactic Odyssey Mind Breakers
Gambara versus Barugon Gamera versus Barugon
Gamera: Daikaiju Kuchu Kessen Gamera: Guardian of the Universe
Gamera Tai Barugon Gamera versus Barugon
Gamera tai Gaos Gamera versus Gaos
Gamera Tai Giuron Gamera versus Guiron
Gamera tai uchu kaiju Bairasu Gamera versus Viras
Gamera Tai Viras Gamera versus Viras
Gamera versus Gyaos Gamera versus Gaos
Gamera Versus Outer Space Monster Viras Gamera versus Viras
Gamera vs Devil-Beast Giron Gamera versus Guiron
Gammo Sango Uchu Daisakusen The Green Slime
Gandahar Light Years
Gangster World The Outsider
The Gargon Terror Teenagers from Outer Space
Gasu Ningen Daiichigo The Human Vapour
Gekko Kamen Moonbeam Mask
Gendarme et les Extra-Terrestres, Le The Spacemen of St Tropez
Gene Roddenberry's Andromeda Andromeda
Gene Roddenberry's Battleground Earth Earth: Final Conflict
Gene Roddenberry's Earth: Final Conflict Earth: Final Conflict
Ghidora, the Three-Headed Monster Ghidrah, the Three-Headed Monster
Ghidrah: the Greatest Battle on Earth Ghidrah, the Three-Headed Monster
Gift from a Red Planet The Alpha Incident
Gigantis, the Fire Monster Godzilla Raids Again
Gill Woman Voyage to the Planet of Prehistoric Women
Gill Women of Venus Voyage to the Planet of Prehistoric Women
Girara The X from Outer Space
Girl in the Moon The Woman in the Moon
The Girl on the Moon The Woman in the Moon
Girls on the Moon Nude on the Moon
Gladiatorerna The Peace Game
The Gladiators The Peace Game
Godzilla and Mothra: The Battle for Earth Godzilla vs Mothra
Godzilla Fights the Giant Moth Godzilla vs Mothra
Godzilla, King of the Monsters Godzilla
Godzilla 1985 Godzilla
Godzilla on Monster Island Godzilla vs Gigan
Godzilla versus Cosmic Monster Godzilla vs the Cosmic Monster
Godzilla versus Mechagodzilla Godzilla vs the Cosmic Monster
Godzilla vs Monster Zero Invasion of the Astro-Monster
Godzilla versus the Bionic Monster Godzilla vs the Cosmic Monster
Godzilla versus the Sea Monster Ebirah, Horror of the Deep
Godzilla vs the Smog Monster Godzilla vs Hedora
Godzilla vs the Thing Godzilla vs Mothra
Godzilla's Counterattack Godzilla Raids Again
Godzilla's Leverage Godzilla's Revenge
Gojira Godzilla
Gojira ni-sen Mireniamu Godzilla 2000
Gojira no Gyakushu Godzilla Raids Again
Gojira tai Hedora Godzilla vs Hedora
Gojira Tai Meka-Gojira Godzilla vs the Cosmic Monster
Gojira vs Mosura Godzilla vs Mothra
Goke the Vampire Goke, Bodysnatcher from Hell
Golddigger A Robot Called Golddigger
Gomar – the Human Gorilla Night of the Bloody Apes
Grand Tour: Disaster in Time Timescape
Grave Robbers from Outer Space Plan 9 from Outer Space
Graveyard Tramps Invasion of the Bee Girls
Great Charge of All Monsters Godzilla's Revenge
Great Monster Yongkari Yongkari Monster of the Deep
Great Planet War War of the Planets
The Great Rat Swarm Gamera the Invincible
The Great Space War Battle in Outer Space
The Great Undersea War Terror beneath the Sea
Green Monkey Blue Monkey
Grey Matter The Brain Machine
La Grieta Endless Descent

Gritos en la Noche The Awful Dr Orloff
Die Grosse Verhau The Big Mess
Guerre Planetari Battle of the Worlds
Guilala The X from Outer Space
Guirara The X from Outer Space

H

HG Wells' Invisible Man The Invisible Man
HG Wells' The Shape of Things to Come The Shape of Things to Come
Hands of a Killer The Planets against Us
Hands of a Strangler The Hands of Orlac
The Hands of Orlac Mad Love
He, She or It The Doll
A Head for the Devil The Head
The Head That Wouldn't Die The Brain That Wouldn't Die
The Heavens Call Battle beyond the Sun
Hector Servadac's Ark On the Comet
Helden: Operation Ganymed Operation Ganymed
Hell of the Living Dead Zombie Creeping Flesh
Hell's Bells Murder by Phone
Der Herr der Welt Master of the World
Herrin der Welt Mistress of the World
The Hills Have Eyes III: the Outpost Wes Craven's Mind Ripper
El Hombre Invisible The Invisible Man
El Hombre Que Logro Ser Invisible The Invisible Man
El Hombre Que Vino de Ummo Assignment Terror
El Hombre y la Bestial The Strange Case of the Man and the Beast
L'Homme au Cerveau Greffé The Man with the Transplanted Brain
L'Homme sans Visage Shadowman
La Horriplante Bestia Humana Night of the Bloody Apes
The Horror Chamber of Dr Faustus Eyes without a Face
Horror Creatures of the Prehistoric Planet Horror of the Blood Monsters
The Horror of Death The Asphyx
Horror Planet Inseminoid
Host Virtual Obsession
Hothouse Habitat
The House at the End of the World Die, Monster, Die!
House of Fright The Two Faces of Dr Jekyll
Howard the Duck Howard, a New Breed of Hero
The Human Vapor The Human Vapour
Humanoids from the Deep Monster
The Hunters High Desert Kill
Hydra The Sea Serpent
Hyper Sleep Alien Cargo
Hyperspace Gremloids

I

I Come in Peace Dark Angel
I Was a Teenage Gorilla Konga
Icarus XB-1 Voyage to the End of the Universe
Ich Liebe Dich Ich Toete Dich I Love You I Kill You
Ido Zero Daisakusen Latitude Zero
Ikarie XB 1 Voyage to the End of the Universe
Immediate Disaster Stranger from Venus
L'Inafferrabile Invincibile Mr Superinvisible
Incident at Raven's Gate Encounter at Raven's Gate
The Incredible Invasion Alien Terror
The Incredible Praying Mantis The Deadly Mantis
The Incredibly Strange Creatures The Incredibly Strange Creatures Who Stopped Living and Became Mixed-up Zombies
The Indestructible Man Indestructible Man
Inferno dei Morti-Viventi Zombie Creeping Flesh
Infested Ticks
The Infra Superman Infra-Man
Inhumanoid Circuit Breaker
Intruder Moon 44
Invader Lifeform
The Invasion The Starlost
Invasion Robin Cook's Invasion
Invasion Earth: They Came from Outer Space Invasion Earth: the Aliens Are Here!
Invasion Earth 2150 AD Daleks – Invasion Earth 2150 AD
Invasion Force Hangar 18
Invasion from Mars War of the Worlds
Invasion from the Moon Mutiny in Outer Space
Invasion of Planet X Invasion of the Astro-Monster
Invasion of the Astros Invasion of the Astro-Monster
Invasion of the Body Stealers The Body Stealers
Invasion of the Flying Saucers Earth vs the Flying Saucers
La Invasion Siniestra The Incredible Invasion
El Invencible Hombre Invisible Mr Superinvisible
Invention Diabolique Invention of Destruction
An Invention for Destruction Invention of Destruction
Invincible Mr Invisible Mr Superinvisible
The Invisible Man Becomes the Gemini Man The Gemini Man
The Invisible Spy The Invisible Agent
Island of the Alive It's Alive III: Island of the Alive
Island of the Burning Damned Night of the Big Heat
The Island of the Fishmen Island of the Fish Men
L'Isola degli Uomini Pesce Island of the Fish Men
It Came without Warning Without Warning
It Fell From the Sky The Alien Dead
It Stalked the Ocean Floor Monster from the Ocean Floor
It! the Vampire from beyond Space It! The Terror from beyond Space
It's Alive II It Lives Again
Izbavitelj The Rat Saviour

J

James A Michener's Space Space
James Cameron's Dark Angel Dark Angel
Jet Jackson, the Flying Commando Captain Midnight
Jikan no Kyofu The Final War
J.O.E. and the Colonel Humanoid Defender
John Carpenter's Escape from LA Escape from LA
Journey into Primeval Times Voyage into Prehistory
Journey into Space: A Tale of the Future Journey into Space: Operation Luna
The Journey that Shook the World Jules Verne's Rocket to the Moon
Journey to the Beginning of Time Voyage into Prehistory
Journey to the Unknown Out of the Unknown
Judas Goat Xtro
July 13th Without Warning
Jurassic Park 2 The Lost World: Jurassic Park

K

Kaiju Daisenso Invasion of the Astro-Monster
Kaiju Soshingeki Destroy All Monsters
Kaitei Daiseno Terror beneath the Sea
Kaitei Gunkan Atragon
Kdo Chce Zabit Jessu? Who Killed Jessie?
Kessen Nankai No Daikaiju The Space Amoeba
Killer Bats Devil Bat
King Kong no Gyakushu King Kong Escapes
King Kong versus Godzilla King Kong vs Godzilla
King Kong's Counterattack King Kong Escapes
Kingu Kongu no Gyakushu King Kong Escapes
Kingu Kongu Tai Gojira King Kong vs Godzilla
The Knight of the Dragon Star Knight
Knights of the Dragon Star Knight
Knoflikari Buttoners
Knuckle-Men Terminal Island
Kokaku Kidotai Ghost in the Shell
Kong King Kong
Kosmichesky Reis The Space Ship
Kosmitchesky Reis The Space Ship
Die Kreuzritter The High Crusade
The Krofft Superstar Hour The Krofft Supershow
Kurt Vonnegut's Harrison Bergeron Harrison Bergeron
Kyuketsuki Gokemidoro Goke, Bodysnatcher from Hell

L

The Last Combat The Last Battle
The Last Days of Man on Earth The Final Programme
The Last War The Final War
Legend in Leotards The Return of Captain Invincible
Let Sleeping Corpses Lie The Living Dead at the Manchester Morgue
Lethal Orbit Orbit
Lethal Terminator The Glove
De Lift The Lift
Lost Planet Airmen King of the Rocket Men
Lost Women Mesa of Lost Women
Lost Women of Zarpa Mesa of Lost Women
Lou Costello and His 30 Foot Bride The 30 Foot Bride of Candy Rock
The Love Factor Zeta One
Love Is Strange The Mysterious Island
Lugosi Meets a Brooklyn Gorilla Bela Lugosi Meets a Brooklyn Gorilla
Lunar Cop Solar Force
Lunarcop Solar Force

M

MST3K: The Movie Mystery Science Theater 3000: The Movie
The Man and the Beast The Strange Case of the Man and the Beast
The Man He Found The Whip Hand
The Man in the Moonlight Mask Moonbeam Mask
The Man Who Lived Again The Man Who Changed His Mind
The Man Who Stole the Moon The Sky Ranger
The Man Who Wanted to Live Forever The Only Way Out Is Dead
The Man with the Yellow Eyes The Planets against Us
The Man without a Face Shadowman
Manden der Taenkte Ting The Man Who Thought Life
Mandragore Alraune
Mandrake Alraune
The Manster – Half Man, Half Monster The Manster
Marabunta Legion of Fire: Killer Ants!
Le Martien de Noël The Christmas Martian
Master of Terror 4D Man
Mastermind QED
Masters of the Universe II: The Cyborg Cyborg
Matango: Fungus of Terror Matango
Matt Riker Mutant Hunt
Mauvais Sang The Night Is Young
Mein Ist die Welt An Invisible Man Goes through the City
Men in White National Lampoon's Men in White
Men with Steel Faces Phantom Empire
Metalbeast Metal Beast
Meteor Monster Teenage Monster
Mighty Morphin Alien Rangers Mighty Morphin Power Rangers
Milczaca Gwiada First Spaceship on Venus
Mind Games Brainwaves
Mind Machine The Brain Machine
Mind Ripper Wes Craven's Mind Ripper
The Mind Snatchers The Happiness Cage
Mind Warp The Brain Machine
Mindwarp: an Infinity of Terrors Galaxy of Terror
Minya, Son of Godzilla Godzilla's Revenge
Missile Monsters Flying Disc Man from Mars
Mission Genesis Deepwater Black
Mister, You Are a Widower Sir, You Are a Widower
Il Mistero dei Tre Continenti Mistress of the World
Mizu no naka no hachigatsu August in the Water
Molchaniye Doktora Ivens The Silence of Dr Evans
La Momia Azteca contra el Robot Humano The Robot vs the Aztec Mummy
Il Mondo di Yor Yor, the Hunter from the Future
Monkey Boy Chimera
The Monster and the Lady The Lady and the Monster
The Monster and the Woman Four-Sided Triangle
Monster from a Prehistoric Planet Gappa the Trifibian Monster
Monster Maker Monster from the Ocean Floor
Monster of Monsters Ghidrah, the Three-Headed Monster
Monster of Terror Die, Monster, Die!
The Monster with Green Eyes The Planets against Us
Monster Yongkari Yongkari Monster of the Deep
Monster Zero Invasion of the Astro-Monster
The Monster's Castle The Lady and the Monster
Monsters from the Moon Robot Monster
El Monstruo de la Montana Hueca The Beast of

Hollow Mountain
El Monstruo Resucitado Doctor Crimen
The Moonbeam Man Moonbeam Mask
The Moondolls Nude on the Moon
Moonshot Countdown
La Mort en Direct Deathwatch
La Morte Viene Dalla Spazio The Day the Sky Exploded
Mosura tai Gojira Godzilla vs Mothra
Mothra vs Godzilla Godzilla vs Mothra
Mothra vs Gojira Godzilla vs Mothra
Murder by Moonlight Murder on the Moon
Mutant Forbidden World
Mutant 2 Alien Predator
Les Mutants de la Duexième Humanité Rats Night of Terror
Mutronics The Guyver
Mutronics: the Movie The Guyver
My Friend Frank Frankenstein: the College Years
Les Mystères d'Angkor Mistress of the World
The Mysterious Dr R Man Made Monster
The Mysterious Dr X Man Made Monster
Mysterious Invader The Astounding She-Monster

N

Na Komete On the Comet
Die Nackte und der Satan The Head
Naked Robot 4 1/2 Invader
Naked Space The Creature Wasn't Nice
Nankai No Daikaiju The Space Amoeba
Nash's Vision Steel Justice
Nathaniel Hawthorne's "Twice Told Tales" Twice Told Tales
Nature Girls on the Moon Nude on the Moon
Ne Jouez Pas avec les Martiens Don't Play with Martians
Nebo Zovyot Battle beyond the Sun
Nemesis III: Prey Harder Nemesis 3 – Time Lapse
The Neptune Disaster The Neptune Factor
The New Adventures of Batman and Robin Batman and Robin
The New Adventures of Swamp Thing Swamp Thing
The New Adventures of Wonder Woman Wonder Woman
The New, Original Wonder Woman Wonder Woman
Night Breed Nightbreed
The Night Crawlers The Navy vs the Night Monsters
Night Man NightMan
Night of the Flesh Eaters Night of the Living Dead
Night Shadows Mutant
Nightfliers Nightflyers
No Cause for Alarm Project: Alien
Non Si Seve Profanare Ol Sonne Die Morte The Living Dead at the Manchester Morgue
Norman's Awesome Experience A Switch in Time
Nosutoradamusu no Daiyogen Last Days of Planet Earth
Nuclear Run The Chain Reaction
Nude in His Pocket Amour de Poche
Nudes on the Moon Nude on the Moon
Nuits Rouges Shadowman
Nuke Nukie
Nuke 'em High Class of Nuke 'Em High

O

Occhi Senza Volto Eyes without a Face
Ocean Odyssey Ocean Girl
The Octave of Claudius A Blind Bargain
Odeon Alien from LA
On the Sixth Day The 6th Day
One Clear Moment Mysterious Ways
One Hour to Doomsday City beneath the Sea
1,000 Years from Now Captive Women
Operation Blue Book The Bamboo Saucer
Operation Monsterland Destroy All Monsters
Operation Terror Assignment Terror
L'Or Gold
Orbita Mortal Mission Stardust
The Original Fabulous Adventure of Baron Munchausen Baron Munchhausen
Orlacs Hände Hands of Orlac
Orlak, el Infierno de Frankenstein Orlak, the Hell of Frankenstein
Le Orme Primal Impulse
Oru Kaiju Daishingeki Godzilla's Revenge
Otel U Pogibshego Alpinista The Dead Mountaineer Hotel
Out of the Darkness Teenage Caveman
Outpost Wes Craven's Mind Ripper
Over My Dead Body The Brain

P

PT Barnum's Rocket to the Moon Jules Verne's Rocket to the Moon
Pane, Vy Jste Vdova! Sir, You Are a Widower
Parade sur un Air de Charleston Charleston
Paranoia Brain Dead
The Parasite Murders Shivers
Parts: the Clonus Horror The Clonus Horror
Per Aspera ad Astra Humanoid Woman
Perhaps Maybe
Perry Rhodan – SOS aus dem Weltall Mission Stardust
Personal Choice Beyond the Stars
La Perversa Caricia de Satan The Devil's Kiss
Peut-être Maybe
The Phantom Menace Star Wars Episode I: the Phantom Menace
I Pianeta degli Uomini Spenti Battle of the Worlds
I Pianeti contro di Noi The Planets against Us
Planet of Blood Planet of the Vampires
Planet of Horrors Galaxy of Terror
Planet of Incredible Creatures Fantastic Planet
Planet of Storms Planeta Burg
Planet of the Lifeless Men Battle of the Worlds
The Planet of the Women Invaders El Planeta de las Mujeres Invasoras
Planeta Bur Planeta Burg
La Planète Sauvage Fantastic Planet
The Plants Are Watching The Kirlian Witness
Pocket of Love Amour de Poche
The Pocket Venus Amour de Poche
Poliziotto Superpiu Supersnooper
La Poupée The Doll
Power.com Menno's Mind
Power Rangers Mighty Morphin Power Rangers
Power Rangers Ninja Mighty Morphin Power Rangers
Power Rangers 2 Turbo: a Power Rangers Adventure
I Predatori dell'Anno Omega Warrior of the Lost World
Prehistoric Adventure Voyage into Prehistory
Prehistoric Planet Women Women of the Prehistoric Planet
Prehistoric World Teenage Caveman
Programmed for Murder Homewrecker
Programmed to Kill The Retaliator
Project Genocide Starship Invasions
Project: Metalbeast Metal Beast
Project Metalbeast: DNA Overload Metal Beast
Project Moon Base Project Moonbase
Prophecies of Nostradamus Last Days of Planet Earth
Prototype Prototype X29A

Q

Qatilon Ke Qatil Katilon Ke Katil
The Quatermass Conclusion Quatermass
4...3...2...1 Morte Mission Stardust
Queen of Atlantis Siren of Atlantis
Queen of Blood Planet of Blood
Quest Galaxy of Terror

R

Radio Ranch Phantom Empire
Les Rats de Manhattan Rats Night of Terror
Rats Notte di Terrore Rats Night of Terror
Raumschiff Venus antwortet Nicht First Spaceship on Venus
Raw Meat Death Line
Le Rayon Diabolique Paris Qui Dort
Le Rayon Invisible Paris Qui Dort
Re-Animator 2 Bride of Re-Animator
The Reactor Deadly Reactor
Rebel Storm Rising Storm
Rebel Waves Rising Storm
Red Neck Zombies Redneck Zombies
The Redeemer The Rat Saviour
Redneck County Rape Redneck Zombies
Regenerator Metamorphosis
Rejuvenatrix The Rejuvenator
Retik, the Moon Menace Radar Men from the Moon
The Return of Batman Batman and Robin
The Return of Godzilla Godzilla Raids Again
The Return of Godzilla Godzilla
The Return of the Giant Monsters Gamera versus Gaos
Return of the Jedi Star Wars Episode VI: Return of the Jedi
Return of the Six Million Dollar Man and the Bionic Woman Bionic Showdown: the Six Million Dollar Man and the Bionic Woman
The Revenge of King Kong King Kong Escapes
Revenge of the Ape Man Return of the Ape Man
Revolt of the Humanoids The Creation of the Humanoids
La Revolte des Vivants Le Monde Tremblera
Riffs III Die Ratten von Manhattan Rats Night of Terror
The Rift Endless Descent
The Road Warrior Mad Max 2
Robert A Heinlein's The Puppet Masters The Puppet Masters
Formula for Death Robin Cook's Formula for Death
Robin Cook's Virus Robin Cook's Formula for Death
Robo Man Who?
Robocop – The Future of Law Enforcement Robocop: the Series
Roboman Who?
Robosaurus Steel Justice
El Robot Humano The Robot vs the Aztec Mummy
Robot in the Family A Robot Called Golddigger
Robotjox Robot Jox
Rocket Man Rocketman
Rocket Ship Flash Gordon
Rocket to the Moon Jules Verne's Rocket to the Moon
Rocket to the Moon Cat-Women of the Moon
Rod Serling's A Town Has Turned to Dust A Town Has Turned to Dust
Rodon the Flying Monster Rodan
Roger Corman Presents Not of This Earth Not of This Earth
Roger Corman Presents Piranha Piranha
Roger Corman Presents Welcome to Planet Earth Welcome to Planet Earth
Roger Corman Presents Suspect Device Suspect Device
Roger Corman's Frankenstein Unbound Frankenstein Unbound
Rojin Z Roujin Z
Roswell High Roswell
The Roswell Project Roswell: the Aliens Attack
Ruler of the World Master of the World
Ruusujen Aika Time of Roses
Rymdinvasion I Lappland Invasion of the Animal People

S

SF Shinseiki Lensman Lensman
SOS Spaceship The Invisible Boy
Salvage Terror Island
San Daikaiju Chikyu Saidai no Kessen Ghidrah, the Three-Headed Monster
Santa Claus Conquers Mars Santa Claus Conquers the Martians
Santa Claus Defeats the Aliens Santa Claus Conquers the Martians
Satan's Satellites Zombies of the Stratosphere
Satellite of Blood First Man into Space
Satellite Police Space Patrol
The School That Stole My Brain Zombie High
Der Schweigende Stern First Spaceship on Venus
Screamers Island of the Fish Men
The Screaming Head The Head
seaQuest 2032 seaQuest DSV
Secret Abduction Visitors of the Night
The Secret Bride of Candy Rock The 30 Foot Bride of Candy Rock
Secrets of FP1 FP1

Seddok, L'Ereda di Sarona Atom Age Vampire
Seed People Seedpeople
Sekai Daisenso The Final War
Seksmisja The Sex Mission
Il Seme dell'Uomo The Seed of Man
Semi-automatic The Outsider
Sengoku Jietai Time Slip
El Sensacional y Extrano Caso del Hombre y la Bestia The Strange Case of the Man and the Beast
Serpiente de Mar The Sea Serpent
Seven Cities to Atlantis Warlords of Atlantis
Sexmission The Sex Mission
The Shadow Webmaster
Shadowchaser Project: Shadowchaser
Sharad of Atlantis Undersea Kingdom
Shocker: No More Mr Nice Guy Shocker
Shockwave The Arrival
Shockwave Stranded
Sieriebristaya Pyl Silver Dust
The Silent Star First Spaceship on Venus
The Sinister Invasion Alien Terror
Sir Arthur Conan Doyle's The Lost World The Lost World
Six Inches Tall Attack of the Puppet People
The Sky Calls Battle beyond the Sun
The Sky Is Calling Battle beyond the Sun
Skyggen Webmaster
Slapstick Slapstick of Another Kind
Slapstick of a Different Kind Slapstick of Another Kind
Solarbables Solarwarriors
Something Is Waiting Dark Side of the Moon
Something Waits in the Dark Island of the Fish Men
Son of Blob Beware! The Blob
Sora no Daikaiju Radon Rodan
Space Apeman Gori Spectreman
Space Avenger Alien Space Avenger
Space Challenge Men into Space
Space Devils The Snow Devils
Space Family Robinson Lost in Space
Space Invasion from Lapland Invasion of the Animal People
Space Invasion of Lapland Invasion of the Animal People
Space Men Appear in Tokyo The Mysterious Satellite
Space Monster Dogora Dogora the Space Monster
Space Rage – Breakout on Prison Planet Space Rage
Space Soldiers Flash Gordon
Space Station X Mutiny in Outer Space
Space Station X-14 Mutiny in Outer Space
The Space Vampires The Astro-Zombies
Spacemaster X 7 Space Master X 7
Spaceship The Creature Wasn't Nice
Spaceship to the Unknown Flash Gordon
Spaziale K! The Human Duplicators
Spear of Death Future Hunters
Spectralman Spectreman
The Spider Earth vs the Spider
Spirit of the Dead The Asphyx
The Split The Manster
Sputnik A Dog, a Mouse and a Sputnik
The Spy Spies
Spy Kids SPYkids
Star Crash Starcrash
Star Quest Terminal Voyage
Star-Rock The Apple
Star Wars Star Wars Episode IV: a New Hope
Starflight: the Plane That Couldn't Land Starflight One
Starknight Star Knight
Starquest II Mind Breakers
Starship Lorca and the Outlaws
Steel Force Legion of Iron
Stella Star Starcrash
Stephen King's Golden Years Golden Years
Stephen King's The Langoliers The Langoliers
Stephen King's The Stand The Stand
Stephen King's The Tommyknockers The Tommyknockers
The Stolen Airship The Stolen Dirigible
Storm Planet Planeta Burg
The Strange Case of the Man and the Beast The Strange Case of the Man and the Beast
Strange Holiday Jules Verne's Strange Holiday
Strike Me Deadly The Crawling Hand
Sub-a-Dub-Dub Hello Down There
Supekutoruman Spectreman
Super Fuzz Supersnooper
The Super Infra-Man Infra-Man
Superman and the Strange People Superman and the Mole Men
Sur un Air de Charleston Charleston
Survival Run Damnation Alley
Swamp of the Blood Leeches The Alien Dead
Synapse Memory Run

T

Tainstvenni Ostrov Mysterious Island
Tangents Time Chasers
Teenage Dracula Dracula vs Frankenstein
Teenage Psycho Meets Bloody Mary The Incredibly Strange Creatures Who Stopped Living and Became Mixed-up Zombies
The Telegian The Secret of the Telegian
Le Temps de Mourir Twice Upon a Time
Terminal Force Galaxis
Terror at Halfday Monster a Go-Go!
Terror en el Espacio Planet of the Vampires
The Terror Factor Scared to Death
Terror in the Midnight Sun Invasion of the Animal People
Terror of Frankenstein Victor Frankenstein
Terrore nello Spazio Planet of the Vampires
Test Pilot Pirx The Test of Pilot Pirx
Test Pilota Pirxa The Test of Pilot Pirx
These Are the Damned The Damned
They Came From Within Shivers
They're Coming to Get You Dracula vs Frankenstein
The Thing The Thing from Another World
This Air The Body Stealers
Thor Wes Craven's Mind Ripper
Thorny Way to the Stars Humanoid Woman
Those Fantastic Flying Fools Jules Verne's Rocket to the Moon
3 Minutes to Impact Falling Fire
3,000 AD Captive Women
Time for Terror Flesh Feast
Time Lock Timelock
Time of the Beast Mutator
The Time Shifters Thrill Seekers
The Time to Die Twice Upon a Time
Time Trap The Time Travelers
The Time Travellers The Time Travelers
Time Warp The Day Time Ended
Timerider Timerider: the Adventure of Lyle Swann
To the Stars by Hard Ways Humanoid Woman
Tomorrow You Die The Crawling Hand
Toto nella Luna Toto in the Moon
Toxic Spawn Alien Contamination
Trackers Space Rage
Transatlantic Tunnel The Tunnel
The Traveler Night Visitors
Trip to the Centre of the Earth Where Time Began
Trip to the Moon Le Voyage dans la Lune
Der Tunnel The Tunnel
2084 Lorca and the Outlaws
The Two-Headed Monster The Manster
Two Years' Holiday The Stolen Dirigible

U

Uchu Daikaiju Guilala The X from Outer Space
Uchu Daisenso Battle in Outer Space
Uchu Kara No Messeji Message from Space
Uchudai Dogora Dogora the Space Monster
Uchujin Tokyo ni Arawaru The Mysterious Satellite
Ukradena Vzducholod The Stolen Dirigible
El Ultimo de su Sexo It's Great to Be Alive
L'Ultimo Uomo della Terra The Last Man on Earth
Ultraman G Ultraman Great
Ultraman: Towards the Future Ultraman Great
L'Umanoide The Humanoid
An Undersea Odyssey The Neptune Factor
Unholy Love Alraune
Unidentified Flying Oddball The Spaceman and King Arthur
Unknown Origin The Alien Within
Unknown Satellite over Tokyo The Mysterious Satellite
Unnatural Alraune
Unsichtbare Gegner Invisible Adversaries
Ein Unsichtbarer Geht durch die Stadt An Invisible Man Goes through the City
Uomini H The H-Man
L'Uomo Puma The Puma Man

V

The Vampire-Beast Craves Blood The Blood Beast Terror
Vampire Men of the Lost Planet Horror of the Blood Monsters
La Venganza del Saxo Curious Dr Humpp
Vengeance The Brain
Vengeance Alraune
The Venusian Stranger from Venus
Viaje al Centro de la Tierra Where Time Began
Virtual Combat Grid Runners
Virus Robin Cook's Formula for Death
Virus Zombie Creeping Flesh
Vital Contact Orbit
Viva la vie! Long Live Life
The Volcano Monster Godzilla Raids Again
Vortex The Day Time Ended
The Voyage Home – Star Trek IV Star Trek IV: the Voyage Home

W

Wakusei Daisenso War of the Planets
War-Gods of the Deep City under the Sea
War in Space War of the Planets
War of the Aliens Starship Invasions
War of the Monsters Godzilla vs Gigan
The War of the Monsters Gamera versus Barugon
War of the Worlds: the Second Invasion War of the Worlds
Warlords of the 21st Century Battletruck
Warning from Space The Mysterious Satellite
Water Cyborgs Terror beneath the Sea
The Watts Monster Dr Black and Mr Hyde
Die Welt Ohne Maske The World without a Mask
Wes Craven Presents Mind Ripper Wes Craven's Mind Ripper
What Waits Below Secrets of the Phantom Caverns
What Would You Say to Some Spinach A Nice Plate of Spinach
Who Wants to Kill Jessie? Who Killed Jessie?
Who Would Kill Jessie? Who Killed Jessie?
Winged Serpent Starship Invasions
Winter Angel Doomwatch: Winter Angel
W.O.G. World of Giants
Wojna Swiatow – Nastepne Stulecie The War of the Worlds – Next Century
The Woman on the Moon The Woman in the Moon
The World Is Mine An Invisible Man Goes through the City
The World of Space Battle in Outer Space
The World of Yor Yor, the Hunter from the Future
World War III Breaks Out The Final War

XYZ

X The Man with the X-Ray Eyes
The X Files Movie The X Files
X: the Man with X-Ray Eyes The Man with the X-Ray Eyes
Les Yeux sans Visage Eyes without a Face
Yog – Monster from Space The Space Amoeba
Yosei Gorasu Gorath
Yosei Gorath Gorath
Zeiramu Zeram
Zero Population ZPG: Zero Population Growth
Zombie Zombie Flesh Eaters
Zombie 2 Zombie Flesh Eaters
Zombie Inferno Zombie Creeping Flesh
Zombies Dawn of the Dead

SciQ answers

1. Chris Barrie, whose voice featured in ITV's *Spitting Image*, and who starred in both *Brittas Empire* and the long-running *Red Dwarf* on BBC TV

2. The music composed by Arthur Bliss for *The Shape of Things to Come* proved so popular with audiences that it became the first movie score to be recorded commercially and released in record stores

3. Nicholas Hammond, who played Friedrich von Trapp and grew up to be the Amazing Spider-Man

4. *Captain Video and His Video Rangers* spawned *Captain Video Master of the Stratosphere*, a 15-chapter movie serial in 1951

5. *A for Andromeda*, the 1961 BBC seven-part serial

6. *Invasion: Earth*, BBC TV's most expensive sci-fi series to date

7. The *Millennium Falcon* spacecraft flown by Han Solo in the *Star Wars* films

8. Despite the appearance of scores of alien assailants, in total only six creature suits were used – the rest is down to editing

9. Picked at random from the telephone directory. "It had the unusual quality that seemed to fit the director of a rocket group which was to send a man-carrying missile into space and bring it back to Earth."

10. The rocket-launching sequences in Fritz Lang's 1929 classic *The Woman in the Moon* were considered so realistic that Hitler ordered all prints to be destroyed to protect his war preparations

11. The silent 1925 classic, *The Lost World*, directed by Harry O Hoyt

12. Charles Chilton

13. *King Kong*, the classic monster adventure from 1933

14. There are 9, but only 7 are used regularly when dialling from a gate.

15. In *Fireball XL5*, Anderson provided the voice of Robby the robot

16. *The Bridge on the River Kwai*

17. Britt Reid aka The Green Hornet, is the son of Dan Reid, who was the Lone Ranger's nephew (John Reid). For TV it was suggested that John Reid is Britt's great-grand uncle

18. *Mork & Mindy*. Mork from Ork appeared in two episodes of the popular series early in 1978

19. Sam Peckinpah

20. ET the Extra-Terrestrial

21. James Cameron – he made his "actors" writhe by secretly wiring a prop severed arm to the mains (he was working second unit on *Galaxy of Terror* at the time)

22. David Vincent (Roy Thinnes) in *The Invaders*; they were headed up by Edgar Scoville, played by Kent Smith

23. *The Chronic Argonauts*

24. Metal Mickey, in LWT's eighties family sci-fi comedy.

25. *Star Trek II: the Wrath of Khan* – specifically, the "Genesis" sequence (before this, however, there were instances of computer-generated wire-frame imagery etc being seen on TV monitors within a shot).

26. Thermoman, aka Gary Sunday (comedian Ardal O'Hanlon) in BBC1's *My Hero*.

27. Boris Karloff, who is supposed to have been the inspiration for the first illustrations of the Incredible Hulk.

28. Steve Bochco, creator of *Hill Street Blues*, *LA Law* et al. He shares the writing credit for *Silent Running* with Deric Washburn and Michael Cimino. Washburn would later write *The Deer Hunter* for Cimino to direct.

29. The time-travelling Marshalls in the original *Land of the Lost* TV series.

30. *Star Wars Episode VI: Return of the Jedi.*

31. 1988's *Earth Girls Are Easy*

32. *Honey I Shrunk the Kids*

33. Claudia Christian

34. Paul McCrane, now familiar as Dr Romano in *ER*.

35. *Videodrome*

36. *Star Trek VI: the Undiscovered Country.* It's Tiberius

37. *Star Trek V: the Final Frontier.*

38. *Split Second* (1991).

39. *Hackers* (1995)

40. Michelle Williams, who played the young Sil in 1995's *Species* (it was her second movie after a small part in a Lassie remake)

41. *Deep Rising*

42. Bruce Willis in *Armageddon*

43. *Island of Lost Souls*

PICTURE CREDITS Aquarius pg 105, 119, 203, 212, 251, 281 **BBC** 49, 104, 105, 153, 265, 269 **Ronald Grant Archive** 13, 19, 61, 72, 85, 91, 128, 191, 193, 245, 280, 281, 311, 312, 322 (top left and right), 349, 379 **Jim Henson Company** 122 **Hulton Archive** 363 **Kobal Collection** 33, 36, 38, 58, 82, 100, 140, 154, 165, 169, 181, 185, 277, 281, 285, 322 (bottom), 325, 333, 351, 355, 369 **London Features International** 334 **Moviestore Collection** 35, 39, 76, 111, 120, 139, 177, 198, 202, 207, 257, 280, 281, 308, 310, 375, 376, 376, 381 **Pictorial Press** 51, 65, 219, 231, 235, 323, 340 **Warner Bros** 15